Ideas and Diplomacy

# Ideas and Diplomacy

Readings in the Intellectual Tradition
of American Foreign Policy

EDITED WITH COMMENTARY BY
## NORMAN A. GRAEBNER

UNIVERSITY OF ILLINOIS

New York   OXFORD UNIVERSITY PRESS   1964

To My Father and Mother

This volume is essentially a study in ideas. As such it comprises a conceptual rather than a narrative approach to the record of American diplomacy. It recognizes the significant relationship between the intellectual milieu in which a foreign policy is conducted and the foreign policy itself. Concepts transcend space and time, but they determine how a nation will react in a given circumstance and what a national leadership will regard as legitimate and acceptable diplomatic behavior. Specific problems abroad eventually disappear into history, leaving a legacy of success or failure, depending upon their contribution to the nation's permanent interests. But the concepts and assumptions underlying policy decisions live on as the country's true diplomatic tradition, remaining to serve and guide future generations as they attempt to dispose of new challenges which confront them. Specifically, this volume is concerned with the intellectual conflict provoked by a series of major issues which have troubled the United States since the eighteenth century. It endeavors, moreover, through the study of competing concepts of proper diplomatic action in precise episodes, to account for the varying successes in the nation's diplomatic experience. The readings themselves have been selected largely, and often exclusively, because of the fundamental ideas which they expound. Because they represent an attempt to illustrate the genuine intellectual history of American diplomacy, they have been extracted from the unfolding record itself. They reveal that American diplomatic thought has had moments of brilliance not surpassed elsewhere in the modern world.

Innumerable issues of general significance have confronted the United States in every decade of its history, but the fundamental concepts which have determined the nation's responses have been basically two. The first might be termed the *analytical* approach to external affairs. It suggests that a foreign policy serves the nation. It discovers the ends of prudent action in the country's historic traditions, its geographical location, its security requirements, and the economic, social, and political welfare of its citizens. These, taken together, create the

vii

national interests which foreign policy seeks to defend. But only for the omnipotent are ambitions synonymous with achievement. For this reason national leaders must distinguish between the essential interests of the nation, upon which hinge its security and welfare, and demands of secondary importance which are always proper questions for negotiation and compromise. The primary task of leadership consists in determining the hierarchy of the nation's interests, measured always against the traditional interests of other countries. Each nation, according to the realist image of the world, is suspended in a multistate system in which all members are engaged in a continuing struggle to enhance or defend their own territories and security. Diplomacy and power serve as the necessary and only means available for defending a nation's interests abroad. War as the continuance of diplomacy by other means is senseless unless attached to political objectives that are clearly achievable through the process of destruction alone.

The second and competing approach to foreign policy, one that has had a profound effect on American diplomacy in the twentieth century, is the *ideological*. This school of thought views external affairs largely in philosophical and psychological terms. Measured by this standard, foreign policies reflect not a nation's hierarchy of interests but rather its prevailing political, social, and religious beliefs. Diplomacy thus becomes one function of a political system; it serves an idea, not a nation. It looks beyond nations to individuals, not to the multistate system but to the world community and the people that compose it. Its accent is less on national interests than on the common interests of mankind—peace, freedom, justice, and self-government. The school of idealism seeks not to understand and control the use of power with countering power but to eliminate it from world affairs completely. It reflects, therefore, a deep faith in reason and progress, in the perfectibility of human society. Its optimistic assumptions regarding humankind were expressed well by the English philosopher Joseph Priestley, when he wrote: "Whatever was the beginning of this world, the end will be glorious and paradisiacal beyond what our imaginations can now conceive. Extravagant as some people may suppose these views to be, I think I could show them to be fairly suggested by the true theory of human nature and to arise from the natural course of human affairs." If the world is perfectible and if liberty and democracy, as the most rational of all governmental ideals, represent humanity's ultimate goals, then why should not a nation's foreign policies be devised to serve such transcendent human ends?

Within each of these two bodies of diplomatic thought have been some variations, yet in practice they have tended to be quite fundamental and mutually exclusive. A nation cannot pursue simultaneously its national interest and what it imagines to be the cause of humanity, for a nation and its ideology are not synonymous. One is a geographic, economic, political, and military entity; the other is a concept that resides in the minds of men. When the two converge, as indeed they may, one policy will serve them both. When they diverge, as generally they do, the nation must choose. In a crisis it can measure its interests with some precision and attempt to defend them, or it can place the nation's destiny on the altar of its principles, assuming that the nation, with its vast resources, can take care of itself.

For the Founding Fathers the automatic preference for the analytical over the ideological approach to foreign policy was dictated by their fundamental conservatism. They accepted without question all the assumptions of the great European statesmen from Richelieu to Bismarck regarding the nature of international society. All nations, they agreed, pursued their interests in a universal system of power politics. Beginning with the war for American independence, they defined the interests of the United States in specific, not general, terms. They accepted both the clash of interests and the danger of conflict as normal, and they recognized, therefore, the necessity of a sizable army and navy, as well as a strong central government, to maintain the nation's position in an ever-changing and often-threatening state system. They established the nation's freedom of action less to guarantee the country's insulation from the conflicts of Europe than to escape those wars which could not serve the national interests of the United States.

That such realistic notions of prudent diplomatic action continued to guide American foreign policy during the nineteenth century is clear from the consistency of thought from John Adams, Alexander Hamilton, George Washington, and Thomas Jefferson to John Quincy Adams, James K. Polk, and William H. Seward. Nowhere was the great American conservative tradition, with its limited view of human progress and thus of legitimate national action, more apparent than in its application to foreign affairs. What those who question the uniform realism of the eighteenth and nineteenth century American diplomatic tradition overlook is that early American democratic idealism did not, in a single instance, determine the fundamental policies of the nation. Without exception, those charged with the responsibility for American action abroad condemned those who attempted to identify the national interest with the cause of humanity.

Not until 1898 did the struggle between the realists and the idealists for control of American foreign policy become serious. Under William B. McKinley the established American tradition began to falter, largely because of the ease with which the United States achieved such allegedly humanitarian goals as the freedom of Cuba, the acquisition of the Philippines, and the establishment of the Open Door for China. The older tradition was shattered completely when Woodrow Wilson led a successful intellectual assault on every assumption that had guided the nation's early leaders. In identifying American purpose with the establishment of a world free of power politics and anchored to the democratic principle of self-determination, Wilson created a vision so grand in terms of American idealism and self-interest and so undemanding in terms of national power that scarcely one American diplomatist who wielded authority after Wilson cared to question the new assumptions.

Wilson's view pervaded the writings and speeches of such powerful spokesmen for American foreign relations as William E. Borah, Cordell Hull, Arthur H. Vandenberg, and John Foster Dulles. With variations in detail and phraseology they all denied that diplomacy played a limited and specific role of settling affairs among nations through negotiation and compromise. They regarded it rather as a means of exhorting nations to accept the new principles of peaceful change or of condemning aggressors for pursuing goals achievable only within

the context of the older principles of power politics. Unfortunately, the Wilsonian system, with its pretensions to peace, contained one major fallacy which
subsequent American leadership refused to recognize. As Arnold Wolfers has
written, "[though] peace-loving nations wish for peace, they also wish to preserve what in the past they as individual nations have acquired or helped to
establish. When their valued possessions come to include a wide circle of values
reaching far beyond the national boundaries, as they do in the days of ideological or religious conflict, the occasions for power competition and violence are
further enhanced." Neither Wilson nor his successors could eliminate conflict
from the world. Peace after 1919 obviously hinged less on the attitudes of the
satisfied powers toward one another than on the ability of the *status quo* nations
to manage the areas of major tension in international politics. Wilson's optimism had no place in world affairs as long as nations with the power to wage
war desired what they did not possess.

In practice, the evils which American idealists in this century have sought to
identify and destroy have been specific challenges to the *status quo* which existed
at the turn of the century, a *status quo* which represented a balance of power
and a world-wide stability that assured the United States a maximum of security
at a minimum of cost. In the Orient the nation identified its fundamental interests with the Open Door in China, in Europe with a hierarchy of power which
placed England in a sufficiently dominant position to control the shifting align-
ments among France, Germany, Russia, Austria, and Italy. The United States
eventually fought World War II to prevent Germany and Japan from destroying
what remained of the older structure. When after that war the nation faced
similar threats to its established interests in Europe and Asia, it perpetuated,
through its refusal to recognize the Soviet hegemony in Eastern Europe and the
Peiping regime in China, the American dream of recalling into being the lost
world of the 'twenties in which Japan, China, Germany, and Russia had apparently assumed their proper places in a peaceful world order. Because these
recurrent challenges have finally exceeded the capacity of Western Europe to
control, they have gradually forced the United States to the forefront of world
affairs. Locked in a massive struggle, partially political and partially ideological,
the United States, under idealists such as John Foster Dulles, while still allegedly
pursuing the transcendent goals of humanity, has thought less in terms of conciliation and more in terms of countering power to preserve the peace. Having
attempted for one long generation to conduct a successful diplomacy without
power, the nation's leadership finally arrived after World War II at the opposite pole of concentrating on power to the exclusion of diplomacy and other
conciliatory devices.

National greatness is determined as much by wisdom as by power. No writer
ever laid this charge before the American nation with greater cogency than did
Thomas Huxley: "I cannot say that I am in the slightest degree impressed by
your bigness, or your material resources as such. Size is not grandeur, and territory does not make a nation. The great issue, about which hangs a true sub-
limity and the terror of overhanging fate, is what are you going to do with all
these things?" To employ its power wisely a nation must learn from experience.

And that experience, if it is to be helpful (for precise situations seldom reoccur), must lie in the general concepts of diplomacy, power, national interest, and world society which determined the actual decisions and against which their results must then be measured. It is in such testing alone that nations grow in wisdom.

In this extensive search for significant readings I have benefited from the suggestions of many people, including a number of my graduate students at the University of Illinois. My indebtedness to Edward M. Bennett, Richard D. Burns, Marguerite Fallucco, Richard P. Mahany, Frederick B. Misse, and Arvarh E. Strickland is quite beyond measure. I am especially grateful also to the staff of the University of Illinois Library whose co-operation has always exceeded the call of duty. Betty Hampel aided in the preparation of the manuscript with her customary care. For remaining errors of judgment, interpretation, and fact I alone am responsible.

*Urbana, Illinois*                                                      NORMAN A. GRAEBNER
*October, 1963*

# Contents

# Ideas and Diplomacy

# I

## Evolution of the National Interest

Historians customarily begin any survey of the American diplomatic experience by stressing its uniqueness—a uniqueness embodied in the single word "isolationism." This tendency has the support of logic if not of fact. It appears totally reasonable that the English colonists should have wanted to elude the the radiating influence of European politics. They had shared the dangers of a long and usually terrifying ocean voyage to create a new civilization on the North American continent. They subsequently attributed their success in building a "New Zion" not only to the riches and opportunities afforded by an unexploited wilderness but also to the absence of war. Peace seemed essential for their uninterrupted expansion, and it was not to be jeopardized by involvement in the rivalries of Europe, which geographical separation had assuredly rendered unnecessary. When the French and Indian wars disturbed the tranquillity of the New World, resentful Americans, so the standard isolationist argument continues, viewed themselves as pawns of Europe's diplomacy. Eventually such infringements on their interests prompted them to seek political independence from England. This growing determination to escape Europe's quarrels was summed up well by John Adams in 1775 when he wrote: "[W]e ought to lay it down, as a first principle and maxim never to be forgotten, to maintain an entire neutrality in all future European wars." The Treaty of Paris, which in 1783 recognized the new Republic, was symbolic of both the final release from the aggressions, tyrannies, and rivalries of the Old World and the creation of a unique political, social, and moral order in the New.

American isolationism suggests a national diplomatic tradition at variance with that of the modern world. That American behavior in the external realm did not always follow the established pattern of European *Realpolitik* is demonstrated repeatedly by the record itself. Yet that divergence was always limited in nature and degree. Geographic isolation, for example, has been a lesser determinant than commercial empire in affairs among nations. This is amply illustrated by the fact that the American people were involved from the

3

eighteenth century onward—and not against their will—in every European war that ventured onto the Atlantic. Whatever differences from the European standard actually existed in American diplomatic practice hinged less on conceptual uniqueness than on the greater freedom of action permitted by the absence of contiguous nations which possessed the power to challenge the United States at every turn. The American people, moreover, inherited from Europe a diplomatic tradition, thoroughly established by experience and common sense, which stressed flexibility as the foundation of successful national policy. Washington's Farewell Address, with its emphasis on complete diplomatic independence from Europe, unencumbered by any ideological or political preferences, was a classic exposition of eighteenth-century diplomatic doctrine. Not even as a form of escapism did isolationism create national responses necessarily strange, for the nation, in attempting to hoard its energy by limiting its transatlantic commitments, pursued policies universally accepted by prudent statesmen. Thus to accentuate the uniqueness of the American diplomatic experience is to distort the record and to disregard the complexity of the concepts which governed that experience.

## II

At no time after the seventeenth century could the North American colonies escape the intellectual and diplomatic influence of the European state system. That system was dominated by five closely related and generally equal nations—Great Britain, France, Russia, Prussia, and Austria. Europe contained a larger number of secondary and lesser nations, including Turkey, which often played definable roles in the European balance of power, but the Big Five managed the system and determined its fundamental activities. What contributed to the success of this balancing system was both Europe's common culture and the concept of a common destiny which gave the nations a certain unity of outlook despite their continuing differences. G. F. von Martens, in his *Summary of the Law of Nations* (1795), stressed Europe's essential unity when he wrote that

> . . . the resemblance in manners and religion, the intercourse of commerce, the frequency of traders of all sorts, and the ties of blood between sovereigns, have so multiplied the relations between each particular state and the rest, that one may consider Europe (particularly the Christian states of it) as a society of nations and states, each of which has its laws, its customs, and its maxims, but which it cannot put in execution without observing a great deal of delicacy towards the rest of society.

Despite its many tensions, Europe was tied together by a common experience and common institutions. All member states in the European system shared similar diplomatic and economic practices, similar military organizations, and a group consciousness which gave all a common interest in the perpetuation of the balance of power structure itself.

In operation, the system sought to check the universal selfishness of men and nations with counterchecks composed of opposing combinations of power. The fundamental aim in preserving the balance was to ensure the survival of each individual state, for each nation was essential for the preservation of the system. Thus to a master diplomatist such as Metternich the perpetuation of the European state system was the ultimate goal of wise statesmanship. Metternich wrote in his *Memoirs*:

> Politics is the science of the vital interests of States in its widest meaning. Since, however, an isolated state no longer exists, and is found only in the annals of the heathen world . . . we must always view the society of states as the essential condition of the modern world. . . . The great axioms of political science proceed from the knowledge of the true political interests of all states; it is upon these general interests that rests the guarantee of their existence. . . . What characterizes the modern world and distinguishes it from the ancient is the tendency of states to draw near each other and to form a kind of social body based on the same principle as human society. . . . In the ancient world isolation and the practice of the most absolute selfishness without other restraint than that of prudence was the sum of politics. . . . Modern society on the other hand exhibits the application of the principle of solidarity and of the balance of power between states. . . . The establishing of international relations, on the basis of reciprocity under the guarantee of respect for acquired rights . . . constitutes in our time the essence of politics.

Nothing would destroy the system so completely as the predominance of one of its members. On the day that one nation became powerful enough to challenge all others combined, the system would cease to exist. Writers on the balance of power assumed that each nation would seek to enhance, if not to maximize, its power. Every member state, therefore, in its own interest and in the interest of the entire system, carried the obligation to prevent any one country from becoming too powerful.

European diplomatists recognized the movement of history, the rise and decline of national power and ambition. The constant change in the relationship of nations demanded the vigilance necessary to detect the tendencies within international society, to judge their consequences in terms of the general good, and, if necessary, to form those alliances which might preserve the balance. Diplomatic flexibility was of the essence, for, as Abbé de Pradt suggested, in any threat to the system it was imperative that "enemies come together for common defense, and allies momentarily separate for the same reason." There was no room in a balanced system for partiality; therefore the system was fundamentally amoral. Maintaining the equilibrium was more important than peace, pledges, treaties, or friendships. As Lord Brougham once observed: "All particular interests, prejudices, or partialities must be sacrificed to the higher interest . . . of uniting against oppression or against the measures which appear to place the security of all in jeopardy. No previous quarrel with any given state, no existing condition even of actual hostility, must be suffered to interfere with the imperative claims of the general security."

Lastly, the European state system required moderation. It was an eighteenth-century maxim that victors never crush an aggressor nation but rather permit it to play its necessary role in the general balance. Montesquieu once asserted that the "law of nations is naturally founded on this principle, that different nations ought in time of peace to do one another all the good they can and in time of war as little injury as possible, without prejudicing their real interest." The essential purpose of the balance of power system was to contain the power of nations within the bounds of moderation, never to annihilate the power of any state in the interest of stern justice. Within the limits imposed by this context each nation was free to pursue its own national interests.

## III

That fateful half-century from 1750 to 1800 was a period of trial and opportunity for the American people. Throughout most of that period American leaders pursued policies of involvement, not isolation, ever mindful of the close relationship between their prospective success in achieving American interests and the necessity of exploiting the rivalries of Europe. Only when they had gained a succession of positive goals in the New World did they identify their interests with complete diplomatic independence from the Old.

During the early eighteenth century the vast majority of English colonists in America, as faithful subjects of the British Empire, were content with imperial diplomatic policy. Their outlook was continental, and their search for opportunity and security was scarcely touched by British activity elsewhere, especially since the entire burden of that involvement was carried by English taxpayers. This general unawareness of European politics evaporated with the outbreak of the French and Indian wars. Suddenly it became clear to the seaboard colonies from Massachusetts to Virginia that the French, with their Indian allies, challenged their access to the continent as well as their traditional security. Following La Salle's overland journey of 1682 the French had built a series of posts which followed the arc of their claims through the Great Lakes country and down the Mississippi River to the Gulf of Mexico. To the English colonists, the inland empire, by charter rights, belonged to them; they regarded the French as intruders. The struggle for the wilderness was primarily an issue between the English colonies and the French in the New World. Not until its final stages did this contest become part of the world-wide imperial competition between the two great European rivals.

At Utrecht in 1713 the British ignored the colonial demands and permitted the French to maintain their control of the St. Lawrence and the Great Lakes. The two powers created an Indian buffer zone, which they soon penetrated with additional forts in preparation for an eventual showdown. The French established their key fort at Detroit in 1701, but added strategic Fort Niagara in 1720. New York, on its own initiative, countered almost immediately with the erection of Fort Oswego on Lake Ontario. The Indians divided sharply into pro-British and pro-French factions. The barrier was no longer a source of stability but rather a source of friction and strife. These bitter rivalries along the frontier created a violent reaction in New England, New York, and Virginia. To northern leaders, determined to secure their borders and control the fur trade, it had become essential to capture Quebec and break the French hold on the St. Lawrence and Great Lakes trading routes. For the Virginians the issue was one of title, for the French challenged their legal claims to the Ohio Valley.

To protect New England's interests on the Atlantic, Governor William Shirley of Massachusetts determined to dislodge the French from their position along the upper St. Lawrence. His immediate objective was Fort Louisbourg on Cape Breton Island at the mouth of the St. Lawrence, a powerful fortress from which the French conducted raids on British shipping. The fortress, moreover, commanded the entrance to the St. Lawrence Valley. With the renewal of war Shirley acted swiftly. He captured the fort in 1745 and made preparations for an immediate assault on Quebec. It appeared that New England at last had reached the point of driving France from the North American continent. Shirley wrote from Louisbourg in October 1745: "The reduction of Canada seems to be the most effectual means of securing . . . not only Nova Scotia . . . but the whole northern continent as far back as the French settlements on the . . . Mississippi, which are about 2,000 miles distance from Canada. . . ." Shirley's hopes collapsed when the British refused to underwrite his program and, instead, returned Louisbourg to France. Britain was not prepared to dispossess the French of their North American empire merely to satisfy the interests of her colonies.

Meanwhile the leaders of Pennsylvania and Virginia pressed the British for the establishment of forts in the Ohio Valley. In 1751 the Virginia planter Lewis Burwell complained to the Board of Trade in London that occupancy alone could convey the right of ownership and that the British government, therefore, should open up the trans-Appalachian lands for settlement to prevent their acquisition by the French. Benjamin Franklin, the key spokesman for Pennsylvania's interests, added his own warning. If England failed to establish colonies in the Ohio Valley, he wrote,

> . . . [the French] will both in time of peace and war (as they have always done against New England) set the Indians on to harass our frontiers, kill and scalp our people, and drive in the advanced settlers; and so, in preventing our obtaining more subsistence by cultivating of new lands, they discourage our marriages, and keep our people from increasing. . . .

Another American imperialist, Robert Livingston of New York, warned the British that the colonies were an inexhaustible source of national wealth and "if suffered to fall into the hands of the French, such will be the accession to their already extended commerce and marine strength, that Great Britain must not only lose her former lustre, but, dreadful even in thought! cease to be any longer an independent power." For, declared Livingston, if France gained control of the seas she could reduce all Europe to her control. The Reverend

Jonathan Mayhew in 1754 expressed the typical preferences of the English colonists for British institutions when he urged his fellow countrymen to protect their way of life against the danger of French domination:

> And what horrid scene is this, which restless, roving fancy, or something of an higher nature, presents to me, and so chills my blood! Do I behold these territories of freedom, become the prey of arbitrary power? . . . Do I see a protestant, there, stealing a look at his bible, and being tak[en] in the fact, punished like a felon! . . . Do I see all liberty, property, religion, happiness, changed, or rather transubstantiated, into slavery, poverty, superstition, wretchedness!

After 1750, the French, conscious of the colonial threat to their empire, began to prepare for the inescapable British-American assault on their New World possessions. American traders had established a post on the Great Miami, which the French destroyed in 1751. Then, in 1754, the French moved south from Lake Erie to the forks of the Ohio to strengthen their claims to the Ohio watershed. Virginia accepted the challenge by dispatching George Washington and a small military force to argue the French into retreat. Instead, the French drove Washington and his men from the vicinity. But this threat to the empire in America was too patent to be ignored by the London government. It sent General Braddock with a British army to drive the French from the Ohio Valley. French ambition, when it encompassed the Ohio Valley, had overreached what the British could tolerate. This at last forced the British to consider the American program. During the six subsequent years of fighting in America, which culminated with the recapture of Louisbourg in 1758 and the fall of Quebec in 1760, American spokesmen endeavored to convince the British officials that England's imperial interests lay in the removal of the French from the North American continent. No one carried the argument as far as Franklin did. (*Reading No. 1.*)

This time the American imperialists had their way. The Treaty of Paris marked the final triumph of the first major involvement of the American people in external affairs. With good reason the war years from 1754 to 1760 provoked an unprecedented burst of good will and patriotism toward the British Empire. Franklin expressed the feeling well when he wrote in 1760:

> No one can more sincerely rejoice than I do, on the reduction of Canada; and this not merely as I am a colonist, but as I am a Briton. I have long been of [the] opinion, that the foundations of the future grandeur and stability of the British empire lie in America; and though, like other foundations, they are low and little seen, they are nevertheless, broad and strong enough to support the greatest political structure human wisdom ever erected. . . . All the country from the St. Lawrence to the Mississippi will in another century be filled with British people. Britain itself will become vastly more populous, by the immense increase of its commerce; the Atlantic sea will be covered with your trading ships; and your naval power, then continually in-

creasing, will extend your influence round the whole globe, and awe the world!

### IV

Until 1763 the Empire had served the mutual interests of Britain and her American colonies. With a fair distribution of the financial burden required to maintain the imperial structure and a general relaxation of those commercial policies which might have crippled American trade, membership in the British Empire had been far from onerous. Britain, in the process of defeating the French, however, had overextended herself so enormously that her new postwar obligations multiplied the burdens of maintaining her world-wide commitments. To guarantee the Indians the possession of their lands in payment for their wartime support, the British government established the notorious Proclamation Line of 1763, despite the obvious antagonism that such a restriction would create in America. To relieve the British taxpayers and to control the empire commerce for the benefit of British merchants, investors, and processors, the British Parliament, between 1764 and 1767, passed such regulatory and revenue measures as the Sugar Act, the Stamp Act, and the Townshend Act. Whether these acts were fair was hardly the issue. For a people accustomed to the benefits of membership in the British Empire at relatively little cost to themselves, any controls or taxes were dangerous precedents, especially when enacted by Parliament. Their appeals to the principles of charter and natural rights, plus their occasional rioting to escape the new restrictions, were not without effect. After 1767 most British controls were lifted and the profitable empire commerce returned to its established pattern.

Refusing to pay for the recent war which had served their interests so well, spokesmen for the colonial cause now charged that it has been a British war fought for British, not American, interests. Thus Franklin could declare before a committee of the House of Commons in 1766:

> We had . . . no particular concern or interest in that dispute. As to the Ohio, the contest there began about your right of trading in the Indian country, a right you had by the Treaty of Utrecht, which the French infringed. . . . they took a fort which a company of your merchants . . . had erected there to secure that trade. Braddock was sent with an army to retake the fort . . . and to protect your trade. It was not until after his defeat that the colonies were attacked. They were before in perfect peace with both French and Indians.

Daniel Dulany, another vigorous partisan in the colonial assault on Parliament, raised the same issue of British motivation in the great war for empire: "An *American*, without justly incurring the imputation of ingratitude, may doubt, whether some other motive, besides pure generosity, did not prompt the *British Nation* to engage in the defense of the colonies." Britain had fought the French in America, Dulany added, to protect her own colonies because she needed them for her own prosperity and independence. John Dickinson asserted in his *Letters from a Farmer in Pennsylvania* (1768) that the war was purely an English war, fought for the selfish purpose of imperial expansion, and therefore of no concern to the colonies. There was a touch of irony in this new spirit of independence and resistance, for the feeling of American security from which it sprung was dependent upon the removal of France from Canada. No one saw the British dilemma more clearly than did Thomas Hutchinson, the loyal governor of Massachusetts Bay, when he wrote to the Earl of Dartmouth late in 1773: "Before the peace [of Paris] I thought nothing so much to be desired as the cession of Canada. I am now convinced that if it had remained to the French none of the spirit of opposition to the Mother Country would have yet appeared & I think the effect of it [the cession of Canada] worse than all we had to fear from the French or Indians."

Britain's coercion of Massachusetts Bay in 1774, in retaliation for the destruction of East India Company tea in Boston harbor, raised anew and in increasingly strident form the issue of colonial rights. The atmosphere became even more charged when fighting broke out in the environs of Boston. In the crisis thoughtful Americans were trapped between their traditional and willing reliance on Britain and their determination to destroy the control of Parliament over the colonies. Thomas Jefferson, writing to John Randolph in August 1775, saw the issue clearly. "I would rather," he admitted, "be in dependence on Great Britain, properly limited, than on any nation upon earth. . . . But I am one of those too who rather than submit to the right of legislating for us assumed by the British parliament . . . would lend my hand to sink the whole island in the ocean."

By 1776 the American people were submerged in a massive search for their true interests in a faltering transatlantic relationship. At one extreme, conservative men of wealth and distinction, great merchants and landowners especially, identified their interests solely with membership in the British Empire. Others—the true eighteenth-century isolationists—had little interest in imperial affairs, for nowhere did British policy touch their interests or their sentiments directly. If they vaguely resented British restrictions, they were concerned only with the end of removing the immediate problem, not with the means required to establish a more stable and satisfactory relationship with England. A third group, unclear as to its ultimate objectives, recognized the need of force to gain even the recognition of their rights by the London government. To that end they were willing to seek actively the support of Europe, especially that of France. Even a negotiated compromise would require some American military successes. The final group, powerfully led but numerically weak, were convinced that British and American interests had become totally incompatible. For them the American interest lay in independence, and they were willing to pay any price, even the involvement of Europe in war, to achieve that goal. It was left for Thomas Paine, in his *Common Sense,* to argue with force and conviction the second major interest of the American people in the eighteenth century—independence from the British Empire. (*Reading No. 2.*) After January 1776 the movement for independence began to sweep the more conservative forces aside.

V

Independence, like the earlier removal of the French from Canada, hinged on the European balance of power as it existed in the late eighteenth century. So stupendous had been British success in the wars which culminated in the Treaty of Paris that her unprecedented dominance in European affairs would of necessity initiate the formation of an opposing coalition to right the balance. American leaders understood the European system perfectly and thus quite naturally looked to the continent for support. Nor were they disappointed. Agents of the French Foreign Office had reported the tensions between England and her New World colonies. At the same time the Count de Vergennes, the able and energetic French Minister, was determined to employ all means at hand to retrieve the fallen glory of the French monarchy. "The deplorable peace of 1763," he reminded his king, "the partition of Poland, and in fact, other causes equally disastrous, have struck the greatest blows to the respect for your crown." The restoration of French prestige required, above all, the humiliation of England. To achieve this Vergennes was eager to aid the colonies in their opposition to the British government. Yet France and England in the mid-'seventies were formally at peace. France could not with prudence break the peace without the assurance that she had in America a staunch and effective ally. Perhaps no American saw more clearly than John Adams the importance of the Anglo-French rivalry for the colonial cause. In his autobiography Adams analyzed in detail the relationship of America to the European balance of power:

> Some gentlemen doubted of the sentiments of France; thought she would frown upon us as rebels, and be afraid to countenance the example I replied to those gentlemen, that I apprehended they had not attended to the relative situation of France and England; that it was the unquestionable interest of France that the British Continental Colonies should be independent; that Britain, by the conquest of Canada and her naval triumphs during the last war, and by her vast possessions in America and the East Indies, was exalted to a height of power and pre-ëminence that France must envy and could not endure. But there was much more than pride and jealousy in the case. Her rank, her consideration in Europe, and even her safety and independence, were at stake. . . . that interest could not lie; that the interest of France was so obvious, and her motives so cogent, that nothing but a judicial infatuation of her councils could restrain her from embracing us; that our negotiations with France ought, however, to be conducted with great caution, and with all the foresight we could possibly obtain; that we ought not to enter into any alliance with her, which should entangle us in any future wars in Europe; that we ought to lay it down, as a first principle and maxim never to be forgotten, to maintain an entire neutrality in all future European wars; that it never could be our interest to unite with France in the destruction of England, or in any measures to break her spirit, or reduce her to a situation in which

she could not support her independence. On the other hand, it could never be our duty to unite with Britain in too great a humiliation of France, that our real, if not our nominal, independence, would consist in our neutrality. . . . The opening of American trade to her [France], would be a vast resource for her commerce and naval power, and a great assistance to her in protecting her East and West India possessions, as well as her fisheries; but the bare dismemberment of the British empire would be to her an incalculable security and benefit, worth more than all the exertions we should require of her, even if it should draw her into another eight or ten years' war.

Colonial leaders such as Adams who favored foreign help, whether to secure independence or their rights as Englishmen, moved slowly, for it was obvious that aid would require some commitment to Europe without the benefit of British power and counsel. Adams's views were characteristic of American hesitancy. He recognized the French interest in the American cause, but he believed the colonies so lacking in coercive power that he doubted if they could negotiate and sustain a favorable agreement with a nation as powerful as France. In March 1776 he argued for a commercial treaty whereby the colonies might exchange tobacco, rice, indigo, and fur for such military stores as arms, saltpeter, powder, and steel. But Adams continued to oppose an alliance. Even if France helped the Americans to achieve their independence, he warned, she would soon desert them to the British under conditions far less acceptable than those which the American people had enjoyed as members of the British Empire.

Richard Henry Lee, the Virginia planter, represented a more venturesome approach to Europe. He wrote to a fellow Virginian, Patrick Henry, that only "by a timely alliance with proper and willing powers in Europe" could the colonial leaders "secure America from the despotic aims of the British Court." He pointed out with considerable realism, however, that no European power would extend special favors to the American people as long as they regarded themselves members of the British Empire. *"It is not choice then,"* he wrote to Landon Carter on June 2, 1776, *"but necessity that calls for Independence, as the only means by which foreign Alliance can be obtained. . . ."* Lee's famous independence resolution, offered to the Continental Congress on June 7, included the charge that it forthwith "take the most effectual measures for forming foreign alliances." On July 2 the Congress declared the United States an independent nation, but Adams, in the Plan of 1776 which followed in September, managed again to confine American objectives in Europe to military assistance and free commercial arrangements.

Slowly the pressure of necessity undermined the American colonial mentality and drove the new nation toward an active participation in European affairs. In the Plan of 1776 the United States asked France to support independence openly and thus run the risk of war in exchange for American trade and the mere promise that, should England declare war on France, the United States would not assist Britain with men, money, or ships. In October, Congress selected three men, including Franklin, to represent the United States in France. It instructed them to remind the French government of the limited strength and resources of the United States and "to press for the immediate and explicit declaration of France in our Favour, upon a Suggestion that a Re-union with Great Britain may be the Consequence of a delay." By the end of the year Congress recognized at last the need of a stronger American commitment to France. In its instructions of December 30, 1776, it authorized the American commissioners "to make such tenders to France and Spain as they hope will prevent any longer delay of an event that is judged so essential to the well-being of North America." Meanwhile the commissioners, cognizant of the need for stronger guarantees to France, offered, in exchange for direct French involvement in the war against England, to sustain the full military exertion of the United States until the conclusion of the war. The French interest in an American military victory was clear, and when Vergennes was convinced by the decisive American victory at Saratoga in 1777 that the United States was a potentially successful ally, he pushed Franklin for an alliance. (*Reading No. 3.*) The two nations signed treaties of commerce and alliance on February 6, 1778. Article II of the alliance treaty declared that the "essential and direct End of the present defensive alliance is to maintain effectually the liberty, Sovereignty, and independence absolute and unlimited of the said United States, as well as in Matters of Gouvernement as of commerce."

In large measure the French alliance assured the triumph of the American interest in independence. But the prospect of victory created a new interest for the United States not shared by the French at all. What were to be the boundaries of the new nation? Would the French and Americans together subjugate Canada and annex it to the United States? Some Americans predicted that a British Canada would be a source of constant friction. George Mason wrote to Richard Henry Lee in July 1778 that if "G. Britain possesses Canada & west Florida, she will be continually setting the Indians upon us, & while she holds the harbours of Augustine & Halifax, especially the latter, we shall not be able to protect our trade or coasts from her depredations; at least for many years to come. . . ." Franklin knew that France would not underwrite such a broad objective, but he attempted to convince the British government privately that a cession of Canada would re-establish the friendship between England and her former colonies and create the basis for a solid peace. Britain would eventually pay a price to break the United States-French Alliance, but not one that extensive.

In its instructions of August 14, 1779, Congress defined the boundaries of the United States to be incorporated in any future peace treaty with England. (*Reading No. 4.*) These proposals included the hinterland extending northward into the Great Lakes and westward to the Mississippi. France had little interest in the nation's future boundaries. Spain, allied to France but not to the United States, dreaded the creation of an independent United States which touched the Spanish holdings in the southwest. Vergennes was forced to carry the burden of Spanish fears. In August 1779 he dispatched the Chevalier de la Luzerne to Philadelphia to argue Congress into accepting either the Alleghenies or some compromise line between the mountains and the Mississippi as the future boundaries of the United States. Eventually Congress gave in, but it mattered little. For Franklin and his colleagues in Paris were in complete control of American diplomacy. Franklin continued to press the British government for Nova Scotia and Canada. Lord Shelburne, the British Minister, countered with the cession of all British claims west of the mountains to the Mississippi. Franklin thereupon terminated the French and Spanish pressures for reduced boundaries by accepting the British offer. This permitted Franklin, in the final negotiations, to present Vergennes with a *fait accompli*. Pursuing limited and concrete objectives, Franklin thus secured the American interest in the Mississippi boundary as well as the interest in independence itself.

## VI

With the Treaty of Paris of 1783 the United States entered the family of nations as an independent and sovereign state. Independence did not bring into being a strong, determined nation agreed on its objectives and the means to accomplish them. The country's population scarcely reached three million; it had no army or navy worthy of the name or the national income required to create them. The government under the Articles of Confederation, adopted in 1781, was hardly designed to achieve national efficiency and purpose. The states, in full command of the essential powers of commerce and taxation, tended to reduce the United States to a league of sovereigns. So negligible was the concern for national activity that only with difficulty could Congress assemble a quorum to ratify the treaty which conveyed independence. There was no central authority which could concentrate and give direction to the nation's limited resources. With apathy and bankruptcy threatening a national government which lacked the powers of coercion, the United States was in no position to command respect abroad.

It mattered little to Europeans whether the United States succeeded or failed. Monarchs and aristocrats, if not disinterested, were generally apprehensive of the new experiment in democracy. If too successful, it could, by the force of its example, topple thrones in Europe. To thoughtful Spaniards, fearful for the future of Spain's North American empire, the new nation was a potential monster which would revolutionize the balance of power in the New World. Britain and France were committed to the independence but not to the success of the United States. The French alliance appeared to convey sufficient guarantees and mutual advantages that Shelburne, in his negotiations with Franklin, had tried to terminate the arrangement as a threat to British interests. His failure was of no significance, for after the achievement of American independence, the only question on which the French and Americans really agreed, the alliance was a dead issue. After 1783 the United States quickly returned to its accustomed commercial relationships with England. British merchants and financiers, offering credit and marketing facilities with which the French could not compete, began to re-create a genuine *rapprochement* between England and her former colonies. In this relationship lay the real riches of commerce. The

French alliance, built originally on the prospects of trade, now lost its reason for existence. The French government, moreover, was not inclined during the 'eighties to support the treaty claims of the United States against Britain and Spain. Thomas Jefferson in Paris placed the issues of the British posts and the fur trade before Vergennes. He provoked no reaction except indifference. Alliances have meaning only to the extent that they represent clearly demonstrable mutual interests, and after 1783 those mutual interests between France and the United States were nowhere in evidence.

Most problems involved in establishing the nation's diplomatic position in the European world fell heavily on the shoulders of John Adams, who, after the spring of 1785, represented the United States as minister to London. His subsequent dispatches revealed an accurate judgment of the American dilemma. His acceptance, in June 1785, at the Court of St. James's was propitious. (*Reading No. 5.*) But at the same time Adams was conscious of his lack of coercive power in forcing more equitable treaty agreements from the British government. He criticized the New England merchants for their willingness to conform to British regulations and realized from the beginning of his mission that the American answer lay primarily in a strong central government. (*Reading No. 6.*) While in London, Adams was oppressed by the problem of the Tripoli pirates, and engaged in a vigorous correspondence with Jefferson, then in Paris, over the issue. Both men were concerned with the necessity of protecting American commerce in the Atlantic and the Mediterranean; they disagreed over the means. Adams favored bribery in lieu of any Congressional determination to destroy the pirates through force; Jefferson saw no alternative to continued submission but war itself. (*Reading No. 7.*)

After 1785 the Articles of Confederation were under general fire from American conservatives who, like John Adams, believed that the interests of the nation would be better served by a more powerful central authority. The discord at the Constitutional Convention of 1787 was so great that the sessions were conducted in profound secrecy. The resulting Constitution was the product of compromise. Because of its vagueness, it could be subjected to an infinite variety of interpretations. But to Alexander Hamilton, whose notions regarding society and government dominated Federalist thought, the Constitution was the agency for creating the leviathan state demanded by his unlimited vision of the nation's potentiality for economic greatness. His domestic program as Secretary of the Treasury was designed to promote a powerful capitalistic order which, in turn, would create national power. To build the nation's capital fund he favored tariffs, the National Bank, and the full use of the commerce and taxing powers now centered in the Federal government. To Hamilton, the National Bank, created in 1791, by encouraging the country's domestic trade and investment, would "have the most beneficial influence upon its future commerce, and be a source of national wealth and strength."

For Hamilton it was the means that mattered—the wielding of power through a consolidated governmental system. The ends of policy comprised wealth, public and private. Like Adams, Hamilton had little faith in ideals. For these men, villainy, corruption, ambition, avarice, intrigue, and revenge were interwoven in all human affairs. To control such tendencies within mankind required a vast system of checks and balances which operated within government and law. Nor had these Federalist philosophers any greater interest in equality or democracy. For them there existed an eternal aristocracy among men. "The world is, always has been, and ever will be governed by it," wrote Adams. "All that policy and legislation can do is to check force by force." Passions were universal, and democracies were no less selfish or avaricious than monarchies. Unless checked with counterforce they would produce everywhere the same unfortunate results. In a world geared to the use of force, only as a consolidated nation, wielding adequate power, could the United States establish its interest successfully beyond its own shores. "Let the thirteen states," Hamilton exhorted, ". . . concur in erecting one great American system, superior to the control of all transatlantic force or influence, and able to dictate the terms of connection between the old and the new world!" In *The Federalist* Hamilton reminded his readers of the persistence of force in international affairs and suggested the means necessary to defend the nation's commercial and security interests in a world of everlasting conflict. (*Reading No. 8.*)

After 1792 the French Revolution threatened again to involve the United States in the vicissitudes of European politics. The product of recent revolution itself, the United States was in no position to question the legitimacy of other governments. In November 1792 Secretary of State Thomas Jefferson rationalized the recognition of the French revolutionary government and thus established the pattern of American policy. (*Reading No. 9.*) When France and England went to war in 1793, the nation divided immediately between those who favored a pro-French involvement on the side of France and those who preferred a pro-British policy of official neutrality. President Washington, in April, submitted a circular to his cabinet for advice. Jefferson argued that the United States was obligated by the alliance treaty to support France. (*Reading No. 10.*) Hamilton retorted that the United States had no obligation to support the French revolutionary government. When Washington's proclamation of official neutrality provoked the condemnation of the powerful pro-French elements in the country, Hamilton rushed to the defense of the administration with his famous "Pacificus" papers. (*Reading No. 11.*) James Madison, leader of the anti-Federalist forces in Congress, responded with his "Helvidius" letters which raised the issue of Congressional *vs.* Executive leadership in foreign affairs. (*Reading No. 12.*) Hamilton, early in 1794, resolved the debate for the moment with his "Americanus" papers. (*Reading No. 13.*)

Hamilton's brilliance in arguing for the national interest has hardly been exceeded anywhere in the modern world. Unfortunately that brilliance was not matched by the wisdom of his actions. So completely did he identify American interests with British dominance on the high seas that when Jefferson in 1791 sought full satisfaction from the London government for infractions of the peace treaty, Hamilton undermined the Secretary of State by assuring the British minister privately that Jefferson did not speak for the administration. When the British defied American neutrality and restricted American trade in the West Indies, Hamilton again informed London officials that Jefferson's condemnation of British policy did not reflect American sentiment. Such meddling in diplomatic affairs finally prompted Jefferson to resign from the cabinet. When in 1794 Hamilton favored the mission of John Jay to England to wrest control of policy from the hands of an anti-British Congress, he again undermined the bargaining power of an official American diplomat by assuring a British agent that the United States would under no circumstances go to war against England. Hamilton's concept of the national interest, although narrowly conceived, did not serve the nation badly. Eventually he managed to defend even the unpopular Jay's Treaty with considerable success.

Washington's Farewell Address was the culminating declaration of diplomatic independence from Europe. Its accent was less on isolationism than on the flexibility which would permit the nation to pursue its interests whenever and wherever it saw them challenged. The clear substitution of independence from all nations for the principle of alliance served the British interest well and advanced further the *rapprochement* between the two nations. (*Reading No. 14.*) Adams, as President, emphasized the role of flexibility in keeping the nation at peace. When the insulting XYZ Affair precipitated a naval war against France in 1798, Adams would not permit Hamilton's allies to force him into a strong anti-French policy. Instead, he dispatched his own secret mission to France. After successful negotiations, his agent signed the convention of 1800 and thus secured an honorable peace with Napoleon. To Adams this comprised the outstanding achievement of his career. He once observed: "I desire no other inscription over my gravestone than: 'Here lies John Adams, who took upon himself the responsibility of the peace with France in the year of 1800.'"

# 1 | The American Interest in the Removal of France from the North American Continent, 1760 *

Perhaps no spokesman for mid-eighteenth century American interests detected more clearly the advantages that would accrue to the American people from the removal of French power from Canada and the Mississippi Valley than did Benjamin Franklin. Quite conscious of the fact that the removal of the French barrier to the westward expansion of the English colonists lay with British power and British diplomacy, Franklin sought to argue the London government into employing its diplomatic advantage after 1760 to acquire Canada from France. In a long pamphlet published during the French and Indian War, Franklin attacked the popular notion that Britain should retain Guadeloupe rather than Canada, especially since the American people, unless limited by the French in Canada, would become dangerous to England. By removing the French from the North American continent, Franklin assured the British, they would render France no great injury and would serve the cause of peace everywhere by eliminating the necessity of future costly wars for the defense of British interests in the New World.

✍

. . . *Canada,* in the hands of *Britain,* will endanger the kingdom of *France* as little as any other cession; and from its situation and circumstances cannot be hurtful to any other state. Rather, if peace be an advantage, this cession may be such to all *Europe.* The present war teaches us, that disputes arising in *America* may be an occasion of embroiling nations who have no concerns there. If the *French* remain in *Canada* and *Louisiana,* fix the boundaries as you will between us and them, we must border on each other for more than 1500 miles. The people that inhabit the frontiers are generally the refuse of both nations, often of the worst morals and the least discretion, remote from the eye, the prudence, and the restraint of government. Injuries are therefore frequently, in some part or other of so long a frontier, committed on both sides, resentment provoked, the colonies are first engaged, and then the mother countries. And two great nations can scarce be at war in *Europe,* but some other prince or state thinks it a convenient opportunity to revive some ancient claim, seize some advantage, obtain some territory, or enlarge some power at the expence of a neighbour. The flames of war once kindled, often spread far and wide, and the mischief is infinite. Happy it prov'd to both nations, that the *Dutch* were prevailed on finally to cede the *New Netherlands* (now the province of *New York*) to us at the peace of 1674; a peace that has ever since continued between us, but must have been frequently disturbed, if they had retained the

* Benjamin Franklin, "The Interest of Great Britain Considered with Regard to Her Colonies," *The Writings of Benjamin Franklin,* Albert Henry Smyth, ed. (New York, 1906), IV: 40–41, 44–6, 50–51, 53–4, 66, 69–73, 75–6, 81.

possession of that country, bordering several hundred miles on our colonies of *Pensilvania* westward, *Connecticut* and the *Massachusetts* eastward. Nor is it to be wondered at that people of different language, religion, and manners, should in those remote parts engage in frequent quarrels, when we find, that even the people of our own colonies have frequently been so exasperated against each other in their disputes about boundaries, as to proceed to open violence and bloodshed. . . .

The security desirable in America may be considered as of three kinds. 1. A security of possession, that the *French* shall not drive us out of the country. 2. A security of our planters from the inroads of savages, and the murders committed by them. 3. A security that the *British* nation shall not be obliged, on every new war, to repeat the immense expence occasion'd by this, to defend its possessions in *America*.

Forts in the most important passes, may, I acknowledge, be of use to obtain the first kind of security: but as those situations are far advanc'd beyond the inhabitants, the expence of maintaining and supplying the garrisons, will be very great even in time of full peace, and immense on every interruption of it; as it is easy for skulking parties of the enemy in such long roads thro' the woods, to intercept and cut off our convoys, unless guarded continually by great bodies of men.

The second kind of security will not be obtained by such forts, unless they were connected by a wall like that of *China,* from one end of our settlements to the other. . . .

As to the third kind of security, that we shall not, in a few years, have all we have now done to do over again in *America;* and be obliged to employ the same number of troops, and ships, at the same immense expence, to defend our possessions there, while we are in proportion weaken'd here: such forts, I think, cannot prevent this. During a peace, it is not to be doubted the *French,* who are adroit at fortifying, will likewise erect forts in the most advantageous places of the country we leave them, which will make it more difficult than ever to be reduc'd in case of another war. We know by the experience of this war, how extremely difficult it is to march an army through the *American* woods, with its necessary cannon and stores, sufficient to reduce a very slight fort. The accounts at the treasury will tell you what amazing sums we have necessarily spent in the expeditions against two very trifling forts, *Duquesne* and *Crown Point.* While the *French* retain their influence over the *Indians,* they can easily keep our long-extended frontier in continual alarm, by a very few of those people; and with a small number of regulars and militia, in such a country, we find they can keep an army of ours in full employ for several years. We therefore shall not need to be told by our colonies, that, if we leave *Canada,* however circumscrib'd, to the *French,* "we have done nothing"; we shall soon be made sensible ourselves of this truth, and to our cost. . . .

Now all the kinds of security we have mentioned are obtain'd by subduing and retaining *Canada.* Our present possessions in *America* are secur'd; our planters will no longer be massacred by the *Indians,* who depending absolutely on us for what are now become the necessaries of life to them, guns, powder, hatchets, knives, and clothing; and having no other *Europeans* near, that can either supply them, or instigate them against us; there is no doubt of their being always dispos'd, if we treat them with common justice, to live in perpetual peace with us. And with regard to *France,* she cannot, in case of another war, put us to the immense expence of defending that long-extended frontier; we shall then, as it were, have our backs against a wall in *America,* the seacoast will be easily protected by our superior naval power; and here "our own watchfulness and our own strength" will be properly, and cannot but be successfully employed. In this situation the force now employ'd in that part of the world, may be spar'd for any other service here or elsewhere; so that both the offensive and defensive strength of the *British* empire, on the whole, will be greatly increased. . . .

Our *North American* colonies are to be considered as the frontier of the *British* empire on that side. The frontier of any dominion being attack'd, it becomes not merely *"the cause"* of the people immediately affected, (the inhabitants of that frontier) but properly "the cause" of the whole body. Where the frontier people owe and pay obedience, there they have a right to look for protection. No political proposition is better established than this. It is therefore invidious to represent the "blood and treasure" spent in this war, as spent in "the cause of the colonies" only, and that they are "absurd and ungrateful" if they think we have done nothing unless we "make conquests for them," and reduce Canada to gratify their "vain ambition," &c. It will not be a conquest for them, nor gratify any vain ambition of theirs. It will be a conquest for the whole; and all our people will, in the increase of trade, and the ease of taxes, find the advantage of it.

Should we be obliged at any time to make a war for the protection of our commerce, and to secure the exportation of our manufactures, would it be fair to represent such a war merely as blood and treasure spent in the cause of the weavers of *Yorkshire, Norwich,* or the *West,* the cutlers of *Sheffield,* or the button-makers of *Birmingham?* I hope it will appear before I end these sheets, that if ever there was a *national war,* this is truly such a one: a war in which the interest of the *whole* nation is directly and fundamentally concerned. . . .

A reader of the remarks [against which Franklin's essay was directed] may be apt to say; "If this writer would have us restore *Canada* on principles of moderation, how can we, consistent with those principles, retain *Guadaloup,* which he represents of so much greater value!" I will endeavour to explain this, because by doing it I shall have an opportunity of showing the truth and good sense of the answer to the interested application I have just supposed. The author, then, is only *apparently* and not *really* inconsistent with himself. If we can obtain the credit of moderation by restoring *Canada,* it is well: but we should, however, restore it at all events; because it would not only be of no use to us, but "the possession of it (in his opinion) may in its consequences be dangerous." As how? Why, plainly, (at length it comes out) if the *French* are not left there to check the growth of our colonies, "they will extend themselves almost without bounds into the inland parts, and increase infinitely from all causes; becoming a numerous, hardy, *independent* people; possessed of a strong country, communicating little or not at all with *England,* living wholly on their own labour, and in process of time knowing little and inquiring little about the mother country."

In short, according to this writer, our present colonies are large enough and numerous enough; and the *French* ought to be left in *North America* to prevent their increase, lest they become not only *useless,* but *dangerous* to *Britain.* I agree with the gentleman, that, with *Canada* in our possession, our people in *America* will increase amazingly. I know, that their common rate of increase, where they are not molested by the enemy, is doubling their numbers every twenty-five years, by natural generation only; exclusive of the accession of foreigners. I think this increase continuing would probably, in a century more, make the number of *British* subjects on that side the water more numerous than they now are on this; but, I am far from entertaining, on that account, any fears of their becoming either *useless* or *dangerous* to us; and I look on those fears to be merely imaginary, and without any probable foundation. . . .

Our trade to the *West India* islands is undoubtedly a valuable one: but whatever is the amount of it, it has long been at a stand. Limited as our sugar planters are by the scantiness of territory, they cannot increase much beyond their present number; and this is an evil, as I shall show hereafter, that will be little helped by our keeping *Guadaloupe.*

The trade to our *Northern Colonies* is not only greater, but yearly increasing with the increase of the people: and even in a greater proportion, as the people increase in wealth and the ability of spending, as well as in numbers. . . .

In fact, the occasion for *English* goods in *North America,* and the inclination to have and use them, is, and must be for ages to come, much greater than the ability of the people to pay for them; they must therefore, as they now do, deny themselves many things they would otherwise chuse to have, or increase their industry to obtain them; and thus, if they should at any time manufacture some coarse article, which on account of its bulk or some other circumstance, cannot so well be brought to them from *Britain,* it only enables them the better to pay for finer goods that otherwise they could not indulge themselves in: So that the exports thither are not diminished by such manufacture, but rather increased. . . .

Thus much as to the apprehension of our colonies becoming *useless* to us. I shall next consider the other supposition, that their growth may render them *dangerous.* Of this, I own, I have not the least conception, when I consider that we have already fourteen separate governments on the maritime coast of the continent, and if we extend our settlements shall probably have as many more behind them on the inland side. Those we now have, are not only under different governors, but have different forms of government, different laws, different interests, and some of them different religious persuasions, and different manners.

Their jealousy of each other is so great, that however necessary an union of the colonies has long been, for their common defence and security against their enemies, and how sensible soever each colony has been of that necessity, yet they have never been able to effect such an union among themselves, nor even to agree in requesting the mother country to establish it for them. Nothing but the immediate command of the crown has been able to produce even the imperfect union, but lately seen there, of the forces of some colonies. If they could not agree to unite for their defence against the *French* and *Indians,* who were perpetually harassing their settlements, burning their villages, and murdering their people; can it reasonably be supposed there is any danger of their uniting against their own nation, which protects and encourages them, with which they have so many connections and ties of blood, interest and affection, and which 'tis well known they all love much more than they love one another?

In short, there are so many causes that must operate to prevent it, that I will venture to say, an union amongst them for such a purpose is not merely improbable, it is impossible; and if the union of the whole is impossible, the attempt of a part must be madness: as those colonies, that did not join the rebellion, would join the mother country in suppressing it. When I say such an union is impossible, I mean without the most grievous tyranny and oppression. People who have property in a country which they may lose, and privileges which they may endanger, are generally dispos'd to be quiet; and even to bear much, rather than hazard all. While the government is mild and just, while important civil and religious rights are secure, such subjects will be dutiful and obedient. The waves do not rise but when the winds blow.

What such an administration, as the Duke of *Alva's* in the *Netherlands,* might produce, I know not; but this I think I have a right to deem impossible. And yet there were two very manifest differences between that case and ours; and both are in our favour. The first, that *Spain* had already united the seventeen provinces under one visible government, tho' the states continued independent: The second, that the inhabitants of those provinces were of a nation, not only different from, but utterly unlike the *Spaniards.* Had the *Netherlands* been peopled from *Spain,* the worst of oppression had probably not provoked them to wish a separation of government. . . .

To this I shall only add the observation of *Machiavel,* in his *Prince,* that a government seldom long preserves its dominion over those who are foreigners to it; who, on the other hand, fall with great ease, and continue inseparably annexed to the government of their own nation, which he proves by the fate of the *English conquests in France.* Yet with all these disadvantages, so difficult is it to overturn an established government, that it was not without the assistance of *France* and *England,* that the *United Provinces* supported themselves: which teaches us, that if the visionary danger of independence in our colonies is to be feared, nothing is more likely to render it substantial than the neighbourhood of foreigners at enmity with the sovereign government, capable of giving either aid or an asylum, as the event shall require. . . .

We have already seen in what manner the *French* and their *Indians check the growth* of our colonies. 'Tis a modest word, this, *check,* for massacring men, women and children. The writer would, if he could, hide from himself as well as from the public, the horror arising from such a proposal, by couching it in general terms: 'tis no wonder he thought it a "subject not fit for discussion" in his letter, tho' he recommends it as "a point that should be the constant object of the minister's attention!"

But if *Canada* is restored on this principle, will not *Britain* be guilty of all the blood to be shed, all the murders to be committed, in order to check this dreaded growth of our own people? Will not this be telling the *French* in plain terms, that the horrid barbarities they perpetrate with their *Indians* on our colonists are agreeable to us; and that they need not apprehend the resentment of a government with whose views they so happily concur? Will not the colonies view it in this light: Will they have reason to consider themselves any longer as subjects and children, when they find their cruel enemies halloo'd upon them by the country from whence they sprung, the government that owes them protection as it requires their obedience? Is not this the most likely means of driving them into the arms of the *French,* who can invite them by an offer of that security their own government chuses not to afford them? . . .

I have before said I do not deny the utility of the conquest, or even of our future possession of *Guadalupe,* if not bought too dear. The trade of the *West Indies* is one of our most valuable trades. Our possessions there deserve our greatest care and attention. So do those of *North America.* I shall not enter into the invidious task of comparing their due estimation. It would be a very long and a very disagreeable one, to run through every thing material on this head. It is enough to our present point, if I have shown, that the value of *North America* is capable of an immense increase, by an acquisition and measures, that must necessarily have an effect the direct contrary of what we have been industriously taught to fear; and that *Guadalupe* is, in point of advantage, but a very small addition to our *West India* possessions, rendered many ways less valuable to us, than it is to the *French,* who will probably set more value upon it than upon a country that is much more valuable to us than to them. . . .

## 2 | The American Interest in Independence, 1776 *

That spirit of loyalty toward the British Empire, provoked by the removal of the French threat in 1763, was dissipated during the decade which followed because of the growing conflict between England and her American colonies over matters of trade and investment. As this conflict approached its climax in 1774, American leaders disagreed violently on the central issue of whether the American interest lay in securing the recognition of American rights from the

* *The Life and Works of Thomas Paine,* William M. Van der Weyde, ed. (10 vols., New Rochelle, N. Y., 1925) II: 93–182.

London government or in complete independence from England. Thomas
Paine, an English journalist who arrived in Philadelphia in November 1774
with a letter of introduction from Benjamin Franklin, grasped the fundamental
issue confronting the American people. Paine was editor of the *Pennsylvania
Magazine* when war broke out in the environs of Boston in 1775. For him it
was imperative that the colonists fight for their independence, not their rights.
This cause he argued eloquently in *Common Sense,* published in January 1776.

✍

. . . Volumes have been written on the subject of the struggle between
England and America. Men of all ranks have embarked in the controversy,
from different motives, and with various designs; but all have been ineffectual,
and the period of debate is closed. Arms as the last resource decide the contest;
the appeal was the choice of the King, and the Continent has accepted the
challenge. . . .

The Sun never shined on a cause of greater worth. 'Tis not the affair of a
City, a County, a Province, or a Kingdom; but of a Continent—of at least one
eighth part of the habitable Globe. 'Tis not the concern of a day, a year, or
an age; posterity are virtually involved in the contest, and will be more or less
affected even to the end of time by the proceedings now. Now is the seed-time
of Continental union, faith, and honor. The least fracture now will be like a
name engraved with the point of a pin on the tender rind of a young oak; the
wound would enlarge with the tree, and posterity read it in full grown characters.

By referring the matter from argument to arms, a new era for politics is
struck—a new method of thinking hath arisen. All plans, proposals, *etc.*, prior
to the nineteenth of April, *i.e.*, to the commencement of hostilities [at Lexing-
ton], are like the almanacs of the last year; which though proper then, are
superseded and useless now. Whatever was advanced by the advocates on either
side of the question then, terminated in one and the same point, *viz.*, a union
with Great Britain; the only difference between the parties was the method of
effecting it; the one proposing force, the other friendship; but it hath so far
happened that the first hath failed, and the second hath withdrawn her influence.

As much hath been said of the advantages of reconciliation, which, like an
agreeable dream, hath passed away and left us as we were, it is but right that
we should examine the contrary side of the argument, and inquire into some
of the many material injuries which these Colonies sustain, and always will sustain, by being connected with and dependent on Great Britain. To examine
that connection and dependence, on the principles of nature and common
sense, to see what we have to trust to, if separated, and what we are to expect,
if dependent.

I have heard it asserted by some, that as America has flourished under her
former connection with Great Britain, the same connection is necessary towards
her future happiness, and will always have the same effect. Nothing can be more

fallacious than this kind of argument. We may as well assert that because a child has thrived upon milk, that it is never to have meat, or that the first twenty years of our lives is to become a precedent for the next twenty. But even this is admitting more than is true; for I answer roundly, that America would have flourished as much, and probably much more, had no European power taken any notice of her. The commerce by which she hath enriched herself are the necessaries of life, and will always have a market while eating is the custom of Europe.

But she has protected us, say some. That she hath engrossed us is true, and defended the Continent at our expense as well as her own, is admitted; and she would have defended Turkey from the same motive, *viz.,* for the sake of trade and dominion.

Alas! we have been long led away by ancient prejudices and made large sacrifices to superstition. We have boasted the protection of Great Britain, without considering that her motive was *interest* not *attachment;* and that she did not protect us from *our enemies* on *our account;* but from *her enemies* on *her own account,* from those who had no quarrel with us on any *other account,* and who will always be our enemies on the *same account.* Let Britain wave her pretensions to the Continent, or the Continent throw off the dependence, and we should be at peace with France and Spain, were they at war with Britain. The miseries of Hanover's last war ought to warn us against connections.

It hath lately been asserted in parliament that the Colonies have no relation to each other but through the Parent Country, *i.e.,* that Pennsylvania and the Jerseys, and so on for the rest, are sister Colonies by the way of England; this is certainly a very roundabout way of proving relationship, but it is the nearest and only true way of proving enmity—or enemyship, if I may so call it. France and Spain never were, nor perhaps ever will be, our enemies as *Americans,* but as our being the *subjects of Great Britain.* . . .

Much hath been said of the united strength of Britain and the Colonies, that in conjunction they might bid defiance to the world: But this is mere presumption; the fate of war is uncertain, neither do the expressions mean any thing; for this continent would never suffer itself to be drained of inhabitants, to support the British arms in either Asia, Africa, or Europe.

Besides, what have we to do with setting the world at defiance? Our plan is commerce, and that, well attended to, will secure us the peace and friendship of all Europe; because it is the interest of all Europe to have America a free port. Her trade will always be a protection, and her barrenness of gold and silver secure her from invaders.

I challenge the warmest advocate for reconciliation to show a single advantage that this continent can reap by being connected with Great Britain. I repeat the challenge; not a single advantage is derived. Our corn will fetch its price in any market in Europe, and our imported goods must be paid for, buy them where we will.

But the injuries and disadvantages which we sustain by that connection are without number; and our duty to mankind at large, as well as to ourselves, instruct us to renounce the alliance: because, any submission to, or dependence on, Great Britain, tends directly to involve this Continent in European wars and quarrels, and set us at variance with nations who would otherwise seek our friendship, and against whom we have neither anger nor complaint. As Europe is our market for trade, we ought to form no partial connection with any part of it. It is the true interest of America to steer clear of European contentions, which she never can do while, by her dependence on Britain, she is made the makeweight in the scale of British politics.

Europe is too thickly planted with Kingdoms to be long at peace, and whenever a war breaks out between England and any foreign power, the trade of America goes to ruin, *because of her connection with Britain*. The next war may not turn out like the last, and should it not, the advocates for reconciliation now will be wishing for separation then, because neutrality in that case would be a safer convoy than a man of war. Everything that is right or reasonable pleads for separation. The blood of the slain, the weeping voice of nature cries, 'Tis Time To Part. Even the distance at which the Almightly hath placed England and America is a strong and natural proof that the authority of the one over the other was never the design of Heaven. The time likewise at which the Continent was discovered, adds weight to the argument, and the manner in which it was peopled increases the force of it. The Reformation was preceded by the discovery of America: As if the Almighty graciously meant to open a sanctuary to the persecuted in future years, when home should afford neither friendship nor safety.

The authority of Great Britain over this continent is a form of government which, sooner or later, must have an end: And a serious mind can draw no true pleasure by looking forward, under the painful and positive conviction that what he calls "the present constitution" is merely temporary. As parents, we can have no joy, knowing that this government is not sufficiently lasting to insure any thing which we may bequeath to posterity: And by a plain method of argument, as we are running the next generation into debt, we ought to do the work of it, otherwise we use them meanly and pitifully. In order to discover the line of our duty rightly, we should take our children in our hand, and fix our station a few years farther into life; that eminence will present a prospect which a few present fears and prejudices conceal from our sight. . . .

As to government matters, 'tis not in the power of Britain to do this continent justice: the business of it will soon be too weighty and intricate to be managed with any tolerable degree of convenience by a power so distant from us, and so very ignorant of us; for if they cannot conquer us, they cannot govern us. To be always running three or four thousand miles with a tale or a petition, waiting four or five months for an answer, which, when obtained, requires five or six more to explain it in, will in a few years be looked upon as folly and childishness. There was a time when it was proper, and there is a proper time for it to cease.

Small islands not capable of protecting themselves are the proper objects for government to take under their care; but there is something absurd in supposing a Continent to be perpetually governed by an island. In no instance hath nature made the satellite larger than its primary planet; and as England and

America, with respect to each other, reverse the common order of nature, it is evident that they belong to different systems. England to Europe: America to itself.

I am not induced by motives of pride, party, or resentment to espouse the doctrine of separation and independence; I am clearly, positively, and conscientiously persuaded that it is the true interest of this Continent to be so; that everything short of *that* is mere patchwork, that it can afford no lasting felicity—that it is leaving the sword to our children, and shrinking back at a time when a little more, a little further, would have rendered this Continent the glory of the earth. . . .

## 3 | The French Interest in American Independence, 1778 *

Having identified American purpose with independence, the Revolutionary leaders could make that purpose effective only with the support of one of the major nations of Europe. Fortunately for the United States, the French government recognized the interest of France in the independence of the new Republic. This interest in supporting the American cause, reflected in the treaties of alliance and commerce dated February 6, 1778, was rationalized clearly in a Memorandum of the French Foreign Ministry dated January 13, 1778, advocating French support for the American cause.

✍

The quarrel which exists between England and the Colonies of North America is as important to France as to Great Britain, and its issue will have equal influence on the reputation and power of those two Crowns. It is, therefore, essential that France should decide upon and fix the policy it is advisable she should adopt in such a conjuncture.

The Americans have been struggling for the last three years against the efforts of Great Britain, and they have up to the present maintained a sort of superiority; but the war which they wage fatigues and exhausts them, and must necessarily weary the people and awaken in them a desire for repose.

England, for her part, crushed by the expenditure occasioned by this same war, and convinced of the impossibility of reducing the Colonies, is occupied with the means of re-establishing peace. With this view she is taking the most urgent and animated steps with the Deputies from Congress, and it is natural that the United States should at last decide to listen to their proposals.

* Quoted in Edward S. Corwin, *French Policy and the American Alliance of 1778* (Princeton, N.J., 1916), 398–403. Reprinted by permission of Princeton University Press.

In this state of affairs it is desirable to examine what course it is proper for France to take.

There exist two courses only,—that of abandoning the Colonies, and that of supporting them.

If we abandon them, England will take advantage of it by making a reconciliation, and in that case she will either preserve her supremacy wholly or partially, or she will gain an ally. Now it is known that she is disposed to sacrifice that supremacy and to propose simply a sort of family compact, that is to say, a league against the House of Bourbon.

The result of this will be that the Americans will become our perpetual enemies, and we must expect to see them turn all their efforts against our possessions, and against those of Spain, This is all the more probable as the Colonies require a direct trade with the sugar islands. England will offer them that of our islands after having conquered them, which will be easy for her.

Thus the coalition of the English and the Americans will draw after it our expulsion, and probably that of the Spaniards, from the whole of America; it will limit our shipping and our commerce to the European seas only, and even this trade will be at the mercy of English insolence and greed.

It would be a mistake to suppose that the United States will not lend themselves to the proposals of the Court of St. James's. Those States took up arms only in order to establish and defend their independence and the freedom of their commerce; if, therefore, England offers them both, what reason will they have for refusing? Their treaty with that Power will give them more safety than the engagements which they might make with other Powers, or than all the guarantees which we might offer them. Indeed, what opinion can they have of our means, and even of our good-will, since we have not dared to co-operate in securing an independence of which we would afterwards propose the empty guarantee? Their surest guarantee will be in the community of interests and views which will be established between them and their former mother-country; we have nothing to offer which can counterbalance that.

Such will be the effects of the independence of the United States of America, if it is established without our concurrence.

It follows from this that the glory, the dignity and the essential interest of France demand that she should stretch out her hand to those States, and that their independence should be her work.

The advantages which will result are innumerable; we shall humiliate our natural enemy, a perfidious enemy who never knows how to respect either treaties or the right of nations; we shall divert to our profit one of the principal sources of her opulence; we shall shake her power, and reduce her to her real value; we shall extend our commerce, our shipping, our fisheries; we shall ensure the possession of our islands, and finally, we shall re-establish our reputation, and shall resume amongst the Powers of Europe the place which belongs to us. There would be no end if we wished to detail all these points; it is sufficient to indicate them in order to make their importance felt.

In presupposing that the independence of the Americans is to be the work of France, it is necessary to examine what line of conduct it is desirable for us to observe in order to attain that end; there is but one,—to assist the colonies.

But in order to determine the sort of assistance to be given, it is essential not to deviate from the two following truths: 1st, that whatever sort of assistance we give the Americans, it will be equivalent to a declaration of war against Great Britain: 2nd that when war is inevitable, it is better to be beforehand with one's enemy than to be anticipated by him.

Starting with these two principles, it appears that France cannot be too quick in making with the Americans a treaty of which recognized independence will be the basis, and that she should take her measures for acting before England can anticipate her.

It is all the more urgent to hasten the arrangements to be made with the Americans, as the Deputies are hard pressed by emissaries of the English Ministry, and as, if we are not the first to bind them, they will give the Court of London a foundation for proposing a plan of reconciliation at the reassembly of Parliament, which will take place on the 20th instant, and then all will be over with us, and it will only remain for us to prepare to undertake war against the English and against the insurgents, whereas we could and ought to have begun it in concert with the latter.

In all that has just been said, the co-operation of Spain has been presupposed.

But in the event of that Power not adopting the principles and plan of France, or of her judging the moment of putting it into execution not yet arrived, what course will France, thus isolated, have to follow?

The independence of the Colonies is so important a matter for France, that no other should weaken it, and France must do her utmost to establish it, even if it should cost her some sacrifices; I mean that France must undertake the war for the maintenance of American independence, even if that war should be in other respects disadvantageous. In order to be convinced of this truth, it is only necessary to picture to ourselves what England will be, when she no longer has America.

Thus France must espouse the American cause, and use for that purpose all her power, even if Spain should refuse to join her. From this one of two things will happen; either that Power will still remain neutral, or she will decide to join France. In the first case, although she will be passive, she will nevertheless favour our operations, because she will be armed, and England will see her constantly placed behind us, and ready, if need be, to assist us: but in order to maintain this opinion, we must also maintain that of a good understanding between the two Courts. The second case has no need of development.

But Spain is awaiting a rich fleet from Vera Cruz, and that fleet will not arrive until about next spring. Its arrival must unquestionably be ensured, and that may be done in two ways; 1st by prolonging the period of our operations, or else, 2nd, by sending a squadron to meet the fleet. Spain has vessels at Cadiz and Ferrol; they are armed and ready to put to sea. A cruise might be given as a pretext in order to mask their real destination.

If the King adopts the course of going forward without the participation of

Spain, he will take away from that Power all just reason for complaint, by stipulating for her eventually all the advantages which she would have claimed, had she been a contracting party. These advantages will be the same as those which His Majesty will ask for himself.

— | "France is the natural ally of the United States." *

In May 1778 the Continental Congress ratified the French treaties. American leaders, both political and military, received the news of the alliance with enthusiasm, for it made victory possible if not probable. John Adams, despite his earlier reluctance to accept the necessity of an alliance, wrote to his cousin Samuel Adams that France and the United States were natural allies and that the two nations together could maintain the balance of power in the Atlantic against England.

It is an observation that I have often heard you make, that "France is the natural ally of the United States." This observation is, in my opinion, both just and important. The reasons are plain. As long as Great Britain shall have Canada, Nova Scotia, and the Floridas, or any of them, so long will Great Britain be the enemy of the United States, let her disguise it as much as she will.

It is not much to the honor of human nature, but the fact is certain that neighboring nations are never friends in reality. In the times of the most perfect peace between them their hearts and their passions are hostile, and this will certainly be the case forever between the thirteen United States and the English colonies. France and England, as neighbors and rivals, never have been and never will be friends. The hatred and jealousy between the nations are eternal and ineradicable. As we therefore, on the one hand, have the surest ground to expect the jealousy and hatred of Great Britain, so on the other we have the strongest reasons to depend upon the friendship and alliance of France, and no reason in the world to expect her enmity or jealousy, as she has given up every pretension to any spot of ground on the continent. The United States, therefore, will be for ages the natural bulwark of France against the hostile designs of England against her, and France is the natural defense of the United States against the rapacious spirit of Great Britain against them. France is a nation so vastly eminent, having been for so many centuries what they call the dominant power of Europe, being incomparably the most powerful at land, that united in a close alliance with our States, and enjoying the benefit of our

* The Revolutionary Diplomatic Correspondence of the United States, Francis Wharton, ed. (Washington, 1889), II: 667–8.

trade, there is not the smallest reason to doubt but both will be a sufficient curb upon the naval power of Great Britain.

This connection, therefore, will forever secure a respect for our States in Spain, Portugal, and Holland, too, who will always choose to be upon friendly terms with powers who have numerous cruisers at sea, and indeed in all the rest of Europe. I presume, therefore, that sound policy as well as good faith will induce us never to renounce our alliance with France, even although it should continue us for some time in war. The French are as sensible of the benefits of this alliance to them as we are, and they are determined as much as we to cultivate it.

## 4 | National Objectives in the War for Independence, 1779 *

Walter Lippmann has written that "a foreign policy consists in bringing into balance, with a comfortable surplus of power in reserve, the nation's commitments and the nation's power. The constant preoccupation of the true statesman is to achieve and maintain this balance. Having determined the foreign commitments which are vitally necessary to his people, he will never rest until he has mustered the force to cover them. In assaying ideals, interests, and ambitions which are to be asserted abroad, his measure of their validity will be the force he can muster at home combined with the support he can find abroad among other nations which have similar ideals, interests, and ambitions."

That the diplomacy of the American Revolution comprises a classic example of successful negotiation suggests at the outset that it resulted from a clear balance between ends and means. Franklin and his distinguished colleagues in Paris benefited from the ambitions of France in the Atlantic world, for this alone forced the British to seek the re-establishment of cordial relations with the United States based on a wide spectrum of mutual interests. British officials, therefore, were not averse to creating a nation in the New World that had a chance at political and economic greatness. Yet even such diplomatic advantage could serve the national interest only to the extent that American diplomats limited their objectives to the means available. Those wartime goals of American diplomacy which the Congress defined in its instructions to its ministers in Paris on August 14, 1779, lay well within the realm of the achievable. They were later modified by the Congress itself under French pressure, but they remained the guide to American negotiations in Paris and formed the basis of the Treaty of Paris of 1783.

✎

* Instructions of Congress relative to a peace treaty with England, August 14, 1779, *The Revolutionary Diplomatic Correspondence of the United States*, III: 300–302.

You will herewith receive a commission, giving you full power to negotiate a treaty of peace with Great Britain; in doing which you will conform to the following information and instructions:

1. The United States are sincerely desirous of peace, and wish by every means consistent with their dignity and safety to spare the further effusion of blood. They have, therefore, by your commission and these instructions, labored to remove the obstacles to that event before the enemy have evidenced their disposition for it. But as the great object of the present defensive war on the part of the allies is to establish the independence of the United States, and as any treaty whereby this end can not be obtained must be only ostensible and illusory, you are therefore to make it a preliminary article to any negotiation that Great Britain shall agree to treat with the United States as sovereign, free, and independent.

2. You shall take especial care also that the independence of the said States be effectually assured and confirmed by the treaty or treaties of peace according to the form and effect of the treaty of alliance with his most Christian majesty; and you shall not agree to such treaty or treaties unless the same be thereby so assured and confirmed.

3. The boundaries of these States are as follows, viz: These States are bounded north by a line to be drawn from the north west angle of Nova Scotia along the highlands which divide those rivers which empty themselves into the river St. Lawrence from those which fall into the Atlantic Ocean to the northwesternmost head of Connecticut River; thence down along the middle of that river to the forty-fifth degree of north latitude; thence due west in the latitude of forty-five degrees north from the equator to the north westernmost side of the river St. Lawrence or Cadaraqui; thence straight to the south end of Nepissing; and thence straight to the source of the river Mississippi. West by a line to be drawn along the middle of the river Mississippi from its source to where the said line shall intersect the thirty-first degree of north latitude. South by a line to be drawn due east from the termination of the line last mentioned in the latitude of thirty-one degrees north from the equator to the middle of the river Appalachicola, or Catahouchi; thence along the middle thereof to its junction with the Flint River; thence straight to the head of St. Mary's River; and thence down along the middle of the St. Mary's River to the Atlantic Ocean. And east by a line to be drawn along the middle of the St. John's River from its source to its mouth in the Bay of Fundy; comprehending all islands within twenty leagues of any part of the shores of the United States and lying between lines to be drawn due east from the points where the aforesaid boundaries between Nova Scotia on the one part and East Florida on the other part shall respectively touch the Bay of Fundy on the Atlantic Ocean. You are therefore strongly to contend that the whole of the said countries and islands lying within the boundaries aforesaid, and every citadel, fort, post, place, harbor, and road to them belonging be absolutely evacuated by the land and sea forces of his Britannic majesty and yielded to the powers of the States to which they respectively belong in such situation as they may be at the termination of the war. But notwithstanding the clear right of these states and the importance of

the object, yet they are so much influenced by the dictates of religion and humanity, and so desirous of complying with the earnest request of their allies, that if the line to be drawn from the mouth of the lake Nepissing to the head of the Mississippi can not be obtained without continuing the war for that purpose, you are hereby empowered to agree to some other line between that point and the river Mississippi, provided the same shall in no part thereof be to the southward of latitude forty-five degrees north. And in like manner, if the eastern boundary above described cannot be obtained, you are hereby empowered to agree that the same shall be afterwards adjusted by commissioners to be duly appointed for that purpose according to such line as shall be by them settled and agreed on as the boundary between that part of the State of Massachusetts Bay, formerly called the Province of Maine, and the colony of Nova Scotia, agreeably to their respective rights; and you may also consent that the enemy shall destroy such fortifications as they may have erected.

4. Although it is of the utmost importance to the peace and commerce of the United States that Canada and Nova Scotia should be ceded, and more particularly that their equal common right to the fisheries should be guaranteed to them, yet a desire of terminating the war has induced us not to make the acquisition of these objects an ultimatum on the present occasion.

5. You are empowered to agree to a cessation of hostilities during the negotiation, provided our ally shall consent to the same, and provided it shall be stipulated that all the forces of the enemy shall be immediately withdrawn from the United States.

6. In all other matters not above mentioned you are to govern yourself by the alliance between his most Christian majesty and these States, by the advice of our allies, by your knowledge of our interests, and by your own discretion, in which we repose the fullest confidence.

## 5 | John Adams at the Court of St. James's, June 1785 *

Much of the burden of conducting the foreign relations of the United States after the establishment of independence fell to the experienced John Jay, who had revealed his diplomatic skill in the Paris negotiations of 1782. It was Jay whom Congress appointed Secretary for the Department of Foreign Affairs in May 1784. Under his leadership the office acquired prominence and prestige, for he succeeded at least partially in wresting direct control of policy from Congress. In 1785 the Congress selected John Adams, an associate of Franklin and Jay in Paris, to represent the United States at the Court of St. James's in

* John Adams to John Jay, June 2, 1785, *The Works of John Adams*, Charles Francis Adams, ed. (Boston, 1853), VIII: 255-9.

London. From London, Adams engaged in a lengthy and enlightening correspondence with Jay which revealed clearly the difficulties of creating an effective balance between ends and means under the agency of the Articles of Confederation. Yet Adams's reception by George III was propitious. Following Adams's gracious speech, the King responded with equal grace. Adams soon discovered, however, that successful foreign relations hinged on more than proper rhetoric.

&

. . . At one, on Wednesday, the master of ceremonies called at my house, and went with me to the secretary of state's office, in Cleveland Row, where the Marquis of Carmarthen received me, and introduced me to his under secretary, Mr. Fraser, who has been, as his Lordship told me, uninterruptedly in that office, through all the changes in administration for thirty years, having first been appointed by the Earl of Holderness. After a short conversation upon the subject of importing my effects from Holland and France free of duty, which Mr. Fraser himself introduced, Lord Carmarthen invited me to go with him in his coach to Court. When we arrived in the antechamber, the *aeil de boeuf* of St. James's, the master of the ceremonies met me and attended me, while the secretary of state went to take the commands of the King. While I stood in this place, where it seems all ministers stand upon such occasions, always attended by the master of ceremonies, the room very full of ministers of state, lords, and bishops, and all sorts of courtiers, as well as the next room, which is the King's bedchamber, you may well suppose I was the focus of all eyes. I was relieved, however, from the embarrassment of it by the Swedish and Dutch ministers, who came to me, and entertained me in a very agreeable conversation during the whole time. Some other gentlemen, whom I had seen before, came to make their compliments too, until the Marquis of Carmarthen returned and desired me to go with him to his Majesty. I went with his Lordship through the levee room into the King's closet. The door was shut, and I was left with his Majesty and the secretary of state alone. I made the three reverences,—one at the door, another about half way, and a third before the presence,—according to the usage established at this and all the northern Courts of Europe, and then addressed myself to his Majesty in the following words:—

"Sir,—The United States of America have appointed me their minister plenipotentiary to your Majesty, and have directed me to deliver to your Majesty this letter which contains the evidence of it. It is in obedience to their express commands, that I have the honor to assure your Majesty of their unanimous disposition and desire to cultivate the most friendly and liberal intercourse between your Majesty's subjects and their citizens, and of their best wishes for your Majesty's health and happiness, and for that of your royal family. The appointment of a minister from the United States to your Majesty's Court will form an epoch in the history of England and of America. I think myself more fortunate than all my fellow-citizens, in having the distinguished honor to be the first to stand in your Majesty's royal presence in a diplomatic character; and I shall esteem myself the happiest of men, if I can be instrumental in recommending my country more and more to your Majesty's royal benevolence, and of restoring an entire esteem, confidence, and affection, or, in better words, the old good nature and the old good humor between people, who, though separated by an ocean, and under different governments, have the same language, a similar religion, and kindred blood.

"I beg your Majesty's permission to add, that, although I have some time before been intrusted by my country, it was never in my whole life in a manner so agreeable to myself."

The King listened to every word I said, with dignity, but with an apparent emotion. Whether it was the nature of the interview, or whether it was my visible agitation, for I felt more than I did or could express, that touched him, I cannot say. But he was much affected, and answered me with more tremor that I had spoken with, and said:—

"Sir,—The circumstances of this audience are so extraordinary, the language you have now held is so extremely proper, and the feelings you have discovered so justly adapted to the occasion, that I must say that I not only receive with pleasure the assurance of the friendly dispositions of the United States, but that I am very glad the choice has fallen upon you to be their minister. I wish you, sir, to believe, and that it may be understood in America, that I have done nothing in the late contest but what I thought myself indispensably bound to do, by the duty which I owed to my people. I will be very frank with you. I was the last to consent to the separation; but the separation having been made, and having become inevitable, I have always said, as I say now, that I would be the first to meet the friendship of the United States as an independent power. The moment I see such sentiments and language as yours prevail, and a disposition to give to this country the preference, that moment I shall say, let the circumstances of language, religion, and blood have their natural and full effect." . . .

The King then asked me whether I came last from France, and upon my answering in the affirmative, he put on an air of familiarity, and, smiling, or rather laughing, said, "there is an opinion among some people that you are not the most attached of all your countrymen to the manners of France." I was surprised at this, because I thought it an indiscretion and a departure from the dignity. I was a little embarrassed, but determined not to deny the truth on one hand, nor leave him to infer from it any attachment to England on the other. I threw off as much gravity as I could, and assumed an air of gayety and a tone of decision as far as was decent, and said, "that opinion, sir, is not mistaken; I must avow to your Majesty, I have no attachment but to my own country." The King replied, as quick as lightning, "an honest man will never have any other."

The King then said a word or two to the secretary of state, which, being between them, I did not hear, and then turned round and bowed to me, as is customary with all kings and princes when they give the signal to retire. I retreated, stepping backward, as is the etiquette, and, making my last reverence at the door of the chamber, I went my way. The master of ceremonies joined me the moment of my coming out of the King's closet, and accompanied me through the apartments down to my carriage, several stages of servants, gentlemen-porters and under-porters, roaring out like thunder, as I went along, "Mr. Adams's servants, Mr. Adams's carriage, &c." I have been thus minute, as it may be useful to others hereafter to know.

The conversation with the King congress will form their own judgment of. I may expect from it a residence less painful than I once expected, as so marked an attention from the King will silence many grumblers; but we can infer nothing from all this concerning the success of my mission.

There are a train of other ceremonies yet to go through, in presentations to the Queen, and visits to and from ministers and ambassadors, which will take up much time, and interrupt me in my endeavors to obtain all that I have at heart,—the objects of my instructions. It is thus the essence of things is lost in ceremony in every country of Europe. We must submit to what we cannot alter. Patience is the only remedy.

## 6 | John Adams and the National Interest in a Stronger Government, 1785 *

Under the Articles of Confederation the Federal Congress was granted all the powers over external affairs normally possessed by central authority—to despatch and receive ambassadors, to enter treaties or alliances, to determine the conditions of peace and war. Each state retained the essential powers of commerce and taxation and thus could deprive Congress of the engines of coercion which might force satisfactory commercial arrangements with the nations of Europe. The British government after 1783 imposed arbitrary regulations on American commerce without fear of retaliatory legislation, for it was clear that the thirteen states would never agree on any program. As early as May 1785, Adams complained that the British would never modify their partial regulations until the Congress enjoyed the power to govern the commerce of the entire nation.

🖎

The Britons boast that all the prophecies of the loss of the American trade from the independence of the United States have proved false; that the experiment has been tried, and the contest decided; that there was at the peace a competition of the commercial nations of Europe for the prize; that the superior abilities of the British manufacturers, and the greater capitals of their merchants, have enabled them to give our traders better bargains and longer credit than any others in Europe; that, as we love our interest and have small for-

* John Adams to John Jay, May 5, 1785, *The Works of John Adams*, VIII: 240–42.

tunes, we must come to them who can furnish us with goods of the best qualities, at the cheapest rates, and allow us the longest time to pay; that Britain has monopolized our trade beyond credibility; that all the foreign merchants,—French, Dutch, and even Spanish and Portuguese,—who had engaged in our trade have failed, while few of theirs have suffered.

While, on the one hand, it is certain that in all this there is much exaggeration, it must be confessed, on the other, that there is too much truth; and the success of your mission to London will depend very much upon the researches of congress and the States into this subject, and the measures they may take in consequence of their inquiries. You will negotiate for reciprocities in commerce to very little purpose, while the British ministers and merchants are certain that they shall enjoy all the profits of our commerce under their own partial regulations.

It behoves the whole people of America, then, to turn their attention to this subject. It would be presumption in me to discuss the question, whether it is necessary that the States should give to congress a plenary power to govern the commerce of the whole confederation. I have been too long absent, and at too great a distance, to be able to form a judgment, even to my own satisfaction. But I can see numberless mischiefs and inconveniences arising from the want of unity and system, in the direction of such complicated interests, and every State will find itself necessitated frequently to apply to congress for their interposition, either by recommendations or decisions.

You will give me leave, then, to inquire, whether it may not be proper for congress to call upon the States, in such manner as they may judge constitutional, to furnish them with authentic accounts of all the exports and imports of every State since the peace, of the vessels which have entered or cleared out, the nation to which they belong, and all other particulars which may be thought proper. It should seem impossible that the Union can be preserved without some such general repository of the commercial interests and knowledge. The information to be derived from it would bring the States to act in concert, by showing the necessity of it to all, and congress or the States might take such measures as would insure them justice against the English; from such a view, they might lay such discouragements on British ships and manufactures, and procure such advantages to their own, as would be beneficial to our country, while it would show the English their own weakness; heavy duties might be laid upon articles of luxury wrought in England and imported from thence, which would discourage the extravagant use of them among ourselves, place other nations upon as good or a better footing than the English, and raise a revenue for the public out of that enthusiasm for England which has been, and is still, so unwise in itself, and so hurtful to our country. Such measures as these would discover to the English that we know our own strength and their weakness, and would have probably a greater tendency to influence the ministry, by preparing the nation, than any reasoning which can be used. It is a diplomatic axiom, "that he always negotiates ill who is not in a condition to make himself feared;" but measures for this purpose must be taken by the people of America. Our army will be no terror to them, because they think at present they shall never send an army to fight us in our own country, and they do not believe that ours will go abroad to attack them; they are too proud of their own navy, and have too much disregard of ours, to dread us upon the sea, although experience should have taught them that their commerce might be much endangered by our cruisers. So that we have no means to make an impression on them but by commercial regulations, which the vulgar may see strike essentially at their interests without injuring our own.

— | "We ought to attend to considerations of strength and defence." *

Three days later Adams wrote to Jay again, suggesting that since the United States would not automatically enjoy the benefits of the balance of power, as did Switzerland and Holland, the nation must look to its own defenses.

. . . The last year must have been a prosperous period in the United States. The high prices of their produce, and the low prices of foreign merchandises, are a demonstration of it. Yet our shipping, our seamen, our carrying trade, have been discouraged. Present ease, and even wealth, should not be our only object.

We ought to attend to considerations of strength and defence. Our situation is different from some of the powers of Europe who have neglected their own defence. Switzerland is situated so, that if she should be attacked by one neighbor, she would infallibly be defended by two others. If attacked by Sardinia, she would be defended by France and the Emperor; if by the Emperor, France and Sardinia would support her; and if by France, the Emperor and Sardinia would unite to protect her. This is so fully known to her and all her neighbors, that she fears nothing, and is at no expense. Holland, if attacked by France, found a friend in England, when attacked by England, France supports her; when the Emperor threatened her, she found a friend in France, too, and she will forever be sure that neither of these three great powers can ever suffer her to fall a prey to any of the others. She has relied so much upon this, as to neglect her defence, to her great regret at present. But what are Switzerland and Holland,— small powers limited by nature, so that they never can be great,—to the United States of America, destined beyond a doubt to be the greatest power on earth, and that within the life of man? This is so well known, that, instead of being overlooked among the powers, like Holland and Switzerland, we shall be more an object of jealousy than any other upon earth. All the powers know that it is impossible for any, the proudest of them, to conquer us; and, therefore, if we should be attacked by any one, the others will not be fond of undertaking our defence; knowing we can defend ourselves, they will leave us to do it, and, if

* John Adams to John Jay, May 8, 1785, *The Works of John Adams*, VIII: 245–6.

they assist us at all, it will not be until we have done the work, and then it will be feebly, and only with a view of deriving more benefit and reputation from it than they do us good. They will be pleased to see us weakened, and our growth a little retarded. It behoves the United States, then, to knit themselves together in the bands of affection and mutual confidence, search their own resources to the bottom, form their foreign commerce into a system, and encourage their own navigation and seamen, and to these ends their carrying trade; and I am much afraid we shall never be able to do this, unless congress are vested with full power, under the limitations prescribed of fifteen years, and the concurrence of nine States of forming treaties of commerce with foreign powers.

— | "We shall have no treaty of commerce until this nation [England] is made to feel the necessity of it." *

Again, in June and July 1785, Adams complained that the British would continue to exploit the political weakness of the United States by imposing unfair commercial restrictions on American merchants until "vigorous measures are taken by all the States in concert."

✍

By the ninth article of the confederation, the United States, in congress assembled, have the sole and exclusive right and power of entering into treaties and alliances, provided that no treaty of commerce shall be made whereby the legislative power of the respective States shall be restrained from imposing such imposts and duties on foreigners as their own people are subjected to, or from prohibiting the exportation or importation of any species of goods or commodities whatsoever.

I have ventured, sir, in some former letters to you, notwithstanding the delicacy of tampering with the confederation, to suggest to your consideration, whether it may not be necessary for the States to reconsider this proviso, and give to congress unlimited authority to enter into treaties of commerce with foreign powers, at least for a limited term of years. I have also inquired, whether it might not be necessary for the States to confer upon congress authority to regulate the external commerce of all the members of the confederation for a like term of years.

If the States should hesitate at this, I am persuaded they would readily comply with recommendations of congress to this effect. For example, if congress should recommend to the legislatures of the States to lay duties, heavy duties, upon all British vessels entering into or clearing out of their ports, especially upon all vessels coming from or bound to the West India Islands, Nova Scotia, Canada,

* John Adams to John Jay, June 26, July 19, 1785, *The Works of John Adams*, VIII: 273–5, 281–3.

or Newfoundland, and upon all merchandises imported from, or exported to, any part of the British dominions, I can scarcely doubt that every legislature would immediately comply; and by this means our own navigation would be encouraged, and the British discouraged to such a degree as to compel the British government to enter into an equitable treaty; nay, I cannot doubt the readiness of the States to comply with a recommendation of congress wholly to prohibit British vessels and merchandises.

Although I have been received here, and continue to be treated, with all the distinction which is due to the rank and title you have given me, there is, nevertheless, a reserve, which convinces me that we shall have no treaty of commerce until this nation is made to feel the necessity of it. I am every day astonished at the ignorance of all ranks of people of the relation between this country and ours. *"Cui bono?"* they cry, "to what end a treaty of commerce, when we are sure of as much American trade as we have occasion for, without it? The experiment has been tried, and the Americans have found that they cannot supply themselves elsewhere; there must be *quid pro quo*; and what have the United States to give in exchange for the liberty of going in their own ships to our sugar colonies and our colonies upon the continent?" These smart reasoners are answered, "The Americans allow Britons to come in their own vessels to all their ports in the United States, and this is more than a *quid* for your *quo*. This is the true reciprocity; and while we allow you this liberty, we have a right to demand it in return."

"But," replies the Briton, "you cannot avoid this; you have no government; you cannot agree to prohibit our ships and goods, or to lay duties on them." "Then," says the American, "you give up the argument of reciprocity; you confess that you are not willing to allow us a *quid* for your *quo*, and that you are disposed to take advantage of our supposed disunion to get unequal benefits from us; but you will find yourselves disappointed in this disunion that you build so much upon. Nothing but too much good nature to you, and too high an opinion of your wisdom, has prevented the States hitherto from uniting in a reciprocal discouragement of your ships and goods; but when the Americans find themselves deceived, you will soon see them too much united for your purposes."

Such have been the dialogues in conversation for a year or two, and these ignorant sophisms of the Britons will never be confuted to any effect, until vigorous measures are taken by all the States in concert. . . .

With independence the United States lost whatever protection membership in the British Empire afforded against the Barbary pirates. The North African states of Morocco, Algiers, Tripoli, and Tunis preyed upon the Mediterranean commerce of the weak nations, elevating ransom and blackmail to legitimate national industries. Even the powerful maritime nations of Europe paid tribute as the cheapest method of ensuring the passage of their vessels through the Mediterranean. By the mid-1780's these pirates had almost driven American commerce, which lacked the benefits of bribery, from the Mediterranean. Some British spokesmen scarcely concealed their pleasure at the efficiency with which the pirates removed American competition from many of Europe's lucrative markets. As Franklin wrote to Robert Livingston in July 1783, "I think it not improbable that those rovers may be privately encouraged by the English to fall upon us, and to prevent our interference in the carrying trade; for I have in London heard it is a maxim among the merchants that *if there were no Algiers it would be worth England's while to build one.*" In December, 1784, Adams suggested to Jay that the United States follow the other powers of Europe in paying tribute to the pirates as the only means available for dealing effectively with the problem.

❦

. . . The Emperor of Morocco sent an ambassador last winter to Holland to demand materials for some frigates, and as none of the great maritime powers have the courage or the will to refuse such requisitions, obtained them. It now appears probable that they have been employed in corsairs against American trade, and one Virginia vessel appears to have been taken and carried to Tangiers. This has spread an alarm, and raised the insurance on American vessels, and rendered it necessary that something should be soon done.

There is danger of our making mistakes upon this occasion. Some are of opinion that our trade in the Mediterranean is not worth the expense of the presents we must make the piratical states to obtain treaties with them. Others think it humiliating to treat with such enemies of the human race, and that it would be more manly to fight them. The first, I think, have not calculated the value of our Mediterranean trade, in which every one of our States is deeply interested. But this is not all. The piratical corsairs will go all over the ocean, and will even raise the insurance upon all our commerce so high, as to cost us more in this single article than all the presents exacted would amount to. The last have more spirit than prudence. As long as France, England, Holland, the Emperor, &c., will submit to be tributary to these robbers, and even encourage them, to what purpose should we make war upon them? The resolution might

* John Adams to John Jay, December 15, 1784, *The Works of John Adams*, VIII: 217–19.

be heroic, but would not be wise. The contest would be unequal. They can injure us very sensibly, but we cannot hurt them in the smallest degree. We have, or shall have, a rich trade at sea exposed to their depredations; they have none at all upon which we can make reprisals. If we take a vessel of theirs, we get nothing but a bad vessel fit only to burn, a few guns and a few barbarians, whom we may hang or enslave if we will, and the unfeeling tyrants, whose subjects they are, will think no more of it than if we had killed so many caterpillars upon an apple-tree. When they take a vessel of ours, they not only get a rich prize, but they enslave the men, and, if there are among them men of any rank or note, they demand most exorbitant ransoms for them. If we could even send a force sufficient to burn a town, their unfeeling governors would only insult and deride. Unless it were possible, then, to persuade the great maritime powers of Europe to unite in the suppression of these piracies, it would be very imprudent for us to entertain any thoughts of contending with them, and will only lay a foundation, by irritating their passions, and increasing their insolence and their demands, for long and severe repentance. I hope, therefore, we shall think of nothing but treating with them.

But how? where is the money? France calls upon us to fulfill our engagements with her, both for interest and principal, and our creditors in Holland, who are very numerous, will soon be uneasy, unless something is done for their security. Holland is the only place where we can borrow money, and there it will be impracticable, unless our European debt at least be consolidated.

If congress, therefore, think of borrowing in Holland, they must begin by laying duties at home to pay the interest.

I have not time to enlarge at present on any subject. This is the most pressing, and deserves the immediate attention of congress and their ministers, of whom I hope you are one, as I am very sure no man is better qualified or better disposed; but if, unfortunately, you should not be in office, let me pray you to transmit the substance of this letter to congress.

— | "The policy of Christendom has made cowards of all their sailors before the standard of Mahomet." *

In July 1786 Adams repeated in a letter to Thomas Jefferson, then in Paris, his argument that the United States bribe the Barbary pirates since the nation lacked the power to punish the North African states.

---

* John Adams to Thomas Jefferson, July 3, 1786, *The Works of John Adams*, VIII: 406–7.

. . . There is no intelligence from America of armies marching to take the posts from the English. The news was made, as I suppose, against the opening of the three per cents; and it had the intended effect, to beat down the stocks a little.

Although the posts are important, the war with the Turks is more so. I lay down a few simple propositions.

1. We may at this time have peace with them, in spite of all the intrigues of the English or others to prevent it, for a sum of money.

2. We never shall have peace, though France, Spain, England, and Holland should use all their influence in our favor, without a sum of money.

3. That neither the benevolence of France, or the malevolence of England, will be ever able materially to diminish or increase the sum.

4. The longer the negotiation is delayed, the larger will be the demand.

From these premises, I conclude it to be wisest for us to negotiate and pay the necessary sum without loss of time. Now, I desire you, and our noble friend the Marquis, to give me your opinion of these four propositions. Which of them do you deny or doubt? If you admit them all, do you admit the conclusion? Perhaps you will say, fight them, though it should cost us a great sum to carry on the war, and although, at the end of it, we should have more money to pay as presents. If this is your sentiment, and you can persuade the southern States into it, I dare answer for it that all from Pennsylvania, inclusively northward, would not object. It would be a good occasion to begin a navy.

At present we are sacrificing a million annually, to save one gift of £200,000. This is not good economy. We might, at this hour, have two hundred ships in the Mediterranean, whose freights alone would be worth £200,000 besides the influence upon the price of our produce. Our farmers and planters will find the price of their articles sink very low indeed, if this peace is not made.

The policy of Christendom has made cowards of all their sailors before the standard of Mahomet. It would be heroical and glorious in us to restore courage to ours. I doubt not we could accomplish it, if we should set about it in earnest; but the difficulty of bringing our people to agree upon it, has ever discouraged me. . . .

— | "[War against the Barbary states] will procure us respect in Europe, and respect is a safe-guard to interest." *

Jefferson, responding to Adams's letter, favored the employment of force through a small navy as the only permanent and honorable method of resolving the problem of the Barbary pirates.

Our instructions relative to the Barbary states having required us to proceed by way of negotiation to obtain their peace, it became our duty to do this to the best of our power. Whatever might be our private opinions, they were to be suppressed, and the line marked out to us, was to be followed. It has been so honestly, and zealously. It was therefore never material for us to consult together on the best plan of conduct towards these states. I acknolege I very early thought it would be best to effect a peace thro' the medium of war. Tho' it is a question with which we have nothing to do, yet as you propose some discussion of it I shall trouble you with my reasons. Of the 4 positions laid down in your letter of the 3d. instant, I agree to the three first, which are in substance that the good offices of our friends cannot procure us a peace without paying it's price, that they cannot materially lessen that price, and that paying it, we can have the peace in spight of the intrigues of our enemies. As to the 4th. that the longer the negotiation is delayed the larger will be the demand, this will depend on the intermediate captures: if they are many and rich the price may be raised; if few and poor it will be lessened. However if it is decided that we shall buy a peace, I know no reason for delaying the operation, but should rather think it ought to be hastened. But I should prefer the obtaining it by war. 1. Justice is in favor of this opinion. 2. Honor favors it. 3. It will procure us respect in Europe, and respect is a safe-guard to interest. 4. It will arm the federal head with the safest of all the instruments of coercion over their delinquent members and prevent them from using what would be less safe. I think that so far you go with me. But in the next steps we shall differ. 5. I think it least expensive. 6. Equally effectual. I ask a fleet of 150. guns, the one half of which shall be in constant cruise. This fleet built, manned and victualled for 6. months will cost 450,000 £ sterling. . . . Were we to charge all this to the Algerine war it would amount to little more than we must pay if we buy peace. But as it is proper and necessary that we should establish a small marine force (even were we to buy a peace from the Algerines,) and as that force laid up in our dockyards would cost us half as much annually as if kept in order for service, we have a right to say that only 22,500 £ sterl. per ann. should be charged to the Algerine war. 6. It will be as effectual. To all the mismanage-

* Thomas Jefferson to John Adams, July 11, 1786, *The Adams–Jefferson Letters*, Lester J. Cappon, ed. (Chapel Hill, N.C., 1959), I: 142–3. Reprinted by permission of the University of North Carolina Press.

ments of Spain and Portugal urged to shew that war against those people is ineffectual, I urge a single fact to prove the contrary where there is any management. About 40. years ago, the Algerines having broke their treaty with France, this court sent Monsr. de Massac with one large and two small frigates, he blockaded the harbour of Algiers three months, and they subscribed to the terms he dictated. If it be admitted however that war, on the fairest prospects, is still exposed to incertainties, I weigh against this the greater incertainty of the duration of a peace bought with money, from such a people, from a Dey 80. years old, and by a nation who, on the hypothesis of buying peace, is to have no power on the sea to enforce an observance of it.

So far I have gone on the supposition that the whole weight of this war would rest on us. But 1. Naples will join us. The character of their naval minister (Acton), his known sentiments with respect to the peace Spain is officiously trying to make for them, and his dispositions against the Algerines give the greatest reason to believe it. 2. Every principle of reason tells us Portugal will join us. I state this as taking for granted, what all seem to believe, that they will not be at peace with Algiers. I suppose then that a Convention might be formed between Portugal, Naples and the U. S. by which the burthen of the war might be quotaed on them according to their respective wealth, and the term of it should be when Algiers should subscribe to a peace with all three on equal terms. This might be left open for other nations to accede to, and many, if not most of the powers of Europe (except France, England, Holland and Spain if her peace be made) would sooner or later enter into the confederacy, for the sake of having their peace with the Pyratical states guarantied by the whole. I suppose that in this case our proportion of force would not be the half of what I first calculated on.

These are the reasons which have influenced my judgment on this question. I give them to you to shew you that I am imposed on by a semblance of reason at least, and not with an expectation of their changing your opinion. You have viewed the subject, I am sure in all it's bearings. You have weighed both questions with all their circumstances. You make the result different from what I do. The same facts impress us differently. This is enough to make me suspect an error in my process of reasoning tho' I am not able to detect it. It is of no consequence; as I have nothing to say in the decision, and am ready to proceed heartily on any other plan which may be adopted, if my agency should be thought useful. . . .

— | "We ought not to fight them at all, unless we determine to fight them forever." *

Adams agreed with Jefferson that war against the pirates would best protect American commerce in the Mediterranean, but he doubted that Congress would agree to such stern and costly measures. Adams concluded that Congress would neither fight nor treat and thus would continue to expose American commerce to the mercy of foreign powers. The heart of the problem, Adams saw, was the nation's refusal to balance its intentions with the means required to achieve them.

✍

. . . There are great and weighty considerations urged . . . in favor of arming against the Algerines, and, I confess, if our States could be brought to agree in the measure, I should be very willing to resolve upon external war with vigor, and protect our trade and people. The resolution to fight them would raise the spirits and courage of our countrymen immediately, and we might obtain the glory of finally breaking up these nests of banditti. But congress will never, or at least not for years, take any such resolution, and in the mean time our trade and honor suffers beyond calculation. We ought not to fight them at all, unless we determine to fight them forever.

This thought, I fear, is too rugged for our people to bear. To fight them at the expense of millions, and make peace, after all, by giving more money and larger presents than would not procure perpetual peace, seems not to be economical. Did Monsieur de Massac carry his point without making the present? Has not France made presents ever since? Did any nation ever make peace with any one Barbary state without making the presents? Is there an example of it? I believe not, and fancy you will find that even Massac himself made the presents.

I agree in opinion of the wisdom and necessity of a navy for other uses, but am apprehensive it will make bad worse with the Algerines. I will go all lengths with you in promoting the navy, whether to be applied to the Algerines or not. But I think, at the same time, we should treat. Your letter, however, has made me easier upon this point. Nevertheless, to humble the Algerines, I think you have undercalculated the force necessary. They have now fifty gun-boats, which, being small objects against great ships, are very formidable. None of these existed in the time of Monsieur Massac. The harbor of Algiers, too, is fortified all round, which it was not in M. Massac's time, which renders it more difficult and dangerous to attempt a blockade. I know not what dependence is to be put upon Portugal and Naples, in case of a war with the barbarians; perhaps they might assist us in some degree. Blocking Algiers would not obtain peace with Morocco; so that our commerce would still be exposed.

After all, though I am glad we have exchanged a letter on the subject, I perceive that neither force nor money will be applied. Our States are so backward,

* John Adams to Thomas Jefferson, July 31, 1786, *The Works of John Adams*, VIII: 410–12.

that they will do nothing for some years. If they get money enough to discharge the demands upon them in Europe already incurred, I shall be agreeably disappointed. A disposition seems rather to prevail among our citizens to give up all ideas of navigation and naval power, and lay themselves consequently at the mercy of foreigners, even for the prices of their produce. It is their concern, and we must submit; for your plan of fighting will no more be adopted, than mine of treating. This is more humiliating to me than giving the presents would be. . . .

## 8 | The Persistence of Power Politics: *The Federalist* *

By 1786 the impotence of Congress, under the Articles of Confederation, to resolve the challenges confronting the government from its detractors at home and abroad drove the nation's conservative leadership toward the demand for a new constitution. "Your sentiments, that our affairs are drawing rapidly to a crisis," Washington wrote to Jay in August 1786, "accord with my own. . . . Experience has taught us, that men will not adopt and carry into execution measures best calculated for their own good, without the intervention of a coercive power. I do not conceive that we can exist long as a nation without having lodged somewhere a power, which will pervade the whole Union in as energetic a manner as the authority of the State governments extends over the several States." Such widespread conviction led in 1787 to the calling of a constitutional convention. In defending the jurisdiction of the new constitution over foreign affairs, Alexander Hamilton in *The Federalist No. 6* pointed to the persistence of conflict in world affairs, even among commercial nations, and the resultant requirement of national power in sustaining adequate relations with other countries. Nor did democracy, Hamilton noted, guarantee the peaceful disposition of one country toward another.

. . . A man must be far gone in Utopian speculations who can seriously doubt that, if these States should either be wholly disunited, or only united in partial confederacies, the subdivisions into which they might be thrown would have frequent and violent contests with each other. To presume a want of motives for such contests as an argument against their existence, would be to forget that men are ambitious, vindictive, and rapacious. To look for a continuation of harmony between a number of independent, unconnected sovereignties

* Alexander Hamilton, John Jay, and James Madison, *The Federalist*, Edward Mead Earle, ed. (New York, 1937), 27–33.

in the same neighborhood, would be to disregard the uniform course of human events, and to set at defiance the accumulated experience of ages.

The causes of hostility among nations are innumerable. There are some which have a general and almost constant operation upon the collective bodies of society. Of this description are the love of power or the desire of preeminence and dominion—the jealousy of power, or the desire of equality and safety. There are others which have a more circumscribed though an equally operative influence within their spheres. Such are the rivalships and competitions of commerce between commercial nations. And there are others, not less numerous than either of the former, which take their origin entirely in private passions; in the attachments, enmities, interests, hopes, and fears of leading individuals in the communities of which they are members. Men of this class, whether the favorites of a king or of a people, have in too many instances abused the confidence they possessed; and assuming the pretext of some public motive, have not scrupled to sacrifice the national tranquillity to personal advantage or personal gratification. . . .

But notwithstanding the concurring testimony of experience, in this particular, there are still to be found visionary or designing men, who stand ready to advocate the paradox of perpetual peace between the States, though dismembered and alienated from each other. The genius of republics (say they) is pacific; the spirit of commerce has a tendency to soften the manners of men, and to extinguish those inflammable humors which have so often kindled into wars. Commercial republics, like ours, will never be disposed to waste themselves in ruinous contentions with each other. They will be governed by mutual interest, and will cultivate a spirit of mutual amity and concord.

Is it not (we may ask these projectors in politics) the true interest of all nations to cultivate the same benevolent and philosophic spirit? If this be their true interest, have they in fact pursued it? Has it not, on the contrary, invariably been found that momentary passions, and immediate interests, have a more active and imperious control over human conduct than general or remote considerations of policy, utility, or justice? Have republics in practice been less addicted to war than monarchies? Are not the former administered by men as well as the latter? Are there not aversions, predilections, rivalships, and desires of unjust acquisitions, that affect nations as well as kings? Are not popular assemblies frequently subject to the impulses of rage, resentment, jealousy, avarice, and of other irregular and violent propensities? Is it not well known that their determinations are often governed by a few individuals in whom they place confidence, and are, of course, liable to be tinctured by the passions and views of those individuals? Has commerce hitherto done any thing more than change the objects of war? Is not the love of wealth as domineering and enterprising a passion as that of power or glory? Have there not been as many wars founded upon commercial motives since that has become the prevailing system of nations, as were before occasioned by the cupidity of territory or dominion? Has not the spirit of commerce, in many instances, administered new incentives to the appetite, both for the one and for the other? Let experience, the least fallible guide of human opinions, be appealed to for an answer to these inquiries.

Sparta, Athens, Rome, and Carthage were all republics; two of them, Athens and Carthage, of the commercial kind. Yet were they as often engaged in wars, offensive and defensive, as the neighboring monarchies of the same times. Sparta was little better than a well-regulated camp; and Rome was never sated of carnage and conquest.

Carthage, though a commercial republic, was the aggressor in the very war that ended in her destruction. Hannibal had carried her arms into the heart of Italy and to the gates of Rome, before Scipio, in turn, gave him an overthrow in the territories of Carthage, and made a conquest of the commonwealth.

Venice, in later times, figures more than once in wars of ambition, till, becoming an object to the other Italian states, Pope Julius II. found means to accomplish that formidable league, which gave a deadly blow to the power and pride of this haughty republic.

The provinces of Holland, till they were overwhelmed in debts and taxes, took a leading and conspicuous part in the wars of Europe. They had furious contests with England for the dominion of the sea, and were among the most persevering and most implacable of the opponents of Louis XIV.

In the government of Britain the representatives of the people compose one branch of the national legislature. Commerce has been for ages the predominant pursuit of that country. Few nations, nevertheless, have been more frequently engaged in war; and the wars in which that kingdom has been engaged have, in numerous instances, proceeded from the people.

There have been, if I may so express it, almost as many popular as royal wars. The cries of the nation and the importunities of their representatives have, upon various occasions, dragged their monarchs into war, or continued them in it, contrary to their inclinations, and sometimes contrary to the real interests of the state. In that memorable struggle for superiority between the rival houses of Austria and Bourbon, which so long kept Europe in a flame, it is well known that the antipathies of the English against the French, seconding the ambition, or rather the avarice, of a favorite leader, protracted the war beyond the limits marked out by sound policy, and for a considerable time in opposition to the views of the court.

The wars of these two last-mentioned nations have in a great measure grown out of commercial considerations,—the desire of supplanting and the fear of being supplanted, either in particular branches of traffic or in the general advantages of trade and navigation.

From this summary of what has taken place in other countries, whose situations have borne the nearest resemblance to our own, what reason can we have to confide in those reveries which would seduce us into an expectation of peace and cordiality between the members of the present confederacy, in a state of separation? Have we not already seen enough of the fallacy and extravagance of those idle theories which have amused us with promises of an exemption from the imperfections, weaknesses, and evils incident to society in every shape? Is it not time to awake from the deceitful dream of a golden age, and to adopt as a practical maxim for the direction of our political conduct that we, as well as the other inhabitants of the globe, are yet remote from the happy empire of perfect wisdom and perfect virtue?

Let the point of extreme depression to which our national dignity and credit have sunk, let the inconveniences felt everywhere from a lax and ill administration of government, let the revolt of a part of the State of North Carolina, the late menacing disturbances in Pennsylvania, and the actual insurrections and rebellions in Massachusetts, declare————!

So far is the general sense of mankind from corresponding with the tenets of those who endeavor to lull asleep our apprehensions of discord and hostility between the States, in the event of disunion, that it has from long observation of the progress of society become a sort of axiom in politics, that vicinity, or nearness of situation constitutes nations natural enemies. An intelligent writer expresses himself on this subject to this effect: "NEIGHBORING NATIONS [says he] are naturally enemies of each other, unless their common weakness forces them to league in a CONFEDERATIVE REPUBLIC, and their constitution prevents the differences that neighborhood occasions, extinguishing that secret jealousy which disposes all states to aggrandize themselves at the expense of their neighbors." This passage, at the same time, points out the EVIL and suggests the REMEDY.

— | "A nation, despicable by its weakness, forfeits even the privilege of being neutral." *

In *The Federalist No. 11* Hamilton warned that the great maritime nations of Europe would attempt to curtail the commercial greatness of the United States. To meet this challenge, wrote Hamilton, the government would require a variety of coercive powers to force the Europeans into granting favorable commercial privileges. He suggested that American interests lay not alone in the creation of a navy to protect American commerce but also in aiming "at an ascendant in the system of American affairs." The success of American diplomacy abroad required above all a strong national Union.

✒

. . . There are appearances to authorize a supposition that the adventurous spirit, which distinguishes the commercial character of America, has already excited uneasy sensations in several of the maritime powers of Europe. They seem to be apprehensive of our too great interference in that carrying trade, which is the support of their navigation and the foundation of their naval strength. Those of them which have colonies in America look forward to what this country is capable of becoming, with painful solicitude. They foresee the

* *The Federalist,* 62–9.

dangers that may threaten their American dominions from the neighborhood of States, which have all the dispositions, and would possess all the means, requisite to the creation of a powerful marine. Impressions of this kind will naturally indicate the policy of fostering divisions among us, and of depriving us, as far as possible, of an ACTIVE COMMERCE in our own bottoms. This would answer the threefold purpose of preventing our interference in their navigation, of monopolizing the profits of our trade, and of clipping the wings by which we might soar to a dangerous greatness. Did not prudence forbid the detail, it would not be difficult to trace, by facts, the workings of this policy to the cabinets of ministers.

If we continue united, we may counteract a policy so unfriendly to our prosperity in a variety of ways. By prohibitory regulations, extending, at the same time, throughout the States, we may oblige foreign countries to bid against each other, for the privileges of our markets. This assertion will not appear chimerical to those who are able to appreciate the importance of the markets of three millions of people—increasing in rapid progression, for the most part exclusively addicted to agriculture, and likely from local circumstances to remain so—to any manufacturing nation; and the immense difference there would be to the trade and navigation of such a nation, between a direct communication in its own ships, and an indirect conveyance of its products and returns, to and from America, in the ships of another country. Suppose, for instance, we had a government in America, capable of excluding Great Britain (with whom we have at present no treaty of commerce) from all our ports; what would be the probable operation of this step upon her politics? Would it not enable us to negotiate, with the fairest prospect of success, for commercial privileges of the most valuable and extensive kind, in the dominions of that kingdom? When these questions have been asked, upon other occasions, they have received a plausible, but not a solid or satisfactory answer. It has been said that prohibitions on our part would produce no change in the system of Britain, because she could prosecute her trade with us through the medium of the Dutch, who would be her immediate customers and paymasters for those articles which were wanted for the supply of our markets. But would not her navigation be materially injured by the loss of the important advantage of being her own carrier in that trade? Would not the principal part of its profits be intercepted by the Dutch, as a compensation for their agency and risk? Would not the mere circumstance of freight occasion a considerable deduction? Would not so circuitous an intercourse facilitate the competition of other nations, by enhancing the price of British commodities in our markets, and by transferring to other hands the management of this interesting branch of the British commerce? . . .

A further resource for influencing the conduct of European nations towards us, in this respect, would arise from the establishment of a federal navy. There can be no doubt that the continuance of the Union under an efficient government, would put it in our power, at a period not very distant, to create a navy which, if it could not vie with those of the great maritime powers, would at least be of respectable weight if thrown into the scale of either of two contending parties. This would be more peculiarly the case in relation to operations in the West Indies. A few ships of the line, sent opportunely to the reinforcement of either side, would often be sufficient to decide the fate of a campaign, on the event of which interests of the greatest magnitude were suspended. Our position is, in this respect, a most commanding one. And if to this consideration we add that of the usefulness of supplies from this country, in the prosecution of military operations in the West Indies, it will readily be perceived that a situation so favorable would enable us to bargain with great advantage for commercial privileges. A price would be set not only upon our friendship, but upon our neutrality. By a steady adherence to the Union, we may hope, erelong, to become the arbiter of Europe in America, and to be able to incline the balance of European competitions in this part of the world as our interest may dictate.

But in the reverse of this eligible situation, we shall discover that the rivalships of the parts would make them checks upon each other, and would frustrate all the tempting advantages which nature has kindly placed within our reach. In a stage so insignificant our commerce would be a prey to the wanton intermeddlings of all nations at war with each other; who, having nothing to fear from us, would with little scruple or remorse supply their wants by depredations on our property as often as it fell in their way. The rights of neutrality will only be respected when they are defended by an adequate power. A nation, despicable by its weakness, forfeits even the privilege of being neutral.

Under a vigorous national government, the natural strength and resources of the country, directed to a common interest, would baffle all the combinations of European jealousy to restrain our growth. This situation would even take away the motive to such combinations, by inducing an impracticability of success. An active commerce, an extensive navigation, and a flourishing marine would then be the offspring of moral and physical necessity. We might defy the little arts of the little politicians to control or vary the irresistible and unchangeable course of nature.

But in a state of disunion, these combinations might exist and might operate with success. It would be in the power of the maritime nations, availing themselves of our universal impotence, to prescribe the conditions of our political existence; and as they have a common interest in being our carriers, and still more in preventing our becoming theirs, they would in all probability combine to embarrass our navigation in such a manner as would in effect destroy it, and confine us to a PASSIVE COMMERCE. We should then be compelled to content ourselves with the first price of our commodities, and to see the enemies and persecutors. That unequalled spirit of enterprise, which signalizes the genius of the American merchants and navigators, and which is in itself an inexhaustible mine of national wealth, would be stifled and lost, and poverty and disgrace would overspread a country which, with wisdom, might make herself the admiration and envy of the world. . . .

There are other points of view in which this subject might be placed, of a striking and animating kind. But they would lead us too far into the regions of futurity, and would involve topics not proper for a newspaper discussion. I shall briefly observe, that our situation invites and our interests prompt us to aim at an ascendant in the system of American affairs. The world may politically, as well as geographically, be divided into four parts, each having a distinct set of interests. Unhappily for the other three, Europe, by her arms and by her negotiations, by force and by fraud, has, in different degrees, extended her dominion over them all. Africa, Asia, and America, have successively felt her domination. The superiority she has long maintained has tempted her to plume herself as the Mistress of the World, and to consider the rest of mankind as created for her benefit. Men admired as profound philosophers have, in direct terms, attributed to her inhabitants a physical superiority and have gravely asserted that all animals, and with them the human species, degenerate in America—that even dogs cease to bark after having breathed awhile in our atmosphere. Facts have too long supported these arrogant pretensions of the Europeans. It belongs to us to vindicate the honor of the human race, and to teach that assuming brother, moderation. Union will enable us to do it. Disunion will add another victim to his triumphs. Let Americans disdain to be the instruments of European greatness! Let the thirteen States, bound together in a strict and indissoluble Union, concur in erecting one great American system, superior to the control of all transatlantic force or influence, and able to dictate the terms of the connection between the old and the new world!

# 9 | Jefferson and the American Principle of Recognition, 1792 *

Americans were stirred to the depths by the outbreak of the French Revolution in July 1789. For many Americans, convinced that the French were merely responding to the American precedent, the events in France merited the nation's full approbation. By 1792 the succession of revolutionary governments in France, each more radical than the one that preceded it, raised the question of recognition. Secretary of State Thomas Jefferson resolved the issue with his statement of American policy on recognition in November 1792.

&

. . . I am perfectly sensible that your situation must, ere this reaches you, have been delicate & difficult: and tho' the occasion is probably over, and your part taken of necessity, so that instructions now would be too late, yet I think it just to express our sentiments on the subject as a sanction of what you have

* Jefferson to Gouverneur Morris, United States Minister to France, November 7, 1792, *The Writings of Thomas Jefferson,* Paul Leicester Ford, ed. (New York, 1895), VI: 131.

probable done. Whenever the scene became personally dangerous to you, it was proper you should leave it, as well from personal as public motives. But what degree of danger should be awaited, to what distance or place you should retire, are circumstances which must rest with your own discretion, it being impossible to prescribe them from hence.—With what kind of government you may do business, is another question. It accords with our principles to acknolege any government to be rightful which is formed by the will of the nation substantially declared. The late government was of this kind, & was accordingly acknoleged by all the branches of ours. So any alteration of it which shall be made by the will of the nation substantially declared, will doubtless be acknoleged in like manner. With such a government *every kind* of business may be done. But there are *some matters* which I conceive might be transacted with a government *de facto;* such for instance as the reforming the unfriendly restrictions on our commerce & navigation. . . .

10 | Jefferson and the Concept of Moral Obligation in Diplomacy, April 1793 *

Despite the vociferous partisanship for the French cause in the United States, the nation managed to avoid involvement in the affairs of Europe. When in February 1793 France and England went to war, however, the pro-French elements in American society, led by Jefferson himself, discovered in the alliance treaty of 1778 an American obligation to support France against England. Washington sought the advice of his cabinet. Hamilton argued that the treaty was negotiated with the French monarchy, not with the French revolutionary government. Thus it was no longer binding. Jefferson countered in April 1793 with an impressive document which insisted that the United States had a binding commitment to France and that the nation's foreign policies should be guided by its moral obligations.

𝒦

    . . . In the Consultation at the President's on the 19th inst. the Secretary of the Treasury took the following positions & consequences. France was a monarchy when we entered into treaties with it: but it has now declared itself a Republic, & is preparing a Republican form of government. As it may issue in a Republic, or a Military despotism, or in something else which may possibly render our alliance with it dangerous to ourselves, we have a right of election

* Jefferson's opinion of the French treaties, April 23, 1793, *The Writings of Thomas Jefferson,* VII: 219–31.

to renounce the treaty altogether, or to declare it suspended till their government shall be settled in the form it is ultimately to take; and then we may judge whether we will call the treaties into operation again, or declare them forever null. Having that right of election now, if we receive their minister without any qualifications, it will amount to an act of election to continue the treaties; & if the change they are undergoing should issue in a form which should bring danger on us, we shall not be then free to renounce them. To elect to continue them is equivalent to the making a new treaty at this time in the same form, that is to say, with a clause of guarantee; but to make a treaty with a clause of guarantee, during a war, is a departure from neutrality, and would make us associates in the war. To renounce or suspend the treaties therefore is a necessary act of neutrality.

If I do not subscribe to the soundness of this reasoning, I do most fully to its ingenuity.—I shall now lay down the principles which according to my understanding govern the case.

I consider the people who constitute a society or nation as the source of all authority in that nation, as free to transact their common concerns by any agents they think proper, to change these agents individually, or the organisation of them in form or function whenever they please: that all the acts done by those agents under the authority of the nation, are the acts of the nation, are obligatory on them, & enure to their use, & can in no wise be annulled or affected by any change in the form of the government, or of the persons administering it. Consequently the Treaties between the U.S. and France, were not treaties between the U.S. & Louis Capet, but between the two nations of America & France, and the nations remaining in existence, tho' both of them have since changed their forms of government, the treaties are not annulled by these changes.

The Law of nations, by which this question is to be determined, is composed of three branches. 1. The Moral law of our nature. 2. The Usages of nations. 3. Their special Conventions. The first of these only, concerns this question, that is to say the Moral law to which Man has been subjected by his creator, & of which his feelings, or Conscience as it is sometimes called, are the evidence with which his creator has furnished him. The Moral duties which exist between individual and individual in a state of nature, accompany them into a state of society & the aggregate of the duties of all the individuals composing the society constitutes the duties of that society towards any other; so that between society & society the same moral duties exist as did between the individuals composing them while in an unassociated state, their maker not having released them from those duties on their forming themselves into a nation. Compacts then between nation & nation are obligatory on them by the same moral law which obliges individuals to observe their compacts. There are circumstances however which sometimes excuse the non-performance of contracts between man & man: so are there also between nation & nation. When performance, for instance, becomes *impossible,* non-performance is not immoral. So if performance becomes *self-destructive* to the party, the law of self-preservation overrules the laws of obligation to others. For the reality of these principles I appeal to the true fountains of evidence, the head & heart of every rational & honest man. It is there Nature has written her moral laws, & where every man may read them for himself. He will never read there the permission to annul his obligations for a time, or for ever, whenever they become "dangerous, useless, or disagreeable." Certainly not when merely *useless* or *disagreeable*, as seems to be said in an authority which has been quoted, Vattel. 2. 197, and tho he may under certain degrees of *danger,* yet the danger must be imminent, & the degree great. . . .

. . . Obligation is not suspended till the danger is become real, & the moment of it so imminent, that we can no longer avoid decision without forever losing the opportunity to do it. But can a danger which has not yet taken it's shape, which does not yet exist, & never may exist, which cannot therefore be defined, can such a danger I ask, be so imminent that if we fail to pronounce on it in this moment we can never have another opportunity of doing it? . . .

If in withholding a compliance with any part of the treaties, we do it without just cause or compensation, we give to France a cause of war, and so become associated in it on the other side. An injured friend is the bitterest of foes, & France had not discovered either timidity, or over-much forbearance on the late occasions. Is this the position we wish to take for our constituents? It is certainly not the one they would take for themselves. . . .

The doctrine . . . of Grotius, Puffendorf & Wolf is that "treaties remain obligatory notwithstanding any change in the form of government, except in the single case where the preservation of that form was the object of the treaty." There the treaty extinguishes, not by the election or declaration of the party remaining in statu quo; but independently of that, by the evanishment of the object. Vattel lays down, in fact, the same doctrine, that treaties continue obligatory, notwithstanding a change of government by the will of the other party, that to oppose that will would be a wrong, & that the ally remains an ally notwithstanding the change. So far he concurs with all the previous writers. But he then adds what they had not said, nor would say "but if this change renders the alliance *useless,* dangerous, or *disagreeable* to it, it is free to renounce it." It was unnecessary for him to have specified the exception of *danger* in this particular case, because that exception exists in all cases & it's extent has been considered. But when he adds that, because a contract is become merely *useless* or *disagreeable,* we are free to renounce it, he is in opposition to Grotius, Puffendorf, & Wolf, who admit no such licence against the obligation of treaties, & he is in opposition to the morality of every honest man, to whom we may safely appeal to decide whether he feels himself free to renounce a contract the moment it becomes merely *useless* or *disagreeable,* to him? . . .

After evidence so copious & explicit of the respect of this author for the sanctity of treaties, we should hardly have expected that his authority would have been resorted to for a wanton invalidation of them whenever they should become merely *useless* or *disagreeable*. We should hardly have expected that, rejecting all the rest of his book, this scrap would have been culled, & made the hook whereon to hang such a chain of immoral consequences. Had the passage accidentally met our eye, we should have imagined it had fallen from the author's pen under some momentary view, not sufficiently developed to found a conjecture what he meant: and we may certainly affirm that a fragment like this cannot weigh against the authority of all other writers, against the uniform & systematic doctrine of every work from which it is torn, against the moral feelings & the reason of all honest men. If the terms of the fragment are not misunderstood, they are in full contradiction to all the written & unwritten evidences of morality: if they are misunderstood, they are no longer a foundation for the doctrines which have been built on them.

But even had this doctrine been as true as it is manifestly false, it would have been asked, to whom is it that the treaties with France have become *disagreeable?* How will it be proved that they are *useless?*

The conclusion of the sentence suggests a reflection too strong to be suppressed "for the party may say with truth that it would not have allied itself with this nation, if it had been under the present form of it's government." The Republic of the U. S. allied itself with France when under a despotic government. She changes her government, declares it shall be a Republic, prepares a form of Republic extremely free, and in the meantime is governing herself as such, and it is proposed that America shall declare the treaties void because "it may say with truth that it would not have allied itself with that nation, if it had been under the present form of it's government!" Who is the American who can say with truth that he would not have allied himself to France if she had been a republic? or that a Republic of any form would be as *disagreeable* as her antient despotism?

Upon the whole I conclude

That the treaties are still binding, notwithstanding the change of government in France: that no part of them, but the clause of guarantee, holds up *danger,* even at a distance.

And consequently that a liberation from no other part could be proposed in any case: that if that clause may ever bring *danger,* it is neither extreme, nor *imminent,* nor even probable: that the authority for renouncing a treaty, when *useless* or *disagreeable,* is either misunderstood, or in opposition to itself, to all their writers, & to every moral feeling: that were it not so, these treaties are in fact neither useless nor disagreeable.

That the receiving a Minister from France at this time is an act of no significance with respect to the treaties, amounting neither to an admission nor a denial of them, forasmuch as he comes not under any stipulation in them:

That were it an explicit admission, or were an express declaration of this obligation now to be made, it would not take from us that right which exists at all times of liberating ourselves when an adherence to the treaties would be *ruinous* or *destructive* to the society: and that the not renouncing the treaties now is so far from being a breach of neutrality, that the doing it would be the breach, by giving just cause of war to France.

When Washington's Proclamation of Neutrality, April 22, 1793, appeared to divide the nation as had no previous issue in its brief history, Hamilton defended the decision of the administration with a series of brilliant essays, published under the name "Pacificus" in July 1793. These writings constitute the most penetrating examination of the diplomatic principles guiding the young Republic to come from the pen of any of the nation's early leaders. Hamilton argued that the United States had neither the power nor the obligation to come to the aid of France, that its first obligation was to itself. Unlike individuals, continued Hamilton, a nation had no right to "indulge in emotions of generosity and benevolence" at the expense of its own interests. Nor had it the right to endanger its own welfare in pursuing the cause of liberty.

## No. III

### July 6, 1793

France, at the time of issuing the proclamation, was engaged in war with a considerable part of Europe, and likely to be embroiled with almost all the rest, without a single ally in that quarter of the globe.

In such a situation, it is evident, that however she may be able to defend herself at home, of which her factions and internal agitations furnish the only serious doubt, she cannot make external efforts in any degree proportioned to those which can be made against her.

This state of things alone discharges the United States from an obligation to embark in her quarrel.

It is known that we are wholly destitute of naval force. France, with all the great maritime powers united against her, is unable to supply this deficiency. She cannot afford us that species of co-operation which is necessary to render our efforts useful to her, and to prevent our experiencing the destruction of our trade, and the most calamitous inconveniences in other respects.

Our guaranty does not look to France herself. It does not relate to her immediate defence, but to the defence and preservation of her American colonies; objects of which she might be deprived, and yet remain a great, a powerful, and a happy nation.

In the actual situation of this country, and in relation to a matter of only secondary importance to France, it may fairly be maintained that an ability in her to supply, in a competent degree, our deficiency of naval force, is a condition of our obligation to perform the guaranty on our part.

* *The Works of Alexander Hamilton*, Henry Cabot Lodge, ed. (New York, 1885), **IV**: 157–71, 175, 178–80, 183.

Had the United States a powerful marine, or could they command one in time, this reasoning would not be solid; but circumstanced as they are, it is presumed to be well founded.

There would be no proportion between the mischiefs and perils to which the United States would expose themselves, by embarking in the war, and the benefit which the nature of their stipulation aims at securing to France, or that which it would be in their power actually to render her by becoming a party.

This disproportion would be a valid reason for not executing the guaranty. All contracts are to receive a reasonable construction. Self-preservation is the first duty of a nation; and though in the performance of stipulations relating to war, good faith requires that its ordinary hazards should be fairly met, because they are directly contemplated by such stipulations, yet it does not require that extraordinary and extreme hazards should be run, especially where the object to be gained or secured is only a partial or particular interest of the ally, for whom they are to be encountered.

As in the present instance, good faith does not require that the United States should put in jeopardy their essential interests, perhaps their very existence, in one of the most unequal contests in which a nation could be engaged, to secure to France—what? Her West India islands and other less important possessions in America. For it is always to be remembered, that the stipulations of the United States do, in no event, reach beyond this point. If they were, upon the strength of their guaranty, to engage in the war, and could make any arrangement with the belligerent Powers, for securing to France those islands and those possessions, they would be at perfect liberty instantly to withdraw. They would not be bound to prosecute the war one moment longer.

They are under no obligation in any event, as far as the faith of treaties is concerned, to assist France in defence of her liberty; a topic on which so much has been said, so very little to the purpose, as it regards the present question.

The contest in which the United States would plunge themselves, were they to take part with France, would possibly be still more unequal than that in which France herself is engaged. With the possessions of Great Britain and Spain on both flanks, the numerous Indian tribes under the influence and direction of those Powers, along our whole interior frontier, with a long extended sea-coast, with no maritime force of our own, and with the maritime force of all Europe against us, with no fortifications whatever, and with a population not exceeding four millions; it is impossible to imagine a more unequal contest than that in which we should be involved in the case supposed. From such a contest we are dissuaded by the most cogent motives of self-preservation, no less than of interest. . . .

If too, as no sensible and candid man will deny, the extent of the present combination against France is in a degree to be ascribed to imprudences on her part, the exemption to the United States is still more manifest and complete. No country is bound to partake in hazards of the most critical kind, which may have been produced or promoted by the indiscretion and intemperance of another. This is an obvious dictate of reason, with which the common sense and common practice of mankind coincide. . . .

No. IV

July 10, 1793

A third objection to the proclamation is, that it is inconsistent with the gratitude due to France for the services rendered to us in our revolution.

Those who make this objection disavow, at the same time, all intention to maintain the position that the United States ought to take part in the war. They profess to be friends to our remaining at peace. What then do they mean by the objection?

If it be no breach of gratitude to refrain from joining France in the war, how can it be a breach of gratitude to declare that such is our disposition and intention?

The two positions are at variance with each other; and the true inference is, either that those who make the objection really wish to engage this country in the war, or that they seek a pretext for censuring the conduct of the Chief Magistrate, for some purpose very different from the public good. . . .

If the objectors mean that the United States ought to favor France, in things relating to war, and where they are not bound to do it by treaty, they must in this case also abandon their pretension of being friends to peace. For such a conduct would be a violation of neutrality, which could not fail to produce war.

It follows then, that the proclamation is reconcilable with all that those who censure it contend for; taking them upon their own ground, that nothing is to be done incompatible with the preservation of peace.

But though this would be a sufficient answer to the objection under consideration, yet it may not be without use to indulge some reflections on this very favorite topic of gratitude to France, since it is at this shrine that we are continually invited to sacrifice the true interests of the country; as if "all for love, and the world well lost," were a fundamental maxim in politics.

Faith and justice between nations are virtues of a nature the most necessary and sacred. They cannot be too strongly inculcated, nor too highly respected. Their obligations are absolute, their utility unquestionable; they relate to objects which, with probity and sincerity, generally admit of being brought within clear and intelligible rules.

But the same cannot be said of gratitude. It is not very often that between nations it can be pronounced with certainty that there exists a solid foundation for the sentiment; and how far it can justifiably be permitted to operate, is always a question of still greater difficulty.

The basis of gratitude is a benefit received or intended, which there was no right to claim, originating in a regard to the interest or advantage of the party on whom the benefit is, or is meant to be, conferred. If a service is rendered from views relative to the immediate interest of the party who performs it, and is productive of reciprocal advantages, there seems scarcely, in such a case, to be an adequate basis for a sentiment like that of gratitude.

The effect at least would be wholly disproportioned to the cause, if such a service ought to beget more than a disposition to render in turn a correspondent good office, founded on mutual interest and reciprocal advantage. But gratitude would require much more than this: it would exact to a certain extent even a sacrifice of the interest of the party obliged to the service or benefit of the one by whom the obligation had been conferred.

Between individuals, occasion is not unfrequently given for the exercise of gratitude. Instances of conferring benefits from kind and benevolent dispositions or feelings toward the person benefited, without any other interest on the part of the person who renders the service, than the pleasure of doing a good action, occur every day among individuals. But among nations they perhaps never occur. It may be affirmed as a general principle, that the predominant motive of good offices from one nation to another is the interest or advantage of the nation which performs them.

Indeed, the rule of morality in this respect is not precisely the same between nations as between individuals. The duty of making its own welfare the guide of its actions, is much stronger upon the former than upon the latter; in proportion to the greater magnitude and importance of national compared with individual happiness, and to the greater permanency of the effects of national than of individual conduct. Existing millions, and for the most part future generations, are concerned in the present measures of a government; while the consequences of the private actions of an individual ordinarily terminate with himself, or are circumscribed with a narrow compass.

Whence it follows that an individual may, on numerous occasions, meritoriously indulge the emotions of generosity and benevolence, not only without an eye to, but even at the expense of, his own interest. But a government can rarely, if at all, be justifiable in pursuing a similar course; and, if it does so, ought to confine itself within much stricter bounds. Good offices which are indifferent to the interest of a nation performing them, or which are compensated by the existence or expectation of some reasonable equivalent, or which produce an essential good to the nation to which they are rendered, without real detriment to the affairs of the benefactors, prescribe perhaps the limits of national generosity or benevolence.

It is not here meant to recommend a policy absolutely selfish or interested in nations; but to show, that a policy regulated by their own interest, as far as justice and good faith permit, is, and ought to be, their prevailing one; and that either to ascribe to them a different principle of action, or to deduce, from the supposition of it, arguments for a self-denying and self-sacrificing gratitude on the part of a nation which may have received from another good offices, is to misrepresent or misconceive what usually are, and ought to be, the springs of national conduct. . . .

## No. V

July 13, 1793

France, the rival, time immemorial, of Great Britain, had, in the course of the war which ended in 1763, suffered from the successful arms of the latter the severest losses and the most mortifying defeats. Britain from that moment had acquired an ascendant in the affairs of Europe, and in the commerce of the world, too decided and too humiliating to be endured without extreme impatience, and an eager desire of finding a favorable opportunity to destroy it, and to repair the breach which had been made in the national glory. The animosity of wounded pride conspired with calculations of interest to give a keen edge to that impatience, and to that desire.

The American revolution offered the occasion. It early attracted the notice of France, though with extreme circumspection. As far as countenance and aid may be presumed to have been given prior to the epoch of the acknowledgment of our independence, it will be no unkind derogation to assert, that they were marked neither with liberality nor with vigor; that they wore the appearance rather of a desire to keep alive disturbances which might embarrass a rival, than of a serious design to assist a revolution, or a serious expectation that it could be effected.

The victories of Saratoga, the capture of any army, which went a great way toward deciding the issue of the contest, decided also the hesitations of France. They established in the government of that country a confidence of our ability to accomplish our purpose, and, as a consequence of it, produced the treaties of alliance and commerce.

It is impossible to see in all this any thing more than the conduct of a jealous competitor, embracing a most promising opportunity to repress the pride and diminish the power of a dangerous rival, by seconding a successful resistance to its authority, with the object of lopping off a valuable portion of its dominions. The dismemberment of this country from Great Britain was an obvious and a very important interest of France. It cannot be doubted that it was both the determining motive and an adequate compensation for the assistance afforded to us.

Men of sense, in this country, derived encouragement to the part which their zeal for liberty prompted them to take in our revolution, from the probability of the co-operation of France and Spain. It will be remembered that this argument was used in the publications of the day; but upon what was it bottomed? Upon the known competition between those nations and Great Britain, upon their evident interest to reduce her power and circumscribe her empire; not certainly from motives of regard to our interest, or of attachment to our cause. Whoever should have alleged the latter, as the grounds of the expectation held out, would have been then justly considered as a visionary or a deceiver. And whoever shall now ascribe to such motives the aid which we did receive, would not deserve to be viewed in a better light.

The inference from these facts is not obscure. Aid and cooperation, founded upon a great interest, pursued and obtained by the party rendering them, is not a proper stock upon which to engraft that enthusiastic gratitude which is claimed from us by those who love France more than the United States.

This view of the subject, extorted by the extravagancy of such a claim, is not meant to disparage the just pretensions of France to our good-will. Though neither in the motives to the success which she furnished, nor in their extent (considering how powerfully the point of honor, in such war, reinforced the considerations of interest when she was once engaged), can be found a sufficient basis for that gratitude which is the theme of so much declamation, yet we shall find, in the manner of affording them, just cause for our esteem and friendship.

France did not attempt, in the first instance, to take advantage of our situation to extort from us any humiliating or injurious concessions as the price of her assistance; nor afterwards, in the progress of the war, to impose hard terms as the condition of particular aids.

Though this course was certainly dictated by policy, yet it was a magnanimous policy, such as always constitutes a title to the approbation and esteem of mankind, and a claim to the friendship and acknowledgment of the party in whose favor it is practised.

But these sentiments are satisfied on the part of the nation, when they produce sincere wishes for the happiness of the party from whom it has experienced such conduct, and a cordial disposition to render all good and friendly offices which can be rendered without prejudice to its own solid and permanent interests.

To ask of a nation so situated, to make a sacrifice of substantial interest; to expose itself to the jealousy, ill-will, or resentment of the rest of the world; to hazard, in an eminent degree, its own safety for the benefit of the party who may have observed towards it the conduct which has been described, would be to ask more than the nature of the case demands, more than the fundamental maxims of society authorize, more than the dictates of sound reason justify. . . .

## No. VI

July 17, 1793

. . . But we are sometimes told, by way of answer, that the cause of France is the cause of liberty; and that we are bound to assist the nation on the score of their being engaged in the defence of that cause. How far this idea ought to carry us, will be the subject of future examination.

It is only necessary here to observe that it presents a question essentially different from that which has been in discussion. If we are bound to assist the French nation, on the principle of their being embarked in the defence of liberty, this is a consideration altogether foreign to that of gratitude. Gratitude has reference only to kind offices received. The obligation to assist the cause of liberty must be deduced from the merits of that cause and from the interest we have in its support. It is possible that the benefactor may be on one side; the defenders and supporters of liberty on the other. Gratitude may point one way, the love of liberty another. It is therefore important to just conclusions, not to confound the two things.

A sentiment of justice, more than the importance of the question itself, has led to so particular a discussion respecting the proper object of whatever acknowledgment may be due from the United States, for the aid which they received from France during their own revolution.

The extent of the obligation which it may impose is by far the most interesting inquiry. And though it is presumed, that enough has been already said to evince, that it does in no degree require us to embark in the war, yet there is another and a very simple view of the subject, which is too convincing to be omitted.

The assistance derived from France was afforded by a great and powerful nation, possessing numerous armies, a respectable fleet, and the means of rendering it a match for the force to be encountered. The position of Europe was favorable to the enterprise; a general disposition prevailing to see the power of Britain abridged. The co-operation of Spain was very much a matter of course, and the probability of other Powers becoming engaged on the same side not remote. Great Britain was alone, and likely to continue so; France had a great and persuasive interest in the separation of this country from her. In this situation, with much to hope and little to fear, she took part in our quarrel.

France is at this time singly engaged with the greatest part of Europe, including all the first-rate Powers except one; and in danger of being engaged with the rest. To use the emphatic language of a member of the national convention, she has but one enemy, and that is all Europe. Her internal affairs are, without doubt, in serious disorder; her navy comparatively inconsiderable. The United States are a young nation: their population, though rapidly increasing, still small; their resources, though growing, not great; without armies, without fleets; capable, from the nature of the country and the spirit of its inhabitants, of immense exertions for self defence, but little capable of those external efforts which could materially serve the cause of France. So far from having any direct interest in going to war, they have the strongest motives of interest to avoid it. By embarking with France in the war, they would have incomparably more to apprehend than to hope.

This contrast of situations and inducements is alone a conclusive demonstration, that the United States are not under an obligation, from gratitude, to join France in the war. The utter disparity between the circumstances of the service to be rendered, and of the service received, proves that the one cannot be an adequate basis of obligation for the other. There would be a manifest want of equality, and consequently of reciprocity.

But complete justice would not be done to this question of gratitude, were no notice to be taken of the address which has appeared in the public papers (the authenticity of which has not been impeached), from the convention of France to the United States, announcing the appointment of the present Minister Plenipotentiary. In that address the convention informs us, that "the support which the ancient French court had afforded the United States to recover their independence, was only the fruit of a base speculation; and that their glory offended its ambitious views, and the ambassadors of France bore the criminal orders of stopping the career of their prosperity.". . .

The information which the address of the convention contains ought to serve as an instructive lesson to the people of this country. It ought to teach us not to overrate foreign friendships, and to be upon our guard against foreign attachments. The former will generally be found hollow and delusive; the latter will have a natural tendency to lead us aside from our own true interest, and to make us the dupes of foreign influence. Both serve to introduce a principle of action which in its effects, if the expression may be allowed, is anti-national. Foreign influence is truly the Grecian horse to a republic. We cannot be too careful to exclude its entrance. Nor ought we to imagine that it can only make its approaches in the gross form of direct bribery. It is then most dangerous when it comes under the patronage of our passions, under the auspices of national prejudice and partiality.

I trust the morals of this country are yet too good to leave much to be apprehended on the score of bribery. Caresses, condescensions, flattery, in unison with our prepossessions, are infinitely more to be feared; and as far as there is opportunity for corruption, it is to be remembered that one foreign Power can employ this resource as well as another, and that the effect must be much greater when it is combined with other means of influence than where it stands alone.

## 12 | James Madison's Argument for Congressional Leadership in Foreign Affairs: "Helvidius" *

Jefferson, recognizing the strength of Hamilton's "Pacificus" papers, urged his disciple, James Madison, to take up the pen and answer Hamilton lest his views remain unchallenged. Madison, under the pseudonym "Helvidius," avoided a direct assault on Hamilton's concept of national interest, but questioned instead Washington's right, as President, to issue the Neutrality Proclamation. He argued that the Executive, in issuing a proclamation which had the force of law and committed the nation to a specific relationship with other countries over questions of peace and war, had infringed upon powers belonging to Congress.

Having seen that the executive has no constitutional right to interfere in any question, whether there be or be not a cause of war, and the extensive consequences flowing from the doctrines on which such a claim has been asserted, it remains to be inquired, whether the writer is better warranted in the fact which he assumes, namely, that the proclamation of the executive has undertaken to decide the question whether there be a cause of war or not, in the article of guaranty between the United States and France, and in so doing has exercised the right which is claimed for that department.

Before I proceed to the examination of this point, it may not be amiss to advert to the novelty of the phraseology, as well as of the doctrines espoused by

* *Letters and Other Writings of James Madison* (Philadelphia, 1865), I: 646–54.

this writer. The source from which the former is evidently borrowed may en-
lighten our conjectures with regard to the source of the latter. It is a just
observation, also, that words have often a gradual influence on ideas, and when
used in an improper sense may cover fallacies which would not otherwise
escape detection.

I allude particularly to his application of the term *government* to the *executive authority alone.* The proclamation is a "manifestation of the sense of the
government.". . . The reader will probably be struck with the reflection, that
if the proclamation really possessed the character, and was to have the effects,
here ascribed to it, something more than the authority of *the government,* in
the writer's sense of government, would have been a necessary sanction to the
act; and if the term "government" be removed, and that of "president" substituted, in the sentence quoted, the justice of the reflection will be felt with
peculiar force. But I remark only on the singularity of the style adopted by the
writer, as showing either that the phraseology of a foreign government is more
familiar to him than the phraseology proper to our own, or that he wishes to
propagate a familiarity of the former in preference to the latter. . . . "The
government" unquestionably means, in the United States, the whole government, not the executive part, either exclusively or *pre-eminently;* as it may do
in a monarchy, where the splendor of prerogative eclipses, and the machinery
of influence directs, every other part of the government. In the former and
proper sense, the term has hitherto been used in official proceedings, in public
discussions, and in private discourse. It is as short and as easy, and less liable
to misapprehension, to say the executive or the president, as to say the government. In a word, the new dialect could not proceed either from necessity,
conveniency, propriety, or perspicuity; and being in opposition to common
usage, so marked a fondness for it justifies the notice here taken of it. It shall
no longer detain me, however, from the more important subject of the present
paper.

I proceed, therefore, to observe, that as a "proclamation," in its *ordinary* use,
is an address to citizens or subjects only; as it is always understood to relate to
the law *actually in operation,* and to be an act *purely* and *exclusively* executive,
there can be no implication in the *name* or the *form* of such an instrument,
that it was meant principally for the information of foreign nations; far less
that it related to an *eventual stipulation* on the subject *acknowledged* to be
within the *legislative province.* . . .

If there be anything in the proclamation of which the writer could have
made a handle, it is the part which declares the *disposition,* the *duty,* and the
*interest* of the United States, in relation to the war existing in Europe. As the
legislature is the only competent and constitutional organ of the will of the
nation, that is, of its disposition, its duty, and its interest, in relation to a
commencement of war, in like manner as the president and senate *jointly,* not
the president *alone,* are in relation to peace, after war has been commenced, I
will not dissemble my wish that a language less exposed to criticism had been
preferred; but taking the expressions, in the sense of the writer himself, as
analogous to the language which might be proper on the reception of a public

minister or any similar occasion, it is evident that his construction can derive no succour even from this source.

If the proclamation, then, does not *require* the construction which this writer has taken the liberty of putting on it, I leave it to be decided whether the following considerations do not forbid us to suppose that the president could have intended, by that act, to embrace and prejudge the legislative question, whether there was, or was not, under the circumstances of the case, a cause of war in the article of guaranty.

It has been shown that such an intention would have usurped a prerogative not vested in the executive, and even *confessedly* vested in another department.

In exercising the constitutional power of deciding a question of war, the legislature ought to be as free to decide, according to its own sense of the public good, on one side as on the other side. Had the proclamation prejudged the question on either side and *proclaimed its decision to the world,* the legislature, instead of being as free as it ought, might be thrown under the dilemma of either sacrificing its judgment to that of the executive, or, by opposing the executive judgment, of producing a relation between the two departments extremely delicate among ourselves, and of the worst influence on the national character and interests abroad. A variance of this nature, it will readily be perceived, would be very different from a want of conformity to the mere recommendations of the executive in the measures adopted by the legislature. . . .

There are reasons of another sort which would have been a bar to such a proceeding. It would have been as impolitic as it would have been unfair and unkind.

If France meant not to insist on the guaranty, the measure, without giving any present advantage, would have deprived the United States of a future claim which may be of importance to their safety. It would have inspired France with jealousies of a secret bias in this country toward some of her enemies, which might have left in her breast a spirit of contempt and revenge of which the effects might be felt in various ways. It must in particular have tended to inspire her with a disinclination to feed our commerce with those important advantages which it already enjoys, and those more important ones, which it anxiously contemplates. The nation that consumes more of the fruits of our soil than any other nation in the world, and supplies the only foreign raw material of extensive use in the United States, would not be unnecessarily provoked by those who understand the public interest, and make it their study, as it is their interest to advance it. . . .

On the supposition that France might intend to claim the guaranty, a hasty and harsh refusal before we were asked, on a ground that accused her of being the aggressor in the war against every power in the catalogue of her enemies, and in a crisis when all her sensibility must be alive towards the United States, would have given every possible irritation to a disappointment which every motive that one nation could feel towards another and towards itself, required to be alleviated by all the circumspection and delicacy that could be applied to the occasion.

The silence of the Executive since the accession of Spain and Portugal to the

war against France throws great light on the present discussion. Had the proclamation been issued in the sense, and for the purposes ascribed to it, that is to
say, as a declaration of neutrality, another would have followed, on that event.
If it was the right and duty of the *Government,* that is, the *President,* to manifest to Great Britain and Holland, and to the American merchants and citizens,
his *sense,* his *disposition,* and his *views* on the question, whether *the United
States were under the circumstances of the case, bound or not, to execute the
clause of guaranty, and not to leave it uncertain whether the Executive did or
did not believe a state of neutrality,* to be consistent with our treaties, the *duty*
as well as the right prescribed a similar manifestation to all the parties concerned
after Spain and Portugal had joined the other maritime enemies of France. The
opinion of the Executive with respect to a consistency or inconsistency of neutrality with treaties in the *latter case,* could not be *inferred* from the proclamation in the former, because the *circumstances might be different.* Taking the
proclamation in its proper sense, as reminding all concerned, that as the United
States were at peace, (that state not being affected by foreign wars, and only
to be changed by the legislative authority of the country,) the laws of peace
were still obligatory and would be enforced, and the inference is so obvious and
so applicable to all other cases *whatever circumstances* may distinguish them,
that another proclamation would be unnecessary. Here is a new aspect of the
whole subject, admonishing us in the most striking manner at once of the
danger of the prerogative contended for, and the absurdity of the distinctions
and arguments employed in its favour. It would be as impossible in practice, as
it is in theory, to separate the power of judging and concluding that the obligations of a treaty do not impose war from that of judging and concluding that
the obligations *do impose war.* In certain cases, silence would proclaim the
latter conclusion, as intelligibly as words could do the former. . . .


13 | Hamilton on the Foundations of Prudent Action
      in Foreign Affairs: "Americanus" *


In his "Americanus" papers, published early in 1794, Hamilton continued the
argumentation of "Pacificus" against involvement in the wars of Europe on the
side of France. Prudence demanded, he wrote, that the United States measure
not only its limited power to influence the affairs of Europe but also the limited
power of Europe to interfere in affairs purely American. The European
balance of power guaranteed the existence of the United States, for the
great nations would never permit one of their number to destroy its freedom.

* *The Works of Alexander Hamilton,* IV: 272, 274–82.

Nor did France, in the throes of violence and bloodshed, comprise for Hamilton the cause of liberty.

✍

## II

February 8, 1794

. . . The certain evils of our joining France in the war are sufficient dissuasives from so intemperate a measure. The possible ones are of a nature to call for all our caution, all our prudence.

To defend its own rights, to vindicate its own honor, there are occasions when a nation ought to hazard even its existence. Should such an occasion occur, I trust those who are most averse to commit the peace of the country, will not be the last to face the danger, nor the first to turn their backs upon it.

But let us at least have the consolation of not having rashly courted misfortune. Let us have to act under the animating reflection of being engaged in repelling wrongs, which we neither sought nor merited; in vindicating our rights, invaded without provocation; in defending our honor, violated without cause. Let us not have to reproach ourselves with having voluntarily bartered blessings for calamities.

But we are told that our own liberty is at stake upon the event of the war against France—that if she falls, we shall be the next victim. The combined powers, it is said, will never forgive in us the origination of those principles which were the germs of the French Revolution. They will endeavor to eradicate them from the world.

If this suggestion were ever so well founded, it would perhaps be a sufficient answer to it to say, that our interference is not likely to alter the case; that it would only serve prematurely to exhaust our strength.

But other answers more conclusive present themselves.

The war against France requires, on the part of her enemies, efforts unusually violent. They are obliged to strain every nerve, to exert every resource. However it may terminate, they must find themselves spent in an extreme degree; a situation not very favorable to the undertaking anew, and even to Europe combined, an immense enterprise.

To subvert by force republican liberty in this country, nothing short of entire conquest would suffice. This conquest, with our present increased population, greatly distant as we are from Europe, would either be impracticable, or would demand such exertions as, following immediately upon those which will have been requisite to the subversion of the French Revolution, would be absolutely ruinous to the undertakers.

It is against all probability that an undertaking, pernicious as this would be, even in the event of success, would be attempted against an unoffending nation, by its geographical position little connected with the political concerns of Europe.

But impediments would arise from more special causes. Suppose France subdued, and a restoration of the monarchy in its ancient form, or a partition effected—to uphold either state of things, after the general impulse in favor of liberty which has been given to the minds of twenty-four millions of people, would in one way or another find occupation for a considerable part of the forces which had brought it about.

In the event of an unqualified restoration of the monarchy, if the future monarch did not stand in need of foreign legions for the support of his authority, still the powers which had been concerned in the restoration could not sufficiently rely upon the solidity of the orders of things re-established by them, not to keep themselves in a posture to be prepared against the disturbance of it, till there had been time to compose the discordant interests and passions produced by the revolution, and bring back the nation to ancient habits of subordination. In the event of a partition of France, it would of course give occupation to the forces of the conquerors to secure the submission of the dismembered parts.

The new dismemberment of Poland will be another obstacle to the detaching of troops from Europe for a crusade against this country—the fruits of that transaction can only be secured to Russia and Prussia by the agency of large bodies of forces, kept on foot for the purpose, within the dismembered territories.

Of the powers combined against France, there are only three whose interests have any material reference to this country—England, Spain, Holland. As to Holland, it will be readily conceded that she can have no interest or feeling to induce her to embark in so mad and wicked a project. Let us see how the matter will stand with regard to Spain and England.

The object of the enterprise against us must be, either the establishment in this country of a royal in place of our present republican government, the subjugation of the country to the dominion of one of the parties, or its division among them.

The establishment of an independent monarchy in this country would be so manifestly against the interests of both those nations, in the ordinary acceptation of this term in politics, that neither of them is at all likely to desire it.

It may be adopted as an axiom in our political calculations, that no foreign power which has valuable colonies in America, will be propitious to our remaining one people under a vigorous government.

No man, I believe, but will think it probable, however disadvantageous the change in other respects, that a monarchical government, from its superior force, would ensure more effectually than our present form our permanent unity as a nation. This at least would be the indubitable conclusion of European calculators; from which may be confidently inferred a disinclination in England and Spain to our undergoing a change of that kind.

The only thing that can be imagined capable of reconciling either of those powers to it would be the giving us for monarch a member of its own royal family, and forming something like a family compact.

But here would arise a direct collision of interests between them. Which of them would agree that a prince of the family of the other should, by reigning over this country, give to that other a decided preponderancy in the scale of American affairs?

The subjugation of the United States to the dominion of those powers would fall more strongly under a like consideration. 'T is impossible that either of them should consent that the other should become master of this country, and neither of them without madness could desire a mastery which would cost more than 'twas worth to maintain it, and which, from an irresistible course of things, could be but of very short duration.

The third, namely, the division of it between them, is the most colorable of the three suppositions. But even this would be the excess of folly in both. The dominion of neither of them could be of any permanency, and while it lasted, would cost more than it was worth. Spain on her part could scarcely fail to be sensible that, from obvious causes, her dominion over the part which was allotted to her would be altogether transient.

The first collision between Britain and Spain would indubitably have one of two effects, either a temporary reunion of the whole country under Great Britain, or a dismission of the yoke of both.

The latter, by far the most probable and eventually certain, would discover to both the extreme absurdity of the project. If the first step was a reunion under Great Britain, the second, and one not long deferred, would be a rejection of her authority.

The United States, rooted as are now the ideas of independence, are happily too remote from Europe to be governed by her; dominion over any part of them would be a real misfortune to any nation of that quarter of the globe.

To Great Britain, the enterprise supposed would threaten serious consequences in more ways than one. It may safely be affirmed, that she would run by it greater risks of bankruptcy and revolution than we of subjugation. A chief proportion of the burthen would unavoidably fall upon her as the monied and principal maritime power, and it may emphatically be said, that she would make war upon her own commerce and credit. There is the strongest ground to believe that the nation would disrelish and oppose the project. The certainty of great evils attending it, the dread of much greater, experience of the disasters of the last war, would operate upon all; many, not improbably a majority, would see in the enterprise a malignant and wanton hostility against liberty, of which they might themselves expect to be the next victim. Their judgments and their feeling would easily distinguish this case from either that of their former contest with us or their present contest with France. In the former they had pretensions to support which were plausible enough to mislead their pride and their interest. In the latter there were strong circumstances to rouse their passions, alarm their fears, and induce an acquiescence in the course which was pursued.

But a future attack upon us, as is apprehended, would be so absolutely pretextless, as not to be understood. Our conduct will have been such as to entitle us to the reverse of unfriendly or hostile dispositions, while powerful motives of self-interest would advocate with them our cause.

But Britain, Spain, Austria, Prussia, and perhaps even Russia, will have more need and a stronger desire of peace and repose, to restore and recruit their wasted strength and exhausted treasures, to reinvigorate the interior order and industry of their respective kingdoms, relaxed and depressed by war, than either means or inclination to undertake so extravagant an enterprise against the liberty of this country.

If there can be any danger to us, it must arise from our voluntarily thrusting ourselves into the war. Once embarked, nations sometimes prosecute enterprises of which they would not otherwise have dreamt. The most violent resentment, as before intimated, would no doubt in such a case be kindled against us, for what would be called a wanton and presumptuous intermeddling on our part; what this might produce, it is not easy to calculate.

There are two great errors in our reasoning upon this subject: one, that the combined powers will certainly attribute to us the same principles which they deem so exceptionable in France; the other, that our principles are in fact the same.

If left to themselves they will all . . . naturally see in us a people who originally resorted to a revolution in government, as a refuge from encroachments on rights and privileges *antecedently* enjoyed, not as a people who from choice sought a radical and entire change in the established government, in pursuit of new privileges and rights carried to an extreme, irreconcilable perhaps with any form of regular government. They will see in us a people who have a due respect for property and personal security; who, in the midst of our revolution, abstained with exemplary moderation from every thing violent or sanguinary, instituting governments adequate to the protection of persons and property; who, since the completion of our revolution, have in a very short period, from mere reasoning and reflection, without tumult or bloodshed, adopted a form of general government calculated, as well as the nature of things would permit, to remedy antecedent defects, to give strength and security to the nation, to rest the foundations of liberty on the basis of justice, order, and law; who have at all times been content to govern themselves without intermeddling with the affairs or governments of other nations; in fine, they will see in us sincere republicans, but decided enemies to licentiousness and anarchy; sincere republicans, but decided friends to the freedom of opinion, to the order and tranquillity of all mankind. They will not see in us a people whose best passions have been misled, and whose best qualities have been perverted from their true direction by headlong, fanatical, or designing leaders, to the perpetration of acts from which humanity shrinks, to the commission of outrages over which the eye of reason weeps, to the profession and practice of principles wihch tend to shake the foundations of morality, to dissolve the social bands, to disturb the peace of mankind, to substitute confusion to order, anarchy to government.

Such at least is the light in which the reason or the passions of the powers confederated against France lead them to view her principles and conduct. And it is to be lamented, that so much cause has been given for their opinions. If, on our part, we give no incitement to their passions, facts too prominent and too decisive to be combated will forbid their reason to bestow the same character upon us.

It is therefore matter of real regret, that there should be an effort on our part to level the distinctions which discriminate our case from that of France, to confound the two cases in the view of foreign powers, and to pervert or hazard our own principles by persuading ourselves of a similitude which does not exist.

Let us content ourselves with lamenting the errors into which a great, a gallant, an amiable, a respectable nation has been betrayed, with uniting our wishes and our prayers that the Supreme Ruler of the world will bring them back from those errors to a more sober and more just way of thinking and acting, and will overrule the complicated calamities which surround them, to the establishment of a government under which they may be free, secure, and happy. But let us not corrupt ourselves by false comparisons or glosses, nor shut our eyes to the true nature of transactions which ought to grieve and warn us, nor rashly mingle our destiny in the consequences of the errors and extravagances of another nation.

## 14 | Washington's Farewell Address: The National Interest in Diplomatic Freedom, September 17, 1796 *

Washington's famous valedictory to the nation was the fitting culmination of Federalist writings on the subject of government, politics, and foreign affairs. It contained the essence of the views expressed earlier by Hamilton in both *The Federalist* and the "Pacificus" and "Americanus" papers. Washington argued, as had Hamilton, for separation from the politics of Europe and for policies that would avoid all concepts of moral and ideological preference which might prejudice the nation's freedom of choice by universalizing its interests under a blanket of abstract ideals. Washington's address was, therefore, a declaration of diplomatic independence, and as such was condemned by those who still insisted that the United States had special obligations to France.

### ✍

. . . Observe good faith and justice toward all nations. Cultivate peace and harmony with all. Religion and morality enjoin this conduct. And can it be that good policy does not equally enjoin it? It will be worthy of a free, enlightened, and at no distant period a great nation to give to mankind the magnanimous and too novel example of a people always guided by an exalted justice and benevolence. Who can doubt that in the course of time and things

* *Messages and Papers of the Presidents,* James D. Richardson, ed. (Washington, 1896), I: 221–3.

the fruits of such a plan would richly repay any temporary advantages which might be lost by a steady adherence to it? Can it be that Providence has not connected the permanent felicity of a nation with its virtue? The experiment, at least, is recommended by every sentiment which ennobles human nature. Alas! is it rendered impossible by its vices?

In the execution of such a plan nothing is more essential than that permanent, inveterate antipathies against particular nations and passionate attachments for others should be excluded, and that in place of them just and amicable feelings toward all should be cultivated. The nation which indulges toward another an habitual hatred or an habitual fondness is in some degree a slave. It is a slave to its animosity or to its affection, either of which is sufficient to lead it astray from its duty and its interest. Antipathy in one nation against another disposes each more readily to offer insult and injury, to lay hold of slight causes of umbrage, and to be haughty and intractable when accidental or trifling occasions of dispute occur.

Hence frequent collisions, obstinate, envenomed, and bloody contests. The nation prompted by ill will and resentment sometimes impels to war the government contrary to the best calculations of policy. The government sometimes participates in the national propensity, and adopts through passion what reason would reject. At other times it makes the animosity of the nation subservient to projects of hostility, instigated by pride, ambition, and other sinister and pernicious motives. The peace often, sometimes perhaps the liberty, of nations has been the victim.

So, likewise, a passionate attachment of one nation for another produces a variety of evils. Sympathy for the favorite nation, facilitating the illusion of an imaginary common interest in cases where no real common interest exists, and infusing into one the enmities of the other, betrays the former into a participation in the quarrels and wars of the latter without adequate inducement or justification. It leads also to concessions to the favorite nation of privileges denied to others, which is apt doubly to injure the nation making the concessions by unnecessarily parting with what ought to have been retained, and by exciting jealousy, ill will, and a disposition to retaliate in the parties from whom equal privileges are withheld; and it gives to ambitious, corrupted, or deluded citizens (who devote themselves to the favorite nation) facility to betray or sacrifice the interests of their own country without odium, sometimes even with popularity, gilding with the appearances of a virtuous sense of obligation a commendable deference for public opinion, or a laudable zeal for public good the base or foolish compliances of ambition, corruption, or infatuation.

As avenues to foreign influence in innumerable ways, such attachments are particularly alarming to the truly enlightened and independent patriot. How many opportunities do they afford to tamper with domestic factions, to practice the arts of seduction, to mislead public opinion, to influence or awe the public councils! Such an attachment of a small or weak toward a great and powerful nation dooms the former to be the satellite of the latter. Against the insidious wiles of foreign influence ( I conjure you to believe me, fellow-citizens) the jealousy of a free people ought to be *constantly* awake, since history and experience prove that foreign influence is one of the most baneful foes of republican government. But that jealousy, to be useful, must be impartial, else it becomes the instrument of the very influence to be avoided, instead of a defense against it. Excessive partiality for one foreign nation and excessive dislike of another cause those whom they actuate to see danger only on one side, and serve to veil and even second the arts of influence on the other. Real patriots who may resist the intrigues of the favorite are liable to become suspected and odious, while its tools and dupes usurp the applause and confidence of the people to surrender their interests.

The great rule of conduct for us in regard to foreign nations is, in extending our commercial relations to have with them as little *political* connection as possible. So far as we have already formed engagements let them be fulfilled with perfect good faith. Here let us stop.

Europe has a set of primary interests which to us have none or a very remote relation. Hence she must be engaged in frequent controversies, the causes of which are essentially foreign to our concerns. Hence, therefore, it must be unwise in us to implicate ourselves by artificial ties in the ordinary vicissitudes of her politics or the ordinary combinations and collisions of her friendships or enmities.

Our detached and distant situation invites and enables us to pursue a different course. If we remain one people, under an efficient government, the period is not far off when we may defy material injury from external annoyance; when we may take such an attitude as will cause the neutrality we may at any time resolve upon to be scrupulously respected; when belligerent nations, under the impossibility of making acquisitions upon us, will not lightly hazard the giving us provocation; when we may choose peace or war, as our interest, guided by justice, shall counsel.

Why forego the advantages of so peculiar a situation? Why quit our own to stand upon foreign ground? Why, by interweaving our destiny with that of any part of Europe, entangle our peace and prosperity in the toils of European ambition, rivalship, interest, humor, or caprice?

It is our true policy to steer clear of permanent alliances with any portion of the foreign world, so far, I mean, as we are now at liberty to do it; for let me not be understood as capable of patronizing infidelity to existing engagements. I hold the maxim no less applicable to public than to private affairs that honesty is always the best policy. I repeat, therefore, let those engagements be observed in their genuine sense. But in my opinion it is unnecessary and would be unwise to extend them.

Taking care always to keep ourselves by suitable establishments on a respectable defensive posture, we may safely trust to temporary alliances for extraordinary emergencies.

Harmony, liberal intercourse with all nations are recommended by policy, humanity, and interest. But even our commercial policy should hold an equal and impartial hand, neither seeking nor granting exclusive favors or preferences; consulting the natural course of things; diffusing and diversifying by gentle means the streams of commerce, but forcing nothing; establishing with powers so disposed, in order to give trade a stable course, to define the rights of our merchants, and to enable the Government to support them, conventional rules of intercourse, the best that present circumstances and mutual opinion will permit, but temporary and liable to be from time to time abandoned or varied as experience and circumstances shall dictate; constantly keeping in view that it is folly in one nation to look for disinterested favors from another; that it must pay with a portion of its independence for whatever it may accept under that character; that by such acceptance it may place itself in the condition of having given equivalents for nominal favors, and yet of being reproached with ingratitude for not giving more. There can be no greater error than to expect or calculate upon real favors from nation to nation. It is an illusion which experience must cure, which a just pride ought to discard. . . .

# II

## The Foundations of American Foreign Policy

Thomas Jefferson inherited from his Federalist predecessors a body of diplomatic thought and practice rooted firmly in the realistic traditions of the modern world. Washington and Hamilton had established the principles which guided the nation's behavior. "In every act of my administration," Washington wrote in 1795, "I have sought the happiness of my fellow citizens. My system for the attainment of this object has uniformly been to overlook all personal, local, and partial considerations; to contemplate the United States as one great whole, . . . and to consult only the substantial and permanent interest of our country." He warned the nation to aspire to no more than this, declaring that "it is a maxim, founded on the universal experience of mankind, that no nation is to be trusted further than it is bound by its interest; and no prudent statesman or politician will venture to depart from it." Regarding as dangerous the intrusion of morality and ideology in affairs among nations, the Federalists committed the United States to a genuinely flexible, amoral world view, which would maximize the country's freedom to pursue its own requirements. Washington warned the Republic in his Farewell Address: "The nation which indulges toward another an habitual hatred or an habitual fondness is in some degree a slave. It is a slave to its animosity or to its affection, either of which is sufficient to lead it astray from its duty and its interest."

To guarantee the nation's independence from European politics the Founding Fathers expanded the concept of geographical isolation into a fundamental theory of national policy. Except for the French alliance the United States would not have gained its independence. But few Americans anticipated that this involvement in Europe's rivalries, entered into only through necessity, would extend beyond the achievement of independence itself. As early as 1780 John Adams warned Congress against future American entanglements with the powers of Europe. "Our business with them, and theirs with us," he wrote, "is commerce, not politics, much less war. America has been the sport of European wars and politics long enough." During the peace negotiations of November

77

1782, Adams explained to Oswald, the British plenipotentiary, his fear of any permanent American commitment to Europe:

> It is obvious that all the powers of Europe will be continually manoeuvering with us, to work us into their real or imaginary balance of power. . . . They will all wish to make us a makeweight-candle, when they are making out their pounds. Indeed it is not surprising, for we shall very often, if not always, be able to turn the scale. But I think it ought to be our rule not to meddle, and that of all the powers of Europe, not to desire us nor perhaps even to permit us to interfere, if they can help it.

After 1783 American officials made the avoidance of entangling alliances the keystone of their diplomacy. "It is our true policy," wrote Washington, "to steer clear of permanent alliances with any portion of the foreign world, so far, I mean, as we are now at liberty to do it." In 1796 Washington was still troubled by the French alliance. But eight years earlier John Jay had attempted to consign the alliance to history. On the arrival of the French Minister, the Marquis de Moustier, Jay insisted that the compact had been created to secure American independence, and that, having attained that purpose, it could no longer serve any useful object. The French refused to negotiate a formal abrogation of the treaty, and thus it continued nominally in force. But when President Adams negotiated his understanding with the French government, the two nations seized the occasion to terminate the arrangement. By the Treaty of Morfontaine of 1800 the alliance ceased to exist. Adams had no great interest in substituting for this alliance a new one with England. When the House of Representatives passed a resolution to entrust the nation's security to its own resources and energy, Adams replied: "The genuine disdain which you so coolly and deliberately express, of a reliance on foreign protection, wanting no foreign guarantee of our liberties, resolving to maintain our national independence against every attempt to despoil us of this inestimable treasure, will meet the . . . exulting applauses from the heart of every faithful American." Even the pro-British Hamilton opposed an alliance treaty with Britain as an unnecessary entanglement. Jefferson, in carrying forward this established policy, phrased its essentials best when he wrote, ". . . peace, commerce, and honest friendship with all nations, entangling alliances with none."

That balance of power which had made independence possible would also preserve it. As long as that balance remained, the United States could have no vital interest at stake in the wars of Europe. Prudent policy, therefore, would limit the political interests of the United States to the Western Hemisphere, where the nation's geographical insulation would contribute to the defense of those interests. In his Farewell Address, Washington acknowledged the diplomatic and military benefits that accrued from distance. "Why forego the advantages of so peculiar a situation?" he asked. "Why quit our own to stand on foreign ground?" Washington's convictions reflected a realistic judgment of European power and the conclusion that the young Republic would only waste its energies if it engaged in struggles abroad which it could not control.

Jefferson, in his First Inaugural Address, restated the advantage of America's isolation from the strife of Europe:

> Kindly separated by nature and a wide ocean from the exterminating havoc of one quarter of the globe; too high-minded to endure the degradations of the others; possessing a chosen country, with room enough for our descendants to the thousandth and thousandth generation; entertaining a due sense of our equal right to the use of our own faculties, to the acquisitions of our own industry, to honor and confidence from our fellow-citizens, resulting not from birth, but from our actions . . . ; enlightened by a benign religion, professed, indeed, and practiced in various forms, yet all of them inculcating honesty, truth, temperance, gratitude, and the love of man . . . with all these blessings, what more is necessary to make us a happy and a prosperous people?

In their preoccupation with diplomatic flexibility, the nation's early leaders reinforced the doctrine of no entangling alliances with the principle of complete neutrality in relation to Europe's wars. No nation could be totally free that had bartered away its right to be neutral. Nor could a nation be free that lacked the strength to enforce its neutrality. Washington recognized the role of force in the country's noninvolvement when he wrote: "If we remain one people, under an efficient government, the period is not far off when we . . . may take such an attitude as will cause the neutrality we may at any time resolve upon to be scrupulously respected; when belligerent nations . . . will not lightly hazard the giving us provocation. . . ." But always the avoidance of strife was less important than preserving the nation's freedom to carry out its own decisions. By maintaining a close balance between its commitments and its power, the nation could choose, in Washington's words, "peace or war, as our interest, guided by justice, shall counsel."

If the United States during the wars of the French Revolution maintained its independence of action more successfully than did the powers of Europe, it did not do so because of differences in concept or even of geographical insulation, but rather because the precise political conditions of Europe in the late eighteenth century seemed to assure American security. American diplomacy could pursue a policy of isolationism without undermining the nation's interests only as long as the European balance of power suited the country's needs. As Thomas Boylston Adams wrote with remarkable perception in October 1799: "It must always happen, so long as America is an independent Republic or nation, that the balance of power in Europe will continue to be of the utmost importance to her welfare. The moment that France is victorious and Great Britain with her allies depressed, we have cause for alarm ourselves. The same thing is true when the reverse of this happens."

One essential adjunct to the nation's isolationist policies was the principle of nonintervention in the affairs of other nations. This doctrine was held commonly by all the Founding Fathers, and entered the phraseology of Adams, Hamilton, and Washington. But its most consistent and outspoken advocate was

John Quincy Adams. When the Jacobin societies demanded that the United States rescue, in the name of humanity, the French victims of war and repression, young Adams gave the principle of abstention classic form in his letters of "Marcellus," published in April and May 1793:

> As men, we must undoubtedly lament the effusion of human blood, and the mass of misery and distress which is preparing for the great part of the civilized world; but as the citizens of a nation at a vast distance from the continent of Europe; of a nation whose happiness consists in a real independence, disconnected from all European interests and European politics, it is our duty to remain, the peaceable and silent, though sorrowful spectators of the sanguinary scene.

For the nation to involve itself in the revolutions of Europe, declared Adams, would doom it to inevitable destruction and ruin. "We are therefore commanded by . . . that uncontrolable law of nature, which is paramount to all human legislation, . . . to remain at peace, and to content ourselves with wishing that laureled Victory may sit upon the sword of justice, and that smooth success may always be strewed before the feet of virtuous Freedom."

Isolationism and nonintervention were not the only determinants in the evolution of American policy. For the United States could not and would not escape the forces of international involvement which characterized the traditional struggles and conflicts of Europe. Isolationism was more than a response to geographic factors or the basis of a thoughtless preoccupation with internal concerns and self-sufficient pursuits. The United States never sought the solitude of such hermit nations as Japan and Korea; from its republican beginnings it created and maintained a commercial empire that blanketed much of the globe. American isolationism was always political and military, never commercial or intellectual. Fundamentally, three pressures warred on American noninvolvement in external affairs: the nation's commercial and trading interests abroad; its democratic idealism, which could, under certain circumstances, assign to diplomacy the task of promoting American ideals throughout the world; and the country's interest in eliminating dangerous and competing centers of power and influence from the North American continent or threats to the balance of power in Europe which might involve the security of the United States. There could be little genuine isolation, whether in mind or in action, from the major trends and events in world affairs.

## II

In 1800 no hemispheric dangers threatened to involve the United States in the power politics of Europe. In Jay's Treaty the British had promised to withdraw their "troops and garrisons from all posts and places within the boundary lines assigned by the treaty of peace to the United States." Spain, fearing that Jay's Treaty might bring an alignment between the United States and England against France, agreed in 1795 to free navigation of the Mississippi and the right of deposit at New Orleans. For pioneers of the Ohio Valley this agreement assured access to the necessary markets of the Atlantic world. Unknown to American officials, the Directory had given instructions to the French Minister at Madrid to seek the relinquishment of Louisiana. "We alone," it declared, "can trace with strong hands the bounds for the power of the United States and the limits for their territory." Finally, in October 1800, Spain retroceded Louisiana to France. Napoleon believed that province, with San Domingo in the West Indies, would form the foundation of a new French empire in America. When, late in 1801, President Jefferson received a copy of the French treaty, his anxiety was aroused. The French did not occupy New Orleans immediately, and they continued to deny that they had acquired title to the region. Then, in October, 1802, the Spanish Intendant closed the American deposit at New Orleans. Suddenly the Federalists, in a massive bid for Western support, accused Jefferson of neglecting the nation's commercial and security interests and demanded that the administration seize New Orleans. Jefferson responded to this political pressure by dispatching James Monroe to Paris on a special mission to resolve the Mississippi question.

Historians have often described the Louisiana Purchase as a calculated maneuver by Jefferson to serve the interests of the American farmer. Jefferson had written repeatedly that he regarded agriculture the true foundation of the Republic. "Cultivators of the earth," he once wrote, "are the most valuable citizens. They are the most vigorous, the most independent, the most virtuous, and are tied to their country, and wedded to its liberty and interests, by the most lasting bonds."

Jefferson was also an expansionist. In a letter of 1801 to Monroe he wrote, "However our present interests may restrain us within our own limits, it is impossible not to look forward to distant times, & cover the whole northern if not the southern continent, with people speaking the same language, governed in similar forms, and by similar laws. . . ." But Jefferson did not necessarily anticipate the expansion of the Republic. For him the United States would comprise a parent nation, nothing more, scattering its people and institutions over the continent. He favored the annexation of Canada, but only if the Canadians approved. Even after the purchase of Louisiana he did not assume that the far Northwest would be other than a separate nation. He wrote to John Jacob Astor in November 1813, "I view it [the Oregon country] as the germ of a great, free, and independent empire on that side of our continent. . . ."

Jefferson was interested in commerce as well as in agriculture. From an early date he sought a trade route across the continent to exploit the potential riches of the Orient. While serving as United States Minister in Paris he dispatched young John Ledyard, a Yankee sailor, to find a continental route by entering Nootka Sound from Kamchatka and eventually following the Missouri River to St. Louis. The Russian empress ruined this mission by refusing Ledyard authority to cross Siberia. But Jefferson continued his search. What he asked of André Michaux in conducting his western explorations was that he "seek for and pursue that route which shall form the shortest and most convenient communication between the high parts of the Missouri and the Pacific Ocean."

His instructions to Meriwether Lewis in 1803 showed his commercial motivation in unmistakable terms. "The object of your mission," he charged the frontiers-man, "is to explore the Missouri River, and such principal streams of it, as by its course and communication with the waters of the Pacific Ocean, may offer the most direct and practicable water communication across the continent for the purposes of commerce." For Jefferson the object of continental expansion was as much the acquisition of a passage through Oregon as it was the acquisition of land for the American farmers.

The Louisiana Purchase was a diplomatic windfall, neither anticipated nor sought. In his famous letter to Robert Livingston, of April 18, 1802, Jefferson admitted his deep concern for the acquisition of New Orleans by the French. He hoped that France, in the interest of international harmony, would cede New Orleans and Florida to the United States. (*Reading No. 1.*) In explaining the Monroe mission to Livingston in February, 1803, Jefferson again pointed to New Orleans as the area of friction and the object of his diplomacy. (*Reading No. 2*) Napoleon's failure to reconquer San Domingo, the weakness of his power on the North American continent, and his desire to establish a better rapport with the United States prompted him to sell all of Louisiana. This un-expected offer caught the American diplomats in Paris, as well as the entire administration, by surprise. Livingston argued that the United States wanted only New Orleans and Florida. When the French government insisted on selling all of Louisiana, he proceeded to haggle over the price. Livingston's reluctance placed the Marquis de Barbé-Marbois, the French negotiator, in the strange role of explaining the advantages that would accrue to the United States from the acquisition of all Louisiana. (*Reading No. 3.*) Eventually the diplomats agreed on the bargain price of fifteen million dollars. The purchase not only assured the United States control of the Mississippi Valley, it also gave the na-tion claims to frontage on the Pacific. It pushed the areas of conflict with Euro-pean power on the North American continent westward to regions bordering the distant ocean.

### III

With the adoption of the Constitution in 1789 the foreign commerce of the United States became a matter of primary concern to the nation. There had been some trade expansion under the Articles, especially in the Orient, but the general inefficiency of the government discouraged foreign nations from entering into commercial treaties which alone might open to American merchants the potential markets of the European world. John Jay analyzed the problem with considerable accuracy in 1785: "This being the state of things, you may depend upon it, the commerce of America will have no relief at present nor, in my opinion, ever, until the United States shall have generally passed navigation acts. If these measures are not adopted, we shall be derided, and the more we suffer, the more will our calamities be laughed at." The Constitution, by grant-ing the Federal government exclusive control over the foreign commerce of the United States, removed the artificial obstacles to commercial expansion by placing in the hands of that government the power to encourage, control, and retaliate. Congress, in July 1789, promoted the building of a large merchant fleet by extending a discount on duty for goods carried in American vessels. Not until November 1794 did Britain sign a commercial treaty with the United States, but similar treaties with France and Prussia soon followed. During the late 'nineties Congress provided for the creation of a navy to protect American shipping, and so effectively did the new ships of war deal with the Barbary pirates that by 1805 the United States had negotiated satisfactory trade agreements with Tripoli, Algiers, and the Barbary States. The wars of the French Revolution destroyed the normal channels of trade so effectively that all the warring nations looked to the United States as the leading neutral carrier of the Atlantic world. Despite considerable English and French interference with the free movement of United States vessels into European waters, American foreign commerce entered a period of remarkable growth. This expanding trade met its first serious impediment in Napoleon's "continental system."

In an effort to gauge the American interest Jefferson paid close attention to the constantly shifting balance of power in Europe. As early as 1801 he was concerned with the "necessity of restoring freedom to the ocean," but he believed that the achievement of that purpose would vastly exceed in cost the benefits to be derived from involvement in an armed European confederacy. Jefferson continued to follow the struggle between England and France with outward aloofness. Conscious of the protection afforded by a mighty ocean, he wrote: 'Tremendous times in Europe! How mighty this battle of lions & Tygers! With what sensations should the common herd of cattle look on it? With no partialities, certainly. If they can so far worry one another as to destroy their power of tyrannizing, the one over the earth, the other over the waters, the world may perhaps enjoy peace, till they recruit again." For Jefferson, each of the great warring powers was a needed check on the tyrannizing propensities of the other. But by 1805 he began to fear Napoleon's success. He considered an alliance with Britain despite the fact that Napoleon had surrendered Louisiana in part to strengthen the United States as a counterweight to British sea power. British insolence forced Jefferson back into a posture of neutrality, although he asserted in 1806 that "an English ascendancy on the ocean is safer for us than that of France." It was not until the United States was outraged by the *Chesapeake* affair in 1807—a classic example of impressment—that Jefferson found himself "under the necessity of wishing success to Bonaparte. . . . The English being equally tyrannical at sea as he is on land, and that tyranny bearing on us in every point of either honor or interest, I say, 'Down with England,' and as for what Bonaparte is then to do to us, let us trust to the chapter of accidents."

The disastrous policies employed by Britain and France in their attempts to eliminate the neutral commerce each of the other persuaded Jefferson to respond with the embargo of December 1807. His objective was the preservation of American peace and neutrality; the balance of power itself he entrusted to the progress of war. By depriving both Britain and France of the benefits of American commerce, even at the price of destroying the nation's trade and its mer-

chant marine. Jefferson hoped to force one or both of the great European rivals
to recognize American neutral rights. The policy was doomed to failure from
the outset, simply because it had no appreciable effect on the attitudes of the
belligerents. Responding to bitter opposition within the United States, Jefferson
and the Congress retreated to the Non-Intercourse Act of March 1, 1809, which
reopened American commerce with all nations except England and France.
When either of these two powers modified its edicts against neutral trade, the
United States would re-establish normal commercial relations with that nation.
When this failed to influence the warring states, Congress, in May 1810, passed
Macon's Bill Number 2. This reopened commerce with both England and
France but promised that if one of the two belligerents ceased its restrictions
against American trade, the United States would close its shipping to the
opponent of that nation. These repeated and ineffectual retreats brought forth
the ridicule of those realists who had doubted from the beginning the power
of American commerce to coerce the great powers of Europe. No one attacked
Jefferson's policies more savagely than did the conservative John Randolph of
Virginia. (*Reading No. 4.*)

Ultimately the United States had no choice but to give up its neutral rights
or enter the war in their defense. Yet the forces that propelled the nation into
war after the passage of Macon's Bill were extremely involved. In the summer
of 1810 Napoleon announced the repeal of the French restrictions on trade.
President James Madison and his administration immediately cut off all commerce with England. Eventually Britain withdrew her offending decrees, but
this was still unknown in Washington in June 1812. The United States had no
interest at stake in a French victory. But Britain, commanding the seas, had
created far greater pressures on American neutral rights than had France.
Britain, moreover, held territory in North America where she was vulnerable
to American attack. If England was to be fought, why in 1812? British assaults
on American shipping and other maritime rights had been continuous for
twenty years; they were probably less in 1812 than they had been five years
earlier. But other anti-British pressures were determining the mood of Congress.
Western Congressmen attributed the Indian troubles along the frontier to British machinations. (*Reading No. 5.*) Yet Congressmen from New England, New
York, and Pennsylvania favored war, and they faced no Indian problems at all.
The West, following the embargo, faced a deepening depression, but Western
prosperity required trade with England rather than war. Behind the war spirit
of 1812 was less a rational design than a broad conviction that England had
dealt dishonorably with the United States. This, in large measure, was the
burden of Madison's war message of June 1, 1812. (*Reading No. 6.*) Those who
opposed the war pointed both to the greater national interest in Napoleon's
defeat and to the nation's lack of preparedness for war. (*Reading No. 7.*)

For Jefferson what mattered was the balance of power. In April 1812 he still
wished a plague on both the British and French houses. By 1814 he feared the
consequences of Napoleon's conquest of Russia. In June 1815 he hoped "that
a salutary balance may ever be maintained among nations and that our peace,
commerce, and friendship, may be sought and cultivated by all." (*Reading*

*No. 8.*) With the Peace of Ghent and the Congress of Vienna, Jefferson witnessed the return of Europe to what he, in 1812, had believed the nation
should pray for—"that the powers of Europe may be so poised and counter-
poised among themselves that their own security may require the presence of all
their forces at home, leaving the other quarters of the globe in undisturbed
tranquility." On that new balance of power hinged the nation's security and
the validity of its reasserted policies of isolationism and nonentanglement.

## IV

American idealism, always vulnerable to exploitation in behalf of revolutionary
causes abroad, was a powerful factor that threatened on occasion to drag the
nation from its diplomatic isolation. Jefferson's original draft of the Declaration of Independence comprised a classic statement of that idealism: "We hold
these truths to be sacred and undeniable; that all men are created equal and
independent, that from that equal creation they derive rights inherent and inalienable, among which are the preservation of life, liberty and the pursuit of
happiness." For the Jeffersonians the essential meaning of this doctrine was
clear: Man possessed by the laws of nature the right of equal access to the
freedom and opportunity required to develop his personal nature as fully as
possible. For each person to reach his full potential it was required that he
possess the power to decide when and how to act. His decisions, whether right
or wrong, must reflect the preferences of his own mind. This was the essence of
freedom. As Jefferson once wrote: "I have sworn upon the altar of God, eternal
hostility against every form of tyranny over the mind of man."

Unlike Hamilton, whose emphasis on power stressed the importance of means,
Jefferson and Madison were concerned primarily with ends. Their writings
dwelt less on the bases of human action than on the vision of a good society.
They accepted the role of force in human affairs, for not even the ideals of liberty could be promoted without it. To them, however, force was potentially
corrupt unless combined with moral purpose. "What a perversion of the natural
order of things," wrote Madison, ". . . to make power the primary and central
object of the social system, and Liberty but its satellite." Madison agreed with
Hamilton that men responded to interests; he believed only that interests need
not be narrow and selfish. They could encompass the general interests of mankind. Power and liberty, held in proper balance, comprised the essence of the
democratic tradition. Power without liberty was tyrannical; liberty without
power was utopian. In his eightieth year Jefferson summarized his philosophy
of democracy:

> We believed . . . that man was a rational animal, endowed by nature
> with rights, with an innate sense of justice; that he could be restrained
> from wrong and protected in right, by moderate powers, confided to
> persons of his own choice, and held to their duties by dependence on
> his own will. We believed that the complicated organization of kings,
> nobles, and priests, was not the wisest nor the best to effect the happi-

ness of associated man; that wisdom and virtue were not hereditary; that the trappings of such a machinery, consumed by their expense, those earnings of industry they were meant to protect and, by the inequalities they produced, exposed liberty to sufferance. We believed that men, enjoying in ease and security the full fruits of their own industry, enlisted by all their interests on the side of law and order, habituated to think for themselves, and to follow their reason as their guide, would be more easily and safely governed, than with minds nourished in error, and vitiated and debased . . . by ignorance, indigence and oppression. The cherishment of the people then was our principle.

Such concepts, embodied, if imperfectly, in an established constitutional and political system, created within the nation the tendency toward a messianic consciousness. This messianism, when applied to America's relations with the external world, took two forms: the liberal and expansive desire to remake the world in the American image, and the conservative, but no less idealistic, view that the nation fulfilled its obligations to humankind when it created an example which other nations would choose to follow. Both Jefferson and Madison, despite their almost limitless expectations for American society, took a decidedly limited view of what the country might achieve abroad. Jefferson believed that the United States would serve humanity both by example and by remaining a sanctuary for the oppressed and misruled. "A single good government," he could write, "becomes thus a blessing to the whole earth." Madison claimed a similar mission for America:

The free system of government we have established is so congenial with reason, with common sense, and with a universal feeling, that it must produce approbation and a desire of imitation, as avenues may be found for truth to the knowledge of nations. Our Country, if it does justice to itself, will be the workshop of liberty to the Civilized World, and do more than any other for the uncivilized.

Unfortunately, this mission, so universally acceptable to a democratic people, confronted editors and political leaders with the constant temptation to exploit its emotional appeal by transforming its conservative function of example into the transcendent purpose of underwriting the cause of liberty abroad. Jefferson and his fellow Virginians, Madison and Monroe, inaugurated this practice themselves when, in the name of liberty, they led a dramatic assault on the conservative and limited goals of the Washington administration. They preached the doctrine, amid popular acclaim, that the United States should seek the fulfillment of its democratic mission by supporting revolution. Jefferson opposed Washington's proclamation of Neutrality and defended his pro-French policy on the bases of such abstract principles as treaty obligations, gratitude, and preference for republican institutions. Monroe, his disciple, declared before the French Convention in 1794 that "republics should approach near to each other." Such continuing, and often embarrassing, efforts to identify the nation's interests with revolution never altered in practice the fundamental policies of Washington and Hamilton. Nor is it clear that the Jeffersonians had any such intention. The ideals they professed were shams, having no relationship to their actual motivation or to the power at their disposal. These men carried no responsibility for the country's actions abroad. Indeed, they were free to criticize because they had calculated the power and determination of the Washington administration to defend its actions and objectives. It is significant that Jefferson, as President, followed the dictum of Washington closely and employed his diplomatic authority to pursue only the interests of the United States as he understood those interests.

When revolution swept across Latin America following the Napoleonic wars, American idealism again burned brightly. Secretary of State John Quincy Adams predicted, in December 1817, that enemies of the Monroe administration would soon attempt to embarrass the government by demanding that it openly support the cause of Latin American liberty. (Reading No. 9.) During 1818 Henry Clay in the House of Representatives pressed the administration for a recognition of the new revolutionary governments of South America. (Reading No. 10.) Monroe, then President, chided Clay for his demand that the nation, in the interest of freedom, officially recognize the independence movement of Latin America before it had achieved complete success. To Andrew Jackson, another enthusiast, Monroe wrote that he would recognize Latin American independence when the aspiring nations to the south had demonstrated their ability to cast off Spanish rule, for, he continued, "if they cannot beat Spain, they do not deserve to be free." Yet Monroe, much to Adams's discomforture, responded to Congressional pressure sufficiently to include the subject of Latin American revolution in his annual messages. (Reading No. 11.) When the new Latin American nations by 1821 had established beyond doubt their power to remain independent, Adams took the lead in supporting their recognition by the United States, but he never ceased to uphold the validity of his earlier conservatism. Nor did he alter his limited view of Latin America's political future. (Reading No. 12.)

## V

Meanwhile, Adams continued the process, inaugurated by Jefferson, of defining and extending the nation's boundaries. Like Jefferson, Adams regarded Florida a natural appendage of the United States and, under Spain, a constant source of friction if not insecurity. Spain's weakening control had permitted the American seizure of both the Baton Rouge district in 1810 and the region about Mobile during the War of 1812. Spanish impotence was demonstrated again in 1818 when United States forces, in pursuit of the rampaging Seminoles, occupied portions of Florida without facing any reprisals. Secretary Adams, exploiting Spain's collapsing power on the Continent, negotiated a settlement with the Spanish minister in Washington, which not only acquired all of Florida for the United States but also defined the transcontinental boundary line which separated the Louisiana Purchase from Spanish Mexico. This treaty established the northern boundary of California at 42° and left the United States in possession of the old Spanish claims north of that line.

Unlike Jefferson, Adams recognized no limit to the continental expansion of the Republic. In 1818 he accepted an agreement with Britain which established the 49th parallel as the northern boundary of the Louisiana Purchase between Lake of the Woods and the Rocky Mountains. But he preferred to leave the boundary beyond the mountains unmarked rather than accept the British offer to extend the line along the Columbia River to the Pacific Ocean. Adams considered it essential that the United States acquire no less than access to the Strait of Juan de Fuca if it would achieve its dream of commercial empire in the Pacific. But he would not permit even such objectives to set the limits of the nation's ultimate expansion. (*Reading No. 13.*) It was his desire to keep the Northwest as an American preserve that prompted him to assert the principle of *noncolonization* against both British and Russian encroachment. He expressed this determination to Richard Rush, the United States Minister in London, during July 1823:

> It is not imaginable that in the present condition of the world, *any* European Nation should entertain the project of settling a *Colony* on the Northwest Coast of America—That the United States should form establishments there with views of absolute territorial right, and inland communication is not only to be expected, but is pointed out by the fingers of Nature, and has been for years a subject of serious deliberation in Congress. . . .

Meanwhile American idealism again threatened to drag the nation into European affairs. For some Americans the world of the early 1820's appeared especially oppressive. The Greeks had staged an independence movement only to be suppressed by Turkish barbarities. Hezekiah Niles of *Niles' Register* and Edward Everett of the *North American Review*, joined by Daniel Webster in Congress, assailed the Monroe administration for its apparent indifference to human suffering in other parts of the world. At one philhellenic meeting at Albany, New York, Benjamin F. Butler extolled Greece as the land "where the voice of liberty is heard. . . ." But John Quincy Adams, in his famous address of July 4, 1821, read a lecture to those who demanded that the nation underwrite a policy of liberation abroad:

> America . . . has abstained from interference in the concerns of others, even when the conflict has been for principles to which she clings, as to the last vital drop that visits the heart. She has seen that probably for centuries to come, all the contests of that Aceldama, the European world, will be contests of inveterate power and emerging right. Wherever the standard of freedom and independence has been or shall be unfurled, there will her heart, her benedictions, and her prayers be. But she goes not abroad in search of monsters to destroy. She is the well-wisher to the freedom and independence of all. She is the champion and vindicator only of her own. . . . She well knows

that by once enlisting under other banners than her own, were they
even the banners of foreign independence, she would involve herself beyond the power of extrication, in all the wars of interest and intrigue,
of individual avarice, envy, and ambition, which assume the colors and
usurp the standard of freedom.

Responding to the enthusiasm for the Greek cause, Monroe lauded Greece
publicly as the cradle of civilization and expressed the hope that her people
would soon "recover their independence and resume their equal station among
the nations of the earth." Adams, always the realist, objected violently to such
displays of sentiment which had no counterpart in action. (*Reading No. 14.*)
Adams favored the independence of Greece, but he would have the nation
assume no responsibility for bringing it about.

Adams's conservatism became even more apparent when the cabinet, late in
November 1823, contemplated the danger posed by the Holy Alliance to the
continued independence of Latin America. Earlier, Adams had praised the concert of Europe as a source of European stability. When France invaded Spain in
1823 to suppress a Spanish revolution, Adams warned the Madrid government
that the United States would *oppose the transfer* of any remaining colony of
Spain in the New World, such as Cuba, to another continental power. (*Reading
No. 15.*) By November the central challenge facing the Monroe administration,
first raised by the British government, was the threatened reconquest of the
Spanish Empire by France. Again it was Adams who argued for a conservative
declaration which would avoid the tone of a crusade against the reactionary
forces of Europe. He favored a *firm, unilateral declaration against the military
reconquest of Latin America* by the power of Europe. Adams believed that
Britain alone could and would defend Latin America from the Holy Alliance,
but such a victory would throw that vast region into the arms of England. It
was essential, therefore, that the United States act promptly and decisively.
Adams reminded the cabinet that any public expression of sympathy for the
revolutionary causes of Europe, either in Spain or in Greece, would defy the
established principle of *nonintervention*. It would be difficult enough, he
warned, to meet the European powers on American soil without "going to bid
them defiance in the heart of Europe." (*Reading No. 16.*) The Secretary had
his way. Monroe, in his famous message of December 1823, repeated forcefully
the doctrine of abstention. Adams had helped to formulate the principles of
hands-off and noncolonization for the Western Hemisphere where the United
States held the strategic advantage, but he opposed commitments to Europe
which exceeded the nation's power to defend. (*Reading No. 17.*)

Monroe's message did not resolve the debate over Greece. In October 1823,
Everett published in the *North American Review* the Greek Appeal of May
1821, a document which sought an alliance, based on freedom and virtue, with
the United States. In his long editorial which followed, Everett called upon
the American people, as individuals, to support the Greek cause. (*Reading
No. 18.*) On December 8, Webster introduced a resolution in the House of
Representatives which called for a declaration of sympathy for the oppressed

Greeks. Finally, on January 19, 1824, the day that the motion came before the House, Webster, before a packed gallery, launched into one of the great oratorical efforts of his life. The resolution would benefit the Greeks, he said, by giving them courage and spirit and would "teach them that they are not wholly forgotten by the civilized world, and inspire them with constancy in the pursuit of their great end." Five days later John Randolph answered the American Demosthenes. In the name of liberty and religion, he charged, the United States was asked to go on a crusade in another hemisphere when there was much to crusade for within the Republic itself. He called the nation back to its old policy of "peace, commerce, and honest friendship with all nations, entangling alliances with none," for, he said, "to entangling alliances we must come, if you once embark in projects such as this." (*Reading No. 19.*) Randolph spoke the mind of the country. After a quarter-century of deep involvement in the affairs of Europe, the American people were prepared to accept the credo of Monroe and Adams that there were two distinct worlds and that they were separated by the Atlantic.

After the announcement of the Monroe Doctrine, American foreign policy ceased to have its traditional unity. No longer did it revolve around questions purely European or react almost solely to the constant shifts in the balance of power. During the decades that followed, Europe's relative stability permitted American diplomacy to pursue the national interest on three separate fronts— the continent, the hemisphere, and the world at large. (Parts III, IV, and V of this volume are concerned with these three major areas of American policy.) The remarkable solvency of United States diplomacy during the seventy-five years from 1823 until 1898 was based on the mutuality of British and American interest in both the European balance of power and the political stability of the Western Hemisphere. This unwritten alliance covered the essential commitments of the nation.

# 1 | Jefferson and the French Threat to New Orleans, April 1802 *

Jefferson regarded the French acquisition of Louisiana as a major threat to the nation's security, for along the Mississippi frontier it replaced the declining power of Spain with the might of the strongest nation on the European continent. Jefferson, traditionally an enthusiastic Francophile, wrote to Robert R. Livingston on April 18, 1802, explaining why France, in possession of New Orleans, had ceased to be a natural friend of the United States. Livingston was then the American Minister in Paris.

The cession of Louisiana and the Floridas by Spain to France, works most sorely on the United States. On this subject the Secretary of State has written to you fully, yet I cannot forbear recurring to it personally, so deep is the impression it makes on my mind. It completely reverses all the political relations of the United States, and will form a new epoch in our political course. Of all nations of any consideration, France is the one which, hitherto, has offered the fewest points on which we could have any conflict of right, and the most points of a communion of interests. From these causes, we have ever looked to her as our *natural friend,* as one with which we never could have an occasion of difference. Her growth, therefore, we viewed as our own, her misfortunes ours. There is on the globe one single spot, the possessor of which is our natural and habitual enemy. It is New Orleans, through which the produce of three-eighths of our territory must pass to market, and from its fertility it will ere long yield more than half of our whole produce, and contain more than half of our inhabitants. France, placing herself in that door, assumes to us the attitude of defiance. Spain might have retained it quietly for years. Her pacific dispositions, her feeble state, would induce her to increase our facilities there, so that her possession of the place would be hardly felt by us, and it would not, perhaps, be very long before some circumstance might arise, which might make the cession of it to us the price of something of more worth to her. Not so can it ever be in the hands of France: the impetuosity of her temper, the energy and restlessness of her character, placed in a point of eternal friction with us, and our character, which, though quiet and loving peace and pursuit of wealth, is high-minded, despising wealth in competition with insult or injury, enterprising and energetic as any nation on earth; these circumstances render it impossible that France and the United States can continue long friends, when they meet in so irritable a position. They, as well as we, must be blind if they do not see this; and we must be very improvident if we do not begin to make arrangements on that hypothesis. The day that France takes possession of New Orleans, fixes

* Thomas Jefferson to Robert Livingston, April 18, 1802, *The Writings of Thomas Jefferson,* Paul Leicester Ford, ed. (New York, 1897), VIII: 144–7.

the sentence which is to restrain her forever within her low-water mark. It seals the union of two nations, who, in conjunction, can maintain exclusive possession of the ocean. From that moment, we must marry ourselves to the British fleet and nation. We must turn all our attention to a maritime force, for which our resources place us on very high ground; and having formed and connected together a power which may render reinforcement of her settlements here impossible to France, make the first cannon which shall be fired in Europe the signal for the tearing up any settlement she may have made, and for holding the two continents of America in sequestration for the common purposes of the United British and American nations. This is not a state of things we seek or desire. It is one which this measure, if adopted by France, forces on us as necessarily, as any other cause, by the laws of nature, brings on its necessary effect. It is not from a fear of France that we deprecate this measure proposed by her. For however greater her force is than ours, compared in the abstract, it is nothing in comparison of ours, when to be exerted on our soil. But it is from a sincere love of peace, and a firm persuasion, that bound to France by the interests and the strong sympathies still existing in the minds of our citizens, and holding relative positions which insure their continuance, we are secure of a long course of peace. Whereas, the change of friends, which will be rendered necessary if France changes that position, embarks us necessarily as a belligerent power in the first war of Europe. In that case, France will have held possession of New Orleans during the interval of a peace, long or short, at the end of which it will be wrested from her. Will this short-lived possession have been an equivalent to her for the transfer of such a weight into the scale of her enemy? Will not the amalgamation of a young, thriving nation, continue to that enemy the health and force which are at present so evidently on the decline? And will a few years' possession of New Orleans add equally to the strength of France? She may say she needs Louisiana for the supply of her West Indies. She does not need it in time of peace, and in war she could not depend on them, because they would be so easily intercepted. I should suppose that all these considerations might, in some proper form, be brought into view of the Government of France. Though stated by us, it ought not to give offence; because we do not bring them forward as a menace, but as consequences not controllable by us, but inevitable from the course of things. We mention them, not as things which we desire by any means, but as things we deprecate; and we beseech a friend to look forward and to prevent them for our common interest.

If France considers Louisiana, however, as indispensable for her views, she might perhaps be willing to look about for arrangements which might reconcile to it our interests. If anything could do this, it would be the ceding to us the island of New Orleans and the Floridas. This would certainly, in a great degree, remove the causes of jarring and irritation between us, and perhaps for such a length of time, as might produce other means of making the measure permanently conciliatory to our interests and friendships. It would, at any rate, relieve us from the necessity of taking immediate measures for countervailing such an operation by arrangements in another quarter. But still we should consider New Orleans and the Floridas as no equivalent for the risk of a quarrel with France, produced by her vicinage. . . .

— | "We see all the disadvantageous consequences of taking a side, and shall be forced into it only by a more disagreeable alternative . . ." *

Jefferson wrote to Livingston again on October 10, 1802, and admitted that all of his earlier assumptions regarding the mutuality of interest between the United States and France had proven erroneous. Yet he insisted that, while the United States could expect little of the French government, it was essential that the most cordial relations possible be maintained with the new French Empire.

🖋

The departure of Made Brugnard for France furnishes me a safe conveyance of a letter, which I cannot avoid embracing, altho I have nothing particular for the subject of it. It is well, however, to be able to inform you, generally, through a safe channel, that we stand, compleately corrected of the error, that either the government or the nation of France has any remains of friendship for us. The portion of that country which forms an exception, though respectable in weight, is weak in numbers. On the contrary, it appears evident, that an unfriendly spirit prevails in the most important individuals of the government, towards us. In this state of things, we shall so take our distance between the two rival nations, as, remaining disengaged till necessity compels us, we may haul finally to the enemy of that which shall make it necessary. We see all the disadvantageous consequences of taking a side, and shall be forced into it only by a more disagreeable alternative; in which event, we must countervail the disadvantages by measures which will give us splendor & power, but not as much happiness as our present system. We wish, therefore, to remain well with France. But we see that no consequences, however ruinous to them, can secure us with certainty against the extravagance of her present rulers. I think, therefore, that while we do nothing which the first nation on earth would deem crouching, we had better give to all our communications with them a very mild, complaisant, and even friendly complexion but always independent. Ask no favors, leave small & irritating things to be conducted by the individuals interested in them, interfere ourselves but in the greatest cases, & then not push them to irritation. No matter at present existing between them & us is important enough to risk a breach of peace; peace being indeed the most important of all things to us, except the preserving an erect & independent attitude. . . .

* Thomas Jefferson to Robert Livingston, October 10, 1802, *The Writings of Thomas Jefferson,* VIII: 172-3.

When the Spanish Intendant closed the right of deposit at New Orleans in October 1802, the demands of Western farmers for action gave the Federalists, then out of power, an unforeseen opportunity to embarrass the Jefferson administration and to pose as the protectors of Western interests by prodding the President to employ force if necessary to obtain a satisfactory settlement of the Mississippi question. Jefferson was trapped between the necessity of countering the Federalist appeal to the West and the necessity of avoiding a war with France. In this extremity he appointed James Monroe, a hero to Western Jeffersonians, as a special emissary to France to negotiate, if possible, a satisfactory settlement with Napoleon relative to New Orleans. Writing to Livingston on February 3, 1803, Jefferson explained why he was dispatching Monroe to Paris.

. . . A late suspension by the Intendant of N Orleans of our right of deposit there, without which the right of navigation is impracticable, has thrown this country into such a flame of hostile disposition as can scarcely be described. The western country was peculiarly sensible to it as you may suppose. Our business was to take the most effectual pacific measures in our power to remove the suspension, and at the same time to persuade our countrymen that pacific measures would be the most effectual and the most speedily so. The opposition caught it as a plank in a shipwreck, hoping it would enable them to tack the Western people to them. They raised the cry of war, were intriguing in all the quarters to exasperate the Western inhabitants to arm & go down on their own authority & possess themselves of New Orleans, and in the meantime were daily reiterating, in new shapes, inflammatory resolutions for the adoption of the House. As a remedy to all this we determined to name a minister extraordinary to go immediately to Paris & Madrid to settle this matter. This measure being a visible one, and the person named peculiarly proper with the Western country, crushed at once & put an end to all further attempts on the Legislature. From that moment all has become quiet; and the more readily in the Western country, as the sudden alliance of these new federal friends had of itself already began to make them suspect the wisdom of their own course. The measure was moreover proposed from another cause. We must know at once whether we can acquire N Orleans or not. We are satisfied nothing else will secure us against a war at no distant period; and we cannot press this reason without beginning those arrangements which will be necessary if war is hereafter to result. For this purpose it was necessary that the negotiators should be fully possessed of every idea we have on the subject, so as to meet the propositions of the opposite party, in whatever form they may be offered; and give them a shape admissible

---

* Thomas Jefferson to Robert Livingston, February 3, 1803, *The Writings of Thomas Jefferson*, VIII: 209–10.

by us without being obliged to await new instructions hence. With this view, we have joined Mr. Monroe to yourself at Paris, & to Mr. Pinkney at Madrid, altho' we believe it will be hardly necessary for him to go to this last place. Should we fail in this object of the mission, a further one will be superadded for the other side of the channel. On this subject you will be informed by the Secretary of State, & Mr. Monroe will be able also to inform you of all our views and purposes. By him I send another letter to Dupont, whose aid may be of the greatest service, as it will be divested of the shackles of form. The letter is left open for your perusal, after which I wish a wafer stuck in it before it be delivered. The official and the verbal communications to you by Mr. Monroe will be so full and minute, that I need not trouble you with an inofficial repetition of them. The future destinies of our country hang on the event of this negotiation, and I am sure they could not be placed in more able or more zealous hands. On our parts we shall be satisfied that what you do not effect, cannot be effected. Accept therefore assurances of my sincere & constant affection and high respect. . . .

## 3 | Negotiations for the Purchase of Louisiana, 1803 *

On April 11, 1803, Talleyrand, the French Foreign Minister, caught Livingston by surprise by offering to sell to the United States the entire French claim to Louisiana. Two days later Monroe joined Livingston in Paris. On that day, April 13, Livingston reported his conversations with the French to Secretary of State James Madison. This letter revealed clearly the workings of traditional diplomacy even when questions of momentous significance were at issue.

I have just come from the Minister of the Treasury. Our conversation was so important, that I think it necessary to write it, while the impressions are strong upon my mind; and the rather, as I fear I shall not have time to copy and send this letter, if I defer it till morning.

By my letter of yesterday, you learned that the Minister has asked me whether I would agree to purchase Louisiana, etc. On the 12th, I called upon him to press this matter further. He then thought proper to declare that his proposition was only personal, but still requested me to make an offer; and, upon my declining to so do, as I expected Mr. Monroe the next day, he shrugged up his

* Robert Livingston to James Madison, April 13, 1803, *House Ex. Docs. No. 4531,* 57th Congress, 2nd Sess., (1902–3) 159–63.

shoulders, and changed the conversation. Not willing, however, to lose sight of it, I told him I had been long endeavoring to bring him to some point; but, unfortunately, without effect; that I wished merely to have the negotiation opened by any proposition on his part; and, with that view, had written him a note which contained that request, grounded upon my apprehension of the consequence of sending General Bernadotte without enabling him to say a treaty was begun. He told me he would answer my note, but that he must do it evasively, because Louisiana was not theirs. I smiled at this assertion, and told him I had seen the treaty recognizing it; that I knew the Consul had appointed officers to govern the country, and that he had himself told me that General Victor was to take possession; that, in a note written by the express order of the First Consul, he had told me that General Bernadotte was to treat relative to it in the United States, etc. He still persisted that they had it in contemplation to obtain it, but had it not. I told him that I was very well pleased to understand this from him, because, if so, we should not commit ourselves with them in taking it from Spain, to whom, by his account, it still belonged; and that, as we had just cause of complaint against her, if Mr. Monroe concurred in opinion with me, we should negotiate no further on the subject, but advise our Government to take possession. He seemed alarmed at the boldness of the measure, and told me he would answer my note, but that it would be evasively. I told him I should receive with pleasure any communication from him, but that we were not disposed to trifle; that the times were critical, and though I did not know what instructions Mr. Monroe might bring, I was perfectly satisfied that they would require a precise and prompt notice; that I was very fearful, from the little progress I had made, that my Government would consider me as a very indolent negotiator. He laughed, and told me that he would give me a certificate that I was the most importunate he had met with. . . .

This day Mr. Monroe passed with me in examining my papers; and while he and several other gentlemen were at dinner with me, I observed the Minister of the Treasury walking in my garden. I sent out Colonel Livingston to him; he told him he would return when he had dined. While we were taking coffee he came in; and, after being some time in the room, we strolled into the next room, when he told me he heard I had been at his house two days before, when he was at St. Cloud; that he thought I might have something particular to say to him, and had taken the first opportunity to call on me. I saw that this was meant as an opening to one of those free conversations which I had frequently had with him. I accordingly began on the subject of the debt, and related to him the extraordinary conduct of the Minister, etc. He told me that this led to something important, that had been cursorily mentioned to him at St. Cloud; but as my house was full of company, he thought I had better call on him any time before 11 that night. He went away, and, a little after, when Mr. Monroe took leave, I followed him. He told me that he wished me to repeat what I had said relative to M. Talleyrand's requesting a proposition from me as to the purchase of Louisiana. I did so; and concluded with the extreme absurdity of his evasions of that day, and stated the consequence of any delay on this subject,

as it would enable Britain to take possession, who would readily relinquish it
to us. He said that this proceeded upon a supposition of her making so successful a war as to be enabled to retain her conquests. I told him that it was probable that the same idea might suggest itself to the United States; in which case,
it would be their interest to contribute to render her successful, and I asked
whether it was prudent to throw us into her scale? This led to long discussions
of no moment to repeat. We returned to the point: he said, that what I had
told him led him to think that what the Consul had said to him on Sunday, at
St. Cloud, (the day on which, as I told you, the determination had been taken
to sell,) had more of earnest than he thought at the time; that the Consul had
asked him what news from England? . . .

He (Marbois) then took occasion to mention his sorrow that any cause of difference should exist between our countries. The Consul told him, in reply,
"Well, you have the charge of the treasury; let them give you one hundred millions of francs, and pay their own claims, and take the whole country." Seeing,
by my looks, that I was surprised at so extravagant a demand, he added that he
considered the demand as exorbitant, and had told the First Consul that the
thing was impossible; that we had not the means of raising that. The Consul
told him that we might borrow it. I now plainly saw the whole business: first, the
Consul was disposed to sell; next, he distrusted Talleyrand, . . . and meant to
put the negotiation into the hands of Marbois, whose character for integrity is
established. I told him that the United States were anxious to preserve peace
with France; that, for that reason, they wished to remove them to the west side
of the Mississippi; that we would be perfectly satisfied with New Orleans and
the Floridas, and had no disposition to extend across the river; that, of course,
we would not give any great sum for the purchase; that he was right in his idea
of the extreme exorbitancy of the demand, which would not fall short of one
hundred and twenty-five millions; that, however, we would be ready to purchase,
provided the sum was reduced to reasonable limits. He then pressed me to name
the sum. I told him that this was not worth while, because, as he only treated
the inquiry as a matter of curiosity, any declaration of mine would have no
effect. If a negotiation was to be opened, we should (Mr. Monroe and myself)
make the offer after mature reflection. This compelled him to declare, that,
though he was not authorized expressly to make the inquiry from me, yet, that,
if I could mention any sum that came near the mark, that could be accepted,
he would communicate it to the First Consul. I told him that we had no sort
of authority to go to a sum that bore any proportion to what he mentioned; but
that, as he himself considered the demand as too high, he would oblige me by
telling me what he thought would be reasonable. He replied that, if we would
name sixty millions, and take upon us the American claims, to the amount of
twenty more, he would try how far this would be accepted. I told him that it
was vain to ask anything that was so greatly beyond our means; that true policy
would dictate to the First Consul not to press such a demand; that he must
know that it would render the present Government unpopular, and have a
tendency, at the next election, to throw the power into the hands of men who

were most hostile to a connection with France; and that this would probably happen in the midst of a war. I asked him whether the few millions acquired at this expense would not be too dearly bought?

He frankly confessed that he was of my sentiments; but that he feared the Consul would not relax. I asked him to press this argument upon him, together with the danger of seeing the country pass into the hands of Britain. I told him that he had seen the ardor of the Americans to take it by force, and the difficulty with which they were restrained by the prudence of the President; that he must easily see how much the hands of the war party would be strengthened, when they learned that France was upon the eve of a rupture with England. He admitted the weight of all this: "But," says he, "you know the temper of a youthful conqueror; everything he does is rapid as lightning; we have only to speak to him as an opportunity presents itself, perhaps in a crowd, when he bears no contradiction. When I am alone with him, I can speak more freely, and he attends; but this opportunity seldom happens, and is always accidental. Try, then, if you can not come up to my mark. Consider the extent of the country, the exclusive navigation of the river, and the importance of having no neighbors to dispute you, no war to dread." I told him that I considered all these as important considerations, but there was a point beyond which we could not go, and that fell far short of the sum he mentioned. . . .

Mr. Monroe will be presented to the Minister to-morrow, when we shall press for as early an audience as possible from the First Consul. I think it will be necessary to put in some proposition to-morrow: the Consul goes in a few days to Brussels, and every moment is precious.

4 | John Randolph's Conservative Argument Against the
Restriction of American Commerce, 1809–11 *

Jefferson's effort to coerce England and France by depriving them, as well as the American people themselves, of the benefits of United States commerce created a continuous storm of criticism from the Federalists and their merchant allies. Yet perhaps the most vociferous and caustic critic of Jeffersonian policy was the conservative Virginian, John Randolph. On February 20, 1809, Randolph attacked the Non-Intercourse Act as an unnecessary exposure of American weakness in the face of the power and determination of the warring nations of Europe. For Randolph the answer rested in the building of military strength without which the United States could never make its will felt in European counsels.

* Annals of Congress, 10th Congress, 2nd Sess., Columns 1465–6, 1470, 1473–4.

. . . No question can exist, it would appear to me, in the mind of any practical man, that the embargo must be repealed; and this vote for a partial repeal of the embargo is a proof that there exists a conviction in this House that some way or other the embargo must be gotten rid of. I look upon the embargo as the most fatal measure that ever happened to this country—as the most calamitous event. On account of pecuniary loss? No. Great as that is, I do not view it so on that account. On account of the vexations to which our citizens have been exposed under it, not only from officers of Government, but from their fellow-citizens—from one another—tearing one another to pieces in the courts, where they were open, and unable to satisfy each other's just demands? Not, sir, on that account. Suppose we had answered, in November last, the almost unanimous expectation of America, how different would have been the result! But, by that blind perseverance in this most unfortunate measure, we have lifted the veil which concealed our weakness—we have exposed our imbecility. The veil of the temple of the Constitution is rent in twain; the nakedness of the fathers of the country has been exposed to their unnatural, impious children. That is our situation. You never can redeem it. The Constitution has received a wound that ages cannot heal. But, if we had only come up to the expectation of our suffering people—if we had been content with a twelve month's embargo, instead of an embargo *ad eternum,* the nation would have obeyed, would have been united. . . .

On the subject of the embargo, sir, I have always understood it, like a vessel for holding liquor, to derive all its value from its tightness; and whenever you begin to drill holes in the bottom, no matter of what diameter, it is good for nothing. We have trusted our most precious interests in this leaky vessel; and now, by way of amendment, we are going to bore additional holes in this machine, which, like a cask, derives all its value, if it have any, from being water-tight. From some notion of honor or dignity, quite incomprehensible to me, we are to stick to this thing; it is to be hung around our necks, or to be trailed after us like a canister tied to the tail of a miserable persecuted dog. This is not all; we are not content to lift the covering which hid, I will not say our nakedness, but we are, I fear, breaking up from the very foundation every principle and maxim of policy which governed the country from the institution of the Federal Constitution to the present moment. . . .

. . . One of the principal objections urged by me on the night when the first embargo bill passed, was, that hitherto the people had been obedient to the laws—not in the sense of not making insurrection against the laws—I mean voluntary obedience, from the heart as well as the hand. The character of a smuggler was disreputable on the exchange and in the coffee-house: this is an honorable trait in the character of our merchants. I anticipated from the embargo that we should put men to a school of smuggling *out,* and, after the embargo was repealed, they would keep their hand in by smuggling *in;* more especially, as, after having put them apprentices to the business, we have given them an additional premium of 50 per cent. Lest they should not set up for themselves in it. We have given them a stock—lent them a lift. I was going to say that I am surprised, but I am not, cannot, be surprised. . . .

But, sir, it seems that to repeal this embargo wholly would be to descend from our dignity. The committee of exterior relations told us as much at the beginning of the session. I will thank any gentleman, who has it, for a copy of the report. The report being handed to him by a member, Mr. R. quoted the following passage:

> There is no other alternative than war with both nations, or a continuance of the present system. For war with one of the belligerents only would be submission to the edicts and will of the other; and a repeal in whole or in part of the embargo must necessarily be war or submission. A general repeal without arming, would be submission to both nations. A general repeal and arming of our merchant vessels would be war with both, and war of the worst kind, suffering the enemies to plunder us without retaliation upon them. A partial repeal——

. . . It seems that we are neither to have war with both nations nor a continuance of the present system; which will bring the Committee into a dilemma —but as to *me*, (I speak in the singular) my withers are unwrung. Suppose, sir, that, instead of this indecisive state of acting, this House had, at the commencement of the present session, repealed the embargo, and armed in our defence *instanter*—what would have been the consequence? That you must have had at this moment, whilst I am speaking, war with both nations, or an accommodation with one, and war with the other, or an accommodation with both; and I believe that the last would have ensued.

Will gentlemen hint, that arming the merchantmen is not a dignified resistance, and that the embargo, or this wretched thing, is? What is the embargo? It compels your own produce to die on your hands. It has been said, that our merchants would go to England and pay tribute. The embargo is tribute, and of the most destructive sort. It leaves your own produce to perish—to rot—permitting your adversary to throw in her own goods to any amount, and saddle you with a debt which you will be able to pay no one. Two years' importations are to be met with one year's crop. This is a tribute, sir. I am against any tribute; but if we must pay it, I had rather pay it with a full pocket than one nearly empty. A system of resistance to the belligerents, by arming and defending yourself, is paying tribute; but going out under this bill to London, and taking a license, is not tribute. Going to St. Bartholomew's, and disposing of your produce to British capitalists for what you can get, is not paying tribute; but actual fighting is paying tribute. That is all right, sir; for we ought to have a new nomenclature; everything is left-handed. The political heart is in the wrong place, where the mock-doctor placed it in the play. This bill, however, is at least as much resistance as the embargo, and more so: for the embargo runs you in debt, destroys your produce, and levies a contribution on you to an amount which cannot be calculated. . . .

— | "Against foreign aggression we want nothing more to support our rights than the spirit of ordinary man." *

In March and April 1810, Randolph again challenged the entire program of trade restrictions against England and France and demanded the immediate repeal of the Non-Intercourse Act. He accused some members of Congress of attaching foreign policy, not to the nation's power and interests, but to its sentiments and easily aroused hatreds, especially toward England. The spirit of '76, he insisted, was the resistance to tyranny at home, not resistance to specific nations abroad. The Declaration of Independence, added Randolph, had no place in the foreign relations of the United States.

. . . This act has been reprobated and reviled by every man, of every political description, in this House and out of it, from one end of the continent to the other; and yet, sir, strange as it may appear, Congress has been in session near five months, and this law in relation to which every one seems to concur, indeed, vie with each other in its reprobation, still remains upon our statute books. To answer what end, I beseech you, sir? Is it a sort of scarecrow, set up to frighten the great belligerents of Europe; or, is it a toy, a rattle, a bare plaything, to amuse the great children of our political world? On whatsoever measures the nation may ultimately resolve, be it peace, be it war, be it (if there be such a thing) an intermediate state between these two, there is no difference of opinion as to the deleterious operation of this unfortunate law. I ought, perhaps to call it fortunate; for, although it was introduced into the House without a single friend, although no man was found to lift up his voice in its defence, it actually passed by a majority of two to one, and is found nearly as difficult to repeal as the old sedition law of a former majority, even after all its abettors have become convinced of its mischievous tendency. I hope, sir, we shall profit of former experience, and not pertinaciously adhere to a measure which is daily diminishing the resources of the nation, and very justly impairing the public confidence in the wisdom and patriotism of the Legislature. . . . If any member of the House will figure to himself the fair and *bona fide* American merchant whose ship has been lying at the wharf the greater part of the winter, laden with a cargo perishable in its nature, say flaxseed, which, if not exported now, becomes utterly worthless, he will conceive of the situation of those whom I wish to relieve. How our resources are to be enlarged, or the belligerents to be acted on by our produce perishing here, I cannot conceive. I mean the produce of the fair and *bona fide* trader, for the other description of men, we know, all send their produce when and where they please. We have had official information, near five months ago, that the law is wholly inoperative, except as to men of high character for probity and honor, who cannot gain their own consent to violate the law. . . .

* Remarks of Randolph on the Non-Intercourse Act of 1809, March 31, April 2, 1810, *Annals of Congress*, 11th Congress, 2nd Sess., Columns 1702–3, 1710, 1726–7.

. . . Now, sir, it is fair to take for granted that the President of the United States has done his duty; that he has recommended such measures as he may judge necessary and expedient. What are they, sir? If the President of the United States, who is charged with the execution of the laws, whose knowledge respecting all our foreign relations is perfect as that of finite man can be—if he, on whom (do what you will) the execution of these measures must ultimately rest, has recommended no measures as necessary and expedient, it hardly becomes— I will not say a member of this House, but me, to step in "where angels fear to tread." And until the President of the United States who stands at the helm of our Government, shall disclose his plan of operations to this House—until the efficient Prime Minister of this country, who has an almost omnipotent control over our foreign affairs, and nearly as great over our domestic, shall disclose his sentiments, it is idle and ridiculous for members of this House to be popping up in their seats with shreds and patches and disjointed members of systems which can never make a whole one. System supposes connexion and sympathy of parts; and, after giving as much credit as you please to the independence of the two Houses of Congress—I speak now of no undue influence, but of Fair Constitutional influence, and duty too—the members of this House cannot make a system of foreign policy which shall seem good in the eyes of the President, and which he can execute beneficially to the State, unless he be consulted in some way, directly or indirectly, as to the nature and extent of that system. It becomes a question whether the direct influence of the President shall not supersede an influence, if such there be, of a worse kind. The President has a great duty to perform. I conclude that he is unable to devise any system, or that he thinks none necessary, because if he had been able to devise such a system, he would, as in duty bound, have submitted it to Congress. There is then no system. Far be it from me to attempt to make one, especially out of discordant materials. But surely, sir, when a law has existed on our statute book for months, an acknowledged excrescence, I may move its repeal. If the non-intercourse be this manly resistance which some gentlemen seem to suppose it, let us have a resolution to continue it—let us re-enact it. If not, let us repeal it now, when the merchants and planters may receive some benefit from it. Instead of letting it die what may be called a natural death (although it will die on the gibbet) at the end of the session, I hope it will be now repealed. However the House may act, no part of the responsibility for its continuance can attach to me. . . .

. . . If the system be prolonged, my anxiety is, that it shall be no conduct of mine, passive or active, and I hope to have a direct vote on the question. The House can as well act on the subject in one day as in seven years. There is nothing *de novo*; every man's mind is long ago made up upon it. If gentlemen see something so charming in this system that they will not give it up till death do them part, so be it. With respect to all the rest, as to the amendment proposed, for bolstering up our independence, etc. I have not a word to utter. I really could wish that less was said in this House about the independence of the United States. I do not think it creditable to us. It looks as if we had not an assurance of our independence—as if we doubted or were afraid of some flaw in our title; and I should be sorry to see that spirit which dictated it invoked, not for the purpose for which alone it should be called up, but to answer the ordinary occasions of political life. A great deal has been said, sir, about the spirit of seventy-six. What is it? A spirit which calls upon the nation to guard against abuse in Government—a spirit which resisted the unconstitutional and arbitrary measures of the Government of that day, a spirit which darts its penetrating eye always into abuses of Government at home. It is the genius of investigation—the spirit of resistance—it has nothing to do with foreign prejudices and partialities. The very moment the Treaty of '83 was signed, the spirit of the American Revolution became, as to foreign nations, neutralized. We took our rank among the nations of the earth, and stood upon equal ground with any of them. I am sorry, sir, to be hurried into these observations: but I do think that the public mind ought not to be artfully led away, under a cry of the spirit of '76, from objects to which that spirit would direct us—the union of military and civil offices in a single individual—a tyrannical Governor Gage at Boston, rendering the military superior to the civil power, and protecting them by mock trial from punishment; arbitrary and oppressive laws, cutting off our trade to all parts of the world—a Legislature turning a deaf ear to petitioning citizens. These, sir, are the objects to which the spirit of '76, and of the Revolution, naturally guide us. The moment you invoke it to support your independence against Great Britain or any foreign Power, you do by a sort of *ex post facto* act bastardize your own pedigree—you seem willing to concede that we are not an independent people. The spirit of the Revolution is invoked to induce you to resist—what? Great Britain. Sir, it is not a spirit of opposition to foreign nations, but a spirit of resistance to corruption and tyranny at home. We want no Revolutionary spirit to rouse us to assert and defend our right to a place among the nations of the earth, but to induce us to sift carefully and pertinaciously every abuse of the Government at home. It is not worth while in a foreign contest to be repeating our Declaration of Independence. It is a black catalogue of crimes which never were nor never can be committed by a foreign Government upon an independent State, but by a Government upon its own people, and against these we ought to guard. Against foreign aggression we want nothing more to support our rights than the spirit of ordinary man.

— | "I want, sir, to relieve the Virginia planter, and not to settle questions of good or bad faith . . . with the French Emperor . . ." *

In February 1811, Randolph attacked the tendency of Congress, under Macon's Bill Number 2, to drive the nation into the arms of Napoleon. The Virginian again favored the repeal of a system which, he said, had no effect on the enemy and injured the commerce and shipping of the United States.

. . . We once had, if I recollect right, a report before this House declaring that only three possible alternatives presented themselves to the country—war, embargo, or disgrace. I put it emphatically to the advocates of that position— are those, who would have neither war, or embargo, willing to concede that by their act the nation has been disgraced? I put it to the gentlemen whether any pledge of this kind, given by a vote of this House, can at a subsequent time be conjured up, to terrify us into the adoption of measures, which every man acknowledges to be pregnant with great public detriment, if not with ruin.

My object in bringing forward this motion was to give that practical relief to the people whom I represent which they now do, or soon will stand in need of— to do away a system which has no effect upon their enemies, whose deleterious operation is confined to themselves alone. I want, sir, to relieve the Virginia planter, and not to settle questions of good or bad faith, or of mode or courtesy, with the French Emperor or his courtiers. We do appear to me to have involved ourselves in a most embarrassing situation. I am sometimes inclined to doubt whether some frenzy has not seized upon us. Gentlemen get up and depict in the strongest colors that they can command the injuries we have received from both belligerents. It seems to be the unanimous sentiment that they cannot be disguised or palliated, that they are self evident, and that it is a waste of time to attempt to describe, much more to demonstrate them. When, *hey-presto!* in the next breath we stand in such a relation to the Emperor of France that it is sacrilege to doubt—what? His disposition to injure us? No. That in fact he has injured us? Not at all—to doubt that he has in any one instance, although the proof is all the while staring us in the face—that in any one instance, this Imperial and Royal Personage has been found to depart from his imperial and royal word! God bless us! and is this the man of whom and of whose acts such pictures are drawn on all sides of this House, by men of all descriptions? Are the practical wrongs which the people of this country have received to be salved over with douceurs of etiquette? If that be the case we should send some dancing-master, some master of the ceremonies; if any such we have among us, to exchange bows with Duroc, the Imperial Grand Chamberlain; things might be settled in the style of the old *minuet de la cour;* they might make their honors,

* Remarks of Randolph on Macon's Bill Number 2. February 2, 1811, *Annals of Congress,* 11th Congress, 3rd Sess., Columns 890–92.

go all around the room in great state, and would, no doubt, end precisely where they began.

. . . An honorable gentleman from New York (Mr. Fisk) had proposed to get over this difficulty. How? Not by repealing the act regulating commercial inter-course with the belligerents, but, forsooth, by suspending its operation. It is said, that on this second day of February, in the year of our Lord—(we still count by the Christian era in this country, I thank God!) one thousand eight hundred and eleven—you stand bound to carry into effect a rigorous non-intercourse with England. You cannot repeal it—but then you may say suspend it! How long? From session to session, as some laws have been suspended, ever since I had a seat in this House? I take the gentleman at his word and agree so to suspend. I am for substantial relief, and if the term suspension will operate as a salve on the conscience of the gentleman from New York, no doubt it will be equally potent and operative with others.

Again, listen to my worthy colleague near the door (Mr. Eppes.) He too con-ceived that we were pledged to France. In redemption of that pledge he had brought in a bill for the rigorous enforcement of non-intercourse with England. He now moved to recommit the bill. Why? "There hung," he said, "a cloud over that quarter"—it was, however, but a "speck" in the horizon, not of war, but of treachery and ill faith. What, sir, had the Committee of Foreign Relations proposed to do? It was to carry into effect with good faith his contract which they say we have made with France, and which I say we did not make. Was it not the object of the bill, which the gentleman this morning moved to recommit, to carry into effect the stipulations said to have been entered into between us and France? Unquestionably it was. The gentleman, then, by his own showing, has found cause in the conduct of the French Government for failing to do that which by his own argument the United States are bound in good faith to exe-cute; over which they have not any discretionary power whatever. The question is surrendered, sir, entirely on the other side. The expedient of the gentleman from New York to suspend the operation of the law—the proposition of the gentleman from Virginia to delay carrying it into execution, as he had con-templated before the late intelligence from Paris, are virtually and substantially, in principle, the same with my own, which has excited so much reprehension. The power to suspend of the gentleman from New York implies the power, prac-tically, to repeal; and it is admitted by the gentleman from Virginia that a state of things has arisen in which he feels, if not released from his obligation, yet that it hangs so loosely about him, that he will desist from carrying it into effect. Upon the argument of either gentleman, the question is yielded. If the honor of the United States is mortgaged, let it be forthwith redeemed. If it be indeed pledged let us not come halting to this House with the national faith in one hand and expedients to evade it in the other. There can be on such a question no recurrence to expedients. This is the second of February. The time has arrived—the hour now is, when gentlemen, by their own arguments, if their arguments be just, are bound to fulfil the contract, which I do not under-take to expound, but which they say has been made, certainly in a manner very novel to our Constitution, between the House of Representatives on the one hand, and Bonaparte on the other—a bargain which, like the bargains of old, with the devil, there is no shaking off. It is a bargain which credulity and imbecility enters into with cunning and power: it is like the stock in a neighboring turnpike, which you can neither sell nor give away, but which operates as an eternal lien upon every shilling of your property. . . .

## 5 | Western Interests and the War of 1812 *

Ultimately the War of 1812 must be explained in terms of Western interests, for it was a group of Western Congressmen, led by Henry Clay of Kentucky, who carried the responsibility for the war resolution. Historians have never agreed on the precise anti-British motivation of Western leaders, but in large measure the immediate cause for their antagonism lay in the alleged British complicity in the Indian wars along the Wabash frontier. Perhaps no Western Congressman stated his section's case against England with more vehemence and emotion than did Richard Mentor Johnson of Kentucky, on December 11, 1811.

. . . For the first time since my entrance into this body, there now seems to be but one opinion with a great majority—that with Great Britain war is inevitable; that the hopes of the sanguine as to a returning sense of British justice have expired; that the prophecies of the discerning have failed; and, that her infernal system has driven us to the brink of a second revolution, as important as the first. Upon the Wabash, through the influence of British agents, and within our territorial sea by the British navy, the war has already commenced. Thus, the folly, the power, and the tyranny of Great Britain, have taken from us the last alternative of longer forbearance.

Mr. J. said we must now oppose the farther encroachments of Great Britain by war, or formally annul the Declaration of our Independence, and acknowledge ourselves her devoted colonies. The people whom I represent will not hesitate which of the two courses to choose; and, if we are involved in war, to maintain our dearest rights, and to preserve our independence, I pledge myself to this House, and my constituents to this nation, that they will not be wanting in valor, nor in their proportion of men and money to prosecute the war with effect. Before we relinquish the conflict, I wish to see Great Britain renounce the piratical system of paper blockade; to liberate our captured seamen on board her ships of war; relinquish the practice of impressment on board our

* *Annals of Congress,* 12th Congress, 1st Sess., Columns 456–7, 459–61, 463, 465–7.

merchant vessels; to repeal her Orders in Council; and cease, in every other respect, to violate our neutral rights; to treat us as an independent people. The gentleman from Virginia (MR. RANDOLPH) has objected to the destination of this auxiliary force—the occupation of the Canadas, and the other British possessions upon our borders where our laws are violated, the Indians stimulated to murder our citizens, and where there is a British monopoly of the peltry and fur trade. I should not wish to extend the boundary of the United States by war if Great Britain would leave us to the quiet enjoyment of independence; but, considering her deadly and implacable enmity, and her continued hostility, I shall never die contented until I see her expulsion from North America, and her territories incorporated with the United States. . . .

The gentleman from Virginia says we are identified with the British in religion, in blood, in language, and deeply laments our hatred to that country, who can boast of so many illustrious characters. This deep rooted enmity to Great Britain arises from her insidious policy, the offspring of her perfidious conduct towards the United States. Her disposition is unfriendly; her enmity is implacable; she sickens at our prosperity and happiness. If obligations of friendship do exist, why does Great Britain rend those ties asunder, and open the bleeding wounds of former conflicts? Or does the obligation of friendship exist on the part of the United States alone? I have never thought that the ties of religion, of blood, of language, and of commerce, would justify or sanctify insult and injury—on the contrary, that a premeditated wrong from the hand of a friend created more sensibility, and deserved the greater chastisement and the higher execration. What would you think of a man, to whom you were bound by the most sacred ties, who would plunder you of your substance, aim a deadly blow at your honor, and in the hour of confidence endeavor to bury a dagger in your bosom? Would you, sir, proclaim to the world your affection for this miscreant of society, after this conduct, and endeavor to interest your audience with the ties of kindred that bound you to each other? So let it be with nations, and there will be neither surprise nor lamentation that we execrate a Government so hostile to our independence—for it is from the Government that we meet with such multiplied injury, and to that object is our hatred directed. As to individuals of merit, whether British or French, I presume no person would accuse the people of the United States of such hatred to them, or of despising individuals, who might not be instrumental in the maritime despotism which we feel; and this accounts for the veneration we have for Sidney and Russell, statesmen of whom the gentleman has spoken; they are fatal examples, why we should love the British Government. The records of that Government are now stained with the blood of these martyrs in freedom's cause, as vilely as with the blood of American citizens; and certainly we shall not be called upon to love equally the murderer and the victim. For God's sake let us not again be told of the ties of religion, of laws, of blood, and of customs, which bind the two nations together, with a view to extort our love for the English Government, and more especially, when the same gentleman has acknowledged that we have ample cause of war against that nation—let us not be told of the freedom of that corrupt Government whose hands are washed alike in the blood of her

own illustrious statesmen, for a manly opposition to tyranny, and the citizens of
every other clime. But I would inquire into this love for the British Government
and British institutions, in the gross, without any discrimination. Why love her
rulers? Why kiss the rod of iron which inflicts the stripes without a cause? When
all admit we have just cause of war, such attachments are dangerous, and encourage encroachment. I will venture to say, that our hatred of the British
Government is not commensurate with her depredations and her outrages on
our rights, or we should have waged a deadly war against her many years
past. . . .

. . . Now I shall attend to the charge of partiality in our measures towards
France. It is an insinuation not founded in fact, and can only exist in the
imagination of those who may insinuate it. We are not driven to mere declarations—the truth of the assertion is bottomed upon the statute records of the
United States; and we appeal to the character of every measure relative to foreign relations, since the adoption of the embargo, in consequence of the violation of neutral rights upon the high seas. . . .

The British Minister has insinuated that we have suffered our commerce to
be moulded by France to the annoyance of the British trade, and attempts have
been made to conjure up the idea of an alliance with France against Great
Britain, because we have made arrangements with France that our neutral rights
shall be regarded. The idea of an alliance is as idle as it is unfounded. Thank
Heaven we are under no obligations to any Power to go to war, nor to continue that war after the objects for which we contend shall be accomplished.
The non-importation law is the cause of complaint with Great Britain, and she
knows if the Orders in Council and her blockade of May were repealed, that
our non-importation law would cease to operate against her. But instead of
this, sir, every day our merchant ships fall a prey to the Orders in Council, and
we are menaced with retaliation for the non-importation, which does not capture and condemn British ships and cargoes, but prevents the importation of
British property into our markets. . . .

The gentleman from Virginia has called the military regular forces mer-
cenaries. If by this appellation any reproach or degradation is intended, its
justice and propriety is denied. In times like the present, when dangers thicken
upon us, at the moment when we are compelled by most wanton tyranny upon
the high seas, and upon land may be added, to abandon our peaceful habits for
the din of arms, officers and soldiers in this country are governed by the noble
feelings of patriotism and of valor. The history of the world may be ransacked;
other nations may be brought in review before us, and examples of greater
heroism cannot be quoted, than shall be performed in battle by our officers and
soldiers, military, and naval, and marine. The deeds of their ancestors would be
before them; glory would animate their bosoms, and love of country would
nerve the heart to deeds of mighty fame. If, therefore, there should not be a
diminution of respect for those who entertain an opinion so degrading to our
army, it should at least be understood that such opinions do not lessen the
confidence due to those who faithfully serve their country, and who would lay
down their life for it. This reflection brings to memory the late memorable

conflict upon the Wabash. Governor Harrison pitched his tents near the Prophet's town; and although this fanatic had his followers collected, and the American forces were anxious to finish work by an open and day-light engagement, if there was a necessity to resort to arms, their impetuous valor was easily stayed, when they were informed that the white flag of peace was to be hoisted next morning, and the effusion of blood was to be spared. But in the silent watches of the night, relieved from the fatigues of valor, and slumbering under the perfidious promises of the savages, who were infuriated and made drunk by British traders, dreaming of the tender smile of a mother, and the fond embraces of affectionate wives, and of prattling children upon their knees, on their return from the fatigues of a campaign!—the destroyers came with the silent instruments of death, the war club, the scalping knife, the tomahawk, and the bow and arrow; with these they penetrate into the heart of our forces—they enter the tents of our officers—many close their eyes in death—it was a trying moment for the rest of our heroes, but they were equal to the dreadful occasion. The American forces flew to arms; they rallied at the voice of their officers, and soon checked the work of death. The savages were successively and successfully charged and driven until day-light, when they disappeared like the mist of morning. . . . So long as the records of this transaction remain, the 9th of November will not be forgotten, and time shall only brighten the fame of the deeds of our army, and a tear shall be shed for those who have fallen. But the loss will not be felt by the public alone: the friends of their social hours will regret their loss; the widow will mourn her disconsolate situation; the orphan shall cry for the return of his father in vain; and the mother carry her sorrow to the grave. Let this ornamented hall be clothed with the symbols of mourning, although our army proved victorious in war; and to their memory let a monument be erected in the hearts of a grateful country.

— | "The coast is to be left defenceless, whilst men of the interior are revelling in conquest and spoil." *

Randolph, pro-British and opposed to war, answered the Western Representatives with equal determination. He questioned the evidence that British policy lay behind the battle of Tippecanoe in November, 1811. He accused the Westerners of attempting to commit the nation to a war of conquest without realizing what a conflict with England would cost the American people. Even if the United States managed to conquer Canada, he added, it would still not have touched Britain or British sea power. And if the United States succeeded in disposing of Britain completely, it would destroy the only power of Europe that held Napoleon in check.

* Remarks against the war resolution, December 10, 16, 1811, *Annals of Congress,* 12th Congress, 1st Sess., Columns 441, 445–9, 453–4, 529–30.

. . . The Committee of Foreign Relations had indeed decided that the subject of arming the militia (which he had pressed upon them as indispensable to the public security) did not come within the scope of their authority. On what ground he had been and still was unable to see, they had felt themselves authorized (when that subject was before another committee) to recommend the raising of standing armies, with a view (as had been declared) of immediate war—a war not of defence, but of conquest, of aggrandizement, of ambition; a war foreign to the interest of this country, to the interests of humanity itself. . . .

An insinuation had fallen from the gentleman from Tennessee, (Mr. Grundy,) that the late massacre of our brethren on the Wabash had been instigated by the British Government. Has the President given any such information? has the gentleman received any such, even informally, from any officer of this Government? Is it so believed by the Administration? He had cause to think the contrary to be the fact; that such was not their opinion. This insinuation was of the grossest kind—a presumption the most rash, the most unjustifiable. Show but good ground for it, he would give up the question at the threshold—he was ready to march to Canada. It was indeed well calculated to excite the feelings of the Western people particularly, who were not quite so tenderly attached to our red brethren as some modern philosophers; but it was destitute of any foundation, beyond mere surmise and suspicion. What would be thought, if, without any proof whatsoever, a member should rise in his place and tell us, that the massacre in Savannah, a massacre perpetrated by civilized savages, with French commisisons in their pockets, was excited by the French Government? There was an easy and natural solution of the late transaction on the Wabash, in the well known character of the aboriginal savage of North America, without resorting to any such mere conjectural estimate. He was sorry to say that for this signal calamity and disgrace the House was, in part, at least, answerable. Session after session, their table had been piled up with Indian treaties, for which the appropriations had been voted as a matter of course, without examination. Advantage had been taken of the spirit of the Indians, broken by the war which ended in the Treaty of Greenville. Under the ascendency then acquired over them they had been pent up by subsequent treaties into nooks, straightened in their quarters by a blind cupidity, seeking to extinguish their title to immense wildernesses, for which, (possessing, as we do already, more land than we can sell or use) we shall not have occasion, for half a century to come. It was our own thirst for territory, our own want of moderation, that had driven these sons of nature to desperation, of which we felt the effects. . . .

This war of conquest, a war for the acquisition of territory and subjects, is to be a new commentary on the doctrine that Republics are destitute of ambition—that they are addicted to peace, wedded to the happiness and safety of the great body of their people. But it seems this to be a holiday campaign—there is to be no expense of blood, or treasure, on our part—Canada is to conquer herself—she is to be subdued by the principles of fraternity. The people of that country are first to be seduced from their allegiance, and converted into traitors, as preparatory to the making them good citizens. Although he must acknowledge that some of our flaming patriots were thus manufactured, he did not think the process would hold good with a whole community. It was a dangerous experiment. We were to succeed in the French mode by the system of fraternization—all is French! but how dreadfully it might be retorted on the Southern and Western slaveholding States. He detested this subornation of treason. No—if he must have them, let them fall by the valor of our arms, by fair, legitimate conquest; not become the victims of treacherous seduction. . . .

. . . Go! march to Canada! leave the broad bosom of the Chesapeake and her hundred tributary rivers—the whole line of seacoast from Machias to St. Mary's, unprotected! You have taken Quebec—have you conquered England? Will you seek for the deep foundations of her power in the frozen deserts of Labrador? . . .

Will you call upon her to leave your ports and harbors untouched, only just till you can return from Canada, to defend them? The coast is to be left defenceless, whilst men of the interior are revelling in conquest and spoil. But grant for a moment, for mere argument's sake, that in Canada you touched the sinews of her strength, instead of removing a clog upon her resources—an encumbrance, but one, which, from a spirit of honor, she will vigorously defend. In what situation would you then place some of the best men of the nation? As Chatham and Burke, and the whole band of her patriots, prayed for her defeat in 1776, so must some of the truest friends to their country deprecate the success of our arms against the only Power that holds in check the archenemy of mankind. . . .

. . . If it were allowable to entertain partialities, every consideration of blood, language, religion, and interest, would incline us towards England; and yet, shall they be alone extended to France and her ruler, whom we are bound to believe a chastening God suffers as the scourge of a guilty world! On all other nations he tramples—he holds them in contempt—England alone he hates; he would, but he cannot despise her—fear cannot despise. . . .

. . . Suppose France in possession of the British naval power—and to her the Trident must pass should England be unable to wield it—what would be your condition? What would be the situation of your seaports and their seafaring inhabitants? Ask Hamburg, Lubec? Ask Savannah? What, sir! when their privateers are pent up in our harbors by the British bull-dogs, when they receive at our hands every rite of hospitality, from which their enemy is excluded—when they capture within our own waters, interdicted to British armed ships, American vessels; when such is their deportment towards you, under such circumstances, what could you expect if they were the uncontrolled lords of the ocean? . . .

But we are told, and by men of honor too, that we stand pledged to France. I was not surprised, sir, to see this asserted by factious journalists, but I confess my astonishment; nay, my grief and indignation, when I hear it asserted on this floor, by men whom I honor, whom I love, whom I revere! Bound to France, as Sinbad the sailor was bound to the putrifying corpse of his deceased wife. If so, then have we sealed our perdition. Will any man contend that we have the right to transfer to a foreign Despot the power of making war for us, upon whom and when he shall please? No, sir, I deny it; such is not our miserable, our hopeless condition. We are not bound to France, and, so help me God, with my consent, we never shall be so bound. What will your constituents say to this? Suppose they crowd your table with memorials and instructions against this measure, will you reply to them with the coolness of a modern duellist—"we are bound in honor; we are sorry for it, but cannot help it. The sacred trust which you reposed in us we have betrayed; the high attributes of sovereignty, the power of war and peace with which you clothed us for your own good, we have made over, by legislative legerdemain, to the great oppressor of our name and race. We are spell bound, under incantation, and must obey." Will the people endure this? Is the power of making war transferred from the American Congress to France? and by chicanery too? *Bound to France!* By what? By a contrivance, an artifice the most bungling—by a quibble which a Newgate solicitor would blush to plead in bar of an indictment for felony. But, sir, if you have sold yourselves into foreign bondage I pray you to show me the equivalent, the *quid pro quo.* What have you got in exchange from the tyrant of the earth? Where is the mess of pottage, the miserable dish of French broth, of soup maigre, for which you have bartered away your birthright; the birthright of a whole people; the right of self-government; the power over war and peace! . . .

## 6 | Madison's War Message, June 1, 1812 *

In his war message, President Madison listed the "progressive usurpations" and "accumulated wrongs" perpetrated by the British government against the nation's neutral rights on the high seas and the peace of its Western frontier.

↙

. . . Without going back beyond the renewal in 1803 of the war in which Great Britain is engaged, and omitting unrepaired wrongs of inferior magnitude, the conduct of her Government presents a series of acts hostile to the United States as an independent and neutral nation.

British cruisers have been in the continued practice of violating the American flag on the great highway of nations, and of seizing and carrying off persons sailing under it, not in the exercise of a belligerent right founded on the law of nations against an enemy, but of a municipal prerogative over British subjects. British jurisdiction is thus extended to neutral vessels in a situation where no laws can operate but the law of nations and the laws of the country to which the vessels belong, and a self-redress is assumed which, if British subjects were wrongfully detained and alone concerned, is that substitution of force for a

* *Messages and Papers of the Presidents,* James D. Richardson, ed. (Washington, 1896), I: 499–505.

resort to the responsible sovereign which falls within the definition of war. Could the seizure of British subjects in such cases be regarded as within the exercise of a belligerent right, the acknowledged laws of war, which forbid an article of captured property to be adjudged without a regular investigation before a competent tribunal, would imperiously demand the fairest trial where the sacred rights of persons were at issue. In place of such a trail these rights are subjected to the will of every petty commander.

The practice, hence, is so far from affecting British subjects alone that, under the pretext of searching for these, thousands of American citizens, under the safeguard of public law and of their national flag, have been torn from their country and from everything dear to them; have been dragged on board ships of war of a foreign nation and exposed, under the severities of their discipline, to be exiled to the most distant and deadly climes, to risk their lives in the battles of their oppressors, and to be the melancholy instruments of taking away those of their own brethren.

Against this crying enormity, which Great Britain would be so prompt to avenge if committed against herself, the United States have in vain exhausted remonstrances and expostulations, and that no proof might be wanting of their conciliatory dispositions, and no pretext left for a continuance of the practice, the British Government was formally assured of the readiness of the United States to enter into arrangements such as could not be rejected if the recovery of British subjects were the real and the sole object. The communication passed without effect. . . .

Not content with these occasional expedients for laying waste our neutral trade, the cabinet of Britain resorted at length to the sweeping system of blockades, under the name of orders in council, which has been molded and managed as might best suit its political views, its commercial jealousies, or the avidity of British cruisers.

To our remonstrances against the complicated and transcendent injustice of this innovation the first reply was that the orders were reluctantly adopted by Great Britain as a necessary retaliation on decrees of her enemy proclaiming a general blockade of the British Isles at a time when the naval force of that enemy dared not issue from his own ports. She was reminded without effect that her own prior blockades, unsupported by an adequate naval force actually applied and continued, were a bar to this plea; that executed edicts against millions of our property could not be retaliation on edicts confessedly impossible to be executed; that retaliation, to be just, should fall on the party setting the guilty example, not on an innocent party which was not even chargeable with an acquiescence in it.

When deprived of this flimsy veil for a prohibition of our trade with her enemy by the repeal of his prohibition of our trade with Great Britain, her cabinet, instead of a corresponding repeal or a practical discontinuance of its orders, formally avowed a determination to persist in them against the United States until the markets of her enemy should be laid open to British products, thus asserting an obligation on a neutral power to require one belligerent to encourage by its internal regulations the trade of another belligerent, contradicting her own practice toward all nations, in peace as well as in war, and betraying the insincerity of those professions which inculcated a belief that, having resorted to her orders with regret, she was anxious to find an occasion for putting an end to them.

Abandoning still more all respect for the neutral rights of the United States and for its own consistency, the British Government now demands as prerequisites to a repeal of its orders as they relate to the United States that a formality should be observed in the repeal of the French decrees nowise necessary to their termination nor exemplified by British usage, and that the French repeal, besides including that portion of the decrees which operates within a territorial jurisdiction, as well as that which operates on the high seas, against the commerce of the United States should not be a single and special repeal in in relation to the United States, but should be extended to whatever other neutral nations unconnected with them may be affected by those decrees. And as an additional insult, they are called on for a formal disavowal of conditions and pretensions advanced by the French Government for which the United States are far from having made themselves responsible that, in official explanations which have been published to the world, and in a correspondence of the American minister at London with the British minister for foreign affairs such a responsibility was explicitly and emphatically disclaimed. . . .

Anxious to make every experiment short of the last resort of injured nations, the United States have withheld from Great Britain, under successive modifications, the benefits of a free intercourse with their market, the loss of which could not but outweigh the profits accruing from her restrictions of our commerce with other nations. And to entitle these experiments to the more favorable consideration they were so framed as to enable her to place her adversary under the exclusive operation of them. To these appeals her Government has been equally inflexible, as if willing to make sacrifices of every sort rather than yield to the claims of justice or renounce the errors of a false pride. Nay, so far were the attempts carried to overcome the attachment of the British cabinet to its unjust edicts that it received every encouragement within the competency of the executive branch of our government to expect that a repeal of them would be followed by a war between the United States and France, unless the French edicts should also be repeated. Even this communication, although silencing forever the plea of a disposition in the United States to acquiesce in those edicts originally the sole plea for them, received no attention. . . .

There was a period when a favorable change in the policy of the British cabinet was justly considered as established. The minister plenipotentiary of His Britannic Majesty here proposed an adjustment of the differences more immediately endangering the harmony of the two countries. The proposition was accepted with the promptitude and cordiality corresponding with the invariable professions of this Government. A foundation appeared to be laid for a sincere and lasting reconciliation. The prospect, however, quickly vanished. The whole proceeding was disavowed by the British Government without any explanations which could at that time repress the belief that the disavowal proceeded from a spirit of hostility to the commercial rights and prosperity of the

United States; and it has since come into proof that at the very moment when the public minister was holding the language of friendship and inspiring confidence in the sincerity of the negotiation with which he was charged a secret agent of his Government was employed in intrigues having for their object a subversion of our Government and a dismemberment of our happy union.

In reviewing the conduct of Great Britain toward the United States our attention is necessarily drawn to the warfare just renewed by the savages on one of our extensive frontiers—a warfare which is known to spare neither age nor sex and to be distinguished by features peculiarly shocking to humanity. It is difficult to account for the activity and combinations which have for some time been developing themselves among tribes in constant intercourse with British traders and garrisons without connecting their hostility with that influence and without recollecting the authenticated examples of such interpositions heretofore furnished by the officers and agents of that Government.

Such is the spectacle of injuries and indignities which have been heaped on our country, and such the crisis which its unexampled forbearance and conciliatory efforts have not been able to avert. . . .

Whether the United States shall continue passive under these progressive usurpations and these accumulating wrongs, or, opposing force to force in defense of their national rights, shall commit a just cause into the hands of the Almighty Disposer of Events, avoiding all connections which might entangle it in the contest or views of other powers, and preserving a constant readiness to concur in an honorable reestablishment of peace and friendship, is a solemn question which the Constitution wisely confides to the legislative department of the Government. In recommending it to their early deliberations I am happy in the assurance that the decision will be worthy the enlightened and patriotic councils of a virtuous, a free, and a powerful nation.

Having presented this view of the relations of the United States with Great Britain and of the solemn alternative growing out of them, I proceed to remark that the communications last made to Congress on the subject of our relations with France will have shown that since the revocation of her decrees, as they violated the neutral rights of the United States, her Government has authorized illegal captures by its privateers and public ships, and that other outrages have been practiced on our vessels and our citizens. It will have been seen also that no indemnity had been provided or satisfactorily pledged for the extensive spoliations committed under the violent and retrospective orders of the French Government against the property of our citizens seized within the Jurisdiction of France. I abstain at this time from recommending to the consideration of Congress definitive measures with respect to that nation, in the expectation that the result of unclosed discussions between our minister plenipotentiary at Paris and the French Government will speedily enable Congress to decide with greater advantage on the course due to the rights, the interests, and the honor of our country.

Although both houses of Congress eventually adopted the war resolution, several members opposed any declaration of war against England as an act contrary to the true interests of the United States. None touched the essential issues with more realism than did Senator Obadiah German of New York. On June 13, 1812, he reminded the Congress that Britain controlled the seas and had never been more powerful, while the United States was obviously not prepared for war. Nor had the American people, he added, any intention of paying the taxes required to conduct a successful war. German, more than those who favored the war, saw that successful national action required some balancing of ends and means.

💫

. . . I will first call the attention of the Senate to the ability and strength of the nation we are about, by this bill, to declare war against. Gentlemen ought to recollect, that Great Britain has been almost constantly engaged in war for twenty years past against one of the most powerful nations that ever existed; and for a considerable part of that time, the energies of her enemy have been directed by war's favorite genius—Napoleon, who has succeeded in uniting nearly the whole force of the Continent of Europe against her: against that very nation which we are about to assail; and what has been the effect? Is Great Britain less powerful now, than she was twenty years ago? No, sir, this constant warfare has increased her powers instead of diminishing them. At the commencement of the war, France was nearly her equal on the ocean, and several other nations of Europe maintained a powerful naval force. But what is their situation at present? Has not Great Britain driven them all from the ocean? And does she not remain sole mistress? I ask, gentlemen, if her ability to carry on a distant war by land or sea, has diminished? The answer must be that it has increased with her navy, and extended with her dominion. Great Britain now commands the strength and resources of most of the West India islands, and many of the islands in the Indian Ocean. She controls the destinies of more than thirty millions of people on the Continent of Asia. And she has, at this time, or will have, if we engage in a war with her, the exclusive benefit of the trade of the world; and under these circumstances possesses the ability to carry on a war in distant countries across the ocean, beyond any nation ever heard of. . . .

. . . Far be it from me that I should wish to become the apologist for any of the aggressions of the British upon our rights, or any of their unfriendly conduct towards us, but I think, if our Executive instead of carping and scolding about the vigilance of the British, in inducing the Indians to join them, in the event of a war between the two countries, had been more vigilant in furnishing the Indians with the necessaries they had been in the habit of receiving from

* *Annals of Congress*, 12th Congress, 1st Sess., Columns 272, 275–82.

our public trading houses and other sources, and had seasonably recommended to Congress to have authorized the Executive to make the Indians some suitable presents, at proper times, it would have been productive of more good to our western frontier. It is said that the British furnish the Indians with arms and ammunition; well, do not our public stores and traders do the same? And do not the Indians depend upon their arms and ammunition for their daily subsistence? It should be recollected that they are a people who live by hunting, and they must be supplied with arms and ammunition from some quarter or other. While I am on this subject, Mr. President, I will beg leave just to notice the Indian war between the troops under the command of Governor Harrison, and the Prophet and his adherents—I mean the famous battle of Tippecanoe; and I will ask, sir, for what purpose was Governor Harrison and the army under his command sent against those people?

If there was any disagreement between the Indians and our Government, why were not discreet commissioners sent to treat with them first, and let them know that the Government was willing to do them justice? It is natural to suppose that the Prophet and his four or five hundred associates would never have calculated on coercing the Government of the United States out of much more than what was their just right to receive. And, upon what authority was this war waged? Was not our army collected and marched two or three hundred miles, in a threatening manner, and without any declaration of war? And did not Governor Harrison plant his army in a menacing attitude before the Indian town, on their own lands, and in their own territory? And had not the Prophet and his party sufficient reason to believe that everything dear to them was at stake? Yes, sir, their homes, their firesides, and their all, was about to be destroyed, except they submitted unconditionally to the commander who had, perhaps, been the cause of all the difficulty which subsisted between the Indians and our Government. And I must here ask, Mr. President, if any one can blame the Indians for fighting, under such circumstances? No, sir, I conceive if they had not fought they would have debased human nature itself. Since, then, this flame is kindled, and that, too, by ourselves, is it prudent to wage a premature war with Great Britain, and bring her force in reality and openly in aid of the savage tomahawk and scalping-knife, already raised against our innocent frontier settlements? I think the more prudent course would be first to treat with the Indians, to send some two or three discreet and proper men among them to promise them justice and friendship, and really to perform what is just and right towards them; and, then, my word for it, they would be willing to remain at peace with us. In the mean time let us raise and discipline our army and fortify our seaports and harbors. And when we are prepared, if Great Britain does not, in the mean time, do us justice we can then attack her colonies with more certain prospects of success; and, with the satisfaction, too, of having first detached from her the aid of a savage enemy, whose known rule of warfare is to spare neither age nor sex.

I will next, Mr. President, take a view of our real effective disposable force, which, in the event of immediate war, is to protect and defend the vast extent of our Northern and Western frontier, which will be exposed to the incursions of the enemy, especially if we have war with the British and Western Indians, both at the same time. If we may consider the statement obtained from the head of the War Department, as correct, what a discouraging appearance does it afford us! The records in the War Office tell us that, including officers, there are between six and seven thousand men in the two old armies; but as to the new army of 25,000 men, it is difficult to give any certain account of the number recruited. It is, however, said, that orders have been issued directing the recruiting officers to make monthly returns; but, from information which cannot be doubted, it seems that these orders have not been observed; so that the War Department are quite in the dark as to the number actually enlisted in the new army. I understand, however, that an estimate, by the head of the War Department, sets them down at about five thousand, more or less, I suppose, as the case may be. But, supposing our three distinct armies to actually consist of nine thousand men, exclusive of the sick, (which will be found a very liberal estimate,) they do not then give you men enough to man the guns in the works for the defence of the Western frontier and seaports. The most of the six thousand men of the old army appear to be spread over the whole extent of the United States and their Territories; and, this being the case, where is the army to come from for the invasion of Canada? If gentlemen calculate on the new army of 25,000 men for that purpose, I will ask them to show me the army or inform me where it may be found? Is it under the direction and daily discipline of the Commander-in-Chief on the grand rendezvous at Albany; or is it only an army on paper; or is it the small part which may be recruited, and are spread over the Union at the different recruiting places, following the recruiting sergeant, and the drum and fife, in the rags which happen to cover them when they enlist; and not knowing how long they may remain in that forlorn condition, for the want of provident care in the War Department? . . .

Before we take the step proposed by the bill before us, I think we ought also to make some calculation on the general state of the nation. Except some trifling Indian war, it will be recollected we have been twenty-nine years at peace, and have become a nation, in a great degree, of active money-makers. We have lost much of the spirit of war and chivalry possessed by our Revolutionary fathers; and we are a people, also, not over fond of paying taxes to the extent of our ability, and this because our purses have been sweated down by our restrictive system, till they have become light. . . .

It will be necessary, Mr. President, to take a view of the subject of ways and means on this occasion, and see what aspect of the finances of the nation afford. It is well known to every member of the Senate, that our Treasury is empty, and that the Government has been under the necessity of authorizing loans in time of peace; but has the sanguine expectations relative to the subscriptions for the eleven million loan, authorized this session, been at all answered? I believe not. If my recollection serves me faithfully, there is about five millions still wanting to complete the subscription to the loan for the current year's expenditures; and here it is worthy of remark, what quarter of the Union has been most remiss on this patriotic occasion. If I were to inquire how much the States beyond the Alleghany mountains have subscribed to this loan, I believe the answer would be, not one dollar; but, sir, if the people in those States have not been found forward in their subscriptions towards carrying on the war, their Representatives have made up for this deficiency by being forward and liberal enough in their war speeches. They have raised the war-whoop equal to those of any section of the Union, and particularly the representation from the State of Kentucky, one of the gentlemen, in this Senate, only excepted. After the war is once commenced, however, I presume gentlemen will find something more forcible than empty war speeches will be necessary. It will not be sufficient, then, to rely on war speeches, documents, nor proclamations, to repel the attack of an enemy, or to carry war into their territory. And I have understood that the people of those States are not extremely partial to internal and direct taxes, nor were they very promptly collected and paid there, when formerly laid, under the Administration of Mr. Adams. . . .

Mr. President, I have now taken a view of the ability of the country we are about to make war upon, to sustain that war, and make it terrible to us; I have also shown the wretched unprepared situation my country is in, to repel the attacks of an enemy, much less of carrying war into the enemy's territory with a probability of success. . . . Can we look for a blessing without the use of rational means? Does God in his providence ever dispense his blessings on any but those who are vigilant in the use of means? Can we expect to reap, if we neglect to sow? If we do, the crop will surely be briars, thorns, and thistles. I must call on every member of this Senate to pause before he leaps into or crosses the Rubicon—declaring war is passing the Rubicon in reality, and you cannot recross it when you please. It must be remembered, that when you once declare war, you must obtain the consent of your enemy before you can make peace. And gentlemen may be assured that if we do not pause and reflect, before we act, the people will reflect and examine our deeds after we have acted; and if, contrary to every principle of prudence and common sense, we at this time declare war, the people, who are always governed by the rules of common sense, deduced from practical observation, will, after they have had time to reflect, dismiss us as unprofitable servants. . . .

If the taking of Canada, Mr. President, is the real object of the war, no discreet Executive would wish that war declared, until he saw a force raised, concentrated, and disciplined, that would warrant the calculation of Montreal's being in our possession within six weeks after the declaration; for if Canada is not assailed in this manner, the conflict must be lengthy and consequently more bloody if not doubtful. If you commence the attack at Fort Malden, and pursue the enemy down the lakes and rivers, they will be falling back or retreating on their reinforcements, and constantly increasing and concentrating their forces; and would perhaps be able to hold your army in check before it reaches Montreal; but let your army be enabled by its strength to first possess itself of Montreal, and all the upper country must fall of course; you would then soon be able to draw the line dividing your army and that of your enemy between Montreal and Quebec, and when this is accomplished you have put an end to the Indian war, by cutting the Indians off from any further succor from the British. Did I wish, sir, to embarrass the Executive at the expense of the blood

and treasure of my country, I would vote for the immediate passage of this bill;
I would strive to bring on premature war, especially since he has recommended
it; and I must, sir, be here permitted to ask, who displays the greatest friendship
for the President, those that wish to plunge him and the nation down the
precipice which presents itself to us, or those who wish to check this hazardous—
this uncertain step?

I do not, Mr. President, draw all these discouraging pictures, or relate these
lamentable facts, because I would shrink from the conflict or terrors of war, for
the defence of the rights of my injured country, sooner than any gentleman of
this Senate, nor with a wish that all these evils may be realized; my object is to
avert them from my country. I do it, sir, to check the precipitate step of plunging my country prematurely into a war, without any of the means of making
the war terrible to our enemy; and with the certainty that it will be terrible to
ourselves, or at least to our merchants, our seaports, and cities. Yes, sir; the
millions that your merchants will lose in consequence of this rash, this premature step, will strike them with terror and dismay from New Orleans to Maine;
and how lamentable it is that a war, which has for its avowed object the protection of commercial rights, should be commenced at a time and in a manner
which will prove more destructive to commerce itself than all the plunderings
and burnings of both France and England. But I conclude the ostensible object
of this war is to force the cotton and tobacco trade into the continent of Europe,
and to support the Executive in the declaration, that the Berlin and Milan decrees are revoked; but it should be recollected, that it will not only be necessary
in order to enforce a market for our cotton and tobacco upon the Continent, to
obtain a repeal of the British orders; but it will be also necessary to force Napoleon to give up his continental system, or make an exception in it in our
favor; and even if he permits us to go to the Continent with the produce of our
soil, his tariff of duties is an exclusion to our trade, for cotton and tobacco will
scarcely pay freight and charges. I must now ask, sir, with what force we are to
effectuate all these desirable objects? Are our six thousand men, and the few
raw recruits of the new army spread over the vast extent of these United States
and their Territories, and our little fleet of four or five frigates, equal to the
invasion of the Canadas, and the protection of our maritime frontiers, and to
strike the British Government and the inflexible Napoleon with such terrors,
that we are to expect they will abandon their system of warfare against each
other? I presume no one will pretend to say they are. Well, then, why declare
war at this time; why will gentlemen not defer until your new army of twenty-
five thousand men are raised and disciplined fit for service? It must be believed,
sir, if we now declare war, that the object of it is not for the reduction of Canada,
because we have not the means provided; and I am somewhat at a loss to discover
the real object, but if I dare indulge a suspicion that the real and avowed objects are different, I should say this war is to be declared, but not prosecuted,
other than in a defensive manner, and consequently altogether within our own
territory, and to operate as an enforcement of the restrictive system, and may
with propriety be called the terrapin war, and be by some considered more
popular than a continuance of the embargo. . . .

That Jefferson, despite the language of his First Inaugural Address, harbored no dogmatic prejudice against alliances when American interests were at stake is illustrated repeatedly by his observations on the European balance of power. His deep concern as President for the relative position of Britain and France in European affairs reveals how little he clung to the dogma of isolationism. Throughout the Napoleonic wars Jefferson was obsessed with the problem of maintaining a balance between the power of England and that of France. In April 1812 he wrote to an English friend that the United States had no more interest in Napoleon's dominance on land than in Britain's dominance on the high seas, for both nations sought to impose their will on others.

🖎

. . . Our two countries are to be at war, but not you and I. And why should our two countries be at war, when by peace we can be so much more useful to one another? Surely the world will acquit our government from having sought it. Never before has there been an instance of a nation's bearing so much as we have borne. Two items alone in our catalogue of wrongs will forever acquit us of being the aggressors: the impressment of our seamen, and the excluding us from the ocean. The first foundations of the social compact would be broken up, were we definitively to refuse to its members the protection of their persons and property, while in their lawful pursuits. I think the war will not be short, because the object of England, long obvious, is to claim the ocean as her domain, and to exact transit duties from every vessel traversing it. This is the sum of her orders of council, which were only a step in this bold experiment, never meant to be retracted if it could be permanently maintained. And this object must continue her in war with all the world. To this I see no termination, until her exaggerated efforts, so much beyond her natural strength and resources, shall have exhausted her to bankruptcy. The approach of this crisis is, I think, visible in the departure of her precious metals, and depreciation of her paper medium. We, who have gone through that operation, know its symptoms, its course, and consequences. In England they will be more serious than elsewhere, because half the wealth of her people is now in that medium, the private revenue of her money-holders, or rather of her paper-holders, being, I believe, greater than that of her land-holders. Such a proportion of property, imaginary and baseless as it is, cannot be reduced to vapor but with great explosion. She will rise out of its ruins, however, because her lands, her houses, her arts will remain, and the greater part of her men. And these will give her again that place among nations which is proportioned to her natural means, and which we all wish her to hold. We believe that the just standing of all nations is the health

* Thomas Jefferson to James Maury, April 25, 1812, *The Writings of Thomas Jefferson*, IX: 348–9.

and security of all. We consider the overwhelming power of England on the ocean, and of France on the land, as destructive of the prosperity and happiness of the world, and wish both to be reduced only to the necessity of observing moral duties. We believe no more in Bonaparte's fighting merely for the liberty of the seas, than in Great Britain, fighting for the liberties of mankind. The object of both is the same, to draw to themselves the power, the wealth and the resources of other nations. We resist the enterprises of England first, because they first come vitally home to us. And our feelings repel the logic of bearing the lash of George the III for fear of that of Bonaparte at some future day. When the wrongs of France shall reach us with equal effect, we shall resist them also. But one at a time is enough; and having offered a choice to the champions, England first takes up the gauntlet. . . .


— | "It cannot be to our interest that all Europe should be reduced to a single monarchy." *

In January 1814, Jefferson was distressed at the power of Napoleon on the Continent. Napoleon, he said, was useful to America only as a restraint on British power. Jefferson feared especially a French conquest of Russia, for this would lay at the feet of Napoleon the entire European continent.

✍

. . . That Bonaparte is an unprincipaled tyrant, who is deluging the continent of Europe with blood, there is not a human being, not even the wife of his bosom, who does not see: nor can there, I think, be a doubt as to the line we ought to wish drawn between his successes and those of Alexander. Surely none of us wish to see Bonaparte conquer Russia, and lay thus at his feet the whole continent of Europe. This done, England would be but a breakfast; and, although I am free from the visionary fears which the votaries of England have effected to entertain, because I believe he cannot effect the conquest of Europe; yet put all Europe into his hands, and he might spare such a force to be sent in British ships, as I would as leave not have to encounter, when I see how much trouble a handful of British soldiers in Canada has given us. No. It cannot be to our interest that all Europe should be reduced to a single monarchy. The true line of interest for us, is, that Bonaparte should be able to effect the complete exclusion of England from the whole continent of Europe, in order, as the same letter said, "by this peaceable engine of constraint, to make her renounce her views of dominion over the ocean, of permitting no other nation to navigate it but with her license, and on tribute to her, and her aggressions on the persons of our citizens who may choose to exercise their right of passing over that ele-

* Thomas Jefferson to Thomas Leiper, January 1, 1814, *The Writings of Thomas Jefferson*, IX: 445–6.

ment." And this would be effected by Bonaparte's succeeding so far as to close the Baltic against her. This success I wished him the last year, this I wish him this year; but were he again advanced to Moscow, I should again wish him such disasters as would prevent his reaching Petersburg. And were the consequences even to be the longer continuance of our war, I would rather meet them than see the whole force of Europe wielded by a single hand. . . .

— | "For my part, I wish that all nations may recover and retain their independence. . . ." *

Again, in June 1815, Jefferson hoped that Napoleon would wear down the maritime power of England to safe dimensions. Beyond that he hoped only for the perpetuation of a balance of power in Europe that would guarantee the independence and security of the United States.

. . . We concur in considering the government of England as totally without morality, insolent beyond bearing, inflated with vanity and ambition, aiming at the exclusive dominion of the sea, lost in corruption, of deep-rooted hatred towards us, hostile to liberty wherever it endeavors to show its head, and the eternal disturber of the peace of the world. In our estimate of Bonaparte, I suspect we differ. I view him as a political engine only, and a very wicked one; you, I believe, as both political and religious, and obeying, as an instrument, an unseen hand. I still deprecate his becoming sole lord of the continent of Europe, which he would have been, had he reached in triumph the gates of St. Petersburg. The establishment in our day of another Roman empire, spreading vassalage and depravity over the face of the globe, is not, I hope, within the purposes of Heaven. Nor does the return of Bonaparte give me pleasure unmixed; I see in his expulsion of the Bourbons, a valuable lesson to the world, as showing that its ancient dynasties may be changed for their misrule. Should the allied powers presume to dictate a ruler and government to France, and follow the example he had set of parcelling and usurping to themselves their neighbor nations, I hope he will give them another lesson in vindication of the rights of independence and self-government, which himself had heretofore so much abused, and that in this contest he will wear down the maritime power of England to limitable and safe dimensions. So far, good. . . . Whether the war we have had with England, and the achievements of that war, and the hope that we may become his instruments and partisans against that enemy, may induce him, in future, to tolerate our commercial intercourse with his people, is still to be seen. For my part, I wish that all nations may recover and retain their inde-

* Thomas Jefferson to Thomas Leiper, June 12, 1815, *The Writings of Thomas Jefferson*, IX: 519-20.

pendence; that those which are overgrown may not advance beyond safe measures of power, that a salutary balance may be ever maintained among nations, and that our peace, commerce, and friendship, may be sought and culti-vated by all. It is our business to manufacture for ourselves whatever we can, to keep our markets open for what we can spare or want; and the less we have to do with the amities or enmities of Europe, the better. Not in our day, but at no distant one, we may shake a rod over the heads of all, which may make the stoutest of them tremble. But I hope our wisdom will grow with our power, and teach us, that the less we use our power, the greater it will be. . . .

# 9 | Latin American Revolution and a New Crusade for Liberty, 1817 *

John Quincy Adams, as Secretary of State, predicted in December 1817 that the revolutions of Latin America against Spanish rule would motivate another great crusade for liberty among the American people, much as the French Revolution had done in the days of Washington's Presidency. This would occur, observed Adams, because American political leaders would discover the opportunity for partisan advantage by demanding that the government support the cause of revolution.

✍

   There are, however, several subjects of no small importance upon which opinions are not well settled, and some upon which the divisions will soon awaken the *antagonizing* feelings of party spirit. The Abbé de Pradt, whose pamphlet on the Bourbon restoration you have read, has since published, in July last, another pamphlet called *Les trois derniers mois de l'Amérique Méridionale,* in which he says that South America has now taken in the world the place which the French Revolution had held for twenty years before. It is very much so here. The republican spirit of our country not only sympathizes with people struggling in a cause, so nearly if not precisely the same which was once our own, but it is working into indignation against the relapse of Europe into the opposite principle of monkery and despotism. And now, as at the early stage of the French Revolution, we have ardent spirits who are for rushing into the conflict, without looking to the consequences. Others are for proceeding more deliberately, and for waiting to ascertain what the nature and character of the governments in South America are to be, with whom we are to associate

* J. Q. Adams to John Adams, December 21, 1817, *Writings of John Quincy Adams,* Worthington C. Ford, ed. (New York, 1916), VI: 275-6.

as members of the community of nations. Spain. on the one hand, by her mode of negotiating provokes us to take a part against her; and the colonies, by the irregular and convulsive character of their measures, and by their internal elements of the exterminating war between black and white, present to us the prospect of very troublesome and dangerous associates, and still more fearful allies. Such are the ingredients of the caldron, *which will soon be at boiling heat.* . . .

— | "[N]o feeble exertion is now making to rouse a party in this country against the government of the Union. . . ." *

Several days later Adams concluded that the revolutions of Latin America, unlike that of the United States, sought political independence but not civil rights for the Latin Americans themselves. Despite the absence of genuine political promise in the region, Adams complained, many Americans were becoming critical of the United States government for not supporting the cause of Latin American revolution.

. . . The mention of Buenos Ayres brings to my mind an article that I have lately seen in the *Boston Patriot* and which I concluded was from your pen. Its tendency was to show the inexpediency and injustice there would be in our taking sides with the South Americans in their present struggle against Spain. It was an excellent article, and I should be glad to see the same train of thought further pursued. As for example by a discussion of the question in political [*blank*] by what *right* we could take sides? and who in this case of civil war has constituted us the *judges* which of the parties has the righteous cause? Then by an inquiry what the cause of the South Americans is, and whether it really be, as their partisans here allege, the same as our own cause in the war of our Revolution? Whether for instance, if Buenos Ayres has formally offered to accept the Infant Don Carlos as their absolute monarch, upon condition of being politically independent of Spain, their cause is the same as ours was? Whether if Bolivar, being at the head of the republic of Venezuela, has solemnly proclaimed the absolute and total emancipation of the slaves, the cause of Venezuela is precisely the same as ours was? Whether in short, there is any other feature of identity between their cause and ours, than that they are, as we were, colonies fighting for independence? In our Revolution there were two distinct stages, in the first of which we contended for our civil rights, and in the second for our *political independence.* The second, as we solemnly declared to the world, was imposed upon us as a necessity after every practicable effort had been made in vain to secure the first.

* J. Q. Adams to Alexander Hill Everett, December 29, 1817, *Writings of John Quincy Adams*, VI: 281-3.

In South America civil rights, if not entirely out of the question, appear to have been equally disregarded and trampled upon by all parties. Buenos Ayres has no constitution, and its present ruling powers are establishing [themselves] only by the arbitrary banishment of their predecessors. Venezuela, though it has emancipated all its slaves, has been constantly alternating between an absolute military government, a capitulation to Spanish authority, and guerillas black and white, of which every petty chief has acted for purposes of war and rapine as an independent sovereign. There is finally in South America, neither unity of cause nor unity of effort, as there was in our Revolution. Neither was our Revolution disgraced by that buccaneering and piratical spirit which has lately appeared among the South Americans, not of their own growth, but I am sorry to say chiefly from the continuation of their intercourse with us. Their privateers have been for the most part fitted out and officered in our ports, and manned from the sweeping of our streets. It was more effectually to organize and promote their patriotic system that the expeditions to Galveston and Amelia Island were carried into effect, and that the successive gangs of desperadoes, Scotch, French, Creole, and North Americans, that no public exertions have been constituting the republic of the Florida. Yet such is the propensity of our people to sympathize with the South Americans, that no feeble exertion is now making to rouse a party in this country against the government of the Union, and against the President, for having issued orders to put down this host of freebooters at our doors. . . .

## 10 | Henry Clay on the Independence of Latin America, 1818 *

Clay, a critic of the Monroe administration, demanded on March 25, 1818, that the United States recognize the independence of the United Provinces of the Rio de la Plata and other revolutionary republics of South America. The occasion for this speech, which attempted to bind foreign policy to the nation's liberal sentiment, was the proposition to amend the annual general appropriation bill by inserting a clause to allow $18,000 for the outfit and one year's salary for a mission to Buenos Aires. Clay agreed with Adams that the United States had no interest in the revolutions of Europe, but argued that the United States had a primary interest in the success of the Latin American independence movements. Clay believed that the character of the Latin American governments was not the concern of the United States.

🖎

. . . In the establishment of the independence of Spanish America, the United States have the deepest interest. He had no hesitation in asserting his

* *Annals of Congress*, 15th Congress, 1st Sess., II, Columns 1481–2, 1487–9.

firm belief, that there was no question, in the foreign policy of this country, which had ever arisen, or which he could conceive as ever occurring, in the decision of which we had so much at stake. This interest concerned our politics, our commerce, our navigation. There could not be a doubt that Spanish America, once independent, whatever might be the form of the governments established in its several parts, those governments would be animated by an American feeling, and guided by an American policy. They would obey the laws of the system of the New World, of which they would compose a part, in contradistinction to that of Europe. Without the influence of that vortex in Europe, the balance of power between its several parts, the preservation of which had so often drenched Europe in blood, America is sufficiently remote to contemplate the new wars which are to afflict that quarter of the globe, as a calm, if not a cold and indifferent spectator. In relation to those wars, the several parts of America will generally stand neutral. And as, during the period when they rage, it would be important that a liberal system of neutrality should be adopted and observed, all America will be interested in maintaining and enforcing such a system. The independence, then, of Spanish America is an interest of primary consideration. Next to that, and highly important in itself, was the consideration of the nature of their governments. That was a question, however, for themselves. They would, no doubt, adopt those kinds of governments which were best suited to their condition, best calculated for their happiness. Anxious as he was that they should be free governments, we had no right to prescribe for them. They were, and ought to be, the sole judges for themselves. . . . We were their great example. Of us they constantly spoke as of brothers, having a similar origin. They adopted our principles, copied our institutions, and, in some instances, employed the very language and sentiments of our revolutionary papers. . . .

It was not necessary for their interest, it was not expedient for our own, that we should take part in the war. All they demanded of us was a just neutrality. It was compatible with this pacific policy—it was required by it, that we should recognise any established Government, if there were any established Government in Spanish America. Recognition alone, without aid, was no just cause of war. With aid it was, not because of the recognition, but because of the aid, as aid without recognition was cause of war. The truth of these propositions he would maintain upon principle, by the practice of other States, and by the usage of our own. There was no common tribunal among the nations, to pronounce upon the fact of the sovereignty of a new State. Each Power must and does judge for itself. It was an attribute of sovereignty so to judge. A nation, in exerting this incontestable right—in pronouncing upon the independence in fact of a new State, takes no part in the war. It gives neither men, nor ships, nor money. It merely pronounces that in so far as it may be necessary to institute any relations or to support any intercourse, with the new Power, that Power is capable of maintaining those relations and authorizing that intercourse. . . .

. . . We had constantly proceeded on the principle, that the government *de facto* was that which we could alone notice. Whatever form of government any society of people adopt; whoever they acknowledge as their sovereign, we consider that government or that sovereign as the one to be acknowledged by

us. We have invariably abstained from assuming a right to decide in favor of
the sovereign *de jure,* and against the sovereign *de facto.* That is a question for
the nation in which it arises to determine. And, so as far as we are concerned,
the sovereign *de facto* is the sovereign *de jure.* Our own revolution stands on the
basis of the right of a people to change their rulers. . . .

   If, then, there be an established Government in Spanish America, deserving
to rank among the nations, we were morally and politically bound to acknowledge it, unless we renounced all the principles which ought to guide, and which
hitherto had guided, our councils. . . .

## 11 | John Quincy Adams on Sentiment and Politics in Foreign Policy, 1820 *

Adams again revealed his conservatism and his deep opposition to the intrusion
of sentiment into foreign policy when he, in November 1820, criticized Monroe
in his diary for responding to the demands of Clay for the recognition of Latin
American independence by admitting partiality for the Latin American revolutionaries in his annual messages.

   . . . This is the analysis of a session-opening message. Mr. Monroe's messages
have always had a long paragraph upon the civil war between Spain and her
Colonies, and there is one in the present message. There was some discussion
about it. I have always thought these paragraphs exotics to the proper region
of the message; which might just as well descant upon the wars of the English
in India, or more suitably upon the treaties and Congresses of the European
allies. The only difference is, that Mr. Clay having attempted to raise an opposition party upon a sympathetic feeling in the people of this country favorable
to the South Americans, and having insinuated that Mr. Monroe's Administration was partial against the South Americans, the President has thought it necessary to counteract this party manoeuvring by professions of favor to them,
repeated at every session of Congress. This course of policy has perhaps been
necessary; it has been hitherto successful. There were some passages in the
draft this day much more favorable to the colonists than the facts would warrant. Objections were made to them by Mr. Calhoun, and the President altered
several of them. I raised none of these objections, repeating what I had said at
the drafting of a former message, that whatever the President would strike out

* Entry for November 12, 1820, *Memoirs of John Quincy Adams,* Charles Francis
Adams, ed. (Philadelphia, 1875), V: 200.

or soften upon that subject would be so much of improvement to the message. My objection to it is, that, our system being professedly neutrality, any avowal of partiality for the South Americans was inconsistent with it, and liable to raise doubts of our sincerity. I believe that these paragraphs of the message have been the principal real cause of the delay of Spain to ratify the Florida Treaty. . . .

## 12 | Adams on the Recognition of Latin American Independence, 1821–22 *

On March 9, 1821, Adams, in conversation with Clay, revived their quarrel over the issue of American policy toward Latin American independence. Adams admitted that the new nations would not be reconquered by Spain, but he doubted that any of them would develop free or liberal institutions.

. . . [Clay] said he regretted that his views had differed from those of the Administration in relation to South American affairs. He hoped, however, that this difference would now be shortly over. . . .

. . . I also regretted the difference between his views and those of the Administration upon South American affairs. That the final issue of their present struggle would be their entire independence of Spain I had never doubted. That it was our true policy and duty to take no part in the contest I was equally clear. The principle of neutrality to all foreign wars was, in my opinion, fundamental to the continuance of our liberties and of our Union. So far as they were contending for independence, I wished well to their cause; but I had seen and yet see no prospect that they would establish free or liberal institutions of government. They are not likely to promote the spirit either of freedom or order by their example. They have not the first elements of good or free government. Arbitrary power, military and ecclesiastical, was stamped upon their education, upon their habits, and upon all their institutions. Civil dissension was infused into all their seminal principles. War and mutual destruction was in every member of their organization, moral, political, and physical. I had little expectation of any beneficial result to this country from any future connection with them, political or commercial. We should derive no improvement to our own institutions by any communion with theirs. Nor was there any appearance of a disposition in them to take any political lesson from us. As to the commercial connection, I agreed with him that little weight should be allowed to argu-

* Memoirs of John Quincy Adams, V: 324–5.

ments of mere pecuniary interest; but there was no basis for much traffic between us. They want none of our productions, and we could afford to purchase very few of theirs. Of these opinions, both his and mine, time must be the test; but, I would candidly acknowledge, nothing had hitherto occurred to weaken in my mind the view which I had taken of this subject from the first. . . .

— | "This recognition . . . is the mere acknowledgment of existing facts. . . ." *

In 1822 Adams defended the right of the United States to recognize the Latin American states. On January 22 the House of Representatives requested that the President lay before it such communications as it might have received from agents of the United States in the revolutionary countries of Latin America which might illustrate the state of Spanish power in the region. Monroe responded on March 8 with a message which stated that "it merits the most profound consideration whether their right to the rank of independent nations . . . is not complete." When this message appeared in the Washington *National Intelligencer,* the Spanish Minister, Joaquin de Anduaga, registered a diplomatic protest. On April 6 Adams explained to Anduaga why the United States regarded the recognition of the new nations as legitimate national policy.

Your letter of the 9th of March was immediately after I had the honor of receiving it laid before the President of the United States, by whom it has been deliberately considered, and by whose direction I am replying to it, to assure you of the earnestness and sincerity with which the government desires to entertain and to cultivate the most friendly relations with that of Spain.

This disposiion has been manifested, not only by the uniform course of the United States in their direct political and commercial intercourse with Spain, but by the friendly interest which they have felt in the welfare of the Spanish nation, and by the cordial sympathy with which they have witnessed their spirit and energy, exerted in maintaining their independence of all foreign control, and their right of self-government.

In every question relating to the independence of a nation two principles are involved, one of *right,* and the other of *fact;* the former depending upon the determination of the nation itself, and the latter resulting from the successful execution of that determination. This right has been recently exercised as well by the Spanish nation in Europe, as by several of those countries in the American hemisphere, which had for two or three centuries been connected as colonies with Spain. In the conflicts which have attended these revolutions, the United

* J. Q. Adams to Joaquin de Anduaga, April 6, 1822, *Writings of John Quincy Adams,* VII: 216–19.

States have carefully abstained from taking any part, respecting the right of
the nations concerned in them to maintain or new organize their own political
constitutions, and observing, whereon it was a contest by arms, the most impartial neutrality. But the civil war, in which Spain was for some years involved
with the inhabitants of her colonies in America, has in substance ceased to
exist. Treaties equivalent to an acknowledgment of independence have been
concluded by the commanders and viceroys of Spain herself, with the Republic
of Colombia, with Mexico, and with Peru; while in the provinces of La Plata
and in Chile, no Spanish force has for several years existed, to dispute the independence which the inhabitants of those countries had declared [and which has
already been formally recognized by their immediate neighbor and ally of Spain,
the king of Portugal].

Under these circumstances the government of the United States far from
consulting the dictates of a policy questionable in its morality, has yielded to an
obligation of duty of the highest order, by recognizing as independent states,
nations, which after deliberately asserting their right to that character, have
maintained and established it against all the resistance which had been or could
be brought to oppose it. This recognition is neither intended to invalidate any
right of Spain, nor to affect the employment of any means which she may yet be
disposed or enabled to use, with the view of reuniting those provinces to the
rest of her dominions. It is the mere acknowledgment of existing facts, with the
view to the regular establishment with the nations newly formed of those relations, political and commercial, which it is the moral obligation of civilized and
Christian nations to entertain reciprocally with one another.

It will not be necessary to discuss with you a detail of facts, upon which your
information appears to be materially different from that which has been communicated to this government, and is of public notoriety; nor the propriety of
the denominations which you have attributed to the inhabitants of the South
American provinces. It is not doubted that other and more correct views of the
whole subject will very shortly be taken by your government, and that it, as well
as the other European governments, show that deference to the example of the
United States, which you urge it as the duty or the policy of the United States
to show to theirs. The effect of the example of one independent nation upon
the councils and measures of another, can be just only so far as it is voluntary;
and as the United States desire that their example should be followed, so it is
their intention to follow that of others upon no other principle. They confidently rely that the time is at hand when all the governments of Europe
friendly to Spain, and Spain herself, will not only concur in the acknowledgment
of the independence of the American nations, but in the sentiment that nothing
will tend more effectually to the welfare and happiness of Spain than the universal concurrence in that recognition.

# 13 | Adams's Territorial Pretensions to the North American Continent, 1819 *

One of Adams's great achievements as Secretary of State was that of defining, through negotiation, the boundaries of the Louisiana Purchase. That those boundaries were vague at the time of the actual purchase in 1803, even in the French mind, was made clear by Robert Livingston's report to Madison on May 20, 1803: "I asked the [French] minister what were the east bounds of the territory ceded to us? He said he did not know; we must take it as they received it. I asked him how Spain meant to give them possession? He said . . . I do not know. Then you mean that we shall construe it our own way? I can give you no direction; you have made a noble bargain for yourselves, and I suppose you will make the most of it."

Having negotiated the boundary treaties of 1818 and 1819, Adams recognized the general criticism of American ambition among European diplomats. But he saw clearly that the protection of the United States on the North American continent hinged less on its naval power than on its relative supremacy in the New World. Those territorial advances that the nation had achieved appeared to Adams completely logical, and because they revealed vast discrepancies of power and interest between the United States and the nations of Europe in North America, Adams believed that the United States would ultimately control what remained of the continent.

. . . Great Britain, after vilifying us twenty years as a mean, low-minded, peddling nation, having no generous ambitions and no God but gold, had now changed her tone, and was endeavoring to alarm the world at the gigantic grasp of our ambition. Spain was doing the same; and Europe, who, ever since the commencement of our Government under the present Constitution, had seen those nations intriguing with the Indians and negotiating to bound us by the Ohio, had first been startled by our acquisition of Louisiana, and now by our pretension to extend to the South Sea, and readily gave credit to the envious and jealous clamor of Spain and England against our ambition. Nothing that we could say or do would remove this impression until the world shall be familiarized with the idea of considering our proper dominion to be the continent of North America. From the time when we became an independent people it was as much a law of nature that this should become our pretension as that the Mississippi should flow to the sea. Spain had possessions upon our southern and Great Britain upon our northern border. It was impossible that centuries should elapse without finding them annexed to the United States; not that any spirit of encroachment or ambition on our part renders it necessary, but because it is a physical, moral, and political absurdity that such fragments of territory, with

* Entry for November 16, 1819, *Memoirs of John Quincy Adams*, IV: 438–9.

sovereigns at fifteen hundred miles beyond sea, worthless and burdensome to their owners, should exist permanently contiguous to a great, powerful, enterprising, and rapidly-growing nation. Most of the Spanish territory which had been in our neighborhood had already become our own by the most unexceptionable of all acquisitions—fair purchase for a valuable consideration. This rendered it still more unavoidable that the remainder of the continent should ultimately be ours. But it is very lately that we have distinctly seen this ourselves; very lately that we have avowed the pretension of extending to the South Sea; and until Europe shall find it a settled geographical element that the United States and North America are identical, any effort on our part to reason the world out of a belief that we are ambitious will have no other effect than to convince them that we add to our ambition hypocrisy. . . .

## 14 | Adams's Opposition to the Crusade for Greek Liberation, 1823 *

Adams was deeply opposed to any policy that did not measure the interests of the United States or consider the costs involved in pursuing a specific program. It was for this reason that he ridiculed pro-Greek sentiment within the cabinet, for none of the adherents of that cause, Adams noted in his diary, had any interest in effective action at all. The American crusade in behalf of Greek liberty merely confirmed Adams's belief in the principle of nonintervention.

✍

Cabinet meeting at the President's at one. . . . The subject first mentioned by the President for consideration was a letter to me from Andreas Luriottis at London, styling himself Envoy of the Provisional Government of the Greeks, a copy of which was sent me some months since by R. Rush. This letter, recommending the cause of the Greeks, solicited of the United States recognition, alliance, and assistance. It was proper to give a distinct answer to this letter, and I had asked the President's directions what the answer should be.

The President now proposed the question. Mr. Gallatin had proposed in one of his last dispatches, as if he was serious, that we should assist the Greeks with our naval force in the Mediterranean—one frigate, one corvette, and one schooner. Mr. Crawford and Mr. Calhoun inclined to countenance this project. Crawford asked, hesitatingly, whether we were at peace with Turkey, and seemed only to wait for opposition to maintain that we were not. Calhoun descanted upon his great enthusiasm for the cause of the Greeks; he was for taking no heed

* Entry for August 15, 1823, *Memoirs of John Quincy Adams,* VI: 172-3.

of Turkey whatever. In this, as in many other cases, these gentlemen have two sources of eloquence at these Cabinet meetings—one with reference to sentiment, and the other to action. Their enthusiasm for the Greeks is all sentiment, and the standard of this is the prevailing popular feeling. As for action, they are seldom agreed; and after two hours of discussion this day the subject was dismissed, leaving it precisely where it was—nothing determined, and nothing practicable proposed by either of them. Seeing their drift, I did not think it necessary to discuss their doubts whether we were at peace with Turkey, their contempt for the Sublime Porte, or their enthusiasm for the cause of the Greeks. I have not much esteem for the enthusiasm which evaporates in words; and I told the President I thought not quite so lightly of a war with Turkey. I said I would prepare an answer to Mr. Luriottis, and an instruction to Mr. Rush for his consideration. . . .

## 15 | Adams and the Principle of No-Transfer, 1823 *

In his letter to Richard Rush of July 1823 relative to the Northwest coast of America, Adams established the principle of noncolonization by a European power of any portion of the North American continent not already in that nation's possession. But Adams, in his effort to guarantee the security of the United States in the Western Hemisphere, faced another serious challenge. The declining Spanish Empire still possessed such strategic territories in the New World as Cuba, and there existed the danger that Spain would transfer such regions to a more powerful European nation for equal advantages elsewhere. In warning the Spanish government against such a decision, Adams reaffirmed the American doctrine of no-transfer. In a letter to Hugh Nelson, the United States Minister at Madrid, the Secretary assured the officials of Spain that the United States would join no cause detrimental to their country, but he also reminded them that Cuba in the possession of either Britain or France would be an unacceptable danger to American security. In this letter Adams discussed at length the proper relationship between the United States and Europe.

ϟ

. . . It has been a maxim in the policy of these United States, from the time when their independence was achieved, to keep themselves aloof from the political systems and contentions of Europe. To this principle it is yet the purpose of the President to adhere: and in the war about to commence, the atti-

* J. Q. Adams to Hugh Nelson, April 28, 1823, *Writings of John Quincy Adams,* VII: 370–81.

tude to be assumed and maintained by the United States will be that of neutrality.

But the experience of our national history has already shown that, however sincerely this policy was adopted, and however earnestly and perseveringly it was maintained, it yielded ultimately to a course of events by which the violence and injustice of European powers involved the immediate interests and brought in conflict the essential rights of our own country.

Two of the principal causes of the wars between the nations of Europe since that of our own Revolution, have been, indeed, the same as those in which that originated—civil liberty and national independence. To these principles, and to the cause of those who contend for them, the people of the United States can never be indifferent. A feeling of sympathy and of partiality for every nation struggling to secure or to defend these great interests, has been and will be manifested by this Union; and it is among the most difficult and delicate duties of the general government, in all its branches, to indulge this feeling so far as it may be compatible with the duties of neutrality, and to withhold and restrain from encroaching upon them. So far as it is indulged, its tendency is to involve us in foreign wars, while the first and paramount duty of the government is to maintain *peace* amidst all the convulsions of foreign wars, and to enter the lists as parties to no cause, other than our own.

In the *maritime* wars of Europe, we have, indeed, a direct and important interest of our own; as they are waged upon an element which is the common property of all; and as our participation in the possession of that property is perhaps greater than that of any other nation. The existence of maritime war, itself, enlarges and deepens the importance of this interest; and it introduces a state of things in which the conflict of neutral and belligerent rights becomes itself a continual and formidable instigation to war. To all maritime wars Great Britain can scarcely fail of becoming a party; and from that moment arises a collision between her and these states, peculiar to the situation, interests and rights of the two countries, and which can scarcely form a subject of discussion between any other nation and either of them.

This cause then is peculiarly our own: and we have already been once compelled to vindicate our rights implicated in it by war. It has been too among the dispensations of Providence, that the issue of that war should have left that question unsettled for the future; and that the attempts which on the part of the United States have been repeatedly made since the peace for adjusting it by amicable negotiation, have in like manner proved ineffectual. There is therefore great reason to apprehend, that if Great Britain should engage in the war, now just kindled in Europe, the United States will again be called to support by all their energies, not excepting war, the rights of their national independence, enjoyed in the persons of their seamen.

But in the war between France and Spain now commencing, other interests, peculiarly ours, will in all probability be deeply involved. Whatever may be the issue of this war, as between those two European powers, it may be taken for granted that the dominion of Spain upon the American continents, North and South, is irrecoverably gone. But the islands of Cuba and of Porto Rico still remain nominally and so far really dependent upon her, that she yet possesses the power of transferring her own dominion over them, together with the possession of them, to others. These islands, from their local position, are natural appendages to the North American continent; and one of them, Cuba, almost in sight of our shores, from a multitude of considerations has become an object of transcendent importance to the political and commercial interests of our Union. Its commanding position with reference to the Gulf of Mexico and the West India seas; the character of its population; its situation midway between our southern coast and the island of San Domingo; its safe and capacious harbor of the Havana, fronting a long line of our shores destitute of the same advantage; the nature of its productions and of its wants, furnishing the supplies and needing the returns of a commerce immensely profitable and mutually beneficial; give it an importance in the sum of our national interests, with which that of no other foreign territory can be compared, and little inferior to that which binds the different members of this Union together.

Such indeed are, between the interests of that island and of this country, the geographical, commercial, moral, and political relations, formed by nature, gathering in the process of time, and even now verging to maturity, that in looking forward to the probable course of events for the short period of half a century, it is scarcely possible to resist the conviction that the annexation of Cuba to our federal republic will be indispensable to the continuance and integrity of the Union itself. It is obvious however that for this event we are not yet prepared. Numerous and formidable objections to the extension of our territorial dominions beyond the sea present themselves to the first contemplation of the subject. Obstacles to the system of policy by which it alone can be compassed and maintained are to be foreseen and surmounted, both from at home and abroad. But there are laws of political as well as of physical gravitation; and if an apple severed by the tempest from its native tree cannot choose but fall to the ground, Cuba, forcibly disjoined from its own unnatural connection with Spain, and incapable of self-support, can gravitate only towards the North American Union, which by the same law of nature cannot cast her off from its bosom. . . .

Whether the purposes of France, or of her continental allies, extend to the subjugation of the remaining ultramarine possessions of Spain or not, has not yet been sufficiently disclosed. But to confine ourselves to that which immediately concerns us, the condition of the island of Cuba, we know that the republican spirit of freedom prevails among its inhabitants. The liberties of the constitution are to them rights in possession: nor is it to be presumed that they will be willing to surrender them, because they may be extinguished by foreign violence in the parent country. As Spanish territory the island will be liable to invasion from France during the war: and the only reasons for doubting whether the attempt will be made are the probable incompetency of the French maritime force to effect the conquest, and the probability that its accomplishment would be resisted by Great Britain. In the meantime and at all events, the condition of the island in regard to that of its inhabitants, is a condition of great, imminent, and complicated danger: and without resorting to speculation upon what such a state of things must produce upon a people so situated, we know that its approach has already had a powerful effect upon them, and that the question what they are to do upon contingencies daily pressing upon them and ripening into reality, has for the last twelve months constantly excited their attention and stimulated them to action.

Were the population of the island of one blood and color, there could be no doubt or hesitation with regard to the course which they would pursue, as dictated by their interests and their rights. The invasion of Spain by France would be the signal for *their* Declaration of Independence. That even in their present state it will be imposed upon them as a necessity is not unlikely; but among all their reflecting men it is admitted as a maxim fundamental to all deliberation upon their future condition, that they are not competent to a system of permanent self-dependence. They must rely for the support of protection upon some force from without; and as, in the event of the overthrow of the Spanish constitution, that support can no longer be expected from Spain, their only alternative of dependence must be upon Great Britain, or upon the United States. . . .

Great Britain has formally withdrawn from the councils of the European Alliance in regard to Spain. She disapproves the war which they have sanctioned, and which is undertaken by France: and she avows her determination to defend Portugal against the application of the Principles, upon which the invasion of Spain raises its only pretence of right. To the war as it commences, she has declared her intention of remaining neutral; but the spirit of the British nation is so strongly and with so much unanimity pronounced against France, their interests are so deeply involved in the issue, their national resentments and jealousies will be so forcibly stimulated by the progress of the war, whatever it may be, that unless the conflict should be as short and the issue as decisive as that of which Italy was recently the scene, it is scarcely possible that the neutrality of Great Britain should be long maintained. The prospect is that she will be soon engaged on the side of Spain; but in making common cause with her, it is not to be supposed that she will yield her assistance upon principles altogether disinterested and gratuitous. As the price of her alliance the two remaining islands of Spain in the West Indies present objects no longer of much possible value or benefit to Spain, but of such importance to Great Britain, that it is impossible to suppose her indifferent to the acquisition of them.

The motives of Great Britain for desiring the possession of Cuba are so obvious, especially since the independence of Mexico, and the annexation of the Floridas to our Union; the internal condition of the island since the recent Spanish revolution, and the possibility of its continued dependence upon Spain, have been so precarious; the want of protection there; the power of affording it possessed by Great Britain, and the necessities of Spain to secure, by some equivalent, the support of Great Britain for herself; have formed a remarkable concurrence of predispositions to the transfer of Cuba; and during the last two years rumors have been multiplied, that it was already consummated. . . .

The transfer of Cuba to Great Britain would be an event unpropitious to the interest of this Union. This opinion is so generally entertained, that even the groundless rumors that it was about to be accomplished, which have spread abroad and are still teeming, may be traced to the deep and almost universal feeling of aversion to it, and to the alarm which the mere probability of its occurrence has stimulated. The question both of our right and our power to prevent it, if necessary, by force, already obtrudes itself upon our councils, and the administration is called upon, in the performance of its duties to the nation, at least to use all the means within its competency to guard against and forefend it. . . .

While disclaiming all disposition on our part, either to obtain possession of Cuba, or of Porto Rico, ourselves, you will declare that the American government had no knowledge of the lawless expedition undertaken against the latter of those islands last summer. This was one among many subjects upon which the Spanish minister residing here, Anduaga, remonstrated in a style of complaint to which, from respect for Spain, and that alone, no answers were returned to him. . . .

You will not conceal from the Spanish government the repugnance of the United States to the transfer of the island of Cuba by Spain to any other power. The deep interest which would to them be involved in the event gives them the right of objecting against it; and as the people of the island itself are known to be averse to it, the right of Spain herself to make the cession, at least upon the principles on which the present Spanish constitution is founded, is more than questionable. Informal and verbal communications on this subject with the Spanish Minister of Foreign Affairs will be most advisable. In casual conversation, and speaking as from your own impressions, you may suggest the hope, that if any question of transferring the island to any other power is, or shall be in agitation, it will not be withheld from your knowledge, or from ours; that the condition of Cuba cannot be changed without affecting in an eminent degree the welfare of this Union, and consequently the good understanding between us and Spain; that we should consider an attempt to transfer the island, against the will of its inhabitants, as subversive of their rights, no less than of our interests; and that, as it would give them the perfect right of resisting such transfer, by declaring their own independence, so if they should, under those circumstances, resort to that measure, the United States will be fully justified in supporting them to carry it into effect. . . .

# 16 | Adams and the Formulation of the Monroe Doctrine, November 1823 *

Adams's major role in the final structuring of the Monroe Doctrine was that of stripping Monroe's rhetoric of all idealistic overtones that might commit the United States to liberal causes everywhere and thus needlessly place the nation at odds with the reactionary powers of Europe. Specifically, he argued against the President's sentimental references to the revolutionary movement in Greece. The Secretary favored only what became the fundamental theme of the Monroe Doctrine—that the United States assume a position of "earnest remonstrance against the interference of the European powers by force with South America, but to disclaim all interference on our part with Europe; to make an American cause, and adhere inflexibly to that." Adams recorded the crucial discussions of November 21, 22, and 24, 1823, in his diary.

≮

21st. . . . The President approved of this idea; and then taking up the sketches that he had prepared for his message, read them to us. Its introduction was in a tone of deep solemnity and of high alarm, intimating that his country is menaced by imminent and formidable dangers, such as would probably soon call for their most vigorous energies and the closest union. It then proceeded to speak of the foreign affairs, chiefly according to the sketch I had given him some days since, but with occasional variations. It then alluded to the recent events in Spain and Portugal, speaking in terms of the most pointed reprobation of the late invasion of Spain by France, and of the principles upon which it was undertaken by the open avowal of the King of France. It also contained a broad acknowledgment of the Greeks as an independent nation, and a recommendation to Congress to make an appropriation for sending a Minister to them.

Of all this Mr. Calhoun declared his approbation. I expressed as freely my wish that the President would reconsider the whole subject before he should determine to take that course. I said the tone of the introduction I apprehended would take the nation by surprise and greatly alarm them. It would come upon them like a clap of thunder. There had never been in the history of this nation a period of so deep calm and tranquillity as we now enjoyed. We never were, upon the whole, in a state of peace so profound and secure with all foreign nations as at this time. This message would be a summons to arms—to arms against all Europe, and for objects of policy exclusively European—Greece and Spain. It would be as new, too, in our policy as it would be surprising. For more than thirty years Europe had been in convulsions; every nation almost of which it is composed alternately invading and invaded. Empires, kingdoms, principalities, had been overthrown, revolutionized, and counter-revolutionized, and we had looked on safe in our distance beyond an intervening ocean, and avowing a total forbearance to interfere in any of the combinations of European politics. This message would at once buckle on the harness and throw down the gauntlet. It would have the air of open defiance to all Europe, and I should not be surprised if the first answer to it from Spain and France, and even Russia, should be to break off their diplomatic intercourse with us. I did not expect that the quiet which we had enjoyed for six or seven years would last much longer. The aspect of things was portentous; but if we must come to an issue with Europe, let us keep it off as long as possible. Let us use all possible means to carry the opinion of the nation with us, and the opinion of the world. . . .

22nd. . . . Mr. Gallatin was with the President, but withdrew on my going in. I left with the President my draft for a second dispatch to R. Rush on South American affairs. And I spoke to him again urging him to abstain from everything in his message which the Holy Allies could make a pretext for construing into aggression upon them. I said there were considerations of weight which I could not even easily mention at a Cabinet meeting. If he had determined to retire from the public service at the end of his present term, it was now drawing to a close. It was to be considered now as a whole, and a system of administration for a definite term of years. It would hereafter, I believed, be looked back to as the golden age of this republic, and I felt an extreme solicitude that its end might correspond with the character of its progress; that the Administration might be delivered into the hands of the successor, whoever he might be, at peace and in amity with all the world. If this could not be, if the Holy Alliance were determined to make up an issue with us, it was our policy to meet, and not to make it. We should retreat to the wall before taking to arms, and be sure at every step to put them as much as possible in the wrong. I said if the Holy Alliance really intended to restore by force the Colonies of Spain to her dominion, it was questionable to me whether we had not, after all, been overhasty in acknowledging the South American independence. It had pledged us now to take ground which we had not felt at all bound to take five years ago. At the Congress of Aix-la-Chapelle the allies had discussed what they should do with South America, and we had not even thought of interfering with them. If they intend now to interpose by force, we shall have as much as we can do to prevent them, without going to bid them defiance in the heart of Europe. Something had been said yesterday, that if the President did not recommend the recognition of the independence of the Greeks it would be pressed in the House of Representatives. What would be Mr. Clay's course in this case I could not foresee. But he (the President) well knew that at the time when Mr. Clay so urgently pushed for the South American independence, his main object was popularity for himself and to embarrass the Administration. It did not appear that this object was now so important to him, and, as he had some prospect of coming to the succession himself, I should not suppose he would wish it encumbered with a quarrel with all Europe. But, be that as it may, it was infinitely better that the impulse should come from Congress than that it should go from the Executive. Congress are responsible for their own acts. Foreign powers are apt to take less notice of them than of Executive measures, and if they put us in attitudes of hostility with the allies, be the blame upon them. The ground that I wish to take is that of earnest remonstrance against the interference of the European powers by force with South America, but to disclaim all interference on our part with Europe; to make an American cause, and adhere inflexibly to that.

The President said he had spoken of the Greeks and of the Spaniards in his last year's message. I said I should not object to paragraphs of a like description, in general terms and pledging nothing, but I would be specially careful to avoid anything which may be construed as hostility to the allies. . . .

24th. Mr. Gallatin was here, and talked much upon the topics to be touched upon in the President's message. His views coincided entirely with those which I have so earnestly urged upon the President, excepting as to the Greeks, to whom he proposes, as if he was serious, that we should send two or three frigates to assist them in destroying the Turkish fleet, and a loan or a subsidy of two millions of dollars. I told Gallatin that I wished he would talk to the President as he had done to me, upon everything except the Greeks. . . .

I called at the President's, and found Mr. Gallatin with him. He still adhered to his idea of sending a naval force and a loan of money to the Greeks; and as he is neither an enthusiast nor a fool, and knows perfectly well that no such thing will be done, I look for the motives of this strange proposal, and find them not very deeply laid. Mr. Gallatin still builds castles in the air of popularity, and, being under no responsibility for consequences, patronizes the Greek cause for the sake of raising his own reputation. His measure will not succeed, and, even if it should, all the burden and danger of it will bear not upon him, but upon the Administration, and he will be the great champion of Grecian liberty. 'Tis the part of Mr. Clay towards South America acted over again. After he withdrew, the President read me his paragraphs respecting the Greeks, Spain, Portugal, and South America. I thought them quite unexceptionable, and drawn up altogether in the spirit that I had so urgently pressed on Friday and Saturday. I was highly gratified at the change, and only hope the President will adhere to his present views.


# 17 | The Monroe Doctrine, December 2, 1823 *

Monroe's famous declaration of the principles which guided American foreign policy was a fitting climax to a quarter-century of Jeffersonian rule. Like Hamilton and Washington, Adams and Monroe sought to limit the nation's political and military commitments to Europe while guaranteeing American predominance in the Western Hemisphere. There was little in the diplomatic experience of the young Republic to distinguish Federalists from Jeffersonians in

* *Messages and Papers of the Presidents,* II: 209, 217-19.

either concept or performance. Those in power from 1789 to 1823 focused on the central problem of limiting the nation's interests to its power. They avoided sentimentality and abstractions, and they condemned the intrusion of domestic politics into matters of diplomacy. By confining direct American commitments to the Western Hemisphere, the Monroe Doctrine was a realistic document. Yet even these limited objectives would have exceeded the power of the United States in the face of a genuine threat from the Holy Alliance. What made the Monroe Doctrine a viable basis of policy was, in effect, the unacknowledged alliance with England which it created.

. . . At the proposal of the Russian Imperial Government, made through the minister of the Emperor residing here, a full power and instructions have been transmitted to the minister of the United States at St. Petersburg to arrange by amicable negotiation the respective rights and interests of the two nations on the northwest coast of this continent. A similar proposal had been made by His Imperial Majesty to the Government of Great Britain, which has likewise been acceded to. The Government of the United States has been desirous by this friendly proceeding of manifesting the great value which they have invariably attached to the friendship of the Emperor and their solicitude to cultivate the best understanding with his Government. In the discussions to which this interest has given rise and in the arrangements by which they may terminate the occasion has been judged proper for asserting, as a principle in which the rights and interests of the United States are involved, that the American continents, by the free and independent condition which they have assumed and maintain, are henceforth not to be considered as subjects for future colonization by any European powers. . . .

A strong hope has been long entertained, founded on the heroic struggle of the Greeks, that they would succeed in their contest and resume their equal station among the nations of the earth. It is believed that the whole civilized world take a deep interest in their welfare. Although no power has declared in their favor, yet none, according to our information, has taken part against them. Their cause and their name have protected them from dangers which might ere this have overwhelmed any other people. The ordinary calculations of interest and of acquisition with a view to aggrandizement, which mingles so much in the transactions of nations, seem to have had no effect in regard to them. From the facts which have come to our knowledge there is good cause to believe that their enemy has lost forever all dominion over them; that Greece will become again an independent nation. That she may obtain that rank is the object of our most ardent wishes.

It was stated at the commencement of the last session that a great effort was then making in Spain and Portugal to improve the condition of the people of those countries, and that it appeared to be conducted with extraordinary moderation. It need scarcely be remarked that the result has been so far very different from what was then anticipated. Of events in that quarter of the globe, with which we have so much intercourse and from which we derive our origin, we have always been anxious and interested spectators. The citizens of the United States cherish sentiments the most friendly in favor of the liberty and happiness of their fellow-men on that side of the Atlantic. In the wars of the European powers in matters relating to themselves we have never taken any part, nor does it comport with our policy so to do. It is only when our rights are invaded or seriously menaced that we resent injuries or make preparation for our defense. With the movements in this hemisphere we are of necessity more immediately connected, and by causes which must be obvious to all enlightened and impartial observers. The political system of the allied powers is essentially different in this respect from that of America. This difference proceeds from that which exists in their respective Governments; and to the defense of our own, which has been achieved by the loss of so much blood and treasure, and matured by the wisdom of their most enlightened citizens, and under which we have enjoyed unexampled felicity, this whole nation is devoted. We owe it, therefore, to candor and to the amicable relations existing between the United States and those powers to declare that we should consider any attempt on their part to extend their system to any portion of this hemisphere as dangerous to our peace and safety. With the existing colonies or dependencies of any European power we have not interfered and shall not interfere. But with the Governments who have declared their independence and maintained it, and whose independence we have, on great consideration and on just principles, acknowledged, we could not view any interposition for the purpose of oppressing them, or controlling in any other manner their destiny, by any European power in any other light than as the manifestation of an unfriendly disposition toward the United States. In the war between those new Governments and Spain we declared our neutrality at the time of their recognition, and to this we have adhered, and shall continue to adhere, provided no change shall occur which, in the judgment of the competent authorities of this Government, shall make a corresponding change on the part of the United States indispensable to their security.

The late events in Spain and Portugal shew that Europe is still unsettled. Of this important fact no stronger proof can be adduced than that the allied powers should have thought it proper, on any principle satisfactory to themselves, to have interposed by force in the internal concerns of Spain. To what extent such interposition may be carried, on the same principle, is a question in which all independent powers whose governments differ from theirs are interested. even those most remote, and surely none more so than the United States. Our policy in regard to Europe, which was adopted at an early stage of the wars which have so long agitated that quarter of the globe, nevertheless remains the same, which is, not to interfere in the internal concerns of any of its powers; to consider the government *de facto* as the legitimate government for us; to cultivate friendly relations with it, and to preserve those relations by a frank, firm, and manly policy, meeting in all instances the just claims of every power, submitting to injuries from none. But in regard to those continents circumstances are eminently and conspicuously different. It is impossible that the allied powers should extend their political system to any portion of either continent without endangering our peace and happiness; nor can anyone believe that our southern brethren, if left to themselves, would adopt it of their own accord. It is equally impossible, therefore, that we should behold such interposition in any form with indifference. If we look to the comparative strength and resources of Spain and those new Governments, and their distance from each other, it must be obvious that she can never subdue them. It is still the true policy of the United States to leave the parties to themselves, in the hope that other powers will pursue the same course. . . .

# 18 | Edward Everett and the Cause of Greek Independence, October 1823 *

Edward Everett's long crusade for the liberation of the Greeks from Turkish rule culminated in his noted editorial of October 1823, which appeared in the *North American Review*. In his defense of the American crusade Everett presented a standard statement of the proposition that the people of the United States could exert themselves effectively in behalf of oppressed peoples in distant lands. In terms of precise action he recommended no more than a system of individual subscriptions of money and material for the Greek liberty fighters. Everett prefaced this major effort to enlist support for the Greek cause with the publication of the Greek Appeal to the American people, dated May 25, 1821.

ʁ

To the citizens of the United States of America [began the Greek Appeal]— Having formed the resolution to live or die for freedom, we are drawn toward you by a just sympathy; since it is in your land that Liberty has fixed her abode, and by you that she is prized as by our fathers. Hence, in invoking her name, we invoke yours at the same time, trusting that in imitating you, we shall imitate our ancestor, and be thought worthy of them if we succeed in resembling you.

Though separated from you by mighty oceans, your character brings you near us. We esteem you nearer than the nations on our frontiers; and we possess, in you, friends, fellow-citizens, and brethren, because you are just, humane and generous;—just because free, generous and liberal because christian. Your liberty is not propped on the slavery of other nations, nor your prosperity on their calamities and sufferings. But, on the contrary, free and prosperous yourselves, you are desirous that all men should share the same blessings; that all should enjoy those rights, to which all are by nature equally entitled. It is you, who

* Edward Everett, "Affairs of Greece," *North American Review*, XVII (October 1823), 417–24.

first proclaimed these rights; it is you who have been the first again to recognize them, in rendering the rank of men to the Africans degraded to the level of brutes. It is by your example, that Europe has abolished the shameful and cruel trade in human flesh, from you that she receives lessons of justice, and learns to renounce her absurd and sanguinary customs. This glory, Americans, is yours alone, and raises you above all the nations which have gained a name for liberty and laws.

It is for you, citizens of America, to crown this glory, in aiding us to purge Greece from the barbarians, who for four hundred years have polluted the soil. It is surely worthy of you to repay the obligations of the civilized nations, and to banish ignorance and barbarism from the country of freedom and the arts. You will not assuredly imitate the culpable indifference or rather the long in- gratitude of some of the Europeans. No, the fellow-citizens of Penn, of Wash- ington, and of Franklin, will not refuse their aid to the descendants of Phocion, and Thrasybulus, of Aratus, and of Philopoemen. You have already shown them esteem and confidence in sending your children to their schools. You know with what pleasure they were welcomed, and the steady kindness and attentions which they received. If such has been their conduct when enslaved; what friendship and zeal will they not manifest to you, when through your aid they shall have broken their chains. Greece will then furnish you advantages, which you can in vain seek from her ignorant and cruel tyrants; and the bands of gratitude and fraternity will forever unite the Greeks and the Americans. Our interests are of a nature more and more to cement an alliance founded on freedom and virtue.

. . . Though we do not consider [commented Everett] the foregoing address to be in very good taste, nor in every part perfectly intelligible, it shows at least how soon and how spontaneously the eyes of Greece were turned to this country as the great exemplar of states in the agonies of contest for inde- pendence. Such an appeal from the anxious conclave of self-devoted patriots, in the inaccessible cliffs of the Morea, must bring home to the mind of the least reflecting American, the great and glorious part, which this country is to act, in the political regeneration of the world. It must convince us that what Burke originally said in eulogy of his own land, is going into its literal fulfilment here; and in a wider sense than he dared to speak it. Wheresoever the chosen race, the sons of liberty shall worship freedom, they will turn their faces to us.—We have seen, in our own days, the oldest and most splendid monarchy in Europe, cast- ing off its yoke, under the contagion of liberty caught from us; and why should the excesses of that awful crisis be ascribed to the new found remedy rather than to the inveterate disease? Through France, the influence of our example has been transmitted to the other European states, and in the most enslaved and corrupted of them, the leaven of freedom is at work. Meantime, at one and the same moment, we perceive in either hemisphere the glorious work of emancipa- tion going on; and the name and the example of the United States alike invoked by both. From the earliest abodes of European civilization, the venerated plains of Greece, and from the scarcely explored range of the Cordilleras, a voice of salutation and a cry for sympathy are resounding in our ears. While the great

states of Europe, which for centuries have taken the lead in the affairs of the
world, stand aghast at this spectacle, and know not if they shall dare to sanction
what they cannot oppose, our envoys have already climbed the Andes and
reached the Pacific, with the message of gratulation. We devoutly trust that
another season will find them on their way to Greece. . . .

Meantime there is something for the people of this country in their private
capacity, to do for Greece. In Germany, and in France, large numbers of enthusiastic young men have devoted themselves personally to the cause, and
flocked to Greece, as the same class of generous spirits did to this country, in the
revolutionary war. Considerable sums of money have also been raised in those
countries, and supplies of arms and ammunition sent to the Grecian armies. In
England a benevolent association has been formed under the presidency of Lord
Milton, a nobleman of one of the wealthiest and most powerful British families; and this association has entered into a correspondence with the Grecian
authorities. Local political dissensions have unfortunately mingled themselves
with the counsels adopted in England for the relief of the Grecians. Still, however, large subscriptions have been made and forwarded to that country. We are
sorry for the fact, that America did not set this example also. The experience of
our own revolutionary war is so recent, that we ought to have felt, how precious
would be any aid from a distant land, however insignificant in amount. Who
does not know that there were times in our own revolutionary war, when a few
barrels of gunpowder, the large guns of a privateer, a cargo of flour, a supply of
clothing, yea, a few hundred pairs of shoes, for feet that left in blood the tracks
of their march, would have done essential service to the cause of suffering
liberty. . . .

America has done something for Greece. Our missionary societies have their
envoys to the Grecian church, with supplies of bibles and religious tracts for
their benighted flocks. But in the present state of this unhappy people, this is
not the only succor they require. They are laying the foundations of civil freedom, without which even the blessings of the Gospel will be extended to them
in vain. . . .

. . . At this crisis the messenger of the gospel fraternity should come in other
guise than the distributer of the word; and could the broad and deep current of
religious bounty be turned into a channel to reach the seat of the principal
distress, it is not going too far to say, that it might be the means of giving
another independent country to the church of Christ; and do more to effect the
banishment by the crescent to the deserts of Tartary, than all that has yet been
achieved by the counsels of christendom.

The same considerations call upon our wealthy citizens to extend their aid to
the citizens of a country possessed of more than one bond of community with
ours. The common council of London have voted £1000 for the relief of the
sufferers in Greece. Let Boston appropriate ten thousand dollars for the same
object; New York, and Philadelphia, and Baltimore, and the cities of the South
in proportion to their means, will heartily unite in the cause; and a sum of
money may be transmitted to Greece, either directly or through the English

committee, which will teach those who are now toiling and bleeding for freedom, that we prize the blessing too highly, not to aid them in attaining it. . . .

. . . It is the great curse of a despotism like that of the Turks, that it inverts the laws of conduct for its subjects, and connects suffering and death with those principles and actions, to which providence attaches the rewards of life in a healthy state of society. We are able to pity individuals among us, so unfortunately born and bred, as to be surrounded with corrupting examples, and taught to find occupation and pleasure in vice. What a spectacle do not the Greeks present in this connection, to the practical philanthropist! Are they zealous in the profession of their religion and in the observance of its rights, they jeopardize the continuance of the jealous and contemptuous toleration beneath which they live. Do they love and serve the land of their birth, they are guilty of treason against its barbarous master. Do they with industry and enterprize acquire wealth, it is necessary studiously to conceal it from unprincipled extortion, and to invest it in foreign countries. Do they found schools and make provision for education, they expose themselves to exaction and their children to outrage, and are obliged to proceed with the greatest possible secrecy and circumspection. What a monstrous complication of calamity, to have the best, the worthiest, the purest designs and actions, loaded with all the consequences of vice and crime; to be deprived not only of all that makes life joyous, but to be punished for doing well, and to be forced to go privately about those good deeds, to which men, in other countries, are exhorted as to a source of praise and honor. These things ought to be considered; and a reprehensible apathy prevails as to their reality. If liberty, virtue, and religion, were not words on our lips, without a substance in our hearts, it would be hardly possible to pursue our little local interests with such jealousy; to be all on fire in one state, for fear Congress should claim the power of internal improvements, and up in arms in another against a change of the tariff, and carried away in all, with a controversy between rival candidates for an office, which all would administer in much the same way; if a narrow selfishness did not lie at the bottom of our conduct, we could not do all this, while men, christians as good as we, who have nerves to smart, minds to think, hearts to feel, like ourselves, are waging unaided, single-handed, at perilous odds, a war of extermination against tyrants, who deny them not only the blessings of liberty, but the mercies of slavery.

But we hope better things of our country. In the great Lancastrian school of the nations, liberty is the lesson, which we are appointed to teach. Masters we claim not, we wish not, to be, but the Monitors we are of this noble doctrine. It is taught in our settlement, taught in our revolution, taught in our government; and the nations of the world are resolved to learn. It may be written in sand and effaced, but it will be written again and again, till hands now fettered in slavery shall boldly and fairly trace it, and lips, that now stammer at the noble word, shall sound it out in the ears of their despots, with an emphasis to waken the dead. Some will comprehend it and practice it at the first; others must wrestle long with the old slavish doctrines; and others may abuse it to excess, and cause it to be blasphemed awhile in the world. But it will still be taught and still be repeated, and must be learned by all; by old and degenerate communities to revive their youth; by springing colonies to hasten their progress. With the example before them of a free representative government—of a people governed by themselves,—it is no more possible that the nations will long bear any other, than that they should voluntarily dispense with the art of printing or the mariner's compass. . . .

## 19 | Debate on the Greek Resolution in Congress, January 1824 *

Among Everett's converts in support of the Greek cause was Daniel Webster, then Congressman from Massachusetts. Webster, a spokesman for New England's business interests, had been cautious in his public statements because the Smyrna trade of the Turkish Empire was one of the most lucrative in the world for Boston merchants. Indeed, the nation's tangible interest in Turkish trade far outweighed its abstract interest in Greek independence. Nevertheless, Webster introduced a resolution into the House in December 1823 which provided: "That provision ought to be made by law, for defraying the expense incident to the appointment of an Agent or Commissioner to Greece, whenever the President shall deem it expedient to make such appointment." On this seemingly noncommittal text Webster, on January 19, 1824, launched into his celebrated and eloquent appeal to American humanitarian sentiment. He asked nothing of Congress. Courage and spirit, properly encouraged by the passage of the resolution, would, he said, achieve more than money.

✒

. . . This magnificent edifice, these columns, with their stately proportions, this fine architecture by which we are surrounded, what are these but so many witnesses of what Greece once was, and what she has taught us to be? Yet, sir, . . . I have not introduced the resolution, now on your table, with any view towards repaying aught of the debt, which we, in common with the civilized world, owed to that land of science, freedom, arts, and arms. It is a debt that never can be paid. Whatever may be our feelings of gratitude for these gifts, we are constrained to act with a view alone to the present state of the world, and of our relations to it. What I propose, and what I shall say, has reference to modern, not to ancient Greece—to the living, not to the dead.

I am aware, sir, that it is a very easy thing to turn over common places on

* *Annals of Congress*, 18th Congress, 1st Sess., Columns 1085–99.

the subject of this resolution; to call it a visionary and Quixotic measure, and to urge the good old maxim of its being the soundest policy for each one to take care of his own concerns. That maxim, sir, is very true, but very inapplicable to the present occasion. The question which is now to be discussed is the American question in relation to this affair—what is it best for us to do in the present aspect of things respecting Greece? And surely, sir, this is a question that comprehends something more than a mere pecuniary calculation. Whenever my mind turns to that question, I cannot forget the age I live in, as well as the peculiar position of our own country. . . .

. . . There has occurred no age that may be compared with the present, whether in the interest excited by what now is, or the prospects it holds out as to what shall be. The attitude of the United States, meanwhile, is solemn and impressive. Ours is now the great Republic of the earth; its free institutions are matured by the experiment of half a century; nay, as a free Government, it goes farther back—the benefits of a free Constitution have virtually been enjoyed here for two centuries. As a free Government, as the freest Government, its growth and strength compel it, willing or unwilling, to stand forth to the contemplation of the world. We cannot obscure ourselves, if we would; a part we must take, honorable or dishonorable, in all that is done in the civilized world. Now, it will not be denied, that, within the last ten years, there has been agitated, in that world, a question of vast moment—a question pregnant with consequences favorable or unfavorable to the prevalence, nay, to the very existence, of civil liberty. It is a question which comes home to us. It calls on us for the expression of our opinion on the great question now before us. Assuredly, if there is any general tendency in the minds and affairs of men, which may be said to characterize the present age, it is the tendency to limited Governments. The enlightened part of mankind have very distinctly evinced a desire to take a share, at least, in the government of themselves. The men of this age will not be satisfied even with kind masters. They have shown, (except where force has been interposed to crush them,) that they will not be contented without a participation in the Government. This is so strongly marked a feature in the social condition of this age, that it can have escaped the observation of none to whom I address myself. . . .

. . . The age we live in, and our own active character, have connected us with all the nations of the world, and we, as a nation, have precisely the same interest in international law as a private individual has in the laws of his country.

But, apart from the soundness of the policy, on general principles there is a ground of duty in this matter. What do we not, as a people, owe to the principle of lawful resistance? to the principle that society shall govern itself? These principles have raised us to a state of prosperity, in which our course is rapid and irresistible. We are borne on as by a mighty current, and if we would stop long enough to take an observation, that we may measure our national course, before we can effect it, we find we have already moved a vast distance from the point at which it was commenced. This course we cannot check; it is the course of things and it will go on. Shall we not, thus situated, give to others who are struggling for these very principles, the cheering aid of our example and opinion? . . .

. . . This thunder is at a distance—the wide Atlantic rolls between—we are safe: would you have us go to war? Would you have us send armies into Europe? No: I would not. But this reasoning mistakes the age. Formerly, indeed, there was no making an impression on a nation but by bayonets, and subsidies, by fleets and armies: but the age has undergone a change: there is a force in public opinion which, in the long run, will outweigh all the physical force that can be brought to oppose it. Until public opinion is subdued, the greatest enemy of tyranny is not yet dead. What is the soul, the informing spirit of our institutions, of our entire system of government? Public opinion. While this acts with intensity, and moves in the right direction, the country must ever be safe—let us direct the force, the vast moral force of this engine, to the aid of others. . . .

I shall not detain this Committee by laying before it any statistical, geographical, or commercial account of Greece. . . . This people, a people of intelligence, ingenuity, refinement, spirit, and enterprise, have been for centuries under the most atrocious, unparalleled Tartarian barbarism that ever oppressed the human race. This House is unable to estimate duly, it is unable even to conceive or comprehend it. It must be remembered that the character of the force which has so long domineered over them is purely military. . . . Despotic power is there, if the phrase may be allowed, formed into a regular system of anarchy. The power delegated to the inferior tyrant is as absolute within its sphere, as the power of the Sultan himself—and hence, there is scarcely a great post under the whole government whose incumbent is not virtually, often actually, at war with the Porte. Between these two opposite Powers, both despotic, it is dangerous to take sides, and yet sides must be taken: in all the empire there is no property, no security. The well known and undisguised sale of all offices, is, of itself, a sufficient index of the state of society. In the whole world no such oppression is felt as that which has crushed down the wretched Greeks. . . .

It may now be asked, will this resolution do them any good? Yes, it will do them much good. It will give them courage and spirit, which is better than money. It will assure them of the public sympathy, and will inspire them with fresh constancy. It will teach them that they are not forgotten by the civilized world, and to hope one day to occupy, in that world, an honorable station. . . .

Do gentlemen fear the result of this resolution in embroiling us with the Porte? Why, sir, how much is it ahead of the whole nation, or rather let me ask how much is the nation ahead of it? Is not this whole people already in a state of open and avowed excitement on this subject? Does not the land ring from side to side with one common sentiment of sympathy for Greece, and indignation towards her oppressors? Nay more sir, are we not giving money to this cause? More still, sir, is not the Secretary of State in open correspondence with the President of the Greek Committee in London? The nation has gone as far as it can go, short of an official act of hostility. This resolution adds nothing beyond what is already done; nor can any of the European Governments take offence at such a measure. But, if they would, shall we be withheld from an honest expression of liberal feelings in the cause of freedom for fear of giving

umbrage to some member of the Holy Alliance? We are not, surely, yet prepared to purchase their smiles by a sacrifice of every manly principle. Dare any
Christian Prince even ask us not to sympathize with a Christian nation struggling
against Tartar tyranny? We do not interfere—we break no engagements—we
violate no treaties—with the Porte we have none.

Mr. Chairman, there are some things which, to be well done, must be promptly
done. If we even determine to do the thing that is now proposed, we may do it
too late. Sir, I am not one of those who are for withholding aid when it is most
urgently needed, and when the stress is past, and the aid no longer necessary,
overwhelming the sufferer with caresses. I will not stand by and see my fellow
man drowning without stretching out a hand to help him, till he has by his
own efforts and presence of mind reached the shore in safety, and then en-
cumber him with aid. With suffering Greece, now is the crisis of her fate—her
great, it may be, her last struggle. Sir, while we sit here deliberating, her destiny
may be decided. The Greeks, contending with ruthless oppressors, turn their
eyes to us, and invoke us by their ancestors, by their slaughtered wives and
children, by their own blood, poured out like water, by the hecatombs of dead
they have heaped up as it were to heaven, they invoke, they implore of us some
cheering sound, some look of sympathy, some token of compassionate regard.
They look to us as the great Republic of the earth—and they ask us by our
common faith, whether we can forget that they are struggling, as we once
struggled, for what we now so happily enjoy? I cannot say, sir, that they will
succeed: that rests with Heaven. But for myself, sir, if I should to-morrow hear
that they have failed—that their last phalanx had sunk beneath the Turkish
scimetar, that the flames of their last city had sunk in its ashes, and that naught
remained but the wide melancholy waste where Greece once was, I should still
reflect, with the most heartfelt satisfaction, that I have asked you, in the name of
seven millions of freemen, that you would give them at least the cheering of
one friendly voice.

— | "We are absolutely combatting shadows." *

Randolph's reply to Webster on January 24 revealed the conservatism that the
nation had learned to expect of him. He attacked especially Webster's effort,
through the employment of sentimental appeals, to commit the nation abroad to
what it could not accomplish except at the destruction of its own interests. Why,
he wondered, would Webster launch a crusade against slavery in the eastern
Mediterranean when slavery existed by law within the United States itself. His
argument against the pursuit of liberal causes abroad, embellished with a touch
of his inimitable style, remains a classic presentation of American conservative
doctrine.

✍

* *Annals of Congress,* 18th Congress, 1st Sess., Columns 1182–90.

. . . It is with serious concern and alarm . . . that I have heard doctrines broached in this debate, fraught with consequences more disastrous to the best interests of this people, than any that I ever heard advanced during the five and twenty years since I have been honored with a seat on this floor. They imply, to my apprehension, a total and fundamental change of the policy pursued by this Government, *ab urbe condita*—from the foundation of the Republic, to the present day. Are we, sir, to go on a crusade, in another hemisphere, for the propagation of two objects as dear and delightful to my heart as to that of any gentleman in this, or in any other assembly—Liberty and Religion—and, in the name of those holy words—by this powerful spell, is this nation to be conjured and beguiled out of the high way of Heaven—out of its present comparatively happy state, into all the disastrous conflicts arising from the policy of European Powers, with all the consequences which flow from them? Liberty and Religion, sir! Things that are yet dear, in spite of all the mischief that has been perpetrated in their name. I believe that nothing similar to this proposition is to be found in modern history, unless in the famous decree of the French National Assembly, which brought combined Europe against them, with its united strength, and, after repeated struggles, finally effected the downfall of the French power. . . .

. . . Among other cases forcibly put by the gentleman from Massachusetts, why he should embark in this incipient crusade against Mussulmen, he stated this as one—that they hold human beings as property. Ah, sir, . . . and what says the Constitution of the United States on this point? unless, indeed, that instrument is wholly to be excluded from consideration—unless it is to be regarded as a mere useless parchment, worthy to be burnt, as was once actually proposed. Does not that Constitution give its sanction to the holding of human beings as property? Sir, I am not going to discuss the abstract question of liberty or slavery, or any other abstract question. I go for matters of fact. But I would ask gentlemen in this House, who have the misfortune to reside on the wrong side of a certain mysterious parallel of latitude, to take this question seriously into consideration—whether the Government of the United States is prepared to say, that the act of holding human beings as property is sufficient to place the party so offending under the ban of its high and mighty displeasure?

Sir, the objections to this resolution accumulate as I proceed—*vires acquirit eundo*. If I should attempt to go through with a statement of them all, and had strength to sustain me, I should do what I promised I would not do—I should worry and exhaust the patience of this Committee. . . .

Permit me, sir, to ask why, in the selection of an enemy to the doctrines of our Government, and a party to those advanced by the Holy Alliance, we should fix on Turkey? She, at least, forms no party to that alliance; and I venture to say, that, for the last century, her conduct, in reference to her neighbors, has been much more Christian than that of all the "Most Christian," "Most Catholic," or "Most Faithful" Majesties of Europe—for she has not interfered, as we propose to do, in the internal affairs of other nations.

But, sir, we have not done. Not satisfied with attempting to support the Greeks, one world, like that of Pyrrhus or Alexander, is not sufficient for us. We have yet another world for exploits: we are to operate in a country distant from us eighty degrees of latitude, and only accessible by a circumnavigation of the globe, and to subdue which we must cover the Pacific with our ships, and the tops of the Andes with our soldiers. Do gentlemen seriously reflect on the work they have cut out for us? Why, sir, these projects of ambition surpass those of Bonaparte himself. . . .

Sir, I am afraid, that, along with some most excellent attributes and qualities —the love of liberty, jury trial, the writ of habeas corpus, and all the blessings of free government, that we have derived from our Anglo-Saxon ancestors, we have got not a little of their John Bull, or rather John Bull Dog spirit—their readiness to fight for anybody, and on any occasion. Sir England has been for centuries the game cock of Europe. It is impossible to specify the wars in which she has been engaged for contrary purposes; and she will, with great pleasure, see us take off her shoulders the labor of preserving the balance of power. We find her fighting, now, for the Queen of Hungary—then, for her inveterate foe, the King of Prussia—now at war for the restoration of the Bourbons—and now on the eve of war with them for the liberties of Spain. These lines on the subject were never more applicable than they have now become—

> Now Europe's balanced—neither side prevails;
> For nothing's left in either of the scales.

If we pursue the same policy, we must travel the same road, and endure the same burdens, under which England now groans. . . .

Let us adhere to the policy laid down by the second, as well as the first founder of our Republic—by him who was the Camillus, as well as the Romulus, of the infant state;—to the policy of peace, commerce and honest friendship with all nations, entangling alliances with none: for to entangling alliances we must come, if you once embark in projects such as this. . . .

. . . We are absolutely combatting shadows. The gentleman would have us to believe his resolution is all but nothing; yet again it is to prove omnipotent, and fills the whole globe with its influence. Either it is nothing, or it is something. If it is nothing, let us lay it on the table, and have done with it at once; but, if it is that something which it has been on the other hand represented to be, let us beware how we touch it. For my part, I would sooner put the shirt of Nessus on my back, than sanction these doctrines—doctrines such as I never heard from my boyhood till now. They go the whole length. If they prevail, there are no longer any Pyrenees—every bulwark and barrier of the Constitution is broken down; it is become *tabula rasa—a carte blanche,* for every one to scribble on it what he pleases.

# III

## Continental Expansion

Broad generalizations that defy accurate definition often cloud the meaning of events. Manifest Destiny is such a phrase, suggesting as it does that the United States had a "manifest destiny" to expand during the 1840's. The fact that the nation reached the shores of the Pacific at relatively little cost to itself further suggests that national sentiment and emotion comprised the basic ingredient in that expansion. Such notions lead nowhere; they deny all the elements of successful national action. The acquisition of a continental empire between 1845 and 1848 represented a series of highly effective national policies, none of which can be explained by the concept of manifest destiny. The mere urge to expand, if indeed such an urge is meaningful in the context of actual policy formulation, cannot in itself result in expansion. What matters in successful diplomacy is the accurate definition of ends and the wielding of means sufficient to achieve those ends. Manifest destiny—a phrase denoting national sentiment and nothing more —merely obfuscates the essential factors involved in national expansion. To identify American interests with such abstractions as "expanding the area of freedom" ignores the existence or even the requirement of specific, limited objectives. And because such abstractions reveal no concern for defining the ends of policy in terms that are readily achievable, they cannot embrace any real interest in the means of policy at all.

Manifest destiny comprised a body of democratic ideals, not a set of concrete national interests. To exploit the Texas and Oregon issues in American politics during the mid-'forties, Democratic politicians and editors fused expansionism with the latent messianism in American thought to maximize its emotional impact on the nation. Since the founding of the Republic, and especially after the presidency of Andrew Jackson, many citizens had viewed their political system with a messianic consciousness, convinced that they held the future of republican government in their hands. Jackson had asserted in his Farewell Message that Providence had selected the American people to be "the guardians of freedom to preserve it for the benefit of the human race." John L. O'Sullivan, editor of the *Democratic Review*, attached this democratic faith to the idea of national expansion. "We are the nation of human progress," he wrote in 1839, "and who will, what can, set limits to our onward march?" America's mission of humanity was not new, but the generation of the 'forties was the first to tie it to territorial extension.

That the doctrine of manifest destiny, as a powerful Democratic appeal in the 1844 campaign, played a significant role in the annexation of Texas does not suggest its relevancy to the successful conduct of diplomacy. For Texas, unlike Oregon and California, confronted the nation with a purely internal political question. Texas was a free agent in control of its own destiny. As early as 1836 the Lone Star Republic had won its independence from Mexico. France, Holland, and Belgium had recognized that independence before Captain Charles Elliot arrived in Texas in August 1842, as British chargé d'affaires. Even thereafter the Texas Republic faced neither internal nor external crises, and many Texans appeared willing to continue their experiment in democracy. British officials sought to encourage this spirit of independence by pressing Mexico both to recognize the independence and to refrain from further molestation of Texas. At the same time they assured the Texas government that continued independence would bring certain privileges and advantages in the Republic's relations with the nations of Europe. British policy had no chance of success, for it was clear that the overwhelming sentiment of the Anglo-Americans in Texas favored annexation to the United States. What mattered, therefore, was the relationship of the annexation question to the political factions struggling for power within the United States itself.

President John Tyler commenced his promotion of the Texas issue as early as 1843, assured that it would seize the imagination of the nation and thus repair his battered political fences. His personal efforts to control the question culminated in an annexation treaty, negotiated with the Texas Republic, which he submitted to the Senate in April 1844. His reasoned message of transmittal reminded all sections of the nation of their special interests in Texas. If the treaty were rejected, he warned the Senate, Texas would seek the friendship of others. "In contemplating such a contingency," he continued, "it can not be overlooked that the United States are already almost surrounded by the possessions of European powers. The Canadas, New Brunswick, and Nova Scotia, the islands in the American seas, with Texas trammeled by treaties of alliance or of a commercial character differing in policy from that of the United States, would complete the circle." (*Reading No. 1.*) Similarly Jackson in his famous letter to Aaron V. Brown in 1843 had advocated extending "the area of freedom" to Texas to terminate British ambition and intrigue along the southwestern frontier of the United States.

For John C. Calhoun, Texas comprised less a national than a Southern issue. As Secretary of State in 1844 he promoted annexation with the sectional fervor expected of him. For pro-slavery politicians and editors Texas was an issue upon which hinged the very existence of Southern institutions. It was British abolitionism that rendered annexation so essential for Southern security. Lord Aberdeen, the British Foreign Minister, had made clear the attitudes of the British government toward slavery. Reassuring the United States in December 1843 of Britain's honorable intentions toward Texas, Aberdeen added the disturbing comment that "Great Britain desires and is constantly exerting herself to promote the general abolition of slavery throughout the world." Whereas England would do nothing secretly or underhandedly to accomplish it, continued Aberdeen, she hoped to see that institution abolished in the United States. In his reply Calhoun not only defended the right of the United States to annex Texas but also reminded the British government that slavery was a Southern question and beyond the jurisdiction of the Federal government. (*Reading No. 2.*)

Southern politicians, for whom Texas annexation would not only guarantee Southern institutions but also strengthen Calhoun's chances for the Democratic presidential nomination, soon discovered that they could not control the Texas question at all. Agrarian Democrats, centering in the Midwest, with allies in the Southwest and the East, gradually captured the issue, nationalized it, carried expansionism to its highest pitch of the decade, and eventually rode to power on its emotional impact. These men had no interest in the extension of slavery. They defended annexation on broad national grounds, reassuring the nation that the further expansion of the United States would strengthen rather than weaken its political institutions. As nationalists they reminded the North that slavery was a local matter, far removed from the struggle for control of the Federal government. (*Reading No. 3.*) But the proponents of annexation faced two powerful anti-annexationist forces. Northern abolitionists dreaded the extension of the slave power within the United States; conservative Whigs, North and South, recognized the narrow political balance of power in the country and feared the addition of another large Democratic state. Joshua R. Giddings, the determined Ohio abolitionist and Whig, introduced both these fears of annexation into his argument against expansion of May 21, 1844. (*Reading No. 4.*)

With the rejection of the treaty of annexation by the Senate, Texas quickly dominated the campaign of 1844. The election of the expansionist Democratic nominee, James K. Polk, was interpreted by President Tyler, as well as by both the Southern and national factions of the Democratic party, as a mandate for consummating the movement for annexation. After a strong debate that raged through January and February 1845, Congress on March 1 passed a joint resolution for annexation. To the extent that manifest destiny doctrines strengthened the pro-annexationist forces in Congress, they contributed to American expansion, for no one would deny the relevance of public opinion to the actions of Congress.


II

Along the distant Pacific, where the lands were not for the taking, the doctrines of manifest destiny played a decreasingly significant role. Here public opinion, whatever its unanimity (and it was really never united), could achieve nothing unless it was transformed into national policies that recognized the interests and claims of other nations. That American expansionism embraced regions along the Pacific by 1844 was obvious enough. American pioneers, pouring across the Rockies, seemed capable of resolving alone the perennial quarrel with England over the Oregon country. Nothing, predicted the confident David R. Atchison of Missouri, would prevent them from occupying the whole territory. "You might as well attempt to turn the waters of the Missouri River back upon its sources in the Rocky Mountains as to turn back the flood of population from the shores of the Pacific Ocean," he declared. "[T]he Alleghenies may be piled upon the Rocky Mountains, and our people will scale them. The march of empire is westward; nothing will, nothing can check it." Clearly the United States was destined to reach the Pacific—the boundary prescribed by the God of nature.

But as a determinant in national policy the concept of manifest destiny was scarcely helpful. It represented an expanding force with no clear territorial objectives. By the mid-'forties, when democratic idealism had reached its most vociferous stage of public expression, American expansionism looked far beyond Texas, Oregon, and California. Indeed, it had no visible limit. The New York *Herald* prophesied that the American Republic would in due course embrace all the land from the Isthmus of Panama to the polar regions and from the Atlantic to the Pacific. One Texas correspondent wrote that "the fact must be no longer disguised, that we, the people of the United States must hold, and govern, under free and harmonious institutions, the continent we inhabit." Others suggested that the area of freedom be extended to Cape Horn. Many looked beyond the continent to Cuba, the Sandwich Islands, the far-flung regions of the Pacific, and even to the Old World itself. Again the New York *Herald* declared in September 1845:

> American patriotism takes a wider and loftier range than heretofore. Its horizon is widening every day. No longer bounded by the limits of the confederacy, it looks abroad upon the whole earth, and into the mind of the republic daily sinks deeper and deeper the conviction that the civilization of the earth—the reform of the governments of the ancient world—the emancipation of the whole race, are dependent, in a great degree, on the United States.

This was a magnificent vision for a democratic purpose, but it could not, because it lacked precision, guide the United States across the continent or serve as the basis of national policy.

Successful diplomacy, the past had revealed, necessitated concrete goals, limited and precisely defined, plus the means required to encourage or compel agreement from other nations. America's expansionist program succeeded because it was guided not by the idealism of manifest destiny but rather by the specific and mundane. United States diplomatic and military policy that secured the acquisition of both Oregon and California was controlled by men who never defined their expansionist purpose in terms of democratic idealism. The vistas of all were maritime; they were invariably anchored to specific waterways along the Pacific coast. Land was important only as the necessary right of way to ocean ports—a barrier to be spanned by improved avenues of commerce. Traders and seamen who visited the Pacific coast of North America during the decade before 1845 had created a precise vision of those coasts—a vision always born of the sea. Whatever their mission on that great ocean, they were without exception struck by the excellent quality of three inlets—the three which ultimately guided American expansion across the continent. All agreed that the Columbia River, which marked the northern extremity of American settlements in Oregon, was useless as an ocean port. Running the bar at its entrance was always hazardous and often disastrous. By contrast, travelers agreed that the Fuca Strait and the sea arms to the east of it comprised one of the finest harbors in the world. Charles Wilkes, the American naval officer, presented this characteristic description: "Nothing can exceed the beauty of these waters, and their safety; not a shoal exists within the Straits of Juan de Fuca, Admiralty Inlet, Puget Sound, or Hood's Canal, that can in any way interrupt their navigation by a seventy-four gun ship. I venture nothing in saying, there is no country in the world that possesses waters equal to these." Here were the harbors of Oregon that could be entered or left under any wind or during any season. These waters were the objective of every American diplomatist—from John Quincy Adams to James K. Polk—who carried responsibility for the Oregon negotiations.

For travelers and sea captains of the early 'forties two inlets gave special significance to the California coast—the bays of San Francisco and San Diego. They viewed San Francisco harbor with wonderment. Wilkes assured the readers of his *Narrative* that California could boast "one of the finest, if not the very best harbor in the world." It was sufficiently extensive, he added, to shelter the combined navies of Europe. Thomas J. Farnham, the American traveler and writer, called it simply "the glory of the Western world." All agreed that the bay was the unqualified answer to American hopes for commercial greatness in the Pacific world. To the south lay San Diego Bay—the rendezvous of the California hide trade. Here all Boston firms maintained their coastal depots for cleaning, drying, and storing the hides until a full cargo of thirty to forty thousand had been collected for the long journey to Boston. The processing and storing of hides required a warm port, free from rain, fog, and heavy surf. San Diego alone met all these requirements. This beautiful bay, so deep and placid that ships could lie a cable's length from the smooth, hard-packed, sandy beach, became the chief point of New England's interest on the California coast. Protected for its entire length of fifteen miles, except for its narrow, deep entrance, the bay was exposed to neither wind nor surf. Richard Henry Dana observed in his *Two Years Before the Mast* (1840) that San Diego harbor was comparable in value and importance to San Francisco Bay. The noted sea captain, Benjamin Morrell, once termed San Diego "as fine a bay for vessels under three hundred tons as was ever formed by Nature in her most friendly mood to mariners."

### III

With the essential interests of the United States along the Pacific so accurately defined, what was required to achieve their incorporation into the territorial limits of the United States was the accumulation of pressures, internal and external, which might create the occasion for diplomatic settlements. On Oregon the initial impulse that suddenly, in 1846, resolved the issue came from within the nation itself. From the moment that Oregon became a matter of diplomatic concern in 1818, Britain had offered a settlement along the Columbia River—a boundary which John Quincy Adams, with his New England interest in the Fuca Strait, refused to accept. Thereafter the issue lay dormant under the provision that both nations could occupy the region until one gave a year's notice that it intended to terminate the agreement for joint occupancy. By 1844 the rapid movement of pioneers into Oregon had raised the issue of a permanent settlement of the Northwest boundary. Immediately the political factions within the nation divided sharply over the question of goals. Western Democrats, led by such men as Lewis Cass of Michigan and Stephen A. Douglas of Illinois, seized the issue as another great political bonus. Employing the patriotic appeals of manifest destiny, they claimed Oregon as a Western issue to be settled, by war if necessary, at the Alaska line of 54° 40'. (*Reading No. 5.*) That this extreme demand was meaningless in the context of diplomacy mattered little. It carried the desired political appeal and thus forced the issue of Oregon into the Democratic platform of 1844.

Whig conservatives, led by such men as Robert Winthrop of Massachusetts, denied that Oregon was a Western issue. It was a commercial question, national in scope, one on which the East had an equal right to be heard. (*Reading No. 6.*) For them the nation's interests were limited to the acquisition of the Strait of Fuca and Puget Sound—objectives that could be obtained by the continuation of the boundary line along the 49th parallel to the Pacific Ocean. Since this matter, as one between two nations, lay solely within the realm of diplomatic competence, the Whigs denied the relevance of the political debate over Oregon to the ultimate resolution of the issue. They denounced the Democrats for speaking lightly of war against England and accused them of interfering with purely diplomatic questions for political ends. This Congressional interference Rufus Choate of Massachusetts described as a menace to peace, and he concluded that only his "sincere respect and regard for senators who propose and urge it prevents my saying, still further, that it is the most indecent, indecorous, unintelligible proceeding the world of civilization ever witnessed." Perhaps no New Englander summarized better the conservative, commercial view of Oregon than did William Sturgis, the noted Boston merchant, in his address of January 22, 1845. (*Reading No. 7.*)

President Polk, responsible after March 4, 1845, for the conduct of American foreign policy, was trapped between two clearly distinguishable notions regarding the Oregon question. Politically he was committed to the whole of Oregon, and in his Inaugural Address he proclaimed it his duty "to assert and maintain by all constitutional means the right of the United States to that portion of our territory which lies beyond the Rocky Mountains." The title of the United States to the Oregon country, he added, was "clear and unquestionable." Intellectually and diplomatically, however, Polk was committed from the beginning to the Whig position. This he made clear when he authorized Secretary of State James Buchanan to offer England, on July 12, 1845, a compromise along the line of 49° and rationalized the offer in commercial terms. (*Reading No. 8.*) Such a settlement would not, Buchanan informed Minister Louis Mc-Lane in London, materially injure the interests of the United States. "The entrance of the Straits of Fuca, Admiralty Inlet, and Puget's Sound, with their fine harbors and rich surrounding soil, are all south of this parallel," wrote Buchanan. "We know but little of the country north of it; but, from all the information we have obtained, it is, with the exception of a few spots, wholly unfit for agriculture, and incapable of sustaining any considerable population."

Thereafter what stood in the path of a diplomatic settlement was not British policy, for Aberdeen as early as 1844 had agreed privately to this distribution of Oregon's waterways. Polk's dilemma lay at home—in the extreme demands of his own party to which he had contributed. There could be no Oregon settlement until the partisan campaign for 54°40' had run its course in American politics. The President, in this extremity, had the support of the Whig party, the powerful Calhoun and Martin Van Buren factions of the Democratic party, and the bulk of the important metropolitan press. Perhaps no publication cast more scorn on the partisan pressures preventing compromise or argued more effectively for a settlement than did the *North American Review* in January 1846. (*Reading No. 9.*) "We have been arguing the question for thirty years," charged the writer, "and stand precisely where we did when the discussion commenced." The debate, he declared, sounded like a "solemn mummery" in which too many ambitious politicians were preventing the vast majority from regarding the issue with perfect indifference. Continued the writer: "Not one in ten thousand . . . would be immediately affected by the successful assertion of our claim to the whole of Oregon."

Eventually the pressures for compromise broke the power of the ultras over American policy. By April 1846 it was clear that a negotiated settlement along the 49th parallel would receive the overwhelming endorsement of the Senate. Polk, still bound politically to the Western Democrats, permitted England to assume the diplomatic initiative. The British proposal, varying only in minor detail from the President's own offer of July 1845, proved to be completely acceptable. On June 10 Polk sent the British formula to the Senate for its prior approval. The Senate responded with an affirmative vote of 38 to 12. Thereupon the diplomats prepared a final treaty which was quickly ratified. To the end the President posed as a proponent of "54–40" and accused the Senate of forcing the compromise on the United States government.

IV

Events moved rapidly in the mid-'forties. Long before the United States acquired title to the seven degrees of Pacific Ocean frontage from the 42nd to the 49th parallel, Polk had embarked on a dual course to gain additional ocean frontage south of 42° in the Mexican province of California. In 1845 Mexico's title to California was as clear as her hold on the distant province was tenuous. The acquisition of this derelict necessitated bargaining with its owner. Unfortunately Mexico had responded to the Joint Resolution to annex Texas by severing diplomatic relations with the United States. Buchanan had assured General Juan Almonte, the Mexican Minister to the United States, that the new administration would make every effort to adjust amicably all outstanding complaints. But to Mexico the move to annex Texas was an unbearable affront. Polk was determined to pursue the matter of California with the Mexican government. Aboard the *Anahuac,* which carried Almonte to Vera Cruz in April 1845, was William S. Parrott, long-time resident of Mexico, now serving as Polk's special agent to Mexico City.

Polk's acquisitiveness toward California reflected his conviction that the United States faced the competition of Great Britain for possession of the province. From London, Mexico City, and California the administration received rumors of British interests in California. Even the French were known to have cast covetous eyes toward San Francisco Bay. Thomas O. Larkin, the American merchant at Monterey, reported that the French and British governments maintained consuls in California although neither nation had any commercial interests along the Pacific coast. "Why they are in Service their Government best know and Uncle Sam will know to his cost," Larkin warned in July 1845. Larkin's reports produced a wave of excitement in the administration. "The appearance of a British Vice Consul and French Consul in California at this present crisis without any apparent commercial business," Buchanan answered Larkin, "is well calculated to produce the impression that their respective governments entertained designs on that country. . . ." On October 17 Buchanan drafted special instructions to Larkin:

> The future destiny of that country is a subject of anxious solicitude for the government and people of the United States. The interests of our commerce and our whale fisheries on the Pacific Ocean demand that you should exert the greatest vigilance in discovering and defeating any attempts which may be made by foreign governments to acquire a control over that country. . . . On all proper occasions, you should not fail prudently to warn the government and people of California of the danger of such an interference to their peace and prosperity; to inspire them with a jealousy of European dominion, and to arouse in their bosoms that love of liberty and independence so natural to the American continent.

Polk appointed Larkin as his confidential agent in California to encourage the Californians, should they separate from Mexico, to cast their lot with the United States. "While the President will make no effort and use no influence to induce California to become one of the free and independent states of the Union, yet," continued Buchanan's instructions, "if the people should desire to unite their destiny with ours, they would be received as brethren, whenever this can be done without affording Mexico just cause of complaint." Larkin was told to let events take their course unless Britain or France should attempt to take California against the will of its residents.

During November 1845 Polk initiated the second phase of his California policy—an immediate effort to purchase the province from Mexico. On November 9 Parrott returned to Washington with confirming information that the officials in Mexico City would receive an American envoy. As early as September, Polk and his cabinet had agreed to tender such a mission to John Slidell of Louisiana. In his instructions to Slidell, dated November 10, Buchanan clarified the administration's objectives in California. In a variety of boundary proposals Polk was adamant only on the Rio Grande. Those that applied to California were defined solely in terms of California ports. They started with San Francisco and Monterey, the capital of the province, but they included also a suggested boundary line which would reach westward from El Paso along the 32nd parallel to the Pacific, this to include the harbor of San Diego. (*Reading No. 10.*) Unfortunately Slidell was not received by the Mexican government. The administration's program of acquiring at least one of the important harbors along the California coast by purchase from Mexico had failed. Yet for an influential minority of American writers, merchants, and party leaders, California had become a national interest of the United States. So limitless was the potential contribution of San Francisco Bay, as an American port, to the nation's future wealth and power, that no longer could the United States government suppress the national effort to acquire it. (*Reading No. 11*).

That Polk eventually achieved the acquisition of California through the agency of the Mexican War suggests that he purposely maneuvered United States-Mexican relations into a crisis from which only open conflict could extricate them. General Zachary Taylor's presence on the Rio Grande, not regarded by Polk as an act of aggression but merely the occupation of contested territory, left sufficient doubt in the minds of his Whig opposition to make the Mexican War the most bitterly criticized in American history. Actually, from the moment of Texas annexation a wide variety of pressures had been driving the two nations toward war. Annexation itself was only the most serious in a long succession of diplomatic crises. The causes of the Mexican War lay deep in the web of diplomatic and commercial relations covering fully two decades. At the close of the war, Lt. Robert S. Ripley wrote, with remarkable insight, that "the controversies in arms in which great nations of modern times have engaged have almost invariably been brought about by a long series of circumstances, so connected, that in their succession the danger of the conflict could hardly be perceived until its occurrence was inevitable."

American victories in Mexico were essential to the success of the expansionist program only because they increased the bargaining power of the Polk administration. That the war served the interest of the United States hinged less upon the nation's predominant military power than in the precise and limited goals which that war was meant to achieve. These objectives the President and his advisers had defined initially in Slidell's instructions. They attached those goals—the acquisition of San Francisco and San Diego harbors—to the war effort as early as June 1846. They repeated them in April 1847, in the instructions issued to Nicholas P. Trist, who was to become the administration's private negotiator in Mexico. It was Trist who, in his subsequent negotiations, secured the southern boundary of California—a line which joined the mouth of the Gila River on the Colorado with a point on the Pacific one league south of San Diego Bay. (*Reading No. 12.*) This line completed the American quest for frontage on the Pacific. Polk, in appraising his diplomatic successes, pointed only to the ports along the distant coast which would "enable the United States to command the already valuable and rapidly increasing commerce of the Pacific." Polk's diplomacy triumphed, not because it was anchored to a vague but optimistic national messianism, but because it, like the diplomacy of the American Revolution, was ever focused on the specific and the achievable.

# 1 | President John Tyler's Argument for the Annexation of Texas, April 1844 *

John Tyler, a Virginia states' rightist who had broken politically with Andrew Jackson, was nominated as a no-principle candidate by the Whig party for the vice presidency in 1840 to strengthen that party's appeal in the South. When Tyler succeeded to the presidency in 1841 upon the death of William Henry Harrison, it became evident that Tyler was a Whig in name only, for he soon began to veto the Whig measures of a Whig Congress. By 1843 he was a man without a party but still politically ambitious. To sustain his political life he required an issue of great potential popularity; he discovered it in the Texas question. Tyler, although a Southerner and under direct Southern influence, cast his appeal in national terms. In his message to Congress on April 22, 1844, transmitting the annexation treaty which his Secretary of State, John C. Calhoun, had negotiated with the Texas Republic, the President made it clear that Texas, as a part of the American Union, would serve all sections of the nation.

🖋

. . . The country thus proposed to be annexed has been settled principally by persons from the United States, who emigrated on the invitation of both Spain and Mexico, and who carried with them into the wilderness which they have partially reclaimed the laws, customs, and political and domestic institutions of their native land. They are deeply indoctrinated in all the principles of civil liberty, and will bring along with them in the act of reassociation devotion to our Union and a firm and inflexible resolution to assist in maintaining the public liberty unimpaired—a consideration which, as it appears to me, is to be regarded as of no small moment. The country itself thus obtained is of incalculable value in an agricultural and commercial point of view. To a soil of inexhaustible fertility it unites a genial and healthy climate, and is destined at a day not distant to make large contributions to the commerce of the world. . . . A new and powerful impulse will thus be given to the navigating interest of the country, which will be chiefly engrossed by our fellow-citizens of the Eastern and Middle States, who have already attained a remarkable degree of prosperity by the partial monopoly they have enjoyed of the carrying trade of the Union, particularly the coastwise trade, which this new acquisition is destined in time, and that not distant, to swell to a magnitude which can not easily be computed, while the addition made to the boundaries of the home market thus secured to their mining, manufacturing and mechanical skill and industry will be of a character the most commanding and important. Such are some of the many advantages which will accrue to the Eastern and Middle States by the ratification of the treaty—advantages the extent of which it is impossible

* Messages and Papers of the Presidents, James D. Richardson, ed. (Washington, 1897), IV: 308–13.

to estimate with accuracy or properly to appreciate. Texas, being adapted to the culture of cotton, sugar, and rice, and devoting most of her energies to the raising of these productions, will open an extensive market to the Western States in the important articles of beef, pork, horses, mules, etc., as well as in breadstuffs. At the same time, the Southern and Southeastern States will find in the fact of annexation protection and security to their peace and tranquillity, as well against all domestic as foreign efforts to disturb them, thus consecrating anew the union of the States and holding out the promise of its perpetual duration. Thus, at the same time that the tide of public prosperity is greatly swollen, an appeal of what appears to the Executive to be of an imposing, if not of a resistless, character is made to the interests of every portion of the country. Agriculture, which would have a new and extensive market opened for its produce; commerce, whose ships would be freighted with the rich productions of an extensive and fertile region; and the mechanical arts, in all their various ramifications, would seem to unite in one universal demand for the ratification of the treaty. But important as these considerations may appear, they are to be regarded as but secondary to others. Texas, for reasons deemed sufficient by herself, threw off her dependence on Mexico as far back as 1836, and consummated her independence by the battle of San Jacinto in the same year, since which period Mexico has attempted no serious invasion of her territory, but the contest has assumed features of a mere border war, characterized by acts revolting to humanity. In the year 1836 Texas adopted her constitution, under which she has existed as a sovereign power ever since, having been recognized as such by many of the principal powers of the world; and contemporaneously with its adoption, by a solemn vote of her people, embracing all her population but ninety-three persons, declared her anxious desire to be admitted into association with the United States as a portion of their territory. This vote, thus solemnly taken, has never been reversed, and now by the action of her constituted authorities, sustained as it is by popular sentiment, she reaffirms her desire for annexation. This course has been adopted by her without the employment of any sinister measures on the part of this Government. No intrigue has been set on foot to accomplish it. Texas herself wills it, and the Executive of the United States, concurring with her, has seen no sufficient reason to avoid the consummation of an act esteemed to be so desirable by both. . . . The documents now transmitted along with the treaty lead to the conclusion, as inevitable, that if the boon now tendered be rejected Texas will seek for the friendship of others. In contemplating such a contingency it can not be overlooked that the United States are already almost surrounded by the possessions of European powers. The Canadas, New Brunswick, and Nova Scotia, the islands in the American seas, with Texas trammeled by treaties of alliance or of a commercial character differing in policy from that of the United States, would complete the circle. Texas voluntarily steps forth, upon terms of perfect honor and good faith to all nations, to ask to be annexed to the Union. As an independent sovereignty her right to do this is unquestionable. In doing so she gives no cause of umbrage to any other power; her people desire it, and there is no slavish transfer of her sovereignty and independence. She has for eight years maintained her independence against all efforts to subdue her. She has been recognized as independent by many of the most prominent of the family of nations, and that recognition, so far as they are concerned, places her in a position, without giving any just cause of umbrage to them, to surrender her sovereignty at her own will and pleasure. The United States, actuated evermore by a spirit of justice, has desired by the stipulations of the treaty to render justice to all. They have made provision for the payment of the public debt of Texas. We look to her ample and fertile domain as the certain means of accomplishing this; but this is a matter between the United States and Texas, and with which other Governments have nothing to do. Our right to receive the rich grant tendered by Texas is perfect, and this Government should not, having due respect either to its own honor or its own interests, permit its course of policy to be interrupted by the interference of other powers, even if such interference were threatened. The question is one purely American. In the acquisition, while we abstain most carefully from all that could interrupt the public peace, we claim the right to exercise a due regard to our own. This Government can not consistently with its honor permit any such interference. With equal, if not greater, propriety might the United States demand of other governments to surrender their numerous and valuable acquisitions made in past time at numberless places on the surface of the globe, whereby they have added to their power and enlarged their resources.

To Mexico the Executive is disposed to pursue a course conciliatory in its character and at the same time to render her the most ample justice by conventions and stipulations not inconsistent with the rights and dignity of the Government. It is actuated by no spirit of unjust aggrandizement, but looks only to its own security. It has made known to Mexico at several periods its extreme anxiety to witness the termination of hostilities between that country and Texas. Its wishes, however, have been entirely disregarded. It has ever been ready to urge an adjustment of the dispute upon terms mutually advantageous to both. It will be ready at all times to hear and discuss any claims Mexico may think she has on the justice of the United States and to adjust any that may be deemed to be so on the most liberal terms. There is no desire on the part of the Executive to wound her pride or affect injuriously her interest, but at the same time it can not compromit by any delay in its action the essential interest of the United States. Mexico has no right to ask or expect this of us; we deal rightfully with Texas as an independent power. The war which has been waged for eight years has resulted only in the conviction with all others than herself that Texas can not be reconquered. . . .

In full view, then, of the highest public duty, and as a measure of security against evils incalculably great, the Executive has entered into the negotiation, the fruits of which are now submitted to the Senate. Independent of the urgent reasons which existed for the step it has taken, it might safely invoke the fact (which it confidently believes) that there exists no civilized government on earth having a voluntary tender made it of a domain so rich and fertile, so replete with all that can add to national greatness and wealth, and so necessary to its peace and safety that would reject the offer. Nor are other powers, Mexico inclusive, likely in any degree to be injuriously affected by the ratification of the treaty.

The prosperity of Texas will be equally interesting to all; in the increase of the general commerce of the world that prosperity will be secured by annexation.

But one view of the subject remains to be presented. It grows out of the proposed enlargement of our territory. From this, I am free to confess, I see no danger. The federative system is susceptible of the greatest extension compatible with the ability of the representation of the most distant State or Territory to reach the seat of Government in time to participate in the functions of legislation and to make known the wants of the constituent body. Our confederated Republic consisted originally of thirteen members. It now consists of twice that number, while applications are before Congress to permit other additions. This addition of new States has served to strengthen rather than to weaken the Union. New interests have sprung up, which require the united power of all, through the action of the common Government, to protect and defend upon the high seas and in foreign parts. Each State commits with perfect security to that common Government those great interests growing out of our relations with other nations of the world, and which equally involve the good of all the States. Its domestic concerns are left to its own exclusive management. But if there were any force in the objection it would seem to require an immediate abandonment of territorial possessions which lie in the distance and stretch to a far-off sea, and yet no one would be found, it is believed, ready to recommend such an abandonment. Texas lies at our very doors and in our immediate vicinity.

## 2 | John C. Calhoun's Southern View of Texan Annexation, April 1844 *

For Southern sectionalists, led by John C. Calhoun of South Carolina, Texas annexation was never more than a Southern issue—a program to expand the plantation system and slave labor into the Southwest. Only with the addition of Texas as slave territory could the South maintain some balance between free and slave states. "I only ask the south to stand by me," Calhoun wrote while negotiating the Texas treaty. "Now is the time to vindicate and save our institutions." Calhoun's letter to Richard Pakenham of April 1844 was more than a defense of United States annexationist diplomacy; it was a moral and constitutional defense of slavery against the assaults of British abolitionism. Calhoun made it clear that the domestic institutions of the United States were not the proper concern of British diplomacy.

✍

* Calhoun to Pakenham, April 18, 1844, *Diplomatic Correspondence of the United States: Inter-American Affairs, 1831–1860*, William R. Manning, ed. (Washington, 1936), VII: 18–22.

The Undersigned Secretary of State of the United States, has laid before the President the note of the Right Honorable Mr. Pakenham, Envoy Extraordinary and Minister Plenipotentiary of Her Britannic Majesty. . . .

In reply, the Undersigned is directed by the President to inform the Right Honorable Mr. Pakenham that, while he regards with pleasure the disavowal of Lord Aberdeen of any intention on the part of Her Majesty's Government "to resort to any measures, either openly or secretly, which can tend to disturb the internal tranquillity of the slave-holding States, and thereby affect the tranquillity of this Union," he, at the same time, regards with deep concern, the avowal, for the first time made to this Government, "that Great Britain desires, and is constantly exerting herself to procure the general abolition of slavery throughout the world."

So long as Great Britain confined her policy to the abolition of slavery in her own possessions and colonies, no other country had a right to complain. It belonged to her, exclusively, to determine according to her own views of policy whether it should be done or not. But when she goes beyond, and avows it as her settled policy, and the object of her constant exertions, to abolish it throughout the world, she makes it the duty of all other countries, whose safety or prosperity may be endangered by her policy, to adopt such measures as they may deem necessary for their protection.

It is with still deeper concern the President regards the avowal of Lord Aberdeen of the desire of Great Britain to see slavery abolished in Texas; and, as he infers, is endeavoring, through her diplomacy, to accomplish it, by making the abolition of slavery one of the conditions on which Mexico should acknowledge her independence. It has confirmed his previous impressions as to the policy of Great Britain in reference to Texas, and made it his duty to examine with much care and solicitude, what would be its effects on the prosperity and safety of the United States should she succeed in her endeavors. The investigation has resulted in the settled conviction that it would be difficult for Texas, in her actual condition, to resist what she desires, without supposing the influence and exertions of Great Britain would be extended beyond the limits assigned by Lord Aberdeen; and that, if Texas could not resist, the consummation of the object of her desire would endanger both the safety and prosperity of the Union. Under this conviction, it is felt to be the imperious duty of the Federal Government, the common representative and protector of the States of this Union, to adopt, in self-defence, the most effectual measures to defeat it.

This is not the proper occasion to state at large the grounds of this conviction. It is sufficient to say, that the consummation of the avowed object of her wishes in reference to Texas, would be followed by hostile feelings and relations between that country and the United States, which could not fail to place her under the influence and control of Great Britain. That, from the geographical position of Texas, would expose the weakest and most vulnerable portion of our frontier to inroads, and place, in the power of Great Britain, the most efficient means of effecting in the neighboring States of this Union, what she avows it to be her desire to do in all countries, where slavery exists. To hazard consequences which would be so dangerous to the prosperity and safety of this Union, without resorting to the most effective measures to prevent them, would be, on the part of the Federal Government, an abandonment of the most solemn obligation imposed by the guaranty, which the States, in adopting the constitution, entered into to protect each other against whatever might endanger their safety, whether from without or within. Acting in obedience to this obligation, on which our Federal System of Government rests, the President directs me to inform you that a treaty has been concluded between the United States and Texas, for the annexation of the latter to the former, as a part of its territory, which will be submitted without delay to the Senate for its approval. This step has been taken as the most effectual, if not the only, means of guarding against the threatened danger, and securing their permanent peace and welfare.

It is well known that Texas has long desired to be annexed to this Union; that her People, at the time of the adoption of her constitution, expressed by an almost unanimous vote, her desire to that effect; and that she has never ceased to desire it, as the most certain means of promoting her safety and prosperity. The United States have heretofore declined to meet her wishes; but the time has now arrived when they can no longer refuse consistently with their own security and peace, and the sacred obligation imposed by their constitutional compact, for mutual defence and protection. Nor are they any way responsible for the circumstances which have imposed this obligation on them. They had no agency in bringing about the state of things which has terminated in the separation of Texas from Mexico. It was the Spanish Government and Mexico herself which invited and offered high inducements to our citizens to colonize Texas. That, from the diversity of Character, habits, religion, and political opinions, necessarily led to the separation, without the interference of the United States in any manner whatever. It is true, the United States, at an early period, recognised the independence of Texas; but, in doing so, it is well known, they but acted in conformity with an established principle to recognise the Government *de facto*. They had previously acted on the same principle in reference to Mexico herself, and the other Governments which have risen on the former dominions of Spain, on this continent. They are equally without responsibility for that state of things already adverted to as the immediate cause of imposing on them, in self-defence, the obligation of adopting the measure they have. They remained passive, so long as the policy on the part of Great Britain, which has led to its adoption, had no immediate bearing on their peace and safety. While they conceded to Great Britain the right of adopting whatever policy she might deem best, in reference to the African race, within her own possessions, they, on their part, claim the same right for themselves. The policy she has adopted, in reference to the portion of that race in her dominions, may be humane and wise; but it does not follow, if it prove so with her, that it would be so in reference to the United States and other countries, whose situation differs from hers. But, whether it would be or not, it belongs to each to judge and determine for itself. With us, it is a question to be decided, not by the Federal Government, but by each member of this Union for itself, according to its own views of its domestic policy; and without any right on the part of the Federal Government to interfere, in any manner whatever. Its rights and duties are limited to protecting, under the guaranties of the constitution, each member of this Union, in whatever policy it may adopt, in reference to the portion within its respective limits. A large number of the States has decided, that it is neither wise nor humane to change the relation, which has existed from their first settlement, between the two races; while others, where the African is less numerous, have adopted the opposite policy.

It belongs not to this Government to question whether the former have decided wisely or not; and if it did, the Undersigned would not regard this as the proper occasion to discuss the subject. He does not, however, deem it irrelevant to state, that, if the experience of more than half a century is to decide, it would be neither humane nor wise in them to change their policy. The census and other authentic documents show that, in all instances in which the States have changed the former relation between the two races, the condition of the African, instead of being improved, has become worse. . . .

Taking the two extremes of North and South, in the State of Maine the number of negroes returned as deaf and dumb, blind, insane and idiots, by the census of 1840, is one out of every twelve; and in Florida, by the same returns, it is one out of every eleven hundred and five; or ninety-two to one in favor of the slaves of Florida, as compared with the free blacks of Maine.

In addition, it deserves to be remarked, that, in Massachusetts, where the change in the ancient relation of the two races was first made, (now more than sixty years since), where the greatest zeal has been exhibited in their behalf, and where their number is comparatively few, (but little more than eight thousand in a population of upwards of seven hundred and thirty thousand,) the condition of the African is amongst the most wretched. By the latest authentic accounts, there was one out of every twenty-one of the black population in jails or houses of correction; and one out of every thirteen was either deaf and dumb, blind, idiot, insane, or in prison. On the other hand, the census and other authentic sources of information establish the fact, that the condition of the African race throughout all the States, where the ancient relation between the two has been retained, enjoys a degree of health and comfort which may well compare with that of the laboring population of any country in christendom; and it may be added, that in no other condition, or in any other age or country has the negro race ever attained so high an elevation in morals, intelligence, or civilization.

If such be the wretched condition of the race in their changed relation, where their number is comparatively few, and where so much interest is manifested for their improvement, what would it be in those States where the two races are nearly equal in numbers, and where, in consequence, would necessarily spring up mutual fear, jealousy, and hatred, between them? It may, in truth, be assumed as a maxim, that two races differing so greatly, and in so many respects, cannot possibly exist together in the same country, where their numbers are nearly equal, without the one being subjected to the other. Experience has proved, that the existing relation in which the one is subjected to the other in the slave-holding States, is consistent with the peace and safety of both, with great improvement to the inferior; while the same experience proves, that the relation which it is the desire and object of Great Britain to substitute in its stead, in this and all other countries, under the plausible name of the abolition of slavery, would, (if it did not destroy the inferior by conflicts to which it would lead,) reduce it to the extremes of vice and wretchedness. In this view of the subject, it may be asserted that what is called slavery, is, in reality, a political institution, essential to the peace, safety, and prosperity of those States of the Union in which it exists. Without, then, controverting the wisdom and humanity of the policy of Great Britain, so far as her own possessions are concerned, it may be safely affirmed, without reference to the means by which it would be effected, that, could she succeed in accomplishing in the United States, what she avows it to be her desire, and the object of her constant exertions to effect throughout the world, so far from being wise or humane, she would involve in the greatest calamity the whole country, and especially the race which it is the avowed object of her exertions to benefit.

## 3 | The Nationalistic Defense of Texas Annexation, April 1844 *

Texas fused within the Democratic party two powerful streams of agrarian expansionism, one Southern and sectional in outlook, the other Western and national in sentiment. The latter faction, led by such men as Lewis Cass of Michigan and Stephen A. Douglas of Illinois, eventually captured control of the issue and rode it into power. For them the burden of argument lay in convincing the nation that Texas annexation would serve the entire nation, not merely the South, and that expansion would strengthen rather than undermine the American constitutional system. Perhaps no single document illustrated better the nationalist appeal for Texas annexation than did the following article, which appeared in the *Democratic Review* of April 1844.

ε

. . . That Texas is to be, sooner or later, included in the Union, we have long—nay, ever since the battle of San Jacinto—regarded as an event already indelibly inscribed in the book of future, fate and necessity. The questions of time and mode we have looked upon as comparatively of minor moment. As for the latter, the question of *mode*—even if the case had presented any serious obstacle of political formality, he has read all history in vain who may yet imagine that in the larger transactions of nations there is ever much difficulty about a *way* when there is any very earnest *will* to find one. And as for the former question,

* "The Texas Question," *Democratic Review*, XIV (April 1944), 423, 428–30.

that of *time*, it has all along been manifest that the time would be on the day when the South should arouse itself to a combined and determined demand for the reception of Texas into the Confederation; and when that just jealousy of English power and English ambition on our Continent, which is a strong pervading sentiment throughout all the sections of the Union, should become sufficiently alarmed, to counter-balance the repugnance with which the first suggestion of the proposition would be received by the North. These two conditions would probably be pretty nearly coincident, mutually connected as they indeed are with each other. Their conjunction must fix the date of the inevitably future annexation;—that the conjunction is now close at hand, if not already arrived, the signs are neither few nor equivocal. . . .

It is very certain that the reasons which caused the settled opposition of Jefferson and Madison to any relinquishment of Texas, and which, after that unlucky mistake, caused the earnest desire of all the succeeding administrations to retrace and retrieve it, by getting back the lost territory by treaty with Mexico, even though it should be at the expense of a liberal price, have not ceased to exist. This is no new thing. It is no sudden experiment of the South, as it is alleged, to recruit a political strength felt to be failing before the rapid growth and extension of the free States. It is simply the revival of an old question, established by the emphatic authority of many of the elder and the most eminent sages of the Republic, as one of high national importance, and which has for a few past years been kept in abeyance or temporary suspension only by a peculiar state of circumstances. Whether the proper period for its revival has arrived, may perhaps be a subject of difference of opinion. Those who regard the length of time for which Texas has maintained her independence, together with the manifest and utter hopelessness of any possible reconquest by Mexico, as now sufficient to justify disregard of the nominal rights still absurdly pretended by the latter, may certainly claim that the proper period is fully mature. And when to those considerations is added that of the danger of England's acquiring the possession of, or a dominant control over, the young State, we can feel no surprise at the earnestness of their interest in the prompt settlement of the question. Mr. Tyler has seen fit to precipitate it, in a manner much more eager than dignified, to a point which now compels an early and decisive action upon it. What may have been his personal motives in thus arguing it, we little care to inquire. Perhaps they were entirely disinterested and upright,—perhaps, in the forlorn position to which his administration had sunk, he was prompted by a desire, according to the common phrase, to make "political capital" for himself,—perhaps, as in the greater proportion of men's actions, his motives were a tangled web of the good and the evil. At any rate the thing is done; the question is forced upon us; it must be fully met, and it may as well be settled promptly and quietly, on the basis to which it is perfectly palpable that it must come at last.

The two common objections against the Annexation have but little real weight,—namely, that of unwieldy and dangerous extension of territory, and that of its alleged bearing upon the institution of Slavery. To the first a sufficient answer might be found in the peculiar reasons . . . of geographical and political fitness, if not necessity. But independently of these—independently, too, of those derived from the worse evils of an English possession,—independently of the commercial advantages to the rest of the Union involved in the measure—independently of the boundless facilities for smuggling, by which Texas could be made the avenue for the supply of the whole West with foreign goods—independently of the evils of a hostile commercial rivalry between two contiguous countries so similar in climate, soil, productions and population, instead of that unity of nationality and policy, in all respects properly befitting them,—independently of all these reasons, we say, the objection has no force for us. Our system of government is one which, rightly administered,—administered on the principles of the State-Rights theory—will bear indefinite extension; nor do we doubt but that in the fulness of time it is destined to embrace within its wide sweep every habitable square inch of the continent. Our rapid ratio of increase in population, together with that *diffusiveness* which appears to be a principle of our national character, and which will never permit our fast multiplying millions to confine themselves within territorial limits so long as their movement remains unchecked by any great natural barriers of division, insures the arrival of a not very distant day that shall witness this consummation.

And as for what may be termed the Anti-Slavery objection, this has no greater force that the other. The question of slavery is not a federal or national, but a local question. The Abolition movement has erroneously assumed for it the former character, and has chosen the federal government as the point or avenue of attack against the institution. Hence the desire of those whose conscientious views of duty make them participators in that movement, to strengthen the ascendency of the Free States in the general government; and on the other hand that of the South to maintain as long as possible the equilibrium of which it has always been so jealous. The one hopes, and the other fears, that the federal government will fall under the control of the Abolition party, who are urging with zeal and confidence the propagandism which they expect to extend successfully over all the Free States. For ourselves, we repeat that we do not regard the question as a *federal* but as a *local* one—not as a political but a moral and economical one, the decision of which must rest, voluntarily, with the Slave States themselves. This balance of political power between the two sections, we regard as of little consequence. The controlling predominance of the Free States in the national government, even supposing it to be in the hands of the Abolition party itself, though it might dissolve the Union, would not dissolve the bonds of slavery within the Slave States. Nor, on the other hand, would that institution be prolonged by the reverse state of things. The eventual settlement of that unhappy question will be through the operation of much deeper and broader influences than any of these mistaken and injurious political efforts. . . .

But while we thus assent to the reception of Texas into the Union, seeing little force in the objections urged against it, and viewing it as a necessary political and geographical fact, let us not be supposed willing to witness its adoption in the violent and hasty manner in which Mr. Tyler, without regard either to the claims of Mexico, or to political decency, appears to have urged it on. It is far too important a matter to be thus sprung upon us, and hurried summarily into effect by a Vice-President and Senate, in the form of a treaty, without consultation with the Representatives of the People, and before time or opportunity for any popular discussion of the question and the formation of any distinct public opinion on the subject. That such process of discussion would result in general acquiescence, we have little doubt, but the precedent would be altogether too dangerous to dispense with the former in a confident reliance upon the latter.

Nor ought the Annexation to be made without the consent of Mexico, or her recognition of the independence of her successfully revolted province. We must avoid even the appearance of evil. It is not enough that we may be abundantly certain that Mexico can never again even hope to shake the established independence of Texas. The nominal, theoretical right is still asserted, which we cannot disregard without incurring a just liability to declaration of war by Mexico. . . .

## 4 | Joshua Giddings's Dual Argument Against the Annexation of Texas, May 1844 *

Texas annexation posed a special threat to both the conservative and abolitionist elements within the Whig party. For twenty years the most ardent opposition to the Whig doctrines of high tariffs and internal improvements had come from Southern Democratic leadership. The Whig and abolitionist forces of the North thus combined to oppose annexation on two counts: the expansion of slavery and the extension of Democratic power. Philip Hone, the New York merchant, detected clearly why the Texas issue was rocking the Republic to its foundations. Southern demagogues, he recorded in his diary, were promoting their personal objectives and those of the South by solidifying their power through the addition of four or five slave states (to be carved out of Texas.) It was left for Joshua Giddings, Ohio abolitionist and Whig, to demonstrate the dual nature of the expansionist conflict in American politics, and nowhere did he do so with more vehemence than in his speech before the House of Representatives on May 21, 1844.

𝄢

. . . The President and his cabinet, and the southern democrats, aver that this nation shall take upon itself the support and perpetuation of slavery in Texas, and of the slave trade between our slave-breeding States and the people of that government. They urge that our army and navy shall be employed, and our national energies put forth; our character disgraced before the civilized

* *Congressional Globe,* 28th Congress, 1st Sess., Appendix, 704–5, 707.

world, in order to attain that object. They insist that we shall violate our treaty stipulations with Mexico; that we shall abandon our principles in favor of human liberty; acknowledge ourselves a nation of political hypocrites; bring dishonor upon the memory of our revolutionary patriots; turn traitors to the sacred cause of freedom; and wage an unceasing war upon humanity itself. These are the matters urged on one side, and objected to by the other. This is the issue to be determined by the people—by the electors of the North and of the South, of the East and of the West. On this issue the whigs, the democrats, and liberty men are to pass judgment.

It is true that the annexation of Texas to these United States is brought forward as the proposed means by which we may extend and perpetuate slavery, and continue the slave trade; but that object is merely collateral to the great and ulterior design of supporting slavery and the slave trade. The object and purpose for which it is now sought to annex Texas to the United States is clearly and unequivocally set forth in the official correspondence between the Secretary of State and Mr. Everett, our minister at the court of St. James; between said Secretary and our "charge de affaires" in Texas, and between him and the British minister resident in this city. In every letter of that correspondence the object is frankly avowed, without any apparent delicacy or attempt at concealment. The same object of maintaining the slave trade between the slave-breeding States of this Union and Texas, and the perpetuating slavery in Texas, is the avowed object of nearly every democratic paper south of Mason and Dixon's line, by nearly every address upon that subject, and by the proceedings of nearly all the public meetings held in the slave States for the purpose of promoting the cause of annexation. . . .

And now what say our democrats of New England, and New York, and Ohio? I call upon them to come forth and show their colors; play the man, meet the issue, and let us have no dodging. We shall soon return to our constituents, and must meet this question before the people. Will the gentleman from Indiana then stand forth frankly and say to the democrats of his district "you must work hard, and live cheap, and be economical, for we have agreed to pay the debts of Texas, and every laboring man in the nation must contribute a portion of his earnings?" And then suppose the honest farmer, in the true Yankee fashion, should inquire for the benefits which this nation is to derive from the payment of this twenty millions of Texas debts; will that gentleman frankly and boldly declare to him, that, by paying that amount of money, we have established true democratic slavery in Texas, and have secured a first rate market for the democratic slave dealers of the South? . . .

It is well known, Mr. Chairman, that, since the formation of this confederacy, there has long been a supposed conflict between the interests of free labor and of slave labor, between the southern and northern States. I do not say that the conflict is real; I only say that in the minds of the people, both north and south, and in this hall, such conflict exists. This supposed conflict has given rise to difference of policy in our national councils. I refer to the tariff in particular, as being a favorite measure of the North, while free trade is advocated by the South. I refer also to our harbor improvements, and the improvement of our river navigation, as another measure in which the northwest and west have felt great interest and much anxiety, and to which the south have been constantly opposed. But so equally balanced has been the political power between these opposing interests, that for five years past our lake commerce has been entirely abandoned; and such were the deficits of the tariff, that for many years our revenues were unequal to the support of government. Time eventually gave the friends of northern interests power to amend the tariff, and, by the fixed order of nature's law, our population at the north has increased so much faster than it has in the slave States, that under the late census, the North and West now hold the balance of political power; and at the present session we have passed a bill for the protection of our lake and river commerce, which now awaits the action of the Senate, and will soon become a law. But let us admit Texas, and we shall place the balance of power in the hands of the Texians themselves. They, with the southern states, will then be held at the will of the Texian advocates of free trade. Are our friends of the north prepared to deliver over this great national policy to the people of Texas? Are the liberty-loving democrats of Pennsylvania ready to give up our tariff?—to strike off all protection from the articles of iron, and coal, and other productions of the State, in order to purchase a slave market for their neighbors, who, in the words of Thomas Jefferson Randolph, "breed men for the market like oxen for the shambles?" . . .

And I appeal to the whole population of the western States—of all classes and conditions, and political parties—to say whether they are willing to give up their harbor improvements, and the improvement of our river navigation, for the purpose of improving the southern slave trade, and of perpetuating slavery in Texas? What say my democratic colleagues on this point—will they go it? Will the democracy of Ohio march up to that point with firm and unflinching step? I think not. If they do, they had better settle their political affairs, and make their political bequests before election, or they will take their departure from the political world unprepared. . . .

Mr. Chairman, we at this moment appear before the civilized world in the disgraceful attitude of making war upon Mexico, an unoffending nation, in the obvious violation of our treaty stipulations and our national faith solemnly pledged, for the purpose of extending slavery and perpetuating the slave trade. And I am exceedingly desirous of knowing whether any political party, or any respectable portion of any political party, intend to support and maintain this policy? What say our democratic friends? Has the gentleman from Indiana [Mr. Owen] spoken the sentiments of his party? Are the democrats of our free States prepared to follow his lead? Will they enter the field with "democracy and slavery, Texas and the slave-trade," inscribed upon their banners? If so, I ask them to come forth boldly, unfurl your banners, not to the breeze, but to that whirlwind of indignation which shall scatter you to the four winds of heaven, and which will leave no other memorial of you than the disgraceful cause that shall have exterminated your party. But, sir, I have too much respect for gentlemen of that party in our free States to indulge apprehensions of this kind. I hope, on the contrary, to see them treating this odious, this treasonable proposition, with that scorn and contempt which it justly merits. . . .

. . . I will now proceed to examine the proposed means of effecting the permanent establishment of slavery in Texas, and the slave trade between our slave States and the people of that government. To effect these objects the President proposes to annex Texas to the Union of these States. I, for one, deny the constitutional power of this government to amalgamate the political destinies of this people with those of Texas or any other foreign government. . . . The ability to purchase territory without inhabitants is one thing; but to annex a foreign government—that is, the people of a foreign government, with their habits, their moral and political views—is another and a different subject. . . .

The old thirteen States had each borne a portion of the burdens, and had shared in the dangers, of the revolution. Their people understood the objects for which they had contended. And I should like to find the man who will say, that he really believes the framers of that instrument intended to give authority to the federal government to annex the people of these States to Mexico, or to Brazil, or to Great Britain, by which our institutions would be subverted, and all the blood and treasure expended in the revolution would be lost to posterity? . . . Would the descendants of the pilgrim fathers—of those who had been driven from the land of their nativity by oppression, and who encountered the dangers of the sea, and sought freedom in the new world, amid the perils that awaited them; who, in the cabin of the Mayflower, while speeding her way from the land of oppression, concocted and arranged the first code of American popular government, and who carried it into practical operation at Plymouth, and inculcated its principles into the minds of their children? Would the descendants of those pilgrim heroes, reared and educated in the religious and political faith of their fathers, and who had manifested their unmitigated hatred of oppression, and their own devotion to the doctrines of civil liberty at Concord, at Lexington, at Bunker's hill, and on all the glorious battlefields of the revolution—would they have been likely to enter into any compact by which this federal government might transfer them or their descendants to the dominion of Texas, or Mexico, or Brazil, or to England itself? Sir, the assertion that such powers exist in the constitution is a reproach upon the New England character; it is offensive to New England feeling, an imputation upon New England honor; it is an insult to the common feelings of our people, and must inevitably call forth a corresponding indignation in the breast of every true son of the North.

But, Mr. Chairman, by adopting our federal constitution, a union was voluntarily formed of the old thirteen States. This was the act of each State; for each determined for itself upon the propriety of adopting the constitution. The compact made provisions for admitting by act of Congress new States, to be formed out of the territory included within the boundaries dividing our government from foreign nations. That union, formed by the wisdom of our fathers, and consecrated by the blood and suffering which had marked their recent struggle for independence we love and cherish. To it we shall adhere in all of its stipulations. We regard it as the sanctuary of American liberty. We shall defend it, if necessary, with our treasure and our lives. But we shall not surrender this Union, sanctioned and sanctified by half a century of national prosperity, in order to try a new union, and that, too, with slaveholding Texas! Sir, every school boy must see, that to form a new union with any foreign power, would be, *ipso facto,* a dissolution of our present Union. Now, I would say to an imbecile President, and a demented cabinet, that they have not the power to form a union between our people of the free States and Texas. If such a union be ever formed, it will be the voluntary acts of the people of our States and those of Texas. The President and his cabinet may enter into as many treaties as they please, and make such stipulations as they please, and form such unions for themselves as they please—we shall adhere to our present Union. If they wish to leave this Union and go to Texas, I, for one, will bid them "God speed." And if any of our southern sister States are desirous of leaving our present Union to form a new compact with Texas, let them say so with generous frankness. But if northern States prefer adhering to our present Union, and refuse to follow them into such new confederacy, do not let them attempt to charge us with dissolving the Union. I regret that any northern man should speak of dissolving the Union, if Texas be annexed. Such expressions are an abuse of language. The act of uniting with Texas would itself be the dissolution; and refusal to unite with that government would be to maintain the present Union. . . .

## 5 | The Western Claim to the Oregon Question, March 1844 *

Throughout 1844, Congress was locked in a bitter struggle for control of Oregon policy. Congressmen from the Middle West, demanding no less than a settlement on the line of 50° 40′, claimed Oregon as an issue of vital concern to the Western states. It was a question, declared John C. McClernand of Illinois, "of border safety, of territorial limits, and of relative political . . . influence, wealth, and power." Westerners in speech after speech declared that the West would experience no security until the British were removed from the Oregon country. Perhaps no Western representative stated the case for his region in more sectional terms than did Andrew Kennedy of Indiana in March 1844.

🖎

MR. CHAIRMAN: The inquiry has been made, What are the feelings of the western people on this subject? It is not my intention to detain the committee but a few moments; but, coming from that section, I feel bound to respond to this inquiry. Mr. Chairman, the western people believe that this Oregon country belongs to the United States; and so believing, they expect to occupy it. We were taught to believe that the territory in dispute between this Government and

* *Congressional Globe,* 28th Congress, 1st Sess., Appendix, 264-5.

Great Britain, on our northeastern boundary, was ours, and the West was pre-pared to stand by the State of Maine, in whose boundary it fell, in her assertion of her right thereto. In our primary assemblies, in our conventions and legis-lative halls, we pledged ourselves so to do; and as long as Maine stood up to her own rights, we stood ready to back her to the death. But, when Maine con-sented to be dismembered, we yielded—with a wry face, I admit; but still we submitted; supposing it was her business rather than ours. But, sir, if you suppose that the West will yield one acre—ay, one inch—of our northwestern territory, as long as there is a man left to defend it, then, sir, you or I have mistaken the character of that western people, who have driven the red man before them like the morning mist before the rays of a clear, cloudless sun. We have no objection to your negotiating, if you will negotiate speedily. But these negotiations must be made with the full, plain, and distinct understanding that not one inch of what is ours is to be given away, either with or without equivalents. This, sir, is what I take to be western feeling on this subject. But if any government on God's footstool presumes to make the conditions of our occupying that territory a war, or the surrendering one acre of that territory the conditions of the peace—though that acre might be as poor as the sandy deserts of Arabia, and as distant as the North Pole—we take war to the knife, and the knife to the hilt—infinitely preferring extermination to national dishonor. . . .

Mr. Chairman, I have spoken of what I have good reason to believe the feel-ings of almost the entire people of the West. It is the spontaneous feeling of patriotism which burns in the bosoms of the whole western people, whigs and democrats. But let no man be deceived as to what will be the effect of the avowal which I dread, and the action for which I now look by the whigs of this House and the Senate. Let them, as a party, take the stand which I fear they will, and the consequence will be, to some extent, to make it a party question; and, although you will not be able to smother the flame in the bosoms of western whigs now in favor of it, yet many are the tongues you will stop. . . . Would to God, Mr. Chairman, that it might turn out that our western people could and would break loose from these miserable party shackles with which the leaders hope to bind them to this modern Juggernaut, at the price of the loss of this fair heritage. And it may be so. For my country's glory, I will hope and believe that it will. I will hope to see their patriotism rise like a whirlwind at this effort to make what should be a national question, a party one. God grant that it may be so. If it should, I tell those men who are playing this political game, that they are trampling on the verge of a volcano. If they once pull the party cords so tight as to snap them, woe be to the political wireworkers who attempt to turn the patriotism of our western people into the channel of promo-tion to a political chief at the expense of their country! The storm of indigna-tion which will overtake them will be as terrible as one of those wonderful tornadoes, which sometimes leave our vast forests a trackless waste of mangled ruins.

# 6 | Robert Winthrop on the Commercial Interest in Oregon, March 1844 *

Eastern Whigs challenged the Western Democrats for control of Oregon policy, claiming that it was a commercial question, national in scope, and not a Western question at all. The East, with its specific, if limited, goal of gaining access to the Strait of Fuca and Puget Sound, had an equal right to be heard on the Oregon question. No one emphasized the commercial aspect of the issue with more clarity than Robert Winthrop of Massachusetts in his speech before the House of Representatives on March 18, 1844. Winthrop could force an agreement from Democrats on the commercial value of Oregon, but he could not establish a bipartisan approach in Congress to the question of the Far Northwest. Western Democrats were in quest of votes, and the broad avenue of nationalism that led to "54–40" could not be closed. The Whigs and their Democratic allies who believed that the Oregon waterways comprised the limits of the American interest in Oregon as well as a goal achievable through diplomacy alone, condemned as unnecessarily provocative the tendency of Western Democrats to force the issue of the whole of Oregon on Britain, for this was an objective achievable only through war. The Whigs preferred that the Oregon question remain within the jurisdiction of Executive decision where it might be resolved by diplomacy alone. They challenged, therefore, the very right of Congress to debate the question of Oregon at all.

🖎

. . . It has been often said that the question about Oregon is a western question; and a disposition has been manifested to charge hostility to western interests and western rights upon all who are not ready to draw the sword, without further delay, in defence of this territory. I deny this position altogether. It is a national question. It is a question for the whole country. The North have as much interest in it as the West, and as much right to be heard upon it: indeed, there are some views in which it is more a northern than a western question. I cannot forget that the American claim to Oregon, so far as it rests upon discovery, dates back to Massachusetts adventure and Boston enterprise. It was a Boston ships which gave its name to the Columbia river. It was Captain Robert Gray, of Boston, who first discovered that river. It was the Hancock and the Adams of Massachusetts—the proscribed patriots of the revolution—whose names were inscribed on those remote capes. And if we turn from the early history of Oregon to its present importance, and to the immediate interests which are involved in its possession, the North will be found no less prominently concerned in the question. The great present value of this Territory has relation to the commerce and navigation of the Pacific ocean. The whale fishery of this country requires safe stations and harbors on the Northwest coast. And

* Congressional Globe, 28th Congress, 1st Sess., Appendix, 318–19.

by what part of the nation is this fishery carried on? Why, sir, the State of Massachusetts owns nine-tenths of all the whale ships of the United States. The single town of New Bedford (the residence of my honorable friend Mr. Grinnell) sends out 92,000, out of a little more than 130,000, tons of the American shipping employed in this business; and three other towns in the same district employ 31,170 tons of the remainder. So far, then, as the whaling interest is to be regarded, the Oregon question is emphatically a Massachusetts question. I feel bound to add, however, that the whole coast of Oregon can hardly furnish one really good harbor. South of the forty-ninth degree of latitude, (a boundary which we have once offered to compromise upon,) there is not one which a ship can get safely into or out of, during three-quarters of the year. The harbor of San Francisco, in northern California, would be worth the whole Territory of Oregon to the whaling fleet of the nation.

A mere western interest! Sir, I doubt whether the West has a particle of real interest in the possession of Oregon. It may have an interest—a momentary, seeming, delusive interest—in a war for Oregon. Doubtless, the western States might reap a rich harvest of spoils in the prosecution of such a war. Doubtless, there would be fat contracts of all sorts growing out of such a contest, which would enure to their peculiar advantage. Doubtless, the characteristic spirit of the western people—that spirit of restless adventure, and roving enterprise, and daring conflict, which the honorable gentleman has just eulogized—would find ample room and verge enough for its indulgence, even to satiety, in such a campaign. Whether that spirit, indomitable as it is in any ordinary encounter, would not be found stumbling upon the dark mountains, or fainting in the dreary valleys, or quenched beneath the perpetual snows which nature has opposed to the passage to this disputed territory, remains to be seen. A march to Oregon, I am inclined to believe, would take the courage out of not a few who now believe themselves incapable of fatigue or fear. But suppose the war were over, successfully over, and Oregon ours: what interest, let me ask—what real, substantial, permanent interest—would the West have in its possession? Are our western brethren straitened for elbow-room, or likely to be for a thousand years? Have they not too much land for their own advantage already? I verily believe that, if land were only half as abundant and half as cheap as it is, the prosperity of the West would be doubled. . . .

. . . The Oregon question . . . , Mr. Chairman, as now presented to us, is not a question of interest, but of right; not a question as to the ultimate reach of our federal union, but as to the existing extent of our territorial title. Upon this point I shall say little. An argument to this House in favor of our title to Oregon, would be words thrown away. If any man can convince the British government that the territory is ours, his labor will be well employed, and the sooner he sets about it the better. But we are convinced already. For myself, certainly, I believe that we have a good title to the whole twelve degrees of latitude. I believe it, not merely because it is the part of patriotism to believe one's own country in the right, but because I am unable to resist the conclusions to that effect, to which an examination of the evidence and the authorities have brought me. In saying this, however, I would by no means be understood to concur in the idea which has recently been advanced in some quarters, that our title is of such a character that we are authorized to decline all negotiation on the subject. Why, sir, with what face can we take such a stand, with the history of this question before us and before the world? Nothing to negotiate about! Has not every administration of our government, since we had a government to be administered, treated this as an open question? Have we not at one time expressly offered to abandon all pretension to five-twelfths of the Territory, and to allow our boundary line to follow the forty-ninth degree of latitude? Have we not united a convention of joint occupancy for thirty years, in order to keep it an open question? What, pretence have we for planting ourselves in our presumed rights at this late day, and for shutting our ears to all overtures of negotiation, and all assertion or argument of the rights of others? None; none whatever. Such a course would subject us to the just reproach and scorn of the civilized world. . . .

## 7 | William Sturgis's Lecture on the Commercial Importance of Oregon, January 1845 *

William Sturgis, at one time New England's leading merchant in the California hide trade and in 1845 still actively a member of Boston's commercial aristocracy, was as knowledgable as any other United States citizen on the question of American interests along the Pacific coast. His intense activity in Pacific trade, covering at least three decades, had focused his attention on ports and not on land. In his famous lecture to the citizens of Boston in January 1845, Sturgis admitted that the Willamette Valley of Oregon was both attractive and productive, but he added that he had not heard of lands in Oregon superior to millions of uncultivated acres east of the Rocky Mountains. Sturgis indicated what ports in Oregon would be required to assure the nation's future position in the commerce of the Orient. He agreed with conservative members of Congress that a settlement at the 49th parallel, with the granting of Vancouver Island to the British, would secure the necessary maritime objectives of the United States in Oregon and still not deny to England the navigation of Fuca Strait, a right which she would not relinquish without war.

. . . The people of this country are both covetous and ambitious in regard to territory. They covet and are ready to grasp at all that lies upon their borders,

* William Sturgis, *The Oregon Question: Substance of a Lecture Before the Mercantile Library Association, Delivered January 22, 1845* (Boston, 1845), 23–32.

and are ambitious of extending their empire from sea to sea—from the shores of the Atlantic to the borders of the Pacific. I do not participate in this feeling, and have little sympathy with those who cherish it. Settlements scattered over a vast extent of territory—very likely to be badly governed in time of peace, and certain to present remote and exposed points to be defended in time of war—will not, in my belief, add to the power or promote the prosperity of the United States. The true policy of the country is tersely and forcibly expressed by that veteran statesman, Andrew Jackson, in a letter to President Monroe: "Concentrate our population, confine our frontier to proper limits, until our country, to those limits, is filled with a dense population. It is the denseness of our population that gives strength and security to our frontier." . . .

I will add, as my own views, that rather than have new States formed beyond the Rocky Mountains, to be added to our present Union, it would be a lesser evil, so far as that Union is concerned, if the unoccupied portion of the Oregon Territory should sink into Symmes's Hole, leaving the western base of those Mountains and the borders of the Pacific Ocean one and the same. But as this consummation—however devoutly it may be wished—can hardly be expected, I deem it very desirable that the question of boundary should be speedily adjusted, and that the limits and the rights of each party be so clearly established and defined as to prevent all danger of collision hereafter. . . . [A]nd it seems to me that each party will attain their object, and justice be done to both, by adopting as the boundary a continuation of the parallel of 49° across the Rocky Mountains, to tide-water, say to the middle of the "Gulf of Georgia;" thence by the northernmost navigable passage (not north of 49°) to the Straits of Juan de Fuca, and down the middle of these Straits to the Pacific Ocean; the navigation of the Gulf of Georgia and the Straits of Juan de Fuca to be forever free to both parties—all the islands and other territory lying South and East of this line to belong to the United States, and all North and West to Great Britain. By this arrangement we should yield to Great Britain the portion of Quadra and Vancouver's Island that lies South of Latitude 49°, which, in a territorial point of view, is of too little importance to deserve a moment's consideration; and both parties would secure, for a considerable extent, a well-defined natural boundary, about which there could hereafter be no doubt or dispute. Will Great Britain accede to this? I think she will. Up to the close of the last negotiation, in 1827, the free navigation of the Columbia was declared to be indispensable to Great Britain, by the British Commissioners; but subsequent developments will probably render the British less pertinacious upon this point. The "summary" presented by the Commissioners in 1827, shows that the Columbia was then supposed to be the most convenient—in fact the only—navigable channel of communication between the Ocean and most of the numerous establishments of the Hudson Bay Company, West of the Rocky Mountains. Within a few years past, however, several rivers, of considerable magnitude, have been explored from the interior to the seas into which they empty, North of Latitude 49°. . . . All these would be within the British territory, or are so situated that the British, by their Convention with Russia, would have the right of navigating them; and they would afford convenient communication with most of their establishments

North of 49°; and if this adjustment should be made they would retain none South of that line. . . . But Great Britain will not relinquish the right to the free navigation and use of the Straits of Juan de Fuca if she retains the territory North of 49°. The use of these Straits would, in fact, be indispensable to her, for through them is the only convenient access to a considerable portion of this territory. The Strait of Juan de Fuca is about three leagues wide at its entrance, within which the width increases. Near its head are numerous islands, and some of the finest harbors in the world. "Admiralty Inlet" branches off to the South, and runs towards the main stream of the Columbia to the Latitude of 47°, and all these islands, harbors and inlets would be within our limits. This Strait, with all its branches, being easy of access, safe, and navigable at all seasons and in any weather, while the mouth of the Columbia is at all times dangerous to enter, and for a considerable part of the year almost inaccessible, I cannot but think that the Strait will ultimately be the great channel through which will pass most of the products of the whole region drained by the Columbia and its branches—both that part of it which would fall to us in the proposed division, and a considerable portion of that which would fall to Great Britain, lying North of 49°.

Very different and conflicting representations have been made by different writers in regard to the general aspect of the whole territory, and its adaptation to agricultural purposes: some have described it as a perfect paradise, while by others it has been represented as wild and sterile. According to my observation both have exaggerated. . . . South of the parallel of 49°, near the borders of Admiralty Inlet and Puget's Sound, and in the valley of the Wallammette, or Multnomah River, which empties into the Columbia, and upon the banks of which the principal settlements of emigrants from the United States have been made, and in some other places, the appearance of the country is attractive, the soil good, and well adapted to agricultural purposes; and so likewise is the eastern side of Queen Charlotte's Islands, and some other places North of 49°. But I have neither seen nor heard of lands in any part of this territory that are superior to the millions upon millions of uncultivated acres within the limits of the United States, on this side of the Rocky Mountains; and I doubt if those who are dissatisfied with the state of things eastward of these mountains, will find their condition much improved by emigration to the Oregon Territory. . . .

I have thus endeavored to give you the material facts in relation to our claim to territory West of the Rocky Mountains, and to the present state of the dispute with Great Britain in relation to it. There is evidently a lamentable ignorance upon the subject, both among those who call loudly for action and those whose position gives them the power to act; and it seems to me that many, both in and out of Congress, who are most clamorous for taking immediate possession of the "whole Territory of Oregon," know little if anything about the real merits of the question. . . . Can any man in his sober senses believe that Great Britain will stand tamely by and see such a measure carried out? She has repeatedly claimed and maintained rights in this territory before the whole civilized world —she has enjoyed these rights, and exercised undisturbed authority within the disputed limits, nearly half a century. . . . There are, I doubt not, in some parts of the Union, political aspirants and political demagogues—men of desper-

ate fortunes—who believe that any change would, to them, be for the better, and
therefore desire to provoke a war with Great Britain, reckless of consequences to
the country so long as their individual interests are promoted. But I hope that
the number of such is small, and trust that their counsels will not be listened
to. This controversy may easily be made the pretext for a war with Great Britain,
if war is desired; but I repeat that it is eminently one to be settled by negocia-
tion. If this cannot be done, let no other steps be taken at present. The British
have now a decided superiority in that quarter, but emigration is constantly
changing the relative situation of the parties in favor of the United States; and
a few years hence she will be better able to support her pretensions by force
than she is at the present time. But it is idle to speak of force. A resort to it
can never be necessary. Let the able negociators, who now have this matter in
charge, examine it with reference solely to its own merits,—regardless of the
clamors of ignorance, or the suggestions of selfishness,—and let them discuss it
with the manly frankness and concilatory spirit that guided the distinguished
diplomatists who settled the Northeastern boundary, and it can scarcely fail to
be adjusted to the satisfaction of a vast majority of the intelligent people of both
nations. . . .

# 8 | James K. Polk and the American Interest in Oregon, July 1845 *

James K. Polk, a Tennessee Democrat, was the successful candidate of a party
that had campaigned in 1844 for the whole of Oregon. Yet as President his views
regarding the proper disposal of the Oregon question coincided with those of
Winthrop, Sturgis, and other spokesmen for Boston's commercial interests.
That he also viewed the diplomatic issues raised by the Far Northwest in terms
of ports, not land, was apparent from the lengthy dispatch of July 12, 1845, in
which his Secretary of State, James Buchanan, offered Britain a compromise of
the Oregon boundary based on an equitable distribution of ports.

‰

   Although the President does not intend to transfer the Oregon negotiation
from Washington to London, yet, as Her Britannic Majesty's Ministers will
doubtless afford you frequent opportunities of conversing upon the subject, it is
proper that you should be well informed of the present state of the question.
For this purpose it is necessary to furnish you with a brief historical sketch of

* Buchanan to Louis McLane, July 12, 1845, *The Works of James Buchanan,* John
Bassett Moore, ed. (Philadelphia, 1909), VI: 186–94.

the propositions for its adjustment which have been heretofore made and rejected by the respective Governments.

The first negotiation was that of 1818, which terminated in the convention of the 20th October of that year. It was conducted by Messrs. Gallatin and Rush, as American Plenipotentiaries, in obedience to instructions from Mr. Adams, then Secretary of State, under Mr. Monroe's administration. Our Plenipotentiaries inform us that they did not, on that occasion, "assert that the United States had a perfect right to the country; but insisted that their claim was at least good against Great Britain." They, therefore, offered to compromise by adopting the parallel of 49° as the dividing line between the two countries, and by surrendering to Great Britain the free navigation of the rivers (the Columbia of course included) which might be intersected by this line. The British Plenipotentiaries, (Messrs. Robinson and Goulburn) in answer, "did not make any formal proposition for a boundary; but intimated that the river itself was the most convenient that could be adopted, and that they would not agree to any that did not give them the harbor at the mouth of the river in common with the United States." But although they did not propose a permanent boundary, they did make a most extraordinary proposition to the American Plenipotentiaries, which was instantly and properly rejected. This was no less in effect than that the United States should surrender to Great Britain the exclusive sovereignty over the whole territory north of 49°, whilst that portion of it which lies between the 45th and the 49th parallels, embracing the mouth, and nearly the whole course of the Columbia river, should "be free and open to the subjects and citizens of the two States respectively, for the purpose of trade and commerce," reserving the claims of the respective parties, not to the whole territory, but to this section of it merely.

This negotiation resulted in the adoption of the third article of the convention of the 20th October, 1818, under which the United States so far yielded to the claims of Great Britain as to agree that the whole territory should "be free and open for the term of ten years from the date of the signature of the present convention, to the vessels, citizens, and subjects of the two Powers."

The second negotiation on this subject, during the administration of Mr. Monroe, was conducted in 1824 by Mr. Rush as the American Plenipotentiary, under the instructions of Mr. Adams. In the meantime the United States had acquired the Spanish title, embracing the whole territory in dispute, under the Florida treaty of the 22d February, 1819; and Mr. Monroe had made his celebrated declaration to the world that the American continent should no longer be subject to colonization. Notwithstanding this change in the relative position of the parties, Mr. Monroe, anxious to settle the conflicting claims of Russia, Great Britain, and the United States to the territory on the Northwest Coast of America, and knowing that this could only be done by compromise, authorized Mr. Rush, through the instructions from Mr. Adams, dated the 22d July, 1823, "with a view to draw a definite line of demarcation for the future, to stipulate that no settlement shall be made on the Northwest Coast or on any of the islands thereto adjoining, by Russian subjects, south of latitude 55; by citizens of the

United States north of latitude 51°, or by British subjects either south of 51 or north of 55. I mention, (says Mr. Adams,) the latitude of 51 as the bound within which we are willing to limit the future settlement of the United States because it is not to be doubted that the Columbia river branches as far north as 51." "As, however, the line already runs in latitude 49° to the Stony Mountains, should it be earnestly insisted upon by Great Britain, we will consent to carry it in continuance on the same parallel to the sea."

Mr. Rush, with great ability, attempted to execute his instructions. He first proposed 51°, and afterwards 49°; but in vain. . . .

The third negotiation in this subject took place in 1826–'7, during the administration of Mr. Adams, and was conducted by Mr. Gallatin, as American Plenipotentiary, under instructions from Mr. Clay, then Secretary of State. . . .

The next notice of this question will be found under the administration of General Jackson. It is contained in the instructions of Mr. Livingston to Mr. Van Buren, dated on the 1st August, 1831, with a copy of which, so far as they relate to this subject, you shall be furnished. From this you will perceive that General Jackson's administration, so far from objecting to the occupation of the whole territory by the British in common with ourselves, were entirely satisfied to suffer this state of things to continue. . . .

From the 1st of August, 1831, the date of Mr. Livingston's instructions to Mr. Van Buren, until the 9th of October, 1843, no further notice of the Oregon question was taken in any instructions from this Department. On that day, Mr. Upshur, then the Secretary of State under Mr. Tyler's administration, addressed instructions to Mr. Everett on the subject. Following in the course of compromise pointed out by his predecessors, Mr. Upshur says: "The offer of the 49th parallel of latitude, although it has once been rejected, may be again tendered, together with the right of navigating the Columbia, upon equitable terms. . . .

Next came the existing negotiation, which the President found pending on his accession to office.

This negotiation, like all which had preceded it, was based upon the principle of compromising the claims of the parties and not of demanding the whole territory for the United States. The first protocol signed by Messrs. Calhoun and Pakenham, on the 23d August last, states that it was instituted "to treat of the respective claims of the two countries to the Oregon territory with the view to establish a permanent boundary between the two countries westward of the Rocky Mountains to the Pacific Ocean."

The President, at a very early period of his administration, was called upon to decide whether he would break off or continue this negotiation. Placed in such a responsible position, he first inquired whether the national honor required that he should abruptly terminate it by demanding the whole territory in dispute. War before dishonor is a maxim deeply engraven upon the hearts of the American People; and this maxim ever shall regulate his conduct towards foreign nations. But it was impossible for him to conceive that there could be dishonor in pursuing the course which had been adopted by Mr. Monroe, his patriot Revolutionary predecessor, more than a quarter of a century ago, and had been either expressly sanctioned or acquiesced in by all succeeding administrations.

His next inquiry was, would a compromise of the claims of the parties, by adopting the parallel of 49°, materially injure the interest of the United States. The entrance of the Straits of Fuca, Admiralty Inlet, and Puget's Sound, with their fine harbors and rich surrounding soil, are all south of this parallel. We know but little of the country north of it; but, from all the information we have obtained, it is, with the exception of a few spots, wholly unfit for agriculture, and incapable of sustaining any considerable population. Its chief, indeed almost its only value consists in the furs which may yet be collected upon it; and, even in this particular, it is not of much importance.

Arbitration being out of the question, the alternatives which remained were either to compromise the claims of the parties upon terms similar to those which had often been proposed by the Government of the United States and rejected by that of Great Britain, or to demand the exclusive sovereignty over the whole territory in dispute, and thus to render war almost inevitable. In the present enlightened and Christian age, war ought to be the very last alternative of nations, and should never be resorted to unless for a cause which renders it imperatively necessary. To rush into hostilities, if this can be honorably avoided, would subject the United States to the condemnation of all Christendom. The President doubts whether the judgment of the civilized world would be in our favor in a war waged for a comparatively worthless territory north of 49°, which his predecessors had over and over again offered to surrender to Great Britain, provided she would yield her pretensions to the country south of that latitude. Besides, a war for such a cause, whilst it would doubtless be sustained by the patriotism, might not meet the approbation, of a large portion of our own fellow-citizens.

On the other hand, suppose the American proposition of the 49th degree of latitude should be again made by the United States and again rejected by Great Britain, and war then be the consequence, we might appeal to all mankind for the justice and moderation of our demand: the voice of an impartial world would pronounce our cause to be righteous, and our own citizens would be enthusiastically united in sustaining such a war. Should the negotiation end in disappointment, the President, having done all that can be required of him for the preservation of peace, will afterwards feel himself perfectly free to insist upon our rights in their full extent up to the Russian line.

Influenced by these important considerations, you will perceive, from my note to Mr. Pakenham, a copy of which I now enclose you, that the President has once more proposed to the Government of Great Britain that the territory west of the Rocky Mountains which has been, under existing treaties, "free and open" to the occupation of nations ever since 1818, shall now be divided between them by the forty-ninth parallel of north latitude, offering at the same time to make free to Great Britain any port or ports on Vancouver's Island, south of this parallel, which the British Government may desire.

You will observe that the proposition is silent in regard to the navigation of the Columbia river—a privilege which has heretofore been repeatedly offered to Great Britain in former attempts to settle this question. Such a privilege the President cannot concede, although he is well aware of the serious if not insuperable obstacles which this may present to the success of the negotiation. The tenacity with which Great Britain will adhere to the free navigation of the Columbia which she now enjoys is manifest from the note of Mr. Pakenham to Mr. Calhoun of the 12th September last, with a copy of which you have been furnished.

If the free navigation of the Columbia were granted to Great Britain, this would be a perpetual source of strife and cause of collision between the citizens and subjects of the two nations in those remote regions. . . .

Whilst denying this privilege which has been hitherto so often offered, it may be asked what reason have we to hope that Great Britain may now accede to the naked parallel of 49°. There would be little or none, unless our proposition had contained such a concession in some other particular as to enable her to retreat with honor from her former demands. This will be found in our offer to make free to Great Britain any port or ports on Vancouver's Island south of 49°, which the British Government may desire. It is true this is but a trifling concession, considering the small portion of the cap of Vancouver's Island which lies south of that parallel; and although no equivalent, it is yet something, which may be a refuge for British pride, whilst surrendering the free navigation of the Columbia. Besides, as they have, in their last proposition, so far gone beyond that of 1827 as to offer to make free to the United States any port or ports which they might desire, either on the main land or Vancouver's Island south of latitude 49°, our offer to them of free ports on the southern cap of that island may be deemed a reciprocal concession. . . .

From what has been said, you will perceive how wholly impossible it is for the President to accept any terms of compromise which would bring the British south of the parallel of 49°; and this you may intimate to the British Ministers in conversation, should you deem it wise under all the circumstances. The only exception to this rule which could possibly be made might be the concession, for an adequate equivalent, of the small cap of Vancouver's Island south of this latitude, which would be of no importance to the United States, whilst it is of considerable value to Great Britain.

You will enforce our proposition upon the British Ministry with all the enlightened ability of which you are so eminently the master. Should it be rejected, the President will be relieved from the embarrassment in which he has been involved by the acts, offers, and declarations of his predecessors. Afterwards, if the difficulty can only be resolved by the sword, we may then appeal with confidence to the world for the equity and justice of our cause, and may anticipate the smiles of Heaven upon the right.

# 9 | Partisan Politics and the Oregon Question, January 1846 *

By January 1846 the movement within the United States for compromise on the Oregon question had effectively challenged the power of the extremists. It was already becoming evident that any compromise treaty which established a boundary along the 49th parallel would receive the overwhelming support of the Senate. It was equally clear that England had dropped her earlier demand for the Columbia River boundary and would also accept a compromise at 49°. What stood in the path of a popular settlement, therefore, was less the diplomatic position of the two nations than the internal pressures on the Polk administration, which still demanded nothing less than the whole of Oregon. Polk, for political reasons, could not accept a compromise settlement until the movement for "54-40" had run its course. Of the many writings which condemned the Western Democrats for perpetuating the Oregon dispute from purely partisan motives, none was more effective than a long essay which appeared in the January 1846 issue of *The North American Review*.

🖎

. . . The country of Oregon, lying between the Rocky mountains and the Pacific Ocean, is bounded on the south by the parallel of 42° of latitude, and on the north by the parallel of 54° 40′. On a rough estimate, therefore, it occupies a space of about thirteen degrees of latitude, and fifteen of longitude, reckoning from the meridian of 110° to that of 125° west from Greenwich. Besides the great range of the Rocky mountains, forming its eastern boundary, there are two other chains of mountains, one called the Far-West, or the Cascade range, and the other the Blue mountains, which run through the country from north to south, and separate it into three great divisions, differing from each other by marked peculiarities of soil and climate; these may be denominated for convenience as Western, Middle, and Eastern Oregon. . . .

To show what are the capacities of the country for agriculture and commerce, and what encouragements generally it offers for emigrants, we will begin with Eastern Oregon, which lies between the Blue and the Rocky mountains. A short quotation from Mr. Greenhow, whose work is a very convenient and faithful summary of all the accessible information upon this subject, will place in a very clear light the true character of this region. His testimony, it may be observed, is unimpeachable, when used for this purpose, as the sole object of his book is to defend the American claim, and to advocate the retention of the country by the United States.

> The country between the Blue mountains and the Rocky mountains appears to be, except in a very few, small, detached, spots, absolutely uninhabitable by those who depend on agriculture for subsistence. It is,

* "The Oregon Question," *The North American Review*, LXII (January 1846), 220-21, 225, 227-30, 232-9, 243-4, 249, 251-2.

in fact, a collection of bare, rocky mountain chains, separated by deep gorges, through which flow the streams produced by the melting of the snows on the summits; for in the lower grounds rain seldom falls at any time. On the borders of the Lewis, and of some of the streams falling into it, are valleys and prairies, producing grass for cattle; but all the attempts to cultivate the esculent vegetables have failed, chiefly, as it is believed, from the great difference in the temperature between the day and the succeeding night, especially in the summer, which is commonly not less than thirty, and often exceeds fifty, degrees of Fahrenheit's thermometer. . . .

This is bad enough, and Middle Oregon, according to the same authority, is but little better. Here, the rain never falls from April to November, and even during the remainder of the year, which is called the wet season, the rains are neither abundant nor frequent. It is impossible to form settlements, then, except upon the borders of the streams, which are not numerous, and the banks of which offer but few attractions in other respects to the emigrant. There are but few trees, chiefly sumach, cotton-wood, and other soft and useless woods. Fuel and building materials can be obtained only from a great distance up the north branch of the Columbia, or from the Pacific region, by few and difficult passes through the mountains. The soil is very unpromising, consisting, in the northern part, generally, of a yellow, sandy clay, covered only with grass and small shrubs. In the valleys farther south it is a little better, as there is more vegetable mould, and a few trees are found of the species above mentioned. Mr. Greenhow's conclusion is, "that little encouragement is offered for the cultivation of this part of Oregon," though cattle may be pastured to advantage, as grass is abundant.

We cannot wonder, then, that emigrants from the United States invariably pass through both the regions which we have described, and seek a home only in Western Oregon. West of the Cascade range is the only portion of this assumed El Dorado on the Pacific which can ever be inhabited except by hunters and their game. . . .

That the American settlers in the most promising part of Oregon can raise enough from the soil for the supply of their own wants is very certain; but it is impossible that they should ever become rich, owing to the want of a market. Of what use is it to raise more grain than they need for themselves, when they are separated from the United States by a desert two thousand miles broad, and from any other customers by thousands of leagues of ocean passage, to say nothing of the difficulty of reaching the seacoast, caused by the numerous falls and sandbanks which obstruct the navigation of the rivers? The mouth of the Columbia is closed by a bar which makes ingress and egress impossible for three fourths of the year, and very dangerous at any other period. . . .

The information which we have here attempted to bring together may be very briefly summed up. Of the whole territory of Oregon, there is but one district, and that not much larger than Pennsylvania, which is habitable except by hunters and Indians, and not more than an eighth part even of this district is arable land. The region actually in dispute contains at the utmost but one half of this improvable ground, and in addition to it an arid and rugged waste on which any considerable colonization is impossible. Parched with drought for nearly three fourths of the year, and drenched with rains for the remainder of the time, the soil and climate alike must baffle what experience the farmer may have gained in more favored regions, and prove a sore trial to any constitutions not inured to such peculiar seasons. Isolated in position, with almost insurmountable obstacles to internal communication, the merchant can expect as little from the country as the agriculturist. In fine, it is hardly too much to say, that what Siberia is to Russia, Oregon is to the United States. The road thither is equally long and wearisome, and even less cheered by the sight of human habitations, though in the one case it is trodden only by the free backwoodsman and the sturdy emigrant, and in the other by the condemned exile who "drags at each remove a lengthening chain." . . .

The truth is, the extravagant notions entertained of Oregon have been nourished by the very cause which should have made men suspicious of all stories respecting it, and have entirely checked the tide of emigration that is now flowing thither. We mean the dispute respecting the ownership of the territory. Politicians and diplomatists, to make their services appear more meritorious, have striven to put a higher value upon the title they were defending. But for this reason, we should have heard little about the fertility of Oregon, the beauty of its climate, the ease of communicating with it, or its importance for commercial purposes. The statesman's shortest and surest road to popularity nowadays consists in an affected zeal and watchfulness for the interests of our country in its foreign relations. There is no risk here of offending one portion of the sovereign people while seeking to please another. There is no divergence, no contrariety, of interests here to care for; if but few are directly interested in the prosecution of a claim against France or England, none are injured by it. The good-will that is thus conciliated is all clear gain. Not one in ten thousand of our vast population would be immediately affected by the successful assertion of our claim to the whole of Oregon. To the vast majority of our people the matter is one of perfect indifference, except so far as it is linked with the interests of a party. But to this party it is of vital importance. Hence the warmth and jealousy of each other which politicians manifest in combating the pretensions of a foreign power. One party makes a merit of having secured so much territory by a successful negotiation, as in the case of the Ashburton treaty; and the other party imputes to it as a fault that it did not obtain more. Lord Palmerston attacks Sir Robert Peel because Great Britain surrendered so much by that treaty; Mr. Benton attacks Mr. Webster because the United States surrendered so much. Both charges cannot be true; but that is of no importance. If similar attacks were not foreseen, the question about Oregon might be settled to-morrow. If the two countries are finally plunged into a war respecting it, it will not be because the bulk of the English or the American people care a straw about the land; but because the dominant party on both sides of the Atlantic wishes to preserve its ascendency over its opponents. In its inception and fundamental character, it will be, as usual, a war not between two nations, but between two political parties. . . .

Since 1818, Oregon has been held under a convention, avowedly temporary in its nature, which provides that the whole country, with its rivers, bays, and harbours, shall remain free and open to the vessels and subjects of both powers, without prejudice to the claims of either to the entire and exclusive sovereignty of the territory. Had it not been for the absurdly exaggerated statements of its value, to which the circumstances that we have mentioned have given currency in this country, the land might have remained under this treaty of joint occupancy for a century to come. Offering some facilities for trade in fur and fish, but hardly any for permanent settlement, both nations might have made free use of it for traffic, in open and manly competition with each other, and have left the land to its only proper owners, a few thousand miserably degraded Indians, who derive a wretched subsistence from it. But the evil is now done; these false reports, disseminated for political purposes, or to answer the private ends of a few persons, have caused an American colony to be established there, and the dominant party in the United States is so deeply pledged to support it by claiming the whole territory for its use, that a compromise seems hardly practicable. On the other hand, Great Britain is bound in honor not to recede so far as to sacrifice the interests of her subjects in that region. *The faith of the government is pledged to support the Hudson's Bay Company in its present location.* . . .

In conformity with this view of the case, the leaders of the two great parties in England, Lord John Russell and Sir Robert Peel, have formally declared in Parliament, that Great Britain has rights in Oregon which must be maintained at all hazards; and this declaration has been supported with the greatest unanimity by the voice of parliament and the public press. If the United States, then, insist upon the whole of their claim, war is inevitable. . . .

It may seem idle to discuss the merits of their respective titles, when it is evident that the parties *cannot* recede. It is useless to stand fencing with arguments, when every body can see that the affair must ultimately be decided by considerations of a totally different character. We have been arguing the question for thirty years, and stand precisely where we did when the discussion commenced. The resources of logic, then, are exhausted, even if it were possible that logic should ever settle a national dispute. We confess, that all the recent negotiations about Oregon seem to us very much like a solemn mummery. A series of well known facts, musty inferences, and venerable arguments are gravely adduced on both sides; each party repeats its conviction that it is entirely in the right, and its opponent is entirely wrong; reciprocal proposiitons for compromise, which had been made and rejected several times before, are again made and rejected; and the plenipotentiaries—so called because nothing is left to their power or discretion—then separate, repeating to each other "the assurances of their distinguished consideration," and leaving the matter precisely when it was before. Such conduct may be very proper for diplomatists, but it would be called very silly for children. . . .

To prevent misapprehension, we may as well repeat here the opinion that has often been expressed, and, as we think, proved, in our pages, that the United States title, though imperfect, is the better of the two. In fact, Great Britain has admitted by implication as much as this; for, while this country asserts its exclusive ownership of Oregon, she has expressly, in several official communications, limited her claim to a right of *joint occupancy* of the territory with the United States, leaving the question of *absolute dominion* in abeyance. . . .

The positive side of the British title may be very quickly discussed; it rests entirely on the Nootka convention of 1790. Up to that period, England and Spain were the only powers that had any claims to the possession of the North Pacific coast. The conflict of their respective claims was put at rest by the convention which Spain was bullied into making in this year, by the threat of a war which she was not prepared for. . . .

By this treaty, both Spain and England consented to forego all their previous claims and rights,—founded on alleged prior discoveries, contiguity of territory, or any other basis,—for the sake of this mutual guaranty of joint occupation. . . .

This is the whole positive side of Great Britain's pretensions to Oregon; the negative side consists in a refutation of the counter pretensions of the United States. By the Florida treaty of 1818, Spain made over all her right to the Pacific coast north of latitude 42°, whatever it might be, to the United States. Of course, she could not cede more than she possessed; she ceded it loaded with all the treaty stipulations and restrictions which she had made respecting it while it was in her possession. She did not *warrant* the goods sold; the purchaser took them for better or worse. Was Oregon, in 1818, still subject to the Nootka Convention of 1790? England maintains that it was, that the treaty was perpetual, that, as no limitation of time is mentioned in it, or even hinted at, it was to last for ever. The United States say that it was not, that Spain and England went to war with each other in 1796, and as war annuls all treaties, that the Nootka convention then ceased. . . .

It is also held, that the United States derive a claim from France, founded on the purchase of Louisiana from that power in 1803. The unquestioned possession of a territory extending to the eastern base of the Rocky mountains affords some title, it is thought, by contiguity at least, to the ownership of Oregon on the western side. To this it is replied, first, that France never pretended that Louisiana reached beyond the Rocky mountains; and secondly, that the same remark applies to this title which has just been made upon the title obtained from Spain; it is covered by the Nootka convention. France ceded Louisiana to Spain in 1762; and it was as the owner not only of California, but of Louisiana, that Spain signed a convention in 1790, which admitted the British to a right of joint occupancy of Oregon. Spain ceded Louisiana back to France in 1802, but not in such a perfect condition as it was when she received it. She returned it burdened with the treaty stipulations which she had made while it was in her hands. And it was with this incumbrance upon it that the United States purchased Louisiana in the following year.

Having considered two branches of the argument in favor of our pretensions to the whole of Oregon,—namely, the rights obtained by purchase from Spain and France,—we now come to the third and only remaining one, which is founded on the proceedings and discoveries of our own citizens. And here one remark is necessary respecting the effect of thus accumulating several distinct titles in the hands of one claimant. Some maintain, that these independent claims, being inconsistent one with another, when united, destroy each other, and leave the claimant who has brought them together without any firm title. Others say, that they mutually confirm and strengthen each other, and in case of a division of the land, entitle the party owning them to as many distinct shares as it possesses claims; that is, that the United States in their own right, and in that of France and of Spain, ought to have three fourths of the territory, while Great Britain, resting only on its own pretensions, can demand but one fourth. Neither position is correct. The United States, by purchasing the French and Spanish titles, gain an advantage, though it is one only of a negative character, by lessening the number of competitors; the agency of Frenchmen or Spaniards in discovering or settling Oregon, or acquiring possessions bordering upon it, cannot be adduced to weaken our claim, though it may be urged against the pretensions of the English. On the other hand, this union of claims does not directly strengthen our title, for, if either of them be assumed to be well founded, our own proper claim disappears entirely; and conversely, if the claim in our own right be good, the French and Spanish titles are of no worth. We cannot pile these pretensions one upon another; their force is not cumulative, but disjunctive. If Spain actually surveyed the coast of Oregon and discovered the mouth of the Columbia in 1775, then Captain Gray in 1792, and Lewis and Clarke in 1805, were only intruders; and on the other hand, if the discoveries of Gray, Lewis, and Clarke make out a perfect right, if their explorations, in fact, can be called *discoveries,* then Oregon was vacant and unappropriated,—a mere *terra incognita,* open to the first comer,—down to 1792, and the antecedent claims of France and Spain are mere nonentities. We may, it is true, elect the strongest out of the three claims, and rest the whole of our title upon that, reserving the other two to be urged against the English, and thereby may weaken or break down their claim, though without demonstrating our own. . . .

We have but one other remark to make upon this subject, but it is applicable to all the grounds upon which the American claim to Oregon is supported. A disputed title, whether it rests on discovery, settlement, or contiguity, is entirely indefinite in respect to the limits of the country claimed. If the subject of dispute be an island, indeed, of moderate magnitude, then discovery or settlement of any portion of it constitutes a good title to the whole. But when the land in question is only a small part of a vast continent, it is impossible to tell where the title ends. Discoveries and settlements are usually made on the seacoast; how far do they extend inland? Not, surely, over the whole breadth of the continent. . . .

But enough of this dry discussion of claims, which has been drawn out much longer than we had intended. We have not sought to disprove the American title to Oregon, but only to show that it is necessarily qualified, indeterminate, and imperfect; and this has been proved so conclusively, that any statesman who shall hereafter declare that this title is perfect and unquestionable will afford good reason to doubt either his soundness of mind or his honesty. That the United States have rights in Oregon, equal in every respect to the British rights, is known by the full and explicit admission of England herself; and thus we have all the needed ground for a compromise, and an equitable division of the territory. . . .

. . . The bulk of the population of either country care nothing about Oregon; why should they? Not one in ten thousand of them would be made richer or poorer, happier or sadder, by a gain of the whole territory. But where shall we put a limit, even in imagination, to the sufferings, the disasters, the horrors, which must follow in the train of an obstinate and protracted, though it be a successful, war? To what fireside, either in England or the United States, will not bring distress, if not a feeling of desolation and despair? . . .

It behooves those who have the power to act at a conjuncture pregnant with such awful consequences to look with a heedful eye to the measure of their own responsibility. . . . If the careless and the unthinking still speak recklessly about a war, it is only because war is not definitely connected in their minds with any idea of the shedding of blood. . . . The news of a great victory, of the old-fashioned kind, attended with the slaughter of thousands on both sides, instead of being received with exultation, as we verily believe, would excite in their minds only the mingled feelings of grief, humiliation, and repentance. Above all, they would hold to a fearful accountability the politicians whose policy had become so deeply stained with blood. Then let the English ministry and the American government look to it; they may carry on this war of words for a while longer, and it will harm no one; they will even deserve and obtain what is the sole object of their ambition, the applause of their countrymen for being so valiant and steadfast in defence of their country's rights. But the outbreak of actual hostilities between England and America about such a contemptible possession will be followed by a storm of popular indignation, that will not only hurl them from their pride of place, but will cover the history of their administrations with disgrace, and leave an indelible blot upon their names.

When the Polk administration, eight months after taking office, discovered an opportunity to open negotiations with the Mexican government over the Texas and California boundary questions, it was clear that its acquisitiveness toward California was motivated by maritime factors as was the case with Oregon. Indeed, Buchanan's instructions to John Slidell, Polk's envoy to Mexico, comprised both a review of the California question as well as an analysis of the historic tensions between the United States and Mexico, especially as they impinged on the issue of outstanding claims of American citizens against the Mexican government. In these claims, moreover, resided that body of moral and economic assets from which Polk hoped to pry a portion of California from Mexico. In a variety of proffered boundary lines between the Rio Grande and the California coast, Polk and his advisers had nothing in mind but a succession of well-known California ports.

. . . In the present crisis of the relations between the two countries, the office for which you have been selected is one of vast importance. To counteract the influence of foreign powers exerted against the United States in Mexico, and to restore those ancient relations of peace and good will which formerly existed between the governments and the citizens of the sister republics, will be principal objects of your mission. . . .

The first subject which will demand your attention is the claims of our citizens on Mexico. It would be useless here to trace the history of these claims, and the outrages from which they spring. The archives of your legation will furnish all the necessary information on this subject. The history of no civilized nation presents, in so short a period of time, so many wanton attacks upon the rights of persons and property as have been endured by citizens of the United States from the Mexican authorities. These never would have been tolerated by the United States from any nation on the face of the earth, except a neighboring and sister republic. . . .

But in what manner can this duty [settlement of claims] be performed consistently with the amicable spirit of your mission? The fact is but too well known to the world, that the Mexican government are not now in a condition to satisfy these claims by the payment of money. Unless the debt should be assumed by the government of the United States, the claimants cannot receive what is justly their due. Fortunately, the joint resolution of Congress, approved 1st March, 1845, "for annexing Texas to the United States," presents the means of satisfying these claims, in perfect consistency with the interests, as well as the honor,

* Buchanan to Slidell, November 10, 1845, Instructions to Mexico MSS, Department of State, National Archives, Vol. XVI.

of both republics. It has reserved to this government the adjustment "of all questions of boundary that may arise with other governments." This question of boundary may, therefore, be adjusted in such a manner between the two republics as to cast the burden of the debt due to American claimants upon their own government, whilst it will do no injury to Mexico. . . .

Besides, it is greatly to be desired that our boundary with Mexico should now be established in such a manner as to preclude all future difficulties and disputes between the two republics. A great portion of New Mexico being on this side of the Rio Grande, and included within the limits already claimed by Texas, it may hereafter, should it remain a Mexican province, become a subject of dispute and a source of bad feeling between those who, I trust, are destined in future to be always friends.

On the other hand, if, in adjusting the boundary, the province of New Mexico should be included within the limits of the United States, this would obviate the danger of future collisions. Mexico would part with a remote and detached province, the possession of which can never be advantageous to her; and she would be relieved from the trouble and expense of defending its inhabitants against the Indians. Besides, she would thus purchase security against their attacks for her other provinces west of the del Norte, as it would at once become the duty of the United States to restrain the savage tribes within their limits, and prevent them from making hostile incursions into Mexico. From these considerations, and others which will readily suggest themselves to your mind, it would seem to be equally the interest of both powers that New Mexico should belong to the United States.

But the President desires to deal liberally by Mexico. You are, therefore, authorized to offer to assume the payment of all the just claims of our citizens against Mexico; and, in addition, to pay five millions of dollars in case the Mexican government shall agree to establish the boundary between the two countries from the mouth of the Rio Grande, up the principal stream to the point where it touches the line of New Mexico; thence west of the river along the exterior line of that province, and so as to include the whole within the United States, until it again intersects the river; thence up the principal stream of the same to its source; and thence due north until it intersects the forty-second degree of north latitude.

A boundary still preferable to this would be an extension of the line from the northwest corner of New Mexico, along the range of mountains until it would intersect the forty-second parallel.

Should the Mexican authorities prove unwilling to extend our boundary beyond the del Norte, you are, in that event, instructed to offer to assume the payment of all the just claims of citizens of the United States against Mexico, should she agree that the line shall be established along the boundary defined by the act of Congress of Texas, approved December 19, 1836, to wit: beginning at "the mouth of the Rio Grande; thence up the principal stream of said river to its source; thence due north to the forty-second degree of north latitude." . . .

There is another subject of vast importance to the United States, which will demand your particular attention. From information possessed by this department, it is to be seriously apprehended that both Great Britain and France have designs upon California. . . .

The possession of the bay and harbor of San Francisco is all important to the United States. The advantages to us of its acquisition are so striking, that it would be a waste of time to enumerate them here. If all these should be turned against our country by the cession of California to Great Britain, our principal commercial rivals, the consequences would be most disastrous.

The government of Californiia is now but nominally dependent upon Mexico; and it is more than doubtful whether her authority will ever be reinstated. Under these circumstances, it is the desire of the President that you shall use your best efforts to obtain a cession of that province from Mexico to the United States. Could you accomplish this object, you would render immense service to your country, and establish an enviable reputation for yourself. Money would be no object, when compared with the value of the acquisition. Still, the attempt must be made with great prudence and caution, and in such a manner as not to alarm the jealousy of the Mexican government. Should you, after sounding the Mexican authorities on the subject, discover a prospect of success the President would not hesitate to give, in addition to the assumption of the just claims of our citizens on Mexico, twenty-five millions of dollars for the cession. Should you deem it expedient, you are authorized to offer this sum for a boundary running due west from the southern extremity of New Mexico to the Pacific Ocean, or from any other point on its western boundary which would embrace Monterey within our limits: If Monterey cannot be obtained, you may, if necessary, in addition to the assumption of these claims, offer twenty millions of dollars for any boundary commencing at any point on the western line of New Mexico and running due west to the Pacific, so as to include the bay and harbor of San Francisco. The larger the territory south of this bay, the better. Of course, when I speak of any point on the western boundary of New Mexico, it is understood that from the del Norte to that point our boundary shall run according to the first offer which you have been authorized to make. I need scarcely add, that in authorizing the offer of five millions or twenty-five millions, or twenty millions of dollars, these are to be considered as maximum sums. If you can accomplish either of the objects contemplated for a less amount, so much more satisfactory will it prove to the President. . . .

Although California had never been an issue in American politics, it had become
by 1846 a significant topic for editorial opinion in the great metropolitan newspapers of the nation. California, with its magnificent harbor of San Francisco,
had become a vital interest of the United States, to be made an integral part of
the country by whatever means came to hand. Why the question of Calfiornia's
future could no longer be escaped was revealed clearly by a long essay on
California which appeared in *The American Review* of January 1846.

Letters from Washington, on which we rely, render it probable that Mr.
Slidell, our newly appointed minister to Mexico, goes clothed with power to
treat with that government for the cession of California to the United States.
The intelligence is vague, but we trust it is true, and that the negotiation may
prove successful. The natural progress of events will undoubtedly give us that
province just as it gave us Texas. Already American emigrants thither are to
be numbered by thousands, and we may, at almost any moment, look for a
declaration, which shall dissolve the slight bonds that now link the province to
Mexico, and prepare the way for its ultimate annexation to the United States.

Regarding, therefore, the accession of California as an event which present
tendencies, if not checked or counteracted, must render inevitable, we should
prefer to see it accomplished by an agency, at once more direct and less questionable in point of national morality. It cannot be disguised that we stand open to
the charge of having colonized Texas, and recognized her independence, for
the express purpose of seizing her soil—that we wrested her territory from
Mexico, peacefully and by a gradual process, to be sure, but as really and as
wrongfully as if we had conquered her by arms in the field of battle. . . .

. . . Texas, it seems not at all unlikely, may yet cost us more than would in
the beginning have bought it outright; and California, it may fairly be presumed, may now be purchased, at least *nemine contradicente,* for a sum which
the country will deem small for so valuable an acquisition.

For, certainly, we do regard it as extremely desirable that California—a part,
at least, of the province known by that name—should become the property, and
remain forever under the exclusive jurisdiction, of the United States. Lower
California, as it is called, embracing the long, narrow peninsula between the
Gulf and the Pacific, stretching from the 21st to the 33d degree of latitude, a
distance of above eight hundred miles, with an average breadth of about sixty,
is universally represented by travelers as sterile and hopelessly desolate. It consists, indeed, of a chain of volcanic, treeless, barren mountains of rock, broken
only by still more dreary plains of sand, destitute of streams, swept by fierce

* "California," *The American Review,* III (January 1846), 82–99.

tornadoes, and of necessity abandoned almost entirely to sterility and desolation. . . .

With Upper California the case is different. The southern and eastern portions —indeed nearly the whole province except that part bordering on the Pacific— is scarcely more valuable than the lower province. Through the eastern section extends the chain of the Rocky Mountains, broken into fragments, and converting a wide space of the country, through its entire length, into a waste perfectly uninhabitable, producing very little vegetation, and through which the traveler, with danger and difficulty, finds a casual and precarious path. West of this chain lies a vast, sandy plain, nearly seven hundred miles in length, with a width of one hundred miles at its southern, and two hundred at its northern, extremity. The whole valley of the Colorado is utterly barren, and is described by an American traveler as a great burial-place of former fertility, which can never return. Like its branches the river is not navigable. . . .

The remaining part of Upper California—that which lies nearest the Pacific Coast—is not only by far the best portion of the province, but one of the most beautiful regions on the face of the earth. It embraces the whole country drained by the waters which empty into the Bay of San Francisco. . . .

Although agriculture, throughout this vast and fertile region, is of the rudest and most unskillful character, nearly all kinds of grain have been readily raised. In the immediate neighborhood of San Francisco Bay the most extraordinary crops are easily produced. Dr. Marsh, long a resident on the banks of the Sacramento, informed Mr. Farnham that from ten bushels of wheat he had known to be harvested a crop of 3652: though he says that the average yield is from 30 to 50 bushels from one that is sown. The first part of this statement is incredible; but Commodore Wilkes mentions an instance in which 3600 bushels were harvested from 30 sown; and he places the average crop at 80 fold. The most moderate of these statements exhibits a degree of fertility seldom found in the most favored regions of the earth. Indian corn is said to return about 150 fold. The potato thrives; hemp, flax, oats, barley, peas, fruits of all kinds, and indeed all the productions of the temperate zone, are produced in great abundance, and with the greatest ease; while in the southern portion, cotton, tobacco, figs, lemons, olives, oranges, and especially grapes, seem to find a native and most propitious soil; and the marshes about the mouths of the San Joaquin and Sacramento, may easily be turned into some of the richest and most beautiful rice fields in the world.

Here, then, lies upon the Pacific coast, adjoining our western border, included between the parallels which embrace the southern sections of the United States, and stretching northward to the southern boundary of Oregon, a region of country capable of sustaining a greater population than now inhabits the entire American Union. Traversed, through its entire length, and from its most remote corners, by noble rivers all concentrating their waters, and forming at their common mouth, the finest harbor perhaps in the world;—abounding in timber of the best quality for ship-building and all naval purposes, easily floated to a common point, and that the beautiful and capacious harbor of San Francisco;—containing measureless water power, immense agricultural resources, and

all the elements which nature can furnish of national wealth and national consequence—it is yet shut out from the influences of Christian civilization and
abandoned to a people who neither know its capacities, nor feel the pressure
of any obligation to develop and expand them. The aggregate population is
probably below 20,000; the harvested crops in 1839 amounted to 69,000 bushels
of wheat, 22,000 of maize, and 15,000 of barley; and the whole annual merchant-
able production of the country, including cattle and furs, its staple commodities,
is estimated by Capt. Wilkes at less than a million of dollars. Nor is there anything in the history of the country, to induce the hope that, under its present
control, it will ever attain that position, and serve those ends, in the great
scheme of the world's civilization, for which Providence has so clearly designed it.

For more than three hundred years it has been under exclusive Spanish
dominion. Yet up to the present time, notwithstanding its immense advantages
for trade, it has no commerce; in spite of its fertility, it has no agriculture; its
water power and ability to yield a bountiful supply of every raw material, have
not erected a solitary manufacturing establishment within its borders; and the
whole country is even now as far removed from that high and palmy state of
wealth, cultivation and power of which it is susceptible, as it was before the
Spaniard Cobrillo, in 1542, first explored its coast and landed upon its shore. . . .

No one who cherishes a faith in the wisdom of an overruling Providence, and
who sees, in the national movements which convulse the world, the silent operation of an invisible but omnipotent hand, can believe it to be for the interest
of humanity, for the well-being of the world, that this vast and magnificent region
should continue forever in its present state. Capable of sustaining millions of
people, of conferring upon them all the physical comforts of life, and of raising
them to the highest point of mental and moral cultivation, if only they have
the energy and the ability to use its resources—so long as desolation broods
upon it, so long as the shadows of ignorance, indolence and moral degradation
hang around it, the manifest designs of Providence are unfulfilled, and the
paramount interests of the world lack due advancement. While California
remains in possession of its present inhabitants, and under control of its present
government, there is no hope of its regeneration. . . .

California, to become the seat of wealth and power for which Nature has
marked it, must pass into the hands of another race. . . .

This point, then, being conceded, it remains only to inquire, into whose hands
shall California pass? What nation of the earth shall succeed to Mexico, whenever the sovereignty shall pass from her grasp?

There are, we believe, but two powers to whom the design of acquiring
California is ever ascribed. One of these is Great Britain; the other is the
United States. . . .

. . . There has sprung up of late a very general demand from all sides of the
British press, for the prompt accomplishment of these designs. The Foreign
Quarterly Review closes some speculations upon the probable destiny of California, with the remark that "an active minister, who had a forecast of the
future, might secure it as an appendage to Oregon, our unquestionable right to

which is too clear to be surrendered. The Mexicans," it is added, "would not be sorry to part with it to us upon fair terms." . . .

With this evidence before us, it is impossible, or at least unwise, to doubt that Great Britain is striving to secure from Mexico sovereignty in California, absolute, it may be, or perhaps "somewhat in the manner of the East India Company."

The next question naturally suggested relates to the probability of her success. This must be simply a matter of opinion. It would be useless to disguise our fear that, so far as Mexico is concerned, she may accomplish her purpose. We have less confidence than perhaps is just, in the good faith of the friendly disposition towards the Government and people of the United States, which Mexico is said of late to have evinced. Our acquisition of Texas as yet too re-cent—our port towards Mexico has been too commanding—our exactions have been too rigorous, for the wound they inflicted upon this sensitive and resentful race to have yet fully healed. . . .

It seems to us improbable that a government marked and swayed by Mexican temper, which persisted against the advice and example of the leading nations of the earth, in refusing to recognize the independence of Texas, for a long series of years of enforced inaction, which has, from first to last, charged upon the United States the robbery and despoilment of the fairest of her possessions, should now, so soon after the obnoxious deed is finally and fully accomplished, manifest even an intemperate eagerness to resume with us friendly relations, and to nego-tiate for a boundary upon so liberal a basis as she is said to have proposed. We fear these measures are but the fair-seeming dictates of a "necessity of present life." They have already relieved her seaboard from the presence of our squadron, and her Texan frontier from the pressure of our troops. They have averted, or at least deferred, a blow against which she had found it impossible to interpose the shield of British power, and have released her from the fatal necessity of engaging, single-handed, the power of the United States. Of such a struggle the result has repeatedly been predicted in Europe. The French *Journal des Debats* has declared that "the conquest of Mexico would be a wide step towards the en-slavement of the world by the United States, and a levy of bucklers by the Mexicans at this moment would lead the way to this subjection." The London *Times* remarks that Mexico has had the sagacity to perceive that a declaration of war would enable the United States to seize upon and and retain the Mexican territory. . . . "Between the autocracy of Russia on the East, and the democracy of America, aggrandized by the conquest of Mexico, on the West," says the *Journal des Debats,* the official paper of the French government, *"Europe may find herself more compressed than she may one day think consistent with her independence and dignity."* It cannot be disguised that apprehensions of the future power of the American people are arousing the fears, and influencing the policy of the principal nations of Europe. The leading journal of Great Britain but a few days since, declared, that "no European politician can look forward to the power of the United States, within the present century, but with the most *appalling* prospects." And so the Paris *Debats* remarks, that "for the political balance of the world, the conquest of Mexico by the United States may create eventual dangers, which, although distant, it may not be superfluous to *guard against*." And so again, upon another occasion, the same official journal employed this still more emphatic language:

"A cry of war between America and Mexico has been raised: although it is not believed that the threats will be followed by acts, yet it would be well for us to be prepared for anything. North America presents her ambitious plans for conquering all the American continent. She began by the annexation of Texas, by which she divides Mexico, and a war will give her a welcome pretence for possessing herself of all Mexico. Soon the smaller states will follow, and the Isthmus of Panama fall into the hands of North America. *Europe should not tolerate this,* NOR SUFFER NORTH AMERICA TO INCREASE, or the independence of Europe might sooner or later be wedged in by the two colossuses of Russia and North America, and suffer from their oppression.". . .

The existence of this feeling among the sovereigns of Europe towards this country, cannot be cloaked by honied diplomatic assurances of distinguished consideration, nor disproved by angry or contemptuous denial. We look upon it as a fact—a *"fixed fact,"* which must have weight in any speculations, that claim to be intelligent, concerning our present and future foreign relations. We have introduced it here for the purpose of saying that Mexico cannot be ignorant of its existence, and that, in our judgment, she intends, with more of wisdom than we have given her credit for, to make it serviceable in "feeding fat the grudge" she bears us. She cannot lack the sagacity to perceive that, with Great Britain firmly fixed in California, she could not engage in war with the United States without a certainty, or, at the least, a very strong probability of having Great Britain for an active ally. . . .

. . . A glance at a globe, or a Mercator's map, will convince any one that the occupation of that province by Great Britain would give to that power, for all time to come, absolute dominion of the Pacific Ocean, with all its islands, coasts and commerce, and place her in a position which might at any moment become infinitely dangerous to our safety and prosperity. In an individual, self-defence is an instinct. In a nation it becomes a *duty*—one, too, of paramount obligation, far superior in binding force to any other, inasmuch as it lies at the foundation of all others, and as obedience to it is the sole condition upon which other duties can be discharged. As in individual cases, too, the obligation of national self-preservation comprises more than resistance to imminent and actual assault. It enforces in peace preparation for war—that is to say, the adoption of such measures as shall, in the event of war, put the national existence and safety beyond the hazards of any contest, and out of reach of any hostile blow. Though it neither sanctions nor requires injustice or wrong, it often supersedes the common rules of international law and, where clear and undeniable, justifies acts for which no public law exists. This broad but fundamental and essential principle, though it cannot invalidate existing rights, wherever they may exist, will most certainly forbid the extension of European dominion over at least this portion of the American Continent. And upon these grounds, sufficiently broad and perfectly tenable as we believe them to be, we have ventured the assertion that England cannot expect to occupy California with the acquiescence or indifference of the United States.

We have left ourselves but small space for reference to the efforts of the United States to become possessed, by purchase from Mexico, of this portion of her territory; but, fortunately, little is required. . . .

With regard to Mr. Slidell's negotiation, we must repeat, we have misgivings of his success. England stands ready, we doubt not, to give a larger sum for California than our government is likely to offer. If, as she seems to believe her paramount and imperative policy must be to check the further growth of the American Union, and to make perfect her net-work of military posts and stations, from which, at any moment, she may strike with most effect upon every side, her interest certainly lies in the acquisition of the bay and harbor of San Francisco. Nor can we escape the fear that Mexico would greatly prefer such an arrangement to that which we propose. She has not yet abandoned her project of reconquering Texas; and she must feel the need of a powerful ally. . . .

We have endeavored, in the course of this article, to show,

1. That California, a region of vast resources, and destined, at no distant day, to hold important relations to the commerce and politics of the world, must—and ought, in the natural course of events, and for the general good of humanity—pass from its present dominion into the hands of another race, and under the sway of another political system.

2. That Great Britain is seeking the establishment of her sovereignty there, being moved thereto, not only by her general lust for colonial possessions, but by the necessity which, in common with the other monarchies of Europe, she feels, of interposing a barrier to the growth in wealth, dominion and power, of the American Union, and of thus checking the progress of republican liberty, by which she believes her own institutions, and the position of the family of European sovereigns, to be seriously menaced.

3. That the accomplishment of this design would be inconsistent with the interests and the safety of the United States; that it would be in direct hostility to fundamental principles they are pledged to sustain; and that the paramount law of self-preservation will impel them to assume that like the European occupation of Cuba, it is an event which they "CANNOT PERMIT IN ANY CONTINGENCY WHATEVER."

In all its aspects and relations, and from whatever point it may be viewed, this is preeminently an AMERICAN question—one to be decided in the light of the future, and upon the broadest and most essential principles of that American system which is fully discussed in another portion of this Review. We have not allowed ourselves, therefore, to make the remotest party reference in any part of our remarks—though our citations from American authorities, as will have been seen, are entirely from sources connected with that party with whose principles and welfare this Review is fully identified. We hope and trust that a timely purchase of California by the United States, and the adjustment of pending questions of difference between our government and those of Great Britain and Mexico, will avert the necessity of an appeal to the terrible arbiter of irreconcilable international disputes. Should such an appeal, through the madness or selfish ambition of any of the contestant parties, be finally taken, the struggle, as has been remarked by a distinguished Senator of the United States, will involve far more than the questions out of which, as a pretext, it may grow: and not only will the entire territory bordering on the Pacific coast, from the Gulf of California to the Russian frontier, extending over *twenty-three* degrees of latitude, and embracing a region capable of becoming more populous and powerful than is France or the United States at the present day, become the prize of contending nations, but a contest will ensue between opposite systems of political existence—systems in their nature essentially hostile, and between which, in the judgment of many men of foresight and wisdom, there is yet to be a final, and for one or the other a fatal, collision. Most earnestly and sincerely do we hope the prophecy may prove fallacious, and the contest be forever averted. Should, however, the irresistible progress of events throw its tremendous weight upon us, it will not become the American nation, as the only republic of mark on the face of the earth, with timid shrinking or unmanly fear, to decline it, or to tremble for the result. . . .

# 12 | Maritime Objectives in the Mexican War, 1846–48 *

Undaunted by political hostility which accused him of forcing Mexico into a war with the United States, Polk assumed the burdensome task of conducting a victorious war and determining, at the same time, the specific aims of the war, for only to the extent that the objects of the war had some relationship to the power to be expended could it achieve any useful purpose at all. Even while Congress debated the war resolution in May 1846, Polk informed his cabinet that in a treaty the United States "would, if practicable, obtain California and such other portion of the Mexican territory as would be sufficient to indemnify our claimants on Mexico, and to defray the expenses of the war. . . ." Early in the war the American Pacific fleet closed in on California and by the autumn of 1846 the American flag floated over much of the Mexican province. During the early months of the Mexican War the President noted repeatedly in his diary that he would accept no treaty which would not transfer New Mexico and Upper California to the United States. What remained was the determination of the precise territorial objectives. Initially, San Francisco and Monterey were the chief attractions in California to the Polk administration. Secretary of the Navy George Bancroft assured Samuel Hooper, Marblehead merchant and son-in-law of William Sturgis, that by mid-June the United States flag would be floating over these two northern California ports. "I hope California is now in our possession, never to be given up," he added. "We were driven reluctantly to war; we must make a solid peace."

* George Bancroft to Samuel Hooper, June 19, 1846, George Bancroft Papers, Massachusetts Historical Society.

With this promise Hooper would not rest. He prodded the administration to look southward along the coast.

✄

. . . Every one here is exceedingly pleased with the Oregon settlement. In the course of the year I trust the Southern boundary on the Pacific will be as favorably settled by a Mexican treaty, in which I have more personal interest from the fact of having many creditors on the Coast of California as far South as St. Diego, and this I hope will excuse me for troubling you with the question; if Monterey & St. Francisco only will enjoy the benefits of our flag or if it will be extended as far South as St. Diego, which is Lat. 32½, and includes all the good harbours of California? . . .

— | "Write to me exactly . . . what line to insist upon in the event of a treaty of peace." *

Upon receiving Hooper's letter of June 19, Bancroft asked the New England merchant for more specific information regarding American mercantile interests in California.

✄

. . . Write to me exactly your views about California, what order it would be for the mercantile interest to give now, what line to insist upon in the event of a treaty of peace. . . .

I had not enumerated in the orders San Diego, but had said "San Francisco," "Monterey," "Mazatlan" and "Guymas"—& such other ports as he can. I can bid him send a brig into San Diego. Write me fully, giving information & suggestions.

If Mexico makes peace this month the Rio del Norte & the parallel of 35° may do as a boundary; after that 32° which will include San Diego.

— | "I hope you will order a small vessel to St. Diego. . . ." †

Hooper, in response to Bancroft's inquiry, spelled out in detail for the administration the nature of New England's commercial interests in California. To protect those interests, he wrote, the United States should not acquire less than the entire region extending as far south as San Diego Bay.

✄

* George Bancroft to Samuel Hooper, June 22, 1846, George Bancroft Papers.
† Samuel Hooper to George Bancroft, June 25, 1846, George Bancroft Papers.

In your note of the 22d Inst you ask me to write you my views about California, what order it would be for the Mercantile interest to give now and what line to insist on in the event of peace. My business has made me somewhat familiar with that country, and you may gather from this something of the position of things there which may assist you in forming your own judgment.

The paralel [sic] you name if peace is made this month of Lat. 35° includes the most important point, viz. the Bay of St. Francisco and the beautiful country watered by the principal streams that flow into it; Latitude 32° however embraces the whole of Upper California which is good for anything including "Pueblo de los Angellos," the principal settlement of the country, an inland town in Lat. 34 in an extensive and fertile plain covered with beautiful farms & vinyards, many of them owned and cultivated by foreigners who would be certain to revolt against Mexico and join with the northern part of the country if that should become subject to the laws of the United States.

Upper California embraces a great extent of country on the map, but the only part settled except by indian tribes is a narrow strip extending about 300 miles on the coast north from Lat. 32°; if 35 is made the boundary line it leaves about one third of what is called there the "reasonable population" (to distinguish it from the indian) belonging to Mexico and isolated from it by hundreds of miles of almost impassable country; this could not be of any value to Mexico, but a source of annoyance by its revolts; the difference between the Northern under the equal laws of the United States and this Southern portion under the oppressions of Mexican rulers would keep them in a state of revolt, which would be certain to excite sympathy and interference from their Northern neighbours. South of 32 Lat there is no fine land to invite settlers; and if that line is made the boundary, it would for centuries to come leave an almost impassable country between us & Mexico on the Pacific.

Until a peace is made I see no reason why the American flag should not be hoisted at "St. Diego" & "Pueblo de los Angellos"—there is no force at "St. Diego" and but little population; the entrance to the harbour is not safe to vessels drawing over 7 feet, once entered the water is deep & entirely protected from the sea, vessels laying in all parts of it as in a dock. "Pueblo de los Angellos" has more population but no defences; it would cause no trouble or expence to take possession & retain it as a large portion of the population would favor it. It is important to the mercantile interest to have these two places taken as well as Monterey & St. Francisco, as it would ensure a peaceful state of things through the whole country and ennable them to continue their trade as before along the whole coast and to collect their debts as they expected from the crops of this year. If when a treaty is made the boundary line is to be 35, the vessels which have entered and paid duty to trade on the coast as far South as 32 should have that right continued until their voyages are completed.

I suppose Com. Sloat will take possession of the California ports, and only blockade the ports of Mazatlan & Guymas—these two last could be of no importance except to annoy Mexico during the war by interrupting her commerce. I hope you will order a small vessel to St. Diego as it is made the depot for the collection of homeward cargo until the vessels are to be loaded for the homeward voyage. . . .

— | "The extension of our boundaries over New Mexico and Upper California . . . is to be considered a sine qua non of any Treaty." *

In April 1847 the Polk administration dispatched Nicholas P. Trist, Chief Clerk in the Department of State, to Mexico to join the army of General Winfield Scott and handle any possible negotiations with the Mexican government. In his instructions to Trist, Buchanan stressed the importance of acquiring the entire California coast as far south as San Diego Bay.

. . . Considering the heavy expenses and sacrifices of the war on our part, and the brilliant success of our arms, as well as the large amount which, under the projet, this Government has assumed to pay our own citizens for claims due to them by Mexico, justice would seem to require that the Treaty should not stipulate for the payment of any very large sum. You may in conversation with [the Mexican Plenipotentiary] ascertain what change in the terms of the projet the Mexican Government would require: and if this should become indispensable to attain the object, you may modify these terms, including the amount to be paid to Mexico, in the following particulars.

1. Instead of fifteen millions of dollars stipulated to be paid by the fifth article for the extension of our boundary over New Mexico and Upper and Lower California, you may increase the amount to any sum not exceeding thirty millions of dollars, payable by instalments of three millions per annum; provided the right of passage and transit across the Isthmus of Tehuantepec secured to the United States by the eighth article of the projet, shall form a part of the Treaty.

2. Whilst it is of the greatest importance to the United States to extend their boundaries over Lower California as well as New Mexico and Upper California, you are not to consider this as a sine qua non to the conclusion of a Treaty. You will, therefore, not break off the negotiation if New Mexico and Upper California can alone be acquired. In that event, however, you will not stipulate to pay more than twenty millions of dollars for these two Provinces, without the right of passage and transit across the Isthmus of Tehuantepec.

3. You are authorized to stipulate for the payment of any sum not exceeding twenty five millions of dollars for New Mexico and Upper California, without Lower California, provided the stipulation securing the right of passage and transit across the Isthmus of Tehuantepec shall be retained in the Treaty or if this should be stricken out, you are authorized to stipulate for the payment of the like sum of twenty five millions of dollars for Lower California in addition to New Mexico and Upper California.

Should Lower California not be embraced in the Treaty, then it will become necessary to change the delineation of boundary contained in the fourth article of the projet in the following manner: Instead of the concluding words "[down

* Buchanan to Trist, April 15, 1847, Instructions to Mexico MSS, Department of State, National Archives, Vol. XVI.

the middle of the Colorado and the middle of the Gulf of California] to the Pacific Ocean", let it read, "to a point directly opposite the division line between Upper and Lower California; thence, due West, along the said line which runs north of the parallel of 32° and South of San Miguel to the Pacific Ocean: and the vessels and citizens of the United States shall in all time to come have free and uninterrupted access to and from the ocean through the Gulf of California from and to their possessions north of the said division line.". . .

The extension of our boundaries over New Mexico and Upper California for a sum not exceeding twenty millions of dollars, is to be considered a sine qua non of any Treaty. You may modify, change or omit the other terms of the Projet, if needful, but not so as to interfere with this ultimatum. . . .

— | "The bay of San Francisco, and other harbors . . . would in a short period become the marts of an extensive and profitable commerce with China. . . ." *

The publication of Trist's instructions in the American press, revealing the territorial objectives of the Polk administration, no longer made secrecy an issue. Polk in his message to Congress in December 1847 announced publicly that United States wartime diplomacy with Mexico was directed at the acquisition of San Francisco and San Diego.

. . . The doctrine of no territory is the doctrine of no indemnity; and if sanctioned, would be a public acknowledgment that our country was wrong, and that the war declared by Congress with extraordinary unanimity, was unjust, and should be abandoned—an admission unfounded in fact, and degrading to the national character.

The terms of the treaty proposed by the United States were not only just to Mexico, but, considering the character and amount of our claims, the unjustifiable and unprovoked commencement of hostilities by her, the expenses of the war to which we have been subjected, and the success which had attended our arms, were deemed to be of a most liberal character.

The commissioner of the United States was authorized to agree to the establishment of the Rio Grande as the boundary, from its entrance into the Gulf to its intersection with the southern boundary of New Mexico, in north latitude about thirty-two degrees, and to obtain a cession to the United States of the provinces of New Mexico and the Californias, and the privilege of the right of way across the isthmus of Tehuantepec. The boundary of the Rio Grande, and the cession to the United States of New Mexico and Upper California, consti-

* Polk's message to Congress, December 7, 1847, *Congressional Globe*, 30th Congress, 1st Sess., Part I, 5–6.

tuted an ultimatum which our commissioner was, under no circumstances, to yield. . . .

The cession to the United States by Mexico, of the provinces of New Mexico and the Californias, as proposed by the commissioner of the United States, it was believed, would be more in accordance with the convenience and interests of both nations, than any other cession of territory which it was probable Mexico could be induced to make.

It is manifest to all who have observed the action condition of the Mexican Government, for some years past, and at present, that if these provinces should be retained by her, she could not long continue to hold and govern them. Mexico is too feeble a Power to govern these provinces, lying as they do at a distance of more than a thousand miles from her capital, and, if attempted to be retained by her, they would constitute but for a short time, even nominally, a part of her dominions.

This would be especially the case with Upper California. The sagacity of powerful European nations has long since directed their attention to the commercial importance of that province, and there can be little doubt that the moment the United States shall relinquish their present occupation of it, and their claim to it as indemnity, an effort would be made by some foreign Power to possess it, either by conquest or by purchase. If no foreign Government should acquire it in either of these modes, an independent revolutionary government would probably be established by the inhabitants, and such foreigners as may remain in or remove to the country, as soon as it shall be known that the United States have abandoned it. Such a Government would be too feeble long to maintain its separate independent existence, and would finally become annexed to, or be a dependent colony of, some more powerful State. . . .

The provinces of New Mexico and the Californias are contiguous to the territories of the United States, and if brought under the government of our laws, their resources—mineral, agricultural, manufacturing, and commercial—would soon be developed.

Upper California is bounded on the north by our Oregon possessions; and if held by the United States, would soon be settled by a hardy, enterprising, and intelligent portion of our population. The bay of San Francisco, and other harbors along the Californian coast, would afford shelter for our navy, for our numerous whale ships, and other merchant vessels employed in the Pacific ocean, and would in a short period become the marts of an extensive and profitable commerce with China, and other countries of the East.

These advantages, in which the whole commercial world would participate, would at once be secured to the United States by the cession of this territory; while it is certain that as long as it remains a part of the Mexican dominions, they can be enjoyed neither by Mexico herself nor by any other nation. . . .

— | "The excellent harbors of Upper California will, under our flag, afford security and repose to our commercial marine. . . ." *

With the ratification of the Treaty of Guadalupe Hidalgo in the spring of 1848, the President could at last contemplate the success of his expansionist policy. In July he delivered to Congress his personal appraisal of his diplomatic achievement in expanding the borders of the United States to include 1300 miles of frontage on the Pacific Ocean. Again his eyes were only on ports.

✍

. . . New Mexico and Upper California have been ceded by Mexico to the United States, and now constitute a part of our country. Embracing nearly ten degrees of latitude, lying adjacent to the Oregon Territory, and extending from the Pacific Ocean to the Rio Grande, a mean distance of nearly a thousand miles, it would be difficult to estimate the value of these possessions to the United States. They constitute of themselves a country large enough for a great empire, and their acquisition is second only in importance to that of Louisiana in 1803. Rich in mineral and agricultural resources, with a climate of great salubrity, they embrace the most important ports on the whole Pacific coast of the continent of North America. The possession of the ports of San Diego, Monterey, and the bay of San Francisco, will enable the United States to command the already valuable and rapidly increasing commerce of the Pacific. The number of our whale-ships alone, now employed in that sea, exceeds seven hundred, requiring more than twenty thousand seamen to navigate them; while the capital invested in this particular branch of commerce is estimated at not less than forty millions of dollars. The excellent harbors of Upper California will, under our flag, afford security and repose to our commercial marine; and American mechanics will soon furnish ready means of ship-building and repair, which are now so much wanted in that distant sea.

By the acquisition of these possessions, we are brought into immediate proximity with the west coast of America, from Cape Horn to the Russian possessions north of Oregon; with the islands of the Pacific Ocean; and, by a direct voyage in steamers, we will be in less than thirty days of Canton and other parts of China.

In this vast region, whose rich resources are soon to be developed by American energy and enterprise, great must be the augmentation of our commerce; and with it, new and profitable demands for mechanic labor in all its branches, and new and valuable markets for our manufactures and agricultural products. . . .

* Polk's message to Congress, July 6, 1848, *Congressional Globe*, 30th Congress, 1st Sess., Part I, 901.

# IV

## The Monroe Doctrine

If nineteenth-century Americans agreed that the Monroe Doctrine had significance for American foreign policy, they never agreed on the nature of its role. This confusion resulted in large measure from the peculiar conditions which gave rise to the doctrine. These conditions centered in the revolt of the Spanish-American colonies, which involved the future independence of a large portion of the American continents, and in the alleged intention of the Holy Alliance of the continental powers of Europe to reduce Spanish America to its former allegiance through force of arms. To discourage such an attempt the United States and Great Britain acted in common, if not in concert, and with the distinct threat to employ force if necessary. Trivial as was the naval power of the United States, when contrasted with that of Britain, it was welcomed by the London government as evidence of a clear mutuality of interest in eliminating Continental power from the Atlantic. Together the two nations discouraged the proposed involvement of European armies in the American quarrel. Until 1823 the Holy Alliance did not threaten any established American policies. Indeed, European powers had conquered, colonized, and exchanged territories in the Western Hemisphere well into the nineteenth century without provoking any opposition from within the United States. But once the Latin American nations had demonstrated the power to break their ties with Spain, their independence became a matter of deep concern to Britain and America alike, for their reconquest by France would have endangered both the established power structure and the basic commercial relationships of the entire Atlantic world.

In identifying American will with the continued independence of Latin America, the Monroe administration assigned the Monroe Doctrine a dual role. The doctrine represented, first, a fundamental national interest in preserving the nation's unique position of predominant power in the hemisphere. As such it was a policy, effective for the reason that it conformed to the realities of power in the Atlantic and did not overextend the nation's commitments in the New World. So realistic, in fact, was the American purpose in preventing the establishment of rival power in the Western Hemisphere that the United States required neither war nor the threat of war to protect this essential interest. British leaders tended to accept the Monroe Doctrine as a statement of policy, nothing more. The American principle of hands-off, directed against England as well as the European continent itself, served British purpose well. In fact, George Canning, the British Foreign Secretary, took some credit for Monroe's announcement. In 1826 he boasted to Parliament: "I called the New World into existence to redress the balance of the Old."

For some Americans, however, the Monroe Doctrine was a broad declaration of liberal principles. The United States, in defying the Holy Alliance, had not defended the interests of the United States but the liberty of Latin America. Because it appeared to attach American purpose to a universal democratic ideal, the Monroe Doctrine was viewed by many European masters of *Realpolitik* as purely utopian. A number of leading Continental diplomatists condemned the doctrine because, as a body of abstract principle, it would overreach actual American economic and security interests and would attempt to eliminate European influence from Latin American affairs solely on the basis of special rights. For Prince Metternich, the Austrian Chancellor, such claims to political virtue were nothing less than sheer arrogance. "The United States of America," he wrote, ". . . have cast blame and scorn on the institutions of Europe most worthy of respect. . . . In permitting themselves these unprovoked attacks, in fostering revolutions wherever they show themselves, in regretting those which have failed, in extending a helping hand to those which seem to prosper, they lend new strength to the apostles of sedition and reanimate the courage of every conspirator." Baron Von Tuyll, the Russian Minister in Washington, passed similar judgment on the Monroe Doctrine: "The document in question enunciates views and pretensions so exaggerated, it establishes principles so contrary to the rights of the European powers that it merits only the most profound contempt."

In practice the administrations from Monroe to John Tyler recognized the Monroe Doctrine as policy, not principle. Because they measured the political changes wrought by the European nations within Latin America solely in the light of American economic and security interests, they accepted those changes without criticism or complaint. In January 1833 a British warship cast anchor off the Falkland Islands in the southern Atlantic, claimed them for the king, and hoisted the Union Jack in defiance of Argentina's clear title to the islands. President Andrew Jackson and his advisers were totally unconcerned. These islands were remote and their possession by England was no threat to American interests. When the British during the following year encroached on Belize along the Central American coast, the Central American government reminded Washington that British action had defied the words of Monroe's declaration. But the British Minister had already assured the Secretary of State, John Forsyth, that no American interest was involved in the transfer. The British seizure of Ruatan in the Bay Islands off the Honduras coast in 1838 was a clear case of aggression against a Latin American state, but it also aroused no reaction within the United States. In the mid-'thirties France attempted to extend the limits of French Guiana eastward, thus encroaching on the territory of Brazil. It was British rather than American pressure on the French government that secured, in 1840, the evacuation of French troops from the disputed region. On other occasions both Britain and France meddled in the internal affairs of the Latin American nations, usually by establishing blockades to exert pressure on their governments. In none of these affairs did the United States reveal any interest despite occasional appeals from Latin American diplomats in Washington. Until the 'forties the Monroe Doctrine represented policy and as such remained inoperative. In none of the political changes within Latin America had the true interests of the United States been challenged.

## II

For two decades the Monroe Doctrine was all but forgotten when the rumor of European designs on Oregon and California sent Americans scrambling for whatever defense the noncolonization principle of the Monroe declaration might afford. During the autumn of 1845, when the danger of British ambition in North America appeared especially acute, leading proponents of manifest destiny demanded that President Polk reaffirm the superior claims of the United States, under the Monroe Doctrine, to the regions along the Pacific coast. Quite characteristically the New York *Herald* in September urged the President to assume even higher ground than had Monroe by putting "into operation those principles and elements of power, which have been committed to the hands of the American people by the Almighty, for the purpose of regenerating, not only this continent, but the old continent of Europe, in due process of time." In his message of December 1845 Polk challenged the alleged determination of Britain and France to create a "balance of power" on the North American continent for the purpose of checking the expansion of the United States. (*Reading No. 1.*) The President cited only Oregon in his message, but he informed Senator Thomas Hart Benton of Missouri that in his reassertion of the Monroe Doctrine he had "California & the fine bay of San Francisco, as much in view as Oregon."

Polk's message sparked the first significant debate in Congress on the meaning of Monroe's declaration, a debate which quickly touched the very foundations of proper national behavior in the area of external affairs. On January 14, 1846, Senator William Allen of Ohio, chairman of the Senate Committee on Foreign Relations, introduced a resolution designed to commit the Congress to the principles of the Monroe Doctrine. Having asserted that the President had the right and obligation to counter the European concept of the "balance of power" with the principle of European nonintervention in American affairs, Allen declared that Congress had been compelled by events to solemnly declare

> . . . the unalterable resolution of the United States to adhere to and to enforce the principle, that any effort of the Powers of Europe to intermeddle in the social organization or political arrangements of the Independent nations of America, or further to extend the European system of Government upon this continent by the establishment of new Colonies, would be incompatible with the independent existence of

the nations, and dangerous to the liberties of the people of America, and therefore will incur, as by the right of self-preservation it would justify, the prompt resistence of the United States.

This resolution excited the approval of those members of Congress, led by Senator Lewis Cass of Michigan, who viewed American foreign policy as a body of ideals. Cass lauded Allen's motion as an attempt, at last, to identify the Congress with Monroe's declaration and thus make it an essential element in the foreign relations of the United States. The Senator continued: "It is the assertion of a great principle—of an everlasting principle—of the right of the independent nations upon this hemisphere to be free from the control of the powers of Europe, and an assertion by the oldest of the family of nations upon this continent, made by one for the benefit of all."

John C. Calhoun, a leading spokesmen for the nation's conservative tradition in foreign affairs, attacked the resolution as a dangerous overcommitment of American policy since it would invoke United States guardianship for all the nations of the New World against all foreign aggression. If this was to be the settled policy of the United States, then, he warned, "the energies of the country must be concentrated and put forth to enable us to carry out this policy, if we intend that our declaration shall mean anything." Nothing would result from the declaration, he predicted, because the government was not prepared to act. For Calhoun it was essential that ends be determined by the means available. It was, he said, "the part of wisdom to select wise ends in a wise manner. No wise man, with a full understanding of the subject, could pledge himself, by declaration, to do that which was beyond the power of execution, and without mature reflection as to the consequences. There would be no dignity in it. True dignity consists in making no declaration which we are not prepared to maintain. If we make the declaration, we ought to be prepared to carry it into effect against all opposition." Calhoun, in one forceful exchange with Cass, decried as demeaning to the nation's character the tendencies within Congress to pass abstract resolutions designed to govern external affairs. (*Reading No. 2.*)

Two years later Polk inaugurated the most searching examination of the relevance of the Monroe Doctrine to American foreign policy in the nation's history. During the spring of 1848 an agent of the Yucatán government, Don Justo Sierra, appealed to the Polk administration for American military aid against the rebellious Indians of the hinterland who threatened to drive the whites of the region into the sea. He offered the United States, in return for its support, "dominion and sovereignty" over the state of Yucatán, explaining that the same appeal had been extended to England and Spain with the same assurance of "dominion and sovereignty" should they offer protection. On April 29, 1848, Polk, addressing a message to Congress, repeated his earlier sweeping assertion that it was the settled policy of the United States "that no future European colony or dominion shall . . . be planted or established on any part of the American continent." Polk based his appeal for American involvement partially on the moral obligation of the United States to rescue the whites of Yucatán, partially on the danger to American security entailed in the possible reduction of Yucatán to the status of a European colony. The Senate Committee on Foreign Relations quickly reported a bill which provided for the military occupation of Yucatán. In the bitter debate which ensued Congress again divided sharply on the two issues of humanitarian obligation and national security.

Immediately Western Democrats, proclaiming anew the nation's transcendent mission to humanity, rushed to the defense of the President's appeal. Senator Sam Houston of Texas termed the issue raised by the civil war in Yucatán the simple one between civilization and barbarism. "The war raging in Yucatán," he declared, "is not only one of desolation and rapine, but of unheard-of cruelty and extermination." The threat to American security rendered the issue even more vital. If the United States failed to protect Yucatán from European encroachment, he warned, it would give up all pretext for resisting anywhere in the hemisphere the European assault on its free institutions. Again it was Cass who carried the chief burden of argumentation for the interventionists. For the Michigan Senator the alleged European danger to Yucatán carried with it a pervading threat to both American continental security and American political principles. Intervention, therefore, was not improper, "but a high dictate of duty, demanded by the true principles of public safety." England, warned Cass, would accept Yucatán's invitation if the United States did not, and in possession of the Yucatán coast would command the entrance to the Gulf of Mexico as well as the political and economic future of Cuba itself. The question before the Congress was not annexation, but rather the peace and independence of Yucatán itself. (*Reading No. 3.*)

Much of the Whig party and the Eastern metropolitan press condemned the efforts of Democratic leaders to involve the nation in the affairs of Yucatán. Where would the pursuit of humanitarian goals terminate? Representative Joseph Root of Ohio wondered if the United States was committing itself "to go out and aid the weaker party in every war all over the world." Once the nation accepted the dictate of humanity as its guide in foreign affairs, charged one Whig Senator, there would no longer exist any limit to its interference in the affairs of other states. Similarly, the Washington *National Intelligencer,* on May 1, protested against the President's assumption that his interpretation of the Monroe Doctrine was the established policy of the United States. This nation, charged the editor, was not "the Grand Protector of the Continent." Other editors reminded the proponents of abstract principle that none of the European powers were at odds with the United States. Nor did any of them harbor any intent to interfere in the territorial arrangements, or institutions of the New World. Too many Senators, charged the *Baltimore Clipper,* talked as if England could be and should be whipped. "Weak as she may be considered by some who expect to reach the Presidency by exciting enmity to her," charged the editor, "we have no desire to witness another war with that country!"

Conservatives sought to limit the nation's commitments abroad. John M. Niles of Connecticut, for example, observed that the inclination of some Senators to interfere in Yucatán affairs defied two thoroughly established principles of American diplomacy—neutrality and nonintervention. He warned that any departure from these traditions "might be fatal to our best interests, and we might find it difficult to get back into the path in which we have so far walked with safety, and which has given to this country . . . a freedom from disturbances and entanglements which has fallen to the lot of no other nation." Again it was Calhoun who, on May 15, carried the burgeoning assault on Polk's reassertion of the Monroe Doctrine to its ultimate conclusion. The South Carolinian, as a member of Monroe's cabinet in 1823, made it clear that Monroe's message was directed at one specific threat to the independence of Latin America—that of the Holy Alliance. The disintegration of the Holy Alliance had rendered the doctrine meaningless. Since England has been an ally of the United States in 1823, how could the President employ the words of Monroe against that nation, especially when it had revealed no disposition to interfere in the affairs of Yucatán? Monroe's words, declared Calhoun, were declarations, nothing more. Yet Polk, Calhoun complained, had called them the settled policy of the United States. Calhoun concluded his speech with a carefully studied review of the concept of national interest. (*Reading No. 4.*)

Such debates as that which raged over Yucatán settled nothing. For politicians and editors more concerned with the form than the substance of public expression, Calhoun's arguments appeared a needless denial of the nation's transcendent obligation to oppressed mankind. Indiana's ebullient Senator, Edward Hannegan, termed Calhoun "the most deadly and dangerous enemy of Democratic causes who is now to be found in the Republic." During the succeeding decade it became habitual for Americans to interpret the Monroe Doctrine as a statement of liberal purpose and to call upon it to maintain the *status quo* against every European action. Democratic politicians, for example, employed the doctrine to denounce the Whig administration for the Clayton-Bulwer Treaty of 1850 whereby the United States agreed to share with Britain the right to control any future canal across Central America. But the Monroe Doctrine, despite the ubiquitous references to it, was not the determining factor in Latin American affairs. The United States pursued its own limited interests in the Western Hemisphere and until 1860 no European power harbored any ambition in the region which might have challenged the nation's irreducible commitments. What maintained the independence of Latin America was less the rhetoric of Monroe than the clearly recognized power factors in the Atlantic world—the Atlantic itself, rendered formidable as a barrier by British interests and the British navy, the European balance of power, the genuine security interests of the United States, the nationalisms of the Latin American nations themselves, and, lastly, the absence of any overriding incentive among the European governments to interfere in Western Hemispheric affairs.

## III

Not even when the United States was torn by civil war could France establish a puppet monarchy in Mexico with any success. Yet so inviting were conditions within the Mexican Republic that Napoleon III could not resist the temptation to intervene. Mexico was torn by revolution, and the clerical party, favoring a monarchy, assured Napoleon that the Mexican people would welcome his interference in the interest of national stability. By 1862, moreover, Napoleon and the Mexican agents had found an attractive candidate for the Mexican throne in Archduke Maximilian of Austria. For Napoleon himself the establishment of a French-supported monarchy in Mexico promised to improve his relations with the Catholic party in France and to open vast markets and sources of raw material in the New World for French industry. In a letter of October 9, 1861, to the Comte de Flahault, Napoleon summarized the factors which propelled him into his Mexican venture:

> There is no need for me to enlarge upon the common interest which we in Europe have in seeing Mexico pacified and endowed with a stable government. Not only has that country, which enjoys every advantage, attracted much of our capital, and many of our fellow-countrymen, but, if it were regenerated, it would form an impassible barrier to the encroachments of North America, it would afford an important opening for English, Spanish, and French trade, while exploiting its own wealth, and lastly it would render great services to our manufactories by extending its cultivation of cotton. . . . Today unexpected events have arisen and changed the face of affairs. The American war has made it impossible for the United States to interfere, and what is more, the outrages committed by the Mexican government have provided England, Spain, and France with a legitimate motive for interference in Mexico.

The fact that Britain and Spain, as well as France, harbored long-standing grievances against Mexico assured the French government of British co-operation—an essential element in any military excursion across the Atlantic. Clearly, for the moment American policy in Latin America was inoperative.

Napoleon's ambitions vastly exceeded the power that he could bring to bear on affairs so remote from the true interests of France. When it was clear that he had dispatched French forces to Mexico for reasons other than the collecting of debts, Britain and Spain deserted him. In Mexico his army faced a sullen population as well as the determined and effective resistance of Mexican guerrillas under Benito Juárez. Napoleon, trapped by a long series of miscalculations, nevertheless persisted in his misadventure and in 1864 managed to install Maximilian as monarch of Mexico.

Meanwhile, President Abraham Lincoln and his Secretary of State, William H. Seward, refused to confront Napoleon with any threat, for they knew that Mexico, despite its weakness and internal chaos, would generate enough opposition eventually to drive the French forces out of the country. In his letter to Charles Francis Adams in London, dated March 3, 1862, Seward predicted that the French effort would fail simply because it ran counter to all the political trends of the age. (*Reading No. 5.*)

Lincoln and Seward could discover no advantage in antagonizing France and therefore resisted the pressures exerted by their Congressional opponents who condemned the administration's inaction in Mexico with appeals to the Monroe

Doctrine. Matias Romero, the Mexican agent in Washington, convinced members of the House of Representatives that a Congressional resolution, condemning France, would undermine the French position in Mexico without committing the United States to any specific action. It was clear that the Senate would reject any such resolution, but in April 1864 the House passed a resolution, by a vote of 109 to 0, which declared that "the Congress of the United States are unwilling by silence to have the nations of the world under the impression that they are indifferent spectators of the deplorable events now transpiring in the Republic of Mexico, and that they think fit to declare that it does not accord with the policy of the United States to acknowledge any monarchical government erected on the ruins of any republican government in America under the auspices of any European power." This meaningless appeal to patriotic sentiment was part of a political maneuver among Radical Republicans to secure the 1864 Republican nomination for John C. Frémont, whose own condemnation of French intervention in Mexico had been well publicized.

For Seward the American interest in Mexico was governed by policy, not abstractions. To the end of the war the Lincoln administration refused to issue any warning to France. When after Lee's surrender at Appomattox, General U. S. Grant suggested to Lincoln that the Northern armies be employed to drive the French from Mexico, Seward resisted. He repeated his earlier conviction that the French involvement in Mexico was doomed to failure. Seward instructed the special mission to France in 1865 "to see if the French Emperor could not be made to understand the necessity of withdrawing his army from Mexico, and thus save the necessity of expelling it by force." Such was the intimation which Seward conveyed. So devoid of offense was his manner that the ultimate agent, force, hardly appeared in the controversy at all. In his noted dispatch to the French government of February 12, 1866, Seward refused again to condemn the French for engaging Mexico in war. He reasserted, however, the interest of the United States in the principle of self-determination for Mexico and suggested that it would be to the interest of France as well to recognize the validity of that principle. (*Reading No. 6.*) As the administration had predicted, the cost of the Mexican involvement eventually became so high that Napoleon was delighted to withdraw his forces, permitting the Emperor Maximilian to die before a Mexican firing squad. Not again in the nineteenth century was American preponderance in the Western Hemisphere seriously challenged by any European power.

## IV

Two episodes in the late nineteenth century encouraged widespread assertions of the superior claims and unlimited jurisdiction of the United States in Latin American controversies which involved a European nation. In 1879 the French canal company under Ferdinand de Lesseps, emerging from its conquest of Suez, negotiated a contract with the Republic of Colombia to construct a canal across the Isthmus of Panama. For that minority in the United States who regarded the French concession an unwarranted danger to the vital interests of the United States, the words of the Monroe Doctrine provided the immediate stimulus to action. In June 1879, Senator Ambrose Burnside of Rhode Island introduced a resolution which declared that the American people, who had adhered to the Monroe Doctrine for fifty years, "would not view without serious disquietude any attempt of the powers of Europe to establish under their protection and domination a ship-canal across the isthmus of Darien, and such action on the part of any other power could not be regarded in any other light than as the manifestation of an unfriendly disposition towards the United States." In defending his resolution, the Senator termed the Monroe Doctrine "the safeguard of these United States and . . . the club of Hercules and the shield of Telamon." For him it was essential that the United States protect the nation's rights as well as all progress, civil and religious, in the hemisphere. By constructing an interocean canal, he warned, a European government could control the destiny of any state through which the canal passed and thus endanger the security of the United States. Never enacted by Congress, the Monroe Doctrine was the "unwritten law of the land."

Again in this crisis there were realists who restated the original concept of the doctrine as an expression of the national interest of the United States in the Western Hemisphere. President Monroe, declared one former diplomat, had not established a policy. Nor would the repetition of his words by all the Presidents of the United States establish a policy. Not one of the prohibitions listed in Monroe's message, he pointed out, was involved in the building of a canal by a private French company. How could the United States properly restrict the right of Colombia to negotiate with M. Lesseps? "The Monroe Doctrine," he concluded, "culminates and settles itself in the entire absolute sovereignty and independence of the South American states." Similarly E. L. Youmans, the noted social Darwinian, declared in the *Popular Science Monthly* that the Monroe Doctrine was "the very bulwark of De Lesseps' enterprise. Originally designed to guarantee to Colombia her sovereign rights over her own soil, it now becomes a hypocritical pretext for invading and crushing her nationality." To Youmans all the public clamor in behalf of the Monroe Doctrine served only the interests of the rival canal companies of the United States who found the Frenchman a formidable competitor. Perhaps the most remarkable evaluation of the Monroe Doctrine produced by the canal controversey was Gustave Koerner's article which appeared in *The Nation* on January 5, 1882. (*Reading No. 7.*) "The true Monroe Doctrine," he wrote, "is the interest of our country; . . . Practically, we have always so acted, and as long as we have statesmen at the helm of state, and not mere 'doctrinaires' . . . we shall continue so to act, whether our action squares with the Monroe or any other doctrine or not. No doctrine will excuse us when we act unjustly, and none will prevent us from asserting our rights, at any cost, when our interest or our honor is involved."

In 1895 the Venezuela boundary dispute set off the second and final serious controversy over the meaning of the Monroe Doctrine in the late nineteenth century. Despite repeated negotiations, England and Venezuela had never agreed on an acceptable boundary to separate British Guiana from the South American republic. British surveyors had marked a boundary as early as the 'forties—the Schomburgh Line—which even granted Venezuela control of the mouth of the Orinoco River. Venezuela rejected the British proposal and demanded arbitration with the hope of securing a more favorable settlement. Within the disputed area were 40,000 inhabitants who favored British rule. Should the British arbitrate in principle, moreover, their entire empire might become subject to such corroding devices. The British agreed to arbitrate the western portion of the area in dispute—the region beyond which the British subjects resided. Venezuela broke off diplomatic relations with Britain in 1887, determined to enlist the support of the United States by reviving the phraseology of the Monroe Doctrine. Finally in the autumn of 1894 Venezuela brought the boundary dispute to a critical stage when its agent in the United States, former American minister to Venezuela, William L. Scruggs, published a pamphlet which listed the alleged British aggressions against Venezuela. Within months both houses of Congress had adopted resolutions condemning British policy. Senator Henry Cabot Lodge expressed Republican sentiment in *The North American Review:* "If Great Britain is to be permitted to occupy the ports of Nicaragua and, still worse, take the territory of Venezuela, there is nothing to prevent her taking the whole of Venezuela or any other South American state. If Great Britain can do this with impunity, France and Germany will do it also. . . . The supremacy of the Monroe Doctrine should be established at once—peaceably if we can, forcibly if we must."

Faced with a Republican opposition which threatened to turn the Democrats out of office with appeals to the Monroe Doctrine, President Grover Cleveland threw the power and prestige of the United States government behind the Venezuelan claims. In January 1895 his Secretary of State, Richard Olney, dispatched a note to the British government which extended American pretensions under the Monroe Doctrine to include the complete control of the hemisphere. (*Reading No. 8*) "To-day," he wrote, "the United States is practically sovereign on this continent, and its fiat is law upon the subject to which it confines its interposition." The United States was master of the hemisphere, not because of its wisdom and justice, but because of its superior resources and its isolated position. Olney termed Monroe's declaration "a doctrine of American public law, well founded in principle and abundantly sanctioned by precedent. . . ." In his reply of November 26, Lord Salisbury, the British Foreign Minister, challenged the relevance of the Monroe Doctrine to the Venezuelan boundary controversy. His profoundly perceptive evaluation of the unchallengeable foundations of American foreign policy argued that the United States might have interests in Latin America, as it might also have them in China or Japan, and that it had the right and obligation to defend those interests. But the United States, he added, "is not entitled to affirm as a universal proposition, with reference to a number of independent states for whose conduct it assumes no responsibility, that its interests are necessarily concerned in whatever may befall those states simply because they are situated in the Western Hemisphere." (*Reading No. 9.*)

In a sense Olney was correct in his grandiose claims of 1895. Behind the prohibitions aimed at the European powers the Monroe Doctrine could be employed eventually as a rationalization for American imperialism in the Caribbean. The sheer power which the United States could display, especially when contrasted with the abject weakness and disarray of the Caribbean republics, made the Roosevelt Corollary completely feasible as policy. In pursuing its widespread interests in the Caribbean after 1900, the United States engaged in no actions which required more than a limited application of power. Direct American intervention began in Santo Domingo, but continued throughout the area until by World War I the United States had established five protectorates in the region of the Caribbean. By employing its predominant military, economic, political, and diplomatic power it could overthrow recalcitrant governments almost at will. The tragedy in the recurring debate over the meaning of the Monroe Doctrine, then, lay not in the tendency to commit the United States beyond its interests, but in the tendency to perpetuate and strengthen the illusion that abstract doctrine can serve as the legitimate basis of policy. The vast disproportion of power in the New World misled too many Americans into believing that the words of Monroe were law whereas in reality the law resided in the large variety of genuine power factors involved. The ultimate danger of resting foreign policy on abstract statements of public law, such as the Monroe Doctrine, was analyzed dramatically by the noted American conservative, William Graham Sumner, in his famous essay "War." (*Reading No. 10.*) Unfortunately the danger was not easily demonstrable from the history of the Monroe Doctrine, for the claims to the *status quo* in Latin America, as encompassed by the doctrine, were never challenged by the nations of Europe in any fashion sufficiently threatening to require a genuine examination of the doctrine as national interest and not as unilateral public law.

# 1 | Polk's Reaffirmation of the Monroe Doctrine, December 2, 1845 *

In his message to Congress of December 1845 President Polk established what became the traditional and popular concept of the Monroe Doctrine, one that was to be repeated by proponents of the declaration in every succeeding hemispheric crisis throughout the nineteenth century. To Polk the United States and the nations of Latin America possessed the rights of sovereignty and independence, commensurate with the nations of Europe, not because of their intrinsic strength but because they were American, with structures of government that differed from those of Europe. For that reason, declared Polk, the people of the Western Hemisphere alone had the right to determine their destiny. The principle of self-determination, moreover, included the freedom of all New World states to enter the American Confederacy, whatever the effect of such a union on the "balance of power" in the hemisphere.

✍

. . . The rapid extension of our settlements over our territories heretofore un-occupied, the addition of new States to our Confederacy, the expansion of free principles, and our rising greatness as a nation are attracting the attention of the powers of Europe, and lately the doctrine has been broached in some of them of a "balance of power" on this continent to check our advancement. The United States, sincerely desirous of preserving relations of good understanding with all nations, can not in silence permit any European interference on the North American continent, and should any such interference be attempted will be ready to resist it at any and all hazards.

It is well known to the American people and to all nations that this Government has never interfered with the relations subsisting between other governments. We have never made ourselves parties to their wars or their alliances; we have not sought their territories by conquest; we have not mingled with parties in their domestic struggles; and believing our own form of government to be the best, we have never attempted to propagate it by intrigues, by diplomacy, or by force. We may claim on this continent a like exemption from European interference. The nations of America are equally sovereign and independent with those of Europe. They possess the same rights, independent of all foreign interposition, to make war, to conclude peace, and to regulate their internal affairs. The people of the United States can not, therefore, view with indifference attempts of European powers to interfere with the independent action of the nations on this continent. The American system of government is entirely different from that of Europe. Jealousy among the different sovereigns of Europe, lest any one of them might become too powerful for the rest, has caused

* *Messages and Papers of the Presidents,* James D. Richardson, ed. (Washington, 1897), IV: 398–9.

them anxiously to desire the establishment of what they term the "balance of power." It can not be permitted to have any application on the North American continent, and especially to the United States.

We must ever maintain the principle that the people of this continent alone have the right to decide their own destiny. Should any portion of them, constituting an independent state, propose to unite themselves with our Confederacy, this will be a question for them and us to determine without any foreign interposition. We can never consent that European powers shall interfere to prevent such a union because it might disturb the "balance of power" which they may desire to maintain upon this continent. Near a quarter of a century ago the principle was distinctly announced to the world, in the annual message of one of my predecessors, that—

> The American continents, by the free and independent condition which they have assumed and maintain, are henceforth not to be considered as subjects for future colonization by any European powers.

This principle will apply with greatly increased force should any European power attempt to establish any new colony in North America. In the existing circumstances of the world the present is deemed a proper occasion to reiterate and reaffirm the principle avowed by Mr. Monroe and to state my cordial concurrence in its wisdom and sound policy. The reassertion of this principle, especially in reference to North America, is at this day but the promulgation of a policy which no European power should cherish the disposition to resist. Existing rights of every European nation should be respected, but it is due alike to our safety and our interests that the efficient protection of our laws should be extended over our whole territorial limits, and that it should be distinctly announced to the world as our settled policy that no future European colony or dominion shall with our consent be planted or established on any part of the North American continent. . . .

## 2 | Calhoun's Opposition to Congressional Resolutions Designed To Govern External Affairs, January 1846 *

In the following brief exchange with Lewis Cass, Calhoun revealed himself a powerful spokesman of the conservative tradition in American diplomacy. He, like Hamilton and John Quincy Adams, decried the tendency of national leaders to attach the country's external objectives to broad abstract principles which eliminated the essential factor of precision in policy formulation. Declarations of principle, Calhoun observed, were not policies and did not control affairs among nations.

* Calhoun's remarks in the Senate, January 26, 1846, *Congressional Globe*, 29th Congress, 1st Sess., 245–6.

. . . Mr. Monroe was a wise man, and had no design of burdening the country with a task which it could not perform. . . . Our own good sense should teach us that we ought not to undertake what we cannot perform. It should be so with individuals and with nations. By the adoption of the principle of the resolution, we would be called on to interfere whenever a European nation, right or wrong, should bring on a conflict of arms between one or another nation on this continent. I would ask the Senator from Michigan, where is the limitation?

Mr. CASS. Will the gentleman allow me to explain? The principle for which I contend is this: by such a declaration as that contemplated in the resolution, we would merely place our protest on record, not being thereby bound to any definite course of action, but being left free to maintain neutrality or actively engage in enforcing the principle, as we might see fit.

Mr. CALHOUN. Well, would it not be better to wait for the emergency in which we would have sufficient interest to interfere, and sufficient power to make that interference influential? Why make any such declaration now? What good purpose can it serve? Only to show to the men that are to come after us that we were wiser and more patriotic than we feared they might be! I cannot, for my life, see a single good likely to result from this measure. Will it have a tendency to conciliate European powers, who, in case of a collision with Great Britain, might be friendly to us? or will such a declaration prevent these five great European powers, who, he says, have the regulation of the balance of power, and can do their fiat in Europe, from attempting the execution of any of their schemes? Will mere vaporing bravado have any practical effect? No. You must adopt a very different course of policy. You must arm, equip, fit out your navies, raise a powerful revenue, and resist them by practical measures, if you think proper to resist them. Will not the effect of such a declaration be the very reverse of all this practical course of policy? Will it not create jealousy on the part of England? Will it not militate against the formation of alliances on the part of nations favorably disposed towards us? No good effects can come from it. From first to last, in my opinion, it will be followed by unqualified evil consequences. . . .

. . . As to Texas, Mr. President, as far as I had any share in the management of that particular question, I can only say that the declaration of Mr. Monroe had not the weight of that piece of paper; and if a thousand such declarations, in even stronger terms, had been made and passed the Senate, they would not have had that weight. Declarations, sir, are easily made. The affairs of nations are not controlled by mere declarations. If a declaration of opinion were sufficient to change the whole course of events, no nation would be more prompt than we. But we must meet interference in our affairs in another way. We must meet it as it was met in the case of Texas—decidedly, boldly, and practically. We must meet each particular case by itself, and according to its own merits, always taking care not to assert our rights until we feel ourselves able to sustain our assertions. As to general abstract declarations of that kind, I would not give a farthing for a thousand of them. They do more harm than good, or rather no good at all, but a great deal of harm. . . .

# 3 | Debate on the Yucatán Bill, May 1848:
## The Monroe Doctrine as Principle *

The sweeping debate on the applicability of the Monroe Doctrine to the Yucatán issue in May, 1848, again raised the fundamental American disagreement over the nature and role of a nation's diplomacy—whether it is to serve the cause of humanity or the carefully calculated interests of the country. Senator Sam Houston's argument demanding United States involvement in the affairs of Yucatán under the precepts of Monroe was a standard appeal to the nation's humanitarian sentiments.

✒

. . . No case can possibly arise that will more directly appeal to the true policy of the country or the humanity of a nation than that which is now under discussion. Yucatán has appealed to this country for relief. She has offered to us in return her "dominion and sovereignty." Her existence is dependant upon our action. We are to decide in favor of civilization or barbarism. The war raging in Yucatan is not only one of desolation and rapine, but of unheard-of-cruelty and extermination. It seems to me if any circumstance independent of the true policy of this Government could claim our consideration, it would be the sufferings of the unhappy Yucatecos. Laying aside their appeals to our humanity, the highest political considerations present themselves to the patriot's mind. In the desperation of the affairs of those people, they have not only appealed to the Government of the United States, and made a tender of their dominion and their sovereignty, but they have made a similar tender to England and to Spain. They have first appealed to us, and we are now discussing the propriety of interposing in their behalf. Some Power must interpose. It is true, they are not entitled to our consideration as a recognized member of the family of nations, for they have been abandoned by their natural ally, with whom we are at war. If we refuse aid, and England or Spain or any other Power should interpose in their behalf, how can we say to them, you have no right to interpose? If England should acquire peaceable possession, with the right of dominion and sovereignty, will we not be precluded from all interference hereafter in relation to that territory? If, in consequence of delay on the part of this Government, or a want of action, a foreign Power should take possession of it, we are precluded forever from all interference with that country unless by an act of open war, nor will we have a right to question their title to it. No matter whether they are prompted by a love of dominion or feelings of humanity, if they acquire possession of it owing to delinquency on the part of this Government, we never can question their right, as connected with the affairs of this continent, as embraced in the declaration of Mr. Monroe. That declaration either

* Sam Houston's remarks in the Senate, May 8, 1848, *Congressional Globe,* 30th Congress, 1st Sess., Appendix, 604.

meant something or it meant nothing; and if this Government does not take action in behalf of Yucatán, we must regard that proud sentiment of a revolutionary patriot as idle gasconade. It was no idle threat, nor has it been so understood. . . .

If we do not aid Yucatán in this emergency, it will be an abandonment of all pretext for resisting any encroachment that may be made upon this continent upon any territory not within the defined boundary of the United States. Hence, I believe the true policy of this country, aside from motives of humanity, should induce us to act promptly and efficiently. The course which we ought to pursue is consistent with the safety and well-being of our country. No time would be more propitious than the present for the practical application of the principle inhibitory of the intervention of foreign Powers upon this continent. When again will the state of Europe be found so auspicious to the upbuilding of free institutions upon this continent? Since the existence of this Government no such opportunity has been afforded to us in the establishing of our free institutions as the present. Europe is convulsed. England has to guard her own position. She has perplexities at home. Her complicated colonial system must be kept in operation, and will call in requisition all the ability of her most enlightened statesmen. Under these circumstances, we are left to the accomplishment of the great object of our mission here, if she were even disposed to raise objections to our taking possession of Yucatán. But she can have no ground of complaint. Our intervention has been invoked, and I can apprehend no reason why we should withhold it. But gentlemen have discovered imaginary dangers. They apprehend that it may be a cause of war with France or England. A cause of war, if we choose to assist a neighboring people overwhelmed by calamity! Would it be a just cause? Would the community of nations countenance such a pretext? I cannot believe that there is a nation of the earth that would raise its voice against the interference of this country for the protection of Yucatán. If we were to usurp her territory for self-aggrandizement—if we were seeking to conquer them for spoil, then there would be some pretext for supposing that any foreign Power might interpose to prevent the extension of our dominion. I cannot believe that the Executive contemplates any object, unless it is to prevent the intervention of a foreign Power, and to interfere in behalf of humanity. . . .

It is regretted that obstacles are thrown in the way of the proposition to supply a force and means necessary for the alleviation of the sufferings of Yucatán. The President requests this aid and support from Congress. Is it to annex Yucatán to the United States? No, sir. It is to render such aid as may be necessary to defend the white population of that country against the savages, and to enable them to maintain their position until the Indians can be repulsed, or peace is restored, and then to leave the country in the enjoyment of liberty, after making such arrangements as will reimburse the United States for the aid rendered. This I understand to be the object of the President; and whether it be his meaning or not, it is the design which I would entertain myself. . . .

— | "It is a case of overwhelming, overpowering, necessity." *

Cass, entering the debate with his customary demand that the United States accede to the dictates of humanity as well as public safety, advocated the rescue of the citizens of Yucatán from their savage foes. For Cass, Monroe's declaration established a broad principle to be enforced against every European encroachment on the sovereign rights of an American state.

✍

. . . Certainly gentlemen do not desire the same time to discuss such a question as this, as was necessarily consumed in the collection of information. The great points of the case are before us, and the application now comes, not merely from the Yucatánese commissioner, but from the legislative department of the Government in a solemn decree, and from the Executive of the country. It is a case of overwhelming, overpowering, necessity. While we are deliberating, the sad action is going on; and however prompt we may now be, we may not be prompt enough for the circumstances. The fate of the country may be decided before we can send any relief. At any rate, let us redeem ourselves from the reproach of indifference or unnecessary delay. This is one of those great cases for human action, where to do well is to do promptly, and where too much caution will show that we are unequal to the position in which we find ourselves placed.

I need not recall the condition of Yucatán. The message itself, with the accompanying documents, the information which daily reaches us through the public journals, and the discussion here, have put us in possession of the true state of things in that unhappy country. It is divided between the two races of Spanish and of aboriginal descent, and the Indians have obtained the superiority —have descended from the high country upon the low, and are driving the white race before them to death or to the ocean. It is a war, if that can be called a war, where the fighting seems to be all upon one side, of destruction and extermination. . . . We have reached one of those epochs in the progress of nations to which the historian looks back with interest, and whence he traces much of the good or evil they encounter in their career—one of those epochs which impress themselves upon the character of a country, and when vigorous counsels are equally dictated by justice and by wisdom, while timid and irresolute measures are sure to be followed by political weakness and by the contempt of the world.

The principle advanced by Mr. Monroe, many years since, in two of his messages to Congress, which denounced any future attempt of the European Powers to establish new colonies in this country, has been brought into this discussion, and, in fact, necessarily connects itself with it. This principle has been reasserted by the present Executive, upon the same general considerations which influenced the action of his predecessor. It was a wise measure, fully

* Cass's speech on the Yucatán bill, May 10, 1848, *Congressional Globe*, 30th Congress, 1st Sess., Appendix, 613–17.

justified by received principles of the law of nations and by the actual circumstances of our country. . . . Neither of these Presidents, the past nor the present, assumed to interfere with any existing rights of other nations upon this continent. Neither of them called in question their right to hold and improve the colonies they possessed, at their own pleasure. Such an assumption would have been equally obtrusive and ineffectual; and how the opinion could have prevailed that has been advanced, no one can tell; for, in the documents themselves, the true doctrine is cautiously guarded, and existing rights considered as unassailable. The object which these statesmen had in view was to prevent the recolonization of any portion of this hemisphere; to announce to the world, that when any of the colonies planted upon it escaped from European thraldom, they should not be again subjected to that comparatively humiliating condition. The Spanish colonies had shaken off the yoke of Spain, and had asserted their independence. The struggle had been going on some time, and it was apparent to all the world, except to the world of Spanish obstinacy, that, if not prevented by external force, it would terminate, as it has terminated, in their admission into the great family of nations. It was obvious that European complications might arise, in consequence of the necessities of Spain, and of her recklessness in pushing the contest, which might affect the fate of these countries. French or English assistance might be asked for, and rights conveyed which would induce these Powers to take part in the struggle, with a view to take part in the spoils that might result from it. This was the evil foreseen, and the declaration of this country was one of the remedies to avert it. . . .

We desire no union of the American States; no league to involve us in their difficulties, or they in ours; no Panama mission to open a grand negotiation, and to open likewise a career of complicated diplomatic relations, as difficult to define in their principles as to control in their practical operations. We desire the most perfect independence for all of them, and the most amicable relations among themselves and with us. But we are determined, so far as depends on us, that no European family principles shall come to find an abiding place upon this continent, and to involve in wars, that do not interest them, the various States which occupy it. . . .

. . . The entire political separation of this continent from Europe is not a question of fact, but of time. That event must come, and appearances augur that it will come speedily. We may well leave it to its own fullness of time without any improper interference on our part.

But we are now called upon to make a practical application of the great principle I have been considering. The condition of Yucatán, and the considerations connected with it, bring this subject directly before us. We can enforce the doctrine; but we cannot enforce it without discharging the duties which it brings with it. And if we do not enforce it, we shall expose ourselves to eternal self-reproach and to the contumely of the world.

I have already briefly alluded to the condition of Yucatán. Its civilized population is placed, not between the ocean and the frowning battlements which drive it back, and where no human being can live, but between the ocean and ruthless barbarians, possessing as little mercy as the sea into which they are driving their wretched victims. It is one of those great cases in human affairs which override all other considerations. Yucatán has a right to go where she can, with her sovereignty in her hand, and demand protection from the Powers of the earth, and offer her own allegiance in return for it. She has gone to England and to Spain, and she has come to us. She prefers our action to theirs; but if she cannot get the one, she must accept the other. As to Spain, any effective aid or any design of aggrandizement is probably equally out of the question, and we have England alone to look to in the solution of the question presented to us. If we do not act, will she render the assistance demanded, and accept the consideration which may accompany it? That she may do so, without giving us any just cause of offence whatever, and thus accomplish her mission without being involved in any controversy with us, is too clear to be called in question. Interest, therefore, and humanity, as well as the principles which from all time have regulated her political conduct, prompt her to accede to the demands of the Government of Yucatán. . . .

. . . Now, sir, if England possesses the promontory of Yucatán and the island of Cuba, she will build steam vessels suitable to the harbors which may be found there: vessels of a light draught of water, but carrying a few heavy guns, and capable of commanding the outlet of the Gulf—floating batteries, in fact, almost equal in efficiency to permanent batteries, ready to be stationed in the narrow channel, and completely to command it. . . .

. . . From the southern point of Florida to Yucatán, the chord of the arc does not probably exceed two hundred and fifty miles—a shorter distance than that from Yucatán to Vera Cruz. From the southern point of Florida to Cuba, it is not more than forty miles; and from the western extremity of Cuba to the peninsula of Yucatán, it is not more than sixty miles. These two outlets—the latter into the Caribbean sea, and the former into the Atlantic Ocean—do not, therefore, exceed one hundred miles in their united width, and together make the exit and entrance of the Gulf. Opposite the mouth of the Mississippi, is the noble harbor of Havana, almost within sight of which the whole commerce of the Gulf passes. England has already got the Bahama Islands, with the port of Nassau, and other positions. So long as Cuba and Yucatán are held by their present possessors, neither we nor the commercial world have anything to fear from English projects, whatever they may be. But let their dominion be transferred to England, and where are we? The mouth of our great river might at any time be hermetically sealed, and the most disastrous injuries inflicted upon us. One important step in the command of the outlet of the Gulf of Mexico she has already taken by the possession of the Bahamas. If she gets peaceable possession of Yucatán, by our remissness, she will have taken the second. Cuba may be the last. . . .

I do not know, sir, that any one proposes, under existing circumstances, to send forces to Yucatán with any design of holding permanent possession of the country. The President in his message openly disclaims any such view, and our proceedings here are based upon the same determination. We go there to aid the Yucatecos in this their day of extremity; not only in obedience to the dictates of humanity, but as a great measure of public policy, to prevent that region from falling into other hands. Our duty fulfilled, tranquility restored, and the Government of the country placed in the exercise of its legitimate functions, we shall have discharged our trust, and can then retire with safety and with honor. . . .

## 4 | Debate on the Yucatán Bill, May 1848: The Monroe Doctrine as Policy *

Senator John M. Niles of Connecticut, in opposing such Democratic spokesmen as Houston and Cass, denied that the Monroe Doctrine had any applicability to the Yucatán question. He preferred that the foreign policies of the United States follow the traditional principles of Washington, Jefferson, and Monroe. To him the declaration of Monroe was aimed not at the European system of government but at the specific combination of European power, led by France, that in 1823 threatened to reconquer some portion of Latin America.

. . . Mr. President, in whatever light we regard the people of Yucatán, whether as an independent people, or as a dependency upon Mexico, or as in a state of revolution, you cannot pass this bill consistently with what I believe we admit to be the settled principles of policy which have ever governed the conduct of this Government in its intercourse with foreign Powers. In accordance with these principles, it makes no difference whether Yucatán is regarded in any one of these three lights. We have no more right to interfere in the domestic concerns of a State or province under the jurisdiction of some other country—no more right to interfere in domestic affairs, local in their character, than we have to interfere in the domestic affairs of a great independent State. Upon what principle, sir, can this military occupation of this province be justified in reference to the established principles which have governed the action of the United States? View it in whatever aspect you please, I ask upon what ground can it be justified?

Sir, there are two great principles which have been held sacred by this country from its earliest history; and I am not prepared to admit that the declaration of Mr. Monroe, so often referred to, if properly understood, gives any sanction, or recognizes any policy of this Government, which involves a departure from these principles. What are these principles? First, there is the principle of neutrality with regard to belligerents. This principle our Government has ever maintained,

* Address of John M. Niles in the Senate, May 9, 1848, *Congressional Globe*, 30th Congress, 1st Sess., Appendix, 609–10, 613.

and a majority of our most distinguished statesmen have endeavored to impress its importance upon the minds of our people, and upon every other nation in the world, in every possible mode and form. They have held it as one of the most sacred of principles in regard to our intercourse with the other Powers of the world, and the surest guaranty of peace. Can we, consistently with what is due to this great principle, interfere in this civil war, whether we regard Yucatán as an independent State, or as a dependent province? She is no part of the United States; she is a country foreign to us. There is a war there, sir; and can we forcibly interfere in it, without invalidating the great principle of neutrality towards belligerents? I see no answer to this query, and I believe there can be no answer.

The second principle we have hitherto held equally sacred, the principle of non-intervention. It is the principle which this Government, above all others, ought to hold sacred, because it strikes at the very foundations of free government. It is the principle which belongs to a free people; which is, that they should take care of their own affairs. Is it consistent with this principle to take possession of a foreign State, and take part in a civil war in which it is engaged? Why, sir, a proposition of this kind needs but to be fully understood, in order to show its fallacy. It does not admit of argument, because stating it carries with it the argument. Are we to undertake to control by force the destinies of this people? and because they are in a terrible state of tumult and civil anarchy, are we to settle their difficulties by taking possession of the country, putting down one party and setting up another? What sort of government will you give them? Will you attempt to force your own principles of government upon them, or will you consult their wishes, and attempt to set up such a government as they may ask at your hands? Sir, this matter is beset with difficulties at every step.

I wish to say something, Mr. President, in regard to this doctrine which has been said to have been held by President Monroe, and which is very gravely spoken of as the settled and established policy of this country. We must look to the circumstances of the nations in this hemisphere and in Europe at the time the declarations of Mr. Monroe were made, and to which they were applied, to form a correct opinion of them. These were not abstract declarations of principles to govern the action of this Government, but declarations applied to the then existing state of the countries in Europe and America. I have examined the two messages of 1823 and 1824 which contain his doctrines. Some years previous to that, the Spanish colonies in this hemisphere had asserted and declared their independence; but Spain refused to acknowledge them, and still asserted her dominion over them. Mr. Monroe did not deny the right of Spain to reëstablish her dominion over them; much less did he assert the right of the United States to interfere between Spain and her colonies, or to set itself up as the arbitrator and guardian of all the nations in this hemisphere. What he declared was, that the political system of Europe must not be extended to America to control the destinies of these Spanish American countries. He did not mean the monarchical system of Europe, as some seem to suppose, but that combination among the great Powers, sometimes called the Holy Alliance, which divided and disposed of the small States of Europe according to their pleasure. . . . After a while, the combination was broken up, and soon after Spain acknowledged the independence of these States on this continent. This is one of the positions of Mr. Monroe, and has no connection whatever with the right of intervention, as now asserted, in the concerns of foreign Powers—no connection with the idea which seems to be assumed, that Mr. Monroe claimed for the United States, as the principal and only great nation in this hemisphere, the right to dictate to or to control the destinies of all others, or assumed the obligation to protect them. His was not the doctrine of interference, but of resistance to the interference of others. He was a man of too much good sense to have contended for the right of intervention in the manner which is asserted. He had no such idea. . . .

. . . In regard to the request contained in the message, and the appeal made to us, I would go for assisting this suffering people as far as may be consistent with the established principles of this Government—with maintaining our neutrality in this war as in all other wars, and of abstaining from improper interference with the domestic concerns of this as of all other nations. I am of the opinion that something might be done without violating these principles. Whatever measure may be proposed in accordance with those principles for their relief, I assure the honorable chairman I will go as far, if not farther, than himself, in carrying it out. Possibly we might go so far as to supply that people with arms and ammunitions; I am not prepared to say but that I would go to that length, but that would be the extent to which I would go. We have hitherto maintained a prudent, just, and safe course of policy upon this subject, and I earnestly hope that no untoward circumstances, no emergency in neighboring States, no affecting appeal to our feelings, will induce us to depart from it. Any departure might be fatal to our best interests, and we might find it difficult to get back into the path in which we have so far walked with safety, and which has given to this country a degree of prosperity, an exemption from the evils of war, and a freedom from disturbances and entanglements which has fallen to the lot of no other nation. If, then, we have thus far steadily pursued this policy with a success and prosperity almost unequalled, I hope and trust the Senate will consider long and seriously upon the subject before they pass a bill, which, in my judgment, involves a departure from established principles, and which will expose us to new sources of difficulty, and become an example for the future fraught with danger and evils which no one can foresee, and no human sagacity control.

— | "I am not willing to have this task, which does not belong to us, assumed by our Government." *

In what was probably the major foreign policy address of his career, Calhoun restated, in his attack on the Yucatán bill, the conservative view of the Monroe Doctrine as a declaration of policy against the immediate challenge of the Holy Alliance to the continued independence of Latin America. Designed for the exigencies of the moment, the Monroe Doctrine could not establish a policy of universal applicability. For that reason, said Calhoun, it could have no relationship to Yucatán. National interest, not abstract principle, should guide the hemispheric policies of the United States. Calhoun explained why he invariably found himself siding with the Whig Party on matters of foreign affairs.

The President in his message recommends to Congress to adopt such measures as they may deem expedient to prevent, in the first place, Yucatán from becoming a colony of any European Power; and, in the next, to prevent the white inhabitants of that territory from being exterminated or expelled. In support of the latter, he informed the Senate that there is now raging a cruel and devastating war on the part of the Indians against the whites; and that, unless some foreign Power should aid, they will be destroyed or driven from the country. In support of the other recommendation, he states that the Government of Yucatán has offered to the Governments of Great Britain, Spain, and the United States, the dominion over the country, in order to obtain aid. The President also informs the Senate, that unless we grant aid, some other Power will; and that ultimately it may assert its dominion and sovereignty over the territory—a result which, he informs us, would be in contravention of the declaration of Mr. Monroe, and which must on no account be permitted. The Committee on Foreign Relations, in order to carry out these recommendations, have reported a bill which is now before us, the first section of which provides for taking military occupation of Yucatán, as recommended by the President.

Such are the recommendations of the President, and such the measure recommended by the committee. The subject is one of great magnitude. It is pregnant with consequences, both near and remote, which may deeply affect the peace and interests of this country. It demands the most serious deliberation. I have bestowed upon it full attention, and have arrived at a conclusion adverse to the recommendations of the President and the report of the committee. I propose to show, in the first place, that the case of Yucatán, even as stated by the President himself, does not come within the declarations of Mr. Monroe, and that they do not furnish the slightest support to the measure reported by the committee.

In the message referred to, that of 1823, Mr. Monroe makes three distinct

* Calhoun's speech on the Yucatán bill, May 15, 1848, *Congressional Globe*, 30th Congress, 1st Sess., Appendix, 630–33.

declarations. The first, and by far the most important, announces that the United States would regard any attempt on the part of the Allied Powers to extend their system to this country as dangerous to our peace and safety. To show that the case of Yucatán does not come within this declaration, all that will be necessary is, to explain who were the Allied Powers, the object of their alliance, and the circumstances in which the declaration itself was made. The Allied Powers were the four great continental monarchies—Russia, Prussia, Austria, and France. Shortly after the overthrow of Bonaparte these Powers entered into an alliance called the "Holy Alliance," the object of which was to sustain and extend the monarchical principles as far as possible, and to oppress and put down popular institutions. England, in the early stages of the alliance, favored it. The members of the Alliance held several Congresses, attended either by themselves or their ambassadors, and undertook to regulate the affairs of all Europe, and actually interfered in the affairs of Spain for the purpose of putting down popular doctrines. In its progress the Alliance turned its eyes to this continent, in order to aid Spain in regaining her sovereignty over her revolted provinces. . . . The late revolutions in Europe have put an end to all its work, and nothing remains of all that it ever did. Now, by what ingenuity of argument, by what force of sophistry can it be shown that this declaration comprehends the case of Yucatán, when the events which called it forth have passed away forever?

And yet the President has quoted that very declaration in support of his recommendation; but in a manner changing entirely its meaning, by separating it from the context as it stood in the message, and which referred to the Allied Powers; and placing it in connection with a portion of his message which made it refer to Great Britain, Spain, or other European Powers. The change has made the declaration so inconsistent and absurd, that had it been made by Mr. Monroe, as it stands in the President's message, it would have been the subject of the severest animadversion and ridicule instead of receiving, as it did, the approbation and applause of the whole country. It would have placed England in the false position of acting against us and with the Holy Alliance in reference to the Spanish American republics; and it would also have placed us in the position of opposing Spain in her efforts to recover her dominion over those States; and, finally, it would have involved the absurdity of asserting that the attempt of any European State to extend its system of government to this continent, the smallest as well as the greatest, would endanger the peace and safety of our country.

The next declaration was, that we would regard the interposition of any European Power to oppress the Governments of this continent, which we had recently recognized as independent, or to control their destiny in any manner whatever, as manifesting an unfriendly disposition towards the United States. This declaration, also, belongs to the history of that day. It grew out of the same state of circumstances, and may be considered as an appendage to the declaration to which I have just alluded. By the Governments on this continent, which we had recognized, were meant the republics which had grown up after having thrown off the yoke of Spain. They had just emerged from their protracted revolutionary struggles. They had hardly yet reached a point of solidity, and in that tender stage the Administration of Mr. Monroe thought it proper not only to make that general declaration in reference to the Holy Alliance, but to make a more specific one against the interference of any European Power, in order to countenance and encourage these young republics as far as we could with propriety. This, like the other, belonging to the events of the time, has passed away with them; but suppose that not to be the case, I ask, does the case of Yucatán come within this declaration? Has there been any interposition in the affairs of Yucatán on the part of any European Power with the design of oppressing her or changing her destiny? If not, how can the case of Yucatán be comprehended in this declaration?

But, it may be said, although the case of Yucatán is not expressly comprehended in the declaration, yet it is so by implication, as it is mediated by England; for, after all, that is the Government which is meant in the message, under the general term "European Powers." The message indicates that England mediates such interference, and the chairman of the Committee on Foreign Relations distinctly avows that opinion. Has England, then, manifested any disposition to interfere, in order to oppress the people of Yucatán, or to change the character of their Government from a republic to a monarchy? We have no evidence whatever on that point. . . .

The word "colonization" has a specific meaning. It means the establishment of a settlement by emigrants from the parent country in a territory either uninhabited or from which the inhabitants have been partially or wholly expelled. This is not a case of that character. But here it may be proper, in order to understand the force of my argument, to go into a history also of this declaration of Mr. Monroe. It grew out of circumstances altogether different from the other two. At that time there was a question between Great Britain and the United States on one side and Russia on the other. All three claimed settlements on the northwest portion of this continent. Great Britain and ourselves having common interest in keeping Russia as far north as possible, the former Power applied to the United States for cooperation; and it was in reference to that matter that this additional declaration was made. It was said to be a proper opportunity to make it. It had reference specially to the subject of the northwestern settlement, and the other portions of the continent were thrown in, because all the rest of it, with the exception of some settlements in Surinam, Maracaibo, and thereabout, had passed into independent hands.

Now, having stated the history of these transactions, I contend that the word "colonization" does not apply to the case of Yucatán. That is the case of surrendered sovereignty over a people already there—a people who have tendered it, and, if accepted, freely accepted on the other side. Is that "colonization?" Can it be construed to be so by any forced interpretation? No; by accepting it, Yucatán may become a province, or, to use the appropriate term that she employs, a "possession" of Great Britain, but not a colony. . . .

In stating the precise character of these declarations, and the manner in which they originated, I have discharged a double duty; a duty to my country, to whom it is important that these declarations should be correctly understood, and a duty to the cabinet of which I was a member, and am now the only survivor. I remove a false interpretation, which makes safe and proper declarations improper and dangerous.

But it is not only in these respects that these famous declarations are misunderstood by the Chief Magistrate of the country, as well as by others. They were but declarations, nothing more; declarations, announcing in a friendly manner to the Powers of the world that we should regard certain acts of interposition of the Allied Powers as dangerous to our peace and our safety; interposition of European Powers to oppress the Republics which had just arisen upon this continent, as manifesting an unfriendly disposition; and that this continent, having become free and independent, was no longer the subject of colonization by European Powers. Not one word in any one of them in reference to resistance. There is nothing said of it; and with great propriety was it omitted. Resistance belonged to us—to Congress; it is for us to say whether we shall resist or not, and to what extent. But such is not the view taken by the present Chief Magistrate. He seems to hold these declarations as imposing a solemn duty on him as Chief Magistrate to resist on all occasions; and not only to resist, but to judge of the measure of that resistance. He tells us in this very message that it is not to be permitted in any event that any foreign Power should occupy Yucatán. That is language for us to hold, not for the Chief Magistrate. And in conformity with that, he sends in a message, without giving us one particle of evidence as to those great political considerations which influenced the cabinet decisions, as stated on this floor, in declaring whether we shall occupy the country or not. I speak it not in the way of censure. I state it only as a matter of fact deducible from the message itself, and as evincing undoubtedly a great and dangerous misconception of these celebrated declarations. But that is not all. He tells you in the same message, that these declarations have become the settled policy of this country. What! the declarations? Declarations are not policy, and cannot become settled policy. He must mean that it has become the settled policy of this country to resist what these declarations refer to; and to resist, if need be, by an appeal to arms. Is this the fact? Has there been one instance in which these declarations have been carried into effect by resistance? If there be, let it be pointed out. Have there not been innumerable instances in which they have not been applied? Certainly. Still stronger declarations, under this broad interpretation, were disavowed entirely three years afterwards by the vote of the Republican party, when the Administration of Mr. Adams endeavored to apply them by sending ministers to the Congress at Panama, as will be seen by reading the debates and the proceedings on the subject. And let me say—for it is proper that I should make the declaration on this occasion—that there has been an entire revolution between the two parties in this country in reference to our foreign relations. At the commencement of our Government, and down to a late period—I will mark it—the commencement of Jackson's administration, the policy of the Republican party was to avoid war as long as war could be avoided, and to resort to every means to avert its calamities. The opposite party, without being a war party, had not so decided an aversion to war. The thing is now reversed; and hence I, who endeavored to maintain the old ground of the party, have for years on all questions connected with our foreign relations, been compelled to cooperate with gentlemen on the opposite side, and to resist those in the midst of whom I stand. No; it is not, and never has been, the established policy of the country. And if it should ever become so, to the wide extent to which these declarations have been interpreted to go, our peace would ever be disturbed; the gates of our Janus would ever stand open; wars would never cease.

What the President has asserted in this case is not a principle belonging to these declarations; it is a principle which, in his misconception, he attempts to ingraft upon them, but which has an entirely different meaning and tendency. The principle which lies at the bottom of his recommendation is, that when any Power on this continent becomes involved in internal warfare, and the weaker side chooses to make application to us for support, we are bound to give them support for fear the offer of the sovereignty of the country may be made to some other Power and accepted. It goes infinitely and dangerously beyond Mr. Monroe's declaration. It puts it in the power of other countries on this continent to make us a party to all their wars; and hence I say, if this broad interpretation be given to these declarations, we shall forever be involved in wars.

But, in disavowing a principle which will compel us to resist every case of interposition of European Powers on this continent, I would not wish to be understood as defending the opposite, that we should never resist their interposition. That is a position which would be nearly as dangerous and absurd as the other. But no general rule can be laid down to guide us on such a question. Every case must speak for itself—every case must be decided on its own merits. . . . There are cases of interposition where I would resort to the hazard of war, with all its calamities. Am I asked for one? I will answer. I designate the case of Cuba. So long as Cuba remains in the hands of Spain—a friendly Power, a Power of which we have no dread—it should continue to be, as it has been, the policy of all Administrations ever since I have been connected with the Government, to let Cuba remain there; but with the fixed determination, which I hope never will be relinquished, that if Cuba pass from her, it shall not be into any other hands but ours; this, not from a feeling of ambition, not from a desire for the extension of dominion, but because that island is indispensable to the safety of the United States; or rather, because it is indispensable to the safety of the United States that this island should not be in certain hands. . . .

But I was asked by one of the members of the Committee on Foreign Relations, if I would be in favor of resisting Great Britain if she should assert sovereignty and dominion over Yucatán? I answer, I would not; and for irresistible reasons. I would not, because the country is, to a great extent, a most worthless one. Nearly one-half is destitute of a single stream—rocky and barren throughout the greater part; and it is only by means of the artificial reservoirs of water that they are enabled to live through the dry season. I would not, because the possession of Yucatán would contribute nothing to the defence of the passage between it and Cuba, which is represented to be so important to our commerce. It is not without its importance: it is important to the inward trade, but not at all to the outward trade of the Gulf. There is a constant current of wind and water setting in that direction, of which vessels going to New Orleans, or any other port on the Gulf, may avail themselves; but on coming from those ports, they almost invariably take their way between Florida and Cuba, and thus the passage between Yucatán and Cuba is the inlet, to a limited extent, into the Gulf, but not the outlet from it; while the passage between Cuba and Florida is the almost exclusive outlet and the principal inlet. I speak in reference to coasting vessels. In voyages from Europe, they pass south of Cuba into the Gulf.

But I take higher grounds. If it were ever so important, not only as an inlet, but an outlet, the occupation of Yucatán by England would add nothing to her power in cutting off our trade. Yucatán is very destitute of ports; there is not a frigate port laid down in the charts on the whole peninsula, unless that at the Balize be so. But with or without Yucatán, Great Britain possesses an uncontrollable power over the passage whenever she chooses to exert it. . . .

. . . I am in favor of peace, whenever it can be maintained consistently with the honor and the safety of the country. I see no such necessity in this case, even on the supposition stated, as to induce me to incur such hazard, especially at a period like the present. Never was the future more uncertain. Events occur with electric rapidity. No man can tell what may come to-morrow; and never was there a time when caution was more necessary—when there was stronger inducement to husband our resources—to avoid quarrels and wars, or anything that can involve us in difficulty, in order to stand prepared to meet emergencies as they arise. He who looks abroad—he who looks at the eastern horizon, and does not see the necessity for caution, is blind to the future.

I would not take military possession, even under the contingency I have stated, for another reason. It would be a breach of good faith. Not long since, we agreed upon the terms of a treaty with Mexico. That treaty, before this time, has been acted on, or is about ot be acted on, by the Mexican Government; and until it is acted on we are bound in good faith to observe it. If it is acted on favorably, it becomes a permanent obligation. We have considered Yucatán as part of Mexico, as one of the States of the Mexican Republic. It is not comprehended within the line which is proposed to be drawn between us and her. We could not seize upon that State in conformity with good faith; nor could we in conformity with the armistice, for the same reason. The armistice makes some exceptions, but this is not one of them.

I have now stated my reasons against the measure reported by the committee to carry into effect the message of the President, recommending that we should adopt the measure to prevent Yucatán from becoming a colony of a foreign Power. I now proceed to consider the next—to adopt measures to prevent the white population from being exterminated or expelled from Yucatán. And here let me express my regret that the President should, in the same message, unite two measures of such different characters—one an appeal to our humanity, which I would, as far as we could with propriety, act upon promptly, and at once. The other, involving the highest considerations of policy, and which requires much time and much deliberation. It is among the most complicated questions ever presented to this body, and by no means the least important. Why these different questions have been mingled I am not prepared to say. The emergency for the one seems to have existed long before the other. Danger to the white population has been known to exist since the middle of February, but the message has only been recently communicated to us. During this long interval, if the case appealing to our humanity had been brought forward, we might long ere this have rendered efficient aid. But, whatever may be the effects of the delay in reference to the Yucatánese, they are not chargeable to us. Higher considerations in reference to ourselves—considerations of policy—demand of us deliberation, and that deliberation, I trust, will be given, in despite of the charge of unnecessary delay. But I pass on to the question of humanity.

If this be a war of races in reality; if the white race be not responsible for this war; if they have used all manly exertions, and exhibited due courage in repelling the danger, strong indeed would be the appeal to my sympathies. I have no aversion to any race, red or black, but my sympathies are for the white race. . . . If they can maintain themselves, there is some hope that Yucatán may go forward, that intelligence may increase, and that at some future day they may be prepared to take a higher position in civilization than at present. If the white race be overthrown and Indian ascendency established, there will be a directly opposite tendency to end in a despotic government, like that of Hayti. Perhaps a capable man may at first be elevated to power, and may govern tolerably well, but it will undoubtedly follow the course of Hayti. The tendency of power will be downwards, until it come down to the very bottom, and end in a savage state.

But if there are powerful considerations why we should interfere as far as we could with propriety for these reasons, there are very powerful ones why we should act with great caution. The case of Yucatán does not stand alone. All the causes operating there to produce the present state of things are operating in all the portions of this continent south of us, including Mexico, down on the eastern side of the Andes to Buenos Ayres, and on the western to Chili. All, all are in great danger of falling into the condition in which Yucatán is now placed. The history of all has been the same. The white and mixed races led in casting off the yoke of Spain. They, everywhere, elevated the Indian race to an equality with themselves. It was done most imprudently, and inculcates a solemn lesson. . . . All these South American States consist of the same population—whites, mixed, and Indians. The African population is small. All will, I fear, be revolutionized in turn, and the whole of them be subjected to one melancholy fate, in spite of all that we can do. But I trust that it may be otherwise. The magnitude of this subject, however, should teach us caution. . . .

How far ought we go, then, on the score of humanity? I am of the opinion that all the naval force which we can spare should be sent to relieve these helpless people, and that we should supply food and raiment for their present necessities, and convey them wheresoever they desire—to Cuba or elsewhere. In a word, we should do all that humanity requires. But I cannot agree to carry out the provisions of a bill which authorizes the President to use the army and navy to take military occupation of the country. No considerations of humanity, or of the ascendency of the white race in Yucatán, justify, in my opinion, the adoption of such a course of policy. It is now clear that the white population, including the mixed race, is so prostrated and feeble, and the Indians so powerful, that not a hope remains of reestablishing the permanent ascendency of the former. We can, doubtless, by force, subject the Indians and reinstate the whites in power; but the moment that we withdraw, the former state of things will recur. We will thus be perpetually engaged in this work. Now, I am not willing to incur the danger and the cost of maintaining the ascendency of the whites. I am not willing to have this task, which does not belong to us, assumed by our Government. . . .

## 5 | William H. Seward on the Realities of Power in the Western Hemisphere, March 1862 *

Nowhere did Seward reveal his adherence to the conservative tradition of American diplomacy more clearly than in his celebrated letter to Charles Francis Adams, American Minister in London, of March 3, 1862. In the midst of the Civil War, with the course of conflict running hard against the North, Seward calmly reminded the European powers of the effort that would be required to overcome the nationalistic and liberal resistance of the Mexican people. He warned Napoleon III of France especially that he could not sustain sufficient strength in the Western Hemisphere to achieve his goal of establishing a permanent French hegemony in Mexico. The accuracy of Seward's prediction illustrated the fact that the realities of power, not the Monroe Doctrine, guaranteed the interests of the United States in the hemisphere. Seward refused even to refer to the Monroe Doctrine.

We observe indications of a growing opinion in Europe that the demonstrations which are being made by Spanish, French and British forces against Mexico, are likely to be attended by a revolution in that country which will bring in a monarchical government there, in which the crown will be assumed by some foreign Prince. This country is deeply concerned in the peace of nations and aims to be loyal at the same time in all its relations as well to the Allies as to Mexico. The President has therefore instructed me to submit his views on the new aspect of affairs to the parties concerned.

He has relied upon the assurances given to this government by the Allies that they were seeking no political objects, and only a redress of grievances. He does

* Seward to Adams, March 3, 1862, Instructions to Great Britain MSS, Department of State, National Archives, Vol. XVIII.

not doubt the sincerity of the Allies, and his confidence in their good faith, if it could be shaken, would be reinspired by explanations apparently made in their behalf, that the governments of Spain, France, and Great Britain are not intending to intervene, and will not intervene to effect a change of the Constitutional form of government now existing in Mexico, or to produce any political change there in opposition to the will of the Mexican people. Indeed, he understands the Allies to be unanimous in declaring that the proposed revolution in Mexico is moved only by Mexican citizens now in Europe.

The President, however, deems it his duty to express to the Allies, in all candor and frankness, the opinion that no monarchical government which could be founded in Mexico, in the presence of foreign navies and armies in the waters, and upon the soil of Mexico, would have any prospect of security or permanence.

Secondly, that the instability of such a monarchy there, would be enhanced, if the throne should be assigned to any person not of Mexican nativity. That, under such circumstances, the new government must speedily fall, unless it could draw into its support European alliances, which, relating back to the first invasion, would in fact make it the beginning of a permanent policy of armed European monarchical intervention, injurious and practically hostile to the most general system of government on the continent of America, and this would be the beginning rather than the ending of revolution in Mexico.

These views are grounded upon some knowledge of the political sentiments and habits of society in America.

In such a case, it is not to be doubted that the permanent interests and sympathies of this country would be with the other American republics. It is not intended, on this occasion, to predict the course of events which might happen as a consequence of the proceeding contemplated, either on this continent or in Europe. It is sufficient to say that, in the President's opinion, the emancipation of this continent from European control, has been the principal feature in its history during the last century. It is not probable that a revolution in a contrary direction would be successful in an immediately succeeding century, while population in America is so rapidly increasing, resources so rapidly developing, and society so steadily forming itself upon principles of Democratic American government. Nor is it necessary to suggest to the Allies the improbability that European nations could steadily agree upon a policy favorable to such a counter-revolution as one conducive to their own interests, or to suggest that, however studiously, the allies may act to avoid lending the aid of their land and naval forces to domestic revolutions in Mexico, the result would nevertheless be traceable to the presence of those forces there, although for a different purpose, since it may be deemed certain that, but for their presence there, no such revolution could probably have been attempted or even conceived.

The Senate of the United States has not indeed given its official sanction to the precise measures which the President has proposed for lending our aid to the existing government in Mexico, with the approval of the Allies, to relieve it from its present embarrassments. This however, is only a question of domestic administration. It would be very erroneous to regard such a disagreement as indicating any serious difference of opinion in this Government or among the American people, in their cordial good wishes for the safety, welfare and stability of the republican system of government in that country.

# 6 | Seward, Napoleon, and Self-Determination for Mexico, February 1866 *

By February 1866 it was apparent to Seward that Napoleon was tiring of his Mexican venture. No longer was there any prospect that the benefits to France from the Mexican monarchy would match the cost of maintaining a French army in the war-torn Latin American republic. In a letter to the French government, a model in diplomatic language, the Secretary of State explained the interest of the United States in the principle of self-determination for the Western Hemisphere, a principle agreed to by France and yet defied by French policy in Mexico. It remained for Seward to prod Napoleon into acceding to his own words and thus withdraw the remainder of his forces from Mexico. Again Seward refused to include any reference to the Monroe Doctrine.

✍

. . . We are, as we have been, in the relations of amity and friendship equally with France and with Mexico, and therefore we cannot, consistently with those relations, constitute ourselves a judge of the original merits of the war which is waged between them. We can speak concerning that war only so far as we are affected by its bearing upon ourselves and upon republican and American institutions on this continent. . . .

. . . France is entitled, by every consideration of respect and friendship, to interpret for herself the objects of the expedition, and of the whole of her proceedings in Mexico. Her explanation of those motives and objects is, therefore, accepted on our part with the consideration and confidence which we expect for explanations of our own when assigned to France or any other friendly power. Nevertheless, it is my duty to insist that, whatever were the intentions, purposes, and objects of France, the proceedings which were adopted by a class of Mexicans for subverting the republican government there, and for availing themselves of French intervention to establish on its ruins an imperial monarchy, are regarded by the United States as having been taken without the authority, and prosecuted against the will and opinions, of the Mexican people. For these reasons

* Seward to the Marquis de Montholon, February 12, 1866, *The Works of William H. Seward,* George E. Baker, ed. (Boston, 1884), V: 428–43.

it seems to this government, that in supporting institutions thus established in derogation of the inalienable rights of the people of Mexico, the original purposes and objects of the French expedition, though they have not been, as a military demand of satisfaction, abandoned, nor lost out of view by the Emperor of the French, were, nevertheless, left to fall into a condition in which they seem to have become subordinate to a political revolution, which certainly would not have occurred if France had not forcibly intervened, and which, judging from the genius and character of the Mexican people, would not now be maintained by them if that armed intervention should cease. The United States have not seen any satisfactory evidence that the people of Mexico have spoken, and have called into being or accepted the so-called empire which it is insisted has been set up in their capital. The United States, as I have remarked on other occasions, are of opinion that such an acceptance could not have been freely procured or lawfully taken at any time in the presence of the French army of invasion. The withdrawal of the French forces is deemed necessary to allow such a proceeding to be taken by Mexico. . . .

This position is held, I believe, without one dissenting voice by our countrymen. I do not presume to say that this opinion of the American people is accepted or will be adopted generally by other foreign powers, or by the public opinion of mankind. The Emperor is quite competent to form a judgment upon this important point for himself. I cannot, however, properly exclude the observation that, while this question affects by its bearings, incidentally, every republican state in the American hemisphere, every one of those states has adopted the judgment which, on the behalf of the United States, is herein expressed. Under these circumstances it has happened, either rightfully, or wrongfully, that the presence of European armies in Mexico, maintaining a European prince with imperial attributes, without her consent and against her will, is deemed a source of apprehension and danger, not alone to the United States, but also to all the independent and sovereign republican states founded on the American continent and its adjacent islands. . . .

. . . The United States have not claimed, and they do not claim, to know what arrangements the Emperor may make for the adjustment of claims for indemnity and redress in Mexico. It would be, on our part, an act of intervention to take cognizance of them. We adhere to our position that the war in question has become a political war between France and the republic of Mexico, injurious and dangerous to the United States and to the republican cause, and we ask only that in that aspect and character it may be brought to an end. It would be illiberal on the part of the United States to suppose that, in desiring or pursuing preliminary arrangements, the Emperor contemplates the establishment in Mexico, before withdrawing his forces, of the very institutions which constitute the material ground of the exceptions taken against his intervention by the United States. It would be still more illiberal to suppose for a moment that he expects the United States to bind themselves indirectly to acquiesce in or support the obnoxious institutions.

On the contrary, we understand him as announcing to us his immediate purpose to bring to an end the service of his armies in Mexico, to withdraw them, and in good faith to fall back, without stipulation or condition on our part, upon the principle of non-intervention upon which he is henceforth agreed with the United States. We cannot understand his appeal to us for an assurance that we ourselves will abide by our own principles of non-intervention in any other sense than as the expression, in a friendly way, of his expectation that when the people of Mexico shall have been left absolutely free from the operation, effects, and consequences of his own political and military intervention, we will ourselves respect their self-established sovereignty and independence. In this view of the subject only can we consider his appeal pertinent to the case. Regarding it in only this aspect, we must meet the Emperor frankly. He knows the form and character of this government. The nation can be bound only by treaties which have the concurrence of the President and two thirds of the Senate. A formal treaty would be objectionable as unnecessary, except as a disavowal of bad faith on our part, to disarm suspicion in regard to a matter concerning which we have given no cause for questioning our loyalty, or else such a treaty would be refused upon the ground that the application for it by the Emperor of France was unhappily a suggestion of some sinister or unfriendly reservation or purpose on his part in withdrawing from Mexico. . . .

With these explanations I proceed to say that, in the opinion of the President, France need not for a moment delay her promised withdrawal of military forces from Mexico, and her putting the principle of non-intervention into full and complete practice in regard to Mexico, through any apprehension that the United States will prove unfaithful to the principles and policy in that respect which, on their behalf, it has been my duty to maintain in this now very lengthened correspondence. The practice of this government, from its beginning, is a guarantee to all nations of the respect of the American people for the free sovereignty of the people in every other state. We received the instruction from Washington. We applied it sternly in our early intercourse even with France. The same principle and practice have been uniformly inculcated by all our statesmen, interpreted by all our jurists, maintained by all our Congresses, and acquiesced in without practical dissent on all occasions by the American people. It is in reality the chief element of foreign intercourse in our history. Looking simply toward the point to which our attention has been steadily confined, the relief of the Mexican embarrassments without disturbing our relations with France, we shall be gratified when the Emperor shall give to us, either through the channel of your esteemed correspondence or otherwise, definitive information of the time when French military operations may be expected to cease in Mexico.

Here I might, perhaps, properly conclude this note. Some obscurity, however, might be supposed to rest upon the character of the principle of non-intervention, which we are authorized to suppose is now agreed upon between the United States and France as a rule for their future government in regard to Mexico. I shall, therefore, reproduce on this occasion, by way of illustration, some of the forms in which that principle has been maintained by us in our previous intercourse with France. In 1861, when alluding to the possibility that the Emperor might be invoked by rebel emissaries from the United States to intervene in our civil war, I observed: "The Emperor of France has given abundant proofs that he considers the people in every country the rightful source of authority, and that its only legitimate objects are their safety, freedom, and welfare." . . .

In declining the offer of French mediation, on the 8th of June, 1861, I wrote to Mr. Dayton: "The present paramount duty of the government is to save the integrity of the American Union. Absolute, self-sustaining independence is the first and most indispensable element of national existence. This is a republican nation; all its domestic affairs must be conducted and even adjusted in constitutional forms, and upon constitutional, republican principles. This is an American nation, and its internal affairs must not only be conducted with reference to its peculiar continental position but by and through American agencies alone." . . .

On the 8th of May, 1862, Mr. Dayton was instructed to express to Mr. Thouvenel "the desire of the United States that peaceful relations may soon be restored between France and Mexico upon a basis just to both parties, and favorable to the independence and sovereignty of the people of Mexico, which is equally the interest of France and all other enlightened nations."

On the 21st of June, 1862, Mr. Dayton was authorized to speak on behalf of the United States concerning the condition of Mexico in these words: "France has a right to make war against Mexico, and to determine for herself the cause. We have a right to insist that France shall not improve the war she makes to raise up in Mexico an anti-republican or anti-American government, or to maintain such a government there."

# 7 | The Monroe Doctrine and American Interests in the Western Hemisphere, 1882 *

In the following article, Gustave Koerner, the noted political leader of Illinois, challenged the views of John A. Kasson, the American diplomat, on the meaning and significance of the Monroe Doctrine. Koerner acknowledged the validity of Kasson's observation that the doctrine was a popular American dogma. He charged, however, that the power of the Monroe Doctrine to excite the emotions of the nation resulted from a serious misunderstanding. What mattered in the formulation of policy for the Western Hemisphere or elsewhere, he pointed out, were not "doctrines, programmes, or platforms," but the true interests of the nation.

🖋

* Gustave Koerner, "The True Monroe Doctrine," *The Nation*, XXXIV (January 5, 1882), 9–11.

Sir: The Hon. John A. Kasson has devoted an article, in the September number of the *North American Review,* to what he calls the "Monroe Declaration." He gives us the genesis of what is more usually called the "Monroe Doctrine," and, as far as he goes, with that correctness which might have been expected from a gentleman as intelligent and well informed as Mr. Kasson is known to be. But to a proper understanding of what was meant by President Monroe in his celebrated message of December, 1823, we have to take the strictly American view of the political condition of Europe at the time in question. . . .

The occasion for such a declaration as that contained in the message of President Monroe in 1823 will in all probability never arise again. The Monroe Doctrine, as understood by its authors and the statesmen of that time, has passed into the domain of history, furnishing one of its brightest pages for our people, and reflecting the highest credit on President Monroe, his Cabinet, and his advisers, who defied the greatest powers of Europe when supposed to be desirous to extend their system (of intervention for the suppression of liberty) to the American continents. It is obvious that in its true sense that part of the Monroe Declaration which refers to a combined intervention of European governments with American states is just as dead as the other branch of it in regard to colonization. And yet with all this easily accessible documentary evidence before our eyes, coupled with the fact that our Government as such, in its relation with foreign powers, has never since insisted on this doctrine, there having been no occasion for it, there is no subject more misunderstood than this very Monroe Declaration. Even Mr. Kasson, just returned from his mission to Austria, and having made a particular study of the subject—to judge from the opening remarks of his article—seems to share the same loose, vague, and everchanging ideas in regard to it with the great majority of the American people.

> The Monroe Doctrine [he says] is quoted as the supreme, indisputable, and irreversible judgment of our National Union. Among the very few maxims which serve to guide public opinion in our country this ranks as the chief. It has also taken fast hold on the popular mind. A President of the United States, justly appealing to it in an emergency, could not fail of the unanimous following of patriotic citizens, even in presence of a consequently impending war. It touches the instincts of national safety and of pride in our national institutions.

The Monroe Doctrine proper, however, as understood at the time it was made, and with its limitations as applicable to a particular crisis, could have no such stirring effects as Mr. Kasson ascribes to it. But what has been from time to time substituted for it, its misunderstood meaning, may often have excited the American people. Some have taken it to mean that America belongs to the Americans (whatever that may signify); others, that we have a right to extinguish all monarchical governments still found on this continent; others, that we have a right to annex all territories on the continent, republican or otherwise, that we have a mind to. It was invoked in 1836, when the French part of Canada had risen against the English Government; it was invoked to further the annexation of Texas; it was appealed to whenever a filibustering expedition started for Cuba. . . . It was loudly called into requisition when France imported Maximilian and his ephemeral empire into Mexico; and, lastly, now, when a private company, under the auspices of M. Lesseps, has undertaken to dig a canal through the Isthmus of Panama—a corporation, by the way, which offered its stock to any American citizen who had a surplus to invest in a hazardous undertaking.

These appeals, however, were made by the press, by orators in and out of Congress, but never by any act of Congress or by our Government as such. True statesmen do not rule by doctrines, programmes, or platforms. With them the welfare of the people is the supreme law. They do not commit themselves by generalities. Every conflict that arises is judged by them according to the circumstances of the times. If our interests or our honor be threatened in the particular instance, then they protest, then they arm, then they go to war, independent of sentiments, of traditions, of programmes, of doctrines. The highest commercial interests, the permanency of our republican institutions, would have been seriously threatened had Spain, by the help of the allied powers, reduced her revolted provinces to subjection, or ceded them in part to other far more powerful nations. Here was an emergency, and Mr. Monroe met it manfully, but not on philosophical, abstract principles. If allied or single European powers should at this day try to conquer some of our sister republics, and plant monarchical institutions on American soil, so as to endanger our own safety, the American people would calmy weigh the matter, and, without any reference to former action, decide the case for itself, and no President would fail to carry out the decision. It would go to war just as if the Monroe Declaration had never been made.

The invasion of Mexico by the French in 1862, under pretence of enforcing a settlement of claims (most of which were fraudulent and held by the Emperor's intimate associates in crime), but in truth to subvert the Republican Government and to assist the Clerical-Conservative party in Mexico to establish a monarchy, furnished, perhaps, the most plausible reason for an application of the Monroe Doctrine. There was this difference, however, in the case: at the time of the Monroe message Spain was to be assisted in her conquest by the great powers of Europe, and the principle of intervention was to be applied to America, as was feared. In 1862 there was a powerful clerical and monarchical party in Mexico itself, not strong in number, but in wealth, rank, and intelligence. They acted, at least apparently, as the home Government, called a Congress of "Notables" together, proclaimed a monarchy, and called (1864) the Archduke Maximilian to the throne.

Mr. Seward recognized this distinction. Early in February, 1863, a letter of Louis Napoleon's, written in 1862 to General Forey, who, after the French had been at first repulsed from Puebla, had been appointed commander-in-chief of the French army, very unaccountably found its way into the French papers. In an interview which the American Minister in Spain had with Marshal Serrano, Minister of Foreign Affairs, after official business had been disposed of, an unofficial conversation took place, in which the latter expressed his very great surprise at the letter in which Louis Napoleon had foreshadowed his intention to establish a Government in Mexico, and would hereafter protect the Latin races on the American Continent from the dictation and encroachments of the Anglo-Saxons in the North. The American Minister shared this surprise, not so much at the contents of the letter itself, but that it ever should have been made public, and took occasion to say that his Government would not look upon this plan with indifference, but would consider it as highly dangerous to its interests, and would take proper action to prevent it. The American Minister, in his next despatch, called the attention of Mr. Seward to this remarkable letter, and reported also the conversation with General Serrano in regard to it. Mr. Seward, however, in his reply (February 28, 1863) to this despatch, expressed his regret that the Minister should have used this language, remarking that the United States were strictly neutral in this affair, and he desired him to explain to General Serrano that what the Minister had said to him was only his private opinion, and not that of the Government he represented. . . . Later on, when it was well understood that, after the French had taken possession of the City of Mexico and started a provisional government, negotiations had been set on foot to make Mexico a monarchy, and to call Maximilian to the throne, Mr. Motley, our Minister at Vienna, became very much alarmed, considered this conquest of the capital as "fraught with piteous woe to our country" (August 17, 1863), reminded Mr. Seward of the Monroe Doctrine, and asked for the Austrian Minister of Foreign Affairs for explanations; but Mr. Seward most emphatically instructed him to make no representations to the Emperor of Austria, as chief of the House of Austria, regarding Maximilian's acceptance of the crown. To serve, as it were, as a guide for our other ministers, Mr. Seward sent a copy of this despatch to all our chief ministers in Europe. In his despatch (October 9, 1863) to Mr. Motley, Mr. Seward very elaborately repeated those instructions. It contains this remarkable passage:

> France has invaded Mexico, and war exists between the two countries. The United States hold, in regard to these two states and their conflict, the same principle that they hold in relation to all other nations and their mutual wars. *They have neither a right nor any disposition to intervene by force in the internal affairs of Mexico, whether to establish or maintain a republican or even a domestic government there, or to overthrow an imperial or a foreign one if Mexico shall choose to establish or accept it.* (Despatch to Mr. Motley, Oct. 9, 1863.)

Mr. Seward distinctly denied even here the application of the Monroe Doctrine. It would be a very great mistake, however, to infer from this course of Mr. Seward that he for one moment forgot the true interests of our country. We were still in the midst of our troubles, and so he bided his time. His policy was that of opportunity, which, in fact, is the only true one for a statesman. He was determined from the start, if we could, to drive out the French, and to make an end to the empire of Maximilian. In spite of the urgency of the French Government, he declined, in the politest manner, to recognize the new Latin empire. But as soon as he ascertained that the Mexican expedition had become extremely odious in France itself, and we had triumphed over the rebellion, and hundreds of thousands of veterans of the victorious and vanquished armies were ready and anxious at once to spring to arms to restore a republican government in Mexico, he began reminding Louis Napoleon of his promises that the French should evacuate the country after the government of Maximilian was once established, not only once but again, and again, and so pressingly and persuasively invited the French to step out, using always the most courteous language, that France could no longer resist his friendly admonition, and took her leave, being handsomely complimented by Mr. Seward for so doing. The withdrawal of the French army was the end of the unfortunate Mexican empire.

The true Monroe Doctrine is the interest of our country; and what that interest is, and how it is to be protected, and whether it is to be asserted or not, is to be judged by the circumstances existing at the time such judgment is to be exercised, unfettered by any traditions, or programmes, or doctrines, or precedents. Practically, we have always so acted, and as long as we have statesmen at the helm of state, and not mere "doctrinaires" or political "aspirants," we shall continue so to act, whether our action squares with the Monroe or any other doctrine or not. No doctrine will excuse us when we act unjustly, and none will prevent us from asserting our rights, at any cost, when our interest or our honor is involved.


## 8 | Richard Olney's Claims to American Suzerainty over the Western Hemisphere, July 1895 *

In this letter Olney, under the heavy pressure of domestic politics, expanded the nation's presumptions under the Monroe Doctrine to include complete dominance of the Western Hemisphere. He claimed for the United States government the right to interfere in any question which might be termed "American."

🖎

. . . That there are circumstances under which a nation may justly interpose in a controversy to which two or more other nations are the direct and immediate parties is an admitted canon of international law. The doctrine is ordinarily expressed in terms of the most general character and is perhaps incapable of more specific statement. It is declared in substance that a nation may avail itself of this right whenever what is done or proposed by any of the parties primarily concerned is a serious and direct menace to its own integrity, tran-

* Olney to Thomas F. Bayard, July 20, 1895, *Papers Relating to the Foreign Relations of the United States, 1895, Part I* (Washington, 1896), 553–62.

quillity, or welfare. The propriety of the rule when applied in good faith will
not be questioned in any quarter. On the other hand, it is an inevitable though
unfortunate consequence of the wide scope of the rule that it has only too often
been made a cloak for schemes of wanton spoliation and aggrandizement. We
are concerned at this time, however, not so much with the general rule as with
a form of it which is peculiarly and distinctively American. Washington, in the
solemn admonitions of the Farewell Address, explicitly warned his countrymen
against entanglements with the politics or the controversies of European
powers. . . .

During the administration of President Monroe this doctrine of the Farewell
Address was first considered in all its aspects and with a view to all its practical
consequences. The Farewell Address, while it took America out of the field of
European politics, was silent as to the part Europe might be permitted to play
in America. Doubtless it was thought the latest edition to the family of nations
should not make haste to prescribe rules for the guidance of its older members,
and the expediency and propriety of serving the powers of Europe with notice
of a complete and distinctive American policy excluding them from interference
with American political affairs might well seem dubious to a generation to whom
the French alliance, with its manifold advantages to the cause of American independence, was fresh in mind.

Twenty years later, however, the situation had changed. The lately born nation
had greatly increased in power and resources, had demonstrated its strength on
land and sea and as well in the conflicts of arms as in the pursuits of peace
and had begun to realize the commanding position on this continent which the
character of its people, their free institutions, and their remoteness from the
chief scene of European contentions combined to give to it. The Monroe administration therefore did not hesitate to accept and apply the logic of the
Farewell Address by declaring in effect that American non-intervention in European affairs necessarily implied and meant European non-intervention in
American affairs. . . .

That America is in no part open to colonization, though the proposition was
not universally admitted at the time of its first enunciation, has long been
universally conceded. We are not concerned, therefore, only with that other
practical application of the Monroe doctrine the disregard of which by an
European power is to be deemed an act of unfriendliness towards the United
States. The precise scope and limitations of this rule cannot be too clearly apprehended. It does not establish any general protectorate by the United States
over other American states. It does not relieve any American state from its
obligations as fixed by international law nor prevent any European power
directly interested from enforcing such obligations or from inflicting merited
punishment for the breach of them. It does not contemplate any interference
in the internal affairs of any American state or in the relations between it and
other American states. It does not justify any attempt on our part to change the
established form of government of any American state or to prevent the people
of such state from altering that form according to their own will and pleasure.
The rule in question has but a single purpose and object. It is that no European

power or combination of European powers shall forcibly deprive an American state of the right and power of self-government and of shaping for itself its own political fortunes and destinies. . . .

. . . A doctrine of American public law thus long and firmly established and supported could not easily be ignored in a proper case for its application, even were the considerations upon which it is founded obscure or questionable. No such objection can be made, however, to the Monroe doctrine understood and defined in the manner already stated. It rests, on the contrary, upon facts and principles that are both intelligible and incontrovertible. That distance and three thousand miles of intervening ocean make any permanent political union between an European and an American state unnatural and inexpedient will hardly be denied. But physical and geographical considerations are the least of the objections to such a union. Europe, as Washington observed, has a set of primary interests which are peculiar to herself. America is not interested in them and ought not to be vexed or complicated with them. Each great European power, for instance, to-day maintains enormous armies and fleets in self-defense and for protection against any other European power or powers. What have the states of America to do with that condition of things, or why should they be impoverished by wars or preparations for wars with whose causes or results they can have no direct concern? If all Europe were to suddenly fly to arms over the fate of Turkey, would it not be preposterous that any American state should find itself inextricably involved in the miseries and burdens of the contest? If it were, it would prove to be a partnership in the cost and losses of the struggle but not in any ensuing benefits.

What is true of the material, is no less true of what may be termed the moral interests involved. Those pertaining to Europe are peculiar to her and are entirely diverse from those pertaining and peculiar to America. Europe as a whole is monarchical, and, with the single important exception of the Republic of France, is committed to the monarchical principle. America, on the other hand, is devoted to the exactly opposite principle—to the idea that every people has an inalienable right of self-government—and, in the United States of America, has furnished to the world the most conspicuous and conclusive example and proof of the excellence of free institutions, whether from the standpoint of national greatness or of individual happiness. It can not be necessary, however, to enlarge upon this phase of the subject—whether moral or material interests be considered, it can not but be universally conceded that those of Europe are irreconcilably diverse from those of America, and that any European control of the latter is necessarily both incongruous and injurious. If, however, for the reasons stated the forcible intrusion of European powers into American politics is to be deprecated—if, as it is to be deprecated, it should be resisted and prevented—such resistance and prevention must come from the United States. They would come from it, of course, were it made the point of attack. But, if they come at all, they must also come from it when any other American state is attacked, since only the United States has the strength adequate to the exigency.

Is it true, then, that the safety and welfare of the United States are so concerned with the maintenance of the independence of every American state as against any European power as to justify and require the interposition of the United States whenever that independence is endangered? The question can be candidly answered in but one way. The states of America, South as well as North, by geographical proximity, by natural sympathy, by similarity of governmental constitutions, are friends and allies, commercially and politically, of the United States. . . . The people of the United States have a vital interest in the cause of popular self-government. They have secured the right for themselves and their posterity at the cost of infinite blood and treasure. . . . It is in that view more than in any other that they believe it not to be tolerated that the political control of an American state shall be forcibly assumed by an European power. . . .

. . . To-day the United States is practically sovereign on this continent, and its fiat is law upon the subjects to which it confines its interposition. Why? It is not because of the pure friendship or good will felt for it. It is not simply by reason of its high character as a civilized state, nor because wisdom and justice and equity are the invariable characteristics of the dealings of the United States. It is because, in addition to all other grounds, its infinite resources combined with its isolated position render it master of the situation and practically invulnerable as against any or all other powers.

All the advantages of this superiority are at once imperiled if the principle be admitted that European powers may convert American states into colonies or provinces of their own. The principle would be eagerly availed of, and every power doing so would immediately acquire a base of military operations against us. What one power was permitted to do could not be denied to another, and it is not inconceivable that the struggle now going on for the acquisition of Africa might be the partition of all South America. If it were, the weaker countries would unquestionably be soon absorbed, while the ultimate result might be the partition of all South America between the various European powers. The disastrous consequences to the United States of such a condition of things are obvious. The loss of prestige, of authority, and of weight in the councils of the family of nations, would be among the least of them. Our only real rivals in peace as well as enemies in war would be found located at our very doors. . . .

There is, then, a doctrine of American public law, well founded in principle and abundantly sanctioned by precedent, which entitles and requires the United States to treat as an injury to itself the forcible assumption by an European power of political control over an American state. The application of the doctrine to the boundary dispute between Great Britain and Venezuela remains to be made and presents no real difficulty. Though the dispute relates to a boundary line, yet, as it is between states, it necessarily imports political control to be lost by one party and gained by the other. . . .

Thus, as already intimated, the British demand that her right to a portion of the disputed territory shall be acknowledged before she will consent to an arbitration as to the rest seems to stand upon nothing but her own *ipse dixit*. She says to Venezuela, in substance: "You can get none of the debatable land by force, because you are not strong enough; you can get none by treaty, because I will not agree; and you can take your chance of getting a portion by arbitration, only if you first agree to abandon to me such other portion as I may designate." It is not perceived how such an attitude can be defended nor how it is reconcilable with that love of justice and fair play so eminently characteristic of the English race. It in effect deprives Venezuela of her free agency and puts her under virtual duress. Territory acquired by reason of it will be as much wrested from her by the strong hand as if occupied by British troops or covered by British fleets. It seems therefore quite impossible that this position of Great Britain should be assented to by the United States, or that, if such position be adhered to with the result of enlarging the bounds of British Guiana, it should not be regarded as amounting, in substance, to an invasion and conquest of Venezuelan territory.

In these circumstances, the duty of the President appears to him unmistakable and imperative. Great Britain's assertion of title to the disputed territory combined with her refusal to have that title investigated being a substantial appropriation of the territory to her own use, not to protest and give warning that the transaction will be regarded as injurious to the interests of the people of the United States as well as oppressive in itself would be to ignore an established policy with which the honor and welfare of this country are closely identified. While the measures necessary or proper for the vindication of that policy are to be determined by another branch of the Government, it is clearly for the Executive to leave nothing undone which may tend to render such determination unnecessary. . . .

# 9 | Lord Salisbury's Reply to Olney, November 1895 *

Lord Salisbury's carefully worded reply to Olney's extensive claims to American jurisdiction in the Western Hemisphere (under the Monroe Doctrine) comprises a brilliant statement of the traditional and inescapable role of national interest in a nation's foreign policy. He rejected Olney's argument that the United States had special claims in all matters purely American even when they transcended American interests. He suggested rather that the United States, like every other country, had the right and obligation to pursue its interests wherever those interests might exist. It had no right, continued Salisbury, to claim any jurisdiction over questions that did not affect its security or welfare.

* Salisbury to Sir Julian Pauncefote, November 26, 1895, *Papers Relating to the Foreign Relations of the United States, 1895,* Part I, 563–7.

. . . The contentions set forth by Mr. Olney in . . . his despatch are represented by him as being an application of the political maxims which are well
known in American discussion under the name of the Monroe doctrine. As far
as I am aware, this doctrine has never been before advanced on behalf of the
United States in any written communication addressed to the Government of
another nation; but it has been generally adopted and assumed as true by many
eminent writers and politicians in the United States. It is said to have largely
influenced the Government of that country in the conduct of its foreign affairs:
though Mr. Clayton, who was Secretary of State under President Taylor, expressly stated that the Administration had in no way adopted it. But during the
period that has elapsed since the Message of President Monroe was delivered in
1823, the doctrine has undergone a very notable development, and the aspect
which it now presents in the hands of Mr. Olney differs widely from its character when it first issued from the pen of its author. . . .

The dangers against which President Monroe thought it right to guard were
not as imaginary as they would seem at the present day. The formation of the
Holy Alliance; the Congresses of Laybach and Verona; the invasion of Spain by
France for the purpose of forcing upon the Spanish people a form of government which seemed likely to disappear, unless it was sustained by external aid,
were incidents fresh in the mind of President Monroe when he penned his
celebrated Message. The system of which he speaks, and of which he so resolutely
deprecates the application to the American Continent, was the system then
adopted by certain powerful States upon the Continent of Europe of combining
to prevent by force of arms the adoption in other countries of political institutions which they disliked, and to uphold by external pressure those which they
approved. Various portions of South America had recently declared their
independence, and that independence had not been recognized by the Governments of Spain and Portugal, to which, with small exception, the whole of
Central and South America were nominally subject. It was not an imaginary
danger that he foresaw, if he feared that the same spirit which had dictated the
French expedition into Spain might inspire the more powerful Governments of
Europe with the idea of imposing, by the force of European arms, upon the
South American communities the form of government and the political connection which they had thrown off. In declaring that the United States would
resist any such enterprise if it were contemplated, President Monroe adopted
a policy which received the entire sympathy of the English Government of
that date.

The dangers which were apprehended by President Monroe have no relation
to the state of things in which we live at the present day. There is no danger
of any Holy Alliance imposing its system upon any portion of the American
Continent, and there is no danger of any European State treating any part of
the American Continent as a fit object for European colonization. . . .

Great Britain is imposing no "system" upon Venezuela, and is not concerning
herself in any way with the nature of the political institutions under which the
Venezuelans may prefer to live. But the British Empire and the Republic of
Venezuela, are neighbors, and they have differed for some time past, and con-

tinue to differ, as to the line by which their dominions are separated. It is a controversy with which the United States have no apparent practical concern. It is difficult, indeed, to see how it can materially affect any State or community outside those primarily interested, except perhaps other parts of Her Majesty's dominions, such as Trinidad. The disputed frontier of Venezuela has nothing to do with any of the questions dealt with by President Monroe. It is not a question of the colonization by a European Power of any portion of America. It is not a question of the imposition upon the communities of South America of any system of government devised in Europe. It is simply the determination of the frontier of a British possession which belonged to the Throne of England long before the Republic of Venezuela came into existence. . . .

The Government of the United States do not say that Great Britain, or that Venezuela, is in the right in the matters that are in issue. But they lay down that the doctrine of President Monroe, when he opposed the imposition of European systems, or the renewal of European colonization, confers upon them the right of demanding that when a European Power has a frontier difference with a South American community, the European Power shall consent to refer that controversy to arbitration; and Mr. Olney states that unless Her Majesty's Government accede to this demand, it will "greatly embarrass the future relations between Great Britain and the United States." . . .

I will not now enter into a discussion of the merits of this method of terminating international differences. It has proved itself valuable in many cases; but it is not free from defects, which often operate as a serious drawback on its value. It is not always easy to find an Arbitrator who is competent, and who, at the same time, is wholly free from bias; and the task of insuring compliance with the Award when it is made is not exempt from difficulty. It is a mode of settlement of which the value varies much according to the nature of the controversy to which it is applied, and the character of the litigants who appeal to it. Whether, in any particular case, it is a suitable method of procedure is generally a delicate and difficult question. The only parties who are competent to decide that question are the two parties whose rival contentions are in issue. The claim of a third nation, which is unaffected by the controversy, to impose this particular procedure on either of the two others, cannot be reasonably justified, and has no foundation in the law of nations.

In the remarks which I have made, I have argued on the theory that the Monroe doctrine in itself is sound. I must not, however, be understood as expressing any acceptance of it on the part of Her Majesty's Government. It must always be mentioned with respect, on account of the distinguished statesman to whom it is due, and the great nation who have generally adopted it. But international law is founded on the general consent of nations; and no statesman, however eminent, and no nation, however powerful, are competent to insert into the code of international law a novel principle which was never recognized before, and which has not since been accepted by the Government of any other country. The United States have a right, like any other nation, to interpose in any controversy by which their own interests are affected; and they are the judge whether those interests are touched, and in what measure they

should be sustained. But their rights are in no way strengthened or extended by
the fact that the controversy affects some territory which is called American. Mr.
Olney quotes the case of the recent Chilean war, in which the United States
declined to join with France and England in an effort to bring hostilities to a
close, on account of the Monroe doctrine. The United States were entirely in
their right in declining to join in an attempt at pacification if they thought fit;
but Mr. Olney's principle that "American questions are for American decisions,"
even if it receive any countenance from the language of President Monroe
(which it does not), can not be sustained by any reasoning drawn from the law
of nations.

The Government of the United States is not entitled to affirm as a universal
proposition, with reference to a number of independent States for whose conduct it assumes no responsibility, that its interests are necessarily concerned in
whatever may befall those States simply because they are situated in the Western
Hemisphere. It may well be that the interests of the United States are affected
by something that happens to Chile or to Peru, and that that circumstance may
give them the right of interference; but such a contingency may equally happen
in the case of China or Japan, and the right of interference is not more extensive or more assured in the one case than in the other.

Though the language of President Monroe is directed to the attainment of
objects which most Englishmen would agree to be salutary, it is impossible to
admit that they have been inscribed by any adequate authority in the code of
international law; and the danger which such admission would involve is
sufficiently exhibited both by the strange development which the doctrine has
received at Mr. Olney's hands, and the arguments by which it is supported,
in the despatch under reply. In defence of it he says:

> That distance and 3,000 miles of intervening ocean *make any perma-*
> *nent political union between a European and an American State un-*
> *natural and inexpedient* will hardly be denied. But physical and
> geographical considerations are the least of the objections to such a
> union. Europe has a set of primary interests which are peculiar to
> herself; America is not interested in them, and ought not to be vexed
> or complicated with them. . . .

The necessary meaning of these words is that the union between Great
Britain and Canada; between Great Britain and Jamaica and Trinidad; between
Great Britain and British Honduras or British Guiana are "inexpedient and
unnatural." President Monroe disclaims any such inference from his doctrine;
but in this, as in other respects, Mr. Olney develops it. He lays down that the
inexpedient and unnatural character of the union between a European and
American State is so obvious that it "will hardly be denied." Her Majesty's
Government are prepared emphatically to deny it on behalf of both the British
and American people who are subject to her Crown. They maintain that the
Union between Great Britain and her territories in the Western Hemisphere is
both natural and expedient. They fully concur with the view which President
Monroe apparently entertained, that any disturbance of the existing territorial

distribution in that hemisphere by any fresh acquisitions on the part of any European State would be a highly inexpedient change. But they are not prepared to admit that the recognition of that expediency is clothed with the sanction which belongs to a doctrine of international law. They are not prepared to admit that the interests of the United States are necessarily concerned in every frontier dispute which may arise between any two of the States who possess dominion in the Western Hemisphere; and still less can they accept the doctrine that the United States are entitled to claim that the process of arbitration shall be applied to any demand for the surrender of territory which one of those States may make against another. . . .

## 10 | William Graham Sumner's Observations on the Role of Doctrines in Foreign Affairs, 1903 *

In the following essay William Graham Sumner, the noted Yale sociologist, challenged the employment of doctrine—any doctrine, but especially the Monroe Doctrine—as a guide to foreign policy. A doctrine, insisted Sumner, was an "abomination in statecraft" because it lacked any precise reference to actual interests at stake. Yet as a carefully sustained deity it stood as an arbiter of the nation's destiny, for as a deity, whatever the tensions and strife which it created, it could never be rejected in a crisis by a national leadership.

. . . If you want war, nourish a doctrine. Doctrines are the most frightful tyrants to which men ever are subject, because doctrines get inside of a man's own reason and betray him against himself. Civilized men have done their fiercest fighting for doctrines. The reconquest of the Holy Sepulcher, "the balance of power," "no universal dominion," "trade follows the flag," "he who holds the land will hold the sea," "the throne and the altar," the revolution, the faith—these are the things for which men have given their lives. What are they all? Nothing but rhetoric and phantasms. Doctrines are always vague; it would ruin a doctrine to define it, because then it could be analyzed, tested, criticised, and verified; but nothing ought to be tolerated which cannot be so tested. Somebody asks you with astonishment and horror whether you do not believe in the Monroe Doctrine. You do not know whether you do or not, because you do not know what it is; but you do not dare to say that you do not,

* William Graham Sumner, "War," *Essays of William Graham Sumner,* Albert Galloway Keller and Maurice R. Davie, eds. (New Haven, 1934), I: 169–73. Reprinted by permission of Yale University Press.

because you understand that it is one of the things which every good American is bound to believe in. Now when any doctrine arrives at that degree of authority, the name of it is a club which any demagogue may swing over you at any time and apropos of anything. In order to describe a doctrine we must have recourse to theological language. A doctrine is an article of faith. It is something which you are bound to believe, not because you have some rational grounds for believing it true, but because you belong to such and such a church or denomination. The nearest parallel to it in politics is the "reason of state". . . . A policy in a state we can understand; for instance it was the policy of the United States at the end of the eighteenth century to get the free navigation of the Mississippi to its mouth, even at the expense of war with Spain. That policy had reason and justice in it; it was founded in our interests; it had positive form and definite scope. A doctrine is an abstract principle; it is necessarily absolute in its scope and abstruse in its terms; it is a metaphysical assertion. It is never true, because it is absolute, and the affairs of men are all conditioned and relative. The physicists tell us now that there are phenomena which appear to present exceptions to gravitation which can be explained only by conceiving that gravitation requires time to get to work. We are convinced that perpetual motion is absolutely impossible within the world of our experiences, but it now appears that our universe taken as a whole is a case of perpetual motion.

Now, to turn back to politics, just think what an abomination in statecraft an abstract doctrine must be. Any politician or editor can, at any moment, put a new extension on it. The people acquiesce in the doctrine and applaud it because they hear the politicians and editors repeat it, and the politicians and editors repeat it because they think it is popular. So it grows. During the recent difficulty between England and Germany on one side and Venezuela on the other, some newspapers here began to promulgate a new doctrine that no country ought to be allowed to use its naval force to collect private debts. This doctrine would have given us standing-ground for interference in that quarrel. That is what it was invented for. Of course it was absurd and ridiculous, and it fell dead unnoticed, but it well showed the danger of having a doctrine lying loose about the house, and one which carries with it big consequences. It may mean anything or nothing, at any moment, and no one knows how it will be. You accede to it now, within the vague limits of what you suppose it to be; therefore you will have to accede to it to-morrow when the same name is made to cover something which you never heard or thought of. If you allow a political catchword to go on and grow, you will awaken some day to find it standing over you, the arbiter of your destiny, against which you are powerless, as men are powerless against delusions.

The process by which such catchwords grow is the old popular mythologizing. Your Monroe Doctrine becomes an entity, a being, a lesser kind of divinity, entitled to reverence and possessed of prestige, so that it allows of no discussion or deliberation. The President of the United States talks about the Monroe Doctrine and he tells us solemnly that it is true and sacred, whatever it is. He even undertakes to give some definition of what he means by it; but the definition which he gives binds nobody, either now or in the future, any more than what Monroe and Adams meant by it binds anybody now not to mean anything else. He says that, on account of the doctrine, whatever it may be, we must have a big navy. In this, at least, he is plainly in the right; if we have the doctrine, we shall need a big navy. The Monroe Doctrine is an exercise of authority by the United States over a controversy between two foreign states, if one of them is in America, combined with a refusal of the United States to accept any responsibility in connection with the controversy. That is a position which is sure to bring us into collision with other States, especially because it will touch their vanity, or what they call their honor—or it will touch our vanity, or what we call our honor, if we should ever find ourselves called upon to "back down" from it. Therefore it is very true that we must expect to need a big navy if we adhere to the doctrine. What can be more contrary to sound statesmanship and common sense than to put forth an abstract assertion which has no definite relation to any interest of ours now at stake, but which has in it any number of possibilities of producing complications which we cannot foresee, but which are sure to be embarrassing when they arise!

What has just been said suggests a consideration of the popular saying, "In time of peace prepare for war." If you prepare a big army and navy and are all ready for war, it will be easy to go to war; the military and naval men will have a lot of new machines and they will be eager to see what they can do with them. There is no such thing nowadays as a state of readiness for war. It is a chimera, and the nations which pursue it are falling into an abyss of wasted energy and wealth. When the army is supplied with the latest and best rifles, someone invents a new field gun; then the artillery must be provided with that before we are ready. By the time we get the new gun, somebody has invented a new rifle and our rival nation is getting that; therefore we must have it, or one a little better. It takes two or three years and several millions to do that. In the meantime somebody proposes a more effective organization which must be introduced; signals, balloons, dogs, bicycles, and every other device and invention must be added, and men must be trained to use them all. There is no state of readiness for war; the notion calls for never-ending sacrifices. It is a fallacy. It is evident that to pursue such a notion with any idea of realizing it would absorb all the resources and activity of the state; this the great European states are now proving by experiment. A wiser rule would be to make up your mind soberly what you want, peace or war, and then to get ready for what you want: for what we prepare for is what we shall get.

# V

## Nonintervention and the Balance of Power

Toward Europe, the only region of the world with sufficient power to challenge the interests of the United States directly, isolationism remained throughout the nineteenth century the underlying theory of American foreign policy. The effectiveness of that theory appeared obvious enough from the record of non-involvement itself. The years before 1815 had demonstrated the disturbing truth that any major European war that ventured onto the Atlantic eventually encompassed the lands across the sea. What created the illusion—one that grew more convincing with each passing decade—that the Atlantic was a genuine barrier against involvement was the fact that Europe's wars after 1815 were confined to the Continent. Thus it was neither American intent nor American interest, but the European balance of power, that preserved American isolation. The key to that balance, and thus to the security of the United States, especially after the enunciation of the Monroe Doctrine, was the predominance of British naval power. The same factors in the Atlantic world which guaranteed an acceptable balance of power in Europe protected simultaneously the interests of the United States in the Western Hemisphere. Because these factors were the essence of American security, European politics affected American interests, directly and inevitably. The rise of any nation to an unchallengeable position on the European continent would threaten the United States with attack. What gradually removed Europe from the consciousness of the American people as a potential source of danger were the remarkable conditions of stability which flowed from the restoration of the Continent after the Napoleonic wars.

That very stability, because it rested on reaction, would eventually reactivate those liberal enthusiasms which the American people, during the early 'twenties, had directed against the oppressive Turk. Guided by Prince Metternich of Austria, Europe's established ruling classes identified the peace of the Continent with the re-establishment of legitimate authority. Having battled the French Revolution and Napoleon for a quarter-century, they quite reasonably regarded nationalism and liberalism as wicked delusions that would plunge Europe into perennial wars. It was Metternich who attacked the ideas of the French Revolution as "the disease which must be cured, the volcano which must be extinguished. . . ."

Accepting the formula of legitimacy and disregarding the revolutionary concept of self-determination, the Holy Alliance after 1815 faced a series of sporadic revolts in western Europe. So dominant were the forces of reaction throughout Europe, however, that these outcroppings of opposition scarcely revealed the seething revolutionary tendencies among the Slavic minorities in the Austrian, Turkish, and Russian empires, or the mounting liberal and democratic pressures within the great Western powers themselves. The enormous gap between hope and reality on the European scene was not lost on the Democratic leadership of the United States. It was the repressive nature of the great powers of Europe that prompted Lewis Cass of Michigan to denounce so passionately their alleged ambitions in the Western Hemisphere. "But what is this balance of power," he asked the Senate in January 1846, "which is to cross the Atlantic and take up its abode in this New World?" Cass supplied his own answer:

> It is the assumption of a power which has deluged Europe in blood, and which has attempted to stifle the first germs of freedom in every land where they have started up; which has bolted Poland from the map of nations; which has given a moiety of Saxony, in spite of the prayers of the people, to Prussia; which has extinguished Venice and Genoa; which added Belgium to Holland, notwithstanding the repugnance of its inhabitants, who eventually rose in their revolutionary might, and asserted and achieved their own independence; which transferred Norway from Denmark, to which it was attached by old ties and by a mild government, to Sweden, who had to send an army, and to call upon the navy of England to aid her to take possession of this gift of the holy alliance; which keeps Switzerland in eternal turmoil, and which sent a French army into Spain to put down the spirit of liberty, and an Austrian army to Italy for the same purpose; and which watches and wards off the very first instincts of human nature to meliorate its social and political condition.

This deep-seated, but seldom expressed, antagonism toward the European system finally broke loose at the first news of the revolutions which, beginning in France in February 1848, swept rapidly across the whole Continent. The United States Minister in Paris recognized the provisional government of France, and added hopefully that "if the Union gives to others the choice of government without interference, it naturally feels gratified at seeing another nation, under similar institutions, assuring to themselves the benefits of social order and public liberty." In New York an enthusiastic throng at Lafayette Hall adopted a resolution which declared that the establishment of a republic in France "constituted a new and bright era in the world's history . . . and imparts hope and light to the oppressed and toiling nations of Europe."

Upon receiving the official report of the overthrow of the French monarchy and the establishment of a provisional government based on republican principles,

President Polk addressed the Congress on April 3: "The world has seldom witnessed a more interesting and sublime spectacle than the peaceful rising of the French people, resolved to secure for themselves enlarged liberty, and to assert in the majesty of their strength the great truth that, in this enlightened age, man is capable of governing himself." The policy of the United States, Polk reminded the Congress, had always been that of nonintervention in the domestic affairs of other nations; yet, he added, "all our sympathies are naturally enlisted on the side of a great people, who, imitating our example, have resolved to be be free." Three days later Senator Edward Hannegan of Indiana reported a joint resolution from the Committee on Foreign Relations which offered the congratulations of the United States to the people of France "upon the recent change in their form of government, and their successful efforts thus far to found for their country institutions similar to our own."

This congratulatory resolution set off a violent debate in Congress over the propriety of such Congressional behavior. (*Reading No. 1.*) Senator Daniel Dickinson of New York, an earlier proponent of manifest destiny, rushed to the defense of the resolution. The revolution, he declared, had "removed every obstacle between thirty-five millions of king-oppressed people and liberty. If this," he added, "is not an achievement worthy of congratulation, I cannot imagine what would be." To Lewis Cass the continued success of the French Republic, surrounded as it was by monarchical enemies, hinged in large measure on the solicitude and encouragement of the United States. "We cannot halt in our course, and withhold our congratulations," he cried, "without giving the most serious offence to the French people, and without, in fact, announcing to the world that the struggle in which they are engaged will terminate unfortunately. . . ."

Again the Whigs spoke for the American conservative tradition. Senator Arthur P. Bagby of Alabama admitted that he was somewhat afraid of a three-days' revolution. He wanted to know, he said, what it was that Congress was congratulating. To him the French Republic had not demonstrated its ability to last or to prevent the disintegration of the turmoil of Paris into a war of desolation and destruction. R. S. Baldwin of Connecticut likewise reminded the Senate that the French provisional government had been established by the revolutionaries of Paris and had not received the approval of the people of France. The deeply conservative Whig, William L. Dayton of New Jersey, agreed with the Democrats that the resolution did not require the maturation of the French Republic. He believed, however, that the Congress might wait at least until a genuine republic was born. "I consider that a month, more or less," he declared, "will not diminish the value of our congratulations to the French Government; and I hope that when these congratulations shall be tendered, we shall find there a government to receive them."


II

By 1849 the spontaneous uprising of one European people after another had diverted attention from France to Hungary where the Magyar patriots were engaged in a heroic struggle against Austrian rule. That summer, while the nation applauded the successive Hungarian triumphs, Secretary of State John Clayton dispatched Ambrose Dudley Mann to Hungary as a special agent to report the progress of the revolution and to offer the nation's encouragements. Senator John J. Crittenden of Kentucky addressed Clayton: "Your readiness to recognize Hungary is a forward and bold step. I like it for the sentiment and resolution it implies. Go ahead!—it is glorious and will please our people to see the Majesty of our Republic exhibiting itself on all proper occasions, with its dignity and fearless front, in the eyes and to the teeth of misruling kings, or despots of whatever make or title they may be." After winning momentary success under their eloquent leader, Louis Kossuth, the Hungarians were crushed by Russian troops brought to the aid of the Austrian emperor. Later, Americans followed with delight the glorious reception accorded Kossuth by the people of London. Then came the even more exhilarating news that the now legendary hero would visit the United States.

Again the sentimentalists faced the determined opposition of the traditionalists. Early in 1850 Cass proposed a resolution demanding that the national administration sever diplomatic relations with Austria. Henry Clay, the established leader of the Whig party in the Senate, took strong exception to the proposal. The New York *Atlas* commented acidly: "We do not think it is the duty or the province of the United States to undertake to say that Austria is beyond the pale of civilized life, and unentitled to the rights of diplomacy and humanity. . . . The United States cannot afford to make the cause of every broil in which the States of Europe become involved, an affair of their own." With such conservatism President Millard Fillmore agreed. In his message of December 1850 he restated the traditional American doctrine that each nation possesses the right "of establishing that form of government which it may deem most conducive to the happiness and prosperity of its own citizens. . . . The people of the United States claim this right for themselves, and they readily concede it to others." (*Reading No. 2.*)

Meanwhile Chevalier J. G. Hülsemann, chargé d'affaires at the Austrian legation, had lodged a protest with the United States government, accusing it of displaying too much public interest in Hungary's liberation. In his famous reply of December 21, 1850, Secretary of State Daniel Webster claimed for the American people the right to cheer the forces of freedom in Europe. He assured Hülsemann, however, that the United States would engage in no action that might give weight to its words. Nor was the sympathy of the American people for struggling humanity to be interpreted as a sign of hostility toward any of the parties in the great national uprisings of Europe. Indeed, declared Webster, the United States desired amicable relations with them all. (*Reading No. 3.*)

Upon his arrival in New York harbor on December 5, 1851, announced by the booming of cannon, Kossuth received the city's greatest ovation since the visit of Lafayette a quarter-century earlier. Upon hearing him speak, New York editors praised his intellectuality and the subtle qualities of his expression. The New York *Tribune* called him "the greatest of orators now living." This triumphal reception set off a Kossuth craze from the Atlantic to the Great Lakes.

Articles on Hungary filled the press; Hungarian menus and Hungarian wines became the specialties of good restaurants throughout the North. Everywhere the voices of American orators throbbed with sympathy for the oppressed of Europe. At a Washington dinner in Kossuth's honor, attended by over two hundred members of Congress, Webster exclaimed: "We shall rejoice to see our American model upon the Lower Danube and on the mountains of Hungary." At Springfield, Illinois, a public meeting adopted resolutions which praised Kossuth as "the most worthy and distinguished representative of the cause of civil and religious liberty on the continent of Europe," demanded that the nation's sympathy "be exerted in favor of the people of every nation struggling to be free," condemned the Russians specifically for their unwarranted repression of the Hungarian revolt, but then admitted reluctantly that it was not the obligation of the United States to foment or assist revolutions in other countries.

More realistic Americans again reminded the enthusiasts that their effort to create policy out of sympathy alone was worthless to Hungary and dangerous to the United States. Congress had before it a resolution to welcome the Hungarian leader to American shores and to extend "the sympathy of Congress and the people of the United States to the victims of oppression everywhere." William H. Seward of New York attacked the resolution in the Senate as a move that might commit the Congress "to some act of intervention in the affairs of Europe, by which the Government of the United States may be embarrassed in its foreign relations." Clay reminded Kossuth privately that even if the United States declared war on Russia it could not transport men and arms across the sea. It would be far better, warned Clay, to "keep our light burning on this western shore, as a light to all nations, than to hazard its utter extinction amid the ruins of fallen and falling republics in Europe." (*Reading No. 4.*) The Cincinnati *Weekly Gazette,* late in January 1852, regretted, with Clay, Kossuth's effort to involve the United States in affairs beyond the sea and recommended instead that the nation serve Europe's oppressed (including the Hungarian leader himself) in the only manner commensurate with its interests—by giving discovered that he had been victimized by the very enthusiasms which he had them homes in the New World. (*Reading No. 5.*) The Hungarian hero soon unleashed. Politicians, he discovered, toasted him warmly but refused to vote a dollar for his cause. Eventually he returned to England suffering the disillusionment of those who expect too much of sentiment.

But the movement to transform American foreign policy into a giant effort to serve Europe's oppressed millions continued to grow in grandeur and intensity. The search for a genuine policy of liberation began on December 16, 1851, when Democratic Senator I. P. Walker of Wisconsin demanded that the country use its moral and physical power against any nation that interfered in the affairs of another in defiance of public law. The Republic should prepare itself to fight, if necessary, for the freedom of Hungary. Then on January 20, 1852, Cass introduced in the Senate a resolution declaring that the United States could not again witness, without deep concern, the efforts of European powers to crush an independence movement. Cass defended his resolution, pointing to the fact of "twenty-five millions of people looking across the ocean at Europe, strong in power, acquainted with their rights, and determined to enforce them. . . . And the man is now living," he continued, "who will live to see one hundred and fifty millions of people, free, prosperous, and intelligent, swaying the destinies of this country, and exerting a mighty influence upon those of the world." Earlier the Michigan Senator had claimed for the nation the right, based on principle, to control the hemisphere; now he demanded the extension of "the principle of public law" to include the rights and independence of the peoples of Europe—all without enlarging the responsibility or obligation of the government of the United States. Each nation, he admitted, possessed the right to judge for itself when and how it would interpose. (*Reading No. 6.*) But Cass again aroused the fury of the Congressional conservatives, who asserted that words and resolutions such as his demeaned the dignity of the country, for the moral influence they sought to wield was impotent in affairs among nations. (*Reading No. 7.*)

Kossuth, upon sailing for England, reminded his American hosts that the passion for liberty still burned in the hearts of his countrymen, ready to strike again at the bonds of Austrian oppression. For a small, but exceedingly ambitious, group of young Democratic politicians, the cause of Hungary appeared sufficiently powerful to wrest control of the Democratic party away from its old guard leadership and turn the Whigs out of the White House. This group, under the leadership of George N. Sanders of Kentucky, adopted the name "Young America," and chose the popular Stephen A. Douglas of Illinois as its presidential candidate. Sanders became editor of the important *Democratic Review* in January 1852 and turned it into the mouthpiece of the Young America movement.

Clearly this crusade, like others before it, was concerned less with external than with internal objectives. Avowedly the liberation of eastern Europe promised the expansion of American markets as well as the promotion of a better world. But specifically its appeals to sentimentalism and materialism were designed to capture the allegiance of the thousands of European immigrants then settling in the Midwest. For many of its critics the Young America movement was never more than a massive assault of Western Democrats on the German vote. Douglas, as an outspoken proponent of manifest destiny and the Monroe Doctrine, was the ideal spokesman of such a crusade. He had taken the lead in condemning the conservatism of Whig foreign policy. Democratic politicians could recall the ringing appeal of his Jackson Day address in 1852: "I think it is time that America had a foreign policy—a foreign policy predicated upon a true interpretation of the laws of nations—a foreign policy in accordance with the spirit of the age—but not a foreign policy as we have seen attempted to be enforced in this country in the last three years."

Young America had to content itself with the nomination of Franklin Pierce in 1852, but immediately its spokesmen adopted the nominee as their own and campaigned for him with appeals to liberal nationalism. Even Kossuth electioneered for Pierce by urging, through a circular, that the German clubs in America support the Democratic candidate. Pierce's election was interpreted by the European press as a danger to Europe's stability. The deaths of Clay and

Webster made the prospects even more alarming. Sanders could not prevent the appointment of conservative Democrat William L. Marcy as Secretary of State, but he managed to obtain for himself, in June 1853, an assignment as consul at London.

In London Sanders's residence became the headquarters of exiled European revolutionaries, including Kossuth himself. Attending a dinner party at Sanders's London house in company with Kossuth, Mazzini, Garibaldi, Orsini, and Herzen, American Minister James Buchanan asked his hostess "if she was not afraid the combustible materials about her would explode and blow us all up." Kossuth pressed Sanders for an American commitment against Austria, but to no avail. On December 13, 1853, he wrote to Sanders, "God knows how anxiously I have awaited a letter from America. . . . I am sick with excitement and disappointment." Then in February 1854 the Senate rejected overwhelmingly Sanders's nomination as consul to London. Kossuth, Mazzini, and others expressed mortification, but it mattered little. Young America represented a national self-consciousness, nothing more. Its objectives were vague, its means nonexistent. Europeans, to the extent that they responded to American sentimentalism, might better have anchored their hopes and fears to forces purely European.

### III

Major Robert Anderson's surrender of Fort Sumter in April 1861, which inaugurated four years of civil war in America, reversed the normal relationship of the United States to Europe's liberal causes. To prevent the destruction of the Union, the government of the United States found itself in the embarrassing position of employing force to repress the will of a minority of the nation which desired to establish its own independence. Cassius Clay, the American Minister at St. Petersburg, once declared that the United States was fighting for nationality and liberty. To this the London *Times* replied sarcastically that it was difficult to understand how "a people fighting . . . to force their fellow citizens to remain in a confederacy which they repudiated, can be called the champions of liberty and nationalism." The Confederates were fighting for their independence, observed the *Times,* adding, "But with the Northerners all is different. They are not content with their own. They are fighting to coerce others."

Defending his Unionist policies against the jibes of such European critics, Secretary of State William H. Seward employed all the arguments which European spokesmen of the *status quo* had used to defend their right and obligation to stamp out insurrection and revolution, if necessary, by the power of the sword. As early as June 17, 1861, Seward made it clear to the government of France that the United States remained one nation with one foreign policy and should so be regarded by the nations of Europe. It possessed the right, moreover, to protect its sovereignty against any foreign interference in its internal affairs. "This government insists," Seward addressed the American Minister in Paris, "that the United States are one whole undivided nation, especially so far as foreign nations are concerned, and that France is, by the law of nations and by treaties, not a neutral power between two imaginary parties here, but a friend of the United States." (*Reading No. 8.*) In his letter of August 18, 1862, to Charles Francis Adams in London, Seward reasserted the principle of nonintervention against any European power tempted to cast its lot with the Confederacy. "The nation has a right, and it is its duty, to live," he wrote. "Those who favor and give aid to the insurrection, upon whatever pretext, assail the nation in an hour of danger, and therefore they cannot be held or regarded as its friends. In taking this ground, the United States claim only what they concede to all other nations. No state can be really independent in any other position." (*Reading No. 9.*) Thus Seward, at a moment of national crisis, was forced to admit the legality of force to suppress revolution when at issue was a nation's fundamental integrity.

President Abraham Lincoln established a blockade of the Southern ports early in the war to limit the Confederacy's access to Europe's industrial production. The British eventually manufactured and sold commerce raiders to Southern agents, but they defended their own traditional interest in the principles of a blockade by refusing to challenge the President's right to impose one on the South. In the *Trent* case of December 1861, Seward weighed the interest of the United States with equal care. The Union naval officer, Captain Charles Wilkes, had removed four Confederate officials, including John Slidell and James M. Mason, from the British merchant vessel *Trent*. Seward studied the legality of Wilkes's action in terms of established British and American maritime practice and concluded that Wilkes had erred in not taking the *Trent* to a convenient port where the vessel might have been subjected to a judicial prosecution. Instead, he had released the vessel and permitted it to proceed without four of its passengers. To uphold Wilkes would disavow established principles; to maintain the principles would surrender the case. Yet Seward, in making the latter choice, declared emphatically that if the security of the United States had been involved he would not have released the Confederate diplomats. (*Reading No. 10.*)

Lincoln, like his predecessors, avoided moral commitments to Europe which he knew American power could not fulfill. Rather than expose himself and his administration to the psychological and political pressures that always come to bear on leaders when something specific is expected of them, he refused to involve the nation in the effort of the Polish revolutionaries, early in 1863, to throw off the tyranny of the Russian Czar. Napoleon of France sent an appeal to the United States for support in exerting "a moral influence on the Emperor of Russia." Seward responded for the Lincoln administration. In his letter to the French government of March 11, 1863, he acknowledged the American interest in public order and humanity. He admitted that revolutionaries of every country had been attracted to American democratic idealism and had attempted to involve the United States in events abroad. But, declared Seward, the American policy of nonintervention had remained inviolate since the presidency of George Washington. If the United States entertained good wishes for the progress of humanity, it would not defy its own principle of self-determination. *(Reading No. 11.)*

This insurrection of the Poles was the last European uprising of the century which might have aroused the crusading zeal of the American people. Through the first century of its history, therefore, the United States government consistently repulsed the pressures of idealism in the conduct of its foreign relations. It refused to employ either diplomacy or force in the cause of the oppressed or to withhold recognition from *de facto* or *de jure* regimes because their concepts of politics and morality did not conform to those of the United States. Whatever the extent or ambitions of the messianism stimulated inside the nation by European events, there were always national leaders who rebuked those not responsible for national policy, who would raise false hopes abroad through appeals to sentiment at home. Thus established American diplomatic practice followed that of the great conservative statesmen of Europe.

## IV

Despite the vehement interventionist sentiment which at times characterized popular American attitudes toward Europe, the United States, in the name of isolationism and neutrality, continued to avoid military and political commitments abroad. If such negative policies served the nation well, it was because nothing had disturbed the European balance of power. Americans, especially spokesmen of the Democratic party, professed a deep antipathy toward British policy and the British Empire, but off-setting this enmity was the ever-present realization that the United States and England shared a common historical heritage of language, literature, culture, law, politics, and even national interest. Some writers admitted freely that England was the chief source of the nation's security, that without the Atlantic barrier, which British naval supremacy alone rendered effective, the American people would lose their unique freedom to look inward and devote their considerable energies to the development of a rich continent.

Britain was not so predominant, however, that American editors, officials, and diplomatists could ignore the great changes being wrought after 1865 on the European continent. At one time France had loomed as the one serious European threat to the monopoly of power which the United States enjoyed in the Western Hemisphere. But France had entered upon troubled times. Napoleon III, upon becoming Emperor in 1852, had turned to reform. Under his management Paris became one of the world's most beautiful cities. Wide boulevards replaced thousands of narrow, unsanitary, and unlit streets with their vermin-infested dwellings. France's involvement in the Crimean and Austro-Sardinian wars brought Napoleon to the height of his prestige in 1859, but his Mexican venture not only depleted his treasury but also antagonized Austria, the United States, and the French liberals. Napoleon's court remained brilliant and gay, but his propensity for speculation in politics and foreign affairs did not serve him well. By the 'sixties, despite France's general prosperity, his popularity was disintegrating. Suddenly, when it was too late, he discovered that he had ignored the ultimate challenge to France's greatness, the rise of Prussia to a commanding position on the European continent.

Prussia's successful assault on the established balance of power was the triumph of one man—Bismarck, one of the great masters of *Realpolitik* in modern history. As early as 1851 this Prussian *Junker* had seen that German greatness lay not in liberalism but in national union under the Prussian king, to be imposed by force if necessary. In his first essential maneuver, Bismarck, enjoying the full support of the king, defied the liberals to build a magnificent army. By 1864 he was prepared to assert Prussian predominance in Germanic affairs. When Danish nationalists threatened to absorb the duchies of Schleswig and Holstein into the Danish kingdom, Bismarck defied the British bluff that "if Denmark had to fight, she would not fight alone," and quickly resolved the Schleswig-Holstein issue by force. Next by astute diplomacy he isolated Austria from its potential allies and in 1866, by overwhelming this historic rival for the allegiance of the Germanic states, elevated Prussia to an unchallengeable position as the leader of German unification. Having isolated France by similar tactics, he provoked Napoleon to declare war and, in another totally unexpected display of military supremacy, terminated at once France's divisive influence in Germanic affairs and its primacy on the European continent.

Events so dramatic could not escape the evaluation of American observers. During the weeks that preceded the profound German victory at Sedan, editorial opinion in the United States favored the German cause with almost complete unanimity. *Harper's Weekly*, for example, could detect only one party in the United States: "It is a war in which Louis Napoleon is on one side and the rest of the world upon the other." John Sherman commented in the Senate: "Certainly at the beginning of this war the universal sympathy throughout this country was with the German people. Until Sedan I suppose there was very little division of opinion." Most Americans recalled Napoleon's pro-Southern attitudes during the Civil War as well as his Mexican adventure. They remembered with equal clarity the inestimable aid which Germans, both in the United States and in Germany, had rendered the Union cause. Under such circumstances it was not difficult to charge Napoleon with aggression against Germany. Republican politicians had little choice. In 1870 the German-Americans scattered through the North from New York to Wisconsin numbered almost two million. These were the factors which motivated the following editorial in the Cincinnati *Gazette:*

> . . . the German people . . . were our friends because they love liberty. . . . They bought bonds and thus, as we cannot forget, sustained the credit of our Government when it most needed support. . . . They took all the risks, because their sympathies were on the side of freedom and national unity. . . . Of course the Republicans of the United States have not forgotten . . . the sympathy and the assistance that Germany extended to this government in our dark days; nor can they soon forget the treachery of which Louis Napoleon was guilty.

What disturbed many thoughtful Americans after Sedan was the obvious efficiency of the German military machine. Suddenly the new Germany represented not freedom but militarism and despotism centering in both the Prussian Hohenzollern dynasty and the Prussian *Junker* aristocracy. Germany was not only as militaristic as France but far more powerful. Bismarck's success merely intensified the scale of war. "The next power or combination of powers that goes to war with Germany," predicted one American observer, "will have to begin with a million of men in hand." To American diplomats the new German Empire was upsetting the balance of power, but few regarded that nation as a danger to peace. George Bancroft, the United States Minister at Berlin, defended German policy toward France and lauded the creation of German unity as a source of stability in Central Europe. The new German army, Bancroft assured officials in Washington, merely reinforced that stability. Germany, after all, was surrounded by enemies. (*Reading No. 12.*)

Throughout the following two decades American writers and diplomats followed Bismarck's diplomacy with grave attention and generally with unguarded approval. Until 1875 the chief danger to European peace centered in a possible recurrence of war between France and Germany. British leadership eased the growing crisis, and the Earl of Derby, in explaining British policy to the House of Lords, revealed as well the limits of British influence on the continent of Europe. (*Reading No. 13.*) After 1875 the focus of European tension shifted to the Balkans, where the same Russo-Turkish rivalry for Constantinople which had led to the Crimean War continued to dominate the region. (*Reading No. 14.*) To limit Russian expansion following the Russo-Turkish War of 1877, Bismarck called the famed Congress of Berlin to determine the fate of the Balkans. Britain, France, Austria, Russia, Italy, Turkey, and Germany were represented, and all but Germany and Italy departed with territorial gains. For the moment the nationalist aspirations of the Balkan peoples were sacrificed to the greed and rivalries of the great powers. Turkey's friends had despoiled her empire more than had the Russians. Thereafter the Turkish government looked less to France and England and more to Germany as a potential ally.

Of Czarist Russia the American people knew little. Throughout the nineteenth century the United States had enjoyed friendly relations with this remote empire, for the interests of the two nations converged in their mutual desire to limit the ambitions of Western Europe. Yet to some American observers Russian Pan-Slavism loomed as a potential danger to the stability of Eastern Europe. Russia emerged from the Congress of Berlin harboring grievances toward both Germany and Austria. Bismarck responded to Russian animosity by negotiating the Dual Alliance with Austria in 1879. On November 18, Minister Andrew D. White reported these developments from Berlin. To him it seemed clear that the new Austro-German alliance guaranteed the *status quo* in East-Central Europe and therefore strengthened the prospects for peace. This view was affirmed by *The Nation. (Reading No. 15.)*

During the 'eighties American analysts detected further shifts in Europe's power relationships which could, in the long run, disturb the equilibrium of the Continent established by the Dual Alliance. Bismarck's *rapprochement* with

Russia brought the great Slavic empire into the German constellation of power, and by stabilizing even further the political *status quo* in eastern Europe had the effect of directing Russian energies toward Central Asia and Asia Minor. By the late 'eighties England and Italy had settled their differences in the eastern Mediterranean and had formed what *The Nation* termed a natural alliance. (*Reading No. 16.*) The writer, detecting France's continued isolation and convinced that France and Germany would eventually become involved in a new trial of strength, wondered why France did not "draw nearer to England and to Italy, since England and Italy are allied by necessity." What the European system required, most American observers seemed to agree, was the leadership of Bismarck. For that reason his dismissal in 1890 by young Kaiser Wilhelm II appeared a genuine threat to European peace. As Sir Charles W. Dilke observed in the *North American Review* of July 1890: "One great influence on the side of peace, indeed, has lately gone, for Prince Bismarck in the last fourteen years has been a powerful factor on the side of peace preservation throughout the continent of Europe." It was left for *Puck,* on April 2, 1890, to pass final judgment on the passing of Bismarck from the European diplomatic scene:

> Strange ending of it all! The Iron Hand
> That swept up states into an Empire, held
> The hammer of unchallenged power, to weld
> Disunion into strength, make weakness grand,
> And forge the war-sword of a Fatherland—
> This mighty hand whose lightest sign compelled
> The will of Europe; hand that smote and felled,
> Made or unmade, as the stern spirit planned—
> This hand at last is loosed, nor more shall hold
> Its guiding grasp upon a nation's arm,
> Or mark for her the path of peace again.
> Let him go—an Emperor is come too bold
> To need him, or to heed the land's alarm—
> A boy who plays at making over Men!

## V

By the early 'nineties it was apparent to American writers that two fundamental pressures threatened the Bismarckian peace. The first was Russian ambition in southeastern Europe—a danger that could be contained only by a unified Austria allied to a powerful Germany. The destruction of Austria, predicted *The Nation* in October 1890, would inaugurate a secular struggle between the Germanic and Slavic races with results that one could only conjecture. The Russian danger, therefore, rendered the Austro-German alliance a permanent institution, one that could be broken only to the detriment of European stability. So completely did this alliance rest on mutual self-interest that it would continue unchanged despite Bismarck's retirement.

Another, and even more obvious, threat to Europe's peace was the French *revanche.* "Every schoolboy in America must know by this time," declared *The*

*Nation,* "that France will declare war on the first opportunity, and attack Germany with a fury such as she has never shown in any previous war." What made this threat so dangerous was the fact that it could succeed only at the price of unleashing Russia in eastern Europe. It was the French determination to destroy Germany that rendered the Eastern problem so acute. The only hope for peace, therefore, rested in the continuance of dominant power in the hands of the central alliance, which now included Italy. The Triple Alliance appeared so essential to Europe's peace and stability that Britain, it seemed, had no choice but to join it and thus render the Franco-Russian threat inoperative. (*Reading No. 17.*) Having reviewed the intense military preparations of Europe, Theodore Ayrault Dodge, writing in *The Forum* of July 1892, reached the same conclusion. With the armies of Germany, Austria, and Italy almost matched by those of France and Russia, England still commanded the balance of power. European peace demanded, therefore, that England cast her lot with the Triple Alliance, for France and Russia were Europe's dissatisfied and therefore aggressive nations. (*Reading No. 18.*)

Some Americans in the late nineteenth century were not too absorbed in their own domestic affairs to recall that they were part of a global environment. There were intellectuals, editors, political writers, and diplomats who recognized the interrelationship of nations and understood that the affairs of the United States were not being conducted in a power vacuum. They recognized especially the importance of the balance of power principle in preserving the peace of Europe. They knew that the United States had been the chief beneficiary of that system, and that Europe's very stability had permitted the American people to concentrate on domestic concerns. But by the 'nineties, it seemed clear, complex and powerful pressures rendered the concept of isolation obsolete. American interests were becoming too universal, too enmeshed in the affairs of Europe, to be entrusted to the oceans alone. The equilibrium of Europe, moreover, was no longer self-contained. In a narrowly balanced Continental system the policies of such uncommitted nations as England and the United States carried the burden of future peace and security.

Unfortunately, those who viewed America's world relationships in this light could not dispel the illusions created by successive decades of actual noninvolvement in European affairs. The favorable balance, anchored to British power and British diplomacy, was ultimately taken for granted, and its essential contribution to American security all but forgotten. By the 1890's Americans no longer recognized the nation's vital stake in European politics. The restoration of the Continent after the Napoleonic wars created conditions of such stability that the average citizen of the United States, enjoying perennial security at relatively little cost, began to put his faith in the fact of geographic isolation itself. This gradual identification of American security with the Atlantic Ocean rather than with a body of precise political conditions in Europe, which after 1890 were subject to enormous pressures for change, created the foundations of twentieth-century American isolationism, which viewed mere abstinence from European affairs the essence of sound policy. Whatever happened in Europe, ran the burgeoning isolationist argument, it could not challenge the historic security of the American people.

# 1 | The Senate Debate on the French Resolution, March-April 1848 *

In defending the resolution congratulating the French nation on the overthrow of the monarchy, Senator Daniel Dickinson of New York offered the customary argument employed by Congressional leaders to defend such Congressional efforts to identify United States foreign policy with democratic and liberal causes abroad without committing the nation to any specific action.

✍

. . . When asked what France has yet done to justify the congratulations of this Government, I answer that she has solved a great and interesting problem in human government. America demonstrated to the world that man was capable of self-government; but France established another great fact, scarcely less important to the oppressed people of Europe, that the force of opinion is mightier than armed men, and that monarchy can be overthrown and deprived of its ill-gotten power by social convulsion. What, we are asked, has France done? Peaceably and unarmed, by the omnipotence of opinion, her people have broken down one of the most powerful monarchies of modern times, with all its concomitant enormities and abuses, and have removed every obstacle between thirty-five millions of king-oppressed people and liberty. If this is not an achievement worthy of congratulation, I cannot imagine what would be.

The late "citizen king" attained his position by professions of great regard for the rights and interests of the people of France; and, although for a time he did not openly throw off all pretence of regard for popular rights, the last ten years of his despotic reign have been characterized by avarice, tyranny, and usurpation, and every act that can disgrace even a monarch. In the pursuit of his schemes of ambition and aggrandizement, he had practically limited the right of suffrage to about two hundred thousand of his thirty-five millions of people. . . . The liberty of the press and of speech have been abridged from time to time, to suit the royal wishes, until, in attempting to prescribe the number of citizens who might meet at a public dinner, and frankly discuss the measures of Government, he was deposed and driven from his palaces and gardens—driven, too, like our common progenitor, for his sins, forever, and, like him, his return guarded by the sword of liberty. . . .

. . . Thus have the people of France thrown off a powerful, corrupt, and tyrannous reign, and trodden down every barrier between themselves and civil liberty. Thus have they driven into exile the instruments who have enslaved and oppressed them. Thus much have they already achieved for the cause of oppressed humanity. The future is full of hope, and none can doubt of the ultimate success of this brave and chivalrous people. But if we knew they would

* Remarks by Dickinson on the French resolution, April 6, 1848, *Congressional Globe,* 30th Congress, 1st Sess., Appendix, 456.

again be reduced to the vassalage under which they have so long struggled, and that Louis Philippe himself would be again placed upon the throne, and they be subjected to his arbitrary sway, they would be none the less entitled to our congratulations for the great and good work they have already accomplished—for the mighty advance they have made in proclaiming to the world freedom of opinion and the rights of man. They have spoken in a voice and language that has already been heard throughout Europe, inculcating the doctrines of liberty and equality, that has brought the oppressed and plundered masses to their feet, with joyous expectation, and has caused corrupt and stultified monarchy to feel its thrones rocking and the earth trembling beneath it. They have caused industry to hope that it may yet partake of the bread it has earned; and labor, that while it should toil for those whom Providence has taught to look to it for sustenance, no laws, human or divine, can justly require it to support an indolent and beggarly aristicracy, and armed hirelings to enforce obedience. Ireland has already caught up the sound, and is looking forward with renewed hope to her hour of emancipation. Austria is ringing with shouts of liberty from Hungary and the Bohemian hills; throughout Italy, Germany, and even in England herself, under pretence of giving, terrified and dismayed monarchy is restoring to man rights which were wrested from him during physical ages. If there are no precedents for such congratulations, we can easily make one; and we should by all means do so, for the signs of the times clearly indicate that at no distant day, if not during the present session, our congratulations may be extended to other lands than France, upon a like occasion. Let us, then, congratulate this great nation upon an event so auspicious in her history, and leave future events to the future. . . .

— | "We believe that our congratulations . . . will not only be acceptable to them, but useful to the great cause of freedom throughout the world." *

Cass defended the congratulatory resolution as a move that would contribute to the cause of liberty throughout the world. Like Dickinson, he assumed that the February Revolution in Paris was a great triumph for liberty, to be encouraged on its course by a Congressional expression of sympathy.

. . . What do we propose to do, sir? To congratulate the French people upon the liberty which they have just acquired, and the free principles they have established as the basis of their government. We believe that our congratulations at this time will not only be acceptable to them, but useful to the great cause

* Remarks by Cass on the revolution in France, April 6, 1848, *Congressional Globe*, 30th Congress, 1st Sess., Appendix, 465.

of freedom throughout the world. This tribute, from the oldest, and, unfortunately, I may add, from almost the only Republic free from internal dissensions, to a great nation just entering into the career of self-government, will be received and welcomed in France as a proof of interest and solicitude naturally arising out of the past, and encouraging for the future. And especially will it be acceptable at the commencement of the great work, when the new-born Republic finds itself surrounded with powerful monarchical Governments, jealous of the progress of liberty, and whose very existence may be put to hazard by the portentous event which is fixing the gaze of mankind. The expression of our sentiments under these circumstances was a duty due to France, to ourselves, and to the great cause of human freedom; but that duty has become still more imperative by the discussion in which we are now engaged. We cannot halt in our course, and withhold our congratulations, without giving the most serious offence to the French people, and without, in fact, announcing to the world that the struggle in which they are engaged will terminate unfortunately, and that they are unfit for those political blessings which their fathers aided our own to acquire, and which we hope will go down unimpaired to the latest posterity. And what is the objection to the annunciation by Congress of that sympathy which the American people feel so deeply, and express so plainly? I see none, sir. None at all. There is no internal dispute in France as to its government. There is no contest between authority on one side and rebellion or revolution on the other. The old Government has disappeared. The dynasty of the younger branch of the family of the Bourbons has passed into history, as much as the dynasty of the older branch, or as that of Napoleon; aye, as much as the dynasty of the Pharaohs. The wise man tells us, that there is a time for all things. These things have had their time, and that time has passed away. It is with the years beyond the flood. The people of France have resumed that power which belongs to them, and I hope and trust they will exercise it wisely, and provide for the establishment of a Government protecting the rights of all, and securing internal peace and social order. . . .

Mr. President, doubts hang over this revolution as they hang over all the works of man. But it seems to me it would be in very bad taste in a public act of sympathy and congratulation like this, to speak in hesitating terms, and to express our doubts at the very moment we tender our good wishes. Certainly, the French people are making a great experiment; and how long since we were making one? How long since our own Government was an experiment, rather than experience? Mr. Jefferson called it so in his inaugural address; and here in this very Senate, in this sanctuary of liberty, since I have had a seat here, more than once have we heard the most dismal forebodings, the darkest auguries, the wailing, if not the warning cry, that the death-knell of liberty was tolling, and that we had little else to do but to prepare her grave. If no nation is to be congratulated upon its progress in the principles of free government till no clouds of uncertainty rest upon its future, we must content ourselves with being silent spectators of the great and interesting events around us, shutting our hearts to all sympathy, and taking counsel from dishonorable caution, and not from rational hope.

Our desire is to congratulate the French people upon what they have actually done, leaving to Him who holds in his hand the fate of nations to guide their future destiny by his own good pleasure. They have done enough to merit congratulations from every human being who loves liberty or who hopes for its enjoyment by the nations of the earth. They have resisted oppression; a series of efforts which, if not resisted, would have shown that they were fit only for the bonds preparing for them; the least of which would have roused up twenty millions of Americans, as one man, to fight the battle of liberty—and to gain it. They have overturned the late Government and established one of their own, and with a spirit of wisdom and moderation which, under all the circumstances, has been rarely equalled in the world. The act of the Provisional Government —the temporary Fourth of July declaration, I may call it—of the French people lays down many of the just principles of human freedom, which will find a responsive echo in this country. . . .

— | "I had supposed, sir, that everything relating to the foreign inter-
course of the people of the United States pertained . . . to the
Executive." *

In opposing the French resolution, Senator R. S. Baldwin of Connecticut questioned the right of Congress, through the act of passing a resolution, to interfere with the country's foreign relations. The right to congratulate the French, he argued, implied the right to condemn those foreign states whose institutions did not accord with the ideals of the American Republic. Such interference, he warned, would derange the entire conduct of the nation's diplomacy. There were, moreover, domestic issues which might better occupy the attention of Congress.

. . . Personally, sir, as one of the American people, I yield to no Senator in the expression of my sympathy with the great movement which is now going on for the amelioration of the political and social condition of the people of France, and of the other European states. But as a member of this Senate, I am not prepared to act on these resolutions, or to assign a day for that purpose, until I am better satisfied of our right to act in the manner proposed. I want first to be assured, that we are entitled, as Senators—as members of the Congress of the United States, to speak at all in the name and behalf of the American people, in a matter relating to the intercourse of this Government with a foreign nation. I had supposed, sir, that everything relating to the foreign intercourse of the people of the United States pertained, in the first instance, to the Executive. I had supposed that in the distribution of powers and duties among the several

* Baldwin's remarks in the Senate, March 31, 1848, *Congressional Globe*, 30th Congress, 1st Sess., Appendix, 453–4.

departments of our Government, the people had confided to the President, alone, the trust of speaking in their name and behalf to foreign nations; and to Congress, the trust of legislating for their benefit.

I am aware, sir, that questions may arise in relation to our foreign intercourse, on which it may be proper and expedient that the sentiments of Congress should be declared. But these are cases where legislation is required, to enable the Executive to carry out his views in regard to the foreign intercourse of the nation.

If the President, deeming it his duty to recognize the independence of a foreign government, or to send a minister to a nation with which the United States have before had no diplomatic intercourse, calls on Congress to make provision for the exigency, then, sir, the matter comes up legitimately for discussion before Congress acting in its legislative capacity, in deciding upon the expediency of granting or withholding the appropriation required. . . .

Now, sir, I say the American people are able to speak for themselves. They are able to manifest their own sympathies. They are doing it, sir, from one end of the Union to the other; and that is the proper way for the sympathies of the American people to be manifested on this occasion, unless it be done through that organ of the Government, whom they have specially intrusted with the duty of conducting their foreign intercourse. When and how have they ever delegated to us the power to speak in their name, in relation to the concerns of a foreign people?

Sir, if we can tender congratulations in the name of the American people to the republicans of France, on the achievement of their liberties, can we not also tender the expression of their regrets to the downtrodden subjects of other empires, who yet groan beneath the sceptre of a despot? There are many governments with whom we hold diplomatic intercourse, whose institutions are as little accordant with the views and wishes of the American people as those which have just been so signally overthrown; but have they ever authorized Congress to express their disapprobation for those institutions? To what inconsistencies in the action of the Government would not such a course inevitably lead? To what derangement of the system established by the Executive of conducting its foreign intercourse? By what imperfect lights would Congress necessarily be guided in its action, in comparison with the sources of intelligence, which constant and confidential correspondence with our ministers abroad, places at all times at the command of the President? . . .

. . . The resolutions declare, if I understand their true meaning, that the people of France have succeeded in their efforts to consolidate liberty, by imbodying its principles in a republican constitution. Sir, they are only making, now, the first effort to accomplish this purpose. The Government of France is not in the hands of those who have been elected by the people. It is either self-constituted or it derives its power from the spontaneous movement of the people of Paris, with whom the revolution commenced. The Provisional Government is taking its first measures, for obtaining a full representation of the French people in a convention, to lay the foundation for the establishment and maintenance of constitutional liberty. Have they accomplished it? Is liberty consolidated, in the language of the resolution? I do not like the word, sir. It is rather too much in the style of the Holy Alliance to suit my taste. I remember, in the famous declaration of their policy, sent out to the world by the allied monarchs, they spoke of it as the only means of "consolidating human institutions and remedying their imperfections." I should prefer some other word, of less equivocal import. I had much rather see liberty diffused through France, to the utmost limits of the realm, than consolidated in the hands of a Parisian regency. It sounds too much like the consolidation of power that centralizes here. And I think, sir, that the Congress of the United States would be much better employed in taking measures to prevent that consolidation of power which is so rapidly going on within the precincts of this Capitol, by means of the enormous increase of Executive patronage, than in undertaking to conduct, unasked, the foreign intercourse of the American people. . . .

— | "What is done by a government should be done at least decently and in order." \*

William L. Dayton, the conservative Whig spokesman in the realm of foreign affairs, denied that the revolutionary government of France had achieved any legitimacy. Congratulations, therefore, were not called for.

&

. . . I trust I am not wanting in all those kind, generous feelings which have been so well expressed by Senators; but it seems to me as though we were giving way too much to the current of popular sentiment. . . .

If there ever was a season when we, the model republic, as we glory in calling ourselves to the world, should be cautious as to what we do, it is now. There is, perhaps, no paragraph in our past history conveying more wisdom to posterity than the last and parting address of Washington, when he told us to beware of entangling ourselves with European politics. I admit that this is not an entanglement within the letter, but it is at least within the spirit and meaning of the words of the great Father of his Country. I do not mean to say that we may not, under certain circumstances, express our sympathy with any nation in Europe. We may do so in the language of this resolution, mean what it may, for I hardly know what is meant by consolidation of liberty. But, sir, I want first to be sure that the Government does consolidate liberty. I want to have at least a reasonable assurance that when the Government we are about to congratulate shall be sought after, our minister will not have to make a return of *non est inventus*. The honorable Senator from New Hampshire tells us that he would not wait until the child attains to maturity before he tenders his con-

\* Dayton's remarks on the French resolution, April 6, 1848, *Congressional Globe*, 30th Congress, 1st Sess., Appendix, 459–60.

gratulations. Nor I, sir; but I would wait until the child is born. France is *enciente,* only; whether a child will be born, or France have a miscarriage, is a thing to be hereafter determined. Sir, there is no government now in France to whom we can tender our congratulations. We are tendering them to the now Government of France, not to a government that is to be, but to the Provisional Government. What is that Government? What do we mean by Provisional Government? I ask it in all seriousness. It has the name of government, but we cannot regard it as one. With great respect I say it is no government. Its decrees are no decrees. Its laws are no laws. Its official agents are the creatures, in common parlance, of nobody. We cannot shut our eyes to this fact. Here is a government which puts down the old state of things to-day, and sets up a new state of things to-morrow. By whose act is it done? It is done by the people of Paris. Who are the people of Paris? I mean legally, and as compared with the thirty millions of the French people. It is idle, sir, I say with great respect, to look upon this species of *de facto* power which, for the time being, keeps a kind of order in Paris—it is idle, I say, to look upon it as an existing government which should receive our congratulations? And permit me to say that the official agents of this *quasi* government feel by what a slight tenor they hold their places. A mob has put down a monarchy yesterday, and has raised a republic today. . . . Again, sir, if we examine the progress of this *quasi* government, we see it pandering to the passions of the populace—we see it raising the wages of labor, opening the baker's shops to feed the hungry. These are not the ordinary functions of government. We see it redeeming pledges from the pawnbrokers with the funds of the government, converting the Tuileries into a poorhouse, and confiscating the property of the royal family. Can a conservative people like ours be mistaken as to the tendency of these things? The very men who are now legislating thus feel that they hold their power at the frail tenure of the will of a mob. They feel that they must pander to that mob if they would maintain the position they hold. Why, sir, I say it with great respect for those intelligent high-minded gentlemen who now hold a species of *quasi* power—they have done the best they can—but do you call this body of men a government—a government to make laws? Whence comes their authority? And it is to this self-styled government, to this child in *embryo,* that we are to tender our congratulations. Sir, they show their want of confidence in the stability of their government themselves. And there are other indications which show that it has no security for its stability. The French funds at one time went down to twenty-five per cent. And this meeting which is to be held on the 20th of the present month, what is it to be? A meeting of nine hundred men elected by a community who never elected representatives before. Part of them will come from Algeria. There will be some fifteen or sixteen Algerines. Sir, I speak it with great respect, but when we recollect that this great body of men, enough to form a mob of themselves, are to be elected by a people who have had no experience in these matters, I cannot help distrusting the action of that convention. At all events, let it be as able, pure, patriotic as it may, I would, for one, prefer at least that we should wait calmly and deliberately until we shall have seen the matured action of the convention. And if they give a constitution to France having upon it the face and lineaments of our own, I will tender to them the hand of good fellowship and congratulation. Sir, our minister under the circumstances has perhaps done his duty. He has done enough. It seems to me, I speak it with great respect, that it would be more wise, more statesmanlike to wait the development of events. What is done by a government should be done at least decently and in order. I consider that a month, more or less, will not diminish the value of our congratulations to the French Government; and I do hope that when these congratulations shall be tendered, we shall find there a government to receive them. . . .

# 2 | Millard Fillmore's Message to Congress, December 2, 1850 *

President Fillmore, in this message to Congress, rebuked those Americans who sought to embroil the United States in the affairs of Europe to serve the cause of liberty. To him the principle of self-determination belonged to all nations. If the United States claimed the right for itself, it dared not interfere in the internal affairs of other nations.

𝓴

. . . Nations, like individuals in a state of nature, are equal and independent, possessing certain rights and owing certain duties to each other, arising from their necessary and unavoidable relations; which rights and duties there is no common human authority to protect and enforce. Still, they are rights and duties, binding in morals, in conscience, and in honor, although there is no tribunal to which an injured party can appeal but the disinterested judgment of mankind, and ultimately the arbitrament of the sword.

Among the acknowledged rights of nations is that which each possesses of establishing that form of government which it may deem most conducive to the happiness and prosperity of its own citizens, of changing that form as circumstances may require, and of managing its internal affairs according to its own will. The people of the United States claim this right for themselves, and they readily concede it to others. Hence it becomes an imperative duty not to interfere in the government or internal policy of other nations; and although we may sympathize with the unfortunate or the oppressed everywhere in their struggles for freedom, our principles forbid us from taking any part in such

* *Messages and Papers of the Presidents,* James D. Richardson, ed. (Washington, 1897), V: 78.

foreign contests. We make no wars to promote or to prevent successions to thrones, to maintain any theory of a balance of power, or to suppress the actual government which any country chooses to establish for itself. We instigate no revolutions, nor suffer any hostile military expeditions to be fitted out in the United States to invade the territory or provinces of a friendly nation. The great law of morality ought to have a national as well as a personal and individual application. We should act toward other nations as we wish them to act toward us, and justice and conscience should form the rule of conduct between governments, instead of mere power, self-interest, or the desire of aggrandizement. To maintain a strict neutrality in foreign wars, to cultivate friendly relations, to reciprocate every noble and generous act, and to perform punctually and scrupulously every treaty obligation—these are the duties which we owe to other states, and by the performance of which we best entitle ourselves to like treatment from them; or, if that, in any case, be refused, we can enforce our own rights with justice and a clear conscience. . . .

# 3 | Daniel Webster's Note to Chevalier J. G. Hülsemann, December 1850 *

In this oft-quoted dispatch to the Austrian chargé d'affaires in Washington, Webster attempted to rationalize American sentimentalism toward liberal movements in Europe as a natural expression of the national character. He assured the Austrian government, however, that such popular pronouncements of political preference did not constitute any desertion of the established American doctrine of noninterference in the internal affairs of other countries. Webster, as a conservative, recognized the limits of legitimate action abroad. He attempted in this dispatch to make his bargain with the nationalistic emotions coursing through the nation.

𝒦

. . . The undersigned will first observe, that the President is persuaded his Majesty the Emperor of Austria does not think that the government of the United States ought to view with unconcern the extraordinary events which have occurred, not only in his dominions, but in many other parts of Europe, since February, 1848. The government and people of the United States, like other intelligent governments and communities, take a likely interest in the movements and the events of this remarkable age, in whatever part of the

* Webster to Hülsemann, December 21, 1850, *The Works of Daniel Webster* (Boston, 1860), VI: 494-7.

world they may be exhibited. But the interest taken by the United States in those events has not proceeded from any disposition to depart from that neutrality toward foreign powers, which is among the deepest principles and the most cherished traditions of the political history of the Union. It has been the necessary effect of the unexampled character of the events themselves, which could not fail to arrest the attention of the contemporary world, as they will doubtless fill a memorable page in history.

But the undersigned goes further, and freely admits that, in proportion as these extraordinary events appeared to have their origin in those great ideas of responsible and popular government, on which the American constitutions themselves are wholly founded, they could not but command the warm sympathy of the people of this country. Well-known circumstances in their history, indeed their whole history, have made them the representatives of purely popular principles of government. In this light they now stand before the world. They could not, if they would, conceal their character, their condition, or their destiny. They could not if they so desired, shut out from the view of mankind the causes which have placed them, in so short a national career, in the station which they now hold among the civilized states of the world. They could not, if they desired it, suppress either the thoughts or the hopes which arise in men's minds, in other countries, from contemplating their successful example of free government. That very intelligent and distinguished personage, the Emperor Joseph the Second, was among the first to discern this necessary consequence of the American Revolution on the sentiments and opinions of the people of Europe. In a letter to his minister in the Netherlands in 1787, he observes, that "it is remarkable that France, by the assistance which she afforded to the Americans, gave birth to reflections on freedom." This fact, which the sagacity of that monarch perceived at so early a day, is now known and admitted by intelligent powers all over the world. True, indeed, it is, that the prevalence on the other continent of sentiments favorable to republican liberty is the result of the reaction of America upon Europe; and the source and centre of this reaction has doubtless been, and now is, in these United States.

The position thus belonging to the United States is a fact as inseparable from their history, their constitutional organization, and their character, as the opposite position of the powers composing the European alliance is from the history and constitutional organization of the government of those powers. The sovereigns who form that alliance have not unfrequently felt it their right to interfere with the political movements of foreign states; and have, in their manifestoes and declarations, denounced the popular ideas of the age in terms so comprehensive as of necessity to include the United States, and their forms of government. It is well known that one of the leading principles announced by the allied sovereigns, after the restoration of the Bourbons, is, that all popular or constitutional rights are holden no otherwise than as grants and indulgences from crowned heads. . . .

The power of this republic, at the present moment, is spread over a region one of the richest and most fertile on the globe, and of an extent in comparison with which the possessions of the house of Hapsburg are but as a patch on the earth's surface. Its population, already twenty-five millions, will exceed that of the Austrian empire within the period during which it may be hoped that Mr. Hülsemann may yet remain in the honorable discharge of his duties to his government. Its navigation and commerce are hardly exceeded by the oldest and most commercial nations; its maritime means and its maritime power may be seen by Austria herself, in all seas where she has ports, as well as they may be seen, also, in all other quarters of the globe. Life, liberty, property, and all personal rights, are amply secured to all citizens, and protected by just and stable laws; and credit, public and private, is as well established as in any government of Continental Europe; and the country, in all its interests and concerns, partakes most largely in all the improvements and progress which distinguish the age. Certainly, the United States may be pardoned, even by those who profess adherence to the principles of absolute government, if they entertain an ardent affection for those popular forms of political organization which have so rapidly advanced their own prosperity and happiness, and enabled them, in so short a period, to bring their country, and the hemisphere to which it belongs, to the notice and respectful regard, not to say the admiration, of the civilized world. Nevertheless, the United States have abstained, at all times, from acts of interference with the political changes of Europe. They cannot, however, fail to cherish always a lively interest in the fortunes of nations struggling for institutions like their own. But this sympathy, so far from being necessarily a hostile feeling toward any of the parties to these great national struggles, is quite consistent with amicable relations with them all. The Hungarian people are three and four times as numerous as the inhabitants of these United States were when the American Revolution broke out. They possess, in a distinct language, and in other respects, important elements of a separate nationality, which the Anglo-Saxon race in this country did not possess; and if the United States wish success to countries contending for popular constitutions and national independence, it is only because they regard such constitutions and such national independence, not as imaginary, but as real blessings. They claim no right, however, to take part in the struggles of foreign powers in order to promote these ends. It is only in defence of his own government, and its principles and character, that the undersigned has now expressed himself on this subject. But when the people of the United States behold the people of foreign countries, without any such interference, spontaneously moving toward the adoption of institutions like their own, it surely cannot be expected of them to remain wholly indifferent spectators. . . .

# 4 | Henry Clay's Observations on the Mission of America, January 1852 *

In warning Louis Kossuth to expect nothing tangible for the Hungarian cause from American enthusiasm, Clay recalled the conservative messianism of Jefferson and Madison—that the United States would fulfill its mission to humanity, not by interfering in the affairs of other nations, but by maintaining on American shores a nation worthy of imitation.

𝒦

. . . For the sake of my country you must allow me to protest against the policy you propose to her. Waiving the grave and momentous question of the right of one nation to assume the executive power among nations, for the enforcement of international law, or of the right of the United States to dictate to Russia the character of her relations with the nations around her, let us come at once to the practical consideration of the matter. You tell us yourself, with great truth and propriety, that mere sympathy, or the expression of sympathy, can not advance your purposes. You require material aid. . . . Well, sir, suppose that war should be the issue of the course you propose to us, could we then effect anything for you, ourselves, or the cause of liberty? To transport men and arms across the ocean in sufficient numbers and quantities to be effective against Russia and Austria, would be impossible. . . . Thus, sir, after effecting nothing in such a war, after abandoning our ancient policy of amity and non-intervention in the affairs of other nations, and thus justifying them in abandoning the terms of forbearance and non-interference which they have hitherto preserved toward us; after the downfall, perhaps, of the friends of liberal institutions in Europe, her despots, imitating and provoked by our example, may turn upon us in the hour of weakness and exhaustion, and with an almost irresistible force of reason and of arms, they may say to us: "You have set us the example; you have quit your own to stand on foreign ground; you have abandoned the policy you professed in the day of your weakness, to interfere in the affairs of the people upon this continent, in behalf of those principles the supremacy of which you say is necessary to your prosperity, to your existence. We, in our turn, believing that your anarchical doctrines are destructive of, and that monarchical principles are essential to, the peace, security, and happiness of our subjects, will obliterate the bed which has nourished such noxious weeds; we will crush you, as the propagandists of doctrines so destructive of the peace and good order of the world." The indomitable spirit of our people might and would be equal to the emergency, and we might remain unsubdued, even by so tremendous a combination, but the consequences to us would be terrible enough. You must allow me, sir, to speak thus freely, as I feel deeply, though my opinion may be of but

* Quoted in John Bassett Moore, *A Digest of International Law* (Washington, 1906), VI: 51–2.

little import, as the expression of a dying man. . . . By the policy to which we have adhered since the days of Washington we have prospered beyond precedent; we have done more for the cause of liberty in the world than arms could effect; we have shown to other nations the way to greatness and happiness. . . . Far better is it for ourselves, for Hungary and for the cause of liberty, that, adhering to our wise pacific system and avoiding the distant wars of Europe, we should keep our lamp burning brightly on this western shore, as a light to all nations, than to hazard its utter extinction, amid the ruins of fallen and falling republics in Europe. . . .

# 5 | The United States and Foreign Revolution: An Editorial Comment, January 1852 *

Kossuth's visit to the United States and his continuing appeal to American sentimentalism prompted an endless review of his cause and the national obligation to its success in the metropolitan press of the United States. The following editorial from an important Midwestern newspaper comprised a typical conservative reaction to the Kossuth craze. Like other conservatives, the editor limited the nation's obligation to the oppressed of Europe to the maintenance of an expanding democracy at home.

❦

. . . The first speeches of Kossuth at New York—the remarks made there by intelligent men who heard him—and the general belief as to the end and purposes of his visit and exertions, and his future course of action—created alarm and regret throughout the nation. The policy of this Government has long been settled by the wisdom of our fathers of the Revolution, with Washington at their head, and there has been a strict adherence to their course by all wise men of the Union from his day to this, as our only safe and true course. The interest felt in Kossuth for his noble exertions and self-sacrifices in the cause of his country, was sincere—deep—universal. That feeling prompted—induced—the action of our Government to rescue from imprisonment the Ex-Governor—to show him honor for his exertions, and afford him a home, a resting place, in a land of freedom—such as could not be hoped for in his father-land. The ground taken by our Government, in its application to the Turkish Sultan for his release, was, that the fugitive was rendered powerless, the struggle in Hungary was hopeless, and a home in a distant land was all that was desired. And on this application, on these assurances, a release was effected. There was not the remotest idea, at

* Weekly Gazette (Cincinnati), January 29, 1852.

the inception of these proceedings, of any national interference by the United States in the matters at issue between Hungary and Russia, and the adjoining country. We sought but to do Kossuth honor, and to manifest to the wide world our sympathy in behalf of the struggles of his countrymen for liberty.

The first speeches alluded to, struck with surprise and alarm those not participating in the excitement of a first greeting, but who calmly *read* at leisure the words of the exile. Surprise, because it was different from what was purposed; alarm, because they were words likely to excite to ill advised action a multitude, apt to yield to their sympathies. Surrounded as the great Magyar was, and has been, and will be, by men always at hand to avail themselves of any popular breeze to push themselves forward, without regard to the consequences of their actions, it was feared, if such was to be the course of the exile—if he was to excite the sympathies of the people—to take advantage of his position, and use his immense power to forward his own aims and ends, regardless of the matured and uniform policy of our Government—there was reason to fear that the result would be to entangle this Republic into difficulties inconsistent with our welfare, security and interest.

These influences, these fears, *we* have felt in common with vast numbers of others throughout the land. We hesitated to give vent to the natural feelings and promptings of our heart to do honor to this stranger, when we saw that the peace of the country might be jeoparded; and however much we might be willing to concede to his superior attainments and forethought, we could not yield our own judgment of the bad policy of pursuing a course towards which his first words would seem destined to drive us. The late speech of Kossuth at the Congressional Banquet at Washington has shown that his purposes, his aims and views are changed, or that he will no longer persevere in his course. . . . When we find, as we see, that "no encouraging generosity will make him forget where he stands," and that he never had the impious wish to try and entangle this great Republic in difficulties inconsistent with its own welfare, its own security, its own interest; confiding in these promises, all will be ready to aid in giving him such a welcome as is worthy of so distinguished a man, and is suited and suitable to his position, and calculated best to promote the future interest and happiness of himself and his countrymen.

Ere this the hollowness of the idle vauntings of many of those who have surrounded the exile will have been made manifest. The mass of the people of this country have never dreamed of involving our government in a struggle—probably a fruitless struggle—in that distant land. The millions of freemen ready to rush forward and risk thus their lives in battle, has been an illusion—the stands of arms and munitions of war which were to be ready at command, has been found not to be had—the pecuniary free will Offerings of our people, which, when asked for, was to flow in a steady tide of millions to the reservoirs appointed to hold it, has dwindled down to a few insignificant sums, insignificant in proportion to that which would be even *useful*—and these small sums, when traced to their origin have proven in a majority of instances to have been given for interested purposes and personal notoriety. Those who have been the most free to *promise* such—whosoever they may have been, and wheresoever such promises have been made—have as yet personally manifested nothing, given nothing. This all shows that the great mass of citizens did not approve the course suggested and had no faith in any good to result; and Kossuth, has doubtless ere this seen, and he has began to understand, the true sentiment of the intelligence of the land. Having, therefore, got beyond this danger—having made the promises we quote, having taken his position—we feel that we may all unite to do him honor, without endangering the country.

When we review the past history of Kossuth—when we recollect his course of action and read his speeches, we can see no where anything but entire consistency. We see no where a promise broken—no where a stain on his character. We can trust to his plighted faith that the encouraging generosity of his reception will not make him forget where he stands, and that he will entertain no impious wish to entangle this great Republic in difficulties inconsistent with her own welfare, security, and interest.

How then *shall* we best do the Exile honor?—How *best* subserve the great *future* interests for which he hopes and labors? An exile—in a strange land—removed from his country—a country, for a time, in the tyrant's grasp—shall we meet him with empty show—with bon-fire—illuminations—feastings—speech makings—and wasteful, *useless* expenditure, subserving of no good purpose—promotive of no good results? Cannot our good feelings and desires be better, more appropriately, manifested and directed? Of such acts has there not been enough? How then shall we do him proper honor—how best promote and forward his real welfare? Not in a *continuance* of scenes and excitements, such as have been already witnessed. Of these there have been enough—too much. Of speeches, we have had enough to get at a full and true understanding of each other.

In expressing our feelings and our sympathies, we should do all that we can —not because of their personality to him—but as manifesting our interest in the struggle—our sympathy for the oppressed. Of these feelings, of these manifestations, there has been already indubitable, sufficient proof. The *Nation* has spoken, when she sent her national ship and national officers to ask a release and afford a conveyance here, and in offering a safe refuge and a free home. . . .

How then shall we do the Magyar honor, and best subserve the future and *true* interests of himself and his country? Here we can give "protection to the oppressed." Here "is the air of Liberty," "a sanctuary of eternal rights." Here we can give a home free from the oppressor's chains—a welcome to the persecuted, the helpless and the poor, of every clime. Here is the safe abiding place—the refuge for the oppressed, and for all panting for freedom. Hither millions on millions, who thus seek a refuge, have already flocked, and the tide has but began to set in. Here is untold millions of rich, uncultivated lands suited to every constitution and every habit—here are equal laws and equal protection. Here then is *our* mission—the object, a sufficient object for all our exertions and solicitude. Here should be concentrated all our efforts. This should be truly an independent land—a land of freedom—a land independent of aid, or sustenance of any character, from any other land—a land of equality. To preserve this, a land of refuge, we should direct all our energies, and yield to it our constant solicitude. With unwavering firmness we should keep our observations here. This soil should be preserved, forever, as the refuge of the down-trodden and struggling sons of freedom, of every other nation, till, from Atlantic to Pacific, our soil is all occupied, and no more room remains. This is *our* destiny—this our future. Providence has committed this to our care, and no momentary excitement or appeals should seduce us from our trust. If this is lost what hope remains—what nation could have a future if this is lost? Here, then, let us welcome Hungary, Ireland, Germany and France, and all of every nation and every clime. Here let us *tender* a home to those who can buy—let us *give* a home to those who *cannot provide.* Let us rest assured, that this our trust, well guarded, will, in time to come, reflect back on Europe and on every land and every clime, where the oppressor's hand is laid on the people, and in due time break the chains, as sure as there is a future and a just God, to whom we can pray.

How then, we repeat, can we *best* subserve the interest of this exile *for his* country and *to our* country? We say again—not in this show, not in this parade—not in the useless, meaningless expenditures, of which he has had sufficient. Let his mission be forwarded. Let him be carried throughout the length and breadth of the land.—Let him examine our institutions—let him select a home and abiding place for himself and his countrymen, and let that home be secured to him. To that home let us bid him and his countrymen welcome. To and in that home let us give material aid to the needful, and for needful use. Thus we will give a useful, a material, a significant welcome. To this, to such a welcome, let our efforts be directed.

# 6 | Lewis Cass's Defense of the Right of Congress To Pass Resolutions Relative to External Affairs, February 1852 *

In the following speech Cass again asserted the right and obligation of Congress to debate and pass resolutions declaring its disapprobation of political repression abroad. Such action, he insisted, imposed no burden on the United States to act when other governments ignored the opinions of Congress. Whether ignored or not, such expressions of sentiment would have their effect by instructing the public opinion of the world. Cass's argument remains a classic defense of a moralistic approach to foreign affairs, for Cass searched diligently for whatever efficacy might exist in the moral rebuke of other nations.

. . . We believe in the right and in the capacity of man for self-government—not that he is everywhere prepared for institutions like ours. We know, while we regret, that he is not. But we believe that he is everywhere fitted, even now,

* Speech on nonintervention in the Senate, February 10, 1852, *Congressional Globe,* 32nd Congress, 1st Sess., Appendix, 159–64.

for taking some part in the administration of political affairs, greater or less, in proportion to his experience and condition; and that everywhere, with time and practice, he may improve himself and his government till both become as free as the state of society will permit. And certainly the expression of the warm hope that this time will come, and come speedily, is consistent with every respect for other Powers.

We claim no right to interfere in their internal concerns. While we are firm believers in our own political faith, we enter into no crusade to establish it elsewhere. Propagandism is no part of our creed, unless it be that propagandism which works its own way by the force of example, thus inviting the oppressed nations of the earth to do as we have done, and to be as free and happy as we are. But we cannot be indifferent to the condition of the human race, however widely scattered. A desire for its improvement, morally, and materially, is a sentiment natural to man. . . .

Even to the most superficial observer, the signs of the times are as portentous as they are interesting. The accumulated oppressions of ages and the capacity of endurance stretched to its utmost tension, now meet face to face, with existing power, in a struggle for life and death; and the contest will go on, though there may be fitful intervals of apparent repose, still it will go on till one or the other is finally vanquished. Why, sir, is it in human nature, is it in the ordination of a just God, that such tyranny as that which recently made prisoner the aged mother of the illustrious Hungarian exile, now exciting the sympathy of the American people, and was reported by that act to have sent her to the grave, though the report, I believe, was unfounded, and such a consummation of a deed of barbarity is therefore one charge the less in the catalogue of Austrian cruelties, and such tyranny as that which sent his sisters to a dungeon, an *Austrian dungeon,* perhaps to issue from it only to find refuge in that final asylum of the oppressed, where the wrath of man reaches not—can it be that such an unmitigated despotism will be long permitted to revel in the wantonness of its own power and passions? . . .

Now, sir, what we want is that freedom should have a fair battle-field. That whenever a struggle is commenced to overthrow an arbitrary Government, other despotic Powers should not be permitted to take part in the contest, and with foreign bayonets decide the issue. . . .

I am not going into the history of the Hungarian effort to break the yoke of Austrian despotism. Suffice it to say, that the people of Hungary had enjoyed their nationality for a thousand years; and more recently, while acknowledging allegiance, with Austria, to the same common sovereign, have been connected with that country only by this mutual bond, and have been wholly separate in political rights and in the administration of Government. For causes, as just as ever drove a people to arms, the people of Hungary threw off their allegiance to the Austrian Emperor, and, resuming their independence, established a Government of their own, and for a time maintained it to the end, had not the Russian sovereign, making common cause with his Austrian brother, marched his armies across the frontier, and thus extinguished the liberties and the hopes of Hungary. . . .

. . . I suppose a man could hardly be found in this broad land, however sensitive he may be on the subject of our foreign policy, who fears the wrath or the power of the Russian or of the Austrian Emperor, should we assert a great fact, now passed into history, that the right and independence of nations have been flagrantly violated in the case of Hungary, and should we declare the principle of public law which ought to have protected that unfortunate country. Well, then, if we fear no such danger abroad, where is the danger we do fear? It is at home, sir. We cannot shut our eyes to that truth. The signs all around us indicate, with unerring certainty, that the apprehension, felt and avowed, is directed, not to others, but to ourselves.

One would really suppose there was imminent danger, if this claim to assert an equal right to adjust questions of the law of nations, is once established; that this great Republic would deal with war, as a child deals with a plaything, and that it would rush into it with a blind haste, restrained by no considerations of duty or expediency. Let this apprehension be dismissed. This is one of the last dangers, we have to fear. The honor and welfare of the country are safe in the custody of the PEOPLE, and we need not hesitate to assert our just rights, lest the PEOPLE should betray their own trust. Almost seventy years have passed away, since the acknowledgment of our independence, and in that time we have had but two wars, deserving the name of such. Where is there another nation, great or small, which can say the same for its own moderation? So much for the effect of a salutary public opinion upon the policy of a country.

But to return to the erroneous doctrine, which has been so widely and so confidently spread, and which seeks to deter us from expressing any opinion upon the law of nations, by an apprehension of the consequences, and by which it is maintained, that in all cases where a nation makes such a declaration, it is bound to support its views by war, if these are not acquiesced in, or it will lose its own self-respect, and subject itself to the contumely of the world. There is not the least foundation, in reason, or authority, or precedent, for such an assumption. . . .

Mr. President, I have already said, that the particular form in which a nation makes known its views, from the most common diplomatic note to the most solemn protest, neither adds to nor takes from its responsibility or obligation. It appears to be assumed, that there is some peculiar pugnacious quality attached to a protest, which necessarily leads to armed action. This is not so. A public declaration in that form no more imposes on the nation making it the duty of vindicating it by arms, than the every day representations which the usual diplomatic intercourse renders necessary. . . .

We ought neither to mistake our position, nor neglect the obligations it brings with it. We have at length reached the condition of one of the great Powers of the earth, and yet we are but in the infancy of our career. The man yet lives, who was living, when a primitive forest extended from the Allegheny to the Rocky Mountains, trodden only by the Indian, and by the animals, his cotenants of a world of vegetation, whom God had given to him for his support. Then a narrow strip upon the sea-coast, thirteen remote and dependent colonies, and less than three millions of people, constituted what is now this vast Republic, stretching across the continent and extending almost from the Northern

Tropic to the Arctic Circle. And the man is now living, who will live to see one hundred and fifty millions of people, free, prosperous, and intelligent, swaying the destinies of this country, and exerting a mighty influence upon those of the world. . . . But it has been asked, why proclaim your opinion, unless you mean to maintain it by the strong hand? For the same reasons, that countless representations and remonstrances have been made by independent Powers, when they had reason to apprehend the adoption of measures, hostile to the just principles of national intercommunication. To mark their disapprobation of the act and of the doctrine, that there silence might not be construed into acquiescence, and that when, in the mutation of political affairs, the proper time should come, they might interpose effectually, if they should desire it, not concluded by the success of violence nor by the lapse of time, that the Power itself, contemplating the step, might pause and review its position and its pretensions, and the consequences to which it might be led; not knowing, of course, what measures might follow these appeals to its sense of right should they fail to be effectual; and, above all, that the public opinion of the world should be rightly instructed and brought to aid these peaceful efforts to preserve the rights of mankind. And let no man underrate the power of this mighty engine for good. It will go on from conquering to conquer, till its influence is everywhere established and recognized. . . .

It has been said, in condemnation, or in reproach of this effort, that there are many other suffering people and violated principles calling equally for the assertion of this right, and why, it is asked sneeringly, if not triumphantly, why do you not extend your regards and your action to all such cases? And as that is impossible with any useful result, as every one knows, we are, therefore, to sit still and do nothing, because we cannot do everything. . . . There are conditions of the public mind, arising out of passing events, favorable to the consideration of particular questions, while others are cast into the shade, and command no attention. The former is the state of things in relation to Hungary; to her rights and her wrongs; and the principles thus brought up are attracting the attention of the world, and are discussed in conversation, in legislative assemblies, in the public journals, and in diplomatic correspondence, and they thus commend themselves to general consideration. And the facts have been of a nature to impart deep interest to the whole subject, and without some degree of interest it were vain to endeavor to engage the public attention.

Mr. President, what earthly tribunal has a better right than the Congress of the American people to pronounce the opinion of that people upon such subjects? I do not speak, lest I should be accused of patriotic exaggeration, of those qualities, intellectual and moral, which are found here, and which are essential to a sound decision; but I speak of its representative capacity, as the depository of much of the power of a people, whose interest and feelings are intimately connected with the broadest principles of freedom and independence. . . .

Many objections, more or less plausible, have been presented to deter us from any action in this matter, but not one of them, with more confidence or pertinacity, nor with less regard to the true circumstances of our position, than that which warns us, that by such a proceeding we should violate alike the traditions of our policy and the advice of our wisest statesmen, and especially the injunctions of Washington and Jefferson. Never were just recommendations more inappropriately applied, than in this attempt to apply the views of those great men to the circumstances in which we are placed.

Non-intervention, it is said, was the policy they maintained, and the legacy they bequeathed to us; but is it possible that a single American can be found, who believes that either of those patriots would condemn the declaration of his country's opinion upon a great question of public law, because they condemned its interference with the affairs of other nations? Why, this is our affair, sir; an affair as interesting to us as to any other community on the face of the globe; one which involves the safety of independent States, and the true intent and obligation of the code, that regulates their intercourse. . . .

Mr. President, it has often been said, that we have a mission to fulfill, and so, indeed, has every nation; and the first mission of each is to conduct its own affairs honestly and fairly, for its own benefit; but after that, its position and institutions may give to it peculiar influence in the prevailing moral and political controversies of the world, which it is bound to exert for the welfare of all. While we disclaim any crusading spirit against the political institutions of other countries, we may well regard with deep interest the struggling efforts of the oppressed through the world, and deplore their defeat, and rejoice in their success. And can any one doubt, that the evidences of sympathy which are borne to Europe from this great Republic will cheer the hearts, even when they do not aid the purposes, of the downtrodden masses, to raise themselves, if not to power, at least to protection? Whatever duties may be ultimately imposed on us by that dark future which overshadows Europe, and which we cannot foresee, and ought not to undertake to define, circumstances point out our present policy, while, at the same time, they call upon us to exert our moral influence in support of the existing principles of public law, placed in danger, not merely by the ambition, but still more by the fear of powerful monarchs—the fear lest the contagion of liberty should spread over their dominions, carrying destruction to the established systems of oppression. . . .

# 7 | Senator J. C. Jones's Reply to Cass, March 1852 *

Senator J. C. Jones of Tennessee, in his reply to Cass, questioned, as had Adams, Randolph, and Calhoun before him, the usefulness of Congressional resolutions which rebuked other governments for their alleged immorality. How could Congress, through a resolution, he asked, exert moral influence on a government sufficiently evil to merit such moral condemnation? Jones condemned the crusading approach to foreign affairs. To him the passage of resolutions, divorced from actual policy, merely exposed the nation to insult and ridicule. Like Randolph, Baldwin, and others, Jones suggested that Congress devote its attention to the many unsolved problems at home.

. . . The Senator from Michigan, in his able and learned speech, which was filled with beauty, made a declaration to which I freely assent. It is this, in substance: That every nation has a right to determine for itself when its safety demands that it shall interpose. Now, if that be true, (and I am not disposed to controvert it,) I ask, upon what pretext is Russia arraigned at the bar of the enlightened judgment of the world? I am no eulogist of Russia. I am not her advocate. I despise her cruelty; I scorn and condemn her wrongs and outrages; but if that principle which is asserted by the Senator from Michigan be true, then Russia had a right to intervene. If that is the law of nations, and if each nation has a right to judge for itself, then Russia had that right; and judging for herself, and acting upon that judgment, I want to know how the honorable Senator can get up here and arraign her. I believe there was no necessity for the interposition of Russia, but, according to the principles laid down by the Senator from Michigan, she must be the judge of that. She put it upon that express ground, and used the express words that her safety depended upon it.

But have we a right to interfere at all, and is it proper and expedient that we should interfere? My doctrine is, that our best interests would be subserved by having nothing to do with this matter. If we have a right to speak out at all, we have a right to speak boldly, to speak freely, and to speak authoritatively. If it is the policy of this Government to interfere in the affairs of foreign countries, though I shall oppose it at every step, I want to see gentlemen come up and speak boldly, fearlessly, frankly, independently, and authoritatively, and when we have spoken, then, to borrow the language of a distinguished gentleman of your party, let us maintain it, "at all hazards, and to the last extremity." Suppose you make this protest, and it goes to Russia, and Russia receives it, and treats it with scorn and contempt, tramples it under foot, sends back an indignity and an insult, what do you propose to do then? The Senator from Michigan says that the man who is in favor of an armed intervention is a madman. The Senator from New York says we must not go to war except in self-defense. Then

* Speech in the Senate, March 18, 1852, *Congressional Globe,* 32nd Congress, 1st Sess., Appendix, 305–6, 308.

your protest is received with scorn and contempt, and a re-protest is sent back here, full of insolence. How will you receive it? I can speak for you, Mr. President: You would not pocket the insult, you would not submit to the indignity. Now, if we take this step at all, I want to know from the learned Senators from Michigan, and from New York, whether they are ready to take the next step? If Russia treat us with scorn and contempt, and heap odium upon our Government and nation, are we ready to vindicate it? Are we ready to stand up to it, and to vote the men and the money necessary to vindicate the honor of the Government? If they are not ready to do this, in the name of God, in the name of liberty, in the name of the honor of this country, let us stop before we take another step. They have no right to involve the pride and the honor of this country, unless they are willing also to take the necessary steps to vindicate and maintain them. My policy is to let them alone; to let them manage their own affairs in their own way. But if we speak at all, speak like men; speak like Americans; speak as Senators ought to speak. Let us say to Russia, "Hands off; a clear field and a fair fight"; and if she disregards it, and treats it with contempt, we know where duty points the way. I shall oppose it; but if this Government takes the step, if she madly forgets her best interests, for one—though I shall have no agency in it, it may be carried by a majority of the Senate and House—"I am for my country, right or wrong;" and if it should take the last ship that floats upon our seas, the last American ship upon all seas, and every American soldier that wears the insignia of his country's arms, and every dollar in the American Treasury, I would bring them all and lay them down at the footstool of my country, to vindicate the honor of the nation.

But the gentlemen say they will not fight over this. Well, if you do not mean to fight about it, just let it alone. [Laughter.] I am opposed to fighting as much as you are; but if you mean to get us into a quarrel, in which our honor will be at stake, in which our pride will be involved, I want you to stand up and fight it out, and have no dodging.

But, I would like to know why we should go out upon this crusade? This is a wonderful age, Mr. President. Oh! it is a stupendous age! We are to go out upon a crusade for the liberties of the whole world? There is not enough in this broad Union of ours—"ocean bound," I believe my friend from Illinois calls it—to engage the time and the intellect of Senators; but the redemption, the political redemption of the whole world is brought up, and we are to march out upon that grand crusade. I should like to see the world redeemed; but I am no propagandist; and whilst I feel a devotion, amounting to idolatry, for my country and her institutions, and her peculiar form of government, deeply as I am devoted to it, high and holy as I conceive it to be, I would not impose it upon one single, solitary being upon earth. If a man chooses to be a slave, let him be so. I would not force him from any position he might occupy. Let every people choose their own government; and let us choose ours, and take care of it, and guard it, and protect it, and defend it.

But the very distinguished Senator from Michigan claims that the chief virtue which is to be found in his resolution—his protest, I believe, it is called, though I do not know what notary public has signed it; I suppose when you sign it,

Mr. President, it will be—is the moral influence it is to exert upon Russia and the world. Do you remember, Mr. President and Senators, the speech of that learned gentleman, in which he inveighed with such touching and powerful eloquence against the cruelties, the enormities, and the outrages of the Czar of Russia? Why, sir, the veriest monster that ever disgraced the image of his God is an angel transformed into the brightness of light, compared with that miserable wretch, and yet the Senator from Michigan thinks there is virtue enough in this protest to rouse the moral sensibilities of such a devil. It may be so. I cannot tell, but it does seem to me that there is some mistake about the moral influence of such a protest. What amount of moral power and influence is to attach to it? How is it to arise? . . . I would not give a straw for all the moral influences of your declarations, unless there be a power behind the throne greater than the throne. There must be physical power, and force, and will, to execute and require obedience to the protest. . . .

Sir, I love this Union—love of the Union is idolatry with me; and it is because I love and cherish it with the fondness of devoted affection, that I am against any of those Utopian schemes, any of those modern doctrines of progress, or manifest destiny, or higher or lower law, come from what sources they may. Why should we go abroad? Have we not enough to do at home? Have we not a field broad enough for the sympathies of Senators? Are all our sympathies to be exhausted on Hungary? Weep over her wrongs to your heart's content; I will join you in the holy office; but I ask you to come back in the hours of quietude, and look to your own country. Have you not enough here to engage your time, to enlist your talents, to enlist the talents of the loftiest intellect of the age? See your country, with twenty-five millions of population, extending from ocean to ocean; a territory of empires in extent, and yet not enough for the enlarged capacity of some gentlemen. The world itself seems scarcely large enough to contain their boundless sympathies. It is enough for me to know that there are interests here that command and demand my attention. Look at the interests of this country! You have a territory almost boundless; unnumbered millions and hundreds of millions of public domain, that might be made the basis upon which the hopes, the prosperity, the happiness, the grandeur, and the glory of the mightiest nation upon earth might be established. And yet, sir, that is a small matter, that concerns nobody. We must go and weep over Hungary. If your sympathies are so large, go into the valley of the Mississippi, that I have the honor in part to represent. I see the honored representative of my district here now. Go there, and see the unnumbered and numberless lives that are constantly sacrificed to the imbecility and weakness of this Government of ours. There is a hecatomb of living spirits carried down into the deep and angry waters of the Mississippi and its tributaries. There is no sympathy for them. We must go abroad, and shed tears of blood and compassion for the sufferings of Hungary. Better come home, and weep over widows and orphans, left husbandless and fatherless by the neglect of the Government to give protection, and to improve her inland and her external commerce. That is enough to engage the time and the talents of the whole Senate— of the loftiest genius that ever lived. Yet these are very small matters—we may forget them all! We have a sea-coast almost boundless, with harbors to improve, interests to protect, thousands and tens of thousands of American citizens languishing for the want of that paternal regard which the Government ought to extend them, in giving protection to the honest labor of the country. All that moves no sympathetic cord in those hearts that sympathise with the oppressed of all nations. Come home, gentlemen, come home, and let us see if we cannot do something here. When we shall have made our own people happy and prosperous, when the Treasury shall be overflown, when the Navy shall find nothing to do, when the Army shall be a burden upon our hands, then you may go out and fight the battles of other people. But first let us establish ourselves upon a basis, not only honorable, but safe and perpetual. . . .

## 8 | Seward's Argument Against European Recognition of the Southern Confederacy, June 1861 *

With the outbreak of war between the Union and the Confederacy in the spring of 1861, Seward acknowledged the danger of a possible European recognition of Southern independence. In this well-argued statement of American policy, the Secretary of State denied that any government existed within the boundaries of the United States that merited diplomatic recognition except the established government in Washington. Like Adams before him, Seward insisted that insurrectionary governments deserved recognition only when they had established their independence beyond any question of doubt. Until that moment arrived, the government of the United States would insist on the sole right to conduct the foreign relations of the Republic. In this the nation was asking only those rights which all other governments demanded during periods of internal upheaval.

✌

Every instruction which this government has given to its representatives abroad, since the recent change of administration took place, has expressed our profound anxiety lest the disloyal citizens who are engaged in an attempt to overthrow the Union should obtain aid and assistance from foreign nations, either in the form of a recognition of their pretended sovereignty, or in some other and more qualified or guarded manner. Every instruction has expressed our full belief that, without such aid or assistance, the insurrection would speedily come to an end, while any advantage that it could derive from such aid or assistance could serve no other purpose than to protract the existing struggle and aggravate the

* Seward to Dayton, June 17, 1861, *The Works of William H. Seward*, George E. Baker, ed. (Boston, 1884), V: 268–76.

evils it is inflicting on our own country and on foreign and friendly nations. Every instruction bears evidence of an earnest solicitude to avoid even an appearance of menace or of want of comity towards foreign powers; but at the same time it has emphatically announced, as is now seen to have been necessary, our purpose not to allow any one of them to expect to remain in friendship with us if it should, with whatever motive, practically render such aid or assistance to the insurgents. We have intended not to leave it doubtful that a concession of sovereignty to the insurgents, though it should be indirect or unofficial, or though it should be qualified so as to concede only belligerent or other partial rights, would be regarded as inconsistent with the relations due to us by friendly nations. Nor has it been left at all uncertain that we shall, in every event, insist that these United States must be considered and dealt with now, as heretofore, by such nations as exclusively sovereign for all purposes whatsoever within the territories over which the Constitution has been extended. On the other hand, we have not, at any time, been unmindful of the peculiar circumstances which might excite apprehensions on the part of commercial nations for the safety of their subjects and their property in the conflicts which might occur upon sea as well as on land between the forces of the United States and those of the insurgents. . . .

Sometime ago we learned through our legation at St. Petersburg that an understanding had been effected between the governments of Great Britain and France that they should take one and the same course on the subject of the political disturbances in this country, including the possible recognition of the insurgents. At a later period this understanding was distinctly avowed by Mr. Thouvenel to Mr. Sanford, who had been informally introduced by me to the French Minister for Foreign Affairs, and by Lord John Russell to Mr. Dallas, our late minister in London. The avowal in each case preceded the arrival of our newly appointed ministers in Europe, with their instructions for the discharge of their respective missions.

On receiving their avowals I immediately instructed yourself and Mr. Adams "that although we might have expected a different course on the part of these two great powers, yet, as the fact that an understanding existed between them did not certainly imply an unfriendly spirit, we should not complain of it, but that it must be understood by the French and British governments that we shall deal hereafter, as heretofore, in this case, as in all others, with each power separately, and that the agreement for concerted action between them would not at all influence the course we should pursue." The concert thus avowed has been carried out. The ministers came to me together; the instructions they proposed to me differ in form, but are counterparts in effect. . . .

The United States, rightly jealous, as we think, of their sovereignty, cannot suffer themselves to debate any abridgment of that sovereignty with France or with any other nation. Much less can it consent that France shall announce to it a conclusion of her own against that sovereignty, which conclusion France has adopted without any previous conference with the United States on the subject. This government insists that the United States are one whole undivided nation, especially so far as foreign nations are concerned, and that France is, by the law of nations and by treaties, not a neutral power between two imaginary parties here, but a friend of the United States. . . .

It is erroneous, so far as foreign nations are concerned, to suppose that any war exists in the United States. Certainly there cannot be two belligerent powers where there is no war. There is here, as there has always been, one political power, namely, the United States of America, competent to make war and peace, and conduct commerce and alliances with all foreign nations. There is none other, either in fact, or recognized by foreign nations. There is, indeed, an armed sedition seeking to overthrow the government, and the government is employing military and naval forces to repress it. But these facts do not constitute a war presenting two belligerent powers, and modifying the national character, rights, and responsibilities, or the characters, rights, and responsibilities of foreign nations. It is true that insurrection may ripen into revolution, and that revolution thus ripened may extinguish a previously existing state, or divide it into one or more independent states, and that if such states continue their strife after such division, then there exists a state of war affecting the characters, rights, and duties of all parties concerned. But this only happens when the revolution has run its successful course.

The French government says, in the instruction which has been tendered to us, that certain facts which it assumes confer upon the insurgents of this country, in the eyes of foreign powers, all the appearances of a government *de facto,* wherefore, whatever may be its regrets, the French government must consider the two contending parties as employing the forces at their disposal in conformity with the laws of war.

This statement assumes not only that the law of nations entitles any insurrectionary faction, when it establishes a *de facto* government, to be treated as a belligerent, but also that the fact of the attainment of this status is to be determined by the appearance of it in the eyes of foreign nations. If we should concede both of these positions, we should still insist that the existence of a *de facto* government, entitled to belligerent rights, is not established in the present case. We have already heard from most of the foreign nations. There are only two which seem so to construe appearances, and France is one of them. Are the judgments of these two to outweigh those of all other nations? Doubtless each nation may judge and act for itself, but it certainly cannot expect the United States to accept its decision upon a question vital to their national existence. The United States will not refine upon the question when and how new nations are born out of existing nations. They are well aware that the rights of the states involve their duties and their destinies, and they hold those rights to be absolute as against all foreign nations. These rights do not at all depend on the appearances which their condition may assume in the eyes of foreign nations, whether strangers, neutrals, friends, or even allies. The United States will maintain and defend their sovereignty throughout the bounds of the Republic, and they deem all other nations bound to respect that sovereignty until, if ever, Providence shall consent that it shall be successfully overthrown. Any system of public law or national morality that conflicts with this would resolve society, first in this hemisphere and then in the other, into anarchy and chaos. . . .

Of course, it is understood that on this occasion we reserve, as on all others, our right to suppress the insurrection by naval as well as by military power, and for that purpose to close such of our ports as have fallen or may fall into the hands of the insurgents, either directly or in the more lenient and equitable form of a blockade, which for the present we have adopted. It is thus seen that there is no practical subject of difference between the two governments. The United States will hope that France will not think it necessary to adhere to and practise upon the speculation concerning the condition of our internal affairs which she has proposed to communicate to us. But however this may be, the United States will not anticipate any occasion for a change of the relations which, with scarcely any interruption, have existed between the two nations for three quarters of a century, and have been very instrumental in promoting, not merely the prosperity and greatness of each state, but the cause of civil and religious liberty and free institutions throughout the world.

This government understands equally the interest of friendly nations and its own in the present emergency. If they shall not interfere, the attempt at revolution here will cease without inflicting serious evils upon foreign nations. All that they can do by any interference, with a view to modify our action, will only serve to prolong the present unpleasant condition of things, and possibly to produce results that would be as universally calamitous as they would be irretrievable.

The case, as it now stands, is the simple, ordinary one that has happened at all times and in all countries. A discontented domestic faction seeks foreign intervention to overthrow the Constitution and the liberties of its own country. Such intervention, if yielded, is ultimately disastrous to the cause it is designed to aid. Every uncorrupted nation, in its deliberate moments, prefers its own integrity, even with unbearable evils, to division through the power or influence of any foreign state. This is so in France. It is not less so in this country. Down deep in the heart of the American people—deeper than the love of trade, or of freedom—deeper than the attachment to any local or sectional interest, or partizan pride or individual ambition—deeper than any other sentiment—is that one out of which the Constitution of this Union arose, namely, American independence—independence of all foreign control, alliance, or influence. Next above it lies the conviction that neither peace, nor safety, nor public liberty, nor prosperity, nor greatness, nor empire, can be attained here with the sacrifice of the unity of the people of North America. Those who, in a frenzy of passion, are building expectations on other principles do not know what they are doing. Whenever one part of this Union shall be found assuming bonds of dependence or of fraternity towards any foreign people, to the exclusion of the sympathies of their native land, then, even if not before, that spirit will be reawakened which brought the states of this Republic into existence, and which will preserve them united until the common destiny which it opened to them shall be fully and completely realized.

## 9 | Seward on the Right of a Nation To Defend Its Existence, August 1862 *

In this letter Seward argued that a nation has a right and duty to live. Since the majority of Americans favored the Union cause, external involvement in the American civil war would deny the right of self-determination. The choice, whatever the outcome, must remain within the nation itself.

✍

. . . Reviewing the whole course of the existing administration, I may safely claim that it shows that, even if the government had been left at liberty to conduct its foreign relations, altogether irrespectively of the civil war, it would yet have chosen and maintained a policy of peace, harmony, and friendship towards all nations. It is certainly our especial care, under existing circumstances, to do no injustice, to give no offence, and to offer and receive explanations in a liberal spirit whenever they are possible, and thus to make sure that if, at any time, either accidentally or through the intriques of the insurgents, we shall incur the misfortune of collision with foreign states, our position will then be one of pure and reproachless self-defence.

The nation has a right, and it is its duty, to live. Those who favor and give aid to the insurrection, upon whatever pretext, assail the nation in an hour of danger, and therefore they cannot be held or regarded as its friends. In taking this ground, the United States claim only what they concede to all other nations. No state can be really independent in any other position.

Willing, however, to avert difficulties by conciliatory explanations, we frankly confess to the conviction that either the insurrection must be subdued and suppressed or the nation must perish. The case admits of no composition. If we have no fear of failure, it is because we know that no other government than this could stand in this country, and that permanent dismemberment of it is impossible. The principal masses of the population are content with the present system, and cannot be brought to oppose or to surrender it. The faction which is attempting to destroy it, although infatuated and energetic, is, relatively to the whole people, an inconsiderable one. . . .

. . . It may be that the storm may continue one or more years longer, and that there may be a dissolution of society in that unhappy region. But after such a convulsion every state requires repose and again seeks peace, safety, and freedom; and it will have them, if possible, under the political system which is best adapted to those ends. Alexander, Caesar, and Napoleon, each in his time cast down established states and substituted new ones in their places. Yet the hand

* Seward to Adams, August 18, 1862, Instructions to Great Britain MSS, Department of State, National Archives, Vol. XVIII.

that made the violent change had hardly been withdrawn when the subverted states reappeared, standing more firmly than before on their ancient foundations.

It is freely admitted that the salvation of the Union depends on the will and the choice of the American people, and that they are now engaged in a fierce conflict upon that very question. But sooner or later there must come a truce, because civil war cannot be indefinitely endured. Will there then be a reconciliation? It cannot happen otherwise. When such a time arrives, any society will prefer the attainable to the unattainable object, the greater to the lesser advantage, and will bury every domestic difference to save itself from the worst of all political evils—foreign conquest and domination. The object of the insurgents is the fortifying and extending of African slavery. Is the object, under existing circumstances really attainable? Is it not becoming more manifestly impossible every day that the war is prolonged? Is even the continuance of slavery itself worth the sacrifices which the war has brought? It is assumed that the insurgents, however erroneously, are determined upon that point. I reply, that it is always a class, or a sect, or a party, and not the whole country, that provokes or makes civil war, but it is not the same class or sect or party, but the whole country that ultimately makes the peace; and hence it has happened that hardly one out of a hundred attempted revolutions has ever been successful. Is not this the instruction of the civil wars of England, France, and San Domingo?

The consideration that this is a republican state has been heretofore impressed upon the correspondence of this Department, and it cannot be too steadily kept in view by our representatives in Europe. Precisely because it is both a Federal and a republican state, with its cohesion resulting from the choice of the people in two distinct processes, the nation must cease to exist when a foreign authority is admitted to any control over its counsels. It must continue to be jealous of foreign interventions and alliances, as it always heretofore has been.

The nation, moreover, is an American one. It has maintained pleasant and even profitable intercourse with the states of the eastern continent; but it nevertheless is situated in a hemisphere where interests and customs and habits widely differing from those of Europe prevail. Among these differences this one at least is manifest: We neither have sought, nor can we ever wisely seek, conquests, colonies, or allies in the Old World. We have no voice in the congresses of Europe, and we cannot allow them a representation in our popular assemblies. All of the American states once were dependencies of European powers. The fact that it is necessary to discuss the subject of this letter sufficiently proves that even if those powers have relinquished all expectation of recovering a sway here that was so long ago cast off, yet the American nations have nevertheless not realized their safety against European ambition. For this reason, also, we must be left by foreign nations alone, to settle our own controversies and regulate our own affairs in our own American way. If the forbearance we claim is not our right, those who seek to prevent our enjoyment of it can show the grounds upon which foreign intervention or mediation is justified. Will they claim that European powers are so much more enlightened, more just, and more humane than we are, that they can regulate not only their own affairs but ours also, more wisely and more beneficially than we have done? How and where have they proved this superiority?

I cannot avoid thinking that the ideas of intervention and mediation have their source in an imperfect conception in Europe of the independence of the American nation. Although actual foreign authority has so long passed away, yet the memory of it, and the sentiment of dictation, still linger in the parental European states. Perhaps some of the American nations have by their willingness to accept of favors, lent some sanction to the pretension. But certainly this will not be urged against the United States. We have too many proofs that our independence is by no means pleasing to portions of European society. They would, however, find it difficult to justify their dislike. That independence was lawfully won, and it has been universally acknowledged. . . .

What plea for intervention or mediation remains? Only this, that our civil war is inconvenient to foreign states. But the inconvenience they suffer is only incidental, and must be brief; while their intervention or mediation might be fatal to the United States. Are not all civil wars necessarily inconvenient to foreign nations? Must every state, when it has the misfortune to fall into civil war, forego its independence and compromise its sovereignty because the war affects its foreign commerce? Would not the practice upon that principle result in the dissolution of all political society? But it is urged that the war is protracted. What if it were so? Do our national rights depend on the time that an insurrection may maintain itself? It has been a war of fifteen months. The battlefield is as large as Europe. The dynamical question involved is as important as any that was ever committed to the issue of civil war. The principles at issue are as grave as any that ever were intrusted to the arbitration of arms. The resources opened by the government, the expenditures incurred, the armies brought into the field, and the vigor and diligence with which they are manoeuvred, have never been surpassed; nor has greater success, having due regard to the circumstances of the case, ever been attained. Notwithstanding these facts, Europeans tell us that the task of subduing the insurrection is too great, that the conclusion is already foregone, and the Union must be lost. They fail, however, to satisfy us of either their right or their ability to advise upon it, while they no longer affect to conceal the prejudices or the interests which disqualify them for any judgment in the case.

Finally, the advocates of intervention are shocked by the calamities we are enduring, and concerned by the debts we are incurring, yet they have not one word of remonstrance or discouragement for the insurgents, and are busy agents in supplying them with materials of war. We deplore the sufferings which the war has brought, and are ready and anxious to end the contest. We offer the simple terms of restoration to the Union, and oblivion of the crimes committed against it so soon as may be compatible with the public safety. I have expressed these views of the President to our representatives at this time, when I think there is no immediate danger of foreign intervention, or attempt at mediation, to the end that they may have their due weight whenever, in any chances of the war, apprehensions of foreign interference may recur.

## 10 | Seward, the National Interest, and the *Trent* Case, December 1861 *

In explaining to the British government his reasons for releasing the Confederate diplomats removed from aboard the *Trent* by an American naval officer, Seward revealed his deep concern for long-range national interests. Here as elsewhere Seward's diplomacy had but one objective—to maintain the integrity of the Union.

🖎

. . . The British government has rightly conjectured, what it is now my duty to state, that Captain Wilkes, in conceiving and executing the proceeding in question, acted upon his own suggestions of duty, without any direction or instruction, or even foreknowledge of it, on the part of this government. No directions had been given to him, or any other naval officer, to arrest the four persons named, or any of them, on the *Trent* or on any other British vessel, or on any other neutral vessel, at the place where it occurred or elsewhere. The British government will justly infer from these facts that the United States not only have had no purpose, but even no thought, of forcing into discussion the question which has arisen, or any other which could affect in any way the sensibilities of the British nation. . . .

Your lordship will now perceive that the case before us, instead of presenting a merely flagrant act of violence on the part of Captain Wilkes, as might well be inferred from the incomplete statement of it that went up to the British government, was undertaken as a simple legal and customary belligerent proceeding by Captain Wilkes to arrest and capture a neutral vessel engaged in carrying contraband of war for the use and benefit of the insurgents.

The question before us is, whether this proceeding was authorized by and conducted according to the law of nations. It involves the following inquiries: . . .

I address myself to the first inquiry, namely, Were the four persons mentioned, and their supposed despatches, contraband?

Maritime law so generally deals, as its professors say, *in rem,* that is with property, and so seldom with persons, that it seems a straining of the term contraband to apply it to them. But persons, as well as property, may become contraband, since the word means broadly "contrary to proclamation, prohibited, illegal, unlawful.". . .

The second inquiry is, whether Captain Wilkes had a right by the law of nations to detain and search the *Trent.*

The *Trent,* though she carried mails, was a contract or merchant vessel—a common carrier for hire. Maritime law knows only three classes of vessels—

* Seward to Lord Lyons, December 26, 1861, *The Works of William H. Seward,* V: 295–309.

vessels of war, revenue vessels, and merchant vessels. The *Trent* falls within the latter class. Whatever disputes have existed concerning a right of visitation or search in time of peace, none, it is supposed, has existed in modern times about the right of a belligerent in time of war to capture contraband in neutral and even friendly merchant vessels, and of the right of visitation and search, in order to determine whether they are neutral, and are documented as such according to the law of nations.

I assume in the present case what, as I read British authorities, is regarded by Great Britain herself as true maritime law: That the circumstance that the *Trent* was proceeding from a neutral port to another neutral port does not modify the right of the belligerent captor.

The third question is whether Captain Wilkes exercised the right of search in a lawful and proper manner.

If any doubt hung over this point, as the case was presented in the statement of it adopted by the British government, I think it must have already passed away before the modifications of that statement which I have already submitted.

I proceed to the fourth inquiry, namely: Having found the suspected contraband of war on board the *Trent,* had Captain Wilkes a right to capture the same?

Such a capture is the chief, if not the only recognized, object of the permitted visitation and search. The principle of the law is, that the belligerent exposed to danger may prevent the contraband persons or things from applying themselves or being applied to the hostile uses or purposes designed. The law is so very liberal in this respect that when contraband is found on board a neutral vessel, not only is the contraband forfeited, but the vessel which is the vehicle of its passage or transportation, being tainted, also becomes contraband, and is subjected to capture and confiscation.

Only the fifth question remains, namely: Did Captain Wilkes exercise the right of capturing the contraband in conformity with the law of nations?

It is just here that the difficulties of the case begin. What is the manner which the law of nations prescribes for disposing of the contraband when you have found and seized it on board of the neutral vessel? The answer would be easily found if the question were what you shall do with the contraband vessel. You must take or send her into a convenient port, and subject her to a judicial prosecution there in admiralty, which will try and decide the questions of belligerency, neutrality, contraband, and capture. So, again, you would promptly find the same answer if the question were, What is the manner of proceeding prescribed by the law of nations in regard to the contraband, if it be property or things of material or pecuniary value? . . .

In the present case, Captain Wilkes, after capturing the contraband persons and making prize of the *Trent* in what seems to be a perfectly lawful manner, instead of sending her into port, released her from the capture, and permitted her to proceed with her whole cargo upon her voyage. He thus effectually prevented the judicial examination which might otherwise have occurred.

If, now, the capture of the contraband persons and the capture of the contraband vessel are to be regarded, not as two separate or distinct transactions under the law of nations, but as one transaction, one capture only, then it follows that the capture in this case was left unfinished, or was abandoned. Whether the United States have a right to retain the chief public benefits of it, namely, the custody of the captured persons on proving them to be contraband, will depend upon the preliminary question whether the leaving of the transaction unfinished was necessary, or whether it was unnecessary, and therefore voluntary. If it was necessary, Great Britain, as we suppose, must, of course, waive the defect, and the consequent failure of the judicial remedy. On the other hand it is not seen how the United States can insist upon her waiver of that judicial remedy, if the defect of the capture resulted from an act of Captain Wilkes, which would be a fault on their own side.

Captain Wilkes has presented to this government his reasons for releasing the *Trent*. "I forbore to seize her," he says, "in consequence of my being so reduced in officers and crew, and the derangement it would cause innocent persons, there being a large number of passengers who would have been put to great loss and inconvenience, as well as disappointment, from the interruption it would have caused them in not being able to join the steamer from St. Thomas to Europe. I therefore concluded to sacrifice the interest of my officers and crew in the prize, and suffered her to proceed after the detention necessary to effect the transfer of those commissioners, considering I had obtained the important end I had in view, and which affected the interest of our country and inter-rupted the action of that of the Confederates.". . .

We are thus brought directly to the question whether we are entitled to re-gard the release of the *Trent* as involuntary, or whether we are obliged to con-sider that it was voluntary. Clearly the release would have been involuntary had it been made solely upon the first ground assigned for it by Captain Wilkes, namely, a want of a sufficient force to send the prize vessel into port for adjudi-cation. It is not the duty of a captor to hazard his own vessel in order to secure a judicial examination to the captured party. No large prize crew, however, is legally necessary, for it is the duty of the captured party to acquiesce, and go willingly before the tribunal to whose jurisdiction it appeals. If the captured party indicate purposes to employ means of resistance which the captor cannot with probable safety to himself overcome, he may properly leave the vessel to go forward; and neither she nor the state she represents can ever afterwards justly object that the captor deprived her of the judicial remedy to which she was entitled.

But the second reason assigned by Captain Wilkes for releasing the *Trent* differs from the first. At best, therefore, it must be held that Captain Wilkes, as he explains himself, acted from combined sentiments of prudence and gener-osity, and so that the release of the prize vessel was not strictly necessary or involuntary. . . .

I have not been unaware that, in examining this question, I have fallen into an argument for what seems to be the British side of it against my own country. But I am relieved from all embarrassment on that subject. I had hardly fallen into that line of argument when I discovered that I was really defending and maintaining, not an exclusively British interest, but an old, honored, and cherished American cause, not upon British authorities, but upon principles that constitute a large portion of the distinctive policy by which the United States have developed the resources of a continent, and, thus becoming a considerable maritime power, have won the respect and confidence of many nations. These principles were laid down for us in 1804, by James Madison, when secretary of state in the administration of Thomas Jefferson, in instructions given to James Monroe, our minister to England. Although the case before him concerned a description of persons different from those who are incidentally the subjects of the present discussion, the ground he assumed then was the same I now occupy, and the arguments by which he sustained himself upon it, have been an inspiration to me in preparing this reply. . . .

If I decide this case in favor of my own government, I must disavow its most cherished principles, and reverse and forever abandon its essential policy. The country cannot afford the sacrifice. If I maintain those principles, and adhere to that policy, I must surrender the case itself. It will be seen, therefore, that this government could not deny the justice of the claim presented to us in this respect upon its merits. We are asked to do to the British nation just what we have always insisted all nations ought to do to us.

The claim of the British government is not made in a discourteous manner. This government, since its first organization, has never used more guarded language in a similar case.

In coming to my conclusion I have not forgotten that, if the safety of this Union required the detention of the captured persons, it would be the right and duty of this government to detain them. But the effectual check and waning proportions of the existing insurrection, as well as the comparative unimportance of the captured persons themselves, when dispassionately weighed, happily forbid me from resorting to this defence.

Nor am I unaware that American citizens are not in any case to be unnecessarily surrendered for any purpose into the keeping of a foreign state. Only the captured persons, however, or others who are interested in them, could justly raise a question on that ground. . . .

The four persons in question are now held in military custody at Fort Warren, in the State of Massachusetts. They will be cheerfully liberated. Your lordship will please indicate a time and place for receiving them.

# 11 | Seward and the American Doctrine of Nonintervention, May 1863 *

When France and other European powers invited the United States to join them in denouncing the Russian repression of Poland in 1863, Seward restated the American doctrine of nonintervention in the affairs of other nations. His letter to William L. Dayton, American Minister in Paris, comprised a remarkable exposition of traditional United States diplomacy toward the cause of liberty abroad. Again Seward revealed his deeply conservative attitude toward matters of external affairs.

𝒦

This government is profoundly and agreeably impressed with the consideration which the Emperor has manifested towards the United States by inviting their concurrence in a proceeding having for its object the double interests of public order and humanity. Nor is it less favorably impressed with the sentiments and the prudential considerations which the Emperor has in so becoming a manner expressed to the court of St. Petersburg. They are such only as appeal to the just emotions and best sympathies of mankind. The enlightened and humane character of the Emperor of Russia, so recently illustrated by the enfranchisement of a large mass of the Russian people from inherited bondage, and the establishment of an impartial and effective administration of justice throughout his dominions, warrant a belief that the appeal will be received and responded to by him with all the favor that is consistent with the general welfare of the great state over which he presides with such eminent wisdom and moderation.

Notwithstanding, however, the favor with which we thus regard the suggestion of the Emperor of the French, this government finds an insurmountable difficulty in the way of any active cooperation with the governments of France, Austria, and Great Britain, to which it is thus invited.

Founding our institutions upon the basis of the rights of man, the builders of our Republic came all at once to be regarded as political reformers, and it soon became manifest that revolutionists in every country hailed them in that character, and looked to the United States for effective sympathy, if not for active support and patronage. Our invaluable Constitution had hardly been established when it became necessary for the government of the United States to consider to what extent we could, with propriety, safety, and beneficence, intervene, either by alliance or concerted action with friendly powers or otherwise, in the political affairs of foreign states. An urgent appeal for such aid and sympathy was made in behalf of France, and the appeal was sanctioned and enforced by the treaty then existing of mutual alliance and defence, a treaty without which it may even now be confessed, to the honor of France, our own

* Seward to Dayton, May 11, 1863, *Works of William H. Seward*, V: 382–4.

sovereignty and independence could not have been so early secured. So deeply did this appeal touch the heart of the American people, that only the deference they cherished to the counsels of the Father of our Country, who then was at the fulness of his unapproachable moral greatness, reconciled them to the stern decision that, in view of the location of this republic, the characters, habits, and sentiments of its constituent parts, and especially its complex yet unique and very popular Constitution, the American people must be content to recommend the cause of human progress by the wisdom with which they should exercise the powers of self-government, forbearing at all times, and in every way, from foreign alliances, intervention, and interference.

It is true that Washington thought a time might come when, our institutions being firmly consolidated and working with complete success, we might safely and perhaps beneficially take part in the consultations held by foreign states for the common advantage of the nations. Since that period occasions have frequently happened which presented seductions to a departure from what, superficially viewed, seemed a course of isolation and indifference. It is scarcely necessary to recur to them. One was an invitation to a congress of newly emancipated Spanish-American states; another an urgent appeal to aid Hungary in a revolution aiming at the restoration of her ancient and illustrious independence; another, the project of a joint guarantee of Cuba to Spain in concurrence with France and Great Britain; and more recently, an invitation to a cooperative demonstration with Spain, France, and Great Britain in Mexico; and, later still, suggestions by some of the Spanish-American states for a common council of the republican states situated upon the American continent. These suggestions were successively disallowed by the government, and its decision was approved in each case by the deliberate judgment of the American people. Our policy of non-intervention, straight, absolute, and peculiar as it may seem to other nations, has thus become a traditional one, which could not be abandoned without the most urgent occasion, amounting to a manifest necessity. Certainly it could not be wisely departed from at this moment, when the existence of a local, although as we trust only a transient disturbance, deprives the government of the counsel of a portion of the American people, to whom so wide a departure from the settled policy of the country must in any case be deeply interesting.

The President will not allow himself to think for a single moment that the Emperor of the French will see anything but respect and friendship for himself and the people of France, with good wishes for the preservation of peace and order, and the progress of humanity in Europe, in the adherence of the United States on this occasion to the policy which they have thus far pursued with safety, and not without advantage, as they think, to the interests of mankind.

Bancroft's dispatches on the rise of the German Empire inaugurated what became the generally accepted pro-German outlook of the United States toward
European politics during the final twenty years of Bismarck's leadership. Bancroft accepted German primacy on the Continent as essential to European
stability and thus a guarantee of the American interest in the balance of power.
He argued that Germany had the right to seek its security against France
through both a revision of the French-German boundary and the maintenance
of its military superiority.

✍

. . . The majority of the French chamber, the senate, and the organs of
public opinion through the press have demanded a war of conquest against
Germany so loudly that the insulated friends of peace lost all courage to oppose,
and the Emperor may have thought himself justified in asserting that he had
been forced into the war by public opinion. In view of these facts the German
allied governments cannot find a guarantee of peace in the disposition of the
French people. They must not therefore deceive themselves into the belief that
there is no reason to expect after this peace a speedy renewal of an attack,
whatever may be the conditions which may be demanded from France. The
French nation will never forgive the series of defeats which have attended their
present war of aggression. Even though the Germans were to demand no cession
of territory, no indemnity, no advantage, except the glory of their arms, there
would remain the wounded self-love of the French people and their hereditary
desire of conquest, and they would only wait for a day when they might hope
to renew the war with success. The forbearance of the German government in
1867 was due to their desire not to conjure up an era of bitterness and angry
passions, but by patience and the careful culture of friendly relations between
the two nations to lay the foundations of an era of peace and reciprocal good
will. As this moderation failed of its effect, and as the Germans, against all
their efforts, have been compelled to encounter a war of aggression, they regard
it henceforward as necessary to look for some securities against the next attack
other than can be found in the good will of France. The guarantees which
were established in 1815 against the same ambition of the French people have
lost their effect, and Germany must now rely on its own strength and its own
resources. The Germans ought not to be continually exposed to the necessity
of again making the same exertions which they have done at this time, and
material securities are therefore needed for their own protection and for the
preservation of the peace of Europe. These securities are to be demanded, not

* Bancroft to Hamilton Fish, September 21, 1870, *Papers Relating to the Foreign Relations of the United States, 1870* (Washington, 1870), 207–8.

from any transient government of France, but from the French nation, which has shown itself ready, as the history of past centuries proves, to follow any government into war, and under any government to seek acquisitions of territory from Germany. In order, therefore, to establish peace, securities must be obtained against the next imminent attack from France, and these can be found only in the change of the present defenseless boundary of South Germany, so that the point from which future attack may emanate may be more remote, and the fortresses with which France has hitherto threatened Germany may so far be brought into the power of Germany as to constitute hereafter defensive bulwarks against invasion.

The views which I have detailed to you I know to be those which are entertained in the cabinets of the German princes. They also exist in all but irresistible strength in the minds of the German people. I will add but one remark of my own. A true guarantee for Germany against future attacks from France would be the political union of Germany itself; and the most earnest negotiations are now pending between North Germany on the one side and South Germany, especially Wurtemberg and Bavaria on the other, for the accomplishment of that object; Germany, being united, will have nothing to fear from France on the one side or Prussia on the other.

— | "No plans of future conquest are now cherished. . . . I have met no one who wants territory occupied by men of another race and language." *

Early in 1871, as the German Empire neared its final triumph, Bancroft's dispatches to Hamilton Fish, the American Secretary of State, confirmed his earlier optimism.

The new year opens a new era; North Germany disappears and Germany rises into being. To the December address of the North German Diet, inviting the King of Prussia to accept the title of Emperor of Germany, offered him by the princes and free cities, the King wisely answered that he would wait for the decision of the people of South Germany, through their respective legislatures. The concurrence of all the legislatures, except Bavaria, has been given. The constitution of the United States of Germany went into effect on New Year's day. There was no ringing of bells, no salvo of artillery, no military parade, no proclamation, and the revolution which makes of United Germany the strongest power on the continent of Europe came in as still and noiselessly as the falling of dew on a summer's afternoon. The German Union has at this moment

* Bancroft to Fish, January 7, February 1, and March 22, 1871, *Foreign Relations of the United States, 1871* (Washington, 1871), 365–6, 374, 379–80.

but four and twenty members, but no one doubts that Bavaria will join within a few days. The young commonwealth comes into being with every wish to maintain the most friendly relations with the United States of America. I am sorry to see that this disposition troubles British statesmen. . . .

The relations between the new empire and Austro-Hungary involve questions of the highest political importance. On the 14th of last month Count Bismarck, through the North German minister at Vienna, announced to Count Beust the impending change in the most conciliatory manner, deduced its rightfulness from the peace of Prague, and opened the way for establishing the most friendly relations between the two powers. I annex Count Bismarck's dispatch to the German minister in Vienna, in German and in English. The answer of Count Beust was awaited with the greatest interest. Now, that it is published, it excites universal satisfaction that the Austrian chancellor, in his dispatch of December 26, to the Austrian minister at Berlin, putting aside all consideration of the peace of Prague, treats the union of Germany, under Prussian lead, as a fact of the first importance in the modern development of Europe.

He gives assurances of the sincerest wish of all influential circles in Austro-Hungary to cultivate the best and most friendly relations with the mighty state whose establishment approaches its completion. He joins the German government in the wish that Germany and Austro-Hungary may extend to one another the hand for the advancement of the welfare and prosperity of both countries. In this he sees a pledge for permanent peace. The emperor, he adds, recalling the ennobling recollections which united his dynasty for centuries with the destinies of the German people, promises to cherish the warmest sympathies for the further development of that people, and expresses his unreserved wishes that its new form as a body-politic may give genuine securities for its own happiness and the welfare of the ancient imperial state with which it is in so many ways connected by tradition, language, manners, and laws. . . .

With regard to Germany, present appearances indicate that, after the close of this war, it will devote itself exclusively to the employments of peace. Compared with the great objects of this war, which involved the question of national existence, all conceivable causes for a future war will appear trivial and indifferent. This war has carried sorrow into almost every family, alike into the houses of that class from which the officers are chiefly taken, and those of the poor. Two hundred of the students of Konigsberg University are serving for the most part in the ranks, and the other universities have contributed to the army in the same proportion, so that for the future no motive to war that is likely to occur can seem worthy of a repetition of equal sacrifices.

Indeed, people of every degree long for peace, and long for its continuance. I am, therefore, of the opinion that Germany in the coming years will devote its immense energies to the improvement of its laws, the establishment of its liberties, and the development of its great resources. . . .

The new empire contains a little more than forty millions of people, who are almost exclusively of one nationality; even in the new provinces of Alsace and Lorraine 1,350,000 are Germans, and only about 300,000 are of French descent. In Posen, in the eastern part of the empire, a majority of the people are Polish;

and about half a million of Jews are scattered through the country, but these all speak the German language and have for centuries been resident in Germany.

This unity of nationality already gives evidence that it will control the policy of the empire. It is held in memory that in centuries long gone by the German Emperor professed to be the successor of the Roman, and as such was constantly involved in foreign, especially Italian, wars, to the ruin of the country. No plans of future conquest are now cherished, but, instead of it, the culture and development of the homogeneous population are the great ends which are proposed. The unity of nationality shows itself already as a guarantee of a policy of peace. I have met no one who wants territory occupied by men of another race and language. Another guarantee of peace is the character of the army, composed as it is of the people, and, as with us, disinclined to any war except for self-defense. Still another guarantee is found in the federal constitution of the empire, the several governments having reserved to themselves the right of being consulted before war can be declared.

The President in his message to Congress expressed his confidence that the body which represents the people would be marked by a love of liberty, and it has proved so. The Grand Duchy of Baden is entitled to twelve representatives in the German Diet, and, though the majority of the people of Baden are Catholics, the national party has elected ten of the representatives, the ultramontanes only two. The victory of the liberal national party in Wurtemburg is still more remarkable. Three years ago it did not elect to the German customs parliament one single national member, while in the present election, out of seventeen to which Wurtemburg is entitled, all are national and liberal except two. Bavaria was looked upon by the ultramontanes as their stronghold, and in Bavaria, where the Catholics compared with the Protestants, are as five to two, the ultramontanes and the separatists combined are left in a decided minority. Thus South Germany comes into the German Parliament with all of its states on the side of union, and with a great majority for the development of the country on the principle of freedom. Yesterday the Parliament of Germany had its first sitting. The day began with divine service in the royal chapel, after which the speech of the Emperor was delivered in a large hall in the palace to the members of the two houses of Parliament, of whom nearly every one seemed to be present. It was addressed to them as the representatives of the German people, who have at last attained to consciousness of life and unity; and the object of the constitution was declared to be the protection of justice in Germany and the fostering of the welfare of the German people. Next to the recognition of the union of Germany as the result of the efforts of the nation, the most remarkable point in the speech is the pledge which it gives for the maintenance of peace, for respect for the rights of all other powers, whether strong or weak, and for emulation in the victories of peace. Before the day closed the Emperor, as King of Prussia, not as Emperor of Germany, raised Count Bismarck to the rank of prince.

## 13 | Great Britain and the European Balance of Power: A Model for American Policy, June 1875 *

For thoughtful Americans the relationship of Britain to the European balance of power was a matter of major concern. The Earl of Derby, a spokesman for British policy during the Franco-German crisis of 1875, analyzed the British interest in the peace and stability of the Continent. He emphasized that freedom of action which permitted England to operate as the effective balancer of the European system. He made it clear that the mere avoidance of continuous involvement in affairs across the Channel was secondary in importance to the protection of British interest in each succeeding crisis. What the Earl of Derby said of the English outlook toward Continental politics applied with equal validity to the judgment of those citizens of the United States who understood that it was the balance of power and not the Atlantic that lay at the foundation of America's security.

✍

. . . Every one knows that great uneasiness existed a few weeks ago in respect of the relations of the governments of France and Germany. Language had been held by persons of the highest authority and position—statements had been made by the semi-official press of Germany—to the effect that the French army was being increased to a degree which was dangerous to Germany and exceeded the requirements of France, and that the course being pursued in respect of that army manifested a determination on the part of France to renew the war of 1870-'71 at the earliest period at which she would be in a position to do so. It was further said that if such was to be taken as the object which France had in view, it might not be the duty of the German government to wait until France had made her preparations, but that government might feel itself called upon to take the initiative. It was said that Germany did not desire war, but that if war was to be avoided, it seemed necessary that the French armaments should be discontinued. My lords, those statements were, as I have observed, made by persons in high position in Germany, and they were repeated in other countries. In France, of course, they caused great uneasiness, and the French government disclaimed all such intentions as those which were thus attributed to them. I am bound to say that I accepted, and I still accept, that disclaimer as one made in all sincerity. I do not believe that any public man in France contemplated a renewal of the war of 1870-'71. After the misfortunes which they have undergone and the humiliations which they have endured, the French very naturally desire to keep up such an army as shall not only give them security at home, but shall give them such power and influence in Europe as they feel their importance as a great nation entitles them to. The existence of such

* "The Peace of Europe," *The Times* (London), June 1, 1875, quoted in *Foreign Relations of the United States, 1875*, Part I (Washington, 1875), 638-9.

a feeling on the part of the French cannot be disputed, nor is there any reason why it should not exist. [Hear, hear.] But it is one thing to desire to be safe and even strong at home, and it is another to be arming with ulterior motives. We believe that the apprehensions that have been entertained on this point have been unfounded. [Cheers.] One of the greatest difficulties that we had to encounter in the matter was that the French on their side seemed hardly able to understand or to conceive that these apprehensions, which were felt on the part of the German government, were genuine or sincere, and that they—I won't say the French government—but the French people, undoubtedly looked upon these apprehensions as being put forward by Germany as a mere pretext for a fresh attack. Now, that was the situation with which we had to deal, and it appeared to Her Majesty's government that in such a state of things a mutual misunderstanding existed which might lead to the very gravest consequences. On the one hand, if the German government continued to entertain these apprehensions of the designs of France which they expressed, the next step on their part might be a formal request to France to discontinue arming. Had such a request been made it would have been very difficult to preserve peace, and the cause of quarrel between the two nations might have been revived. On the other hand, it will be obvious to your lordships that if the French statesmen believed that the apprehensions entertained by Germany were not genuine and were merely put forward as a pretext for war, such a belief on their part was not unlikely to lead to most undesirable complications. Under these circumstances, therefore, it appeared to Her Majesty's government that much good might be done by their endeavoring, quietly and unostentatiously, to calm down these feelings of mutual suspicion and distrust entertained by the two countries. [Cheers.] It appeared to Her Majesty's government that when two great nations are determined upon going to war with each other it is of very little use for their neighbors to attempt to interpose in the cause of peace; but that when the feeling between them is not so much one of the violent irritation as of extreme mutual suspicion and distrust, there is room for the friendly offices of their neighbors. We did not think that France was contemplating a renewal of the war, neither did we believe that the German government were contemplating an act so entirely repugnant to the moral sense of Europe as that of running into an unprovoked war with the intention of completing the destruction of her former foe. [Cheers.] We found that the Russian government were determined to use their best efforts in the interests of peace, and the late visit of the Emperor of Russia to Berlin furnished us with a convenient opportunity of supporting, as far as support appeared necessary, the representations in favor of peace which we were led to believe the Emperor of Russia intended to make in the course of his visit to the German capital. That is substantially what has occurred in reference to this question as far as we are concerned. I can assure the house that I did not in any way wish to exaggerate the part Her Majesty's government have played in the matter, neither do I wish to claim any particular merit for them. We have only done what it seems to me it was our obvious duty to do, and what we could not have avoided doing in the interest of peace and in the interest of justice. [Hear, hear.] My lords, it has been asked in some quarters whether the results which I am happy to say have been brought about were secured by any sacrifice on our part of our freedom of action, either present or prospective, and whether we had entered into any engagements which may bind us in future. I am glad to have this opportunity of stating that such is not the case. [Cheers.] We have used no language, we have entered into no engagement, and we have given no pledges that will fetter our freedom of action in the future, and if we were to quit office to-morrow we should leave our successors neither embarrassed nor committed by anything said or done by us in reference to this matter. I will not enter into the wide and deep-rooted question as to the rule which the noble earl said ought to guide our foreign policy. I do not believe that it is possible for us to lay down any formula or any general rule which shall bind us in our foreign policy for all time and on all occasions. We must deal with the circumstances of each case as it arises. I believe that the policy of non-intervention in general in continental disputes is the one which finds most favor with the people of this country; but a policy of non-intervention does not mean a policy of isolation and indifference, and it does not mean that England either is or can be indifferent to the maintenance of European peace. . . .

## 14 | The Russo-Turkish Rivalry and the European Balance of Power, 1876 *

The following article analyzes simply and clearly the conflicting interests of Russia, England, France, and Austria in the slow disintegration of the Turkish Empire in the region of the Balkans. It explains why, therefore, the great powers of western Europe would not tolerate the Treaty of San Stefano, signed in March 1878, whereby Russia created from former Turkish possessions a huge Bulgaria which appeared to give Russia control of the Balkan peninsula. Only by submitting the treaty to revision at the Congress of Berlin (1878) did Czar Alexander II avoid a major war with Austria and Britain.

✍

The war which is now going on in European Turkey is in the strictest sense of the term an insurrectionary war. It commenced in the Herzegovina, an outlying province of the Turkish empire, and bordering closely upon Austrian territory on the shores of the Adriatic. The anti-Turkish sentiment has since found more forceful expression in Montenegro and in Servia, both of them princi-

* "The Insurrection in Turkey," *Frank Leslie's Illustrated Weekly*, XLII (August 12, 1876), 370–71.

palities and enjoying a quasi-independence, but still owing allegiance, and held
under certain obligations, pecuniary and otherwise, to the Sultan at Constantinople. The dominant religion in these provinces which have gone to war
with the Sultan is Christianity. Considerably more than four-fifths of the population of Turkey in Europe are attached to the Christian faith; and that form
of the Christian faith which most extensively prevails is the Greek Church.
There were a large number of Roman Catholics and a considerable number
who were members of the Armenian Church; but the so-called Greek Church
counts by far the largest number of adherents. The religion of the dominant
race is Mohammedanism—a religion which is radically opposed to Christianity;
and this is the reason why the sympathy of Europe and America is so largely
and so generously extended to the provinces now in open revolt.

It has always been regarded as a blot on European civilization that the Turk
should be allowed to hold in unwilling bondage so many millions of Christians.
It has seemed to argue a lukewarmness in matters of faith on the part of the
governing powers, and it has always been apparent that the people of the different nations were more opposed to Moslem domination, and consequently
more in sympathy with the Christians, than were the governments. State policy,
begotten of national jealousy and national rivalry, has always held the governments in check. The people, overlooking or despising reasons of state, have
seen only the injustice. But for the jealousies of what have been called the
Great Powers, there can be no doubt that Mohammedan rule would long since
have ceased to exist. Russia has from time immemorial been covetous of Constantinople, and she has never lost an opportunity to encourage disaffection in
those provinces which happen to be of the same race and the same religion
with her own people. England has always been jealous of Russia, and has always thwarted her measures regarding Turkey, because Russia, enthroned at
Constantinople, would seriously affect the balance of power, and would greatly
reduce the influence of England in the Mediterranean. France has in general
sympathized with England, and taken the same course for substantially the
same reasons. Austria, the only other power seriously interested, has been opposed to Russia not so much because she favored the policy of France and England as because the dismemberment of Turkey might prove detrimental to the
integrity of her own dominions. These were the reasons—these the motives which
brought about the Crimean war. These are the reasons—these the motives which
at this time have made active interference in the affairs of Turkey by the Great
Powers impossible, and which have induced them all to stand aloof and allow
the Sultan and his subjects to settle their own difficulties—the Great Powers
reserving to themselves the right to interfere at the proper time in the interests
of peace, and with a view to effect an amicable arrangement. . . .

For Bismarck, architect of the foreign policy of the new German Empire from 1870 until 1890, nothing would serve German consolidation better than a long period of peace. To his mind France, nursing the sentiment of revenge, was the chief threat to Europe's stability. Bismarck, therefore, applied his considerable skill to the diplomatic isolation of France from any potential allies. Britain presented no problem, for her "splendid isolation" would continue as long as developments on the Continent did not challenge British security. Italy was too weak to matter. Bismarck, therefore, concentrated on Austria and Russia, for only with the support of one of these two nations would France ever embark on war. As early as 1872 the German Chancellor secured an agreement with both Austria and Russia called the League of the Three Emperors. When the Russo-Turkish war and the Congress of Vienna placed Russia and Austria on opposite sides, forcing Bismarck to support Austria, the Russians withdrew from their former co-operation. Bismarck, then, in 1879, negotiated the famous Dual Alliance with Austria. The reaction of Andrew D. White, the able American Minister in Berlin, was clear from the following dispatch.

✒

. . . Close as may have been the understanding between the Prussian and Russian Governments since 1812, a feeling of distrust has long been growing between the two peoples. I became aware of this as long ago as 1855–'56, when I was attached to the United States legation at St. Petersburg; for although at that time the friendship between the two governments was so close that abuse was lavished upon the Prussian sovereign by the English and French press, and although the Emperor Alexander, in his first reception of the diplomatic body, took especial pains to dwell upon the warmness of the friendship between himself and the Prussian King, it was not less evident that the thorough Russians greatly disliked Germany and the German element in their government, which, by its thrift and vigor, had taken such a great share of Russian positions of profit and honor. On the other hand, the thorough German, while he had no such personal dislike to Russia, naturally distrusted that Russian influence which, from the days of the Holy Alliance, had opposed the entire forward movement in his own country.

The Berlin treaty of 1878 rendered this chronic trouble acute. The organs of Russian Panslavism, in discussing that treaty, declared that it utterly failed to recognize the Russian friendliness toward Prussia in the wars of 1866 and 1870 and the Russian victories over the Turks in 1877. Prince Bismarck, it was said, was to blame for this—he, it was alleged, having at the conference given the

\* White to William Evarts, November 18, 1879, *Foreign Relations of the United States, 1880* (Washington, 1880), 391–3.

support of Germany to Austria and England rather than to Russia. Thus began a series of journalistic attacks upon Germany more vigorous than any hitherto known. As the provisions of the treaty were carried into effect, and Austria, which had remained peaceful, was seen to be receiving fruits of victories which had cost Russia so dear, these utterances became more and more bitter. That they were subdued at intervals, was probably due to the protests of the German Government.

That the old kindly feeling between the heads of the two empires still continued, was evident at the interview between the Emperors at Alexandrowno in the beginning of September; but it is now seen that personal considerations were not to determine the course of events. Last summer, when it was announced that the German chancellor was about to visit Vienna, the Panslavistic press was aroused to new activity. . . .

A fortnight afterward, that is, toward the close of September last, Prince Bismarck went to Vienna. The cordiality with which he was received by the Emperor and Count Andrássy, who was just at that time about to hand over his authority as premier to Baron Haymerle, and the enthusiasm with which the populace greeted him, were eagerly commented upon in every political circle. It soon became understood that an alliance between Germany and Austria-Hungary had been completed. As regards internal affairs, it was hailed with joy by liberals of every shade in Germany as putting an end to that Russian influence which, in their opinion, had been so injurious for many generations. As regards external affairs, it was received by all parties as another great step toward the consolidation of German-speaking peoples against Panslavism, and, therefore, as giving strength to German ideas and a more peaceable development to German civilization. . . .

The first result was a cloud of rumors of war. An acknowledged authority assured me at that time that, in his belief, a general European war would begin early next spring. The argument was, war must come sooner or later, and every one feels that, relatively, Germany is stronger now than she may be a few years hence. But opinion rapidly changed, and there now seems a general impression that the new alliance has done much to strengthen the prospects of a continuance of peace. Russia, it is believed, will never attack Germany and Austria, with whom England would then be leagued, without powerful alliances; and to secure these further diplomatic action and the lapse of considerable time are indispensable. . . .

While no one can doubt that the logical result of this German-Austrian alliance is a league which shall embrace England, the best opinion here just now seems to be that great care is taken by the German Government to avoid any appearances of any such league at present. It is believed here by persons who seemed to me well worthy of confidence that the present English Government has already, in its Turkish policy, presumed too much on an immediate prospect of such an alliance. There seems to be a strong desire on the part of those in power here to have it understood that the alliance made at Vienna is strictly what it claims to be, that is, one between the two German speaking nations with reference to dangers which may beset them, and that it shall not be developed into anything more offensive to Russia than it now is. It is felt that the Emperor of Germany, in view of his close personal connection with the Russian Imperial family, has gone quite as far as he can be expected to go; that his sacrifice of personal feeling is very great, and that he would oppose the idea of pressing this policy any further than is absolutely necessary, or making this change in the time-honored political alliance of Prussia and Russia any more unpleasant to Russia than it is at present. . . .

— | "There is still too great a distance between the dreams of Russia and the stern reality—between the cup and the lip." *

The following analysis of the Dual Alliance, which appeared in *The Nation,* noted the central importance of the pact—that it held Russia at bay and transformed Austria into an eastern European power. Thereafter the Austrian Empire became the key to the stability of much of Slavic Europe, and its destruction could only contribute to the influence of Russia in the affairs of that important region.

The visit of Prince Bismarck to Vienna has excited the greatest interest throughout Europe, and is clearly a political event of the first importance. It is impossible not to look at it at first from what may be called the dramatic point of view. Can anything show better the changing nature of man than the reception given in Vienna to the stern diplomat who, after Sadowa, signed the preliminaries of Nikolsburg and turned the Austrian Empire out of the Bund of German Princes? It is quite true that even at Nikolsburg Bismarck was careful not to inflict on Austria wounds that cannot well be cured; he offended the pride of the Emperor more than the interests of the people. The Prussian military party was very anxious to keep the battle-fields of Bohemia, and to annex this province to Prussia, as the great Frederick had once annexed Silesia. Bismarck, who was not then as powerful as he is now with his sovereign, had the greatest difficulty in imposing moderation on the leaders of the conquering army. His secretary tells us, in those curious memoirs where the true Bismarck is found, that his *patron,* as he always calls him, left the room where Moltke and the others were, retired to an adjoining room, and had become so nervous with his discussion that he began to sob; the generals heard him, and renounced an annexation which would have been a perpetual obstacle to a reconciliation with Austria. Bismarck's object was to give to his own sovereign the undoubted leadership of the German race; meanwhile he considered, as Metternich and Gentz and all the German political philosophers have done, that Austria had a special mission in the East. She was to represent German civilization and cul-

* "The German-Austrian Alliance," *The Nation,* XXIX (October 23, 1879), 269–70.

ture in the valley of the Danube, in the peninsula of the Balkans, and to stand
as a living obstacle to the growing influence of Panslavism, a force which is yet
hardly defined in its character and ambitions, but which has always inspired the
German mind with a profound and mysterious awe.

The occasion has come for Prince Bismarck to give effect to the German
theories about Austria. By the Treaty of Berlin, Austria was allowed to occupy
Bosnia, Herzegovina, and the outlying district of Novi-Bazar. This occupation
has met with no serious opposition, while it has given great satisfaction to the
military party in Austria. The extension of Austria-Hungary towards the East
has begun. It is obvious that the occupation of Bosnia and Herzegovina will be
indefinitely prolonged. This district is placed between Montenegro on one side
and Servia on the other, and these two countries will fall by necessity under the
influence of the Austrians. There will be, in consequence, in the peninsula of
the Balkans, in the direction of Salonica, a group of states placed under the
direct or indirect administration of Austria. Prince Bismarck has in this way
given a mission to Austria-Hungary; it will be a long time before all these
provinces are well intersected with railroads, and before the effects of the government of the Turks are effaced. Austria has always shown much capacity for
governing half-civilized countries; she will accomplish much for the Oriental
races, and confer on them benefits which will prove the most effectual barrier
against Panslavism. Has Russia the right to complain of these changes? It would
seem so, according to the Russian papers, the tone of which has lately become
excessively hostile to Germany. . . .

Prince Bismarck not only allowed Russia to enter upon the Eastern war, but
he protected her against all the other Powers while the war was going on. There
were hours of trial for Russia. Her armies were not well organized, the trans-
ports were slow, the army of Osman Pasha was inflicting enormous losses on the
army commanded by the Czar in person. Who can tell what thoughts came
across the minds of Austrian statesmen during that period? During the siege
of Plevna one single Austrian *corps d'armée* entering Turkey would have turned
the Russian campaign into a disaster. But Count Andrássy was ruling the policy
of Austria, and there was already at that time a thorough understanding between the German and the Austrian chancellors. Russia was, in fact, protected
against Austria during the war, and the neutrality of Europe allowed the Russian armies to arrive before Constantinople. Why they did not enter Stamboul,
why they did not use the force of accomplished facts and strike one of those
blows which seem the blows of destiny and which seldom meet with any
resistance, is a mystery which has hitherto not been solved. It seemed almost
incredible that Russia should not give her people and the Christian world of
the East the pride of occupying Constantinople. When the Congress of Berlin
was opened it was clear that Prince Bismarck had repaid, and had repaid generously, the debt of gratitude which Germany owed to Russia. Prince Gortchakoff may now be speaking with bitterness of the ingratitude of Germany; he
may regret that he allowed France to be too much humbled and weakened in
1870. . . . The Russians entered into the war with the greatest audacity, not to say
imprudence, and when everything had become easy they became timid. They

allowed the Powers which had not made the war to draw more prizes than Russia herself. She is left with slices of Armenia and Bessarabia, while England has taken Cyprus, and Austria is now quietly taking possession of Bosnia, of Herzegovina, and of the district of Novi-Bazar. The understanding between Count Andrássy and Prince Bismarck is of long standing. Bismarck has often said that Andrássy was necessary, not only to Austria, but to Europe; but since the visit to Vienna this understanding has become more apparent, and it may have taken the form of some practical arrangements, not to say treaties. These arrangements principally concern France, Italy, and Russia.

As for France, there is little to say. There was a deep-seated irony in the declaration which Prince Bismarck made to M. Teisserenc de Bort, the French Ambassador to Vienna, when he paid him his visit. He said that France had nothing to fear; that Germany was satisfied, quite satisfied. Perhaps this was a distant allusion to a famous saying of Napoleon III in his days of glory "Quand la France est satisfaite, l'Europe est tranquille."

As for Italy, she cannot see with much satisfaction the alliance of Austria with the strongest power in Europe. . . . It is quite clear that Austria, backed by Prince Bismarck, will only look with contempt on the "Italia irredenta" party. Italy can get nothing out of the present situation; she was used to obtaining a province after each European war, whether she had herself been beaten or victorious on the battlefield. . . . The establishment of the Austrian rule all along the opposite coast of the Adriatic is not pleasant to the Italians; but they must submit to the inevitable.

Russia looks, of course, with much concern on the alliance which has been made at Vienna, and in which she is more interested than any other power. She feels now more isolated from Europe; she found it difficult to carry on a war against the Turks, how could she carry on a war against Germany and Austria-Hungary? In case Russia should begin, a few years hence, a war against Turkey, it would be easy for the Austrians, starting from Novi-Bazar, to reach Constantinople before the Russian armies had crossed the Danube and arrived before the Balkans. Austria has now a flank position which allows her to go straight to Constantinople without encountering great difficulties. Russia is not and cannot be well pleased with such a state of things; she comes out of the war tired, discontented, disappointed; there are in the empire many germs of discontent. Russia must do again what she did after the Crimean war—reconstitute her army, build up railways, civilize her people, develop her immense natural resources. She has a vast future before her; but she needs financiers, engineers, economists, professors more than diplomats. Prince Gortchakoff has done as well as he could; he is a true Russian patriot; but he must have found that there is still too great a distance between the dreams of Russia and the stern reality—between the cup and the lip.

# 16 | Europe's Shifting Alignments, 1885 *

So completely did the Dual Alliance isolate Russia that the Czar renewed the League of the Three Emperors in 1881. That same year a clash between Italy and France over Tunis in the Mediterranean sent Italy in search of an ally. This situation permitted Bismarck to negotiate the Triple Alliance among Germany, Austria, and Italy in 1882. As the following article in *The Nation* suggests, the Dual Alliance remained the central factor in European politics. The writer observed that Italy was not completely incorporated into the German system, that France and Russia were still isolated, and that in a new trial of strength between Germany and France, the French would find their natural allies in Britain and Italy.

✍

. . . We have now before us in Europe a constellation which may be called of the first magnitude—it is the constellation of Germany, of Austria, and of Russia; a recent interview has again shown it to the world, "et nunc erudimini gentes." We know that in this aggregation of imperial Powers Prussia is the centre of gravity; Austria at first was somewhat reluctantly drawn into it, but since the journey of Prince Bismarck to Vienna, the alliance, founded on the sentiment, if not of German unity, at least of German solidarity, has become the most important factor in European politics. It is felt that in certain emergencies Germany would bring together such a host as has never been seen since Napoleon invaded Russia with the "grande armee"; from the Baltic to the Adriatic there would be an overwhelming obstacle opposed to all effort coming from the west or from the east. This alliance is so formidable that, by the mere force of gravity, as it were, Russia has been drawn into the German constellation. The Slavophiles have struggled in vain—in vain have appeals been made to the national sentiment by enthusiastic generals, by writers, by journalists; these spasmodic efforts have been futile. The leading minds in Russia have, so to speak, disarmed; they understand that Russia, irresistible and perhaps invincible at home, has no great offensive powers. She has an inexhaustible supply of men, but, in one sense, she is still in the inorganic state. "On the frontier of Germany," a Russian once said to me, "we can open a door and let out any number of horsemen; we can make a sort of inundation of men, but where? In enormous and thinly-inhabited provinces. It will be like a river spreading over an immense plain. We cannot get possession of any vital points, and should soon have to retire as the water recedes after an inundation and disappears by evaporation." In Russia there is a sort of electric light at St. Petersburg, a very powerful light, which throws its rays to a great distance: it is the court, the central government, the guard, the great powers of the state; but outside of the circle of this electric light all is obscurity, silence, and death. Immense regions remain

* "England and Italy," *The Nation*, XL (March 5, 1885), 197–8.

in a sort of social and political darkness. Germany is now, as it has always been, the civilizing element. The Russians like to quarrel with their civilizers, as a boy likes to quarrel with his master; but, after a while, the court influences, the ruling powers, always incline again toward Germany. The late interview of the three Emperors did not place Russia exactly on the same footing as Austria in the great Continental constellation: Russia remains a little in the background. Her hands have been tied; she has made sacrifices, and in return she has obtained distinct promises. . . .

. . . Many rumors are abroad, but they are mere rumors. It is said that Russia has been allowed to extend herself to her heart's content in Central Asia and in Asia Minor; that Austria is free to extend her influence in the direction of Salonica, and of the Aegean Sea; that in case Salonica should fall into her hands, the character of Trieste might be changed, and this great port might become more German than Austrian, perhaps by a new boundary of Bavaria. This question of Trieste brings us naturally to consider the role of Italy. There was a time when Italy expected to be drawn into the German constellation. There had been approaches made by her and to her. The old feud with Austria seemed to be forgotten, guarantees had been given against "Italia irredenta," the names of Trentino and of Trieste were no longer to be pronounced. This was the time when, to the great disgust of Italy, France set foot in the province of Tunis. It seemed as if Rome had been despoiled of Carthage, as if Italy had been robbed of one of her legitimate possessions. The ill will against France took the form of friendship for the Germans. These Germanic demonstrations, however, had not much effect; Italy wasted her time, and she felt angry and disgusted on finding out that her alliance was not more valued by the great Continental Powers. She was not deemed, perhaps, a very safe friend; the Germans did not think enough of her navy or her army; it was perhaps thought necessary in Berlin to spare the feelings of Vienna, and a close alliance with Rome would certainly have offended Vienna. Whatever the reasons may have been, the German enthusiasm of the Italians was allowed to cool down. But as Italy is quite determined to have her influence felt, and as she can change her position very rapidly, she soon remembered that England could be no more satisfied than she was herself with the existence in the midst of Europe of a nucleus of political forces almost overwhelming in their united strength. England seemed to be ignored, like herself, by the new arbiters of the Continent. It seemed as if she was put out of Europe. Italy remembered that though England had given to her neither men nor money in her great struggle for independence and unity, she had always lent her moral support. Gladstone, Lord Palmerston, Lord John Russell, had been her warmest friends. . . .

The question now arises, Is there a distinct understanding between England and Italy, or does Italy seize the opportunity of England's troubles in Egypt to offer her help and to take a part of the spoils? This question has been asked in the Italian Parliament and has not been distinctly answered. One thing is certain: Italy has taken possession of a point on the coast of the Red Sea, she is making great preparations at home, she is arming her heaviest ships. It seems as if she was undertaking a great task, still undefined and obscure. . . .

Under ordinary circumstances it would be natural that France—a Republic, a Government apparently founded on liberal principles—should fall into the constellation of England and of Italy. But who can say what will happen in France? The question of Tunis has made a wide breach between her and Italy. The energies of France are spent in a distant enterprise in Tonquin, which has not been looked upon with much favor by England. If we regarded only appearances, nothing would be more unlikely than a triple alliance of England, Italy, and France; at the same time, it would be clearly the advantage of France to emerge from her present isolation. The Continental alliance of the Emperors is directed especially against her, it is like a dagger perpetually aimed at her head. The frivolous encouragements of Germany, her caresses, her demonstrations on all colonial questions, cannot blind a serious mind to the brutal fact that sooner or later there must be a new trial of strength between France and Germany. It would be therefore for the interest of France, without committing herself to any important course, to draw nearer to England and to Italy, since England and Italy are allied by necessity. . . .

## 17 | The Russo-French Threat to European Stability, 1890 *

In a brilliant analysis of the pressures endangering the peace of Europe in 1890, *The Nation* cited two: the Russian drive toward southeastern Europe and the French determination to recover the lost provinces of Alsace-Lorraine. But the fundamental conflict in Europe, noted the writer, was the German-Russian rivalry over the future of eastern Europe, a struggle which would break out into the open with the destruction of Austria. French *revanche* had meaning only in the context of the Russo-German rivalry, for France would not attack Germany without the support of Russia.

✑

. . . The peace of Europe is in danger from two probable aggressive movements, and no more. The first and most menacing of these is the attempt of the Russians to regain their control of Bulgaria, Servia, and the South Slavic tribes generally, and the other is the determination of France to recover the lost provinces of Alsace and Lorraine. I defy the worst alarmist in France to point out any other tendency which can be considered as a present danger for Europe. The former threatens the destruction of Austria, for nothing is clearer than that if Russia once gets established in the Balkan [Peninsula], it is only a question of time how she shall undermine and destroy the polyglot empire. This, *per se*,

* "Italy and the Triple Alliance," *The Nation*, LI (October 30, 1890), 340–41.

would not cause so great grief in the Western world were it to stop there; but when the general character of Russian propaganda is considered, and that it has already to a very large extent undermined not merely Herzegovina and Bosnia, but the original Serb provinces of Austria-Hungary, so that it is a boast of the Russian agents that the Serb regiments in the army will go over to the Russians if it comes to a war between the empires—and that this game, once played success-fully, is certain to go on till the German and Slav elements are face to face—we come in sight of a conflict which is fraught with greater dangers to European peace than any which is now above the horizon of actual politics. Russia is in effect today an Asiatic country; but with her entry into European politics at Constantinople, or as the mistress of Bulgaria (which amounts in the end to the same thing), she will become an aggressive Power, with elements of invasive strength which no other nation now in Europe possesses. The slow and certain destruction of Austria would be only the prelude to a secular struggle between the German and Slavic races, the issue of which can be only conjectured. It was the perception of this which made Austria persist in the Germanizing policy of the past half century, and the incapacity to realize it which led the Hungarians under Kossuth to play into the hands of Russia by opposing, in their blind egoism, the unification of Austria. It is the same foresight which makes Germany and Austria-Hungary allies against any advance of Russia westward, and which will always prevent any pact between Germany and Russia to the injury of Austria. This is the necessity of the situation. The sound and traditional policy of England which seconds this policy, has no direct relation to the triple alliance, and I need only allude to it as an element in the position which rather confirms the idea that the alliance is really defensive. The Austro-German alliance is a permanent institution.

The French *revanche* is a menace which is serious only as it can ally with it some other element of conflict, *e.g.*, Russia. The nation was foolish enough to provoke a war unprepared, and paid for it by the loss of two provinces, the recovery of which justifies it, in its own eyes, in keeping Europe in a state of perpetual alarm and financial depletion, and, if it is attempted by force of arms, will cost France more lives than there are inhabitants in the two provinces. Every schoolboy in America must know by this time that France will declare war on the first convenient opportunity, and attack Germany with a fury such as she has never shown in any previous war. Frenchmen are rather proud of this determination. But for this the Eastern danger might be met with comparative ease, and perhaps kept back till the Balkan States were organized for their self-defence, and effectively. It is the fact that the two dangers will break on Central Europe at the same moment, that constitutes the peculiar nature of the present impending crisis. The only hope of averting the conflict lies in the possibility of drawing into the central alliance enough of the Powers interested in peace more than in any possible gains by war, to make the confederation clearly master of the situation. This is the interest which the central Powers have in drawing Italy into the alliance, and this addition has no doubt made France less con-fident of victory, and retarded the outbreak of hostilities for which the French believe they were ready last year; but there is still another weight in the scale of peace in the well-founded conviction that the power of England would be thrown in against the party that began hostilities.

It is, however, against Italy that the French journals launch their deadliest shafts, because Italy is the make-weight which gives a preponderant force to the central alliance, and prevents France from attacking Germany. . . .

So far from contemplating any attack on France, Italy is very far yet from being prepared for a purely defensive campaign, and the fixed belief that the triple alliance is sufficient to avert war is so potent that all the pressure of Germany to get the army into condition for entering into one has not yet produced the desired result. Italy is far from ready for war, and, but for the English determination that she should not be the victim of an unprovoked aggression by sea, hostilities would probably have long ago begun. The consciousness that as long as the Conservatives in England are in power, and, perhaps, even if the Liberals come in, England will take part in the fray against the Power that disturbs the peace, makes it morally certain that neither Germany nor Italy can afford to take the initiative. If, indeed, England were frankly to accede to the triple alliance, and then to induce, as she alone could, the minor Powers, Holland, Belgium, Denmark, and Scandinavia, to enter it, a partial disarmament would at once take place, because the attack on such a combination would be hopeless.

The present policy of France is to exhaust the finances of the triple alliance by the necessity of constantly increasing its armaments to keep pace with hers; and, trusting to her greater wealth to hold out longest, she goes on increasing her army and spending for new guns. The consequences of her success in the game which she is playing would be such that the contemplation of them ought to deprive her of the sympathy of the entire civilized world, for they mean the extension of Siberia over eastern Europe, and the loss of all its independence by western; interminable wars till Russia and France meet, and then, perhaps, a mortal struggle between the Republic and the Cossack. Meanwhile it becomes doubtful if the Powers who favor peace will not be driven to finish with the ruinous condition of affairs by compelling France to disarm or fight. This probably would have taken place the autumn that the Emperor of Germany was here had Italy been prepared; but as Italy had never taken the danger of war seriously to heart, and was most unprepared for it, nothing came of it.

The following description of Europe's military preparations for war in 1892 provides an illuminating review of the ultimate impact of imperialism, nationalism, and militarism on the state of European politics. In a close balance of military might between the power of France and Russia at the extremities and the strength of Germany, Austria, and Italy across the heart of Europe, England held the key to the Continent's future peace and stability. Since Germany and Austria represented the *status quo,* as did England, the writer believed that peace would be better guaranteed if England cast her lot with the Central Powers.

✍

. . . Europe has never been so perfectly prepared for war; nor, curiously, has she ever seen a time when soldiers were more loath to fight. There exists a marked and universal dread of war, coupled with an unexampled ability to wage it. Not that there is a lack of stomach; the *morale* of the leading armies is of the best. But Europe stands aghast at her own weapons. War is *quasi*-suicide; and Europe gazes at the blade she holds against her vitals and shrinks from the thrust. The dread is born of certainty that a war will be a general one, of the uncertainty of its issue. Even France, despite her unquenched thirst for revenge, will do nothing to provoke war. But an accident, the foolish demonstration of a mob in Paris or the ill-considered utterance of the German *Kaiser,* may precipitate war at any moment. Can we gauge the chances of any of the probable combatants?

There are twenty countries contributing to the eighteen millions of troops. Of these, two antagonistic groups monopolize the situation. In the centre of the Continent stands the German colossus, with its allies, Austria-Hungary and Italy. On either hand are France and Russia, a political Scylla and Charybdis between which the bark freighted with European peace must be steered. Possessing all they can properly claim, the members of the Triple Alliance are directly interested in steadying the helm, while France yearns for her old boundary and Russia proposes—when the time is ripe—to seize the Golden Horn. The lesser powers, in case of war, can complicate the situation by joining either the Double or the Triple Alliance; but immediate danger lurks in the statecraft—one might say simply craft—of the five powers named. England, by the necessity of maintaining her supremacy in the Mediterranean, is drawn to closer relations with Italy. She looks askance at the encroachments in Africa of France and dreads the influence in Asia of Russia. The key of the situation has been thrust upon her. The substantial powers of Europe are three or four against two, in case of a general war. What are their relative abilities?

England stands by herself in not having adopted the rule of universal service.

* Theodore Ayrault Dodge, "A Glance at the European Armies," *The Forum,* XIII (July 1892), 561–73.

While still ruling the waves so long as there is no combination against her, Britannia cannot claim to be a military power. She alone takes herself seriously as such. Since the Napoleonic struggle she has had no war which has taxed her stanchness to the utmost, and this is the only test of military force. In view of the gigantic proportions of our rebellion and of the Franco-Prussian war, is it not droll to see her "point with pride" to such pigmy operations as the Abyssinian, Ashantee, Zulu, Transvaal, Afghanistan, or Egyptian campaigns? Yet to the average Englishman these are clad with more splendor than the wars of the giants. . . .

The gravest danger to England's position as a great power is not in Europe. It may be difficult for her to keep out of the next war, for France views with alarm her occupation of Egypt, yet redolent with the elder Napoleon's lustre; but this is a minor matter. It is in Russia's restless pushing across the great Aryan plateau toward the confines of the Indian empire that lurks the nearest peril. The Orientals have a cognate liking for Russia; they understand the stable autocracy of the Czar; but a change in the British ministry is always an enigma. Were it not for the wonderful personal force of many English officials in the East, England could not long retain her prestige in rivalry with the insinuating policy of Russia. Since Turkestan fell under Russia's sway, Bokhara, Khiva, Kokhand, Merv, have slowly but surely followed. Just when Russia will feel strong enough to make an actual bid for control dangerous to England's holding in India depends upon many contingencies. But she can at almost any moment advance along the line Herat-Kandahar with a force sufficient to prevent England from interfering too seriously with her Bosphorus projects. By fortifying Quetta, England shows that she fears this. It seems as if Great Britain must side with the Triple Alliance and against France and Russia.

The aspirations of Russia in Europe extend only to the Balkan Peninsula. She cares little for the politics which sway the other powers. Her destiny pushes her toward a Mediterranean outlet for her potential commerce and toward the control of inner Asia. In whichever direction she can the more safely tread at any given time will be her path. She does not seek war, but she will not rest from encroachment. Her next step in Asia will be to control Persia, or she may attack the Turkish problem from Asia Minor. Russia is active in the Baltic, though in case of war the more mobile and active German fleet could probably neutralize hers. In the Black Sea she is not doing so much. As fearless of conquest as the United States, she is more troubled by her present finances than by fears of her future growth. She can bide her time, certain that she will gain ground to the south and east. But that a war which appealed to the restless element might quiet her internal politics does not make for peace.

Russia is rich in material for an army, since eight years ago she fell into line by adopting universal service. The material has excellent physical qualities, but it lacks intelligence. The Russian soldier has always been a dangerous opponent; Kunersdorf and Borodino tell a story of undaunted heroism. Brave, of wonderful endurance, uncomplaining, easily subjected to discipline, requiring little, he has been a pattern soldier. But to-day, when the intelligence of the enlisted man is so marked a factor in the efficiency of an army, it is a query whether the

Russian can hold his own in Europe; for 73 per cent of the army in Europe can neither read nor write, of that in Asia, 82 per cent. The minor officers are, moreover, of low grade, a fact scarcely compatible with efficiency. The Russian army has always been proud of its ability to stand hammering at close quarters; but this is not of the essence of modern war—when actual annihilation may follow a false manoeuvre. It is the intelligent initiative that keeps out of false positions which is demanded. . . .

The French army has never been in so prime a condition as it now is. Napoleon's, as an army, was at no time as sound throughout. It can pass almost any test. Even the best German authorities acknowledge this. *"Frankreicht steht mit uns in den Waffen gleich,"* says General von Leszczynsky. Sir Charles Dilke's summary of the French armies goes too far—not in actual, but in comparative praise. The French army is not the best in Europe. It is highly commended when put on the same level as the German. There are still some serious points of criticism. The spirit which animates the army is the same as that which produces the restless ambition of the leaders and the changeableness of the people. Jealousies with many attendant evils come frequently to the surface. There is lacking the quiet pose of subordination to one central autocratic permanent power for which discipline, however severe, will not make up. No man is more patriotic than the Gaul; but his patriotism is of a different order from the *Vaterlandsliebe* of the Teuton. No more splendid example of patient, intelligent, consistent work than the recent reorganization of the French army adorns the pages of history. The infantry is excellent, the artillery of the best, and the two arms work admirably together—the most important of modern demands. The cavalry did not shows its capacity in the last manoeuvres, but it is well mounted and taught. The engineers did remarkable work; the telegraph and telephone service was perfect; the balloon corps promised results; the train management was not to be criticised. But there was no attempt to combine the workings of the three arms, nor was the cavalry used in its proper *role*. . . .

Despite excellent preparation, the French are not eager for war. *"Revanche"* is not now as keen-scented a cry as it was ten years ago. Though his spurs are sharper, the Gallic cock's crow is less shrill. France recognizes the uncertainties of the situation, and though in better financial condition than Germany, is not going to war for a shadow. At an opening which promised success, however, she would immediately thrust. It is wiser for France not to strike for Alsace and Lorraine too soon; better use her means in developing her enormous African colonies and protectorates by the trans-Saharan railway. By and by she will be proportionately stronger than she now is. If her government remains stable, she will gain by every year's delay.

If the status of France is difficult to determine, that of Germany is a very maze. Those who in 1870 knew Prussia well had no doubt as to the issue of a war with France, though no one expected a walk-over. The case to-day is different. The German army is not the superior of the French. Whoever estimates at their true value the homogeneous organization, the diligence, and the subordination of self to the general result which have always characterized the Germans, may cast his vote in their favor. But it is a narrow choice. The next war will call out national individualities. According as each views the qualities of the Teuton or the Gaul, each may divine results. Some conditions are to be noted. So long as an army is a despotic body, so long will service due to a single chief, which cannot be complicated by professional intrigues, be the better rendered. In the German army officers are put where they can do the work they are best fitted for. This is not always possible in France. The discipline of the French army is more severe; the training of the German is superior, and individual training is worth more in the field than severity. The latter work harder and more hours; they will go into a campaign more seasoned. All Germans work together; nation and army are interchangeable terms. Manoeuvres lately introduced into France and Russia are a generation old in Prussia. The knowledge and individual initiative of the German officers of all ranks are higher than those which any body of military men has ever had; and they believe in and rely on the exceptional intelligence which permeates the ranks. That despite their penury the quality of the German officers does not slacken, speaks well. The Germans will bear up under initial disaster; a first defeat might dishearten the French—it might work a change in their commanders or even affect the government, a result which could not follow in Germany. Assuming that the armies are equal, it is method and race characteristics which will yield superiority. That army which has the best *morale,* other things being equal, will win. What may be said about the Germans in no wise detracts from the value of their opponents. No army can possess more *esprit de corps* than the French, nor be sounder through and through. And keen military observers have more than once expressed their preference for the present military status of *la belle France*. . . .

The Triple Alliance is strong. Austria has made a great gain in her military status. Professional pride is higher, instruction is more diligent, discipline and *morale* are excellent, and the armament better than it has been. The intelligence of the troops is not as high as in Germany, but decidedly higher than in Russia. Her interests are identical with Germany's, but she fears no attack except from Russia, while Germany may have to meet Russia and France. Though with but half her force, Austria ought to be able to hold head against a Russian attack, especially as Roumania can lend a hand and keep at least two Russian army corps idle. Austria can more quickly mobilize, and is well placed strategically. She is strong in some arms. The cavalry and field artillery are all but the equal of Germany's; her infantry force is, however, on the whole, inferior to that of any of the greater powers. Her officers are poorly paid, and though the cadet school is gaining, are not so able as the French or German; and the non-commissioned officers are of lower grade. Little is done to make the soldier's life attractive or honorable. His pay, rations, and clothing are all poor, and the instruction cannot be called good. But a marked improvement is being scored every year. The magazine rifle and smokeless powder will do wonders, and the new equipment is lighter and better adapted to modern requirements. There has been added to the army-trains a system of portable railways which can be quickly laid along otherwise poor roads for the transport of army material, a thing important in southeastern Europe; and field telegraphy is now part of the staff equipment. To fend off Russia's attack, Galicia has been strongly fortified and garrisoned, but it has an open frontier. Nothing short of the Carpathian Mountains could well arrest a pronounced onset; but Austria could no doubt confine the early campaign to the lowlands of Galicia, which would act as a bumper for the nonce, while the second line was coming up.

The value of Italy in the Triple Alliance is that she holds in check all the French forces which lie in the districts of Lyons, Marseilles, and Nice, as well as the Alpine divisions. To have Italy join with Germany and Austria was imperative. The three are scarcely stronger than France and Russia. Indeed, France believes that as Germany must put up against Russia, on account of her naturally open frontier, a much larger force than France need put up against Italy, she can largely outnumber her old opponent with the sixteen army corps she proposes to unleash in the Vosges region on the first cry of war. Italy adds no inconsiderable strength to the Triple Alliance, though despite severe economy she is financially bankrupt. Her army is very big on paper—a war strength of 2,700,000 men. But she cannot mobilize more than a portion of this force. Her coast lays her open to sudden and disastrous descents, and her length makes mobilization slow, despite the three railways running up and down the peninsula. France could put a large force on the Po before Italy could meet it. In twelve days several French corps could be at the defile of Stradella, while it would take Italy over twenty days to meet them. Such a movement is, however, highly improbable. France is led to expend her energy against Germany by every reason of pride and safety. Italy will not invade French territory; Germany will sweep over it as in 1870, unless France is on hand in overwhelming force. . . .

It is, then, a question of France and Russia on exterior lines against Germany, Austria, and Italy on interior ones. And happily the powers holding interior lines most desire peace. There is some doubt as to whether Russia will join France in a fight for mere revenge. The Alsace-Lorraine question has no importance for Russia, said Prince Gortchakoff long ago, and the policy of Russia is not noted for unselfishness. The most important question is what England will do. All her leanings are, it would seem, to the side of the Triple Alliance. What could induce her to side with France, the increase of whose fleet is a disturbing element, if not a subject of fear, it is hard to say; and as to Russia, England can be counted as certainly on the other side. England's neutrality would leave the scales very evenly balanced between the rival alliances; England casting in her lot with the Triple Alliance would make this the stronger and tend toward peace, which England has also every motive to desire. Germany would like to feel herself abreast of the situation with England neutral, but she manifestly feels its doubtfulness as never before. . . .

# VI

## The Reluctant World Power

America's explosive rise to industrial greatness during the closing decades of the nineteenth century produced ambivalent reactions in the minds of European statesmen. A nation's significance in world politics hinges not only upon its intrinsic power but also upon the judgment of others as to how and under what circumstances that power will be employed. That the United States possessed a unique capacity to sustain a determined and large-scale military action was demonstrated by the American Civil War itself. That it possessed enormous productive energy was illustrated not only by its amazing internal development but also by its burgeoning commercial activities all over the globe. The profound significance of the nation's territorial expansion, moreover, had not escaped the attention of British and French officials. Indeed, the acquisition of Texas and California rendered the United States so completely dominant in the Western Hemisphere that some European editors and diplomats favored direct European intervention and the establishment of a balance of power in the New World. In April 1862, Cassius Clay could observe with some truth that it was "useless to deceive ourselves with the idea that we can isolate ourselves from European interventions. We became in spite of ourselves—the Monroe Doctrine—Washington's farewell—and all that—a part of the 'balance of power.'" The United States had become by 1895 a nation of consequence in world affairs.

Still the United States as a nation among nations was an unknown quantity. Despite its energy and latent power, it had engaged in no actions abroad which proved its willingness to recognize and defend economic, political, or moral commitments distant from its own shores. The United States had once disposed of the Barbary pirates, but its involvement in the War of 1812 had been less than impressive. Thereafter the nation pursued its interests, quite isolated from the politics of Europe and the Far East. Thus for most European diplomats the United States remained a remote and comparatively unimportant country whose foreign policies mattered little. As late as 1895 the United States as a potentially first-class military nation and the United States as an active and predictable component in a world-wide balance of power presented a profound dichotomy.

334

Even then events in the Pacific and the Caribbean were slowly, almost imperceptibly, pushing the United States onto the world stage. American commercial expansionists of the 'forties had predicted accurately the impact which the acquisition of San Francisco Bay and the Strait of Juan de Fuca would have on American relations with the Pacific. By mid-century trading vessels, emerging from these harbors, sailed the entire region. The French consul at San Francisco predicted in 1852 that "all the archipelagoes of the Pacific Ocean, the entire American continent from Sitka to the Strait of Magellan, China, Japan, are destined to submit to the influence of this state [and] to be attracted into the sphere of its commercial activity." In China, American merchants, under the most-favored-nation principle, continued to gain all the commercial and extraterritorial rights which British and French arms extracted from the Chinese government. Also, by mid-century, Boston traders, with their missionary allies, had transformed the Hawaiian Islands, with their port of Honolulu, into an important Pacific depot. The American Hawaiians were not annexationists, but the strategic significance of the islands to the future importance of the United States in the Pacific Ocean was obvious. Eugene Duflot de Mofras, French explorer of the early 'forties, regarded Hawaii as an appendage of California and predicted that the nation which controlled one would also control the other. Sir George Simpson, in his *Narrative of a Journey Round the World* (1847), described the island group as "a stepping-stone from the whole of the American coast to the Celestial Empire. . . ."

Meanwhile the invasion of the north Pacific by New England whalers, the increased traffic between California and China, the projected San Francisco-Shanghai steamship line, plus Commodore Matthew C. Perry's own penchant for expansion, led to the breakdown of Japanese isolation under United States pressure in 1854. Perry's treaty with Japan was devoid of the conventional unequal clauses which had been imposed on China; it anticipated a United States-Japanese relationship based on the concept of two equal and independent nations. Four years later the Townsend Harris treaty reverted in phraseology to the older pattern of extraterritoriality and treaty ports, but this imposition merely drove Japan toward the modernization of its legal, administrative, and economic systems in its determination to achieve equality with the West. This intense effort at modernization culminated during the 'nineties in the emergence of Japan as the first Asian nation to achieve the status of world power. Such achievements in human progress won the overwhelming approval of the American people.

By the 'eighties expanding American commercial interests in the Pacific had involved the United States in a scramble with other powers for position in a variety of strategic areas. As early as 1867 an American naval officer had claimed Midway for the United States. Another naval captain successfully opened Korea to American influence in 1882. Within a year the State Department instructed the American Minister in Korea to "secure for our citizens the privileges granted to the Chinese in the Commercial Regulations [and] to inform this Department fully as to all matters of political importance or of interest to those engaged in commerce." Soon the United States faced the competition of Britain, Russia, and Japan, for Korea was located too strategically to pass the notice of other powers. Similarly, United States naval officials in 1878 secured special privileges in the harbor of Pago Pago on one of the south Pacific islands in the Samoan group in return for an American promise to protect the island from the encroachments of other foreign countries. This effort to monopolize Samoa antagonized the British and Germans, who also had commercial and political ambitions in the island. Eventually the three nations agreed to recognize one another's interests, but the United States concern was illustrated by the report of an American agent to the Secretary of State in December 1886:

> It is now quite certain that an interoceanic canal across the Isthmus of Panama is one of the possibilities of the not very distant future, and it needs only a glance at the map to see that when that fact is accomplished the key of maritime domination in the Pacific, and to some extent the intercontinental commerce of the world, will be held, not alone by Hawaii, but jointly by Hawaii and Samoa.

Expanding American interests in Hawaii reached their consummation in the Hawaiian revolution of 1893. Through three generations of missionary and commercial encroachment a small group of American investors gained a dominant position in the islands' sugar industry as well as their foreign trade. Then, in 1890, the McKinley tariff, in terminating reciprocal tariff arrangements with Hawaii, apparently doomed the islands to lowered property values and continued depression. Many planters, however, feared annexation to the United States because of the possible effect of American labor and immigration laws on the importation of cheap contract labor from China and Japan. As late as 1893 the large planters opposed annexation, but they acquiesced in the overthrow of the queen because of their primary need for sound and stable government, a need which ultimately prompted them to take their chances on the labor question rather than on the continued independence of the islands.

Expansionists within the United States accepted the possible consequences of the American invasion of the Pacific without equivocation. Imperialism was the order of the day. Britain, France, Belgium, and a more reluctant Germany had commenced their partition of Africa and the islands of the Pacific into colonies and spheres of influence. Western industrialism had developed an insatiable demand for markets, raw materials, and areas for investment. These, in turn, had exposed the need for strategic naval bases. Yet the new colonialism was as much a quest for prestige as it was a search for expanding economic opportunity. Thus it projected onto the world scene the international rivalries within Europe itself. Darwinism encouraged the spirit of imperialism by insisting that only the fittest could survive the struggle for existence.

Nowhere did such motives for expansion receive more fervid attention than in the United States. For John Fiske, Josiah Strong, and other American Darwinians, the nation's superior power, energy, and governmental forms resulted from natural selection and compelled the United States, as the more fit, to join the powers of western Europe in ruling the backward, less fit peoples of the world. In the Benjamin Harrison administration of the early 'nineties the United

States had a leadership ready to inaugurate policies which would capitalize the opportunities made possible by previous American activity in the Pacific. Under the direction of Secretary of the Navy Benjamin F. Tracy, the United States between 1890 and 1893 launched its new steel battleships *Maine, Oregon,* and *Olympia.* Tracy declared in an interview of November 1891 that "the sea will be the future seat of empire. And we shall rule it as certainly as the sun doth rise!" Colonies would help to give the United States a pre-eminent rank among nations.

Other Americans denounced such expansionist tendencies as an unwarranted departure from the nation's established policies. In March 1893, *Harper's Weekly* passed judgment on the attitudes of the Harrison administration in its attempt to multiply the nation's entanglements abroad. "Are we ready," demanded the writer, "to alter the whole character of the government, with its beneficent traditional policies, to impose upon the people the burdens entailed by the building up and maintaining of immense armaments, and to expose this republic to all the political and economic consequences which such a policy would bring in its train . . . ?" Similarly Carl Schurz, the noted Republican leader, writing in *Harper's New Monthly Magazine* in October 1893, warned that the United States, should it annex Hawaii, would be giving up the advantages of geographic insulation which gave it a security possessed by no other nation on the globe. (*Reading No. 1.*)

## II

As late as the mid-'nineties such conservatism governed the policies of the United States in the Pacific area. The administration of Grover Cleveland which entered office in March 1893, for example, refused to consider the annexation of Hawaii. Yet between 1895 and 1898 two series of events tended to drag the United States into broad commitments in the western Pacific. The first began with Japan's successful assault on China in 1894, which demonstrated China's internal weakness as well as Japan's new Asiatic ambitions. Following Japan's victory, the great European powers, at China's request, deprived Japan of her wartime territorial gains, but soon inaugurated the process of dividing China into spheres of influence. In March 1897, France assumed economic control of the island of Hainan. In November, German troops seized Kiaochow, and shortly thereafter a Russian fleet entered Port Arthur. To American business groups operating in China, such as the American-China Development Company and the American exporters of cotton goods, these developments were matters of grave concern. If unopposed, they would destroy the equal trading and investment privileges which Americans enjoyed in China. Speaking for the American business interests in China, the New York Chamber of Commerce memorialized the federal government in February 1898:

> That there are important changes now going on in the relations of European powers to the Empire of China . . . affecting the privileges enjoyed under existing treaty rights by American citizens trading in and

with China. That the trade of the United States to China is now rapidly increasing, and is destined, with the further opening of that country, to assume large proportions unless arbitrarily debarred by the action of foreign governments. . . . That, in view of the changes threatening to future trade development of the United States in China, the Chamber of Commerce . . . respectfully and earnestly urge that such proper steps be taken as will commend themselves to your wisdom for the prompt and energetic defence of the existing treaty rights of our citizens in China, and for the preservation and protection of their important commercial interests in that Empire.

Late in January 1898, the American Minister to China, Charles Denby, warned the administration in Washington that partition would tend to destroy American markets in China. "The Pacific Ocean," he wrote, "is destined to bear on its bosom a larger commerce than the Atlantic. . . . Here are diverse and varied sources of interest in the Far East which directly touch us. . . . We should urge on China the reform of all evils in her government which touch American interests, and the adoption of vigorous measures in the line of material progress. . . . We should not hesitate, also, I think, to announce our disapproval of acts of brazen wrong, and spoilation, perpetrated by other nations towards China— should any such occur." Denby reminded the government that the United States had fifteen hundred missionaries in China. These, he added, were also entitled to the protection of the United States government.

Of more immediate consequence was the Cuban revolt that broke out in February 1895. Without delay the Cuban *Junta,* with headquarters in New York, supported by the Cuban League, its American counterpart, with branches in all the large cities of the nation, launched a campaign to involve the United States in the Cuban struggle for independence. The *Junta* promoted mass meetings to exploit American humanitarianism and thus create a powerful anti-Spanish sentiment in the United States. The newspaper press supported the Cuban cause, stressing not only Spain's inhumanity but also that nation's threat to American trade, financial, and property interests in the Caribbean. By midsummer the *Junta*'s demand for action had won the support of Republican editors who discovered the political implications in the nation's latest humanitarian crusade. Meanwhile Cleveland, resentful of the *Junta*'s filibustering activities and embarrassed by the legitimacy of the Spanish complaints, announced, in June 1895, a policy of strict neutrality. In his annual message of December, the President explained to the nation why he refused to be guided by liberal sentiment. It was the plain duty of the government, he said, "to observe in good faith the recognized obligations of international friendship." (*Reading No. 2.*)

But after another year of continuing insurrection on the island of Cuba, Cleveland was less sanguine. The utter ruin of an adjoining territory, he admitted in his December 1896 message to Congress, was not only a question of philanthropic concern but also one of pecuniary interest, for American investments in Cuba were second only to those of Spain. Both issues, he continued, had led to vehement demands that the strife in Cuba "be terminated by our intervention, even at the cost of war between the United States and Spain. . . ." Should the insurrection degenerate into a hopeless struggle which promised nothing but useless destruction, the President concluded, "a situation will be presented in which our obligations to the sovereignty of Spain will be superseded by higher obligations, which we can hardly hesitate to recognize and discharge."

President William B. McKinley had no greater desire than his predecessor to fight for Cuban rights. But during the spring of 1898 he found it exceedingly difficult to withstand the pressure of events. The Spanish government, to be sure, had recognized its failure in Cuba and by 1898 had done much to alleviate conditions on the island. It desired to avoid war with the United States and moved forward as rapidly as Spanish opinion would permit in meeting the demands of American leadership. But the government at Madrid faced odds with which it could not cope. Within the United States the Cuban *Junta* continued its sustained and successful assault on the American mind. By 1898 editors advocated overwhelmingly the independence of Cuba as the only means remaining to protect the interests of the United States in the Caribbean. They assumed, generally, that this objective could be achieved through diplomacy alone. But the yellow press, after the destruction of the *Maine* in Havana harbor, demanded war. Thereafter, as the crisis mounted, both Democratic and Republican spokesmen concluded that a war against Spain would redound to the glory of the party which promoted it.

When Republican Congressmen made this clear to the cabinet, McKinley, in the interest of party unity and executive leadership, assumed the responsibility for involving the nation in war. After March, his demands on Spain included the independence of Cuba. On April 5, American Minister to Spain, Stewart L. Woodford, reported to McKinley that the Queen had agreed to proclaim an "immediate and unconditional suspension of hostilities in the island of Cuba." This suspension would continue for six months to provide time for the establishment of permanent peace between the Spanish government and the insurgents. "I believe that this means peace," added Woodford, "which the sober judgment of our people will approve long before next November, and which must be approved at the bar of final history." To Woodford it was clear that the United States could eventually achieve Cuban independence without resort to war. Two days after McKinley learned of the Spanish capitulation to all his demands, save independence itself, he sent his war message to Congress. (*Reading No. 3.*)

Few Americans attempted to justify the war against Spain except in terms of humanitarianism. Such motives were not strange to American liberal thought, but before 1898 they had never governed action. With the Spanish American War moral abstraction as a mass phenomenon was substituted for the political realism which had circumscribed previous American diplomacy. This was a people's war, forced on a reluctant administration. It was not the result of any deliberate weighing of interests and responsibilities. "Our own direct interests [in Cuba] were great . . ." observed Theodore Roosevelt in his *Autobiography*. "But even greater were our interests from the standpoint of humanity. Cuba was at our very doors. It was a dreadful thing for us to sit supinely and watch her death agony." For Theodore Marburg of the Baltimore *American* the destruction of Spanish power in Cuba was proper because Spain had "failed to keep abreast of the world in moral and intellectual progress, and must pay the penalty. . . . we cannot escape the conclusion that man's express duty is the uplifting of man. The duty to improve and elevate himself and his fellows thus becomes an end in itself and a justification of life. . . . Any nation which blocks the way of human progress must expect to be brushed aside by some more powerful and vigorous blood." A previous generation of American idealists had sought in vain a new deal for the Poles and the Hungarians. In 1898 such idealism mattered, for at last it was directed at oppression adjacent to the nation's shores where the United States, not reactionary Europe, held the clear strategic advantage.

### III

To destroy Spanish power on the high seas and thus protect American commerce, the McKinley administration ordered Commodore George Dewey to Manila Bay, where on May 1, 1898, his squadron destroyed the Spanish Pacific fleet without any loss of American life. The President next dispatched an expeditionary force to reduce Spanish power and guarantee order and security in the islands. Suddenly the nation faced an unanticipated problem. What was to be the disposition of the Philippines now in American hands? For weeks the press debated the question while the administration searched for a policy. In July 1898 the annexation of Hawaii placed the nation on an expansionist course and, in a sense, settled the fate of the Philippines. McKinley's ultimate decision to annex the islands, like the war itself, was rationalized in terms of the nation's obligation to humanity. In his instructions of September 16 to his peace commission the President wrote:

> Without any original thought of complete or even partial acquisition, the presence and success of our arms at Manila imposes upon us obligations which we can not disregard. The march of events rules and overrules human action. . . . we cannot be unmindful that, without any desire or design on our part, the war has brought us new duties and responsibilities which we must meet and discharge as becomes a great nation on whose growth and career from the beginning the Ruler of Nations has plainly written the high command and pledge of civilization.

During his speaking tour of the Midwest in October 1898 to test the nation's support for annexation, McKinley dwelt only on the theme of the country's responsibility to the Filipinos. (*Reading No. 4.*) His remarks at Columbus, Ohio, were typical: "We know what our country is now in its territory, but we do not know what it may be in the near future. But whatever it is, whatever obligation shall justly come from this for humanity, we must take up and perform, and as free, strong, brave people, accept the trust which civilization puts upon us." The President simply refused to dwell on the burdens of empire at all. In destroying the nation's historic political isolation from the Eastern Hemisphere, all in the name of humanitarianism, McKinley divorced the foreign policies of the United States from their established course. The nation thus deserted, in the process of acquiring the Philippine Islands, those principles of statecraft which had guided it through its first century of independence. The splendid victory over the Spanish fleet at Manila merely obscured the magnitude of that departure.

Even at that the nation's conservative tradition in diplomacy died hard. McKinley and the expansionist bloc in Congress were soon confronted by a powerful anti-imperialist movement, led by many of the nation's political and intellectual leaders. This movement comprised two distinct groups which agreed only on their opposition to annexation. For some the issue was purely the suppression of a conquered people. Annexation was wrong because it defied the nation's democratic principles. David Starr Jordan, the noted American educator, told a San Francisco audience that there was great danger that in their easy victory the American people "might lose sight of the basal principles of the Republic, a co-operative association in which 'all just government is derived from the consent of the governed.'" Former President Cleveland professed amazement in November 1898 at the extent to which the nation tolerated "the fatal un-American idea of imperialism and expansion. . . . The extent of this," he added, "presents to me a new startling phase in our national character, and a craze which, like a fever, must have its course." Senator George F. Hoar of Massachusetts anchored his speech of January 9, 1899, against annexation to this sentiment. (*Reading No. 5.*)

American conservatives, who opposed Philippine annexation with equal vigor, were concerned less with self-determination than with McKinley's defiance of the nation's traditional concern for means as well as ends. For them the United States possessed neither the naval forces adequate for the defense of its new far-flung commitments to Guam and the Philippines nor the necessary interest in building them. Both Andrew Carnegie, the American industrialist, and William Graham Sumner, the sociologist, challenged American expansion into the western Pacific as a needless and dangerous commitment of the United States to obligations which exceeded its interests and its power. (*Reading No. 6.*) Eventually, by a narrow margin, the annexationists had their way. The arguments of such expansionists as Senator Albert J. Beveridge carried the day (*Reading No. 7.*) The suddenness and completeness of the changes in the nation's outlook wrought by expansion measured the extent to which illusions emanating from the habit of easy success had supplanted analysis in the conduct of the nation's foreign affairs.

## IV

Having extended the United States commitments so easily and satisfactorily to the Philippines, the McKinley administration found no difficulty in rationalizing the further extension of the nation's Far Eastern political involvements to include China itself. During March 1898, before the outbreak of the Spanish American War, the United States government had rejected a British request for United States co-operation "in opposing any action of foreign powers which would tend to restrain the opening of China to the commerce of all nations." The American tradition of noninvolvement was still sufficiently powerful to urge caution. Both Germany and Russia, moreover, had assured the United States government that they had no intention of defying the principle of open trade in China. The Secretary of State rejected the British proposal, reminding the British Foreign Office that the immediate problem of Cuba was sufficient to occupy the energies of the nation.

When the United States, in the summer of 1899, finally issued the Open Door notes, its action was largely unilateral. The British no longer sought American support, for British officials themselves had become committed to the concept of special privilege. Nor is it certain that the influence in Washington of Alfred E. Hippisley, an officer of the Chinese Imperial Maritime Customs Service and a private British citizen, was significant. Secretary of State John Hay required no conversion to the principle of the Open Door. United States commercial diplomacy had always pursued equal trading privileges for Americans abroad, and United States merchants in China had long condemned the tendencies toward commercial exclusiveness in Chinese markets. Neither Hay nor his Far Eastern adviser, W. W. Rockhill, had any intention of serving the interest of any nation except the United States. Indeed, the phraseology of the Open Door notes so completely ignored British policy in China that the London government accepted the notes only with extreme reluctance and some modifications.

Hay's circular letter of September 6, 1899, committed the United States to the concept of commercial equality for all nations in the ports of China. This obligation to protect the amorphous Chinese Empire from external economic encroachment Hay expanded in July 1900 to encompass political and territorial encroachment as well. When the Boxer Rebellion compelled the powers to dispatch armed forces to China to rescue their nationals besieged in Peking, the Secretary declared American purpose in China to include the preservation of Chinese territorial and administrative integrity as well as the safeguarding for all nations "the principle of equal and impartial trade with all parts of the Chinese Empire." The sheer grandeur of Hay's apparent achievement merely confirmed the new illusion of omnipotence. Never before had the United States gained such unlimited commercial and humanitarian objectives at such negligible cost. For many Americans, Hay's contribution of the Open Door ranked him with the greatest of nineteenth-century American diplomatists. The eulogy by Senator Shelby M. Cullom of Illinois was characteristic:

> The magnitude of the man [Hay] will only appear in the magnitude of his work when it reaches its colossal proportions in the proper perspective of the past. . . . It is claiming nothing not fully accorded to him to say that at home he has long held a position beside John Quincy

Adams, Daniel Webster and Seward, the greatest of our Secretaries of
State. . . . It is suggestively true that his genius for statecraft has
gained fuller recognition in the Old World than among his own countrymen.

Actually the Open Door policy committed the nation politically and even
militarily to the *status quo* in a disorganized region remote from the United
States, concerning which other countries harbored deeper ambitions and where
they wielded greater power. Russia placed the Open Door in jeopardy as early
as 1901, when it made demands on Manchuria. Supported by the other Far
Eastern powers, including Japan, Hay managed through moral pressure alone
to prevent the establishment of Russian dominion in the Chinese province.
Yet the final sentence of the Russian note of April 5, 1901, contained a warning
for the future: "Remaining immovably faithful to its original program, which
has been so many times declared, the Imperial Government will quietly await
the further march of events."

That the nation was vastly overcommitted in the Far East was apparent to
American officials and analysts alike. Rockhill admitted to Hay: "I do not look
to the future with any great hopefulness. I greatly fear that under present
Chinese rule things will not improve; reforms will not be seriously undertaken
except under strong outside pressure. Trade will improve . . . but disintegration will go on, for there is no life, energy, or patriotism throughout the whole
governing class. It looks to me very dark ahead for China." During the Boxer
crisis of 1900, Josiah Quincy, a former First Assistant Secretary of State, warned
in the *North American Review* that Russia had far greater interests in China
than did the United States. (*Reading No. 8.*) Alfred Thayer Mahan, the well-
known naval historian and diplomatic analyst, in *The Problem of Asia* (1900),
pointed specifically to Russia and Japan as the two dominant nations in the
Far East. To defend the Open Door against such odds, he asserted, required
American naval power in evidence. (*Reading No. 9.*) Tragically, the new determination to maintain the *status quo* in eastern Asia brought Japan and
Russia into the focus of American concern and automatically rendered them
potential enemies of the United States. This proved to be especially true for
Japan. Perhaps no writer laid bare with such precision the crux of the American
problem in the Far East as did Sidney Brooks in *The Living Age,* February 6,
1904. His conclusion analyzed the nature of Hay's diplomacy:

> Diplomacy, to be successful, must ultimately rest on the implication
> of force. But the beginning and end of Mr. Hay's diplomacy in des-
> patch-writing. So astute a statesman in his heart of hearts must feel a
> sort of final impotence when he reflects that public opinion will sup-
> port him only so long as he spills ink, but no blood, and that his
> "protests" and "demands" are founded on nothing but bluff. One can-
> not bluff forever; even a Bismarck needs a Moltke in the background;
> and Mr. Hay, I suspect, may one of these days find himself manoeuvred
> into a position essentially that of the French at Fashoda.

V

No American was more aware of the pitfalls confronting United States diplomacy in the Far East than was Theodore Roosevelt. Like Mahan and other intellectuals of the day, Roosevelt possessed a deep sense of realism in foreign affairs. As a member of the McKinley administration he had been a leading proponent of expansion; as President he was mindful of the gap between the limited prospects of the nation's new commitments and the potential price required to maintain them. He upheld the Open Door in principle, but he recognized its limits as national policy. He wrote to Hay in May 1903: "As for China, I do not see that there is anything we can say, even by way of suggestion. The mendacity of the Russians is something appalling. The bad feature of the situation from our standpoint is that as yet it seems that we cannot fight to keep Manchuria open. I hate being in the position of seeming to bluster without backing it up. . . . I would like to try to get some idea of what we are to do in the future." To bring some balance between ends and means in Far Eastern policy, Roosevelt favored the augmentation of the country's naval power and the elimination of its crusading spirit. To Congressman Theodore Burton of Ohio he wrote, "To be rich, aggressive, and yet helpless in war, is to invite destruction." Roosevelt favored a naval base at Subig Bay in the Philippines as well as the fortification of Hawaii as essential for conserving the nation's interests in the Pacific. (*Reading No. 10.*) To impress Japan with the superiority of American naval power he sent the battle fleet on its historic cruise around the world in March 1907.

Roosevelt sought a realistic balance of power in the Far East. To this purpose he negotiated an end to the Russo-Japanese War in 1905. (*Reading No. 11.*) Thereafter he believed that United States policy in the Far East should avoid needlessly antagonizing the rising Japanese Empire with insulting anti-Japanese practices in the United States and defying its genuine interests in the Far East with an uncompromising adherence to the principle of the Open Door in China. (*Reading No. 12.*) He attempted to eliminate the Japanese threat to the Philippines with the Taft-Katsura agreement of 1905, and to the Open Door in China with the Root-Takahira agreement of 1908. To that end Roosevelt recognized the Japanese gains in Korea. But when his successor, William Howard Taft and Taft's Secretary of State, Philander C. Knox, resorted to the "neutralization" scheme to deprive Japan of its controlling interest in the Manchurian railroads, Roosevelt reminded them that Japan had far greater interests in Manchuria than did the United States and that only at the price of war could the nation maintain the Open Door in that portion of China. (*Reading No. 13.*)

Roosevelt likewise harbored a deep concern for the European balance of power. Like Hay and Mahan, he favored a closer *rapprochement* with Britain. On one occasion he wrote to British Minister Cecil Spring Rice: "I feel that England and the United States, beyond any other two powers should be friendly with one another, and what I can legitimately do to increase this friendliness will be done." After some reluctance he agreed to serve as honest broker at the Algeciras Conference, but his sympathies were decidedly with the British and

French. These powerful pro-British tendencies in the American outlook, so well represented by Roosevelt himself, were evidence of that vast revolution in European politics occasioned by the new German naval program which aimed at replacing England as master of the seas. Mahan detected the full impact of German ambition on the established balance of power and the relationship of the United States to Europe:

> In the determination of Germany to assert for herself a leading position in world politics, and in her avowed plan to build a navy which, when completed, will exceed in strength that which Great Britain now possesses, and be superior to any as yet contemplated by any other nation, including the United States, she is exercising her indisputable right as an independent state, answerable to no other for her actions; but in so doing she places herself in a position of preponderant force over every other state singly, and that not only with reference to local defense, but in respect to her contentions wherever they may arise throughout the whole world.

Tragically, German naval and diplomatic aggressiveness forced the British to re-evaluate their interests on the Continent and eventually drove them into an alliance with France and Russia. The dominant opinion within the United States followed the same anti-German course. As late as the 1890's American observers had lauded German policy as Europe's chief source of stability; after 1900 they viewed it as a danger to Europe's peace and security. (*Reading No. 14.*) Herbert Croly in his book *The Promise of American Life* (1909) presented a mature and comprehensive evaluation of the world-wide interests and commitments of the United States. He concurred with Roosevelt that the nation could no longer rationalize away its responsibilities under such popular beliefs as the Monroe Doctrine. (*Reading No. 15.*) "That idea," he wrote, "has given a sort of religious sanctity to the national tradition of isolationism; and it will survive its own utility because it flatters American democratic vanity. . . ." For Croly it was essential that the nation mark well its obligations in Europe and Asia and create policies to meet them. What mattered in Europe, he pointed out, was the fact that three powers—England, France, and Italy—had much more to lose than to gain by war. Any threat to these *status quo* nations, therefore, would demand a sound and well-informed American response. Such advice was lost, however, on the Taft administration, which married national policy to the requirements of business. Influenced by such proponents of expanding American investments in China as William Straight, it drew away from Europe and re-instituted the United States's pro-Chinese mission in the Far East which Roosevelt, in his concern for Japanese interests, had abandoned. (*Reading No. 16.*)

That American expansion into the Pacific failed to challenge the nation's isolationist tradition reflects fundamentally the ease whereby the acquisition of Hawaii, Guam, and the Philippines, as well as the establishment of the Open Door in China, were achieved. Even in the Caribbean, where the nation faced no competing power, the new commitments created the illusion of huge accomplishment at a minimum of financial and military expenditure. Thus the nation could underwrite enthusiastically the policies of expansion while refusing to assume an imperial outlook. As Sidney Brooks wrote early in the century, "An empire is easier to come by than the spirit of empire, and we altogether overrate American Conservatism, if we think that because they have the former they must also have the latter." The new sense of obligation to expand did not include, except on the part of a brilliant minority of American writers, any gauging of the forces being unleashed by British-German rivalry, or any evaluation of the meaning of that rivalry for the American future. Perhaps the noted English student of American politics, James Bryce, described the pre-war attitudes of the American people with some precision when he wrote: "America lives in a world of her own. . . . Safe from attack, safe even from menace, she hears from afar the warring cries of European races and faiths, as the gods of Epicurus listened to the murmurs of the unhappy earth spread out beneath their golden dwellings. . . . Had Canada or Mexico grown to be a great power, had France not sold Louisiana, or had England, rooted on the American continent, become a military despotism, the United States could not indulge the easy optimism which makes them tolerate the faults of their government. As it is, that which might prove to a European state a mortal disease is here nothing worse than a teasing ailment. Since the War of Secession ended, no serious danger has arisen either from within or from without to alarm transatlantic statesmen. Social convulsions from within, warlike assaults from without, seem now as unlikely to try the fabric of the American Constitution, as an earthquake to rend the walls of the Capitol. . . . The vessel may not be any better built, or found, or rigged than are those which carry the fortunes of the great nations of Europe. She is certainly not better navigated. But for the present at least—it may not always be so—she sails upon a summer sea."

# I | The Conservative Argument Against Expansion, October 1893 *

American penetration of the Pacific after 1870 entailed a steady expansion of the nation's political and military commitments. All of this was in defiance of an established policy of hoarding American power by limiting American obligations that might demand war to the Western Hemisphere itself. No American writer or political leader opposed more forcefully the expansionist pressures of the early 'nineties, especially as they incorporated Hawaii, than Carl Schurz.

✍

. . . In our present condition we have over all the great nations of the world one advantage of incalculable value. We are the only one that is not in any of its parts threatened by powerful neighbors; the only one not under any necessity of keeping up a large armament either on land or water for the security of its possessions; the only one that can turn all the energies of its population to productive employment; the only one that has an entirely free hand. This is a blessing for which the American people can never be too thankful. It should not be lightly jeoparded.

This advantage, I say, we have *in our present condition*. We occupy a compact part of the American Continent, bounded by great oceans on the east and west, and on the north and south by neighbors neither hostile in spirit nor by themselves formidable in strength. We have a population approaching seventy millions and steadily growing, industrious, law-abiding, and patriotic; not a military, but, when occasion calls for it, a warlike, people, ever ready to furnish to the service of the country an almost unlimited supply of vigorous, brave, and remarkably intelligent soldiers. Our national wealth is great, and increases rapidly. Our material resources may, compared with those of other nations, be called inexhaustible. Our territory is large, but our means of interior communication are such as to minimize the inconveniences of distance. In case of war a hostile naval power might, indeed, sweep what maritime commerce we have from the seas—a compliment we could return with a comparatively small number of cruisers—and it might blockade some of our seaports and molest some of our coasts, without, however, seriously impairing our strength or doing more than excite the war spirit among our people to greater heat. But no European enemy could invade our soil without bringing from a great distance a strong land force; and no force that could possibly be brought from such a distance, were it ever so well prepared, could hope to strike a crippling blow by a sudden dash, and thus to force us to a peace, or to effect a lodgement within our boundaries without the certainty of being soon overwhelmed by an easy concentration of immensely superior numbers. Nor could a European enemy hope

* Carl Schurz, "Manifest Destiny," *Harper's New Monthly Magazine*, LXXXVII (October 1893), 743–4.

to raise a sufficient land force by alliances on this continent, for neither north nor south of us can armies be mustered strong enough seriously to threaten us. In other words, in our compact continental stronghold we are substantially unassailable. We present no vulnerable point of importance. There is nothing that an enemy can take away from us and hope to hold. We can carry on a defensive warfare indefinitely without danger to ourselves, and meanwhile, with our enormous resources in men and means, prepare for offensive operations.

The prospect of such a war will be to any European nation, or any league of European nations, extremely discouraging, especially as not one of them has the same free hand that we have. Every one of them is within the reach of dangerous rivals, whom a favorable opportunity might tempt to proceed to hostilities, and such an opportunity would certainly be presented by a long and exhausting war with the United States. And this very circumstance would afford to this republic in such a case the possibility of alliances which would enable it to pass from its defensive warfare to a most vigorous offensive one.

Seeing the impossibility, under existing conditions, of striking against us a quick blow that would have any decisive consequences, and seeing also that a war carried on upon our own ground would, owing to our unlimited staying power, be practically a war without end, and present chances of combinations most dangerous to them—recognizing these obvious facts, all those powers will be naturally disposed to go to the extreme of honorable concession in order to avoid hostilities with the United States. In fact, we can hardly get into a war unless it be of our own seeking. And this inestimable advantage of commanding among the nations of the world the greatest degree of consideration and deference without any necessity on our part of keeping up burdensome military and naval establishments we enjoy now and shall continue to enjoy so long as we are so situated that in case of war we can defend all our possessions without leaving our own continental ground, on which we can fight with every condition in our favor.

This advantage will be very essentially impaired if we present to a possible enemy a vulnerable point of attack which we have to defend, but cannot defend without going out of our impregnable stronghold, away from the seat of our power, to fight on ground on which the enemy may appear in superior strength, and have the conditions in *his* favor. Such a vulnerable point will be presented by the Hawaiian Islands if we annex them, as well as by any outlying possession of importance. It will not be denied that in case of war with a strong naval power the defence of Hawaii would require very strong military and naval establishments there, and a fighting fleet as large and efficient as that of the enemy; and in case of a war with a combination of great naval powers, it might require a fleet much larger than that of any of them. Attempts of the enemy to gain an important advantage by a sudden stroke, which would be entirely harmless if made on our continental stronghold, might have an excellent chance of success if made on our distant insular possession, and then the whole war could be made to turn upon that point, where the enemy might concentrate his forces as easily as we, or even more easily, and be our superior on the decisive field of operations. It is evident that thus the immense advantage we now enjoy of a substantially unassailable defensive position would be lost. We would no longer possess the inestimable privilege of being stronger and more secure than any other nation without a large and costly armament. Hawaii, or whatever other outlying domain, would be our Achilles' heel. Other nations would observe it, and regard us no longer as invulnerable. If we acquire Hawaii, we acquire not an addition to our strength, but a dangerous element of weakness. . . .

## 2 | Grover Cleveland and the Conservative Tradition of American Diplomacy, December 1895 *

In resisting the humanitarian sentiment which demanded United States intervention in the Cuban revolution, President Cleveland reminded Congress of the established American diplomatic tradition, characterized by Secretary of State Seward's refusal to engage in any crusade in behalf of the Poles, that external objectives be limited to the national interest alone.

✍

. . . Cuba is again gravely disturbed. An insurrection in some respects more active than the last preceding revolt, which continued from 1868 to 1878, now exists in a large part of the eastern interior of the island, menacing even some populations on the coast. Besides deranging the commercial exchanges of the island, of which our country takes the predominant share, this flagrant condition of hostilities, by arousing sentimental sympathy and inciting adventurous support among our people, has entailed earnest effort on the part of this Government to enforce obedience to our neutrality laws and to prevent the territory of the United States from being abused as a vantage ground from which to aid those in arms against Spanish sovereignty.

Whatever may be the traditional sympathy of our countrymen as individuals with a people who seem to be struggling for larger autonomy and greater freedom, deepened, as such sympathy naturally must be, in behalf of our neighbors, yet the plain duty of their Government is to observe in good faith the recognized obligations of international relationship. The performance of this duty should not be made more difficult by a disregard on the part of our citizens of the obligations growing out of their allegiance to their country, which should restrain them from violating as individuals the neutrality which the nation of which they are members is bound to observe in its relations to friendly sovereign

* Cleveland's message to Congress, December 2, 1895, *Messages and Papers of the Presidents,* James D. Richardson, ed. (Washington, 1898), IX: 636.

states. Though neither the warmth of our people's sympathy with the Cuban insurgents, nor our loss and material damage consequent upon the futile endeavors thus far made to restore peace and order, nor any shock our humane sensibilities may have received from the cruelties which appear to especially characterize this sanguinary and fiercely conducted war, have in the least shaken the determination of the Government to honestly fulfill every international obligation, yet it is to be earnestly hoped on every ground that the devastation of armed conflict may speedily be stayed and order and quiet restored to the distracted island, bringing in their train the activity and thrift of peaceful pursuits. . . .

## 3 | William McKinley's War Message, April 1898 *

Cleveland's effort to retain the realistic tradition of American diplomacy under McKinley gave way to a giant crusade in behalf of the downtrodden people of Cuba. The oppression of the Cubans was too close at hand, and the power required to liberate them was too negligible to warrant or encourage any close calculation of national interest. Previously the United States avoided any commitment to a revolutionary movement until that movement had established beyond question its capacity to maintain itself in power. In the Cuban crisis, as McKinley noted in his war message of April 11, 1898, the United States would interfere in the imperial affairs of another nation to assure the success of a revolutionary upheaval. McKinley's humanitarian motivation in recommending war emanated from his conviction that neither Spain nor the Cuban insurgents possessed the power, of themselves, to terminate the struggle for Cuba. Peace for the Cuban people was the cause of humanity, and it could be achieved only through American military involvement. Only in the final two paragraphs did the President acknowledge the receipt of Minister Woodford's communication of April 5 which announced the Spanish capitulation.

✍

Obedient to that precept of the Constitution which commands the President to give from time to time to the Congress information of the state of the Union and to recommend to their consideration such measures as he shall judge necessary and expedient, it becomes my duty now to address your body with regard to the grave crisis that has arisen in the relations of the United States to Spain by reason of the warfare that for more than three years has raged in the neighboring island of Cuba.

* *Messages and Papers of the Presidents* (Washington, 1899), X: 139–50.

I do so because of the intimate connection of the Cuban question with the state of our own Union and the grave relation the course which it is now incumbent upon the nation to adopt must needs bear to the traditional policy of our Government if it is to accord with the precepts laid down by the founders of the Republic and religiously observed by succeeding Administrations to the present day.

The present revolution is but the successor of other similar insurrections which have occurred in Cuba against the dominion of Spain, extending over a period of nearly half a century, each of which, during its progress, has subjected the United States to great effort and expense in enforcing its neutrality laws, caused enormous losses to American trade and commerce, caused irritations, annoyance, and disturbance among our citizens, and, by the exercise of cruel, barbarous, and uncivilized practices of warfare, shocked the sensibilities and offended the humane sympathies of our people.

Since the present revolution began, in February, 1895, this country has seen the fertile domain at our threshold ravaged by fire and sword in the course of a struggle unequaled in the history of the island and rarely paralleled as to the numbers of the combatants and the bitterness of the contest by any revolution of modern times where a dependent people striving to be free have been opposed by the power of the sovereign state. . . .

The efforts of Spain were increased, both by the dispatch of fresh levies to Cuba and by the addition to the horrors of the strife of a new and inhuman phase happily unprecedented in the modern history of civilized Christian peoples. The policy of devastation and concentration, inaugurated by the Captain-General's bando [edict] of October 21, 1896, in the Province of Pinar del Rio was thence extended to embrace all of the island to which the power of the Spanish arms was able to reach by occupation or by military operations. The peasantry, including all dwelling in the open agricultural interior, were driven into the garrison towns or isolated places held by the troops.

The raising and movement of provisions of all kinds were interdicted. The fields were laid waste, dwellings unroofed and fired, mills destroyed, and in short, everything that could desolate the land and render it unfit for human habitation or support was commanded by one or the other of the contending parties and executed by all the powers at their disposal. . . .

In this state of affairs my Administration found itself confronted with the grave problem of its duty. My message of last December reviewed the situation and narrated the steps taken with a view to relieving its acuteness and opening the way to some form of honorable settlement. The assassination of the prime minister, Canovas, led to a change of government in Spain. The former administration, pledged to subjugation without concession, gave place to that of a more liberal party, committed long in advance to a policy of reform, involving the wider principle of home rule for Cuba and Puerto Rico.

The overtures of this Government, made through its new envoy, General Woodford, and looking to an immediate and effective amelioration of the condition of the island, although not accepted to the extent of admitted mediation in any shape, were met by assurances that home rule, in advanced phase, would be forthwith offered to Cuba, without waiting for the war to end, and that more humane methods should thenceforth prevail in the conduct of hostilities. Coincidentally with these declarations, the new Government of Spain continued and completed the policy already begun by its predecessor, of testifying friendly regard for this nation by releasing American citzens held under one charge or another connected with the insurrection, so that by the end of November not a single person entitled in any way to our national protection remained in the Spanish prison. . . .

Thousands of lives have already been saved. The necessity for a change in the condition of the reconcentrados is recognized by the Spanish Government. Within a few days past the orders of General Weyler have been revoked; the reconcentrados, it is said, are to be permitted to return to their homes and aided to resume the self-supporting pursuits of peace. Public works have been ordered to give them employment, and a sum of $600,000 has been appropriated for their relief.

The war in Cuba is of such a nature that short of subjugation or extermination a final military victory for either side seems impracticable. The alternative lies in the physical exhaustion of one or the other party, or perhaps of both—a condition which in effect ended the ten years' war by the truce of Zanjon. The prospect of such a protraction and conclusion of the present strife is a contingency hardly to be contemplated with equanimity by the civilized world, and least of all by the United States, affected and injured as we are, deeply and intimately, by its very existence.

Realizing this, it appeared to be my duty, in a spirit of true friendliness, no less to Spain than to the Cubans who have so much to lose by the prolongation of the struggle, to seek to bring about an immediate termination of the war. To this end I submitted, on the 27th ultimo, as a result of much representation and correspondence, through the United States minister at Madrid, propositions to the Spanish Government looking to an armistice until October 1 for the negotiation of peace with the good offices of the President.

In additon, I asked the immediate revocation of the order of reconcentration, so as to permit the people to return to their farms and the needy to be relieved with provisions and supplies from the United States, cooperating with the Spanish authorities, so as to afford full relief.

The reply of the Spanish cabinet was received on the night of the 31st ultimo. It offered, as the means to bring about peace in Cuba, to confide the preparation thereof to the insular parliament, inasmuch as the concurrence of that body would be necessary to reach a final result, it being, however, understood that the powers reserved by the constitution to the central Government are not lessened or diminished. As the Cuban parliament does not meet until the 4th of May next, the Spanish Government would not object, for its part, to accept at once a suspension of hostilities if asked for by the insurgents from the general in chief, to whom it would pertain, in such case, to determine the duration and conditions of the armistice.

The propositions submitted by General Woodford and the reply of the Spanish Government were both in the form of brief memoranda, the texts of which are before me, and are substantially in the language above given. The function of the Cuban parliament in the matter of "preparing" peace and the manner of its doing so are not expressed in the Spanish memorandum; but from General Woodford's explanatory reports of preliminary discussions preceding the final conference it is understood that the Spanish Government stands ready to give the insular congress full powers to settle the terms of peace with the insurgents—whether by direct negotiation or indirectly by means of legislation does not appear.

With this last overture in the direction of immediate peace, and its disappointing reception by Spain, the Executive is brought to the end of his effort. . . .

I said in my message of December last, "It is to be seriously considered whether the Cuban insurrection possesses beyond dispute the attributes of statehood which alone can demand the recognition of belligerency in its favor." The same requirement must certainly be no less seriously considered when the graver issue of recognizing independence is in question, for no less positive test can be applied to the greater act than to the lesser; while, on the other hand, the influences and consequences of the struggle upon the internal policy of the recognizing State, which form important factors when the recognition of belligerency is concerned, are secondary, if not rightly eliminable, factors when the real question is whether the community claiming recognition is or is not independent beyond peradventure.

Nor from the standpoint of expediency do I think it would be wise or prudent for this Government to recognize at the present time the independence of the so-called Cuban Republic. Such recognition is not necessary in order to enable the United States to intervene and pacify the island. To commit this country now to the recognition of any particular government in Cuba might subject us to embarrassing conditions of international obligation toward the organization so recognized. In case of intervention our conduct would be subject to the approval or disapproval of such government. We would be required to submit to its direction and to assume to it the mere relation of a friendly ally.

When it shall appear hereafter that there is within the island a government capable of performing the duties and discharging the functions of a separate nation, and having, as a matter of fact, the proper forms and attributes of nationality, such government can be promptly and readily recognized and the relations and interests of the United States with such nation adjusted.

There remain the alternative forms of intervention to end the war, either as an impartial neutral by imposing a rational compromise between the contestants, or as the active ally of the one party or the other.

As to the first it is not to be forgotten that during the last few months the relation of the United States has virtually been one of friendly intervention in many ways, each not of itself conclusive, but all tending to the exertion of a potential influence toward an ultimate pacific result, just and honorable to all interests concerned. The spirit of all our acts hitherto has been an earnest, unselfish desire for peace and prosperity in Cuba, untarnished by differences between us and Spain, and unstained by the blood of American citizens.

The forcible intervention of the United States as a neutral to stop the war, according to the large dictates of humanity and following many historical precedents where neighboring States have interfered to check the hopeless sacrifices of life by internecine conflicts beyond their borders, is justifiable on rational grounds. It involves, however, hostile constraint upon both the parties to the contest as well to enforce a truce as to guide the eventual settlement.

The grounds for such intervention may be briefly summarized as follows:

First. In the cause of humanity and to put an end to the barbarities, bloodshed, starvation, and horrible miseries now existing there, and which the parties of the conflict are either unable or unwilling to stop or mitigate. It is no answer to say this is all in another country, belonging to another nation, and is therefore none of our business. It is specially our duty, for it is right at our door.

Second. We owe it to our citizens in Cuba to afford them that protection and indemnity for life and property which no government there can or will afford, and to that end to terminate the conditions that deprive them of legal protection.

Third. The right to intervene may be justified by the very serious injury to the commerce, trade, and business of our people, and by the wanton destruction of property and devastation of the island.

Fourth, and which is of the utmost importance. The present condition of affairs in Cuba is a constant menace to our peace, and entails upon this Government an enormous expense. With such a conflict waged for years in an island so near us and with which our people have such trade and business relations; when the lives and liberty of our citizens are in constant danger and their property destroyed and themselves ruined; where our trading vessels are liable to seizure and are seized at our very door by war ships of a foreign nation, the expeditions of filibustering that we are powerless to prevent altogether, and the irritating questions and entanglements thus arising—all these and others that I need not mention, with the resulting strained relations, are a constant menace to our peace, and compel us to keep on a semiwar footing with a nation with which we are at peace.

These elements of danger and disorder already pointed out have been strikingly illustrated by a tragic event which has deeply and justly moved the American people. I have already transmitted to Congress the report of the naval court of inquiry on the destruction of the battle ship *Maine* in the harbor of Havana during the night of the 15th of February. The destruction of that noble vessel has filled the national heart with inexpressible horror. Two hundred and fifty-eight brave sailors and marines and two officers of our Navy, reposing in the fancied security of a friendly harbor, have been hurled to death, grief and want brought to their homes, and sorrow to the nation.

The naval court of inquiry, which, it is needless to say, commands the unqualified confidence of the Government, was unanimous in its conclusion that the destruction of the *Maine* was caused by an exterior explosion, that of a submarine mine. It did not assume to place the responsibility. That remains to be fixed.

In any event the destruction of the *Maine,* by whatever exterior cause, is a patent and impressive proof of a state of things in Cuba that is intolerable. That condition is thus shown to be such that the Spanish Government can not assure safety and security to a vessel of the American Navy in the harbor of Havana on a mission of peace, and rightfully there.

Further referring in this connection to recent diplomatic correspondence, a dispatch from our minister to Spain, of the 26th ultimo, contained the statement that the Spanish minister for foreign affairs assured him positively that Spain will do all that the highest honor and justice require in the matter of the *Maine.* The reply above referred to of the 31st ultimo also contained an expression of the readiness of Spain to submit to an arbitration all the differences which can arise in this matter, which is subsequently explained by the note of the Spanish minister at Washington of the 10th instant, as follows:

> As to the question of fact which springs from the diversity of views between the reports of the American and Spanish boards, Spain proposes that the facts be ascertained by an impartial investigation by experts, whose decision Spain accepts in advance.

To this I have made no reply. . . .

The long trial has proved that the object for which Spain has waged the war can not be attained. The fire of insurrection may flame or may smolder with varying seasons, but it has not been and it is plain that it can not be extinguished by present methods. The only hope of relief and repose from a condition which can no longer be endured is the enforced pacification of Cuba. In the name of humanity, in the name of civilization, in behalf of endangered American interests which give us the right and the duty to speak and to act, the war in Cuba must stop.

In view of these facts and of these considerations, I ask the Congress to authorize and empower the President to take measures to secure full and final termination of hostilities between the Government of Spain and the people of Cuba, and to secure in the island the establishment of a stable government, capable of maintaining order and observing its international obligations, insuring peace and tranquility and the security of its citizens as well as our own, and to use the military and naval forces of the United States as may be necessary for these purposes. . . .

The issue is now with the Congress. It is a solemn responsibility. I have exhausted every effort to relieve the intolerable condition of affairs which is at our doors. Prepared to execute every obligation imposed upon me by the Constitution and the law, I await your action.

Yesterday, and since the preparation of the foregoing message, official information was received by me that the latest decree of the Queen Regent of Spain directs General Blanco, in order to prepare and facilitate peace, to proclaim a suspension of hostilities, the duration and details of which have not yet been communicated to me.

This fact with every other pertinent consideration will, I am sure, have your just and careful attention in the solemn deliberation upon which you are about to enter. If this measure attains a successful result, then our aspirations as a Christian, peace-loving people will be realized. If it fails, it will be only another justification for our contemplated action.

4 | McKinley's Address at the Trans-Mississippi Exposition at Omaha, Nebraska, October 12, 1898 *

This address, delivered on McKinley's tour of the Midwest to test public senti- ment on the Philippine issue, revealed with remarkable clarity the changes being wrought in the nation's diplomatic tradition by the events of 1898. At Omaha the President stressed both the sacrifice of the country in the cause of humanity and the necessity of continuing along the path of duty in settling the issues of the Philippines and Puerto Rico. The applause which greeted McKinley's humanitarian sentiment, now applied to actual American policies abroad for the first time in the Republic's history, was carefully recorded by a secretary. It convinced McKinley that the American people would support an expansionist policy.

✍

. . . It has been said by some one that the normal condition of nations is war. That is not true of the United States. We never enter upon a war until every effort for peace without it has been exhausted. Ours has never been a military government. Peace, with whose blessings we have been so singularly favored, is the national desire and the goal of every American aspiration. [Ap- plause].

On the 25th of April, for the first time for more than a generation, the United States sounded the call to arms. The banners of war were unfurled; the best and bravest from every section responded; a mighty army was enrolled; the North and the South vied with each other in patriotic devotion; science was invoked to furnish its most effective weapons; factories were rushed to supply equipment; the youth and the veteran joined in freely offering their services to their country; volunteers and regulars and all the people rallied to the support of the republic. There was no break in the line, no halt in the march, no fear in the heart [great applause]; no resistance to the patriotic impulse at home, no successful resistance to the patriotic spirit of the troops fighting in distant water or on a foreign shore. [Continued applause.]

What a wonderful experience it has been from the standpoint of patriotism

* New York *Tribune,* October 13, 1898.

and achievement! The storm broke so suddenly that it was here almost before we realized it. Our navy was too small, though forceful with its modern equipment, and most fortunate in its trained officers and sailors. Our army had years ago been reduced to a peace footing. We had only twenty-eight thousand available troops when the war was declared, but the account which officers and men gave of themselves on the battlefield has never been surpassed. . . .

The heroes of Manila and Santiago and Porto Rico have made immortal history. They are worthy successors and descendants of Washington and Greene; of Paul Jones, Decatur, and Hull, and of Grant, Sheridan, Sherman, and Logan; of Farragut, Porter, and Cushing, of Lee, Jackson, and Longstreet. [Tremendous applause.]

New names stand out on the honor-roll of the nation's great men, and with them, unnamed, stand the heroes of the trenches and the forecastle, invincible in battle and uncomplaining in death. [Great applause.] The intelligent, loyal, indomitable soldier and sailor and marine, regular and volunteer, are entitled to equal praise as having done their whole duty, whether at home or under the baptism of foreign fire. [Applause.]

Who will dim the splendor of their achievements? Who will withhold from them their well-earned distinction? Who will intrude detraction at this time to belittle the manly spirit of the American youth and impair the usefulness of the American army? Who will embarrass the government by sowing seeds of dissatisfaction among the brave men who stand ready to serve and die, if need be, for their country? Who will darken the counsels of the republic in this hour, requiring the united wisdom of all? [Cheers and prolonged applause.]

Shall we deny to ourselves what the rest of the world so freely and so justly accords to us? [General cry of "No!"] The men who endured in the short but decisive struggle its hardships, its privations, whether in field or camp, on ship or in the siege, and planned and achieved its victories, will never tolerate impeachment, either direct or indirect, of those who won a peace whose great gain to civilization is yet unknown and unwritten. [Tremendous applause.]

The faith of a Christian nation recognizes the hand of Almighty God in the ordeal through which we have passed. Divine favor seemed manifest everywhere. In fighting for humanity's sake we have been signally blessed. We did not seek war. To avoid it, if this could be done in honor and justice to the rights of our neighbors and ourselves, was our constant prayer. The war was no more invited by us than were the questions which are laid at our door by its results. [Great applause.] Now as then we will do our duty. [Continued applause.] The problems will not be solved in a day. Patience will be required—patience combined with sincerity of purpose and unshaken resolution to do right, seeking only the highest good of the nation, and recognizing no other obligation, pursuing no other path, but that of duty. . . .

Senator Hoar, leader of the anti-imperialist forces in Congress, rebelled at the defiance of the principles of the Declaration of Independence involved in the forcible annexation of the Philippine populace to the United States.

🖎

. . . There are two lessons our fathers learned from the history of Greece which they hoped their children would remember—the danger of disunion and domestic strife and an indulgence in the greed and lust of empire. The Greeks stood together against the power of Persia as the American States stood together against the tyranny of England. For us the danger of disunion has happily passed by. Our Athenians and our Spartans are bound and welded together again, each lending to the other the strength of their steel and the sharpness of their tempered blade in an indissoluble Union. Our danger to-day is from the lust of empire. It is a little remarkable that the temptation that besets us now lured and brought to ruin the Athenian people in ancient times. I hope that we may be able to resist and avert that danger as we resisted and averted the peril of disunion. . . .

I hope not to weary the Senate by reiteration. But this is the greatest question, this question of the power and authority of our Constitution in this matter, I had almost said, that had been discussed among mankind from the beginning of time. Certainly it is the greatest question ever discussed in this Chamber from the beginning of the Government. The question is this: Have we the right, as doubtless we have the physical power, to enter upon the government of ten or twelve million subject people without constitutional restraint? . . .

Mr. President, I am no strict constructionist. I am no alarmist. I believe this country to be a nation, a sovereign nation. I believe Congress to possess all the powers which are necessary to accomplish under the most generous and liberal construction the great objects which the men who framed the Constitution and the people who adopted it desired to accomplish by its instrumentality. I was bred, I might almost say I was born, in the faith, which I inherited from the men whose blood is in my veins, of the party of Hamilton and Washington and Webster and Sumner, and not in that of Madison or Calhoun or the strict constructionists. . . .

. . . The powers of the United States must be affirmatively delegated or they do not exist. The powers claimed by the States must be expressly prohibited or they do exist. And there are other powers not delegated to the United States and prohibited to the States which are reserved up to the people; that is, there are powers which the people of the United States mean shall not be exercised

* *Congressional Record,* 55th Congress, 3rd Sess., Part I, 494–6, 498, 503.

by anybody on the face of the earth, so far as their jurisdiction and authority extend, unless they shall hereafter change their mind and grant them. . . .

But the question with which we now have to deal is whether Congress may conquer and may govern, without their consent and against their will, a foreign nation, a separate, distinct, and numerous people, a territory not hereafter to be populated by Americans, to be formed into American States and to take its part in fulfilling and executing the purposes for which the Constitution was framed, whether it may conquer, control, and govern this people, not for the general welfare, common defense, more perfect union, more blessed liberty of the people of the United States, but for some real or fancied benefit to be conferred against their desire upon the people so governed or in discharge of some fancied obligation to them, and not to the people of the United States.

Now, Mr. President, the question is whether the men who framed the Constitution, or the people who adopted it, meant to confer that power among the limited and restrained powers of the sovereign nation that they were creating. . . .

I declare not only that this is not among the express powers conferred upon the sovereignty they created, that it is not among the powers necessarily or reasonably or conveniently implied for the sake of carrying into effect the purposes of that instrument, but that it is a power which it can be demonstrated by the whole contemporaneous history and by our whole history since until within six months they did not mean should exist—a power that our fathers and their descendants have ever loathed and abhorred—and that they believed that no sovereign on earth could rightfully exercise it, and that no people on earth could rightfully confer it. They not only did not mean to confer it, but they would have cut off their right hands, every one of them, sooner than set them to an instrument which should confer it. . . .

Mr. President, the persons who favor the ratification of this treaty without conditions and without amendment differ among themselves certainly in their views, purposes, and opinions, and as they are so many of them honest and well-meaning persons, we have the right to say in their actual and real opinions. In general, the state of mind and the utterance of the lips are in accord. If you ask them what they want, you are answered with a shout; "Three cheers for the Flag! Who will dare to haul it down? Hold on to everything you can get. The United States is strong enough to do what it likes. The Declaration of Independence and the counsel of Washington and the Constitution of the United States have grown rusty and musty. They are for little countries and not for great ones. There is no moral law for strong nations. America has outgrown Americanism."

Mr. President, when I hear from some of our friends this new doctrine of constitutional interpretation, when I hear attributed to men in high places, counselors of the President himself, that we have outgrown the principles and the interpretation which were sufficient for our 13 States and our 3,000,000 of people in the time of their weakness, and by which they have grown to 75,000,000 and 45 States, in this hour of our strength, it seems to me these counselors would have this nation of ours like some prosperous thriving youth who reverses suddenly all the maxims and rules of living in which he has been educated and says to himself, "I am too big for the Golden Rule. I have outgrown the Ten Commandments. I no longer need the straight waistcoat of the moral Law. Like Jeshuron, I will wax fat and kick." . . .

Now, Mr. President, there are Senators here yet hesitating as to what their action may be in the future, who will tell you that they loathe and hate this doctrine that we may buy nations at wholesale; that we may acquire imperial powers or imperial regions by conquest; that we may make vassal states and subject peoples without constitutional restraint, and against their will, and without any restraint but our own discretion.

Now, I appeal to those gentlemen whenever and wherever they may be called to act to answer to themselves as the one great proposition, the greatest question that has ever been or ever will be put to them in their lives, the question, not of a year or of a Congress, not of a generation, not of a century, but a question pertaining rather to the great period of a national life, I might almost say to the great eternity of national life, whether—even if that action be permitted or not by the letter of the Constitution—it be not repugnant to its form and spirit. Will they commit themselves in principle and in doctrine to such a policy, and then say that they will consider hereafter the question of how they will act under it? . . .

. . . Is it true, or is it a falsehood, that the doctrine that governments derive their just power from the consent of the governed is to be applied in interpreting the Constitution of the United States, and controlling the action of the legislature it creates, as if the words were written between the lines of the Constitution itself? . . .

Is it true that liberty-loving Vermont, that up to this moment has never uttered a thought or spoken a word or given a vote but for freedom, is to repudiate these golden utterances now? Why, Mr. President, I should think the insulted eagles would forsake her mountains if it were reported that her vote had been cast to trample under foot these mighty doctrines of liberty.

Are the thought and the spirit to prevail, and the interpretation we are to give the great document that which secures liberty to the people of the United States, or to people everywhere where the flag floats?

Now, I claim that under the Declaration of Independence you can not govern a foreign territory, a foreign people, another people than your own, that you can not subjugate them and govern them against their will, because you think it is for their good, when they do not; because you think you are going to give them the blessings of liberty. You have no right at the cannon's mouth to impose on an unwilling people your Declaration of Independence and your Constitution and your notions of freedom and notions of what is good. . . .

# 6 | The Conservative Argument Against Annexation of the Philippines, 1898–99 *

Throughout the seventy-five years preceding 1898 the American concert with Britain had provided an adequate force to cover the foreign commitments of the United States. It was clear in 1898 and 1899, however, that the nation was undertaking a series of commitments in the Far East without any thought of developing a sustained or even remotely adequate policy to bring its power into balance with its new obligations. American foreign policy was fast losing its solvency. In the following article Andrew Carnegie argued against annexation on the basis of American interest. To Carnegie's mind the Philippines would contribute nothing to American commerce. Like Carl Schurz, he believed that all United States commitments should be limited to the Western Hemisphere, where the nation possessed a clear strategic advantage. With deep reluctance Carnegie accepted the acquisition of Hawaii, but for him the annexation of the Philippines marked the parting of the ways.

✒

. . . In considering the issue now before us, the agitator, the demagogue, has no part. Not feeling, not passion, but deliberate judgment alone should have place. The question should be calmly weighed; it is not a matter of party, nor of class; for the fundamental interest of every citizen is a common interest, that which is best for the poorest being best for the richest. Let us, therefore, reason together and be well assured, before we change our position, that we are making no plunge into an abyss. . . .

Some of the organs of manufacturing interests, we observe, favor foreign possessions as necessary or helpful markets for our products. But the exports of the United States this year are greater than those of any other nation in the world. Even Britain's exports are less, yet Britain "possesses," it is said, a hundred "colonies" and "dependencies" scattered all over the world. The fact that the United States has none does not prevent her products and manufactures from invading Japan, China, Australia, New Zealand, Canada, and all parts of the world in competition with those of the British. "Possession" of colonies or dependencies is not necessary for trade reasons. What her colonies are valued for, and justly so, by Britain, is the happiness and pride which the mother feels in her children. The instinct of motherhood is gratified, and no one living places a higher estimate upon the sentiment than I do. Britain is the kindest of mothers, and well deserves the devotion of her children.

If we could establish colonies of Americans, and grow Americans in any part of the world now unpopulated and unclaimed by any of the great powers, and thus follow the example of Britain, heart and mind might tell us that we should

* Andrew Carnegie, "Distant Possessions—The Parting of the Ways," *The North American Review*, CLXVII (August 1898), 239–48.

have to think twice, yea, thrice, before deciding adversely. Even then our decision should be adverse; but there is at present no such question before us. What we have to face is the question whether we should embark upon the difficult and dangerous policy of undertaking the government of alien races in lands where it is impossible for our own race to be produced. . . .

Up to this time we have disclaimed all intention to interfere with affairs beyond our own continent, and only claimed the right to watch over American interests according to the Monroe Doctrine, which is now firmly established. This carries with it serious responsibilities, no doubt, which we cannot escape. European nations must consult us upon territorial questions pertaining to our Continent, but this makes no tremendous demand upon our military or naval forces. We are at home, as it were, near our base, and sure of the support of the power in whose behalf and on whose request we may act. If it be found essential to possess a coaling station at Porto Rico for future possible, though not probable, contingencies, there is no insuperable objection. Neither would the control of the West Indies be alarming, if pressed upon us by Britain, since the islands are small and the populations must remain insignificant and without national aspirations. Besides, they are upon our own shores, American in every sense. Their defense by us would be easy. No protest need be entered against such legitimate and peaceful expansion in our own hemisphere, should events work in that direction. I am no "Little" American, afraid of growth, either in population or territory, provided always that the new territory be American and that it will produce Americans, and not foreign races bound in time to be false to the Republic in order to be true to themselves.

As I write, the cable announces the annexation of Hawaii, which is more serious, but the argument for this has been the necessity for holding the only coaling station in the Pacific so situated as to be essential to any power desirous of successfully attacking our Pacific coast. Until the Nicaragua Canal is made, it is impossible to deny the cogency of this contention. We need not consider it a measure of offense or aggression, but as strictly defensive. The population of the islands is so small that national aspirations are not to be encountered, which is a great matter, nor is it obtained by conquest. It is ours by a vote of its people, which robs its acquisition of many dangers. Let us hope that our far outlying possessions may end with Hawaii.

To reduce it to the concrete, the question is: Shall we attempt to establish ourselves as a power in the Far East and possess the Philippines for glory? The glory we already have, in Dewey's victory overcoming the power of Spain in a manner which adds one more to the many laurels of the American navy, which, from its infancy till now, has divided the laurels with Britain upon the sea. The Philippines have about seven and a half millions of people, composed of races bitterly hostile to one another, alien races, ignorant of our language and institutions. Americans cannot be grown there. The islands have been exploited for the benefit of Spain, against whom they have twice rebelled, like the Cubans; but even Spain has received little pecuniary benefit from them. The estimated revenue of the Philippines in 1894–95 was £2,715,980, the expenditure being £2,656,026, leaving a net result of about $300,000. The United States could obtain even this trifling sum from the inhabitants only by oppressing them as Spain has done. But, if we take the Philippines, we shall be forced to govern them as generously as Britain governs her dependencies, which means that they will yield us nothing, and probably be a source of annual expense. Certainly, they will be a grievous drain upon revenue if we consider the enormous army and navy which we shall be forced to maintain upon their account. . . .

Let another phase of the question be carefully weighted. Europe is to-day an armed camp, not chiefly because the home territories of its various nations are threatened, but because of fear of aggressive action upon the part of other nations touching outlying "possessions." France resents British control of Egypt and is fearful of its West African possessions; Russia seeks Chinese territory, with a view to expansion to the Pacific; Germany also seeks distant possessions; Britain, who has acquired so many dependencies, is so fearful of an attack upon them that this year she is spending nearly eighty millions of dollars upon additional warships, and Russia, Germany and France follow suit. Japan is a new element of anxiety; and by the end of the year it is computed she will have 67 formidable ships of war. The naval powers of Europe, and Japan also, are apparently determined to be prepared for a terrific struggle for possessions in the Far East, close to the Philippines—and why not for these islands themselves? Into this vortex the Republic is cordially invited to enter by those powers who expect her policy to be of benefit to them, but her action is jealously watched by those who fear that her power might be used against them.

It has never been considered the part of wisdom to thrust one's hand into the hornet's nest, and it does seem as if the United States must lose all claim to ordinary prudence and good sense if she enter this arena, and become involved in the intrigues and threats of war which make Europe an armed camp.

It is the parting of the ways. We have a continent to populate and develop; there are only 23 persons to the square mile in the United States. England has 370, Belgium 571, Germany 250. A tithe of the cost of maintaining our sway over the Philippines would improve our internal waterways; deepen our harbors; build the Nicaraguan Canal; construct a waterway to the ocean from the Great Lakes; an inland canal along the Atlantic seabord; a canal across Florida, saving 800 miles distance between New York and New Orleans; connect Lake Michigan with the Mississippi; deepen all the harbors upon the lakes; build a canal from Lake Erie to the Allegheny River, slackwater through movable dams the entire length of the Ohio River to Cairo; thoroughly improve the Lower and Upper Mississippi, and all our seaboard harbors. All these enterprises would be as nothing in cost in comparison to the sums required for the experiment of possessing the Philippine Islands, 7,000 miles from our shores. If the object be to render our Republic powerful among nations, can there be any doubt as to which policy is the better? To be more powerful at home is the surest way to be more powerful abroad. To-day the Republic stands the friend of all nations, the ally of none; she has no ambitious designs upon the territory of any power upon another continent; she crosses none of their ambitious designs, evokes no jealousy of the bitter sort, inspires no fears; she is not one of them, scrambling for "possessions;" she stands apart, pursuing her own great mission, and teaching all nations by example. Let her become a power annexing foreign territory, and all is changed in a moment.

If we are to compete with other nations for foreign possessions we must have a navy like theirs. It should be superior to any other navy, or we play a second part. It is not enough to have a navy equal to that of Russia or of France, for Russia and France may combine against us just as they may against Britain. We at once enter the field as a rival of Britain, the chief possessor of foreign possessions, and who can guarantee that we shall not even have to measure our power against her?

What it means to enter the list of military and naval powers having foreign possessions may be gathered from the following considerations. First, look at our future navy. If it is only to equal that of France it means 51 battleships; if of Russia, 40 battleships. If we cannot play the game without being at least the equal of any of our rivals, then 80 battleships is the number Britain possesses. We now have only 4, with 5 building. Cruisers, armed and unarmed, swell the number threefold, Britain having 273 ships of the line built or ordered, with 308 torpedo boats in addition; France having 134 ships of the line and 269 torpedo boats. All these nations are adding ships rapidly. Every armor and gun making plant in the world is busy night and day. Ships are indispensable, but recent experience shows that soldiers are equally so. While the immense armies of Europe need not be duplicated, yet we shall certainly be too weak unless our army is at least twenty times what it has been—say 500,000 men.

To-day two great powers in the world are compact, developing themselves in peace throughout vast coterminous territories. When war threatens they have no outlying "possessions" which can never be really "possessed," but which they are called upon to defend. They fight upon the exposed edge only of their own soil in case of attack, and are not only invulnerable, but they could not be more than inconvenienced by the world in arms against them. These powers are Russia and the United States. The attempt of Britain to check Russia, if the wild counsels of Mr. Chamberlain were followed, could end in nothing but failure. With the irresistible force of the glacier, Russia moved upon the plains below. Well for Russia, and well for the world, is her advance over pagan China, better even for Britain from the standpoint of business, for every Russian to-day trades as much with Britain as do nine Chinamen. Britain, France, Germany, Belgium, Spain, are all vulnerable, having departed from the sagacious policy of keeping possessions and power concentrated. Should the United States depart from this policy, she also must be so weakened in consequence as never to be able to play the commanding part in the world, disjointed, that she can play whenever she desires if she remain compact.

Whether the United States maintain its present unique position of safety or forfeit it through acquiring foreign possessions, is to be decided by its action in regard to the Philippines; for, fortunately, the independence of Cuba is assured, for this the Republic has proclaimed to the world that she has drawn the sword. But why should the less than two millions of Cuba receive national existence and the seven and a half millions of the Philippines be denied it? The United States, thus far in their history, have no page reciting self-sacrifice made for others; all their gains have been for themselves. This void is now to be grandly filled. The page which recites the resolve of the Republic to rid her neighbor Cuba from the foreign "possessor" will grow brighter with the passing centuries, which may dim many pages now deemed illustrious. Should the coming American be able to point to Cuba and the Philippines rescued from foreign domination and enjoying independence won for them by his country, and given to them without money and without price, he will find no citizen of any other land able to claim for his country services so disinterested and so noble.

We repeat there is no power in the world that could do more than inconvenience the United States by attacking its fringe, which is all that the world combined could do, so long as our country is not compelled to send its forces beyond its own compact shores to defend worthless "possessions." If our country were blockaded by the united powers of the world for years, she would emerge from the embargo richer and stronger, and with her own resources more completely developed. We have little to fear from external attack. No thorough blockade of our enormous seaboard is possible; but even if it were, the few indispensable articles not produced by ourselves (if there were any such) would reach us by way of Mexico or Canada at slightly increased cost.

From every point of view we are forced to the conclusion that the past policy of the Republic is her true policy for the future; for safety, for peace, for happiness, for progress, for wealth, for power—for all that makes a nation blessed. . . .

— | "Patriotism is being prostituted into a nervous intoxication which is fatal to an apprehension of truth." *

William Graham Sumner was equally opposed to the acquisition of the Philippines. Recalling the closely guarded tradition of realism in American diplomacy, he condemned the easy departure of the nation's leadership, supported by successful appeals to American patriotism, from the established policies of limited commitment abroad. He warned that the nation would eventually pay a heavy price for this disregard of the limits of the American democratic system to perform in the external realm, especially when democracy had demonstrated its inability to resolve many of the most obvious political and economic problems within the country itself.

✍

. . . War, expansion, and imperialism are questions of statesmanship and of nothing else. I disregard all other aspects of them and all extraneous elements which have been intermingled with them. I received the other day a circular of

* William Graham Sumner, "The Conquest of the United States by Spain," *Yale Law Journal,* VIII (January 1899), 168–93.

a new educational enterprise in which it was urged that, on account of our new possessions, we ought now to devote especial study to history, political economy, and what is called political science. I asked myself, Why? What more reason is there for pursuing these studies now on behalf of our dependencies than there was before to pursue them on behalf of ourselves? In our proceedings of 1898 we made no use of whatever knowledge we had of any of these lines of study. The original and prime cause of the war was that it was a move of partisan tactics in the strife of parties at Washington. As soon as it seemed resolved upon, a number of interests began to see their advantage in it and hastened to further it. It was necessary to make appeals to the public which would bring quite other motives to the support of the enterprise and win the consent of classes who would never consent to either financial or political jobbery. Such appeals were found in sensational assertions which we had no means to verify, in phrases of alleged patriotism, in statements about Cuba and the Cubans which we now know to have been entirely untrue.

Where was the statesmanship of all this? If it is not an established rule of statecraft that a statesman should never impose any sacrifices on his people for anything but their own interests, then it is useless to study political philosophy any more, for this is the alphabet of it. It is contrary to honest statesmanship to imperil the political welfare of the state for party interests. It was unstatesman-like to publish a solemn declaration that we would not seize any territory, and especially to characterize such action in advance as "criminal aggression," for it was morally certain that we should come out of any war with Spain with conquered territory on our hands, and the people who wanted the war, or who consented to it, hoped that we should do so.

We talk about "liberty" all the time in a big and easy way, as if liberty was a thing that men could have if they want it, and to any extent to which they want it. It is certain that a very large part of human liberty consists simply in the choice either to do a thing or to let it alone. If we decide to do it, a whole series of consequences is entailed upon us in regard to which it is exceedingly difficult, or impossible, for us to exercise any liberty at all. The proof of this from the case before us is so clear and easy that I need spend no words upon it. Here, then, you have the reason why it is a rule of sound statesmanship not to embark on an adventurous policy. A statesman could not be expected to know in advance that we should come out of the war with the Philippines on our hands, but it belongs to his education to warn him that a policy of adventure and of gratuitous enterprise would be sure to entail embarrassments of some kind. . . .

The war with Spain was precipitated upon us headlong, without reflection or deliberation, and without any due formulation of public opinion. Whenever a voice was raised in behalf of deliberation and the recognized maxims of states-manship, it was howled down in a storm of vituperation and cant. Everything was done to make us throw away sobriety of thought and calmness of judgment and to inflate all expressions with sensational epithets and turgid phrases. It can-not be denied that everything in regard to the war has been treated in an exalted strain of sentiment and rhetoric very unfavorable to the truth. At present the whole periodical press of the country seems to be occupied in tickling the national vanity to the utmost by representations about the war which are extravagant and fantastic. There will be a penalty to be paid for all this. Nervous and sensational newspapers are just as corrupting, especially to young people, as nervous and sensational novels. The habit of expecting that all mental pabulum shall be highly spiced, and the corresponding loathing for whatever is soberly truthful, undermines character as much as any other vice. Patriotism is being prostituted into a nervous intoxication which is fatal to an apprehension of truth. It builds around us a fool's paradise, and it will lead us into errors about our position and relations just like those which we have been ridiculing in the case of Spain.

There are some now who think that it is the perfection of statesmanship to say that expansion is a fact and that it is useless to discuss it. We are told that we must not cross any bridges until we come to them; that is, that we must discuss nothing in advance, and that we must not discuss anything which is past because it is irretrievable. No doubt this would be a very acceptable doctrine to the powers that be, for it would mean that they were relieved from responsibility, but it would be a marvelous doctrine to be accepted by a self-governing people. Senator Foraker has told us that we are not to keep the Philippines longer than is necessary to teach the people self-government. How one man can tell what we are to do before the constitutional authorities have decided it, I do not know. Perhaps it is a detail in our new method of self-government. If his assurances are to be trusted, we are paying $20,000,000 for the privilege of tutoring the Tagals up to liberty and self-government. I do not believe that, if the United States undertakes to govern the islands, it will ever give them up except to superior force, but the weakening of imperialism shown by this gentleman's assurances, after a few days of mild debate in the senate, shows that agitation of the subject is not yet in vain. Then again, if we have done anything, especially if we have acted precipitately, it is a well-recognized course of prudent behavior to find out where we are, what we have done, and what the new situation is into which we have come. Then, too, we must remember that when the statesman lays a thing down the historian takes it up, and he will group it with historical parallels and contrasts. There is a set of men who have always been referred to, in our Northern states, for the last thirty years, with especial disapproval. They are those Southerners who, in 1861, did not believe in secession, but, as they said, "went with their states." They have been condemned for moral cowardice. Yet within a year it has become almost a doctrine with us that patriotism requires that we should hold our tongues while our interests, our institutions, our most sacred traditions, and our best established maxims have been trampled underfoot. There is no doubt that moral courage is the virtue which is more needed than any other in the modern democratic state, and that truckling to popularity is the worst political vice. The press, the platform, and the pulpit have all fallen under this vice, and there is evidence that the university also, which ought to be the last citadel of truth, is succumbing to it likewise. I have no doubt that the conservative classes of this country will yet look back with great regret to their acquiescence in the events of 1898 and the doctrines and precedents which have been silently established. . . .

Another answer which the imperialists make is that Americans can do anything. They say that they do not shrink from responsibilities. They are willing to run into a hole, trusting to luck and cleverness to get out. There are some things that Americans cannot do. Americans cannot make $2 + 2 = 5$. You may answer that that is an arithmetical impossibility and is not in the range of our subject. Very well; Americans cannot collect two dollars a gallon tax on whisky. They tried it for many years and failed. That is an economic or political impossibility, the roots of which are in human nature. It is as absolute an impossibility on this domain as the former on the domain of mathematics. So far as yet appears, Americans cannot govern a city of one hundred thousand inhabitants so as to get comfort and convenience in it at a low cost and without jobbery. The fire department of this city is now demoralized by political jobbery—and Spain and all her possessions are not worth as much to you and me as the efficiency of the fire department of New Haven. The Americans in Connecticut cannot abolish the rotten borough system. The English abolished their rotten borough system seventy years ago, in spite of nobles and landlords. We cannot abolish ours in spite of the small towns. Americans cannot reform the pension list. Its abuses are rooted in the methods of democratic self-government, and no one dares to touch them. It is very doubtful indeed if Americans can keep up an army of one hundred thousand men in time of peace. Where can one hundred thousand men be found in this country who are willing to spend their lives as soldiers; or if they are found, what pay will it require to induce them to take this career? Americans cannot disentangle their currency from the confusion into which it was thrown by the Civil War, and they cannot put it on a simple, sure, and sound basis which would give stability to the business of the country. This is a political impossibility. Americans cannot assure the suffrage to negroes throughout the United States; they have tried it for thirty years and now, contemporaneously with this war with Spain, it has been finally demonstrated that it is a failure. . . . The ballot, we are told, was an educator and would solve all difficulties in its own path as by magic. Worse still, Americans cannot assure life, liberty and the pursuit of happiness to negroes inside of the United States. . . . The laws of nature and of human nature are just as valid for Americans as for anybody else, and if we commit acts we shall have to take consequences, just like other people. Therefore prudence demands that we look ahead to see what we are about to do, and that we gauge the means at our disposal, if we do not want to bring calamity on ourselves and our children. We see that the peculiarities of our system of government set limitations on us. We cannot do things which a great centralized monarchy could do. The very blessings and special advantages which we enjoy, as compared with others, bring disabilities with them. That is the fundamental cause of what I have tried to show throughout this lecture, that we cannot govern dependencies consistently with our political system, and that, if we try it, the State which our fathers founded will suffer a reaction which will transform it into another empire just after the fashion of all the old ones. That is what imperialism means. That is what it will be; and the democratic republic, which has been, will stand in history, like the colonial organization of earlier days, as a mere transition form.

And yet this scheme of a republic which our fathers formed was a glorious dream which demands more than a word of respect and affection before it passes away. . . . Our fathers would have an economical government, even if grand people called it a parsimonious one, and taxes should be no greater than were absolutely necessary to pay for such a government. The citizen was to keep all the rest of his earnings and use them as he thought best for the happiness of himself and his family; he was, above all, to be insured peace and quiet while he pursued his honest industry and obeyed the laws. No adventurous policies of conquest or ambition, such as, in the belief of our fathers, kings and nobles had forced, for their own advantage, on European states, would ever be undertaken by a free democratic republic. Therefore the citizen here would never be forced to leave his family or to give his sons to shed blood for glory and to leave widows and orphans in misery for nothing. Justice and law were to reign in the midst of simplicity, and a government which had little to do was to offer little field for ambition. In a society where industry, frugality, and prudence were honored, it was believed that the vices of wealth would never flourish.

We know that these beliefs, hopes, and intentions have been only partially fulfilled. We know that, as time has gone on and we have grown numerous and rich, some of these things have proved impossible ideals, incompatible with a large and flourishing society, but it is by virtue of this conception of a commonwealth that the United States has stood for something unique and grand in the history of mankind and that its people have been happy. It is by virtue of these ideals that we have been "isolated," isolated in a position which the other nations of the earth have observed in silent envy; and yet there are people who are boasting of their patriotism, because they say that we have taken our place now amongst the nations of the earth by virtue of this war. My patriotism is of the kind which is outraged by the notion that the United States never was a great nation until in a petty three months' campaign it knocked to pieces a poor, decrepit, bankrupt old state like Spain. To hold such an opinion as that is to abandon all American standards, to put shame and scorn on all that our ancestors tried to build up here, and to go over to the standards of which Spain is a representative.

# 7 | Albert J. Beveridge's Defense of American Imperialism, January 1900 *

Beveridge, in defending the decision to annex the Philippines, assigned to the United States a moral mission to regenerate the world, not as Henry Clay would suggest, by establishing a democratic model in America worthy of emulation, but by reaching outward with military and naval power. In rescuing the Philippines from Spanish misrule, declared Beveridge, the United States served humanity as well as its own expanding commercial empire in the Orient. Beveridge represented those American imperialists who, at the turn of the century, swept all conservative opposition aside through their successful identification of the new American policies of expansion with the powerful emotions of nationalism and patriotism.

. . . Mr. President, the times call for candor. The Philippines are ours forever, "territory belonging to the United States," as the Constitution calls them. And just beyond the Philippines are China's illimitable markets. We will not retreat from either. We will not repudiate our duty in the archipelago. We will not abandon our opportunity in the Orient. We will not renounce our part in the mission of our race, trustee, under God, of the civilization of the world. And we will move forward to our work, not howling out regrets like slaves whipped to their burdens, but with gratitude for a task worthy of our strength, and thanksgiving to Almighty God that He has marked us as His chosen people, henceforth to lead in the regeneration of the world.

This island empire is the last land left in all the oceans. If it should prove a mistake to abandon it, the blunder once made would be irretrievable. If it proves a mistake to hold it, the error can be corrected when we will. Every other progressive nation stands ready to relieve us.

But to hold it will be no mistake. Our largest trade henceforth must be with Asia. The Pacific is our ocean. More and more Europe will manufacture the most it needs, secure from its colonies the most it consumes. Where shall we turn for consumers of our surplus? Geography answers the question. China is our natural customer. She is nearer to us than to England, Germany, or Russia. the commercial powers of the present and the future. They have moved nearer to China by securing permanent bases on her borders. The Philippines give us a base at the door of all the East.

Lines of navigation from our ports to the Orient and Australia; from the Isthmian Canal to Asia; from all Oriental ports to Australia, converge at and separate from the Philippines. They are a self-supporting, dividend-paying fleet, permanently anchored at a spot selected by the strategy of Providence, command-

---

* Beveridge's speech in the Senate, January 9, 1900, *Congressional Record*, 56th Congress, 1st Sess., 704–12.

ing the Pacific. And the Pacific is the ocean of the commerce of the future. Most future wars will be conflicts for commerce. The power that rules the Pacific, therefore, is the power that rules the world. And, with the Philippines, that power is and will forever be the American Republic. . . .

Nothing is so natural as trade with one's neighbors. The Philippines make us the nearest neighbors of all the East. Nothing is more natural than to trade with those you know. This is the philosophy of all advertising. The Philippines bring us permanently face to face with the most sought-for customers of the world. National prestige, national propinquity, these and commercial activity are the elements of commercial success. The Philippines give the first; the character of the American people supply the last. It is a providential conjunction of all the elements of trade, of duty, and of power. If we are willing to go to war rather than let England have a few feet of frozen Alaska, which afford no market and commands none, what should we not do rather than let England, Germany, Russia, or Japan have all the Philippines? And no man on the spot can fail to see that this would be their fate if we retired. . . .

Here, then, Senators, is the situation. Two years ago there was no land in all the world which we could occupy for any purpose. Our commerce was daily turning toward the Orient, and geography and trade developments made necessary our commercial empire over the Pacific. And in that ocean we had no commercial, naval, or military base. To-day we have one of the three great ocean possessions of the globe, located at the most commanding commercial, naval, and military points in the eastern seas, within hail of India, shoulder to shoulder with China, richer in its own resources than any equal body of land on the entire globe, and peopled by a race which civilization demands shall be improved. Shall we abandon it? That man little knows the common people of the Republic, little understands the instincts of our race, who thinks we will not hold it fast and hold it forever, administering just government by simplest methods. We may trick up devices to shift our burden and lessen our opportunity; they will avail us nothing but delay. We may tangle conditions by applying academic arrangements of self-government to a crude situation; their failure will drive us to our duty in the end. . . .

But, Senators, it would be better to abandon this combined garden and Gibraltar of the Pacific, and count our blood and treasure already spent a profitable loss, than to apply any academic arrangement of self-government to these children. They are not capable of self-government. How could they be? They are not of a self-governing race. They are Orientals, Malays, instructed by Spaniards in the latter's worst estate.

They know nothing of practical government except as they have witnessed the weak, corrupt, cruel, and capricious rule of Spain. What magic will anyone employ to dissolve in their minds and characters those impressions of governors and governed which three centuries of misrule has created? What alchemy will change the oriental quality of their blood and set the self-governing currents of the American pouring through their Malay veins? How shall they, in the twinkling of an eye, be exalted to the heights of self-governing peoples which required a thousand years for us to reach, Anglo-Saxon though we are? . . .

Mr. President, self-government and internal development have been the dominant notes of our first century; administration and the development of other lands will be the dominant notes of our second century. And administration is as high and holy a function as self-government, just as the care of a trust estate is as sacred an obligation as the management of our own concerns. Cain was the first to violate the divine law of human society which makes of us our brother's keeper. And administration of good government is the first lesson in self-government, that exalted estate toward which all civilization tends. . . .

The Declaration of Independence does not forbid us to do our part in the regeneration of the world. If it did, the Declaration would be wrong, just as the Articles of Confederation, drafted by the very same men who signed the Declaration, was found to be wrong. The Declaration has no application to the present situation. It was written by self-governing men for self-governing men. . . .

Senators in opposition are estopped from denying our constitutional power to govern the Philippines as circumstances may demand, for such power is admitted in the case of Florida, Louisiana, Alaska. How, then, is it denied in the Philippines? Is there a geographical interpretation to the Constitution? Do degrees of longitude fix constitutional limitations? Does a thousand miles of ocean diminish constitutional power more than a thousand miles of land? . . .

No; the oceans are not limitations of the power which the Constitution expressly gives Congress to govern all territory the nation may acquire. The Constitution declares that "Congress shall have power to dispose of and make all needful rules and regulations respecting the territory belonging to the United States." Not the Northwest Territory only; not Louisiana or Florida only; not territory on this continent only, but any territory anywhere belonging to the nation. The founders of the nation were not provincial. Theirs was the geography of the world. They were soldiers as well as landsmen, and they knew that where our ships should go our flag might follow. They had the logic of progress, and they knew that the Republic they were planting must, in obedience to the laws of our expanding race, necessarily develop into the greater Republic which the world beholds today, and into the still mightier Republic which the world will finally acknowledge as the arbiter, under God, of the destinies of mankind. And so our fathers wrote into the Constitution these words of growth, of expansion, of empire, if you will, unlimited by geography or climate or by anything but the vitality and possibilities of the American people: "Congress shall have power to dispose of and make all needful rules and regulations respecting the territory belonging to the United States. . . ."

Mr. President, this question is deeper than any question of party politics; deeper than any question of the isolated policy of our country even; deeper even than any question of constitutional power. It is elemental. It is racial. God has not been preparing the English-speaking and Teutonic peoples for a thousand years for nothing but vain and idle self-contemplation and self-admiration. No! He has made us the master organizers of the world to establish system where chaos reigns. He has given us the spirit of progress to overwhelm the forces of reaction throughout the earth. He has made us adepts in government that we may administer government among savage and senile peoples. Were it not for such a force as this the world would relapse into barbarism and night. And of all our race He has marked the American people as His chosen nation to finally lead in the regeneration of the world. This is the divine mission of America, and it holds for us all the profit, all the glory, all the happiness possible to man. We are trustees of the world's progress, guardians of its righteous peace. The judgment of the Master is upon us: "Ye have been faithful over a few things; I will make you ruler over many things."

What shall history say of us? Shall it say that we renounced that holy trust, left the savage to his base condition, the wilderness to the reign of waste, deserted duty, abandoned glory, forgot our sordid profit even, because we feared our strength and read the charter of our powers with the doubter's eye and the quibbler's mind? Shall it say that, called by events to captain and command the proudest, ablest, purest race of history in history's noblest work, we declined that great commission? Our fathers would not have had it so. No! They founded no paralytic government, incapable of the simplest acts of administration. They planted no sluggard people, passive while the world's work calls them. They established no reactionary nation. They unfurled no retreating flag. . . .

Blind indeed is he who sees not the hand of God in events so vast, so harmonious, so benign. Reactionary indeed is the mind that perceives not that this vital people is the strongest of the saving forces of the world; that our place, therefore, is at the head of the constructing and redeeming nations of the earth; and that to stand aside while events march on is a surrender of our interests, a betrayal of our duty as blind as it is base. Craven indeed is the heart that fears to perform a work so golden and so noble; that dares not win a glory so immortal. . . .

# 8 | Josiah Quincy's Argument Against the Open Door Policy, October 1900 *

John Hay's Open Door Note of July 1900, which vaguely committed the United States to the defense of the territorial integrity of China, destroyed whatever remained of the older foreign policy of Jefferson, Madison, Monroe, and Adams. The United States now had commitments, which ultimately would be supported by war, reaching far into the western Pacific and onto the mainland of Asia itself. With the Open Door policy Hay committed the nation to the task of transforming China into a modern, efficient power. This objective, when achieved, would serve Asian stability, limit Japanese and Russian ambition, and satisfy the new American paternalistic and humanitarian sentiments for the

* Josiah Quincy, "China and Russia," *The North American Review*, CLXXI (October 1900), 529–32, 534–5, 537–8, 541–2.

Chinese people. Josiah Quincy, formerly First Assistant United States Secretary of State, criticized the Open Door policy as an American commitment which could not be sustained if challenged by another Pacific power. He argued, furthermore, that Russia, with its long common border with China and its memory of two centuries of Tartar rule, had far greater interests in China than had the other powers, and that the true interests of the United States in the Pacific rested on cordial relations with Russia, not China.

. . . The action of our own Government for the last year in connection with Chinese affairs, beginning with the circular note of Secretary Hay relative to the "open door" policy, in September, 1899, has certainly, in the main, been wise and conservative, and it may well be conceded that if the record closes equally well, a creditable chapter will have been added to the annals of American diplomacy. But the critical period of the real difficulties is just upon us, and this may last even for years before any final settlement is effected—if, indeed, the Chinese puzzle is to be solved at all in our day, which is by no means certain. It may not, therefore, be out of place to point out, in a spirit of considerate criticism, two mistakes, perhaps not unnatural ones, and fortunately not of the gravest importance or incapable of correction, which the present Administration seems to have made.

In the first place, the programme outlined in Secretary Hay's note of July 3d, while excellent ideally, was too ambitious and comprehensive in its scope, and too political in its character, differing radically in the latter respect from the policy embodied in his negotiations for the maintenance of the "open door" for commerce. His promise to hold the responsible authors of wrongs to American citizens to "the uttermost accountability" can easily be seen, in the light of recent developments, to have been somewhat too sweeping, and a more intimate knowledge of existing conditions in China would, doubtless, have prevented it from being made. It is never wise to threaten punishment which cannot be inflicted; and even on July 3d it should have been sufficiently evident that the difficulties in the way of even ascertaining, to say nothing of punishing, the "responsible authors" of outrages would be so great as to make threats worse than idle; and a great nation cannot but suffer some loss of dignity if unable to make good its solemn words. . . .

In further declaring it to be the policy of the United States to seek a solution of the existing troubles which should "prevent a recurrence of such disasters, bring about permanent safety and peace in China," Secretary Hay plainly implied the intention of our Government to join in political action for the radical reconstruction of Chinese administration. Fortunately, his language is general and does not hold us to any specific programme, and when it suits our convenience we can dismiss it as a mere expression of pious good will toward the Chinese people; but taking the then existing conditions in connection with the context, it is sufficiently clear that the intention was to commit the United States to political action for the reform of Chinese government—an object quite outside the scope of previous American policy in the Far East, impossible of attainment by our own independent action and, if pursued in common with other Powers, fraught with the gravest possibilities of those international entanglements with European nations, which it is our historical policy to keep out of. The Chinese government is, indeed, in the most crying need of reconstruction, whether from within or from without. But if this reform is to come from within, we have no more right to interfere with the internal politics of China than she has to take sides in our Presidential election; if from without, we had much better leave this huge, if not impossible, task to such nations as Russia or Japan, which could alone attempt it with any hope of success. It is not the mission of the United States to set right everything that is amiss all over the world, even if we have interests involved, or to take part in remodelling the government of some four hundred millions of people who deeply resent foreign interference with their affairs. The idea of joining a syndicate of nations for the establishment of a political trust to regulate the affairs of the world may be a dazzling one, but when it seriously appeals to the United States, the whole character of our government and of our institutions will have to be changed; for world-empire and democracy are inconsistent with each other and cannot co-exist. Fortunately, the territory and power of the whole eastern hemisphere have already been so far divided up or preempted among the older nations that the share which a new political partner would now receive would not be a very tempting one, in comparison with their great empires and dependencies—and perhaps we have our share in the political hegemony of the whole American hemisphere under the Monroe doctrine, to say nothing of our newly acquired islands.

The second mistake of the Administration was its assent to the appointment of a Commander-in-Chief of the forces of the allied Powers. No exception can, of course, be taken to the eminent fitness of Count von Waldersee to assume a military position of such delicacy and importance; and if, as appears to be the case, the selection of any German officer for this command was somewhat unfortunate—owing to the aggressive attitude of the German Emperor and the probability, to say the least, that his designs in China are too comprehensive— no part of this responsibility seems to attach to our own Government. But a willingness to place American troops under any foreign officer implied a closer alliance with other Powers in China than was consistent with the independent attitude of the United States in Asiatic affairs in the past, and involved unknown risks of entangling us in political complications. . . . If our sole military object was to relieve our own legation and citizens, and to take part in a longer or shorter occupation of Pekin—and it should not have been, and probably was not, any more comprehensive, as we took pains to disclaim being at war with China—then we should have replied that if this purpose had not been attained by the time Count von Waldersee arrived on the scene of action, we should be very glad to place our troops under an officer of such high qualifications. As things have turned out, this appointment, no doubt intended to secure greater harmony between the Powers, seems to be a threatening source of discord, and at least one of the obstacles in the way of a speedy re-establishment of peace seems to lie in the difficulty of saving the dignity of the Commander-in-Chief (not, be it noted, in China, but only in the Province of Pechili,) and of the country which he represents, and of finding something for him to do consistent with his high rank and functions. The United States at least might, by a little prudence, and without any discourtesy to Germany, have kept out of this complication and the jealousies which it may engender. . . .

We should never lose sight of the cardinal fact in the Chinese situation, so far as we are concerned—namely, that we have no present or prospective territorial or political interests, "spheres of influence," or "leases" of ports, in China, and that we do not want any—in which respects we are in a radically different position from all the other Powers represented in the concert. If we have joined with other nations in forcing our missionaries and our trade on China, we have not, at least, participated in the exaction of those cessions of territory and comprehensive privileges which seem to have been the direct cause of the present outbreak. We may, therefore, well leave the main task of quelling the storm to those Powers which have raised it, merely safeguarding our own special interests, so far as that is possible.

In another respect, also, the position of the United States in China is fundamentally different from that of the other allied Powers. Every one of these has such important interests at stake or such political alliances in Europe, that it must unfortunately consider becoming involved in war over the issues to be settled in Asia as at least a possibility—and each is at present practically on a war footing, though this can only be said of Great Britain owing to the conflict in South Africa. Doubtless, the tremendous disasters which would be involved in any war carried on between two great Powers under modern conditions— disasters which would fall only less heavily upon the victors than upon the vanquished—are fully realized by responsible statesmen and rulers, and this knowledge makes their action most careful and conservative. Yet to the European Powers and Japan the dread possibility of armed conflict is always present in the background. Fortunately for the United States, in spite of our large army in the Philippines and our troops now in China, no sane American thinks that we will fight with any other member of the concert, whatever may be our policy or our interests, either to prevent the dismemberment of China or to secure any share in the partition for ourselves, or to reform the Chinese government, or even to maintain the "open door" for our trade. This certainly affords another cogent consideration in favor of keeping out of the threatening complications which may lead to war between the Powers; for, if we do not mean to fight, neither do we want to suffer any loss of dignity or prestige. . . .

The simple fact that Russia has a frontier coterminous with that of China for some four thousand miles requires that her policy toward that Empire should be based on very different considerations from those which the other nations need take into account. No other Power represented in the concert is a territorial neighbor of China, except through distant dependencies—France through Tongking, and Great Britain through Burma; and of these two frontiers, that of France, the ally of Russia, is by far the more important. Russia is uniting her empire with China by railroads; the other Powers must always be dependent upon communications by sea. Japan, indeed, is a near neighbor of China; but the fact that she is separated from the Celestial Empire by water makes her necessary relations to the problem differ as much from those of Russia as the situation of England with reference to France is distinguished from that of Germany. The difference between sea and land relations of offense and defense between nations is fundamental. With Russia the security of a frontier of enormous extent must be a primary consideration, and recent events prove that its liability to attack is by no means merely a theoretical one. The last thing that she desires, or can afford, is to have to maintain this frontier in a perpetual state of defense against possible attack. For this reason alone, if for no other, the maintenance of friendly relations with China must be a cardinal point in her policy in Asia.

China cannot strike other nations except through their interests on her coasts, or within her borders; she can strike Russia within the Empire of the Czar, and it is at least conceivable and possible, even if quite unlikely, that she might some day organize out of her teeming population armies which would repeat the Tartar invasion. Russia has not yet forgotten that these fierce Asiatics ruled her people for over two centuries, and the overthrow of their domination is of as recent date as the discovery of America. While all the conditions of warfare have changed since Genghis Khan started the career of Asiatic conquest to the westward, the marvelous history of Japanese development within a single generation proves that, under some circumstances, Orientals can assimilate the material side of Western civilization, including its methods of fighting, with extraordinary rapidity and success. The striking military progress made by the Chinese themselves in the few years since the close of their war with Japan affords another illustration of this fact. Russians believe that, if Japan were once allowed to organize and arm the Chinese, their own great Asiatic Empire would be in imminent peril, if not their European territory as well; and it must be admitted that their fears seem to be well founded. A cardinal point in Russian policy is, therefore, to keep Japan out of China at all hazards, and out of Corea, if possible; hence her alarm at the cession of the Liao-tung peninsula to Japan after the war, and her coercion of that Power, in combination with France and Germany, to give up this important part of the fruits of her victory. . . .

The natural and legitimate character of the expansion of Russia to the Pacific, the fact that she has a real civilizing mission in Asia, however her own civilization may fall below the European standard in some respects; the service which she is rendering to the future commerce of the world by the great continental railroad which she is building at such an enormous cost; the pacific character of her policy—these are points which cannot be treated within the limits of this article. The maintenance of friendly relations with Russia should be as cardinal a point in our diplomatic policy as the cultivation of similar relations with us is in her own programme. Each nation has expanded across a continent, from one ocean to another; we meet as friends upon the shores of the Pacific—the great arena in which, perhaps, is to be fought out, in war or in peace, the struggle for political or commercial supremacy.

# 9 | Alfred Thayer Mahan on the Problem of Asia, 1900 *

Alfred Thayer Mahan was among that coterie of American writers who sensed that the United States, at the turn of the century, was neglecting the conservative principle of maintaining a clear balance between commitments and power. Without that balance the nation's influence would be ineffectual in settling controversies and forcing decisions. Unfortunately, in the assumptions of McKinley and the imperialists there was no room for such concepts of diplomacy. After 1900 it was no longer possible to conduct a practical, nation-wide discussion of foreign affairs, for such a discussion, to lead anywhere, must revolve around the question of balancing ends and means. Without a general consensus that a nation can have only that for which it is willing to pay there can be no foreign policy at all.

In his book, *The Problem of Asia*, Mahan reminded his readers of the need of reintroducing the genuine ingredients of traditional diplomacy into the nation's new Pacific policies. To guarantee the Open Door in China against such powers of Asia as Russia and Japan required not only greater American naval power in the western Pacific but also the building of a canal through Central America and the defense of the commercial routes to the Orient. To Mahan the new American commitments in the Pacific, if supported by adequate naval power, did not exceed the limits of legitimate national policy. At the heart of American policy in the Far East, Mahan saw, was the growing mutuality of interest between the United States and Britain. Mahan favored, however, a retrenchment of American responsibility for the *status quo* in South America through the abrogation of the traditional United States commitment under the Monroe Doctrine.

✒

. . . The altered conditions in the East have doubtless resulted—as did American expansion—from certain preparative antecedents, less obvious at the time of their occurrence, and which therefore then escaped particular notice; but the incidents that have signalized the change have been compacted into a very few years. Hence they possess the attribute of suddenness, which naturally entails for a time a lack of precise comprehension, with the necessary consequence of vagueness in opinion. Neverhteless, there they are; matters of grave international moment to those older nationalities, from whom heretofore we have held ourselves sedulously aloof. Side by side with them is our own acceptance of the Philippines, an act which we could not rightly avoid, and which carries with it opportunity. Opportunity, however, can never be severed from responsibility; for, whether utilized or neglected, a decision, positive or negative, is made, which cannot be dissociated from the imputation of moral right or wrong, of intellectual mistake or of wisdom.

* Alfred Thayer Mahan, *The Problem of Asia* (Boston, 1900), 11–18, 47–8, 106–7, 179–81, 187–91, 201–2.

It may be well here to consider for a moment the charge, now often made, that by the acceptance of the Philippines, and, still more, by any further use of the opportunities they may give us, we abandon the Monroe doctrine. The argument, if it can be allowed that name, derives such force as it has from appeal to prejudice; a word which, although it has an invidious association, does not necessarily imply more than opinion already formed, and which, if resting on solid basis, is entitled to full respect, unless, and until, it refuses to face new conditions. The Monroe doctrine, however, commits us only to a national policy, which may be comprehensively summarized as an avowed purpose to resist the extension of the European system to the American continents. As a just counterweight to this pretension, which rests in no wise upon international law, but upon our own interests as we understand them, we have adopted, as a rule of action, abstention from interference—even by suggestion, and much more by act—in questions purely European.

Of these complementary positions, neither the one nor the other possesses any legal standing, any binding force, of compact or of precedent. We are at liberty to abandon either at once, without incurring any just imputation of unlawful action. Regarded, however, purely as a matter of policy, and as such accepted as wise, by what process of reasoning is to to be established that either the one rule or the other bars us, on the ground of consistency, from asserting what we think our rights in Asia? . . . It has never, that I know, been seriously wished to compass our ends by the acquisition of European territory, for it would be neither expedient nor justifiable, even if possible, to unsettle conditions the permanency of which is the secure evolution of centuries of racial and national history; but we have had no scruples of justice or of expediency as to extension of territory in this hemisphere, where no such final adjustments had been reached. Now in Asia we are confronted at this moment by questions in which our interests will probably be largely involved. There is no more inconsistency in taking there such action as the case demands than there has been in any international difference we have hitherto had with a European power; while if such action should involve use of territory, directly or incidentally, by possession or by control—sphere of influence—it will only be because decadent conditions there shall hereafter have resulted in a lack of power, either to perpetuate a present system or to resist encroachments which the progress of the world under the impulse of more virile states is sure to entail. . . .

In the relation of land power to the future of Middle Asia—between the parallels of thirty and forty north—natural conditions have bestowed upon Russia a pre-eminence which approaches exclusiveness. The share of other states, where any exists, is incidental; and with one conspicuous exception, which will be indicated later, is deficient either in numbers, position, or organization. This predominance will enable Russia to put forth her strength unopposed, directly, by any other of the same nature, in quarters outside of the extreme range that can with any probability be predicated of sea power. But where immediate opposition is not feasible, adequate restraint is frequently imposed by force exerted, or capable of exertion, in other quarters, by land or by sea—dependent, as all force is, partly upon its own intrinsic value and partly upon positions occupied. Such pressure is possible, more or less, in all conditions of life, where interests are extensive, various, or scattered. It is notably so in international life, where action in one quarter is continually hindered by the consciousness of weakness elsewhere. Brought into action for military ends, this means of constraint is known technically as "diversion.". . .

There remains to consider Japan, the importance of whose part is evident, because she is the one nation, Asiatic in genius as in position, which by efficiency of action, internal as well as external, has established and maintained its place as a fully equipped member of the commonwealth of states, under recognized international law. . . . The essential elements of her strength, being insular, place her inevitably in the ranks of the Sea Powers, and whatever ambitions of territorial acquisition upon the continent she may entertain must be limited in extent, because of the limited number of her own population compared to that of the mainland adjacent; farther than which, of course, it is not supposable that she can wish to extend her activities. Western Asia and the Mediterranean, for example, though inseparably a part of the broad world question which centres just now about China, are clearly beyond the scope of Japan. Like the United States, local conditions emphasize her primary interests in a particular region and in one continent. Unlike the United States, the contractedness of her area denies the expectation of a superfluity of force, disposable in remoter quarters; while the nearness, in Asia, of great rival powers diminishes still further the possibility of distant enterprises. Narrow restriction in local territorial occupancy, however, is common to all the interested states; except, perhaps, Russia. The others, on account of their distance, as Japan on account of her size, must expect to affect China by impulses imparted to the inhabitants through commercial and political relations, supported militarily by sea power, which, from its mobility, will be operative not only in the immediate locality, but wherever else throughout the world its force can be felt in checking an opposing influence—as, for instance, in the control of commerce to its own advantage and to the injury of an enemy. . . .

To assure the open door in its fullest sense, requires power in evidence, not merely localized in China itself, but asserted over the maritime lines of communication; especially over the shortest. This inevitable extension of effort shows at once the necessity of cooperation among states; a division of labor, mutually, if tacitly, recognized. In the antagonism of policy between land and sea power which now exists, no one nation of those dependent upon the latter is competent to develop and sustain the whole gigantic scheme. Narrowed down even to the decisive points, which all control must be in politics as in war, the task overpasses the strength of any one state.

In final analysis the great lines of communication to the farther East are two, from Europe and from America. The former is by way of Suez, the latter by the Pacific; but the present distribution of our national wealth, and its communications with our seaboard, require, and doubtless will insure, the opening of access for our Atlantic slope by way of the Central American Isthmus. In that case the American line of communications to China may be correctly said to be by Nicaragua,—or Panama,—as that of Europe is by way of Suez; and as the Mediterranean, Egypt, Asia Minor, the Red Sea, and Aden, designate the points decisive of control by the one route, so do the Caribbean Sea and the continental surroundings of the future canal, with Hawaii and the Philippines, fix those of the other, the importance of which to ourselves make it our especial interest.

That it should be our special interest, however, is not all. It is also our charge, from the standpoint of international relations, as well as from that of our duty to the present and future of our own country. I do not mean here to affirm an obligation of benevolence to other nations, strong enough to take care of themselves. I mean, on the contrary, that because of great common interests—with Great Britain especially, though not solely—in the Pacific commerce of the future, and in the nature of the development of China, we need to receive and to give support, and should be ashamed to receive more than we give, in proportion to our means and opportunities. Gradually, as we have grown in strength, we have made good our claims to preponderant consideration in the Caribbean and at the Isthmus; we have obtained acquiescence where we once met opposition—from Great Britain herself. Is this a mere selfish, and in so far barren, triumph of national diplomacy, or an opportunity involving further duty? Certainly the latter; not because British welfare, regarded alone, is a concern for our action, but because community of interests, and duty to the world's future, centring about China, impose mutual support. This cannot be assured in matters pertaining to the East merely by accord localized there. It requires also such a grip upon our special great line of communications thither, from both our coasts, as shall give assurance that the force of our distant action cannot be impaired by any weakening of a link essential to its continuity.

From the conditions, we must be in effective naval force in the Pacific. We must similarly be in effective force on the Atlantic; not for the defence of our coasts primarily, or immediately, as is commonly thought,—for in warfare, however much in defence of right, the navy is not immediately an instrument of defence but of offence,—but because the virtual predominance of our naval power in the Caribbean is essential to preserve the use of the Isthmian Canal to our commerce, and to give our navy quick access to the Pacific. . . .

. . . Great Britain no longer has occasion to feel antagonism towards us in the Caribbean, and any traditional sentiment of that sort which may remain in her older men must disappear from popular consciousness, because contradicted by the facts. Antagonism, resting once on real opposition of interest, is being displaced by realization of the community of interest known as the open door, and of community in political principles, the outgrowth of traditions which, having been not stagnant but progressive, have now by evolution reached the stage of willing the integrity of China and its free development from within. From this, it is but a short step to a national support of China against foreign domination, or annexation, or partition,—a policy identical in principle with the Monroe Doctrine; but to take this, either state needs a reasonable security of the other's co-operation. As far as community of interest and of standard goes, the assurance is there, nor is the evidence of national feeling absent; but there is wanting on our part the assurance of the national purpose,—not by compact, but by action,—of which action a first instalment is the provision of force. We cannot expect the nations, friendly or the reverse, to take our purpose seriously, unless they see us firm in provision as well as in speech.

It may be objected, in Great Britain as well as here, that if there be among some of our citizens a clear appreciation of the advantage of common, though mutually independent, action, there is in very many of us a loudly expressed bitterness of feeling towards her; and that this will impede, if not prevent, mutual support in external matters of common interest. It is possible to admit the fact of the bitterness expressed, without accepting the conclusion. Sentiment is mighty, mightier at moments than interests; but where interest rests on real and permanent conditions, and sentiment on impressions which are transient and unreal, there can be no doubt which will prevail with the victory ever won by truth. The interest is real. The open door expresses a policy as important to us as to Great Britain; more important to us than to her, if our export trade take on the superior proportions anticipated by some serious thinkers. The standards also really exist. We, like her, and she, like us, at the present time shrink from partition and annexation as evils,—evil in principle, and evil in the consequent burden entailed. . . . The sentiment in the United States which to-day withstands movement in the direction of our common interests is partly traditional, like that which survives in Great Britain concerning the Caribbean; partly, as is notorious, it is the transference to United States politics of foreign prepossessions by citizens foreign-born, in their own persons or in those of their parents. Such sentiment is transient; for it is unreal in that it does not correspond to the facts of the United States' interests. A sagacious statesman will see in this the assurance of the ultimate trend of sentiment. But such an one will also reckon, with very different certitude, upon our national backwardness to provide the organized force,—especially the naval,—without which the attempted expression of national will, on emergency, becomes the clumsy and abortive gestures of a flabby and untrained giant. . . .

Coincidently with the development of our power, we should, in order to effectiveness of action, consider also the retrenchment of responsibility. Briefly, this remark is intended to raise the question, in view of the tremendous advance in importance of the Pacific and Asia, whether the extension of the Monroe Doctrine to the extent of supporting the independence of the states of extreme South America against all European interference, is a position now either wise or tenable? Great Britain suffers many strains by the dispersion of her Empire, but it is at least her Empire,—bone of her bone and flesh of her flesh. But what part have we, naturally or politically, in the foreign communities—foreign in blood and in tradition—south of the valley of the Amazon. That they do not love us is notorious; probably, indeed, they love us less because of our supposed purpose of interposition, which they doubtless would welcome in a strait, but which in ordinary times causes them chiefly mortification and apprehension. Within range of effect upon the Isthmus, certainly, our clear interest forbids toleration of any acquisition, through possession or through influence, by a great foreign state—more so now than ever before; but for the American communities beyond that range, our professed political concern is to us a waste of strength, as it is to them distasteful. The great valley of the Amazon, not unlike that of the Yang-tse, though far more practicable, indicates easily a great commercial zone in which the "open door" might profitably be assured by international understanding, and which also might very wisely be accepted in our national consciousness as interposing a broad effectual belt between the region where the Monroe Doctrine is applicable, and that where, for any useful purpose, it ceases to apply.

## 10 | Theodore Roosevelt and the Conservative Foundations of Diplomacy, 1904–5 *

Roosevelt's correspondence as President of the United States reveals a mind which appreciated the traditional conservatism of American foreign policy. It was this that compelled him to become a severe critic of the tendencies within American behavior relative to external affairs during the early years of the twentieth century. Unfortunately Roosevelt was trapped politically by the absence of that sense of proportion among the American people which his own letters advocated. The America of Roosevelt's day no longer found its security in the genuine elements of national power—the British navy, the balance of power in Europe and Asia, and the absence of competing strength in the Western Hemisphere. Americans after 1900 discovered their security in their geographic isolation and the superiority of their economic and politcial institutions.

Against such illusions Roosevelt battled, not always ineffectually, to create some sense of balance in American foreign policy. He insisted on the building of the Panama Canal so that a single navy could patrol both oceans. He knew that the British navy, facing the threat of a German naval program after the mid-'nineties, had lost much of its freedom to maneuver, especially in the Pacific. Rosevelt understood that Germany was jealous of the new American possessions in the Far East and that, therefore, the United States required allies. For this reason he favored a stronger *rapprochement* with Britain. On the other hand, Roosevelt sought to limit American commitments abroad to the clear interests of the United States. In a letter to the noted English historian, George Otto Trevelyan, Roosevelt condemned crusades of liberation abroad as fundamentally immoral because they were never supported by a willingness to perform.

* Roosevelt to Trevelyan, May 13, 1905, *The Letters of Theodore Roosevelt*, Elting E. Morison, ed. (Cambridge, Mass., 1951), IV: 1174–5. Copyright 1951, 1952, 1954 by the President and Fellows of Harvard College. Reprinted by permission.

. . . I have recently been reading with much interest de La Gorce's *History of the Second Empire*. I wonder if you will agree with me when I say that it seems to me that the England of Palmerston and Russell, like the United States of today, is too apt to indulge in representations on behalf of weak peoples which do them no good and irritate the strong and tyrannical peoples to whom the protest is made. It seems to me that the protest on behalf of the Poles to Russia in '63, and the protest on behalf of the Danes to Germany about the same time, were harmful rather than beneficial. Out in the west we always used to consider it a cardinal crime to draw a revolver and brandish it about unless the man meant to shoot. And it is apt to turn out sheer cruelty to encourage men by words and then not back up the words by deeds. I am all the time being asked to say something on behalf of the Jews in Russia, of the Armenians in Turkey, of the people of the Congo Free State, etc., etc. It does not do always to refuse. England rendered a real and great service to Italy by her sympathy and championship, for instance. But it certainly does harm to be always harping on the sympathy which finds expression only in words. I think that by speaking, though very gently and cautiously, for the Jews in Russia we were able to accomplish a little, a *very* little, toward temporarily ameliorating their conditions. As for the Armenians in Turkey, if I could get this people to back me I really think I should be tempted to go into a crusade against the Turk. But as this is of course a sheer impossibility I simply dare not give expression to my sympathy and indignation, lest harm and not good should result.

Moreover, I have plenty of evils to fight here at home, evils connected with race prejudice, especially against the negro, evils connected with the tyranny of corporations and the tyranny of the labor unions. Corporations are indispensable and I believe in labor unions; but both are potent weapons for evil, when under the control of unscrupulous men. However, this letter has run to a dreadful length already; as you won't come to this side of the water, when I am through being President I shall have to come to your side of the water, and then there will be many things I shall wish to talk over with you and tell you about. . . .

— | "To be rich, aggressive, and yet helpless in war, is to invite destruction." *

Roosevelt again expressed his conservative outlook on foreign affairs in his letter of February 1904 to Congressman Theodore E. Burton of Ohio. The President declared that the United States could render its policies solvent by either giving up its new commitments or building the naval power to underwrite them. To do neither, he warned, would result in disaster.

* Roosevelt to Burton, February 23, 1904, *The Letters of Theodore Roosevelt*, IV: 736–7.

. . . Let me point out very briefly what I regard as the fundamental error in the position of those who now wish to stop our building up the navy, and who nevertheless belong to the republican party. The one unforgivable crime is to put one's self in a position in which strength and courage are needed, and then to show lack of strength and courage. This is precisely the crime committed by those who advocate or have acquiesced in the acquisition of the Philippines, the establishment of naval stations in Cuba, the negotiation of the treaty for building the Panama Canal, the taking of Porto Rico and Hawaii, and the assertion of the Monroe Doctrine, and who nevertheless decline to advocate the building of a navy such as will alone warrant our attitude in any one, not to say all, of these matters. It is perfectly allowable, although I think rather ignoble, to take the attitude that this country is to occupy a position in the New World analogous to that of China in the Old World, to stay entirely within her borders, not to endeavor to assert the Monroe Doctrine, incidentally to leave the Philippines, to abandon the care of the Panama Canal, to give up Hawaii and Porto Rico, etc., etc., and therefore to refuse to build up any navy. It is also allowable, and as I think, in the highest degree far-sighted and honorable, to insist that the attitude of the republican party in all these matters during the last eight years has been the wise and proper attitude, and to insist therefore that the navy shall be kept up and built up as required by the needs of such an attitude. But any attempt to combine the two attitudes is fraught with the certainty of hopeless and ignominious disaster to the Nation. To be rich, aggressive, and yet helpless in war, is to invite destruction. If everything that the republican party has done during the past eight years is all wrong; if we ought not to have annexed Hawaii, or taken the Philippines, or established a kind of protectorate over Cuba, or started to build the Panama Canal, then let us reverse these policies and give up building a navy; but to my mind it is to inflict a great wrong on the generations who come after us if we persevere in these policies and do not back them up by building a navy. Mr. Williams, for instance, is against the fortification of Subig Bay. He affects to regard the fortification of Subig Bay as a menace to the independence of the Philippines; with which it has nothing in the world to do. . . . Mr. Williams' attitude about Subig Bay is monstrous in view of what we have seen happen before our eyes to the Russians at Port Arthur because of their unpreparedness. If we are to have a naval station in the Philippines; if we are to have a fleet in Asiatic waters, or to exert the slightest influence in eastern Asia where our people hope to find a market, then it is of the highest importance that we have a naval station at Subig Bay. If we are not to have that station, and are not to have a navy, then we should be manly enough to say that we intend to abandon the Philippines at once; not to try to keep a naval station there; and not to try to exercise that influence in foreign affairs which comes only to the just man armed who wishes to keep the peace. . . .

Roosevelt recognized, as did Mahan, that Japan and Russia comprised the two major threats to the balance of power in the Far East. For that reason he took a profound interest in the course of the Russo-Japanese War of 1904. In a letter to his son, Theodore Jr., he revealed why he favored Japanese success.

🖋

. . . I am greatly interested in the Russian and Japanese war. It has certainly opened most disastrously for the Russians, and their supine carelessness is well-nigh incredible. For several years Russia has behaved very badly in the far East, her attitude toward all nations, including us, but especially toward Japan, being grossly overbearing. We had no sufficient cause for war with her. Yet I was apprehensive lest if she at the very outset whipped Japan on the sea she might assume a position well-nigh intolerable toward us. I thought Japan would probably whip her on the sea, but I could not be certain; and between ourselves—for you must not breathe it to anybody—I was thoroughly well pleased with the Japanese victory, for Japan is playing our game.

— | "We should treat her [Japan] courteously, generously and justly, but we should keep our navy up and make it evident that we are not influenced by fear." †

Roosevelt continued to view Japan as a "formidable counterpoise to Russia in the Far East," as he wrote in January 1898. Eventually, after a succession of brilliant Japanese victories, he favored, in the interest of the balance of power, a compromise settlement between Japan and Russia. At the request of the Japanese government, Roosevelt arranged a peace conference at Portsmouth, New Hampshire, between Russian and Japanese diplomats. During the negotiations, in a letter to Henry Cabot Lodge, Roosevelt expressed his views regarding Russia and Japan as Pacific powers, noting especially the ingredients of a proper United States policy toward Japan.

🖋

. . . I have treated both Takahira and Cassini with entire frankness, saying the same things in effect to each, except that I have of course concealed from everyone—literally everyone—the fact that I acted in the first place on Japan's

* Roosevelt to Theodore Roosevelt, Jr., February 10, 1904, *The Letters of Theodore Roosevelt*, IV: 724.
† Roosevelt to Lodge, June 16, 1905, *The Letters of Theodore Roosevelt*, IV: 1229–31.

suggestion. I told Russia that it was nonsense for her to stick at trifles, that if the war went on she would lose all her possessions in eastern Asia and that the blow to her would be well-nigh irreparable; that while I had not sympathized with her at the outset I should be very sorry, because of my real regard for the Russian people and because of my regard for the interests of the world generally, to see her driven out of territory which had been hers for a couple of centuries; and that I had hoped she would make up her mind that she would have to make concessions in order to obtain peace because her military position was now hopeless, and that however future wars might come out this war was assuredly a failure. To the Japanese I have said that if they made such terms that Russia would prefer to fight for another year, they would without doubt get all eastern Siberia, but that in my opinion it would be an utterly valueless possession to them while they would make of Russia an enemy whose hostility would endure as long as the nation herself existed and that to achieve this result at the cost of an additional year of loss of blood and money and consequent strain upon Japanese resources seems to me to be wholly useless. Japan now has Port Arthur and Korea and the dominance in Manchuria, and I should feel that the less she asked for in addition the better it would be. . . .

In short, the more I see of the Czar, the Kaiser, and the Mikado the better I am content with democracy, even if we have to include the American newspaper as one of its assets—liability would be a better term. Russia is so corrupt, so treacherous and shifty, and so incompetent, that I am utterly unable to say whether or not it will make peace, or break off the negotiations at any moment. Japan is, of course, entirely selfish, though with a veneer of courtesy, and with infinitely more knowledge of what it wants and capacity to get it. I should not be surprised if the peace negotiations broke off at any moment. Russia, of course, does not believe in the genuineness of my motives and words, and I sometimes doubt whether Japan does.

It is for the real interest of Japan to make peace, if she can get suitable terms, rather than fight on for a year at a great cost of men and money and then find herself in possession of eastern Siberia (which is of no value to her) and much strained by the struggle. Russia had far better make peace now, if she possibly can and find her boundaries in east Asia left without material shrinkage from what they were ten years ago, than to submit to being driven out of east Asia. While for the rest of us, while Russia's triumph would have been a blow to civilization, her destruction as an eastern Asiatic power would also in my opinion be unfortunate. It is best that she should be left face to face with Japan so that each may have a moderative action on the other. As for Japan, she has risen with simply marvelous rapidity, and she is as formidable from the industrial as from the military standpoint. She is a great civilized nation; though her civilization is in some important respects not like ours. There are some things she can teach us, and some things she can learn from us. She will be as formidable an industrial competitor as, for instance, Germany, and in a dozen years I think she will be the leading industrial nation of the Pacific. The way she has extended her trade and prepared for the establishment of new steamship lines to all kinds of points in the Pacific has been astonishing, for it has gone right on even through the time of this war. Whether her tremendous growth in industrialism will in course of time modify and perhaps soften her wonderful military spirit she has inherited from the days of the Samurai supremacy it is hard to say. Personally, I think it will; but the effect will hardly be felt for a generation to come. Still, her growing industrial wealth will be to a certain extent a hostage for her keeping the peace. We should treat her courteously, generously and justly, but we should keep our navy up and make it evident that we are not influenced by fear. I do not believe she will look toward the Philippines until affairs are settled on the mainland of Asia in connection with China even if she ever looks toward them, and on the mainland in China her policy is the policy to which we are already committed. . . .

— | "The peace negotiations were entered into by me at the instance of Japan." *

Roosevelt later explained his role in the Portsmouth negotiations, which terminated the Russo-Japanese War, in a letter to journalist George Kennan. Kennan had written that Roosevelt's interference in the Russo-Japanese War, encouraging negotiations before Japanese predominance in eastern Asia could be demonstrated on the battlefield, had deprived Japan of the indemnity and additional territory which she deserved. Roosevelt made it clear that he had acted only on the written request of the Japanese government.

. . . I very much like your first article on Korea, in the *Outlook;* but at present I wish to write you as to your article called "The Sword of Peace in Japan." As far as I am concerned it is of exceedingly little importance what anyone says about the peace negotiations. My object in bringing them was not my own personal credit or even the advancement of this country, but the securing of peace. Peace was secured. Personally I believe that the credit of this country was greatly increased by it, and as far as I am personally affected I have received infinitely more praise for it than in my opinion I deserved; and I have not been very greatly concerned as to whether I was praised or blamed. But you are writing as a man supposed to know the facts at first hand. Your writings will be read here and read in Japan, and while you may not do much damage to America you may do some to Japan if you get your facts crooked. They are crooked in this article. You say that it seems to you that "it would have been much better both for Russia and Japan if President Roosevelt had waited until the close of this campaign before he had proposed a peace conference." What I am about to say is for your own information and not for the public. I acted at the time I did at the written request of Japan, and when Japan made the request I ex-

* Roosevelt to Kennan, October 15, 1905, *The Letters of Theodore Roosevelt*, V: 56–60.

plained to the Japanese Government that in my judgment she would not get an indemnity. . . . You say that Marshal Oyama, if I had waited, would probably have defeated General Linevitch. Your guess is probably as good as anyone else's, and no better. Personally I should make the same guess; but the ugly fact remains that after winning the battle of Mukden Marshal Oyama instead of being able to press his demoralized foe, had let four months and over go by without being able to strike him, and that the Russian army had recovered its morale, was in good position, was reinforced, and was very anxious to be allowed to try the chances of another battle before peace was declared. As I say, I personally think you are right in your guess, and I took this view in my communications with the Russians; but it is not a matter about which anyone can be sure. The parallel you draw between what has happened to Russia and an imaginary case of what might happen if we were engaged in a war with Germany is thoroughly misleading, if only from the simple fact that in drawing it you were ignorant that it was not the "suggestion of an outsider" but the immediate need of Japan, and the earnest wish of the Japanese Government (expressed in writing) which brought about the peace conference. Your fancied analogy would have to be corrected by supposing that every serious American statesman knew that America would be terribly exhausted by further war, and that, if she should retain what she had gained, peace was urgently necessary; while there was nothing she wanted which it was possible for her to gain by further war. It is simply nonsense for anyone to talk of the Japanese being in a position to demand an indemnity. No nation that does not give up anything ever gets an indemnity in such circumstances or ever could get it unless the other nation was hopelessly frightened. In recent times no sensible nation has made such a request. Moreover, your whole comparison is vitiated by the fact (which, my dear Mr. Kennan, it is extraordinary that you do not know) that the prime motive influencing Japan to wish peace was not any one of those that you give, but her great personal interest in obtaining peace on the very terms that finally were obtained and at that very time. You were on the ground. There may be reasons why you do not choose to make public the fact; but if these reasons do not exist, it is extraordinary that you should not know the fact, that the head men of many villages and country communities in Japan were notifying the government that they could not spare any more of their young men; that if more of their young men were drawn for the army the rice fields would have to be partially abandoned and a partial famine would ensue, and that moreover the little savings of their people had all been exhausted. I believe that Japan was partly influenced by proper motives of humanity and by the desire to have the respect of the nations as a whole, and that this feeling had its weight in influencing the Japanese statesmen who knew the facts to disregard the views held by the Tokyo mob and which are substantially the views set forth by you. But the main factor in influencing Japan was undoubtedly the fact that to go on with the war meant such an enormous loss, such an enormous cost to her, that she could not afford to incur it save from dire need. For example, you speak about her not having obtained the north half of Sakhalin Island. She had not reduced to possession this north half of Sakhalin, and there were Russian forces still there, a fact of which you do not seem to be aware. But this is not important. It may interest you to know, again for your own private use, the following facts. Do what I could I was unable to get the Czar to yield more than the south half of Sakhalin. On the point of honor he insisted on keeping the comparatively valueless northern half. So far from advising the Japanese to give up on the question of Sakhalin, I explicitly told and wrote them that in my judgment they would be justified in fighting for Sakhalin. I did not appreciate quite how urgent their need of peace was. They, as I think with eminent propriety, went a little beyond what I advised and made peace without getting the northern half of Sakhalin. I had told them all along that to fight for an indemnity merely, would forfeit the respect of everybody whose respect was worth having, and would be an act of wicked folly, for it would mean at the very best at least another year of war, and mortgaging the future of Japan for a generation to come, while they would get nothing of any value to them. They would certainly not get any money, and if, as I thought was likely, they conquered East Siberia, they would get what they explicitly assured me that they did not want and what would cost them an immense amount to administer; while there would always be the risk that some reverse would occur, in which case the damage done to Japan might well be irreparable.

The above are the facts, They are for your private information. I do not intend to make public any of the details about this peace, because the Japanese have asked me not to make public those details which they think would in any way embarrass them, and I am anxious to do what they desire. But I do intend, privately, to keep intelligent observers sufficiently enlightened to prevent their going wrong. I think it is wise that a man of your standing who is supposed to speak with knowledge, should for his own information merely, know what the facts are and thereby avoid taking a position as wholly mistaken as you have taken in the part of your article to which I have referred.

Let me repeat. The peace negotiations were entered into by me at the instance of Japan. The treaty of peace was finally made by Japan because it was greatly to her interest to make it then, and in the shape in which it was made. Japan was not entitled to an indemnity, and in my judgment it is so absurd to suppose that she was entitled to an indemnity as to mark the man making the claim as either utterly ignorant of the facts or not competent to pass upon the facts. Japan gained everything she was entitled to. She was entitled to much and she gained much. It would have been (from the standpoint of her own interest) criminal, as well as foolish to the last degree, for her to continue the war under these circumstances, and she owes a great debt of gratitude to her statesmen who disregarded the feelings of the mob at home and of their well-meaning but most ill-advised counselors abroad who desired her to take any other course. The peace was made on pratically exactly the terms on which it should have been made. It was for the interest of Japan; it was for the interest of Russia; it was for the interest of the world. . . .

Let me again say that while it was even more to Russia's interest than to Japan's that peace should come on the terms, upon which it actually came, yet that it was very greatly to Japan's interest also, and that while Japan went a little further than I had advised her to go, in yielding the north half of Sakhalin without getting anything for it, yet as this north half of Sakhalin was a trivial matter, and the amount she could have gotten would have been very small, I think she was wise in doing so.

## 12 | Roosevelt on the Essentials of a Solvent Policy Toward Japan, 1905–9 *

Roosevelt's bitterness toward California's measures of repression against Japanese residents reflected his concept of a balanced policy toward an increasingly powerful and potentially dangerous Japan. The Californians, he noted, antagonized Japan and at the same time opposed the building of effective United States naval power in the Pacific. For Roosevelt prudent policy demanded the opposite course.

✍

. . . That Japan will have her head turned to some extent I do not in the least doubt, and I see clear symptoms of it in many ways. We should certainly as a nation have ours turned if we had performed such feats as the Japanese have in the past sixteen months; and the same is true of any European nation. Moreover, I have no doubt that some Japanese, and perhaps a great many of them, will behave badly to foreigners. They cannot behave worse than the State of California, through its Legislature, is now behaving toward the Japanese. The feeling on the Pacific slope, taking it from several different standpoints, is as foolish as if conceived by the mind of a Hottentot. These Pacific Coast people wish grossly to insult the Japanese and to keep out the Japanese immigrants on the ground that they are an immoral, degraded and worthless race; and at the same time that they desire to do this for the Japanese and are already doing it for the Chinese they expect to be given advantages in Oriental markets; and with besotted folly are indifferent to building up the navy while provoking this formidable new power—a power jealous, sensitive and warlike, and which if irritated could at once take both the Philippines and Hawaii from us if she obtained the upper hand on the seas. Most certainly the Japanese soldiers and sailors have shown themselves to be terrible foes. There can be none more dangerous in all the world. But our own navy, ship for ship, is I believe at least as efficient as theirs, although I am not certain that our torpedo boats would be handled as well as theirs. At present we are superior to them in number of ships, and this superiority will last for some time. It will of course come to an

* Roosevelt to Lodge, June 5, 1905, *The Letters of Theodore Roosevelt*, IV: 1205–6.

end if Hale has his way, but not otherwise. I hope that we can persuade our people on the one hand to act in a spirit of generous justice and genuine courtesy toward Japan, and on the other hand to keep the navy respectable in numbers and more than respectable in the efficiency of its units. If we act thus we need not fear the Japanese. But if as Brooks Adams says, we show ourselves "opulent, aggressive and unarmed," the Japanese may sometime work us an injury. In any event we can hold our own in the future, whether against Japan or Germany, whether on the Atlantic or the Pacific, only if we occupy the position of the just man armed—that is, if we do the exact reverse of what the demagogues on the one hand and the mugwumps on the other would like to have us do.

— |  "The peace societies, and Senators and Congressmen . . . oppose the navy and hamper its upbuilding, while doing nothing whatever to prevent insult to Japan." *

Shortly before his successor, William Howard Taft, took office, Roosevelt, in a long letter to Taft's choice as Secretary of State, Philander Chase Knox, restated his concept of a solvent policy toward Japan. To Roosevelt it was clear that there was not a semblance of balance between ends and means in American Far Eastern policies.

✍

. . . It is utterly impossible to foretell as regards either foreign or domestic policy what particular questions may appear as at the moment of most engrossing interest. It may be that there will be no ripple of trouble between Japan and the United States during your term of service. It may very well be that you will have acute trouble about Cuba, or with Venezuela or in Central America, or with some European power; but it is not likely that grave international complications—that is, complications which can possibly lead to serious war—can come from any such troubles. . . .

But with Japan the case is different. She is a most formidable military power. Her people have peculiar fighting capacity. They are very proud, very warlike, very sensitive, and are influenced by two contradictory feelings, namely, a great self-confidence, both ferocious and conceited, due to their victory over the mighty empire of Russia; and a great touchiness because they would like to be considered as on a full equality with, as one of the brotherhood of, Occidental nations, and have been bitterly humiliated to find that even their allies, the English, and their friends, the Americans, won't admit them to association and citizenship, as they admit the least advanced or most decadent European peoples.

* Roosevelt to Knox, February 8, 1909, *The Letters of Theodore Roosevelt*, VI: 1510–14.

Moreover, Japan's population is increasing rapidly and demands an outlet, and the Japanese laborers, small farmers, and petty traders would, if permitted, flock by the hundred thousand into the United States, Canada, and Australia.

Now for our side. The events of the last three years have forced me to the clear understanding that our people will not permit the Japanese to come in large numbers among them; will not accept them as citizens; will not tolerate their presence as large bodies of permanent settlers. This is just as true in Australia and Columbia as in our Rocky Mountain and Pacific States; but at present the problem is more acute with us because the desire of the Japanese to come here has grown. The opposition to the presence of the Japanese, I have reluctantly come to feel, is entirely warranted, and not only must be, but ought to be, heeded by the national Government in the interest of our people and our civilization; and this in spite of the fact that many of the manifestations of the opposition are unwise and improper to the highest degree. To permit the Japanese to come in large numbers into this country would be to cause a race problem and invite and insure a race contest. It is necessary to keep them out. But it is almost equally necessary that we should both show all possible courtesy and consideration in carrying out this necessarily disagreeable policy of exclusion, and that we should be thoroly armed, so as to prevent the Japanese from feeling safe in attacking us. Unfortunately, great masses of our people show a foolish indifference to arming, and at the same time a foolish willingness to be offensive to the Japanese. Labor unions pass violent resolutions against the Japanese and almost at the same moment protest against strengthening our military resources on land or sea. Big corporations seek to introduce Japanese coolies, so as to get cheap labor, and thereby invite agitation which they are powerless to quell. The peace societies, and Senators and Conrgessmen like Burton of Ohio, Perkins of California, Perkins of New York, Tawney of Minnesota, McCall of Massachusetts, and Bartholdt of Missouri, blatantly or furtively oppose the navy and hamper its upbuilding, while doing nothing whatever to prevent insult to Japan. The California Legislature is threatening to pass the most offensive kind of legislation aimed at the Japanese, and yet it re-elects a wretched creature like Perkins to the Senate altho he has opposed, with his usual feeble timidity and so far as he dared, the upbuilding of the navy, following Hale's lead. . . .

As regards the mainland, our policy should have three sides, and should be shaped not to meet the exigencies of this year or next, but to meet what may occur for the next few decades. Japan is poor and is therefore reluctant to go to war. Moreover, Japan is vitally interested in China and on the Asiatic mainland and her wiser statesmen will if possible prevent her getting entangled in a war with us, because whatever its result it would hamper and possibly ruin Japan when she came to deal again with affairs in China. But with so proud and sensitive a people neither lack of money nor possible future complications will prevent a war if once they get sufficiently hurt and angry; and there is always danger of a mob outbreak there just as there is danger of a mob outbreak here. Our task therefore is on the one hand to meet the demands which our own people make and which cannot permanently be resisted and on the other to treat Japan so courteously that she will not be offended more than is necessary; and at the same time to prepare our fleet in such shape that she will feel very cautious about attacking us. Disturbances like those going on at present are certain to occur unless the Japanese immigration, so far as it is an immigration for settlement, stops. For the last six months under our agreement with Japan it has been stopped to the extent that more Japanese have left the country than have come into it. But the Japanese should be made clearly to understand that this process must continue and if there is relaxation it will be impossible to prevent our people from enacting drastic exclusion laws; and that in such case all of us would favor such drastic legislation. Hand in hand with insistence on the stopping of Japanese immigration should go insistence as regards our own people that they be courteous and considerate, that they treat the Japanese who are here well; and above all that they go on with the building of the navy, keep it at the highest point of efficiency, securing not merely battleships but an ample supply of colliers and other auxiliary vessels of every kind. . . .

There is no more important continuing feature of our foreign policy than this in reference to our dealing with Japan; the whole question of our dealings with the Orient is certain to grow in importance. I do not believe that there will be war, but there is always the chance that war will come, and if it did come, the calamity would be very great, and while I believe we would win, there is at least a chance of disaster. We should therefore do everything in our power to guard against the possibility of war by preventing the occurrence of conditions which would invite war and by keeping our navy so strong that war may not come or that we may be successful if it does come.


13 | Roosevelt and the Open Door for China,
     December 1910 *


Fundamental to Roosevelt's realistic approach to foreign policy in the Far East was his conviction that the United States could not avoid war with Japan unless it modified its commitment to China under the Open Door. That Roosevelt favored such a modification in the interest of long-term peace with Japan he made clear in the following letter to Taft in December 1910.

🖋

. . . Our vital interest is to keep the Japanese out of our country, and at the same time to preserve the good will of Japan. The vital interest of the Japanese,

* Roosevelt to Taft, December 22, 1910, *The Letters of Theodore Roosevelt*, VII: 189–90.

on the other hand, is in Manchuria and Korea. It is therefore peculiarly our interest not to take any steps as regards Manchuria which will give the Japanese cause to feel, with or without reason, that we are hostile to them, or a menace—in however slight a degree—to their interests. Alliance with China, in view of China's absolute military helplessness, means of course not an additional strength to us, but an additional obligation which we assume; and as I utterly disbelieve in the policy of bluff, in national and international no less than in private affairs, or in any violation of the old frontier maxim, "Never draw unless you mean to shoot," I do not believe in our taking any position anywhere unless we can make good; and as regards Manchuria, if the Japanese choose to follow a course of conduct to which we are adverse, we cannot stop it unless we are prepared to go to war, and a successful war about Manchuria would require a fleet as good as that of England, plus an army as good as that of Germany. The "open-door" policy in China was an excellent thing, and will I hope be a good thing in the future, so far as it can be maintained by general diplomatic agreement; but as has been proved by the whole history of Manchuria, alike under Russia and under Japan, the "open-door" policy, as a matter of fact, completely disappears as soon as a powerful nation determines to disregard it, and is willing to run the risk of war rather than forego its intention. How vital Manchuria is to Japan, and how impossible that she should submit to much outside interference therein, may be gathered from the fact—which I learned from Kitchener in England last year—that she is laying down triple lines of track from her coast bases to Mukden, as an answer to the double tracking of the Siberian Railway by the Russians. However friendly the superficial relations of Russia and Japan may at any given time become, both nations are accustomed to measure their foreign policy in sections of centuries; and Japan knows perfectly well that sometime in the future, if a good occasion offers, Russia will wish to play a return game of bowls for the prize she lost in their last contest. . . .

## 14 | Germany and American Public Opinion, August 1905 *

After 1900 the established order of power in Europe no longer conformed to the actuality of power. To establish a new order, with a minimum of stress, required a series of massive adjustments. Of these the most complex and dangerous was that of finding a place for Germany in European affairs which reflected German strength and efficiency. In the Far East, Roosevelt was willing to permit Japan some room for expansion, even at the expense of China, to prevent

* "Germany and American Public Opinion," *The Living Age*, CCXLVI (August 12, 1905), 436–7.

an explosion. Yet long before 1914 such notions of tolerance toward Japan ceased to characterize the American outlook. In Europe the adjustments in the hierarchy of power which might avoid a resort to force were even more illusive, for the traditional interests of France, England, and the United States were attached to the *status quo* on the Continent (with the exception of France's desire to recover Alsace-Lorraine). That American opinion by 1905 viewed the rise of German power on land and sea with some alarm was illustrated by the following article. Yet unless a predominant position could be assigned to Germany in European affairs the world could look forward to a new cycle of wars until the intrinsic strength of nations was again registered in the order of power. This article reveals to what extent world events after 1890 had revolutionized American attitudes toward Germany.

✍

. . . The recent action of Germany on the Moroccan question has been a revelation to many persons here, and has had a remarkable effect on public opinion. Those who were inclined to think that the need for watchfulness in regard to German policy, and the belief that German ambitions were antagonistic to the British Empire, were exaggerated have undergone a complete mental change. The spectacle presented by the brutal threats of the German Government levelled at France has moved men's minds far more than any amount of cautionary leading articles. It was almost at once realized here that the Germans cared little or nothing about Morocco, and that what they were doing was in reality punishing France for daring to make an agreement with Britain. In effect, if not in so many words, the Germans told the French:—"We will teach you to make a friend of Britain! It is true we cannot touch Britain directly, but, nevertheless, we mean to isolate her, and if you dare to work with her you must take the consequences. No one can be friendly to Britain without feeling the weight of our arm." Such an attitude so plainly shown has produced a great awakening here, and it is now difficult to find men who do not agree that as long as Germany is in the hands of those who now control her destinies the peace of the world is endangered. Three months ago the majority of the British people would not admit that there was any such peril. But though there is so great a change of feeling in regard to the need of watching German policy and being on our guard, there is, as we have said, not the slightest indication of any desire to attack Germany or to treat her as an enemy. It would be just as hard now as it was before the Morocco incident to induce our people to wage anything but a defensive war against Germany. The British people were never more profoundly anxious to keep the peace than at the present moment. Nothing but proof of the absolute necessity for self-protection, or for carrying out their obligations to their friends, would induce them to enter upon hostilities.

A word must be said as to "An Old Berliner's" suggestion that the efforts on the part of Germany to influence public opinion in America may prove successful. For ourselves, we entertain no such dread. We quite admit that if the

German Government take sufficient trouble, as no doubt they will, they will be able to get American newspapers to print a great deal of cleverly concocted anti-British stuff, the object of which will be to induce the Americans to believe that we are a dangerous and aggressive Power bent on attacking Germany, and that Germany in self-defence may some day be obliged to organize a coalition to destroy us as a mad dog is destroyed. But between such suggestions being freely cabled to American newspapers and their really influencing American public opinion there is all the difference in the world. The Americans like sensational telegrams, but when it comes to forming a practical judgment on public affairs these is no people less easily "taken in." Serious-minded Americans realize perfectly well the anti-liberal character of the German Government, and have noted once and for all the German Emperor's autocratic views and his dislike of free institutions. The American people, we are glad to think, have strong German sympathies. They are not, however, in sympathy with the autocrat who allows the officer to cut down the civilian who does not bow his head before the Imperial uniform, or who permits imprisonment for *lèse-majesté*, but with the democracy who desire that the German people shall be allowed to lift their heads to the light, and who want to loosen the chains of militarism and bureaucratic oppression. The American nation have an unfailing political instinct, and that political instinct is in favor of what for want of a better expression we must call liberal political ideas. When they realize, as they will realize the moment they are called upon to reflect seriously on the matter, that Britain and France stand for liberal ideas, and that the Germans as at present organized stand for the reverse, we have not the slightest fear as to which side their sympathies will incline to. The thing an American hates most in the world is the tone of Frederick the Great's drill-sergeant when he cut the recruit across the mouth with his cane, with a "Hound! you mutiny." As long as that is the attitude of the German autocracy at home and abroad, it will take an eternity of interviews with Professor Schiemann to "rectify" American public opinion.

# 15 | Herbert Croly's Observations on American Foreign Policy, 1909 *

After 1900 the new American commitments in the Far East—achieved with a negligible expenditure of effort and unsupported by adequate naval power—added to a continuing lack of concern for the shifting European balance of power, gave to American isolationism a decidedly Asia-first orientation. Herbert Croly, in an effort to frame a realistic policy for the United States, suggested that the nation beware of its Far Eastern commitments and turn its attention to

* Herbert Croly, *The Promise of American Life* (New York, 1911), 306–14. Copyright 1909 by The Macmillan Company. Reprinted by permission.

Europe, where it faced a more genuine challenge to its interests and security. Geographical isolation in itself, he warned, was no guarantee against involvement in any future European war. Only through a prudent involvement in Europe's affairs could the United States preserve the traditional balance.

Any systematic development of the foreign policy of the United States, such as proposed herewith, will seem very wild to the majority of Americans. They will not concede its desirability, because the American habit is to proclaim doctrines and policies, without considering either the implications, the machinery necessary to carry them out, or the weight of the resulting responsibilities.

A genuinely national foreign policy for the American democracy is not exhausted by the Monroe Doctrine. The United States already has certain colonial interests; and these interests may hereafter be extended. I do not propose at the present stage of this discussion to raise the question as to the legitimacy in principle of a colonial policy on the part of a democratic nation. The validity of colonial expansion even for a democracy is a manifest deduction from the foregoing political principles, always assuming that the people whose independence is thereby diminished are incapable of efficient national organization. On the other hand, a democratic nation cannot righteously ignore an unusually high standard of obligation for the welfare of its colonial population. It would be distinctly recreant to its duty, in case it failed to provide for the economic prosperity of such a population, and for their educational discipline and social improvement. It by no means follows, however, that because there is no rigid objection on democratic principles to colonial expansion, there may not be the strongest practical objection on the score of national interest to the acquisition of any particular territory. A remote colony is, under existing international conditions, even more of a responsibility than it is a source of national power and efficiency; and it is always a grave question how far the assumption of any particular responsibility is worth while.

Without entering into any specific discussion, there can, I think, be little doubt that the United States was justified in assuming its existing responsibilities in respect to Cuba and its much more abundant responsibilities in respect to Porto Rico. Neither can it be fairly claimed that hitherto the United States has not dealt disinterestedly and in good faith with the people of these islands. On the other hand, our acquisition of the Philippines raises a series of much more doubtful questions. These islands have been so far merely an expensive obligation, from which little benefit has resulted to this country and a comparatively moderate benefit to the Filipinos. They have already cost an amount of money far beyond any chance of compensation, and an amount of American and Filipino blood, the shedding of which constitutes a grave responsibility. Their future defense against possible attack presents a military and naval problem of the utmost difficulty. In fact, they cannot be defended from Japan except by the maintenance of a fleet in Pacific waters at least as large as the Japanese fleet; and it does not look probable that the United States will be able to afford for another generation any such concentration of naval strength in the Pacific. But even though from the military point of view the Philippines may constitute a source of weakness and danger, their possession will have the political advantage of keeping the American people alive to their interests in the grave problems which will be raised in the Far East by the future development of China and Japan.

The future of China raises questions of American foreign policy second only in importance to the establishment of a stable American international organization; and in relation to these questions, also, the interests of the United States and Canada tend both to coincide and to diverge (possibly) from those of Great Britain. Just what form the Chinese question will assume, after the industrial and the political awakening of China has resulted in a more effective military organization and in greater powers both of production and consumption, cannot be predicted with any certainty; but at present, it looks as if the maintenance of the traditional American policy with respect to China, viz., the territorial integrity and the free commercial development of that country, might require quite as considerable a concentration of naval strength in the Pacific as is required by the defense of the Philippines. It is easy enough to enunciate such a policy, just as it is easy to proclaim a Monroe Doctrine which no European Power has any sufficient immediate interest to dispute; but it is wholly improbable that China can be protected in its territorial integrity and its political independence without a great deal of diplomacy and more or less fighting. During the life of the coming generation there will be brought home clearly to the American people how much it will cost to assert its own essential interests in China; and the peculiar value of the Philippines as an American colony will consist largely in the fact that they will help American public opinion to realize more quickly than it otherwise would the complications and responsibilities created by Chinese political development and by Japanese ambition. . . .

The increasingly strenuous nature of international competition and the constantly higher standards of international economic, technical, and political efficiency prescribe a constantly improving domestic political and economic organization. The geographical isolation which affords the United States its military security against foreign attack should not blind Americans to the merely comparative nature of their isolation. The growth of modern sea power and the vast sweep of modern national political interests have at once diminished their security, and multiplied the possible sources of contact between American and European interests. No matter how peaceably the United States is inclined, and no matter how advantageously it is situated, the American nation is none the less constantly threatened by political warfare, and constantly engaged in industrial warfare. The American people can no more afford than can a European people to neglect any necessary kind or source of efficiency. Sooner than ever before in the history of the world do a nation's sins and deficiencies find it out. . . .

The inference inevitably is that the isolation which has meant so much to the United States, and still means so much, cannot persist in its present form. Its geographical position will always have a profound influence on the strategic situation of the United States in respect to the European Powers. It should always emancipate the United States from merely European complications. But, while the American nation should never seek a positive place in an exclusively European system, Europe, the United States, Japan, and China must all eventually take their respective places in a world system. While such a system is still so remote that it merely shows dimly through the obscurity of the future, its manifest desirability brings with it certain definite but contingent obligations in addition to the general obligation of comprehensive and thorough-going national efficiency. It brings with it the obligation of interfering under certain possible circumstances in what may at first appear to be a purely European complication; and this specific obligation would be the result of the general obligation of a democratic nation to make its foreign policy serve the cause of international peace. Hitherto, the American preference and desire for peace has constituted the chief justification for its isolation. At some future time the same purpose, just in so far as it is sincere and rational, may demand intervention. The American responsibility in this respect is similar to that of any peace-preferring European Power. If it wants peace, it must be spiritually and physically prepared to fight for it. Peace will prevail in international relations, just as order prevails within a nation, because of the righteous use of superior force—because the power which makes for pacific organization is stronger than the power which makes for a warlike organization. It looks as if at some future time the power of the United States might well be sufficient, when thrown into the balance, to tip the scales in favor of a comparatively pacific settlement of international complications. Under such conditions a policy of neutrality would be a policy of irresponsibility and unwisdom.

The notion of American intervention in a European conflict, carrying with it either the chance or the necessity of war, would at present be received with pious horror by the great majority of Americans. Non-interference in European affairs is conceived, not as a policy dependent upon certain conditions, but as absolute law—derived from the sacred writings. If the issue should be raised in the near future, the American people would be certain to shirk it; and they would, perhaps, have some reason for a failure to understand their obligation, because the course of European political development has not as yet been such as to raise the question in a decisive form. All one can say as to the existing situation is that there are certain Powers which have very much more to lose than they have to gain by war. These Powers are no longer small states like Belgium, Switzerland, and Holland, but populous and powerful states like Great Britain, Italy, and France. It may be one or it may be many generations before the issue of a peaceful or a warlike organization is decisively raised. When, if ever, it is decisively raised, the system of public law, under which any organization would have to take place, may not be one which the United States could accept. But the point is that, whenever and however it is raised, the American national leaders should confront it with a sound, well-informed, and positive conception of the American national interest rather than a negative and ignorant conception. And there is at least a fair chance that such will be the case. The experience of the American people in foreign affairs is only beginning, and during the next few generations the growth of their traffic with Asia and Europe will afford them every reason and every opportunity to ponder seriously the great international problem of peace in its relation to the American national democratic interest. . . .

# 16 | The Asia-First Policies of William Howard Taft, December 1912 *

President Taft characterized the foreign policies of his administration in his message to Congress in December 1912. Under the general principle of "Dollar Diplomacy" he rationalized an expanding American financial involvement in China which gave "new life and practical application" to the Open Door policy. He cited the role of diplomacy in broadening the trade and investment opportunities in the Caribbean. Toward Europe he revealed no interest at all.

ß

The foreign relations of the United States actually and potentially affect the state of the Union to a degree not widely realized and hardly surpassed by any other factor in the welfare of the whole Nation. The position of the United States in the moral, intellectual, and material relations of the family of nations should be a matter of vital interest to every patriotic citizen. The national prosperity and power impose upon us duties which we can not shirk if we are to be true to our ideals. The tremendous growth of the export trade of the United States has already made that trade a very real factor in the industrial and commercial prosperity of the country. With the development of our industries the foreign commerce of the United States must rapidly become a still more essential factor in its economic welfare. Whether we have a far-seeing and wise diplomacy and are not recklessly plunged into unnecessary wars, and whether our foreign policies are based upon an intelligent grasp of present-day world conditions and a clear view of the potentialities of the future, or are governed by a temporary and timid expediency or by narrow views befitting an infant nation, are questions in the alternative consideration of which must convince any thoughtful citizen that no department of national polity offers greater

* Taft's message to Congress, December 3, 1912, *Papers Relating to the Foreign Relations of the United States, 1912* (Washington, 1919), vii–viii, x–xii, xvi–xvii, xxvii.

opportunity for promoting the interests of the whole people on the one hand, or greater chance on the other of permanent national injury, than that which deals with the foreign relations of the United States.

The fundamental foreign policies of the United States should be raised high above the conflict of partisanship and wholly dissociated from differences as to domestic policy. In its foreign affairs the United States should present to the world a united front. The intellectual, financial, and industrial interests of the country and the publicist, the wage earner, the farmer, and citizen of whatever occupation must cooperate in a spirit of high patriotism to promote that national solidarity which is indispensable to national efficiency and to the attainment of national ideals.

The relations of the United States with all foreign powers remain upon a sound basis of peace, harmony, and friendship. A greater insistence upon justice to American citizens or interests wherever it may have been denied and a stronger emphasis of the need of mutuality in commercial and other relations have only served to strengthen our friendships with foreign countries by placing those friendships upon a firm foundation of realities as well as aspirations.

Before briefly reviewing the more important events of the last year in our foreign relations, which it is my duty to do as charged with their conduct and because diplomatic affairs are not of a nature to make it appropriate that the Secretary of State make a formal annual report, I desire to touch upon some of the essentials to the safe management of the foreign relations of the United States and to endeavor, also, to define clearly certain concrete policies which are the logical modern corollaries of the undisputed and traditional fundamentals of the foreign policy of the United States. . . .

The diplomacy of the present administration has sought to respond to modern ideas of commercial intercourse. This policy has been characterized as substituting dollars for bullets. It is one that appeals alike to idealistic humanitarian sentiments, to the dictates of sound policy and strategy, and to legitimate commercial aims. It is an effort frankly directed to the increase of American trade upon the axiomatic principle that the Government of the United States shall extend all proper support to every legitimate and beneficial American enterprise abroad. How great have been the results of this diplomacy, coupled with the maximum and minimum provision of the tariff law, will be seen by some consideration of the wonderful increase in the export trade of the United States. Because modern diplomacy is commercial, there has been a disposition in some quarters to attribute to it none but materialistic aims. How strikingly erroneous is such an impression may be seen from a study of the results by which the diplomacy of the United States can be judged.

In the field of work toward the ideals of peace this Government negotiated, but to my regret was unable to consummate, two arbitration treaties which set the highest mark of the aspiration of nations toward the substitution of arbitration and reason for war in the settlement of international disputes. Through the efforts of American diplomacy several wars have been prevented or ended. I refer to the successful tripartite mediation of the Argentine Republic, Brazil, and the United States between Peru and Ecuador; the bringing of the boundary dispute between Panama and Costa Rica to peaceful arbitration; the staying of warlike preparations when Haiti and the Dominican Republic were on the verge of hostilities; the stopping of a war in Nicaragua; the halting of internecine strife in Honduras. The Government of the United States was thanked for its influence toward the restoration of amicable relations between the Argentine Republic and Bolivia. The diplomacy of the United States is active in seeking to assuage the remaining ill-feeling between this country and the Republic of Colombia. In the recent civil war in China the United States successfully joined with the other interested powers in urging an early cessation of hostilities. An agreement has been reached between the Governments of Chile and Peru whereby the celebrated Tacna-Arica dispute, which has so long embittered international relations on the west coast of South America, has at last been adjusted. Simultaneously came the news that the boundary dispute between Peru and Ecuador had entered upon a stage of amicable settlement. The position of the United States in reference to the Tacna-Arica dispute between Chile and Peru has been one of nonintervention, but one of friendly influence and pacific counsel throughout the period during which the dispute in question has been the subject of interchange of views between this Government and the two Governments immediately concerned. In the general easing of international tension on the west coast of South America the tripartite mediation, to which I have referred, has been a most potent and beneficent factor.

In China the policy of encouraging financial investment to enable that country to help itself has had the result of giving new life and practical application to the open-door policy. The consistent purpose of the present administration has been to encourage the use of American capital in the development of China by the promotion of those essential reforms to which China is pledged by treaties with the United States and other powers. The hypothecation to foreign bankers in connection with certain industrial enterprises, such as the Hukuang railways, of the national revenues upon which these reforms depended, led the Department of State early in the administration to demand for American citizens participation in such enterprises, in order that the United States might have equal rights and an equal voice in all questions pertaining to the disposition of the public revenues concerned. The same policy of promoting international accord among the powers having similar treaty rights as ourselves in the matters of reform, which could not be put into practical effect without the common consent of all, was likewise adopted in the case of the loan desired by China for the reform of its currency. The principle of international cooperation in matters of common interest upon which our policy had already been based in all of the above instances has admittedly been a great factor in that concert of the powers which has been so happily conspicuous during the perilous period of transition through which the great Chinese nation has been passing.

In Central America the aim has been to help such countries as Nicaragua and Honduras to help themselves. They are the immediate beneficiaries. The national benefit to the United States is twofold. First, it is obvious that the Monroe doctrine is more vital in the neighborhood of the Panama Canal and the zone of the Caribbean than anywhere else. There, too, the maintenance of that doctrine falls most heavily upon the United States. It is therefore essential that the countries within that sphere shall be removed from the jeopardy involved by heavy foreign debt and chaotic national finances and from the ever-present danger of international complications due to disorder at home. Hence the United States has been glad to encourage and support American bankers who were willing to lend a helping hand to the financial rehabilitation of such countries because this financial rehabilitation and the protection of their custom-houses from being the prey of would-be dictators would remove at one stroke the menace of foreign creditors and the menace of revolutionary disorder.

The second advantage to the United States is one affecting chiefly all the southern and Gulf ports and the business and industry of the South. The Republics of Central America and the Caribbean possess great natural wealth. They need only a measure of stability and the means of financial regeneration to enter upon an era of peace and prosperity, bringing profit and happiness to themselves and at the same time creating conditions sure to lead to a flourishing interchange of trade with this country. . . .

As illustrating the commercial benefits to the Nation derived from the new diplomacy and its effectiveness upon the material as well as the more ideal side, it may be remarked that through direct official efforts alone there have been obtained in the course of this administration, contracts from foreign Governments involving an expenditure of $50,000,000 in the factories of the United States. Consideration of this fact and some reflection upon the necessary effects of a scientific tariff system and a foreign service alert and equipped to cooperate with the business men of America carry the conviction that the gratifying increase in the export trade of this country is, in substantial amount, due to our improved governmental methods of protecting and stimulating it. . . .

Congress should fully realize the conditions which obtain in the world as we find ourselves at the threshold of our middle age as a Nation. We have emerged full grown as a peer in the great concourse of nations. We have passed through various formative periods. We have been self-centered in the struggle to develop our domestic resources and deal with our domestic questions. The Nation is now too mature to continue in its foreign relations those temporary expedients natural to a people to whom domestic affairs are the sole concern. In the past our diplomacy has often consisted, in normal times, in a mere assertion of the right to international existence. We are now in a larger relation with broader rights of our own and obligations to others than ourselves. A number of great guiding principles were laid down early in the history of this Government. The recent task of our diplomacy has been to adjust those principles to the conditions of to-day, to develop their corollaries, to find practical applications of the old principles expanded to meet new situations. Thus are being evolved bases upon which can rest the superstructure of policies which must grow with the destined progress of this Nation. The successful conduct of our foreign relations demands a broad and a modern view. We can not meet new questions nor build for the future if we confine ourselves to outworn dogmas of the past and to the perspective appropriate at our emergence from colonial times and conditions. The opening of the Panama Canal will mark a new era in our international life and create new and world-wide conditions which, with their vast correlations and consequences, will obtain for hundreds of years to come. We must not wait for events to overtake us unawares. With continuity of purpose we must deal with the problems of our external relations by a diplomacy modern, resourceful, magnanimous, and fittingly expressive of the high ideals of a great nation.

# VII

## The Great Crusade

The successive crises which brought a general war to Europe during the summer of 1914 challenged the American doctrines of isolationism and neutrality as had no previous series of events in the nation's history. The rise of the German Empire threatened, for the first time in a century, the traditional hierarchy of European power to which the American people had grown accustomed and with which they identified their security. That the United States possessed the physical strength to assure a victory for Britain and France, and thus right the balance, was obvious long before the United States entered the war against Germany. But far more important for the twentieth century than American involvement itself were the nature and purpose of that involvement. Would it be guided by the limited purpose of entering an established international system on terms which that system imposed? Or would it pursue purposes that transcended the nation's limited power to achieve? Wars accomplish far more than the mere separation of the quick from the dead, but whether they bring any genuine gains to civilization depends upon the manner in which they are fought. The inescapable challenge of the war years was less to the nation's productive capacity than to its political wisdom.

Every prospect that America's role in the war would reflect some appreciation for Europe's political and diplomatic traditions was prejudiced even before the war began. The utopian assumptions of nineteenth-century rationalism had already weakened the American powers of critical analysis. For countless American intellectuals the forces of reason had triumphed over the tendency toward war. As late as 1913 David Starr Jordan, director of the World Peace Foundation, declared: "What shall we say of the Great War of Europe, ever threatening, ever impending and which never comes? We shall say that it will never come. Humanly speaking, it is impossible." That same year William Jennings Bryan observed, "I believe there will be no war while I am Secretary of State, and I believe there will be no war as long as I live." During the events of July 1914, following the murder of the Austrian archduke at Sarajevo, Americans continued to look at Europe in disbelief. On July 28 the *New York Times* proclaimed: "That [war] is too dreadful for imagining, and because it is too dreadful it cannot happen." The *New York World* added emphatically: "The stakes are too enormous, the issue of the game too uncertain, for civilized Europe . . . to risk its future well-being at the caprice of military gamblers."

Having discounted the possibility of war, the purveyors of American thought could perceive in the outbreak of the European conflict no challenge to their assumptions that war had ceased to be a rational and legitimate national endeavor. This war, like all wars, was the creation of evil men and evil institutions—imperialism, militarism, and monarchy. For some Americans, such as Henry Ford, it was the imperial lust for markets that had driven Europe into war. For others it was the deepening struggle of militarism against the rising tide of social democracy. The *New York Tribune* put forth the latter view with remarkable precision. "It must be," ran its editorial, "that military castes [in Germany and Austria] feel that war, with all its dangers, is better for them than the slowly losing struggle they are now making against the oncoming democratic revolution. . . . Militarism has come to be accepted by a large element as the only safe barrier against the encroachment of social democracy." But ultimately the responsibility for the war, in the American mind, rested on monarchy, specifically on the three great war lords of Europe—Kaiser Wilhelm of Germany, Czar Nicholas of Russia, and Emperor Franz Joseph of Austria. As *The Nation* summarized:

> . . . after this most awful and most wicked of all wars is over, the power of life and death over millions of men, the right to decree the ruin of industry and commerce and finance . . . will be taken away from three men. . . . But whatever happens, Europe—humanity—will not settle back again into a position enabling three Emperors—one of them senile, another subject to melancholia, and the third often showing signs of disturbed mental balance—to give, on their individual choice or whim, the signal for destruction and massacre.

For American idealists, unmindful and contemptuous of the vast complexities of European politics, the war represented the twilight of the kings. The European masses, predicted the *New York Times,* would cast off such feudal institutions as monarchy and militarism. Thereafter they would have peace. Meanwhile the United States was safe in its isolation. For many of its citizens the American relationship to the European war was well exemplified by the cartoon in *Harper's Weekly* which depicted Uncle Sam with a consoling arm around a weeping Civilization, looking across the water at a burning Europe. Recognizing the war's enormous tug on American emotions, President Woodrow Wilson admonished the nation to be "impartial in thought as well as in action." To provide for the country's peace and safety, the President favored the strengthening of the National Guard. More than this, he declared, "would mean merely that we had lost our self-possession, that we had been thrown off our balance by a war with which we have nothing to do, whose causes can not touch us, whose very existence affords us opportunities of friendship and disinterested service which should make us ashamed of any thought of hostility or fearful preparations for trouble."


## II

Not all Americans shared these detached and simplistic notions regarding the European war. For half a decade a distinguished group of American and British writers had dissected and exposed for the American public the burgeoning trends in European affairs and their possible impact on the interests of the United States. What was at stake, they agreed, was the traditional balance of power. Some found the answer to the challenge of Germany and Austria in the rebuilding of British naval supremacy. (*Reading No. 1.*) Others predicted that American power would ultimately be thrown into the struggle, for inasmuch as the European balance was no longer self-contained, the German naval program endangered the security of the United States. In July 1909, Sidney Brooks, the well-known British writer, presented a thoughtful evaluation of the revolution which had occurred in United States-German relationships since the turn of the century. Outside the ranks of the German-Americans and Irish-Americans, he wrote, there existed little sentiment in the United States that favored Germany's naval ambitions. (*Reading No. 2.*) Perhaps no American writer predicted more alarmingly the consequences of German naval supremacy in the Atlantic than did Alfred Thayer Mahan. Since it seemed clear to such critics that the United States would never permit the defeat of Britain in war, they argued that the nation should desert its isolationist habits of mind while it could still influence the inescapable tendencies in European politics in defense of its own interests.

For Lewis Einstein the issue was no longer a simple matter of sustaining British predominance. His fundamental concern lay in the perpetuation of the entire European balance of power, threatened in the long run as much by Russia as by Germany, and the essential role of the United States in preserving that balance. To him the American mind was less than promising. In his noted essay of January 1913, published anonymously in *The National Review,* this perceptive member of the United States Foreign Service pointed to the deep, but generally unrecognized, American interest in the European balance. The intense and somewhat irrational rivalry between England and Germany, he predicted accurately, would terminate in war--a war in which the vital interests of the United States would become involved. Whatever occurred in Europe, he warned, the Republic had "a distinct and legitimate duty in the family of great nations in contributing to preserve those elements which compose the balance of power, and to which it can only be blind at a later cost." (*Reading No. 3.*) Einstein wrote again in November 1914, following the outbreak of war, that although the crushing of France would be a misfortune, the United States could not prevent it. But the defeat of England, he added, would be intolerable. To guarantee British survival, wrote Einstein, the United States had no choice but to extend the Monroe Doctrine to England, "not on grounds of common civilization or race, or tongue, but on grounds of solid interest reinforced by the weight of tradition and sentiment. . . ."

Theodore Roosevelt, writing in *The Outlook* of September 23, 1914, believed it essential that the United States, in responding to the European crisis, maintain a posture of traditional courtesy toward all nations while it measured its interests in the struggle and prepared to defend them. To this former President, speaking softly was still as essential as carrying the big stick. Roosevelt harbored a deep concern for the European balance of power. Like Lewis Einstein, he identified American security in both the Atlantic and the Western Hemisphere with British predominance in Europe. Shortly before the outbreak of war he informed Baron Hermann von Eckhardstein, a friend in the German Foreign Service, that

> as long as England succeeds in keeping up the balance of power in Europe, not in principle but in reality, well and good. Should she, however, for some reason or other fail in doing so, the United States would be obliged to step in, at least temporarily, in order to re-establish the balance of power in Europe, never mind against which country or group of countries our efforts may have to be directed. In fact, we are becoming, owing to our strength and geographical situation, more and more the balance of power of the whole globe.

It was imperative, Roosevelt wrote in November 1914, that the war not terminate in the destruction of either England or Germany, for both nations were essential to Europe's stability. The total destruction of Germany, he warned, would force the entire Western world into a contest with Russia. (*Reading No. 4.*)

Roosevelt's initial response to Germany's predominant position on the European continent followed conceptually his earlier reaction as President to the rise of Japan as a major power in the Pacific. Roosevelt in 1914 represented the sober, conservative tradition in modern diplomacy, with its emphasis on both civility and power as the necessary means for preserving the national interest.

### III

For Woodrow Wilson such mundane objectives as the preservation of the national interest and the balance of power simply underestimated the moral and intellectual resources of the nation to reform the entire international order. Wilson, in practice, could not discount the national interests of the United States completely. Yet he was unable to conceive of international relations except in moral terms, and there is little evidence that even his later opposition to a German victory was motivated by a desire to preserve the European balance of power. Before the outbreak of war in 1914 Wilson had paid scant attention to foreign affairs. He had displayed no knowledge or interest in the tensions which were propelling Europe into a general war. Even after the war arrived he disclaimed any concern for its origins. His thinking on external issues was faddish. His acceptance of the current nonpower approaches to international settlements, such as arbitration conventions and cooling-off treaties, was reinforced by his own deep faith in democratic processes. To Wilson democracy was more than a system of government; it was a set of moral principles which exemplified the highest ideals of human society. Wilson never doubted, moreover, the capacity of all peoples to develop the necessary habits of democracy. "When properly directed," he wrote, "there is no people not fitted for self-government." To such assumptions Wilson eventually attached his expectations of a democratically governed international society.

Wilson's concepts relative to world affairs were molded as well by his unshakable allegiance to the nineteenth-century idea of progress. The modern school of utopian politics found its ultimate source of truth in individual human reason. And since it was a fundamental characteristic of human nature to seek pleasure and avoid pain, Jeremy Bentham, the British philosopher, concluded early in the century that the ultimate human objective was the greatest happiness for the greatest number. Moreover, Bentham observed, the capacity to achieve this goal of human happiness rested less in monarchy than in the simple common sense of the masses. Perhaps no nineteenth-century writer attributed greater infallibility to public opinion than did Bentham's pupil, James Mill, who wrote:

> Every man possessed of reason is accustomed to weigh evidence and to be guided and determined by its preponderance. When various conclusions are, with their evidence, presented with equal care and with equal skill, there is a moral certainty, though some few may be misguided, that the greatest number will judge right, and that the greatest force of evidence, whatever it is, will produce the greatest impression.

Thus nineteenth-century optimism was anchored, as Edward H. Carr has written, to the conviction that "the pursuit of good was a matter of right reasoning, that the spread of knowledge would soon make it possible for everyone to reason rightly on this important subject, and that anyone who reasoned rightly on it would necessarily act rightly." When applied to international affairs, such principles ruled out the necessity of war and other irrational uses of power. War was simply a failure of understanding; an educated, informed people, desiring good, would regard international anarchy as absurd and put an end to it.

European political philosophers had, in large measure, deserted these utopian assumptions long before the end of the century. With the outbreak of World War I in 1914, however, men began to search for the foundations of some new world order which might protect human society from the curse of war. It was Woodrow Wilson, the admirer of such nineteenth-century British rationalists as John Bright and William E. Gladstone, who resurrected the rationalist faith and applied it to international politics. Yet Wilson's determination to create an international order based on the power of world opinion had some precedent in the plan of his predecessor, William Howard Taft, to negotiate compulsory arbitration treaties between the United States and other major countries. When asked how the award of an arbitral court would be enforced, Taft replied lightly that in a democracy the enforcement of legal decisions never gave rise to any difficulty. Nor would it in an international judicial system. "After we have gotten the cases into court and decided, and the judgments embodied in a solemn declaration of a court thus established," he predicted, "few nations will care to face the condemnation of international public opinion and disobey the judgment."

The Senate rejected Taft's arbitration proposals, but in 1913 Bryan, as Wilson's first Secretary of State, negotiated a group of cooling-off treaties which substituted the principle of conciliation for arbitration. Under these treaties the signatories agreed not to resort to war for at least twelve months after the beginning of a dispute. "The sum and substance [of these treaties]," declared Wilson in October 1914, three months after Europe went to war, "is that whenever any trouble arises the light shall shine on it for a year before anything is done; and my prediction is that after the light has shone on it for a year, it will not be necessary to do anything; that after we know what happened, then we will know who was right and who was wrong." In vain Mahan and others attacked as utopian and fallacious the notion that either arbitration or conciliation, supported only by legal or moral judgments, could resolve basic conflicts of interest. For them there existed among nations no mutual interest in peace sufficiently strong to eliminate the continuing necessity of employing force in the management of international relationships. (*Reading No. 5.*)

## IV

Ignoring the warnings of the nation's realists, Wilson, following the outbreak of war in July 1914, identified America's role in world affairs with the creation of a rational, peaceful international system. At the core of Wilson's thought was the conviction that the nation's political, social, and moral uniqueness had assigned to it a transcendent mission to serve humanity. America had been born, said Wilson, that man might be free. His exhortation to the nation on Independence Day, 1914, was characteristic: "America has lifted high the light which will shine unto all generations and guide the feet of mankind to the goal of justice, and liberty, and peace."

As the struggle on the Western front moved from trench to trench and the contestants became locked in a process of futile destruction, Wilson informed the American people that Europe beckoned, not for material aid, but for leadership in creating a better world. "Why is it that all nations turn to us with the instinctive feeling that if anything touches humanity it touches us?" he asked; then he answered his own question: "Because it knows that ever since we were born as a Nation we have undertaken to be the champions of humanity and the rights of men." Even in war, he said, the United States would struggle only for the rights of mankind. Thus Wilson could address a Chicago audience in January 1916: "America has no reason for being unless her destiny and her duty be ideal. It is her incumbent privilege to declare and stand for the rights of men. Nothing less is worth fighting for."

Eventually Wilson, in his effort to establish the intellectual bases of a new world order, warred on every vestige of the established state system. For him the special villains which kept the world at war were secret diplomacy, the balance of power, and the concept of national interest. His continued search for alternatives to these accouterments of power politics upon which to build the foundations of peace culminated in his message to the Senate of January 22,

1917. (*Reading No. 6.*) Future peace, Wilson declared, must be secured, not by the warring nations alone, but by the organized force of mankind. Having assigned to the silent masses of the world the power and the right to control world affairs, he committed the United States to the support of a new postwar organization which would carry out the universal interest of mankind in sustaining the peace. It was essential, therefore, that the European war be fought to achieve "a just and secure peace" and not "a new balance of power. . . . There must be, not a balance of power, but a community of power; not organized rivalries, but an organized common peace."

Whether Wilson required actual United States involvement in the European conflict if he would become the arbiter of peace mattered little, for by January 1917 the nation was drifting rapidly toward war. Many pressures had warred on American neutrality—British propaganda, economic interests, and submarine warfare—but none of these forces, in themselves, would have carried the United States into war had the nation exhibited any genuine neutrality toward the struggle for Europe. But for the pro-British sympathies harbored by the American people, British propaganda would have been resented or ignored. Had American business leaders not favored a British victory, they would not have forced on the national administration policies which created a vested United States interest in the Allied cause. Had Wilson, supported by his advisers, not desired the eventual triumph of the British effort, he would have given up, at least temporarily, the American concept of freedom of the seas, or at least applied the concept equally to the British and German nations. It was this profound absence of neutrality in American thought that drove the nation steadily toward involvement. After the outbreak of war in Europe it made considerable difference to the administration, to leading members of Congress, and to the public at large who would emerge victorious. There existed throughout the Republic, as many writers had predicted, a deep-seated conviction that the destruction of both British naval supremacy and British leadership in European affairs would leave the United States far less secure than it had been in the past. Against this predominant sentiment Germany had no chance. Every German innovation, whether reasonable within the context of technological advancement or not, was held against that nation. This decreed from the beginning that the submarine issue eventually would become critical.

When the great European war ventured onto the Atlantic in 1915, the United States could no more avoid the buffeting of the struggling nations on the high seas than could Thomas Jefferson's America after the renewal of the Napoleonic wars in 1806. Jefferson employed the economic weapon of the embargo to defend the American principle of freedom of the seas, and eventually, if futilely, he was willing to pay the price of the destruction of American commerce and the American merchant marine to defend the nation's rights. It is significant that Wilson, a century later, attempted to achieve the protection of United States commerce, if not an actual British victory, by the simple and inexpensive expedient of declaring the submarine illegal and immoral. Undoubtedly the submarine rendered obsolete the tradition of rescue on the high seas. It did not comprise some new, unprecedented depravity on the part of the user. Nor did it alter the basic nature of sea warfare, in which the object had always been the sinking of ships. In a total war, moreover, it was the one method available to Germany for creating sea power sufficient to challenge British control of the sea lanes leading to the key English ports. The iniquitous character of the submarine was less important than the new weapon's threat to British naval supremacy in the Atlantic.

Eventually Wilson's legalistic methods of bridging the gap between his goal of a British victory and the actuality of German power proved ineffective, for the German interest in victory was too great to be jeopardized by Wilson's precepts of right and wrong. When the Berlin government announced a program of unrestricted submarine warfare late in January 1917, Wilson rationalized his decision for war against Germany, not by identifying American interest with the balance of power, but rather by designating Germany as the final barrier to the achievement of his dreams of building a peaceful future. In his war message of April 2, the President repeated unequivocally the goals of his earlier speeches. "Our object now, as then," he said, "is to vindicate the principles of peace and justice in the life of the world as against selfish and autocratic power and to set up amongst the really free and self-governed peoples of the world such a concert of purpose and of action as will henceforth insure the observance of those principles. . . . The world must be made safe for democracy." (Reading No. 7.)

Not all members of Congress accepted Wilson's decision for war or the purity of his motives. Perhaps Senator George Norris of Nebraska summarized as accurately as any the fundamental arguments of those who opposed the war. For him the nation had failed to maintain its neutrality; this failure, in turn, he attributed to the influence of bankers and munitions makers who had a vested interest in a British victory. (Reading No. 8.)

## V

Wilson's every military and diplomatic decision through the period of American involvement in World War I was designed to maximize his voice in world affairs once the fighting had ended. By 1917 the war had degenerated into a meaningless slaughter. On June 7, two months after the United States entered the war, Sir Douglas Haig, commander of the British forces on the Western front, ordered the British troops forward into the morass that separated them from the German machine guns. During the next three months the British suffered a quarter of a million casualties in the battle. To remove the control of the war from generals so devoid of imagination, British Prime Minister David Lloyd George attempted in 1918 to divert a larger portion of the Western military effort to other fronts. But Wilson sided with the Allied commanders who preferred to concentrate the fighting on the Western front to achieve the earliest possible defeat of the German armies. It was on this front that the United States expeditionary forces would make their bid for glory, thus enabling the President as peacemaker to enjoy the power and prestige of the leader of that nation which had made victory possible.

When General John J. Pershing, commander of the American forces in France, opposed those European generals who wanted the American troops integrated into British and French units so that they might be prepared for battle more quickly, Wilson supported his commander's purpose of keeping the American forces intact so that their achievements might be more easily measured and demonstrated. When European diplomats in 1918 favored preliminary Allied negotiations in anticipation of an armistice, again Wilson objected. He preferred to avoid all diplomatic commitments until the end of the fighting when, backed by the general acknowledgment that American arms, matériel, and credit had turned the tide, he might dictate the terms of peace. Instead, his decision to postpone all genuine negotiations until the peace conference at Versailles merely assured the President a declining voice in international affairs. When it became apparent in Paris that he could not command the allegiance of even the United States Senate, Wilson became as common clay among Allied diplomatists.

Throughout his ordeal as wartime leader of the Republic, Wilson sustained his vision of a new international order based upon the reasoned judgment of mankind. In January 1918 he promulgated his famous "Fourteen Points" which promised a postwar peace founded on a League of Nations. This would mobilize the conscience of mankind against any future aggressor. The League of Nations, once considered theoretical and idealistic, he declared, had turned out to be practical and necessary. "What we seek," he emphasized on July 4, 1918, "is the reign of law, based on the consent of the governed and sustained by the organized opinion of mankind." In his address opening the Fourth Liberty Loan campaign, delivered in New York on September 27, 1918, Wilson continued his assault on the notion that power politics and the balance of power still governed international affairs:

> It is the peculiarity of this great war that while statesmen have seemed to cast about for definitions of their purpose and have sometimes seemed to shift their ground and their point of view, the thought of the mass of men, whom statesmen are supposed to instruct and lead, has grown more and more unclouded; more and more certain of what it is that they are fighting for. National purposes have fallen more and more into the background and the common purpose of enlightened mankind has taken their place. The counsels of plain men have become on all hands more simple and straightforward and more unified than the counsels of sophisticated men of affairs, who still retain the impression that they are playing a game of power and playing for high stakes. That is why I have said that this is a peoples' war, not a statesmen's. Statesmen must follow the clarified common thought or be broken. . . .

Wilson's idealism continued to mount after the Versailles Conference and reached its epitome during his swing across the nation in September 1919, when he attempted to take the issue of the League of Nations before the people after the Senate's rejection of the Versailles Treaty. The most notable of these speeches were those delivered at San Diego and Los Angeles on September 19 and 20. (*Reading No. 9.*) Wilson's words again carried the burden of his long-run expectations for a world of universal freedom and justice. Their immediate purpose, however, was that of undermining the administration's opposition in the Senate. Nothing that Wilson might say in defense of the Versailles Treaty and the League of Nations, however, could undo the force of the intellectual and political assault on his leadership, whether that assault was an expression of nationalism, isolationism, realism, or simple partisanship. (*Reading No. 10.*) Perhaps no democratic leader offered a more concise and perceptive critique of Wilson's "monism" than did one British Tory who declared:

> The world moves on differences; polarity is the law of life, and political monism sins against it. In any case, the grouping of nations dependent on their resources and fixed ideas is likely to be shaped for another half century, not by the League of Nations with its academic dialogues, but by the real Balance of Power. In that combination if America will bind herself to stand with what is now the Entente, she may compel Germany to keep the peace, not by eloquent discourses, but by the constantly active energies of more than a hundred millions, prepared to go to war on behalf of their ideals. . . . The Balance of Power corresponds to forces and interests duly weighed; but Mr. Wilson's Monism will prove to be a legal fiction on both sides of the "estranging sea."

Nowhere was Wilson's adherence to the principle of self-determination more clearly demonstrated, and more potentially disastrous, than in his wartime policies toward Japan. World War I, by weakening British, French, Russian, and German influence in Asia, presented Japan with an unprecedented opportunity to complete her expansionist program at the expense of China. It was quickly apparent that the United States, following the outbreak of the European war, faced the task of defending alone the principle of the Open Door. In August 1914 the Wilson administration accepted the Chinese request for support against external aggression and informed the British government that it intended "to preserve the *status quo* in China." When Japan entered the war against Germany on August 19, Secretary Bryan reminded that nation of its pledge to support "the independence and integrity of China and the principle of equal opportunities for the commerce and industry of all nations in China."

Japan defied these warnings early in 1915 by secretly presenting to China her famous Twenty-one Demands. These conditions, if accepted by the Chinese government, would have transformed the celestial empire into a virtual protectorate of Japan. Through procrastination alone China was able to achieve some drastic modifications in the original Japanese demands. When Washington learned of these transactions, Bryan, in a note to the Japanese government, restated the traditional United States policy toward China. He acknowledged, however, that "territorial contiguity" created special relationships between China and Japan. Then on May 11, 1915, in an effort to defend China against all Japanese encroachment, Bryan notified Tokyo and Peking that the United States "cannot recognize any agreement or undertaking which has been entered into or which may be entered into between the Governments of Japan and China, impairing the political or territorial integrity of the Republic of China, or the international policy relative to China commonly known as the Open Door policy." In the Lansing-Ishii Agreement of November 2, 1917, signed during the tenure of Robert Lansing as Secretary of State, the United States and Japan again reaffirmed their mutual respect for the principle of the Open Door. At Versailles, Wilson, vigorously but unsuccessfully, attempted to counter the secret wartime treaties of Japan with the European Allies and prevent all Japanese gains at the expense of China. By 1919 it was apparent that the events of World War I had substituted for the former balance of power in the Far East an all-pervading and determined antagonism between the United States and Japan. There was little doubt in the minds of Far Eastern observers that Wilson's repeated demands on Japan had ignored the fundamental questions posed by Japanese expansionism and had placed United States–Japanese relations on a collision course. (*Reading No. 11.*)

Nor were the settlements in eastern Europe any more hopeful of permanent peace and security. The nationalistic aspirations of Slavic Europe, released during the war and confirmed by the Versailles settlement, destroyed much of Europe's traditional equilibrium. The Austro-Hungarian, the Turkish, the German, and the Russian empires gave way to numerous self-contained national states, inexperienced in government and beset by grievous economic and minority problems. For Winston Churchill the breakup of the Austro-Hungarian Empire was especially tragic. "For centuries," he wrote in *The Gathering Storm,* "this surviving embodiment of the Holy Roman Empire had afforded a common life, with advantages in trade and security, to a large number of peoples, none of whom in our own time had the strength or vitality to stand by themselves in the face of pressure from a revivified Germany or Russia. . . . There is not one of the peoples or provinces that constituted the Empire of the Hapsburgs to whom gaining their independence has not brought the tortures which ancient poets and theologians had reserved for the damned." To the east in 1919 lay Russia, a Communist state that controlled an international political movement which intensified everywhere in East-Central Europe the social unrest which followed in the wake of the war.

It is significant that Wilson never applied the principle of self-determination to the European victors of World War I. In practice the principle became a device for punishing the losers, and the territorial arrangements which consigned purely German areas to the new Slavic nations hardly served the principle of self-determination or the cause of peace. As David Lloyd George declared prophetically, "I cannot conceive any greater cause of future war than that the German people . . . should be surrounded by a mob of small States, many of them consisting of peoples who have never previously set up a stable government for themselves, but each of them containing large masses of Germans." No longer, finally, was there a Franco-Russian-British alliance capable of restricting the tensions that would surely emanate from the eastern European settlements.

## VI

Wilson's designation of America's proper role in international affairs, enunciated with deep conviction and appealing phraseology, gave American idealism a new birth and fastened it unshakably to the nation's attitudes and expectations in the realm of foreign relations. Wilson's speeches more than his actions carried the intent and had the effect of undermining completely an established diplomatic tradition that had, through much of the nation's history, taken its strength, consciously or unconsciously, from the words and policies of all American statesmen from Washington to Lincoln. What was tragic in Wilson's leadership was not that he warred on the finest traditions of the Founding Fathers, but that he warred with such remarkable success. Wilson had attached the nation's diplomacy to the unachievable. Thus his idealism, in assigning to the United States a revolutionary role in world affairs, carried the seeds of vanity and disappointment. In divorcing the country from its load of original sin and placing it morally above all others, Wilson incurred the resentment of much of the world's leadership. Despite his impressive rhetoric, he could never demonstrate how one nation's foreign policies could achieve such transcendent goals as the establishment and maintenance of freedom and justice for all mankind. Such purposes not only separated the nation's objectives from the limited means of politics and diplomacy, but also undermined its capacity to render humanity some genuine, if limited, service. It would have been no betrayal of American idealism or American moral purpose to have accepted the established rules of European diplomacy as had all the nation's early diplomatists.

Wilson eventually committed the errors of all leaders who ignore the limits of politics. He proposed a body of thought which had little or no relationship to the political realities with which he was forced to contend. At Versailles he became the embodiment of his self-created problem. Even while proclaiming the virtues of open diplomacy and self-determination he was forced to engage in deliberations of profound secrecy week after week. Like all idealists in power, Wilson eventually over-promised every group that attributed some precise meaning to his words—the Germans, the Allies, and the American people. (*Reading No. 12.*)

Ironically, Wilson's failure to fasten his concepts of world politics to the continuing existence of the old diplomacy in no way shattered the attachment of his followers to the views he had proclaimed. Perhaps the reason is clear. Wilson, whether purposefully or not, had devised an international system which, if accepted by all the major powers of the world, would have fastened the *status quo* on the international order of power, thus assuring the United States and the victorious democracies their predominant position in world affairs at little or no cost to themselves. Wilson's principles, tragically, were less concerned with justice than with the prevention of change. Their virtue flowed from that morality which he and other Allied leaders assigned to the Versailles system itself. Any attack on that system would be by definition immoral and a defiance of the principles embodied in Wilsonian thought. Had the President defended the Versailles Treaty as a proper definition of the interests of the United States around the world and thus an arrangement to be protected by force if necessary, he might have established the foundations of a viable national response to postwar world politics. But by defending his system as an expression of the sentiments of mankind, to be guaranteed by the universal acceptance of his principles of justice and self-determination, he led his followers to reject as either immoral or nonexistent the inescapable reality of a state system operating through the traditional means of power politics and the balance of power.

# 1 | The New European Balance of Power, January 1910 *

European peace and security rested after 1890, first, on the close balance of military power between the Triple Alliance and that of Russia and France and, second, on the unquestioned naval supremacy of Great Britain. By 1910 the vast expansion of the German army and navy challenged both foundations of the traditional European balance. This burgeoning threat to the customary position and security of France and Russia, as well as of England, drove these three nations into a defensive alliance, the Triple Entente. To Archibald R. Colquhoun, a contemporary writer of world affairs, analyzing the European balance of power in January 1910, Germany had become a danger to peace because only by some assault on the *status quo* could the German leadership present some tangible gain for the justification of the enormous German military expenditure. Peace hinged on the willingness of Britain to make sacrifices sufficient to discourage German aggression.

✑

It is essential for the maintenance of the balance of power that the great States of Europe should be grouped in such a manner as to prevent any one from becoming the supreme arbiter of the continent. This is no academic or theoretic proposition to be artificially maintained in the interests of symmetry, but is the outcome of the law of self-preservation which applies to nations as well as to individuals. Therefore, while the political manoeuvres of the European governments and their diplomatists may at times be puzzling, not merely to the man in the street, but to the student of world affairs, yet it will be found that on certain broad lines it is possible to disentangle the threads and to understand the drift of affairs. At the same time the growth and change inevitable in all States which are living organisms render any permanent grouping of the Powers unlikely, and, moreover, the psychological element which can never be fully reckoned with in the history of nations, may at any time provide surprises which alter the whole course of events.

For the greater part of the lifetime of most of us certain dominating features have determined the current of European politics. First, the Triple Alliance, the work of Bismarck; second, the great military power of Russia and her alliance with France; and third, the unquestioned naval supremacy of Great Britain. These three factors, by the balance of interests which they established and maintained, have secured peace to Europe, and have prevented any serious war between European States since the struggle of 1870, which founded the German Empire. But the last few years have seen changes which go to the foundations of that peace by striking at all these bulwarks. The Triple Alliance still exists,

* Archibald R. Colquhoun, "The New Balance of Power in Europe," *The North American Review*, CXCI (January 1910), 18–28.

but under circumstances which constitute a menace rather than a guarantee. Russia's military power has received an extraordinary check. Great Britain's naval supremacy is challenged. To older diplomatists it may well seem that the very foundations on which the European system has rested since the end of the Napoleonic wars is crumbling before their eyes. But, as it crumbles, another system will arise, and Europe, which has seen the decay of so much, will once more begin to build up. . . .

The actual position of Germany is, of course, of primary importance in discussing the balance of Power, because it is the growth of that country in armaments which, to borrow a phrase from Cecil Rhodes, has "upset the apple-cart," and apart from her internal strength Germany has consolidated her position by cementing, in the closest possible way, her alliance with Austria-Hungary. When Bismarck initiated the Triplice he was anxious not to draw the cords so tightly as to preclude the idea of understandings in other quarters of Europe as well—notably in St. Petersburg, but then Austria was but a weak ally, and Russia a powerful potential enemy. To-day Austria-Hungary has an army second only to that of Germany in size and training, and together the two constitute a military weapon such as Napoleon never dreamed of. . . . Italy, the third party in the Triplice, is in a very different position to her partners. The enmity between her people and Austria is always ready to break out, as was evidenced recently when an eminent General in presenting new colors to a regiment practically told them that he hoped the flags would lead Italian soldiers to the recovery of their lost lands. Italy's acquiescence in the Bosnian annexation was secured by timely concessions on the coast of the Adriatic, but at the present moment the relations of Italy and Austria, though officially unruffled, are disturbed by two events. The first is the Isvolsky-Aerenthal dispute, in which the two statesmen try to throw on each other the onus for the steps leading to the annexation of Bosnia-Herzegovina, and on the top of this the Emperor of Russia visits the King of Italy and rather pointedly avoids Austrian territory en route. There is little doubt that Italy remains within the Triplice chiefly because the policy of her King is to secure his throne against republicanism by alliance with strongly monarchical countries, and also because Italy, whose fleet is only in its infancy, has an extended coast-line extremely difficult to defend. Italy has, however, attempted an insurance through an entente with Great Britain and is contemplating an extension of this understanding to France, but neither of these Powers, however good their will may be, can afford Italy protection in the quarter where she needs it. On her nothern frontier the Trentino, lying on the southern slope of the Austrian Alps, and belonging not only racially but lingually and geographically to the kingdom of Italy, is a second Alsace to Italian patriots. Trieste and the eastern Adriatic Coast are partly Latin by tradition and sympathy, and the Irridentist faction in Italy has a popular following when it talks of the lost provinces which should once more be joined to the motherland. The Italian government cannot risk any expression of sympathy with these views, knowing too well the weakness of their position, with the great military combination of Germany and Austria-Hungary hanging over them.

Between the devil of this menace and the deep sea of socialism and irridentism (two schools of thought far apart, yet united in embarrassing the government by their propaganda) the King of Italy and his advisers are obliged to cling desperately to the Triple Alliance long after it has ceased to be acceptable to the people or of service in the direction for which it was originally formed. In estimating the balance of Power, therefore, Italy's influence is neutralized by the conflict between her sympathies and her needs. . . .

Against this consolidation of Central Europe into one vast armed camp we find a regrouping of the other Powers. Great Britain has composed her long differences with Russia and France, and the three now enjoy what is known as an *entente cordiale*. Practical politicians are sceptical as to the actual value of these somewhat indefinite understandings, and if their worth is to be computed in men or ships probably they are not very useful. But the moral element cannot be left out of account in international relations, and there is no doubt that the friendship between three great Powers, founded on a common danger—by far the most effectual tie—is of real use in maintaining the equilibrium of Europe. Unfortunately the new Triple Entente is composed of Powers geographically separated, and all three in a peculiar condition of unpreparedness, and the danger of the situation lies in the fact that the next few years offer to Germany an opportunity which may never occur again. Given the moment of weakness on the part of opponents and the necessity for some signal success to justify William II in his military and naval policy and to demonstrate the advantages of the system of government which he typifies, is it conceivable that the opportunity will be allowed to pass without any attempt to take advantage of it to increase German power and prestige?

German writers like Professor Hans Delbrück have been busy demonstrating that the naval power of Britain was a menace to the world, which Germany felt obliged to check in the interests of peace. The fact that the British navy has not, with the exception of the bombardment of Alexandria, been engaged in war since Napoleonic times, is not alluded to or explained. The most significant, and indeed the conclusive, feature in the case is, however, the fact that German naval construction took on its most feverish aspect just at the time when the Government of England was cutting down naval expenditure, and when the Prime Minister had openly declared in favor of the limitation of armaments. This was represented as hypocrisy in German newspapers, but official Germany knew better. Sir Henry Campbell Bannerman was incapable of the particular form of duplicity, and he actually received a deputation of one hundred and forty-four members of the British Parliament desiring the reduction of the Navy. While the naval estimates were accordingly reduced, and all attempts to maintain the "two-power" standard were abandoned, Germany accelerated her rate of construction. . . .

In considering the balance of power, therefore, we have to take into account the evidence that one Power, at all events, is not satisfied with her share, and is forging a powerful weapon in order to get more. The writer does not believe that the creator of that weapon has any definite plan as to when and how it will be used, but from his first master in strategy, Bismarck, he learned the important lesson that one must be prepared for any eventuality and must seize the first favorable opportunity. One thing is quite certain, he will be unable to maintain the heavy expenditure on naval and military matters and the martial ardor which has been stirred up without giving his people some tangible result for their money.

The situation, which is now fairly well understood by the small minority of people in Great Britain who give serious attention to foreign affairs, does not appeal in the same way to that democracy, which, like all democracies, is hardly capable of seeing through foreign eyes. It is so unlikely to the average Englishman, who is in a serenely pacific frame of mind, that any one should attack him, that he cannot be made to take the matter seriously. To the German, carefully taught by his teachers and his press to regard the Englishman as an aggressive animal before everything, it is equally obvious that he, with his predominance on the sea, blocks the way to a fresh world which, otherwise, Germany could easily conquer. Without any immediate territorial designs, beyond coaling stations, Germany desires to be the first world-power, the arbiter of Europe—an ambition only to be realized by such a blow to England's Navy as would break its present predominance once and forever.

The balance of power in Europe therefore, in the judgment of the present writer, depends upon the immediate action taken by Great Britain towards National Defence. Her Fleet needs to be not only strong but superlatively strong, equipped in every detail. While believing that such a condition can be attained, if her Government will undertake the work in earnest, there is ground to fear that at present much remains to be done, especially in detail. The enthusiasm of her overseas Dominions in the cause of Imperial Defence is a pledge for the future, but not a shield against present dangers. Finally, the great movement in favor of National Service, the compulsory military training of every able-bodied British citizen, must be placed in the forefront of her programme, because only by securing an adequate second line of defence can she free her Fleet for the work it ought to do. As a nation in Arms she should never have to face invasion, for it is one thing to invade a people defended by a paid army—beat the army and the people are conquered—but no one yet has attempted to invade a nation in Arms. In the interests of Peace, in the interests of the Balance of Power on which Peace depends, the British nation is called upon to make certain sacrifices, but these are as nothing compared to what she may be called on to pay if she does not make these sacrifices. . . .

## 2 | The United States and the European Balance of Power, July 1909 *

At issue for the United States in the shifting European balance of power was the significance of German naval might for British and American security in the Atlantic. On this question writers and opinion leaders were not in agreement. Addressing the Lake Mohonk Conference on International Arbitration in 1909, Nicholas Murray Butler, the president of Columbia University, asked, "what reason is to be found in the nature of the German people, in the declarations of their responsible rulers, or in the political relations between Germany and any other nation, for the belief that the German navy alone, among all modern navies, is building for a warlike purpose?" It was the duty of the friends of England and Germany, declared Butler, "to exert every possible influence to promote a better understanding of each of these people by the other, a fuller appreciation of the services of each to modern civilization, and to point out the folly, not to speak of the wickedness, of permitting the seeds of discord to be sown between them by any element in the population of either."

Such a view of German naval ambition did not reflect the intellectual trends of the age. In the essay that follows Sidney Brooks analyzed the continuing revolution in American attitudes toward Germany and its weakening effect on American isolationism. Few Americans, wrote Brooks, believed that Germany could challenge British naval supremacy in the North Sea and not challenge the *status quo* in the entire Atlantic world. The writer predicted with perfect accuracy the conditions under which the United States would engage actively in some future war between England and Germany.

🖋

In much of the discussion that has recently been stirred up by Germany's naval expansion, it has been either assumed or openly stated that the matter is not one that concerns Great Britain and Germany alone, and that the United States is remotely but none the less unescapably affected by it. Put in this moderate form the proposition is, I think, indisputable, infinitely more so, at any rate, than some of the inferences drawn from it. The Americans, indeed, have not been slow to recognize and express their very real, if indirect, interest in the situation which threatens to throw Great Britain and Germany into an antagonism as sharp as that of two gladiators in a Roman arena. The gravity of the crisis has impressed them far more than our way of meeting it. We could not, as a matter of fact, have done more to alienate American sympathy than by the humiliating panics we have indulged in over phantom torpedo-boats, invisible airships, and belligerent German waiters. Like the rest of the

* Sidney Brooks, "Great Britain, Germany, and the United States," *The Living Age,* XLIV (July 31, 1909), 259–66.

world, Americans have noted our attack of "nerves" with ridicule and contempt, wondering, as they well might, what has come over us, and half-inclined to conclude that if we fail in the ordeal that awaits us it will be because we deserve to fail. But they have not on that account disguised from themselves that between American interests and the ultimate outcome, whatever it may be, of the prodigious preparations for war on both sides of the North Sea, there exists a tangible, and possibly a vital, connection. . . . Considering the self-contentment and isolation of American life, its happy or harmful immunity from the fierce juxtapositions and imminent contentions of Europe and the lack of anything in the nature of a constant education in the realities of world-politics, one could not expect the ordinary, busy, and complacent citizen to feel much more than a purely spectacular interest in the successive phases of a distant old-world rivalry. That he should feel any sort of interest at all is, however, something; and that the better sort of American journals and of American politicians and publicists should not only discern but proclaim the fact that the German question is an American as well as a British question, is little less than revolutionary. Thirteen years ago, at any rate, when I first visited America, nothing like it would have been possible. . . . Had the Anglo-German situation in its present or anything like its present form developed a decade and a half ago, Americans would have discussed it, as they discussed the Graeco-Turkish war, with a wholly impersonal detachment, and would have repudiated with the most ingenuous incredulity any suggestion that its issue could possibly affect or involve themselves. In those untroubled days they agreed with St. Paul that it is only the fool whose eyes are on the ends of the earth. International politics had no meaning for them; they were a hermit nation, eminently self-centered and incurious, surveying the outer world with an almost comical pity as an institution whose one office of utility was to serve as a foil to the singular blessedness of American conditions. To-day, as the reflex of those breathless events that in the last twelve years have transformed the American Republic into an Empire, established her as an Asiatic Power, given her knowledge and experience, and brought her at more than one point into somewhat hazardous contact with the nations of the Orient and Occident alike, the old instinctive attitude of provincialism and disdain has been, not destroyed, but sensibly weakened. The discussion of the Anglo-German problem throughout the United States has been far wider, better informed, and more realistic than would have been possible before the Spanish-American war; and the number of Americans who perceive and acknowledge its bearings on American interests is far greater and far more authoritative than it could have been in the days when, apart from the Monroe Doctrine, the United States had virtually no external policy or commitments whatever.

But the change which has come over America's position and outlook is visible not merely in the amount and quality of the attention directed toward the gathering stringency of Anglo-German relations, but also in the whole tone of American comment and criticism. A decade and a half ago, it is not too much to say, Americans were incapable of a calm consideration of any fact or incident that concerned, however remotely, their relations with Great Britain. . . . It is enough to register the fact that the whole spirit of American comment on the recent developments in the North Sea attests a change that has all the sweep of a revolution in the national attitude towards the people and policies of Great Britain. You will hardly anywhere find in the United States, outside the ranks of the Irish-Americans and German-Americans, a single journal that favors Germany's naval ambitions, or that does not regard the growth of the German Navy as a direct challenge to Great Britain's supremacy at sea, or that does not perceive that if maritime ascendancy were to pass into German hands American interests of all kinds would not be merely prejudiced, but severely and perhaps permanently dislocated. There is a renewed and a more vivid consciousness of the innumerable bonds that link the United States to Great Britain and of the staggering shock that American commerce and power—to say nothing of other and rarer possessions—would experience if the might of Great Britain were to be suddenly humbled. However much Americans might gird at our diplomacy and our Empire and the form of our civilization, I have never got the impression that they grudged us, or conceived themselves menaced by, our command of the sea. . . . I hardly think it an exaggeration to say that so long as they do not themselves care to be the first naval Power in the world, Americans would rather see Great Britain than any other nation at the head of the list.

Least of all, in my judgment, would they relish the prospect of Germany reaching that position. During the past twelve years a certain suspiciousness of Germany has permeated American opinion. It is founded perhaps at bottom on incompatibility of temper. There are two instincts derived from their past which have struck firm roots in the national character and outlook of the American people. One is their dislike of kingship; the other is their dislike of bureaucracy. Germany offends against both instincts. Great Britain does not, partly because while those Americans who regard the British Crown as a useful institution are comparatively few, and those who regard it with a more or less kindly amusement are very many, there is a general recognition that democracy in Great Britain, in spite of the monarchy, is the real and dominating fact. In Germany the case is held to be very different. Whereas Americans believe they detect in our form of government the veritable rule of the people, by the people, for the people, operating behind the veil of a constitutional monarchy, in Germany they are persuaded that Parliamentary institutions serve merely as trappings for something little less than an effective and ubiquitous absolutism—an absolutism all the more offensive to their way of thinking because it appears to rest on a military, aristocratic, and bureaucratic caste. The whole system which the Kaiser personifies, his whole conception of the State and of the respective parts that the people and the Sovereign should play in it, revolt not merely the opinion but the political conscience of the American people, and rasp unceasingly on their perfectly sincere and exalted sense of the worth and dignity of the individual and of the moral efficacy of "free institutions."

There exists, in short, between the genius of the two countries a permanent conflict of ideas and aspirations. . . . There has never been anything, except the slender bond of an interchange of educational ideas, to bridge the gulf of spiritual antipathy of which Americans never wholly lose the consciousness. On the contrary, whenever events, at any rate during the past ten or twelve years, have brought the two peoples into contact they have also brought them into conflict. The attitude, the decidedly waspish attitude, of Germany during the war with Spain, was one, and by no means the least startling, of the many surprises which that episode sprung upon the American people. The futile rudeness of the German squadron in Manila Bay, the Kaiser's swoop down upon the *disjecta membra* of the Spanish Empire in the Pacific, the clash over Samoa, and many smaller but not less irritating incidents, expanded the distrust of German policy into a national prepossession. . . . All the doubts and apprehensions, the wilful misunderstandings, and irrational animosities that Americans used to project into their dealings with us, they have, since 1908, brought to bear against Germany. I do not say that the new enmity has any more root in reason than had the old. International likes and dislikes rarely are determined by broad principles of reason. As a rule, they are nothing but the outcome of caprice, and accident, and uninquiring prejudice—which is one of the causes why one should doubt whether anything is of so little consequence as not to have its influence in shaping national preferences and aversions. I merely state the fact that in American eyes at the beginning of the twentieth century it was no longer Great Britain but Germany that was "the enemy.". . .

. . . Those Americans who think at all about foreign affairs realize perfectly well that, next to the security and well-being of their own country, there is and can be no higher American interest than the preservation of the British Empire on its present footing; that its downfall would react nowhere so disastrously as upon the United States; and that the rise of a Greater Germany in its place would be little less, in the long run, than a challenge to their position and freedom as a World-Power.

Captain Mahan, as one would expect, has been quick to seize on the essential point. In an article that appeared in *Collier's Weekly* a few weeks ago, he endeavored to rouse his countrymen to the duty of pondering the "portentous international fact and factor—that is, maker of further facts—" that had come so rapidly into existence. "It is surely incumbent upon us," he wrote, "to recognize that there is now visible in the near future a foreign fleet decisively superior to our own in the class of vessel accepted at present by preponderant naval opinion as the determinative factor in naval war." It was unthinkable, he argued, that Great Britain should ever wish to contravene the Monroe Doctrine. Nobody, of course, had the right to impute any such intention to Germany either. "But we must look facts straight in the face, and see that, in case of future offence given by some future Castro—a condition almost sure to arise—such superiority at sea as Germany is now establishing puts it in her power to exact whatever reparation she may please, irrespective of the Monroe Doctrine"; and he went on to pose to Americans the tremendous question whether they were willing "to have a permanent element of national policy dependent upon the uncertain indulgence of a foreign State, which is notoriously thirsting for colonization in the supposed interest of racial development. . . ." The great bulk of his countrymen have not, of course, Captain Mahan's vision or his grasp of principles and consequences, or his sense of the complexity and inter-dependence of all human affairs. I quote his words less as a *précis* of what Americans are thinking to-day than as a forecast of what they will most likely be thinking ten or fifteen years hence. Very few, probably, of the readers of *Collier's Weekly* understood his argument or accepted his conclusions, or re-garded his sombre elucidation of America's concern in Germany's naval ambi-tions as other than fanciful. The average citizen has not yet been educated quite so far as all that in the realities of *Weltpolitik*. But that he would prefer not to see Great Britain disappear before the mailed fist, that sentiment and self-interest both incline his sympathies, as between Germany and Great Britain, towards the latter Power, and that he is conscious, or half conscious, with a sort of vague disquietude, that complications not wholly favorable to the United States might ensue if Germany were to acquire command of the Sea—this I be-lieve to be the fact.

But it is a fact to which, in my judgment, little political moment can at present be attached. . . . The course of American action in external affairs, depending, as it does, very largely upon the personality of the President and upon the incalculable conditions of domestic politics, is always difficult to fore-cast; but I think it fairly safe to assert that except in one contingency there is no possibility whatever of the United States taking sides in an Anglo-German conflict or of her departing from an attitude of strict neutrality—an attitude that might be relaxed here and there, if occasion offered and no risk of trouble was to be feared, in our favor, that would certainly be compatible with the heartiest wishes for our success, but that on the whole would be unfalteringly maintained till the struggle was over and whatever its issue. The contingency to which I have alluded, the contingency that might force America into the arena, would arise if Germany were to attempt any interference with the supply of food and grain from the United States to Great Britain. Any such attempt Americans would resist if necessary by force of arms. Short of that I can conceive no circumstance that would be likely to move the United States one inch beyond her traditional policy of non-interference. She would remain neutral partly because the political influence of the German-American and Irish-American "vote" would make it a most hazardous enterprise for any President to suggest to Congress an alliance with Great Britain, but chiefly because the great majority of Americans would look upon an Anglo-German conflict as primarily a European question in which their concern stopped far short of the point of intervention and participation.

. . . The operative opinion of the Commonwealth still desires to have as few dealings as possible with foreign Powers, still quotes and abides by Washing-ton's warning against "entangling alliances," still shrinks from any course that threatens "complications," still clings to the policy of isolation as the one that most adequately squares with the needs of American conditions. This is so, even though facts and necessity have out-run many of the formulae, prejudices, and traditions that a decade and a half ago were all but omnipotent. The peculiarity of America's position in the general scheme of *Weltpolitik* is, indeed, precisely this, that her people are unconsciously engaged in adapting their mental outlook to their achievements. The Spanish war launched them on a stream of tendencies that has already carried them far beyond their old confines, and is inexorably destined to carry them further still. But the instinct of many millions of American citizens is still to pretend that nothing essential has been changed. They have overthrown Spanish power in Cuba and the Philippines, but the far harder task of overthrowing the mental habits and prepossessions of a hundred years' growth they have not yet accomplished. They have an Empire, but they have not yet become Imperial. They have expanded physically, but they have still to expand mentally. They are a World-Power in fact, but not in consciousness, in breadth of vision, in a resolute acceptance of new conditions, in a not less resolute emancipation from the precepts of an outworn past. They are multiplying every year fresh points of diplomatic contact with the outer world, and yet no American statesman would dare to proclaim it as a fact that the days of America's isolation are over. Without quite realizing it, they are undergoing a course of education in the realities of their new international position. Events are teaching them, but the progress of enlightenment will be arduous and protracted.

Americans, for instance, have not yet put tradition so far behind them as to admit the word "alliance" or any word pointing in that direction, into their political vocabulary. . . . Americans as a whole are still far from realizing how much their prejudice against any kind of formal understanding and cooperation with other Powers militates against their effectiveness in world-politics. They do not see that a Power that automatically and unreflectingly rules out the possibility of alliances in any circumstances whatsoever is a Power that wilfully handicaps its freedom of action and runs the risk of sacrificing its interests to a theory. In the broader field on which the United States has now entered, immutable rules and cast-iron systems are a hindrance, not a help. That nice adaptation of means to ends which is the essence of diplomacy cannot possibly be effected if the choice of means is abridged beforehand by a hard and fast formula. Americans will understand this in time, but they do not understand it now. Happily, we in Great Britain can well afford to wait while they are gathering wisdom from experience—and to wait with an assurance that prevents anxiety as decisively as it forbids over-precipitancy. It is simply a question of time before the bonds that already link British and American policy on more than one international field are formally cemented. Temporary circumstances and accidental events may hasten that consummation or retard it; it may be evolved from America's necessity or from our own; no one can foresee how or when it will come. But that come it ultimately will, that the permanent currents of national interests and sentiment are setting full and fair towards it, is no longer, I think, open to question.

## 3 | Lewis Einstein on the Bases of a Realistic American Foreign Policy, January 1913 *

In the following essay Lewis Einstein challenged American isolationism vis-à-vis Europe by recounting the role of the balance of power in the nation's remarkable internal development in the nineteenth century. For him the Anglo-German rivalry dominated European politics. What made this rivalry so dangerous was the absence of any conflicts of interest that could be adjusted diplomatically. In a struggle for prestige there could be no solution but war. Such a war, he predicted, would affect the interests of the United States at many points. Thus the challenge to American policy was clear.

✍

American life is still too intense, the problems of its economic development, and the relations between the individual and the State, still too unsettled, to have fostered an interest in the nation at large, in questions of foreign policy which are no less far-reaching in their nature, because not visibly oppressive. Yet the recent vast extension in foreign trade, and the gradual industrial evolution of the country, coupled with the growth of population, causing American exports to be increasingly manufactures, and decreasingly agricultural, must inevitably bring about an augmenting attention to questions of external order. Already, within the last decade, this has become noticeable in the importance which the so-called "Open Door" in China, and the relations with Latin America have assumed before the public eye. In both instances, trade, present and future, has been the foundation and the objective of interest. The political cloak assumed, in the one case, by often repeated formulas regarding the integrity of China, in the other by the Monroe Doctrine and American sisterhood, has covered the very legitimate self-interest presented by the extension of commercial relations and the growth of the nation's influence.

Beyond this, however, watchfulness ceased. The affairs of Europe, picturesque and weighty as they appeared, yet seemed to have no immediate visible relation to the United States. In whatever direction might lie natural sympathies, the country as a whole remained unaware that its own interests were in any way concerned or affected by the future of the European problem and indifferent thereto. A traditional disinterestedness continued as potent a formula of statecraft as half a century ago, without Americans realising that altered conditions rendered necessary a modification of this attitude, and that the vast extension of international interests and the complexity of modern life no longer permitted former isolation. While the country had consciously altered its political, strategical and economic situation in the world by the creation of new oversea

* "The United States and Anglo-German Rivalry," *The National Review*, LX (January 1913), 736–50. Reprinted by permission.

interests and the industrial growth of a century, it yet cherished the illusion of being able to preserve intact diplomatic ideas that had long since served their time. The belief prevailed that since in Europe, America had no territorial interests nor ambition, it had likewise no solicitude and could with impunity remain indifferent to whatever occurred on its political plane.

A brief retrospect suggests, however, ample proof to the contrary. The European balance of power has been such a permanent factor since the birth of the republic that Americans have never realised how its absence would have affected their political status. The national existence was first brought about by European dissension. When Pitt resisted Napoleon, the justifiable irritation felt against British high-handedness at sea caused Americans to forget that England's fight was in reality their own, and that the undisputed master of Europe would not have been long in finding pretexts to reacquire the Louisiana territory which, except for England, he would never have relinquished. When the Holy Alliance endeavoured to concentrate the power of Europe under the banner of legitimacy and divine right, Canning, by inspiring the Monroe Doctrine, interposed an effective restraint in the Western Hemisphere, and in the often-quoted phrase, "called in the New World to redress the balance of the Old."

Fifty years later, had England joined France in recognising the Confederacy or in her abortive Mexican adventure, the history of the United States might have run a different course. At no time since the foundation of the Republic could a change materially altering the ancient European balance of power have been brought about without perceptibly affecting American interests and the position of the United States. Even to-day, in spite of the enormous increase in the country's resources and population, this political axiom holds as true as it did in the period of national formation and weakness. The undisputed paramountcy of any nation, both by land and sea, must inevitably make that Power a menace and a peril to every other country. . . . It may therefore be of interest to survey the forces of war and peace today at work in Europe and see if there lies any menace to that balance of power, the preservation of which is essential to its national security. . . .

The sources of European unrest could, however, be more lightly dismissed without the antagonism between Great Britain and Germany. In spite of the attempts made on both sides to explain it away, and to dwell on the pacific disposition animating the construction of new "Dreadnoughts," this remains as an irreducible fact obscuring the political horizon. Nor should it be regarded as a mere contest for commercial supremacy on the part of two countries, one seeking to preserve, the other to gain new markets. Intelligent Germans are the first to recognise that neither their merchants nor their trade suffer in British Colonies. Beneath it lies the deeply conscious rival ambitions of two great nations, the one to maintain undiminished the heritage conquered by its forebears, the other to obtain the place "under the sun" which it regards as its right. And the magnitude of this issue is enhanced by the hardly lesser constellations gravitating around the rivals, each with its own historic traditions and interests, but who have realised comparative security in a system which finds its political expression in the series of alliances and understandings forming the balance of modern Europe.

Paradoxical as it may seem, the grave danger of the present relations between Great Britain and Germany lies in the fact that there is no real difficulty between the two Powers. Where a concrete obstacle stands in the way, by compromise and mutual goodwill it may be removed. In recent years, the Anglo-French and Anglo-Russian negotiations, by a judicious policy of give-and-take, smoothed out through diplomatic means the colonial rivalry of a century. But between Germany and England similar adjustment is impossible. Their antagonism presents nothing concrete save rival ambition. . . .

Whatever be the future of this situation a far-sighted statesmanship compels the United States, as it does every other nation, to take cognisance of the possibility of a conflict breaking out in the near future between Great Britain and Germany, and to consider in what manner its interests would be affected. It is an easy remedy to repeat the old adage about American proverbial non-interference in European affairs. With all respect toward a policy which in the past has been thoroughly sound, it cannot be said in this instance to offer a complete panacea. A struggle between the two nations, even though it did not set ablaze the rest of Europe, cannot leave America indifferent. In too many regions of the world would its interests be affected by such reality.

It would withal be absurd to deduce from this, that the United States would be dragged into a war against all inclination. The alternative of arms is no necessary consequence of diplomatic interest, and in such a conflict direct participation would with proper precautions be most unlikely. This should not, however, excuse any neglect on the part of Americans to consider the various political, strategic, and economic points of view in different regions of the world, where such struggle would react upon them, or how the balance of power, which it should be the policy of the United States to preserve in Europe, would be affected by the contest. An indication of its wide-reaching nature independent of the actual field of hostilities, would, for instance, be presented in the Far East, where the even temporary withdrawal of European influence would leave America face to face with a commensurately more powerful Japan. To say nothing of the Philippines the situation thus created depends on the degree of stability and strength attained by China. It is not difficult, however, to conceive of circumstances where to ensure respect for the often pledged integrity of that State would lead the United States toward a course of action which it would be obliged to adopt single-handed, and without the benefit of such diplomatic support as in the past it has received from friendly Powers.

Omitting from consideration the extent to which the almost inevitable conflagration would affect the world in a conflict between Great Britain and Germany, three general possibilities are open: (1) The victory of the former; (2) The reverse; (3) A war of indefinite result.

So far as America is concerned, the first alternative would be the least likely to materially alter the existing status. England might conceivably recover a pecuniary indemnity and deal a death-blow to German oversea commerce. But the German Colonies are not such as to sensibly attract a conqueror, nor would a change in their title affect other nations in any way. While the predominant position of Germany upon the European Continent would be shattered, the balance of power would hardly be affected, even though the disposition of its weight were altered. The insular position of Great Britain debars her from continental ambitions, and any attempt to assert herself in such manner would both run counter to all her traditions and be stoutly resisted by former allied States. It is fortunate that in modern times no nation has succeeded in being paramount on both land and sea. Great Britain has hitherto refrained from unduly developing her military strength and there is no reason to anticipate that flushed by victory she would adopt a different course. Her naval superiority, which is a matter of life and death, menaces no one though it bars the way to Germany already supreme on land. But for America it represents an essential element in the maintenance and stability of the European balance of power.

If the terms of peace after such a war were to be dictated in London, the situation as it affected the United States would be radically reversed. While defeat for Germany might prove disastrous to the dynasty, for Great Britain it would be fatal to the Empire whose disintegration would almost inevitably ensue. It is apparent that the fate of Canada and the British possessions in America immediately concern the Republic. . . . [I]f the fortune of war prove adverse, there is no reason to suppose that Canada would long continue under the control, however nominal, of a parent State deprived of prestige and authority, and ruined by an unsuccessful war. . . .

Without going to the length of such extreme conclusions, a third and more likely possibility would be that of a contest long drawn out between the two countries wherein neither could obtain decisive advantage. In spite of the paper proof that a lengthy war presents to-day an economic impossibility there is no practical evidence to substantiate this theory, and there are distinguished economists who believe that the modern system of credit is peculiarly adopted to facilitate the prolongation of war. When poor countries, like Japan and Russia, have been able to maintain in the field for a considerable duration armies of almost unprecedented size, there is no reason to suppose that the pinch of poverty alone would materially hasten the conclusion of a contest between England and Germany. The financial aspect of this is also likely to concern America. If the struggle should be protracted, extensive borrowing will have to be undertaken, and New York is more and more becoming one of the money markets of the world. It is probable that it will be called upon, possibly by both sides, to furnish pecuniary assistance, even though the obligations of strict neutrality are somewhat questionable on this point. . . .

If this remains a remote though possible contingency it is otherwise with the effect of a great struggle upon economic interests. As all industry in the belligerent nations would be brought to a virtual standstill it is likely that while American manufactured exports in Europe suffered there would be a greatly increased demand for food-stuffs as well as for whatever might be of utility in the conduct of war. Such commercial losses as would be experienced in Europe could be more than counterbalanced by the opportunity presented elsewhere to acquire new markets and supplant former rivals. This would give an unwonted impetus to trade. American commerce should find before it in Latin America, South Africa, Australia, and the Far East, new outlets and new opportunities as the consequence of such a struggle.

Without a merchant marine under the American flag no adequate benefit would be derived from this situation. The export of American products would be rendered increasingly difficult by the few remaining neutral bottoms with the consequent increase in freight rates. The creation of an American Merchant Navy thus becomes a primary necessity whether affected by postal subventions, direct subsidies, or the admission of foreign-built ships. . . .

Even more important than the creation of an American merchant marine is that at a time of uncertainty like the present, with the future still befogged, no efforts be spared to maintain its relative naval strength. Already the United States has fallen from the second place which, for a decade, it had occupied, and without greater exertion is likely to sink still further in the scale. . . .

In the event of a European conflagration the American fleet, even if maintained at its present relative strength, might find difficulty in accomplishing its double task of preserving the *status quo* in the Far East, and enforcing the neutrality of the Caribbean, where the presence of hostilities would certainly embarrass and possibly endanger American interests. The preservation of the *Pax Americana* as a corollary to the Monroe Doctrine should be its goal at all times. The United States has everything to gain by the peaceful and orderly evolution of existing conditions on the Western Hemisphere and nothing by sudden or violent changes, even where its interests do not appear to be immediately affected. Hence any attempt to make of American waters the scene of war would be extremely distasteful to its policy. . . .

An Anglo-German conflict would thus affect the United States at various points and in various ways. There is hardly a branch of American national activity, governmental or economic, which would not feel its consequences in varying degree or be concerned by its outcome. While the American attitude in such contest would in the beginning be one of strict neutrality, which would be maintained as long as possible, this does not mean that a far-sighted policy might not under certain contingencies impose a different course of action. However considerable the responsibility incurred, however great the bait offered, it would hardly be wise statesmanship to remain passive if England should by any series of disasters be crushed. Even though the immediate consequence would be to throw Canada and the British Antilles into the lap of the United States, it would leave the latter confronted by an Empire supreme on land and sea, and would force it to pursue a preparation of armaments which for its own preservation could not be inferior to what it might be called upon to face. Unperceived by many Americans, the European balance of power is a political necessity which can alone sanction on the Western Hemisphere the continuance of an economic development unhandicapped by the burden of extensive armaments. At no time, even unknown to the United States, were European politics a matter of indifference to its vital interests. But if hitherto it was impotent to alter their march, a fortunate destiny preserved the existing balance.

Seeking, as little as in the past, any selfish benefit in the Old World, even though it were possible, America has to-day a distinct and legitimate duty in the family of great nations in contributing to preserve those elements which compose the balance of power, and to which it can only be blind at a later cost. The disappearance or diminution of any one State in Europe would be a calamity, varying with its degree. But while the importance of such extinction might not in most instances be sufficiently close to warrant or provoke active intervention, this would not be true with Great Britain. The disintegration of the British Empire would be a defeat for America by the erection of a Power supreme on land and sea. A German historian of reputation, Professor Oncken, of Heidelberg, has lately, with reason, expounded the view that in 1864 in the war over the Duchies, England was unconsciously defeated. "Had Schleswig-Holstein remained Danish, the right bank of the Elbe up to the gates of Hamburg not been German territory, and the Canal from the Baltic to the North Sea an impossibility, all the conditions of Germany's maritime position would have been non-existent." French historians have similarly traced the beginnings of their disasters in 1870 to their non-interference in the affair of the Duchies. The lesson of how a failure to act later reacts should not be lost.

To consider the possible contingency of such intervention by the United States as tantamount to an alliance with Great Britain would be untrue. Where there is no treaty there is no alliance. America does not keep England from war nor push her toward a conflict. In the event of hostilities the assertion of its neutrality would at once be made and strictly lived up to. If Germany and England choose to indulge in the luxury of war such is their right. However much one may lament the loss of life, it is no affair of the United States even though England were defeated, so long as the general balance is preserved. But if ever decisive results are about to be registered of a nature calculated to upset what has for centuries been the recognised political fabric of Europe, America can remain indifferent thereto only at her own eventual cost. If it then neglects to observe that the interests of the nations crushed are likewise its own, America will be guilty of political blindness which it will later rue. To guard against this danger the diplomatic role of the United States in Europe should be far more active than in the past. Properly understood and carried out by skilful agents it would be one which instead of being resented should entitle it to the gratitude of all lovers of peace, since it would be apparent that without selfish designs of its own it aimed to preserve the rights of all.

It is mistaking the nature of diplomacy to think that this would involve America in entanglements wherein it had no concern. But it is likewise mistaking its scope for national utility to accord by an attitude of indifferent passivity a free field to the forceful ambition of any single State. Great Britain, by upholding the European balance of power, has contributed toward American development. If misfortune in arms await her it would be as politically unwise as it would be ungenerous to allow her to suffer unduly. A disastrous defeat inflicted by an opponent unwilling to use moderation in his victory should invite on the part of America a friendly mediation which in the last extremity might have to be converted into more effective measures. Hence the advisability for the United States of preserving its strength in such a way as ever to make its counsel welcome and its action unnecessary.

## 4 | Theodore Roosevelt and the European Balance of Power, 1914 *

Writing in September 1914, shortly after the outbreak of war, Roosevelt elaborated on his slogan, "Speak softly and carry a big stick." He urged on the nation an attitude of courtesy and the avoidance of a crusade against any nation of Europe, a recognition of conflicting interests among nations, and the maintenance of adequate power to influence the actions of others.

✍

. . . One of the main lessons to learn from this war is embodied in the homely proverb, "Speak softly and carry a big stick." Persistently only half of this proverb has been quoted in deriding the men who wish to safeguard our National interest and honor. Persistently the effort has been made to insist that those who advocate keeping our country able to defend its rights are merely adopting "the policy of the big stick." In reality, we lay equal emphasis on the fact that it is necessary to speak softly; in other words, that it is necessary to be respectful toward all people and scrupulously to refrain from wronging them, while at the same time keeping ourselves in condition to prevent wrong being done to us. If a nation does not in this sense speak softly, then sooner or later the policy of the big stick is certain to result in war. But what befell Luxemburg six weeks ago, what has befallen China again and again during the past quarter of a century, shows that no amount of speaking softly will save any people which does not carry a big stick.

I earnestly believe in peace. I respect every sincere and upright man who with wisdom and proper sense of perspective does all he can at peace conferences, or by the negotiation of reasonable arbitration treaties, or by the utilization of the Hague International Court in proper cases, to minimize the chances of war among civilized nations, and to give the opportunity to use other means than war for the settlement of international disputes. A little good can come

* Theodore Roosevelt, "The World War: Its Tragedies and Its Lessons," *The Outlook*, CVIII (September 23, 1914), 175-6.

from all these movements, but only on condition that there is no attempt made
to erect shams and say they are truths or to pretend to be doing what we are
not doing. A little good can come, but only on condition that nations remember that as yet arbitration treaties, neutrality treaties, treaties for the erection
of independent tribunals, treaties of all kinds, can do nothing to save a nation
in great crises unless that nation is able to defend its own honor, its own vital
interests.

America should have a coherent policy of action toward foreign powers, and
this should primarily be based on the determination never to give offense when
it can be avoided, always to treat other nations justly and courteously, and, as
long as present conditions exist, to be prepared to defend our own rights ourselves. No other nation will defend them for us. No paper guarantee or treaty
will be worth the paper on which it is written if it becomes to the interest of
some other power to violate it, unless we have strength, and courage and ability
to use that strength, back of the treaty. Every public man, every writer who
speaks with wanton offensiveness of a foreign power or of a foreign people,
whether he attacks England or France or Germany, whether he assails the
Russians or the Japanese, is doing an injury to the whole American body politic.
We have plenty of shortcomings at home to correct before we start out to criti-
cise the shortcomings of others. Now and then it becomes imperatively necessary
in the interests of humanity, or in our own vital interest, to act in a manner
which will cause offense to some other power. This is a lamentable necessity;
but when the necessity arises we must meet it and act as we are honorably bound
to act, no matter what offense is given. We must always weigh well our duties
in such a case, and consider the rights of others as well as our own rights, in
the interest of the world at large. If after such consideration it is evident that
we are bound to act along a certain line of policy, then it is mere weakness to
refrain from doing so because offense is thereby given. But we must never act
wantonly or brutally, or without regard to the essentials of genuine morality—a
morality considering our interests as well as the interests of others, and considering the interests of future generations as well as of the present generation.
We must so conduct ourselves that every big nation and every little nation that
behaves itself shall never have to think of us with fear, and shall have confidence
not only in our justice but in our courtesy. Submission to wrong-doing on our
part would be mere weakness and would invite and insure disaster. We must
not submit to wrong done to our honor or to our vital National interests. But
we must be scrupulously careful always to speak with courtesy and self-restraint
to others, always to act decently to others, and to give no nation any justification
for believing that it has anything to fear from us as long as it behaves with
decency and uprightness.

Above all, let us avoid the policy of peace with insult, the policy of unpreparedness to defend our rights, with inability to restrain our representatives
from doing wrong to or publicly speaking ill of others. The worst policy for the
United States is to combine the unbridled tongue with the unready hand. . . .

— | "It would be a disaster to mankind if Germany were reduced to the condition in which she was after the end of the Thirty Years War." *

In the following letter, written in November 1914, Roosevelt again favored an American policy of moderation designed to preserve the balance of power in Europe.

. . . I entirely agree with you that most Germans are actuated by a genuine fear of what will befall them if they are left helpless before Russian aggression, and I would believe in making it evident that in such case you could count upon the active support of the United States. At the outset of this war I happened to have visiting me half a dozen of our young men, including for instance Herbert Croly. Belgium had just been invaded. We all of us sympathized with Belgium, and therefore with England and France in their attitude toward Belgium, but I was interested to find that we all of us felt that the smashing of Germany would be a great calamity, and would result in the entire western world being speedily forced into a contest against Russia.

I am delighted to find that you take the view that you do about Germany's sea power. I do not agree with you as to your statement that it is impossible that England can be smashed in this war. I most cordially admire and respect German efficiency, and if I must choose between the ruthless ability of the neo-Bismarckians and the milk-and-water or diluted-mush policy of Wilson, Bryan, Taft and the like, I am certainly in favor of the neo-Bismarckians. If Germany pushes the French back beyond Calais, then I think that with the extraordinary efficiency the German navy as well as the German army have shown, that an invasion of England and the destruction of London, either or both, are quite possible. The British Empire might then fly to pieces, but such an event would be a disaster to mankind just as it would be a disaster to mankind if Germany were reduced to the condition in which she was after the end of the Thirty Years War.

I am very much interested at what you say as to the possible basis of peace if Austria breaks up. I believe that Russia is advancing towards civilization, and while I think she still holds menace, I think this menace will gradually disappear as the years go on, if only we can prevent her at the present time from becoming anything like the world mistress. One way of checking this would be the establishment of such independent Slav powers as those of which you speak. I am absolutely certain that these independent Slav powers would violently resist any kind of dominion of Russia over them if only once they could be definitely assured that Russian dominion over them was not to be accepted as the necessary alternative to some kind of dominion to which they would object even more. . . .

* Roosevelt to Hugo Münsterberg, November 2, 1914, *The Letters of Theodore Roosevelt*, Elting E. Morison, ed. (Cambridge, Mass., 1954), VIII: 826. Copyright 1951, 1953, 1954, by the President and Fellows of Harvard College.

# 5 | Alfred Thayer Mahan on the Role of Power in International Life, November 1911 *

By 1914 two approaches to the problem of international conflict were struggling for possession of the American mind. One sought to replace the traditional methods of diplomacy, operating in the context of a hierarchy of national power, with arbitration, conciliation, and other peaceful and democratic devices for resolving conflicts among nations. These methods of settling disputes hinged less on the relative power and energy of nations than on the absolute justice, determined by international law, in any dispute. The distinguished American jurist, Elihu Root, for example, favored a legal system, administered by a small, permanent world court, for the peaceful settlement of international conflict. He opposed diplomatic compromise because it substituted expediency for absolute justice. "Peace," Root warned, "can never be except as it is founded upon justice. And it rests with us in our own country to see to it that the idea of justice prevails. . . ." For Root world public opinion was the final arbiter of peace.

Mahan argued that compromise and expediency not only reflected the true nature of the international system but also that they would often assure greater justice than a resort to legality. He once wrote: "In the conflicting relations of independent states a particular action may be lawful—legal—yet not expedient; it may be both lawful and expedient; or it may not square with exact law, yet be essentially just because possessing the highest degree of expediency, that, namely, of doing essential justice between all the parties concerned." In the following essay Mahan observed that arbitration and law were hopeful bases of settlement only for *status quo* powers, because nations which desired to alter the established arrangement of power and possession seldom enjoyed the advantages of legality. For Mahan national strength, reflecting national efficiency, was "entitled to claim its sphere of extension and of opportunity."

✍

. . . If we are to think accurately concerning the sphere of Arbitration, as propounded by its extreme and most logical advocates, we must recognize that the object of their attack necessarily is not Armament, but Diplomacy. The attempt is to carry all cases into court instead of arranging them outside by compromise or adjustment. It is true that as the case stands the proposition is diplomacy first, arbitration only in case of diplomacy failing; but diplomacy will fail more readily when one of the parties think that it will gain substantially by insisting on arbitration—going into court. . . .

. . . National power is surely a legitimate factor in international settlements;

* Alfred Thayer Mahan, "The Deficiencies of Law as an Instrument of International Adjustments," *The North American Review*, CXCIV (November 1911), 677–84.

for it is the outcome of national efficiency, and efficiency is entitled to assert its fair position and chance of exercise in world matters, not restricted unduly by mere legal tenures dependent for their existing legality upon a prior occupancy, which occupancy often represents an efficiency once existent but long since passed away. The colonial empire of Spain, unimpaired a bare century ago, now wholly disappeared, is a familiar instance. The Empire of the Turks is another. The present intervention of Italy in Tripoli is but a further step in a process of which Bosnia, Herzegovina, Bulgaria are merely the most recent examples. The supplanting of preceding dynasties in India by Great Britain, and her supervision over administration in Egypt, are again illustrations. By what system of law is provision to be made for solving such questions?

Can that which has just been said be condemned fairly as simply a less bald way of affirming that might makes right? No; although certainly it does affirm that the existence of might is no mere casual attribute, but the indication of qualities which should, as they assuredly will, make their way to the front and to the top in the relations of States. Once Prussia counted for less than Holland in international balances. Such qualities, capabilities, not only confer rights, but entail duties, none the less real because not reducible to legal definition; such as the interference of the United States and of Great Britain in 1823 on behalf of South American independence, and of the United States alone, backed by the silent arms of Great Britain, in Cuba in 1898. It is only when opposition between national forces ceases, because one or more nations become exhausted, or are recreant to duty, that the might of some one, becoming unconditioned, incurs the risk, and the imminent probability of excess and decay, like all absolute power. Rome and Carthage, Louis XIV., Napoleon, are familiar instances. Great Britain after Trafalgar illustrated the same on the seas; but she was saved by the opposing forces of the Continent. The Monroe Doctrine itself is such an instance of national force opposing the intrusion of other force in settlements such as have been cited. It is local power asserting that it will withstand the beginnings; will not permit distant power, perhaps mightier than itself, to be established at its very doors in a position involving national danger. This also illustrates the safeguard against the consequences which might be inferred from the proposition that national power, being essentially national efficiency, is entitled to claim its sphere of extension and of opportunity. The coordination and balance of international factors, like the balances of powers in a constitution, secure a firmer basis of general welfare than mere legal adjudication, which can be only partially applicable to the community of nations. . . .

Curiously and interestingly, simultaneous with the framing of the recent treaties of general arbitration, in the brief interval between their final conclusion and the signature in Washington, the British Government, dealing with the current dispute between France and Germany about Morocco, found itself compelled to a most deliberate and formal pronouncement of its purpose, in all events, to protect "vital interests and national honor," by force if necessary, although the case might present no legal ground for such contingent action. . . .

After expressing, incidentally, his satisfaction at the prospect of a happy issue to the negotiations for a Treaty of General Arbitration with the United States, Mr. Lloyd-George continued:

> But I am also bound to say this—that I believe it is essential in the highest interests, not merely of this country, but of the world, that Britain should at all hazards maintain her place *and her prestige* amongst the Great Powers of the World. Her potent influence has many a time been in the past, and may yet be in the future, invaluable to the cause of human liberty. It has more than once in the past redeemed Continental nations, who are sometimes too apt to forget that service, from overwhelming disaster and even from national extinction. I would make great sacrifices to preserve peace. I conceive that nothing would justify a disturbance of international good-will except questions of the gravest national moment. But if a situation should be forced upon us in which peace could only be preserved by the *surrender of* the great and beneficent *position* Britain has won by centuries of heroism and achievement, by allowing Britain to be treated where her *interests are vitally affected* as if she were of no account in the Cabinet of nations, then I say emphatically that peace at that price would be a humiliation intolerable for a great country like ours to endure. *National honor* is no party question.

The phrases "vital interests" and "national honor," carefully excluded from the recent treaties of general arbitration—the exclusion of which was indeed a chief object of the treaties—appear here again in terms and in full force; not by mere implication, but in distinct assertion relatively to a pending political situation unsettled at the moment of speaking. Nor this alone. Equal stress is laid upon the right of the nation to play its part in the world, to assert itself as a factor in international relations; to sustain by force, by national efficiency, its position—"prestige"—and its influence among States; to assert the qualities which entitle it to a place in the front; all which are attributes distinct from, and in excess of, such simply inherent rights as vital interests and national honor. No inefficient State could take the same position. . . .

The solid basis upon which general arbitration may produce beneficial results was well expressed in another speech of Sir Edward Grey's. In this, without formal definition, he indicates the limits which Great Britain feels that expediency places upon treaties having this object in view.

> Anything like war between the United States and the British Empire would be so violently opposed to the deepest sentiments and feelings of the people in both countries as to be unthinkable. This made the ground between the two nations especially favorable for an arbitration treaty of an extended kind. If they wished to build a house which was to be secure, he imagined that they would choose to build it on a site which was not liable to earthquakes. There were political as well as territorial earthquakes, but the *respective national policies* of the two countries made it *certain* that they were not liable to political earth-

quakes; *that there was no conflict of national policy*. . . . If it be, as I
think it must be, *a postulate of any successful arbitration treaty* of an
extended kind that there should be no conflict or possibility of conflict
between the national policies of the nations which are parties to it,
this condition is assured between us.

In like spirit the London *Spectator* comments:

> The United States is the one country in the world our differences
> with which we can commit to arbitration without any reserve or mis-
> giving, because she is the only country besides our own which is content
> with the *status quo*.

Most Americans will gladly accept this hopeful prognostic concerning the
future relations of the two nations; yet Sir Edward Grey's speech by its reservations sufficiently shows that in his judgment the General Arbitration Treaty
between Great Britain and the United States cannot safely be accepted in
Great Britain as a type for all occasions and all nations. As to Great Britain herself, it may be well to remember a recent very distinct divergence of political
view, in which the Senate of the United States prevented the nation from committing itself to a treaty which might have proved extremely awkward at the
present moment. . . .

Historical illustration, which is simply the citation of cases and precedents,
amply shows the insufficiency of law as an instrument in composing differences.
By insufficient I do not mean that it is not sufficient in many instances, possibly
in most; but that the exceptions are so numerous that legal classification cannot
fully embrace them, and therefore another instrument than law, than arbitration, is in such cases required. In the matter of instruction, no theoretic discussion, however ample and lucid, affords a substitute for historical illustration.

Several such illustrations of very recent date have been adduced in this and
previous articles. One much more ancient, yet entirely analogous, and demon-
strative that the instrument used must be adapted to the end in view, is afforded
by the history of liberty in England. The early Stuart kings, notably Charles I.,
with great care based their oppressive actions upon law; upon law obsolete in
the sense that the progress of the nation had rendered inapplicable methods
which in previous years had been applicable, but still law existing unrepealed.
International Law, as law, has similarly to treat as legal a claim which may have
issued in intolerable conditions. Claims of such character could have been alleged for the forcible retention of the American colonies by Great Britain, and
of the Spanish colonies by Spain, up to and including the deliverance of Cuba;
and such law must govern any tribunal. The judge decides what the law is, not
what it should be.

Concerning the Stuart oppression, the latest and most distinguished historian
of the period, Dr. Rawson Gardiner, after remarking that "it was impossible to
allow any mere interpretation of the law to decide the question at issue" between King and Parliament, used an illustration which in the light of this
year's events is singularly striking.

Suppose it should happen that the House of Lords placed itself in deliberate opposition to the House of Commons, even after a general election had shown that the House of Commons was in accord with the feelings of the constituencies. Suppose that the House of Lords rejected every bill sent up to it by the Commons. What would be the use of applying to the judges as arbitrators? They could but decide that the Lords were legally in the right. They could not decide whether they were politically in the right.

The imagined case has occurred, not in all particulars, but in substance. The inadequacy of the law has been recognized; and the British Government of the day has obtained by political action, of the nature of threatened violence, that to which law as an instrument, proved inadequate. A political instrument was employed when the legal instrument—recourse to a court—could not but fail. In the case of the Stuarts the political instrument used was armed resistance.

In the intercourse of nations diplomacy is the analogue of the discussions out of Parliament which preceded the recent use of force by one party to this dispute. In the one kind of contention as in the other, recognized force lay in the background. It is in neither a principal; in both it is an agent. The positiveness inherent in the very idea of law, its lack of elasticity, renders it too frequently inadequate to the settlement of certain classes of disputes, because in the cases an accepted law exists, decision in accordance with which would simply perpetuate injustice or sustain intolerable conditions.

# 6 | Woodrow Wilson's Address to the Senate, January 22, 1917 *

This noted address summarized the Wilsonian answer to the problem of world peace. Its substitution of world opinion and a League of Nations for national interest and the traditional accouterments of power politics comprised a complete intellectual break from the conservative traditions of American diplomacy.

🖎

. . . I have sought this opportunity to address you because I thought that I owed it to you, as the counsel associated with me in the final determination of our international obligations, to disclose to you without reserve the thought and purpose that have been taking form in my mind in regard to the duty of our Government in the days to come when it will be necessary to lay afresh and upon

* The Public Papers of Woodrow Wilson: The New Democracy, Ray Stannard Baker and William E. Dodd, eds. (New York, 1926), II: 407–14.

a new plan the foundations of peace among the nations.

It is inconceivable that the people of the United States should play no part in that great enterprise. To take part in such a service will be the opportunity for which they have sought to prepare themselves by the very principles and purposes of their polity and the approved practices of their Government ever since the days when they set up a new nation in the high and honorable hope that it might in all that it was and did show mankind the way to liberty. They cannot in honor withhold the service to which they are now about to be challenged. They do not wish to withhold it. But they owe it to themselves and to the other nations of the world to state the conditions under which they will feel free to render it.

That service is nothing less than this, to add their authority and their power to the authority and force of other nations to guarantee peace and justice throughout the world. Such a settlement cannot now be long postponed. It is right that before it comes this Government should frankly formulate the conditions upon which it would feel justified in asking our people to approve its formal and solemn adherence to a League for Peace. I am here to attempt to state those conditions.

The present war must first be ended; but we owe it to candor and to a just regard for the opinion of mankind to say that, so far as our participation in guarantees of future peace is concerned, it makes a great deal of difference in what way and upon what terms it is ended. The treaties and agreements which bring it to an end must embody terms which will create a peace that is worth guaranteeing and preserving, a peace that will win the approval of mankind, not merely a peace that will serve the several interests and immediate aims of the nations engaged. We shall have no voice in determining what those terms shall be, but we shall, I feel sure, have a voice in determining whether they shall be made lasting or not by the guarantees of a universal covenant, and our judgment upon what is fundamental and essential as a condition precedent to permanency should be spoken now, not afterwards when it may be to late. . . .

I do not mean to say that any American government would throw any obstacle in the way of any terms of peace the governments now at war might agree upon, or seek to upset them when made, whatever they might be. I only take it for granted that mere terms of peace between the belligerents will not satisfy even the belligerents themselves. Mere agreements may not make peace secure. It will be absolutely necessary that a force be created as a guarantor of the permanency of the settlement so much greater than the force of any nation now engaged or any alliance hitherto formed or projected that no nation, no probable combination of nations could face or withstand it. If the peace presently to be made is to endure, it must be a peace made secure by the organized major force of mankind.

The terms of the immediate peace agreed upon will determine whether it is a peace for which such a guarantee can be secured. The question upon which the whole future peace and policy of the world depends is this: Is the present war a struggle for a just and secure peace, or only for a new balance of power? If it be only a struggle for a new balance of power, who will guarantee, who can guarantee the stable equilibrium of the new arrangement? Only a tranquil Europe can be a stable Europe. There must be, not a balance of power, but a community of power; not organized rivalries, but an organized common peace.

Fortunately we have received very explicit assurances on this point. The statesmen of both of the groups of nations now arrayed against one another have said, in terms that could not be misinterpreted, that it was no part of the purpose they had in mind to crush their antagonists. But the implications of these assurances may not be equally clear to all—may not be the same on both sides of the water. I think it will be serviceable if I attempt to set forth what we understand them to be.

They imply, first of all, that it must be a peace without victory. It is not pleasant to say this. I beg that I may be permitted to put my own interpretation upon it and that it may be understood that no other interpretation was in my thought. I am seeking only to face realities and to face them without soft concealments. Victory would mean peace forced upon the loser, a victor's terms imposed upon the vanquished. It would be accepted in humiliation, under duress, at an intolerable sacrifice, and would leave a sting, a resentment, a bitter memory upon which terms of peace would rest, not permanently, but only as upon quicksand. Only a peace between equals can last. Only a peace the very principle of which is equality and a common participation in a common benefit. The right state of mind, the right feeling between nations, is as necessary for a lasting peace as is the just settlement of vexed questions of territory or of racial and national allegiance.

The equality of nations upon which peace must be founded if it is to last must be an equality of rights; the guarantees exchanged must neither recognize nor imply a difference between big nations and small, between those that are powerful and those that are weak. Right must be based upon the common strength, not upon the individual strength, of the nations upon whose concert peace will depend. Equality of territory or of resources there of course cannot be; nor any other sort of equality not gained in the ordinary peaceful and legitimate development of the peoples themselves. But no one asks or expects anything more than an equality of rights. Mankind is looking now for freedom of life, not for equipoises of power.

And there is a deeper thing involved than even equality of right among organized nations. No peace can last, or ought to last, which does not recognize and accept the principle that governments derive all their just powers from the consent of the governed, and that no right anywhere exists to hand peoples about from sovereignty to sovereignty as if they were property. I take it for granted, for instance, if I may venture upon a single example, that statesmen everywhere are agreed that there should be a united, independent, and autonomous Poland, and that henceforth inviolable security of life, of worship, and of industrial and social development should be guaranteed to all peoples who have lived hitherto under the power of governments devoted to a faith and purpose hostile to their own. . . .

And the paths of the sea must alike in law and in fact be free. The freedom of the seas is the *sine qua non* of peace, equality, and cooperation. No doubt a somewhat radical reconsideration of many of the rules of international practice hitherto thought to be established may be necessary in order to make the seas indeed free and common in practically all circumstances for the use of mankind, but the motive for such changes is convincing and compelling. There can be no trust or intimacy between the peoples of the world without them. The free, constant, unthreatened intercourse of nations is an essential part of the process of peace and of development. It need not be difficult either to define or to secure the freedom of the seas if the governments of the world sincerely desire to come to an agreement concerning it.

It is a problem closely connected with the limitation of naval armaments and the co-operation of the navies of the world in keeping the seas at once free and safe. And the question of limiting naval armaments opens the wider and perhaps more difficult question of the limitation of armies and of all programs of military preparation. Difficult and delicate as these questions are, they must be faced with the utmost candor and decided in the spirit of real accommodation if peace is to come with healing in its wings, and come to stay. Peace cannot be had without concession and sacrifice. There can be no sense of safety and equality among the nations if great preponderating armaments are henceforth to continue here and there to be built up and maintained. The statesmen of the world must plan for peace and nations must adjust and accommodate their policy to it as they have planned for war and made ready for pitiless contest and rivalry. The question of armaments, whether on land or sea, is the most immediately and intensely practical question connected with the future fortunes of nations and of mankind. . . .

. . . I would fain believe that I am speaking for the silent mass of mankind everywhere who have as yet had no place or opportunity to speak their real hearts out concerning the death and ruin they see to have come already upon the persons and the homes they hold most dear.

And in holding out the expectation that the people and Government of the United States will join the other civilized nations of the world in guaranteeing the permanence of peace upon such terms as I have named I speak with the greater boldness and confidence because it is clear to every man who can think that there is in this promise no breach in either our traditions or our policy as a nation, but a fulfilment, rather, of all that we have professed or striven for.

I am proposing, as it were, that the nations should with one accord adopt the doctrine of President Monroe as the doctrine of the world: that no nation should seek to extend its polity over any other nation or people, but that every people should be left free to determine its own polity, its own way of development, unhindered, unthreatened, unafraid, the little along with the great and powerful.

I am proposing that all nations henceforth avoid entangling alliances which would draw them into competitions of power; catch them in a net of intrigue and selfish rivalry, and disturb their own affairs with influences intruded from without. There is no entangling alliance in a concert of power. When all unite to act in the same sense and with the same purpose all act in the common interest and are free to live their own lives under a common protection.

I am proposing government by the consent of the governed; that freedom of the seas which in international conference after conference representatives of the United States have urged with the eloquence of those who are the convinced disciples of liberty; and that moderation of armaments which makes of armies and navies a power for order merely, not an instrument of aggression or of selfish violence.

These are American principles, American policies. We could stand for no others. And they are also the principles and policies of forward looking men and women everywhere, of every modern nation, of every enlightened community. They are the principles of mankind and must prevail.

# 7 | Woodrow Wilson's War Message, April 2, 1917 *

In his war message Wilson assumed that Germany, with its unrestricted submarine warfare, acted in bad faith. He accepted the simple notion that the Prussian autocracy alone stood between a world of conflict and war and a world of peace, justice, and freedom. By committing the nation not to the mere curtailment of German power and ambition but to the establishment of a new world order, Wilson embarked on a goal which he could never reach. Thus American involvement, instead of balancing the ends and means of national policy, as Einstein and others had hoped, left the foreign policies of the United States even less solvent than they had been during the previous decade.

✍

. . . When I addressed the Congress on the twenty-sixth of February last I thought that it would suffice to assert our neutral rights with arms, our right to use the seas against unlawful interference, our right to keep our people safe against unlawful violence. But armed neutrality, it now appears, is impracticable. Because submarines are in effect outlaws when used as the German submarines have been used against merchant shipping, it is impossible to defend ships against their attacks as the law of nations has assumed that merchantmen would defend themelves against privateers or cruisers, visible craft giving chase upon the open sea. It is common prudence in such circumstances, grim necessity indeed, to endeavor to destroy them before they have shown their own intention. They must be dealt with upon sight, if dealt with at all. The German

* The Public Papers of Woodrow Wilson: War and Peace, Baker and Dodd (eds.) (New York, 1927), I: 6–16.

Government denies the right of neutrals to use arms at all within the areas of the sea which it has proscribed, even in the defense of rights which no modern publicist has ever before questioned their right to defend. The intimation is conveyed that the armed guards which we have placed on our merchant ships will be treated as beyond the pale of law and subject to be dealt with as pirates would be. Armed neutrality is ineffectual enough at best; in such circumstances and in the face of such pretensions it is worse than ineffectual: it is likely only to produce what it was meant to prevent; it is practically certain to draw us into the war without either the rights or the effectiveness of belligerents. There is one choice we cannot make, we are incapable of making: we will not choose the path of submission and suffer the most sacred rights of our Nation and our people to be ignored or violated. The wrongs against which we now array ourselves are no common wrongs; they cut to the very roots of human life.

With a profound sense of the solemn and even tragical character of the step I am taking and of the grave responsibilities which it involves, but in unhesitating obedience to what I deem my constitutional duty, I advise that the Congress declare the recent course of the Imperial German Government to be in fact nothing less than war against the government and people of the United States; that it formally accept the status of belligerent which has thus been thrust upon it; and that it take immediate steps not only to put the country in a more thorough state of defense but also to exert all its power and employ all its resources to bring the Government of the German Empire to terms and end the war.

What this will involve is clear. It will involve the utmost practicable cooperation in counsel and action with the governments now at war with Germany, and, as incident to that, the extension to those governments of the most liberal financial credits, in order that our resources may so far as possible be added to theirs. It will involve the organization and mobilization of all the material resources of the country to supply the materials of war and serve the incidental needs of the Nation in the most abundant and yet the most economical and efficient way possible. It will involve the immediate full equipment of the navy in all respects but particularly in supplying it with the best means of dealing with the enemy's submarines. It will involve the immediate addition to the armed forces of the United States already provided for by law in case of war at least five hundred thousand men, who should, in my opinion, be chosen upon the principle of universal liability to service, and also the authorization of subsequent additional increments of equal force so soon as they may be needed and can be handled in training. It will involve also, of course, the granting of adequate credits to the Government, sustained, I hope, so far as they can equitably be sustained by the present generation, by well conceived taxation.

I say sustained so far as may be equitable by taxation because it seems to me that it would be most unwise to base the credits which will now be necessary entirely on money borrowed. It is our duty, I most respectfully urge, to protect our people so far as we may against the very serious hardships and evils which would be likely to arise out of the inflation which would be produced by vast loans. . . .

While we do these things, these deeply momentous things, let us be very clear, and make very clear to all the world what our motives and our objects are. My own thought has not been driven from its habitual and normal course by the unhappy events of the last two months, and I do not believe that the thought of the Nation has been altered or clouded by them. I have exactly the same things in mind now that I had in mind when I addressed the Senate on the twenty-second of January last; the same that I had in mind when I addressed the Congress on the third of February and on the twenty-sixth of February. Our object now, as then, is to vindicate the principles of peace and justice in the life of the world as against selfish and autocratic power and to set up amongst the really free and self-governed peoples of the world such a concert of purpose and of action as will henceforth insure the observance of those principles. Neutrality is no longer feasible or desirable where the peace of the world is involved and the freedom of its peoples, and the menace to that peace and freedom lies in the existence of autocratic governments backed by organized force which is controlled wholly by their will, not by the will of their people. We have seen the last of neutrality in such circumstances. We are at the beginning of an age in which it will be insisted that the same standards of conduct and of responsibility for wrong done shall be observed among nations and their governments that are observed among the individual citizens of civilized states.

We have no quarrel with the German people. We have no feeling towards them but one of sympathy and friendship. It was not upon their impulse that their government acted in entering this war. It was not with their previous knowledge or approval. It was a war determined upon as wars used to be determined upon in the old, unhappy days when peoples were nowhere consulted by their rulers and wars were provoked and waged in the interest of dynasties or of little groups of ambitious men who were accustomed to use their fellow men as pawns and tools. Self-governed nations do not fill their neighbor states with spies or set the course of intrigue to bring about some critical posture of affairs which will give them an opportunity to strike and make conquest. Such designs can be successfully worked out only under cover and where no one has the right to ask questions. Cunningly contrived plans of deception or aggression, carried, it may be, from generation to generation, can be worked out and kept from the light only within the privacy of courts or behind the carefully guarded confidences of a narrow and privileged class. They are happily impossible where public opinion commands and insists upon full information concerning all the nation's affairs.

A steadfast concert for peace can never be maintained except by a partnership of democratic nations. No autocratic government could be trusted to keep faith within it or observe its covenants. It must be a league of honor, a partnership of opinion. Intrigue would eat its vitals away; the plottings of inner circles who could plan what they would and render account to no one would be a corruption seated at its very heart. Only free peoples can hold their purpose and their honor steady to a common end and prefer the interests of mankind to any narrow interest of their own. . . .

One of the things that has served to convince us that the Prussian autocracy was not and could never be our friend is that from the very outset of the present war it has filled our unsuspecting communities and even our offices of government with spies and set criminal intrigues everywhere afoot against our national unity of counsel, our peace within and without, our industries and our commerce. Indeed, it is now evident that its spies were here even before the war began; and it is unhappily not a matter of conjecture but a fact proved in our courts of justice that the intrigues which have more than once come perilously near to disturbing the peace and dislocating the industries of the country have been carried on at the instigation, with the support, and even under the personal direction of official agents of the Imperial Government accredited to the Government of the United States. Even in checking these things and trying to extirpate them we have sought to put the most generous interpretation possible upon them because we knew that their source lay not in any hostile feeling or purpose of the German people towards us (who were no doubt as ignorant of them as we ourselves were), but only in the selfish designs of a Government that did what it pleased and told its people nothing. But they have played their part in serving to convince us at last that that Government entertains no real friendship for us and means to act against our peace and security at its convenience. That it means to stir up enemies against us at our very doors the intercepted note to the German Minister at Mexico City is eloquent evidence.

We are accepting this challenge of hostile purpose because we know that in such a Government, following such methods, we can never have a friend; and that in the presence of its organized power, always lying in wait to accomplish we know not what purpose, there can be no assured security for the democratic Governments of the world. We are now about to accept gage of battle with this natural foe to liberty and shall, if necessary, spend the whole force of the Nation to check and nullify its pretensions and its power. We are glad, now that we see the facts with no veil of false pretense about them, to fight thus for the ultimate peace of the world and for the liberation of its peoples, the German peoples included: for the rights of nations great and small and the privilege of men everywhere to choose their way of life and of obedience. The world must be made safe for democracy. Its peace must be planted upon the tested foundations of political liberty. We have no selfish ends to serve. We desire no conquest, no dominion. We seek no indemnities for ourselves, no material compensation for the sacrifices we shall freely make. We are but one of the champions of the rights of mankind. We shall be satisfied when those rights have been made as secure as the faith and the freedom of nations can make them. . . .

It will be all the easier for us to conduct ourselves as belligerents in a high spirit of right and fairness because we act without animus, not in enmity towards a people or with the desire to bring any injury or disadvantage upon them, but only in armed opposition to an irresponsible government which has thrown aside all considerations of humanity and of right and is running amuck. We are, let me say again, the sincere friends of the German people, and shall desire nothing so much as the early reestablishment of intimate relations of mutual advantage between us,—however hard it may be for them, for the time being, to believe that this is spoken from our hearts. We have borne with their present Government through all these bitter months because of that friendship,—exercising a patience and forbearance which would otherwise have been impossible. We shall, happily, still have an opportunity to prove that friendship in our daily attitude and actions towards the millions of men and women of German birth and native sympathy who live amongst us and share our life, and we shall be proud to prove it towards all who are in fact loyal to their neighbors and to the Government in the hour of test. They are, most of them, as true and loyal Americans as if they had never known any other fealty or allegiance. They will be prompt to stand with us in rebuking and restraining the few who may be of a different mind and purpose. If there should be disloyalty, it will be dealt with with a firm hand of stern repression; but, if it lifts its head at all, it will lift it only here and there and without countenance except from a lawless and malignant few.

It is a distressing and oppressive duty, Gentlemen of the Congress, which I have performed in thus addressing you. There are, it may be, many months of fiery trial and sacrifice ahead of us. It is a fearful thing to lead this great peaceful people into war, into the most terrible and disastrous of all wars, civilization itself seeming to be in the balance. But the right is more precious than peace, and we shall fight for the things which we have always carried nearest our hearts,—for democracy, for the right of those who submit to authority to have a voice in their own Governments, for the rights and liberties of small nations, for a universal dominion of right by such a concert of free peoples as shall bring peace and safety to all nations and make the world itself at last free. To such a task we can dedicate our lives and our fortunes, everything that we are and everything that we have, with the pride of those who know that the day has come when America is privileged to spend her blood and her might for the principles that gave her birth and happiness and the peace which she has treasured. God helping her, she can do no other.

## 8 | George W. Norris's Speech Against the War Resolution, April 4, 1917 *

The opposition of Norris and others to the American declaration of war against Germany contributed nothing to the formulation of a genuine national policy. Their preference for continued neutrality, like the anti-imperialism of Senator Hoar, was anchored primarily to questions of morality. To Norris the United

* *Congressional Record,* 65th Congress, 1st Sess., 212–14.

States, profoundly unneutral, was responding to the dictates of gold. He, like others, avoided the central issues confronting the nation's leaders—the relationship of a possible German victory to the security of the United States and the postwar role of American economic and military power in the maintenance of a reconstituted European balance. For him the tradition of isolationism was sufficient to serve the country's needs.

✒

. . . The resolution now before the Senate is a declaration of war. Before taking this momentous step, and while standing on the brink of this terrible vortex, we ought to pause and calmly and judiciously consider the terrible consequences of the step we are about to take. We ought to consider likewise the route we have recently traveled and ascertain whether we have reached our present position in a way that is compatible with the neutral position which we claimed to occupy at the beginning and through the various stages of this unholy and unrighteous war.

No close student of recent history will deny that both Great Britain and Germany have, on numerous occasions since the beginning of the war, flagrantly violated in the most serious manner the rights of neutral vessels and neutral nations under existing international law as recognized up to the beginning of this war by the civilized world. . . .

. . . [W]e have the two declarations of the two Governments, each declaring a military zone and warning neutral shipping from going into the prohibited area. England sought to make her order effective by the use of submerged mines. Germany sought to make her order effective by the use of submarines. Both of these orders were illegal and contrary to all international law as well as the principles of humanity. Under international law no belligerent Government has the right to place submerged mines in the high seas. Neither has it any right to take human life without notice by the use of submarines. If there is any difference on the ground of humanity between these two instrumentalities, it is certainly in favor of the submarines. The submarine can exercise some degree of discretion and judgment. The submerged mine always destroys without notice, friend and foe alike, guilty and innocent the same. In carrying out these two policies, both Great Britain and Germany have sunk American ships and destroyed American lives without provocation and without notice. There have been more ships sunk and more American lives lost from the action of submarines than from English mines in the North Sea: for the simple reason that we finally acquiesced in the British war zone and kept our ships out of it, while in the German war zone we have refused to recognize its legality and have not kept either our ships or our citizens out of its area. If American ships had gone into the British war zone in defiance of Great Britain's order, as they have gone into the German war zone in defiance of the German Government's order, there would have been many more American lives lost and many more American ships sunk by the instrumentality of the mines than the instrumentality of the submarines.

We have in the main complied with the demands made by Great Britain. Our ships have followed the instructions of the British Government in going not only to England but to the neutral nations of the world, and in thus complying with the British order American ships going to Holland, Denmark, Norway, and Sweden have been taken by British officials into British ports, and their cargoes inspected and examined. All the mails we have carried even to neutral countries have been opened and censored, and oftentimes the entire cargo confiscated by the Government. Nothing has been permitted to pass to even the most neutral nations except after examination and with the permission of the officials of the British Government. . . .

The only difference is that in the case of Germany we have persisted in our protest, while in the case of England we have submitted. What was our duty as a Government and what were our rights when we were confronted with these extraordinary orders declaring these military zones? First, we could have defied both of them and could have gone to war against both of these nations for this violation of international law and interference with our neutral rights. Second, we had the technical right to defy one and to acquiesce in the other. Third, we could, while denouncing them both as illegal, have acquiesced in them both and thus remained neutral with both sides, although not agreeing with either as to the righteousness of their respective orders. We could have said to American shipowners that, while these orders are both contrary to international law and are both unjust, we do not believe that the provocation is sufficient to cause us to go to war for the defense of our rights as a neutral nation, and, therefore, American ships and American citizens will go into these zones at their own peril and risk. Fourth, we might have declared an embargo against the shipping from American ports of any merchandise to either one of these Governments that persisted in maintaining its military zone. We might have refused to permit the sailing of any ship from any American port to either of these military zones. In my judgment, if we had pursued this course, the zones would have been of short duration. England would have been compelled to take her mines out of the North Sea in order to get any supplies from our country. When her mines were taken out of the North Sea then the German ports upon the North Sea would have been accessible to American shipping and Germany would have been compelled to cease her submarine warfare in order to get any supplies from our Nation into German North Sea ports.

There are a great many American citizens who feel that we owe it as a duty to humanity to take part in this war. Many instances of cruelty and inhumanity can be found on both sides. Men are often biased in their judgment on account of their sympathy and their interests. To my mind, what we ought to have maintained from the beginning was the strictest neutrality. If we had done this I do not believe we would have been on the verge of war at the present time. We had a right as a nation, if we desired, to cease at any time to be neutral. We had a technical right to respect the English war zone and to disregard the German war zone, but we could not do that and be neutral. I have no quarrel to find with the man who does not desire our country to remain neutral. While many such people are moved by selfish motives and hopes of gain, I have no

doubt but that in a great many instances, through what I believe to be a misunderstanding of the real condition, there are many honest, patriotic citizens
who think we ought to engage in this war and who are behind the President in
his demand that we should declare war against Germany. I think such people
err in judgment and to a great extent have been misled as to the real history
and the true facts by the almost unanimous demand of the great combination of
wealth that has a direct financial interest in our participation in the war. We have
loaned many hundreds of millions of dollars to the allies in this controversy.
While such action was legal and countenanced by international law, there is
no doubt in my mind but the enormous amount of money loaned to the allies in
this country has been instrumental in bringing about a public sentiment in
favor of our country taking a course that would make every bond worth a hundred cents on the dollar and making the payment of every debt certain and
sure. Through this instrumentality and also through the instrumentality of
others who have not only made millions out of the war in the manufacture of
munitions, etc., and who would expect to make millions more if our country can
be drawn into the catastrophe, a large number of the great newspapers and news
agencies of the country have been controlled and enlisted in the greatest
propaganda that the world has ever known, to manufacture sentiment in favor
of war. It is now demanded that the American citizens shall be used as insurance
policies to guarantee the safe delivery of munitions of war to belligerent nations.
The enormous profits of munition manufacturers, stockbrokers, and bond
dealers must be still further increased by our entrance into the war. This has
brought us to the present moment, when Congress, urged by the President and
backed by the artificial sentiment, is about to declare war and engulf our country in the greatest holocaust that the world has ever known. . . .

. . . War brings no prosperity to the great mass of common and patriotic
citizens. It increases the cost of living of those who toil and those who already
must strain every effort to keep soul and body together. War brings prosperity
to the stock gambler on Wall Street—to those who are already in possession of
more wealth than can be realized or enjoyed. . . .

Their object in having war and in preparing for war is to make money.
Human suffering and the sacrifice of human life are necessary, but Wall Street
considers only the dollars and the cents. . . . The stock brokers would not, of
course, go to war, because the very object they have in bringing on the war is
profit, and therefore they must remain in their Wall Street offices in order to
share in that great prosperity which they say war will bring. The volunteer
officer, even the drafting officer, will not find them. They will be concealed in
their palatial offices on Wall Street, sitting behind mahogany desks, covered up
with clipped coupons—coupons soiled with the sweat of honest toil, coupons
stained with mothers' tears, coupons dyed in the lifeblood of their fellow men.

We are taking a step to-day that is fraught with untold danger. We are
going into war upon the command of gold. We are going to run the risk of
sacrificing millions of our countrymen's lives in order that other countrymen may coin their lifeblood into money. And even if we do not cross the
Atlantic and go into the trenches, we are going to pile up a debt that the toil-

ing masses that shall come many generations after us will have to pay. Unborn millions will bend their backs in toil in order to pay for the terrible step we are now about to take. We are about to do the bidding of wealth's terrible mandate. By our act we will make millions of our countrymen suffer and the consequences of it may well be that millions of our brethren must shed their lifeblood, millions of broken-hearted women must weep, millions of children must suffer with cold, and millions of babes must die from hunger, and all because we want to preserve the commercial right of American citizens to deliver munitions of war to belligerent nations.

## 9 | Wilson's Crusade for the League of Nations, September 1919 *

What characterized the evolution of Wilson's wartime thought was its progressive retreat from reality. Fighting for the Versailles Treaty and the League of Nations during his Western tour of September 1919, the President assigned to the achievements at Versailles a virtue unprecedented in the annals of diplomacy. Ignoring the fact that the empires of the victors had not been touched, Wilson declared in the stadium at San Diego on September 19 that the Versailles Treaty set "at liberty people all over Europe and in Asia who had hitherto been enslaved by powers which were not their rightful sovereigns and masters." Indeed, there could be no peace until all peoples were free. To guarantee that freedom required above all that the United States accept the League of Nations. Wilson, in declaring universal war against oppression, completely transcended the purpose of even such idealists as Jefferson and Madison.

✍

. . . One of the most unexpected things that I have found on my journey is that the people of the United States have not been informed as to the real character and scope and contents of the great treaty of peace with Germany. Whether by omission or by intention, they have been directed in all of the speeches that I have read to certain points of the treaty which are incidental, and not central, and their attention has been drawn away from the real meaning of this great human document. For that, my fellow citizens, is just what it is. It not only concludes a peace with Germany and imposes upon Germany the proper penalties for the outrage she attempted upon mankind, but it also concludes the peace in the spirit in which the war was undertaken by the nations opposed to Germany. The challenge of war was accepted by them not with the

* *The Public Papers of Woodrow Wilson: War and Peace*, II: 277–92.

purpose of crushing the German people but with the purpose of putting an end once and for all to such plots against the free governments of the world as had been conceived on Wilhelmstrasse, in Berlin, unknown to the people of Germany, unconceived by them, advised by little groups of men who had the military power to carry out private ambitions.

We went into this war not only to see that autocratic power of that sort never threatened the world again but we went into it for even larger purposes than that. Other autocratic powers may spring up, but there is only one soil in which they can spring up, and that is the wrongs done to free peoples of the world. The heart and center of this treaty is that it sets at liberty people all over Europe and in Asia who had hitherto been enslaved by powers which were not their rightful sovereigns and masters. So long as wrongs like that exist in the world, you cannot bring permanent peace to the world. I go further than that. So long as wrongs of that sort exist, you ought not to bring permanent peace to the world, because those wrongs ought to be righted, and enslaved peoples ought to be free to right them. For my part, I will not take any part in composing difficulties that ought not to be composed, and a difficulty between an enslaved people and its autocratic rulers ought not to be composed. We in America have stood from the day of our birth for the emancipation of people throughout the world who were living unwillingly under governments which were not of their own choice. The thing which we have held more sacred than any other is that all just government rests upon the consent of the governed, and all over the world that principle has been disregarded, that principle has been flouted by the strong, and only the weak have suffered. The heart and center of this treaty is the principle adopted not only in this treaty but put into effect also in the treaty with Austria, in the treaty with Hungary, in the treaty with Bulgaria, in the treaty with Turkey, that every great territory in the world belongs to the people who are living on it, and that it is not the privilege of any authority anywhere—certainly not the privilege of the peace conference at Paris—to impose upon those peoples any government which they accept unwillingly and not of their own choice. . . .

. . . The heart of humanity beats in this document. It is not a statesman's arrangement. It is a liberation of the peoples and of the humane forces of the world, and yet I never hear the slightest intimation of any of these great features in the speeches of the gentlemen who are opposing this treaty. They never tell you what is really in this treaty. If they did your enthusiasm would sweep them off their feet. If they did they would know that it was an audacity which they had better not risk to impair the peace and the humane conditions of mankind.

At the very front and heart of the treaty is the part which is most criticized, namely, the great Covenant for a League of Nations. This treaty could not be executed without such a powerful instrumentality. Unless all the right-thinking nations of the world are going to concert their purpose and their power, this treaty is not worth the paper that it is written on, because it is a treaty where peace rests upon the right of the weak, and only the power of the strong can maintain the right of the weak. If we as a nation indeed mean what we have always said, that we are the champions of human right, now is the time when we shall be brought to the test, the acid test, as to whether we mean what we said or not. I am not saying that because I have the least doubt as to the verdict. I am just as sure of it as if it had been rendered already. I know this great people among whom I was born and bred and whom I have had the signal honor to serve, whose mouthpiece it has been my privilege to be on both sides of the water, and I know that I am speaking their conscience, when I speak in the name of my own conscience that that is the duty of America and that it will be assumed and performed. . . .

What are those who advise us to turn away from it afraid of? In the first place, they are afraid that it impairs in some way that long traditional policy of the United States which was embodied in the Monroe Doctrine, but how they can fear that I cannot conceive, for the document expressly says in words which I am now quoting that nothing in this Covenant shall be held to affect the validity of the Monroe Doctrine. The phrase was inserted under my own eye, at the suggestion—not of the phrase but the principle—of the Foreign Relations Committees of both Houses of Congress. I think I am justified in dismissing all fear that the Monroe Doctrine is in the least impaired. And what is the Monroe Doctrine? It is that no outside power shall attempt to impose its will in any form upon the Western Hemisphere, and that if it does the United States, acting upon its own initiative and alone, if it chooses, can resist and will resist the attempt. Could anything leave the United States freer as a champion of the independence of the Western Hemisphere than this world acknowledgment of the validity and potency of the Monroe Doctrine?

They are afraid that the League will in some way deal with our domestic affairs. The Covenant expressly says that it will have no right to deal with the domestic affairs of any member of the League, and I cannot imagine anything more definite or satisfactory than that. There is no ambiguity about any part of this Covenant, for the matter of that, but there is certainly no ambiguity about the statement concerning domestic affairs, for it is provided that if any matter brought before the council is found to be a matter which, under international law, lies within the exclusive jurisdiction of the State making the claim, the council shall dismiss consideration of it and shall not even make a report about it. And the subjects which are giving these gentlemen the most concern are agreed by all students of international law to be domestic questions; for example, immigration, naturalization, the tariff—these are the subjects most frequently spoken of. No one of those can be dealt with by the League of Nations, so far as the sovereignty of the United States is concerned. We have a perfectly clear field there, as we have in regard to the Monroe Doctrine. . . .

. . . You have heard a great deal about Article X of the Covenant. Very well, after you have read it suppose you read Article XI. Article XI provides that it shall be the friendly right of any member of the League, big or little, strong or weak, to call attention to anything, anywhere, which is likely to disturb the peace of the world or the good understanding between nations upon which the peace of the world depends. When anybody of kin to us in America is done wrong by any foreign government, it is likely to disturb the good understanding between nations upon which the peace of the world depends, and thus any one of the causes represented in the hearts of the American people can be brought to the attention of the whole world. One of the most effective means of winning a good cause is to bring it before that great jury. A bad cause will fare ill, but a good cause is bound to be triumphant in such a forum. Until this, international law made it an unfriendly act for any nation to call attention to any matter which did not immediately affect its own fortunes and its own right. I am amazed that so many men do not see the extraordinary change which this will bring in the transaction of human affairs. I am amazed that they do not see that now, for the first time, not selfish national policy but the general judgment of the world as to right is going to determine the fortunes of peoples, whether they be weak or whether they be strong, and I myself glory in the provisions of Article XI more than I glory in any other part of the Covenant, for it draws all men together in a single friendly court, where they may discuss their own affairs and determine the issues of justice—just exactly what was desired in the hearts of the men from whom I have read extracts of opinion.

But what disturbs me, perhaps the only thing that disturbs me, my fellow countrymen, about the form which the opposition to the League is taking is this: Certain reservations, as they are called, are proposed which in effect—I am not now stopping to form an opinion as to whether that is the intention or not; I have no right to judge the intention of a man who has not stated what his intention is—which in effect amount to this, that the United States is unwilling to assume the same obligations under the Covenant of the League that are assumed by the other members of the League; that the United States wants to disclaim any part in the responsibility which the other members of the League are assuming. I want to say with all the emphasis of which I am capable that that is unworthy of the honor of the United States. The principle of justice, the principle of right, the principle of international amity is this, that there is not only an imaginary but a real equality of standing and right among all the sovereign peoples of the world. . . .

I will not join in claiming under the name of justice an unjust position of privilege for the country I love and honor. Neither am I afraid of responsibility. Neither will I scuttle. Neither will I be a little American. America, in her make-up, in her purposes, in her principles, is the biggest thing in the world, and she must measure up to the measure of the world. I will be no party in belittling her. I will be no party in saying that America is afraid of responsibilities which I know she can carry and in which in carrying I am sure she shall lead the world. Why, if we were to decline to go into this humane arrangement we would be declining the invitation which all the world extends to us to lead them in the enterprise of liberty and of justice. I, for one, will not decline that invitation. I, for one, believe more profoundly than in anything else human in the destiny of the United States. I believe that she has a spiritual energy in her which no other nation can contribute to the liberation of mankind, and I know that the heart of America is stronger than her business calculations. That is what the world found out when we went into the war. When we went into the war there was not a nation in the world that did not believe we were more interested in making money out of it than in serving the cause of liberty. And when we went in, in those few months the whole world stood at amaze and ended with an enthusiastic conversion. They now believe that America will stand by anybody that is fighting for justice and for right, and we shall not disappoint them. . . .

. . . There is nothing that softens the attitude of men like really, frankly laying their minds alongside of each other and their characters alongside of each other and making a fair and manly and open comparison. That is what all the great fighting nations of the world agree to with every matter of difference between them. They put it either before a jury by whom they are bound or before a jury which will publish all the facts to mankind and express a frank opinion regarding it.

You have here what the world must have, what America went into this war to obtain. You have here an estoppel of the brutal, sudden impulse of war. You have here a restraint upon the passions of ambitious nations. You here have a safeguard of the liberty of weak nations, and the world is at last ready to stand up and in calm counsel discuss the fortunes of men and women and children everywhere. Why, my fellow citizens, nothing brings a lump into my throat quicker on this journey I am taking than to see the thronging children that are everywhere the first, just out of childish curiosity and glee, no doubt, to crowd up to the train when it stops, because I know that if by any chance we should not win this great fight for the League of Nations it would be their death warrant. They belong to the generation which would then have to fight the final war, and in that final war there would not be merely seven and a half million men slain. The very existence of civilization would be in the balance, and I for one dare not face the responsibility of defeating the very purpose for which we sent our gallant men overseas. Every mother knows that her pride in the son that she lost is due to the fact, not that he helped to beat Germany, but that he helped to save the world. It was that light the other people saw in the eyes of the boys that went over there, that light as of men who see a distant horizon, that light as of men who have caught the gleam and inspiration of a great cause, and the armies of the United States seemed to those people on the other side of the sea like bodies of crusaders come out of a free nation to give freedom to their fellows, ready to sacrifice their lives for an idea, for an ideal, for the only thing that is worth living for, the spiritual purpose of redemption that rests in the hearts of mankind.

— | "The world will be absolutely in despair if America deserts it." *

At the Hotel Alexandria in Los Angeles, on September 20, Wilson declared that the Versailles Treaty, with its principle of self-determination, was a triumph not for the world's leadership, but for humanity. To preserve the great gains for liberty achieved by the war required the continuance of the postwar *status quo.*

* *The Public Papers of Woodrow Wilson: War and Peace,* II: 304–10.

For Wilson the proper choice of the American people in upholding the freedom of the world lay in a national rejection of isolationism and an identification of American policy with the League of Nations.

✒

. . . For the first time in the history of civilized society, a great international convention, made up of the leading statesmen of the world, has proposed a settlement which is for the benefit of the weak and not for the benefit of the strong. It is for the benefit of peoples who could not have liberated themselves, whose weakness was profitable to the ambitious and imperialistic nations, whose weakness had been traded on by every cabinet in Europe; and yet these very cabinets represented at the table in Paris were unanimous in the conviction that the people's day had come and that it was not their right to dispose of the fortunes of people without the consent of those people themselves.

At the front of this great settlement they put the only thing that will preserve it. You cannot set weak peoples up in independence and then leave them to be preyed upon. You cannot give a false gift. You cannot give to people rights which they never enjoyed before and say, "Now, keep them if you can." That is an Indian gift. That is a gift which cannot be kept. If you have a really humane purpose and a real knowledge of the conditions of peace in the world, you will have to say, "This is the settlement and we guarantee its continuance." There is only one honorable course when you have won a cause, to see that it stays won and nobody interferes with or disturbs the results. That is the purpose of the much-discussed Article X in the Covenant of the League of Nations. It is the Monroe Doctrine applied to the world. Ever since Mr. Monroe uttered his famous doctrine we have said to the world, "We will respect and preserve as against external aggression the territorial integrity and the political independence of every State in the Western Hemisphere," and those are practically the words of Article X. Under Article X all the members of the League engage to respect and preserve as against external aggression the territorial integrity and existing political independence of the other member States, and if that guarantee is not forthcoming the whole structure of peace will crumble, because you cannot point out a great war that has not begun by a violation of that principle; that has not begun by the intention to impair the territorial integrity or to interfere with the political independence of some body of people of some nation. . . .

You have no choice, my fellow citizens, because the peoples of the world, even those that slept, are awake. There is not a country in the world where the great mass of mankind is not now aware of its rights and determined to have them at any cost, and the present universal unrest in the world, which renders return to normal conditions impossible so long as it continues, will not stop until men are assured by some arrangement they can believe in that their rights will be protected and that they can go about the normal production of the necessaries of life and begin to enjoy the ordinary pleasures and privileges of life without the constant shadow of some cloud of terror over them, some threat of injustice, some tyranny of control. Men are not going to stand it. If you want to quiet the world, you have got to reassure the world, and the only way in which you can reassure it is to let it know that all the great fighting powers of the world are going to maintain that quiet, that the fighting power is no longer to be directed toward aggression, but is to be directed toward protection. And every great fighting nation in the world will be in the League—because Germany for the time being is not a great fighting power. That great nation of over 60,000,000 people has consented in the treaty to reduce its standing armed force to 100,000 men and to give up all the war material over and above what is necessary to maintain an army of 100,000 men; so that for the time being we may exclude Germany from the list of the fighting nations of the world. The whole power of the world is now offered to mankind for the maintenance of peace, and for the maintenance of peace by the very processes we have all professed to believe in, by substituting arbitration and discussion for war, by substituting the judgment of mankind for the force of arms. I say without qualification that every nation that is not afraid of the judgment of mankind will go into this arrangement. There is nothing for any nation to lose whose purposes are right and whose cause is just. The only nations that need fear to go into it are those that have designs which are illegitimate, those which have designs that are inconsistent with justice and are the opposite of peace.

The whole freedom of the world not only, but the whole peace of mind of the world, depends upon the choice of America, because without America in this arrangement the world will not be reassured. I can testify to that. I can testify that no impression was borne in deeper upon me on the other side of the water than that no great free peoples suspected the United States of ulterior designs, and that every nation, the weakest among them, felt that its fortunes would be safe it intrusted to the guidance of America; that America would not impose upon it. . . .

. . . The world will be absolutely in despair if America deserts it. But the thing is inconceivable. America is not going to desert it. The people of America are not going to desert it. The job is to get that into the consciousness of men who do not understand it. The job is to restore some of our fellow citizens to that large sort of sanity which makes a man bigger than himself. We have had a great many successful men in America, my fellow citizens, but we have seldom erected a statue to a man who was merely successful in a business way. Almost all the statues in America, almost all the memorials, are erected to men who forgot themselves and worked for other people. They may not have been rich, they may not have been successful in the worldly sense, they may have been deemed in their generation dreamers and idealists, but when they were dead America remembered that they loved mankind, America remembered that they embodied in those dreamy ideals of theirs the visions that America had had, America remembered that they had a great surplus of character that they spent not upon themselves but upon the enterprises of humanity. A man who has not got that surplus capital of character that he spends upon the great enterprises of communities and of nations will sink into a deserved oblivion, and the only danger is that in his concentration upon his own ambitions, in his centering of everything that he spends upon himself, he will lead others astray and work a disservice to great communities which he ought to have served. It is now an enterprise of infection ahead of us—shall I call it? We have got to infect those men with the spirit of the Nation itself. We have got to make them aware that we will not be led; that we will not be controlled; that we will not be restrained by those who are not like ourselves; and that America now is in the presence of the realization of the destiny for which she has been waiting.

You know, you have been told, that Washington advised us against entangling alliances, and gentlemen have used that as an argument against the League of Nations. What Washington had in mind was exactly what these gentlemen want to lead us back to. The day we have left behind us was a day of alliances. It was a day of balances of power. It was a day of "every nation take care of itself or make a partnership with some other nation or group of nations to hold the peace of the world steady or to dominate the weaker portions of the world." Those were the days of alliances. This project of the League of Nations is a great process of disentanglement. I was reading only this morning what a friend of mine reminded me of, a speech that President McKinley made the day before he was assassinated, and in several passages of that speech you see the dawn of this expectation in his humane mind. Hhis whole thought was against isolation. His whole thought was that we had by process of circumstance, as well as of interests, become partners with the rest of the world. His thought was that the world had grown little by quickened methods of intercommunication. His whole thought was that the better we knew each other and the closer we drew together, the more certain it would be that the processes of arbitration would be adopted; that men would not fight but would talk things over; that they would realize their community of interest; and shot all through that speech you see the morning light of just such a day as this. It would look as if the man had been given a vision just before he died—one of the sweetest and most humane souls that have been prominent in our affairs, a man who thought with his head and with his heart. This new day was dawning upon his heart, and his intelligence was beginning to draw the lines of the new picture which has been completed and sketched in a constructive document that we shall adopt and that, having adopted it, we shall find to reflect a new glory upon the things that we did. Then what significance will attach to the boy's sword or the boy's musket over the mantelpiece—not merely that he beat Germany, but that he redeemed the world.

— | "Autocratic governments are excluded henceforth from respectable society." *

Continuing his defense of the League of Nations at the Los Angeles Auditorium on September 20, Wilson assigned to the economic boycott and the "jury of mankind" the power to enforce the peace. Through such moral pressures, declared

* *The Public Papers of Woodrow Wilson: War and Peace*, II: 310–25.

Wilson, the world, under the League of Nations, would enjoy a 99 per cent assurance of peace. The exclusion of autocratic governments from the League merely guaranteed the effective performance of the organization.

. . . Do not for a moment suppose that the universal unrest in the world at the present time, my fellow citizens, is due to any whim, to any newborn passion, to any newly discovered ambition. It is due to the fact, the sad, the tragic fact, that great bodies of men have throughout the ages been denied the mere rights of humanity. The peoples of the world are tired of a time with governments that exploit their people, and they are determined to have, by one process or another, that concerted order of conciliation and debate and conference which is set up in the great document that we know as the Covenant of the League of Nations. The heart of that document is not in the mere details that you have heard about. The heart of that document is that every great fighting nation in the world—for Germany at present is not a great fighting nation—solemnly engages that it will never resort to war without first having done one or other of two things, either submit the matter in dispute to arbitration, in which case it agrees to abide by the verdict, or, if it does not choose to submit it to arbitration, submit it to the discussion and examination of the council of the League of Nations, before whom it promises to lay all the documents, to whom it promises to disclose all the pertinent facts, by whom it agrees all the documents and facts shall be published and laid before the opinion of the world. It agrees that six months shall be allowed for the examination of those documents and facts by the council of the League and that, even if it is dissatisfied with the opinion finally uttered, it will still not resort to war until three months after the opinion has been rendered. All agree that there shall be nine months of deliberate discussion and frank weighing of the merits of the case before the whole jury of mankind before they will go to war.

If any one of them disregards that promise and refuses to submit the question in dispute either to arbitration or to discussion, or goes to war within less than the nine months, then there is an automatic penalty that is applied, more effective, I take leave to say, than war itself, namely, the application of an absolute boycott. The nation that disregards that promise, we all agree, shall be isolated; shall be denied the right to ship out goods or to ship them in, to exchange telegraphic messages or messages by mail, to have any dealings of any kind with the citizens of the other members of the League. First, the pressure of opinion and then the compelling pressure of economic necessity—those are the great bulwarks of peace. Do you say they are not sufficient? I put this proposition to you: You want insurance against war. Wouldn't you rather have ten per cent insurance than none? If you could get twenty per cent insurance, wouldn't you be delighted? If you got fifty per cent insurance, wouldn't you think it Utopian? Why, my fellow citizens, if you examine the provisions of this League of Nations, I think you will agree with me that you have got ninety-nine per cent insurance. That is what we promised the mothers and wives and sweethearts of these men that they should have—insurance against the terrible danger of losing those who were dear to them, slain upon the battlefield because of the unhallowed plots of autocratic governments. Autocratic governments are excluded henceforth from respectable society. It is provided in the Covenant of the League of Nations that only self-governing peoples shall be admitted to its membership, and the reason that Germany is for the time being excluded is that we want to wait and see whether she really has changed permanently her form of constitution and her habit of government. If she has changed her mind in reality, if her great people have taken charge of their own affairs and will prove it to us, they are entitled to come into respectable society and join the League of Nations. Until then they are on probation, and to hear some of them talk now you would think the probation had to be rather long, because they do not seem to have repented of their essential purpose. . . .

10 | The Nationalist and Isolationist Arguments Against the League of Nations, 1919 *

Despite his prodigious effort, Wilson never explained to the American people the kind of world which they required and the kind which they could have. His rationalization of American involvement in the war, like his rationalization of the League of Nations, was legalistic, moralistic, and idealistic. Because he fought the war without having defined the national interest, he could never impress upon the nation the necessity of a continued defense of the European balance of power. In his failure to identify the League of Nations with the vital interests of the United States, his program appeared at once utopian and a vast and unnecessary overcommitment of the United States to a great philanthropic cause which contributed nothing to the country's security. In the following article Albert J. Beveridge, spokesman for American nationalism, appealed to the alleged isolationist tradition of the Founding Fathers to counter Wilson's defense of the League of Nations. For Beveridge, American security lay in geographic isolation and the uniqueness of the American political and economic system.

⚐

. . . Once more let us make the inquiry as to what beneficial result can come to us from membership in any international combination whatever? Would not the inevitable consequence be that we involve ourselves in racial and historic

* Albert J. Beveridge, "Pitfalls of a 'League of Nations,' " *The North American Review,* CCIX (March 1919), 312–14.

antagonisms and complications from which thus far we have kept ourselves free? Would we not surrender every advantage which our situation on the globe, our history, our one unbroken traditional policy, and our resources afford us? Would we not place ourselves in the position of an integral, physical part of the continents of Europe and Asia?

It is said that steam and electricity have eliminated the oceans and that nations no longer are separated by water barriers. Is this true? The English Channel is now as effective a bulwark to the United Kingdom as it ever was. That narrow strip of water and a strong fleet have saved England from invasion for nearly a thousand years. From the military point of view, it would appear, then, that after all the Atlantic has not been abolished.

We are told that we must no longer be "isolated." How are we "isolated"? How have we ever been "isolated"? Not commercially. Not financially. Not socially. We have been "isolated" only in the political sense—only in the sense that we have not bound ourselves by alliance to mix up in the quarrels of others —only in the sense that we have attended to our own business. Is not that kind of "isolation" the very thing that is best for us and for the world? If so, why abandon it? Does anybody imagine that, if any European Nation were situated as we are, it would surrender its peculiar advantages?

The points that I have suggested are only a few of those involved in the present day recrudescence of the ancient scheme for a League of Nations. But do not the ones enumerated show that the international journey which we are asked to take is through an unexplored and perilous jungle?

Is it not better for the American people to advance along the highway of America's traditional foreign policy? That policy was formulated after years of thought, experience and consultation by all the wonderful company of constructive statesmen who laid the foundations of the American Nation. No such group of far-visioned men ever blessed with their wisdom any country at a given time. Call the roll of them—Washington, Hamilton, Jefferson, Adams, Madison, Marshall, and the others of that galaxy of immortals.

The foreign policy announced by Washington was the product of the combined and profoundly considered judgment of all these men. It was the only policy, foreign or domestic, on which all of them were united. On every other they disagreed. For that alone they stood as a single man. Several years after Washington formally declared this American policy, Jefferson restated it still more broadly and emphatically. Also that policy has been maintained from that day to this by every American statesman and every American political party.

For more than a hundred and thirty years the American Nation has progressed along the plain, safe course these men marked out. It has kept us from disastrous foreign entanglements and ruinous foreign complications. It has saved us hundreds of thousands of lives and hundreds of billions of dollars. Why leave it now to wander through a pathless wilderness of alien interests, racial hatreds, historic animosities?

Do not the wellbeing of a great people and the development of a mighty continent present problems hard enough to tax all the strength of the ablest men in the whole Republic? If the concerns of a few million people occupying a strip of seaboard engrossed all the energy, thought and time of men like "the fathers" whom I have just named, have any intellects now appeared capable of caring not only for the affairs of one hundred and ten million human beings covering an area that stretches from ocean to ocean, but also capable of adjusting all the differences of all the variegated peoples of the entire globe?

The situation of the American Nation is unique. Geographically it sits on the throne of the world. Its history is that of the evolution of a distinct, separate, and independent people. Its mission is no less than to create a new race on the earth and to present to mankind the example of that happiness and well-being which comes from progressive, self-disciplined liberty.

This was the faith of our fathers. By that faith ought we not still to abide?—the American Nation the supreme love of our hearts, the highest object of our effort and our thought—the American Nation free of hand and unmanacled of foot, marching steadily onward toward the destiny to which it is entitled by reason of its place on the globe, the genius of its people, and its orderly institutions of freedom.

— | "There is grave danger in an unshared idealism." *

In his studied attack on Article X of the League of Nations, which to him appeared to commit the United States to involvement in every infraction of the Versailles Treaty, Senator Henry Cabot Lodge challenged the apparent defiance, in such involvements, of the older American principle of absolute freedom of action. Unfortunately there appeared in Lodge's argument no identification of American interests with any precise conformation in European or world politics. The nation's purpose, beyond the avoidance of meddling in everlasting foreign quarrels, remained, in Lodge's mind, vague and indefinite. Thus the Senator, despite his plea for conservatism, contributed no more to the formation of a genuine American foreign policy than did Wilson.

✍

Turn to the preamble of the covenant of the league of nations now before us, which states the object of the league. It is formed "in order to promote international cooperation and to achieve international peace and security by the acceptance of obligations not to resort to war, by the prescription of open, just, and honorable relations between nations, by the firm establishment of the understandings of international laws as the actual rule of conduct among governments and by the maintenance of justice and a scrupulous respect for all treaty obligations in the dealings of organized peoples with one another."

No one would contest the loftiness or the benevolence of these purposes. Brave words, indeed! They do not differ essentially from the preamble of the treaty of Paris, from which sprang the Holy Alliance. But the covenant of this league

* Lodge's speech in the Senate against the League of Nations, August 12, 1919, *Congressional Record*, 66th Congress, 1st Sess., 3779–84.

contains a provision which I do not find in the treaty of Paris, and which is as follows:

> The assembly may deal at its meetings with any matter within the sphere of action of the league or affecting the peace of the world.

There is no such sweeping or far-reaching provision as that in the treaty of Paris, and yet able men developed from that treaty the Holy Alliance, which England, and later France were forced to abandon and which, for 35 years, was an unmitigated curse to the world. England broke from the Holy Alliance and the breach began three years after it was formed, because English statesmen saw that it was intended to turn the alliance—and this league is an alliance—into a means of repressing internal revolutions or insurrections. There was nothing in the treaty of Paris which warranted such action, but in this covenant of the league of nations the authority is clearly given in the third paragraph of article 3, where it is said:

> The assembly may deal at its meetings with any matter within the sphere of action of the league or affecting the peace of the world.

No revolutionary movement, no internal conflict of any magnitude can fail to affect the peace of the world. The French Revolution, which was wholly internal at the beginning, affected the peace of the world to such an extent that it brought on a world war which lasted some 25 years. Can anyone say that our Civil War did not affect the peace of the world? At this very moment, who would deny that the condition of Russia, with internal conflicts raging in all parts of that great Empire, does not affect the peace of the world and therefore come properly within the jurisdiction of the league? "Any matter affecting the peace of the world" is a very broad statement which could be made to justify almost any interference on the part of the league with the internal affairs of other countries. . . . If Europe desires such an alliance or league with a power of this kind, so be it. I have no objection, provided they do not interfere with the American Continents or force us against our will but bound by a moral obligation into all the quarrels of Europe. If England, abandoning the policy of Canning, desires to be a member of a league which has such powers as this, I have not a word to say. But I object in the strongest possible way to having the United States agree, directly or indirectly, to be controlled by a league which may at any time, and perfectly lawfully and in accordance with the terms of the covenant, be drawn in to deal with internal conflicts in other countries, no matter what those conflicts may be. We should never permit the United States to be involved in any internal conflict in another country, except by the will of her people expressed through the Congress which represents them.

With regard to wars of external aggression on a member of the league, the case is perfectly clear. There can be no genuine dispute whatever about the meaning of the first clause of article 10. In the first place, it differs from every other obligation in being individual and placed upon each nation without the intervention of the league. Each nation for itself promises to respect and preserve as against external aggression the boundaries and the political independence of every member of the league. . . . In article 10 the United States is bound on the appeal of any member of the league not only to respect but to preserve its independence and its boundaries, and that pledge, if we give it, must be fulfilled.

There is to me no distinction whatever in a treaty between what some persons are pleased to call legal and moral obligations. A treaty rests and must rest, except where it is imposed under duress and securities and hostages are taken for its fulfillment, upon moral obligations. No doubt a great power impossible of coercion can cast aside a moral obligation if it sees fit and escape from the performance of the duty which it promises. The pathway of dishonor is always open. I for one, however, cannot conceive of voting for a clause of which I disapprove because I know it can be escaped in that way. Whatever the United States agrees to, by that agreement she must abide. Nothing could so surely destroy all prospects of the world's peace as to have any powerful nation refuse to carry out an obligation, direct or indirect, because it rests only on moral grounds. . . .

I return, then, to the first clause of article 10. It is, I repeat, an individual obligation. It requires no action on the part of the league, except that in the second sentence the authorities of the league are to have the power to advise as to the means to be employed in order to fulfill the purpose of the first sentence. But that is a detail of execution, and I consider that we are morally and in honor bound to accept and act upon that advice. The broad fact remains that if any member of the league suffering from external aggression should appeal directly to the United States for support the United States would be bound to give that support in its own capacity and without reference to the action of other powers, because the United States itself is bound, and I hope the day will never come when the United States will not carry out its promises. If that day should come, and the United States or any other great country should refuse, no matter how specious the reasons, to fulfill both in letter and spirit every obligation in this covenant, the United States would be dishonored and the league would crumble into dust, leaving behind it a legacy of wars. . . .

Article 11 carries this danger still further, for it says:

> Any war or threat of war, whether immediately affecting any of the members of the league or not, is hereby declared a matter of concern to the whole league, and the league shall take any action that shall be deemed wise and effectual to safeguard the peace of nations.

"Any war or threat of war" means both external aggression and internal disturbance, as I have already pointed out in dealing with article 3. "Any action" covers military action, because it covers action of any sort or kind. Let me take an example, not an imaginary case, but one which may have been overlooked because most people have not the slightest idea where or what a King of the Hedjaz is. The following dispatch appeared recently in the newspapers:

#### HEDJAZ AGAINST BEDOUINS.

The forces of Emir Abdullah recently suffered a grave defeat, the Wahabis attacking and capturing Kurma, east of Mecca. Ibn Savond is believed to be working in harmony with the Wahabis. A squadron of the royal air force was ordered recently to go to the assistance of King Hussein.

Hussein I take to be the Sultan of Hedjaz. He is being attacked by the Bedouins. . . . Under article 10, if King Hussein appealed to us for aid and protection against external aggression affecting his independence and the boundaries of his Kingdom, we should be bound to give that aid and protection and to send American soldiers to Arabia. It is not relevant to say that this is unlikely to occur; that Great Britain is quite able to take care of King Hussein, who is her fair creation, reminding one a little of the Mosquito King, a monarch once developed by Great Britain on the Mosquito Coast of Central America. The fact that we should not be called upon does not alter the right which the King of Hedjaz possesses to demand the sending of American troops to Arabia in order to preserve his independence against the assaults of the Wahabis or Bedouins. I am willing to give that right to King Hussein, and this illustrates the point which is to me the most objectionable in the league as it stands; the right of other powers to call out American troops and American ships to go to any part of the world, an obligation we are bound to fulfill under the terms of this treaty. I know the answer well—that of course they could not be sent without action by Congress. Congress would have no choice if acting in good faith, and if under article 10 any member of the league summoned us, or if under article 11 the league itself summoned us, we should be bound in honor and morally to obey. . . .

Let me now briefly point out the insuperable difficulty which I find in article 15. It begins: "If there should arise between members of the league any dispute likely to lead to a rupture." "Any dispute" covers every possible dispute. It therefore covers a dispute over tariff duties and over immigration. Suppose we have a dispute with Japan or with some European country as to immigration. I put aside tariff duties as less important than immigration. This is not an imaginary case. Of late years there has probably been more international discussion and negotiation about questions growing out of immigration laws than any other one subject. It comes within the definition of "any dispute" at the beginning of article 15. In the eighth paragraph of that article it is said that "if the dispute between the parties is claimed by one of them, and is found by the council to arise out of a matter which, by international law, is solely within the domestic jurisdiction of that party, the council shall so report and shall make no recommendation as to its settlement." . . . I wish somebody would point out to me those provisions of international law which make a list of questions which are hard and fast within the domestic jurisdiction. No such distinction can be applied to tariff duties or immigration, nor indeed finally and conclusively to any subject. . . .

Article 21 says:

Nothing in this covenant shall be deemed to affect the validity of international engagements, such as treaties of arbitration or regional understandings like the Monroe doctrine for securing the maintenance of peace.

The provision did not appear in the first draft of the covenant, and when the President explained the second draft of the convention in the peace conference he said:

"Article 21 is new."

And that was all he said. No one can question the truth of the remark, but I trust I shall not be considered disrespectful if I say that it was not an illuminating statement. The article was new, but the fact of its novelty, which the President declared, was known to everyone who had taken the trouble to read the two documents. . . .

The Monroe doctrine was the corollary of Washington's neutrality policy and of his injunction against permanent alliances. It reiterates and reaffirms the principle. We do not seek to meddle in the affairs of Europe and keep Europe out of the Americas. It is as important to keep the United States out of European affairs as to keep Europe out of the American Continents. Let us maintain the Monroe doctrine, then, in its entirety, and not only preserve our own safety, but in this way best promote the real peace of the world. Whenever the preservation of freedom and civilization and the overthrow of a menacing world conqueror summon us we shall respond fully and nobly, as we did in 1917. He who doubts that we could do so has little faith in America. But let it be our own act and not done reluctantly by the coercion of other nations, at the bidding or by the permission of other countries. . . .

Another point in this covenant where change must be made in order to protect the safety of the United States in the future is in article 1, where withdrawal is provided for. This provision was an attempt to meet the very general objection to the first draft of the league, that there was no means of getting out of it without denouncing the treaty; that is, there was no arrangement for the withdrawal of any nation. As it now stands it reads that—

> Any member of the league may, after two years' notice of its intention to do so, withdraw from the league, provided that all its international obligations, and all its obligations under this covenant shall have been fulfilled at the time of its withdrawal.

The right of withdrawal is given by this clause, although the time for notice, two years, is altogether too long. Six months or a year would be found, I think, in most treaties to be the normal period fixed for notice of withdrawal. But whatever virtue there may be in the right thus conferred is completely nullified by the proviso. The right of withdrawal cannot be exercised until all the international obligations and all the obligations of the withdrawing nations have been fulfilled. The league alone can decide whether "all international obligations and all obligations under this covenant" have been fulfilled, and this would require, under the provisions of the league, a unanimous vote so that any nation desiring to withdraw could not do so, even on the two years' notice, if one nation voted that the obligations had not been fulfilled. Remember that this gives the league not only power to review all our obligations under the covenant but all our treaties with all nations for every one of those is an "international obligation."

Are we deliberately to put ourselves in fetters and be examined by the league of nations as to whether we have kept faith with Cuba or Panama before we can be permitted to leave the league? This seems to me humiliating to say the least. The right of withdrawal, if it is to be of any value whatever, must be absolute, because otherwise a nation desiring to withdraw could be held in the league by objections from other nations until the very act which induces the nation to withdraw had been completed; until the withdrawing nation had been forced to send troops to take part in a war with which it had no concern and upon which it did not desire to enter. It seems to me vital to the safety of the United States not only that this provision should be eliminated and the right to withdraw made absolute but that the period of withdrawal should be much reduced. . . .

Article 10 I have already discussed. There is no question that the preservation of a State against external aggression can contemplate nothing but war. In article 11, again, the league is authorized to take any action which may be necessary to safeguard the peace of the world. "Any action" includes war. We also have specific provisions for a boycott, which is a form of economic warfare. The use of troops might be avoided but the enforcement of a boycott would require blockades in all probability, and certainly a boycott in its essence is simply an effort to starve a people into submission, to ruin their trade, and, in the case of nations which are not self-supporting, to cut off their food supply. The misery and suffering caused by such a measure as this may easily rival that caused by actual war. Article 16 embodies the boycott and also, in the last paragraph, provides explicitly for war. We are told that the word "recommends" has no binding force; it constitutes a moral obligation, that is all. But it means that if we, for example, should refuse to accept the recommendation, we should nullify the operation of article 16 and, to that extent, of the league. It seems to me that to attempt to relieve us of clearly imposed duties by saying that the word "recommend" is not binding in an escape of which no nation regarding the sanctity of treaties and its own honor would care to avail itself. The provisions of article 16 are extended to States outside the league who refuse to obey its command to come in and submit themselves to its jurisdiction; another provision for war.

Taken altogether, these provisions for war present what to my mind is the gravest objection to this league in its present form. We are told that of course nothing will be done in the way of warlike acts without the assent of Congress. If that is true, let us say so in the covenant. But as it stands there is no doubt whatever in my mind that American troops and American ships may be ordered to any part of the world by nations other than the United States, and that is a proposition to which I for one can never assent. It must be made perfectly clear that no American soldiers, not even a corporal's guard, that no American sailors, not even the crew of a submarine, can ever be engaged in war or ordered anywhere except by the constitutional authorities of the United States. . . .

Those of us, Mr. President, who are either wholly opposed to the league or who are trying to preserve the independence and the safety of the United States by changing the terms of the league and who are endeavoring to make the league, if we are to be a member of it, less certain to promote war instead of peace, have been reproached with selfishness in our outlook and with a desire to keep our country in a state of isolation. So far as the question of isolation goes, it is impossible to isolate the United States. I well remember the time, 20 years ago, when eminent Senators and other distinguished gentlemen who were opposing the Philippines and shrieking about imperialism, sneered at the statement made by some of us, that the United States had become a world power. I think no one now would question that the Spanish War marked the entrance of the United States into world affairs to a degree which had never obtained before. It was both an inevitable and an irrevocable step, and our entrance into the war with Germany certainly showed once and for all that the United States was not unmindful of its world responsibilities. We may set aside all this empty talk about isolation. Nobody expects to isolate the United States or to make it a hermit Nation, which is a sheer absurdity. But there is a wide difference between taking a suitable part and bearing a due responsibility in world affairs and plunging the United States into every controversy and conflict on the face of the globe. By meddling in all the differences which may arise among any portion or fragment of humankind we simply fritter away our influence and injure ourselves to no good purpose. We shall be of far more value to the world and its peace by occupying, so far as possible, the situation which we have occupied for the last 20 years and by adhering to the policy of Washington and Hamilton, of Jefferson and Monroe, under which we have risen to our present greatness and prosperity. The fact that we have been separated by our geographical situation and by our consistent policy from the broils of Europe has made us more than any one thing capable of performing the great work which we performed in the war against Germany, and our disinterestedness is of far more value to the world than our eternal meddling in every possible dispute could ever be. . . .

I am as anxious as any human being can be to have the United States render every possible service to the civilization and the peace of mankind, but I am certain we can do it best by not putting ourselves in leading strings or subjecting our policies and our sovereignty to other nations. The independence of the United States is not only more precious to ourselves but to the world than any single possession. Look at the United States to-day. We have made mistakes in the past. We have had shortcomings. We shall make mistakes in the future and fall short of our own best hopes. But none the less is there any country today on the face of the earth which can compare with this in ordered liberty, in peace, and in the largest freedom? I feel that I can say this without being accused of undue boastfulness, for it is the simple fact, and in making this treaty and taking on these obligations all that we do is in a spirit of unselfishness and in a desire for the good of mankind. But it is well to remember that we are dealing with nations every one of which has a direct individual interest to serve and there is grave danger in an unshared idealism. Contrast the United States with any country on the face of the earth to-day and ask yourself whether the situation of the United States is not the best to be found. I will go as far as anyone in world service, but the first step to world service is the maintenance of the United States. You may call me selfish if you will, conservative or reactionary, or use any other harsh adjective you see fit to apply, but an American I was born, an American I have remained all my life. I can never be anything else but an American, and I must think of the United States first, and when I think of the United States first in an arrangement like this I am thinking of what is best for the world, for if the United States fails the best hopes of mankind fail with it. I have never had but one allegiance—I cannot divide it now. I have loved but one flag and I cannot share that devotion and give affection to the mongrel banner invented for a league. Internationalism, illustrated by the Bolshevik and by the men to whom all countries are alike provided they can make money out of them, is to me repulsive. National I must remain, and in that way I, like all other Americans, can render the amplest service to the world. The United States is the world's best hope, but if you fetter her in the interests and quarrels of other nations, if you tangle her in the intrigues of Europe, you will destroy her power for good and endanger her very existence. Leave her to march freely through the centuries to come as in the years that have gone. Strong, generous, and confident, she has nobly served mankind. Beware how you trifle with your marvelous inheritance, this great land of ordered liberty, for if we stumble and fall, freedom and civilization everywhere will go down in ruin. . . .

No doubt many excellent and patriotic people see a coming fulfillment of noble ideals in the words "league for peace." We all respect and share these aspirations and desires, but some of us see no hope, but rather defeat, for them in this murky covenant. For we, too, have our ideals, even if we differ from those who have tried to establish a monopoly of idealism. Our first ideal is our country, and we see her in the future, as in the past, giving service to all her people and to the world. Our ideal of the future is that she should continue to render that service of her own free will. She has great problems of her own to solve, very grim and perilous problems, and a right solution, if we can attain to it, would largely benefit mankind. We would have our country strong to resist a peril from the West, as she has flung back the German menace from the East. We would not have our politics distracted and embittered by the dissensions of other lands. We would not have our country's vigor exhausted or her moral force abated by everlasting meddling and muddling in every quarrel, great and small, which afflicts the world. Our ideal is to make her ever stronger and better and finer, because in that way alone, as we believe, can she be of the greatest service to the world's peace and to the welfare of mankind.

# 11 | Wilson and the Problem of Japan, November 1919 *

Wilson's Japanese policy, based on a firm application of the Open Door principle to Sino-Japanese relations, was in large measure a continuation and tightening of the Far Eastern policies of the Taft administration. In the thoughtful essay which follows, Arthur Bullard stressed the influence of Japan's internal problems on Japanese external policies. He pleaded for an American attitude of tolerance toward Japan based on a scrupulously fair and generous application of the concept of the Open Door. Like Roosevelt, the writer saw clearly that Japan faced the simple choice between starvation, on the one hand, and commercial and industrial expansion on the other. Unless Japan were permitted all legitimate economic opportunities in the Orient, he predicted, there would be no peace in the Pacific.

🖎

Talk of war with Japan has recently been heard in our Senate. Just as we were relaxing from the great effort against Germany, this old bugaboo has been raised again. The ostrich policy of ignoring danger never prevented any war. "Drift" is what we have most to fear. If we want peace, we must prepare to prevent war. We must think about it.

An important element in our relations with Japan is relative size. Not only in mileage is our country larger than the Japanese Islands; in almost every sense it is more spacious. Masses of statistics could be marshaled to emphasize this contrast. . . .

However, there is no reason for a clash over this difference in scale. If there is to be a fight, there must be an "issue." The sword-wavers are trying to make one out of Japan's tendency to expand at the expense of China. It is a serious matter for us, for under some circumstances it will surely lead to war. But first let us try to state the "issue" clearly.

However threatening Japanese ambitions may be to us, they have to face a worse menace at home. They have a baby-peril, more dangerous than Oriental immigration ever was to us. Each new child born to them increases the desperate pressure of over-population. And no workable Exclusion Laws against babies have yet been devised.

Famine. Emigration. Industrial Expansion. There are no other choices for Japan. The first will never be accepted as a governmental policy. We forbid emigration to the districts where the pressure on the food-supply is less. If ever *force majeure* controlled the destiny of a nation, it drives Japan to expanding industrialism. If her factories can produce what the overfed nations of Christendom will buy, she can feed her people—not otherwise. But goods, exchangeable for food, cannot be manufactured out of thin air or pious wishes. The demand

* Arthur Bullard, "Expanding Japan," *Harper's Monthly Magazine,* CXXXIX (November 1919), 857–66.

for imitation antiques or modern lacquerware is scant. The graceful products of her soul will not keep Japan alive. Her string of rocky islands is not rich in the raw materials of modern industry. The resources of metal and fuel are limited. The crops of wool and cotton and silk are not large enough to keep her looms busy. . . .

. . . The economic situation of Japan is as black midnight compared to our sunny noontide. To check the development of Japanese trade and industry is to push her to suicide—gradual death from famine or such a spectacular climax as has overwhelmed Germany. . . .

The Japanese have tried to meet their need for raw material—just as in so many other cases—by close imitation of the Christian Powers. They have developed a colonial policy; they have annexed territory, against the will of the inhabitants, where they hoped to find the things they needed.

Their first venture was Formosa. There they were after tropical products. But the military expenses incurred in "educating" the head-hunters has wiped out any profit from the enterprise. With this experience to guide them, they did better in the administration of Korea. They have tried in many ways to benefit the "natives." One thing which all tourists notice is the elaborate program of reforestation. The barren and denuded hills of Korea are growing up to a new wealth for the profit of future generations.

Enlightened Japanese were more hopeful about Korea than Formosa. It was very expensive, but rich in promise. However, the present Independence movement is rolling up staggering expenses. They feel about Korea very much as we did about the Philippines, when Aguinaldo was noisily insisting that we were not wanted there. In those days the Spanish priests filled the European press with indignant letters about our brutality to the Filipinos, just as our missionaries are now writing home unpleasant truths about Korea. . . .

In China, Japan does not profess to seek colonies. She wants "spheres of influence." Perhaps this results from her own experiences, her not too successful experiments in colonization. Perhaps it is pure imitation. France is the only one of the European Powers which has carved a colony out of the body of China. It has been more fashionable to grab a "Treaty Port" and secure economic concessions. The dangers involved in "dismemberment" are apparent to the Japanese, and they are probably as sincere as the other Powers in their renunciation of colonial ambitions in China. But economic penetration is a different matter, and they insist that it is their manifest destiny to share largely in the industrial development of China. . . .

The war has quickened economic processes everywhere; it has turned Japan into a vortex of complicated strains. The old feudal control is weakening. The munition business has made many new millionaires. And the cost of rice has gone up. There is immense strain in the conflict between the immemorial customs of the coolies and the desperate new efforts to which they are spurred by the rising cost of food. There have been rice riots in Japan.

That all these internal strains and new adjustments will cause some change in foreign policy is probable, but it would take a very bold prophet to forecast its effect on Japan's relations to us. Mr. Hara's plebeian Cabinet may be less subservient to the General Staff, less hungry for military glory, but it may well be more industrially minded, more influenced by commercial greed. It may prove only a change from the frying-pan of militarism to the fire of capitalistic imperialism. This old world of ours has suffered as much from one as from the other. But of one thing we may be sure. This new mercantile element, which has control, will be more intent than ever on securing access to raw material for the factories. They are face to face with Japan's labor problem—the feeding of the masses.

Another thing is sure. The attitude of America is more important to Japan than ever before. No other country has watched our military development more intently. None has been more impressed, few more surprised. . . .

Now that Russia and Germany are impotent and the other nations exhausted, America is the only country to stand in the way of Japanese ambitions. They are giving us a great deal of thought. The new element, under the leadership of Hara, want "to do business." They need many American products and want to sell to us, but they also want the raw material of Asia and we have always resisted their expansion in China. They are a hard-headed people. Our co-operation would be very valuable, our enmity dangerous. If they could come to terms with us, their future would be more hopeful. There has been much talk of late of a new "American orientation" in foreign policy. . . .

In Tokio, our State Department is faced by a bizarre triangle. It is a three-party affair. British diplomacy is jealous of American-Japanese co-operation, and the Tories of Tokio have everything to gain by making trouble between Washington and London. . . .

"Incidents"—uncontrollable, exasperating—take place generally on the periphery of the circle where conflicting interests clash. "Accords" are achieved by statesmanship at the center of the circle. The French and British residents of North Africa hated one another cordially, partly from memories of Agincourt, partly from trade rivalry. If their advice had been listened to—the famous "advice of the man on the spot," "who knows the real facts"—the Entente would never have been signed.

So, in our relations with Japan, there is every prospect of long-continued and unpleasant "incidents" out on the periphery. In the Far East our traders and diplomats meet in rivalry. The bases of an understanding will not be discovered by competing Japanese and American merchants in Siberia and China. The student of diplomacy will be more interested in the developments at the center of the circle. The "Lansing-Ishii Agreement" shows that an effort is being made to reach an accord. It is quite possible that this beginning may—in spite of the jingoes in both countries—develop into a new and more fruitful *entente cordiale* for the Pacific.

But this is dependent on our attitude toward Japan's policy of expansion. The destinies of nations are not decided on precise dates. Definite decisions, clearcut crises, are the rarest things in history. But ten years hence we will probably be able to look back on the decade following the Great War and tell how a policy —gradually and with many hesitations—took shape. The oscillations of discord will be damped to a point manageable and insignificant, or the vibrations will increase in violence till the structure of peace is wrecked.

No one in America wants war. Most of us want a real friendship with Japan, but some of us would like the spoils of war, without fighting for them. This is the dangerous element on our side of the problem. If a desire for unfair commercial advantages determines our policy, we cannot hope for decent relations. Japan may be too weak to fight us. Like the government of Bogota, her fear of our strength may overshadow her hatred. But such a "peace" is little better than war. If we want friendship we must not use pious phrases to cloak a commercial *realpolitik,* which would strangle Japan. We must help her to find some solution for her problems, which are very real and very pressing.

We have come out officially for the Open Door in the Far East. We will insist —and rightly—that no door of commercial opportunity opened to others shall be closed to us. We must—if we would be fair—insist that no door open to us in China shall be closed on Japan.

If we decide to enforce this rule both ways in China, it means a very real commercial advantage to Japan. We are far from this market, unfamiliar with its language and customs. We have many other markets to interest us. The Japanese will center their efforts in Asia. The Open Door means their commercial predominance in China. If we try to close the door on the Japanese there because it profits them more than us, if our policy is motivated by commercial jealousy, we will lose all moral force in the argument. If we veto projects of theirs in China, which are similar to those we launch there and elsewhere, we shall be the veriest hypocrites. . . .

What rule shall we use in judging Japanese expansion? Our unrealized ideals of perfection? Or accustomed practice? A gentleman tries to observe a higher standard himself than he demands of others. The "accustomed practice" ought not to satisfy us in our own enterprises, but we can hardly expect a higher morality from others.

A thoroughgoing reformer, wishing to arrange a perfect world, could not be content with a mere change in human nature. He would have to undertake geographical and geological reforms. There will be no perfect justice so long as some people are congested in barren districts and others are "chosen" to monopolize the lands flowing with milk and honey. Why did not the Children of Israel—to take an unnecessarily ancient, but still potent, precedent—respect the "political sovereignty and territorial integrity" of Philistia? They might have stayed in the desert.

Nature has been "unjust" to the Japanese. And the monotony of their increasing hunger is not relieved by any miraculous showers of manna. We might somewhat right this natural wrong by sharing our plenty with them. We might encourage them to find an outlet from their misery in the undeveloped regions under our control. Until we do, we cannot—in the name of Justice—ask them to develop perfection and consent to starve in pious peace. We have refused to recognize their "racial equality" and so cannot expect moral superiority.

We could greatly relieve the pressure on China if we were unselfishly willing to allow Japan to expand in our direction, to our detriment. But this is hardly "practical politics." Unless we want to "smash" Japan, we must facilitate her commercial access to China. . . .

We have a right to insist that Japan respect her pledges. But we haven't a leg to stand on, in any attempt to prevent the purely commercial expansion of the Japanese in China. Their Foreign Office knows a great deal more about our mercantile ventures in Central America than most of us do. We cannot pretend to protect the Chinese from commercial exploitation by the Japanese, when we are unwilling or unable to protect our nearer neighbors from the greed of our own capitalistic interests.

We may not be conscious of making up our minds in this matter, but within a decade or so all the world will know that we, as a nation, have decided to befriend Japan or bully her. It is hard to conceive a middle course.

To-day the browbeating would be rather easy. In every way we are so much the stronger. We could probably veto every one of Japan's projects of expansion, by the mere threat of war. It would be wiser for her to submit and continue to starve—until she could find allies.

It would be difficult to enlist a corporal's guard in America for a frank campaign to strangle Japan. With practical unanimity we want peace. Peace in Europe. Peace on our southern border. Peace on the Pacific. But it will take hard work, consistent effort—eternal vigilance—to realize the dream. The friendship of Japan is a necessary element. . . .

We cannot win the friendship of Japan with words. We must deal justly with her. We must co-operate with her in working out plans for her national wellbeing which do not depend on the old method of brutal domination, which we want to see discarded—on the kind of diplomacy, which she learned from the practice of Christendom. If we want Japan to be more considerate to her weaker neighbor than other nations have been—or are—we must give her active and cordial assistance. There is no other policy for us, if we wish the Pacific Ocean to deserve its attractive name.

## 12 | Woodrow Wilson: A Contemporary Critique, 1915–20 *

Wilson reflected the intellectual tendencies of a nation that had achieved much materially at little cost to itself and intended somehow to maintain its predominant position in world affairs at less than the normal price. Wilson extended the humanitarian ends of American policy to include the world at large, but to achieve such limitless goals he recommended little beyond membership in

* "The Other-Worldliness of Wilson," *The New Republic*, II (March 27, 1915), 194–5. Reprinted by permission of *The New Republic*.

the League of Nations. The weakness of his system lay in Article X which, Wilson insisted, would "preserve as against external aggression the territorial integrity and existing political independence" of League members and would prevent absolutely any "ambitious and aggressive war." This article would not only prevent change detrimental to the United States but would prevent it at no cost. It was this vast discrepancy between ends and means in the Wilsonian approach to world politics that led to an endless criticism of his concepts even by his contemporaries. To *The New Republic*, in March 1915, Wilson's views were simply too clean to be meaningful in the context of the world as it existed.

Woodrow Wilson is on the side of the angels. Whether he is writing a Presidential message, a note to Carranza, or a little sermon in essay form, such as the reprinted "When a Man Comes to Himself," Mr. Wilson is unequivocally righteous. His references to this world of strife and woe are faint allusions only, thrown out with that discreet grace which no doubt characterizes the best dinner-table conversation on Olympus. His style has the air of dealing lightly with the disagreeable. Mankind and its gross appetites appear under none too descriptive adjectives like "selfish" or "cynical." Having appeared shyly, they are soon lost to sight again, as the style in ascending rhythm begins to soar into the regions where all is love and law and sweetness and light.

Mr. Wilson seems to be one of those people who shuffle off their mortal coil as soon as they take pen in hand. They become tremendously noble. They write as the monuments of great men might write. They write only upon brass, and for nothing shorter than a millennium. They utter nothing which might sound trivial at the Last Judgment, or embarrass them in the most august company. For a time they are impressive. It is magnificent to hear the accents of greatness, but for human beings it is something of a strain. It is a strain because Ideals, Souls, Spirituality, Unselfishness, Freedom and other aspects of Nobility and Purity languish unless they are nourished by the earth. Intellectually Mr. Wilson realizes this. In fact, his essay is a preachment upon finding the boundaries of the earth. "Moral enthusiasm," he says, somewhat careless of the opinions of his Cabinet, "is not, uninstructed and in itself, a suitable guide to practicable and lasting reformation." And yet moral enthusiasm is what he gives us, redeemed only by the most abstract reference to living.

It is the quality of Mr. Wilson's thinking to make even the most concrete things seem like abstractions. Technically he is perfectly aware that ideals are good for what they are good for, in the real world of moving men; actually he conveys only the most remote view of that world. His mind is like a light which destroys the outlines of what it plays upon; there is much illumination, but you see very little. What you see is certain large, crude symbols; rich men seeking power, not gold; reformers becoming statesmen; energetic small business men making good; a nation struggling for democracy. You do not see Messrs. Rockefeller, Morgan, Bryan, Hearst, Debs, Tumulty, McAdoo, Colonel House, the Guggenheim managers or Pancho Villa. The thinking of Mr. Wilson is always cleaner, more sterilized, than life itself.

The world, like an iceberg, is mainly submerged. Yet you feel when you read Mr. Wilson that he is interested almost exclusively in the fragment that points toward heaven and glistens in the sun. By his reticence he achieves a fine-looking style, but a style as remote as a Sunday morning. The excellence of his intentions no one can dare to deny; their relevance, however, is often difficult to discover. Has he taken into account, let us say, Mr. Roger Sullivan, or found a place for Senator Vardaman? Has he quite squared the idealized Democratic party of service with the Actual Democratic party of the pork barrel? After fastening his career to a machine, is it altogether fair of him to talk as if he had hitched his wagon to a star?

Being too noble is dangerous business. It is the fault of most Sabbath moralities, and the cause of their sterility. When you have purged and bleached your morality into a collection of abstract nouns, you have something which is clean and white, but what else have you? Surely nothing comparable to the usefulness of that wisdom which retains the odor of the world, which shrinks from proclaiming superlatives, is sparing in grandiose phrase, and rich in tumbled experience. The makers of human wisdom put a little clay into the feet of their gods. They seem to know that mankind cannot live by golden affirmations, and when they come to themselves they come to something which is not rhetoric, but life.

— | "Mr. Wilson is a man with narrow boundaries." *

Daniel Halévy, in an article which appeared originally in the French publication, *L'Opinion,* December 6, 1919, attempted to analyze the character and failure of Woodrow Wilson. Though one of Wilson's earliest champions in France, Halévy in 1919 found Wilson's strange blend of realism and idealism beyond comprehension. Wilson's error, believed Halévy, lay in the fact that he was intoxicated by his own words, which led him to promise what he could not achieve.

✍

. . . That magnificent tide of American youth that swept across mourning France in July, 1918, was due to the energy and the foresight of President Wilson alone. I am grateful to him, and I admire him for it.

This does not mean that I regard him as a man of first calibre. A truly great man is something different—something peculiarly rare. I have never viewed nor described Mr. Wilson in this character. I buried myself for four or five months in his writings. I found them interesting but not inspiring. I was never moved by them to that profundity of sentiment, that exaltation of mind which indubitably

* Daniel Halévy, "In Regard to President Wilson," *The Living Age,* CCCIV (January 24, 1920), 192–3.

announce the presence of true greatness. Mr. Wilson reveals no freedom—no elasticity of spirit, no clarity of vision in the higher regions of the mind. Worse than that, his mind seems to me hardly to possess such higher regions. His purely humanitarian theology, after all, leaves us cold. It lacks inspiration. Mr. Wilson is a man with narrow boundaries. The estimate which I formed of him and which inspired my description, is of a politician, an expert in a certain trade, capable and efficient in his specialty.

Two years have passed. What has become of my hero? For a time he carried everything before him. That will remain permanently to his credit. But after the task of war came the more delicate task of peace. What was he aiming at? What did he desire? We do not clearly know. We are brought face to face with this strange fusion of realism and idealism so difficult to elucidate and comprehend. Our embarrassment is increased by the President's vacillation. He does not seem to be complete master of the great ideal which was of such service to him in 1917. His words have evoked it; his rhetoric has carried away the people. But he has raised hopes which he cannot fulfill and created situations which he cannot control. Is he, like the magician in the *Thousand and One Nights,* a prisoner and a victim of the forces which he has conjured? Or again, was he captivated by his own idealism, carried away by his own propaganda, dazzled by his papal role, so as to become the mere servant of his formulas? Another possibility. He has a certain gift of logic, of system. Has this possibly impaired his clearness of vision and his tactical skill? Still another thought. May not the slight tendency to self-worship—a failing from which he is not exempt—have carried him away from securer moorings? The answer to all this lies in obscurity. The history of the Peace Conference is unknown. Long labor and minute study will be necessary to reveal the truth.

Meanwhile, I stick to my theory and search a solution by its light. I still think that Wilson the realist rules Wilson the idealist. I think that Wilson the realist wished to assure the permanent predominance of America in the affairs of Europe, Africa, and Asia. I think that he planned to ally his country with England and France in such a way as to make it the master influence in the group, and thus to insure peace to the world—an Anglo-Saxon peace or an allied peace and not a visionary peace. But America, ignorant of these great purposes, still cherishing its isolation, was not ripe for such a radical change of policy. Its traditions and habits, its political indolence, and its old instinctive desire to keep clear of European embroilments, were too strong to be overcome. President Wilson tried to lead his country into the path of this new peace as he had led it into the path of war, by again employing those methods of a political Messiah which had succeeded so brilliantly before. That is why he desired that the Covenant of the League of Nations should be an integral part of the Treaty, and of the alliance with France. America, taken by surprise, is trying to resist these new entanglements. We do not know yet whether it will succeed. . . .

— | It is . . . the unwillingness to be strictly bound by laws and agree-
ments to which no penalty is attached, that vitiate[s] Mr. Wilson's
whole theory of government and official duty." *

Former United States diplomat David Jayne Hill, writing in October 1920,
attributed the rapid decline of American prestige during the two postwar years
to Wilson's propensity to overpromise those with whom he was forced to deal.
For this reason, noted Hill, nothing but disappointment could flow from Wilson's diplomacy. Through the argument of Senator Warren G. Harding, soon
to become President, Hill exposed the central fallacy in Wilson's concepts of
"moral obligation" and "world opinion."

✍

. . . That the prestige of the United States has suffered greatly during the last
two years is undeniable. In 1918 our armies were battling to drive the German
invaders from the soil of France and Belgium. Their arms were triumphant and
released Europe from the peril of subjugation; and yet, when today we contemplate the lack of esteem in which America is held, it almost seems as if the cause
for which our soldiers fought had not been won, and that universal confidence
in the United States had been changed to general distrust. To what are we to
attribute this failure of complete victory and this loss of national prestige?

If we turn to the record of what has happened, it is not difficult to answer this
question; but it is necessary to review the course of events with some detail.
Such an examination reveals the fact that, at the great turning points of international action, instead of a clear facing of the actual situation and a direct
manner of dealing with it, Mr. Wilson introduced some element of unreality,
obscuring the truth by phraseology having no essential relation to the state of
fact.

As evidence of this I shall cite three instances when the personal decisions
and influence of President Wilson deflected the course of events from the direction which they would otherwise have taken, and raised expectations which
have not been fulfilled.

In October, 1918, the Central Powers, in a military sense, had been defeated
by the joint action of the Allied and Associated Powers. The prompt admission
of this defeat, had it been immediately enforced by unconditional surrender,
would have prepared the German people for expecting a penalty commensurate
with their offense; which would have been regarded as a natural result of the
fortunes of war, in which they had always thought of the victor as possessing a
right of dictation in proportion to his strength.

This natural consequence of military defeat, with its salutary lesson on the
perils incurred by military aggression, was deprived of its disciplinary value by
a determination on the part of President Wilson to impose terms of peace which

* David Jayne Hill, "A Question of Honor," *The North American Review*, CCXII
(October 1920), 433–46.

he had outlined long before Germany was conquered, and while "a peace without victory" was still in his mind. The Central Powers, although finally vanquished, were thus given ground for expecting the privilege of open negotiation on equal terms in the settlements of peace. Under a new form of government, which they had set up for the purpose, they expected to be judged and treated as victims of an autocracy which they had in the end helped to overthrow by a demand for the Kaiser's immediate abdication. Neither the armistice nor the final terms of peace bore out these expectations. As a result, penalties which, though severe, are not so burdensome as the Germans themselves, in case of their victory, would have inflicted, and in fact not essentially different from those which might have followed an unconditional surrender, are now regarded by the German people as having been imposed upon them in violation of an understanding.

This was not a good beginning for the reorganization of the world. If it accelerated the conclusion of an armistice which defeat had necessitated, the only reason why it can be held to have done so is that hopes were awakened that were not realized; and it introduced conditions of procedure which, as Colonel House has recently alleged, resulted in postponing a preliminary peace which could have been made, he thinks, before Christmas of 1918, thus promptly releasing a starving Europe for its difficult task of recuperation. . . .

The President went to Paris avowedly to give the Peace Conference the benefit of his "counsel," not in any way to assume new and unprecedented obligations for the United States. No definite plan of international organization had ever been proposed to the country or to the Senate by Mr. Wilson; but, as we now know, he had prepared a plan before he left the United States which he did not disclose. The composition of the delegation he had personally selected and of which he was the self-appointed head, the size and character of the retinue that accompanied him including more than a thousand subordinates, and above all the studied silence concerning what was intended, not only toward the public but his partner the Senate and even members of his Cabinet, awakened at the time much general comment, and in some quarters created serious disquietude concerning the President's purposes. . . .

At the end of 1918, on account of what the United States forces had accomplished in the war, the prestige of the President in Europe was immense, far greater than it had ever been in America.

If ever, it was a time for "open covenants, openly arrived at." But the President celebrated his departure by having his Postmaster General take over the ocean cables, which had not been thought necessary during the war. Suddenly, while the President in silence put the Atlantic between him and his country, all the means of communication with Europe were placed under Government control!

While the newspapers were filled with the President's speeches to the public in his circular tour as an apostle of peace in Europe, nothing was known of what he was promising in the Supreme Council regarding the future obligations of the United States.

In the fourteenth of the President's "Fourteen Points," he had spoken of "a general association of nations under specific covenants for the purpose of affording mutual guarantees of political independence and territorial integrity to great and small States alike." Precisely what this was intended to mean was not clear, but no one supposed that the United States would ever assent to become the guarantor of the boundaries and independence of all the countries in the world.

That France would be willing to enter into any such general association of which Germany was to be a member, or England to accept international control to maintain the "freedom of the seas, alike in peace and war," as the President hoped, no well informed person in the United States believed; but, even after Clemenceau had made the position of France on this point evident, Mr. Wilson, on December 30, 1918, at Manchester, speaking of America, said:

> I want to say very frankly to you that she is not now interested in European politics, but she is interested in the partnership of right between America and Europe. If the future had nothing for us but a new attempt to keep the world at right poise by a balance of power the United States would take no interest, because she will join no combination of power which is not a combination of all of us. She is not interested merely in the peace of Europe, but in the peace of the world.

In this statement Mr. Wilson, no doubt, voiced the sentiments of the American people so far as peace is concerned. They desired the peace of the world. They were ready to see the Great War through to a triumphant finish, but they had no wish to become entangled in European politics.

Nothing would have given the American people greater satisfaction than for the President to have said: This war arose from a European quarrel. Its settlement is a European question. You have accepted certain principles as a basis of peace. I trust you will make a peace so just and effectual that you can maintain it without reliance upon the intervention of America. But this was no part of Mr. Wilson's programme. He had conceived the idea that he, personally, was to superintend the entire proceedings at Paris. He continued to urge the "general association," even when it was clear that it could not be made general; with the result that it became precisely that entanglement in European politics which he had professed his intention to avoid. . . .

Claiming to speak officially, and understood as so speaking, Mr. Wilson informed the plenipotentiaries of the Conference that, unless there was to be the continuous superintendence of the peace of the world by the associated nations of the world, the United States could not take part in "guaranteeing the European settlements." On the other hand, if such superintendence were organized, in order to make it "a vital and not merely a formal thing," he was empowered to pledge to it the support of the United States. With great intensity of feeling, he declared:

> You can imagine, gentlemen, I dare say, the sentiments and the purpose with which representatives of the United States support this great project for a League of Nations. We regard it as the keystone of the

whole programme, which expresses our purposes and ideals in this war and which the associated nations accepted as the basis of the settlement. If we return to the United States without having made every effort in our power to realize this programme, we should return to meet the merited scorn of our fellow-citizens.

And then, as if exhibiting full powers to make the pledges incident to this programme, Mr. Wilson added impressively:

We have no choice but to obey their mandate. But it is with the greatest pleasure that we accept that mandate; and because this is the keystone of the whole fabric, we have pledged our every purpose to it, as we have to every item of the fabric. We would not dare abate a single item of the programme which constitutes our instruction. . . .

After the use of such technical words in the vocabulary of diplomacy as "mandate" and "instruction," of which the delegates "would not dare abate a single item," the one certain conclusion in the minds of the plenipotentiaries was that the President was delivering to the Conference America's authorized ultimatum regarding her participation in its further deliberations. . . .

On February 14th, the first finished draft of "The Constitution of the League of Nations" was read to the full Conference and commented upon by President Wilson. It was not left in doubt that what had been constituted was a new form of sovereign power which the nations were expected to obey, and if necessary would be forced to obey. In unmistakable language Mr. Wilson himself described this new international authority as "the union of wills in a common purpose, a union of wills which cannot be resisted, and which I dare say no nation will run the risk of attempting to resist." And to leave no doubt regarding the compelling power of the League, if any nation attempted to resist it, he added: "Armed force is in the background of this programme, but it *is* in the background, and if the moral force of the world will not suffice, the physical force of the world shall."

No such words as those of the President of the United States had ever been uttered in any international conference by any responsible statesman. To those who heard them they could have but one meaning. The United States, with resources but slightly impaired by the war and a great army in the field, was ready to dedicate them to the execution of Mr. Wilson's one distinctive contribution to the substance of the League, the guarantee pledge contained in Article X. This, they were assured, was "the only security for peace"; and it was the "mandate" and the "instruction" of the United States! . . .

For a second time, Mr. Wilson thus introduced into the international situation an element of unreality which seriously confused it and diverted the thought of the time from the prompt conclusion of a victorious war to an expectation that by every test of actuality was illusory.

While it must be conceded that Mr. Wilson at Paris proposed pledges that he had no authority to make for his own country, it cannot be contended that the European Powers can justly complain that in so grave a matter they were deceived. With less plausibility but not with less assurance, Mr. Wilson assumed to speak for all the peoples of Europe, and to declare their purpose, also, to insist upon this League of Nations or overthrow their governments.

"The nations of the world," he said in his speech at Boston, on revisiting America, "have set their heads to do a great thing, and they are not going to slacken in their purpose." He was as sure that he represented the people of Europe in America as he was that he represented the people of America in Europe. "When I speak of the nations," he continued, "I do not speak of the governments of the world. I speak of the peoples who constitute the nations of the world. They are in the saddle and they are going to see to it that if their present governments do not do their will some other governments shall. And the secret is out and the present governments know it."

The plenipoteniaries at Paris should have seen—it it probable that they did see—that the references to "mandates" and "instruction" from America were as imaginary as the revolutions that were to upset their governments. But they felt that they could not assert this when the President of the United States was the person with whom they had to deal. The protest of thirty-nine Senators against the President's procedure clearly indicated that the Senate was yet to be reckoned with, but there could be no negotiation by or with the Senate. The President must be taken at his word, for otherwise there could be no business with the United States. . . .

There was, however, further and conclusive evidence that Mr. Wilson's proposal of mutual guarantees in which the United States should share was a purely personal and wholly unauthorized proposition. When he returned to the United States with the final draft of "The Constitution of a League of Nations" under the name of a "Covenant," he had nothing further to say about "mandates" or "instructions." His efforts were then directed toward convincing the Senators and the people of the entirely innocuous character of this document; which, far from guaranteeing anything by really effective means, was now represented as producing universal peace by common consent!

This third element of unreality was fully exploited in the conference of the President with the Foreign Relations Committee of the Senate, at the White House, on August 19, 1919.

In an introductory statement the President undertook to disarm opposition by diminishing as much as possible the extent of the obligations contained in the Covenant. The Council of the League, he said, could only "advise upon" the means by which the obligations were to be given effect. The unanimous vote of the Council, he declared, was required before any advice could be given, and the United States had a vote on this subject. As there is no "sanction"—that is, no penalty is imposed upon non-fulfillment—there is only a "moral," not a "legal," obligation to execute the Treaty, which "leaves our Congress absolutely free to put its own interpretation upon it in all cases that call for action."

This subtle distinction between different forms of obligation in a treaty evoked expressions of astonishment from several Senators.

As to the privilege of withdrawal in Article I, the President held that the United States would have the right to decide for itself when its obligations had been fulfilled. When Senator Borah inquired if the President was expressing the view entertained by the commission which drew the League, he replied: "That view was not formulated, but I am confident that was the view." "Would there be any objection, then," asked Senator McCumber, "to a reservation declaring that to be the understanding?" Mr. Wilson emphatically declined to have his interpretation thus recorded. . . .

The President having stated that "with regard to the method of fulfilling the obligations of a covenant like that under consideration there is freedom of judgment on the part of the individual members of the League," Senator Harding said:

> The President expressed a while ago surprise that I raised a question as to the value of this compact because of the moral obligation feature. Let me premise by the statement that I look upon a moral obligation as that which the conscience of the contracting party impels. The conscience of any nation in Europe, for example, may be warped by its prejudices, racial, geographical, and otherwise. If that be true and any nation may put aside or exercise its judgment as to the moral obligation in accepting any recommendation of the League, really what do we get out of this international compact in the enforcement of any decree?

The President having answered, that we would "get the centering upon it generally of the definite opinion of the world," Senator Harding replied, "That is surrendering the suggestion of a moral obligation for this Republic to the prejudices or necessities of the nations of the Old World, is it not?" and intimated that it would be quite as moral for this Republic itself to determine its moral obligations! Finally, the President having taken refuge in the statement that we are at liberty to reject the judgment of the world as to a moral obligation, "if our moral judgment honestly differs from the moral judgment of the world," Senator Harding exposed the sophistry of Mr. Wilson's whole theory of obligation by asking, since any other nation may take the same position, "What permanent value is there, then, to this compact?"

After a refutation so decisive, it would be useless, in any case, to pursue this subject further, so far as Mr. Wilson personally is concerned; but it is not a person, it is a doctrine, which we now have to combat.

It is this constant appeal to purely subjective standards and the unwillingness to be strictly bound by laws and agreements to which no penalty is attached, that vitiate Mr. Wilson's whole theory of government and official duty. There was no legal penalty attached to his shifting utterances during the war or to his merely personal proposals in the negotiations for peace. He recognized no obligations but those of a "moral" nature, which, he considers, contain nothing explicitly binding, since a personal judgment may determine what the obligation really is. At Paris, not being subject to what he regarded as a legal "sanction," he was under no obligation to consider the constitutional rights of his partners in the process of treaty-making; and could, therefore, freely speak of "mandates" and "instructions" in any way he judged expedient. At Washington, he could interpret Article X as calling for no action, until a country had been invaded, devastated and subjugated, when the question of preserving its territorial integrity and political independence would for the first time arise; and even then each country could take its own advice about it!

Moral obligations do not require treaties to make them binding. They are binding from their very nature. Treaties are intended to make understandings clear, definite, and objectively verifiable. Private judgment does not enter into the interpretation of laws, treaties, and constitutions. They are designed to render accepted obligations imperative. When these are once undertaken honor requires that they must be discharged as they are written. . . .

# VIII

## The Retreat to Utopia

For the traditionally isolationist United States the First World War provided lessons in profusion. Involvement itself demonstrated that with policies for the most part passive or legalistic the nation could not influence the tendencies in European politics in defense of its own interests. Nor, as the past had illustrated with perfect consistency, would it escape any future European war which endangered its security in the Atlantic. On the other hand, Woodrow Wilson's failure at Versailles to exorcise from Europe's diplomacy any of its established characteristics made it clear that the great countries of the world had less interest in Wilson's idealism than in the power which he wielded as President of a nation which possessed a remarkable capacity to conduct war. American strength alone, it was apparent to all, could guarantee the continued predominance of Britain and France in European affairs. The Great War had redistributed power; it had achieved nothing more. Thus, sound American policy, in the future as in the past, would of necessity avoid the extreme goals of either escaping all world responsibilities or rescuing oppressed humanity everywhere. It would be directed rather toward the recognition and protection of a wide variety of specific national interests in competition with nations that could discover in the international system no effective substitute for the traditional rules of power politics.

That the American people drew precisely the wrong conclusions from the two essential lessons of the war was a tribute to Wilson's influence over the nation's emotions. Indeed, so powerful was the Republic's reaction to Wilson's leadership that it drove American thought toward the extremes against which the recent diplomatic past had warned. That Wilson should have produced this dichotomy in the nation's outlook was predicted by the character of his own views. In promising the transformation of the world in accordance with his principles, the President laid the foundations for the rebirth of a pervading postwar isolationism. The nation could measure his success by his own standards alone, and by those standards he had failed. If few Americans asked themselves what influence a German victory might have had on United States security, it was because the country's wartime leadership had failed to formulate American purpose in terms of the balance of power. Indeed, Wilson had succeeded in eliminating that concept from the main currents of the nation's thought and in the process had managed to transform, through promises of a new world order which he could not fulfill, a great and successful national effort into failure.

Millions of Americans concluded that the United States had gained little more from its trans-Atlantic experience than Prohibition and the flu, or, as Henry L. Mencken suggested, American Legion parades and a new Russian colossus. In their revulsion against the war which had cost so much and gained so little, they condemned Wilson and Versailles as well as those European Allies who had seemingly drawn the United States into the war to serve their imperial interests. American isolationism, as it rapidly demolished the country's wartime pro-British sentiment, annexed the powerful support of the Irish and German minorities which had resented Wilson's decision to redeem the British cause. Similarly, Far Eastern minorities in the United States, Indians, Chinese, and Koreans, condemned the Versailles Treaty because it neglected to apply the principle of self-determination in the vast regions belonging to the victors. Isolationism took strength in large measure from a traditional American nationalism and a national feeling of security. For an allegedly self-sufficient country it mattered little what happened to Europe. Sinclair Lewis caught the spirit of the postwar decade when his George Babbitt informed the Zenith Real Estate Board that the real American was "the ideal type to which the entire world must tend if there is to be a decent, well-balanced, Christian, go-ahead future for this little old planet."

Internationalism, as embodied in the Wilsonian tradition itself, was equally antagonistic to the conservative tradition of American diplomacy. Like isolationism, it refused to face political reality. It denied, as did isolationism, that the United States need be concerned with any specific configuration of military or political power in Europe or Asia. Whereas isolationism insisted that the nation had no interests outside the Western Hemisphere (although it never recognized any necessity for curtailing the country's commitments in the Far East), internationalism declared that American interests were nowhere in particular but everywhere where human rights or peace might be challenged. Isolationism preached that events outside the hemisphere were inconsequential; internationalism insisted that they mattered, but that they could be controlled through the universal acceptance of democratically inspired principles of peaceful change. Every program fostered by American internationalists during the 'twenties—membership in the League of Nations or the World Court, the employment of arbitration conventions, the resort to consultation in the event of a crisis, collective security, naval disarmament, and the outlawry of war—denied the need of any precise definition of ends and means in American foreign policy and anchored the effectiveness of that policy to the power of world opinion to bring aggressors before the bar of justice.

II

Perhaps the tragedy in the postwar American response to world affairs required only the memory that it was the military strength of the United States which had created the power structure of Europe as reflected in the Versailles settlement.

If that treaty defined, at least in some general manner, the interests of the United States, then the nation had no choice but to concern itself with any threat to its specific provisions. Any forthright American response might either agree to the defense of those arrangements or to their dissolution as conditions no longer required by the interests of the United States. Only within the context of a constant preparedness to make such decisions could the nation really possess a foreign policy at all.

No country understood better the necessary role of United States power in maintaining the stability of Europe than did France. From the moment of its establishment in 1870–71 the German Empire had outdistanced France militarily. For that reason French supremacy on the Continent required nothing less than the dismemberment of Germany. Having failed to achieve this objective at Versailles, the French negotiators extracted from Wilson a Guaranty Treaty whereby the United States assured the protection of France against future aggression. Britain offered the French government similar guarantees contingent upon the ratification of the Franco-American treaty. At Versailles these pacts were the means whereby Wilson and Lloyd George encouraged France to give up her extreme demands for the separation of the Rhineland from Germany. The subsequent failure of the United States Senate to accept either the Guaranty or the Versailles Treaty threw France on her own resources and contributed to that nation's postwar bitterness and insecurity. (*Reading No. 1.*)

Thereafter France pursued a vindictive course in world affairs. Her unrealistic demands for reparations, followed by her occupation of the Ruhr in 1923, contributed to the creation of a vengeful and aggressive nationalism in Germany and prepared the way for the rise of Hitler. The Socialist Leon Blum criticized President Raymond Poincaré for the French action in the Chamber of Deputies. "You have upset world opinion," he said, "you have weakened German democracy." France approved the Geneva Protocol of 1924 which defined aggression and bound all members of the League of Nations to submit their disputes to compulsory arbitration. Sir Austen Chamberlain, Foreign Minister of the new conservative British government, however, rejected the Protocol as an overextension of British power. French policy after 1919 was less antagonistic toward her wartime allies than toward Germany only in degree. United States and British officials condemned France's refusal to disarm as well as her restrictive policies toward the rehabilitation of the German economy. (*Reading No. 2.*) They questioned France's system of alliances with the new states of eastern Europe, in defiance of the spirit of the Versailles Treaty, when Germany had been disarmed. Whether France was motivated in her postwar policies by insecurity or by the determination to regain an unchallengeable first-rank position in European affairs, denied for half a century by German unification, remained a matter of conjecture. But policies designed to limit an aggressive Germany which did not then exist and which could hardly have been predicted succeeded merely in alienating much of the Western world.

United States policy revealed no greater concern for the future of eastern Europe than it did for France although French primacy on the Continent and the independence of the Slavic states comprised the heart of the Versailles settle-

ment. Nor could Western interests among the new Slavic nations survive for long
the lapse of French military dominance on the Continent. By the mid-'twenties
both Russia and Germany had made clear their ultimate intentions toward the
regions of eastern Europe.

Russia began her assault on the eastern European settlement as early as 1920
when the new Bolshevik regime, recoiling from the unsuccessful invasion of
White armies into Soviet territory during the previous year, despatched the Red
Army into Poland. Immediately J. Pierrepont Moffat, a member of the American
embassy staff in Warsaw, warned Washington that a Russian triumph over Poland
would ignite revolutions in Germany, Austria, and perhaps even Italy. Hugh
Wilson, another distinguished American diplomat, observed regarding the Soviet
advance into Poland that "we have to go back to the defense of Vienna against
the Turks and other crucial battles in world's history to find one of equal significance." France sent token aid to the Warsaw government; the United States and
England sent none. The American Secretary of State, Bainbridge Colby, placed
his reliance solely on another Russian revolution. Poland held by a narrow margin
and the crisis passed. But the lessons were clear. Having only recently created at
Versailles the political structure of eastern Europe as a great democratic achievement, the Western democracies revealed no intention to fight for its preservation.
The dilemma, if unrecognized, was not unlike that which confronted John Hay
and Theodore Roosevelt earlier in the century when they attempted to maintain
the principle of the Open Door in China—recently heralded as a great diplomatic
achievement—in the face of Russian aggressiveness.

German resentment and ambition after Versailles also focused on eastern
Europe. The treaty's Eastern provisions, especially those regarding Austria,
Czechoslovakia, Danzig, and the Polish Corridor, had the effect of directing
German attention toward Slavic Europe, where the obviously minimal interests
of the Western powers, added to the internal confusion of the new states, created
opportunities for unlimited political and military advance. Beyond the new
nations, it is true, loomed Russia, but Germany came to terms with the Soviet
colossus in the Rapallo Treaty of 1922. Perhaps no one stated with greater precision Germany's long-term interest in destroying the Versailles settlement in
eastern Europe than did Hitler in 1924. In his ideal world Britain would exist as
a great nation, but would abandon her balance of power policies on the Continent and maintain only her maritime and imperial interests. France would retain
her national integrity and her colonial empire, but would return to the status of
a secondary power in European affairs. These changes, coming with time, would
permit Germany the freedom to pursue her real interests—the occupation and
colonization of eastern Europe.

Such unhidden threats to the Versailles structure, emanating from both Russia
and Germany, would eventually demand of the United States and England a
willingness either to employ force to maintain the political integrity of eastern
Europe or to accept diplomatically whatever changes appeared consonant with
their interests and security. Such inescapable questions regarding Europe's future
were far too precise and potentially troublesome for the vagaries in American
thought. In February 1925 Sir James Headlam-Morley, historical adviser of the

British Foreign Office, warned his government that the Vistula, not the Rhine, was the real danger point in Europe and could not be ignored with impunity by the Western powers. In a prophetic memorandum to Chamberlain he posed a critical question:

> Has anyone attempted to realize what would happen if there were to be a new partition of Poland, or if the Czechoslovak state were to be so curtailed and dismembered that in fact it disappeared from the map of Europe? The whole of Europe would at once be in chaos. There would no longer be any principle, meaning, or sense in the territorial arrangements of the continent. Imagine, for instance, that under some improbable condition, Austria rejoined Germany; that Germany using the discontented minority in Bohemia, demanded a new frontier far over the mountains, including Carlsbad and Pilsen, and that at the same time, in alliance with Germany, the Hungarians recovered the southern slope of the Carpathians. This would be catastrophic, and, even if we neglected to interfere in time to prevent it, we should afterwards be driven to interfere, probably too late.

### III

In the Far East the United States already possessed a long record of involvement, but its guiding principle of the Open Door for China was scarcely helpful after 1919 in determining a diplomatic course that measured the nation's genuine interests in that critical region of the world. Nor was it probable that in the utopian atmosphere of the 'twenties American policies vis-à-vis China and Japan would assume any greater realism. Yet American and Japanese writers stressed repeatedly in the early 'twenties the inescapable factors in the Chinese-Japanese equation. (*Reading No. 3.*)

Three objectives, largely self-contradictory, determined the nature of United States Far Eastern policy after the war. First and foremost, American leadership desired a further guarantee of the Open Door in China to counter Japan's dominant position in the western Pacific. But the fundamental purpose of undoing the Japanese gains of the war years and preventing their repetition was largely negated by a second powerful factor in American intent—the negotiation of a world-wide program of naval reduction. Many Americans, including Secretary of State Charles Evans Hughes and Senator William E. Borah of Idaho, were convinced that armaments had caused the World War and that naval expansion, continuing unabated into the postwar years, would eventually undermine the peace of the world again. (*Reading No. 4.*)

Thirdly, United States officials, in their determination to resolve the quarrel with Japan without expenditure or compromise, favored the annulment of the Anglo-Japanese Treaty of 1902. This treaty had neutralized British opposition to Japanese expansion during the war and thus appeared to Washington as one element which encouraged Japan's existing enroachment on Chinese territorial integrity. British officials differed among themselves as to the value of the alliance. Some had no interest in the Open Door principle and believed that Japan should not be prevented from seeking her destiny, even at the expense of China. To deny Japan her interests on the mainland might require another major war. The British knew, moreover, that for many Japanese the Anglo-Japanese Treaty was an essential element in that nation's prestige and security. Secretary Hughes, however, transformed the issue of the alliance into a simple one of moral and political choice. England, he declared, must support either the United States or Japan; it could not do both. Pressure by the United States brought the British government into line.

To achieve such conflicting purposes as naval reduction, the abrogation of the Anglo-Japanese Treaty, and the leashing of Japan was diplomatically impossible. Yet on the surface Hughes gained all of these objectives at the Washington Conference of 1921–22. Through the Five Power Pact he forced on Japan, with his famous 5-5-3 ratio, the acceptance of a permanently inferior naval position, as compared with Britain and the United States. In the Nine Power Pact he secured another Japanese acceptance of the principle of the commercial and territorial integrity of China. Then in the Four Power Pact Hughes managed to replace the older Anglo-Japanese alliance with a vague agreement among the United States, Britain, France, and Japan to consult in case any question of aggression should arise in the Orient.

As a parchment arrangement the Washington Treaties were magnificent. That there was no relationship between the actual treaty agreements and the realities of international politics in the Far East was seen by naval and press observers even before the pacts were signed. The naval treaty granted Japan unlimited freedom to expand, in many important categories, the number of its naval vessels. Nor did it prevent any nation from increasing the range and fire-power of its existing warships. The Four Power Pact, whereby the four major Far Eastern powers guaranteed the *status quo* in the Far East, denied the Western nations the right to fortify those islands in the western Pacific from which an effective campaign might be launched against the Japanese homeland. For the United States this meant the elimination of naval bases on Guam or in the Philippines. For the United States Senate this was no sacrifice since it had no interest in such distant fortifications anyway. The Senate declared, moreover, that the treaty implied "no commitment to armed force, no alliance, no obligation to join in any defense." For some naval analysts the Four Power Pact comprised an unprecedented diplomatic victory for Japan (*Reading No. 5.*) Elmer Davis, the well-known journalist and critic, observed in the *New York Times* of February 6, 1922:

> An estimate of the success or failure of the conference can hardly be made until some decades have passed. . . . As the score stands at present, it seems hardly too much to say that this conference has been the greatest success in Japanese diplomatic history. Japan has won more at other conferences, but always at the expense of hard feelings left behind. Her triumphs have usually been conditioned by the certainty that the defeated nation was only waiting its chance to start a fight. . . . Japan retains her strategic supremacy, military and political, on

the continent of Asia, and is reasonably sure that if ever this supremacy should be challenged by Russia or China, Russia or China would have to fight alone. . . . Japan has Asia to herself.

What was gained by the dissolution of the Anglo-Japanese alliance is not clear. As Winston Churchill was to write in *The Gathering Storm:* "The annulment caused a profound impression in Japan and was viewed as the spurning of an Asiatic Power by the Western World. Many links were sundered which might afterwards have proved of decisive value to peace." The Japanese at Washington gave up their claims to Shantung as they had agreed in advance. What remained after 1922 to guarantee the *status quo* in the Pacific was the Nine Power Pact, whereby Japan agreed to uphold the Open Door. For the fulfillment of this ultimate American objective in the Far East the nation could only rely on the moderation of future Japanese policy on the Asiatic mainland.

## IV

This American reliance on paper—stocks and bonds at home and treaty arrangements abroad—culminated in the late 'twenties with the Kellogg-Briand Peace Pact. Aristide Briand, the French Foreign Minister, created an unprecedented stir in American peace circles when, in April 1927, he proposed a pact between the United States and France for the bilateral renunciation of force in any future conflict in which the two nations might become involved. By the mid-'twenties the concept of outlawry, as the ultimate means of applying rationality to international affairs, had caught the national mood. Senator Borah quickly emerged as a leading champion of the idea, arguing that as all human evils were vulnerable to an outraged public sentiment, supported by law, so war could be banished from the earth by educating the peoples of the world that it was wrong. (*Reading No. 6.*)

Secretary of State Frank B. Kellogg resisted the pressures within the nation that the government of the United States accept the opportunity to eliminate war as a legitimate course of national action. To him, as he explained to a number of Senators, the Briand proposal was nothing less than a bilateral alliance. Suddenly, during the spring of 1928, the idea of a general outlawry pact, to include all nations, began to push all opposition aside, for a multilateral treaty would eliminate the danger of war everywhere and at the same time would universalize the American commitment so completely that it would destroy all sense of specific national obligation for the peace of the world. So popular was this new approach to outlawry that Kellogg eventually claimed it as his own. Some Washington realists, however, found the trend disheartening. William R. Castle, a State Department official, visited his office one Sunday late in May 1928 and discovered the Secretary in an adjoining office involved in a discussion of multilateral treaties. Castle confided his opposition to his diary:

> They think that they are remaking the world and actually it is nothing but a beautiful gesture while the Jugoslavs tear down Italian consular flags and the Chinese fight and the Japanese stand at attention. The

gesture is worth while if it is made just right and with a little guidance in wording the Secretary would make it right. . . . [But otherwise it] may seriously tie our hands, as the originators of the plan, if the time comes when as honorable people we must step in with force . . . words can never take the place of actions . . . the only way to achieve peace is by quietly and steadily standing for the right and the fair thing. We could change the whole sentiment of Latin America toward the United States by getting other nations to cooperate with us in our police measures. We have stood for moderation in China and we can be careful not to suspect and offend the Japanese. We can learn courtesy in our dealings without losing any of our firmness. We cannot remake humanity in a day. We cannot abolish war with a pen but we can take the lead in making war unnecessary.

Eventually the proponents of outlawry achieved their triumph in the Kellogg-Briand Peace Pact, signed with appropriate pomp in Paris on August 27, 1928. President Calvin Coolidge's observations on the pact carried the utopian spirit of the decade to a new high. "Had an agreement of this kind been in existence in 1914," he informed a Wausau, Wisconsin, throng, "there is every reason to suppose that it would have saved the situation and delivered the world from all the misery which was inflicted by the great war. . . . It holds a greater hope for peaceful relations than was ever before given to the world. . . . It is a fitting consummation of the first decade of peace." With varying degrees of enthusiasm, the Senate ratified the treaty in January 1929 by a vote of 85 to 1.

For most Americans the Pact of Paris comprised a successful assault of a democratically led world on the institution of war. The fact that Japan had signed the treaty was further assurance that Tokyo had accepted the *status quo* in the Far East or, at any rate, had abjured the use of force in changing it. Still the pact was not without its critics. Some regarded it merely worthless; others viewed it as a positive danger to peace because, like all utopian proposals, it eliminated the need of either diplomatic precision or military commitment. (*Reading No. 7.*) As Salvador de Madariaga observed with remarkable perception, the outlawry-of-war scheme enabled the United States to "bridge over the gap between its two favorite tendencies: the tendency to isolation (from Europe, at any rate) , and the tendency to see itself as a leading nation in moral as well as in material progress." Frank H. Simonds, the noted American journalist, feared that the American involvement in the pact would mistakenly encourage Europeans to believe that the United States had deserted its isolationism. The ultimate impact of the Kellogg-Briand Peace Pact on the foreign policies of the United States was negligible.

Herbert Hoover, who became President in March 1929, was one American official who regarded the new world-wide peace structure with profound seriousness. For him the United States naval establishment was quite adequate, and since the Kellogg-Briand treaty had indeed eliminated war, except for defense, the continued drain of naval expenditures from more useful and humane projects had lost its rationality. Armaments not only comprised an unconscionable burden for mankind but also generated ill-will and rivalries among nations. During his first month in office Hoover initiated discussions with British officials on the question of further naval reduction. In his Armistice Day address of November 11, 1929, he recounted the progress in disarmament achieved since the war. He assured the American people that the key to world peace lay not in preparedness or diplomacy but in the existence of a spirit of goodwill among nations. (*Reading No. 8.*)

Hoover's actual negotiations with J. Ramsay MacDonald, the British Prime Minister, during August and September 1929 illustrated the extent to which American naval power was divorced from policy. For the Prime Minister England possessed an empire which required nothing less than a global defense effort. For Britain, moreover, the United States fleet was a source of security, not a threat of war. Thus MacDonald had little interest in either British or American naval reduction. (*Reading No. 9.*) Eventually at Hoover's prodding the London government called the famous London Naval Conference of 1930. Its five delegations represented the United States, Britain, France, Italy, and Japan. From the outset the conference ran into insurmountable difficulties. All the nations present, except the United States, pointed to specific interests and potential rivals which necessitated either adequate naval power or other security guarantees. The Japanese, for example, made it painfully clear that they had interests and ambitions in the Pacific which demanded a higher naval ratio than that imposed on them by the Washington treaties. The United States, too, had its distant and vulnerable commitments; it simply refused to recognize any relationship between those outposts and the power which it wielded. The United States alone among the great nations refused to be burdened by the obligations of empire.

At length the United States, Britain, and Japan signed a new naval agreement which failed to limit. Indeed, the United States required a major naval-building program if it would reach its quota. France held the key to genuine naval reduction, but French officials established early one immutable condition to any naval agreement—a security pact with the United States. The United States delegation, headed by Secretary of State Henry L. Stimson, hoped to coerce France by arousing public sentiment against the French demands. They discovered, as did Wilson eleven years earlier, that the French government, whatever its views on naval reduction, had the full support of French public opinion. Eventually Stimson had to choose between the collapse of the conference and a consultative pact for France. He chose the latter course only to be repudiated in Washington. Thereafter agreement became impossible. At the end of the conference France and Italy refused to sign any treaty at all. Frank H. Simonds, writing in *The Review of Reviews* of May 1930, summarized the American situation at London:

> Hoover and Stimson had started where Wilson started, with the idea that there was a potency in American ideas which would sweep Europe away from its traditional conceptions, persuade it to renounce its idea of military guarantees, and adopt the American idea of moral assurances. But Stimson like Wilson found Europe stiffly insisting that it would reduce its own armament only as it was assured of the protection of

British and American arms, or at the least of American cooperation. . . .
There in a nutshell was the basic trouble with the London Naval Conference. Before it met, the French said squarely, "Give us a guarantee
and we will reduce our program. Failing that we shall fulfil it." But the
British and the Americans from first to last were on the one hand resolved against guarantees, and on the other determined to get a reduction of French figures. Always the discussion revolved about these
points. . . . The British and Americans were always seeking formulae
which would give the French the semblance of security without the
reality, the French were always demanding the reality and rejecting the
semblance. . . .

## V

From Versailles to the London Conference of 1930 the predominant foreign policy
mood of the United States had gradually conformed to a pattern of utopian
internationalism which found its ultimate expression in the Kellogg-Briand Peace
Pact and in the diplomatic homilies of Herbert Hoover. Lewis Einstein, writing
in the *North American Review* of September 1931, predicted that the outbreak
of another war in Europe would find the United States as unprepared physically
and emotionally as it had been in 1914. For him, in that depression year, American foreign policy was nonexistent. "Beyond current platitudes of peace and
good-will, beyond a predilection for forms of legal remedy which we are only
ready to accept for questions of secondary interest, beyond pushing our dwindling
exports on an impoverished Europe," he wrote, "what more has been our recent
foreign policy?" (*Reading No. 10.*)

Even the internationalists who believed that the United States should play a
leading role in world affairs seldom accepted the obligation that the nation act
responsibly—that it measure events carefully to judge how and where its interests
were involved, that it be prepared to negotiate on matters of secondary importance and engage in the immediate defense of positions of vital concern. At times
the attention which Americans gave to international bodies and conferences
created a semblace of genuine world leadership whereas the utopian methods
employed permitted the total avoidance of responsibility. The perennial escape
from hard political settlements turned the concepts of conciliation, co-operation,
consultation, and peaceful adjustment into ends in themselves. For a leadership
that had led a nation to expect perfection in diplomacy at little expense to itself
it was easier and cheaper to permit potentially costly issues to drift. The nation's
predominant power alone guarded the national interest and sustained the illusion that the foreign policies of the United States were brilliant in concept and
performance. No European or Asiatic state in the 'twenties cared to challenge
the power or the interests of the United States. It was American power, especially
when contrasted with the lack of preparedness within the dissatisfied nations, and
not American moral leadership, that created the unshakable impression that the
world had adopted the principles of Wilson in rejecting the employment of force.

No one saw the error in such assumptions more clearly than did Edwin L. James of the *New York Times*. (*Reading No. 11.*)

That American policy had become divorced from reality was demonstrated during 1931 by events in Manchuria. Japan, having at last rejected her obligations to the Nine Power Pact, presented the United States with two realistic choices, neither of which was acceptable to the Hoover administration. The Japanese assault on Manchuria and the incorporation of that region into the Japanese empire as the puppet state of Manchukuo comprised no threat to the vital interests of the United States. It was for this reason that Washington officials revealed no greaer enthusiasm than the League of Nations for applying stringent economic sanctions against Japan which might have led to direct military involvement in the Sino-Japanese quarrel. On the other hand, both Hoover and Stimson resisted every pressure to negotiate a new *status quo* in the Far East, for any compromise would recognize changes wrought by military force. On January 7, 1932, the United States government dispatched identical notes to China and Japan, informing both nations that it would not recognize the existence of any new territorial or financial arrangement in Manchuria that resulted from the recent aggression.

Beyond this initial response the administration was divided. Stimson preferred stronger American action, perhaps an economic embargo against Japan, which might have encouraged a similar program within the League of Nations. Hoover, relying on moral force alone to terminate Japanese aggression, believed sanctions both dangerous and unnecessary. As a result, neither the League nor the United States adopted any retaliatory measures against Japan more effective than moral condemnation. What this achieved was not clear, but Stimson regarded his success in securing a general condemnatory judgment against Japan perhaps the most constructive achievement of his public career. The United States, he recalled later, had through its leadership "secured a united front against approval of conquest by military force. The united front did not prevent aggression or punish it or even act as an effective discouragement to further aggression. But it prevented any acquiescence by peace-loving powers in a return to the jungle law of international diplomacy before the First World War."

In this observation, Stimson, while praising the moral leadership of the United States which prevented the Western recognition of Japanese expansion, illustrated the ultimate futility of attempting to prevent change through a purely moralistic response. For his moralism permitted the Japanese no choice but to accept as permanent the *status quo* in the Far East (for they would never alter it through peaceful negotiations with the Chinese government), or to stand condemned before the world—a condemnation which entailed the veiled threat that on some propitious occasion the righteously indignant countries might resort to force to undo the accumulation of wrongs. Stimson thus designated Japan an outlaw nation without making any genuine effort to secure the interests of China or to understand the half-century accretion of fears and animosities that underlay the Manchurian crisis of 1931. Nor was he conscious of the magnitude of the obligation which the phraseology of nonrecognition created in Asia for the United

States. As Nathaniel Peffer observed in *Harper's* of February 1933: "The pronouncements of the American government with reference to Manchuria, so glibly
hailed by liberals, will constitute, unless revoked, a pledge and policy no less
binding than the Monroe Doctrine but infinitely harder to effectuate. . . . And
of this fact the American people remain singularly unaware and wholly uncritical." What, Peffer wondered, caused the United States to assume such vast
commitments in Asia which had so little relationship to its own vital interests?
(*Reading No. 12.*)

Nonrecognition, as a logical and popular expression of national thought, became the ultimate American response to the challenge posed by Japanese aggression. In large measure the deep, but hidden, confusion which this posture of
defiant inaction created in the American mind fell heavily on Stimson himself.
The Secretary admitted during the Manchurian crisis that the Nine Power
Treaty no longer reflected the political and military realities in the Far East. But
to him it was law and as law could not be discarded as a scrap of paper. His
concept of justice demanded, moreover, that those who defied the law must be
punished. On the other hand, Stimson's acceptance of the Open Door for China
as a sacred dogma, to be preserved against every encroachment by the Japanese,
defied even his own judgment of legitimate national policy toward the problem
of change. Stimson's private admissions suggested, moreover, why the behavior of
the United States toward Japan would of necessity lead to open conflict. For
Stimson wrote:

> This world of ours is a growing, developing community. In such a world
> a reign of law, however desirable, cannot be used as a strait jacket to
> prevent growth and change and still less to protect injustice and per-
> petuate hardship. Any attempt to make use of such a system of war
> prevention will ultimately cause explosions which may well destroy the
> system itself. I fear Europe will never achieve a permanent system of
> war prevention, no matter how sound a judicial system she may devise,
> until she has provided methods of relieving fundamental causes of
> pressure resulting in discontent.

# 1 | France, the United States, and the Versailles Treaty, November 1919 *

For France in 1919 the Versailles Treaty and the United States acceptance of that treaty were all that remained between the *status quo* and the power of a resurrected Germany. For some French writers the prospects for French security were not bright. Stéphane Lauzanne, editor-in-chief of *Le Matin*, condemned the Versailles Treaty as a compromise between a Wilsonian idealism and a Napoleonic realism which irritated Germany without offering France any security guarantees. The League of Nations was merely a debating society, without any means of action or force. The author questioned the American attitude at Versailles toward Germany and Japan, and reminded the great democracies that France had paid a supreme price for Western civilization in its war dead. For that reason, wrote Lauzanne, French security merited the consideration of the American nation.

✍

In what spirit does France look upon the peace treaty? And in what light does France look upon America?

I want to set down the answer to these two questions with perfect freedom, truth and independence.

For those whose privilege it is to wield a pen, there is no finer task than that of ever seeking truth, pursuing it in the midst of passions and prejudices, trying to seize it, and showing it in the full light of the sun fearlessly, without hesitation or false shame.

France, who has hundreds of faults but at least one quality—that of clearness —was of the opinion at the time of the armistice that there could be one of two treaties: either a Wilsonian treaty, that is, a treaty embodying an abstract ideal, or a Napoleonic treaty, that is, a treaty of practical force.

Each of them had advantages and disadvantages. The Wilsonian treaty amounted to practically the following: "Let us forget hate, ill-feeling and dissension; let us bring together all the peoples of the earth. On the ruins around us, let us build up a new humanity. Let all nations associate in a common effort. Let nothing remain that may divide them or that may set one of them against the other." . . .

The other treaty, the Napoleonic treaty, stated as follows: "An unprecedented crime has been committed against civilization, against the right of nations, against humanity. It has been committed by a race who has other dark deeds to its credit, who stealthily and slowly prepared for aggression, and whose dream it is to dominate and subdue the world. The punishment must fit the crime. The guilty nation shall be placed where it cannot wreak harm for several generations. It shall be tamed, broken in by forcible means and put under perpetual surveillance." . . .

* Stéphane Lauzanne, "France and the Treaty," *The North American Review*, CCX (November 1919), 604–12.

Now, if we take the treaty that was signed at Versailles on the 28th of June, 1919, we find that it does not come under the head of either of the two treaties we have just examined. It is neither Wilsonian nor Napoleonic, neither one thing nor the other. It is a compromise between the principle of idealism and the priciple of strength, the principle of punishment and the principle of forgiveness, that is, between fire and water, between night and day. At least, such is the feeling of Frenchmen of every party and of every shade of opinion. Socialists look upon it as "a treaty made by capitalists and imperialists." The bourgeoisie thinks of it as "a treaty of concession to visions and internationalism." No one will recognize it as his child. Even those who declare they are ready to adopt it—and that is the case of the majority of Frenchmen—deplore that it bears such or such a disfiguring mark, such or such a flaw which threatens to cripple it for ever. . . .

Now for the question of guarantees. The treaty does call for interallied occupation of the left bank of the Rhine and of its bridges for 15 years, with the right of extending the time limit and reoccupying the territory. It does stipulate that the military forces of Germany shall be reduced to an army of 200,000 men. It does provide that the military frontier of Germany shall extend to 50 kilometers on the east of the Rhine, and that Germany shall not be allowed to have any fortifications on this side of that frontier, nor to assemble, maintain or drill armed troops. But who can guarantee that after fifteen years, when the Allies have left, and the French have returned to France, these provisions shall be lived up to? Who can guarantee that if, in 1950, America and Europe hear that garrisons have been organized in the Palatinate or bulwarks built around Coblenz, they shall send their troops forward and declare war, as is provided by Articles 42 and 44, so as to drive out the garrisons and overthrow the bulwarks? Who can guarantee that the German army shall not be secretly increased beyond the 200,000 allowed? Napoleon also claimed that he had enclosed the Prussian army within a narrow circle, and yet, unknown to him, in spite of the fact that his armies were occupying Germany, the Prussian army broke through that narrow circle. Here again, the treaty is a source of irritation and vexation to Germany, lays obligations on the Allies and gives neither France nor the world those lasting guarantees of peace they had a right to expect.

Shall we now examine the question of the League of Nations? The treaty does not give birth to a true League of Nations with a charter, court, army, police, and means of coercion. As a matter of fact it constitutes little more than a debating Society. The covenant is not a social contract, but merely the by-laws of a club. The two parts of the structure which have been given the largest development are the committee room and writing room. There will be much talk, much writing, but little or no action. There will be no means of action: no force, no international police to see that the decisions of the League are carried out. . . .

I could go on ad infinitum to show that the treaty of Versailles does not fully satisfy any Frenchmen; neither the dreamers of the extreme Left, nor the imperialists of the extreme Right, nor the practical minds of the Centre. Above all, it does not satisfy that love of clearness, logic and common sense which lies at the very core of French minds. It is full of complications and delays. It has been necessary to publish a special pamphlet simply to enumerate the long series of dates of the various stages of execution.

However, such as it is, with all its contradictions, dangers and confusion, France accepts this treaty. She accepts it, because one part of it puts an end to a great injustice: Alsace-Lorraine is given back to France, and she is once again whole. She accepts it, because one other point of it opens to France every hope and every possibility: the treaty of Algeciras is repealed as well as the treaty of Frankfort, and Morocco is given unconditionally and unreservedly to France. Now, Morocco has a tremendous development and enormous resources. There, perhaps, lies the chance that will save France from being crippled under the burden of her financial debt and the weight of her ruins.

And then France possesses an inexhaustible fund of philosophy and common sense. Her philosophy tells her that perfect justice, like perfect happiness, is not of this world. Her common sense reminds her that if she is victorious, she did not win alone. She feels obliged therefore to accept the cooperation of the Allies who won with her. The peace treaty does not belong to her alone; it also belongs to America, England, Italy. It is a collective treaty, just as the war was a collective war.

So even if the peace which this treaty gives us is a peace bringing with it heavy burdens, dangerous weaknesses and the pressing necessity of working and watching, it is none the less peace with honor and with hope!

Now that I have stated clearly and simply what France thinks of the peace treaty, I would like to state just as clearly and simply what France thinks of the United States in connection with the peace treaty.

There is no need for me to enter into the feeling of France for America: it is compounded of affection, gratitude and admiration. France has a profound love for her sister beyond the Ocean; she will never forget that America helped her to win the war; she admires the latter's youthful energy and marvelous efficiency. Petty friction, slight misunderstanding, can never alter one great fact: that twice the two nations have fought side by side for the noblest of causes. Their blood has been shed together and their hearts shall ever beat in unison.

But if France loves and admires America, she does not always claim to understand her.

After the armistice, France heard America, or a great part of America, preaching to her the virtues of moderation, generosity, burying of race hatred and conciliation among nations, for the sake of the future happiness of America. France very well knew that this was disinterested language, and she yielded to it. The moderation of the treaty towards Germany, the consideration which has been shown the aggressors of 1914, is all due to America's action at the Peace Conference.

But when at that same Conference, the question of the relations of other nations besides France and Germany came up, when the rights of another than the German race were dealt with, American principles underwent a sudden change. When, for instance, in April, Japan asked for the insertion in the preliminary project of the League of Nations of a simple sentence proclaiming the equality of every nation, the American delegation met the request with a peremptory "No!"

There, France fails to understand. If America asks for the admission of guilty Germany into the League of Nations on an absolutely equal footing, how can America object to the admission of guiltless Japan on the same equal footing? If America cannot lay aside a certain distrust and prejudice towards a country with which she has never been at war, which has never invaded her territory, never laid waste her soil, how can she ask France, assaulted, trampled on, half strangled by Germany, to forget her feelings, her rancor, her hatred? What distinguishes the races of the earth is not the more or less blue blood in their veins, but their manner of conducting themselves, their degree of civilization, the more or less respect they have for their word, their conception of honor. From this point of view, what can Japan be reproached with? Can there be urged against her one hundredth part of what can be proved against Germany? So America—or a part of America—is also prejudiced against another great nation, and her prejudice is a hundred times less justified than that of France against Germany.

And then, when the question of guarantees was brought up at the Conference and there was submitted the remarkable document drawn up on the 10th of January, 1919, by Marshal Foch, asking for the permanent occupation of the left bank of the Rhine and its bridges by Allied troops, the President of the United States sided against the best military judge of France, and refused to give the project America's adhesion. It was at this point that there was substituted for the Foch memorandum what has been called the Franco-Anglo-American pact, that is, a promise made to France that if she was ever attacked by Germany, England and America would immediately send to her help their military forces. For nearly every Frenchman, such a guarantee is sufficient. It is every bit as good as the guarantee Foch wanted. It is of such a nature as to cause Germany to pause and reflect, should she feel inclined once more to become aggressive. But now that same guarantee, suggested by the American delegation, is being opposed by certain elements in America.

Again, France fails to understand. France has nothing to do with Republicans or Democrats in America; she recognizes, and only can recognize, Americans. If she is refused the guarantees asked for by her, because such guarantees are a source of displeasure to some; if she is refused the guarantees that the President of the United States offered her personally, because they do not suit others, what *are* the guarantees she is to have or take? Must France suffer the consequences because Americans disagree? Is she not entitled to ask them to call a truce on the question of home politics, so that she may obtain the security she has a right to expect? When two drivers fight, is it fair that those inside the car should receive the blows?

I am asking these questions in all simplicity and frankness, in the first place because a great many people in France are asking them, and in the second place because, knowing all that is in America's heart for France, I know the answer beforehand.

When Gabriel Hanotaux had the honor of being received in Paris by President Wilson, he said to him:

"We cannot offer every year to the world a battle of the Marne."

It is the plain truth. And neither can we offer to the world the sacrifices which followed the battle of the Marne. The security of France is therefore the condition of the peace and liberty of the world. To give that security is to provide for the security of civilized Europe and of America. . . .

## 2 | French Military Policy and Its American Critics, December 1921 *

Aristide Briand, in explaining French reluctance to disarm in a speech before the Washington Conference, pointed to France as the great defender of Western civilization on the European continent. In this reply, Oswald Garrison Villard, the noted American journalist, declared that the German problem had ceased to exist. Germany, he wrote, had been effectively disarmed. This article revealed how far French policy had isolated France from British and American opinion.

🖋

A masterpiece of falsehood and misrepresentation, and abject confession of fear of Germany and a deliberate slap at the British—this was M. Briand's long-awaited declaration of the French reasons why their country cannot disarm. To hear him was, moreover, to listen to a fire-cracker where a bomb was expected. Aristide Briand can speak much better than he did at the third session of the Washington Conference—as I can testify of personal knowledge. He, moreover, weakened the force of his presentation by permitting himself to be stopped twice for the translation of what he had said. Again, he ended on a dull and quiet note, whereas he had a superb climax for the end of the second portion of his address. It was as if the consciousness of his bad cause fatally handicapped him. . . .

One thing M. Briand unquestionably did—he widened the breach between England and France. Mr. Wells's vigorous characterization of it is mild and gentle as a summer zephyr compared with what the Britishers said of it privately, after they left the hall. One of the most brilliant women in the diplomatic corps here has asked me not to dwell upon this phase of it in my correspondence. But it is necessary to set forth the truth and, more than that, her own assurance that the breach is now about complete is another reason why the facts should be written—no harm can now be done by so doing. But to realize what M. Briand did to the British, one must note the fact that in his speech he *never once* referred to them or to their frightful sacrifices during the war, or to the "holy alliance" between them. On the contrary he dwelt upon the isolation of the French; he presented the case as if there were no other nations on earth

* Oswald Garrison Villard, "Briand's Failure," *The Nation,* CXIII (December 7, 1921), 641–2.

save the French, Russians, and Germans. France, in his eyes, is the sole defender of morality and justice and liberty. It must have a huge army—his promises of reductions in size and of the term of service were as vague as Mr. Hughes's disarmament proposals were clear-cut and specific, and, apparently, simmer down to only 39,000 men—as if France alone would have to bear the whole brunt of another attack by "Huns" or Bolsheviks; as if France alone had saved the world when Lenin fought the Poles. As for Upper Silesia, nothing that he said cut the British more than his references to that imbroglio, where British and French troops all but came to blows.

When M. Briand sat down we were treated to an orgy of insincere flattery and lip-service. Probably not since Shakespeare gave us Marc Antony's oration over the body of Julius Caesar has there been a more brilliant example of that type of speech which praises while scarifying than that afforded by Mr. Balfour's reply. There is a *double entendre* in several paragraphs of that speech in which, after praising a mediocre address as one of the greatest of orations, a master-piece, etc., he spoke of it as also a complete laying bare of the real inwardness of the French thought upon this subject—the heart of a nation. Mr. Balfour rose to bury M. Briand, not to praise him. He easily turned M. Briand's position by simply referring to the million British dead and two million disabled and wounded. France was not alone in defending liberty and justice, he said. If menacing imperialism should raise its head again England would once more be on hand to bear her share. . . .

Mr. Hughes, of course, in behalf of America spoke his share of meaningless platitudes. He was happy to assure M. Briand that France must not fear isolation —"there is no isolation for the defenders of liberty and justice." But fair words no more make defensive and offensive alliances than they butter parsnips. According to Mr. Hughes's phrases, the United States might go to the rescue of Germany some day if she should appear to be on the side of liberty and justice. What an atmosphere of cant and insincerity and hypocrisy! It was good to get out of the hall into clear and pure air again.

As for the mendacity of M. Briand's statements, five minutes of cross-examin-ation would have revealed it. If what he said is true, members of the Interallied Commission for the Disarmament of Germany ought to be court-martialed not only for dereliction of duty but for endless falsehoods. But they have not failed at their tasks. I take, for example, the following from the weekly *Manchester Guardian* of November 9 as to what M. Briand's own French General Nollet has achieved:

> General Nollet, president of the Commission for the Disarmament of Germany, interviewed recently in Paris by a number of political per-sonalities, set the scaremongers at rest. He says that after eighteen months in Germany, visiting every hole and corner up and down the country where arms could be concealed, he is convinced that Germany today is really effectively disarmed. . . .

Now, General Nollet is French and he is M. Briand's subordinate. One or the other is misstating; there is no alternative. It is M. Briand; he knows full well that quite aside from the question of armament Germany is deprived of her old allies and is economically crushed, with her laboring classes on the verge of starvation, her currency debased, her treasury practically bankrupt, the mark sinking out of sight, with food at prohibitive prices. Danger of a German attack there may be fifty years from now, if civilization has survived, but not sooner. And, of course, there would be no danger at all if France's attitude had been forgiving and generous to the Germans. She could not rise to such heights, and as for M. Briand, as my diplomatic friend said: "He *had* to make that speech or lose his job. And if he goes we shall get a worse one." But what an abject confession of French fear of Germany it is to so dread a beaten, wrecked, disorganized, and discredited foe!

## 3 | The Problem of Japan: A Japanese View, November 1921 *

To this Japanese author it seemed clear that the perennial Japanese threat to the *status quo* of East Asia had motivated the calling of the Washington Conference. He questioned the fairness and sincerity of the Western powers when Europe and the United States controlled over ten million square miles of Asia and yet condemned Japan for her limited ambitions, dictated by necessity, on the mainland.

✍

At the coming Disarmament Conference at Washington Japan will be the cynosure of all eyes. Apparently she is the *raison d'être* of the Conference, although a keen observer will not fail to detect various motives, not entirely pleasing, beneath the professed intentions of its promoters. Japan becomes a question because the great Powers of the Occident seem reluctant to observe the principle of live and let live in dealing with the peoples of the Orient. The Japanese problem is, in the last analysis, naught but an aspect of the broad and fundamental question of the inequitable distribution of the world's land and natural resources. This basic question few seem courageous enough to discuss.

Before discussing the specific case of Japan, let us consider Asia as a whole. Asia's total area measures some 17,206,000 square miles, of which 10,000,000 were before the war controlled by Western Powers as follows: Russia 6,495,970 square miles, England 1,998,220, Holland 586,980, France 247,580, America 114,370, Germany 193. As the outcome of the war the small German possessions in China have been wiped out, but British and French possessions in Asia have

---

* K. K. Kawakami, "A Japanese Liberal's View," *The Nation,* CXIII (November 9, 1921), 530–31.

increased by more than 100,000 square miles. Today, therefore, Europe and America control 10,100,000 square miles of Asia with vast mineral resources.

Roughly speaking, the land area of the earth measures 52,825,000 square miles, supporting 1,751,700,000 inhabitants. Of this total area the Caucasian peoples occupy or control about 46,146,084 square miles. It will be seen that the Caucasian race, having completed the occupation of Europe and the Americas, has conquered and secured control of the whole of Australasia, almost all Africa, the greater part of Asia, as well as the adjacent islands. And the Caucasian peoples who control so vast a territory number only 623,000,000. . . .

On the other hand, the native population of Asia numbers no less than 900,000,000. And yet they control only 6,679,000 square miles of territory, because Siberia and Turkestan are occupied by Russia, India by Great Britain, and Tongking and Cochin-China by France, while Tibet, Chinese Turkestan, Mongolia, and Northern Manchuria, aggregating 2,655,000 square miles, are fast passing under British or Russian control. In other words, there are 134.8 Asiatics to each square mile of Asiatic land.

It may, therefore, be safely said that Asia's 900,000,000 souls have been expropriated of most of their territory and are today permitted to possess only 6,679,000 square miles. This, of course, does not mean that Asiatics have been evicted from the Asiatic territories controlled by Europeans, and that 900,000,000 people are actually compelled to live within the area of 6,679,000 square miles, i.e., 134.8 to the square mile. It is true that the natives of Asia are permitted to continue their habitation in India, Cochin-China, Siberia, and other Asiatic territories which have passed under the European scepter. But the fact remains that Asiatic nations are, by this process of expropriation, deprived of the opportunity to utilize the vast resources lying at their very doors.

It must be remembered that the Caucasian nations are always on the alert to exclude outside enterprises, and especially those of non-Caucasian peoples, from the territories they control. Even where they profess to follow the principles of free trade, they set up a barrier against non-Caucasian immigration. Moreover, by reason of their priority and their accumulated wealth, they have so firmly intrenched themselves that outsiders, most of all non-Caucasian outsiders, find little chance to launch new enterprises in competition with them.

Now let us consider the particular case of Japan. Even schoolchildren know that Japan consists of volcanic ranges. The country is virtually filled with mountains, affording but 15,000,000 acres of tillable land, or only 16 per cent of the total area. This allows each inhabitant only one-quarter of an acre of farm land. In California farm land per capita of population is about nine acres. In Great Britain 77 per cent of its land area is agricultural land; in Italy 76 per cent; in France 70 per cent, and in Germany 65 per cent. Because of the peculiar topography of Japan the country appears, and as a matter of fact is, much more crowded than may be judged from statistics on paper. No traveler, not even the most unobserving, can fail to get this impression. . . .

But it is not only the question of land shortage and overpopulation that weigh heavily upon Japan. Equally depressing is the fact that she has not within her own confines adequate mineral resources essential to modern industry. She depends almost entirely upon foreign countries for iron ores. Of coal she has little that can be used in the steel industry. But the most serious handicap is the lack of petroleum, a material which is becoming more and more important in transportation and in manufacturing industries. If you watch the chessboard of European and American diplomacy, you cannot fail to see how each nation is trying to outwit the other in gaining control of oil resources in different parts of the world.

And here is Japan, struggling to solve, partly at least, her population problem by becoming an industrial and trading nation, and yet harassed by the lack of three essential materials of industry—oil, iron, and coal. If she steps an inch out of her narrow precincts and tries to obtain, say in Siberia or China, the privilege of working such mineral resources, down comes the sword of Damocles in the shape of protest, official or otherwise, from the Western nations.

It is obvious that the great Powers of the West have accumulated more land than they should rightly own—than they can hold without doing injustice to the smaller nations, which find themselves in sad plight, due to the impossibility of finding room for their surplus population. The injustice of holding such vast territories would not be so obvious if they were to recognize, in favor of the small nations, the principle of unhindered immigration and of unrestricted enterprise within those territories. It is when they adopt a hide-bound policy of exclusion that they become a menace to the welfare of the human race.

A program to establish permanent peace with justice should contain one of two propositions, namely, a more equitable distribution of territory or the removal of the exclusive policy adopted by Western colonial Powers against Asiatic peoples. To the staid thinkers of the Occident this must seem a picturesque and Quixotic proposition. It is no more picturesque than were trade unionism or woman suffrage at their inception. Just as the political and economic theories which were denounced as visionary and perverted less than a century ago have since gradually been woven into the practical policies of various nations, so the above proposition will in time be seriously considered, not only by thinkers and theorists, but by practical men of affairs in all parts of the world. Unless we make supreme efforts to realize this ideal there remains but one alternative—the perpetuation of the savage "law of the survival of the fittest," which is equivalent to the Bismarckian axiom "Might is right."

4 | William E. Borah on the Necessity for Naval
Disarmament, September 1921 *

Condemning a national tax burden, especially one devoted to armaments, as wasteful, Senator Borah asserted that military preparations were a source of weakness rather than a source of strength. For that reason, he predicted, defeated

* William E. Borah, "Disarmament," *Nation's Business,* IX (September 1921), 7–8. Copyright 1921 by *Nation's Business.* Reprinted by permission.

Germany, stripped of her military burdens, would again become the economically dominant nation of Europe. Borah, disagreeing with those who believed that armaments were the result of existing tensions in world politics, declared that armaments were the cause of the tensions. Reason and justice, not power, continued Borah, could be the chief determinants in world affairs if provided the opportunity. The Washington Conference, therefore, must appeal, not to armaments, but to the public opinion of the world. But nowhere did Borah suggest how specific adjustments in the *status quo* were to be achieved.

✒

Despite her military defeat, Germany, by reason of the shortsighted and blundering policies of the allied and associated powers, may yet secure economic dominance in Europe. Defeat has resulted in Germany's being deprived of her army and her navy. The burden of armaments has ben forced from the backs of the German people. They may now devote their energies and their talents to agriculture, to industry, to the arts, to the things which constitute the real wealth and strength of a people. Their genius will find expression, not in arms or on the military field, but in improved machinery and cooperative industry. Every ounce of effort which they put forth will be along lines which produce something, which add wealth to the community, which make for contentment and prosperity to the people, which insure greater physical prowess and a higher brain power.

On the other hand, the allied and associated powers are carrying a vast burden because of their great armies and navies. These burdens are being increased upon a stupendous scale. Hundreds of thousands of their people are to be engaged in lines which produce nothing, add no wealth to the community, make not for health, growth and happiness, but for display, parade and possibly for destruction and death. The German people are compelled to preserve their energies for things which count. The allied and associated powers are burying their people under intolerable taxes, discouraging industry, sterilizing human energy, and breeding discontent through their ever-enlarging plans for increased armaments. . . .

France has an army of 800,000 men. The exact cost for maintaining this great army I do not know, but one can imagine how stupendous it is. The British army and navy combined call for an expenditure much larger than our own. Thus, while Germany has her billions of reparation, the allied and associated powers are spending their billions for their armies and navies—we alone expending as much for our army and navy as the entire reparation claims against Germany.

The business men of this country must realize, more keenly, perhaps, than anyone else just now, what these armament expenditures and the taxes thereby imposed mean to business of the future. There is little encouragement for men of business capacity to plan and strive for success when they realize, as they must, that their profits are to be taken for taxes, and that those taxes, when collected, are to be expended, not for things which make for wealth and development, but for sheer waste and sterility. We shall not enjoy that resiliency and revival in business which we are entitled to experience in this country until taxes are brought within reason. And taxes can not be reduced until expenditures are brought within reason. And public expenditures can not be reduced until outlays for armaments are brought within reason.

All that is being done and said just now about reducing the expenses of the Government in other departments and along other lines will amount to very little so far as lifting the burden of the taxpayer is concerned, unless we also cut most savagely the expenditures for armaments, for there is where the vast sum of money goes.

Neither can we wait, nor need we wait, until all questions about which nations may hold differing views are settled before we begin to limit our armament expenditures. There are now three nations in absolute dominance of the seas— the United States, Great Britain and Japan. These three nations are the only nations which are building vast navies. They are now actually engaged in a naval race. They are building navies with mad speed and piling taxes upon the people at a rate and to an amount never before dreamed of in time of peace, and seldom in time of war. To say that these building programs shall go forward, that these taxes shall continue to be increased, and the burdens under which the people are breaking shall be augmented until all international questions about which nations and peoples may hold different views are settled, is to say that there is to be no disarmament.

Disarmament should not be postponed, or subordinated, or made incident to the settling and adjusting of all international questions. It should be made the controlling, dominating question. It is the most vital problem in the world today. Unless disarmament is effectuated, there is no possible relief from the economic conditions under which we are now suffering. And any plan, or any program, which makes the question of disarmament a subordinate, or incidental proposition, rather than the main and controlling proposition, will result in the future, as it has in the past, in no relief to the taxpayers and no relief from war.

There are many obstacles to overcome before we can achieve disarmament, or any pronounced limitation of armaments. I do not underestimate the difficulty of overcoming these obstacles. But the obstacle which seems to me the greatest, the obstacle which seems to me the most difficult to master, is one which we will not admit exists, and that is the reliance which we have come to have on force as the only power left on earth with which to govern men.

Mr. Hughes, the Premier of Australia, declared in an interview that we must adjust every question touching the Pacific before we can consider the question of disarmament—that there can be no disarmament until all these questions are amicably arranged and settled. This is to declare in another way that we propose to settle these questions ultimately by force in case we fail to settle them satisfactorily to ourselves through negotiations. It is the old practice attributed to the Kaiser of rattling the sword at the conference table. It is, as everyone understands, a threat. In other words, the real reliance for ultimate settlement is upon force and the covert threat of its use is, as of old, at hand. As a conferee thinketh in his heart, so is he.

This is the system which has been tried by the diplomats for three hundred years, and instead of resulting in disarmament, it has resulted in continued and increasing armaments. If all nations having interest in the Pacific would disarm, or limit their armaments to a point of real defense—or, at least, to the point where it could no longer be said that an actual naval race was on—might it not be possible to adjust these questions more satisfactorily, more effectually, and more easily in the court of reason and conscience and under the compelling power of public opinion? Is it necessary to have this threat of ultimate force pronouncedly a part of every conference? Is it wise to have the hammers and anvils going on the outside of the conference to the extent that the din of building battleships will deafen the voices of the conferees?

The fact is that while we thought we had conquered militarism, it has apparently conquered us. The barbarous creed of Bernhardi has become the accepted rule of the parliaments and congresses and conferences of the new world, as well as the old. The thing which is paralyzing the energies and dissipating the moral forces of the whole human family today and retarding every effort toward peace, driving us to the very brink of chaos and barbarism, is the fact that governments are still worshipping at the throne of militarism. There is to them no God but force. Before the war we had great faith in the commanding influence of justice and the power of public opinion.

I have before me now an interesting editorial in which it is urged that it is useless to talk of disarming until the causes of war are removed. One of the most prolific causes of war is huge armaments. An armed world is a fighting world. Naval competition engenders suspicion, fear, hatred, war. If there should be twenty years of intense naval rivalry between the United States and Japan, any sterile, promontory or irrelevant rock in the Pacific might give rise to war.

There will always be questions of commercial rivalry, matters of difference between nations, and this rivalry and these differences will always lead easily to war when the nations are armed for war. If you wish to make it improbable that differences will lead to conflict, first reduce armaments, which always inspire war, and prevent naval competition which is a daily, ever-present, taunting suggestion of war.

I understand fully that there may be circumstances and conditions in which an appeal to force is not only necessary but righteous. But to deify force, to make it the dominating factor, to have it ever present, to sit at conference with your finger pointing back over your shoulder to your armies and navies, to intrude into every settlement, and to announce to the world that it is your ultimate reliance, is barbaric—and it is none the less barbaric when it is practiced by professedly Christian nations.

For myself, I refuse to concede that force is the only power left, or that it should be the dominating and controlling power. It cannot be possible. Reason and justice must still have their place in the affairs of the world, and if leaders and statesmen are strong enough to place their reliance upon them, they will go far. I venture to declare, in the face of professional militarists, that no nation can long defy the public opinion of the civilized world—and especially no government can long defy the public opinion of their own people. And if this conference is conducted as an appeal to the public opinion of the world and to the public opinions of the peoples of the respective countries, it will accomplish far more than if it is conducted under the constant threat of dominating armaments. . . .

# 5 | A Naval View of the Washington Treaties, April 1922 *

Having recognized Japan as a potential enemy in the Far East, American officials at the Washington Conference attempted to reduce the naval power of England and France as if these two nations were rivals of the United States. What disturbed many naval writers, however, was less the naval clauses of the Washington Treaties (which really failed to limit) than the provisions of the Four Power Pact whereby the United States denied itself the right to fortify Corregidor, Cavite, and Guam. This agreement gave Japan naval supremacy in the western Pacific and thus endangered the American commitments not only to the islands but also to the Chinese mainland, all of which lay under the guns of the Japanese fleet. Again at Washington the Japanese demonstrated that they had a foreign policy with a series of objectives for which they were willing to pay. The United States, on the other hand, had no genuine foreign policy in the western Pacific at all. It sustained its obligations in the region within a military and policy vacuum. Beginning in 1922 the United States and Great Britain together began to lose control of the sea lanes of the Far East. Yet so thoroughly had the American people lost their sense of realism in foreign affairs that the Harding administration could pass off the Washington Treaties as a great diplomatic victory for the United States. For William Howard Gardiner, an advocate of naval preparedness, the Washington Treaties gave Japan a free hand in the western Pacific and thus reduced international relations in that strategic area to a matter of Japanese goodwill.

✍

. . . The general objective of the United States—which was the objective of the Conference as a whole—was (1) to improve policies and consequent conditions in the Far East so as (2) to reduce a specific expectancy of war in the Pacific, and (3) thus permit of a general limitation of armaments.

With this general objective Great Britain was in hearty sympathy—under the very natural proviso that nothing offensive to her close ally, Japan, should transpire in such a way as to endanger the great British interests in the Far East or

* William Howard Gardiner, "A Naval View of the Conference," *The Atlantic Monthly*, CXXIX (April 1922), 522–39. Reprinted by permission.

the security of British India and Australasia. And it was well understood that Great Britain came to the Conference with the particular hope that the aversion of the United States to the Anglo-Japanese alliance might result in expanding that alliance to an Anglo-American-Japanese alliance. For to bring the United States into alliance with herself has been a more or less persistent item of Great Britain's foreign policy, at least since George Canning proposed it in 1823. With respect to this policy—of increasing moment as the United States grew in power—the "Four Party Treaty" between the United States, Great Britain, Japan, and France is an interesting development.

The particular objectives of France at the Conference were twofold. Her paramount concern was that nothing should be done at Washington that would limit the military power of France on the Continent of Europe *vis-à-vis* Germany; and M. Briand's remarks on this subject summarily deleted the entire subject of the limitation of land armaments from any further consideration by the Conference. An evident corollary to this desire for military security on the part of France was her desire to strengthen her naval power in the Mediterranean for the purpose, stated by her representatives, of being able, in the event of war in Europe, to draw with assurance on the great manpower of her vast African possessions. . . .

Of Italy it need only be said that her Far Eastern concerns are less even than those of France; and that her Mediterranean interests, though less extensive, are more vital to her because of her position. But that is not to say that they were parallel with those of France. On the contrary, it appears that Italy found her advantage in sympathy with Great Britain and, by securing the right to a fleet equal in size to that of France, quietly secured a potential naval advantage over the latter because the Italian peninsula does not divide Italy's two coasts to the extent that the Iberian peninsula divides the two coasts of France.

The fact that, of late, Japan has been spending very nearly one half of her national revenues on her navy, while the United States has been spending less than a tenth of the Federal revenue on the American navy, led Japan to welcome with enthusiasm the call of the United States to a conference for the limitation of naval armament *per se*. But the fact that the proposed limitation of naval armament was predicated on arriving at "a common understanding with respect to principles and policies in the Far East" led the militarist press of Japan to characterize the invitation to Japan to attend the Conference as "the greatest calamity that has ever overtaken the Japanese Empire." To reduce naval competition might save Japan from ruin or from the internal necessity of going to war prematurely in order to justify naval expenditures and prevent internal revolt; but policies in the Far East were matters of which, in the view of some Japanese, the least said the better. Yet it was realized that, if Japan declined to attend the Conference, she might be diplomatically isolated and could not hope to save herself from the internal dangers of her excessive naval expenditures.

Finding herself forced by internal as much as by external conditions to attend the Washington Conference, it became the duty of the Japanese Government to make such an estimate of the situation and to devise such a plan of procedure as would give the best promise of protecting and, if possible, advancing Japanese policy while relieving Japan of her unparalleled burden of naval expenditure. . . .

It was natural for Japan to suppose that, having called the Conference, the United States would be prepared to pay a high price to make it a success and might, therefore, be induced to a commitment that would constitute a positive improvement of Japan's politico-naval situation. The problem was to determine on an objective of great naval advantage to Japan, such an objective as would render unnecessary further expansion of Japan's navy while protecting her political policy, and such an objective as might be attained by astute diplomacy at the Conference.

From the course pursued by the Japanese from the moment of their arrival at Washington it was evident that they came with such a plan, prepared by the cooperation of statesmen who understood naval strategy with naval strategists who understood statecraft. It was a plan that should have been apparent before the Conference opened to anyone really conversant with the strategy of the Pacific; for it was a plan that was obvious from the outset to all but those who did not understand both statecraft and naval strategy. Yet the Japanese put it through—as will appear hereunder—with results far transcending such a detail as whether the ratio of capital fleets were to be 10–10–6 or 10–10–7, all the talk over this detail being merely a cloud of dust thrown in the air to conceal the real objective. And, as will appear, they thereby gained an unprecedented naval victory, pregnant with political possibilities for which it would be difficult to find a parallel in history.

To the foregoing very brief outline of the particular objectives of some of the Powers at the Washington Conference, it should be added that some of the Chinese seemed to have entertained hopes of territorial restitution—in addition to Shantung—and hopes of political and economic independence which the issue has proved to have been exaggerated. They seem to have recalled the American idealism that inaugurated the Open Door Doctrine, not only to assure the openness of all China to the trade of all the world without discrimination, but also to assure the territorial integrity and political entity of China; and they seem to have expected that this same idealism would insist on the taking of material steps to correct incursions that had been made during the last twenty years against this doctrine. . . .

It was not to be expected that public interest would concern itself first with such particular objectives as have been suggested, even though they were important factors underlying the primary problem of putting in effect in the Far East such policies as would ensure fair practices by all and to all in that field; and this to the end that the likelihood of further aggressions there—or of a war of defense against further aggression—would be so reduced that it would be safe for the Powers, and for those dependent on them for security, to limit armaments.

On the contrary, public interest centred on the tangible objective of limiting armaments. And this natural centering of public interest on this objective was particularly emphasized because the Conference, though dealing with conditions in the Far East, occurred soon after the great war in Europe and, consequently, at the height of such a popular reaction against armaments as usually follows the close of every great war—especially if it has been one of the wars fought to end war.

From this it followed that the greatest popular interest was accorded to the proposal to destroy over half of the aggregate tonnage of American, British, and Japanese capital ships, built or building, to stop forthwith all building of such ships, and to set up the ratio of 10–10–6 as that to be maintained for ten years between the capital fleets of these Powers. But the Japanese insisted on retaining their brand-new Mutsu which is the greatest battleship in the world and which was built largely by popular subscription; and in order to do this they contended for a ratio of 10–10–7. This was adjusted by allowing Japan to retain the 33,800-ton Mutsu while earmarking her 20,800-ton Settsu for the scrap heap. But this increase in Japanese tonnage compelled the United States to undertake to complete the 32,600-ton Colorado and West Virginia as substitutes for the 20,000-ton Delaware and North Dakota; and this in turn caused Great Britain to desire to undertake the building of two entirely new ships of not over 35,000 tons each, whereupon the Thunderer, King George V, Ajax, and Centurion, aggregating 91,500 tons, would go to the scrap heap. This readjustment caused by the Japanese retention of the Mutsu retained virtually the ratio of 10–10–6 or 5–5–3; but it prevented the putting in practice of the plan to stop forthwith all building of capital ships. . . .

Of the total of 1,645,810 tons to be destroyed, over half is constituted by ships almost all of which are so old, so slow, or are so comparatively weakly armed, that they can no longer be considered fit to fight in an up-to-date battle-fleet. In this connection it is appropriate to recall that, before 1910,—and as a measure of naval efficiency in expectation of war by Germany,—Admiral Lord Fisher got rid of 160 British naval vessels "that could neither fight nor run away." To this it may be added, on personal knowledge of the present writer, that, for several years past, some American naval authorities have been advocating disposing of 15 out of the 17 American battleships to be scrapped; and this not as a measure of reducing the power of the American fleet, but as a way of increasing the efficiency of the American navy by relieving it of practically useless deadwood. As somewhat the same holds true for almost all the British and Japanese ships afloat and to be scrapped, it is difficult to see in this doing away with 51 obsolete or obsolescent battleships any *reduction* in fleet power. . . .

It may be said, in short, that the naval limitations agreement does not limit the extent to which future competition may be carried in building submarines, destroyers, cruisers, or any other type of combatant naval vessel in any number, except capital ships and airplane carriers. It virtually does not reduce the present effective force of capital fleets in themselves, but merely provides against their further expansion; and it makes specific provision for expansions of the present airplane-carrier forces. . . .

Such considerations lead us to the conclusion that the most important thing for us to attempt to estimate is whether or not the naval limitations agreed on will tend to spread righteousness in the Far East; and, subsidiary to that, whether or not they will tend to maintain peace in the Pacific. But, in order to make such an estimate, we shall have to consider the functions of naval force in the Pacific as modified by the Washington Conference, political conditions in the Far East, and the very promising results to be expected from some of the non-naval agreements reached at Washington.

It may conduce to a clearer appreciation of the more important naval consequences of the Washington Conference, as they affect the functions of naval force in the Pacific, if first we consider some of the functions and limitations of modern navies. Then we can apply general principles to the specific situation in the Pacific. . . .

The basic mission of a navy is to defend its country and those for whose defense its country is responsible. The defense of British overseas domains by the British navy and the defense of the Philippines by the American navy are instances wherein a Power, by assuming suzerainty, has incurred the concomitant and unavoidable moral responsibility for the defense of its dependents. Collateral to this primary mission of defense, there rests upon a navy the duty of supporting the external policies of its country. The Monroe Doctrine and the Open Door Doctrine are instances of such policies. . . .

As naval warfare, like chess, is primarily a question of location and then a matter of the timely movement of forces of different strengths, we must first picture to ourselves the very simple geography of the principal strategic points in the Pacific. Hawaii is 2100 miles west-southwest of San Francisco. With adequate base facilities—which do not yet exist—in both places, the American battle-fleet could be supplied from San Francisco if it were based on Hawaii. And from there it could protect the western coast of the United States from enemy operations other than of a touch-and-run cruiser nature—except for the fact that Japan is building large submarines of such great cruising radius that they will be able to cross the Pacific, operate off our western coast for a month and then return to Japan without refueling.

Guam is 3300 miles slightly south of west from Hawaii; and Manila is 1523 miles west beyond Guam. . . . [I]t is clear that neither Guam nor the Philippines could be defended by a fleet based on Hawaii. But if a fleet could be sure of finding fuel and other base facilities at Guam, it could easily advance from Hawaii to Guam, for the distance is less than 4000 miles; though from Hawaii a fleet could not reach the Philippines without refueling somewhere, as they are nearly 5000 miles distant; and a fleet of superior power, based in the region of Guam, could defend the Philippines, as they are only 1500 miles from Guam, although both the Philippines and Guam are less than 1400 miles to the southward of the great naval bases in Japan proper. It will be seen from this that Guam occupies a pivotal position in the strategic geography of the Western Pacific, giving to the possessor of an adequate and secure base region, with Guam as a nucleus, what are known as "interior lines." For not only would a fleet based in the region of Guam command the northern and eastern approaches to the Philippines, but it would command the lines of communication between

Japan and the Marshall, Caroline, and Pelew archipelagoes, which lie to the southward along the line of communications between Hawaii and the Philippines, and in close proximity to this line. . . .

From what has been said the conclusion seems inevitable that the single question that has the most influence on the naval situation in the Western Pacific is, whether or not the United States has secure tenure of Guam. If at Guam there are merely adequate naval stores and such defenses that it cannot be taken by a battle-fleet, then, in the event of war, the American battle-fleet could proceed there and, after refueling, cut the lines of communication the Japanese had extended to the Philippines—if the Japanese had been venturesome enough to attempt to take the latter with Guam securely in American hands. During the early stages of the war, Guam and other appropriately placed islands in the Western Pacific could be provided with adequate base facilities and then the war would proceed to a reasonably quick end.

But if Guam is not strongly enough defended to stand off a battle-fleet, then Japan can take also the Philippines and hold all the Far Eastern possessions of the United States, secure in the knowledge that it will take the latter about three years to regain from Hawaii a base in the Far East by a certain series of operations. . . .

As already may have been inferred, the pivotal point of both the naval and the political conclusions of the Conference was the question of fortifications and naval bases in the Far East—and most particularly the status of the fortifications and such beginnings of naval bases as the United States has in her insular possessions in the Far East. Article XIX of the Naval Treaty provides that these latter fortifications and so-called naval bases shall remain *in statu quo* as at the time of the signing of the Treaty. That is to say that they shall remain in such a status that the Japanese battle-fleet could take Guam and most of the Philippines within about a fortnight of the outbreak of hostilities, and that thereupon, the American battle-fleet being without a Far Eastern base, would be powerless beyond its range of about 2000 miles west of Hawaii—this irrespective of its size relative to that of the Japanese battle-fleet, and for reasons similar to those that make the biggest gun conceivable literally powerless at a distance about twice as great as it can shoot its projectile. Whatever factors led to this pivotal conclusion may be viewed in two entirely different lights.

It was said early in this article that it was clearly evident to strategists that the Japanese came to the Conference with a definite plan designed (1) to safeguard their present politico-naval status in the Far East, and (2) to use the responsibility of the United States for the popular success of the Conference so as to exact concessions that would improve the politico-naval status of Japan in the Far East. A thorough knowledge of the strategy of the naval situation, which has been merely outlined above, made it extremely easy for strategists to forecast what would be the main element or objective in such a Japanese plan. One had only to determnie on that factor in the strategic situation which would be of the greatest advantage to Japan, and yet be attainable by negotiations carried out under all the circumstances qualifying the Washington Conference. So there was no surprise among those who understood the strategic factors involved when, in the very first week of the Conference, rumors developed to the effect that the Japanese, as well as objecting most positively to the proposed scrapping of their peerless new battleship, the Mutsu, were raising questions as to the fortifications and so-called naval bases in the Far Eastern possessions of the United States—and this as a factor of the proposed limitation of naval fleets, and although it had not been mentioned in the original proposals made by Secretary Hughes as to the limitation of fleets. . . .

The conclusion seems unavoidable, therefore, that the naval effect of this whole arrangement is not the establishment of a 5–3 ratio of naval power between the United States and Japan with respect to the Far East. On the contrary, it means virtually complete disarmament by the United States in the Far East while Japan—though statistically less heavily armed at home than the United States is at home—is left overwhelmingly armed in the Far East. And about the same thing might be said with respect to Great Britain's power to express naval force in the Far East *vis-à-vis* Japan. Consequently, in the Far Eastern situation, a region of international interest has been delimited in which Japan is omnipotent as far as arms go, and in which the other interests relatively are powerless. So in the Far East we have a region in which virtually the equivalent of disarmament of all Powers, except Japan, is proposed—a region in which, therefore, the only reliance will be in the validity of such diplomatic agreements as those in which the advocates of complete disarmament repose so much confidence. Consequently, this region may be looked upon in the immediate future as a localized experiment in disarmament wherein, in spite of Japan's armaments, the world is trying the experiment of relying merely on agreements. . . .

In the light of all the circumstances just stated, or implied, it would seem difficult to support the contention that the naval agreement, *considered by itself,* tends to spread righteousness in the Far East—unless Japan chooses, without forceful compulsion, to bring to a definite end the general policy she has been pursuing in recent years. And if she does not so choose, it is difficult to see how peace will be maintained in the Pacific—unless the Powers pharisaically abandon all responsibility for the maintenance of righteousness in the Far East. But it may well be that the entirely new freedom accorded Japan in the Far East will result in an entirely new policy on her part, especially under the stimulus of the purely diplomatic agreements drawn up by the Washington Conference.

The underlying task before the Washington Conference really was to find a diplomatic prospect of solving the problem occasioned by the expansive course Japan has been following during the last sixteen years—and to find this in view of the depleted condition of the European Powers and in view of the popularity of the movement for disarmament in the United States. Of first importance in this respect is the Four Power Treaty which supersedes the Anglo-Japanese alliance and which binds the United States, Great Britain, France, and Japan to each respect the insular possessions of the others in the Pacific. Alongside of this is the treaty regarding China, wherein Japan joins the other Powers that participated in the Conference in categorical promises to respect the Open Door Doctrine, this latter being elaboarted in such great detail that an evasion of it would seem difficult—otherwise than by a patent breach.

In the light of these treaties it would seem that the great accomplishment of the Washington Conference has been to reach something of "a common understanding with respect to principles and policies in the Far East"—in principle. The value of the entire accomplishment will depend on the spirit with which each and all concerned put these principles into practice. Only as, in the course of years, it becomes manifest that principle is or is not being put into practice, will it be possible to decide whether America and Britain have been wise in virtually withdrawing their great naval police power from the Far East and in giving to Japan an unchecked opportunity to choose her course. . . .

## 6 | The Outlawry of War: A Debate Between Robert Lansing and William E. Borah, 1924 *

During the mid-'twenties much of American utopianism in the international realm focused on the crusade to outlaw war. Robert Lansing, Secretary of State under Woodrow Wilson, writing in *The Independent* of August 16, 1924, compared the movement to the Children's Crusade. The process of declaring war illegal would have no influence on international affairs, he predicted, because all law gained its effectiveness from the moral or physical sanction which underlay it. There were possible conditions, added Lansing, which rendered war the only means available to protect the national interest.

✍

During the five years which have passed since the Treaty of Peace was signed at Versailles on June 28, 1919, there has been an enormous increase of organizations in the United States with the laudable object of finding a way to prevent the recurrence of a terrible disaster like the World War. These associations are generally national, but some of them are international. They approach the subject from many angles and suggest many ways of achieving the common object which all are seeking. Some of these suggested ways appear to be based on rational and pratical grounds, but the majority are without merit because impracticable and unworkable. . . .

Among the more recent proposals for the insurance of world peace is the one calling upon the nations to make war illegal. Certain organizations have raised a standard inscribed with the words, "Outlaw War." And to that standard have flocked many supporters with the same fatuous enthusiasm that made possible the Children's Crusade. The idea has even won favor with some American states-

* Robert Lansing, "The Fallacy of 'Outlaw War,'" *The Independent*, CXIII (August 16, 1924), 95–6.

men who ought to be endowed with sufficient reason to appreciate the utter futility of such a demand. One can forgive and pity hysterical women and illogical sentimentalists adopting such a motto, but for men, chosen to public office presumably because of their superior mental attainments, to subscribe to it and acclaim it causes one to doubt their intelligence.

The effectiveness of any law is the moral or physical sanction which underlies it. Physical sanctions are the common and prevailing means of law enforcement in view of the frailties of human nature. It is the physical might of government which prevents crime and protects the individual in the enjoyment of his natural rights and liberties. Moral sanctions are those imposed by an individual upon himself and depend on his sense of justice and duty to do what is right. In international law, moral sanctions prevail since there is no supernational power to exert physical sanctions. It is then the good faith of nations, their high sense of obligation, and their standard of international morality that give vitality to the law of nations and justify the word "law" being applied to the principles and precepts which have come to be recognized as those which should regulate the intercourse between civilized states.

If, however, a nation does not respond to moral obligation, or if a government is inspired by immoral motives which place its own selfish interests above the rights of others, what remedy is there but an appeal to arms? Is there any other means by which a nation can maintain the rights of itself and of its nationals? It is the only way to prevent an unscrupulous and ambitious neighbor or rival from wresting from it its independence and sovereignty. All the declarations in the world as to the wickedness and lawlessness of war will not prevent the use of force. Submission and passive resistance will not save the life of a nation if it is invaded by the armies and navies of an enemy seeking its destruction. There is but one way in such a case to preserve the national safety, and that is by matching force against force, by resisting with all the physical might possessed by a nation the invasion of its territory and the infringement of its rights.

War cannot be outlawed, because under certain conditions it is the only means of preserving national life, because it is often the only means of protecting the rights to which a nation and its people are entitled by every principle of justice and morality. The law, which far transcends any man-made law, is the supreme law of self-preservation.

If all nations were moral and responsive to moral sensibilities, there might be something to the cry, "Outlaw War." But, unfortunately for the peace of the world and the welfare of mankind, civilization has not attained so high a plane, nor does such a condition seem imminent. It would mean the millennium, and that is far in the future. Many nations among those which we term civilized show themselves covetous and selfish and disposed to take every advantage in international affairs, provided it will increase their power and prestige. Recent years have given ample evidence of this aggressive spirit which has persisted in human relations since the very dawn of history. . . .

One may deplore the fact that wars take place. One may agree that war is an evil and contrary to the highest ideals of modern thought, but under existing conditions to attempt to abolish it by proclaiming it illegal is utterly futile.

And, when these dreamers suggest that it can be accomplished by binding themselves as individuals to take no part in any way in arming their country against attack or in resisting foreign aggression, they assume an attitude as irrational and indefensible as it is unpatriotic. They not only preach a pernicious and dangerous doctrine, but they invite the contempt and ridicule of all thinking men.

Until human nature changes and all nations become uniformly virtuous, war cannot be abolished by mandate. The way to stop wars under present conditions is to remove as far as possible their causes. Mutual confidence and cooperation between nations should be cultivated, friendly and fair economic competition practiced, while diplomatic intercourse should be frank and unequivocal and founded on the immutable principles of justice. . . .

As a civilized nation will never at the present time admit to the world that it wages an aggressive war, but invariably asserts that it was justified in taking up arms because its rights were threatened, its legal right to make war is declared. Who is to pass judgment on the rightfulness of that declaration and on the legality of the war? Where rests the authority to decide which belligerent is guilty of aggression and deserving of condemnation? How, then, can either party to an international conflict be denounced as employing force illegally and without justification? Only world public opinion and history yet to be written can determine which party was in the wrong, and that an appeal to force was in violation of legal right and moral obligation.

In the face of these actualities, the present cry, "Outlaw War," becomes an absurdity, an empty demand from unthinking though well-meaning pacifists, who ignore real conditions and the application to them of logic and reason, and loudly clamor for something which common sense and rational thought perceive to be as impracticable as it is vain. No man or woman possessing even average intellect will listen seriously to the words, "Outlaw War."

— |  "There is not a government on the face of the earth strong enough to declare and carry on war against the aroused and sustained public opinion of the people." *

Senator William E. Borah, whose views embodied much of the legalism current in the 'twenties, answered Lansing in the September 13, 1924, issue of *The Independent*. Borah placed his faith in the "invincible force of public opinion." He cited examples of reform achieved through an aroused sense of justice, but he, of necessity, limited his examples to the realm of domestic affairs. Borah insisted, however, that a "code of international law declaring war a crime and making criminally liable those who foment war could be carried out as successfully as any provision of domestic law in the United States." By stripping war

* William E. Borah, "Public Opinion Outlaws War," *The Independent*, CXIII (September 13, 1924), 147–9.

of its legality and glory, by educating the world to its destructiveness and use-lessness, believed Borah, nations could be led to the acceptance of peaceful and legal methods for the settlement of international disputes. It was Borah's failure, here and elsewhere, that he thought purely in terms of means and never in terms of the proper ends to be pursued.

✍

. . . If force be the ultimate arbiter in international affairs, as the ex-Secre-tary plainly argues, then it should be the business of each and every nation to develop its instruments of force to the highest point of perfection. Instead of discussing international law, world courts, and thus deluding the minds of the people and leading them into unsafe paths, it should be our business to spur our experts to the invention of yet more deadly instruments of death, to in-crease our armies and our navies, and to bring force to its highest degree of perfection. It is absolutely certain that there will always be controversies between nations, and equally certain that such controversies must be adjusted, either through orderly, legal methods and under the direction of law and a sense of justice, or by force. Mr. Lansing clearly accepts the latter. The idea of peace, therefore, from his standpoint is a fallacy, an annoying and impossible ideal. All plans and schemes for peace are not only futile, but delusive and dangerous. With great respect for the ex-Secretary, I reject any such savage and destructive doctrine and the theory upon which it is based. . . .

There have been other instances in which imperious intellects and massive minds have turned with a pitying eye upon the sentimentalists and the hysterical. One recalls how the great Webster stood upon the steps of the Revere House in Boston and, in pitying tones, spoke of those hysterical women and illogical sentimentalists—the abolitionists—as irresponsible and dangerous and denounced the whole abolition movement as "rub-a-dub" agitation, fit only for little minds and fatuous disturbers. Mr. Webster's powerful intellect, his remorseless logic, failed to properly measure the uplifting and directing power of an aroused sense of justice, failed to comprehend the invincible force of public opinion. He thought only of physical force, that governments rest at last upon force, that slavery was protected by the Constitution and that back of the Constitution was force. Garrison and Phillips and their hysterical followers were appealing to a power which rewrites constitutions and reforms continents. There is not a gov-ernment on the face of the earth strong enough to declare and carry on war against the aroused and sustained public opinion of the people. If we are to end war, we must get back of governments and diplomats and ex-secretaries, back of leagues and courts, to that educated, aroused, and well-directed public opinion upon which all agreements, all laws, all leagues, and all courts must ultimately seek foundation. . . .

I am unable to determine from Mr. Lansing's article whether he wants an end of war or not. But I must presume he does. If so, does he think that he will turn men and leaders from war more readily by recognizing war as a legitimate institution for the settlement of international disputes, or by declaring it a crime and pointing the way to settlement through lawful procedure? Assuming that the principles we contend for were invoked in international law, accepted by the leading nations, with public opinion behind them, would it not seem certain that it would have a staying effect upon all those who appeal to war for the acquisition of territory and to gratify ambition? If we are to prevent war or to reduce the chances of war, every means known, moral, educational, arbitral, legal, must be harnessed for the struggle.

We must bear in mind also that wars seldom come by reason of mass movements. They are the result of selfish policies and personal scheming. "Peoples do not make war," declared Mr. Lansing's great leader. The peoples of the different nations were not responsible for the late war. Had the peoples of the different nations been consulted, or even informed of the real facts, there would have been no war. It was forced upon the world with all its attendant sacrifices and misery by a few men. Lord Loreburn, ex-Chancellor of England, declared: "We went to war in a Russian quarrel because we were tied to France in the dark." Lord Hugh Cecil declared: "When war was decided upon, it was not decided upon by the House of Commons, or the electorate, but by a concurrence of ministers and ex-ministers." A code of international law declaring war a crime and making criminally liable those who foment war could be carried out as successfully as any provision of domestic law in the United States. Under our Constitution, Congress may punish violations of international law, and so could other nations.

"Until all nations stand on the same high plane of morality . . . this talk and discussion of outlawing war is as useless as it is foolish." This has been the plea of timid souls in every great struggle against wrong and injustice, against every great reform in the history of the world. They say: "Wait until nations stand on the same high plane, wait until the world and the people are all good," but propose to do nothing to bring the nations to the same plane or to lead the people to a higher life. The hoary antiquity of this argument ought to encourage men to leave it undisturbed. It was the argument invoked in the first instance against international law itself, against making piracy a crime, against outlawing dueling. The question is: What do we propose to do to bring these nations to the same high plane? The outlawry of war seems to us to be the one vital, essential, and indispensable first step to attain that end. To treat war as a crime in international law, to remove its legal shield, to shear it of its glory, to educate the world to believe that war is wrong, that force is destructive, that it settles nothing—this is a part of the program to bring the nations to this high plane.

Does the ex-Secretary think that we will make any headway by pursuing the old course and treading the old slippery, bloody paths? For three thousand years we have experimented with his theory and adjusted our minds to this cruel creed of force. We have seen peace schemes and plans and alliances, all recognizing war as a legitimate institution for the settlement of international disputes, all based in the last analysis upon force organized to prevent or minimize war. As a result, we are on the very verge of universal breakdown. Another chapter in Mr. Lansing's philosophy, another "step toward peace" along his way would destroy civilization. With ten million killed on the field of battle, with three hundred billion dollars' worth of property destroyed, with the hospitals from Petrograd to Peking and from Berlin to San Francisco still crowded with the diseased and the insane, with nations more heavily armed now than at the beginning of the late war, with the experts of the different nations industriously scheming for more deadly instruments of torture and destruction—with all these we seem to be gathering the fruits of the philosophy, the theory, the creed of Mr. Lansing. Is it not time to lay the ax at the root of the tree, to recognize war no longer as legitimate, to declare nations and men criminals who engage in this supercrime? It is the moral and educational and legal foundation upon which all plans and schemes and hopes of peace must rest.

The Ex-Secretary of State seems to have a sensitiveness about being regarded as an idealist. "The way to stop wars . . . is to remove as far as possible their causes," he says. But in this proposal he suffers himself to ascend to the higher level. Greed is one of the great causes of war. Can we ever remove it? Ambition, love of power, territorial acquisition, are causes of war. Can we ever remove them? Ex-President Wilson declared at St. Louis that commercial rivalry was the cause of the World War. Does anyone expect to remove commercial rivalry? Does anyone desire to remove commercial rivalry? Certainly not. But you can bring men to understand that commercial rivalry must be waged within the compass of established laws and within the rules of reason, that controversies concerning matters of commerce may not be settled by force, that these things should be settled as disputes relative to commercial rivalry in private affairs are settled, under the law and through the courts.

Is there any law upon the statute books which awaited its enactment for the removal of all causes of crime with which the law was intended to deal? Did we remove the cause of piracy before we outlawed it? Have we removed the causes of murder or theft? Certainly not. We pass laws that men may not push causes to the point of violence. There will always be causes for war. There will always be controversies. There will always be ambitious men and blundering criminal diplomats. And the supreme question is: Shall we adjust these matters and restrain the actors by means of and under the influence of law? Shall we settle such controversies by appeal to violence or to law? Shall men who appeal to violence be protected in the belief and the knowledge that they have a legal right to make such an appeal? If we are ever going to reach a time when these controversies and conflicts are to be settled under and through the process of the law, certainly we must begin by outlawing the opposite of law—war. We must repudiate the antithesis of law—violence. . . .

# 7 | The Kellogg-Briand Peace Pact: A Contemporary Criticism, 1928–29 *

Because the Pact of Paris, in outlawing change in international life through force, appeared to assure the United States its privileged position in the world without the necessity of defending and preserving it through war, it had the effect of reinforcing the utopianism of the American people. Henry Cabot Lodge, in the following article, criticized the treaty on several grounds—that it comprised nothing but an appeal to public sentiment, that it contained reservations in such profusion as to render the pact almost meaningless, and that despite its uselessness Europe desired the pact in order to involve the United States in the protection of the Versailles system. What was basically wrong with the treaty, declared Lodge, was that Secretary Kellogg refused to accept any special responsibility for the United States under his signature at the same time that he and other American spokesmen attributed to the pact some unique power to protect the national interest in peace. In short, the document promised too much for too little.

🖎

. . . What is the Kellogg treaty? It is a brief and simply worded declaration that the nations which sign it agree to "renounce war as an instrument of national policy." It is a statement of intentions, signed by fifteen nations—the United States; Great Britain and the six British dominions; France and her three allies—Czechoslovakia, Poland, and Belgium; and Italy, Germany, and Japan. These nations have signed this statement, and it is this statement which the United States Senate is expected to ratify by a two-thirds vote. But, as will soon be shown, there are other questions connected with this treaty, having co-equal importance with it, which will never come before the Senate. . . .

France, naturally, as the proposer of the original treaty, led the European concert where reservations were concerned, and a long exchange of notes between Paris and Washington was the result. At first France desired the amendment of the simple draft treaty so as to make it clear in the first place that wars of "self-defense" would not be banned; secondly, that the violation of the treaty by any of the signatory powers automatically released the other signatories; and, finally, that nothing in the treaty impaired the covenant of the League of Nations, the Locarno treaties, and the "treaties of neutrality"—the pacts which created the Little Entente in Central Europe.

The State Department thought that if these amendments were secured, there would be nothing left of the Kellogg proposal. A high official of the department

* Henry Cabot Lodge, "The Meaning of the Kellogg Treaty," *Harper's Magazine,* CLVIII (December 1928), 32–41. Reprinted by permission of Henry Cabot Lodge.

told the writer, for instance, that if these points were even admitted the treaty would be made "ridiculous." But here is what finally happened. The treaty itself was not amended, but the French points were virtually admitted by Secretary Kellogg in his address before the American Society of International Law in Washington on April 28, 1928.

Out of it a curious state of affairs arose whereby these points actually became reservations, although they are not part of the pact itself. This is made possible by the fact that the treaty is so loosely worded as to be nothing more than a "moral" pledge and so as to mean very little in international law. Normally, reservations which are not part and parcel of a treaty and which are only to be found in a diplomatic note would have scant standing in a court of law. But in this case it was felt that the sole value of the treaty lay not in its binding effect—which admittedly is practically nil—but in the "moral" effect which the knowledge of its existence would have on public opinion—which, it was hoped, would be very great. Therefore, it was argued, the special interests of the parties concerned would be adequately cared for if they were incorporated in diplomatic notes, provided that these notes received the same attention from the public as did the treaty itself. It thus follows that these reservations demanded by France are actually, if not legally, co-equal with the pact itself. But the Senate will not pass on them. The Senate has only the pact before it, and this is so simple and so general as to make reservations, in the old sense, impossible. The Senate can either ratify or refuse to do so. In the case of this pact, whose only significance is "moral," the Senate can pass on only a fraction—and not the most important fraction at that. . . .

There is another French reservation which has not attracted so much attention in Europe, but which seems to be a rather dubious one for the United States to sanction. That is the reservation which, in effect, excepts from the scope of the treaty the so-called "treaties of neutrality" which France has concluded with the new countries of Central Europe and which are frequently referred to as constituting the "Little Entente."

France has agreements with Czechoslovakia, Rumania, Jugoslavia, and Poland. They are designed to carry out a sort of *Einkreisungspolitik* of Germany. They aim to prevent Germany from realizing whatever expansionist ambitions she may have and, in general, to insure the maintenance of the territorial arrangements of the Versailles treaty. . . .

These "treaties of neutrality" are very close to France. They are cardinal points in her foreign policy. She has virtually agreed to go to war in support of them, for on them she places her reliance that she can keep Germany down. We have no quarrel with that, but should we, even by the slightest gesture, accept French plans and policies in that direction? France, in effect, says to us, "Yes, we agree never to go to war except in those cases where we are most likely to have to go to war." Is it proper for us to give official sanction to such a statement? Does it not really "cut the heart" out of the Kellogg treaty?

I have just analyzed the two principal reservations to the Kellogg pact—that which excepts wars of "self-defense" and which makes each nation its own judge of what constitutes "self-defense" and that which excepts from the scope of the treaty all questions pertaining to the chief danger spots of the world. There are others—notably Great Britain's representation enunciating in effect a British Monroe Doctrine zone, where no interference is to be tolerated. This adds to the exceptions to the treaty; it removes from its scope another wide area whence international complications might spring; and seems to help reduce the pact to nonentity. Moreover, there are no reservations for the zones of American interest, such as the Panama Canal. Indeed, there are no American reservations at all. . . .

I have tried to show that the Kellogg treaty has no binding force, and this is admitted even by its strongest supporters; that it is so surrounded by exceptions as to be robbed of its value; and that connected with it are reservations, such as that pertaining to self-defense, which are sources of danger and provide official, international loopholes for waging wars of conquest. Why, then, is it desired?

The nations of Europe seem to desire it most, in spite of the fact that their representatives in this country certainly realize the impossibility of its fulfilling its purpose. They want it because to them it means American participation in their affairs. This has been shouted from the house-tops; it has been proclaimed in many public ways; it really needs no proof. The Paris correspondent of the New York *Times,* for instance, in one of his many dispatches on the subject says:

> It cannot be overemphasized that the European nations accept the Kellogg treaty as a means to let or get the United States into the world councils. . . . They count on America to help handle and suppress conditions which might cause violation of the American-made compact.

An experienced foreign office reporter, M. Jules Sauerwein, foreign editor of *Le Matin,* writes from Paris on the same subject and in the same American newspaper. M. Sauerwein has for many years been in intimate touch with the French foreign office and his writings are consequently of at least a semi-official character. He says:

> The United States takes a world-wide responsibility which she shunned the risk of during the last ten years. Inasmuch as it is now agreed that all existing treaties, especially the covenant of the League, are confirmed and strengthened, and considering that the signatory nations regain liberty of action against violators of the compact, the United States government becomes the moral guardian of the Peace Treaty and subsequent treaties.

The "moral" phase of the question has, as I have said, great force. On another point this reporter is also instructive.

> M. Briand [he says] in the latter part of the negotiations was very skillful in bringing the United States to recognize as valid all existing treaties. Now France and America stand as charter members of this new moral association of nations.

Is this realized in the United States? Does the Senate intend to "recognize as valid all existing treaties"? It refused to do so ten years ago. I shall quote M.

Sauerwein again, for his view seems so typical of why Europe considers it to her self-interest to have us sign this treaty.

> One should not exaggerate nor belittle [he continues] the risks and entanglements which may result for the United States from this new burden she assumes in international politics. . . . One should not underestimate the responsibilities and duties which will fall on the United States. Especially the citizens of that country should avoid the illusion that risks of war can be eliminated by contagion of pacific ideals. One must indeed be optimistic not to see in different corners of Europe real possibilities of war.

After discussing in some detail Lithuania's desire to seize Vilna, Hungary's ambition to enlarge her frontiers, Germany's hope to abolish the Danzig Corridor, Italy's dream to win Tunis, Corsica, Nice, and Savoy, Jugoslavia's plan to hold Saloniki, and Bulgarian plots to secure Constantinople, he concludes:

> If one adds the fact that the Bolsheviki work constantly to create conflicts, we can see what a grave thing, but what a magnificent thing, the United States has undertaken in seeking to prevent another war in Europe.

Candidly, is this understood in this country? Do Americans intend to take this role in Europe or Asia or South America or in any other corner of the globe? Would they approve of the Kellogg treaty if they saw it in this light? I think it not unreasonable to say that they would not.

The same thing has been expressed in different ways. Sir Austen Chamberlain, foreign minister of Great Britain, discussing the treaty, said in the House of Commons on July 30:

> If the American nation ranges itself behind its own treaty, then indeed the signature of the treaty will be an additional and most formidable deterrent of war, and it will be in addition a most valuable security for peace.

The New York *World* on the same day uttered a similar warning:

> Americans must not think that Mr. Kellogg's treaty brings us to a goal; what it brings us to is merely a good starting point.

In this editorial it explains that membership in the World Court is the logical next step.

What, if anything, has Secretary Kellogg said about this? The New York *Herald Tribune,* in an editorial on July 19th, charged that the treaty involved us in the quarrels of Europe and entailed great sacrifices on our part without bringing us anything in return. On July 21st Secretary Kellogg, in a press interview, indicated that it did no such thing, arguing that since it is without sanctions it is similarly free of legal commitments. Is this not a plain *non sequitur* in view of his belief that the importance of the treaty is not legal but moral?

The fact is that "European public opinion believes that as a consequence of the new treaty the United States will join in any League action to employ military and naval force against any nation pronounced by the League authority to be an aggressor or, at the very least, will respect the naval blockade and the financial and economic boycott which the same body may pronounce against any power. In either case we should become, legally, co-belligerents with the League powers." The above is quoted from a letter written to the New York *Times* by Mr. Frank H. Simonds on August 6th. His standing as an utterly unbiased observer of European affairs needs no comment. Mr. Simonds continues:

> Thus the distinction between President Wilson's proposal and that of Secretary Kellogg would appear to lie in the fact that while the former legally bound us to share in European operations, having participated in the discussions which led to undertaking them, the latter would bind us morally to share the similar operations which had been decided upon in our absence. As between the two, it seems hardly to be questioned that the former was the less dangerous.

> . . . Europe has given us clear and unmistakable proof that she regards the Kellogg treaty as obliging us to interfere and that her interpetation of it is totally different from ours. And interpretations, where so vague a pact is concerned, are of prime importance. Formally to agree to such a pact, when opinions on both sides of the water are so wholly different, is really not to agree at all, but to sow the seeds of more trouble and misunderstanding.

> It is difficult to see how the Senate can disregard such clear warning. If it ratifies the treaty it justifies inevitable criticism from Europe later on—criticism which will be far more severe than any which would attend its refusal to ratify. It has been argued that Europe would be very much distressed if the Senate should refuse to ratify, and would loudly criticize us for refusing to back up "our own treaty." This cry would undoubtedly be raised if the Senate refused. But it would have only the scantest foundation in fact and so could not be persistent. . . .

> If the question of ratification be considered solely from the standpoint of incurring European anger, must it not be set down that it would be better to refuse to ratify it now rather than wait till later? And from the standpoint of historic American foreign policy, does not rejection seem the one intelligent course to follow? The treaty may be a good enough thing for Europe; but it cannot be repeated too often that the position of the United States in world affairs is wholly different from that of the individual European state. This statement does not seek to deny the assertion that we have an interest in what happens in Europe. But our interest is bound to be peculiar and our actions are certain to be different. We are so happily situated by geography that what happens in Asia or Oceania or South America is of nearly equal interest to us with what happens in Europe. Being so far away and so remote from strife, we can apply ourselves to improving our civilization and, perhaps, setting a real example to mankind. In any case, our influence in the affairs of others should not be fettered and predetermined. On the contrary, should we not adhere strictly to the simple rule

that the United States should never agree in advance to support or oppose any Power or group of Powers? . . .

I have tried to show in the foregoing the dangers to world peace contained in the Kellogg treaty and the sacrifices which it would compel us to make to Europe without receiving anything in return. These are in themselves ample argument for the Senate to refuse to ratify. But there is one last argument, which seems to me more impressive than all the rest.

As I have said at the beginning, the last few years have seen a widespread interest in and deep desire for peace. It was for our public servants in Washington to take advantage of this sentiment, interpret it, and give it effect. It was a grand opportunity, with the public in a highly receptive mood, to clear up some of the misconceptions about war. In my judgment they wasted that opportunity.

They could have said, for instance, that so great a luxury as the abolition of war—and what luxury could conceivably be greater?—cannot be obtained without sacrifice. They could have pointed out in some public and impressive way that these sacrifices must be made by those who would benefit most from the abolition of war—the rank and file of the people.

They might have suggested, for instance, that those newspapers which increase their circulation and their revenue by sensationalizing war stop doing so. They might have pointed to the ever-increasing number of business houses, which since the War have been promoting American foreign trade at the expense of such nations as Great Britain, for instance, to whom foreign trade is far more essential than it is to us. They might have made it clear that there are certain business men who, by asking the Department of Commerce for aid in promoting the foreign sale of their product, are actually building up causes of war. These very business men, to be sure, would hotly deny such a charge. They would be perfectly sincere in so doing. But in some cases at least they are making for economic pressure, and their activities are, in fact, contributing causes of war. Yet they do not realize it and neither do the most active and energetic pacifists. That is the worst of it: the chief causes of war are unconscious and unthinking; they spring from apparently peaceful pursuits. But are they not far more dangerous than the navy, which is merely an obvious symbol of the treasure to be defended? Is not the ending of war dependent on a brave and clear realization of ultimate responsibility and, truthfully, can it be said that the Kellogg treaty even contributes to such a realization?

If these and similar commercial activities were curtailed, real sacrifices in money, production, and employment would be the result. Perhaps this curtailment would not be worth doing; perhaps war is cheaper in the end. But why not face the real facts and, after facing them, make the decision? An active, growing state collides with its neighbors. The vast ferment of life and of human activity brings war on—not the neatly worded understandings of diplomatists. To have pointed this out would have been realistic and courageous.

I do not suggest that any attempt should have been made actually to cut down those activities which make for economic pressure and so often result in hostilities. Such an attempt, at this stage, would have been doomed to failure.

Education is necessary, but the government could have called attention to the situation, and so have paved the way for reducing the activities of our growing nation if it saw fit to do so. Instead, they gave us the Kellogg treaty which is an attempt to get something for nothing—and that, as every child knows, is impossible.

In the meantime hundreds of newspapers are hailing the treaty as a great step towards permanent peace, and thousands of persons are being made to believe that something really has been done, when, of course, nothing has or can be until a price is paid. A sense of false security is thus created and official sanction is thereby given to a most portentous misconception.

The conception of renouncing war by governmental fiat seems inherently absurd. The great forces in modern society—and especially American society— are quite independent of the government. We are in great measure our own masters. The banks, the newspapers, the great organizations of business—that whole body of influences which affect our thoughts, our food, our clothes, and our incomes goes forging along no matter what Washington says. We, as individuals, cannot dodge the responsibility for war; we cannot put it off on a few office holders, no matter how conscientious or well-meaning they may be. That may have been possible once; it is no longer possible to-day.

It seems to me that this attempt to get something for nothing, which is actually a program to give something for nothing, entrenches war more solidly than ever. War fears truth and realism; only understanding and mutual sacrifice can end it. Is it not apparent that the Kellogg treaty, with its many textual dangers, only thickens the haze, deepens the pitfalls, and once again postpones the day when some really clear thinking is done? . . .

— | "The outlawry-of-war doctrine is the best-meaning red herring that ever navigated in the waters of international thoughts and politics, but a red herring for all that." *

Salvador de Madariaga, the Spanish writer and diplomat, in his criticism of the Kellogg Pact which appeared in the April 1929 issue of the *The Atlantic Monthly*, stressed the vast discrepancy between American idealism which supported the pact, and thus the *status quo*, and the actual persistence of American isolationism. Outlawry met the requirements of the United States, noted Madariaga, because it permitted the nation "to bridge over the gap between its two favorite tendencies: the tendency to isolation (from Europe, at any rate), and the tendency to see itself as a leading nation in moral as well as in material progress." Madariaga criticized the United States for remaining outside the

* Salvador de Madariaga, "Disarmament—American Plan," *The Atlantic Monthly*, CXLIII (April 1929), 525–38. Reprinted by permission.

League of Nations and accused the nation, whatever its claims to superior virtue, of being more responsible than any other for the slow development of peace.

✒

. . . What is . . . the value of the Kellogg Pact? First, it must be made quite clear that as a pact for the outlawry of war, as a psychological method for driving war out of human possibilities, the Pact is as good as nonexistent. Not only in its reservations and interpretations, but in its very essence, the Pact does not outlaw all wars. It must therefore be considered merely as one of the systems before the world whereby a certain number of wars are forbidden by collective treaty. Viewed in this light, the Pact presents quite a different efficiency, according to whether it is considered in its effects on League members or on non-League members.

From another point of view the Kellogg Pact has often been considered as an important step in international politics, because statesmen and critics of international affairs have seen it as the beginning of an evolution of the United States of America toward the organized world-community and the League. This argument calls in question the whole genesis and evolution of the Pact from the American side. The Pact was evidently born of the outlawry-of-war school. This school, we know, is led by idealists of transparent honesty, who, however, hold strong prejudices about Europe and about the League. Their opposition to political conciliation as distinct from judicial settlement is inspired in noble if, I believe, mistaken conceptions. Theirs is the all-or-nothng attitude about outlawry without qualification. The obvious step following the initial suggestion of a multilateral treaty should therefore have been a round-table conference—the conciliatory international method put at the service of the conciliatory international aim. The idea was of course mooted in Europe. Mr. Kellogg frowned hard. For the chief attraction of his Pact was that America could contribute a magnificent "unqualified" idea to the peace movement without paying a cent in loss of international liberty and independence in its conduct. The Pact, therefore, though aiming at peace and cooperation, was transacted by methods of power and isolation. Hence the maze of speeches, declarations, notes, reservations, and silences which obscure its meaning. And on the day the thought was mooted that it might be considered as the first step to further collaboration between the United States and Europe the most authoritative voices in the State rose to put down the error severely. America was ready to promise that she would not go to war unless she wanted and that she would arbitrate whenever she thought fit on the points which her Senate would define (and that is ultimately what the Pact means), but she was not going to give up one inch of her international sovereignty. America thus took back in the spirit what she gave in the letter, and in the Kellogg Pact she showed the world a magnificent example of splendid isolation and power in terms of idealism.

The result was felt soon enough. The American President, after having congratulated himself and his nation on the idealism of the Kellogg Pact outlawing war, proceeded to advocate a strong navy to guarantee American defense. . . .

In our opinion the chief responsibility for the stagnant state of disarmament lies with the nations which remain outside the League. The League is a courageous attempt at solving world problems in a world way, and those who remain out of it are badly crippling this effort without contributing any positive alternative of a true constructive character.

We have heard many a so-called reason for the United States to remain outside. There is no reason whatsoever for such a thing. There are explanations of the fact; but though the fact may be explained, the act cannot be justified.

The American reader, however, may say that America has contributed an alternative and a better alternative in the doctrine of the outlawry of war. The outlawry-of-war doctrine is the best-meaning red herring that ever navigated in the waters of international thoughts and politics, but a red herring for all that. The worst about it is the high standing, the generosity, and even the intellectual distinction of its trainers and inspirers. Let us briefly recapitulate the tenets of the school and confront them with our own conclusions.

1. War must be outlawed as an institution—all wars without exception. But self-defense remains. No general guarantees are given of what a nation may come to consider as self-defense. For instance, if Mexico granted Japan a ninety-nine years' lease on a comfortable little bay in Lower California, the outlawry-of-war school does not tell us what would happen. Curiously enough, the outlawry-of-war school, while allowing self-defense, condemns sanctions. Yet sanctions, we know, is but another name for collective self-defense. We are therefore entitled to define the outlawry-of-war school as a party which condemns all wars except irresponsible self-defense; and the Covenant as a system which condemns all wars including irresponsible self-defense, except wars fought after collective self-defense has broken down.

2. There is going to be a world court with affirmative jurisdiction, "with a code of law of peace based upon equality and justice between all nations." This is excellent; but alas, we are told that "the greater nations know that compulsory arbitration is for them fraught with grave dangers." And moreover, "there are some questions which, in the present state of the world, or in any conceivable state of this world, cannot be decided by a tribunal of any sort. In the case of the United States we have only to think of tariffs, and immigration, and the Monroe Doctrine, and prohibition, and the allied debts, to see how a meddlesome nation, under cover of our pledge to arbitrate any dispute whatsoever, could provocatively precipitate an issue which was none of its business—in any sense which an independent country like the United States would acknowledge —and then demand that we go to arbitration with it." It is difficult to choose the brightest in such a string of pearls. We notice the "independent" nation (there's the rub—independent, yes, not merely in law but in spirit, cut loose, isolated from the commonalty of the world); we notice the imposing list of examples, for they are only examples, of the questions on which the United States would refuse to arbitrate; we observe that the Monroe Doctrine is one of these questions, and, knowing the admirable elasticity of this expression, we begin to wonder whether its scope can be limited even to the vast American continent.

Imagine France or Germany suggesting that she would arbitrate everything but European affairs!

This simple, nay, simple-minded panacea—the outlawry of war—holds the imagination of many an American citizen. You outlaw wars and you submit your differences to a court. What more perfect? This bald form is that under which it circulates and gathers converts. The holes, the gaps, the abysses, opened out in it by further elaboration do not appear before the public eye. They are believed to be just slight qualifications of the general principle, and not what they really are—its utter negation.

Then the outlawry-of-war school enables the American nation to bridge over the gap between its two favorite tendencies: the tendency to isolation (from Europe, at any rate), and the tendency to see itself as a leading nation in moral as well as in material progress. There is no question that the ethical urge is an earnest and sincere element in American psychology; hence the implicit demand of the public for moral international leadership on the part of the government. Now the government's task is not particularly easy. It must satisfy the public's pride in being 'good'; their pride in being strong; their romantic attachment to the no-entanglement advice which Washington is supposed to have given them; their mystical belief in the mystery of the Monroe Doctrine. In these circumstances is it strange that the government should have adopted this admirable pact, which gives everything in a magnificent general public principle, safeguards everything by means of rather intricate judicial-political inferences, and enables the United States to remain outside the Covenant of the League?

Unfortunately, the people of the United States have but few opportunities to hear a straightforward statement of the position. The immense majority of them honestly think that the United States is the only peace-loving nation with decent standards of international life. Few realize that their nation bears per-- haps the heaviest responsibility for the slow development of international peace. The absence of the United States from the League would suffice to justify this statement. It is sometimes argued on its behalf that it cooperates in nearly all the activities of the League. The observation is correct but irrelevant, for the main point is not movement, work, activity; it is trust, confidence, moral tone. And what is wanted is not merely that the United States should be represented in all the League commissions, but that it should assume all the League obligations. The issue has been befogged both by well-meaning fools and by ill-meaning knaves with an argument representing Europe as anxious to entangle America in European wars: "Europe wants your boys again." Such an argument leaves us cold. We, at any rate, want no American "boys" to come to Europe. We should be delighted if they stayed at home. We should be even delighted if they declined to go to Nicaragua. Our wish is that American boys should not go to war at all in any continent whatsoever. For it is all very well to speak of European politics as squabbles, intrigues, and wars; but had a European nation carried out in regard to another European nation exactly the policy which the United States has carried out in half a dozen Central American countries, there would have been a grave European war. The reason why the American continent is peaceful is not that the United States has succeeded in maintaining a higher level of international politics in it than in Europe, but that the United States, being incomparably stronger than any other of the American nations, has been free to develop whatever policy, high or low, it wished, without fear of endangering the peace of the continent.

It is not that we want America as an ally in Europe; we want her as a peaceful nation in America. We do not want her to strengthen League armies for League wars; we want her to strengthen the League's peace by bowing before the Covenant and submitting to the courts.

The responsibility of America is due to the fact that she gives the world a lesson of unlimited and irresponsible sovereignty every day. She does not accept the Court except under her own conditions, which fifty-five other nations consider inadmissible; she does not arbitrate except in a few cases, and when her Senate has carefully defined the issue; she does not join the League, but picks and chooses whichever points she wishes for cooperation, according to her own ideals, wishes, whims, or interests; she ignores the Covenant and brings forward an alternative scheme, as if the ten years of work done by practically all of the remaining nations had been the futile cackle of hens.

I am not—never was—of the opinion that America may be made to glide into the League in a kind of absent-minded way. I hold that the American people must face the issue squarely; that the nation must realize, on the one hand, the immense gravity of its responsibility while it remains outside, on the other the full meaning of its obligations if it joins. I believe that the very breadth and difficulty of the true position, once it is put squarely before the American people, are of a kind to appeal to their imagination. The American people have a remarkable psychology, a mobility amounting almost to fluidity; a genuine desire for what is good; an enterprising, an almost adventurous spirit, ready to experiment with new ideas; and, finally, a readiness to be led. That is why, though in my opinion the United States is the blackest obstacle in the path toward disarmament, I believe it to be also our brightest hope.

# 8 | Herbert Hoover's Armistice Day Address, Washington, November 1929 *

President Hoover, in his armistice day address of November 11, 1929, accepted the utopian assumptions of the age regarding peace and the means for its preservation. He lauded the decline of secret diplomacy and the recent world-wide renunciation of war. He admitted that peace was not static and that its mainte-

* *The State Papers and Other Public Writings of Herbert Hoover*, William Starr Myers, ed. (Garden City, N.Y., 1934), I: 125–32. Reprinted by permission of Herbert Hoover.

nance required effort, for international friction could not be eliminated from world relationships. But he found the answer to the tendency among nations to employ force in the power of an enlightened public opinion. Peace required above all, declared Hoover, the creation of "the spirit of good will and friendliness" among nations. Armed with this spirit, nations in conflict could not fail to discover a just formula for the settlement of any issue. Since armaments had lost their meaning, the President announced hopefully that he had inaugurated a new round of discussions on naval reduction.

. . . The world to-day is comparatively at peace. The outlook for a peaceable future is more bright than for half a century past. Yet after all it is an armed peace. The men under arms including active reserves in the world are almost 30,000,000 in number, or nearly 10,000,000 more than before the Great War. Due to the Washington Arms Conference and the destruction of the German Navy, the combatant ships in the world show some decrease since the war. But aircraft and other instruments of destruction are far more potent than they were even in the Great War. There are fears, distrusts, and smouldering injuries among nations which are the tinder of war. Nor does a single quarter of a century during all the ages of human experience warrant the assumption that war will not occur again.

Gloomy as this picture may be, yet we can say with truth that the world is becoming more genuinely inclined to peace; that the forces of imperial domination and aggression, of fear and suspicion are dying down; that they are being replaced with the desire for security and peaceful development. The old objectives of tortuous diplomacy are being replaced with frank and open relations directed to peace. There is no more significant step in this progress than the solemn covenant that civilized nations have now entered, to renounce war and to settle disputes by pacific means. It is this realignment of the mind of the world that gives the hope of peace.

But peace is not a static thing. To maintain peace is as dynamic in its requirements as is the conduct of war. We can not say "Let there be peace" and go about other business. Nor are the methods by which peace is to be maintained and war prevented to be established by slogans or by abstract phrases or by academic theory. Progress toward peace can be attained only as a result of realistic practical daily conduct amongst nations. It can be the result only of a frank recognition of forces which may disturb peace. For instance, we must realize that our industrial life, our employment, our comfort, and our culture depend greatly upon our interchange of goods and ideas with other nations. We must realize that this interchange can not be carried on unless our citizens are flung into every quarter of the globe and the citizens of every other nation are represented in our country.

We must realize that some of them will get into trouble somewhere. Certainly their troubles will multiply if other nations are at war. We have an obligation and every other nation has an obligation to see to the protection of their lives, and that justice is done to them so long as they comply with the laws of the countries in which they reside. From all these relationships frictions and controversies will arise daily.

By our undertaking under the Kellogg Pact, to use only pacific means to settle such controversies as these, we have again reaffirmed the doctrine enunciated by that far-sighted statesman, Mr. Elihu Root, in his famous declaration at Rio de Janeiro in 1907. At that time he announced that we would not use war or warlike means to enforce or collect upon private business contracts. It is our settled policy.

But there are other more deep-seated and more dangerous forces which produce friction and controversy than these eruptions over the rights of citizens. We must realize that there are many unsolved problems of boundaries between nations. There are peoples aspiring to a greater measure of self-government. There are the fears of invasion and domination bequeathed to all humanity from its former wars. There are a host of age-old controversies whose specters haunt the world, which at any time may touch the springs of fear and ill will.

We must frankly accept the fact, therefore, that we and all the nations of the world will be involved, for all future time, in small or great controversies and frictions arising out of all of these multiple causes. In these controversies lurks the subtle danger that national temper at any moment may become a heat and that emotion may rise to the flaming point. Therefore, peace must be the result of unceasing endeavor.

I have said that recently we have covenanted with other civilized nations not only to renounce war as an instrument of national policy but also we have agreed that we shall settle all controversies by pacific means. . . .

We are also interested that other nations shall settle by pacific means the controversies arising between them. From every selfish point of view the preservation of peace among other nations is of interest to the United States. In such wars we are in constant danger of entanglement because of interference with the widespread activities of our citizens. But of far more importance than this, our ideals and our hopes are for the progress of justice through the entire world. We desire to see all humanity relieved of the hideous blight of war and of the cruelties and injustices that lead to war. We are interested in all methods that can be devised to assure the settlement of all controversies between nations.

There are today two roads to that end. The European nations have, by the covenant of the League of Nations, agreed that if nations fail to settle their differences peaceably then force should be applied by other nations to compel them to be reasonable. We have refused to travel this road. We are confident that at least in the Western Hemisphere public opinion will suffice to check violence. This is the road we propose to travel. What we urgently need in this direction is a further development of methods for reference of unsettled controversies to joint inquiry by the parties assisted by friendly nations, in order that action may be stayed and that the aggressor may be subjected to the searchlight of public opinion.

And we have another task equally great as the settlement of incidental controversies. We must, where opportunity offers, work steadfastly to remove the deeper causes and frictions which lead to disputes and ill will. One of those causes is competition in armament. In order to stir a nation to the expenditures and burdens of increased armament, some danger and some enemy must be envisaged. Fears and distrust must be used as a goad to stir the Nation forward to competitive effort. No one denies that the maintenance of great armament is a burden upon the backs of all who toil. The expenditure for it curtails vast projects of human betterment which governments might undertake. Every man under arms means that some other man must bear an extra burden somewhere. But a greater cost is the ill will resulting from rivalry between nations in construction of armaments.

It is first and foremost to rid ourselves of this danger that I have again initiated naval negotiations. I have full confidence in the success of the conference which will assemble next January. In setting up this conference we have already agreed with Great Britain that there shall be a parity in naval strength between us. I am in hopes that there will be a serious reduction in navies as a relief to the economic burdens of all peoples. And I believe that men and women throughout the world demand such reduction. We must reduce and limit warships by agreement only. I have no faith in the reduction of armaments by example alone. . . .

Men of good will throughout the world are working earnestly and honestly to perfect the equipment and preparedness for peace. But there is something high above and infinitely more powerful than the work of all ambassadors and ministers, something far more powerful than treaties and the machinery of arbitration and conciliation and judicial decision, something more vital than even our covenants to abolish war, something more mighty than armies and navies in defense.

That is to build the spirit of good will and friendliness, to create respect and confidence, to stimulate esteem between peoples—this is the far greatest guaranty of peace. In that atmosphere, all controversies become but passing incidents of the day. Nor does this friendliness, respect, and esteem come to nations who behave weakly or supinely. It comes to those who are strong but who use their strength not in arrogance or injustice. It is through these means that we establish the sincerity, the justice, and the dignity of a great people. That is a new vision of diplomacy that is dawning in the world.

The colossal power of the United States overshadows scores of freedom-loving nations. Their defense against us is a moral defense. To give to them confidence that with the high moral sense of the American people this defense is more powerful than all armies or navies, is a sacred duty which lies upon us.

It has been my cherished hope to organize positively the foreign relations of the United States on this high foundation and to do it in reality, not simply in diplomatic phrases. The establishment of that relationship is vastly more important than the mere settlement of the details of any of our chronic international problems. In such pure air and in that alone can both sides with frankness and candor present their points of view and either find just formulas as for settlement, or, alternatively, agree to disagree until time finds a solution. We have in recent years heard a vast chatter of enmity and criticism both within and without our borders where there is no real enmity and no conflict of vital interest and no unsolvable controversy.

It is a homely parallel but equally true that relations between nations are much like relations between individuals. Questions which arise between friends are settled as the passing incidents of a day. The very same questions between men who distrust and suspect each other may lead to enmity and conflict.

It was in this endeavor that I visited the Presidents of the South American Republics. That is why I welcomed the visit of the Prime Minister of Great Britain to the United States.

All these men have talked of their problems in a spirit charged with the gravest responsibility, not only for our own relations but for the peace and safety of the world. We have thought out loud together as men can not think in diplomatic notes. We made no commitments. We drove no discussion to final conclusion. We explored the areas of possible constructive action and possible controversy. We examined the pitfalls of international relations frankly and openly. With this wider understanding of mutual difficulties and aspirations we can each in our own sphere better contribute to broaden good will, to assist those forces which make for peace in the world, to curb those forces which make for distrust. Thereby do we secure the imponderable yet transcendent spiritual gains which come from successful organization of peace and confidence in peace. That is why I have endeavored to meet the leaders of their nations, for I have no fear that we are not able to impress every country with the single-minded good will which lies in the American heart.

# 9 | Naval Reduction and the Commitments to Empire, 1929 *

During the summer of 1929 President Hoover pressed the British government for an agreement on the reduction of cruiser strength, an important category of vessel ignored by the Washington Treaties. The close relationship between naval power and British imperial policy, and by contrast the absence of that relationship in American policy, was revealed clearly by two letters of J. Ramsay MacDonald, the British Prime Minister, to the American Ambassador, Charles G. Dawes, in August and September 1929. MacDonald made it clear that he had no interest in naval parity with the United States, for he did not regard the American nation as a possible enemy of England; nor did he regard British involvement in a war of defense impossible.

✍

* MacDonald to Dawes, August 9, September 24, 1929, *Papers Relating to the Foreign Relations of the United States, 1929* (Washington, 1943), I: 186–8, 254–6.

. . . I have been studying very closely whilst in Lossiemouth the recent despatches sent to me in reply to my letter to you last week with a view to discovering whether I am able to meet Mr. Hoover's double desire to get parity as well as reduction. The crux of the problem is the cruiser category and upon that it is necessary for me to make one or two observations because I do not think that Mr. Hoover sees in detail what my position is and it is necessary that it should be understood.

1. Were the question of cruiser tonnage one between the United States and us alone there would be no difficulty. You could build as much as you like or as little as you like. I should not trouble, because the Government declines to make any provisions for the possibility of the United States being an enemy. Therefore I think that Washington is pressing me unduly when it asks me to reduce naval figures compiled solely on account of our needs in relation to the rest of the world.

2. American building however does affect me indirectly. Japan may say, were your cruisers much in excess of theirs, that whatever ratio it accepts must be in relation to the larger and not the smaller fleet. That owing to the United States building would compel me to retain a Japanese relationship which would impose a heavy program upon theirs [sic].

3. In order that an idea may be had of why our cruiser figures appear to be high, the following facts should in fairness be kept in mind.

(a) The British fleet is not one unit. If it were, I could reduce considerably. It is scattered into different and remote divisions each with functions to perform relating to peace and not to war conditions. I know that if war broke out concentration would naturally take place but that cannot be helped. I really cannot neglect peace duties in order to avoid the suspicion that war is in our minds all the time. . . .

(b) Put it another way. Australia, New Zealand and the numerous islands for which we are responsible in the southern Pacific, are policed by four cruisers in commission and two in reserve, and remember these are the only resources we have in the event of civil trouble or lawlessness breaking out. India, Burma, the Malay Straits, Somaliland, Kenya, the Persian Gulf, the Indian Ocean islands are policed by three cruisers and a few sloops which barely can make one visit a year to necessary ports. When one visualizes what the function and necessary work of the cruisers are and when my high figures are apportioned to duties, one begins to see the difficulty of a drastic reduction.

(c) The cruiser category for me is therefore only partly a fighting category and is to a considerable extent a police category. . . .

4. I have been working at a scheme which would make British figures in 1936 the standard of parity. Then without replacement in the meanwhile we should have fifteen 8-inch and thirty-four 6-inch ships, a total of forty-nine. I hope that you will see in the light of the above functions of cruisers that there is not much margin for reduction unless in the meantime by our united efforts we can make the world feel [differently toward?] peace. But I must deal with today and it is quite impossible for me to think of figures now which are remote from today—say beyond 1936. I shall, however, steadily reduce as national

security is found by other means than arms and I shall continue to work for that other security. . . .

5. If your President would agree to this 1936 position as being a temporary maximum goal to be worked for I can see my way to meet him, subject to the proviso I have made. . . .

6. I ought to say that that will leave me in a bit of a fix between 1936 and 1940 as cruisers fall out in bunches during these years to a total of no less than twenty-three but again that would be a matter of arrangment in manipulation of building. That might at times appear to be an increase but of course the whole scheme would be published so that mischief makers might be disarmed.

7. I again press for the production of some yardstick to let us see where we are in actual effective strength. Every text book and naval report I have consulted in order to be prepared for these conversations show that the 8-inch cruisers are worth in the event of a fight almost an infinity of smaller craft and guns. . . .

8. I emphasize the obligations placed upon me by my geographical position which the United States does not have to bear. That makes the Five-Power Conference so important to me, and I could only go as far as I have proposed if that conference is a success.

9. It has been suggested that we might come to a covering political agreement by which after settling figures between ourselves we might provide that, in the event of other powers building so as to [cause] either party disquiet, our agreement might be varied in consequence. We may have to resort to this, but (a) it would leave uncertainty and a possibility of serious disagreement, and (b) would lay both of us open to press stunts and manufactured panics. It should be used only as a last expedient.

10. I have explained the need we have for cruisers to a minimum figure irrespective of programs which compete with any other nation; I have made another suggestion for solving the problem, what the standard of parity should be, and understand that Mr. Gibson has some suggestions to advance upon that in relation to the yardstick and a transfer of destroyer tonnage to cruiser denominations that however may be dangerous in the light of the Five-Power Conference problems. I am also examining the possibility of smaller police craft. I hope I have made it clear that I shall go to the utmost possible length to meet Mr. Hoover. But there are things I cannot do. I cannot take the necessary police off the seas and I cannot make an agreement with America alone which leaves me at the mercy of powers with which I have no agreement or a very imperfect one. I believe that our somewhat different requirements can be met but give and take and a yardstick are required.

. . . This parity business is of Satan himself. I am sure it has struck the President as it has me as being an attempt to clothe unreality in the garb of mathematical reality. Opinion in the United States demands it and the Senate will accept nothing which does not look like it. On my side I am not interested in it at all. I give it to you with both hands heaped and running down. When I am forced to scrutinize your program which you say embodies it, I turn from you altogether and have to think of things which, but for my importunities, you would not think much about, viz., the fleets of other nations. Therefore, although in our talks with each other, we assume that the discussion takes place between us two, that is really not the case. There are shadowy entities behind me. A spirit photograph would show you unaccompanied, but round me would be the ghosts of the other nations. In its ultimate, the parity we are trying to devise is one between you and the rest of the world in relation to the British position in it. If the appearance of parity is to be obtained, neither of us can get away from the fact that the standard must be fixed by British needs. The tides of events swelling upwards and downwards, backwards and forwards, change our defense problems every year and with that the figures change.

Now what am I trying to do? First and foremost, I am trying to stop the daily swell so that we may fix levels which cannot be exceeded and then create a confidence which will permit those levels to be steadily lowered. I want to substitute the security of peace for that of military preparation. But if in the lowering we act impatiently there will be a break back. That psychological fact fixes my present limits. Stabilization downwards is the only road by which Europe will move to disarmament. . . .

The major difficulty is indeed with the 8-inch cruiser. If the three biggest naval powers would agree first of all to a ratio of 6.5.4 (18.15.12) that, as I am advised, would be a world equilibrium unless some of the other powers disturbed it. But Japan wishes instead of two-thirds of the largest cruiser fleet, 70 percent, though, on an American force of eighteen, it might be induced to build no more than twelve. It would certainly want more than twelve on twenty-one and then we should have to move up our figure of fifteen by four or five and the whole plan would fall to the ground.

This is so important that I must emphasize it. If I had the shadow of dread that the United States and ourselves would ever be at war, it would be impossible for me to agree to parity being expressed by any number of 8-inch cruisers beyond our own, e.g., 15. I should be willing to refer the inclosures [issue?] to any body of able and impartial authorities on sea warfare to decide between us and I should be assured of their verdict. But that is not in my mind at all. Everybody here is anxious to accommodate themselves to an agreement with you on the assumption that there will be no war and no interference in which our fleets are involved. But I am not justified in making the same assumption as regards the rest of the world, and Mr. Kellogg himself used language which justifies that.

He referred to the possibilities of wars of defense. I may regret it, but he did it, and if I am to get Parliament to agree to our programs I cannot at the moment overlook that fact. . . .

Perhaps no American in the early 'thirties saw more clearly the absence of realism in the nation's foreign policies than did Lewis Einstein. Whereas Hoover spoke of the bright outlook for peace, Einstein pointed to the almost universal tendency toward war which centered in Europe itself. Should these tendencies lead to war, the United States, predicted Einstein, would be as unprepared as it was in 1914. The problem, he saw, was that of creating a foreign policy acceptable to the American people and still capable of influencing events abroad. The writer attributed the lack of long-range United States foreign policy to the propensity of each administration to employ external policy for the purpose of elevating its own popularity and prestige.

🖋

In his address on Armistice Day last year, President Hoover declared that "the outlook for peace is happier than for half a century." Six and a half million Hitlerites in Germany had just voted for a programme bred by misery and which, if carried out, can only end in war; and four million German Communists had voted for upheaval. Mussolini had repeated his speech of last spring: "Words are beautiful, rifles and cannon are still better," and openly professed his belief in war within the next few years. Soviet Russia remained an outlaw State, planning to bring about World Revolution. Austria was overawed by armed bands and Hungary continued truculent and revengeful. Spain was in the throes of a dangerous crisis; France, Poland and the Little Entente were arming, not without cause, suspicious of their neighbors. Outside Europe, South America had been swept by a wave of revolution, India stirred by dangerous unrest, and in China civil war continued!

It has been said that the only lesson of history is that no nation will profit by it. Today the world is out of joint. If the events which led up to August, 1914, should tomorrow be repeated, as many now believe, we would be found quite as unprepared as we were then. . . .

The average American reads news from abroad without associating this with himself. He is unaware that the question whether Europe is to have peace or war may be decided by our action or inaction during the next few years and that we may pay dearly for our want of foresight. We are building a merchant marine, trying to increase our exports and foreign investments, and remaining blind to the consequences of economic expansion. If American business interests in Europe are unfairly treated, the Administration is expected to defend them. If war breaks out this protection will call for more than words. Even without war we may find that the future basis of European unity will be reached by a common front erected against us.

* Lewis Einstein, "Our Still Dubious Foreign Policy," *The North American Review*, CCXXXII (September 1931), 210–18.

The problem lies in searching for a policy which, while acceptable to the American people, will allow us to exercise an effective influence for peace, and a means of cooperation with other nations, though we have made this more difficult than it need have been by our careless neglect of advantages enjoyed.

When some future Gibbon writes the recent history of the United States he will hardly know whether to be more amazed by the magnitude of American effort in the Great War or the wastage of benefits which victory lavished so bountifully in our favor. An inability to understand our interests beyond their immediate horizon, a timorousness of responsibility, a neglect of diplomacy and an absence of leadership, had caused us to fritter away in recent years the unparalleled ascendancy America had until then enjoyed in Europe. . . .

A qualified belief in disarmament subject to reservations, a qualified belief in arbitration, subject to further reservations, and a qualified desire to adhere to the World Court offers a meagre programme of international expression for the United States. Beyond current platitudes of peace and good-will, beyond a predilection for forms of legal remedy which we are only ready to accept for questions of secondary interest, beyond pushing our dwindling exports on an impoverished Europe, what more has been our recent foreign policy?

This negativeness of attitude has led to an odd divergence between our official and non-official conduct. Not a few American citizens have lent their aid to carry out important duties in which as a nation, since the Dawes Commission met, we disclaimed taking any interest. European powers on several occasions have invited our nationals to participate in affairs which properly belonged to the United States but which the Administration had become too timorous to asume. Officially we took no effective part in conferences like that of the Hague and remained content to send there merely an observer. But Elihu Root, Parker Gilbert and Owen Young, Jeremiah Smith in Hungary and Charles Dewey in Poland have performed tasks of which every American should be proud. The success achieved by our citizens in matters of international importance has not always been viewed at Washington with the favor deserved. Yet if the Administration fears risk in the assumption of duties abroad, these will be performed by private American citizens with fewer disadvantages to the work than to our governmental prestige.

The dread of criticism and the unwillingness to assume any avoidable risk tend to narrow the expression of our foreign policy either to a strict minimum in situations and emergencies which can not be avoided, or to handling only those from which political benefit may be anticipated. Questions arising have been restrained within the narrowest limits and generally reduced to reactions or precautions taken in view of different forms of domestic pressure.

A process of undue restriction unconsciously takes place in an Administration's survey of foreign intercourse. Problems which may not seem of immediate importance are usually left in neglect. Instance of this want of comprehension can be found in the blindness of Washington to the warnings of the Great War. Another Administration was then in power, but almost the only continuity in our policy has been in the similarity of its methods. The self-deception which allows us to justify our want of interest in Europe by our interest in the Western

Hemisphere is a poor defense. The Monroe Doctrine which we continue to brandish from time to time is no more exposed to danger today than the multiplication table. Any pretense to the contrary is a mummery intended to catch the applause of the uninformed but which uselessly alarms our so-called sister republics and suggests arguments to foreign nations which can also be brought against us. . . .

In his recent address before the Bar Association of New York, John Bassett Moore, former judge of the World Court, described our policy toward Latin America as one which "provokes resentment and risks disaster" by its meddlesomeness. He characterized as a violation of the laws of neutrality and of international law Secretary Stimson's placing an embargo on munitions to the Brazilian revolutionists only to find these victorious forty-eight hours later. The same eminent jurist on this occasion described our contradictory relations with the Soviet as approaching "the limit of human incoherence." We invited Russia to sign a pact for the renunciation of war while refusing her recognition.

Since Mr. Hughes left the State Department it is difficult to point to any important achievement in our international relations. Mr. Kellogg's Peace Treaty flashed like a meteor across the sky, seen by all, praised by many, believed in by few and almost forgotten as soon as discussions over naval limitation began. As a Pact it is subordinated to reservations which deprive it of most of its value except as a gesture. Its warmest supporters have recognized the desirability of implementing a treaty officially proclaimed as forming part of our foreign policy. President Hoover on Armistice Day intimated that eventually there may be "the mobilization of world opinion against those who fail when the strain comes," but this suggestion did not meet with any warm response. The President had in mind a consultative pact but refrained from publicly announcing this. That such a pact would really be advantageous is doubtful. Before the Balkan Wars the Concert of the Great Powers in the Near East, which was much the same thing under another name, had become a byword for inaction. Consultation between governments is always feasible, but to stipulate its binding nature beforehand without being able to assure agreement, is to focus attention on dissensions and emphasize every point of discord. A pact of this nature would provide a target to shoot at and guarantee nothing except talk.

At the time of writing it would be premature to judge the effects of the President's plan as the policy which remains to be developed from this is still undivulged. President Hoover, without real risk, could take a step for world peace, the benefits of which would be felt politically and economically and help us regain some of our lost prestige. The fear of war disturbs capital and arrests new undertakings. If this fear can be allayed and we can convince Europe that our wish for peace means something more than words, the first great step will have been taken toward restoring confidence which is at the basis of prosperity.

The President could announce that he would recommend to the Senate holding strictly to account any country which, after signing a solemn Pact for the Renunciation of War, refused to live up to its agreement. We may have no direct interest in the affairs of the Old World or in defending Peace Treaties which two million Americans crossed the ocean to secure, but if revision takes place, this should not be brought about through another World War. The President could solemnly affirm that a heavy responsibility will rest on whoever henceforth disturbs the peace of nations and that we are prepared to decide for ourselves who is the aggressor. With the Senate's approval we should take our part in punishing an international crime and the violation of a treaty to which we are a party.

A declaration of this nature threatens no peaceful State and makes for no entanglement. It reaffirms our traditional independence of action and neither shuts the door on cooperation with other nations whose views are similar to ours, nor compels this. It would be a frank statement of policy which should commend itself to the American people, enhance our prestige and arouse a new interest in our international expression.

On the rare occasions when a problem of foreign policy excites public opinion the violence of discussion at home makes up for its frequently secondary importance. Its true significance is distorted while it is examined with a scrutiny which similar questions meet with in no other nation. Foreign countries have joined the International Court merely as a matter of routine; only in the United States has this threatened to become an issue of grave political consequence.

The feeling aroused can hardly be attributed to an excess of popular interest in foreign policy. Other nations are more dependent on the security of their international situation. Yet rarely does a European opposition seriously criticize the government with respect to foreign affairs. This immunity is not due to the negligible powers of other legislative bodies or to a lesser spirit of partisanship. It comes from greater continuity of policy removed from party strife, and from greater confidence entertained in the permanent officials who in Europe conduct diplomacy.

The controversy which raged in the United States around questions like the Naval Treaty was due more to extraneous causes than to its merits. Outwardly one saw only a fundamentalist attitude of opposition based ostensibly on nationalism and suspicion. President Hoover was deservedly successful in beating down this obstruction and the Naval Treaty was paraded as the greatest success of his foreign policy. Mr. Macdonald in England signed the same treaty but claimed no such result and was frank enough to admit that its provisions did not come up to his expectations. Mr. Hoover's success was not over Great Britain, still less was it over Japan or France or Italy. It could therefore only be over certain United States Senators who had opposed the Treaty. The greatest victory in foreign policy claimed by an Administration has been one obtained over refractory members of a coordinate branch of the Government. . . .

The fact is that every administration assumes a personal rather than a continuous view of those questions of external policy which it chooses to elevate. The conduct of our foreign relations becomes in consequence almost artificially separated between the routine of departmental bureaus in which it remains hidden, and the questions which the President brings forward into prominence to become embellished or distorted from the standpoint of individual or partisan advantage.

As soon as opposition to these develops, it is customary for Administration sympathizers to lay the blame on malice, or the Senate's undue jealousy of its constitutional rights. A legislative body may be little adapted to assuming a dispassionate attitude toward foreign policy, but is not always impressed by the enlightened omniscience of an executive.

Constitutionally the President is able to develop his conduct of foreign affairs with the widest latitude until the doorway of the Senate is reached. It can hardly be maintained that some restrait is undesirable or that an uncontrolled executive will always use its powers wisely. President Wilson tried on his own initiative to saddle America with the Armenian Mandate and failed to grasp its terrifying consequences.

After opposition shows its head, strong Presidents like Roosevelt and Wilson have, at times, obtained enough popular approval behind them to carry out their purpose, but a struggle is always latent between the executive and the Senate in which the protagonists may overweight the issue.

The real losers in these fights are the American people. The spectacle of a nation divided over a question of foreign policy which in no other country could become a party issue, the bandying of invective and the atmosphere of hostility aroused, is little elevating either to our own opinion or in the picture we present to the world. Even materially the diminution in prestige reacts to our detriment abroad. . . .

The undue concentration of powers in a President who can not be a world expert but who is a party chief, is likely to lead to a diplomacy at once amateurish, constipated and unreliable, whenever one Administration reverses what its predecessor had done. Perhaps no President will be ready to divest himself of his apparent responsibility or any shreds of his vast power in order to organize the conduct of foreign policy along more permanent non-partisan lines. At least it is conceivable that if this could be tried, the executive relations with the Senate might also become different. By a paradox, no President will obtain full credit for his direction of our foreign relations until able to persuade the country that he seeks to obtain from these no personal advantage. The Senate may only cease to be obstructive when convinced at last that the Executive expects to derive no personal benefit from foreign policy. Possibly along these lines the real compromise of cooperation between President and Senate must be looked for which will restore the prestige of the American Government to its rightful place, and allow us to assert our proper influence for peace.

## 11 | National Power and Moral Influence: America's Role in the 'Twenties *

That the United States during the 1920's was a nation of enormous influence in world affairs was clear enough from the record. It had taken the lead in such movements as naval disarmament and the outlawry of war. Because of its wealth and demonstrated military power, especially when contrasted to that of the potentially dissatisfied nations of Europe and Asia, the United States had acquired the position in world politics held by England during the century that followed Waterloo. Yet by 1930, noted Edwin L. James, the American journalist, the nation's predominance in international affairs had already begun to decline, for that position had always been anchored to the complete military and political dominance, in Europe especially, of the *status quo* powers. It had been the strength of the great democracies, not their moral influence, that had maintained the stability of the 'twenties. Now that the recovery of Europe again challenged the unique and temporary superiority of the United States and its allies of World War I, it was apparent to James that the world of the next decade would pay decreasing heed to American exhortations.

✎

The material situation of the United States of America is such that the resulting political influence is enormous, so enormous that a failure to place its true value on it may be explained by the circumstance that it has not yet made its real force felt to a degree that will surely materialize.

There is no country where the power of the dollar has not reached. There is no capital which does not take the United States into consideration at almost every turn. Conversely, there is no zone where our interests are not involved. Isolation is a myth. We are not isolated and cannot be isolated. The United States is ever present.

Officially, our government stays out of world organizations. We scorn the League of Nations; we continue to shy at the World Court. But such things count for less and less. We must deal with the world and the world must deal with us. Let there be an international conference, and the imponderable influences bring the United States there. A conference on reparations, we are there. The International Bank is set up, an American is made president. The World Court meets, an American is put on the bench. A naval conference gathers, and the whole business hangs largely on the American position. And so on, ad infinitum.

It is always the case that the American position is among the most important. Such is one of the prices of our power. Few world problems arise in which the

* Edwin L. James, "Our World Power and Moral Influence," *The International Digest,* I (October 1930), 21–4.

influence of the United States will not swing the decision if we take a real interest. Opposition to the United States is a serious undertaking. Our dollars are powerful; there are so many of them.

Take the tariff. Such is the breadth of the trade of the United States that no nation ignores our markets. A higher duty voted in Washington affects work in countless cities abroad. Conversely, higher duties voted in foreign capitals may affect work in our cities from one seaboard to the other.

It is always a question of what the United States does or is going to do. No European nation plans peace without taking America into account. Nor will any European nation plan war without seeking to find out what is the attitude of Washington on the issues at stake. Supplies of credit, food and munitions from the United States mean one situation especially if our navy guarantees our shipments crossing the Atlantic successfully, and the lack of those supplies means quite another thing. Geneva can make no blockade which we do not recognize because there are no League members who will take a serious chance of antagonizing the United States.

Indeed, the position and power of this country is rapidly reaching the point when it will be said that we have gained the relative position which Great Britain held from the Battle of Waterloo up to 1914, which France held for approximately a century preceding and which through history belonged for varying periods to various nations. For all the indications point to this being our century.

To a large degree world greatness has been thrust upon us. It has come to us through the force of circumstances not all of our own making. That, by chance, may explain why nationally we have not come fully to realize where we are.

But there are signs in every direction that the situation which has been so mobile, with everything moving in our direction, is becoming stabilized. The current toward the United States is slackening. Things should tend to stabilize. In other words, in the next decade our progress will not be so great because it cannot bring the same increase in power as we enjoyed in the last ten years.

Furthermore, what we win in the next ten years we shall have to strive for to a much greater degree than since the war. The game of keeping our own markets for ourselves by shutting out foreign goods and at the same time enjoying the markets of other countries is going to be more and more difficult. Europe is back on its feet again and able to compete with us in the world markets.

But if the shake-up is largely over, it was surely to our advantage. The aftermath of the war has left the United States sitting on the top of the world. The predominance of our economic and financial position extends in every direction and is an example being used by the exponents of the movements for a Federated Europe and an economically united British Commonwealth of Nations.

It is generally realized in the United States how great the nation is economically. But there is not yet a realization of the great political power our material position has brought us. And whether we will use that power when we feel it as other nations have or whether we will use it in a new and different manner— there is the greatest question of world politics.

Just as an American observer who has been living in Europe gets the idea, on returning to the United States, that popularly there is an underestimation of the political power which America's material position has given us, he also finds what, looked upon from the other side, seems to be an exaggeration of the moral world influence of the United States.

America's great world political position is not due primarily to our moral leadership but primarily to our wealth and economic position. That is true because it is not to our moral teachings that the rest of the world responds, but to our material power. If we were a poor and weak nation the world would to-day care no more about what we thought than did the world before the Great War.

It is not difficult to understand why the Old World does not take our exhortations to heart any more. There is the old story of the League of Nations. There is the World Court. There are other things, like the International Bank—all of which seem to represent our advice to others as to how to do their business, while we do ours some other way.

Now those who still believe that "the moral sense" of America is a real factor in international affairs will surely cite the Kellogg pact as an example of how we do good and do it altruistically. But no one who has lived in Europe in recent years can believe in the dominant moral effect of the Kellogg pact as an active factor in world affairs. Almost the only attraction Europe ever saw in it was the line the United States signed on. No European nation promised anything in the anti-war pact that it had not already agreed to in the covenant of the League of Nations. But there was the signature of the United States, which seemed to promise the co-operation of our great material power in curbing the aggressor in another war. And that made a powerful appeal. But this appeal lay not in any new religion the Kellogg pact brought to a soul-hungry world. It was based on the great political power of America because of our enormous wealth and potential military and naval power.

Does any one believe seriously that the deference and respect Britain has shown for us in the past decade represent a belief in our moral superiority, a realization of a superior civilization on this side of the Atlantic or a better system of government and social order? Not at all. Britain is extremely practical in foreign affairs. There is no new approval of America and Americans, but there is a realization of our material power as something to be reckoned with seriously, and Britain does just that. . . .

Of course, there have been, in the past, indications pointing to a real influence of our moral advice. In the first five years after the World War the nations of Europe, on their backs and seeking American aid, took all pains to avoid offending us and therefore appeared to give careful and weighty consideration to our altruistic advice. The succeeding five years changed that. To-day, Europe, to a rapidly increasing degree, feels itself getting back to where it may treat with us on a plane of equality. And that puts Europe in a position to do what the Old World likes about our advice. More and more we shall hear that words unaccompanied by acts will not be taken as seriously as in the past.

But Europeans do know the importance of America in the world. Because they are more used to studying and judging world affairs than we are, they realize, perhaps better than we do, just how important is the United States. Their eyes are on us all the time. They must reckon with us; they must do business with us. And so they must know what we are doing and what we may be going to do. That gives us our great importance and out of that grows our influence. Although not exercised as actively as it will be later on, American world political power is interestingly important not only because of its might, but because of its present under-development.

## 12 | Manchuria: A Warning to the United States, February 1933 *

The observations of Einstein and James, that the world was no longer stable or manageable through the techniques of moral exhortation which had appeared so successful throughout the 'twenties, proved to be accurate when the Japanese assaulted Manchuria in 1931. The period of grace for the victorious democracies of World War I had come to a close. The challenge of the 'thirties was clear: these *status quo* powers would either permit a series of major modifications in the Versailles system, both in Europe and in Asia, or fight to preserve that system. Nathaniel Peffer, in an article published in February 1933, demonstrated that this was the essential issue presented by Japanese aggression. Peace in the Far East, warned Peffer, required a willingness of all the Western powers with interests in China to stop their encroachments on that country, for the Japanese would never withdraw their forces from China until they were convinced that the other nations also would abide scrupulously by the principle of the Open Door. The United States, as the leading defender of China, had overreached in the Pacific; now it would pay the price, declared Peffer, of either withdrawing its commitments or engaging in eventual war.

✍

A year has passed since Japan's absorption of Manchuria presented the most serious threat to world peace since 1918 and the first concrete test of all the hopes, plans, and devices contrived for the prevention of war. It is time to take a reckoning.

Two items stand out in such a reckoning.

First America, while clinging to the fiction of isolation from Europe, has become definitely, alarmingly, and perhaps inextricably involved in Asia.

* Nathaniel Peffer, "Manchuria: A Warning to America," *Harper's Magazine,* **CLXVI** (February 1933), 301–8. Reprinted by permission of the estate of Nathaniel Peffer.

Second: The promise of control of war by international machinery has proved illusive. For despite the concurrent ceremonials of League of Nations meetings, international commissions, invocations of peace pacts, and "the technic of peace by conference," Japan has acted as it would have acted before 1914. It wanted Manchuria and has taken it. The League of Nations and the Kellogg Pact might as well not have been.

It is not my intention here to discuss questions of Far Eastern international politics or the Manchurian controversy. They have been sufficiently aired, and the issue has now passed far beyond their intrinsic importance. Nor do I wish to labor the obvious point that the League has failed. For the point is not so much that the League has failed as that it never had a chance to succeed. And in this point lies the innermost truth of the Manchurian controversy, of the whole Far Eastern question, and of all international relations for that matter. The larger significance of the Manchurian episode and its aftermath is just this, that it is the perfect laboratory specimen of how international conflicts are made, how not to attempt to unmake them, and also how they might be averted if we were willing to pay the price. What it shows is that peace cannot be achieved through mechanisms, that there can be no peace so long as the causes of war remain—that is, so long as nations strive for objects which can be attained only by the use of armed force.

This truth, platitudinous and commonly ignored, has never been more completely ignored than in the last year. Underlying all the organized efforts to deal with the Manchurian affair—and never before has so conscious and systematic an effort been made to deal with an international dispute—has been the premise that this was a "crisis," to be "settled" by bringing about a cessation of fighting and a compromise between the disputants, after which peace would be secure. There has been no disposition to face the conditions in the Far East which produce conflicts like this one, which have produced them before, and will do so again unless they are changed.

The Manchurian affair has been treated as an event isolated in time and space, as beginning in 1931, restricted to a region north of the Great Wall of China, and concerning only Japan and China, whereas in fact it has roots running back almost a hundred years and extending to Europe and North America. It is the latest phase of an old struggle and can be understood only in its setting.

This struggle has two aspects, which are interrelated. The first is between China and all the Powers which have appropriated parts of its territory, acquired special privileges on its soil, and otherwise nullified its sovereignty. The issue is whether China will regain its independence or remain the spoils of high politics. The second is among those Powers for the exclusive right to dominate China. The stake is the profits from China's material development. . . .

For Japan the question is not so simple as whether it shall keep Manchuria or China shall have it back. It is whether Japan shall keep Manchuria or China shall have it back or some other Power shall take it. The Japanese came to their second maturity in the harsh and ugly world of the end of the nineteenth century, a world in which the strong took what they could wherever they could. Japan was itself for a generation the victim of the same process to which China was subjected, and if it escaped China's fate, the explanation is partly in its own miraculous effort but mainly in the happy accident that it was near China and China was the bigger prize. To the rival aspirants for Eastern empire Japan was by comparison small pickings. Moreover, Japan watched the relentless approach of the dismemberment of China—until given pause by the outbreak of the World War—knowing that whatever Power appropriated the largest share would have a weapon against Japan itself. Out of the fear begotten by that threat it had to fight Russia in 1904. A definite psychology was formed in the mind of the Japanese. They cannot believe that relinquishment of Manchuria necessarily means its retention by China. They cannot believe that 1914 was more than an interruption. And they may be right. It may be that a new international ethic was born of the lessons of the War and that the race for empire has been abandoned in the East; and it may be that the great powers are only winded and that when they recover their wind the race will be resumed, each spurred now by the redoubled need for foreign markets. If the latter be true, then obviously it would be fatal for Japan not to take advantage of their exhaustion and consolidate its position of mastery when it can. And thus may be explained the motives of Japan's aggressive policy since the Twenty-one Demands of 1915 and its obduracy before world opinion since 1931. Thus may be explained the failure of the League's intervention into the Manchurian conflict and Japan's rejection of the Lytton report.

The League did not fail, however. It did not try. From the first hastily convoked meeting of the Council to the formal debates on the Lytton report it never took cognizance of considerations such as have just been outlined. And without facing them any attempt to deal with the Far East was unreal. It did not touch the root causes of the conflict it was trying to stop. It dealt only with effects. To have gone to the underlying causes might have been unpleasant, since it would have put others besides Japan on the defensive; but without doing so there was no hope of restoring peace in the Far East. . . .

When the balance of all the forces working on history in the Far East is taken, the resultant will be found to be the definitive entry of the United States into the East. The United States has not only intervened but made unequivocal commitments and thereby, with or without deliberate intent, moved to a new position in world affairs. The pronouncements of the American government with reference to Manchuria, so glibly hailed by liberals, will constitute, unless revoked, a pledge and policy no less binding than the Monroe Doctrine but infinitely harder to effectuate. They will embroil us in the most inflammable area in the world; make us the protagonist of the *status quo* in a region where the *status quo* is inherently unstable; enroll us as a partisan in a congeries of crusty international feuds, and, unless revoked, will have a more positive influence on the course of our history than the Monroe Doctrine, since they concern a part of the world more contested than South America and state a position less easy to defend. And of this fact the American people remain singularly unaware and wholly uncritical.

Mr. Stimson, as Secretary of State, has formally announced, not once but twice, that the American government does not recognize what has taken place in Manchuria. He has said that the American government will not recognize political changes brought about by force in contravention of the Kellogg Pact, and by more than inference has so classified the changes in Manchuria. In his studied words before the Council on Foreign Relations in New York he explicitly characterized the formation of the new state of Manchukuo under the aegis of Japan as "fruits of aggression." Mr. Stimson has not said, however, how the American government will implement its declaration.

Unfortunately the occasion will arise when this will have to be determined. It cannot be evaded. Either all the events since September, 1931, are nullified and Manchuria returns to the status it then occupied or Manchuria remains Manchukuo, a fiction for Japanese hegemony. The American government says Manchuria is still a part of China; Japan says it is Manchukuo, an independent state under Japanese advisers. There is no possibility of evasion or compromise. . . .

Saving only the possibility of an economic catastrophe, Japan will not yield. That can be said with dogmatic certainty. Since Japan won South Manchuria from Russia there has been no time when it has not stood ready to fight to extinction to defend its position. On that point there is no division within Japan. There are no Japanese who would not support the government on Manchuria. The so-called Japanese liberals, of whom so much is made by certain elements in America, are a creation of the imagination of finely tempered but innocent Americans who go junketing about the world on good-will tours and believe what they hear at banquets and stageset laymen's conferences. As we understand the word liberal, there are few Japanese liberals, if any. Such as are liberal are without influence. Those commonly designated as liberal are semi-official apologists. The Japanese people will support their government on Manchuria. Against the United States they will support it on anything.

For the United States it will be awkward to yield. For one thing, its prestige is now engaged. More important, the American government has not acted out of caprice or impulse. It has brought into the open a tendency latent for a generation, though but dimly felt and to the American people unknown. With Europe, with which we have racial kinship, cultural affinity, common historical origins and evolution, and economic relations so close that a bank failure on the Danube causes shoe factories in Missouri to go into bankruptcy—with Europe we will not be "involved." But we leap to defiance over the Manchurian plains of Asia, straight into "entanglement" in an area which has produced more wars in the last hundred years than Europe. Our trade there is trifling, our vested interest negligible, our residents there could be housed in a hotel of moderate size. Why, then? It is not our present material stake that draws us. What is it? Nor is this entirely new. For a generation we have been moving in the same direction. For twenty years we have stood squarely in the way of Japan's aggrandizement. Where Japan has been obstructed, as it has been in China, in Manchuria, and in Siberia, the obstruction has been of American making. Whether or not Japan's grandiose dreams imperil world security is another matter. They do, of course, but that is irrelevant in this connection. The point is that America, four thousand miles away and without any tangible interest at stake, takes upon itself the burden of the defense of the *status quo,* deliberately giving the challenge to a militant, determined Power. Why?

Can it be that America has a manifest destiny? Is there some mystic drive that impels us ever westward? As soon as the first settlements had been cleared we started toward the Pacific, reached it, leaped half across to the Hawaiian Islands, and then all the way across to the Philippines. Immediately then our interest in China lifted, and Secretary Hay spoke for the Open Door. Is there in the restless American spirit the unexpressed, inarticulate conviction that Asia is our oyster, ours to open and ours to pluck the pearl? Is that what motivates the otherwise unexplainable determination of our government in the Far East? Have we a destiny, and incidentally do the American people know it, and are they prepared to pay the price that national destinies exact?

These are the questions that are being asked in the Far East and elsewhere, everywhere, in fact, more than in America. Most of all they are being asked in Japan. The cardinal point of reference for Japan's foreign policy is America. China is its theater of action, but toward America is its polarization. When Japanese who think of the political future of their country look out on their world they face America: *voilà l'ennemi.* It is not the attempted restraint by the League of Nations that has aroused Japanese resentment since the beginning of the Manchurian affair; it is the succession of pronouncements by the American government. It is not the League that is held to blame for the strictures on Japan emanating from Geneva, but America for having goaded the League to action. And in that position there is some reason, for Great Britain and France plainly have come as reluctant judges and more reluctant prosecutors.

America and Japan stand at deadlock on Manchuria. Japan will not yield. If America yields it will be for the first time on any important measure of foreign policy on which it has taken a positive stand, and it will be on something, moreover, that lies deeper than prestige or present material interest. What then? By every historical analogy, by all political precedent, Japan and America are to-day where England and Germany were in, say, 1907. If they drift, if the forces now making are allowed to gather, then by every precedent they will come to the same culmination. If we really are concerned about world peace we shall not worry ourselves about machinery and treaties and conferences and commissions. We shall face this fact and deal with it in time.

Concretely, there are two possible courses of action. One is for the American people—not one in five of whom can place Manchuria on a map without search—to ask themselves whether Manchuria means enough to them to risk their fortunes, their future, and the lives of their sons on its disposition. And more is involved than a single war. America would then be caught in a welter of rivalries in what would be worse than the Balkans and from which a succession of wars would result. For no one can be so credulous as to believe that if America should go to war with Japan over Manchuria and win—as it will, by reason of greater economic resources, though only after a long war—it will then return Manchuria to China as before 1931. Instead, it will keep hegemony over Manchuria itself. It will have to; and it will want to. And it will inherit all the resentments, jealousies, and hostilities now Japan's. If the American people

believe that Manchuria means enough for them to be willing to face this prospect, they will let their government proceed on its course and stand behind it,
as the Japanese people do theirs. If not, they will consolidate public opinion to
bring pressure on their government to withdraw from positions which expose
them to risks they are unwilling to take. But this is a counsel of perfection—
or of despair. There is no instrument by which democracies can control their
foreign affairs. The public does not initiate or deliberate and then give its
government mandates for action. Men in governments make commitments,
and then it is a point of honor as well as duty to stand by the government. None
asks then whether the individuals or groups in office made their commitments
with wisdom and with the consent of the governed. By then the hostage of
patriotism has been given.

The second course of action is to do as the League of Nations did not
attempt to do. That is for the great Powers to face the causes of conflict in the
Far East and eradicate them. Fundamentally there is no other course. To deal
with individual incidents like the present one in Manchuria is futile, even if
successful, for there will be others like it. Manchuria is only one phase of a
disorder in the Far East so deep-seated as to be organic. That disorder has been
produced by at least fifty years of competitive aggression on China by the great
nations. In the lust for imperial power which intoxicated the Western world in
the second half of the nineteenth century and plunged it into orgies of conquest in Africa and Asia, China was marked out for spoilation. But there were
many rivals for the spoils and they could neither agree on a division nor eliminate one another. All the great Powers sparred, and Russia and Japan fought it
out. . . .

There can be no peace in the Far East so long as there are rival ambitions for
mastery of China. There can be no peace unless those ambitions are slaked or
renounced. The first can come only as the consummation of a succession of wars.
There is no alternative but the second. What we can do constructively is not
wait for the next eruption and then attempt to deal with it isolated from
the conditions which gave rise to it, but act in advance by way of prevention.
If our desire for peace is truthfully measured by the implications of the Covenant of the League and the Kellogg Pact, the Powers will formally meet and
lay down the foundations of peace in the Far East by first tearing down the
international system built up since relations were established with China in
1842. They will do more than indite amicable generalities of self-denying
ordinances as they did at the Washington Conference. They will implement
them. They will give tokens of good faith. The conflict in the Far East turns on
China's struggle against the Powers to regain its independence and the existence
in China of rival nationalistic outposts of aggression. Each nation wants as
much as any other; none will yield anything lest it handicap itself against the
others. The whole conflict in both its phases can be ended only by removing the
outposts, by giving up fruits of aggression: not just the fruits of aggression since
1931, since that is to penalize Japan alone, but all since 1842. The relations of
the great Powers with China will thereafter be exclusively those of trading
nations, the relations between England and France or between America and

Italy. Such wealth as it to insure to the strong and efficient in dealing with China will come from trade with China on the basis of normal competition. In short, China will be eliminated as a spoils-ground, as an arena for the diplomatic fencing which is a prelude to the larger maneuvers of armies. This will not be for China's sake. It will have no reference to China's advantage or disadvantage. It will be a measure of self-protection, a measure to avert self-destruction in wars by removing the grounds on which each must take the offensive in defense.

Is this impractical? It may be; but if so, then peace is impractical, then it is useless to go through the mummery of League Assemblies and the solemnities of exchanging anti-war treaties and the rhetoric of disarmament meetings. Then it is useless to discuss disarmament; it is foolish even, because if it is impractical to uproot the conditions which must inevitably produce wars then it is the most rudimentary caution to be prepared for defense. If it is impractical, because to give up our concessions, rights, and privileges in China would cause at least a temporary loss of trade, as indeed it would, how much is the loss from wars? Are wars less costly?

It will be said that Japan cannot be induced to renounce anything, least of all now, when it has at last closed its grip on the prize which it has sought for twenty-five years. That is true. But at any rate Japan's primary motive for aggrandizement on the Asiatic continent, its fear that others will entrench themselves, will be left groundless, an indispensable condition to moderating Japan's aggressiveness. Then we can weaken the case of the Japanese military clique in its appeal to the Japanese people for support. It will not be able to plead self-defense so convincingly. We shall be in a position to bring pressure to bear on Japan with greater chance of success. At least we shall give evidence of good faith. The attitude of the Western Powers now is that of invoking the moral law against Japan alone. Other nations may keep what they were able to take. Japan is skeptical, and with reason. If it was obdurate at Geneva, that was because it is moved by a profound skepticism of the motives of other nations, also with reason. It has heard lofty enunciations of the new era; it has seen no signs. Why should it willingly offer itself as the first to make renunciation? The psychology of fear must first be bred out of Japan—the psychology of fear and the aggressiveness which fear begets. Japan's state of mind is that of a small nation which miraculously escaped destruction and now must flaunt its might, if only for its own satisfaction. The fear is still justified. The burden of proof is on the Western Powers. Japan cannot be moved until first it is convinced that other Powers have no ambitions in the Far East. Even then a long time will be required, but a beginning will have been made.

A long time will be required in any case. A situation generations in the making cannot be unmade by resolving. But it will take equally long no matter when we begin. Had we honestly faced the causes of international rancors in the Far East at the Washington Conference in 1921 we might have prevented the outbreak in 1931. If we start now, we may not attain the consummation of our hopes until 1951. If we wait until 1941, we shall not attain it until 1961—provided there is not war in the meantime. A long time will be required; also it will be costly. From that, too, there is no escape. The choice is only between loss voluntarily accepted and the loss imposed by the destruction of war. The rampages of the nineteenth-century conquerors must be paid for. Before there can be a new international society there must be a drastic writing off of old social losses.

There is no easy road to peace. The liberal reliance on treaties and international machinery is part of the deep-seated American faith in mechanical contrivances in all human situations. Peace cannot be had by wishing. If we want peace we must pay for it. We may not get it then. The momentum for war in the East, long gathered, is swift and powerful. But if we get peace at all, it will be only by paying. For America just now the stake is big and worth a risk.

# IX

## The Return to War

Events in Europe and Asia after the mid-'thirties challenged profoundly the entire spectrum of utopian assumptions on which American foreign policy had been erected. Whether the nation, in its various confrontations of the 'twenties, abjured involvement completely or accepted the simple obligation to confer, it invariably identified its interests with the political and military *status quo;* with equal consistency, however, it refused to accept any commitment for the defense of that best of all possible worlds. Yet so favorable was the international environment for the United States that this perennial defiance of the traditional rules of diplomacy scarcely impinged upon the nation's complacency or security. The great democracies throughout the 'twenties held a monopoly of power and the have-not nations were still unprepared to challenge the world created at Versailles. Much of the phraseology of the 'twenties attributed the continuing stability of the international order to the power of world opinion and a universal desire for peace, not to a variety of special circumstances soon to pass away. The delusion, self-inflicted, was complete. Too many Western statesmen, believing their own words, had arrived at the conclusion that power had been eliminated from politics among nations.

When suddenly in the mid-'thirties the Versailles system collapsed under the impact of aggression and war, the democracies could not respond. Whether they suffered from paralysis or from mistaken concepts mattered little. In Europe the two guardians of the *status quo,* France and England, fearful of both Mussolini and Hitler, succeeded, separately and jointly, in giving the two dictators the green light to attack the provisions of the Versailles Treaty. This, however, was never their intention. In March 1935, Hitler announced the reinstitution of universal military conscription and the establishment of a new army of thirty-six divisions with over half a million men. Shortly Hermann Goering apprised the world that Germany would soon create an air force. Thus Germany, without facing any threat of big-power retaliation, managed to subvert the vital military clauses of the Versailles Treaty. Before Hitler could dominate the Continent,

Mussolini, with British and French approval, dispatched his armies to Ethiopia. Then, to secure Germany's support against Italy, the British scrapped the naval clauses of the Versailles Treaty. This action, in large measure, condoned Hitler's entire armament program. In further defiance of the Versailles arrangements Nazi troops occupied the Rhineland in 1936. Ultimately, these diplomatic concessions did not prevent Mussolini from falling into the arms of Hitler. During 1936 the two dictators formed what was to become the Rome-Berlin Axis and openly joined the Spanish Civil War as partisans of Francisco Franco and his rebel forces.

For thoughtful Englishmen the only hope for world stability at that troublesome moment of history lay in a British-American partnership. Indeed, British spokesmen reiterated this quiet hope repeatedly during the 'thirties. Lord Baldwin, for example, declared at the Albert Hall in May 1935:

> I have always believed that the greatest security against war in any part of the world whatever, in Europe, in the East, anywhere, would be the close collaboration of the British Empire with the United States of America. The combined powers of the navies, the potential manpower, the immediate economic power of the combined blockade, and a refusal to trade or lend money would be a sanction that no power on earth however strong dare face. It may be a hundred years before that desirable end may be attained; it may never come to pass. But sometimes we may have our dreams. I look forward to the future, and I see that union of forces for peace and justice in the world, and I cannot but think, even if men cannot advocate it openly yet, that some day and some time those who follow us may see it and know that the peace of the world is guaranteed by those who speak our tongue.

Under the pressure of these world events American isolationism assumed a new militancy. Tinged as it was with pacificism and Anglophobia, isolationism took its chief strength from the broad conviction that a genuinely neutral United States could have avoided involvement in World War I. During 1934 Senator Gerald P. Nye of North Dakota launched his investigation of the munitions industry. His conclusions seemed to prove what many Americans wanted to hear —that Woodrow Wilson had committed the nation to the Allied cause, not to secure the national interest, but rather to underwrite the private interest of the industrialists who had enjoyed such unprecedented profit margins during the early war years. To prevent Wall Street from driving the United States into another European war, Nye, in April 1935, introduced a series of resolutions in the Senate, one of which would impose a mandatory embargo on the shipment of arms to all belligerents in time of war. During August Congress passed the first Neutrality Act which authorized the President, in the event of foreign war, to embargo munitions to all belligerents and warn Americans traveling on the vessels of warring nations that they did so at their own risk. In supporting this measure, Nye repeated what became the standard liberal argument in defense of future American neutrality:

Our experience of twenty years ago is, or should be, a ready reminder of the power of the forces that would drag a great nation into wars not of its own making. We witnessed in our last effort to remain neutral how munitions sales, bankers' loans to the Allies, and Americans sailing upon the vessels of nations at war, such as the *Lusitania,* tended to bring us into a conflict which was in its inception of no relation to us. Had America had a well-defined and strong neutrality policy at the beginning of the World War, she might have escaped participation in that war, and escaped, too, the penalties which we have been bearing and paying ever since, with the end not yet in sight.

For the vast majority of Congressmen, each of whom had become his own historian, the evidence was unshakable. (*Reading No. 1.*) The next year Congress extended the act to prohibit loans to combatants, and in 1937 it made the neutrality legislation permanent. This procedure of determining the character of future American foreign policy through acts of Congress coincided with the dominant intellectual tendencies of the times. Charles A. Beard, the noted American historian, advanced the theory that if the nation would straighten out its domestic economy, it would not require foreign commitments or foreign commerce. For such liberal isolationists as Beard economic involvements abroad were synonymous with war. If the United States concentrated its intelligence and energy on problems at home it could remain at peace.

Confronted at home with the pressures of American isolationism and abroad with the burgeoning aggressions of the dictators, the national administration faced the inescapable obligation, too seldom acknowledged, of creating a series of new external policies that would again bring some balance between ends and means. Eventually President Franklin D. Roosevelt and his Secretary of State, Cordell Hull, in an effort to satisfy the incompatible demands of domestic and international politics, formulated a national response which appeared to meet the requirements of the times but which in reality perpetuated the utopianism of the 'twenties.

Roosevelt's noted address at Chautauqua, New York, in August 1936, contained the fundamental ingredients of an acceptable American response to the disturbing events of that year. After inviting all the nations of the world to accept the American principle of the good neighbor, the President acknowledged with regret that some aggressor nations had rejected such standards of behavior. "It is a bitter experience to us," he said, "when the spirit of agreements to which we are a party is not lived up to. It is an even more bitter experience for the whole company of nations to witness not only the spirit but the letter of international agreements violated with impunity and without regard to the simple principles of honor. Permanent friendships between nations as between men can be sustained only by scrupulous respect for the pledged word." Having noted that some nations were challenging the world's treaty arrangements through force, Roosevelt disposed of the United States obligation to international order by reminding his listeners that the nation had participated in its share of conferences. Thereafter he reaffirmed the country's isolationist intention. "I hate war," he assured the doubters. "I have passed unnumbered hours, I shall pass unnumbered hours thinking and planning how war may be kept from this nation. I wish I could keep war from all nations, but that is beyond my power." The President's diplomatic thought, encompassing both internationalism and isolationism, was characterized by a profound escapism.

## II

American utopianism during the late 'thirties found its most perfect expression in the words and actions of Cordell Hull. For Hull, foreign policy consisted, first, of proclaiming, in response to aggression, a body of international principles and, second, of inviting the aggressor to accept those principles. His precepts rendered legitimate change almost impossible and thus, if complied with, guaranteed both peace and the continuance of the *status quo*, at no cost to the privileged. By merely reiterating them, the Secretary was able to offer a guise of moral leadership without encumbering the nation with any specific or danger-out commitments abroad. When in 1934 the Japanese threatened to assault the financial interests of other countries in China, Hull reminded Tokyo that the United States conducted its relations with other nations in accordance with international law and the provisions of treaties to which the United States was a party; that treaties could be modified lawfully only by processes agreed upon by the parties to them; that no nation could, without the consent of others concerned, rightfully endeavor to make its will conclusive in situations where the rights, obligations, and legitimate interests of other states were involved; and that since the United States always considered the rights of others, it expected of other governments due consideration of its rights. Unfortunately the Secretary's standards of international conduct had meaning only for a satiated power.

When Hitler announced the expansion of the German military machine in 1935, Hull restated his principles before a press conference. "Everybody knows," he said, "that the United States has always believed that treaties must constitute the foundation on which any stable peace structure must rest. . . . I believe that the moral influence of the United States and its people must always encourage living up to treaties." What the United States would do if other governments ignored his preachments he did not say. In his address at Buenos Aires in December 1936, the Secretary found the answer for the growing international anarchy in an educated public opinion. "More than any other factor," he said, "a thoroughly informed and alert public opinion in each country as to the suitable and desirable relationships with other nations and the principles underlying them, enables a government in time of crisis to act promptly and effectually for peace." He believed that a general interest in peace existed among the people of all nations and that therefore the world could anticipate the universal acceptance of his principles. (*Reading No. 2.*)

On July 7, 1937, Japanese and Chinese troops clashed on the Marco Polo Bridge on the outskirts of Peiping. This "Chinese incident" brought a massive invasion of Japanese troops and with it renewed war on a major scale in the

Far East. The American reaction became clear when the Secretary of State issued a carefully worded statement of principles to the press. *(Reading No. 3.)* To Hull this declaration represented such a bold and forceful maneuver at a moment of crisis that he dispatched copies of it to all the governments of the world with the request that they state their reactions. All the nations that replied insisted they were in solid accord with his principles—even those obviously busily engaged in breaking them. It was clear even then that Hull's principles would not control events in Europe or Asia. Nations might accept them, for in the abstract they all favored peace, but they would never permit a body of abstractions to determine their national policies when their interests were at stake. Nor was there any world opinion which would lend force to such principles, whatever the lip service they received from the world's leading governments. Japan subscribed to the peaceful objectives set forth in the note but added that they could "only be obtained, in their application to the Far Eastern situation, by a full recognition and practical consideration of the actual particular circumstances of that region." The one serious objection came from Portugal, a nation which could not be accused of aggression. For the Portuguese government such "vague formulae" were useless if not positively harmful, for they created an impression of policy where in fact none existed. *(Reading No. 4.)* In Japan, American Ambassador Joseph C. Grew recorded in his diary that Hull's declaration of principles, by attaching United States purpose in the Far East firmly to the *status quo,* would not lead to peace but to war. *(Reading No. 5.)*

Hull defended his principles in his *Memoirs.* "They were solid, living, all-essential rules," he recalled. "If the world followed them, the world could live at peace *forever.* If the world ignored them, war would be eternal."

> . . . To me [he continued] these doctrines were as vital in international relations as the Ten Commandments in personal relations. One can argue that the Ten Commandments, too, are "vague formulae." But day after day millions of ministers of God are preaching these formulae, and I believe there is untold value in this preaching. Society would lapse into chaos if the Ten Commandments were universally broken, just as international society lapses into chaos when the principles of right conduct among nations are widely disregarded.

Suddenly in the autumn of 1937 it appeared that United States foreign policy might veer toward a more precise, more committed course of action. On October 5, speaking in Chicago, Roosevelt urged the democratic nations of the world to band together to quarantine the aggressors. *(Reading No. 6.)* To Sumner Welles, who claimed greater knowledge than other members of the State Department regarding the President's personal views toward Germany and Japan, the famed quarantine speech was evidence that Roosevelt did not accept Hull's abstract approach to foreign affairs and preferred a more direct, vigorous policy. If this is true, the President's subsequent actions are puzzling. The speech divided public sentiment sharply, but the bulk of the major American publications supported the President. In his personal correspondence Roosevelt himself accepted the national reaction as favorable. In 1937, however, it was still far easier to announce an intention than to build a policy. At his subsequent press conference the President could not define with any precision the program which his speech suggested. Perhaps it was as much the sheer complexity of the international situation and Roosevelt's own unfamiliarity with foreign affairs as American isolationism that terminated the new approach so abruptly. The President left his followers weakened and confused and thus permitted a powerful recovery of the isolationist forces in the nation. Hull's address in Washington on March 17, 1938, made it clear that American foreign policy had not changed. After reviewing again those principles which for him comprised the foundations of international morality, the Secretary continued: "The objectives of our foreign policy are as easy to grasp as they are fundamental. The means we are using to attain these objectives are the only means approved by reason and by experience." (Reading No. 7.)

### III

This effort to control the world while rejecting involvement in particular events reduced American diplomacy during the critical years of 1938 and 1939 to a state of irrelevancy. As early as November 1937 the Nazi high command had made its fateful decision to strike the territorial arrangements of the Versailles Treaty. For Hitler, Germany's time had arrived, for that nation enjoyed a military advantage that would not survive indefinitely a French and British decision to rearm. Hitler, moreover, had won the test of wills in his reoccupation of the Rhineland; he was convinced that the democratic world would not fight to prevent the reincorporation of the German minorities of central and eastern Europe into the German state. Thereafter Hitler slowly built his forces and with well-timed thrusts seized Austria in March 1938, and the Sudetenland of Czechoslovakia six months later. When, after the final crushing of Czechoslovakia in March 1939, England and France determined belatedly to tolerate no further Nazi incursions into eastern Europe, their warning came too late to be an effective deterrent.

Shocked by the obvious deterioration of European stability, Roosevelt proposed to the British Prime Minister, Neville Chamberlain, in January 1938, that the United States invite to Washington the representatives of all the world's leading nations to discuss the underlying troubles of Europe. Chamberlain rejected the idea as an infringement on his personal diplomacy with Hitler and Mussolini. The Prime Minister was convinced, moreover, that Roosevelt would never take effective action in Europe. He resented, he wrote, the persistent "American lectures on international conduct and American reiteration of moral principles." There existed, in the British estimate, an enormous gap between inspiring words and practical action. Lord Halifax, who was to become British Ambassador to the United States in 1940, likewise condemned the habitual American resort to moral indignation when "there was little likelihood of this indignation being converted into action." The American reaction to the crises of 1938, again limited largely to words, merely convinced the British that they must rely solely on themselves for protection against Hitler. Halifax refused to absolve the United States of responsibility for what occurred at Munich in September 1938. His bitter judgment of American behavior he confided to his memoirs:

> Granted that the danger of Munich was as great, and the policy pursued was as evil, as those who thus judged us affected to think, why was Great Britain to be held morally bound to fight for justice in Czechoslovakia, while the United States was exempt? Three thousand miles of ocean could not dispense with the great obligations of morality, if these were in fact involved. In this business the American critics were like people who had collected to watch a great fight and expressed disappointment that the entertainment was called off. But never had they intended to be more than spectators of the fight.

If official American reaction to the tragic events of 1939 was more pronounced, it had no measurable effect on Europe's drift toward war. In March, when Hitler completed his annihilation of the Czech nation, the State Department issued a statement of principle and high moral rebuke:

> This government . . . cannot refrain from making known this country's condemnation of the acts which have resulted in the temporary extinguishment of the liberties of a free and independent people. . . . The position of the . . . United States has been made consistently clear. It has emphasized the need for respect for the sanctity of treaties . . . and for the non-intervention by any nation in the domestic affairs of other nations; and it has . . . expressed its condemnation of a policy of military aggression.

What remained of Western influence in eastern Europe quickly disintegrated under the pressure of subsequent events. During the weeks which followed the fall of Czechoslovakia, the British and French governments informed Hitler that an assault on Poland would bring a general war. Whatever Hitler's ultimate intentions, he was determined to destroy the Versailles provisions regarding the Polish Corridor. When Warsaw rejected Hitler's demand for a renegotiation of the German-Polish boundary, the stage was set for the final Nazi assault on the Versailles system. With the future of Poland and eastern Europe at stake, Russia could no longer remain isolated from the main currents of European diplomacy. The single remaining hope for Europe's stability in the summer of 1939 lay in the reforging of the Triple Entente of World War I against Germany. Chamberlain, however, shared the general Western misgivings regarding the U.S.S.R. He wrote in March 1939: "I must confess to the most profound distrust of Russia. I have no belief whatever in her ability to maintain an effective offensive, even if she wanted to. And I distrust her motives, which seem to me to have little connection with our ideas of liberty, and to be concerned only with getting everyone else by the ears." Under such circumstances an effective military arrangement between Russia and the Anglo-French entente was impossible. Moreover, to join in the resistance against Hitler would entail severe risks for Russia. Soviet diplomats, therefore, requested the right to reoccupy the ramparts along the

Baltic and to move troops through Poland and Rumania. The Polish government, deeply distrustful of Russia and still hopeful for better alternatives, opposed all military and political agreements between Western Europe and the Soviet Union.

The West, still committed to the territorial integrity of the eastern European states, refused to consign to Russia any portion of the Soviet periphery in exchange for a defensive alliance. Such legalism, though understandable, placed all the trump cards in German hands, for Hitler was not averse to purchasing Soviet neutrality with eastern European territory. He readily authorized the Russians to occupy most of the Baltic states, Bessarabia, and Poland up to the Curzon line. Indeed, Germany was willing to grant the Kremlin much more of eastern Europe than it actually requested. Refusing to negotiate what was beyond their power to maintain, the Western democracies had now completely lost control of eastern Europe's future. Armed with the Nazi-Soviet Non-Aggression Pact of August 1939, which eliminated the immediate danger of a two-front war, Hitler struck Poland early in September, only to provoke a British-French declaration of war. Roosevelt, in his address to the nation on September 3, 1939, assigned to the United States a role of serving humanity not unlike that which Wilson adopted during the months and years that followed the outbreak of war in 1914. "The principle of American policy," said the President, was to seek for humankind "a final peace which will eliminate, as far as it is possible to do so, the constant use of force between nations." (*Reading No. 8.*)

That there was in Roosevelt's definition of national policy a clear dichotomy between the concept of neutrality and the ingredients of security became apparent on September 21 when he asked Congress to repeal the embargo provisions of the neutrality acts on the shipment of goods to belligerents. If American neutrality, security, and peace hinged on keeping the war away from American shores, then they rested on the ability of England and France to resist the power of Germany. After weeks of vituperative debate, Congress eventually repealed the arms embargo. The new neutrality legislation enabled England and France to draw upon the industrial and agricultural productivity of the United States, but only on a cash and carry basis. Thus American nationals would be kept out of the European war zone. Although still officially neutral, the United States had cast its lot with the democracies of Western Europe.

Still, the continuing force of isolationism forced the Roosevelt administration into a contradictory course. Whatever the nation's commitment to a British and French victory, the President's rhetoric merely reinforced American isolationism. On September 9, 1939, the President promised the country: "[As] long as it remains within my power to prevent it, there will be no blackout of peace in the United States." On December 5, Hull added reassuringly: "With the same zeal with which we strove to avert this catastrophe, our Government is now seeking to provide every possible assurance against our being drawn into it. . . . This country should not, and must not, be drawn into war." For Roosevelt and his advisers such professions of neutrality were based on the assumption that France and England, with limited American aid, could maintain the Atlantic defenses. The United States government would not, in the long run, permit a German victory at the expense of England and France. Perhaps no one in Washington detected the fundamental tendencies of American opinion more clearly than did Richard Casey, the Australian Minister. When the Nazis invaded Denmark and Norway in April 1940, the State Department responded with another simple protest against the use of force and a reiteration of the American belief in the right of peoples to govern themselves. But Casey recorded in his diary the true nature of things:

> A wave of pessimism is current in America as to the Allies' chances of winning the war. Not a bad thing. Nothing but such pessimism will bring America to think of the possible repercussions on themselves of a German victory. Until recently it has been widely assumed here that the Allies would win the war easily, and by inference that it was unnecessary for America to come in and help. Public sentiment here is liable to take wide-scale swings. The present pessimism is being accompanied by increasing sympathy for the Allied cause and some thought as to the effect on them of a German victory.

Hitler's dreaded *Wehrmacht* determined America's final course of action. In May 1940 it struck the Netherlands and Belgium and forced the British Expeditionary Force back to the English Channel where only a heroic retreat from Dunkirk by sea saved it from annihilation. By June the famed Nazi Panzer divisions had begun their triumphant assault on France. On June 10, during a tense period of history, the President addressed the graduating class at the University of Virginia at Charlottesville. The United States, he warned, now faced the prospect of becoming a lone island in a world dominated by the philosophy of force. Throwing down the gauntlet to the isolationists, Roosevelt committed the nation's resources to the task of sustaining British resistance. In August the isolationists, now led by the conservative enemies of Roosevelt's New Deal, formed the America First Committee to counter the accumulating pressure for direct American involvement. The United States could not underwrite the British cause, they warned, without drifting into war.

From June 1940 until December 1941 the United States followed a course of gradually increasing commitment to the defeat of Germany. Yet not always was this apparent. Roosevelt and the Republican candidate, Wendell Willkie, eliminated any serious discussion of external affairs from the 1940 presidential campaign by outpromising one another that they would keep the country out of war. Roosevelt declared characteristically before the Irish of Boston, "I have said this before, but I shall say it again and again and again. Your boys are not going to be sent into any foreign wars." Both Republican and Democratic leaders feared the consequences of alienating themselves from the potentially determining isolationist vote. Roosevelt soon had reason to regret such promises.

Following the elections of November 1940 the American involvement in the European struggle became deeper with each passing month. In December Prime Minister Winston Churchill warned the President that American policies of cash and carry were rapidly exhausting England's financial resources. Certainly it could not be in accord with the principles of the people of the United

States, he wrote, "to confine the help which they have so generously promised only to such munitions of war and commodities as could be immediately paid for." Roosevelt responded with a major radio address from Washington on December 29. He recounted the efforts of Britain to resist those forces attempting to enslave the human race. Great Britain and the British Empire, he said, "are putting up a fight which will live forever in the story of human gallantry." (*Reading No. 9.*) Having committed American power to a British victory, he again found the means to achieve this goal in the unlimited capacity of the United States to manufacture the implements of war. By making these weapons available to Britain in sufficient volume and with sufficient speed the American people could still protect themselves from the agony and suffering of war which others had been forced to endure. American purpose would triumph, he assured the nation, without the sending of any United States forces abroad.

To guarantee the uninterrupted flow of American matériel to England, the President, in his annual message of January 6, 1941, presented to Congress the outline of his lend-lease program. After two months of bitter argument in which the Congressional isolationists made their final effort to terminate the drift toward direct American involvement in the European conflict, the Lend-Lease bill passed both houses of Congress with substantial majorities. It provided that the United States "sell, transfer, lease, or lend," to the limit of its financial and industrial resources, military articles to any government "whose defense the President deems vital to the defense of the United States." Isolationists lashed out at the burgeoning British-American alliance. They accused England of dragging the United States into another war, a war which the British themselves should have avoided, for it was the British declaration of war from a posture of unpreparedness that had led to the collapse of Western Europe. For the United States, they argued, there was no vital interest at stake in a British defeat. (*Reading No. 10.*)

From the passage of the Lend-Lease Act it became evident that German submarine warfare threatened to render Roosevelt's entire program of aid to Britain inoperative. The act itself prohibited the use of American convoys or the dispatching of American merchant vessels into combat zones. Rather than inaugurate a system of naval convoys across the Atlantic, the President cabled to Churchill on April 11, 1941, proposing to extend the American patrol areas to cover the north Atlantic west of twenty-five degrees west longitude. Roosevelt requested secret notification of convoys so that United States patrol ships, operating from bases in Greenland, Newfoundland, the United States, Bermuda, and the West Indies, might report the location of enemy ships and aircraft in the area of the western Atlantic. On May 27, the President informed the nation that the Atlantic had become a war zone in which Nazi raiders and submarines were destroying merchant vessels at an alarming rate. Thereupon Roosevelt committed the United States to the delivery of goods to Britain, adding grimly, "This can be done; it must be done; it will be done." In conclusion, the President proclaimed a state of unlimited national emergency.

During July 1941 American forces occupied Iceland and American naval vessels began to convoy British ships halfway across the Atlantic. The results were predictable. On September 11, in another radio address, Roosevelt in-

formed the nation of the increasing destruction of American and British ships
by German submarines. To the United States Navy, he declared, fell the historic
task of protecting the freedom of the seas. "From now on," continued the President, "if German or Italian vessels of war enter the waters the protection of which
is necessary for American defense they do so at their own peril. (*Reading No. 11.*)
At last, in his Navy and Total Defense Day Address, on October 27, 1941, Roosevelt called for full national exertion to eliminate Hitlerism from the earth.
(*Reading No. 12.*) Now the President had committed the nation to the extent of
his prerogatives. All that remained to bring the full might of the United States
into the European war was a formal declaration. Still, between Roosevelt's naval
war in the north Atlantic and full-scale American involvement was the power
and influence of the Congressional isolationists. This final opposition to war
fell before the onslaught of the Japanese.

## IV

Japan's assault on China in 1937 merely intensified the fundamental and inescapable problem which had confronted United States policy in the Far East
since the early twentieth century. The Japanese government, possessed with the
power and intention to alter the *status quo* in East Asia, presented the United
States with two troublesome choices. Either the nation could accept a larger role
for Japan in Far Eastern affairs by giving up the Open Door for China as an
unrealistic and fruitless commitment, or it could fight to prevent the economic
and political changes that defied its will. For the Roosevelt administration
neither alternative was acceptable. It could not, in defiance of the nation's opposition to war, confront the Japanese with force or the threat of force. Nor could
it politically or emotionally abjure the traditional American guardianship of the
Open Door. Indeed, Hull's deeply moralistic outlook on world affairs eliminated
the necessity for such hard decisions. To him the Far Eastern problem was
purely an ethical one, to be exorcised by reminding the Japanese of the error
of their ways.

Subsequent crises in the Far East merely demonstrated the futility of Hull's
inflexible and doctrinaire approach to the Japanese problem. When Hitler's victories of 1940 removed French and Dutch power from the Far East and the south
Pacific, British naval power alone stood between a powerful and determined
Japan and the rice, rubber, and oil of Indochina and the Dutch East Indies. For
the British and Australian ministers in Washington it was clear that the diplomatic cards were all in Japanese hands. They suggested to Hull late in June
1940 that the United States either join England in a show of force or negotiate
a new settlement with Japan in an effort to avoid war. The Secretary replied on
the following day that he would do neither. An alliance with Britain in the Far
East was unthinkable; conciliation would result in an infringement on Chinese
sovereignty. As the crisis approached, the United States confronted Japan with
no policy at all. Availing themselves of a wide range of unanticipated opportunities, the Japanese extracted an arrangement from the Dutch to supply them
with vast quantities of oil from the Dutch East Indies. In August they forced
from the Vichy government of France a recognition of "the preponderance of

Japanese interests" in the region of Southeast Asia, and during the following month they moved troops into northern Indochina.

Not until Japan signed the Tripartite Pact with Germany and Italy on September 27, 1940, did Washington regard Japanese intentions toward Southeast Asia as significant or dangerous. Thereafter United States officials interpreted Japanese aggression in Asia as part of a general assault of the dictators against the free world. It was to counter this tendency that Ambassador Grew warned, in September 1940, that the United States distinguish between its immediate and its long-term goals in the Far East. It was in the immediate interest of the United States, he wrote, to support the British cause in Europe and avoid a conflict with Japan. After the defeat of Germany the United States and England, negotiating from a position of proven strength, might readjust the entire Pacific problem "on a fair, frank, and equitable basis." (*Reading No. 13.*) He wrote again in November:

> We need not aim to drive Japan out of China now. That can be taken care of, perhaps, if and after Britain wins the war with Germany. But stopping Japan's proposed far-flung southward advance and driving her out of China are two different matters. We can tolerate her occupation of China for the time being, just as we have tolerated it for the past three years. I doubt if we should tolerate any great extension of the southward advance.

Grew believed that the Roosevelt administration permitted itself to be guided too much by a sentimental attitude toward China, which in the long run would serve the interests of neither the United States nor China.

When the new Japanese Ambassador, Kichisaburo Nomura, arrived in Washington early in 1941, he faced a determined United States government. Backed by an uncompromising public opinion (for American isolationism had never favored any withdrawal of the United States from the Far East), Hull conducted the critical negotiations with Japan from May to December 1941 from a posture of extreme moral indignation. In a series of preliminary conferences, the Secretary made it clear that the United States government would demand no less than an abandonment of Japan's doctrine of military aggression and a willingness "to adopt the principles which this government has been proclaiming and practicing as embodying the foundation on which all relations between nations should properly rest." On the basis of those principles, Hull reminded Nomura, there could be no change in the *status quo* of the Far East except that achieved by peaceful means. During the succeeding months Hull never varied this principled response to specific Japanese proposals.

Until mid-July 1941 the Japanese government was decidedly aggressive in its demands. Fundamentally it sought the freedom to negotiate an end to the war in China on its own terms. Hull would not agree to this. Early in June he complained that the Japanese government had not revealed any intention to place its relations with China "on a basis which in the opinion of the government of the United States would contribute to a lasting peace and thus to future stability in the Far East. . . ." Hull terminated his conversations with Nomura on July 23 when Japanese forces invaded southern Indochina. At that moment the

American concern was less for China than for the maintenance of the *status quo* in Southeast Asia. At the White House on the following day Roosevelt assured the Japanese Ambassador that the United States, China, England, and the Netherlands would neutralize Indochina if the Japanese would refrain from occupying the region with military forces. Immediately thereafter the President froze all Japanese assets in the United States and instituted a complete embargo on United States commerce with Japan. The Dutch and British promptly followed suit. In forcing Japan to the diplomatic wall, the economic sanctions succeeded far beyond anticipation. With only a year's supply of oil on hand, the Japanese had either to make drastic concessions to the United States or move against the oil-rich Dutch East Indies.

Japanese moderates, favoring the first course, began to recoil. Early in August the Japanese government asked for a personal conference between Premier Konoye and President Roosevelt. Grew regarded the proposal as sincere. Nothing less than an acceptance, he wrote, would keep the Japanese moderates in power. Hull and his political adviser, Stanley Hornbeck, advised the President against acceptance. The Hull-Nomura conversations of August 28, 1941, illustrated again the deepening chasm which separated the Japanese concept of national interest from the American concept of international morality. Hull informed Nomura that no arrangement in the Far East would be acceptable to the United States unless it were equally acceptable to the Chinese government. Since the Japanese government had not agreed to negotiate on the basis of his principles, the Secretary doubted that the President and Konoye could possibly arrive at any settlement acceptable to the Chinese government. Indeed, to Hull any top-level meeting would only ratify agreements already reached in principle. (*Reading No. 14.*)

As the Japanese attempted to extricate themselves from their expanded commitments through a series of less-demanding proposals, Hull went increasingly on the diplomatic offensive, demanding after August a Japanese withdrawal not only from Southeast Asia but also from China itself. The freezing order, issued initially to discourage further Japanese aggression, now became the engine of force to turn the Japanese out of China. The more the Japanese government searched for policies of expediency, the more righteously indignant Hull became. Ultimately he gave Japan no choice but to give up all gains in the Far East, disintegrate economically and militarily before the United States embargo, or fight.

After September Hull and Roosevelt freely admitted that they were continuing negotiations with the Japanese only to gain time. On October 16 the Konoye government fell, to be succeeded by General Hideki Tojo's military cabinet. Tojo made one final, futile effort to reach a compromise. Early in November he dispatched Saburo Kurusu, former Japanese Ambassador to Germany, to aid Nomura in Washington. Having broken the Japanese code, American officials knew that Kurusu's proposals of November 20 comprised the ultimate concession that Japan was prepared to offer. In this dispatch the Japanese agreed to withdraw all their forces from Indochina upon the restoration of peace with China. With the acceptance of the Japanese offer, Japan would withdraw her forces from southern Indochina into the north. The two governments would then co-operate in securing the raw materials Japan desired from the Dutch

East Indies. The United States would restore the commercial relations that existed before the freezing orders, and would not interfere in the restoration of a general peace in China. In response to Hull's prodding, Kurusu repudiated verbally the Tripartite alliance.

What occurred during the following week was crucial. Hull prepared a moderate reply, the *modus vivendi*. This proposal was almost identical to that of Japan—which Hull later termed an ultimatum. It provided for a partial lifting of the embargo on oil if Japan withdrew to northern Indochina, limited her forces there to 25,000, and commenced her negotiations with Chiang Kai-shek. Both the British and the Dutch regarded the proposal as too mild, but Hull retreated essentially from the prospect of facing the Chinese government. At his meeting with Nomura and Kurusu on November 26, Hull presented them with his ten-point program, which demanded that the Japanese, in exchange for the removal of the freezing restrictions, withdraw all military, naval, air, and police forces from China and Indochina. This exchange between Hull and Kurusu revealed the enormous shift that had occurred in the respective diplomatic positions of the two nations during the course of three critical months. In late November the Japanese were no longer granted even the right to negotiate a settlement with Chiang. (*Reading No. 15.*) No Washington official expected the Japanese government to accept the final American offer. On the following day Washington issued a war-warning to American military and naval bases in the Pacific.

Japan's reply to Hull's ten-point program reached Washington piecemeal and was promptly deciphered. Hull and Roosevelt knew its contents before Nomura and Kurusu arrived at the White House in the afternoon of December 7. Upon reading the memorandum, Hull observed: "I have never seen such a document that was more crowded with infamous falsehoods and distortions on a scale so huge that I never imagined until today that any government on this planet was capable of uttering them." In a Secretary of State who had extreme faith in the power and justice of his diplomatic principles such a reaction was understandable. What reinforced his indignation was the knowledge that the Japanese had already attacked Pearl Harbor. But in the Japanese memorandum of December 7 there was an incontrovertible warning for those who preferred to conduct foreign affairs through the universal application of abstract principles. (*Reading No. 16.*) For the Japanese detected what Hull refused to admit—that his principles were designed less to achieve peaceful change in the Far East than to prevent change. Indeed, the sentimental American attachment to Chiang Kai-shek eliminated all possibility of change except through war. Whatever Hull's peaceful intentions, his principles had the effect of protecting the have-nations from any international pressure that threatened or endangered their favored position. As a natural extension of the idea of the Nine Power Treaty, they were calculated to limit Japan's influence in Far Eastern affairs without the necessity of resorting to force. Traditionally, international politics had rested on the rights of the stronger; by the new morality of Hull and other utopians it rested on the rights of possession. Eventually the time arrived when the Japanese preferred war to the acceptance of a permanent status of economic and political inferiority.

# 1 | Bennett Champ Clark's Defense of the First Neutrality Act, December 1935 *

In this well-argued defense of American neutrality legislation, Senator Bennett Champ Clark warned the nation that it was the absence of a well-planned program for safeguarding American neutrality in 1914 that rendered United States involvement in the European war inevitable. The country, believed Clark, could remain out of war if it so desired and if the American people understood the importance of neutrality as the key factor in avoiding war. In outlining the provisions of the Neutrality Act, Clark accepted without question the conclusions of the Nye Committee that the munitions manufacturers had carried the United States into war in 1917. He predicted that, given the opportunity to reap such profits from a future European conflict, the industrialists and financiers would inevitably drag the nation into the struggle again.

🖋

. . . At the present the desire to keep the United States from becoming involved in any war between foreign nations seems practically unanimous among the rank and file of American citizens; but it must be remembered there was an almost equally strong demand to keep us out of the last war. In August, 1914, few could have conceived that America would be dragged into a European conflict in which we had no original part and the ramifications of which we did not even understand. Even as late as November, 1916, President Wilson was reelected because he "kept us out of war." Yet five months later we were fighting to "save the world for democracy" in the "war to end war."

In the light of that experience, and in the red glow of war fires burning in the old countries, it is high time we gave some thought to the hard, practical question of just how we propose to stay out of present and future international conflicts. No one who has made an honest attempt to face the issue will assert that there is an easy answer. But if we have learned anything at all, we know the inevitable and tragic end to a policy of drifting and trusting to luck. We know that however strong is the will of the American people to refrain from mixing in other people's quarrels, that will can be made effective only if we have a sound, definite policy from the beginning.

Such a policy must be built upon a program to safeguard our neutrality. No lesson of the World War is more clear than that such a policy cannot be improvised after war breaks out. It must be determined in advance, before it is too late to apply reason. I contend with all possible earnestness that if we want to avoid being drawn into this war now forming, or any other future war, we must formulate a definite, workable policy of neutral relations with belligerent nations.

* Bennett Champ Clark, "Detour Around War," *Harper's Magazine,* CLXXII (December 1935), 1-9.

Some of us in the Senate, particularly the members of the Munitions Investigation Committee, have delved rather deeply into the matter of how the United States has been drawn into past wars, and what forces are at work to frighten us again into the traps set by Mars. As a result of these studies, Senator Nye and I introduced the three proposals for neutrality legislation which were debated so vigorously in the last session of the Congress. A part of that legislative program was battered through both houses in the closing hours of the session late in August; a very vital part of it was held in abeyance.

Senator Nye and I made no claims then, and make none now, that the neutrality proposals will provide an absolute and infallible guarantee against our involvement in war. But we do believe that the United States can stay out of war if it wants to, and if its citizens understand what is necessary to preserve our neutrality. We feel that the temporary legislation already passed and the legislation we shall vigorously push at the coming session of the Congress point the only practical way. . . .

The act is to terminate February 29, 1936. It is a stop-gap only. But it is pointing the way we intend to go.

The President is empowered to enumerate definitely the arms, munitions, and implements of war, the exportation of which is prohibited by this act. On September 27th President Roosevelt made this enumeration in a proclamation, following closely the list submitted to the disarmament conference at Geneva in our government's proposals for international control of the munitions industry. A National Munitions Control Board has been established, composed of the Secretaries of State, Treasury, War, Navy, and Commerce, with the administration of the board in the Department of State. It is contemplated that by November 29th, when the Act takes effect, the manufacturers and exporters of war implements will all be listed in the office of this board. After that date such materials as are specified may not be exported without a license issued by the board to cover such shipment. This will, obviously, permit the government to prohibit shipments to belligerent nations. The act makes it unlawful for any American vessel to "carry arms, ammunition, or implements of war to any port of the belligerent countries named in such proclamation as being at war, or to any neutral port for transshipment to, or for use in, a belligerent country."

Further provisions of the act empower the President to restrict the use of American ports and waters to submarines of foreign nations in the event such use might disturb our position of neutrality, and to proclaim the conditions under which American citizens on belligerent ships during war must travel entirely at their own risk.

Two provisions from our original program failed to pass: prohibition of loans and credits to belligerent nations, and the application of strict embargoes upon contraband materials other than munitions and war implements. . . .

I have called the present neutrality act a stop-gap. But it has not stopped the activities of our American war-munitions makers anxious for profits from imminent conflicts. Reports from centers of manufacturing and exporting of war implements all tell the same story: there is a boom in war preparations. Chambers of commerce in cities with large war-materials plants proudly report reemployment of skilled munitions makers in large numbers, the stepping up of output to as high as three hundred per cent, the rushing to completion of new additions to plants. Day-and-night shifts in the brass and copper mills, rising prices and large shipments of these metals, and the acquisition of large capital for immediate wartime scale production, all indicate that Mars has waved his magic wand in our direction.

Where are these war-implements shipments going? There is no proof that the munitions makers are trying to "beat the embargo" which will prohibit shipments to belligerents after November 29th, but it stands to reason they are making hay while the sun shines. Our Munitions Investigation Committee has not had time to look into immediate developments, but it needs no stretch of imagination to contemplate the rich profits that would flow from an Italian-Ethiopian war, with England jumping into the fray against Italy, and other European nations following suit on one side or the other.

And, of course, there's lots of war business right here at home. We have increased our expenditures on our Army and Navy in preparation for another and more dreadful war more rapidly than any European country in the period since the World War. . . .

When the Congress meets in January, facing the expiration of the neutrality act on February 29th, the battle for a practical policy of neutrality will have to be fought all over again. We who believe that the detour around another devastating war is to be found only in new conceptions of neutrality will fight for the retention of the present legislation and for the passage of the two items left out in the cold at the adjournment of the Congress.

I firmly believe, whatever the status of the Italo-Ethiopian dispute at that time, whatever the position of other European powers as belligerents or as neutrals, that the United States of America cannot turn back to a policy of so-called neutrality that finally pulls us into conflict with one or all the belligerents. Surely it is obvious that the legislation forcing mandatory embargoes upon war materials will serve to check the growth of another vast munitions trade with warring powers and the dangers that follow a swing of our foreign trade in favor of our munitions customers and against those who cannot purchase the munitions. Why shall we contend for embargoes upon contraband articles as well, and prohibition of loans and credits to belligerents? Because it takes these two items to complete any sort of workable neutrality program. If we are in earnest about neutrality we may as well plan to be neutral. . . .

Let us foresee that under conditions of modern warfare everything supplied to the enemy population has the same effect as supplies to the enemy army, and will become contraband. Food, clothing, lumber, leather, chemicals—everything, in fact, with the possible exception of sporting goods and luxuries (and these aid in maintaining civilian "morale")—are as important aids to winning the war as are munitions. Let us foresee also that our ships carrying contraband will be seized, bombed from the air or sunk by submarines. Let us not claim as a right what is an impossibility. The only way we can maintain our neutral rights is to fight the whole world. If we are not prepared to do that we can only pretend to enforce our rights against one side, and go to war to defend them against the other side. We might at least abandon pretense.

On the matter of loans and credits to belligerents, the train of events which pulled us into the World War is equally significant. Correspondence which our Munitions Investigation Committee discovered in the files of the State Department offers illuminating proof that there can be no true neutrality when our nation is allowed to finance one side of a foreign war. One letter, written by Secretary Robert Lansing to President Wilson, dated September 5, 1915, lucidly points out that loans for the Allies were absolutely necessary to enable them to pay for the tremendous trade in munitions, war materials generally, food stuffs, and the like, or else that trade would have to stop. He declared that the Administration's "true spirit of neutrality" must not stand in the way of the demands of commerce. About one month later the first great loan—the Anglo-French loan of $500,000,000—was floated by a syndicate headed by J. P. Morgan and Company. This company had been the purchasing agents for Allied supplies in the United States since early in 1915. Other loans to the Allied powers quickly followed. . . .

"But, think of the profits!" cry our theorists. "America will never give up her lucrative trade in munitions and necessities of life when war starts!" . . .

Just who profited from the last war? Labor got some of the crumbs in the form of high wages and steady jobs. But where is labor to-day with its fourteen million unemployed? Agriculture received high prices for its products during the period of the War and has been paying the price of that brief inflation in the worst and longest agricultural depression in all history. Industry made billions in furnishing the necessities of war to the belligerents and then suffered terrific reaction like the dope addict's morning after. War and depression—ugly, misshapen inseparable twins—must be considered together. Each is a catapult for the other. The present world-wide depression is a direct result of the World War. Every war in modern history has been followed by a major depression.

Therefore I say, let the man seeking profits from war or the war-torn countries do so at his own risk. . . .

If there are those so brave as to risk getting us into war by traveling in the war zones—if there are those so valiant that they do not care how many people are killed as a result of their traveling, let us tell them, and let us tell the world that from now on their deaths will be a misfortune to their own families alone, not to the whole nation.

The profiteers and others who oppose any rational neutrality shout: "You would sacrifice our national honor!" Some declare we are about to haul down the American flag, and in a future war the belligerents will trample on our rights and treat us with contempt. Some of these arguments are trundled out by our naval bureaucracy. The admirals, I am told, objected strenuously when the State Department suggested a new policy of neutrality somewhat along these lines.

I deny with every fiber of my being that our national honor demands that we must sacrifice the flower of our youth to safeguard the profits of a privileged few.

I deny that it is necessary to turn back the hands of civilization to maintain our national honor. I repudiate any such definition of honor. Is it not time for every lover of our country to do the same thing?

## 2 | Cordell Hull's Address at Buenos Aires, December 5, 1936 *

For Hull the elemental purpose of external policy in 1936 was the avoidance of war. As a guide for the American republics the Secretary of State outlined eight "vitally important principles and proposals for a comprehensive peace program and peace structure." Underlying Hull's principles was the assumption that all peoples of the world had a common interest in peace. What mattered, therefore, was the proper education of public opinion to the ways and necessity of peace, the ample use of conferences and exchange of views, the creation of adequate peace machinery, the will to remain neutral in time of war, the reduction of trade barriers and expenditures for armaments, the revitalization of international law, and the observance of international treaties and agreements. Thus Hull's program was concerned more with form than with substance. It substituted procedure for political settlement. Nowhere did Hull face the fundamental necessity of coming to terms with the demands of nations who were, unlike the United States, dissatisfied with the *status quo* and were willing to employ force to change it. Hull's conviction that his program represented the interest of all nations, equally, ruled out the necessity of force in maintaining world stability.

✗

The primary purpose of this Conference is to banish war from the Western Hemisphere. In its earnest pursuit of this great undertaking it is necessary at the outset to visualize numerous dangerous conditions and practices in general international affairs to the extent that they bear upon and affect the work of this Conference. It is manifest that every country today is faced with a supreme alternative. Each must play its part in determining whether the world will slip backward toward war and savagery, or whether it can maintain and will advance the level of civilization and peace. None can escape its responsibility.

The twenty-one American republics cannot remain unconcerned by the grave and threatening conditions in many parts of the world. Our convocation here in Buenos Aires utters this hemisphere's common voice of its interest in, nay, its intense concern over, the determination of this momentous question. The repercussions of wars and preparations for wars have been so universally disastrous that it is now as plain as mathematical truth that each nation in any

* *Peace and War: United States Foreign Policy 1931–1941* (Washington, 1943), 342–52.

part of the world is concerned in peace in every part of the world. The nations of all the Americas, through their chosen delegates, have assembled to make careful survey and analysis of all aspects of their responsibilities; to take account of their common duties; and to plan accordingly for the safety and welfare of their peoples. . . .

There is no need for war. There is a practical alternative policy at hand, complete and adequate. It is no exclusive policy aimed at the safety or supremacy of a few, leaving others to struggle with distressful situations. It demands no sacrifices comparable to the advantages which will result to each nation and to each individual.

In these circumstances the representatives of the twenty-one American republics should frankly call the attention of the people of this hemisphere to the possibilities of danger to their future peace and progress and at the same time set forth the numerous steps that can well be undertaken as the most effective means of improving and safeguarding the conditions of permanent peace.

While carefully avoiding any political entanglements, my government strives at all times to cooperate with other nations to every practical extent in support of peace objectives, including reduction or limitation of armaments, the control of traffic in arms, taking the profits out of war, and the restoration of fair and friendly economic relationships. We reject war as a method of settling international disputes and favor such methods as conference, conciliation, and arbitration.

Peace can be partially safeguarded through international agreements. Such agreements, however, must reflect the utmost good faith; this alone can be the guaranty of their significance and usefulness. Contemporary events clearly show that, where mutual trust, good-will, and sincerity of purpose are lacking, pacts or agreements fail; and the world is seized by fear and left to the mercy of the wreckers.

The Conference has the duty of considering all peace proposals of merit. Let me enumerate and briefly discuss eight separate and vitally important principles and proposals for a comprehensive peace program and peace structure. They are not designed to be all-inclusive. In considering them we should be guided by guided by the knowledge that other forces and agencies of peace exist besides those made and to be made on our continents; what we do contemplates no conflict with sincere efforts the world over.

*First.* I would emphasize the local and unilateral responsibility of each nation carefully to educate and organize its people in opposition to war and its underlying causes. Support must be given to peace, to the most effective policies for its preservation; and, finally, each nation must maintain conditions within its own borders which will permit it to adopt national policies that can be peacefully pursued. More than any other factor, a thoroughly informed and alert public opinion in each country as to the suitable and desirable relationships with other nations and the principles underlying them, enables a government in time of crisis to act promptly and effectively for peace.

The forces of peace everywhere are entitled to function both through governments and through public opinion. The peoples of the world would be far wiser if they expended more of their hard-earned money in organizing the forces of peace and fewer of the present five billion dollars in educating and training their military forces. . . .

*Second.* Indispensable in their influence for peace and well-being are frequent conferences between representatives of the nations and intercourse between their peoples. Collaboration and the exchange of views, ideas, and information are the most effective means of establishing understanding, friendship, and trust. I would again emphasize that any written pacts or agreements not based upon such relationships as these too often exist on paper only. Development of the atmosphere of peace, understanding, and good-will during our sessions here will alone constitute a vast accomplishment.

*Third.* Any complete program would include safeguarding the nations of this hemisphere from using force, one against the other, through the consummation of all of the five well-known peace agreements, produced in chief part by previous conferences, as well as through the Draft Convention Coordinating the Existing Treaties between the American States and Extending Them in Certain Respects, which the delegation of the United States is presenting for the consideration of this Conference.

In these, virtually all of the essentials of adequate machinery are present. If their operation is somewhat implemented by provisions in the draft proposal I have just mentioned to be considered by this Conference, such machinery would be complete.

The first of these is the Treaty to Avoid and Prevent Conflicts between the American States, which was signed in Santiago in 1923.

The second is the Treaty for the Renunciation of War, known as the Kellogg-Briand pact, or the Pact of Paris, signed at Paris in 1928.

The third is the General Convention of Inter-American Conciliation, signed at Washington in 1929.

The fourth is the General Treaty of Inter-American Arbitration, signed at Washington in 1929.

The fifth is the Anti-War Treaty of Non-Aggression and Conciliation, signed at Rio de Janeiro in 1933.

While the Montevideo Conference in 1933 went on record in favor of the valid execution of these five agreements by each of the twenty-one governments represented, several have not yet completed this ratification. These agreements provide a many-sided and flexible functioning machinery for the adjustment of difficulties that may arise in this hemisphere. A government could not give more tangible proof of its readiness to translate into practicable form its desire to promote and to maintain peace. Swift action by all of us to ratify these agreements should be the natural assertion of our intentions.

*Fourth.* If war should occur, any peace program must provide for the problem then presented. For the belligerent, there is the ruin and suffering of war. For the neutrals, there is the task of remaining neutral, of not being too disturbed in their own affairs, of not having their own peace imperiled, of working in common to restrict the war and bring it to an end. Can we in this Conference work out for ourselves a common line of policy that might be pursued during a period of neutrality? Some first broad approaches toward that end are, I think, possible. If these are to be sound they must be inspired by the determination to stay at peace. When interests are challenged, when minds are stirred, when entry into war in some particular juncture may appear to offer to some country the chance of national advantage, then determination is needed to retain neutrality. The maintenance of neutrality is an achievement to be attained more readily if undertaken jointly. Such agreement would be a tremendous safeguard for each of us. It might be a powerful means of ending war. . . .

*Fifth.* The peoples of this region have a further opportunity. They must make headway with a liberal policy of commerce, which would lower excessive barriers to trade and lessen injurious discriminations as between the trade of different countries. This means the substitution of a policy of economic benefit, good-will, and fair-dealing for one stimulated by greedy and short-sighted calculations of monetary advantage in an impractical isolation. It would have most beneficial effects, both direct and indirect, upon political difficulties and antagonisms.

A thriving international commerce, well-adjusted to the resources and talents of each country, brings benefit to all. It keeps men employed, active, and usefully supplying the wants of others. It leads each country to look upon others as helpful counterparts to itself rather than as antagonists. It opens up to each country, to the extent mutually profitable and desirable, the resources and the organized productive power of other countries; by its benefits small nations with limited territory or resources can have a varied, secure, and prosperous life; it can bring improvement to those who feel their toil too hard and their reward too meager.

Prosperity and peace are not separate entities. To promote one is to promote the other. The economic well-being of peoples is the greatest single protection against civil strife, large armaments, war. Economic isolation and military force go hand in hand; when nations cannot get what they need by the normal processes of trade, they will continue to resort to the use of force. A people employed and in a state of reasonable comfort is not a people among whom class struggles, militarism, and war can thrive. But a people driven to desperation by want and misery is at all times a threat to peace, their conditions an invitation to disorder and chaos, both internal and external.

The intervening years have given added significance to the economic program adopted at the Conference at Montevideo three years ago. That program is today the greatest potential force both for peace and prosperity. Our present Conference should reaffirm and secure action upon this program of economic intelligence. . . .

*Sixth.* The Conference must recognize the all-important principle of practical international cooperation to restore many indispensable relationships between nations, for international relationships, in many vital respects, are at a low ebb. The entire international order is severely dislocated. Chaotic conditions in the relations between nations have appeared. Human progress already has slowed down.

Nations in recent years have sought to live a hermit existence by isolating themselves from each other in suspicion and fear. The inevitable result is not unlike that experienced by a community where individuals undertake to live a hermit existence, with the resultant decline and decay of the spiritual, the moral, the educational, and the material benefits and blessings which spring from community organization and effort. The difference, when nations live apart, is that the entire human race in countless instances suffers irreparable injury—political, moral, material, spiritual, and social. Today, for illustration, through lack of comprehension, understanding, and confidence, we see many nations exhausting their material substance and the vitality of their people by piling up huge armaments. We behold others, in their attempted isolation, becoming more indifferent and less considerate toward the rights, privileges, and honest opinions of others. National character and conduct are threatened with utter demoralization. At no distant time we shall see a state of moral and spiritual isolation, bringing with it the condemnation of the world, covering great parts of the earth, unless peoples halt and turn toward a sane course.

*Seventh.* International law has been in large measure flouted. It should be reestablished, revitalized, and strengthened by general demand. International law protects the peace and security of nations and so safeguards them against maintaining great armaments and wasting their substance in continual readiness for war. Founded upon justice and humanity, the great principles of international law are the source and fountain of the equality, the security, and the very existence of nations. Armies and navies are no permanent substitute. Abandonment of the rule of law would not only leave small or unarmed states at the mercy of the reckless and powerful but would hopelessly undermine all international order. It is inconceivable that the civilized nations would long delay a supreme effort to reestablish that rule of law.

*Eighth.* Observance of understandings, agreements, and treaties between nations constitutes the foundation of international order. May I say here that this is not a time for crimination or recrimination, nor is such in my mind during this discussion. There must be the fullest patience and forbearance, one country with another, as the nations endeavor to climb back to that high ground of wholesome and elevating relationship of loyalty to the given word, of faithful fair-dealing.

International agreements have lost their force and reliability as a basis of relations between nations. This extremely ominous and fateful development constitutes the most dangerous single phenomenon in the world of today; not international law merely, but that which is higher—moral law—and the whole integrity and honor of governments are in danger of being ruthlessly trampled upon. There has been a failure of the spirit. There is no task more urgent than that of remaking the basis of trusted agreement between nations. They must ardently seek the terms of new agreements and stand behind them with unfailing will. The vitality of international agreements must be restored.

If the solemn rights and obligations between nations are to be treated lightly or brushed aside, the nations of the world will head straight toward international anarchy and chaos. And soon, too, the citizen begins to lower his individual standards of personal, moral, and business conduct to those of his government.

Trust in each nation's honor and faith in its given word must be restored by the concerted resolve of all governments.

It is to the interest of everyone that there be an end of treaties broken by arbitrary unilateral action. Peaceful procedure, agreements between the signatories, and mutual understanding must be restored as the means of modifying or ending international agreements.

In the accomplishment of the high aims and purposes of this eight-fold program, the people of every nation have an equal interest. We of this hemisphere have reason to hope that these great objectives may receive the support of all peoples. If peace and progress are to be either maintained or advanced, the time is overripe for renewed effort on each nation's part. There can be no delay. Through past centuries, the human race fought its way up from the low level of barbarism and war to that of civilization and peace. This accomplishment has only been partial, and it may well be but temporary.

It would be a frightful commentary on the human race if, with the awful lesson of its disastrous experience, responsible and civilized governments should now fail.

The nations of this continent should omit no word or act in their attempt to meet the dangerous conditions which endanger peace. Let our actions here at Buenos Aires constitute the most potent possible appeal to peacemakers and warmakers throughout the world. . . .

3 | Hull on the Foundations of American Foreign Policy, July 16, 1937 *

To Hull the following succinct statement of principles comprised the essence of United States foreign policy. Issued in response to the accumulating pressures abroad, they entailed an appeal to reason. If the United States fostered and sustained peaceful relations with the rest of the world, he could detect no reason why other nations should not do so. There was no room in Hull's concept of a moral and peaceful world order for the vast variety of historic and environmental problems and incentives which had always driven nations to war. Like Wilson, Hull assumed that peace was the ultimate good, recognized by all, and that as a guide to national action a country's specific ambitions abroad paled by comparison. Hull's principles, by circumscribing the area of legitimate change, assigned a special morality to the rights of possession.

* *Foreign Relations of the United States, 1937*, I (Washington, 1954), 699–700.

I have been receiving from many sources inquiries and suggestions arising out of disturbed situations in various parts of the world.

Unquestionably there are in a number of regions tensions and strains which on their face involve only countries that are near neighbors but which in ultimate analysis are of inevitable concern to the whole world. Any situation in which armed hostilities are in progress or are threatened is a situation wherein rights and interests of all nations either are or may be seriously affected. There can be no serious hostilities anywhere in the world which will not one way or another affect interests or rights or obligations of this country. I therefore feel warranted in making—in fact, I feel it a duty to make—a statement of this Government's position in regard to international problems and situations with respect to which this country feels deep concern.

This country constantly and consistently advocates maintainence of peace. We advocate national and international self-restraint. We advocate abstinence by all nations from use of force in pursuit of policy and from interference in the internal affairs of other nations. We advocate adjustment of problems in international relations by processes of peaceful negotiation and agreement. We advocate faithful observance of international agreements. Upholding the principle of the sanctity of treaties, we believe in modification of provisions of treaties, when need therefore arises, by orderly processes carried out in a spirit of mutual helpfulness and accommodation. We believe in respect by all nations for the rights of others and performance by all nations of established obligations. We stand for revitalizing and strengthening of international law. We advocate steps toward promotion of economic security and stability the world over. We advocate lowering or removing of excessive barriers in international trade. We seek effective equality of commercial opportunity and we urge upon all nations application of the principle of equality of treatment. We believe in limitation and reduction of armament. Realizing the necessity for maintaining armed forces adequate for national security, we are prepared to reduce or to increase our own armed forces in proportion to reductions or increases made by other countries. We avoid entering into alliances or entangling commitments but we believe in cooperative effort by peaceful and practicable means in support of the principles hereinbefore stated.

# 4 | Portugal's Critique of Hull's Statement of Principles, August 1937 *

In this reply to Hull's statement of principles, the Portuguese government pointed to the fact that all nations believed in peace, provided that peace served their national interests. If, however, a nation were determined to employ force to reach its ends, Hull's principles would not restrain it. To the Portuguese government the international problems of 1937 were genuine and would not be exorcised by appeals to abstract principles.

✍

On general grounds, it . . . seems that no objection can be raised against the assertions, advices or wishes as a whole, of the Secretary of State: everyone desires peace, everyone proclaims the sanctity of treaties and the faithful compliance therewith, everyone desires that there be less difficulties in international trade, and everyone wishes to have the burden of armaments removed or lightened. Difficulties begin only when it is sought to pass from the field of intentions into that of action, or, more concretely, what is to be done so that the events —in the development of which it is very difficult to establish individual or national responsibilities—will not contradict the good intentions.

The repeated affirmation, especially on the part of the great powers, of the principles advocated by the Secretary of State, the intellectual or sentimental adhesion of many to the said principles, their inclusion in many treaties between nations or in a document of greater scope aiming at defining the rules of life common to all states, will have, we believe, the effect of a certain moral pressure, but will produce rather limited practical action. We would be mistaken if we were to expect important results therefrom.

If there exists a danger or preoccupation of war, it is useless to attempt to have the States disarm or reduce the armaments; if there exist grave injustices in the solution of problems of international affairs and no peaceful method is seen to make them disappear, it is useless to dissuade the victims thereof to cause justice to be respected by force, if they have it; if the nations, by virtue of their own excesses or because they are exposed to the mistakes of others, must defend their economy and their financial balance, and deem it necessary to do so by raising tariffs, devaluating currency, or prohibiting the entry of workers or foreign goods, they will do so, even though they should not seek in that policy their true and ultimate interests and even though they should have taken at one time or another the solemn engagement to refrain from doing this. . . .

We believe that one should not forget the difference between the juridical and political field and the sociological field, because one thing is *what is,* and another thing is what it is *ordered to be,* or what it is *wished to be.* International

* The Portuguese reply to Hull's statement of principles, August 20, 1937, *Foreign Relations of the United States, 1937,* I, 791–7.

society has endeavored to solve its difficulties (as many states have done in their internal activity) by means of abstract formulae, declarations of principles, solemn assertions, many texts and treaties, and the uselessness, and at times even the grave inconvenience, of everything, or almost everything, has been seen. At least, everyone is entitled to believe that things would not have happened in a different or worse manner if there had been less law-making. . . .

When it is sought to discover the causes, independent or outside of the will of the peoples and governments, which are at the bottom of today's problems, we find that all, or almost all, the evils from which nations suffer are attributed to the economic crisis of 1929.

Intervention to attenuate or eliminate the effects of the crisis was strong in the national as well as in the international field—it was intense and useless. Remedies and disillusions, conventions, congresses, conferences, and laws came in succession, and finally the passing of time cured the crisis, for outside the general lines of the policy followed as regards gold by Great Britain and the United States, it may be said that, internationally, nothing was accomplished which improved the situation, and in the national sphere, many measures were taken capable of producing adverse results. In the face of the crisis, national egotisms became insensible or hostile, and each one had to take care of himself, merely wishing that the measures taken by others would not constitute too great a burden for each one.

The crisis, or at least, the greater part of its outward signs, has passed, but the universal unrest has continued with the same acuteness, we believe. In the economic and social field, the lack of balance, disorder, and anxiety of the peoples are, thus, not issued from the economic crisis; they come from deeper regions; we feel inclined to assign them to the crisis of economic thought, that is, to the pollution of the fundamental principles of economic affairs.

For those reasons the teachings of that recent past command us to be more modest, if we do not wish to be too daring. At the bottom humanity reacts against an anti-human economy in relation to the essence of which known remedies have to be clearly insufficient. . . .

There is clearly a lack of control in the ambitions of men; there is clearly a lack of proportion between them and the means now existing or which, under present circumstances, might be created for their fulfillment. If this lack of balance is not cured by a return to sentiments of modesty and economy or by a greater capacity of production and greater possibilities of consumption, what will happen to poor mankind?

Now, at the same time that men desire a greater part of an already insufficient wealth, or threaten improvidently to consume treasures accumulated by centuries of work and economy, the uncertainty and nervousness of the international situation cause an ever increasing portion of property to be withdrawn from the consumption of men for the benefit of armaments, deviating into that channel the natural flow of national riches, and causing by this and other means the exhaustion of international credit through which rich countries, more progressive or better endowed, might assist in the economic development of others. Contrary to this, some accumulate useless gold the weight of which depresses still further their own economy.

We are placed in a vicious circle which it is necessary to break for the good of mankind; to find the point where such breaking is easiest is decidedly the problem of problems of our times.

We dare but timidly advance on this path, full of obscurity, but some points are clear: Not all of the problems which face today the generality of the nations offer the same probabilities or risks of being converted into proximate or remote causes of war. Political motives are always more to be feared than others, except when economic difficulties are brought to such a degree of acuteness that nations are condemned to live in misery because the possibilities of work and life are denied them in the world. On the other hand, it is certain that, in present circumstances, violent internal convulsions may bring about conflagrations difficult to localize.

Now, in the political field, it is pertinent to ask whether the internationalism of our days is a factor of peace or of war. It seems to us that internationalism, covering as it does pronounced leanings toward national imperialisms, is a source of complications and dangers. The idea of the supernational organization and the tendency toward "world citizenship" are either essentially erroneous and humanly impossible or are so far removed from present conditions that they can only act—even if the fact noted above did not exist—as perturbing elements.

Furthermore, this would be creating new problems under the pretext of solving those existing, and although at times relief is found in a change of worries, the safest path is that of the closest cooperation between the peoples, on the basis of the national organizations, if, as proposed in the declaration of the Secretary of State, the nations are endowed with the spirit of "mutual assistance" and of absolute respect for the rights of others.

In commenting at length on the note of the Secretary of State, the Portuguese Government did not intend to indicate solutions or the best way to find them. This would be an excessive presumption. However, the nations are attached to false ideas and have taken the habit of entrusting the solution of grave external problems to vague formulae and inconsistent combinations; and to acknowledge by means of an impartial examination the inanity of the efforts made in that direction appears to this Government to be the first step and the indispensable preparation of the ground for any constructive work.

# 5 | Joseph C. Grew's Observations on American Foreign Policy, October 1937 *

For Grew, *Realpolitik,* not idealism, governed international affairs. He recorded in his diary that the United States, whatever its appeal to peaceful methods of

* Joseph C. Grew, *Turbulent Era, A Diplomatic Record of Forty Years, 1904–1945,* Walter Johnson, ed. (Boston, 1952), II: 1167n–8n. Copyright 1952 by Houghton Mifflin. Reprinted by permission of the publisher.

exchange among nations, would not control events or even avoid war unless it demonstrated a will to fight. Grew questioned as well the tendency of the United States to overextend itself in the Far East.

✍

I have no right, as a representative of the Government, to criticize the Government's policy and actions, but that doesn't make me feel any less sorry about the way things have turned. An architect who has spent five years slowly building what he hoped was going to be a solid and permanent edifice and has then seen that edifice suddenly crumble about his ears might feel similarly. Or a doctor who has worked hard over a patient and then has lost his case. Our country came to a fork in the road and, paradoxical as it may seem to a peace-loving nation, chose the road which leads not to peace but potentially to war. Our primary and fundamental concept was to avoid involvement in the Far Eastern mess; we have chosen the road which might lead directly to involvement.

If this sudden turnabout in policy could possibly help the situation either now or in future, if our branding of Japan as an aggressor and our appeal to the Nine Power Treaty and the Kellogg Pact and our support of the League of Nations, could serve to stop the fighting in China or limit its sphere or prevent similar aggression in the world in future, my accord with this step would be complete and wholehearted. But, alas, history and experience have shown that Real Politik and not ethereal idealism should govern our policy and our acts today. With Manchuria, Abyssinia and Spain written in big letters across the pages of history, how can we ignore the practical experience of those events and the hopelessness of deterring them *unless we are willing to fight?* Moral suasion is ineffective; economic or financial sanctions have been shown to be ineffective and dangerous to boot. Once again I fear that we shall crawl out on a limb—and be left there—to reap the odium and practical disadvantages of our course from which other countries will then hasten to profit. Such is internationalism today. Why, oh why, do we disregard the experience and facts of history which stare us in the face?

6 | Franklin D. Roosevelt's Quarantine Speech, Chicago, October 5, 1937 *

For the United States in 1937 the time of reckoning had come. Under the pressure of German and Japanese rearmament and aggressiveness the nation had either to reduce its commitments sharply in both Europe and Asia or prepare for

* *Peace and War,* 383–7.

the coming war. The moralistic preachments of Stimson and Hull had demonstrated conclusively that such devices as nonrecognition and the recital of principles were ineffective in stopping aggression when other nations regarded their interests as involved in change. Roosevelt in his famous Chicago speech of October 1937 commenced his long and halting program to bring some solvency into American foreign policy. He saw the need of expanding United States naval power and supporting the democracies of Europe in their burgeoning struggle against Hitler. Roosevelt reminded the American people that the world was at war and that not all contestants were equally responsible for the death and destruction. Nor would the United States escape unless it combined its resources, moral and physical, with those of the peace-loving nations. It was essential, he declared, that the United States play a role in leading the world to a "triumph of law and moral principles in order that peace, justice, and confidence may prevail in the world." How and at what price the United States could guarantee the sanctity of treaties and respect for the rights and liberties of others he did not say. He suggested only that the will to peace necessitated positive policies which might deter nations from defying international agreements. Even at that Roosevelt spoke not of interests as embodied in the Versailles system, but of abstract principles that were being challenged by aggression. For him any forceful defiance of the *status quo* could result only from immorality. The deeply crusading tone of his speech permitted no distinctions between changes which the nation might or might not accept diplomatically.

I am glad to come once again to Chicago and especially to have the opportunity of taking part in the dedication of this important project of civic betterment.

On my trip across the continent and back I have been shown many evidences of the result of common-sense cooperation between municipalities and the Federal Government, and I have been greeted by tens of thousands of Americans who have told me in every look and word that their material and spiritual well-being has made great strides forward in the past few years.

And yet, as I have seen with my own eyes, the prosperous farms, the thriving factories, and the busy railroads—as I have seen the happiness and security and peace which covers our wide land—almost inevitably I have been compelled to contrast our peace with very different scenes being enacted in other parts of the world.

It is because the people of the United States under modern conditions must, for the sake of their own future, give thought to the rest of the world, that I, as the responsible executive head of the Nation, have chosen this great inland city and this gala occasion to speak to you on a subject of definite national importance.

The political situation in the world, which of late has been growing progressively worse, is such as to cause grave concern and anxiety to all the peoples and nations who wish to live in peace and amity with their neighbors.

Some 15 years ago the hopes of mankind for a continuing era of international peace were raised to great heights when more than 60 nations solemnly pledged themselves not to resort to arms in furtherance of their national aims and policies. The high aspirations expressed in the Briand-Kellogg Peace Pact and the hopes for peace thus raised have of late given away to a haunting fear of calamity. The present reign of terror and international lawlessness began a few years ago.

It began through unjustified interference in the internal affairs of other nations or the invasion of alien territory in violation of treaties and has now reached a stage where the very foundations of civilization are seriously threatened. The landmarks and traditions which have marked the progress of civilization toward a condition of law, order, and justice are being wiped away.

Without a declaration of war and without warning or justification of any kind, civilians, including women and children, are being ruthlessly murdered with bombs from the air. In times of so-called peace ships are being attacked and sunk by submarines without cause or notice. Nations are fomenting and taking sides in civil warfare in nations that have never done them any harm. Nations claiming freedom for themselves deny it to others.

Innocent peoples and nations are being cruelly sacrificed to a greed for power and supremacy which is devoid of all sense of justice and humane consideration.

To paraphrase a recent author, "perhaps we foresee a time when men, exultant in the technique of homicide, will rage so hotly over the world that every precious thing will be in danger, every book and picture and harmony, every treasure garnered through two millenniums, the small, the delicate, the defenseless—all will be lost or wrecked or utterly destroyed."

If those things come to pass in other parts of the world let no one imagine that America will escape, that it may expect mercy, that this Western Hemisphere will not be attacked, and that it will continue tranquilly and peacefully to carry on the ethics and the arts of civilization.

If those days come "there will be no safety by arms, no help from authority, no answer in science. The storm will rage till every flower of culture is trampled and all human beings are leveled in a vast chaos."

If those days are not to come to pass—if we are to have a world in which we can breathe freely and live in amity without fear—the peace-loving nations must make a concerted effort to uphold laws and principles on which alone peace can rest secure.

The peace-loving nations must make a concerted effort in opposition to those violations of treaties and those ignorings of humane instincts which today are creating a state of international anarchy and instability from which there is no escape through mere isolation or neutrality.

Those who cherish their freedom and recognize and respect the equal right of their neighbors to be free and live in peace, must work together for the triumph of law and moral principles in order that peace, justice, and confidence may prevail in the world. There must be a return to a belief in the pledged word, in the value of a signed treaty. There must be recognition of the fact that national morality is as vital as private morality.

A bishop wrote me the other day: "It seems to me that something greatly needs to be said in behalf of ordinary humanity against the present practice of carrying the horrors of war to helpless civilians, especially women and children. It may be that such a protest might be regarded by many, who claim to be realists, as futile, but may it not be that the heart of mankind is so filled with horror at the present needless suffering that that force could be mobilized in sufficient volume to lessen such cruelty in the days ahead. Even though it may take twenty years, which God forbid, for civilization to make effective its corporate protest against this barbarism, surely strong voices may hasten the day."

There is a solidarity and interdependence about the modern world, both technically and morally, which makes it impossible for any nation completely to isolate itself from economic and political upheavals in the rest of the world, especially when such upheavals appear to be spreading and not declining. There can be no stability or peace either within nations or between nations except under laws and moral standards adhered to by all. International anarchy destroys every foundation for peace. It jeopardizes either the immediate or the future security of every nation, large or small. It is, therefore, a matter of vital interest and concern to the people of the United States that the sanctity of international treaties and the maintenance of international morality be restored.

The overwhelming majority of the peoples and nations of the world today want to live in peace. They seek the removal of barriers against trade. They want to exert themselves in industry, in agriculture, and in business, that they may increase their wealth through the production of wealth-producing goods rather than striving to produce military planes and bombs and machine guns and cannon for the destruction of human lives and useful property.

In those nations of the world which seem to be piling armament on armament for purposes of aggression, and those other nations which fear acts of aggression against them and their security, a very high proportion of their national income is being spent directly for armaments. It runs from 30 to as high as 50 percent. The proportion that we in the United States spend is far less—11 or 12 percent.

How happy we are that the circumstances of the moment permit us to put our money into bridges and boulevards, dams and reforestation, the conservation of our soil, and many other kinds of useful works rather than into huge standing armies and vast supplies of implements of war.

I am compelled and you are compelled, nevertheless, to look ahead. The peace, the freedom, and the security of 90 percent of the population of the world is being jeopardized by the remaining 10 percent, who are threatening a breakdown of all international order and law. Surely the 90 percent who want to live in peace under law and in accordance with moral standards that have received almost universal acceptance through the centuries, can and must find some way to make their will prevail.

The situation is definitely of universal concern. The questions involved relate not merely to violations of specific provisions of particular treaties; they are questions of war and of peace, of international law, and especially of principles of humanity. It is true that they involve definite violations of agreements, and especially of the Covenant of the League of Nations, the Briand-Kellogg Pact, and the Nine Power Treaty. But they also involve problems of world economy, world security, and world humanity.

It is true that the moral consciousness of the world must recognize the importance of removing injustices and well-founded grievances; but at the same time it must be aroused to the cardinal necessity of honoring sanctity of treaties, of respecting the rights and liberties of others, and of putting an end to acts of international aggression.

It seems to be unfortunately true that the epidemic of world lawlessness is spreading.

When an epidemic of physical disease starts to spread, the community approves and joins in a quarantine of the patients in order to protect the health of the community against the spread of the disease.

It is my determination to pursue a policy of peace and to adopt every practicable measure to avoid involvement in war. It ought to be inconceivable that in this modern era, and in the face of experience, any nation could be so foolish and ruthless as to run the risk of plunging the whole world into war by invading and violating in contravention of solemn treaties the territory of other nations that have done them no real harm and which are too weak to protect themselves adequately. Yet the peace of the world and the welfare and security of every nation is today being threatened by that very thing.

No nation which refuses to exercise forbearance and to respect the freedom and rights of others can long remain strong and retain the confidence and respect of other nations. No nation ever loses its dignity or good standing by conciliating its differences and by exercising great patience with and consideration for the rights of other nations.

War is a contagion, whether it be declared or undeclared. It can engulf states and peoples remote from the original scene of hostilities. We are determined to keep out of war, yet we cannot insure ourselves against the disastrous effects of war and the dangers of involvement. We are adopting such measures as will minimize our risk of involvement, but we cannot have complete protection in a world of disorder in which confidence and security have broken down.

If civilization is to survive the principles of the Prince of Peace must be restored. Shattered trust between nations must be revived.

Most important of all, the will for peace on the part of peace-loving nations must express itself to the end that nations that may be tempted to violate their agreements and the rights of others will desist from such a cause. There must be positive endeavors to preserve peace.

America hates war. America hopes for peace. Therefore, America actively engages in the search for peace.

# 7 | Hull's Address at Washington, March 17, 1938 *

In this address Hull restated his principles of international morality. He denied specifically that United States policies abroad were based on national interests. What guided American purpose in the Far East and elsewhere, he said, were not financial, commercial, and missionary activities, but rather the desire that "orderly processes in international relationships based on the principles to which I have referred be maintained." For Hull, as for Wilson, American interests were everywhere in principle and nowhere in actuality. The Secretary's speech was another excellent example of the utopian internationalism of the interwar years. The United States had an interest in world stability, completely universalized, but it would maintain that stability, Hull believed, less through power than through the promotion of his principles which would prevent any change not desired by the United States. This speech was another effort of Hull to perpetuate the *status quo* in world affairs at no cost to this nation.

🖎

. . . The primary objectives of our foreign policy are the maintenance of the peace of our country and the promotion of the economic, the social, and the moral welfare of our people. Unfortunately, the means of attaining these objectives involve today so many factors of great complexity that their real significance is frequently misunderstood and misinterpreted.

By instinct and tradition our country has been, throughout its history, sincerely devoted to the cause of peace. Within the limitations imposed by time and circumstance we have earnestly sought to discharge our responsibilities as a member of the family of nations in promoting conditions essential to the maintenance of peace. We have consistently believed in the sanctity of treaty obligations and have endeavored to apply this belief in the actual practice of our foreign relations. In common with all other nations we have, since the end of the World War, assumed a solemn obligation not to resort to force as an instrument of national policy. All this gives us a moral right to express our deep concern over the rising tide of lawlessness, the growing disregard of treaties, the increasing reversion to the use of force, and the numerous other ominous tendencies which are emerging in the sphere of international relations.

On July 16, 1937, I issued a public statement setting forth the fundamental principles to which our Government adheres in the formulation of its foreign policy. On behalf of our Government I transmitted a copy of this statement to every government of the world, requesting such comment as each might see fit to offer. To our profound gratification an overwhelming majority of those governments joined in affirming their faith in these vital principles. . . .

The crucial issue today is whether these principles will be vitalized and be firmly established as the foundation of an international order or whether inter-

* *Peace and War,* 407–19.

national anarchy based on brute force will inundate the world and ultimately sweep away the very bases of civilization and progress. That issue is universal. No more than a community or a nation, can the world base its existence in part on law and in part on lawlessness, in part on order and in part on chaos, in part on processes of peace and in part on methods of violence.

On August 23 I made another public statement reaffirming the principles which should underlie international order, peace, and justice, if the world is to avoid a relapse into another dark night of international anarchy and general retrogression. I called attention again to the fact that if these principles are to be effective they must be universal in their application. This statement was prompted by the fact that the progress and possibilities of armed conflict were becoming more alarming both in the European and the Far Eastern areas and that the basic principles to which I have just referred were being challenged and the doctrine of armed force was gaining supremacy in important regions of the world.

During the early months of the conflict in the Far East I appealed on several occasions, in the name of our Government, to both Japan and China to desist from using armed force and to resort to the well-recognized processes of peaceful settlement for the adjustment of whatever differences existed between them. I said that we would be glad to be of assistance toward facilitating, in any manner that might be practicable and mutually agreeable, resort by them to such processes. . . .

We have affirmed on every possible occasion and have urged upon all nations the supreme need for keeping alive and for practicing sound fundamental principles of relations among civilized nations. We have never entertained and we have not the slightest intention to entertain any such notion as the use of American armed forces for "policing the world." But we equally have not the slightest intention of reversing a tradition of a century and a half by abandoning our deep concern for, and our advocacy of, the establishment everywhere of international order under law, based upon the well-recognized principles to which I have referred. It is our profound conviction that the most effective contribution which we, as a nation sincerely devoted to the cause of peace, can make—in the tragic conditions with which our people, in common with the rest of mankind, are confronted today—is to have this country respected throughout the world for integrity, justice, good will, strength, and unswerving loyalty to principles.

The foregoing is the essence of our foreign policy. The record is an open book. We spare no effort to make known the facts regarding our attitude, our objectives, and our acts. We are always ready to furnish to the members of the Congress essential information. You, gentlemen, have first-hand knowledge of our constant effort to keep the press and the public informed.

There is one thing that we cannot do; and that is, to prepare and to place before every government of the world a detailed chart of the course of policy and action which this country will or will not pursue under any particular set of circumstances. No man, no nation, can possibly foresee all the circumstances that may arise. Moreover, to attempt to make such a detailed chart of future action would merely result in impairing our effectiveness in working for the one objective toward which we constantly strive and on which, I am certain, there is not a vestige of disagreement among the people of our country—the establishment of durable peace.

So strong, indeed, is the desire of this country for peace that many measures have been suggested toward our keeping out of war—some of them in complete disregard of both experience and practicability. It has been urged that we apply the neutrality law automatically in all circumstances, without adequate consideration of the possible consequences of such action for our own peace and for the safety of our citizens. It has been urged that we withdraw precipitately from any part of the world in which violators of international decencies choose to assert themselves. It has even been urged that we change the very basis of our representative form of government in a frantic search for something which the proposers assume would make it more likely that this country avoid war. . . .

Likewise dangerous, from the viewpoint of the preservation of peace, is the proposal that we retire from the Far East, comprising the chief portion of the Pacific area. Unfortunately, many people in this country have wholly misunderstood the position and policy of our Government in relation to that situation. Some have visualized only our trade and investment relationships with China, or our moral and cultural interests there, symbolized by missionary, educational, medical, and similar activities. Some have concentrated their attention solely upon the incidental and exceptional facts of the existence of extraterritoriality and the maintenance of some armed forces to assist in safeguarding our nationals against possible mob violence and similar disorders—special rights which it is our policy to give up and forces which it is our policy to withdraw the moment the unusual conditions disappear.

All these are important. But the interest and concern of the United States— whether in the Far East, in any other part of the Pacific area, in Europe, or anywhere else in the world—are not measured alone by the number of American citizens residing in a particular country, or by the volume of investment and trade, or by exceptional conditions peculiar to the particular area. There is a much broader and more fundamental interest—which is, that orderly processes in international relationships based on the principles to which I have referred be maintained.

As I have already indicated, what is most of all at stake today, throughout the world, is the future of the fundamental principles which must be the foundation of international order as opposed to international anarchy. If we and others were to abandon and surrender these principles in regard to the Pacific area, which is almost one half of the world, we would have to reconcile ourselves to their certain abandonment and surrender in regard to the other half of the world.

It would be absurd and futile for us to proclaim that we stand for international law, for the sanctity of treaty obligations, for nonintervention in internal affairs of other countries, for equality of industrial and commercial rights and opportunities, for limitation and reduction of armaments—but only in one-half of the world, and among one-half of the world's population. The catastrophic developments of recent years, the startling events of the past weeks, offer a tragic demonstration of how quickly the contagious scourge of treaty breaking and armed violence spreads from one region to another.

Those who contend that we can and should abandon and surrender principles in one-half of the world clearly show that they have little or no conception of the extent to which situations and developments in any part of the world of today inevitably affect situations and conditions in other parts of the world. The triumph of this seclusionist viewpoint would inescapably carry the whole world back to the conditions of medieval chaos, conditions toward which some parts of both the eastern and the western worlds are already moving. Such is the fate to which extreme isolationists—isolationists at any price—all those who contend that we should neither protest against abuses nor cooperate with others toward keeping principles alive, those who say that under no circumstances should we insist upon any rights beyond our own territorial waters—such is the fate to which blind extremism of this type would consign this country and the world.

The momentous question—let me repeat—is whether the doctrine of force shall become enthroned once more and bring in its wake, inexorably, international anarchy and a relapse into barbarism; or whether this and other peaceful nations, fervently attached to the principles which underlie international order, shall work unceasingly—singly or in cooperation with each other, as circumstances, their traditional policies and practices, and their enlightened self-interest may dictate—to promote and preserve law, order, morality, and justice as the unshakeable bases of civilized international relations.

We might, if we could reconcile ourselves to such an attitude, turn our backs on the whole problem and decline the responsibility and labor of contributing to its solution. But let us have no illusions as to what such a course of action would involve for us as a nation. . .

It would mean a break with our past, both internationally and domestically. It would mean a voluntary abandonment of some of the most important things that have made us a great nation. It would mean an abject retreat before those forces which we have, throughout our whole national history, consistently opposed.

It would mean that our security would be menaced in proportion as other nations came to believe that, either through fear or through unwillingness, we did not intend to afford protection to our legitimate national interests abroad, but, on the contrary, intended to abandon them at the first sign of danger. Under such conditions the sphere of our international relationships—economic, cultural, intellectual, and other—would necessarily shrink and shrivel, until we would stand practically alone among the nations, a self-constituted hermit state.

Thrown back upon our own resources, we would find it necessary to reorganize our entire social and economic structure. The process of adaptation to a more or less self-contained existence would mean less production and at higher costs; lower living standards; regimentation in every phase of life; economic distress to wage earners and farmers, and to their families; and the dole, on an ever-increasing scale.

All this we would be doing in pursuit of the notion that by so doing we would avoid war. But would these policies, while entailing such enormous sacrifices and rendering the Nation more and more decadent, really give us any such assurance?

Reason and experience definitely point to the contrary. We may seek to withdraw from participation in world affairs, but we cannot thereby withdraw from the world itself. Isolation is not a means to security; it is a fruitful source of insecurity.

We want to live in a world which is at peace; in which the forces of militarism, of territorial aggression, and of international anarchy in general will become utterly odious, revolting, and intolerable to the conscience of mankind; in which the doctrine of order under law will be firmly established; in which there will no longer be one code of morality, honor, justice, and fair play for the individual in his relations with other individuals, and an entirely different code for governments and nations in their relations with each other. We want to live in a world in which fruitful and constructive international relationships can serve as a medium for disseminating throughout the world the benefits of the material, spiritual, and moral progress of mankind.

To that end we will continue to give full and sincere adherence to the fundamental principles which underlie international order; we will continue to urge universal acceptance and observance of these principles; we will continue, wherever necessary and in every practicable and peaceful way, to cooperate with other nations which are actuated by the same desires and are pursuing the same objectives; we will persevere in appropriate efforts to safeguard our legitimate rights and interests in every part of the world; and we will, while scrupulously respecting the rights of others, insist on their respecting our rights.

To that end we will continue to strive, through our reciprocal trade program and through other economic policies, to restore the normal processes and to expand the volume of mutually beneficial trade among the nations, which is indispensable to an increase of production, employment, purchasing power, and general economic well-being here and everywhere; we will continue to promote peace through economic security and prosperity; we will continue to participate in the numerous international scientific, technical, and other conferences and collaborative efforts, which have been such powerful influences in assisting the stream of new ideas, of new discoveries, of learning and culture, to flow throughout the world; and we will continue to urge other nations to give their support to such policies and efforts.

We believe that a world at peace, with law and justice prevailing, is possible, and that it can be achieved by methods to some of which I have referred. That is the cornerstone of our foreign policy—a policy graphically described by President Roosevelt when he said:

> There must be positive endeavors to preserve peace. America hates war. America hopes for peace. Therefore, America actively engages in the search for peace.

The objectives of our foreign policy are as easy to grasp as they are fundamental. The means we are using to attain these objectives are the only means approved by reason and by experience. For the sake of the best interests of our people, we must maintain our strength, our courage, our moral standards, our influence in world affairs, and our participation in efforts toward world progress and peace. Only by making our reasonable contribution to a firm establishment of a world order based on law can we keep the problem of our own security in true perspective and thus discharge our responsibility to ourselves—to America of today and to America of tomorrow. No other course would be worthy of our past or of the potentialities of this great democracy of which we are all citizens and in whose affairs we all participate.

# 8 | Roosevelt's Address on the Outbreak of War in Europe, September 3, 1939 *

After 1937 it was clear that Germany, Italy, and Japan were on the march with designs of undermining and destroying the traditional leadership of the great democracies in world affairs. To prevent another general war, England and France, amply supported by the United States, would have had to possess such power and unity that an assault on them would have threatened an aggressor with absolute disaster. Unfortunately the interwar years, characterized by a profound lack of realism, had witnessed the total disintegration of the alliance which had emerged triumphant from the war itself. Because of their concern for Soviet ideology, the Western democracies had ostracized Russia from their midst. What was left of their traditional alliance with that nation France and England sacrificed in their refusal to defend Czechoslovakia against the encroachment of Hitler. The West had alienated Japan completely by denying it every possibility of creating a new order in Asia. Finally, the great democracies isolated themselves from one another and permitted a powerful alliance to be formed against them, an alliance, which if it lacked the power to win, did have the power to plunge the world into war.

To American leadership any program sufficiently costly and dangerous to meet the challenge of the dictators appeared politically disastrous. In his speech of September 3, 1939, on the outbreak of war in Europe, the President warned the nation that the breaking of peace anywhere endangered the peace everywhere. Yet he assured his listeners that they would not become involved, because the government even then was preparing a proclamation of American neutrality. Roosevelt still identified American safety with the independence of the Western Hemisphere, not the independence of Western Europe. Thus the United States would remain at peace by keeping war from coming to the Americas.

* *Peace and War*, 483–5.

Tonight my single duty is to speak to the whole of America.

Until 4:30 this morning I had hoped against hope that some miracle would prevent a devastating war in Europe and bring to an end the invasion of Poland by Germany.

For 4 long years a succession of actual wars and constant crises have shaken the entire world and have threatened in each case to bring on the gigantic conflict which is today unhappily a fact.

It is right that I should recall to your minds the consistent and at times successful efforts of your Government in these crises to throw the full weight of the United States into the cause of peace. In spite of spreading wars I think that we have every right and every reason to maintain as a national policy the fundamental moralities, the teachings of religion, and the continuation of efforts to restore peace—for some day, though the time may be distant, we can be of even greater help to a crippled humanity.

It is right, too, to point out that the unfortunate events of these recent years have been based on the use of force or the threat of force. And it seems to me clear, even at the outbreak of this great war, that the influence of America should be consistent in seeking for humanity a final peace which will eliminate, as far as it is possible to do so, the continued use of force between nations.

It is, of course, impossible to predict the future. I have my constant stream of information from American representatives and other sources throughout the world. You, the people of this country, are receiving news through your radios and your newspapers at every hour of the day.

You are, I believe, the most enlightened and the best informed people in all the world at this moment. You are subjected to no censorship of news; and I want to add that your Government has no information which it has any thought of withholding from you.

At the same time, as I told my press conference on Friday, it is of the highest importance that the press and the radio use the utmost caution to discriminate between actual verified fact on the one hand and mere rumor on the other.

I can add to that by saying that I hope the people of this country will also discriminate most carefully between news and rumor. Do not believe of necessity everything you hear or read. Check up on it first.

You must master at the outset a simple but unalterable fact in modern foreign relations. When peace has been broken anywhere, peace of all countries everywhere is in danger.

It is easy for you and me to shrug our shoulders and say that conflicts taking place thousands of miles from the continental United States, and, indeed, the whole American hemisphere, do not seriously affect the Americas—and that all the United States has to do is to ignore them and go about our own business. Passionately though we may desire detachment, we are forced to realize that every word that comes through the air, every ship that sails the sea, every battle that is fought does affect the American future.

Let no man or woman thoughtlessly or falsely talk of America sending its armies to European fields. At this moment there is being prepared a proclamation of American neutrality. This would have been done even if there had been no neutrality statute on the books, for this proclamation is in accordance with international law and with American policy.

This will be followed by a proclamation required by the existing Neutrality Act. I trust that in the days to come our neutrality can be made a true neutrality.

It is of the utmost importance that the people of this country, with the best information in the world, think things through. The most dangerous enemies of American peace are those who, without well-rounded information on the whole broad subject of the past, the present, and the future, undertake to speak with authority, to talk in terms of glittering generalities, to give to the Nation assurances or prophecies which are of little present or future value.

I myself cannot and do not prophesy the course of events abroad—and the reason is that because I have of necessity such a complete picture of what is going on in every part of the world, I do not dare to do so. And the other reason is that I think it is honest for me to be honest with the people of the United States.

I cannot prophesy the immediate economic effect of this new war on our Nation, but I do say that no American has the moral right to profiteer at the expense either of his fellow citizens or of the men, women, and children who are living and dying in the midst of war in Europe.

Some things we do know. Most of us in the United States believe in spiritual values. Most of us, regardless of what church we belong to, believe in the spirit of the New Testament—a great teaching with opposes itself to the use of force, of armed force, of marching armies, and falling bombs. The overwhelming masses of our people seek peace—peace at home, and the kind of peace in other lands which will not jeopardize peace at home.

We have certain ideas and ideals of national safety, and we must act to preserve that safety today and to preserve the safety of our children in future years.

That safety is and will be bound up with the safety of the Western Hemisphere and of the seas adjacent thereto. We seek to keep war from our firesides by keeping war from coming to the Americas. For that we have historic precedent that goes back to the days of the administration of President George Washington. It is serious enough and tragic enough to every American family in every State in the Union to live in a world that is torn by wars on other continents. Today they affect every American home. It is our national duty to use every effort to keep them out of the Americas.

And at this time let me make the simple plea that partisanship and selfishness be adjourned, and that national unity be the thought that underlies all others.

This Nation will remain a neutral nation, but I cannot ask that every American remain neutral in thought as well. Even a neutral has a right to take account of facts. Even a neutral cannot be asked to close his mind or his conscience.

I have said not once but many times that I have seen war and that I hate war. I say that again and again. . . .

## 9 | Roosevelt's Radio Address from Washington, December 29, 1940 *

The steady American involvement in the war against Germany was illustrated by the successive speeches by Roosevelt during 1940 and 1941. At the outbreak of war he favored official, if not individual, neutrality. But for him it was unthinkable that the United States would tolerate a Nazi conquest of England. Through 1940 the expanding might of Germany in Western Europe, added to the persistent bombing of London, merely confirmed, for the President, the necessity for an increasing American commitment to England's defense. With the deepening involvement came a changing attitude toward Germany. In his address of December 29, 1940, Roosevelt spelled out the threat that Germany posed for the American people. Should England fall, he warned, the United States would not escape attack. It was for the United States, through its massive productivity, to sustain British resistance. The assumption that by such means alone the United States could achieve a British victory illustrated the continuing gap between the ends and means of American policy. Indeed, the administration's armament rebuilding program progressed too slowly to have any effect on the events of Europe.

✂

This is not a fireside chat on war. It is a talk on national security; because the nub of the whole purpose of your President is to keep you now, and your children later, and your grandchildren much later, out of a last-ditch war for the preservation of American independence and all of the things that American independence means to you and to me and to ours.

Tonight, in the presence of a world crisis, my mind goes back eight years ago to a night in the midst of a domestic crisis. It was a time when the wheels of American industry were grinding to a full stop, when the whole banking system of our country had ceased to function.

I well remember that while I sat in my study in the White House, preparing to talk with the people of the United States, I had before my eyes the picture of all those Americans with whom I was talking. I saw the workmen in the mills, the mines, the factories; the girl behind the counter; the small shopkeeper; the famer doing his spring plowing; the widows and the old men wondering about their life's savings.

I tried to convey to the great mass of American people what the banking crisis meant to them in their daily lives.

Tonight, I want to do the same thing, with the same people, in this new crisis which faces America. . . .

The Nazi masters of Germany have made it clear that they intend not only to dominate all life and thought in their own country, but also to enslave the

* *Peace and War,* 599–608.

whole of Europe, and then to use the resources of Europe to dominate the rest of the world. . . .

In view of the nature of this undeniable threat, it can be asserted, properly and categorically, that the United States has no right or reason to encourage talk of peace until the day shall come when there is a clear intention on the part of the aggressor nations to abandon all thought of dominating or conquering the world.

At this moment, the forces of the states that are leagued against all peoples who live in freedom are being held away from our shores. The Germans and Italians are being blocked on the other side of the Atlantic by the British, and by the Greeks, and by thousands of soldiers and sailors who were able to escape from subjugated countries. The Japanese are being engaged in Asia by the Chinese in another great defense.

In the Pacific is our fleet.

Some of our people like to believe that wars in Europe and in Asia are of no concern to us. But it is a matter of most vital concern to us that European and Asiatic war-makers should not gain control of the oceans which lead to this hemisphere. . . .

Does anyone seriously believe that we need to fear attack while a free Britain remains our most powerful naval neighbor in the Atlantic? Does any one seriously believe, on the other hand, that we could rest easy if the Axis powers were our neighbor there?

If Great Britain goes down, the Axis powers will control the continents of Europe, Asia, Africa, Australasia, and the high seas—and they will be in a position to bring enormous military and naval resources against this hemisphere. It is no exaggeration to say that all of us in the Americas would be living at the point of a gun—a gun loaded with explosive bullets, economic as well as military.

We should enter upon a new and terrible era in which the whole world, our hemisphere included, would be run by threats of brute force. To survive in such a world, we would have to convert ourselves permanently into a militaristic power on the basis of war economy.

Some of us like to believe that even if Great Britain falls, we are still safe, because of the broad expanse of the Atlantic and of the Pacific.

But the width of these oceans is not what it was in the days of clipper ships. At one point between Africa and Brazil the distance is less than from Washington to Denver—five hours for the latest type of bomber. And at the north of the Pacific Ocean, America and Asia almost touch each other.

Even today we have planes which could fly from the British Isles to New England and back without refueling. And the range of the modern bomber is ever being increased. . . .

There are those who say that the Axis powers would never have any desire to attack the Western Hemisphere. This is the same dangerous form of wishful thinking which has destroyed the powers of resistance of so many conquered peoples. The plain facts are that the Nazis have proclaimed, time and again, that all other races are their inferiors and therefore subject to their orders.

And most important of all, the vast resources and wealth of this hemisphere constitute the most tempting loot in all the world.

Let us no longer blind ourselves to the undeniable fact that the evil forces which have crushed and undermined and corrupted so many others are already within our own gates. Your Government knows much about them and every day is ferreting them out.

Their secret emissaries are active in our own and neighboring countries. They seek to stir up suspicion and dissension to cause internal strife. They try to turn capital against labor and vice versa. They try to reawaken long slumbering racial and religious enmities which should have no place in this country. They are active in every group that promotes intolerance. They exploit for their own ends our natural abhorrence of war. These trouble-breeders have but one purpose. It is to divide our people into hostile groups and to destroy our unity and shatter our will to defend ourselves.

There are also American citizens, many of them in high places, who, unwittingly in most cases, are aiding and abetting the work of these agents. I do not charge these American citizens with being foreign agents. But I do charge them with doing exactly the kind of work that the dictators want done in the United States.

These people not only believe that we can save our own skins by shutting our eyes to the fate of other nations. Some of them go much further than that. They say that we can and should become the friends and even the partners of the Axis powers. Some of them even suggest that we should imitate the methods of the dictatorships. Americans never can and never will do that.

The experience of the past two years has proven beyond doubt that no nation can appease the Nazis. No man can tame a tiger into a kitten by stroking it. There can be no appeasment with ruthlessness. There can be no reasoning with an incendiary bomb. We know now that a nation can have peace with the Nazis only at the price of total surrender. . . .

The proposed "new order" is the very opposite of a United States of Europe or a United States of Asia. It is not a government based upon the consent of the governed. It is not a union of ordinary, self-respecting men and women to protect themselves and their freedom and their dignity from oppression. It is an unholy alliance of power and pelf to dominate and enslave the human race.

The British people are conducting an active war against this unholy alliance. Our own future security is greatly dependent on the outcome of that fight. Our ability to "keep out of war" is going to be affected by that outcome.

Thinking in terms of today and tomorrow, I make the direct statement to the American people that there is far less chance of the United States getting into war if we do all we can now to support the nations defending themselves against attack by the Axis than if we acquiesce in their defeat, submit tamely to an Axis victory, and wait our turn to be the object of attack in another war later on.

If we are to be completely honest with ourselves, we must admit there is risk in *any* course we may take. But I deeply believe that the great majority of our people agree that the course that I advocate involves the least risk now and the greatest hope for world peace in the future.

The people of Europe who are defending themselves do not ask us to do their fighting. They ask us for the implements of war, the planes, the tanks, the guns, the freighters, which will enable them to fight for their liberty and our security. Emphatically we must get these weapons to them in sufficient volume and quickly enough, so that we and our children will be saved the agony and suffering of war which others have had to endure.

Let not defeatists tell us that it is too late. It will never be earlier. Tomorrow will be later than today.

Certain facts are self-evident.

In a military sense Great Britain and the British Empire are today the spearhead of resistance to world conquest. They are putting up a fight which will live forever in the story of human gallantry.

There is no demand for sending an American Expeditionary Force outside our own borders. There is no intention by any member of your Government to send such a force. You can, therefore, nail any talk about sending armies to Europe as deliberate untruth.

Our national policy is not directed toward war. Its sole purpose is to keep war away from our country and our people.

Democracy's fight against world conquest is being greatly aided, and must be more greatly aided, by the rearmament of the United States and by sending every ounce and every ton of munitions and supplies that we can possibly spare to help the defenders who are in the front lines. It is no more unneutral for us to do that than it is for Sweden, Russia, and other nations near Germany to send steel and ore and oil and other war materials into Germany every day.

We are planning our own defense with the utmost urgency; and in its vast scale we must integrate the war needs of Britain and the other free nations resisting aggression.

This is not a matter of sentiment or of controversial personal opinion. It is a matter of realistic military policy, based on the advice of our military experts who are in close touch with existing warfare. These military and naval experts and the members of the Congress and the administration have a single-minded purpose—the defense of the United States.

This Nation is making a great effort to produce everything that is necessary in this emergency—and with all possible speed. This great effort requires great sacrifice. . . .

American industrial genius, unmatched throughout the world in the solution of production problems, has been called upon to bring its resources and talents into action. Manufacturers of watches, of farm implements, linotypes, cash registers, automobiles, sewing machines, lawn mowers, and locomotives are now making fuses, bomb-packing crates, telescope mounts, shells, pistols, and tanks.

But all our present efforts are not enough. We must have more ships, more guns, more planes—more of everything. This can only be accomplished if we discard the notion of "business as usual." This job cannot be done merely by superimposing on the existing productive facilities the added requirements for defense.

Our defense efforts must not be blocked by those who fear the future consequences of surplus plant capacity. The possible consequences of failure of our defense efforts now are much more to be feared.

After the present needs of our defense are past, a proper handling of the country's peacetime needs will require all of the new productive capacity—if not more.

No pessimistic policy about the future of America shall delay the immediate expansion of those industries essential to defense.

I want to make it clear that it is the purpose of the Nation to build now with all possible speed every machine and arsenal and factory that we need to manufacture our defense material. We have the men, the skill, the wealth, and above all, the will.

I am confident that if and when production of consumer or luxury goods in certain industries requires the use of machines and raw materials essential for defense purposes, then such production must yield to our primary and compelling purpose.

I appeal to the owners of plants, to the managers, to the workers, to our own Government employees, to put every ounce of effort into producing these munitions swiftly and without stint. And with this appeal I give you the pledge that all of us who are officers of your Government will devote ourselves to the same whole-hearted extent to the great task which lies ahead.

As planes and ships and guns and shells are produced, your Government, with its defense experts, can then determine how best to use them to defend this hemisphere. The decision as to how much shall be sent abroad and how much shall remain at home must be made on the basis of our over-all military necessities.

We must be the great arsenal of democracy. For us this is an emergency as serious as war itself. We must apply ourselves to our task with the same resolution, the same sense of urgency, the same spirit of patriotism and sacrifice, as we would show were we at war.

We have furnished the British great material support and we will furnish far more in the future.

There will be no "bottlenecks" in our determination to aid Great Britain. No dictator, no combination of dictators, will weaken that determination by threats of how they will construe that determination.

The British have received invaluable military support from the heroic Greek Army and from the forces of all the governments in exile. Their strength is growing. It is the strength of men and women who value their freedom more highly than they value their lives.

I believe that the Axis powers are not going to win this war. I base that belief on the latest and best information.

We have no excuse for defeatism. We have every good reason for hope—hope for peace, hope for the defense of our civilization and for the building of a better civilization in the future.

I have the profound conviction that the American people are now determined to put forth a mightier effort than they have ever yet made to increase our

production of all the implements of defense, to meet the threat to our democratic faith.

As President of the United States I call for that national effort. I call for it in
the name of this Nation which we love and honor and which we are privileged
and proud to serve. I call upon our people with absolute confidence that our
common cause will greatly succeed.

10 | Charles A. Lindbergh's Address in New York,
April 23, 1941 *

As late as 1941 Roosevent's policies appeared to many Americans as a needless
meddling in the affairs of other nations. Isolationists condemned every American
involvement in European politics from the repeal of the arms embargo in 1939
to the passage of the lend-lease measures in 1941. Yet they never opposed the
maintenance of American commitments 7000 miles distant in the western Pacific
under the guns of the Japanese fleet. Congressional leaders who favored economic warfare against Japan after 1939 opposed the fortification of Guam or the
support of the British Empire in the Far East. Isolationism never lost its Asia-
first character, for in the Pacific the United States faced no apparent competition
for power.

What disturbed a leading American isolationist such as Charles A. Lindbergh
in April 1941 was the insistence of pro-British elements in the United States
that German power be destroyed. Since England could not recover her traditional
position in world affairs without a victory over Germany, she had no choice but
to draw the United States into her war. To defeat Germany on the European
continent, however, was for Lindbergh quite beyond the capacity of the nation's
military power. He preferred that the United States defend its security in the
Western Hemisphere. The collapse of England would be tragic, he admitted, but
it would entail no irreparable damage to American interests.

🖎

There are many viewpoints from which the issues of this war can be argued.
Some are primarily idealistic. Some are primarily practical. One should, I
believe, strive for a balance of both. But, since the subjects that can be covered
in a single address are limited, tonight I shall discuss the war from a viewpoint
which is primarily practical. It is not that I believe ideals are unimportant, even

* *The New York Times*, April 24, 1941. Copyright 1941 by The New York Times
Company. Reprinted by permission.

among the realities of war; but if a nation is to survive in a hostile world, its ideals must be backed by the hard logic of military practicability. If the outcome of war depended upon ideals alone, this would be a different world than it is today.

I know I will be severely criticized by the interventionists in America when I say we should not enter a war unless we have a reasonable chance of winning. That, they will claim, is far too materialistic a viewpoint. They will advance again the same arguments that were used to persuade France to declare war against Germany in 1939. But I do not believe that our American ideals, and our way of life, will gain through an unsuccessful war. And I know that the United States is not prepared to wage war in Europe successfully at this time. We are no better prepared today than France was when the interventionists in Europe persuaded her to attack the Siegfried Line.

I have said before, and I will say again, that I believe it will be a tragedy to the entire world if the British Empire collapses. That is one of the main reasons why I opposed this war before it was declared, and why I have constantly advocated a negotiated peace. I did not feel that England and France had a reasonable chance of winning. France has now been defeated; and, despite the propaganda and confusion of recent months, it is now obvious that England is losing the war. I believe this is realized even by the British Government. But they have one last desperate plan remaining. They hope that they may be able to persuade us to send another American Expeditionary Force to Europe, and to share with England militarily, as well as financially, the fiasco of this war.

I do not blame England for this hope, or for asking for our assistance. But we now know that she declared a war under circumstances which led to the defeat of every nation that sided with her from Poland to Greece. We know that in the desperation of war England promised to all those nations armed assistance that she could not send. We know that she misinformed them, as she has misinformed us, concerning her state of preparation, her military strength, and the progress of the war.

In time of war, truth is always replaced by propaganda. I do not believe we should be too quick to criticize the actions of a belligerent nation. There is always the question whether we, ourselves, would do better under similar circumstances. But we in this country have a right to think of the welfare of America first, just as the people in England thought first of their own country when they encouraged the smaller nations of Europe to fight against hopeless odds. When England asks us to enter this war, she is considering her own future, and that of her empire. In making our reply, I believe we should consider the future of the United States and that of the Western Hemisphere.

It is not only our right, but is our obligation as American citizens to look at this war objectively and to weigh our chances for success if we should enter it. I have attempted to do this, especially from the standpoint of aviation; and I have been forced to the conclusion that we cannot win this war for England, regardless of how much assistance we extend.

I ask you to look at the map of Europe today and see if you can suggest any way in which we could win this war if we entered it. Suppose we had a large army in America, trained and equipped. Where would we send it to fight? The campaigns of the war show only too clearly how difficult it is to force a landing, or to maintain any army, on a hostile coast.

Suppose we took our Navy from the Pacific, and used it to convoy British shipping. That would not win the war for England. It would at best permit her to exist under the constant bombing of the German air fleet. Suppose we had an air force that we could send to Europe. Where could it operate? Some of our squadrons might be based in the British Isles; but it is physically impossible to base enough aircraft in the British Isles alone to equal in strength the aircraft that can be based on the Continent of Europe.

I have asked these questions on the supposition that we had in existence an Army and an air force large enough and well enough equipped to send to Europe; and that we would dare to remove our Navy from the Pacific. Even on this basis, I do not see how we could invade the Continent of Europe successfully as long as all of the Continent and most of Asia is under Axis domination. But the fact is that none of these suppositions are correct. We have only a one-ocean Navy. Our Army is still untrained and inadequately equipped for foreign war. Our air force is deplorably lacking in modern fighting planes.

When these facts are cited, the interventionists shout that we are defeatists, that we are undermining the principles of democracy, and that we are giving comfort to Germany by talking about our military weakness. But everything I mention here has been published in our newspapers, and in the reports of congressional hearings in Washington. Our military position is well known to the governments of Europe and Asia. Why, then, should it not be brought to the attention of our own people?

I say it is the interventionist in America, as it was in England and in France, who gives comfort to the enemy. I say it is they who are undermining the principles of democracy when they demand that we take a course to which more than 80 per cent of our citizens are opposed. I charge them with being the real defeatists, for their policy has led to the defeat of every country that followed their advice since this war began. There is no better way to give comfort to an enemy than to divide the people of a nation over the issue of foreign war. There is no shorter road to defeat than by entering a war with inadequate preparation. Every nation that has adopted the interventionist policy of depending on some one else for its own defense has met with nothing but defeat and failure.

When history is written, the responsibility for the downfall of the democracies of Europe will rest squarely upon the shoulders of the interventionists who led their nations into war uninformed and unprepared. With their shouts of defeatism, and their disdain of reality, they have already sent countless thousands of young men to death in Europe. From the campaign of Poland to that of Greece, their prophecies have been false and their policies have failed. Yet these are the people who are calling us defeatists in America today. And they have led this country, too, to the verge of war.

There are many such interventionists in America, but there are more people among us of a different type. That is why you and I are assembled here tonight.

There is a policy open to this nation that will lead to success—a policy that leaves us free to follow our own way of life, and to develop our own civilization. It is not a new and untried idea. It was advocated by Washington. It was incorporated in the Monroe Doctrine. Under its guidance, the United States became the greatest nation in the world.

It is based upon the belief that the security of a nation lies in the strength and character of its own people. It recommends the maintenance of armed forces sufficient to defend this hemisphere from attack by any combination of foreign powers. It demands faith in an independent American destiny. This is the policy of the America First Committee today. It is a policy not of isolation, but of independence; not of defeat, but of courage. It is a policy that led this nation to success during the most trying years of our history, and it is a policy that will lead us to success again.

We have weakened ourselves for many months, and still worse, we have divided our own people by this dabbling in Europe's wars. While we should have been concentrating on American defense we have been forced to argue over foreign quarrels. We must turn our eyes and our faith back to our own country before it is too late. And when we do this, a different vista opens before us. Practically every difficulty we would face in invading Europe becomes an asset to us in defending America. Our enemy, and not we, would then have the problem of transporting millions of troops across the ocean and landing them on a hostile shore. They, and not we, would have to furnish the convoys to transport guns and trucks and munitions and fuel across three thousand miles of water. Our battleships and submarines would then be fighting close to their home bases. We would then do the bombing from the air and the torpedoing at sea. And if any part of an enemy convoy should ever pass our Navy and our air force, they would still be faced with the guns of our coast artillery and behind them the divisions of our Army.

The United States is better situated from a military standpoint than any other nation in the world. Even in our present condition of unpreparedness no foreign power is in a position to invade us today. If we concentrate on our own defenses and build the strength that this nation should maintain, no foreign army will every attempt to land on American shores.

War is not inevitable for this country. Such a claim is defeatism in the true sense. No one can make us fight abroad unless we ourselves are willing to do so. No one will attempt to fight us here if we arm ourselves as a great nation should be armed. Over a hundred million people in this nation are opposed to entering the war. If the principles of democracy mean anything at all, that is reason enough for us to stay out. If we are forced into a war against the wishes of an overwhelming majority of our people, we will have proved democracy such a failure at home that there will be little use of fighting for it abroad.

The time has come when those of us who believe in an independent American destiny must band together and organize for strength. We have been led toward war by a minority of our people. This minority has power. It has influence. It has a loud voice. But it does not represent the American people. During the last several years I have traveled over this country from one end to the other.

I have talked to many hundreds of men and women, and I have letters from tens of thousands more, who feel the same way as you and I.

Most of these people have no influence or power. Most of them have no means of expressing their convictions, except by their vote which has always been against this war. They are the citizens who have had to work too hard at their daily jobs to organize political meetings. Hitherto, they have relied upon their vote to express their feelings; but now they find that it is hardly remembered except in the oratory of a political campaign. These people—the majority of hardworking American citizens, are with us. They are the true strength of our country. And they are beginning to realize, as you and I, that there are times when we must sacrifice our normal interests in life in order to insure the safety and the welfare of our nation.

Such a time has come. Such a crisis is here. That is why the America First Committee has been formed—to give voice to the people who have no newspaper, or newsreel, or radio station at their command; to the people who must do the paying, and the fighting, and the dying if this country enters the war.

Whether or not we do enter the war rests upon the shoulders of you in this audience, upon us here on this platform, upon meetings of this kind that are being held by Americans in every section of the United States today. It depends upon the action we take, and the courage we show at this time. If you believe in an independent destiny for America, if you believe that this country should not enter the war in Europe, we ask you to join the America First Committee in its stand. We ask you to share our faith in the ability of this nation to defend itself, to develop its own civilization, and to contribute to the progress of mankind in a more constructive and intelligent way than has yet been found by the warring nations of Europe. We need your support, and we need it now. The time to act is here.


11 | Roosevelt's Radio Address from Washington, September 11, 1941 *


Despite Hitler's decision to undertake a two-front war in 1941 with a massive assault on Russia, the course of war in Western Europe continued to favor Germany. By autumn the President had committed lend-lease aid to Russia as well as to England. He was determined, moreover, to control the sea lanes of the Atlantic sufficiently to guarantee the successful passage of American matériel to the theaters of war. In the following speech Roosevelt condemned the German attacks on American naval and merchant ships and denied German vessels the right to enter those waters designated by the United States government as

* Peace and War, 737–43.

American defense areas. Any German attack on an American ship was for Roosevelt nothing less than international lawlessness, representing a continuing German effort to drive British and American power from the oceans.

⚔

The Navy Department of the United States has reported to me that on the morning of September fourth the United States destroyer *Greer,* proceeding in full daylight towards Iceland, had reached a point southeast of Greenland. She was carrying American mail to Iceland. She was flying the American flag. Her identity as an American ship was unmistakable.

She was then and there attacked by a submarine. Germany admits that it was a German submarine. The submarine deliberately fired a torpedo at the *Greer,* followed later by another torpedo attack. In spite of what Hitler's propaganda bureau has invented, and in spite of what any American obstructionist organization may prefer to believe, I tell you the blunt fact that the German submarine fired first upon this American destroyer without warning, and with deliberate design to sink her.

Our destroyer, at the time, was in waters which the Government of the United States had declared to be waters of self-defense—surrounding outposts of American protection in the Atlantic.

In the north, outposts have been established by us in Iceland, Greenland, Labrador, and Newfoundland. Through these waters there pass many ships of many flags. They bear food and other supplies to civilians; and they bear matériel of war, for which the people of the United States are spending billions of dollars, and which, by congressional action, they have declared to be essential for the defense of their own land.

The United States destroyer, when attacked, was proceeding on a legitimate mission. . . .

This was piracy—legally and morally. It was not the first nor the last act of piracy which the Nazi Government has committed against the American flag in this war. Attack has followed attack.

A few months ago an American-flag merchant ship, the *Robin Moor,* was sunk by a Nazi submarine in the middle of the South Atlantic, under circumstances violating long-established international law and every principle of humanity. The passengers and the crew were forced into open boats hundreds of miles from land, in direct violation of international agreements signed by the Government of Germany. No apology, no allegation of mistake, no offer of reparations has come from the Nazi Government.

In July 1941, an American battleship in North American waters was followed by a submarine which for a long time sought to maneuver itself into a position of attack. The periscope of the submarine was clearly seen. No British or American submarines were within hundreds of miles of this spot at the time, so the nationality of the submarine is clear.

Five days ago a United States Navy ship on patrol picked up three survivors of an American-owned ship operating under the flag of our sister Republic of

Panama—the S. S. *Sessa*. On August seventeenth, she had been first torpedoed without warning and then shelled, near Greenland, while carrying civilian supplies to Iceland. It is feared that the other members of her crew have been drowned. In view of the established presence of German submarines in this vicinity, there can be no reasonable doubt as to the identity of the attacker.

Five days ago, another United States merchant ship, the *Steel Seafarer* was sunk by a German aircraft in the Red Sea two hundred and twenty miles south of Suez. She was bound for an Egyptian port.

Four of the vessels sunk or attacked flew the American flag and were clearly identifiable. Two of these ships were warships of the American Navy. In the fifth case, the vessel sunk clearly carried the flag of Panama.

In the face of all this, we Americans are keeping our feet on the ground. Our type of democratic civilization has outgrown the thought of feeling compelled to fight some other nation by reason of any single piratical attack on one of our ships. We are not becoming hysterical or losing our sense of proportion. Therefore, what I am thinking and saying does not relate to any isolated episode.

Instead, we Americans are taking a long-range point of view in regard to certain fundamentals and to a series of events on land and on sea which must be considered as a whole—as a part of a world pattern.

It would be unworthy of a great nation to exaggerate an isolated incident or to become inflamed by some one act of violence. But it would be inexcusable folly to minimize such incidents in the face of evidence which makes it clear that the incident is not isolated but part of a general plan.

The important truth is that these acts of international lawlessness are a manifestation of a design which has been made clear to the American people for a long time. It is the Nazi design to abolish the freedom of the seas and to acquire absolute control and domination of the seas for themselves.

For with control of the seas in their own hands, the way can become clear for their next step—domination of the United States and the Western Hemisphere by force. Under Nazi control of the seas, no merchant ship of the United States or of any other American republic would be free to carry on any peaceful commerce, except by the condescending grace of this foreign and tyrannical power. The Atlantic Ocean which has been, and which should always be, a free and friendly highway for us would then become a deadly menace to the commerce of the United States, to the coasts of the United States, and to the inland cities of the United States. . . .

To be ultimately successful in world-mastery, Hitler knows that he must get control of the seas. He must first destroy the bridge of ships which we are building across the Atlantic, over which we shall continue to roll the implements of war to help destroy him and all his works in the end. He must wipe out our patrol on sea and in the air. He must silence the British Navy.

It must be explained again and again to people who like to think of the United States Navy as an invincible protection, that this can be true only if the British Navy survives. That is simple arithmetic.

For if the world outside the Americas falls under Axis domination, the shipbuilding facilities which the Axis powers would then possess in all of Europe, in the British Isles, and in the Far East would be much greater than all the shipbuilding facilities and potentialities of all the Americas—not only greater but two or three times greater. Even if the United States threw all its resources into such a situation, seeking to double and even redouble the size of our Navy, the Axis powers, in control of the rest of the world, would have the man-power and the physical resources to outbuild us several times over.

It is time for all Americans of all the Americas to stop being deluded by the romantic notion that the Americas can go on living happily and peacefully in a Nazi-dominated world.

Generation after generation, America has battled for the general policy of the freedom of the seas. That policy is a very simple one—but a basic, fundamental one. It means that no nation has the right to make the broad oceans of the world, at great distance from the actual theater of land war, unsafe for the commerce of others.

That has been our policy, proved time and time again, in all our history.

Our policy has applied from time immemorial—and still applies—not merely to the Atlantic but to the Pacific and to all other oceans as well.

Unrestricted submarine warfare in 1941 constitutes a defiance—an act of aggression—against that historic American policy.

It is now clear that Hitler has begun his campaign to control the seas by ruthless force and by wiping out every vestige of international law and humanity. . . .

And I am sure that even now the Nazis are waiting to see whether the United States will by silence give them the green light to go ahead on this path of destruction.

The Nazi danger to our Western World has long ceased to be a mere possibility. The danger is here now—not only from a military enemy but from an enemy of all law, all liberty, all morality, all religion.

There has now come a time when you and I must see the cold, inexorable necessity of saying to these inhuman, unrestrained seekers of world-conquest and permanent world-domination by the sword—"You seek to throw our children and our children's children into your form of terrorism and slavery. You have now attacked our own safety. You shall go no further."

Normal practices of diplomacy—note-writing—are of no possible use in dealing with international outlaws who sink our ships and kill our citizens.

One peaceful nation after another has met disaster because each refused to look the Nazi danger squarely in the eye until it actually had them by the throat.

The United States will not make that fatal mistake.

No act of violence or intimidation will keep us from maintaining intact two bulwarks of defense: first, our line of supply of matériel to the enemies of Hitler; and second, the freedom of our shipping on the high seas.

No matter what it takes, no matter what it costs, we will keep open the line of legitimate commerce in these defensive waters.

We have sought no shooting war with Hitler. We do not seek it now. But neither do we want peace so much that we are willing to pay for it by permitting him to attack our naval and merchant ships while they are on legitimate business.

I assume that the German leaders are not deeply concerned by what we Americans say or publish about them. We cannot bring about the downfall of Nazism by the use of long-range invective.

But when you see a rattlesnake poised to strike, you do not wait until he has struck before you crush him.

These Nazi submarines and raiders are the rattlesnakes of the Atlantic. They are a menace to the free pathways of the high seas. They are a challenge to our sovereignty. They hammer at our most precious rights when they attack ships of the American flag—symbols of our independence, our freedom, our very life.

It is clear to all Americans that the time has come when the Americas themselves must now be defended. A continuation of attacks in our own waters, or in waters which could be used for further and greater attacks on us, will inevitably weaken American ability to repel Hitlerism. . . .

Upon our naval and air patrol—now operating in large number over a vast expanse of the Atlantic Ocean—falls the duty of maintaining the American policy of freedom of the seas—now. That means, very simply and clearly, that our patrolling vessels and planes will protect all merchant ships—not only American ships but ships of any flag—engaged in commerce in our defensive waters. They will protect them from submarines; they will protect them from surface raiders.

This situation is not new. The second President of the United States, John Adams, ordered the United States Navy to clean out European privateers and European ships of war which were infesting the Caribbean and South American waters, destroying American commerce.

The third President of the United States, Thomas Jefferson, ordered the United States Navy to end the attacks being made upon American ships by the corsairs of the nations of North Africa.

My obligation as President is historic; it is clear; it is inescapable.

It is no act of war on our part when we decide to protect the seas which are vital to American defense. The aggression is not ours. Ours is solely defense.

But let this warning be clear. From now on, if German or Italian vessels of war enter the waters the protection of which is necessary for American defense they do so at their own peril.

The orders which I have given as Commander-in-Chief to the United States Army and Navy are to carry out that policy—at once.

The sole responsibility rests upon Germany. There will be no shooting unless Germany continues to seek it.

That is my obvious duty in this crisis. That is the clear right of this sovereign nation. That is the only step possible, if we would keep tight the wall of defense which we are pledged to maintain around this Western Hemisphere.

I have no illusions about the gravity of this step. I have not taken it hurriedly or lightly. It is the result of months and months of constant thought and anxiety and prayer. In the protection of your Nation and mine it cannot be avoided.

The American people have faced other grave crises in their history—with American courage and American resolution. They will do no less today.

They know the actualities of the attacks upon us. They know the necessities of a bold defense against these attacks. They know that the times call for clear heads and fearless hearts.

And with that inner strength that comes to a free people conscious of their duty and of the righteousness of what they do, they will—with Divine help and guidance—stand their ground against this latest assault upon their democracy, their sovereignty, and their freedom.

## 12 | Roosevelt's Navy and Total Defense Day Address, Washington, October 27, 1941 *

By October 1941 the course of the European war had provided the United States with its ultimate objective—the destruction of Hitlerism. No longer, said the President, could anything required for achieving this goal be spared. Compelled by their single-minded quest for a military victory over Germany, Roosevelt and Hull refused to consider the eventual necessity of facing a victorious Russia across a prostrate Europe.

All of us Americans, of all opinions, in the last analysis are faced with the choice between the kind of world we want to live in and the kind of world which Hitler and his hordes would impose upon us.

None of us wants to burrow under the ground and live in total darkness like a comfortable mole.

The forward march of Hitler and of Hitlerism can be stopped—and it will be stopped.

Very simply and very bluntly—we are pledged to pull our own oar in the destruction of Hitlerism.

And when we have helped to end the curse of Hitlerism we shall help to establish a new peace which will give to decent people everywhere a better chance to live and prosper in security and in freedom and in faith.

Every day that passes we are producing and providing more and more arms for the men who are fighting on actual battlefronts. That is our primary task.

And it is the Nation's will that these vital arms and supplies of all kinds shall neither be locked up in American harbors nor sent to the bottom of the sea. It is the Nation's will that America shall deliver the goods. In open defiance of that will, our ships have been sunk and our sailors have been killed.

I say that we do not propose to take this lying down.

* *The Public Papers and Addresses of Franklin D. Roosevelt,* Samuel I. Rosenman, ed. (New York, 1950), X: 441–4.

That determination of ours not to take it lying down has been expressed in the orders to the American Navy to shoot on sight. Those orders stand.

Furthermore, the House of Representatives has already voted to amend a part of the Neutrality Act of 1937, today outmoded by force of violent circumstances. The Senate Committee on Foreign Relations has also recommended the elimination of other hamstringing provisions in that Act. That is the course of honesty and of realism.

Our American merchant ships must be armed to defend themselves against the rattlesnakes of the sea.

Our American merchant ships must be free to carry our American goods into the harbors of our friends.

Our American merchant ships must be protected by our American Navy.

In the light of a good many years of personal experience, I think that it can be said that it can never be doubted that the goods will be delivered by this Nation, whose Navy believes in the tradition of "Damn the torpedoes; full speed ahead!"

Our Nation will and must speak from every assembly line, from every coal mine—the all-inclusive whole of our vast industrial machine. Our factories and our shipyards are constantly expanding. Our output must be multiplied.

That output cannot be hampered by the selfish obstruction of any small but dangerous minority of industrial managers who perhaps hold out for extra profits, or for "business as usual." And it cannot be hampered by the selfish obstruction of a small but dangerous minority of labor leaders who are a menace—for labor as a whole knows that that small minority is a menace—to the true cause of labor itself, as well as to the Nation as a whole.

The lines of our essential defense now cover all the seas; and to meet the extraordinary demands of today and tomorrow our Navy grows to unprecedented size. Our Navy is ready for action. Indeed, units of it in the Atlantic patrol are in action. Its officers and men need no praise from me.

Our new Army is steadily developing the strength needed to withstand the aggressors. Our soldiers of today are worthy of the proudest traditions of the United States Army. But traditions cannot shoot down dive bombers or destroy tanks. That is why we must and shall provide, for every one of our soldiers, equipment and weapons—not merely as good but better than that of any other army on earth. And we are doing that right now.

For this—and all of this—is what we mean by total national defense.

The first objective of that defense is to stop Hitler. He can be stopped and can be compelled to dig in. And that will be the beginning of the end of his downfall, because dictatorship of the Hitler type can live only through continuing victories and increasing conquests.

The facts of the year 1918 are proof that a mighty German army and a tired German people can crumble rapidly and go to pieces when they are faced with successful resistance.

Nobody who admires qualities of courage and endurance can fail to be stirred by the full-fledged resistance of the Russian people. The Russians are fighting for their own soil and their own homes. Russia needs all kinds of help—planes, and tanks, and guns, and medical supplies and other aids—toward the successful defense against the invaders. From the United States and from Britain, she is getting great quantities of these essential supplies. But the needs of her huge armies will continue—and our help and British help will also continue!

The other day the Secretary of State of the United States was asked by a Senator to justify our giving aid to Russia. His reply was: "The answer to that, Senator, depends on how anxious a person is to stop and to destroy the march of Hitler in his conquest of the world. If he were anxious enough to defeat Hitler, he would not worry about who was helping to defeat him."

Upon our American production falls the colossal task of equipping our own armed forces, and helping to supply the British, the Russians, and the Chinese. In the performance of that task we dare not fail. And we will not fail.

It has not been easy for us Americans to adjust ourselves to the shocking realities of a world in which the principles of common humanity and common decency are being mowed down by the firing squads of the Gestapo. We have enjoyed many of God's blessings. We have lived in a broad and abundant land, and by our industry and productivity we have made it flourish.

There are those who say that our great good fortune has betrayed us—that we are now no match for the regimented masses who have been trained in the Spartan ways of ruthless brutality. They say that we have grown fat, and flabby, and lazy—and that we are doomed.

But those who say that know nothing of America or of American life.

They do not know that this land is great because it is a land of endless challenge. Our country was first populated, and it has been steadily developed, by men and women in whom there burned the spirit of adventure and restlessness and individual independence which will not tolerate oppression.

Ours has been a story of vigorous challenges which have been accepted and overcome—challenges of uncharted seas, of wild forests and desert plains, of raging floods and withering droughts, of foreign tyrants and domestic strife, of staggering problems—social, economic, and physical; and we have come out of them the most powerful Nation—and the freest—in all of history.

Today in the face of this newest and greatest challenge of them all, we Americans have cleared our decks and taken our battle stations. We stand ready in the defense of our Nation and in the faith of our fathers to do what God has given us the power to see as our full duty.

# 13 | Grew on the Requirements of American Policy Toward Japan, September 1940 *

In this judicious survey of American policy toward Japan, Ambassador Grew attempted to bring into American Far Eastern policy some balance between ends

* Grew's dispatch of September 12, 1940, Grew, *Turbulent Era,* II: 1224–9. Reprinted by permission of Houghton Mifflin Company.

and means. Grew viewed Japanese aggression as part of a world problem which found the United States, in its determination to preserve the independence of Britain and the British Empire, becoming vastly overcommitted. Grew favored a Europe-first policy in which the United States would seek to avoid a conflict in the Far East and concentrate its effort on the re-establishment of the traditional balance of power in Europe.

1. The observations of Mr. A. T. Steele concerning Japan, recently received here by mail, have had my careful attention. In general terms I believe that Mr. Steele's observations are well-founded and sound, a belief which applies equally to the important considerations advanced in the final two paragraphs of the summary of Mr. Steele's statement. His thesis that "firmness is the soundest and safest American naval policy" and that "the risks involved are much less than is commonly supposed in the United States" is however of such far-reaching gravity as to deserve carefully studied analysis and comment. In presenting the present trend of my thoughts on this general subject I have constantly in mind the fact that the shaping of our policy vis-à-vis Japan must depend upon the broader viewpoint of the Administration in Washington and upon many factors which may not be apparent to this Embassy.

2. The situation and circumstances which led to the series of exploratory conversations with the former Foreign Minister Arita and to the recommendations for considering steps leading toward the negotiation of a new treaty of commerce with Japan have now obviously passed. I earnestly hope that the time will come when I shall feel justified in renewing those recommendations, but with the fall of the Yonai Cabinet and the radically altered policy and outlook of the present setup in Japan, further initiative on our part in proposing conciliatory measures at the present time would appear to be futile and unwise.

3. Whatever may be the intentions of the present Japanese Government, there can be no doubt that the army and other elements in the country see in the present world situation a "golden opportunity" to carry into effect their dreams of expansion; the German victories have gone to their heads like strong wine; until recently they have believed implicitly in the defeat of Great Britain; they have argued that the war will probably end in a quick German victory and that it is well to consolidate Japan's position in greater East Asia while Germany is still acquiescent and before the eventual hypothetical strengthening of German naval power might rob Japan of far flung control in the Far East; they have discounted effective opposition on the part of the United States although carefully watching our attitude. The ability of the saner heads in and out of the Government to control those elements has been and is doubtful.

4. Now, however, I sense a gradual change in the outburst of exhilaration which greeted the new Government on its inception. The Japanese Government, the army and navy and the public are beginning to see that Germany may not defeat Great Britain after all, a hypothesis which I have constantly emphasized to my Japanese contacts in the plainest language and now to add to that dawning

realization, they see the United States and Great Britain steadily drawing closer together in measures of mutual defense with the American acquisition of naval bases in British possessions in the Atlantic and with our support of the British fleet by the transfer of fifty destroyers. They hear reports of our haste to build a two-ocean navy and of our considering the strengthening of our naval bases in the Pacific and even rumors of our eventual use of Singapore. These developments and rumors are having their logical effect on Japanese consciousness. On the one hand they tend to emphasize the potential danger which Japan faces from eventual positive action by the United States and Great Britain acting together (the danger of combined Anglo-American measures has long been appreciated in Japan as evidenced by efforts to avoid irritating the United States and Great Britain simultaneously) or by the United States alone. On the other hand they furnish cogent arguments for those elements in Japan who seek economic and political security by obtaining markets and sources of raw materials wholly within the control of Japan. As for Germany, the Japanese are beginning to question whether even a victorious Germany would not provide a new hazard to their expansionist program both in China and in the southward advance. Meanwhile the future position and attitude of Soviet Russia is always an uncertain factor in their calculations. These various considerations are beginning to give them concern.

High-pressure diplomacy, especially in the Netherlands East Indies, will continue, but the fact that the Japanese Government was able even temporarily to restrain the military forces from their plans for a headlong invasion of Indochina indicates a degree of caution which I do not doubt was at least partially influenced by the attitude of the United States. What Mr. Steele describes as the "nibbling policy" appears likely to continue until the world situation, and especially the attitude of the United States, becomes clearer.

5. In previous communications I have expressed the opinion that sanctions by the United States would set Japanese-American relations on a downward curve. It is true that our own newly instituted program of national preparedness now justifies measures which need not fall within the realm of outright sanctions. On the other hand we must envisage the probability that drastic embargoes on the export of such important products as petroleum, of which the United States is known to possess a super-abundance, would be interpreted by the Japanese Government and people as actually sanctions which might and probably would lead to some form of retaliation. The risks which Mr. Steele sees as "much less than is commonly supposed in the United States" will depend less upon the careful calculations of the Japanese Government than upon the uncalculated "do or die" temper of the Army and Navy in case they should attribute to the United States the responsibility for the failure of their expansionist plans. Such retaliation might take the form of countermeasures by the Government but there would be even greater likelihood of some sudden stroke by the army or navy without the Government's prior knowledge or authorization. These risks constitute an imponderable factor which cannot at any given moment be weighed with assurance. It would be shortsighted, however, to deny their existence or to proceed with the formulation of policy and the adoption of measures without giving these

potential risks full consideration and determining the wisdom of squarely facing these risks.

6. In the ensuing observations I am carefully considering both of the fundamental purposes of my mission, namely the protection and advancement of American interests and the maintenance of good relations between the United States and Japan. When these two desiderata conflict, the preponderant emphasis to be placed on the one or the other is a matter of high policy which does not lie within my competency. My object is merely to place before the Administration in Washington the oustanding factors in the situation as we see them from the angle of this Embassy. Having carefully set forth the inevitable hazards involved in a strong policy I now respectfully turn to the hazards involved in laissez-faire policy.

7. In discussing the specific question of American-Japanese relations it is impossible to view that problem in its proper perspective without considering it as part and parcel of the world problem which, briefly, presents the following aspects:

> (a) The United States and Great Britain are the leaders of a great group of English speaking nations around the world standing for a "way of life" which is being appallingly threatened today by a group of Germany, Italy, Soviet Russia and Japan whose avowed purpose is to impose by force of arms their will upon conquered peoples. In attempting to deal with such powers the uses of diplomacy are in general bankrupt. Diplomacy may occasionally retard but cannot effectively stem the tide. Force or the display of force can alone prevent these powers from attaining their objectives. Japan today is one of the predatory powers; she has submerged all moral and ethical sense and has become frankly and unashamedly opportunist, seeking at every turn to profit by the weakness of others. Her policy of southward expansion is a definite threat to American interests in the Pacific and is a thrust at the British Empire in the East.

> (b) American security has admittedly depended in a measure upon the existence of the British fleet which in turn has been, and could only have been, supported by the British Empire.

> (c) If we conceive it to be in our interest to support the British Empire in this hour of her travail, and I most emphatically do so conceive it, we must strive by every means to preserve the status quo in the Pacific at least until the European war has been won or lost. In my opinion this cannot be done nor can our interests be further adequately and properly protected by merely registering disapproval and keeping a careful record therof. It is clear that Japan has been deterred from taking greater liberties with American interests only out of respect for our potential power; it is equally clear that she has trampled upon our rights to a degree in precise ratio to the strength of her conviction that the American people would not permit that power

to be used. Once that conviction is shaken it is possible that the uses of diplomacy may again become accepted.

(d) If then we can by firmness preserve the status quo in the Pacific until and if Britain emerges successfully from the European struggle, Japan will be faced with a situation which will make it impossible for the present opportunist philosophy to maintain the upper hand. At a moment it might then be possible to undertake a readjustment of the whole Pacific problem on a fair, frank, and equitable basis to the lasting benefit of both the United States and of Japan. Until such time as there is a complete regeneration of thought in this country [Japan], a show of force, together with a determination to employ it if need be, can alone contribute effectively to the achievement of such an outcome and to our own future security.

8. Passing from the general to the specific problem that now confronts us, and with the foregoing picture in mind, I applauded the timeliness of the instructions from the Department concerning the Shanghai defense sectors. The Department will have seen from my report of September 4 that the Foreign Minister's complaint as to alleged threats on our part was met with the statement that what we have in mind is "a logical reciprocal adjustment of international relations." I feel that the appropriate time has come to proceed, gradually but progressively with that adjustment. In the present situation and outlook I believe that the time has come when continued patience and restraint on the part of the United States may and probably will lead to developments which will render Japanese-American relations progressively precarious. It is my hope that if the Japanese Government and people can be led to believe that their hand is being overplayed, there will eventually ensue a reverse swing of the pendulum in which a reconstruction of good relations between the United States and Japan will be possible. The alternative seems to me to be hopeless.

9. The foregoing analysis, which has been drafted with care over a period of several days, has the expressed complete concurrence of the Naval, Military and Commercial Attachés and all other members of the immediate staff of this Embassy.

## 14 | The Status of United States-Japanese Relations, August 28, 1941 *

In the following statement of the Japanese position in the Far East, the Japanese government emphasized the fact that despite United States claims to peaceful

* *Peace and War*, 722–4.

intentions Japan could only regard herself as threatened by American power. Japan, continued the statement, desired a peaceful settlement in the Far East and for that was willing to make sacrifices. Japan accepted the principles of American foreign policy and wanted them applied around the entire world. Unfortunately for peace, any settlement acceptable to the Japanese required some permanent changes in the *status quo* on the Asian mainland.

. . . The Japanese Government profoundly regrets that despite the pledge it has given heretofore as well as its repeated explanations concerning Japan's actions and measures in the foreign field, the United States Government continues to entertain misgivings.

The United States Government mentions certain situations and measures which it regards as inimical to a peaceful settlement in the Pacific area. In an atmosphere of world crisis and international confusion, it is sometimes difficult to ascertain when an event is a cause and when it is a consequence.

When a nation is obstructed in the path of natural and peaceful development or when the means of its existence is threatened, not only is it imperative that that nation should take defensive measures, but it is also required to do so for the maintenance of a just peace. This was the motivating policy of the Japanese Government.

Meanwhile, the United States has taken certain measures which could be interpreted in Japan as indicative of a continuing unfriendly pressure at variance with the then current amicable conversations.

The United States Government certainly regards some of its actions as merely counter-measures against Japan's policy and procedures which were considered as conflicting with American interests and principles. On the other hand, to the Japanese Government those procedures were determined by considerations of self-protection for meeting national requirements or removing environmental and political obstacles against national security.

With admirable modesty of mind, the Government of the United States has seemed frequently unaware that its words and policies are automatically weighted with the immense power of America's accomplished facts, natural endowment and potential might. The President of the United States, and the Secretary of State, in their own unquestioning adherence to the ways of peaceful procedures, might find it difficult to believe that other nations, anywhere, could consider themselves threatened by the United States.

Yet, as long as there is lacking the assuagement of that possible threat, there will be some less favorably endowed (especially in essential resources) who will feel compelled to consider defensively their relations with the United States.

In consequence, the Japanese Government welcomes the invitation by the Government of the United States to an exchange of views in regard to basic policies and attitudes as the foundation of an understanding that will condition lasting and extensive peace in the Pacific area. For such peace, the Government of Japan is ready: for such a united effort toward a peaceful settlement covering the entire Pacific situation the Government of Japan, like the Government of the United States, would be proud to make sacrifices.

Japan's measure in Indo-China was intended to accelerate the settlement of the China Incident; and at the same time it was calculated to remove all menace to the peace of the Pacific and to secure to Japan an equitable supply of essential materials. It was a measure of self-defense the Japanese Government felt obliged to take. But the Japanese Government has no intention of threatening thereby other countries.

Therefore, the Japanese Government is prepared to withdraw its troops from Indo-China as soon as the China Incident is settled or a just peace is established in East Asia.

Furthermore, in order to remove all possible doubt in this regard, the Japanese Government reaffirms herewith its repeated declaration that its present action in Indo-China is not a preparatory step for military advance into neighboring territories. The Japanese Government believes the above pledge will suffice to clarify also Japan's intentions toward Thailand.

As regards Soviet-Japanese relations, the Japanese Government declares likewise that Japan will take no military action as long as the Soviet Union remains faithful to the Soviet-Japanese neutrality treaty and does not menace Japan or Manchoukuo or take any action contrary to the spirit of the said treaty. On the other hand, the Japanese Government sincerely hopes that the United States Government will avoid any action that might give rise to a fear of menace to Japan through collaboration with the Soviet Union.

In a word, the Japanese Government has no intention of using, without provocation, military force against any neighboring nation.

Quite properly, discussions between the Japanese Government and the Government of the United States directed toward ascertaining if there existed a basis for negotiations for a peaceful settlement covering the entire situation,— such discussions would naturally envisage the working out of a progressive program, obtainable by peaceful methods. The Japanese Government shares fully that view with the Government of the United States.

It is also stated by the United States Government that no proposals or suggestions affecting the rights and privileges of either the United States or Japan would be considered except as these might be in conformity with the basic principles to which the United States has long been committed. The fundamental national policy long cherished by the Japanese Government is again in full agreement on that point.

Regarding the principles and directives set forth in detail by the American Government and envisaged in the informal conversations as constituting a program for the Pacific area, the Japanese Government wishes to state that it considers these principles and the practical application thereof, in the friendliest manner possible, are the prime requisites of a true peace and should be applied not only in the Pacific area but throughout the entire world. Such a program has long been desired and sought by Japan itself.

The Japanese Government now confidently hopes that from the larger viewpoint of a constructive world peace, and in the light of the current international situation, past differences may be merged in an agreement of principles and a cooperative effort based on order and justice. The meeting of the responsible heads of our respective Governments would confirm and give such sanction to our purposes that peace in the Pacific would be instituted by that meeting.

— | "We could not . . . propose that the Chinese negotiate with Japan until we knew what the basic terms were which Japan intended to propose. . . ." *

Hull insisted during his conversation with Japanese Ambassador Nomura on August 28, 1941, that the two nations agree in advance on the principles to be applied to any specific problem at the proposed meeting between Roosevelt and Konoye at Juneau, Alaska. Clearly Hull and Nomura, both claiming allegiance to the same principles, took opposing views toward China's future. Hull's principles, applied to any settlement of the quarrel between China and Japan, would have perpetuated the American version of the Open Door. For Japan, claiming the right to negotiate freely with Chiang Kai-shek on the basis of superior power, the *status quo* was unacceptable. With this conflict between abstract principle and Japanese national interest no agreement was possible.

The Japanese Ambassador called by appointment made at his request at the Secretary's apartment. He expressed his appreciation for the Secretary's having arranged to have the Ambassador see the President that morning. The Ambassador said that he felt much encouraged from his interview with the President to hope for a successful outcome of our common effort to bring about an improvement in the relations between the two countries, and he added that he has telegraphed a full account of that interview to his Government.

The Ambassador said that it was his personal opinion that the suggestion of the President that the meeting between the President and the Japanese Prime Minister be held at Juneau would be agreeable to his Government and that the Prime Minister would probably proceed thither by a Japanese warship, making the journey in about ten days. The Ambassador thought that the Prime Minister would be assisted by a staff of about twenty persons, of whom five each would be from the Foreign Office, the Army, the Navy and the Japanese Embassy at Washington. The Ambassador thought that the inclusion of army and navy representatives in the delegation would be especially beneficial in view of the responsibility which they would share for the settlement reached. . . .

The Secretary then pointed out to the Ambassador the desirability of there being reached in advance of the proposed meeting an agreement in principle on the principal questions which were involved in a settlement of Pacific questions

* *Peace and War*, 724–8.

between the two nations. He dwelt upon the serious consequences from the point of view of both Governments which would ensue if the meeting failed to result in an agreement as a consequence of issues arising which could not be resolved, and he expressed the view that the meeting should therefore have as its purpose the ratification of essential points already agreed to in principle. The Secretary pointed out that in the conversations which had taken place last spring difficulties had been encountered in regard to certain fundamental points which had caused delays which finally culminated in Japan's taking action contrary to the spirit which had animated both the Ambassador and himself in those conversations. The Secretary also pointed out that it would be unfortunate if now, while one half of the Japanese Government was disposed to go along a course of peace the other half should be pulling in the opposite direction.

The Ambassador reviewed the points in regard to which difficulties had been encountered in the conversations, namely: (1) Japan's relations to the Axis, (2) the question of the retention of Japanese troops in North China and Inner Mongolia, and (3) the question of the application of the principle of nondiscrimination in international commercial relations. He noted that only in regard to the question of the retention of Japanese troops in North China, concerning which he had no information that his Government had modified its attitude, did he anticipate real difficulty. He observed that with regard to Japan's relations with the Axis there should be no difficulties, as the Japanese people regarded their adherence to the Axis as merely nominal and as he could not conceive of his people being prepared to go to war with the United States for the sake of Germany. He said he thought our attitude in regard to self-protection was entirely reasonable. The only difficulty that he saw was that to ask that Japan give a blank check for action that the United States might take against Germany in the name of self-defense was equivalent to asking for a nullification of the Tripartite Pact. . . .

The Japanese Ambassador said that with regard to the China question it was the idea of the Japanese Government that we exercise our good offices in bringing the Chinese and Japanese together leaving China and Japan to reach a direct settlement among themselves whereas the United States Government desired to discuss with Japan the basic terms on which peace was to be concluded.

The Secretary said that we were involved in this matter through Japan's requesting this Government to exercise its good offices. In order to exercise such good offices it was necessary for us to have the confidence and friendship of the Chinese Government before and after exercising those good offices. We could not, he said, propose that the Chinese negotiate with Japan until we knew what the basic terms were which Japan intended to propose and it can be imagined what a difficult situation would be created if, after a meeting between Prince Konoye and the President, an explosion should take place in China as a result of dissatisfaction with the results of that meeting. The Secretary explained further that we could not now afford to have the Chinese think that we were ignoring their interests in going ahead with any arrangements and that it was our idea to help the Japanese achieve the purpose of establishing friendship with China on a solid basis. In this way the Secretary said we could work to-

gether, Japan and the United States, in order to make the most of the potentialities of the 500,000,000 people of China as a trading nation. . . .

The Ambassador then recapitulated briefly what the Secretary had said, namely,
that the Secretary considers that there should be an agreement in principle on
the outstanding questions of importance prior to the holding of the meeting,
that the meeting would serve the purpose of ratifying agreement in principle
already reached, that the Secretary considered that the Chinese question was
one of the pivotal subjects calling for settlement, and that this Government in
exercising its good offices between China and Japan would have to consider the
basic terms on which Japan proposed to negotiate. The Secretary said this
represented his views. The Ambassador said that he recognized that what the
Secretary said was quite reasonable. The Ambassador had misgivings as to how
far the Japanese Government could go on account of the internal political
difficulties in Japan. He said, however, that Prince Konoye was a man of great
courage and was prepared to assume great risks in bringing to a successful conclusion an effort to improve relations.


## 15 | The Final Impasse in United States-Japanese Relations, November 26, 1941 *

At the crucial conference with the Japanese representatives in Washington on
November 26, 1941, Hull presented the following ten-point program as the final
United States offer. It demanded that Japan withdraw all its military forces from
China and Indochina, a demand which obviously the Japanese government would
not accept.

✍

The Government of the United States and the Government of Japan propose
to take steps as follows:

1. The Government of the United States and the Government of Japan will
endeavor to conclude a multilateral non-aggression pact among the British
Empire, China, Japan, the Netherlands, the Soviet Union, Thailand and the
United States.

2. Both Governments will endeavor to conclude among the American, British,
Chinese, Japanese, the Netherland and Thai Governments an agreement where-
under each of the Governments would pledge itself to respect the territorial
integrity of French Indochina and, in the event that there should develop a

* *Peace and War,* 811–12.

threat to the territorial integrity of Indochina, to enter into immediate con-sultation with a view to taking such measures as may be deemed necessary and advisable to meet the threat in question. Such agreement would provide also that each of the Governments party to the agreement would not seek or accept preferential treatment in its trade or economic relations with Indochina and would use its influence to obtain for each of the signatories equality of treatment in trade and commerce with French Indochina.

3. The Government of Japan will withdraw all military, naval, air and police forces from China and from Indochina.

4. The Government of the United States and the Government of Japan will not support—militarily, politically, economically—any government or regime in China other than the National Government of the Republic of China with capi-tal temporarily at Chungking.

5. Both Governments will give up all extraterritorial rights in China, including rights and interests in and with regard to international settlements and conces-sions, and rights under the Boxer Protocol of 1901. . . .

6. The Government of the United States and the Government of Japan will enter into negotiations for the conclusion between the United States and Japan of a trade agreement, based upon reciprocal most-favored-nation treatment and reduction of trade barriers by both countries, including an undertaking by the United States to bind raw silk on the free list.

7. The Government of the United States and the Government of Japan will, respectively, remove the freezing restrictions on Japanese funds in the United States and on American funds in Japan.

8. Both Governments will agree upon a plan for the stabilization of the dollar-yen rate, with the allocation of funds adequate for this purpose, half to be supplied by Japan and half by the United States.

9. Both Governments will agree that no agreement which either has concluded with any third power or powers shall be interpreted by it in such a way as to conflict with the fundamental purpose of this agreement, the establishment and preservation of peace throughout the Pacific area.

10. Both Governments will use their influence to cause other governments to adhere to and to give practical application to the basic political and economic principles set forth in this agreement.

— | "Mr. Kurusu . . . went on to say that the Washington Conference Treaties had given a wrong idea to China. . . ." *

As the negotiations between the United States and Japanese officials threatened to give way to force, the Japanese offered their own *modus vivendi* for a tem-porary arrangement while the search for a more permanent settlement continued. This Hull refused to consider. Again it was apparent that China, supported by

* *Peace and War,* 807–10.

the Nine Power Pact and the United States commitment to its territorial and commercial integrity, was the stumbling block to a compromise settlement.

✒

. . . After the Japanese had read the documents, Mr. Kurusu asked whether this was our reply to their proposal for a *modus vivendi*. The Secretary replied that we had to treat the proposal as we did, as there was so much turmoil and confusion among the public both in the United States and in Japan. He reminded the Japanese that in the United States we have a political situation to deal with just as does the Japanese Government, and he referred to the fire-eating statements which have been recently coming out of Tokyo, which he said had been causing a natural reaction among the public in this country. He said that our proposed agreement would render possible practical measures of financial cooperation, which, however, were not referred to in the outline for fear that this might give rise to misunderstanding. He also referred to the fact that he had earlier in the conversations acquainted the Ambassador of the ambition that had been his of settling the immigration question but that the situation had so far prevented him from realizing that ambition.

Mr. Kurusu offered various depreciatory comments in regard to the proposed agreement. He noted that in our statement of principles there was a reiteration of the Stimson doctrine. He objected to the proposal for multilateral non-aggression pacts and referred to Japan's bitter experience of international organizations, citing the case of the award against Japan by the Hague tribunal in the Perpetual Leases matter. He went on to say that the Washington Conference Treaties had given a wrong idea to China, that China had taken advantage of them to flaunt Japan's rights. He said he did not see how his Government could consider paragraphs (3) and (4) of the proposed agreement and that if the United States should expect that Japan was to take off its hat to Chiang Kai-shek and propose to recognize him Japan could not agree. He said that if this was the idea of the American Government he did not see how any agreement was possible.

The Secretary asked whether this matter could not be worked out.

Mr. Kurusu said that when they reported our answer to their Government it would be likely to throw up its hands. He noted that this was a tentative proposal without commitment, and suggested that it might be better if they did not refer it to their Government before discussing its contents further informally here.

The Secretary suggested that they might wish to study the documents carefully before discussing them further. He repeated that we were trying to do our best to keep the public from becoming uneasy as a result of their being harangued. He explained that in the light of all that has been said in the press, our proposal was as far as we would go at this time in reference to the Japanese proposal; that there was so much confusion among the public that it was necessary to bring about some clarification; that we have reached a stage when the public has lost its perspective and that it was therefore necessary to draw up a document which would present a complete picture of our position by making provision for each essential point involved.

The Secretary then referred to the oil question. He said that public feeling was so acute on that question that he might almost be lynched if he permitted oil to go freely to Japan. He pointed out that if Japan should fill Indochina with troops our people would not know what lies ahead in the way of a menace to the countries to the south and west. He reminded the Japanese that they did not know what tremendous injury they were doing to us by keeping immobilized so many forces in countries neighboring Indochina. He explained that we are primarily out for our permanent futures, and the question of Japanese troops in Indochina affects our direct interests.

Mr. Kurusu reverted to the difficulty of Japan's renouncing its support of Wang Ching-wei. The Secretary pointed out that Chiang Kai-shek had made an outstanding contribution in bringing out national spirit in China and expressed the view that the Nanking regime had not asserted itself in a way that would impress the world. Mr. Kurusu agreed with what the Secretary had said about Chiang, but observed that the question of the standing of the Nanking regime was a matter of opinion. His arguments on this as well as on various other points were specious, and unconvincing.

The Ambassador took the occasion to observe that sometimes statesmen of firm conviction fail to get sympathizers among the public; that only wise men could see far ahead and sometimes suffered martyrdom; but that life's span was short and one could only do his duty. The Ambassador then asked whether there was no other possibility and whether they could not see the President.

The Secretary replied that he had no doubt that the President would be glad to see them at any time.

Mr. Kurusu said that he felt that our response to their proposal could be interpreted as tantamount to meaning the end, and asked whether we were not interested in a *modus vivendi*.

The Secretary replied that we had explored that. Mr. Kurusu asked whether it was because the other powers would not agree; but the Secretary replied simply that he had done his best in the way of exploration. . . .

# 16 | The Japanese Decision for War: A Rationale, December 7, 1941 *

This final Japanese communication to the United States government, dispatched almost simultaneously with the attack on Pearl Harbor, revealed the pent-up frustrations of a decade. Pursuing what it had regarded as legitimate goals based on the rights of superior energy, efficiency, and power, the Tokyo government had been confronted with a body of principles, offered in lieu of genuine nego-

* *Peace and War,* 832–8.

tiation, which denied the legitimacy of change except that produced by diplomacy alone. Even such limitations might have served the Japanese interest had the United States and Britain not supported the Chinese position so completely as to nullify the diplomatic advantage which considerable physical effort and military success should have secured for Japan. The Japanese document noted that American principles, advocated in the name of peace, were principles favorable to the United States, as a privileged nation, but were selfishly unmindful of the interests of other nations. No longer would Japan, by observing Hull's principles, sacrifice itself to the prosperity and advantageous position of Great Britain and the United States.

✍

. . . Ever since the China Affair broke out owing to the failure on the part of China to comprehend Japan's true intentions, the Japanese Government has striven for the restoration of peace and it has consistently exerted its best efforts to prevent the extension of war-like disturbances. It was also to that end that in September last year Japan concluded the Tripartite Pact with Germany and Italy.

However, both the United States and Great Britain have resorted to every possible measure to assist the Chungking regime so as to obstruct the establishment of a general peace between Japan and China, interfering with Japan's constructive endeavours toward the stabilization of East Asia. Exerting pressure on the Netherlands East Indies, or menacing French Indo-China, they have attempted to frustrate Japan's aspiration to the ideal of common prosperity in cooperation with these regions. Furthermore, when Japan in accordance with its protocol with France took measures of joint defence of French Indo-China, both American and British Governments, willfully misinterpreting it as a threat to their own possessions, and inducing the Netherlands Government to follow suit, they enforced the assets freezing order, thus severing economic relations with Japan. While manifesting thus an obviously hostile attitude, these countries have strengthened their military preparations perfecting an encirclement of Japan, and have brought about a situation which endangers the very existence of the Empire. . . .

From the beginning of the present negotiation the Japanese Government has always maintained an attitude of fairness and moderation, and did its best to reach a settlement, for which it made all possible concessions often in spite of great difficulties. As for the China question which constituted an important subject of the negotiation, the Japanese Government showed a most conciliatory attitude. As for the principle of non-discrimination in international commerce, advocated by the American Government, the Japanese Government expressed its desire to see the said principle applied throughout the world, and declared that along with the actual practice of this principle in the world, the Japanese Government would endeavour to apply the same in the Pacific Area including China, and made it clear that Japan had no intention of excluding from China economic activities of third powers pursued on an equitable basis. Furthermore, as regards the question of withdrawing troops from French Indo-China, the

Japanese Government even volunteered, as mentioned above, to carry out an immediate evacuation of troops from Southern French Indo-China as a measure of easing the situation.

It is presumed that the spirit of conciliation exhibited to the utmost degree by the Japanese Government in all these matters is fully appreciated by the American Government.

On the other hand, the American Government, always holding fast to theories in disregard of realities, and refusing to yield an inch on its impractical principles, caused undue delay in the negotiation. It is difficult to understand this attitude of the American Government and the Japanese Government desires to call the attention of the American Government especially to the following points:

1. The American Government advocates in the name of world peace those principles favorable to it and urges upon the Japanese Government the acceptance thereof. The peace of the world may be brought about only by discovering a mutually acceptable formula through recognition of the reality of the situation and mutual appreciation of one another's position. An attitude such as ignores realities and imposes one's selfish views upon others will scarcely serve the purpose of facilitating the consummation of negotiations.

Of the various principles put forward by the American Government as a basis of the Japanese-American Agreement, there are some which the Japanese Government is ready to accept in principle, but in view of the world's actual conditions, it seems only a utopian ideal on the part of the American Government to attempt to force their immediate adoption.

Again, the proposal to conclude a multilateral non-aggression pact between Japan, United States, Great Britain, China, the Soviet Union, the Netherlands and Thailand, which is patterned after the old concept of collective security, is far removed from the realities of East Asia.

2. The American proposal contained a stipulation which states—"Both Governments will agree that no agreement, which either has concluded with any third power or powers, shall be interpreted by it in such a way as to conflict with the fundamental purpose of this agreement, the establishment and preservation of peace throughout the Pacific area." It is presumed that the above provision has been proposed with a view to restrain Japan from fulfilling its obligations under the Tripartite Pact when the United States participates in the War in Europe, and, as such, it cannot be accepted by the Japanese Government.

The American Government, obsessed with its own views and opinions, may be said to be scheming for the extension of the war. While it seeks, on the one hand, to secure its rear by stabilizing the Pacific Area, it is engaged, on the other hand, in aiding Great Britain and preparing to attack, in the name of self-defense, Germany and Italy, two Powers that are striving to establish a new order in Europe. Such a policy is totally at variance with the many principles upon which the American Government proposes to found the stability of the Pacific Area through peaceful means.

3. Whereas the American Government, under the principles it rigidly upholds, objects to settle international issues through military pressure, it is exercising in conjunction with Great Britain and other nations pressure by economic power.

Recourse to such pressure as a means of dealing with international relations should be condemned as it is at times more inhumane than military pressure.

4. It is impossible not to reach the conclusion that the American Government desires to maintain and strengthen, in coalition with Great Britain and other Powers, its dominant position it has hitherto occupied not only in China but in other areas of East Asia. It is a fact of history that the countries of East Asia for the past hundred years or more have been compelled to observe the *status quo* under the Anglo-American policy of imperialistic exploitation and to sacrifice themselves to the prosperity of the two nations. The Japanese Government cannot tolerate the perpetuation of such a situation since it directly runs counter to Japan's fundamental policy to enable all nations to enjoy each its proper place in the world.

The stipulation proposed by the American Government relative to French Indo-China is a good exemplification of the above-mentioned American policy. Thus the six countries,—Japan, the United States, Great Britain, the Netherlands, China and Thailand,—excepting France, should undertake among themselves to respect the territorial integrity and sovereignty of French Indo-China and equality of treatment in trade and commerce would be tantamount to placing that territory under the joint guarantee of the Governments of those six countries. Apart from the fact that such a proposal totally ignores the position of France, it is unacceptable to the Japanese Government in that such an arrangement cannot but be considered as an extension to French Indo-China of a system similar to the Nine Power Treaty structure which is the chief factor responsible for the present predicament of East Asia.

5. All the items demanded of Japan by the American Government regarding China such as wholesale evacuation of troops or unconditional application of the principle of non-discrimination in international commerce ignored the actual conditions of China, and are calculated to destroy Japan's position as the stabilizing factor of East Asia. The attitude of the American Government in demanding Japan not to support militarily, politically or economically any regime other than the regime at Chungking, disregarding thereby the existence of the Nanking Government, shatters the very basis of the present negotiation. This demand of the American Government falling, as it does, in line with its above-mentioned refusal to cease from aiding the Chungking regime, demonstrates clearly the intention of the American Government to obstruct the restoration of normal relations between Japan and China and the return of peace to East Asia.

In brief, the American proposal contains certain acceptable items such as those concerning commerce, including the conclusion of a trade agreement, mutual removal of the freezing restrictions, and stabilization of yen and dollar exchange, or the abolition of extra-territorial rights in China. On the other hand, however, the proposal in question ignores Japan's sacrifices in the four years of the China Affair, menaces the Empire's existence itself and disparages its honour and prestige. Therefore, viewed in its entirety, the Japanese Government regrets that it cannot accept the proposal as a basis of negotiation. . . .

# X

## The Grand Alliance

The brief half-decade that spanned the history of the Grand Alliance against Germany was in many respects the most tragic period in the history of American diplomacy. Throughout a successful, and eventually triumphant, military collaboration the United States and the U.S.S.R. could never come to terms on even the most elemental political issues raised by the process of defeating the Nazi enemy. Whatever might have been the ultimate intentions of the Kremlin toward the West, American officials after 1941 refused to accept diplomatically the logical consequences of a quarter-century of Western diplomacy—the wartime establishment of a Soviet hegemony over eastern Europe. What made the situation of the United States particularly ironic was the requirement, created by the military circumstances of the war, of encouraging the Russians to destroy German power and eventually occupy the vast areas of Slavic Europe which had comprised the historic territorial objectives of the Russian nation.

This possessiveness of the United States toward eastern Europe, encompassed in the fundamental wartime decisions to postpone political settlements until the conclusion of the war, had no relationship to the nation's diplomatic past. For American officials the Slavic states of Europe were politically corrupt, economically unstable, and strategically insignificant. The creation of an active American policy toward eastern Europe prior to the outbreak of war in 1939 would have been regarded as madness. During the interwar years United States concern for the region had been limited to occasional statements in behalf of religious freedom and self-determination of peoples. Never had United States officials formulated any specific policies to achieve such aims, for the simple reason that eastern Europe lay outside the region of historic American interest. Neville Chamberlain characterized the Western attitude toward the region when he declared in September 1938, following the Munich crisis: "How horrible, fantastic, incredible, it is that we should be digging trenches and trying on gas-masks here because of a quarrel in a far-away country between people of whom we know nothing."

631

Indeed, the very triumph of self-determination in Slavic Europe in 1919 was an historic anomaly. This region had received its former stability from the four rival empires which controlled it—the Austro-Hungarian, the Turkish, the German, and the Russian. By an extreme historic accident three of these empires, as the defeated powers of World War I, were subject to dismemberment through the simple application of Woodrow Wilson's principle of self-determination. Russia, having sacrificed through revolution the status of a victor, was similarly expected to grant freedom to her eastern European possessions. With the Versailles settlement both Britain and the United States, the nations to whom the Slavs really owed their independence, withdrew their power from the Continent. It was obvious, therefore, that Western influence in the region would not survive any serious German or Russian challenge to French military supremacy in Europe. Actually, the Western democracies gave up their dominant position in eastern Europe when they permitted Nazi power to surpass that of the rest of Western Europe, to destroy Czechoslovakia and Poland in 1939, overrun all eastern Europe in 1940, and finally unleash a massive assault on Russia in June 1941. Only by occupying the Slavic nations ahead of the westward Russian advance in 1944 and 1945 could the West have regained control of their destiny. This feat at all times far exceeded the wartime capabilities of the United States and England. (*Reading No. 1.*)

During those years when Washington displayed a negligible interest in the affairs of eastern Europe, the foundations for a new outlook were being erected within the United States itself. By 1930 the first- and second-generation Americans of eastern European origin, of whom the dominant elements were Polish-American, exceeded seven million. During the New Deal days these urban minorities came into their own in local and national politics; by 1936 they held the political balance of power in many key areas. Throughout the 'thirties, however, none of these domestic factors focused American attention on eastern Europe. Nowhere did United States diplomacy during the fall of Czechoslovakia and Poland and the subsequent Nazi conquest of other Slavic nations actively seek the political independence or economic welfare of the regions from which these millions came. Suddenly the realization in 1941 that the future status of eastern Europe had slipped beyond Western control and hinged on the outcome of the Nazi-Soviet war produced a profound revolution in the nation's diplomatic posture, a revolution in response partly to the wartime moralism of such men as Roosevelt and Hull, partly to the growing influence of eastern European minorities in American politics. It is significant that in his wartime confrontations with Stalin at both Teheran and Yalta Roosevelt reminded the Russian leader that he could not, in his refusal to negotiate territorial changes in eastern Europe, ignore the wishes of his large Polish constituency in the United States.

Even before the United States entered the European war, American leadership had set in motion a program to control the political evolution of the areas dominated by Nazi forces. On August 14, 1941, Roosevelt and British Prime Minister Winston Churchill officially proclaimed their war-time political objectives in the famed Atlantic Charter. The first three principles of the Charter declared that the United States and Great Britain sought "no aggrandisement, territorial or other," that they desired "to see no territorial changes that [did] not accord with the freely expressed wishes of the people concerned," and that they respected "the right of all peoples to choose the form of government under which they will live." In his London broadcast of August 24, Churchill praised the Atlantic Charter as an Anglo-American declaration of unity and purpose. Together, he said, the two great democracies would lead "the toiling masses of all the continents . . . forward out of the miseries into which they have been plunged, back to the broad high road of freedom and justice. . . ." At the same time Churchill assured Parliament that the Atlantic Charter did not apply to the British Empire. As in 1919, the principle of self-determination was meant to apply to the losers, not the victors. Where this left the Soviet Union was not clear. As a purely Anglo-American program, moreover, the Charter could never have meaning beyond the actual reach of British and American armed forces.

Tragically, the Atlantic Charter, based on an abstract principle, ignored the burgeoning interests of the Kremlin in European politics. For Stalin the Charter's repudiation of any alteration in the prewar political and territorial status of eastern Europe—the only region which offered the Soviets any tangible and lasting emoluments of victory—rendered it totally unacceptable as a basis of action. That Russia, unlike both the United States and Britain, eventually suffered incalculable physical destruction and twenty million deaths at the hands of the invading Nazi forces made inevitable vast disagreements over the applicability of the Atlantic Charter to the territories of Germany and eastern Europe. What made the situation even more ironic was the fact that Russia in August 1941 was at least the second strongest partner in the coming Grand Alliance and at that moment the only nation actively fighting Hitler's forces on the battlefronts of Europe. Without the continued and unlimited military effort of the U.S.S.R., moreover, the West could hardly hope to defeat Germany at all. Yet the Atlantic Charter assumed that the two Western democracies, even before the United States had formally entered the war, could dominate the postwar settlements in a region where the Soviet armies might be in actual occupation. It suggested that the Soviets were to bleed but have no authority to determine their own postwar interest vis-à-vis both their proven enemies along Russia's western periphery and the area which had served as the highroad of Nazi invasion.

II

Fortunately for the Grand Alliance, upon which hinged an ultimate victory over Germany, Western leaders managed from the outset to keep hidden the deep East-West rift over the future of eastern Europe. Churchill and Roosevelt, at the conclusion of the Atlantic conference, assured Stalin that they would extend to Russia all possible aid in that nation's conflict with Germany. Stalin demanded an understanding with England on political matters as well. Ivan Maisky, the Soviet Ambassador in London, expressed regret that Roosevelt and Churchill had not consulted the Kremlin before they issued the Atlantic Charter. Yet the Russians, fighting for their existence, were in no position to antagonize their

Western allies. At the Inter-Allied Meeting in London on September 24, 1941, Maisky accepted the principle of self-determination. The Soviet Union, he declared, "defends the right of every nation to the independence and territorial integrity of its country, and its right to establish such a social order and to choose such a form of government as it deems opportune and necessary for the better promotion of its economic and cultural prosperity."

But Maisky quickly gave the principle of self-determination a decidedly Soviet interpretation. It was embodied, he said, in his country's "dealings with various nationalities embraced within the frontiers of the Soviet Union." The Ambassador omitted any reference to the Charter's promise that the signatory powers would "seek no aggrandizement, territorial or other." His bitterness toward the Nazi destruction of Russian farms, villages, and cities conveyed a spirit of revenge that differed widely from the mood of the Atlantic Charter, which anticipated neither victors nor vanquished in the postwar world. Maisky's words predicted that the U.S.S.R. would follow the precepts of the Atlantic Charter only to the extent that they served the security interests of the Soviet Union. That the immediate military requirements far outweighed the matter of ultimate political intention was illustrated when the Soviet Union in January 1942 signed the United Nations Declaration with twenty-five other nations. In the opening paragraph the signatories accepted the purpose and principles of the Atlantic Charter. Officially, at any rate, the U.S.S.R. had been enrolled in the legion of the good.

Actually, Stalin had begun his political assault on the prewar boundaries which separated the Soviet Union from its Slavic neighbors as early as December 1941. He explained his initial territorial objectives to British Foreign Minister Anthony Eden during the latter's visit to Moscow that month. "As regards the special interests of the Soviet Union," ran Eden's report of his Moscow conversations, "M. Stalin desired the restoration of the position in 1941, prior to the German attack, in respect of the Baltic States, Finland, and Bessarabia. The 'Curzon Line' should form the basis for the future Soviet-Polish frontier, and Rumania should give special facilities for bases, etc., to the Soviet Union, receiving compensation from territory now occupied by Hungary."

To Secretary of State Cordell Hull, under enormous pressure from the Polish government-in-exile, which was residing in London, to grant nothing territorially to the Kremlin, any political concession to the Soviet Union was unthinkable. He reminded the British government on December 5, 1941, that the postwar policies of the United States "have been delineated in the Atlantic Charter which today represents the attitude not only of the United States but also of Great Britain and of the Soviet Union." In accordance with the American position, Eden informed Stalin on December 17 that "it was quite impossible for His Majesty's Government to commit themselves at this stage to any post-war frontiers in Europe. . . ."

Churchill agreed. He wrote to Eden three days later that the Soviet proposals defied the principles of the Atlantic Charter. There could be no question whatever of England "making such an agreement, secret or public, direct or implied," wrote Churchill, "without prior agreement with the United States. The time has not yet come to settle frontier questions. . . ." Even to raise the issue with Roosevelt, believed the Prime Minister, would be inexpedient. Writing to Eden on January 8, 1942, Churchill accepted completely the decision of the United States to postpone territorial settlements until the postwar peace conferences. "We have never recognized the 1941 frontiers of Russia except *de facto*," he wrote. "They were acquired by acts of aggression in shameful collusion with Hitler. The transfer of the peoples of the Baltic States to Soviet Russia against their will would be contrary to all the principles for which we are fighting this war and would dishonour our cause." For Churchill the sincerity of the Allied cause required a firm adherence to the precepts of the Atlantic Charter.

During the spring of 1942 Churchill began to relent under the continuing Soviet pressure. If the British government could not defy the wishes of the United States to whom it looked for vital supplies, it could hardly ignore the demands of the U.S.S.R., to whom England's debt at the moment was even greater. British observers were becoming aware of the growing strength of the Red Army, an army with which England would be forced to co-exist on the Continent at the conclusion of the war. British officials as influential as Sir Stafford Cripps, former Ambassador to Russia, believed that Soviet territorial demands were legitimate and no threat to British security. To the London *Times*, also, the Soviet boundaries of 1941 were "in no way incompatible with the security of Europe, which the framework of the Atlantic Charter thought to insure." It was not in the British tradition to be as doctrinaire and uncompromising as the American position dictated, especially when vital British interests were not involved. Indeed, anticipating the forthcoming visit of Foreign Minister V. M. Molotov to negotiate a treaty with the British government, Churchill wrote to Roosevelt on March 7, 1942:

> The increasing gravity of the war has led me to feel that the principles of the Atlantic Charter ought not to be construed so as to deny Russia the frontiers she occupied when Germany attacked her. This was the basis on which Russia acceded to the Charter. . . . I hope therefore that you will be able to give us a free hand to sign the treaty which Stalin desires as soon as possible. Everything portends an immense renewal of the German invasion of Russia in the spring, and there is very little we can do to help the only country that is heavily engaged with the German armies. . . .

Washington officials in the spring of 1942 and throughout the war refused to compromise the principle of postponement. The Polish government-in-exile, supported by spokesmen of the Polish Americans residing in the United States, sustained their determination to hold the United States to the principle of self-determination for the Slavic states. During February and March 1942, Roosevelt and Hull assured representatives of the Polish government that the United States would never consent to any changes in the eastern frontiers of Europe. United States military advisers, motivated by the single-minded purpose of defeating the Axis powers, warned that any advantage derived from political and territorial settlements would be offset by future controversies with the U.S.S.R., which might destroy the alliance completely. Roosevelt, as commander in chief, carried the obligation to permit nothing to interfere with the winning of the war. To maintain national unity he could not antagonize influential minorities by formally ceding portions of eastern Europe to the Soviets. Roosevelt, moreover, was convinced that in due course he could remove the deviations of purpose among the Allies solely by personal diplomacy. At the same time Hull feared that any wartime territorial arrangements would hamper the peace conference. During the critical spring of 1942 Hull held firm to his conviction that there should be no secret accords. "It seemed to me," he recalled in his *Memoirs,*

> we were in great danger of relapsing into the practice of the Allies during the First World War, when they concluded a series of secret treaties splitting up among themselves territories belonging to the Central Powers. These secret treaties had become one of the principal weapons of the isolationists in the United States in the period between the two wars. At least one of the provisions of the Atlantic Charter had been especially devised to prevent the same old device of power politics from being revived.

Molotov reached London on May 20 and opened secret discussions with the British government on the following day. The Soviet Foreign Minister, pressing for the recognition of new Soviet frontiers, faced opposition on all fronts. United States Ambassador John G. Winant, having assimilated the views of Washington, convinced both the British and the Russians that continued American support for the Allied cause required the avoidance of any territorial agreements. Eventually the Russians acceded to British and American demands. The general Anglo-Russian treaty of alliance, signed on May 26, contained no territorial provisions. One day later Churchill reported to Roosevelt that "as Winant will no doubt have informed you, we have completely transformed the treaty proposals. They are now, in my judgment, free from the objections we both entertained, and are entirely compatible with our Atlantic Charter."

When the Germans and Japanese failed to win the required military victory by the autumn of 1942 it was certain that time favored the Allies. Yet even before the Grand Alliance had achieved any of the great advances that eventually destroyed the resistance of the major antagonists, it should have been obvious to American officials that without some recognition of a Soviet sphere of influence in eastern Europe the alliance would not survive the destruction of Nazi power. At no time after 1942 did Stalin hide his intention of creating in eastern Europe a new order which would serve Russia's historic interests. The general Allied agreements on political principles and military strategy achieved at Moscow, Cairo, and Teheran in October and November 1943 created a semblance of East-West unity, but the scarcely guarded observations of Russian leaders exposed a continuing gulf between Soviet and Western views regarding the political reconstruction of Europe. American Ambassador Averell Harriman, reporting from Moscow, described Stalin's postwar ambitions with considerable precision in his secret report to Roosevelt following the Moscow Conference. (*Reading No. 2.*)

III

Clearly, an Anglo-American victory in World War II, similar to that achieved in 1918, was prejudiced even before the entry of the United States into the war. Having been obliged because of military weakness to align themselves with one of the world's leading dictatorships, the two nations were bound to this alliance at the peace table. Unfortunately, their victorious ally did not share their values or their limited interests in re-creating the prewar balance of power, modified only by the imposition of some military and political restrictions on the defeated nations. Whatever the ultimate success of British and American arms, Europe's fate was no longer a matter to be determined solely by the great democracies of the West.

These obvious limitations of American power to remake the world had no effect on the wartime rhetoric of the Roosevelt administration. While acknowledging the danger to the nation's security inherent in a total German victory over Europe, the President turned the war into another giant crusade against the forces of evil, promising with the destruction of Germany and Japan a new world order free from aggression and injustice. In his Columbus Day address in October 1942, for example, Roosevelt assured the American people: "Our cause is not only liberty for ourselves but liberation for others. An American victory will be a United Nations victory and a victory for oppressed and enslaved people everywhere." When Hull returned from the Moscow Conference in October 1943, Roosevelt predicted confidently that a new postwar international organization would mark the end of power politics and usher in a new era of international collaboration. (*Reading No. 3.*)

For the Roosevelt administration, war was scarcely regarded as a means to a political end. What mattered was the rapid and total destruction of the enemy. The fact that the total elimination of Germany and Japan, from the company of major powers, would destroy the former world-wide balance of power, which had served American interests so well, played no role in the President's wartime statements or decisions. Again, as in World War I, the constant assurance of a postwar utopia that would emanate from the unconditional surrender of the enemy, could only disillusion the American people while enhancing the power of the U.S.S.R. vis-à-vis that nation's two historic antagonists, Germany and Japan.

As the Allies in 1944 began to free vast areas of Europe from Nazi control, their political differences could no longer be submerged. When in January the Russian armies rolled into Polish territory, the Kremlin announced that it would correct the injustices of the Riga Treaty, imposed on the U.S.S.R. in 1921, by adopting the Curzon Line as accepted by the Supreme Council of the Allied Powers in 1919. This shifting of the Polish boundary westward would convey both western Ukraine and western Byelorussia to the Soviet Union. As the Russian forces approached the Rumanian border in April 1944, Stalin announced that the U.S.S.R. had removed the question of Bessarabia from further negotiation. What the United States had denied Stalin in December 1941 now fell to the Soviets through a series of rapid military advances. Yet as late as April 1944 Hull not only opposed any negotiation of spheres of influence with the Soviet

Union but also promised the American people a postwar world based on the principles of the Atlantic Charter. (*Reading No. 4.*) Whatever security Stalin required along his western boundaries, said Hull, he could obtain through a strong postwar peace organization. Hull's policy of postponing all territorial settlements had, by 1944, relegated the future of eastern Europe to the simple matter of Soviet power and Soviet intention.

Stalin, in his opposition to the re-establishment of a *cordon sanitaire* of unfriendly states along the Soviet frontier, probably hoped during 1944 that he could come to satisfactory terms with the non-Communist leaders of the Slavic states. When it became clear to him that free governments in such nations as Poland and Rumania would not do his bidding, he employed his military advantage to impose regimes of his own choice. In July the Russians recognized the puppet Polish Committee of National Liberation, which declared Lublin the capital of Poland. This group evolved into Poland's postwar Communist regime. Unfortunately, the Soviet advance across eastern Europe presented Stalin with the extreme choices of accepting without equivocation the principles of the Atlantic Charter or defying Western will totally by establishing his politico-military control throughout Slavic Europe. In giving Soviet leadership such limited choices lay the real tragedy of Western intransigence.

Averell Harriman analyzed Stalin's dilemma in such terms when he recalled:

> The most difficult question to answer is why Stalin took so many commitments which he subsequently failed to honor. . . . I believe that the Kremlin had two approaches to their post-war policies and in my many talks with Stalin I felt that he himself was of two minds. One approach emphasized reconstruction and development of Russia and the other external expansion. On the one hand they were discussing a possible understanding with us which would lead to peaceful relations and result in increased trade and loans from the West for the reconstruction of the terrible devastation left in the wake of the war. . . . On the other hand, we had constant difficulties with them throughout the war and they treated us with great suspicion. Moreover, there were indications that they would take advantage of the Red Army occupation of neighboring countries to maintain control, and they were supporting Communist parties in other countries to be in a position to take control in the post-war turmoil.
>
> The Kremlin took the second course. It is my belief that Stalin was influenced by the hostile attitude of the peoples of Eastern Europe toward the Red Army and that he recognized that governments established by free elections would not be "friendly" to the Soviet Union. In addition, I believe he became increasingly aware of the great opportunities for Soviet expansion in the post-war economic chaos.

Hull's adherence to the doctrine of postponement permitted him to employ the rhetoric of the Atlantic Charter throughout the war years in his definition of American intention. By late 1944, when he resigned his post as Secretary of State, this device for avoiding the hard political decisions confronting the Grand Alliance was fast reaching the end of its usefulness. With victory over Germany,

Hull could no longer assure Stalin an eventual territorial settlement and still promise the people freed from German domination that they would be permitted self-determination. It is not clear that Hull and Roosevelt would ever have been prepared, in the interest of postwar unity, to recognize Soviet control over any portion of eastern Europe, for in their continued insistence on the mood and spirit of the Atlantic Charter they pursued nothing less than the complete withdrawal of the U.S.S.R. to its prewar boundaries. Stalin's ultimate decision to guarantee governments friendly to the Soviet Union through the agency of Communist puppet regimes eliminated the possibility of any serious negotiation on the postwar Soviet frontiers of eastern Europe. By 1945 the Western powers could no longer assure even limited self-determination for the Slavic peoples of Europe. In pushing their way into Germany and Austria, Soviet forces had swept across Poland, Czechoslovakia, Rumania, Bulgaria, and Hungary. Obviously there was no power in Europe that could compel Russia's withdrawal to her boundaries of 1939. What remained for the United States in January 1945 was the cruel choice of compromising the principles of the Atlantic Charter or sacrificing the Grand Alliance itself. (*Reading No. 5.*)

IV

At the Yalta Conference of February 1945, Western spokesmen made a final effort to maintain a modicum of influence in eastern Europe. Even before Roosevelt departed for the Crimea late in January, the State Department assured him that the time had passed when the United States could control the future of the Slavic nations. (*Reading No. 6.*) Clearly, the U.S.S.R. would not give away its victories on the battlefield to comply with a moral promise made to Allies who had no power to force a compliance with that promise. Soviet policy toward Poland had already put the wartime alliance to the test. Early in January a Moscow broadcast announced that the Soviet Union was recognizing the Lublin Committee as the provisional government for all Poland. Roosevelt complained to Stalin on February 6, "It seems to me that it puts all of us in a bad light throughout the world to have you recognizing one government while we and the British are recognizing another in London." Indeed, the question of Poland's future was symbolic of the vast divergence of interest that separated the Allies at Yalta. (*Reading No. 7.*)

Rather than conform to the demands of military and political reality, Western leaders preferred to set the hand of Stalin to another statement of principles, the Declaration on Liberated Europe. Under this agreement the Big Three pledged themselves to assist the former Nazi satellites "to solve by democratic means their pressing political and economic problems" and to acknowledge "the right of all people to choose the form of government under which they will live." This Yalta Charter was Roosevelt's single remaining weapon to prevent the creation of a complete Soviet sphere of influence in eastern Europe. That Stalin signed it when he had no intention of acceding to its demands indicated that the Kremlin, facing the dogged resistance of German forces along the collapsing eastern front and desirous of Western economic co-operation to rebuild their wartorn country, wanted to avoid an open break with the West. So cordial had been

the exchange at Yalta, despite the profound depth of the disagreement, that
Harry Hopkins later recalled: "We really believed . . . that this was the dawn
of a new day. . . . We were *absolutely certain* that we had won the first great
victory of the peace. . . . The Russians had proved that they could be reasonable and farseeing and *there wasn't any doubt* in the minds of the President or
any of us that we could live with them and get along with them peacefully for
as far into the future as any of us could imagine."

Faced with American intransigence on the one hand and continued political
resistance within the Slavic nations on the other, Stalin proceeded to turn liberated Europe into a Soviet sphere of influence. Late in February he dispatched
Soviet diplomat Andrei Vishinski to Bucharest to force King Michael to appoint
the Soviet puppet Petra Groza head of the new Communist-dominated government of Rumania. Early in March, Foreign Minister Molotov demanded that the
Lublin regime form the core of the provisional government of Poland promised
at Yalta. The pattern of Soviet policy was clear. Using his political and ideological identification with local Communist leaders, Stalin gradually established a
series of friendly Communist governments in the areas occupied by Soviet troops.

Differences between the United States and the U.S.S.R. were moving quickly
beyond the point of reconciliation. What disturbed Churchill was the Soviet
policy of creating a distinct zone in eastern Europe. He wired President Harry
Truman on May 12, urging some settlement with the Kremlin even at the cost
of principle:

> I am profoundly concerned about the European situation. I have always
> worked for friendship with Russia, but like you, I feel deep anxiety be-
> cause of their misinterpretation of the Yalta decisions, their attitudes
> toward Poland, their overwhelming influence in the Balkans . . . and
> above all their power to maintain very large armies in the field for a
> long time. . . . Surely it is vital now to come to an understanding with
> Russia, or see where we are with her, before weakening our armies
> mortally or retiring to the zones of occupation. . . . Of course we may
> take the view that Russia will behave impeccably, and no doubt that
> offers the most convenient solution. To sum up, this issue of a settlement
> with Russia before our strength has gone seems to me to dwarf all others.

To discover Soviet motivation and intention at this critical point in the nation's
history, President Truman dispatched Harry Hopkins to Moscow to confer with
Stalin on matters of eastern Europe. The report of the Hopkins-Stalin conversations revealed as did no other official document the widening gulf between
American public opinion (as the administration defined it) and the security
interests of the Soviet Union. (*Reading No. 8.*)

V

What occurred during the eighteen months after Yalta flowed logically and inescapably from the diplomatic and military progress of the war. At no time had
official Washington prepared the nation to accept or deal with Stalin's postwar
behavior. The Soviet Union, augmented in size and authority by its new acquisitions, had decidedly destroyed the prewar balance of power. The challenge

to American security was limited, but unmistakable. Any American response that came to grips with the problem had either to recognize the new Soviet hegemony, in an effort to minimize its scope, or to seek the means to undo it. But Roosevelt's successors, like him unwilling to abandon principle, yet equally unable to dispose of Soviet power in East-Central Europe, could only extend into the postwar era the wartime techniques of evasion.

These limited choices confronting the American people divided public opinion between those who favored recognition of the Soviet sphere of influence and those who believed that continued nonrecognition of the Soviet hegemony would gradually undermine the Kremlin's authority and eventually permit the creation of a Europe built on the program of self-determination. Walter Lippmann voiced the impatience of those who preferred a diplomatic settlement to interminable drift. On May 8 he asserted that Europe was in fact divided into two exclusive spheres of influence, and that the United States and the U.S.S.R. were limited largely to their own spheres. "No nation, however strong," he wrote, "has universal world power which reaches everywhere. The realm in which each state has the determining influence is limited by geography and circumstances. Beyond that realm it is possible to bargain and persuade but not to compel, and no foreign policy is well conducted which does not recognize these invincible realities." (*Reading No. 9.*)

Official Washington had promised too much to follow such advice. In this decision it enjoyed the overwhelming support of those American idealists who believed it the nation's purpose to set men free and those political realists who had no intention of arousing the opposition of any of the powerful minority blocs of eastern European origin by accepting publicly the fact that moral platitudes alone would not reduce the size of the Soviet empire. For many American diplomats, moreover, nothing had ruled out the possibility of deflating the Soviet hegemony through the sheer power of superior legal argumentation and the resultant strengthening of anti-Soviet sentiment throughout the world.

At the Potsdam Conference of July-August 1945 the same issue that had plagued Allied diplomacy again dominated the diplomatic exchange. Stalin remained totally adamant on the question of eastern Europe's future. "A freely elected government in any of these East European countries," he admitted simply, "would be anti-Soviet, and that we cannot allow." The United States, Secretary of State James F. Byrnes assured a suspicious Molotov, "sincerely desires Russia to have friendly countries on her borders, but we believe they should seek the friendship of the people rather than of any particular government." His government, said Byrnes, did not wish to become involved in the elections of other countries; it merely desired to join other nations in observing elections in Italy, Greece, Hungary, Rumania, and Bulgaria. What confused the question of eastern Europe even further was the Soviet insistence that the new governments of that region were democratic. Declared one report of the Soviet claims:

> As far as their present governments are concerned, the Soviet position was that these governments are "democratic" and are such as to have fulfilled the Yalta Declaration on Liberated Areas. (Light is shed on

this characterization by Stalin's remark that "if a government is not Fascist it is democratic.") Stalin on one occasion referred to them as "closer to the people" than the present Government of Italy. Molotov maintained that in all these governments the Communist Party formed only a small minority. The Soviets urged at great length that these governments be recognized either at once or in the very near future by the United States and Great Britain. They were unwilling to accord to Italy more favorable treatment in the easing of the armistice terms and other matters than to Rumania, Bulgaria, Hungary and Finland which they claimed had made a greater contribution to the Allied war effort.

At the London Conference of Foreign Ministers in September 1945, Byrnes again assured Molotov that the United States was interested only in governments friendly to the Soviet Union in eastern Europe. "Our objective," he explained, "is a government both friendly to the Soviet Union and representative of all the democratic elements of the country." The Secretary countered Molotov's continuing demand for security against Germany with an offer binding the United States to German demilitarization for twenty-five years. Such arguments and promises failed to loosen the Soviet grip, and eventually Byrnes returned to the United States, having failed to modify Soviet intransigence on any of the fundamental issues dividing the world. John Foster Dulles, Republican adviser of Byrnes at London, praised the Secretary in a broadcast of October 6, 1945, for not bargaining away American principles of international morality. (*Reading No. 10.*) President Truman, in his Navy Day address of October 27, declared that the United States would never recognize any government established by force against the freely expressed will of the people. (*Reading No. 11.*) In a remarkable speech four days later, Byrnes defined again the fundamental conflict breaking up the Grand Alliance—Soviet security interests vis-à-vis Germany as opposed to American opposition to spheres of influence. (*Reading No. 12.*)

This continuing quest for the triumph of principle weighed heavily on Senator Arthur H. Vandenberg of Michigan, Republican adviser to the administration and chief spokesman for his party on foreign affairs in the Senate. Upon his return to the United States from the opening session of the United Nations in London, he reported to the Senate late in February 1946. In many respects this effort, with its condemnation of power politics and its reliance on moral firmness, to be conveyed largely through the correct choice of rhetoric, was typical of American Congressional leadership. (*Reading No. 13.*) Byrnes, having made several concessions to the Russians at the Moscow Conference of December 1945, attempted to match Vandenberg's toughness in a radio speech the following evening. He then invited the Michigan Senator to accompany him to the Foreign Ministers Conference to open in Paris late in April. There Byrnes, much to the delight of Vandenberg, adopted a tough line of argument to place the onus of deadlock on the Soviets. When the conference recessed in May, Vandenberg again reported to the Senate. "We can compromise within the boundaries of a principle," he admitted. "We can no longer compromise principles themselves." (*Reading No. 14.*)

This "get tough" policy which began in the autumn of 1945 revealed a deep national problem. It never comprised more than a change in style, yet it convinced too many Americans that there was some special power in words and thus created the illusion that the choices confronting the Republic were much broader than the presence of Soviet armies in all regions of dispute suggested. The new attitude gave nothing away, but neither did it assure any settlement on American terms. It was Henry A. Wallace, Secretary of Commerce, who attacked the "get tough" policy in a memorandum to the President on July 23 as "isolationism masquerading as tough realism in international affairs." Then on September 12, at Madison Square Garden, Wallace delivered a strident appeal for the recognition of the Soviet sphere of influence, for mere toughness, he declared, would not secure the fulfillment of any American aspirations. (*Reading No. 15.*) Threatened by the resignation of Byrnes, the President relieved Wallace of his cabinet post for his efforts in the field of foreign affairs.

To Lippmann in December 1946 the pattern of postwar diplomatic failure appeared clear enough. He wondered why fifteen months of intense diplomatic effort since Potsdam had resulted in no effort to reach a general diplomatic settlement. Instead, the diplomats of the Big Three had dealt only with the former German satellites, choosing eastern Europe as the area to begin the resolving of postwar diplomatic issues. "This was a gigantic blunder," concluded Lippmann, "made by men who had had no part in the strategic conduct of the war, and failed to take into account its strategic consequences. For it narrowed the issue between Russia and the West to the very region where the conflict was sharpest and a settlement most difficult." Western leaders had attempted to make a frontal assault on the positions held by the Red Army with weapons no more effective than the Atlantic Charter and the Yalta Declaration. Elsewhere the West had the strength and position to bargain; in eastern Europe it had neither. In an article, "A Year of Peacemaking," which appeared in *Atlantic Monthly,* Lippmann analyzed succinctly why American diplomacy, as long as it concerned itself primarily with the established Soviet hegemony, would reap little but futility. (*Reading No. 16.*)

During the 'thirties the United States had sought to prevent change through the utopian effort to endow the *status quo* of the Versailles system with a special morality which no one would dare to challenge (except through a body of specific procedures which really eliminated the possibility of change). Having lost the world dominated by the victorious democracies because of the ineffectiveness of such methods to prevent a major war, the nation adopted a postwar program, based on the doctrine of self-determination of peoples, to re-create the world of the 'twenties and 'thirties. Certainly this abstraction would no more succeed in returning world politics to the Versailles system than the utopian doctrines of the interwar years had succeeded in preserving it. Again a body of principle had set the United States at odds with other nations. Perhaps those charged with the responsibility for American foreign policy might have recalled the warning of William Graham Sumner, "If you want war, nourish a doctrine. . . ."

# 1 | The Revolution in the Status of Eastern Europe, July 1940 *

*Perhaps no Western writer saw more clearly the significance of the German and Soviet assault on eastern Europe in 1939 and 1940 than did Vera Micheles Dean. Noting the destruction of the principle of self-determination within the Slavic nations, she predicted a revolution in the political structure of eastern Europe no matter what the outcome of the war. The West had lost any possible control of the region's destiny.*

✍

. . . The events of the past week make it increasingly clear that Hitler does not intend to be diverted by any subsidiary clashes on the periphery from his main objective, which is that of crushing Britain and ending all possibility of British intervention on the European continent. Just as the Nazis "prevented the spread of war" to Scandinavia, which might have cut off their imports of iron ore, so now they are endeavoring to check the spread of war to the Balkans, which might interfere with their supplies of oil and foodstuffs. At the conference held in Munich on July 10, Hitler and Count Ciano apparently told the Hungarian delegates, Premier Teleki and Foreign Minister Czaky, that Hungary's territorial claims against Rumania would be ultimately satisfied under a postwar peace settlement, but that meanwhile the Hungarians should abstain from provoking a conflict in the Danubian area, and concentrate on the far more pressing task of getting in the harvest.

Similar advice appears to have been given to Bulgaria, which hopes to obtain the return of territories lost to Rumania and Greece during the Balkan wars of 1912–1913 and the first World War. Germany's insistence on maintenance of the *status quo* in the Balkans for the duration of its war with Britain has had the effect of temporarily stabilizing an explosive situation. From the point of view of the Nazis, it would be disastrous to have war spread to the Balkan countries, which may have to serve as the granary of Europe at a time when great food stringency if not actual famine, is anticipated on the continent. Suspension of Hungarian and Bulgarian claims, moreover, has temporarily halted the advance into the Balkans of the Soviet Union, which would doubtless have claimed a share of the spoils in any reorganization of this region. It is by no means impossible, however, that the Nazis might permit Moscow to obtain additional territory and strategic ports on the Black Sea, in the expectation that, once Britain is crushed or brought to terms, Germany can easily oust Russia.

This possibility is not excluded by Moscow, which has profited by the lull in

* Vera Micheles Dean, "Axis Powers and Russia Reorganize Eastern Europe," *Foreign Policy Bulletin*, XIX (July 19, 1940), 3. Reprinted by permission of the Foreign Policy Association.

the East to consolidate its hold on the Baltic. On July 14 and 15 Lithuania, Latvia and Estonia, where the Soviet Union had already obtained air and naval bases and established its military control, voted for inclusion of their territories in the U.S.S.R., after the leaders of opposition elements had either fled or been placed under arrest. This vote coincided with new Soviet threats against Finland, and with reports in Moscow that Finnish workers were expressing dissatisfaction with deterioration in economic conditions, due in large part to the hardships and territorial losses suffered by Finland as a result of its war with the Soviet Union. It may be expected that, as Germany extends its economic control over Denmark, Norway and Sweden, Moscow will similarly extend its control over what remains of Finland, thus acquiring valuable nickel and lumber resources.

As the triple process of German, Russian and Italian expansion proceeds in Europe, several main trends become increasingly defined. The small countries which had achieved independence in the course of several centuries as a result of the gradual break-up of the Holy Roman, the Hapsburg, and the Romanov Empires, are now being again absorbed into the new empires recreated by the Germans, the Italians and the Russians. Their fate demonstrates that self-determination, unless accompanied by integration of great and small powers into a broad federation based on the principle of mutual assistance, ultimately proves suicidal for weak countries, which are unable to resist the political and economic pressure of powerful neighbors. As a result of this process of re-absorption of small countries into great territorial empires, the concept of national sovereignty, which had proved the principal stumbling-black to the formation of any European union or federation, is being rapidly obliterated. At the same time, the civil conflicts superimposed on international conflicts are undermining the concept of nationalism, which was such a powerful force in the formation of national states on the European continent.

Out of the immense travail which Europe is now undergoing new political and economic forms are bound to emerge, no matter what may be the final result of the war. Most Western observers had assumed for decades that sooner or later Europe would have to achieve unity or perish in the course of suicidal wars. Their principal mistake was to assume that Europe could be unified only under the leadership of the Western democracies, and on lines patterned after Anglo-Saxon institutions. Today Germany and Russia are both ready to impose their programs of political and economic unification on European countries. The principal question is whether these two programs will converge, or whether a victorious Germany will eventually mobilize the rest of Europe in a thrust against Russia.

# 2 | Stalin's Wartime Political Objectives, October 1943 *

That Roosevelt was concerned with Stalin's postwar ambitions in eastern Europe seemed apparent from the following report of the Moscow Conference of Foreign Ministers, held in October 1943. In this private communication Ambassador Averell Harriman was not completely pessimistic over the future of United States-Soviet relations, but he observed with considerable accuracy the attitudes which the Kremlin harbored toward the question of postwar security.

✍

Now that I have had a chance to take a long breath I thought you would want from me a review of the more important impressions of the Soviet attitude we got in and outside of the conference room. Certain of the doubts which some people have had regarding Soviet intentions are now laid to rest. On the other hand the character of certain real difficulties that exist has been more sharply defined.

(1) The Soviet Government before they agreed to the Conference had evidently decided that they would take a shot at working together with the British and ourselves in dealing with war and postwar problems. On the whole the Soviets are delighted with the way the Conference went and it has strengthened their tentative decision. It was interesting to watch how Molotov expanded as the days passed. As he began to realize more and more that we had not come with a united front against him and were ready to expose frankly our preliminary thoughts, he showed increasing enjoyment in being admitted for the first time into the councils as a full member with the British and ourselves. Before the Conference I doubt if they had any intention of allowing the inclusion of China as an original signatory of the Four Nation Declaration. Their acceptance of China is a clear indication that they are genuinely satisfied with the way things went and are ready to make important concessions to further the new intimacy. On the other hand it cannot be assumed that this policy is already so set that we can take liberties with them.

(2) They were unquestionably chagrined by the British and our attitude re Turkey and to a lesser extent regarding Sweden. Eden's final understanding with them on Turkey helped to offset their early disappointment but they are expectantly hopeful that we will join in this agreement at an early date. I am convinced, however, that only Turkey's entry into the war will satisfy them. Without coming to Moscow it is hard to appreciate how differently they view the war from the British and ourselves. The Russians have the primitive view that they have suffered and bled to destroy Hitler and see no reason why the Turks should not do the same if it can help shorten the war. They honestly believe

* Harriman's secret report of the Moscow Conference, November 4, 1943, *Foreign Relations of the United States, Diplomatic Papers: The Conferences at Cairo and Tehran, 1943* (Washington, 1961), 152–5.

that the entry of Turkey will force the Germans to move a considerable number of divisions from the Eastern front. In posing this demand they are entirely indifferent to any moral or actual obligation to assist the Turks in fighting the Germans. Our attitude in this regard is inexplicable to them. The Russians feel that only if the Turks actively fight against Germany now are they entitled to any consideration in the post-war scheme of things. To a somewhat modified degree they feel the same way about the Swedes. In addition to the military value of the entry of these countries into the war, they believe that closing in on Germany from all sides will hasten the deterioration of enemy morale. . . .

(3) The Soviets accepted the explanation of our military plans but our whole permanent relations depend in a large measure on their satisfaction in the future with out [our] military operations. It is impossible to over-emphasize the importance they place strategically on the initiation of the so-called "Second Front" next spring . . .

(4) Their attitude toward Germany as revealed at the Conference is fundamentally satisfactory. There is of course no doubt that they are bent in [on] the complete destruction of Hitler and Nazism. They are ready to deal with Germany on the basis of a three-way responsibility. Our difficulties with them, if any, will be that their present intent toward Germany is tougher than we have in mind, particularly in regard to the magnitude of reparations. Their measure of Germany's capacity to pay reparations in goods and services appears to be based on the concept that the Germans are not entitled to a postwar standard of living higher than the Russians. They definitely did not exclude the possibility of an enforced dismemberment of Germany and are certainly determined to make sure that there will be no military threat from that quarter in any foreseeable future. They convinced me that any public references coming from Moscow or from the free Germany committee showing friendliness to the German people is just propaganda to weaken German resistance.

(5) Their flirtation with the French committee appears to have cooled off as a result of their satisfaction with their new intimacy with the British and ourselves. It may of course be revived if the development of these new relationships is not to their satisfaction.

(6) Although Soviet territorial questions were never raised at the Conference, it can only be inferred that the Soviet Government expects to stand firmly on the position they have already taken in regard to their 1941 frontiers. I believe they have the impression that this has been tacitly accepted by the British, and the fact that we did not bring up the issue may have given them the impression that we would not raise serious objection in the future.

(7) The problem of Poland is even tougher than we believed. They regard the present Polish Government-in-Exile as hostile, and therefore completely unacceptable to them. They are determined to recognize only a Polish government that will be a whole-heartedly friendly neighbor. On the other hand, Molotov told me definitely that they were willing to have a strong independent Poland, giving expression to whatever social and political system the Polish people wanted. They gave us no indication during the Conference that they were inter-

ested in the extension of the Soviet system. I take this with some reservation, particularly if it proves to be the only way they can get the kind of relationships they demand from their western border states.

They are determined to have no semblance of the old "cordon sanitaire" concept in eastern Europe. Molotov told me that the relations they expect to establish with the border countries did not preclude equally friendly relationships with the British and ourselves. In the Conference, however, it was indicated that although they would keep us informed they would take unilateral action in respect to these countries in the establishment of relations satisfactory to themselves. It is my feeling that this rigid attitude may well be tempered in proportion to their increasing confidence in their relations with the British and ourselves in the establishment of overall world security. Although Finland came up only indirectly in our discussions, we sensed a bitter and uncompromising attitude toward her. As to the states west of the areas bordering on the Soviet Union, they appear fully prepared to cooperate with the British and ourselves in working out problems involved, provided they are given full partnership in the decisions.

(8) The discussions on Iran were only on a staff level. One never gets very far on this level in dealing with the Soviets. Although they accepted an unpublished resolution reaffirming their fidelity to their treaty obligations toward Iran, we got no clarification of their real attitude. Because this subject was left to the end, Eden decided not to insist that it be thrashed out in the main conference. . . .

## 3 | The Second Great Crusade, 1941–43 *

Undoubtedly Roosevelt had no desire to carry the American people to the heights of anti-German and anti-Japanese sentiment which the Wilson administration attained through its propaganda program against Germany. Yet beginning with his address of December 9, 1941, on the Pearl Harbor attack, the President stressed the notion that the United States was driven to war, not by conflicts of interests or the need of re-creating a balance of power challenged by aggression, but by the machinations of evil men. Beyond the destruction of their power, he assured the nation, such international immorality would not be permitted to rise again. Neither in this speech nor elsewhere did Roosevelt recognize as legitimate the will of any nation to alter the status of international politics as defined generally by the Versailles Treaty. Where his desire to eliminate the German and Japanese threat to the *status quo* of 1939 left the Soviet Union, with its known territorial ambitions, was not clear.

---

* *Peace and War: United States Foreign Policy 1931–1941* (Washington, 1943), 842–8.

The sudden criminal attacks perpetrated by the Japanese in the Pacific provide the climax of a decade of international immorality.

Powerful and resourceful gangsters have banded together to make war upon the whole human race. Their challenge has now been flung at the United States of America. The Japanese have treacherously violated the long-standing peace between us. Many American soldiers and sailors have been killed by enemy action. American ships have been sunk; American airplanes have been destroyed.

The Congress and the people of the United States have accepted that challenge.

Together with other free peoples, we are now fighting to maintain our right to live among our world neighbors in freedom and in common decency, without fear of assault. . . .

Assembly lines are now in operation. Others are being rushed to completion. A steady stream of tanks and planes, of guns and ships, of shells and equipment —that is what these 18 months have given us.

But it is all only a beginning of what has to be done. We must be set to face a long war against crafty and powerful bandits. The attack at Pearl Harbor can be repeated at any one of many points in both oceans and along both our coast lines and against all the rest of the hemisphere.

It will not only be a long war, it will be a hard war. That is the basis on which we now lay all our plans. That is the yardstick by which we measure what we shall need and demand; money, materials, doubled and quadrupled production—ever-increasing. The production must be not only for our own Army and Navy and Air Forces. It must reinforce the other armies and navies and air forces fighting the Nazis and the war-lords of Japan throughout the Americas and the world.

I have been working today on the subject of production. Your Government has decided on two broad policies.

The first is to speed up all existing production by working on a seven-day-week basis in every war industry, including the production of essential raw materials.

The second policy, now being put into form, is to rush additions to the capacity of production by building more new plants, by adding to old plants, and by using the many smaller plants for war needs.

Over the hard road of the past months, we have at times met obstacles and difficulties, divisions and disputes, indifference and callousness. That is now all past—and, I am sure, forgotten. . . .

I am sure that the people in every part of the Nation are prepared in their individual living to win this war. I am sure they will cheerfully help to pay a large part of its financial cost while it goes on. I am sure they will cheerfully give up those material things they are asked to give up.

I am sure that they will retain all those great spiritual things without which we cannot win through.

I repeat that the United States can accept no result save victory, final and complete. Not only must the shame of Japanese treachery be wiped out, but the sources of international brutality, wherever they exist, must be absolutely and finally broken.

In my message to the Congress yesterday I said that we "will make very certain that this form of treachery shall never endanger us again." In order to achieve that certainty, we must begin the great task that is before us by abandoning once and for all the illusion that we can ever again isolate ourselves from the rest of humanity.

In these past few years—and, most violently, in the past few days—we have learned a terrible lesson.

It is our obligation to our dead—it is our sacred obligation to their children and our children—that we must never forget what we have learned.

And what we all have learned is this:

There is no such thing as security for any nation—or any individual—in a world ruled by the principles of gangsterism.

There is no such thing as impregnable defense against powerful aggressors who sneak up in the dark and strike without warning.

We have learned that our ocean-girt hemisphere is not immune from severe attack—that we cannot measure our safety in terms of miles on any map.

We may acknowledge that our enemies have performed a brilliant feat of deception, perfectly timed and executed with great skill. It was a thoroughly dishonorable deed, but we must face the fact that modern warfare as conducted in the Nazi manner is a dirty business. We don't like it—we didn't want to get in it—but we are in it, and we're going to fight it with everything we've got.

I do not think any American has any doubt of our ability to administer proper punishment to the perpetrators of these crimes. . . .


— | "There never has been—there never can be—successful compromise between good and evil." *

In his State of the Union Message of January 6, 1942, Roosevelt reduced the war to a crusade against "tyranny and cruelty and serfdom." The war, he said, must be pursued to victory, for total victory alone would cleanse the world of its ancient evils. Roosevelt, like Wilson, assigned to the United States the task of bringing universal peace and equality to the peoples of the world.

𝄞

. . . For we are fighting on the same side with the British people, who fought alone for long, terrible months, and withstood the enemy with fortitude and tenacity and skill.

* *Public Papers and Addresses of Franklin D. Roosevelt,* Samuel I. Rosenman, ed. (New York, 1950), XI: 41–2.

We are fighting on the same side with the Russian people who have seen the Nazi hordes swarm up to the very gates of Moscow, and who with almost super-human will and courage have forced the invaders back into retreat.

We are fighting on the same side as the brave people of China—those millions who for four and a half long years have withstood bombs and starvation and have whipped the invaders time and again in spite of the superior Japanese equipment and arms.

Yes, we are fighting on the same side as the indomitable Dutch.

We are fighting on the same side as all the other Governments in exile, whom Hitler and all his armies and all his Gestapo have not been able to conquer.

But we of the United Nations are not making all this sacrifice of human effort and human lives to return to the kind of world we had after the last world war.

We are fighting today for security, for progress, and for peace, not only for ourselves but for all men, not only for one generation but for all generations. We are fighting to cleanse the world of ancient evils, ancient ills.

Our enemies are guided by brutal cynicism, by unholy contempt for the human race. We are inspired by a faith that goes back through all the years to the first chapter of the Book of Genesis: "God created man in His own image."

We on our side are striving to be true to that divine heritage. We are fighting, as our fathers have fought, to uphold the doctrine that all men are equal in the sight of God. Those on the other side are striving to destroy this deep belief and to create a world in their own image—a world of tyranny and cruelty and serfdom.

That is the conflict that day and night now pervades our lives. No compromise can end that conflict. There never has been—there never can be—successful compromise between good and evil. Only total victory can reward the champions of tolerance, and decency, and freedom, and faith.


— | "We are united in our determination to destroy the world-wide forces of ruthless conquest and brutal enslavement." *

Hull, in his radio address of July 23, 1942, described the war as a dire struggle between freedom and slavery. Beyond victory over the enemy, he said, the American people and their allies would face "the great constructive task of building human freedom and Christian morality on firmer and broader foundations than ever before." Hull promised a postwar world of stability based not on power politics but on freer trade and expanding economies.

* *The Department of State Bulletin*, VII (July 25, 1942), 639–47.

The conflict now raging throughout the earth is not a war of nation against nation. It is not a local or regional war or even a series of such wars. On the side of our enemies, led and driven by the most ambitious, depraved, and cruel leaders in history, it is an attempt to conquer and enslave this country and every country. On our side, the side of the United Nations, it is, for each of us, a life-and-death struggle for the preservation of our freedom, our homes, our very existence. We are united in our determination to destroy the world-wide forces of ruthless conquest and brutal enslavement. Their defeat will restore freedom or the opportunity for freedom alike to all countries and all peoples. . . .

Today twenty-eight United Nations are fighting against the would-be conquerors and enslavers of the human race. We know what is at stake. By the barbarian invaders of today nothing is spared—neither life, nor morals, nor honor, nor virtue, nor pledges, nor the customs, the national institutions, even the religion of any people. Their aim is to sweep away every vestige of individual and national rights; to substitute, the world over, their unspeakable tyranny for the ways of life developed each for itself by the various nations; to make all mankind subservient to their will; to convert the two billions of the earth's inhabitants into abject victims and tools of their insatiable lust for power and dominion.

We have seen their work in the countries they have invaded—murder of defenseless men, women, and children; rape, torture, and pillage; mass terrorization; the black system of hostages; starvation and deprivations that beggar description: the most thorough-going bondage the world has ever seen.

This is the so-called "New Order" of Hitler and the Japanese war lords—an order as old as slavery—new only in the calculated thoroughness of its cruelty; in the depth of the degradation to which it subjects its victims; in the degree to which it has revived the worst practices of the darkest ages in history.

From time immemorial attempts at conquest and enslavement have checked and harried the great onward march of men and women toward greater freedom and higher levels of civilized existence. The methods employed have been the same as those which we witness today. Ruthless, ambitious men would succeed in corrupting, coercing, or deceiving into blind obedience enough servile followers to attack or terrify peaceful and law-abiding peoples, too often unprepared to resist. In a few instances whole civilizations collapsed under the impact, and darkness descended on large portions of the world. More often, the attacks were —at great cost—defeated, and mankind resumed its onward march. Yet throughout the ages two lessons have remained unlearned.

The first is that man's innate striving for freedom cannot be extinguished. Since the world began too many men have fought, suffered, and died for freedom —and not in vain—for doubt to remain on that score. And yet, over and over again would-be conquerors and enslavers of mankind have sought to translate their mad dreams of barbarous domination into reality.

The second lesson is that liberty is truly won only when it is guarded by the same watchfulness, the same courage, the same willingness to fight for it which first secured it. Repeatedly throughout history, free men—having won the fight, having acquired precious rights and privileges which freedom brings—have dropped their guard, relaxed their vigilance, taken their freedom for granted. They have busied themselves with many things and have not noticed the beginnings of new tyrannies, the rise of new threats to liberty. They have become so abhorrent of force and cruelty that they have believed the bully and the gangster could be reformed by reason and justice or be defeated by passive resistance. And so they have been surprised and unprepared when the attacks have come again. . . .

After the last war too many nations, including our own, tolerated, or participated in, attempts to advance their own interests at the expense of any system of collective security and of opportunity for all. Too many of us were blind to the evils which, thus loosed, created growing cancers within and among nations—political suspicions and hatreds; the race of armaments, first stealthy and then the subject of flagrant boasts; economic nationalism and its train of economic depression and misery; and finally the emergence from their dark places of the looters and thugs who found their opportunity in disorder and disaster. The shadow of a new war fell across the world. War began in 1931 when Japan invaded China. . . .

Events have demonstrated beyond question that each of the Axis powers was bent on unlimited conquest. As time went on it became manifest that the United States and the whole Western Hemisphere were ultimate targets. Conclusive proof was given by the international desperadoes themselves through the publication on September 27, 1940 of the Tripartite Pact. By that treaty of alliance Germany, Japan, and Italy in effect agreed that, if any country not then at war with one of them placed obstacles in the way of the program of conquest of any of them, the three would unite in political, military, and economic action against that country. This provision was aimed directly at the United States. One of the highest official spokesmen of the Axis powers openly proclaimed that the objective of the three partners was a new world order to be achieved by force. . . .

In this vast struggle, we, Americans, stand united with those who like ourselves, are fighting for the preservation of their freedom; with those who are fighting to regain the freedom of which they have been brutally deprived; with those who are fighting for the opportunity to achieve freedom. . . .

With victory achieved our first concern must be for those whose sufferings have been almost beyond human endurance. When the armies of our enemies are beaten, the people of many countries will be starving and without means of procuring food; homeless and without means of building shelter; their fields scorched; their cattle slaughtered; their tools gone; their factories and mines destroyed; their roads and transport wrecked. Unknown millions will be far from their homes—prisoners of war, inmates of concentration camps, forced laborers in alien lands, refugees from battle, from cruelty, from starvation. Disease and danger of disease will lurk everywhere. In some countries confusion and chaos will follow the cessation of hostilities. Victory must be followed by swift and effective action to meet these pressing human needs. . . .

During this period of transition the United Nations must continue to act in the spirit of cooperation which now underlies their war effort—to supplement and make more effective the action of countries individually in re-establishing public order, in providing swift relief, in meeting the manifold problems of readjustment.

Beyond these there will lie before all countries the great constructive task of building human freedom and Christian morality on firmer and broader foundations than ever before. This task, too, will of necessity call for both national and international action. . . .

For decades all nations have lived in the shadow of threatened coercion or war. This has imposed heavy burdens of armament, which in the cases of many nations has absorbed so large a part of their production effort as to leave the remainder of their resources inadequate for maintaining, let alone improving, the economic, social, and cultural standards of their people. Closely related to this has been a burden less obvious but of immense weight—the inevitable limitation that fear of war imposes on productive activity. Many men, groups of men, and even nations have dared not plan, create, or increase the means of production, fearing lest war come and their efforts thus be rendered vain.

No nation can make satisfactory progress while its citizens are in the grip of constant fear of external attack or interference. It is plain that some international agency must be created which can—by force, if necessary—keep the peace among nations in the future. There must be international cooperative action to set up the mechanisms which can thus insure peace. This must include eventual adjustment of national armaments in such a manner that the rule of law cannot be successfully challenged and that the burden of armaments may be reduced to a minimum.

In the creation of such mechanisms there would be a practical and purposeful application of sovereign powers through measures of international cooperation for purposes of safeguarding the peace. Participation by all nations in such measures would be for each its contribution toward its own future security and safety from outside attack.

Settlement of disputes by peaceful means, and indeed all processes of international cooperation, presuppose respect for law and obligations. It is plain that one of the institutions which must be established and be given vitality is an international court of justice. It is equally clear that, in the process of re-establishing international order, the United Nations must exercise surveillance over aggressor nations until such time as the latter demonstrate their willingness and ability to live at peace with other nations. How long such surveillance will need to continue must depend upon the rapidity with which the peoples of Germany, Japan, Italy, and their satellites give convincing proof that they have repudiated and abandoned the monstrous philosophy of superior race and conquest by force and have embraced loyally the basic principles of peaceful processes. During the formative period of the world organization, interruption by these aggressors must be rendered impossible.

One of the greatest of all obstacles which in the past have impeded human progress and afforded breeding grounds for dictators has been extreme nationalism. All will agree that nationalism and its spirit are essential to the healthy and normal political and economic life of a people, but when policies of nationalism—political, economic, social, and moral—are carried to such extremes as to exclude and prevent necessary policies of international cooperation, they become dangerous and deadly. Nationalism, run riot between the last war and this war, defeated all attempts to carry out indispensable measures of international economic and political action, encouraged and facilitated the rise of dictators, and drove the world straight toward the present war.

During this period narrow and short-sighted nationalism found its most virulent expression in the economic field. It prevented goods and services from flowing in volume at all adequate from nation to nation and thus severely hampered the work of production, distribution, and consumption and greatly retarded efforts for social betterment.

No nation can make satisfactory progress when it is deprived, by its own action or by the action of others, of the immeasurable benefits of international exchange of goods and services. The Atlantic Charter declares the right of all nations to "access, on equal terms, to the trade and to the raw materials of the world which are needed for their economic prosperity." This is essential if the legitimate and growing demand for the greatest practicable measure of stable employment is to be met, accompanied by rising standards of living. If the actual and potential losses resulting from limitations on economic activity are to be eliminated, a system must be provided by which this can be assured.

In order to accomplish this, and to establish among the nations a circle of mutual benefit, excessive trade barriers of the many different kinds must be reduced, and practices which impose injuries on others and divert trade from its natural economic course must be avoided. Equally plain is the need for making national currencies once more freely exchangeable for each other at stable rates of exchange; for a system of financial relations so devised that materials can be produced and ways may be found of moving them where there are markets created by human need; for machinery through which capital may—for the development of the world's resources and for the stabilization of economic activity —move on equitable terms from financially stronger to financially weaker countries. There may be need for some special trade arrangement and for international agreements to handle difficult surplus problems and to meet situations in special areas. . . .

With peace among nations reasonably assured, with political stability established, with economic shackles removed, a vast fund of resources will be released in each nation to meet the needs of progress, to make possible for all of its citizens an advancement toward higher living standards, to invigorate the constructive forces of initiative and enterprise. The nations of the world will then be able to go forward in the manner of their own choosing in all avenues of human betterment more completely than they ever have been able to do in the past. They will do so through their own efforts and with complete self-respect. Continuous self-development of nations and individuals in a framework of effective cooperation with others is the sound and logical road to the higher standards of life which we all crave and seek. . . .

—  |  "The elimination of German, Japanese, and Italian war power . . . means a reasonable assurance of future world peace." *

In his news conference at Casablanca on January 24, 1943, Roosevelt announced the new Allied objective of seeking the unconditional surrender of Germany, Italy, and Japan as the surest means of guaranteeing postwar peace.

This meeting goes back to the successful landing operations last November, which as you all know were initiated as far back as a year ago, and put into definite shape shortly after the Prime Minister's visit to Washington in June.

After the operations of last November, it became perfectly clear, with the successes, that the time had come for another review of the situation, and a planning for the next steps, especially steps to be taken in 1943. That is why we came here, and our respective staffs came with us, to discuss the practical steps to be taken by the United Nations for prosecution of the war. We have been here about a week.

I might add, too, that we began talking about this after the first of December, and at that time we invited Mr. Stalin to join us at a convenient meeting place. Mr. Stalin very greatly desired to come, but he was precluded from leaving Russia because he was conducting the new Russian offensive against the Germans along the whole line. We must remember that he is Commander in Chief, and that he is responsible for the very wonderful detailed plan which has been brought to such a successful conclusion since the beginning of the offensive.

In spite of the fact that Mr. Stalin was unable to come, the results of the staff meeting have been communicated to him, so that we will continue to keep in very close touch with each other.

I think it can be said that the studies during the past week or ten days are unprecedented in history. Both the Prime Minister and I think back to the days of the first World War when conferences between the French and British and ourselves very rarely lasted more than a few hours or a couple of days. The Chiefs of Staffs have been in intimate touch; they have lived in the same hotel. Each man has become a definite personal friend of his opposite number on the other side.

Furthermore, these conferences have discussed, I think for the first time in history, the whole global picture. It isn't just one front, just one ocean, or one continent—it is literally the whole world; and that is why the Prime Minister and I feel that the conference is unique in the fact that it has this global aspect.

The Combined Staffs, in these conferences and studies during the past week or ten days, have proceeded on the principle of pooling all of the resources of the United Nations. And I think the second point is that they have reaffirmed the determination to maintain the initiative against the Axis powers in every part of the world.

* *The Public Papers and Addresses of Franklin D. Roosevelt,* XII: 37–9.

These plans covering the initiative and maintenance of the initiative during 1943 cover certain things, such as united operations conducted in different areas of the world. Second, the sending of all possible material aid to the Russian offensive, with the double object of cutting down the manpower of Germany and her satellites, and continuing the very great attrition of German munitions and materials of all kinds which are being destroyed every day in such large quantities by the Russian armies.

And, at the same time, the Staffs have agreed on giving all possible aid to the heroic struggle of China—remembering that China is in her sixth year of the war —with the objective, not only in China but in the whole of the Pacific area, of ending any Japanese attempt in the future to dominate the Far East.

Another point. I think we have all had it in our hearts and our heads before, but I don't think that it has ever been put down on paper by the Prime Minister and myself, and that is the determination that peace can come to the world only by the total elimination of German and Japanese war power.

Some of you Britishers know the old story—we had a General called U. S. Grant. His name was Ulysses Simpson Grant, but in my, and the Prime Minister's, early days he was called "Unconditional Surrender" Grant. The elimination of German, Japanese, and Italian war power means the unconditional surrender by Germany, Italy, and Japan. That means a reasonable assurance of future world peace. It does not mean the destruction of the population of Germany, Italy, or Japan, but it does mean the destruction of the philosophies in those countries which are based on conquest and the subjugation of other people.

While we have not had a meeting of all of the United Nations, I think that there is no question—in fact we both have great confidence that the same purposes and objectives are in the minds of all of the other United Nations— Russia, China, and all the others. . . .

— | "The doctrine that the strong shall dominate the weak is the doctrine of our enemies—and we reject it." *

That chasm between the realities of world politics and the wartime assumptions of American leadership regarding the objectives and anticipated achievements of the war against Germany and Japan was demonstrated conclusively by Roosevelt's Fireside Chat of December 24, 1943, following the Cairo and Teheran conferences. Recounting his conversations with Churchill and Chiang Kai-shek at Cairo and with Churchill and Stalin at Teheran, the President described accurately the imposing military situation, especially in the Far East, but ignored, in his description of the postwar world, the clear warnings of Soviet ambition in eastern Europe, which Stalin had made no effort to hide. In the utopianism of

* *The Public Papers and Addresses of Franklin D. Roosevelt*, XII: 555–9.

such public statements Roosevelt laid the foundation for eventual disillusionment and conflict.

✑

. . . At Cairo, Prime Minister Churchill and I spent four days with the
Generalissimo, Chiang Kai-shek. It was the first time that we had an opportunity
to go over the complex situation in the Far East with him personally. We were
able not only to settle upon definite military strategy, but also to discuss certain
long-range principles which we believe can assure peace in the Far East for many
generations to come.

Those principles are as simple as they are fundamental. They involve the
restoration of stolen property to its rightful owners, and the recognition of the
rights of millions of people in the Far East to build up their own forms of self-
government without molestation. Essential to all peace and security in the
Pacific and the rest of the world is the permanent elimination of the Empire of
Japan as a potential force of aggression. Never again must our soldiers and
sailors and marines—and other soldiers, sailors, and marines—be compelled to
fight from island to island as they are fighting so gallantly and so successfully
today.

Increasingly powerful forces are now hammering at the Japanese at many
points over an enormous arc which curves down through the Pacific from the
Aleutians to the jungles of Burma. Our own Army and Navy, our Air Forces,
the Australians and New Zealanders, the Dutch, and the British land, air, and
sea forces are all forming a band of steel which is slowly but surely closing in on
Japan.

On the mainland of Asia, under the Generalissimo's leadership, the Chinese
ground and air forces augmented by American air forces are playing a vital part
in starting the drive which will push the invaders into the sea.

Following out the military decisions at Cairo, General Marshall has just flown
around the world and has had conferences with General MacArthur and Admiral Nimitz—conferences which will spell plenty of bad news for the Japs in the
not too far distant future.

I met in the Generalissimo a man of great vision, great courage, and a remarkably keen understanding of the problems of today and tomorrow. We discussed all the manifold military plans for striking at Japan with decisive force
from many directions, and I believe I can say that he returned to Chungking
with the positive assurance of total victory over our common enemy. Today we
and the Republic of China are closer together than ever before in deep friendship and in unity of purpose.

After the Cairo Conference, Mr. Churchill and I went by airplane to Teheran.
There we met with Marshal Stalin. We talked with complete frankness on every
conceivable subject connected with the winning of the war and the establishment
of a durable peace after the war.

Within three days of intense and consistently amicable discussions, we agreed on every point concerned with the launching of a gigantic attack upon Germany.

The Russian Army will continue its stern offensives on Germany's eastern front, the Allied armies in Italy and Africa will bring relentless pressure on Germany from the south, and now the encirclement will be complete as great American and British forces attack from other points of the compass. . . .

During the last two days at Teheran, Marshal Stalin, Mr. Churchill, and I looked ahead to the days and months and years that will follow Germany's defeat. We were united in determination that Germany must be stripped of her military might and be given no opportunity within the foreseeable future to regain that might.

The United Nations have no intention to enslave the German people. We wish them to have a normal chance to develop, in peace, as useful and respectable members of the European family. But we most certainly emphasize that word "respectable"—for we intend to rid them once and for all of Nazism and Prussian militarism and the fantastic and disastrous notion that they constitute the "master race."

We did discuss inernational relationships from the point of view of big, broad objectives, rather than details. But on the basis of what we did discuss, I can say even today that I do not think any insoluble differences will arise among Russia, Great Britain, and the United States.

In these conferences we were concerned with basic principles—principles which involve the security and the welfare and the standard of living of human beings in countries large and small.

To use an American and somewhat ungrammatical colloquialism, I may say that I "got along fine" with Marshal Stalin. He is a man who combines a tremendous, relentless determination with a stalwart good humor. I believe he is truly representative of the heart and soul of Russia; and I believe that we are going to get along very well with him and the Russian people—very well indeed.

Britain, Russia, China, and the United States and their allies represent more than three-quarters of the total population of the earth. As long as these four Nations with great military power stick together in determination to keep the peace there will be no possibility of an aggressor Nation arising to start another world war.

But those four powers must be united with and cooperate with all the freedom-loving peoples of Europe, and Asia, and Africa, and the Americas. The rights of every Nation, large or small, must be respected and guarded as jealously as are the rights of every individual within our own Republic.

The doctrine that the strong shall dominate the weak is the doctrine of our enemies—and we reject it.

But, at the same time, we are agreed that if force is necessary to keep international peace, international force will be applied—for as long as it may be necessary.

It has been our steady policy—and it is certainly a commonsense policy—that the right of each Nation to freedom must be measured by the willingness of that Nation to fight for freedom. And today we salute our unseen allies in occupied countries—the underground resistance groups and the armies of liberation. They will provide potent forces against our enemies, when the day of the counter-invasion comes. . . .

# 4 | Cordell Hull and the Foundations of Postwar Peace, April 1944 *

When the Russian armies began to move across the Balkan states during the spring of 1944, it seemed imperative to the British government that some arrangement be negotiated with the Kremlin on spheres of influence which would permit some Western control over areas whose occupation lay within the power of the Soviet Union. Hull's reaction to the British proposals is recorded in his *Memoirs*.

✍

When the Russian Army began to push into Rumania in April, 1944, the relationship between the Soviet Union and the Balkans came to the forefront of our diplomacy. What were Russia's political intentions in the Balkans? Would she seek to set up a domain of her own in the Balkans? Would she retire completely after victory? Would she work with the other major Allies in solving Balkan questions? . . .

A stir of speculation now arose in the press of many countries as to whether Russia's aim was liberation or acquisition. Suddenly British Ambassador Halifax inquired of me on May 30, 1944, how this Government would feel about an arrangement between the British and Russians whereby Russia would have a controlling influence in Rumania, and Britain a controlling influence in Greece. He said that difficulties had risen between Russia and Britain over the Balkans, especially with regard to Rumania. . . .

The British Foreign Office said that the United Kingdom Government was fully alive to the importance of avoiding even the appearance of carving up the Balkans into spheres of influence. A temporary agreement such as they suggested seemed to them the best chance of amicable cooperation between the Allies in the countries concerned during the military period.

After telling Halifax that I would give this serious consideration, I said point-blank:

"At first blush, in view of the many charges and countercharges now rising—

* *The Memoirs of Cordell Hull* (New York, 1948), II: 1451–5. Copyright 1948 by Cordell Hull. Reprinted by permission of The Macmillan Company.

and which will certainly rise in the future—about encroachments first by one Government and then by another on the economic, political, military, or other internal affairs of the Balkans and other European countries, it would be a doubtful course to abandon our broad basic declarations of policy, principles, and practice. If these are departed from in one or two important instances, such as you propose, then neither of the two countries parties to such an act will have any precedent to stand on, or any stable rules by which to be governed and to insist that other Governments be governed."

I concluded by saying that, in my opinion, this fact should be carefully studied by all concerned before any definite departures took place. Halifax said he appreciated this thought.

I was, in fact, flatly opposed to any division of Europe or sections of Europe into spheres of influence. I had argued against this strongly at the Moscow Conference. It seemed to me that any creation of zones of influence would inevitably sow the seeds of future conflict. I felt that zones of influence could not but derogate from the over-all authority of the international security organization which I expected would come into being.

I was not, and am not, a believer in the idea of balance of power or spheres of influence as a means of keeping the peace. During the First World War I had made an intensive study of the system of spheres of influence and balance of power, and I was grounded to the taproots in their iniquitous consequences. The conclusions I then formed in total opposition to this system stayed with me.

On the following day, May 31, Prime Minister Churchill, to whom Halifax's cable reporting my remarks was undoubtedly communicated, sent the President a telegram direct in which he argued strongly for our approval of the proposed agreement. He emphasized that Britain did not wish to cut up the Balkans into areas of influence, that the arrangement would apply only to war conditions, and that there would be no change in the present collaboration between the American and British Governments in formulating and executing the policy of the Allies toward Greece and Rumania. . . .

Mr. Roosevelt sent this telegram to me for consideration and for the drafting of a reply.

My associates at the State Department agreed with the original attitude I had taken with Lord Halifax; namely, that we could not lend our support to any such agreement and, in fact, should do what we could to discourage it. While we could understand Britain's natural desire to strengthen herself in the Mediterranean through a position of influence in Greece, and to avoid causes of friction with the Russians in the Balkans, we felt that any such arrangement as that proposed, no matter how temporary it might be made to appear, would inevitably conduce to the establishment of zones of influence against which we had been stoutly fighting, and against which I had spoken out at the Moscow Conference.

While this reply was being prepared in the Department, Halifax handed us on June 8 another message from the Prime Minister—this one addressed to him. Mr. Churchill again said there was no question of spheres of influence being involved. But he added that, although we all had to act together, someone must "play the hand." It seemed reasonable to him that the Russians should deal with the Rumanians and Bulgarians, and that Britain should deal with the Greeks, who were in Britain's theater of operations and were Britain's old allies, for whom she had sacrificed 40,000 men in 1941. The same, he added, was true of Yugoslavia. . . .

The President sent our reply to the Prime Minister on June 10. This recalled my conversation with Halifax on May 30 when I communicated to the Ambassador reasons why this Government was unwilling to give its approval. The President acknowledged in his reply that the Government responsible for military actions in any country—Britain was militarily responsible for Greece, and Russia for Rumania—would inevitably make decisions which military developments necessitated. But we were convinced that the natural tendency for such decisions to extend into the political and economic fields would be strengthened by the agreement proposed by the British. The President stated our opinion that this would surely lead to the persistence of differences between Britain and Russia and to the division of the Balkans into spheres of influence, regardless of Mr. Churchill's statement that the agreement would be limited to military matters.

The President concluded that we should prefer to see consultative machinery set up for the Balkans to resolve misunderstandings and to prevent the development of exclusive zones of influence.

The Prime Minister came back the following day, June 11, with a long, forceful telegram saying that the President's message had given him much concern. Action would be paralyzed, he said, if everybody had to consult everybody else before taking action. Events in the Balkans always outstripped the changing situations. . . .

The Prime Minister finally suggested that the arrangement he had proposed should have a three months' trial, following which it would be reviewed by the three Powers.

When this telegram arrived, I was resting for a few days at Hershey, Pennsylvania. The President, without consulting me or the State Department, replied the following day accepting the Prime Minister's three months' proposal, but adding that care should be exercised to make it clear that no postwar spheres of influence were being established.

The President did not inform the State Department of this action. . . .

— | "The [Atlantic] Charter is an expression of fundamental objectives toward which we and our Allies are directing our policies." *

Few speeches of the late war years illustrated more clearly the utopianism in American thought than did Hull's address over the Columbia Broadcasting

* *Documents on American Foreign Relations, July 1943–June 1944,* Leland M. Goodrich and Marie J. Carroll, eds. (Boston, 1945), VI: 25–35.

System on April 9, 1944. For Hull all the increasingly victorious Allies were still seeking a world based on the principle of self-determination of peoples.

✍

. . . In talking about foreign policy it is well to remember, as Justice Holmes said, that a page of history is worth a volume of logic. There are three outstanding lessons in our recent history to which I particularly wish to draw your attention. In the first place, since the outbreak of the present war in Europe, we and those nations who are now our allies have moved from relative weakness to strength. In the second place, during that same period we in this country have moved from a deep-seated tendency toward separate action to the knowledge and conviction that only through unity of action can there be achieved in this work the results which are essential for the continuance of free peoples. And, thirdly, we have moved from a careless tolerance of evil institutions to the conviction that free governments and Nazi and Fascist governments cannot exist together in this world because the very nature of the latter requires them to be aggressors and the very nature of free governments too often lays them open to treacherous and well-laid plans of attack. . . .

The allied strength has now grown to the point where we are on the verge of great events. Of military events I cannot speak. It is enough that they are in the hands of men who have the complete trust of the American people. We await their development with absolute confidence. But I can and should discuss with you what may happen close upon the heels of military action.

As I look at the map of Europe, certain things seem clear to me. As the Nazis go down to defeat they will inevitably leave behind them in Germany and the satellite states of southeastern Europe a legacy of confusion. It is essential that we and our Allies establish the controls necessary to bring order out of this chaos as rapidly as possible and do everything possible to prevent its spread to the German-occupied countries of eastern and western Europe while they are in the throes of reestablishing government and repairing the most brutal ravages of the war. If confusion should spread throughout Europe it is difficult to overemphasize the seriousness of the disaster that may follow. Therefore, for us, for the world, and for the countries concerned, a stable Europe should be an immediate objective of allied policy.

Stability and order do not and cannot mean reaction. Order there must be to avoid chaos. But it must be achieved in a manner which will give full scope to men and women who look forward, men and women who will end Fascism and all its works and create the institutions of a free and democratic way of life.

We look with hope and with deep faith to a period of great democratic accomplishment in Europe. Liberation from the German yoke will give the peoples of Europe a new and magnificent opportunity to fulfill their democratic aspirations, both in building democratic political institutions of their own choice and in achieving the social and economic democracy on which political democracy must rest. It is important to our national interest to encourage the establishment in Europe of strong and progressive popular governments, dedicated like our own to improving the social welfare of the people as a whole —governments which will join the common effort of nations in creating the conditions of lasting peace and in promoting the expansion of production, employment, and the exchange and consumption of goods, which are the material foundations of the liberty and welfare of all peoples. . . .

However difficult the road may be, there is no hope of turning victory into enduring peace unless the real interests of this country, the British Commonwealth, the Soviet Union, and China are harmonized and unless they agree and act together. This is the solid framework upon which all future policy and international organization must be built. It offers the fullest opportunity for the development of institutions in which all free nations may participate democratically, through which a reign of law and morality may arise, and through which the material interests of all may be advanced. But without an enduring understanding between these four nations upon their fundamental purposes, interests, and obligations to one another, all organizations to preserve peace are creations on paper and the path is wide open again for the rise of a new aggressor. . . .

The road to agreement is a difficult one, as any man knows who has ever tried to get two other men, or a city council, or a trade gathering, or a legislative body, to agree upon anything. Agreement can be achieved only by trying to understand the other fellow's point of view and by going as far as possible to meet it.

Although the road to unity of purpose and action is long and difficult we have taken long strides upon our way. The Atlantic Charter was proclaimed by the President and the Prime Minister of Great Britain in August 1941. Then, by the Declaration of the United Nations of January 1, 1942, these nations adopted the principles of the Atlantic Charter, agreed to devote all their resources to the winning of the war, and pledged themselves not to conclude a separate armistice or peace with their common enemies.

After that came the declaration signed at Moscow on October 30, 1943. Here the four nations who are carrying and must carry the chief burden of defeating their enemies renewed their determination by joint action to achieve this end. But they went farther than this and pledged cooperation with one another to establish at the earliest practicable date, with other peace-loving states, an effective international organization to maintain peace and security, which in principle met with overwhelming non-partisan approval by the Congress in the Connally and Fulbright resolutions.

Further steps along the road of united allied action were taken at the conference at Cairo, where the President and Mr. Churchill met with Generalissimo Chiang Kai-shek, and at the conference at Tehran, where they met with Marshal Stalin. At Tehran the three Allies fighting in Europe reached complete agreement on military plans for winning the war and made plain their determination to achieve harmonious action in the period of peace. That concert among the Allies rests on broad foundations of common interests and common aspirations, and it will endure. The Tehran declaration made it clear also that in the tasks of peace we shall welcome the cooperation and active participation of all nations, large and small, which wish to enter into the world family of democratic nations.

The Cairo declaration as to the Pacific assured the liquidation of Japan's occupations and thefts of territory to deprive her of the power to attack her neighbors again, to restore Chinese territories to China, and freedom to the people of Korea. . . .

There has been discussion recently of the Atlantic Charter and of its application to various situations. The Charter is an expression of fundamental objectives toward which we and our Allies are directing our policies. It states that the nations accepting it are not fighting for the sake of aggrandizement, territorial or otherwise. It lays down the common principles upon which rest the hope of liberty, economic opportunity, peace, and security through international cooperation. It is not a code of law from which detailed answers to every question can be distilled by painstaking analysis of its words and phrases. It points the direction in which solutions are to be sought; it does not give solutions. It charts the course upon which we are embarked and shall continue. That course includes the prevention of aggression and the establishment of world security. The Charter certainly does not prevent any steps, including those relating to enemy states, necessary to achieve these objectives. What is fundamental are the objectives of the Charter and the determination to achieve them. . . .

We have found no difference of opinion among our Allies that the organization and purposes of the Nazi state and its Japanese counterpart, and the military system in all of its ramifications upon which they rest, are, and by their very nature must be, directed toward conquest. There was no disagreement that even after the defeat of the enemy there will be no security unless and until our victory is used to destroy these systems to their very foundation. The action which must be taken to achieve these ends must be, as I have said, agreed action. We are working with our Allies now upon these courses.

The conference at Moscow . . . established the European Advisory Commission, which is now at work in London upon the treatment of Germany. Out of these discussions will come back to the governments for their consideration proposals for concrete action.

Along with arrangements by which nations may be secure and free must go arrangements by which men and women who compose those nations may live and have the opportunity through their efforts to improve their material condition. As I said earlier, we will fail indeed if we win a victory only to let the free peoples of the world, through any absence of action on our part, sink into weakness and despair. The heart of the matter lies in action which will stimulate and expand production in industry and agriculture and free international commerce from excessive and unreasonable restrictions. . . .

I shall not on this occasion be able to explain the work which has been done— and it is extensive—in these fields. In many of them proposals are far advanced toward the stage of discussion with members of the Congress prior to formulation for public discussion.

I hope, however, that I have been able in some measure to bring before you the immensity of the task which lies before us all, the nature of the difficulties which are involved, and the conviction and purpose with which we are attacking them. Our foreign policy is comprehensive, is stable, and is known of all men. As the President has said, neither he nor I have made or will make any secret agreement or commitment, political or financial. The officials of the Government have not been unmindful of the responsibility resting upon them, nor have they spared either energy or such abilities as they possess in discharging that responsibility. . . .

## 5 | Arthur H. Vandenberg's Speech in the Senate, January 10, 1945 *

Senator Arthur H. Vandenberg of Michigan, a leading prewar isolationist, appeared to be facing the hard challenge posed by Soviet defiance of the principle of self-determination with stark realism in this speech before the Senate. Vandenberg saw the problem clearly—that the United States had two unpleasant choices before it, either to give up its principles or to give up its alliance with Russia. But having stated the problem, the Senator refused to suggest which course the nation should follow.

✒

Mr. President, there are critical moments in the life of every nation which call for the straightest, the plainest and the most courageous thinking of which we are capable. We confront such a moment now. It is not only desperately important to America, it is important to the world. It is important not only to this generation which lives in blood. It is important to future generations if they shall live in peace.

No man in his right sense will be dogmatic in his viewpoint at such an hour. A global conflict which uproots the earth is not calculated to submit itself to the dominion of any finite mind. . . . Each of us can only speak according to his little lights—and pray for a composite wisdom that shall lead us to high, safe ground. It is only in this spirit that I speak today. . . .

The United Nations, in even greater unity of military action than heretofore, must never, for any cause, permit this military unity to fall apart. . . . We not only have two wars to win, we also have yet to achieve such a peace as will justify this appalling cost. Here again an even more difficult unity is indispensable. Otherwise, we shall look back upon a futile, sanguinary shambles and—God

* The Private Papers of Senator Vandenberg, Arthur H. Vandenberg, Jr. and Joe Alex Morris, eds. (Boston, 1952), 132–8. Reprinted by permission of Houghton Mifflin Company.

save the mark—we shall be able to look forward only to the curse of World War III. . . .

I hesitate, even now, to say these things, Mr. President, because a great American illusion seems to have been built up—wittingly or otherwise—that we in the United States dare not publicly discuss these subjects lest we contribute to international dissension. . . . But I frankly confess that I do not know why we must be the only silent partner in this grand alliance. There seems to be no fear of disunity, no hesitation in Moscow, when Moscow wants to assert unilateral war and peace aims which collide with ours.

There seems to be no fear of disunity, no hesitation in London, when Mr. Churchill proceeds upon his unilateral way to make decisions often repugnant to our ideas and our ideals. Perhaps our allies will plead that their actions are not unilateral; that our President, as Bevin said, has initialed this or that at one of the famous Big Three conferences; that our President, as Churchill said, has been kept constantly "aware of everything that has happened"; in other words, that by our silence we have acquiesced. But that hypothesis would only make a bad matter worse. It would be the final indictment of our silence—the final obituary for open covenants. We, of course, accept no conception that our contribution to unity must be silence, while others say and do what they please, and that our only role in this global tragedy is to fight and die and pay, and that unity for us shall only be the unity which Jonah enjoyed when he was swallowed by the whale.

I hasten to say that any such intolerable conception would be angrily repudiated by every American—from the President down to the last citizen among us. It has not been and is not true. Yet it cannot be denied that our Government has not spoken out—to our own people or to our allies—in any such specific fashion as have the others. It cannot be denied, as a result, that too often a grave melancholy settles upon some sectors of our people. It cannot be denied that citizens, in increasing numbers, are crying: "What are we fighting for?" It cannot be denied that our silence—at least our public and official silence—has multiplied confusion at home and abroad. It cannot be denied that this confusion threatens our unity—yes, Mr. President, and already hangs like a cloud over Dumbarton Oaks. So I venture to repeat, with all the earnestness at my command, that a new rule of honest candor in Washington, as a substitute for mystifying silence or for classical generalities—honest candor on the high plane of great ideals—is the greatest contribution we can make to the realities of unity at this moment when enlightened civilization is our common stake. . . .

I hasten to make my own personal viewpoint clear. I have always been frankly one of those who has believed in our own self-reliance. I still believe that we can never again—regardless of collaborations—allow our national defense to deteriorate to anything like a point of impotence. But I do not believe that any nation hereafter can immunize itself by its own exclusive action. Since Pearl Harbor, World War II has put the gory science of mass murder into new and sinister perspective. Our oceans have ceased to be moats which automatically protect our ramparts. Flesh and blood now compete unequally with winged steel. War has become an all-consuming juggernaut. If World War III ever unhappily arrives, it will open new laboratories of death too horrible to contemplate. I propose to do everything within my power to keep those laboratories closed for keeps.

I want maximum American cooperation, consistent with legitimate American self-interest, with constitutional process and with collateral events which warrant it, to make the basic idea of Dumbarton Oaks succeed. I want a new dignity and a new authority for international law.

I think American self-interest requires it. But, Mr. President, this also requires whole-hearted reciprocity. In honest candor, I think we should tell other nations that this glorious thing we contemplate is not and cannot be one-sided. I think we must say again that unshared idealism is a menace which we could not undertake to underwrite in the post-war world. . . .

The real question always becomes just this: Where does real self-interest lie? Here, Mr. President, we reach the core of the immediate problem. Without remotely wanting to be invidious, I use one of many available examples. I would not presume, even under these circumstances, to use it except that it ultimately involves us. Russia's unilateral plan appears to contemplate the engulfment, directly or indirectly, of a surrounding circle of buffer states, contrary to our conception of what we thought we were fighting for in respect to the rights of small nations and a just peace. Russia's announced reason is her insistent purpose never again to be at the mercy of another German tyranny. That is a perfectly understandable reason. The alternative is collective security. . . . Which is better in the long view, from a purely selfish Russian standpoint: To forcefully surround herself with a cordon of unwillingly controlled or partitioned states, thus affronting the opinions of mankind . . . or to win the priceless asset of world confidence in her by embracing the alternative, namely, full and wholehearted cooperation with and reliance on a vital international organization. . . . Well—at that point, Russia, or others like her, in equally honest candor has a perfect right to reply, "Where is there any such alternative reliance until we know what the United States will do?". . .

I propose that we meet this problem conclusively and at once. There is no reason to wait. America has this same self-interest in permanently, conclusively and effectively disarming Germany and Japan. . . . It should be handled as this present war is handled. There should be no more need to refer any such action [use of force to keep the Axis disarmed] back to Congress than that Congress should expect to pass upon battle plans today. The Commander-in-Chief should have instant power to act and he should act. I know of no reason why a hard-and-fast treaty between the major allies should not be signed today to achieve this dependable end. We need not await the determination of our other post-war relationships. This problem—this menace—stands apart by itself . . . I respectfully urge that we meet this problem now.

From it stem many of today's confusions, doubts and frustrations. I think we should immediately put it behind us by conclusive action. Having done so . . . we shall be able, at least, to judge accurately whether we have found and cured the real hazard to our relationships. We shall have closed ranks. We shall have returned infinitely closer to basic unity.

Then, in honest candor, Mr. President, I think we have the duty and the right to demand that whatever immediate unilateral decisions have to be made in consequence of military need . . . shall all be temporary and subject to final revision in the objective light of the postwar world and the postwar peace league as they shall ultimately develop. . . . Indeed, I . . . would write it in the bond. If Dumbarton Oaks should specifically authorize the ultimate international organization to review protested injustices in the peace itself, it would at least partially nullify the argument that we are to be asked to put a blank-check warrant behind a future status quo which is unknown to us and which we might be unwilling to defend.

We are standing by our guns with epic heroism. I know of no reason why we should not stand by our ideals. If they vanish under ultimate pressures, we shall at least have kept the record straight; we shall have kept faith with our soldier sons; and we then shall clearly be free agents, unhampered by tragic misunderstandings, in determining our own course when Berlin and Tokyo are in Allied hands.

Let me put it this way for myself: I am prepared, by effective international cooperation, to do our full part in charting happier and safer tomorrows. But I am not prepared to guarantee permanently the spoils of an unjust peace. It will not work. . . .

Mr. President, I conclude as I began. We must win these wars with maximum speed and minimum loss. Therefore we must have maximum Allied cooperation and minimum Allied frictions. We have fabulously earned the right to be heard in respect to the basis of this unity. We need the earliest possible clarification of our relations with our brave allies. We need this clarification not only for the sake of total Allied cooperation in the winning of the war but also in behalf of a truly compensatory peace. We cannot drift to victory. We must have maximum united effort on all fronts. We must have maximum united effort in our councils. And we must deserve the continued united effort of our own people.

I realize, Mr. President, in such momentous problems how much easier it is to be critical than to be correct. I do not wish to meddle. I want only to help. I want to do my duty. It is in this spirit that I ask for honest candor in respect to our ideals, our dedications, and our commitments, as the greatest contribution which government can now make to the only kind of realistic unity which will most swiftly bring our victorious sons back home, and which will best validate our aspirations, our sacrifices, and our dreams.

# 6 | The Soviet Challenge in Eastern Europe: A Realistic Appraisal, January 8, 1945 *

In this evaluation of Soviet power and purpose in eastern Europe, John Nickerson, Deputy Director, Office of European Affairs, Department of State, warned the administration that the Slavic states had slipped beyond the control of the West. Unless the United States accepted this fact diplomatically, he wrote, Europe would return to the "diplomacy of the jungle." He preferred that the United States government prepare the American people for a realistic settlement in eastern Europe, especially since the nation required the co-operation of the U.S.S.R. in organizing the peace.

We have a pretty clear idea of the Soviet objectives in Eastern Europe. We know the terms of their settlement with Finland. We know that the three Baltic States have been re-incorporated into the Soviet Union and that nothing which we can do can alter this. It is not a question of whether we like it; I personally don't like it although I recognize that the Soviet Government has arguments on its side. The point is it has been done and nothing which it is within the power of the United States Government to do can undo it. We know that the Russians will insist on the annexation of a substantial portion of East Prussia and a boundary with Poland roughly in accordance with the Curzon line. The Soviet Union has already re-incorporated Bessarabia into its territory. The Soviet Union may insist on minor adjustments in its boundaries with Rumania.

I would favor using any bargaining power that exists in connection with the foregoing matters to induce the Russians to go along with a satisfactory United Nations organization and the proposed Provisional Security Council for Europe to deal with Poland, Greece and other trouble spots. I would favor our agreeing to accept as a fact the re-incorporation of the three Baltic States into the Soviet Union and our recognition of these areas as Soviet territory. This would involve our withdrawing recognition from the three diplomatic representatives of those countries in the United States.

I would favor our agreeing at the appropriate time to accept the transfer of that portion of East Prussia to the Soviet Union which that country insists on having. I would likewise favor our agreeing to accept as a fact at the appropriate time, the Curzon line as a frontier between Poland and the Soviet Union, and to agree to announce publicly such acceptance.

The recognition of the return of Bessarabia to the Soviet Union should present no difficulties to us.

We must have the support of the Soviet Union to defeat Germany. We sorely need the Soviet Union in the war against Japan when the war in Europe is over.

* *Foreign Relations of the United States, Diplomatic Papers: The Conferences of Malta and Yalta, 1945* (Washington, 1955), 94–6.

The importance of these two things can be reckoned in terms of American lives. We must have the cooperation of the Soviet Union to organize the peace. There are certain things in connection with the foregoing proposals which are repugnant to me personally, but I am prepared to urge their adoption to obtain the cooperation of the Soviet Union in winning the war and organizing the peace. By acting on these things, we may be able to work out a regime which will obtain the cooperation of the Soviet Union for the rest of Europe and the rest of the world. There are good arguments from the Soviet point of view in favor of all of these proposals. I am willing to sponsor and support the Soviet arguments if it will save American lives in winning the war and if it will save the rest of Europe from the diplomacy of the jungle which is almost certain to ensue otherwise.

If the proposals set forth in the foregoing paragraphs should be adopted as the policy of the United States Government, a program should be undertaken immediately to prepare public opinion for them. This would involve off-the-record discussions with Congress, with outstanding newspaper editors and writers, columnists and radio commentators.

## 7 | The Yalta Conference: The Debate over Poland, February 6, 1945 *

The question of Poland's future dominated the Big Three political discussions at Yalta. Roosevelt demanded that the government of Poland be representative of all political groups within the country. At the same time he accepted the Soviet contention that the Polish government maintain friendly and co-operative relations with the U.S.S.R. Churchill agreed to the Curzon Line, but, in support of Roosevelt, he declared it a point of honor for Britain that Poland have a free and independent government. Stalin replied that Poland was for Russia a matter of both honor and security. The London Poles, he continued, were the proven enemies of the Soviet state. Only the Lublin Poles, therefore, would give that country a regime friendly to Russia.

✍

The President inquired whether the Polish question should be taken up now or postponed until the next meeting.

The Prime Minister said that he hoped that at least a start could be made today.

* *The Conferences of Malta and Yalta,* 667–71.

The President said that the United States was farther away from Poland than anyone else here, and that there were times when a long distance point of view was useful. He said that at Tehran he had stated that he believed the American people were in general favorably inclined to the Curzon Line as the eastern frontier of Poland, but he felt that if the Soviet Government would consider a concession in regard to Lwow and the oil deposits in the Province of Lwow that would have a very salutary effect. He said that he was merely putting forth this suggestion for consideration and would not insist on it. He said that in regard to the government he wished to see the creation of a representative government which could have the support of all the great powers and which could be composed of representatives of the principal parties of Poland. He said one possibility which had been suggested was the creation of a Presidential Council composed of Polish leaders which could then create a government composed of the chiefs of the five political parties—Workers Party, Peasant Party, Socialist Party, etc. He said that one thing must be made certain and that was that Poland should maintain the most friendly and co-operative relations with the Soviet Union.

Marshal Stalin replied that Poland should maintain friendly relations not only with the Soviet Union but with the other Allies.

The President said he had merely put forth a suggestion but he thought if we could solve the Polish question it would be a great help to all of us. He added he didn't know personally any members of the London government or Lublin government, but he had met Mr. Mikolajczyk who had made a deep impression on him as a sincere and an honest man.

The Prime Minister said that he had consistently declared in Parliament and elsewhere that the British Government would support the Curzon Line, even leaving Lwow to the Soviet Union. He had been criticized for this and so had Mr. Eden, but he felt that after the burdens which Russia had borne in this war the Curzon Line was not a decision of force but one of right. He said he remained in that position. Of course, he added, if the mighty Soviet Union could make some gesture to the much weaker country, such as the relinquishment of Lwow, this act of magnanimity would be acclaimed and admired. He said he was much more interested in sovereignty and independence of Poland than in the frontier line—he wanted to see the Poles have a home where they could organize their lives as they wished. That was an objective that he had often heard Marshal Stalin proclaim most firmly, and he put his trust in those declarations. He said that he therefore had not considered the question of the frontier as a question of vital importance. It must not be forgotten, however, that Great Britain had gone to war to protect Poland against German aggression at a time when that decision was most risky, and it had almost cost them their life in the world. He said Great Britain had no material interest in Poland, but the question was one of honor and that his government would therefore never be content with a solution which did not leave Poland a free and independent state. The freedom of Poland, however, did not cover any hostile designs or intrigue against the U.S.S.R., and none of us should permit this. . . .

Marshal Stalin then gave the following summary of his views on the Polish question: Mr. Churchill had said that for Great Britain the Polish question was one of honor and that he understood, but for the Russians it was a question both of honor and security. It was one of honor because Russia had many past grievances against Poland and desired to see them eliminated. It was a question of strategic security not only because Poland was a bordering country but because throughout history Poland had been the corridor for attack on Russia. We have to mention that during the last thirty years Germany twice was weak. Russia wants a strong, independent and democratic Poland. Since it was impossible by the force of Russian armies alone to close from the outside this corridor, it could be done only by Polands' own forces. It was very important, therefore, to have Poland independent, strong and democratic. It is not only a question of honor for Russia, but one of life and death. It was for this reason that there had been a great change from the policies of the Czars who had wished to suppress and assimilate Poland. In regard to the questions raised here on which we have different opinions, the following might be said:

In regard to the Curzon Line, concessions in regard to Lwow and the Lwow Province, and Mr. Churchill's reference to a magnanimous act on our part, it is necessary to remind you that not Russians but Curzon and Clemenceau fixed this line. The Russians had not been invited and the line was established against their will. Lenin had opposed giving Bialystok Province to the Poles but the Curzon Line gives it to Poland. We have already retreated from Lenin's position in regard to this province. Should we then be less Russian than Curzon and Clemenceau? We could not then return to Moscow and face the people who would say Stalin and Molotov have been less sure defenders of Russian interest than Curzon and Clemenceau. It is, therefore, impossible to agree with the proposed modification of the line. I would prefer to have the war go on although it will cost us blood in order to compensate for Poland from Germany. When he was in Moscow Mr. Mikolajczyk was delighted to hear that Poland's frontier would extend to the West Neisse River and I favor the Polish frontier on the West Neisse and ask the conference to support this proposal.

As to the question of the Polish government, Mr. Churchill has said it would be good to create a Polish government here. I am afraid that was a slip of the tongue, for without participation of the Poles it is impossible to create a Polish government. I am called a dictator and not a democrat, but I have enough democratic feeling to refuse to create a Polish government without the Poles being consulted—the question can only be settled with the consent of the Poles. . . .

As a military man I demand from a country liberated by the Red Army that there be no civil war in the rear. The men in the Red Army are indifferent to the type of government as long as it will maintain order and they will not be shot in the back. The Warsaw, or Lublin, government has not badly fulfilled this task. There are, however, agents of the London government who claim to be agents of the underground forces of resistance. I must say that no good and much evil comes from these forces. Up to the present time they have killed 212 of our military men. They attack our supply bases to obtain arms. Although it has been proclaimed that all radio stations must be registered and obtain permission to operate, agents of the London government are violating these regulations. We have arrested some of them and if they continue to disturb our rear we will shoot them as military law requires. When I compare what the agents of the Lublin government have done and what the agents of the London government have done I see the first are good and the second bad. We want tranquility in our rear. We will support the government which gives us peace in the rear, and as a military man I could not do otherwise. Without a secure rear there can be no more victories for the Red Army. Any military man and even the non-military man will understand this situation.

The Prime Minister said that he must put on record the fact that the British and Soviet Governments have different sources of information in Poland and therefore they obtain different views of the situation there. He said it is possible that their reports are mistaken as it is not always possible to believe everything that anyone tells you. He believed, he added, that with the best of all their information he could not feel that the Lublin government represents more than one third of the people and would not be maintained in power if the people were free to express their opinion. One of the reasons why the British have so earnestly sought a solution had been the fear that the Polish underground army would come into collision with the Lublin government, which would lead to great bloodshed, arrests and deportations which could not fail to have a bad effect on the whole Polish question. The Prime Minister said he agreed that anyone who attacks the Red Army should be punished, but he repeated that the British Government could not agree to recognizing the Lublin government of Poland.

# 8 | The Hopkins-Stalin Conversations over Poland in Moscow, May 1945 *

Harry Hopkins's conversations with Stalin over the future of Poland again revealed the magnitude of the East-West diplomatic impasse. Hopkins repeated emphatically that the United States wanted a Poland friendly to Russia. The fact that Stalin had not permitted a free government in Poland, however, was creating an anti-Soviet sentiment in the United States. Poland, Hopkins assured the Soviet leader, had become the symbol of the ability of the two superpowers to resolve their differences. Stalin reminded Hopkins that twice in one long generation Germany had invaded Russia through Poland because that country was part of an anti-Russian *cordon sanitaire*. Russian security, therefore, required a strong and friendly Poland. To obtain the required stability in Poland

* Charles E. Bohlen's report of the Hopkins-Stalin conversations, May 26–27, 1945, *Foreign Relations of the United States, Diplomatic Papers: The Conference of Berlin* (Washington, 1960), I: 26–8, 37–40.

the Soviet government had been forced to act through the Lublin Committee to establish a responsible regime for that country.

✎

. . . Mr. Hopkins then said that a few days ago President Truman had sent for him and had asked him to come to Moscow to have a talk with Marshal Stalin. There were a number of things that he and Mr. Harriman hoped to discuss wtih Marshal Stalin and Mr. Molotov while he was in Moscow, but before going into those specific questions he wished to tell the Marshal of the real reason why the President had asked him to come, and that was the question of the fundamental relationship between the United States and the Soviet Union. Two months ago there had been overwhelming sympathy among the American people for the Soviet Union and complete support for President Roosevelt's policies which the Marshal knew so well. This sympathy and support came primarily because of the brilliant achievements of the Soviet Union in the war and partly from President Roosevelt's leadership and the magnificent way in which our two countries had worked together to bring about the defeat of Germany. The American people at that time hoped and confidently believed that the two countries could work together in peace as well as they had in war. Mr. Hopkins said there had always been a small minority, the Hearsts and the McCormicks, who had been against the policy of cooperation with the Soviet Union. These men had also been bitter political enemies of President Roosevelt but had never had any backing from the American people as was shown by the fact that against their bitter opposition President Roosevelt had been four times elected President. He said he did not intend to discuss this small minority but to discuss the general state of American opinion and particularly the present attitude of the millions of Americans who had supported President Roosevelt's policy in regard to the Soviet Union and who believed that despite different political and economic ideology of the two countries, the United States and the Soviet Union could work together after the war in order to bring about a secure peace for humanity. He said he wished to assure the Marshal with all the earnestness at his command that this body of American public opinion who had been the constant support of the Roosevelt policies were seriously disturbed about their relations with Russia. In fact, in the last six weeks deterioration of public opinion had been so serious as to affect adversely the relations between our two countries. . . .

Mr. Hopkins said that it was not simple or easy to put a finger on the precise reasons for this deterioration but he must emphasize that without the support of public opinion and particularly of the supporters of President Roosevelt it would be very difficult for President Truman to carry forward President Roosevelt's policy. He said that, as the Marshal was aware, the cardinal basis of President Roosevelt's policy which the American people had fully supported had been the concept that the interests of the United States were world wide and not confined to North and South America and the Pacific Ocean and it was this concept that had led to the many conferences concerning the peace of the world which President Roosevelt had had with Marshal Stalin. President Roosevelt had believed that the Soviet Union had likewise world-wide interests and that the two countries could work out together any political or economic considerations at issue between them. After the Yalta Conference it looked as though we were well on the way to reaching a basic understanding on all questions of foreign affairs of interest to our respective countries, in regard to the treatment of Germany; Japan and the question of setting up a world security organization, to say nothing of the long term interests between the United States and the U.S.S.R. He said in a country like ours public opinion is affected by specific incidents and in this case the deterioration in public opinion in regard to our relations with the Soviet Union had been centered in our inability to carry into effect the Yalta Agreement on Poland. There were also a train of events, each unimportant in themselves, which had grown up around the Polish question, which contributed to the deterioration in public opinion. President Truman feels, and so does the American public, although they are not familiar with all the details, a sense of bewilderment at our inability to solve the Polish question.

Marshal Stalin replied that the reason for the failure on the Polish question was that the Soviet Union desired to have a friendly Poland, but that Great Britain wanted to revive the system of *cordon sanitaire* on the Soviet borders.

Mr. Hopkins replied that neither the Government nor the people of the United States had any such intention.

Marshal Stalin replied he was speaking only of England and said that the British conservatives did not desire to see a Poland friendly to the Soviet Union.

Mr. Hopkins stated that the United States would desire a Poland friendly to the Soviet Union and in fact desired to see friendly countries all along the Soviet borders.

Marshal Stalin replied if that be so we could easily come to terms in regard to Poland.

Mr. Hopkins said that during his visit here there were a number of specific questions that he and Mr. Harriman hoped to discuss with Marshal Stalin and Mr. Molotov but that the general statement he had just made concerning public opinion in the United States was the principal reason for his coming and the principal cause of anxiety at the present time. He said he had wished to state frankly and as forcibly as he knew how to Marshal Stalin the importance that he, personally, attached to the present trend of events and that he felt that the situation would get rapidly worse unless we could clear up the Polish matter. He had therefore been glad to hear the Marshal say that he thought the question could be settled.

Marshal Stalin replied that in his opinion it was best to settle it but not if the British conservatives attempted to revive the *cordon sanitaire*. . . .

Mr. Hopkins then said with the Marshal's permission he would like to review the position of the United States in regard to Poland. He said first of all he wished to assure the Marshal that he had no thought or indeed any right to attempt to settle the Polish problem during his visit here in Moscow, nor was he intending to hide behind American public opinion in presenting the position of the United States.

Marshal Stalin said he was afraid that his remark concerning Soviet public opinion had cut Mr. Hopkins to the quick and that he had not meant to imply that Mr. Hopkins was hiding behind the screen of American public opinion. In fact he knew Mr. Hopkins to be an honest and frank man.

Mr. Hopkins said that he wished to state this position as clearly and as forcibly as he knew how. He said the question of Poland per se was not so important as the fact that it had become a symbol of our ability to work out problems with the Soviet Union. He said that we had no special interests in Poland and no special desire to see any particular kind of government. That we would accept any government in Poland which was desired by the Polish people and was at the same time friendly to the Soviet Government. He said that the people and Government of the United States felt that this was a problem which should be worked out jointly between the United States, the Soviet Union and Great Britain and that we felt that the Polish people should be given the right to free elections to choose their own government and their own system and that Poland should genuinely be independent. The Government and people of the United States were disturbed because the preliminary steps towards the reestablishment of Poland appeared to have been taken unilaterally by the Soviet Union together with the present Warsaw Government and that in fact the United States was completely excluded. He said he hoped that Stalin would believe him when he said that this feeling was a fact. Mr. Hopkins said he urged that Marshal Stalin would judge American policy by the actions of the United States Government itself and not by the attitudes and public expressions of the Hearts newspapers and the *Chicago Tribune*. He hoped that the Marshal would put his mind to the task of thinking up what diplomatic methods could be used to settle this question, keeping in mind the feeling of the American people. He said he himself was not prepared to say how it could be done but that he felt it must be done. Poland had become a symbol in the sense that it bore a direct relation to the willingness of the United States to participate in international affairs on a world-wide basis and that our people must believe that they are joining their power with that of the Soviet Union and Great Britain in the promotion of international peace and the well being of humanity. Mr. Hopkins went on to say that he felt the overwhelming majority of the people of the United States felt that the relations between the United States and the USSR could be worked out in a spirit of cooperation despite the differences in ideology and that with all these factors in its favor he wished to appeal to the Marshal to help find a way to the solution of the Polish problem.

Marshal Stalin replied that he wished Mr. Hopkins would take into consideration the following factors: He said it may seem strange although it appeared to be recognized in United States circles and Churchill in his speeches also recognized it, that the Soviet Government should wish for a friendly Poland. In the course of twenty-five years the Germans had twice invaded Russia via Poland. Neither the British nor American people had experienced such German invasions which were a horrible thing to endure and the results of which were not easily forgotten. He said these German invasions were not warfare but were like the incursions of the Huns. He said that Germany had been able to do this because Poland had been regarded as a part of the *cordon sanitaire* around the Soviet Union and that previous European policy had been that Polish Governments must be hostile to Russia. In these circumstances either Poland had been too weak to oppose Germany or had let the Germans come through. Thus Poland had served as a corridor for the German attacks on Russia. He said Poland's weakness and hostility had been a great source of weakness to the Soviet Union and had permitted the Germans to do what they wished in the East and also in the West since the two were mixed together. It is therefore in Russia's vital interest that Poland should be both strong and friendly. He said there was no intention on the part of the Soviet Union to interfere in Poland's internal affairs, that Poland would live under the parliamentary system which is like Czechoslovakia, Belgium and Holland and that any talk of an intention to Sovietize Poland was stupid. He said even the Polish leaders, some of whom were communists, were against the Soviet system since the Polish people did not desire collective farms or other aspects of the Soviet system. In this the Polish leaders were right since the Soviet system was not exportable—it must develop from within on the basis of a set of conditions which were not present in Poland. He said all the Soviet Union wanted was that Poland should not be in a position to open the gates to Germany and in order to prevent this Poland must be strong and democratic. Stalin then said that before he came to his suggestion as to the practical solution of the question he would like to comment on Mr. Hopkins's remarks concerning future United States interests in the world. He said that whether the United States wished it or not it was a world power and would have to accept world-wide interests. Not only this war but the previous war had shown that with United States intervention Germany could not have been defeated and that all the events and developments of the last thirty years had confirmed this. In fact the United States had more reason to be a world power than any other state. For this reason he fully recognized the right of the United States as a world power to participate in the Polish question and that the Soviet interest in Poland does not in any way exclude those of England and the United States. Mr. Hopkins had spoken of Russian unilateral action in Poland and United States public opinion concerning it. It was true that Russia had taken such unilateral action but they had been compelled to. He said the Soviet Government had recognized the Warsaw Government and concluded a treaty with it at a time when their Allies did not recognize this government. These were admittedly unilateral acts which would have been much better left undone but the fact was they had not met with any understanding on the part of their Allies. The need for these actions had arisen out of the presence of Soviet troops in Poland and it would have been impossible to have waited until such time as the Allies had come to an agreement on Poland. The logic of the war against Germany demanded that the Soviet rear be assured and the Lublin Committee had been of great assistance to the Red Army at all times and it was for this reason that these actions had been taken by the Soviet Government. He said it was contrary to the Soviet policy to set up [a] Soviet administration on foreign soil since this would look like occupation and be resented by the local inhabitants. It was for this reason that some Polish administration had to be established in Poland and this could be done only with those who had helped the Red Army. He said he wished to emphasize that these steps had not been taken with any desire to eliminate or exclude Russia's Allies. . . .

## 9 | The Requirements for Peace in a Divided World, August 1945 *

In a perceptive article John Fischer, one of the editors of *Harper's Magazine*, detected that the world was being divided into two huge spheres of influence, the Anglo-American and the Russian. The world's danger spots, he noted, lay along the margins of the two orbits where the pull of each power center conflicted with that of the other. But the mere dividing up of the earth's surface into two major spheres, he predicted, would not lead to war provided the United States and the U.S.S.R. each recognized the sphere of the other, remained armed and internally prosperous, and obeyed conservative and traditional rules of international conduct. Fischer had little faith in the United Nations.

The hundreds of able reporters who watched the painful carpentry at San Francisco all seem to be agreed on at least one point: the Conference did *not* build world peace. It did not settle the many tensions and conflicts which already have appeared among the victorious Great Powers. It didn't even try. Its sole purpose was to build a kind of arena, in which it might be possible over the course of years to argue out and compromise some international conflicts before they reach the shooting stage.

While the arena was a-building, the conflicts waiting offstage began for the first time to arrange themselves into a clear-cut pattern. Consequently, it is now possible to make some tentative estimate of the kinds of problems which the new World Security Organization must try to handle—and of its chances of solving them before they break out of the arena of peaceful discussion.

It is clear, first of all, that there are now only two nations—America and Russia—of really predominant power. They alone possess the resources to wage

* John Fischer, "Odds Against Another War," *Harper's Magazine*, CXCI (August 1945), 97–106. Copyright 1945 by Harper & Row, Publishers Incorporated. Reprinted by permission of the author.

war on a global scale. If there is another world war, it must be between them. If the conflicts arising between these two can be settled peacefully, there cannot be a truly major war.

Each is deeply suspicious of the other, and neither has any great confidence in the nascent World Security Organization. No doubt both hope earnestly that it may work; but so far they regard it as at best a second line of defense. Both we and the Russians, therefore, are hurriedly building our own regional security systems. As a result, most of the lesser nations are now being drawn by a sort of Law of Political Gravity into the orbits of one or the other of the two Super-Powers. So far neither Russia nor the United States has yet completed its protective belt of satellites. Some areas are being tugged both ways, like small planets caught between two great stars.

The few areas subject to such conflicting pulls are the danger spots. They will remain so until they finally are drawn into the strategic zone either of America or of the U.S.S.R.—or until both big nations agree to quit tugging, and abide honestly by that agreement. (At the moment this latter solution seems rather unlikely.)

While the process of pulling and hauling goes on, relations between America and the Soviets will remain tense, and from time to time quite possibly will get a good deal worse than they are now. This period may last for several years. Such a period of grinding adjustment to the new centers of power follows every great war; and it is always an uncomfortable and hazardous time.

If, however, each of the Super-Powers finally succeeds in putting together a security system which it deems adequate; if this process can be accomplished without an open fight; and if Russia and America each recognizes and accepts the vital sphere of influence of the other—then the prospects for a long-term peace should be reasonably good. From that time on, a major war could occur only if one of the great regional systems mounts a deliberate, full-scale attack on the other. Such an attack—from either side—would be very difficult to organize, and its chances of success would be small. . . .

The shape of the regional system which each of the Super-Powers is trying to build—and the danger spots where the two regions brush together—are already fairly plain.

The American orbit will consist of the entire Western Hemisphere, plus a chain of islands running the length of the oceans on either side. Because we are primarily a naval power, these outlying bases are vital to our whole scheme of defense. . . .

In the Pacific, our strategic island chain will run from New Zealand north to the Aleutians. Its main links will be the Philippines, Hawaii, and the Caroline and Marianas groups which we are taking at such bloody cost from the Japanese; and, until all danger from Japan is clearly past, probably Okinawa as well. . . .

In the Atlantic a similar chain curves from Ascension Island north through the Caribbean, Bermuda, Newfoundland, Greenland, and Iceland to Great Britain. Of all these islands, the British Isles are strategically by far the most important to us. So long as they are available as a base, we can blockade every major water route to Europe. If they are lost, we would lose not only this supremely important advantage; our command of the entire North Atlantic would be threatened as well, and our own northeastern seaboard would be liable to attack. Twice we have gone to war to prevent the islands from falling into the hands of the dominant European power; their protection has become a settled part of our diplomatic and military policy.

Our strategic position in the Atlantic is complicated by the fact that the British Isles (which are vital to our security) trail behind them a long and sometimes embarrassing attachment, the British Empire (much of which is not vital to us at all). . . .

In the British view, it should include all areas commanding the communications lines to distant parts of the Empire, especially India. This means that England will do her utmost to keep strategic control of the key points along the Mediterranean route—Greece, Egypt, the Middle East, Sicily, and, if possible, Italy and Spain. Whenever a dominant Continental power begins to extend its military influence toward the Mediterranean, the British react immediately and with arms—as France learned in the last century, as the Kaiser discovered when he played with the idea of a Berlin-to-Baghdad railway, as the Communist-leaning EAM in Greece and Tito's Partisans at Trieste can testify today. . . .

Finally, Great Britain is working hard to build up a strategic cluster of junior partners in Western Europe, from Scandinavia to Portugal. For five hundred years the very cornerstone of her foreign policy has been to prevent the Channel ports from falling into potentially hostile hands. For this reason, France and the Low Countries, in particular, are tied to the British by the tough cables of strategic geography—just as the British Isles, in turn, are tied to the United States. In practice, the British and American security zones are so closely linked that they form a single—though as yet ill-defined—Anglo-American orbit. . . .

The outline of the regional system which Russia is building also is becoming clear. So far it consists of a chain of small states running across the narrow waist of Europe, from Finland through Poland and the Balkans to the Black Sea. There is every reason to believe that she intends to extend this ring of satellite nations through the Middle East and Asia, until she has "independent but friendly" neighbors on every border. Already the Soviets have announced their intention of negotiating a new treaty of alliance with Turkey. A little to the east, the Iranian government recently was changed under indirect Russian pressure. Still farther east, Communist infiltration apparently is being felt in Sinkiang Province of China. In North China and Outer Mongolia friendly regimes are firmly established. . . .

Once this circle of buffer states is completed, Russia presumably will feel free from that dread of foreign intervention which has obsessed her—with good reason—ever since the founding of the Soviet Republics. And if we have any hope whatever of a durable peace, we must accept in good faith the Russian assurance that she has no intention of aggressive expansion outside her security zone.

A glance at the map and at the latest newspaper indicates the points where friction is likely to arise between the Super-Powers during the period while they are putting together their two regional systems. There are five main danger spots, all lying along the margins where the Soviet and Anglo-American orbits rub together:

1. Poland, where Great Britain and America balked at the installation of a Russian-sponsored regime.

2. The northern shore of the Mediterranean, where one of Russia's junior partners, Yugoslavia, has been reaching toward the ports of Trieste and Salonika against firm British opposition.

3. Iran, where the U.S.S.R. probably will try to get access to a port on the Persian Gulf and a share in the great Iranian oil concessions—again in the face of British opposition.

4. Manchuria and Korea, areas where the United States has attempted to maintain a policy of local independence and the Open Door for more than half a century.

5. Germany, where the two great power systems confront each other across an artificial military boundary.

In the first four instances, at least, the chances for a peaceful settlement seem reasonably good.

In Poland, it appears probable that the Russians ultimately will have their own way. The Red Army is there; Britain and the United States could not possibly bring to bear enough force to affect the issue; and in any case, the Anglo-American stake in the area is negligible beside Russia's. England had to make some protest, because the immediate issue which brought her into war with Germany was Polish independence—and it is now embarrassing to have to acknowledge that unqualified independence for Poland is not feasible. The United States strung along with the British, perhaps in part because Mr. Roosevelt felt the Polish and the Catholic vote was important in last November's election. Sooner or later both of us probably will have to back down with whatever grace we can muster. The Russians apparently are trying to make the process less uncomfortable for us by accepting one or two of the London Poles temporarily into the Lublin government. . . .

In the Trieste and Salonika controversies, Russia has carefully avoided taking an open position in support of Tito. In these areas her stake is minor, while the British interest is relatively great; and here the British navy could bring really important forces to bear. Consequently, it seems likely that England will come out on top; Trieste will remain Italian and Salonika will remain Greek, both under British protection; and the Soviet region will have to get along without a major naval base in the Mediterranean. . . .

In Iran it might be a good guess that some compromise will be worked out under which Russia would get her warm water port plus a special military position, while the British and American oil companies would be assured a share of the Iran petroleum concessions and protection of their investments in the area. . . .

Similar considerations will weigh heavily in the outcome of the Manchuria-Korea issue. Russian dominance in these areas would be hard for Americans to swallow, in view of our traditional Far Eastern policy. Yet we are not apt to try to oust the Red Armies by force. After all, if they come in, their ostensible purpose will be to help us in the struggle against Japan—and to push them right out again would be both ungracious and exceedingly difficult. Moreover, we have never been willing to fight to maintain the integrity of Manchuria and Korea. We have contented ourselves with protests and "non-recognition" of their conquest by Japan. As everybody knows, such a policy has proved not only futile but also rather fussy and undignified. Next time perhaps it would be wiser simply to accept whatever regime the Soviets may install, realistically and without any pious uproar, in the interest of long-term Russo-American relations.

The danger of a conflict over Germany is much more serious, and the means of avoiding it are by no means apparent. If the United States has any policy regarding Germany—aside from reparations and preventing a revival of German military strength—our State Department has not yet announced it. Yet in the absence of a strong, clear-cut Anglo-American policy, Germany is likely to go Communist by default. And a combination of Red Russia and Red Germany—the strongest military and industrial powers of both Europe and Asia—inevitably would be regarded as a grave menace to the Anglo-American system.

Consequently, the working out of a mutually satisfactory policy toward Germany is the most urgent task confronting the Super-Powers. Should we leave Germany split indefinitely into Soviet and Anglo-American zones? Should we try to re-establish it as an intact but much shrunken and largely de-industrialized state? Should we partition it into a number of separate nations, and endeavor by threat of force to prevent their reunion? Each of these alternatives, like several others which have been suggested from time to time, is open to many objections. And we may be sure that whatever solution we adopt, the Germans will try to wreck it by sowing suspicion between the Russians and the Western Powers, and inviting them to bid against each other for German favor. Nevertheless, we must agree with the Soviets on *some* policy, however far from perfect, and try earnestly and in good faith to make it work. If we don't, all the pacts manufactured at San Francisco or at a dozen similar conferences cannot guarantee a lasting peace. . . .

If we assume that some kind of solution can be found to the conflicts of the transitional, region-building period, we can look forward at the end of that time to a world organized on a basis quite different from anything in past history. These probably will be its salient characteristics:

1. For the first time the world will be organized into two great power systems, instead of being split among seven or more major powers and dozens of little ones. Consequently it might be expected to prove a more stable organization. So long as there were several Great Powers, all roughly comparable in strength, there existed an almost infinite opportunity for intrigue and combination. Every nation had to be perpetually uneasy about what its neighbors were doing; they might gang up at any moment. And in real or imagined self-defense, each sought to improve its own system of shifting alliances. In the future there obviously will be far less room for this sort of dangerous maneuver.

2. For the first time the two greatest powers will be widely separated, rather than face to face across a fortified border or narrow seas. War between them

would appear to be less likely, simply because either one would find it almost impossible to reach the vital centers of the other.

3. The *nature* of the military strength of the two Super-Powers is entirely different. America is primarily a naval power, Russia a land power. An American general staff could hardly contemplate an invasion of the vast land masses of the Soviet Union, in the face of Russia's incomparably greater resources in military manpower. (This disparity will continue to grow; long-term population trends will give Russia a sharply increasing proportion of its people within the military age brackets, while the proportion of Americans of military age will decrease.) Conversely, Russia—which has no navy of consequence—could hardly challenge the American fleet, which will come out of the current war stronger than that of all the other navies in the world combined. As Lippmann has suggested, a struggle between the two would be almost as improbable as a fight between an elephant and a whale.

4. Within both Russia and the United States, certain internal factors will tend to discourage a warlike policy. In Russia the memory of the tremendous casualties of World War II should serve as an inhibiting influence for a long while. . . .

5. Finally—as Hanson Baldwin and other military students have pointed out—there is no fundamental strategic conflict between Russia and the United States. Each can build an adequate security zone without threatening the other.

6. Within the great regional systems, minor wars will be far less likely to occur than in the past. Each of the Super Powers has the responsibility for protecting the members of its family; and such responsibility inevitably carries with it the obligation to keep order in the family circle. Normally such intra-regional squabbles will be settled through the machinery of the World Security Organization or such regional agreements as the Act of Chapultepec. In cases of emergency, however, or where no adequate diplomatic apparatus exists, the old-fashioned spanking will have to be used—as it was in the Syrian incident, where Britain (with American support) bluntly ordered France to quit kicking the babies around. . . .

If the world of the future, organized around the two Super-Powers, does turn out to have these six characteristics, then the chances of a long peace would appear to be fairly promising. It is true that the Russian and the Anglo-American orbits will have totally different social and political philosophies; but ideological differences *alone* do not necessarily make war inevitable. After all, America got along on excellent terms with Czarist Russia for several centuries, although the Czars' regime was based on serfdom, tyranny, and terror; our philosophical differences with Stalin certainly are no greater than they were with Nicholas I.

There is an important distinction, however, between the peace of two armed and hostile camps and the peace of friendly neighbors. If the Super-Powers ever hope to get on a footing of mutual confidence and good will, both of them will have to abide by certain fundamental rules of neighborliness.

First of all, each one must convince the other that it has no ambition to expand its orbit. Above all else, both Russia and the United States must resist the temptation to attempt to draw the three key periphereial areas—Germany, Japan, and South China—into their respective spheres. If Russia were to push into Western Europe, for example, the Anglo-American community would be certain to feel gravely alarmed. Similarly, if the United States were to try to convert a conquered Japan into a puppet state aimed at Siberia; or if we encouraged the Chungking government to try to regain Manchuria and the Chinese Communist areas—then Russia could not help but regard us as an implacable enemy. . . .

In the second place, the tension between the Super-Powers is not likely to disappear unless each refrains from meddling in the internal affairs of the other's region. So long as local Communist parties, guided or financed from Moscow, behave as disrupting influences within the Anglo-American orbit, the Western Powers will remain in an irritable and suspicious frame of mind. And so long as the Anglo-American region supports regimes such as the present dictatorships of Spain and Argentina, which agitate openly against Russia and shelter groups of anti-Soviet conspirators, the Russians will continue to be mistrustful. (Incidentally, tempers might be improved all the way around if the Soviet press would quit referring to Wendell Willkie and similar well-meaning people as "fascist," and if certain American newspapers would refrain from calling Stalin "Bloody Joe." The behavior of the Russian newspapers is of course more annoying, since they are official organs, while few people take the screeches of Hearst and McCormick very seriously; but the Russians seem to be abnormally sensitive to press criticism.)

Finally, the cause of peace will be served if each of the great regions keeps its own defenses strong and its own people contented and prosperous—for weakness and disorder always invite aggression. For the United States, this means that we must learn to make our own economy work better than it has in the past. A depression here spells economic collapse in much of Latin America and hardship in England, China, and every other country dependent on American markets. And if we have another full-blown slump, like that of the 'thirties, communism and disunity inevitably will boil up everywhere—with or without Russian encouragement. In the long run, full employment may prove to be the very keystone of our defense policy. . . .

Perhaps the greatest hazard lies in the fact that both we and the Russians are amateurs at world politics. The surge of circumstances has thrust upon these two nations—both isolationist by instinct—the necessity of thinking, consulting, and acting in world terms as never before. If either country, bewildered and perhaps a little heady in its new role, begins to wield its power for power's sake—if it becomes too eager to win minor advantages, and takes advantage of every magnanimous gesture to drive a hard bargain—then we shall be heading for trouble. This does not, of course, mean that either of us should act the appeaser and surrender on every point in disagreement. It does not preclude tough bargaining. But it does mean that both of us must remember that the point at issue in any given bargain is unimportant in comparison with the overwhelming necessity of keeping the peace.

If we and the Russians together can learn this lesson—if we can learn to behave with the responsibility and restraint of true Super-Powers—we may in time build a real peace of mutual confidence instead of an armed truce.

## 10 | John Foster Dulles's Radio Broadcast, October 6, 1945 *

During the autumn of 1945 it became clear that United States foreign policy would reveal expediency in its day-to-day decisions, for the nation had no choice but to co-exist with the Soviet hegemony in eastern Europe. The Republic possessed neither the power nor the intention, supported by actual policy, of bringing self-determination to the Slavic states. On the other hand, it was equally clear that United States diplomacy would remain principled—that it would cling in both its rhetoric and its diplomatic demands on the U.S.S.R. to its established posture of nonrecognition vis-à-vis the Soviet sphere of influence. Precisely what this vast discrepancy between words and actions would achieve was never demonstrated or explained. In his report to the nation, following the London Conference, John Foster Dulles outlined the disagreements which prevented any settlement. To him the U.S.S.R. had attempted to test to what extent the United States would compromise its principles to achieve agreement. Secretary Byrnes, he said, had properly refused to compromise American principles, for the time had come to re-establish principle and morality in world politics. Dulles's views conflicted with the more conservative ones of John Fischer at almost every point. Dulles, like Hull before him, believed that by clinging to principle the United States could make the world conform to its wishes.

✍

At London the Council of Foreign Ministers began the task of peace-making. This is no easy task. It is not a matter of victors imposing their will upon defeated enemies. When we get to that, it will be easy. Before we get to that, the victors must try to agree on what their joint will shall be. So, we are not now negotiating peace with Italy or Rumania or Germany. We are negotiating peace with the Soviet Union, Great Britain, France and other United Nations. These nations have different interests and different ideals. To reconcile them is not a process of coercion but of reason.

I am under no illusion that that will be an easy task. I was at the peace conference which followed the First World War and there learned, at first hand, how difficult it is for a war coalition to maintain unity after victory has been won. It is possible that, this time also, we shall not agree on the post-war settle-

* Vital Speeches of the Day, XII (October 15, 1945), 7–8.

ment. If that happens, it would lead to different nations' carrying out their will in particular areas. That is not necessarily a permanent disaster, but it would be most unfortunate. It would tend to divide the world into blocs and spheres of influence. That would be a bad heritage for the victors to bequeath the United Nations Organization.

So far as the United States delegation to London is concerned, we are determined to preserve in peace the unity we had in war and to apply the lesson we have so painfully learned, that peace is indivisible. There will be no bloc of Western powers if the United States can avoid it. Also, I may say, nothing that has happened so far makes me feel that we may not all come to agree.

I realize that it came as a shock to the American people that the Council of Foreign Ministers ended their first session without producing a public statement of unity and accomplishment. That is because for over four years every meeting of representatives of the great powers was followed by a pronouncement which gave the impression that complete harmony had been achieved. That was a war diet of soothing syrup. The reality was that there was unity in so far as it related to joint effort against common enemies. But behind that there have always been the differences which are now coming to light.

It is not healthy, and I am glad that it is no longer necessary, to try to cover up the fact that we have differences. Only if our people realize the magnitude of the task we face will we put forward the effort and achieve the unity needed for success.

I said that in the task upon which we have embarked the permissible tool is reason, not coercion. The American delegation was alive to that. We presented only propositions which seemed to us to be reasonable.

The basic principles which we espoused were these:

1. Territorial settlements should, as far as possible, conform to the wishes of the peoples concerned. Strategic and economic considerations ought to be subordinated to human considerations. This principle would call for some territorial readjustments. But it would not give to Yugoslavia the large Italian population of Trieste.

2. The treaties should realize the conception of an international bill of rights. At Moscow in 1943 the Big Three had agreed that they sought for Italy a regime which would assure the Italian people freedom of speech, religious worship, political belief and public meeting. We were determined that the treaties of peace should give reality to that goal and make a practical beginning in the great project of assuring to all the enjoyment of human rights and fundamental freedoms.

3. Colonies should be dealt with primarily from the standpoint of the welfare of the colonial peoples and, as in the case of territorial adjustments, human considerations should prevail over strategic and commercial considerations. We called for independence within a fixed term and we proposed trusteeship by the United Nations Organization, rather than by any single power. That was the only solution which would avoid a disastrous struggle between the great powers for colonial prizes. Without it, there was no way to decide the rival claims for the Italian colonies of North Africa.

4. Armament of our ex-enemies should be limited and subjected to a system of supervision which would prevent secret rearmament as occurred after the last war in the case of Germany. This supervision is particularly important in view of the development of modern weapons of vast destructive power. This, we felt, compelled the inauguration of a system, which might later on be extended, whereby the human race would have facilities to protect itself against its own total destruction.

5. Finally we made it clear that we could not negotiate and conclude treaties of peace with governments which, as in Rumania, failed to provide those freedoms which, in conjunction with the Soviet Union and Great Brtiain, we had promised to seek for the liberated peoples of Europe.

The first ten days of the conference were devoted to considering the application of such principles to Italy, Finland, Rumania and Bulgaria. During the course of these discussions it became increasingly evident that the Soviet Union was dissatisfied with the trend of the conference. The American proposals, which in the main were supported by Great Britain, France and China, cut across certain political ends which the Soviet Union sought. For example, the Soviet Union was disposed to support the claim of Yugoslavia to Trieste. It wanted for itself trusteeship of Italy's most valuable colonial area in North Africa in order that it might develop for itself a great warm-water port in the Mediterranean comparable to what it had obtained in the Far East at Port Arthur and Dairen. Above all, the Soviet delegation objected to the refusal of the United States, under existing conditions, to conclude peace treaties with Rumania and Bulgaria.

It was discussion about Rumania on Sept. 21 which led the Soviet Union on Sept. 22 to move to test out the determination of the United States. The means chosen was to insist on a change of procedure. The underlying and understood purpose was to make it appear that the Soviet Union could and would interrupt any procedure which did not lead to results more satisfactory to it.

A great deal has been said, and much more doubtless will be said, as to whether the procedure under which the Conference was operating was in strict conformity with the Berlin agreement, which established the Council. I do not intend tonight to discuss that highly technical matter. It is not really very important. It is enough to say that the procedure which permitted France and China to be present at all Council meetings, though with no power of vote in certain cases, was agreed to by the Soviet Union on Sept. 11 and had been followed for ten days without question. Certainly the Soviet Union would not have accepted and followed a procedure which it believed to be violative of the Berlin agreement. Only when the procedure failed to produce results satisfactory to the Soviet Union did it demand a change which would have eliminated France and China. That change was demanded as a means of indicating Soviet displeasure with the course the negotiations were taking and as a means of finding out whether or not the United States was really determined to hold the basic principles I have described.

The Soviet delegation believed, and rightly believed, that the United States attached great importance to preserving the appearance of unity among the

Big Three. They also knew that we were anxious quickly to conclude peace with Italy. They wanted to find out how much of our principle we would sacrifice to attain these goals. They did find out. They found out that the United States was not willing to sacrifice its principles or its historic friendship with China and France.

That American decision vitally concerned the future of our nation. As Secretary Byrnes said last night, I participated with him in the making of that decision. I unqualifiedly concurred in it. However, he, as the Secretary of State, had to assume the primary responsibility, and he is entitled to the support of the American people, without regard to party, in standing for principle rather than expediency, in keeping with the best American tradition.

Let me hasten to say that I have no feeling that the Soviet delegation, in forcing that decision upon us, did anything that was not within their rights. In every important negotiation, public or private, there comes a moment when the negotiators test each other out. It was inevitable that a time should come when the Soviet Union would want to test us out. It is a good thing that that has happened and that it is now behind us.

The American people should see what has happened in its true proportions. We are at the beginning of a long and difficult negotiation which will involve the structure of the post-war world. The Soviet Union wants to know what our political attitude will be toward the states which border them, particularly in the Balkans. They want to know what our attitude is toward sharing with them the control of defeated Japan. They want to know what our attitude will be toward giving them economic aid. These and other matters must, in due course, be explored, and it may be that until that whole area has been explored, progress will be slow.

Let us be calm and be mature. We have made not a bad, but a good, beginning. That beginning has not created difficulties. It has merely revealed difficulties of long standing, which war has obscured. It is healthy that we now know the facts. Furthermore, we have at the beginning shown that we stand firm for basic principles. That is of transcendent importance.

We are emerging from six years of war, during which morality and principle have increasingly been put aside in favor of military expediency. The war has now ended and with that ending principle and morality must be re-established in the world. The United States ought to take a lead in that. We are the only great nation whose people have not been drained, physically and spiritually. It devolves upon us to give leadership in restoring principle as a guide to conduct. If we do not do that, the world will not be worth living in. Indeed, it probably will be a world in which human beings cannot live. For we now know that this planet will, like others, become uninhabitable unless men subject their physical power to the restraints of moral law.

President Truman, following the lead of such proponents of principle as Hull and Dulles, responded to the pressure of world politics, not with a search for expedient decisions which might create some balance between the ends and means of American policy, but with broad statements of principle which suggested a proper course for all nations to follow. In his Navy Day speech of October 1945 he propounded twelve principles which, if followed by others, would create a world of peace and security. The President, however, did not suggest how these principles were to be put into operation or what the United States would do if other nations continued to ignore them. He assumed, as did Dulles, that the United States could abide by its principles and still maintain a co-operative spirit with all its wartime allies. President Truman's principles, like those of Wilson and Hull, assumed that there were no conflicts of interest in the world which could not be settled by peaceful adjustment and thus largely on American terms.

✍

. . . Why do we seek to preserve this powerful naval and air force, and establish this strong Army reserve? Why do we need to do that?

We have assured the world time and again—and I repeat it now—that we do not seek for ourselves one inch of territory in any place in the world. Outside the right to establish necessary bases for our own protection, we look for nothing which belongs to any other power.

We do need this kind of armed might, however, and for four principal tasks:

First, our Army, Navy and Air Force, in collaboration with our Allies, must enforce the terms of peace imposed upon our defeated enemies.

Second, we must fulfill the military obligations which we are undertaking as a member of the United Nations Organization—to support a lasting peace, by force, if necessary.

Third, we must cooperate with other American nations to preserve the territorial integrity and the political independence of the nations of the Western Hemisphere.

Fourth, in this troubled and uncertain world, our military forces must be adequate to discharge the fundamental mission laid upon them by the Constitution of the United States—to "provide for the common defense" of the United States.

These four military tasks are directed not toward war—not toward conquest—but toward peace.

We seek to use our military strength solely to preserve the peace of the world. For we now know that that is the only sure way to make our own freedom secure.

That is the basis of the foreign policy of the people of the United States.

* Vital Speeches of the Day, XII (November 15, 1945), 66–8.

The foreign policy of the United States is based firmly on fundamental principles of righteousness and justice. In carrying out those principles we shall firmly adhere to what we believe to be right; and we shall not give our approval to any compromise with evil.

But we know that we cannot attain perfection in this world overnight. We shall not let our search for perfection obstruct our steady progress toward international cooperation. We must be prepared to fulfill our responsibilities as best we can, within the framework of our fundamental principles, even though we recognize that we have to operate in an imperfect world.

Let me restate the fundamentals of that foreign policy of the United States.

1. We seek no territorial expansion or selfish advantage. We have no plans for aggression against any other state, large or small. We have no objective which need clash with the peaceful aims of any other nations.

2. We believe in the eventual return of sovereign rights and self-government to all peoples who have been deprived of them by force.

3. We shall approve no territorial changes in any friendly part of the world unless they accord with the freely expressed wishes of the people concerned.

4. We believe that all peoples who are prepared for self-government should be permitted to choose their own form of government by their own freely expressed choice, without interference from any foreign source. That is true in Europe, in Asia, in Africa, as well as in the Western Hemisphere.

5. By the combined and cooperative action of our war allies, we shall help the defeated enemy states establish peaceful democratic governments of their own free choice. And we shall try to attain a world in which nazism, fascism and military aggression cannot exist.

6. We shall refuse to recognize any government imposed upon any nation by the force of any foreign power. In some cases it may be impossible to prevent forceful imposition of such a government. But the United States will not recognize any such government.

7. We believe that all nations should have the freedom of the seas and equal rights to the navigation of boundary rivers and waterways and of rivers and waterways which pass through more than one country.

8. We believe that all states which are accepted in the society of nations should have access on equal terms to the trade and the raw materials of the world.

9. We believe that the sovereign states of the Western Hemisphere, without interference from outside the Western Hemisphere, must work together as good neighbors in the solution of their common problems.

10. We believe that full economic collaboration between all nations, great and small, is essential to the improvement of living conditions all over the world, and to the establishment of freedom from fear and freedom from want.

11. We shall continue to strive to promote freedom of expression and freedom of religion throughout the peace-loving areas of the world.

12. We are convinced that the preservation of peace between nations requires a united nations organization composed of all the peace-loving nations of the world who are willing jointly to use force if necessary to insure peace.

Now that is the foreign policy which guides the United States. That is the foreign policy with which it confidently faces the future.

It may not be put into effect tomorrow or the next day. But none the less, it is our policy, and we shall seek to achieve it. It may take a long time, and it is worth waiting for, and it is worth striving to attain.

The Ten Commandments themselves have not yet been universally achieved over these thousands of years. Yet we struggle constantly to achieve them, and in many ways we come closer to them each year. Though we may meet setbacks from time to time, we shall not relent in our efforts to bring the golden rule into the international affairs of the world.

We are now passing through a difficult phase of international relations. Unfortunately it has always been true after past wars that the unity among allies, forged by their common peril, has tended to wear out as the danger passed.

The world cannot afford any letdown in the united determination of the Allies in this war to accomplish a lasting peace. The world cannot afford to let the cooperative spirit of the Allies in this war disintegrate. The world simply cannot allow this to happen. The people in the United States, in Russia and Britain, in France and China, in collaboration with all the other peace-loving people, must take the course of current history into their own hand and mold it in a new direction—the direction of continued cooperation. It was a common danger which united us before victory. Let it be a common hope which continues to draw us together in the years to come.

The atomic bombs which fell on Hiroshima and Nagasaki must be made a signal, not for the old process of falling apart but for a new era—an era of ever-closer unity and ever-closer friendship among peaceful nations.

Building a peace requires as much moral stamina as waging a war. Perhaps it requires even more, because it is so laborious and painstaking and undramatic. It requires undying patience and continuous application. But it can give us, if we stay with it, the greatest reward that there is in the whole field of human effort.

Differences of the kind that exist today among nations that fought together so long and so valiantly for victory are not hopeless or irreconcilable. There are no conflicts of interest among the victorious powers so deeply rooted that they cannot be resolved. But their solution will require a combination of forbearance and firmness. It will require a steadfast adherence to the high principles which we have enunciated. It will also require a willingness to find a common ground as to the method of applying those principles.

Our American policy is a policy of friendly partnership with all peaceful nations, and of full support for the United Nations Organization. It is a policy that has the strong backing of the American people. It is a policy around which we can rally without fear or misgiving.

The more widely and clearly that policy is understood abroad, the better and surer will be the peace. For our own part, we must seek to understand the special problems of other nations. We must seek to understand their own legitimate urge toward security as they see it.

The immediate, the greatest threat to us is the threat of disillusionment, the danger of an insidious skepticism—a loss of faith in the effectiveness of international cooperation. Such a loss of faith would be dangerous at any time. In an atomic age it would be nothing short of disastrous. . . .

## 12 | James F. Byrnes's Address before the New York *Herald-Tribune* Forum, October 31, 1945 *

Secretary Byrnes, in this speech, recognized the security interests of the U.S.S.R. in East-Central Europe, but suggested that the Kremlin establish relationships with the Slavic states on the same basis of freedom and co-operation which characterized that of the United States and the Latin American republics. What the Soviets required, in short, was a good neighbor policy. The United States, continued Byrnes, recognized the importance of the world community. It opposed, therefore, regional arrangements and spheres of influence as detrimental to both world peace and the principle of the sovereignty and equality of nations. For Byrnes the choice was between one world or no world at all.

⬐

. . . When we consider the principles which govern our inter-American system as it has been worked out in recent years, it is well to remember that these principles were not always recognized by us in our relations with our neighbors. There were times, not so far distant, when we tried dollar diplomacy and intervention and were accused of Yankee imperialism.

But we have learned by experience that to have good neighbors, we must be a good neighbor.

We have discovered that understanding and good will cannot be bought and cannot be forced. They must spring spontaneously from the people. We have learned also that there can be no lasting friendship between Governments unless there is understanding and good-will between their peoples.

In the inter-American system the members do not interfere in the internal affairs of their neighbors nor do they brook interference in those internal affairs by others. Freedom means more than freedom to act as we would like them to act.

But we do want other people to know what our people are thinking and doing. And we want to know what other people are thinking and doing. Only with such knowledge can each people determine for itself its way of life.

* *Vital Speeches of the Day*, XII (November 15, 1945), 68–70.

We believe other nations have a right to know of our own deep attachment to the principles of democracy and human rights, our profound belief that Governments must rest upon the free consent of the governed; and our firm conviction that peace and understanding among nations can best be furthered by the free exchange of ideas.

While we adhere to the policy of non-intervention, we assert that knowledge of what other people are thinking and doing brings understanding and understanding brings tolerance and a willingness to cooperate in the adjustment of differences.

Censorship and blackouts, on the other hand, breed suspicion and distrust. And all too often this suspicion and distrust are justified. For censorship and blackouts are the handmaidens of oppression.

The policy of non-intervention in internal affairs does not mean the approval of local tyranny. Our policy is intended to protect the right of our neighbors to develop their own freedom in their own way. It is not intended to give them free rein to plot against the freedom of others.

We have learned by bitter experience in the past ten years that Nazi and Fascist plans for external aggression started with tyrannies at home which were falsely defended as matters of purely local concern. We have learned that tyranny anywhere must be watched, for it may come to threaten the security of neighboring nations and soon become the concern of all nations.

If, therefore, there are developments in any country within the inter-American system which realistically viewed, threaten our security, we consult with other members in an effort to agree upon common policies for our mutual protection.

We Americans can take genuine pride in the evolution of the good neighbor policy from what in a way were its beginnings in the Monroe Doctrine. We surely cannot and will not deny to other nations the right to develop such a policy.

Far from opposing, we have sympathized with, for example, the effort of the Soviet Union to draw into closer and more friendly association with her Central and Eastern European neighbors. We are fully aware of her special security interests in those countries and we have recognized those interests in the arrangements made for the occupation and control of the former enemy States.

We can appreciate the determination of the people of the Soviet Union that never again will they tolerate the pursuit of policies in those countries deliberately directed against the Soviet Union's security and way of life. And America will never join any groups in those countries in hostile intrigue against the Soviet Union. We are also confident that the Soviet Union would not join in hostile intrigue against us in this hemisphere.

We are concerned to promote friendship not strife among neighbors everywhere. For twice in our generation strife among neighbors has led to world conflict. Lasting peace among neighbors has its roots in spontaneous and genuine friendship. And that kind of friendship among nations depends upon mutual respect for one another.

It is our belief that all peoples should be free to choose their own form of government, a government based upon the consent of the governed and adapted to their way of life.

We have put that belief into practice in our relations with our neighbors. The Soviet Union has also declared that it does not wish to force the Soviet system on its neighbors. The whole-hearted acceptance of this principle by all the United Nations will greatly strengthen the bonds of friendship among nations everywhere.

But the point I wish to emphasize is that the policy of the good neighbor, unlike the institution of marriage, is not an exclusive arrangement. The best neighbors do not deny their neighbors the right to be friends with others.

We have learned that our security interests in this hemisphere do not require its isolation from economic and cultural relations with the rest of the world.

We have freely accepted the Charter of the United Nations, and we recognize the paramount authority of the world community. The Charter, while reserving to us and other nations the inherent right of individual and collective self-defense in case of armed attack, requires that enforcement action taken under regional arrangements be sanctioned by the Security Council of the United Nations Organization.

Moreover, we adhere strictly to the policy that cooperation among the American republics does not justify discrimination against non-American States. The American republics have practiced the policy of equal treatment for all States which respect the sovereignty and integrity of their fellow States.

Inter-American cooperation is not inconsistent with world-wide cooperation among the nations. Regional arrangements like the inter-American system, which respects the rights and interests of other States and fit into the world system, can become strong pillars in the structure of world peace.

But we cannot recognize regional arrangements as a substitute for a world system. To do so would not promote the common and paramount interests of all nations, large and small, in world peace.

We live in one world, and in this atomic age regional isolationism is even more dangerous than is national isolationism.

We cannot have the kind of cooperation necessary for peace in a world divided into spheres of exclusive influence and special privilege.

This was the great significance of the Moscow Declaration of 1943. That joint statement of policy pledged the world's most powerful nations to mutual cooperation in winning the war and maintaining the peace. It was a landmark in our efforts to create a world community of nations and to abandon the discredited system of international relations based upon exclusive spheres of influence.

Out of the Moscow Declaration have come the Dumbarton Oaks, Teheran, Crimea, San Francisco and Potsdam conferences. And the United Nations Organization and the London Council of Foreign Ministers were created in the spirit of that declaration.

International cooperation must—as I emphasized in my recent report on the London council—depend upon intelligent compromise. It does not require us or any other nation to neglect its special relations with its nearer neighbors. But it does require that all neighborly relations be fitted into an organized system of international relations world-wide in scope.

The world system which we seek to create must be based on the principle of the sovereign equality of nations.

That does not mean that all nations are equal in power and in influence any more than all men are equal in power and influence. But it does mean equal respect for the individuality and sovereignty of nations, large and small. Nations, like individuals, should be equal before the law.

That principle is the cornerstone of our inter-American system as it is the cornerstone of the United Nations.

Adherence to that principle in the making of the peace is necessary if we are to achieve enduring peace. For enduring peace is indivisible. It is not the exclusive concern of a few large States or a few large groups of States. It is the concern of all peoples.

Believing this, the position of the United States will continue to be that the nations, large and small, which have borne the burdens of the war must participate in making the peace.

In centuries past powerful nations for various purposes tried to divide the world among themselves. They failed, and in failing left a trail of blood through the centuries. Such efforts have even less chance of success in the modern world where all nations have become neighbors.

Today the world must take its choice. There must be one world for all of us or there will be no world for any of us.

# 13 | Vandenberg's Speech before the Senate, February 27, 1946 *

For Vandenberg the answer to the Soviet challenge in eastern Europe and elsewhere lay less in power and diplomacy than in the proper choice of rhetoric. For him one great hope lay in the United Nations, where all issues could be debated freely. The Senator in 1946, like other leading American spokesmen of the day, insisted that the United States not give up its principles. He suggested that if the nation said only what it meant and did not compromise its position, it could anticipate better relations with the Soviet Union.

✍

. . . Mr. President, I say frankly, at the outset, that I return from London with mixed emotions. I return with no illusion that automatic peace awaits

* *Vital Speeches of the Day,* XII (March 15, 1946), 322–6.

the world just because the machinery of the United Nations is now in gear. But I return also with an over-riding conviction, even more emphatic than before, that the world's only hope of organized peace and security is inseverably linked with the evolution and the destiny of this United Nations Organization. I return in the convinced belief that the more complex or ominous the world's international relations may become, in that same degree the greater becomes the critical need that the peace-loving peoples of the earth shall strive to make this enterprise succeed. I return in the belief that it can succeed unless Russia, Britain, and the United States, individually or collectively, make it impossible.

I can share your disappointments over some phases of the London record. I can share your anxieties over some of the disturbing trends. I can share your desires that the San Francisco Charter should be improved in certain aspects. I intend to speak frankly about some of these things. But I cannot—and I do not—share the melancholy pessimism heard in some quarters, that the United Nations, as a result of this experience, will be unable to cope with world realities as disclosed in current history. It would be silly to ignore the hazards. It would be sillier to ignore vindicated hopes. The amazing thing is not that at London there were vast areas of disagreement but that the areas of agreement were so vast and so significant. . . .

This Charter clearly has its imperfections. We must be constantly alert to opportunities for its improvement. It is helpful that the earnest friends of peace should press these discussions. But it seems clear to me that we must first learn to live with what we have. It seems clear to me that our challenge is to make the United Nations work. It is particularly a challenge to the so-called five great powers. More particularly it is a challenge to three of them. Still more particularly, it is an individual challenge to the Union of Soviet Socialist Republics, upon the one hand, and to our own United States, upon the other. . . .

It would be entirely futile to blink the fact that two great rival ideologies—democracy in the west and communism in the east—here, find themselves face to face with the desperate need for mutual understanding in finding common ground upon which to strive for peace for both. In the final analysis this means that the two great spokesmen for these rival ideologies—Soviet Russia and the United States—find themselves face to face with the same need for mutual understanding, both in and out of the United Nations. Indeed, if this does not oversimplify the problem, it might even be said that the future of the United Nations itself is wrapped up in this equation.

If this be so, Mr. President, I assert my own belief that we can live together in reasonable harmony if the United States speaks as plainly upon all occasions as Russia does; if the United States just as vigorously sustains its own purposes and its ideals upon all occasions as Russia does; if we abandon the miserable fiction, often encouraged by our own fellow travelers, that we somehow jeopardize the peace if our candor is as firm as Russia's always is; and if we assume a moral leadership which we have too frequently allowed to lapse. The situation calls for patience and good will; it does not call for vacillation.

Let me make it wholly clear that I do not complain because Russia speaks—indeed, Mr. Vishinsky probably spoke in this Security Council more than the spokesmen of all the other powers combined. I am glad she speaks. She ought to speak. That is what this forum is for. But it is for others, too, Mr. President— just as Mr. Bevin used it upon more than one eloquent and courageous occasion. It is, I repeat, for others, too. All should feel an equal freedom, an equal duty, and an equivalent responsibility. The governments of the world suddenly find themselves in the presence of a new technique in international relations. It is in this forum of the United Nations where the most dominant of all debates and decisions are hereafter calculated to occur. It would be impossible to over-emphasize the importance of our own role and our own performance in such epochal events, and the need for positive foreign policies as our consistent guide therein.

Speaking in New York last week at a celebration in honor of the great Red Army which Marshal Stalin certifies will be kept at a progressive peak, our new American Ambassador-designate to Moscow, Lt. Gen. Walter Bedell Smith, said: "It is imperative that our national temperatures remain normal." I agree. He said that "both nations want nothing so much as peace and security." I not only agree; but, in addition, if what still bothers Russia is really a security fear against resurgent aggression, I would renew my offer of 1 year ago for a direct treaty of mutual defense, under the United Nations, in the event an aggressor axis ever rises again.

General Smith said that "the United States is willing to go a long way in meeting its international associates, but that it must be watchful of its own vital interests and hold to the line beyond which compromise cannot go." Again I heartily concur. There is a line beyond which compromise cannot go; even if we have previously crossed that line under the pressures of the exigencies of war, we cannot cross it again. But how can we expect our alien friends to know where that line is unless we reestablish the habit of saying only what we mean and meaning every word we say? I have the deep conviction that this way is the dependable way to permanent peace and concord between us, with its inevitable effect upon the United Nations. Indeed, I have the feeling it is the only way. I have the feeling it is the best way to win Soviet respect and Soviet trust. Respect must precede trust; and both are indispensable to peace.

General Smith said that "America and the Union of Soviet Socialist Republics, given honesty and frankness on both sides, can get along together in the future just as well as they have for almost 150 years, in spite of the fact that our Governments and our economic systems have been quite different." Again I associate myself with that sentiment. But the honesty and frankness must be mutual.

Sometimes it is a useful, albeit painful, thing to search our own souls in critical hours like these. Was Sumner Welles, the late President Roosevelt's longtime Under Secretary of State, right in a recent statement from which I quote:

> If the United States is to exercise any potent influence in promoting world peace and in establishing a better international order, other nations must be confident that this Government will abide by our professions. American foreign policy must possess the all-important

quality of dependability. . . . The United States continues to possess the influence in world affairs which is derived from its potential military might and from its material resources. But the moral influence which it possessed during the war years . . . is rapidly vanishing. . . . It would be better far to refrain from giving assurances, however noble they may be, than to fail to carry them out. For the United States cannot exercise any effective leadership until all nations know that it means what it says.

Mr. President, this sort of an analysis does not detract for an instant from the notably loyal and richly helpful record which the United States has made to the foundations of the United Nations. . . . The startling fact at London— I cannot repeat too often—is not that it sometimes trembled in the gale but rather that it so staunchly weathered all the storms. But, sir, we would be dubious mariners if we did not look back upon this pioneering journey to assess the dangers that developed and to put up warning signals for journeys yet to come.

Therefore, in addition to what I have already said, I must add two further admonitions.

I confess that in this first meeting of the United Nations I missed the uplifting and sustaining zeals for a great, crusading, moral cause which seemed to imbue the earlier Charter sessions at San Francisco. Perhaps it was because the agenda was so largely confined to the humdrum routine of organizational details. Perhaps it was the burden of anxiety over the misgivings that are inevitable in launching a peace project which never yet has succeeded in the history of civilization; or, on the other hand, perhaps it was the accumulated tiredness which dampens ardor and easily surrenders to the expedient notion that "all's well." Perhaps it was because, in the aftermath of war, we confront too many grim realities that are utterly at odds with precepts of justice which we presume to defend. In any event, and whatever the cause, we are on notice that the peoples of the earth must never cease to evangelize this struggle for peace if it shall reach full flower.

Again, Mr. President, I sensed at London what seemed to be too great a tendency to relapse into power politics, in greater or less degree, and, as someone has said, to use the United Nations as a self-serving tribune rather than as a tribunal. It will require constant, consistent, courageous guidance to keep the United Nations within the main channel of its obligations—and here again is a clear call to America always to act in its traditional character for liberty and justice, and not to lapse, as I fear we may have done on some occasions.

# 14 | Vandenberg's Report on the Paris Conference, May 28, 1946 *

In this speech before the Senate Vandenberg again upheld the refusal of the United States to make any agreement with the U.S.S.R. that would compromise the principle of self-determination. Paris, he said, was Munich in reverse. The days of appeasement had passed. What he overlooked was the fact that Hitler in 1938 was seeking possession of what he did not have, whereas the U.S.S.R. in 1946 was already in possession of the essential areas that it desired.

It is hard to be *sure* of anything in connection with this desperately important business. Personally, I think we had to do at least one thing at Paris—namely, speaking loosely, to demonstrate that the "appeasement" days are over. Stalin and Molotov had Roosevelt at a perpetual disadvantage in their war conferences because we were afraid the Russians would quit the war and make a separate peace. As a result, I am sure they got the habit (with justification) of believing that they can always "write their own ticket" in these international meetings.

They had a slight but rather successful jolt at San Francisco. They got another at the first meeting of the Council of Foreign Ministers at London. They received considerable self-confidence at the subsequent Council meeting in Moscow where Byrnes gave away more than he should. I think it was absolutely necessary not only to recover lost ground but also to firmly and conclusively establish at the recent Paris meeting a demonstration of a firm but friendly American purpose to stand by its ideals. Appeasement simply feeds the hazard from which it seeks to escape. Paris was Munich in reverse. We now know that Munich was a ghastly mistake. This at least suggests that "Munich in reverse" was wise at Paris.

I may be wrong but I think Byrnes did a magnificently courageous and constructive job. . . . I do not consider that our American position was at all inflexible. . . . We did relentlessly decline to surrender our principles. We can compromise within principles; but we cannot compromise principles themselves.

There is no doubt that Molotov was in a "trading mood." He constantly referred—day after day—to the fact that he had made a "big concession" (namely Tripolitania) and what was he going to get in return. He asked that question a hundred times. We are in a poor position to enter that sort of a bargaining contest because unfortunately America long since has given away everything it has to give away free, gratis, for nothing. Yes; we can still trade away the rights and lives and destinies of many helpless peoples; but in my opinion it would be an ignominious surrender of America's position of moral

* *The Private Papers of Senator Vandenberg*, 285–6. Reprinted by permission of Houghton Mifflin Company.

leadership in the world and it could easily plant the seeds for future wars. Worse; it could encourage the obvious Russian idea that her expansion—in one guise or another—is irresistible. . . .

We shall have to meet events as they develop. I do not believe that Russia wants war—at least not yet. I do not believe that we are in danger of war by reasonably standing our ground with firmness but with patience. If we are in such danger, the continuing appeasement merely postpones and multiplies the hazard. If Russia is bent upon ruthless expansionism then it is only a question of time before we face a showdown in defense of our own democracy.

## 15 | Henry A. Wallace's Speech at Madison Square Garden, September 12, 1946 *

During the year that followed the London Conference of September 1945, the nation's leadership had cast American diplomacy into a peculiarly national pattern of accepting the *status quo* as a matter of political and military necessity while rejecting it diplomatically as an infringement of basic American principles. By 1946 few United States officials were willing to challenge the validity of this clear dichotomy in American policy, but in September Henry A. Wallace attempted to bring greater conformity between American words and American actions by suggesting again that the United States recognize the limits of its power and interests in eastern Europe and negotiate a division of the world on the basis of spheres of influence, provided that the Soviets recognize the paramount position of the United States and Britain, as well as their political and economic values, in the non-Communist world. Wallace hoped that such an agreement would ease world tensions and curtail the arms race.

🖌

. . . Tonight I want to talk about peace—and how to get peace. Never have the common people of all lands so longed for peace. Yet, never in a time of comparative peace have they feared war so much.

Up till now peace has been negative and unexciting. War has been positive and exciting. Far too often, hatred and fear, intolerance and deceit have had the upper hand over love and confidence, trust and joy. Far too often, the law of nations has been the law of the jungle; and the constructive spiritual forces of the Lord have bowed to the destructive forces of Satan.

During the past year or so, the significance of peace has been increased immeasurably by the atom bomb, guided missiles and airplanes which soon will

* *Vital Speeches of the Day*, XII (October 1, 1946), 738–41.

travel as fast as sound. Make no mistake about it—another war would hurt the United States many times as much as the last war. We cannot rest in the assurance that we invented the atom bomb—and therefore that this agent of destruction will work best for us. He who trusts in the atom bomb will sooner or later perish by the atom bomb—or something worse.

I say this as one who steadfastly backed preparedness throughout the Thirties. We have no use for namby-pamby pacifism. But we must realize that modern inventions have now made peace the most exciting thing in the world—and we should be willing to pay a just price for peace. If modern war can cost us $400 billion, we should be willing and happy to pay much more for peace. But certainly, the cost of peace is to be measured not in dollars but in the hearts and minds of men. . . .

I plead for an America vigorously dedicated to peace—just as I plead for opportunities for the next generation throughout the world to enjoy the abundance which now, more than ever before, is the birthright of man.

To achieve lasting peace, we must study in detail just how the Russian character was formed—by invasions of Tartars, Mongols, Germans, Poles, Swedes, and French; by the czarist rule based on ignorance, fear and force; by the intervention of the British, French and Americans in Russian affairs from 1919 to 1921; by the geography of the huge Russian land mass situated strategically between Europe and Asia; and by the vitality derived from the rich Russian soil and the strenuous Russian climate. Add to all this the tremendous emotional powers which Marxism and Leninism gives to the Russian leaders—and then we can realize that we are reckoning with a force which cannot be handled successfully by a "Get tough with Russia" policy. "Getting tough" never bought anything real and lasting—whether for schoolyard bullies or businessmen or world powers. The tougher we get, the tougher the Russians will get.

Throughout the world there are numerous reactionary elements which had hoped for Axis victory—and now profess great friendship for the United States. Yet these enemies of yesterday and false friends of today continually try to provoke war between the United States and Russia. They have no real love of the United States. They only long for the day when the United States and Russia will destroy each other.

We must not let our Russian policy be guided or influenced by those inside or outside the United States who want war with Russia. This does not mean appeasement.

We must earnestly want peace with Russia—but we want to be met half way. We want cooperation. And I believe that we can get cooperation once Russia understands that our primary objective is neither saving the British Empire nor purchasing oil in the Near East with the lives of American soldiers. We cannot allow national oil rivalries to force us into war. All of the nations producing oil, whether inside or outside of their own boundaries, must fulfill the provisions of the United Nations Charter and encourage the development of world petroleum reserves so as to make the maximum amount of oil available to all nations of the world on an equitable peaceful basis—and not on the basis of fighting the next war.

For her part, Russia can retain our respect by cooperating with the United Nations in a spirit of openminded and flexible give-and-take.

The real peace treaty we now need is between the United States and Russia. On our part, we should recognize that we have no more business in the *political* affairs of Eastern Europe than Russia has in the *political* affairs of Latin America, Western Europe and the United States. We may not like what Russia does in Eastern Europe. Her type of land reform, industrial expropriation, and suppression of basic liberties offends the great majority of the people of the United States. But whether we like it or not the Russians will try to socialize their sphere of influence just as we try to democratize our sphere of influence. This applies also to Germany and Japan. We are striving to democratize Japan and our area of control in Germany, while Russia strives to socialize eastern Germany.

As for Germany, we all must recognize that an equitable settlement, based on a unified German nation, is absolutely essential to any lasting European settlement. This means that Russia must be assured that never again can German industry be converted into military might to be used against her—and Britain, Western Europe and the United States must be certain that Russia's German policy will not become a tool of Russian design against Western Europe.

The Russians have no more business in stirring up native communists to political activity in Western Europe, Latin America and the United States than we have in interfering in the politics of Eastern Europe and Russia. We know what Russia is up to in Eastern Europe, for example, and Russia knows what we are up to. We cannot permit the door to be closed against our trade in Eastern Europe any more than we can in China. But at the same time we have to recognize that the Balkans are closer to Russia than to us—and that Russia cannot permit either England or the United States to dominate the politics of that area.

China is a special case and although she holds the longest frontier in the world with Russia, the interests of world peace demand that China remain free from any sphere of influence, either politically or economically. We insist that the door to trade and economic development opportunities be left wide open in China as in all the world. However, the open door to trade and opportunities for economic development in China are meaningless unless there is a unified and peaceful China—built on the cooperation of the various groups in that country and based on a hands-off policy of the outside powers.

We are still arming to the hilt. Our excessive expenses for military purposes are the chief cause for our unbalanced budget. If taxes are to be lightened we must have the basis of a real peace with Russia—a peace that cannot be broken by extremist propagandists. We do not want our course determined for us by master minds operating out of London, Moscow or Nanking.

Russian ideas of social-economic justice are going to govern nearly a third of the world. Our ideas of free enterprise democracy will govern much of the rest. The two ideas will endeavor to prove which can deliver the most satisfaction to the common man in their respective areas of political dominance. But by mutual agreement, this competition should be put on a friendly basis and the Russians should stop conniving against us in certain areas of the world just as we should stop scheming against them in other parts of the world. Let the results of the two systems speak for themselves.

Meanwhile, the Russians should stop teaching that their form of communism must, by force if necessary, ultimately triumph over democratic capitalism—while we should close our ears to those among us who would have us believe that Russian communism and our free enterprise sytsem cannot live, one with another, in a profitable and productive peace.

Under friendly peaceful competition the Russian world and the American world will gradually become more alike. The Russians will be forced to grant more and more of the personal freedoms; and we shall become more and more absorbed with the problems of social-economic justice.

Russia must be convinced that we are not planning for war against her and we must be certain that Russia is not carrying on territorial expansion or world domination through native communists faithfully following every twist and turn in the Moscow party line. But in this competition, we must insist on an open door for trade throughout the world. There will always be an ideological conflict—but that is no reason why diplomats cannot work out a basis for both systems to live safely in the world side by side.

Once the fears of Russia and the United States Senate have been allayed by practical regional political reservations, I am sure that concern over the veto power would be greatly diminished. Then the United Nations would have a really great power in those areas which are truly international and not regional. In the world-wide, as distinguished from the regional field, the armed might of the United Nations should be so great as to make opposition useless. Only the United Nations should have atomic bombs and its military establishment should give special emphasis to air power. It should have control of the strategically located air bases with which the United States and Britain have encircled the world. And not only should individual nations be prohibited from manufacturing atomic bombs, guided missiles and military aircraft for bombing purposes, but no nation should be allowed to spend on its military establishment more than perhaps 15 per cent of its budget. . . .

In brief, as I see it today, the World Order is bankrupt—and the United States, Russia and England are the receivers. These are the hard facts of power politics on which we have to build a functioning, powerful United Nations and a body of international law. And as we build, we must develop fully the doctrine of the rights of small peoples as contained in the United Nations Charter. This law should ideally apply as much to Indonesians and Greeks as to Bulgarians and Poles—but practically, the application may be delayed until both British and Russians discover the futility of their methods.

In the full development of the rights of small nations, the British and Russians can learn a lesson from the Good Neighbor policy of Franklin Roosevelt. For under Roosevelt, we in the Western Hemisphere built a workable system of regional internationalism that fully protected the sovereign rights of every nation—a system of multilateral action that immeasurably strengthened the whole of world order.

In the United States an informed public opinion will be all-powerful. Our people are peace-minded. But they often express themselves too late—for events today move much faster than public opinion. The people here, as everywhere in the world, must be convinced that another war is not inevitable. And through mass meetings such as this, and through persistent pamphleteering, the people can be organized for peace—even though a large segment of our press is propagandizing our people for war in the hope of scaring Russia. And we who look on this war-with-Russia talk as criminal foolishness must carry our message direct to the people—even though we may be called communists because we dare to speak out.

I believe that peace—the kind of peace I have outlined tonight—is the basic issue, both in the Congressional campaign this fall and right on through the Presidential election in 1948. How we meet this issue will determine whether we live not in "one world" or "two worlds"—but whether we live at all.

## 16 | Walter Lippmann's Judgment of Postwar American Diplomacy, December 1946 *

Lippmann, in a survey of postwar East-West diplomacy, pointed to the fact that diplomats had, for the first time, made no effort to negotiate a general settlement following a great war, but had concerned themselves with only one question— that of the former German satellites. Lippmann revealed again the enormous extent to which eastern Europe had preyed on the minds of Western diplomats throughout the period of the Grand Alliance. Ignoring the areas of the world where the West had the better bargaining position, the democratic leaders had concentrated on the one area where Soviet power and interest were must pronounced. Lippmann warned of the dangers of attempting to settle international disputes through voting when the voting could only advertise disagreements at the same time that it settled nothing.

✿

Fifteen months have elapsed, as this article goes to press, since Potsdam, where the Big Three decided to approach the settlement of the world war by negotiating treaties for the European satellite states. A phase of this first chap-

* Walter Lippmann, "A Year of Peacemaking," *The Atlantic*, CLXXVIII (December 1946), 35–40. Reprinted by permission.

ter of the peacemaking ended with the adjournment in Paris on October 15 of the conference of the twenty-one nations. The Big Four, France having been admitted after Potsdam, are now at work in New York trying to conclude these treaties. They have fixed on the end of November as the time to begin to discuss a settlement with Germany. They have no agreement about when they will discuss with Austria. They have not yet begun to discuss when they will begin to discuss the settlement with Japan.

The calendar and the agenda of the peacemaking are extraordinary, indeed astonishing. After no great war of modern times have the victors allowed so much time to pass before treating with their principal enemies. And though this is supposed to be the global settlement of a war that made this "one world," we have thus far confined our peacemaking to one region of the world.

If we ask why there has been this unusually long delay in coming to grips with the main issues of a settlement, why instead there has been this prolonged preoccupation with the satellites, the explanation would, I suppose, be that it is inordinately difficult to deal with Soviet Russia. Now there is no doubt that Mr. Truman and Mr. Byrnes, Mr. Attlee and Mr. Bevin, have found it inordinately difficult to deal with Soviet Russia. But this is not a sufficient explanation. For while it might explain a failure to reach agreement for a general settlement, which would require a settlement for Germany and Japan, it does not explain the fact that fifteen months have passed without a serious attempt to begin to negotiate a general settlement.

We must look for the explanation by asking how it happened, and why, contrary to all precedents in the making of peace, the Allies decided to postpone the settlements with the chief enemy states and to deal instead with the satellites of Germany. They took this decision at Potsdam. They took it, I believe, as the consequence of three considerations which at the time seemed of paramount importance to the Soviet Union, to Britain, and to the United States. The first was that Russia insisted on fixing *de facto* a new eastern frontier for Germany on the line of the Oder and the western Neisse. The second was that Britain had been given the sole control of Northwestern Germany, which contains 70 per cent of the pre-war German heavy industry, and is the most important economic region of Europe. The third was that the United States insisted that we should have the sole control and the deciding vote in the occupation of Japan. By these three decisions each of the Big Three powers got what each of them most wanted immediately. After that a general settlement of the war, which would have had to deal with Germany and Japan, was postponed indefinitely. . . .

When the Potsdam Conference had confirmed the Russian position in Eastern Germany, the British position in the Ruhr, and our position in Japan, the Allies had left on their agenda only the European satellites. And so, contrary to all precedents in settling wars, they chose to begin their peacemaking with the satellites of their principal enemy. . . .

They were confirmed in their choice of the satellites as the subject of their labors by two opposite but complementary purposes. The Soviet Union was interested in dealing with the satellites first. For this meant that the settlements would be made while the Red Army was still near its maximum power and prestige. Excepting Italy, all the satellites were under Russian military occupation, and, therefore, Russia would have the first word and the last in the negotiations. In the case of Italy the Russian and the Yugoslav claims had a better chance if they were pressed before a settlement with Germany had removed the reason for maintaining huge armies in the heart of Europe.

The British and Americans were also preoccupied with the satellites. Mr. Churchill was most particularly concerned about the strength of the Red Army and its advance to the Elbe River. Now Mr. Bevin and Mr. Byrnes were unable to force the Red Army to retire from Central Europe. But they undertook to make the Red Army retire by concentrating on the satellites. The Russians were as far west as they were because they were occupying the satellites. Mr. Byrnes and Mr. Bevin thought that if they could conclude treaties of peace with the satellites, the Russians would then have to evacuate Central and Eastern Europe. This would, they told themselves, arrest the spread of communism, would re-establish democracy and liberty behind the iron curtain, and would restore the balance of power in Germany and in Europe, which had been so radically upset by the advance of the Red Army to the Elbe River.

From the London Conference of September, 1945, through the Paris Conference which closed in October, 1946, they worked on this particular project to the exclusion of all other projects for the settlement of the world war.

The Big Three chose to begin the settlement of the world war in the eastern half of Europe. This was a gigantic blunder, made by men who had had no part in the strategic conduct of the war, and failed to take into account its strategic consequences. For it narrowed the issue between Russia and the West to the very region where the conflict was sharpest and a settlement the most difficult. . . .

I am not saying that it was not a desirable and a necessary thing to reduce the military expansion of Russia. I have no doubt that it is. But I am saying that it was an impossible thing to do immediately, and as our prime object, in the first few months after the war. Mr. Byrnes and Mr. Bevin, armed only with the Atlantic Charter and the Yalta Declaration, were attempting to take by frontal assault the main positions held by the Red Army. These positions are looked upon by all Russians as the British look upon the Low Countries, as we look upon the Caribbean region—as vital to the security of Russia against invasion. Mr. Byrnes and Mr. Bevin picked the one region of the globe where the Soviet Union was the strongest, and we most nearly impotent. In this region the Russians were in possession and could act; Mr. Byrnes and Mr. Bevin could only argue and protest.

In any other region they had power, influence, and possessions with which to bargain. They had two thirds of Germany, much the best part of Germany. They had Japan. They had the leading position in China. They had as their close partners France and the highly civilized nations of Western and Northern and Southern Europe. They had the Mediterranean. They had the Middle East. They had the whole of Africa. They had Southern Asia. They had the whole colonial world. They had the whole democratic world. They had the whole capitalist system. They were preponderant in the organization of the United Nations. They had command of all the seas. They had the atomic bomb.

The one thing they did not have was ground armies to match the Red Army in the region which the Red Army had just conquered triumphantly, and at a terrible cost of blood and treasure. Yet that was the region where they elected to put to the test their relations with the Soviet Union and the whole great business of a world settlement.

Was it not certain that here they must fail, as in fact they have failed, and in the failure to reach a settlement where it was most difficult to reach it, that they must make it infinitely difficult to make any general settlement? Let no one seek to explain away the failure by pointing out how brutal, how stubborn, how faithless, how aggressive the Russians have proved themselves to be. The worse one thinks of the Russians, the greater must be deemed the error of having elected to challenge the Russians first of all on the ground where they were most able to be, and were most certain to be, brutal, stubborn, faithless, and aggressive. . . .

If, as many of Mr. Byrnes's advisers believed, the Russians wished to keep the non-Soviet world unsettled while they consolidated their own conquests behind the iron curtain, then Machiavelli himself could not have devised a plan which served better this Russian purpose. Mr. Byrnes and Mr. Bevin have spent their energies assaulting the strongest position of Russia's vital interests. Thus they have furnished the Soviet Union with reasons, with pretexts, for an iron rule behind the iron curtain, and with ground for believing what Russians are conditioned to believe: that a coalition is being organized to destroy them.

At the same time Mr. Bevin and Mr. Byrnes have subjected the small nations, which they meant to befriend, to the cruel ordeal of having to stand up publicly every day and, in the presence of Messrs. Molotov and Vishinsky, to say whether they are with the Soviet Union or with the Anglo-Americans. As a result we have compromised the political leaders and parties in Poland and elsewhere who wished to be independent of Moscow. We have sponsored them without in fact being able to support them. All this Mr. Byrnes and Mr. Bevin have done with the best of intentions, in the interest of the Atlantic Charter, the Yalta Declaration, and the Four Freedoms. But the strategical plan of their efforts ignored the realities, and was self-defeating: they have led from our own weakness against the strongest position of the Soviet Union, and they became so preoccupied with this unequal struggle that they have neglected to exert our own influence where it was in fact much greater than Russia's.

For the effective answer to the Soviet domination of Eastern Europe was to lay the foundations in Western Europe of a general settlement in which the whole of Europe could eventually be included. Though geographically Europe is divided in half, the western half is, as respects power, population, resources, and its cultural importance, by all odds the more important half. The three western zones of Germany contain three quarters of the German population and nearly three quarters of the industry of Germany. The United Kingdom, France, Belgium, and the Netherlands are incomparably the strongest part of Europe. Had we labored among them and with them for agreements on the political structure of Germany, on the place of German industry in the economy of Europe, the situation would have been radically different today.

The question would not have been whether we can intervene in the Russian orbit. It would have been whether the Soviet Union could prevent the Germans, the Poles, the Czechs, the Hungarians, and the others from participating in the general settlement of Europe. But as long as the future of Trieste, Silesia, and the Danube were separated from the future of Hamburg, the Rhine, and the Ruhr; as long as the political structure of Eastern Europe was debated apart from the political structure of Germany, the peacemakers could have no general plan of a European settlement and reconstruction. They were doomed to treat Europe as the stakes of the diplomacy of the three non-European great powers. . . .

It is most significant, I think, that in this country and in Great Britain, the men who have been trying to settle the war are a different set of men from those who conducted the war. This is most unusual. The leading figures at the Congress of Vienna and at the Paris Conference of 1919 were the leading figures of the war. But this time they have not been. Roosevelt was dead, Churchill was out of office, and Stalin had withdrawn into the recesses of the Kremlin. . . .

As the war was concluded and before it could be settled, Roosevelt and Churchill were replaced by Truman and Attlee, Byrnes and Bevin. The peacemakers for the Western world were men to whom the problems of war and the settlement of war were novel. They had experience only in the internal politics of the two democracies, where the consideration of high strategy and high diplomacy plays no part. The settlement of the war, which was integral with the conduct of the war, was abruptly transferred from the commanders-in-chief to civilian politicians.

Mr. Attlee and Mr. Bevin had, to be sure, been members of the War Cabinet, and had no doubt been kept reasonably well-informed by Mr. Churchill and Mr. Eden about the course of the war. But they had been immersed in domestic affairs and neither of them had, I believe, ever participated in any of the international councils of war before they took over at Potsdam. Mr. Truman had been a Senator who investigated aspects of our own mobilization. He had had no part in the direction of the war. Mr. Byrnes had been at the White House, and therefore much closer to the center of things. But until he attended the Yalta Conference, his task was to act for the President on matters that were not in the field of high policy, so that the President would be free to devote his main attention to the strategy and diplomacy of the war.

The civilian politicians, suddenly and unexpectedly charged with the settlement of the war, were unable to learn quickly the vocabulary and the grammar of diplomacy. Thus they mistook the strategical realities, and committed themselves to the task of negotiating the Soviet Union out of the sphere of its maximum interest and influence. When they found that they could not do this by arguing with M. Molotov, they fell back on the procedure and the tactics which they had learned to use against their opponents in domestic politics.

They tried to operate a peace conference as if it combined the best features of a legislature and a party convention. Mr. Byrnes, Mr. Vandenberg, Mr. Connally, and Mr. Truman had been schooled in the Senate, and Mr. Bevin in the Trades Union Congress and in Parliament. Unable to induce or compel M. Molotov by what they regarded as diplomacy, they sought to outvote him, and to arouse public opinion against him. The theory of this procedure was that by bringing issues to a public vote, an aroused public opinion would do to the Russians what it has done now and then to Tammany Hall and Mayor Hague, to Mr. Joe Martin and Senator Taft.

But to apply the methods of domestic politics to international politics is like using the rules of checkers in a game of chess. Within a democratic state, conflicts are decided by an actual or a potential count of votes—as the saying goes, by ballots rather than bullets. But in a world of sovereign states conflicts are decided by power, actual or potential, for the ultimate arbiter is not an election but war.

To apply among sovereign states the procedures of a democratic state is, therefore, to invite trouble. The voting cannot decide the issue. But the issues are sharply defined by the voting. This causes everyone to speculate on the chances of war. Mr. Byrnes came home from Paris and deplored the amount of talk about war. But if day after day the use of public votes has advertised—the apologists say "clarified"—a conflict among armed states, and if it is demonstrated day after day that a majority of votes does not decide the issue, it is inevitable that men should think about war, which is the only arbiter that can decide an irreconcilable issue among great powers.

So what the world has seen is not the triumph of democracy but a failure of diplomacy. Yet it is only by diplomacy that the interests of sovereign nations can be modified, adjusted, and reconciled.

This failure of diplomacy is not necessarily fatal and irreparable. The first year of peacemaking may prove to have been the hardest and the worst. For while the peacemakers have not advanced towards a settlement, or even conceived in outline the form and structure of a settlement, their peoples realize it. They themselves realize it. What they have come to is a deadlock and a stalemate. But since everywhere the hatred of war is much stronger than the willingness to fight a war, there is a margin of safety in the diplomatic failure. . . .

# XI

## The Strategy of Containment

By 1947 the disintegration of the Grand Alliance demonstrated that the dream of one world, based on the principles of the Atlantic Charter, had ignored the facts of international life. In promising a postwar utopia, managed by the United Nations Organization, Roosevelt and Hull divorced themselves from all rational and historic considerations and, following the lead of Woodrow Wilson, regenerated the latent American passion for remaking the world in the national image, a passion aggravated after 1945 by the growing fear of communism. Charles de Gaulle of France was one European realist who doubted the efficacy of the new messianism. "Mr. Roosevelt's conception," he recalled, "seemed to me an imposing one although disquieting for Europe and for France. It was true that the isolationism of the United States was . . . a great error now ended. But passing from one extreme to the other, it was a permanent system of intervention that he intended to institute by international law."

Somehow the world had refused to conform to American principles of international conduct. Months of fruitless diplomacy, which failed to produce one significant agreement, predicted that international politics in the future as in the past would rest on the fulcrum of power, not ideals. Europe, again living under the shadow of fear and insecurity, could not resist the tug toward bipolarity created by the massive Soviet-Western conflict. The ease and rapidity whereby the United States gained the leadership of the Western world simply reflected the widespread conviction among the war-torn democracies of Europe that a posture of neutrality between the two giants, the United States and the U.S.S.R., was no longer tenable. Whatever the ultimate threat of Soviet policy to the status of Western Europe, the Kremlin's continued assault on the independence of the Slavic nations forced the West to think again in terms of power politics. The events of the decade had given precise meaning to Roosevelt's poignant words of September 1939, "When peace has been broken anywhere, peace of all countries everywhere is in danger."

Postwar Soviet diplomacy had not been reassuring. At the Paris Peace Conference of July 1946 the Soviets compromised sufficiently on tangential issues to permit the negotiation of Allied peace treaties with Italy, Finland, Hungary, Bulgaria, and Rumania. But nowhere did the treaty provisions infringe upon the continuing process of Sovietization across eastern Europe. To eliminate Western influence from the region completely, Stalin gradually established "People's Democracies" in all the occupied states. Communist manipulation of the Polish elections in January 1947 assured the triumph of the Communist-controlled Democratic Bloc. The Communist *coup d'état* of February 1948 in Czechoslovakia erased an important Western salient behind the Iron Curtain. If Soviet policy varied from country to country, the ultimate result conformed to an established pattern. By the end of 1948 eastern Europe had been converted into a Kremlin-controlled monolith. To protect Soviet policies and Soviet troop dispositions behind the Iron Curtain from outside scrutiny, the Kremlin deliberately curtailed all Western contacts with the Soviet world, even to the exclusion of United Nations officials.

Soviet policy toward Germany quite logically sought to deny this nation of proven military capacity to the Western bloc. During 1945 Soviet leaders favored a punitive course of action designed to strip Germany of much of its industrial might. So excessive were Kremlin demands at Potsdam that the West refused to negotiate the German question at all. Then the Soviets, pursuing the consistent objective of isolating Germany from the West, adopted a program of complete conciliation. At Paris in July 1946, Foreign Commissar Molotov demanded that Germany be permitted to become "a democratic and peace-loving state which alongside of agriculture, would have its own industry and foreign trade, but which would be deprived of the economic and military potentiality to rise again as an aggressive force." Secretary of State Byrnes countered this bid for German favor with his famous speech at Stuttgart in September. "The time has come," he declared, "when the zonal boundaries should be regarded as defining only the areas to be occupied for security purposes by the armed forces of the occupying powers and not as self-contained economic and political units." Byrnes openly supported Germany's claims to her "eastern territories" beyond the Neisse River which the Soviets had assigned to Poland as compensation for the regions of eastern Poland annexed to the U.S.S.R. Byrnes implied, furthermore, that if the Soviets refused to co-operate in the formulation of a new policy toward Germany, aimed at national, political, and economic independence, the Western powers would merge their zones and establish a provisional government for West Germany. Thus even before the end of 1946 the Soviet Union and the Western democracies had embarked on antagonistic courses to gain control of Germany, its power and its policies. As Walter Lippmann had predicted in 1943, any quarrel between the United States and the U.S.S.R. over the status of postwar eastern Europe could result only in the eventual revival of German and Japanese power.

Unable to prevent the Western powers from rebuilding an independent and prosperous West Germany, the Kremlin in the spring of 1948 began to restrict the traffic between West Berlin, the last Western outpost behind the Iron Curtain, and West Germany itself. Then in June 1948, in an effort to prevent the actual establishment of a West German government, the Soviets imposed a complete blockade of the historic German capital. The West responded with an expanding air lift which proved so effective that it undermined the Kremlin's bargaining power. By February 1949, Stalin withdrew his opposition to a West German regime. Three months later he lifted the blockade. This Soviet assault on the freedom of West Berlin, like the previous attachment of Czechoslovakia to the Soviet bloc, left the Western world visibly shaken. For the Kremlin had demonstrated its willingness to employ military force to strengthen its political grip on East-Central Europe.

Equally disturbing was the new Soviet rhetoric of ideological conflict attached to the Marxist-Leninist promise of ultimate Communist victory. Unlike the Soviet repression of the Slavic nations, the Soviet dogma of world revolution encompassed as a potential victim the entire free world and all its values. In his radio address of February 9, 1946, Stalin abandoned completely the wartime concept of Allied unity and reopened the Soviet ideological war on the West's capitalistic structure. "Our Marxists declare," said Stalin, "that the capitalist system of world economy conceals elements of crisis and war, that the development of world capitalism does not follow a steady and even course forward, but proceeds through crises and catastrophies." By contrast, he continued, the victory in World War II had demonstrated the superiority of the Soviet system. "The war has shown," the Soviet spokesman declared, "that the Soviet multi-national state system has successfully stood the test, has grown still stronger during the war and has proved a completely vital state system. . . . The point now is that the Soviet state system has proved an example of a multi-national state system where the national problem and the problem of collaboration among nations are solved better than any other multi-national state." The Kremlin confirmed this hard line when Andrei Zhdanov, at the re-establishment of the Cominform in September 1947, recognized the existence of two camps—the anti-imperialist and democratic group of states led by the Soviet Union and the imperialist and anti-democratic bloc led by the United States and Great Britain. One Soviet document of 1948 repeated this theme of a world-wide dichotomy: "The struggle of the two camps now determines the fate of the whole world, the fate of mankind. This struggle emerges more and more as the chief moving force of the development of our age toward communism. Here lies the basic content of the political struggle of our time." No longer was there any legitimacy in nonalignment. Everything outside the Soviet bloc was the enemy.


## II

Soviet behavior confused the West, for the vast disparity between Soviet action, limited largely to a precise region of the globe, and Soviet rhetoric clouded the essential factor of motivation and ultimate intent. That the Kremlin confronted the West with a challenge was clear, but beyond the acknowledgment of a divided world Washington officials seemed incapable of agreeing on either the magnitude or the character of the Russian threat. Churchill, in his noted address at Fulton, Missouri, in March 1946, did not claim to know the limits of the expansive and proselytizing tendencies of the Kremlin. He knew only that the Western world faced another military danger to its security. This challenge, he said, required a "fraternal association of the English-speaking peoples . . . intimate relationships between our military advisers, leading to common study of potential dangers, similarity of weapons and manuals of instruction and inter-change of officers and cadets at colleges . . . [and] joint use of all naval and air-force bases in the possession of either country all over the world." (*Reading No. 1.*)

Prompted by Stalin's ominous speech of February 1946, the State Department asked George F. Kennan, the American chargé d'affaires at Moscow, to prepare an analysis of Soviet policy. Kennan warned the administration that Soviet leadership was motivated by "the traditional and instictive Russian sense of insecurity," that it would exert unrelenting pressure on the international system in an effort to undermine it. There was no escape, he predicted, from a long-term struggle for power and prestige with the Soviet Union.

Quite suddenly in 1947 the United States reached the point of decision. In February the British Embassy in Washington informed the United States government that Britain could no longer afford to carry the economic and military burden of sustaining the Greek government against the Communist rebels in the Greek civil war. Turkey as well was subject to persistent Soviet thrusts. In March the President asked Congress for $400 million in military and economic aid for Greece and Turkey. By May both houses of Congress had approved. In June, Secretary of State George C. Marshall, speaking at Harvard University, urged that the United States "do whatever it is able to do to assist in the return of normal economic health in the world, without which there can be no political stability and no assured peace." Again Congress responded. It created the Marshall Plan, which, with the Truman Doctrine, expressed the new American commitment to the stability and economic regeneration of non-Soviet Europe.

Still, this was only the beginning. The demonstration of open Soviet aggressiveness in 1948 forced another evaluation of Soviet intent. Was the new order in eastern Europe the end of Soviet policy or merely the first step in a general assault on free Europe? Determined to frustrate any conceivable Soviet designs on Western Europe, five nations of the area, in May 1948, signed the Brussels Pact of mutual defense. The government of the United States, responding favorably to their request for military assistance, accepted primary responsibility for maintaining what was left of Europe's security. In April 1949 the United States, Canada, Denmark, Iceland, Italy, Portugal, Norway, and the five signatories of the Brussels Pact—Great Britain, France, the Netherlands, Belgium, and Luxembourg—signed the North Atlantic Treaty with ceremonies in Washington. The old isolationism did not die easily or completely, but the new concept of containment carried the day. The basic decisions of the United States government between 1947 and 1949 determined that thereafter American policies vis-à-vis the U.S.S.R. would include foreign economic and military aid, co-operation with international organizations, and military involvement wherever necessary to maintain the frontiers of the non-Soviet world.

Few Americans would again question the national commitment to world stability, for to do so would bring into question the enormous price, emotional and material, which the new program was exacting of the country. Yet the concept of containment catalyzed rather than terminated the great debate over Soviet intentions and the ingredients of effective countering policy. The debate that accompanied the evolution of American commitments, to Europe especially, often created profound divisions among the nation's writers and officials for the simple reason that much of the argument had little relationship to reality. Containment resurrected the whole past struggle between isolationism and internationalism, between the pragmatism of those who grasped the necessity of involvement in Europe's affairs and the traditionalism of those who rejected Europe from habit. The debate in large measure continued that of the interwar years, and like the earlier debate was characterized by considerable utopianism on both sides. Actually three clearly defined groups after 1947 struggled for possession of the American mind.

### III

George F. Kennan contributed the central statement on containment in his arresting article, "The Sources of Soviet Conduct," published under the pseudonym of Mr. X in the July 1947 issue of *Foreign Affairs*. Kennan offered three postulates regarding Soviet beliefs and expectations: the Kremlin's acceptance of a fundamental antagonism between capitalism and communism, its belief that since capitalism was doomed there was no need of engaging in all-out war, and its assumption of infallibility, which rationalized the total validity of policy decisions at the top level. Kennan characterized the Russian challenge succinctly when he declared that Soviet political action

> is a fluid stream which moves constantly, wherever it is permitted to move, toward a given goal. Its main concern is to make sure that it has filled every nook and cranny available to it in the basin of world power. But if it finds unassailable barriers in its path, it accepts them philosophically and accommodates itself to them. The main thing is that there should always be pressure, unceasing pressure, toward the desired goal.

To meet this challenge, Kennan suggested a program of "direct and vigilant application of counterforce at a series of constantly shifting geographical and political points, corresponding to the shifts and maneuvers of Soviet policy." This was a conservative and restrained program which did not anticipate a massive state of military siege around the Soviet periphery. Nor was it a program without hope. The Russian economy, believed Kennan, was basically weak and would force the Kremlin to concede eventually to Western economic superiority. There was a strong possibility, he continued, "that Soviet power,

like the capitalist world of its conception, bears within it the seeds of its own
decay, and that the sprouting of these seeds is well advanced." His summary
was precise:

> In these circumstances it is clear that the main element of any
> United States policy toward the Soviet Union must be that of a long-
> term, patient but firm and vigilant containment of Russian expansive
> tendencies. It is important to note, however, that such a policy has
> nothing to do with outward histrionics: with threats or blustering or
> superfluous gestures of outward "toughness."

Kennan and his colleagues in the administration accepted the limits of politics and diplomacy. (*Reading No. 2.*) For them the anticipation of a long,
tedious struggle denied the existence of any inexpensive devices which could
assure an ultimate Western triumph, especially one couched in messianic terms.
Their policy recommendations were confined to actions which might exploit the
apparent Soviet weaknesses. Since Kennan believed the Soviet dilemmas genuine, he predicted the eventual weakening of the beleaguered giant. His assumptions proved false. The Soviet Union evolved into a more resilient and
resourceful nation than anyone in 1947 thought possible.

Unlike this coterie of officials and intellectuals who had made some effort to
come to terms with history, the popular proponents of containment quickly
transformed the program into another crusade. To many Washington spokesmen
the struggle for Greece was the proper beginning of a vast Western assault on
the Communist world. So Vandenberg regarded it, and Secretary of the Navy
James V. Forrestal asserted in March 1947 that the United States, to win the
coming competition, would "have to recognize it as a fundamental struggle
between our kind of society and the Russians' and that the Russians would
not respond to anything but power." Truman's famous Truman Doctrine
speech committed the United States to the defense of freedom everywhere.
(*Reading No. 3.*) Kennan's effort to extricate the burgeoning cold war policies
of the United States from their messianic content was reflected in the recommendations of the State Department Policy Planning Staff, established in April
1947 under his leadership, on the question of the Marshall Plan. Unlike the
President's speech, that of Secretary Marshall avoided all ideological implications. "Our policy," Marshall declared, "is directed not against country or
doctrine, but against hunger, poverty, desperation, and chaos." (*Reading No. 4.*)

By mid-century it had become commonplace for national leaders to depict
the Soviet challenge in ideological rather than imperialistic terms. Former Ambassador to Russia Walter Bedell Smith, for example, warned the nation in
January 1949: "It is extremely important for the democracies, and especially
the United States, never to lose sight of the fundamental fact that we are engaged in a constant, continuing, gruelling struggle for freedom and the American way of life that may extend over a period of many years." Dean G. Acheson,
who succeeded Marshall as Secretary of State in January 1949, was largely responsible for molding the power and unity of the Atlantic community during
the critical years that followed. His vigorous defense of his military program

for Europe was characterized by a similar messianic consciousness. (*Reading No. 5.*) Acheson refused to define American objectives in terms other than the traditional American ideal of self-determination. (*Reading No. 6.*)

What disturbed those who expected less of American policy was the tendency of official statements to anchor American purpose to goals that exceeded the capabilities of Western preparedness. Without some willingness to accept the Russian gains of World War II, containment promised only eventual war. Realists concerned with ends as well as means sought to bring the policies down to earth. Arthur M. Schlesinger, Jr., attacked the fundamental moralism in American policy in the *Foreign Policy Bulletin* of February 23, 1951: "The policy of abstract moralism is an honorable and high-minded policy; but it is so concerned with being right in the abstract that it forgets to be effective. . . . The function of foreign policy is not to provide an outlet for moral indignation, however warranted that indignation may be. The function of foreign policy is to produce desired results." Abroad Winston Churchill, convinced that Western power vis-à-vis the Soviet Union was as favorable in 1950 as it was apt to become, argued for a negotiated settlement. (*Reading No. 7.*) Official Washington, committed to the concept of a global conflict of unrelenting hostility, was neither politically nor intellectually prepared to follow such advice.

Postwar American isolationism, too, harbored a messianic vision, but one still anchored to the prospect of creating a perfect society at home. What contributed to the rebirth of a primarily conservative American isolationism at mid-century was the conviction that the Roosevelt administration, through its decision to involve the nation in World War II, had contributed to the creation of the Russian problem which now plagued the country, drained its precious resources, and threatened its economy with disaster. To Senator Robert A. Taft of Ohio, Roosevelt had failed to ensure the nation against the predictable rise of Russia on the ashes of Germany and Japan. The uncontrollable power revolution of the 'forties merely demonstrated that the isolationists of the interwar years had been correct in their judgment of the national interest. The fact that communism rather than fascism was the nation's ideological enemy resurrected the older messianism associated with the sense of American uniqueness and the necessity of protecting that uniqueness from enemies at home and abroad.

For many Americans the containment policies of the Truman administration, because of their enormous expense, were little more than assaults on the nation's values. Committed to tax reduction, they denied that the external threat was serious. Taft, for example, doubted that Russia could conquer the United States. "It would," he said, "take them at least a hundred years to build up their sea power." General Douglas MacArthur contributed to this doctrine the support of his high military reputation. "Talk of imminent threat to our national security through the application of external force," he declared in 1951, "is pure nonsense." The real danger to the nation's welfare, he concluded, came from "the insidious forces rooting from within which have already so drastically altered . . . those institutions we proudly call the American way of life." Taft, believing that the essence of American security lay in the domestic economy, opposed NATO as an overcommitment of American resources to the European continent and as an infringement on the nation's historic freedom of action. "Just as our nation can be destroyed by war," he declared, "it can also be destroyed by a political and economic policy at home which destroys liberty or breaks down the financial and economic structure of the United States." Translated into military terms, postwar isolationism reflected the continuing influence of prewar isolationism with its emphasis on air and sea power. In December 1950, in perhaps the most quoted isolationist speech of the period, former President Herbert Hoover demanded that the United States not send another man or dollar to Europe until that continent manned its own defenses. Instead, he said, the nation should withdraw its defenses to this "Western Hemisphere Gibraltar of Western civilization." (Reading No. 8.)

IV

If the concept of containment, on which there was a general consensus within the nation, could produce a vigorous three-way debate, it was left for events in China to shake the country politically and emotionally as had no other external issue in its history. For at mid-century the nation discovered that a revolution in China had terminated the perennial American effort to create a stable Orient around the China of Chiang Kai-shek. Since the factors in Chiang's fall from power were clear enough, the ensuing debate turned of necessity on the introduction of hypotheticals and the manipulation of symbols. The significance of this debate for the future of American policy in the Far East was beyond calculation.

Throughout the late 'forties it was clear that the United States, having saved Chiang from his Japanese enemies, could not save him from his internal enemies, the Chinese Communists led by the noted Marxist theorist and innovator, Mao Tse-tung. This grinding transferal of power in China had been predicted repeatedly during the war in the Pacific as the inescapable price of victory, for the strains of fighting the Japanese invaders with limited American aid created a burden which the inefficient and increasingly unpopular Kuomintang could not carry. Contrasted to the organization and determination of the Chinese Communists, operating from their bastions in north China, the official Chinese Nationalist government appeared incapable of maintaining the necessary support and devotion of the Chinese people. In what proved to be an accurate forecast of Chinese political developments, American officers in China, such as John Paton Davies, warned the United States government after 1943 that the future of China belonged to Mao and not to Chiang. (Reading No. 9.)

During the long period of Chiang's declining fortunes only two logical choices confronted official Washington. One was massive military intervention to crush the Chinese Communists and suppress perennially the widespread discontent which Chiang refused to allay with any recognizable program of reform. This course of action was rejected by the State Department's Far Eastern advisers as an unwarranted and untenable commitment. To them it was clear that the Kuomintang was incapable of creating an efficient and honest administration. (*Reading No. 10.*) The second course of available action, based on the assumption of an eventual triumph of the Communists, would have reconciled the United States to the inevitable and attempted to defend American interests, to the extent possible, by seeking some *rapprochement* with the ascendant revolutionaries. This approach to the Chinese dilemma was rejected with equal determination as one which could not be explained to the American people at a time when everything Communist was automatically the enemy. Pursuing neither course completely, the government of the United States appeared at times to be pursuing both. General George C. Marshall's diligent effort to establish a coalition government for China throughout 1946 was doomed to failure by the absence of reliability in the Nationalist regime and the aspirations for total control of China within the Communist elite. Thereafter the United States government anticipated the final triumph of Mao Tse-tung at the same time that it supported Chiang Kai-shek, but at a level far below that required to assure his success.

By mid-century China had become the world's second center of Communist power and ideology, but it was no satellite of Russia. Mao and his associates owed nothing to Moscow for their success, and they soon made it clear to the Russians that they would tolerate little outside direction. There could be no certainty, moreover, that these modern spokesmen for traditional Chinese despotism would not turn China into the greatest Asian threat to Russian security since the days of the Mongols.

As Chiang's collapse neared in the early months of 1949, the Truman leadership moved to defend its relations with China against the anticipated onslaught from its enemies at home. No one in Washington appreciated the administration's dilemma more keenly than did Senator Vandenberg. (*Reading No. 11.*) The United States, he saw, could not save Chiang, nor could it desert him for fear that the government of the United States would "never be able to shake the charge that we [were] the ones who gave poor China the final push into disaster." In August 1949 the State Department published the famous Chinese White Paper, a bulky document which attempted to prove that the upheaval in China was the result of massive internal changes, which the United States could not control. Secretary of State Dean Acheson, in an address before the National Press Club in January 1950, analyzed recent events in China in the context of a broad revolutionary movement that was beginning to sweep the Asian continent. If the West could not determine its course in China, he warned, it would not do so elsewhere. (*Reading No. 12.*) Nor did it matter, argued many observers of the Asian scene, for the revolutionary movement was indigenous, lacked ideology, and pursued goals that lay at the heart of the Western tradition—racial equality, self-determination of peoples, and social justice. (*Reading No. 13.*)

Such sophisticated and realistic notions regarding the Orient stood no chance of capturing the American mind against the simple charge that Chiang Kai-shek was the victim of willful pro-Communist decisions within the Department of State. Senator Joseph McCarthy of Wisconsin captured the attention of the nation when at Wheeling, West Virginia, in February 1950, without presenting any evidence, he charged that the State Department was "thoroughly infested" with Communists. (*Reading No. 14*.) The Senator's sensational charges supplied a rationale which tied the unlimited expectations of a counter-revolution in China to the isolationist concept of limited expenditure abroad. If the United States had failed to control the Chinese revolution, it meant simply that the government of the United States was full of Communists. The problem was at home, and it was far cheaper to fight Communists at home than to engage in conflict abroad. Supported by an analysis of Far Eastern affairs which promised Chiang's return from the island of Formosa to the mainland at little cost, as well as by much of the Republican party, which detected in McCarthy's accusations the greatest political asset of the age, the Nationalist China bloc in the United States soon found themselves in an unshakable position to determine American policy toward China.

What was tragic in this successful assault on the past was that the denial of both the existence and the legitimacy of the Chinese revolution destroyed, in large measure, the nation's capacity to recognize the legitimacy and force of the nationalist uprisings beginning to sweep the entire Afro-Asian world. Nor would this corruption of American thought have the compensating advantage of returning Chiang Kai-shek to the mainland. The enormous gap between what was possible and what was held to be possible, moreover, exposed the State Department and the Foreign Service to years of limitless attack, which eventually destroyed its morale and undermined much of its effectiveness. (*Reading No. 15*.)

It required the Korean War to imbue American Far Eastern policies with the same crusading spirit that characterized the containment program in Europe. To the administration the North Korean aggression of June 1950 was nothing less than the beginning of a general Communist assault on the entire free world. "The attack upon the Republic of Korea," the President warned the nation, "makes it plain beyond all doubt that the international Communist movement is prepared to use armed invasion to conquer independent nations." China's entry into the war in November merely confirmed the conviction that Korea represented a global threat. If the new attack were successful, ran a White House press release, "we can expect it to spread through Asia and Europe to this hemisphere. We are fighting in Korea for our own national security and survival." To meet this world-wide danger Congress voted vast increases in military assistance to the free nations. Despite its importance in official American statements, however, the Korean War did not alter the Europe-first orientation of the Truman administration.

Korea created a profound crisis in American thought, for the administration could not follow to its logical conclusion its own estimation of the danger. Future peace and security against a global threat of such magnitude would appear to demand nothing less than total victory, but victory proved elusive indeed. Neither the European nor the Pacific allies had any interest in a general war in the Far East. They had questioned the United States advance to the Yalu in the autumn of 1950 which brought the Chinese actively into the struggle. Thereafter they favored a military stalemate as the best of available choices.

Eventually the administration agreed, for the price of controlling events in the Orient was scarcely commensurate with the expected gains. American military doctrine, moreover, recognized the entire spectrum of military and political involvements, including limited war itself. Even containment, translated into military terms, meant stalemate, not victory. For countless Americans, however, the failure of the nation to have its way in a clash with mainland China for a second time was a bitter experience.

Early in 1951 General Douglas MacArthur, commander of the allied forces in Korea, presented the alternative course of action, which promised the needed victory over China and at reduced cost. Through United States air and naval power, plus the diversionary tactics of the Chinese Nationalists operating from Formosa along the Chinese coast, he would destroy the Chinese and North Korean enemy, reunite Korea, and correct the accumulated errors of American policy in the Far East. When in March the general criticized publicly the limited war strategy of the Truman administration, the President relieved him of his command. This act merely served to demonstrate the gap in strategy and expectation which separated MacArthur from officials in Washington. The ensuing debate again shook the nation's confidence in its leadership, deepened the search for villains in the State Department, and gradually turned the Korean War into a political liability of incalculable proportions.

Explaining his decision to recall MacArthur in a broadcast to the nation in mid-April 1951, the President reaffirmed both the significance of the Korean War and the wisdom of limiting its scope. (*Reading No. 16.*) MacArthur, in his address to both houses of Congress a week later and in his testimony before the Congressional hearing which followed, again asserted that victory lay within the reach of the nation. (*Reading No. 17.*) The time had passed, he believed, for the United States to permit the will of its allies or the fear of Russian intervention to determine its objectives and actions. Yet the general, despite the vigor of his argumentation, did not have his way. For the administration the risks of global conflict remained totally unacceptable. Thus the Korean War ended in a Far Eastern stalemate which reflected the close world-wide balance of power.

During the Korean War the United States government extended its system of military alliances into the Far East. In August and September 1951 it negotiated military defense treaties with the Philippines, Australia, and New Zealand. That same September it also signed a pact with Japan which, although it placed no obligation on the United States, conveyed to the nation the right to maintain land, air, and naval forces in and about Japan. With China allied to Russia in one allegedly monolithic Communist bloc, the United States appeared to have no choice but to include the Chinese periphery in its policies of containment.

# 1 | Winston Churchill's Speech at Fulton, Missouri, March 5, 1946 *

Winston Churchill was one of the first Western leaders to view Russia as a military threat. In his famous "Iron Curtain" address at Westminster College, Fulton, Missouri, he suggested a military response consisting largely of the creation of a joint United States-British military establishment. Churchill made no effort to analyze Soviet intentions, but he accepted the military doctrine that what matters in a potential enemy is not intention but capacity. Russia's superior military power demanded the creation of countering military power within the nations of the West.

✍

. . . The United States stands at this time at the pinnacle of world power. It is a solemn moment for the American democracy. With primacy in power is also joined an awe-inspiring accountability to the future. As you look around you, you must feel not only the sense of duty done but also feel anxiety lest you fall below the level of achievement. Opportunity is here now, clear and shining, for both our countries. To reject it or ignore it or fritter it away will bring upon us all the long reproaches of the aftertime. It is necessary that constancy of mind, persistency of purpose and the grand simplicity of decision shall guide and rule the conduct of the English-speaking peoples in peace as they did in war. We must and I believe we shall prove ourselves equal to this severe requirement.

When American military men approach some serious situation they are wont to write at the head of their directive the words, "over-all strategic concept." There is wisdom in this as it leads to clarity of thought. What, then, is the over-all strategic concept which we should inscribe today? It is nothing less than the safety and welfare, the freedom and progress of all the homes and families of all the men and women in all the lands. . . .

To give security to these countless homes they must be shielded from the two gaunt marauders—war and tyranny. We all know the frightful disturbance in which the ordinary family is plunged when the curse of war swoops down upon the bread winner and those for whom he works and contrives. The awful ruin of Europe, with all its vanished glories, and of large parts of Asia, glares in our eyes. When the designs of wicked men or the aggressive urge of mighty states dissolve, over large areas, the frame of civilized society, humble folk are confronted with difficulties with which they cannot cope. For them all is distorted, broken or even ground to pulp. . . . Our supreme task and duty is to guard the homes of the common people from the horrors and miseries of another war. . . .

I now come to the second danger which threatens the cottage home and ordinary people, namely tyranny. . . . It is not our duty at this time, when diffi·

* *Vital Speeches of the Day,* XII (March 15, 1946), 329–32.

culties are so numerous, to interfere forcibly in the internal affairs of countries whom we have not conquered in war, but we must never cease to proclaim in fearless tones the great principles of freedom and the rights of man, which are the joint inheritance of the English-speaking world and which, through Magna Carta, the Bill of Rights, the habeas corpus, trial by jury and the English common law, find their most famous expression in the Declaration of Independence.

All this means that the people of any country have the right and should have the power by constitutional action, by free, unfettered elections, with secret ballot, to choose or change the character or form of government under which they dwell, that freedom of speech and thought should reign, that courts of justice independent of the executive, unbiased by any party, should administer laws which have received the broad assent of large majorities or are consecrated by time and custom. Here are the title deeds of freedom, which should lie in every cottage home. Here is the message of the British and American peoples to mankind. Let us preach what we practice and practice what we preach. . . .

Neither the sure prevention of war, nor the continuous rise of world organization will be gained without what I have called the fraternal association of the English-speaking peoples. This means a special relationship between the British Commonwealth and Empire and the United States. This is no time for generalities. I will venture to be precise. Fraternal association requires not only the growing friendship and mutual understanding between our two vast but kindred systems of society but the continuance of the intimate relationships between our military advisers, leading to common study of potential dangers, similarity of weapons and manuals of instruction and inter-change of officers and cadets at colleges. It should carry with it the continuance of the present facilities for mutual security by the joint use of all naval and air-force bases in the possession of either country all over the world. This would perhaps double the mobility of the American Navy and Air Force. . . .

A shadow has fallen upon the scenes so lately lighted by the Allied victory. Nobody knows what Soviet Russia and its Communist international organization intends to do in the immediate future, or what are the limits, if any, to their expansive and proselytizing tendencies. I have a strong admiration and regard for the valiant Russian people and for my war-time comrade, Marshal Stalin. . . . We understand the Russians need to be secure on her western frontiers from all renewal of German aggression. We welcome her to her rightful place among the leading nations of the world. Above all we welcome constant, frequent and growing contacts between the Russian people and our own people on both sides of the Atlantic. . . .

From Stettin in the Baltic to Trieste in the Adriatic, an iron curtain has descended across the Continent. Behind that line lie all the capitals of the ancient states of central and eastern Europe. Warsaw, Berlin, Prague, Vienna, Budapest, Belgrade, Bucharest, and Sofia, all these famous cities and the populations around them lie in the Soviet sphere and all are subject in one form or another, not only to Soviet influence but to a very high and increasing measure of control from Moscow. . . .

In front of the iron curtain which lies across Europe are other causes for anxiety. In Italy the Communist party is seriously hampered by having to support the Communist trained Marshal Tito's claims to former Italian territory at the head of the Adriatic. Nevertheless the future of Italy hangs in the balance. Again one cannot imagine a regenerated Europe without a strong France. All my public life I have worked for a strong France and I never lost faith in her destiny, even in the darkest hours. I will not lose faith now. However, in a great number of countries, far from the Russian frontiers and throughout the world, Communist fifth columns are established and work in complete unity and absolute obedience to the directions they receive from the Communist center. Except in the British Commonwealth and in this United States, where Communism is in its infancy, the Communist parties or fifth columns constitute a growing challenge and peril to Christian civilization. . . .

The outlook is also anxious in the Far East and especially in Manchuria. The agreement which was made at Yalta, to which I was a party, was extremely favorable to Soviet Russia, but it was made at a time when no one could say that the German war might not extend all through the summer and autumn of 1945 and when the Japanese war was expected to last for a further eighteen months from the end of the German war. . . .

On the other hand I repulse the idea that a new war is inevitable; still more that it is imminent. It is because I am so sure that our fortunes are in our own hands and that we hold the power to save the future, that I feel the duty to speak out now that I have an occasion to do so. I do not believe that Soviet Russia desires war. What they desire is the fruits of war and the indefinite expansion of their power and doctrines. But what we have to consider here today while time remains, is the permanent prevention of war and the establishment of conditions of freedom and democracy as rapidly as possible in all countries. Our difficulties and dangers will not be removed by closing our eyes to them. They will not be removed by mere waiting to see what happens; nor will they be relieved by a policy of appeasement. What is needed is a settlement and the longer this is delayed the more difficult it will be and the greater our dangers will become. From what I have seen of our Russian friends and allies during the war, I am convinced that there is nothing they admire so much as strength, and there is nothing for which they have less respect than for military weakness. For that reason the old doctrine of a balance of power is unsound. We cannot afford, if we can help it, to work on narrow margins, offering temptations to a trial of strength. If the western democracies stand together in strict adherence to the principles of the United Nations Charter, their influence for furthering these principles will be immense and no one is likely to molest them. If, however, they become divided or falter in their duty, and if these all-important years are allowed to slip away, then indeed catastrophe may overwhelm us all. . . .

If the population of the English-speaking commonwealth be added to that of the United States, with all that such co-operation implies in the air, on the sea and in science and industry, there will be no quivering, precarious balance of power to offer its temptation to ambition or adventure. On the contrary, there will be an overwhelming assurance of security. . . .

Charles Burton Marshall was representative of those officials and intellectuals who at mid-century were concerned that United States foreign policy, under the overdemanding pressure of various foreign policy elites within the nation, was attempting to achieve too much. In the following essay, Marshall, as a member of the State Department staff, reviewed both the world-wide assumptions on which American cold war policy was based and the objectives of that policy in terms of limited power. Like Kennan, he accepted as the end of successful foreign policy the proper management of problems abroad, not their removal.

I shall define the foreign policy of the United States as the courses of action undertaken by authority of the United States in pursuit of national objectives beyond the span of jurisdiction of the United States.

That is a lot of big words. Let me put the idea another way. Our foreign policy unfolds in the things done by the U.S. Government to influence forces and situations abroad. The meaning of the phrase "things done" should not be construed too narrowly. In this field, utterance is a form of action, and pronouncements may be deeds, especially when they convey meaning about intended or possible actions rather than merely expressing abstractions and moralizations.

My definition of foreign policy may sound strange. Let me justify it. Foreign policy may be viewed as something distilled into chapters of a book or as a process involving a lot of daily hard work by many people. I am discussing it in the second sense—in the way that one might talk of a painting as the resultant in a process of putting paint on canvas, rather than as an ultimate effect hanging statically in a museum.

The two elements in my definition to be stressed are these: Foreign policy is generated in actions. The things acted upon in foreign policy are things lying beyond the direct control of this country. Those two things are simple and obvious. Yet they are often overlooked. The overlooking of them leads to a lot of misunderstanding. . . .

Foreign policy consists of what a nation does in the world—not what it yearns for or aspires to. The sphere of doing, as distinguished from the sphere of desire and aspiration, is governed by limits. Adam Smith pointed out that economic behavior derives from imbalance between means and ends and the circumstance that ends therefore tend to conflict. The same is true in foreign policy. . . .

* Charles Burton Marshall, "The Nature of Foreign Policy," *The Department of State Bulletin,* XXVI (March 17, 1952), 415–20.

The world situation concerning us in the recent past and the present has been characterized by five main elements.

The first is the result of complex historic changes, notably two World Wars. A falling away in power among several nations once of primary greatness has occurred. This leaves two states of first magnitude, each with a great geographic span and great resources of power. One of these is our country.

The second relates to the situation of the other main elements in this bipolar world of power, the Soviet Union. It is in the grip of tyrannous rulers. They achieved power by conspiracy. They have never dared risk their hold on power by resort to any procedure of consent. They have remained conspirators after becoming governors. They require tension and conflict within and at the periphery so as to hold onto power. They use in the service of this aim a political doctrine emphasizing the patterns of violence—class conflict, subversion, and so on.

As the third element, I cite the climate of intimidation and fear in much of the world resulting from the circumstance that the Soviet Union has great military forces either under direct control or amenable to its purposes and that these forces are deployed along a huge span bearing on northern and central Europe, the Mediterranean area, the Middle East, southeast Asia, and Japan.

Fourth, the dislocation of economic patterns and the exhaustion and demoralization of peoples in consequence of invasion, occupation, and oppression in World War II have created situations affording special opportunities for Soviet communism working within other countries as a conspiratorial force in the service of the Soviet rulers.

Fifth, the weakening of old restraints in Africa, the Middle East, and east Asia and the impulse to wayward use of freedom among peoples unaccustomed to the usages of responsibility and preoccupied with redressing old grievances, real or fancied, have created opportunities for the Soviet Union, alert as it is to the quest of advantage in the troubles of others.

In these circumstances our endeavor has been along four general lines.

First, we have sought to develop stronger situations in the areas where the choices made by the peoples and governments in the great confrontation coincide with ours. We have done this so as to relieve the sense of anxiety—and with it the intimidatory power of the Kremlin—among the nations disposed to go along with us. In this category I put our alliances, military and economic assistance to our allies, and our efforts to return our former enemies to full relationships with other nations.

Second, we have sought to insure that the areas where the crisis of politics is sharpest—the areas of contest, such as southeast Asia, the Middle East, and the Arab areas—shall not be lost.

Third, we have sought to exercise leadership in working toward the ideas of responsibility and peaceful adjustment in contradistinction to the Soviet pattern of turmoil and conflict. This aim enlightens our attitude of trying to combine responsibility with new found freedom among the Middle Eastern and the southeast Asian countries. It reflects itself in our support of the United Nations pattern, in our confrontation of aggression in Korea, and in our attempts to bring about a system of arms limitation that will not reward faithless perform-ance.

Fourth, we have sought to steer away from the tragedy of another world war.

I am referring here not to objectives divided into neat categories distinct from each other but to concurrent phases of a process. That sounds very bureau-cratic, but I do not know how better to convey the idea that in reality these things do not have such nice separateness as they seem to have when one talks or writes about them. These interrelated aims tend in part to support each other, and in part they also tend to contradict each other.

For example, at a certain point the pace of generating military strength may run counter to the requirements for a sound economic basis among our allies.

In another instance, the effort at countering aggression might be carried to lengths that bear against the aim to avoid a general war.

In still another, the impulse to deal sympathetically with the aspirations of a people new to freedom and not adjusted to its obligations may run counter to the economic necessities of another country which is allied with us or to the strategic necessities of our allies and ourselves.

Again, trying to help with the military needs of one area may require the diversion of arms and supplies from others who also need them.

Such are the dilemmas that arise when our power is not sufficient for doing all the things we want to do.

What requires judgment and timing in the highest degree, along with the fortitude that can defer hopes without surrendering them, is the job of thread-ing a course through such contradictions as these and striving as best one can to find choices of action consistent with all of the aims concurrently.

That is the job of making the best of situations in the knowledge that such is the only way of making them better. The job consists mainly of the rationing of power among aims. There—not in the formulation of aims but in the rationing of power among aims—is where a foreign policy really takes form. . . .

The idea that planning can make everything tidy, answer all problems before they happen, foresee all eventualities, and prepare in advance the pat answer for every exigency is first cousin to the idea that power can be just as great as you want to make it. Power is the capacity to achieve intended results. It is always limited. Not all the elements bearing on a nation's destiny can ever be brought completely within the nation's control. Machiavelli pondered this in *The Prince*. He concluded that a .500 batting average on the field of destiny was about as much as might be hoped for. The figure strikes me as too high, but many persons expect much more than the Florentine did. I refer not to their personal expectations. Most people are not dismayed by having to manage their financial problems along month to month. People go on driving cars year after year without ever permanently solving their parking problems.

Yet some of my friends, and many persons in this country, some of whom write editorials or sit in seats of authority, persist in believing the desirable and achievable situation for the State to be one of perfect efficacy in its world rela-tions. When perfect efficacy is not obtained, these people feel dismay and sense betrayal. . . .

Several things occur to me as sources of the expectation of complete efficacy.

One of them is the consciousness of an extraordinarily successful past. The diplomatic course in the evolution from a colonial beachhead to a power of highest magnitude was one of matchless performance. Just as a man may lose his perspectives in calling up his departed youth, it is all too easy for us to lose a sense of proportion about our national problems by harking back to what we did when horizons were open and distance and the balance of power afforded us a shield.

Another influence I might call faith in engineering. That stems from our natural pride in the physical development of our country. Popular tradition treasures the idea that in the realm of creation all things are possible to those who will them. The margins available to us have made this almost true so far as the development of our own country is concerned.

Some of the popular ideas derived from science reflect this same material optimism. I think these are due not so much to the leaders of science themselves as to the popular interpreters of scientific achievement. From them we get the notion that cumulative knowledge can solve anything and that every problem is by definition solvable. Whatever may be the validity of this notion in the material relations which are the field of science, an error comes in trying to apply it as a universal.

Another contributing circumstance is that so much of foreign policy now stems from legislation. Legislation is law, law is to be obeyed, and an objective expressed in law is bound to be achieved. So goes the notion.

This idea bears particularly on congressional expectations in relation to foreign aid. The Congress has written into foreign aid legislation as conditions upon recipients many purposes whose consummation is devoutly to be wished. Some of these are such that they could be realized only in considerable spans of time and under governments with great margins of political power derived from energized and purposeful public support. The lack of such conditions in Europe is the heart of the difficulty. I find incredible the idea that phrases enacted by one's country's legislature can *ipso facto* solve problems, the solution of which requires redressing the factors of political power in another country. . . .

Besides faith in making laws, let me mention faith in advertising. Where a perfume is marketed not only for its odor but also as a guarantee of domestic bliss, where automobiles are sold as means to capture the esteem of neighbors as well as means of transport, and where life insurance is offered not only as protection but also as a help for insomnia, it is natural to demand of foreign policy not only that it should handle the problems at hand but also that it should lead to a transfiguration of history. . . .

A nation's intentions and its power interact on each other. What we seek is in part determined by what we can do. What we can do is determined in part by what we are after. Furthermore, our own aims and power acting as functions of each other are in an interactive relation with adversary intentions and capabilities, which also relate to each other as interdependent variables.

Foreign affairs are a complex business. Gross errors result in the attempt to treat them on the basis of the misleading notion that all the problems of power can be reduced to the nice simplicity of calculations of force. . . .

It is easy for the unwary to jump to a fallacious conclusion that if all human affairs were laid out with the precision of military plans, then all problems could be brought to as complete solution as can the problem of force in the conduct of a victorious military campaign.

This is the sort of thing one gets to when one tries to find the solution of all of the Nation's problems in the world, instead of taking the historically realistic view that the job is one of managing the problems, not of getting rid of them.

It is only a few steps from the notion of solution to the notion of employing force as a solvent. This is an easy fallacy for those souls anxious for history to be tidy and all conclusions certain. The exercise of force, however, is only an incident. The problems of power are endless. Wars only occur. Politics endures.

Some of my colleagues who bore with me as I tried out these comments thought I discounted too heavily the qualitative importance of objectives in foreign policy and reflected too somber an outlook.

Let me make the proportions clear. I do not disparage the importance of objectives. Only in the light of ultimate purposes can one know how to proceed problem by problem in this field. Moreover, I do not believe that good is forever beyond reach, but I am sure that the way to it is difficult and long.

The young Gladstone was advised by his mentor that politics was an unsatisfactory business and that he would have to learn to accept imperfect results. That advice has wisdom for the conduct of a foreign policy. The never ending dilemmas inherent in measuring what we would like to do against what we can do impose great moral burdens. These are beyond the capacity of some individuals to bear. Sometimes they become intolerable for whole societies.

The rebellion against that burden sometimes takes the form of an abdication of will, and relief is sought in a passive fatalism about the problems of national existence. Again the rebellion may take the form of resorting to the counsel of violence as the solvent for the difficulties and restraints which life imposes. In either form, the rejection is a rejection of life itself, for life imposes on nations, as on men, the obligation to strive without despair even though the way may be long and the burdens heavy. . . .

3 | Truman's Speech to Congress, March 12, 1947 *

In this noted speech, which inaugurated the cold war policies of the United States, President Harry Truman publicized the concept of a global, ideological struggle between the United States and the U.S.S.R. In his request for economic

* *The New York Times,* March 13, 1947.

and military aid for Greece and Turkey, he divided the world into free nations and oppressed nations and committed the United States to support all free governments struggling to maintain themselves against their own minorities or against external pressures.

∠

. . . The United States has received from the Greek Government an urgent appeal for financial and economic assistance. Preliminary reports from the American Economic Mission now in Greece and reports from the American Ambassador in Greece corroborate the statement of the Greek Government that assistance is imperative if Greece is to survive as a free nation. I do not believe that the American people and the Congress wish to turn a deaf ear to the appeal of the Greek Government.

Greece is not a rich country. Lack of sufficient natural resources has always forced the Greek people to work hard to make both ends meet. Since 1940, this industrious, peace loving country has suffered invasion, four years of cruel enemy occupation, and bitter internal strife. . . .

The Greek Government has also asked for the assistance of experienced American administrators, economists and technicians to insure that the financial and other aid given to Greece shall be used effectively in creating a stable and self-sustaining economy and in improving its public administration.

The very existence of the Greek state is today threatened by the terrorist activities of several thousand armed men, led by Communists, who defy the Government's authority at a number of points, particularly along the northern boundaries. A commission appointed by the United Nations Security Council is at present investigating disturbed conditions in Northern Greece and alleged border violations along the frontiers between Greece on the one hand and Albania, Bulgaria, and Yugoslavia on the other.

Meanwhile, the Greek Government is unable to cope with the situation. The Greek Army is small and poorly equipped. It needs supplies and equipment if it is to restore the authority of the Government throughout Greek territory.

Greece must have assistance if it is to become a self-supporting and self-respecting democracy. The United States must supply that assistance. We have already extended to Greece certain types of relief and economic aid but these are inadequate. There is no other country to which democratic Greece can turn. No other nation is willing and able to provide the necessary support for a democratic Greek Government. . . .

Greece's neighbor, Turkey, also deserves our attention. The future of Turkey as an independent and economically sound state is clearly no less important to the freedom-loving peoples of the world than the future of Greece. The circumstances in which Turkey finds itself today are considerably different from those of Greece. Turkey has been spared the disasters that have beset Greece. And during the war, the United States and Great Britain furnished Turkey with material aid. Nevertheless, Turkey now needs our support. . . . I am fully aware of the broad implications involved if the United States extends assistance to Greece and Turkey, and I shall discuss these implications with you at this time.

One of the primary objectives of the foreign policy of the United States is the creation of conditions in which we and other nations will be able to work out a way of life free from coercion. This was a fundamental issue in the war with Germany and Japan. Our victory was won over countries which sought to impose their will, and their way of life upon other nations.

To ensure the peaceful development of nations, free from coercion, the United States has taken a leading part in establishing the United Nations. The United Nations is designed to make possible lasting freedom and independence for all its members. We shall not realize our objectives, however, unless we are willing to help free people to maintain their free institutions and their national integrity against aggressive movements that seek to impose upon them totalitarian regimes. This is no more than a frank recognition that totalitarian regimes imposed on free peoples, by direct or indirect aggression, undermine the foundations of international peace and hence the security of the United States.

The peoples of a number of countries of the world have recently had totalitarian regimes forced upon them against their will. The Government of the United States has made frequent protests against coercion and intimidation, in violation of the Yalta Agreement, in Poland, Rumania and Bulgaria. I must also state that in a number of other countries there have been similar developments. At the present moment in world history nearly every nation must choose between alternative ways of life. The choice is too often not a free one.

One way of life is based upon the will of the majority, and is distinguished by free institutions, representative government, free elections, guarantees of individual liberty, freedom of speech and religion, and freedom from political oppression.

The second way of life is based upon the will of a minority forcibly imposed upon the majority. It relies upon terror and oppression, a controlled press and radio, fixed elections, and the suppression of personal freedoms.

I believe that it must be the policy of the United States to support free peoples who are resisting attempted subjugation by armed minorities or by outside pressures.

I believe that we must assist free peoples to work out their own destinies in their own way.

I believe that our help should be primarily through economic and financial aid which is essential to economic stability and orderly political processes.

The world is not static, and the status quo is not sacred. But we cannot allow changes in the status quo in violation of the Charter of the United Nations by such methods as coercion, or by such subterfuges as political infiltration. In helping free and independent nations to maintain their freedom, the United States will be giving effect to the principles of the Charter of the United Nations. . . .

Should we fail to aid Greece and Turkey in this fateful hour, the effect will be far reaching to the West as well as to the East. We must take immediate and resolute action. . . .

## 4 | George C. Marshall's Speech at Harvard University, June 5, 1947 *

In this speech, which often appears as a natural extension of the Truman Doctrine speech of March 12, 1947, Marshall argued for an expanded economic aid program for Europe, but he also made it clear that United States economic aid, under the new program, would be aimed at poverty and economic dislocation, not at any ideology or nation.

✍

I need not tell you gentlemen that the world situation is very serious. That must be apparent to all intelligent people. I think one difficulty is that the problem is one of such enormous complexity that the very mass of the facts presented to the public by press and radio make it exceedingly difficult for the man in the street to reach a clear appraisement of the situation. Furthermore, the people of this country are distant from the troubled areas of the earth and it is hard for them to comprehend the plight and consequent reactions of the long-suffering peoples, and the effect of those reactions on their governments in connection with our efforts to promote peace in the world.

In considering the requirements for the rehabilitation of Europe, the physical loss of life, the visible destruction of cities, factories, mines and railroads was correctly estimated, but it has become obvious during recent months that this visible destruction was probably less serious than the dislocation of the entire fabric of European economy. For the past ten years conditions have been highly abnormal. . . . The breakdown of the business structure of Europe during the war was complete. Recovery has been seriously retarded by the fact that two years after the close of hostilities a peace settlement with Germany and Austria has not been agreed upon. But even given a more prompt solution of these difficult problems, the rehabilitation of the economic structure of Europe quite evidently will require a much longer time and greater effort than had been foreseen. . . .

The division of labor is the basis of modern civilization. At the present time it is threatened with breakdown. The town and city industries are not producing adequate goods to exchange with the food-producing farmer. Raw materials and fuel are in short supply. Machinery is lacking or worn out. The farmer or the peasant cannot find the goods for sale which he desires to purchase. So the sale of his farm produce for money which he cannot use seems to him an unprofitable transaction. . . . Meanwhile people in the cities are short of food and fuel. So the governments are forced to use their foreign money and credits to procure these necessities abroad. This process exhausts funds which are urgently needed for reconstruction. . . .

* *Documents on American Foreign Relations, January 1–December 31, 1947,* Raymond Dennett and Robert K. Turner, eds. (Princeton, 1949), IX: 9–11. Copyright 1944 by Princeton University Press. Reprinted by permission.

The truth of the matter is that Europe's requirements for the next three or four years of foreign food and other essential products—principally from America—are so much greater than her present ability to pay that she must have substantial additional help, or face economic, social and political deterioration of a very grave character. . . .

It is logical that the United States should do whatever it is able to do to assist in the return of normal economic health in the world, without which there can be no political stability and no assured peace. Our policy is directed not against any country or doctrine but against hunger, poverty, desperation and chaos. Its purpose should be the revival of a working economy in the world so as to permit the emergence of political and social conditions in which free institutions can exist. Such assistance, I am convinced, must not be on a piecemeal basis as various crises develop. Any assistance that this Government may render in the future should provide a cure rather than a mere palliative. Any government that is willing to assist in the task of recovery will find full cooperation, I am sure, on the part of the United States Government. Any government which maneuvers to block the recovery of other countries cannot expect help from us. Furthermore, governments, political parties or groups which seek to perpetuate human misery in order to profit therefrom politically or otherwise will encounter the opposition of the United States.

It is already evident that, before the United States Government can proceed much further in its efforts to alleviate the situation and help start the European world on its way to recovery, there must be some agreement among the countries of Europe as to the requirements of the situation and the part those countries themselves will take in order to give proper effect to whatever action might be undertaken by this Government. It would be neither fitting nor efficacious for this Government to undertake to draw up unilaterally a program designed to place Europe on its feet economically. This is the business of the Europeans. The initiative, I think, must come from Europe. . . . The program should be a joint one, agreed to by a number, if not all, European nations.

An essential part of any successful action on the part of the United States is an understanding on the part of the people of America of the character of the problem and the remedies to be applied. Political passion and prejudice should have no part. With foresight, and a willingness on the part of our people to face up to the vast responsibility which history has clearly placed upon our country, the difficulties I have outlined can and will be overcome.

# 5 | Dean G. Acheson's Speech in Washington, April 22, 1950 *

Acheson's speech before the American Society of Newspaper Editors comprised a good summary of his concept of containment of the Soviet Union. He made it clear that he sought a settlement with Russia, not that country's destruction. He defined the Soviet threat in global, ideological terms, however, and did not here or elsewhere enumerate any achievable conditions for such a settlement. His goals of universal freedom had little relationship to the power at his or the nation's disposal.

✍

I would like to discuss with you the thing that is most important to all of us: the well-being and happiness and security of the United States. I ask you to put aside, for the moment, all considerations that are less important, to forget all differences of opinion that are less than vital. . . .

We are faced with a threat—in all sober truth I say this—we are faced with a threat not only to our country but to the civilization in which we live and to the whole physical environment in which that civilization can exist. This threat is the principal problem that confronts the whole United States in the world today. . . .

There is no miracle that will make it disappear from the earth. Having recognized this truth, we need not for a moment be discouraged or downhearted. We have open to us, and we are now pursuing, many lines of action that will meet the challenge confronting us. May I mention six lines of action.

Our first line of action—and this seems to me the basis of all the others I shall discuss—is to demonstrate that our own faith in freedom is a burning and a fighting faith. We are children of freedom. We cannot be safe except in an environment of freedom. We believe in freedom as fundamentally as we believe anything in this world. We believe in it for everyone in our country. And we don't restrict this belief to freedom for ourselves. We believe that all people in the world are entitled to as much freedom, to develop in their own way, as we want ourselves. . . .

We must use every means we know to communicate the value of freedom to the four corners of the earth. Our message must go out through leaflets, through our free press, radio programs and films, through exchange of students and teachers with other countries, and through a hundred other ways. . . .

Thirdly, it is not enough that one should have a faith and should make that faith articulate. It is also essential that we, and those who think like us, should have the power to make safe the area in which we carry that faith into action.

* The Department of State, *Strengthening the Forces of Freedom: Selected Speeches and Statements of Secretary of State Acheson, February 1949–April 1950* (Washington, 1950), 1–9.

This means that we must look to our defenses. It means that we must organize our defenses wisely and prudently, with all the ingenuity and all the methods in which we are best versed to make ourselves strong.

Every element of promise is present in our situation. We have the ingenuity, we have the productive power, we have the determination, we have the resources. But this is not a subject on which I am competent to dwell at length. The President's chief advisers in this field are our Secretary of Defense and our service secretaries, in whom we can have complete faith and confidence.

Fourthly, beyond faith and preachment and defense there lies the necessity of translating all of these into terms of the daily lives of hundreds of millions of peoples who live in this free world of ours. I am talking about the effort we are now making to help create a better material life for ourselves and for other people in many parts of the world.

One part of this effort has to do with setting in operation again the great workshops of the free world. Since the end of the war we have worked steadily at this problem and we have had a vast measure of success. The chimneys of these factories are smoking again, raw materials are moving into them, finished goods are moving out. Hundreds of millions of people see the specter of insecurity in their daily lives being pushed further back. . . .

Now while we are helping to get workshops going—old and new—and to get people producing in Europe and other parts of the world, we have to do still another thing. And that is to develop a sensible system of trade to exchange the goods which are being and will be produced. . . .

We are going to have to make a great national effort, also, to get our own trade with the rest of the world into balance, to get out of the situation where we are selling abroad much more than we are buying and making up the difference out of the pockets of American taxpayers. Nobody here or abroad wants that situation to continue indefinitely. As part of the remedy we shall have to buy more from abroad, and that will demand a concerted national effort.

The fifth line of action is in the political field. In this political field we have so far only scratched the surface of what can be done to bring the free world closer together, to make it stronger and more secure and more effective.

There are many ways of organizing the free world for common action and many different opinions on how it should be done. But I think it is important in this hour of danger to concentrate our minds and our energies on using the machinery we have at hand, on expanding it and making it work. When you look over the field, you will see that we now have created a great deal of good machinery.

There is the whole machinery of the United Nations which we are continually learning to use more effectively. Within the framework of the United Nations we have other machinery, like the North Atlantic Treaty and the Organization of American States.

The free nations of Europe have banded together in the Council of Europe, in the Marshall Plan organization, and in a smaller group known as the Western Union. We can work with all of these organizations. We can use whichever is best suited to accomplish a particular purpose. What we need to do is to expand the machinery we have, to improve it, to use it with boldness and imagination, and, when necessary, to supplement it with new machinery.

Now our program of action would not be complete if I did not go on to a sixth field, and that is the area of our relations with the Soviet Union and the countries that have fallen under Communist control. In this field, as in our relations with the free nations, we have the machinery of negotiation at hand. In the United Nations we have a dozen or more conference tables at which our differences could be thrashed out, where unfortunately the Soviet chair stands empty at the present time. We shall go on trying to find a common ground for agreement, not perfect or eternal agreement, but at least a better arrangement for living together in greater safety. . . .

We do not propose to subvert the Soviet Union. We shall not attempt to undermine Soviet independence. And we are just as determined that Communism shall not by hook or crook or trickery undermine our country or any other free country that desires to maintain its freedom. That real and present threat of aggression stands in the way of every attempt at understanding with the Soviet Union. For it has been wisely said that there can be no greater disagreement than when someone wants to eliminate your existence altogether.

If, as, and when that idea of aggression, by one means or another, can be ruled out of our relations with the Soviet Union, then the greatest single obstacle to agreement will be out of the way. As the results of our actions become clear and the free world becomes stronger, it will, I believe, become progressively easier to get agreements with the Soviet Union. . . .

# 6 | Acheson's Speech at Berkeley, California, March 16, 1950 *

In this noted speech Secretary Acheson declared the conditions whereby the U.S.S.R. could demonstrate that it was prepared to negotiate in good faith. All that he expected of the Russians, he insisted, were actions which would demonstrate their seriousness in negotiation. The actual conditions which he listed, however, were little removed from a total capitulation of the Soviet Union in its various conflicts around the globe. How the Western alliance, whatever its power, could achieve this capitulation was not clear.

. . . However much we may sympathize with the Soviet citizens who for reasons bedded deep in history are obliged to live under it, we are not attempt-

* Strengthening the Forces of Freedom: Selected Speeches and Statements of Secretary of State Acheson, February 1949–April 1950, 20–28.

ing to change the governmental or social structure of the Soviet Union. The Soviet regime, however, has devoted a major portion of its energies and resources to the attempt to impose its system on other peoples. In this attempt it has shown itself prepared to resort to any method or stratagem including subversion, threats, and even military force.

Therefore, if the two systems are to coexist, some acceptable means must be found to free the world from the destructive tensions and anxieties of which it has been the victim in these past years and the continuance of which can hardly be in the interests of any people.

I wish, therefore, to speak to you about those points of greatest difference which must be identified and sooner or later reconciled if the two systems are to live together, if not with mutual respect, at least in reasonable security. What is it which the leaders of international Communism could do to make such coexistence more tolerable to everyone? . . .

It is now nearly 5 years since the end of hostilities, and the victorious Allies have been unable to define the terms of peace with the defeated countries. This is a grave, a deeply disturbing fact. For our part, we do not intend nor wish, in fact we do not know how, to create satellites. Nor can we accept a settlement which would make Germany, Japan, or liberated Austria satellites of the Soviet Union. The experience in Hungary, Rumania, and Bulgaria has been one of bitter disappointment and shocking betrayal of the solemn pledges by the wartime Allies. The Soviet leaders joined in the pledge at Tehran that they looked forward "with confidence to the day when all peoples of the world may live free lives, untouched by tyranny, and according to their varying desires and their own consciences." We can accept treaties of peace which would give reality to this pledge and to the interests of all in security.

With regard to Germany, unification under a government chosen in free elections under international observation is a basic element in an acceptable settlement. With that need recognized and with a will to define the terms of peace, a German treaty could be formulated which, while not pretending to solve all of the complex and bitter problems of the German situation, would, nevertheless, go far toward a relaxation of a set of major tensions.

With regard to Austria—that unhappy country is still under occupation because the Soviet leaders do not want a treaty. The political and economic independence of Austria is being sabotaged by the determination of the Soviets, camouflaged in technicalities, to maintain their forces and special interests in eastern Austria.

With regard to Japan, we feel that the Soviet leaders could recognize the interest which nations other than the members of the Council of Foreign Ministers have in a Japanese peace treaty and could refrain from taking positions and insisting on procedures which block progress toward a treaty.

In the Far East, generally, there are many points where the Soviet leaders could, if they chose, relax tensions. They could, for example, permit the United Nations Commission in Korea to carry out its duties by allowing the Commission's entry into North Korea and by accepting its report as the basis for a peaceful settlement of that liberated country's problems. They could repatriate

Japanese prisoners of war from Siberian camps. They could refrain from subverting the efforts of the newly independent states of Asia and the native leaders to solve their problems in their own way.

With regard to the whole group of countries which we are accustomed to think of as the satellite area, the Soviet leaders could withdraw their military and police force and refrain from using the shadow of that force to keep in power persons or regimes which do not command the confidence of the respective peoples, freely expressed through orderly representative processes. In other words, they could elect to observe, in practice, the declaration to which they set their signatures at Yalta concerning liberated Euorpe.

In this connection, we do not insist that these governments have any particular political or social complexion. What concerns us is that they should be truly independent national regimes, with a will of their own and with a decent foundation in popular feeling. We would like to feel, when we deal with these governments, that we are dealing with something representative of the national identity of the peoples in question. We cannot believe that such a situation would be really incompatible with the security of the Soviet Union.

This is a question of elementary good faith, and it is vital to a spirit of confidence that other treaties and other agreements will be honored. Nothing would so alter the international climate as the holding of elections in the satellite states in which the true will of the people could be expressed.

The Soviet leaders could drop their policy of obstruction in the United Nations and could instead act as if they believe the United Nations is, as Stalin himself has recently called it, a serious instrumentality for the maintenance of international peace and security. They are simply not acting that way now.

Their policy of walk-out and boycott is a policy that undermines the concept of majority decision. Indeed, they seem deliberately to entrench themselves in a minority position in the United Nations. This was illustrated last fall when they voted against the Essentials of Peace resolution which solemnly restated and reaffrmed the principles and purposes of the United Nations Charter and which pointed to practical steps which members should take to support the peace.

A respect for the expressed will of the majority is as fundamental to international organization as it is to democracy. We know that a majority of the General Assembly has generally not agreed with the Soviet Union, whereas we ourselves have generally been on the majority side. There is nothing artificial about this situation. It has not been the result of any sleight of hand or pressures on our part. We do not have any satellites whose votes we control. The significant fact is that proposals which have commended themselves to a majority of the members of the United Nations have also commended themselves to us. . . .

The Soviet leaders could join us in seeking realistic and effective arrangements for the control of atomic weapons and the limitation of armaments in general. We know that it is not easy for them, under their system, to contemplate the functioning on their territory of an authority in which people would participate who are not of their political persuasion. . . .

The Kremlin could refrain from using the Communist apparatus controlled by it throughout the world to attempt to overthrow, by subversive means, established governments with which the Soviet Government stands in an outward state of friendship and respect. In general, it could desist from, and could cooperate in efforts to prevent, indirect aggression across national frontiers—a mode of conduct which is inconsistent with the spirit and the letter of the United Nations Charter.

The Soviet leaders could cooperate with us to the end that the official representatives of all countries are treated everywhere with decency and respect and that an atmosphere is created in which these representatives could function in a normal and helpful manner, conforming to the accepted codes of diplomacy. . . .

In general, the Soviet leaders could refrain, I think, from systematically distorting to their own peoples the picture of the world outside their borders, and of our country, in particular. . . .

These are some of the things which we feel that the Soviet leaders could do which would permit the rational and peaceful development of the coexistence of their system and ours. They are not things that go to the depths of the moral conflict. They are not things that promise the Kingdom of Heaven. They have been formulated by us, not as moralists but as servants of government, anxious to get on with the practical problems that lie before us and to get on with them in a manner consistent with mankind's deep longing for a respite from fear and uncertainty.

Nor have they been formulated as a one-sided bargain. A will to achieve binding, peaceful settlements would be required of all participants. All would have to produce unmistakable evidence of their good faith. All would have to accept agreements in the observance of which all nations could have real confidence.

The United States is ready, as it has been and always will be, to cooperate in genuine efforts to find peaceful settlements. Our attitude is not inflexible, our opinions are not frozen, our positions are not and will not be obstacles to peace. But it takes more than one to cooperate. If the Soviet Union could join in doing these things I have outlined, we could all face the future with greater security. We could look forward to more than the eventual reduction of some of the present tensions. We could anticipate a return to a more normal and relaxed diplomatic atmosphere and to progress in the transaction of some of the international business which needs so urgently to be done.

I fear, however, that I must warn you not to raise your hopes. No one who has lived through these postwar years can be sanguine about reaching agreements in which reliance can be placed and which will be observed by the Soviet leaders in good faith. . . . We are always ready to discuss, to negotiate, to agree, but we are understandably loath to play the role of international sucker. We will take the initiative in the future as we have in the past in seeking agreement whenever there is any indication that this course would be a fruitful one. What is required is genuine evidence in conduct, not just in words, of an intention to solve the immediate problems and remove the tensions which divide us. I see no evidence that the Soviet leaders will change their conduct until the progress of the free world convinces them that they cannot profit from a continuation of these tensions. . . .

## 7 | Churchill's Speech before the House of Commons, March 28, 1950 *

In this speech Churchill took up the problem of arriving at some settlement with the Soviet Union. He recognized the need of Western preparedness as a deterrent against Soviet aggression, but he believed that the time for arriving at some mutually satisfactory settlement was limited and that the time still left was not necessarily on the side of the West. Power was necessary for successful negotiation, he admitted, but it was not an end in itself.

✑

. . . I come to our relations with Soviet Russia. I will begin by stating the reason why I do not believe that another war is imminent or inevitable, and why I believe that we have more time, if we use it wisely, and more hope of warding off that frightful catastrophe from our struggling, ill-informed and almost helpless human race. Here is the reason. There never was a time when the deterrents against war were to strong. If penalties of the most drastic kind can prevent in our civil life crime or folly, then we certainly have them here on a gigantic scale in the affairs of nations. . . . Moralists may find it a melancholy thought that peace can find no nobler foundations than mutual terror. But for my part I shall be content if these foundations are solid, because they will give us the extra time and the new breathing space for the supreme effort which has to be made for a world settlement.

No one need delude himself by underrating the difficulties which stand in the way of a settlement or by closing his eyes to the gulf which yawns between the two worlds, now facing each other, armed and arming, reaching out for agencies which might eventually destroy the human race. As I said at Boston last year, I think it probable that the Soviet Government fear the friendship of the West even more than they do our hostility. The Soviet regime and the lives of its rulers might be imperiled by allowing free, easy and friendly inter-mingling with the outer world. An endless series of quarrels, a vehement and violent antagonism, the consciousness of an outside enemy in the minds of the masses, may be regarded by the Soviet as a necessary precautionary element in maintaining the

* Hansard's *Parliamentary Debates*, Fifth Series, Vol. 473, March 28, 1950 (London, 1950), 189-202.

existence of the Communist power. There indeed is a gloomy thought. There indeed is a reason for fear. But fear must never be allowed to cast out hope.

During the election I was most anxious that the return of a Conservative Government to power, which was a possibility, should not be taken as involving an exacerbation of the already tense situation that exists, and that we should make it clear above all things that we should strive faithfully for peace. I also felt, and feel, that we owe it to our consciences, all of us, that no door should be closed which may lead to better prospects. I do not, of course, take an over-sanguine view of the position whatever efforts are made, but it is our Christian duty to try our best. Moreover, the democracies of the West must be constantly convinced that those who lead them do not despair of peace if they are to take even the measures which self-preservation demands in case the worst should come to the worst.

Let me repeat what I said at Edinburgh—only a few lines:

> I cannot help coming back to this idea of another talk with Soviet Russia upon the highest level. The idea appeals to me of a supreme effort to bridge the gulf between the two worlds so that each can live their life, if not in friendship at least without the hatreds of the cold war.

I was answered by the Foreign Secretary that all this was a "stunt." . . . But three days later, on 17th February at a Press conference at Lake Success, Mr. Trygve Lie, the Secretary General of U.N.O., said he was in favour of great Power negotiations:

> all the time and on all levels—top level, middle level, and lower level— inside and outside the United Nations. The world would be a lot better today if there had been more real negotiations among the great Powers during the past three years.

He added, what we shall all agree:

> The only people who can rightly judge the timing and form of negotiations and meetings are those who are responsible for conducting the foreign affairs of the countries concerned.

We are all agreed, but those who are responsible, as the right hon. Gentleman and his principal colleagues are, must not fail to seize any opportunities. We cannot go on with a policy of hesitation and drift. Every day is precious if the chance occurs.

I have explained this afternoon the arguments on which I base my belief that a further spell of time will be granted to us. Even at the risk of afterwards being reproached for being wrong, I have not hesitated to state my view that it may well be that several years may pass before a war breaks out. I will take the chance of making that remark although I have no special information at my disposal. Certainly we must seek to negotiate from strength and not from weakness. We all agree on that. Certainly we must move hand in hand with our Allies, and above all with the United States, as the right hon. Gentleman has so far done. . . .

But if there is a breathing space, if there is more time, as I feel and do not hesitate to say, it would be a grave mistake of a different order, perhaps a fatal mistake, to suppose that, even if we have this interlude, it will last for ever, or even last more than a few years. Time and patience, those powerful though not infallible solvents of human difficulties, are not necessarily on our side. When the last Parliament met, I mentioned four years as the period before any other Power but the United States would possess the atomic bomb. That period has already gone by, and our position is definitely worse than it was in this matter both as regards our own safety and as to the conditions which are, I believe, effectively preserving the peace of the world. . . .

Therefore, while I believe there is time for a further effort for a lasting and peaceful settlement, I cannot feel that it is necessarily a long time or that its passage will progressively improve our own security. Above all things, we must not fritter it away. . . .

# 8 | Herbert Hoover's Radio Address, December 20, 1950 *

Throughout 1950 many Americans were growing restive under the evolution of American policy. Herbert Hoover was a key spokesman of this group, and his speech of December 20 served as a catalyst for those who found fault with the nation's foreign relations. As time went on Mr. Hoover's position appeared less and less tenable, and not even a majority of the Republicans in Congress endorsed his views. His military program, concentrating on air and naval power, conformed to the isolationist pattern of the 'thirties.

✑

. . . No appraisal of the world situation can be final in an unstable world. However, to find our national path we must constantly re-examine where we have arrived and at times revise our direction. I do not propose to traverse the disastrous road by which we reached this point.

We may first survey the global military situation. There is today only one center of aggression on the earth. That is the Communist-controlled Asian-European land mass of 800,000,000 people. They have probably over 300 trained and equipped combat divisions with over 30,000 tanks, 10,000 tactical planes, and further large reserves they can put in action in ninety days. But they are

* Herbert Hoover, *Addresses upon the American Road, 1950–1955* (Stanford, Calif., 1955), 3–10. Reprinted by permission of Herbert Hoover.

not a great sea power. Their long range air power is limited. This congeries of over thirty different races will some day go to pieces. But in the meantime they furnish unlimited cannon fodder.

Facing this menace on the Eastern front there are about 100,000,000 non-Communist island people in Japan, Formosa, the Philippines, and Korea. Aside from Korea, which I discuss later, they have probably only 12 effective combat divisions with practically no tanks, air, or navy.

Facing this land mass on the south are the Indies and Middle East of about 600,000,000 non-Communist people. There are about 150,000,000 further non-Communist people in North Africa and Latin America. Except Turkey and Formosa, these 850,000,000 non-Communist people have little military force which they would or could spare. But they could contribute vital economic and moral strength.

Facing this menace on the Continental European front there are about 160,-000,000 further non-Communist people who, excluding Spain, have less than 20 combat divisions now available, few tanks, and little air or naval force. And their will to defend themselves is feeble and their disunities are manifest. Of importance in military weight at this moment there is the British Commonwealth of 150,000,000 people, with probably 30 combat divisions under arms, a superior navy, considerable air force, and a few tanks. And there are 150,000,000 people in the United States preparing 3,500,000 men into a gigantic air force and navy, with about 30 equipped combat divisions.

Thus there are 1,310,000,000 non-Communist people in the world, of whom today only about 320,000,000 have any military potency.

If we weigh these military forces as they stand today we must arrive at certain basic conclusions.

*a*) We must face the fact that to commit the sparse ground forces of the non-Communist nations into a land war against this Communist land mass would be a war without victory, a war without a successful political terminal. The Germans failed with a magnificent army of 240 combat divisions and with powerful air and tank forces. That compares with only 60 divisions proposed today for the North Atlantic Pact Nations. Even were Western Europe armed far beyond any contemplated program, we could never reach Moscow.

Therefore any attempt to make war on the Communist mass by land invasion, through the quicksands of China, India, or Western Europe is sheer folly. That would be the graveyard of millions of American boys and would end in the exhaustion of this Gibraltar of Western Civilization.

*b*) Equally, we Americans alone with sea and air power can so control the Atlantic and Pacific Oceans that there can be no possible invasion of the Western Hemisphere by Communist armies. They can no more reach Washington in force than we can reach Moscow.

*c*) In this military connection we must realize the fact that the Atomic Bomb is a far less dominant weapon than it was once thought to be.

*d*) It is obvious that the United Nations have been defeated in Korea by the aggression of Communist China. There are no available forces in the world to repel them. Even if we sacrifice more American boys to hold the bridgehead, we know we shall not succeed at the present time in the mission given to us by the fifty members of the United Nations.

We may explore our American situation still further. The 150,000,000 American people are already economically strained by government expenditures. It must not be forgotten that we are carrying huge burdens from previous wars including obligations to veterans and $260 billions of bond and currency issues from those wars. In the fiscal year 1952, federal and local expenditures are likely to exceed $90 billions. That is more than our total savings. We must finance huge deficits by further government issues. Inflation is already moving. The dollar has in six months fallen 15 or 20 percent in purchasing power. But we might with stern measures avoid the economic disintegration of such a load for a very few years. If we continued long on this road the one center of resistance in the world will collapse in economic disaster.

We may also appraise the diplomatic front. Our great hope was in the United Nations. We have witnessed the sabotage of its primary purpose of preserving peace. It has been, down to last week, a forum for continuous smear on our honor, our ideals, and our purposes. . . .

Two months ago I suggested a tentative alternate policy for the United States. It received a favorable reception from the large majority of our press.

Since then the crisis in the world has become even more acute. . . . In expansion of my proposals of two months ago, I now propose certain principles and action.

First. The foundation of our national policies must be to preserve for the world this Western Hemisphere Gibraltar of Western Civilization.

Second. We can, without any measure of doubt, with our own air and naval forces, hold the Atlantic and Pacific Oceans with one frontier on Britain (if she wishes to co-operate); the other, on Japan, Formosa, and the Philippines. We can hold open the sea lanes for our supplies. And I devoutly hope that a maximum of co-operation can be established between the British Commonwealth and ourselves.

Third. To do this we should arm our air and naval forces to the teeth. We have little need for large armies unless we are going to Europe or China. We should give Japan her independence and aid her in arms to defend herself. We should stiffen the defenses of our Pacific frontier in Formosa and the Philippines. We can protect this island chain by our sea and air power.

Fourth. We could, after initial outlays for more air and navy equipment, greatly reduce our expenditures, balance our budget, and free ourselves from the dangers of inflation and economic degeneration.

Fifth. If we toil and sacrifice as the President has so well asked, we can continue aid to the hungry of the world. Out of our productivity, we can give aid to other nations when they have already displayed spirit and strength in defense against Communism. We have the stern duty to work and sacrifice to do it.

Sixth. We should have none of appeasement. Morally there is no appeasement of Communism. Appeasement contains more dangers than Dunkirks. We want no more Teherans and no more Yaltas. We can retrieve a battle but we cannot retrieve an appeasement. We are grateful that President Truman has denounced such a course.

Seventh. We are not blind to the need to preserve Western Civilization on the Continent of Europe or to our cultural and religious ties to it. But the prime obligation of defense of Western Continental Europe rests upon the nations of Europe. The test is whether they have the spiritual force, the will, and acceptance of unity among them by their own volition. America cannot create their spiritual forces; we cannot buy them with money. You can search all the history of mankind and there is no parallel to the effort and sacrifice we have made to elevate their spirit and to achieve their unity. . . .

To warrant our further aid they should show they have spiritual strength and unity to avail themselves of their own resources. But it must be far more than pacts, conferences, paper promises, and declarations. Today it must express itself in organized and equipped combat divisions of such huge numbers as would erect a sure dam against the red flood. And that before we land another man or another dollar on their shores. Otherwise we shall be inviting another Korea. That would be a calamity to Europe as well as to us. . . .

These policies I have suggested would be no isolationism. Indeed they are the opposite. They would avoid rash involvement of our military forces in hopeless campaigns. They do not relieve us of working to our utmost. They would preserve a stronghold of Christian civilization in the world against any peradventure.

With the policies I have outlined, even without Europe, Americans have no reason for hysteria or loss of confidence in our security or our future. And in American security rests the future security of all mankind. . . .

9 | John Paton Davies's Observations on the Struggle for Power in China, 1943–44 *

In his wartime communications on the political conditions within China, John Paton Davies, a distinguished and perceptive member of the United States Foreign Service, contrasted the inefficiency and corruption of the Kuomintang with the efficiency and popularity of the Chinese Communists in northern China. He predicted that Chiang Kai-shek would of necessity launch a civil war against his Communist competitors after the defeat of Japan. His only hope for success in such a struggle, wrote Davies, would lay in unlimited quantities

* John Paton Davies's observations on the Kuomintang and the Chinese Communists, June 24, 1943, and November 7, 1944, *United States Relations with China* (Washington, 1949), 566–7, 571, 573.

of foreign military aid. Davies warned the United States government against such an involvement and suggested rather that the nation make some effort to reform the Nationalist government, and, if that failed, to co-operate with the Communists who were destined to control China anyway.

✒

The Chinese Communists are so strong between the Great Wall and the Yangtze that they can now look forward to the postwar control of at least North China. They may also continue to hold not only those parts of the Yangtze valley which they now dominate but also new areas in Central and South China. The Communists have fallen heir to these new areas by a process, which has been operating for seven years, whereby Chiang Kai-shek loses his cities and principal lines of communication to the Japanese and the countryside to the Communists.

The Communists have survived ten years of civil war and seven years of Japanese offensives. They have survived not only more sustained enemy pressure than the Chinese Central Government forces have been subjected to, but also a severe blockade imposed by Chiang.

They have survived and they have grown. Communist growth since 1937 has been almost geometric in progression. From control of some 100,000 square kilometers with a population of one million and a half they have expanded to about 850,000 square kilometers with a population of approximately 90 million. And they will continue to grow.

The reason for this phenomenal vitality and strength is simple and fundamental. It is mass support, mass participation. The Communist governments and armies are the first governments and armies in modern Chinese history to have positive and widespread popular support. They have this support because the governments and armies are genuinely of the people. . . .

. . . The Kuomintang and Chiang Kai-shek recognize that the Communists, with the popular support which they enjoy and their reputation for administrative reform and honesty, represent a challenge to the Central Government and its spoils system. The Generalissimo cannot admit the seemingly innocent demands of the Communists that their party be legalized and democratic processes be put into practice. To do so would probably mean the abdication of the Kuomintang and the provincial satraps.

The Communists, on the other hand, dare not accept the Central Government's invitation that they disband their armies and be absorbed in the national body politic. To do so would be to invite extinction.

This impasse will probably be resolved, American and other foreign observers in Chungking agree, by an attempt by the Central Government to liquidate the Communists. This action may be expected to precipitate a civil war from which one of the two contending factions will emerge dominant. . . .

Chiang Kai-shek and his Kuomintang lieutenants fully realize the risks of an attack on the Communists. This may explain the reported statements of high officials in Chungking that they must prepare not only for the coming civil war but also for the coming war with Russia. Chiang and his Central Government recognize that they cannot defeat the Communists and the Soviet Union without foreign aid. Such aid would naturally be sought from the United States and possibly Great Britain.

. . . We may anticipate that Chiang Kai-shek will exert every effort and resort to every stratagem to involve us in active support of the Central Government. We will probably be told that if fresh American aid is not forthcoming all of China and eventually all of Asia will be swept by communism. It will be difficult for us to resist such appeals, especially in view of our moral commitments to continued assistance to China during the post-war period. . . .

Only if he is able to enlist foreign intervention on a scale equal to the Japanese invasion of China will Chiang probably be able to crush the Communists. But foreign intervention on such a scale would seem to be unlikely. Relying upon his dispirited shambling legions, his decadent corrupt bureaucracy, his sterile political moralisms and such nervous foreign support as he can muster, the Generalissimo may nevertheless plunge China into civil war. He cannot succeed, however, where the Japanese in more than seven years of determined striving have failed. The Communists are already too strong for him.

If the Generalissimo neither precipitates a civil war nor reaches an understanding with the Communists, he is still confronted with defeat. Chiang's feudal China can not long coexist alongside a modern dynamic popular government in North China.

The Communists are in China to stay. And China's destiny is not Chiang's but theirs.

In this unhappy dilemma, the United States should attempt to prevent the disaster of a civil war through adjustment of the new alignment of power in China by peaceful processes. The desirable means to this end is to encourage the reform and revitalization of the Kuomintang so that it may survive as a significant force in a coalition government. If this fails, we must limit our involvement with the Kuomintang and must commence some cooperation with the Communists, the force destined to control China, in an effort to influence them further into an independent position friendly to the United States. We are working against time because, if the U.S.S.R. enters the war against Japan and invades China before either of these alternatives succeeds, the Communists will be captured by the U.S.S.R. and become Soviet satellites.

Nathaniel Peffer, one of the nation's leading students of Far Eastern affairs, predicted that the Kuomintang, hopelessly corrupt and inefficient, would never reform as long as it could anticipate the support of the United States government. He suggested, therefore, that the country withdraw all its military forces from China rather than turn that nation into another battleground of the war against communism. United States policy toward China, like its previous policy toward Japan, was failing, wrote Peffer, because there was no relationship between the goals pursued and the means adopted for achieving the goals.

. . . I have watched China at intervals over the past thirty years. I watched the newly formed republic slowly decline into inanition in the early years of the first World War. I was there in the warlord years which followed, when the country was split into segments, under semiliterate, pseudomilitary men who looted everything within reach, and still later in the seething years of the nationalist revolution. Bad as conditions were in those years, one could hold to perspective and see them as the surface phenomena of social transition, the labor pains of a new society. One actually did discern new forces in the making, young men emerging of a different order.

I have just been in China again, and now I find that one can hold to perspective only by an effort of will and not always successfully. Now the surface conditions are at least as bad as they were—but they can no longer be construed as the painful process of social transformation. Nor can one now discern anything ahead that is better.

There are no new forces in the making (the Communists can only doubtfully be so classified) and the young men of a better order are suppressed. There is still warlordism, but a kind of higher warlordism and therefore a worse one. Twenty years ago the warlords were local satraps, the power and rapacity of each limited to his own locality; now they are organized in a single, centrally controlled machine, with the greater power that centralization and system always give. The rapacity is less crude and less obvious, but in sum it yields as much. The centrally controlled machine is the party called the Kuomintang, which in fact—if no longer in law—is the government of China; and its head is Chiang Kai-shek.

No one who has been in China in the past year will think this picture overdrawn. Nor is it affected by the recent pronouncements about constitutionalism

* Nathaniel Peffer, "Time To Get Out of China," *Harper's Magazine,* CXCV (July 1947), 49–56. Reprinted by permission of the estate of Nathaniel Peffer.

and the broadening of the base of government. I was in Nanking when the new constitution was adopted last December. Among those whose adherence to the government is not bought by political jobs or economic favors there were some who had hopes that it signalized something new in China, but none who had confidence.

There was little reason for confidence. There is nothing much wrong with the constitution itself. From the point of view of a political scientist it is muddled, unclear, and badly thought through; but its merits and demerits from that point of view are irrelevant. As a matter of fact, the constitution *could* serve as a workable basis for responsible representative government—if those who hold power had any desire for such government. The point is that they have no such desire. The constitution was "granted" in order to allay a mounting discontent among the Chinese people on which the Communists were capitalizing, and, still more, in order to meet criticism in America and thus get a large American loan. . . .

The trouble in China is not a matter of the form of government and laws. It is a matter of persons—and not so much the character of persons as their spirit and their political and social attitudes. In theory, the monopolistic rule by the Kuomintang was not particularly unsound. It derived directly from Sun Yat-sen's philosophy of progress toward democracy in stages. The period of Kuomintang monopoly was to be the stage of tutelage; the Kuomintang was to act as trustee, while the people were being educated for democratic government. Had the Kuomintang been what Sun Yat-sen envisaged, this would have been not only logical but ideal; for the Chinese people, who have a long political tradition but one of a different order from democracy, were not prepared to exercise popular rule at once. But the Kuomintang is not, and for twenty years has not been, as Sun Yat-sen envisaged it. It is almost the exact opposite.

The Kuomintang is not a political party in the accepted sense. It is best described as a holding company for a country, with a large number of shareholders (the party members) who have given their proxies to a small number of directors. These directors are self-appointed and self-perpetuating. They may or may not report to the shareholders, but periodically they throw a small dividend to a favored few in order to keep them active in rounding up and delivering proxies. These dividends take the form of jobs for the smaller shareholders and opportunities to make money for the larger ones. But the company is run exclusively by and in the interests of the directors—some of whom take their compensation in wealth, some in power, and some in both. . . .

In any case China has become the private possession of the Kuomintang, and the Kuomintang is controlled by a small coterie of which Chiang Kai-shek is unchallenged chief. The coterie is composed of Chiang himself, his personal associates, military leaders who work with him, the directors of the party's patronage machine, and those big business men and financiers who lend financial support to the Kuomintang when necessary and in return get certain lucrative favors. There is also a group of enlightened, well-meaning and highly-trained men who technically at least are members of the Kuomintang directorate. They are permitted a voice, so long as it is in assent. Many struggle manfully against odds in the hope of accomplishing something, and in small ways they may succeed. They are tolerated so long as they do not interfere unduly—mainly because they make attractive window dressing, especially to the foreign eye.

Government in China is personal government, and the person who counts most is Chiang Kai-shek. He is not easy to classify or understand. It is not accurate to call him a dictator, since words in the lexicon of politics do not carry the same meaning in China as in the West. Not everything that is done in China is what Chiang wants—but nothing can be done that he definitely does not want, and there are few public men in China who are willing to make important decisions without getting Chiang's assent. If they do, they are very likely to find themselves arbitrarily reversed, the law and the formal scheme of government notwithstanding. The legend—more widely disseminated in this country than in China—that Chiang is the victim of the men around him, that he is kept uninformed by them, or that they are so powerful that he must yield to some of them in order to keep their support against the others, is a myth. Chiang is powerful enough to deal with any or all of them if he wants to. . . .

Corruption in China is often exaggerated by foreigners, mainly because standards of public trust vary with social settings. What is graft in one setting may not be graft in another. But judging by China's own standards, one can say that corruption has never in recent times been as brazen as now. There is plenty of positive corruption in the form of private seizure of public funds. Even worse, however, is negative corruption in the form of exemption of the favored few from taxation while the masses are subject to outrageous exactions. In addition, there is the passing on of opportunities for profit from so-called public enterprises to the same favored few.

Furthermore, nothing is done to alleviate the lot of the masses—meaning now not only the peasants and urban workers but also the middle classes, on whom the burden of inflation falls most harshly. Regulations for control of prices and prevention of hoarding are passed in an endless stream, and they flow by as a stream, without even ruffling the surface. This ineffectiveness results in part from the lack of administrative machinery; but it is due even more to the fact that enforcement of the regulations would deprive the favored of their profits.

It is this that has alienated the politically conscious Chinese from the government, and left even the illiterate masses suspicious and distrustful. Still more serious is the system of repression that has been developed to keep the present ruling group in power. This, too, can be exaggerated. It is not nearly so tight and inexorable as repression in ex-Nazi Germany or Communist Russia. The machinery is not so efficient, and the Chinese do not go in for absolutes anyway, either in thought or conduct. But protest is stifled nevertheless, principally because protest has become dangerous. It is not yet necessary to look over one's shoulder before one talks in China, but it is politic to be sure one knows everybody present. . . .

This is the atmosphere in which China now lives—an atmosphere not of terror but of fear. In larger urban centers, especially where foreigners can observe, there is more discretion in imposing repression. In some of the outlying regions there is all but terrorism. Especially in the newspapers, repression is becoming less necessary, because either the Kuomintang buys up newspapers and installs its henchmen as editors, or the editors have seen examples of reprisal—such as, for instance, the withholding of paper stock. Increasingly the men in important posts in media of communication are those who are sure to stand without hitching.

From all this the principal beneficiaries are the Communists. Not Marxism but the perversion of Sun Yat-senism—the original philosophy of the republican and nationalist revolution—has recruited Communists. The young men, the men of spirit or those who despair, see no alternative to the Kuomintang except the Communists. The middle parties are too weak and without hope of succeeding to power, though they contain large numbers of men who carry respect. These are the liberals of whom General Marshall spoke in his farewell statement on leaving China, and they are worthy of respect. But they are at present negligible.

Since that is so and the Kuomintang has repelled them beyond recall, young men of vigor and idealism are turning to the Communists. In many cases they do so regretfully and as a last resort—often not because of the Communist philosophy, but in spite of it. They would be followed by many more, if it were not for a widespread fear of terrorism of another brand and, still more, fear of Russian expansionism. If the Russians had not been shortsighted, if they had not insisted on the restitution of their old imperialistic possessions in Manchuria and had they not looted the industrial properties there, the Communist movement would be far stronger in China today than it is. . . .

Today the Communists appear preferable to their opponents, simply because the Kuomintang leaders are the kind of men from whom no enlightened regime can be expected, while the Communist leaders are the kind from whom it could be. But one can never feel certain of the ultimate purposes of the Communists. Definitely one cannot escape the question whether in power they might not be wholly different from what they are now. Of course they hotly deny that, if successful, they would subordinate themselves to Russia after the fashion of Poland; but in justice to them it should be added that they say bluntly that continued American aid to the Kuomintang would throw them into the arms of Russia.

It is here that the international complications enter—complications of the kind which have produced turmoil in the Far East for generations and a general war in the last decade. By a process of drift rather than reasoned choice, America has entered itself as a major factor in these complications. Legalistic terminology aside, the truth is that America has intervened in China. It has intervened more definitely than any other great power ever did, except Japan. And whatever its original purpose may have been, the effect has been to bring about just those conditions that made civil war inevitable. This war, in turn, produces the kind of international situation in which America has to give its future as hostage.

It was sound analysis of the causes of war in the Far East which made America choose unification in China as the first essential, to be followed by reconstruction and industrialization. With China strong and stable, the Far East would be stable and America would be spared the risk of another war. The choice was sound; the means to give it effect were not.

What we did was to hand a blank check to those elements in China which would make unity impossible. Indeed, we gave unconditional support to the worst elements in China. By 1944 it was already evident that the Kuomintang had alienated a large proportion of the people and that the Communists stood to gain strength thereby. When the war ended with Japan's sudden surrender, American ships and planes moved up the Kuomintang armies to take over the Japanese-occupied areas. This was probably justified, since otherwise both Chinese armies would have rushed in, touching off a civil war at once. But when we presented the country to Chiang Kai-shek and the Kuomintang, it should have been only under stringent conditions—changes in personnel at the top, reform of the army, proof of immediate intention to institute economic and social reforms. We made no conditions. We gave support first, and then expressed hopes; the Chinese returned polite generalities. Why not, since they had already gained what they wanted? . . .

It is unanimously agreed that General Marshall did everything that was humanly possible to induce a compromise. His perception of underlying causes was unfailing, and he pressed for measures that would eliminate them.

But his hands had been tied. We had already forfeited his only means of pressure. Supported by Ambassador Stuart, he could—and did—argue ably and persuasively the merits of democratic government, with representation of all parties. He could even get agreement from Chiang Kai-shek in generalities. Intellectually, no doubt, Chiang was convinced that this was the way of the modern world; but his actions were according to his instincts, which are of an earlier and politically uglier world. Moreover, these instincts were fortified by the persuasions of his friends, for whom there was only one desirable end—continuation of their personal power.

General Marshall's efforts were sabotaged by both sides, but the first and major acts of sabotage were the Kuomintang's. The price of peace was remission of their own absolute power, and the Kuomintang leaders would have none of it. So long as America continued to give support to the Kuomintang, General Marshall had nothing to argue with except logic and appeals to good will. . . .

In the end, of course, General Marshall failed. In publicly acknowledging the completion of his task without result, he acknowledged also that there was a state of war in China. But the American troops remain and the American military mission still remains—in the capital, where in the nature of things it can train only the national army, which means training one side in a civil war. (Even more recently American naval vessels were handed over to the Chinese government.) Now there can be no further pretense that our forces are there only to ensure peace, for we acknowledge that there is no peace. Now we are frankly intervening in a civil war. . . .

Once the Chinese government knew that it could not get further help from America just by playing off Russia against us, it might reform perforce, as a first step introducing into the government the kind of men who understand what reform means.

But if America carrying out what might seem to be the pure logic of the Truman Doctrine, decides to back the present government just because it is anti-Communist, then China will continue to drift further into what will become barely concealed fascism. Then the state of China's politics will deteriorate further, the economy will dissolve, despair will drive more Chinese into the Communist ranks, the civil war will become more intense, America will have to put more strength behind the Kuomintang forces. Then Russia, unwilling to see the Chinese Communists extinguished, may well put force behind them in a way that it has not done so far. And then Communist and Kuomintang forces will confront each other only as skirmishing forces in advance of major armies—American and Russian.

Whatever may be true in Eastern Europe, this does not have to come about in the Far East. America's present policy in China is helping to bring it about. In American self-interest the policy should be reversed. The first step is to withdraw our forces from China entirely and to withhold all further economic help until conditions in China change.

11 | Vandenberg's Observations on China, 1948–50 *

No document revealed more clearly the dilemma posed by events in China than a report of the American Consul General at Tientsin, dated March 15, 1949. Three days earlier the Consul General had forwarded to the State Department the text of a memorandum from the American Chamber of Commerce at that city which strongly opposed further United States aid to Chiang Kai-shek. The Consul General commented on that memorandum: "Americans in Tientsin who had the unhappy experience two months ago of witnessing the capture of Tientsin by Communist armies equipped almost entirely with American arms and other military equipment handed over practically without fighting by Nationalist armies in Manchuria, have expressed astonishment at radio reports from the U.S. during the last two or three days to the effect that a bill may be presented to the Congress to extend further military and economic aid to the Nationalist Government in the sum of a billion and a half dollars.

"Americans in Tientsin feel the only result of further U.S. aid to a Government which has proved so ineffective that most of our previous aid has passed to the Communists will be to further strengthen the Communists. . . . They feel that

* The Private Papers of Senator Vandenberg, Arthur H. Vandenberg, Jr., and Joe Alex Morris, eds. (Boston, 1952), 527, 529–31, 536, 538, 593. Reprinted by permission of Houghton Mifflin Company.

our global policy of opposition to Communism should not oblige us to support a hopelessly inefficient and corrupt government which has lost the support of its people. They believe that at this juncture it would be useless to extend further aid to a government which is so far gone. They feel that the present situation must be solved by the Chinese and that for the time being we should adopt a hands-off policy."

It was against the background of such information that the Truman administration attempted to create an American policy for China. Senator Vandenberg, as a Republican adviser of the government on matters of foreign policy, saw that after 1948 the administration no longer had any choices remaining that contained any promise of success. His observations on the China dilemma he recorded in his diary.

🖋

December 11, 1948

Mr. Landon may be of the opinion that we "gulled" Republicans should have yelled our heads off about China and the Generalissimo during the past year or two, but in my opinion it would only have precipitated and underscored a discussion of Chiang's weaknesses and would have nullified any remnant of his prestige. It is easy to sympathize with Chiang—to respect him . . . —as I always have and still do. But it is quite a different thing to plan resultful aid short of armed American intervention with American combat troops (which I have never favored and probably never shall).

I think our China policy was wrong (and always said so) in striving to force a Communist coalition on Chiang. . . . I think we should have taken realistic steps long ago to sustain the Nationalist Government—but certainly it is now evident that this "realism" also involved an indispensable house-cleaning in Chiang's government. I envy Mr. Landon's freedom to criticize what wasn't done and his freedom of responsibility for deciding specifically what should have been done then and what ought to be done now. When practically all of our American-trained and American-equipped Chinese divisions surrender without firing a shot—where do we go from here? I am afraid I totally miss Mr. Landon's point when he volunteers to take Republican responsibility for these Democratic decisions which never were, and are not now, any part of the bipartisan liaison. . . .

December 14, 1948

We must deal with today's conditions in China as they are and we must be realistic about it. Appropriations alone are not enough. They must implement a plan which offers at least some small degree of hope for success. . . . We have poured more than two billion dollars into China in the last few years. But pouring money is not enough—as we have learned to our sorrow. For example, a number of Chinese divisions—fully trained and equipped by America—have surrendered without firing a shot. And all of the American equipment is in the hands of these Chinese Communists. There can be plenty of argument as to why this happened. But the point is that it did happen—and no plan for the future is any good unless it can avoid such happenings again. This is simply one example out of many to demonstrate the extreme difficulty which the most ardent friends of China (among whom I hope I am enrolled) confront in searching an answer to the current crisis.

[He wrote a month later:]
. . . the situation in China has disintegrated so rapidly that [we] . . . confront the grave question as to how any sort of American aid can be made effective and not be a waste of American resources. . . . It . . . seems to be apparent that this progressive disintegration has cost the National Government the support and sympathy of a large portion of all the Chinese people. Indeed, it is now probable that the Nationalist Government will fall before we could ever sustain it with a new program of aid. . . . If we made ourselves responsible for the Army of the Nationalist Government, we would be in the China war for keeps and the responsibility would be ours instead of hers. I am very sure that this would jeopardize our own national security beyond any possibility of justification. . . .

Saturday, February 5, 1949
Chiang and his Nationalist government may well be on their last legs. They probably will collapse in the near future. Our shipments to them, therefore, might well fall into the hands of the Northern Chinese Communists (as has been the case with American equipment furnished to eight American-trained Nationalist Divisions which surrendered without firing a shot). But there is something here vastly more important than what happens to $60,000,000 worth of supplies. The American Government already is charged with a large share of responsibility for Chiang's Government's fate because of our previous policies and our failure to give it adequate military supplies. (This charge is only partially justified up-to-date.) But if, at the very moment when Chiang's Nationalists are desperately trying to negotiate some kind of a peace with the Communists, we suspend all military shipments to the Nationalists, we certainly shall make any hope of a negotiated peace impossible. We shall thus virtually notify the Communists that they can consider the war ended and themselves as victors. We virtually withdraw our recognition of the Nationalist Government. We seal China's doom. Regardless of the justification of previous charges that our American policy has been largely responsible for China's fate, if we take *this* step at *this* fatefully inept moment, *we* shall never be able to shake off the charge that we are the ones who gave poor China the final push into disaster. Millions of our own people will be shocked; and we shall seriously lose prestige throughout the world. I decline any part of any such responsibility. I beg of you, at the very least, to postpone any such decision for a few more weeks until the China question is settled *by China* and *in China* and not by the *American government in Washington*. This blood must not be on our hands. My point is further emphasized by the fact that the title to almost all of this 60 millions in supplies has already passed to the Nationalist Government which is waiting for these export licenses.

Therefore your order will be much more than a withholding of American supplies in American hands. It will be a ban on the Nationalist Government—and that will be "the last straw." I make it plain that I have little or no hope for stopping the immediate Communist conquest. That is beside the point. I decline to be responsible for the *last push* which makes it possible. . . .

[About August 15, 1949]
. . . [Senator] Alex Smith . . . has a [strong concern] about doing something for China. . . . He doesn't know what—and neither do I, because China aid at the moment is like sticking your finger in the lake and looking for the hole. . . .

January 9, 1950
I . . . deeply dislike the present abrupt abandonment of the Nationalist Government (no matter what its weaknesses) without some sort of alternative program in Formosa (where the Formosans ought to have a right to say a little something about their own fate). I am opposed to recognition of the Communist regime in China at this immediate moment—although realities may force an early abandonment of this position. . . . I may be wrong. But I cannot escape the feeling that the "Ward episode" [detention of U.S. Consul Angus Ward by Communists in Manchuria] and many others require some sort of assurances that the Communist Government in China will respect our rights under international law. Perhaps the assurances (even though given) would prove as futile as the promises in the Roosevelt-Litvinov correspondence preceding our recognition of Soviet Russia. But it seems to me that at least as a matter of self-respect we must keep the record clear. This may prove to be impractical. But I want to explore it to a finality.

January 17, 1950
We must face things as they are and make the best of it. This inevitably requires us to face the total Far Eastern situation rather than China and Formosa by themselves. This means that our policy must concern itself not only with salvaging what we can in China and Formosa, but also in doing what will best keep another billion of Asiatics out of the Soviet order. I am convinced that we would seriously impair our status among the latter billion if we were to join ourselves in any military action. . . . I should . . . like to find a way to give the Formosans some degree of self-determination in respect to their own destiny; and I should like to see some means provided through which the United Nations can take collective action. But the whole thing is desperately complicated and we must proceed (at long last) with prudence as well as courage in this critical area.

Acheson's speech before the National Press Club comprised a complete statement of American Far Eastern policy at mid-century. This policy, he pointed out, was anchored to the assumption of a vast revolutionary upheaval blanketing the Orient. He defined the nation's defense commitment in the Far East, including specifically Japan, the Ryukyus, and the Philippines. Recognizing the force of the Asiatic upheaval, he warned that henceforth the fundamental decisions in Asia would lie in Asian hands. In this speech Acheson clarified the basic Europe-first orientation of American foreign policy under the Truman administration.

. . . I am frequently asked: Has the State Department got an Asian policy? And it seems to me that that discloses such a depth of ignorance that it is very hard to begin to deal with it. The peoples of Asia are so incredibly diverse and their problems are so incredibly diverse that how could anyone, even the most utter charlatan, believe that he had a uniform policy which would deal with all of them. On the other hand, there are very important similarities in ideas and in problems among the peoples of Asia and so what we come to, after we understand these diversities and these common attitudes of mind, is the fact that there must be certain similarities of approach, and there must be very great dissimilarities in action. . . .

There is in this vast area what we might call a developing Asian consciousness, and a developing pattern, and this, I think, is based upon two factors. . . .

One of these factors is a revulsion against the acceptance of misery and poverty as the normal condition of life. Throughout all of this vast area, you have that fundamental revolutionary aspect in mind and belief. The other common aspect that they have is the revulsion against foreign domination. Whether that foreign domination takes the form of colonialism or whether it takes the form of imperialism, they are through with it. They have had enough of it, and they want no more. . . .

Now, may I suggest to you that much of the bewilderment which has seized the minds of many of us about recent developments in China comes from a failure to understand this basic revolutionary force which is loose in Asia. The reasons for the fall of the Nationalist Government in China are preoccupying many people. All sorts of reasons have been attributed to it. Most commonly, it is said in various speeches and publications that it is the result of American bungling, that we are incompetent, that we did not understand, that American aid was too little, that we did the wrong things at the wrong time. . . . Now, what I ask you to do is to stop looking for a moment under the bed and under the chair and under the rug to find out these reasons, but rather to look at the broad picture and see whether something doesn't suggest itself. . . .

* The Department of State Bulletin, XXII (January 23, 1950), 111–19.

What has happened in my judgment is that the almost inexhaustible patience of the Chinese people in their misery ended. They did not bother to overthrow this government. There was really nothing to overthrow. They simply ignored it. . . . They completely withdrew their support from this government, and when that support was withdrawn, the whole military establishment disintegrated. Added to the grossest incompetence ever experienced by any military command was this total lack of support both in the armies and in the country, and so the whole matter just simply disintegrated.

The Communists did not create this. The Communists did not create this condition. They did not create this revolutionary spirit. They did not create a great force which moved out from under Chiang Kai-shek. But they were shrewd and cunning to mount it, to ride this thing into victory and into power. . . .

Now, let me come to another underlying and important factor which determines our relations and, in turn, our policy with the peoples of Asia. That is the attitude of the Soviet Union toward Asia, and particularly towards those parts of Asia which are contiguous to the Soviet Union, and with great particularity this afternoon, to north China.

The attitude and interest of the Russians in north China, and in these other areas as well, long antedates communism. This is not something that has come out of communism at all. It long antedates it. But the Communist regime has added new methods, new skills, and new concepts to the thrust of Russian imperialism. This Communistic concept and techniques have armed Russian imperialism with a new and most insidious weapon of penetration. Armed with these new powers, what is happening in China is that the Soviet Union is detaching the northern provinces [areas] of China from China and is attaching them to the Soviet Union. This process is complete in outer Mongolia. It is nearly complete in Manchuria, and I am sure that in inner Mongolia and in Sinkiang there are very happy reports coming from Soviet agents to Moscow. This is what is going on. It is the detachment of these whole areas, vast areas—populated by Chinese—the detachment of these areas from China and their attachment to the Soviet Union.

I wish to state this and perhaps sin against my doctrine of nondogmatism, but I should like to suggest at any rate that this fact that the Soviet Union is taking the four northern provinces of China is the single most significant, most important fact, in the relation of any foreign power with Asia.

What does that mean for us? It means something very, very significant. It means that nothing that we do and nothing that we say must be allowed to obscure the reality of this fact. All the efforts of propaganda will not be able to obscure it. The only thing that can obscure it is the folly of ill-conceived adventures on our part which easily could do so, and I urge all who are thinking about these foolish adventures to remember that we must not seize the unenviable position which the Russians have carved out for themselves. We must not undertake to deflect from the Russians to ourselves the righteous anger, and the wrath, and the hatred of the Chinese people which must develop. It would be folly to deflect it to ourselves. We must take the position we have always taken —that anyone who violates the integrity of China is the enemy of China and is acting contrary to our own interest. That, I suggest to you this afternoon, is the first and the greatest rule in regard to the formulation of American policy toward Asia.

I suggest that the second rule is very like the first. That is to keep our own purposes perfectly straight, perfectly pure, and perfectly aboveboard and do not get them mixed-up with legal quibbles or the attempt to do one thing and really achieve another. . . .

What is the situation in regard to the military security of the Pacific area, and what is our policy in regard to it?

In the first place, the defeat and the disarmament of Japan has placed upon the United States the necessity of assuming the military defense of Japan so long as that is required, both in the interest of our security and in the interests of the security of the entire Pacific area and, in all honor, in the interest of Japanese security. We have American—and there are Australian—troops in Japan. I am not in a position to speak for the Australians, but I can assure you that there is no intention of any sort of abandoning or weakening the defenses of Japan and that whatever arrangements are to be made either through permanent settlement or otherwise, that defense must and shall be maintained.

The defensive perimeter runs along the Aleutians to Japan and then goes to the Ryukyus. We hold important defense positions in the Ryukyu Islands, and those we will continue to hold. In the interest of the population of the Ryukyu Islands, we will at an appropriate time offer to hold these islands under trusteeship of the United Nations. But they are essential parts of the defensive perimeter of the Pacific, and they must and will be held.

The defensive perimeter runs from the Ryukyus to the Philippine Islands. Our relations, our defensive relations with the Philippines are contained in agreements between us. Those agreements are being loyally carried out and will be loyally carried out. Both peoples have learned by bitter experience the vital connections between our mutual defense requirements. We are in no doubt about that, and it is hardly necessary for me to say an attack on the Philippines could not and would not be tolerated by the United States. But I hasten to add that no one perceives the imminence of any such attack.

So far as the military security of other areas in the Pacific is concerned, it must be clear that no person can guarantee these areas against military attack. But it must also be clear that such a guarantee is hardly sensible or necessary within the realm of practical relationship.

Should such an attack occur—one hesitates to say where such an armed attack could come from—the initial reliance must be on the people attacked to resist it and then upon the commitments of the entire civilized world under the Charter of the United Nations which so far has not proved a weak reed to lean on by any people who are determined to protect their independence against outside aggression. But it is a mistake, I think, in considering Pacific and Far Eastern problems to become obsessed with military considerations. Important as they are, there are other problems that press, and these other problems are not capable of solution through military means. These other problems arise out of the susceptibility of many areas, and many countries in the Pacific area, to subversion and penetration. That cannot be stopped by military means.

The susceptibility to penetration arises because in many areas there are new governments which have little experience in governmental administration and have not become firmly established or perhaps firmly accepted in their countries. They grow, in part, from very serious economic problems. . . . In part this susceptibility to penetration comes from the great social upheaval about which I have been speaking. . . .

So after this survey, what we conclude, I believe, is that there is a new day which has dawned in Asia. It is a day in which the Asian peoples are on their own, and know it, and intend to continue on their own. It is a day in which the old relationships between east and west are gone, relationships which at their worst were exploitations, and which at their best were paternalism. That relationship is over, and the relationship of east and west must now be in the Far East one of mutual respect and mutual helpfulness. We are their friends. Others are their friends. We and those others are willing to help, but we can help only where we are wanted and only where the conditions of help are really sensible and possible. So what we can see is that this new day in Asia, this new day which is dawning, may go on to a glorious noon or it may darken and it may drizzle out. But that decision lies within the countries of Asia and within the power of the Asian people. It is not a decision which a friend or even an enemy from the outside can decide for them.

## 13 | The Nature of Revolt in Asia, October 1951 *

Edgar Ansel Mowrer in the following article posed the central question suggested by the upheaval in Asia: What is it that the peoples of Asia really want? His conclusions conform to the general pattern of analysis to be found in the post-war writings on the Far East. He cited such factors creating pressure on the older *status quo* as the desire for food and land and freedom from the West. He believed, however, that far more fundamental was the Asian revolt against inequality of status.

In a world in ferment, Asia is bubbling most furiously. From the Suez Canal and Iran to Indonesia and the Philippines, what was once the Imperturbable

* Edgar Ansel Mowrer, "What Asia Wants," *Harper's Magazine*, CCIII (October 1951), 67–72. Copyright 1951 by Harper & Brothers. Reprinted by permission of Monica McCall.

Orient now comprises most of the trouble spots of the planet. Violent emotional forces are at work: on that, all observers agree. We Americans should understand them in order to be able to discharge intelligently our vast world responsibilities: that, too, has become a truism. The trouble is that we have great difficulty in comprehending just what these emotional forces are that bring about the malaise of Asia, and the diagnosticians notoriously disagree.

Some trace the trouble primarily to Japan, arguing that the Japanese, with their wartime demonstration that Asians, under favorable circumstances, could defeat the invincible West, and with their Eastern Monroe Doctrine, "Asia for the Asians," started a movement that is now out of control.

Others trace it primarily to Moscow. According to their theory, the ferment in Asia is wholly the result of the Communist crusade. Master minds in the Kremlin, these people claim, have been able, by a mixture of force and fraud, to stir up the vast swarming caldrons of the East and bring some of them to a boil. . . .

Whatever the explanation, the "revolt of Asia" is a fact. Furthermore, this revolt is so formidable that if Moscow succeeds in capturing it, Asia may tip the world balance of power against freedom.

Asia's choice between communism and freedom is, however, not going to be made in a vacuum. Unless the continent is forcibly taken over piecemeal by alien Communist armies, its choice may well depend upon how the West reacts to its revolt—whether with sympathy or with hostility. Moscow advocates the liberation of all colonial peoples (save those within the U.S.S.R.). To match this, the Western peoples have as yet developed no common program or policy toward the new Asia. Until they do, their divided efforts may well cancel out, as they have come tragically close to doing in China.

It is my conviction that Westerners cannot work together until they agree on what it is that the peoples of Asia really want. . . .

Is this revolt—as so many Americans are saying—a revolt against hunger? Not primarily. There is appalling hunger in Asia, permanent hunger of a kind most Americans have never seen. Hundreds of millions of Asians would like to eat oftener and more. Moreover, they have begun to suspect that such a great dream is—or ought to be—possible. Communists and other reformers are using the fact of hunger to transform latent discontent into active rebellion. But in most places they have not succeeded—for the simple reason that most Asians are not yet revolting against underfeeding. If they were, popular discontent would be greatest where hunger is greatest, and least where there is little or no famine.

It is not so. Among the chief foci of rebellion in Asia are Burma and the island of Java, two places where hunger is virtually unknown. . . .

In sober truth, most Asians look upon famine fatalistically. Hunger and premature death disturb them far less than they do Westerners.

Is Asia's revolt directed against "economic exploitation"? Communists and their friends like to think so. Economic-minded Westerners tend to go along. And they all greatly exaggerate.

There is, to be sure, a great deal of vocal protest against "exploitation" almost everywhere. Nobody can deny that one of the best cards the Communists have had has been their promise of "land reform." By this they mean killing landlords and dividing their land without recompense among "deserving"—*i.e.*, pro-Communist—peasants. Obviously such gifts appeal to landless farmers. In China this propaganda unquestionably helped Mao Tse-tung and his friends to get control. A similar land hunger is behind the revolt of the Huks in Central Luzon. It accounts, too, for much of the pro-Communist feeling in the Red River Delta of Viet-Nam where people are overcrowded and hungry.

But actually, in most of Asia the desire for land reform has failed to become overwhelming. Perhaps it is because the peasants—unlike many of the outraged foreigners—realize that with so little land to divide among so many people, mere division of the estates would not solve their problem. I am inclined to attribute it to something else: to the fact that few peasants can imagine a condition, even an improved condition, which they have not seen. Asia still takes its poverty—in land and in everything else—more or less for granted. . . .

Should we then conclude that Asia is in rebellion against the West? Robert Payne says so. In *The Revolt of Asia* he claims that "the world is now clearly divided in to two—Asia and the West."

This explanation does not accurately fit the facts.

To be sure, Asian newspapers and radios systematically blame the Occident for everything the editors and speakers do not like in the world. Uncle Sam, in particular, has become southern Asia's "whipping boy." Great masses of Asians take it for granted—as we observed when the American Congress hesitated to send "neutral" India two million tons of American grain—that the West *owes* them amends for former mistreatment.

Yet no Asian non-Communist leader—not even Mossadegh of Iran—is basically anti-Western. America is widely admired and even liked, even when specific American acts or policies are being blamed. In Burma, for a time, the name of America was synonymous with racial oppression; today, the United States enjoys the particular trust of the Burmese leaders.

As for the Indonesians, their resentment against America seems to be based on nothing more serious than a refusal to forgive the United States for having helped Indonesia to become independent!

In other words, resentment against the West seems to exist in Asia to the precise extent that the West can still be pictured as the headquarters of Western imperialism. Westerners as such are not hated. Throughout non-Communist Asia they are received not only with traditional hospitality but with friendship. . . .

Filipinos generally approve the presence of American soldiers in their country; and Iraqis, Jordanians, Pakistanis, and Burmese are relying upon their former British rulers for various sorts of assistance.

Chief of State Bao Dai and Prime Minister Tran Van Huu, both of Viet-Nam (the largest part of former Indochina), seem almost pathologically fearful lest France violate its promise of full independence. Yet once they are fully reassured, they will, in my judgment, increasingly solicit French advice and make public show of their French education. Meanwhile, they are counting heavily upon French military forces (and American supplies) to save them from being taken over by the Soviet puppet, Ho Chi Minh. . . .

In short, the villain of our time in Asian eyes is not interference with the lives and destinies of other peoples, but interference *by Western colonial powers.*

We approach an answer to our question: Against what is Asia revolting? Asia, I believe, is revolting against *inequality of status*—revolting in the name, not of dialectical materialism, but of human dignity.

This revolt becomes economic wherever an economic fact is seen as discriminatory. It does not entail the claim of each people to live as well as all other peoples but to have a chance to; it need not entail the right of an individual to high wages, or even, so far, to enough to eat. It does include the right to own and operate their own means of production, and the right to earn the same wages as any other fellow doing the same job in the same place receives, or would receive.

Asia's revolt becomes political when a people or an individual is denied equal rights because of some alleged natural inferiority. Thus Iran stands on the same right to nationalize industry as Socialist Britain. Egypt feels it is as justified in controlling the Suez Canal as the United States is in controlling the Panama Canal—indeed, more justified, for the Suez Canal cuts Egyptian territory. . . .

The acute national sensitivity of recently emancipated states like Indonesia, Burma, India, and Pakistan is a perfect example of craving for equality. In fact, the government of Indonesia recently went so far as to protest against having to receive any notes at all from foreign governments on the ground that they violated its sovereignty! . . .

Insistence upon an equality which they have failed to sustain in battle is feeding the ferments in Iraq, Syria, Lebanon, and Egypt. The defeat administered to their joint armies by little Israel was a psychological shock to the Arab rulers. Hence Egypt's desire to break the existing treaty with Great Britain and annex the Anglo-Egyptian Sudan. Hence the assassination of no less than three successive Syrian premiers in a year! Hence Iraq's convulsive expulsion of its Jews, some of whose families had been dwelling there since the Captivity beside the waters of Babylon.

An almost perfect illustration of Asia's revolt against inequality has been furnished by Iran. In expropriating the Anglo-Iranian Oil Company, the Iranian leaders gambled their all. The Cabinet took a potentially suicidal course of action with the apparent approval of the vast majority of citizens.

Why? Not for profit. The Anglo-Iranian Company offered, against reasonable compensation, transfer of ownership to the Iranian state and a bigger share of the profits. Not for national security. In their defiance of Britain, in their repudiation of the World Court, in their reckless willingness to invite internal financial breakdown, the Iranians risked letting the local Communists take over.

They did so in a frantic bid for equality—as a nation and as individuals. Though they charged the company with "robbery" and the squandering of their national resources (which they lacked both the capital and the ability to exploit themselves), the real source of their anger lay deeper. It lay in the contempt for

Iran which they saw in the company's belief that it did not need to pay higher royalties. It lay in the company's failure to place a couple of Iranians on its Board of Directors and in its refusal to submit its books to the Iranian government. Above all, it lay in the habitual segregation—hence discrimination—of employees riding in company busses, one kind for "whites," another for "natives."

Many Americans are puzzled to know what makes the U.S.S.R. attractive to many Asians, attractive despite its lack of democracy, its open cruelty, and its tyrannical—if disguised—colonialism. Generally speaking, the darker peoples are not yet ready for democracy. They are more or less inured to cruelty. (Given a chance, they can be cruel themselves.) They do not see clearly the colonial structure of the Soviet Empire because the Kremlin's tyranny over its many peoples is undiscriminating and relatively equal. What attracts them to the U.S.S.R. is its promise to end political colonialism, foreign economic control, and racial discrimination—everywhere. It is Moscow's claim to have abolished discrimination at home. It is Russia's constant harping upon the theme that the United States in particular, and the Western world in general, still practice discrimination.

That, I believe, is why many Asians who are not by any means Communists look to Moscow for guidance and deliverance. They are not much impressed by its frantic screams against capitalism or economic exploitation. They are not (yet) deeply resentful of their penury and periodic famines. They have not gone very far in embracing any form of collectivism. But they feel that the U.S.S.R. is against inequality of status. . . .

## 14 | Senator Joseph McCarthy's Speech at Wheeling, West Virginia, February 12, 1950 *

This speech of Senator McCarthy not only catapulted him into the limelight of American politics but also inaugurated years of intense anti-Communist agitation within the United States. Its power rested in its very simplicity. Pointing out that the nation, despite its magnificent efforts, had not won World War II, he explained the failure, not in terms of the power revolution in European and Asian politics, but in terms of treason in the Department of State. The speech thus conveyed an illusion of omnipotence, that the United States, under loyal leadership, could always have its way.

🖋

. . . Five years after a world war has been won, men's hearts should anticipate a long peace, and men's minds should be free from the heavy weight that comes

* *Congressional Record*, 81st Congress, 2nd Sess., 1954–7.

with war. But this is not such a period—for this is not a period of peace. This is a time of the "cold war." This is a time when all the world is split into two vast, increasingly hostile camps—a time of a great armaments race. . . .

At war's end we were physically the strongest nation on earth and, at least potentially, the most powerful intellectually and morally. Ours could have been the honor of being a beacon in the desert of destruction, a shining living proof that civilization was not yet ready to destroy itself. Unfortunately, we have failed miserably and tragically to arise to the opportunity.

The reason why we find ourselves in a position of impotency is not because our only powerful potential enemy has sent men to invade our shores, but rather because of the traitorous actions of those who have been treated so well by this Nation. It has not been the less fortunate or members of minority groups who have been selling this Nation out, but rather those who have had all the benefits that the wealthiest nation on earth has had to offer—the finest homes, the finest college education, and the finest jobs in Government we can give.

This is glaringly true in the State Department. There the bright young men who are born with silver spoons in their mouths are the ones who have been the worst. . . . In my opinion the State Department, which is one of the most important government departments, is thoroughly infested with Communists.

I have in my hand 57 cases of individuals who would appear to be either card carrying members or certainly loyal to the Communist Party, but who nevertheless are still helping to shape our foreign policy.

One thing to remember in discussing the Communists in our Government is that we are not dealing with spies who get 30 pieces of silver to steal the blueprints of a new weapon. We are dealing with a far more sinister type of activity because it permits the enemy to guide and shape our policy. . . .

This brings us down to the case of one Alger Hiss who is important not as an individual any more, but rather because he is so representative of a group in the State Department. It is unnecessary to go over the sordid events showing how he sold out the Nation which had given him so much. Those are rather fresh in all of our minds.

However, it should be remembered that the facts in regard to his connection with this international Communist spy ring were made known to the then Under Secretary of State Berle 3 days after Hitler and Stalin signed the Russo-German alliance pact. At that time one Whittaker Chambers—who was also part of the spy ring—apparently decided that with Russia on Hitler's side he could no longer betray our Nation to Russia. He gave Under Secretary of State Berle—and this is all a matter of record—practically all, if not more, of the facts upon which Hiss' conviction was based.

Under Secretary Berle promptly contacted Dean Acheson and received word in return that Acheson (and I quote) "could vouch for Hiss absolutely"—at which time the matter was dropped. . . .

As you know, very recently the Secretary of State proclaimed his loyalty to a man guilty of what has always been considered as the most abominable of all crimes—of being a traitor to the people who gave him a position of great trust. The Secretary of State in attempting to justify his continued devotion to the man who sold out the Christian world to the atheistic world, referred to Christ's Sermon on the Mount as a justification and reason therefor, and the reaction of the American people to this would have made Abraham Lincoln happy.

When this pompous diplomat in striped pants, with a phony British accent, proclaimed to the American people that Christ on the Mount endorsed Communism, high treason, and betrayal of a sacred trust, the blasphemy was so great that it awakened the dormant indignation of the American people. He has lighted the spark which is resulting in a moral uprising and will end only when the whole sorry mess of twisted, warped thinkers are swept from the national scene so that we may have a new birth of national honesty and decency in Government.

## 15 | The Quest for Security: Its Impact on the State Department and Foreign Service, 1954 *

The rationale, fostered by Senator McCarthy and others, that the alleged failures in American foreign policy during the 'forties resulted from treason in high places rendered the United States Department of State and the Foreign Service especially vulnerable to accusations of disloyalty and willful error. Such attacks could only destroy the morale and effectiveness of these important federal agencies, yet few administration officials or members of Congress ever made any effort to defend them publicly. The following letter to *The New York Times,* signed by five former members of the Foreign Service—Norman Armour, Robert Woods Bliss, Joseph C. Grew, William Phillips, and G. Howland Shaw—warned that the sole emphasis on security and the maligning of officers for honest reporting in the past would have the effect of undermining the Service's contribution to the nation.

✍

Since the time when the United States assumed a significant place in international affairs, at the turn of the century, the Foreign Service has been an organization of growing importance. Today it would be impossible to exaggerate that importance, whether it is considered from the angle of the constructive influence of the United States in world affairs or from the more selfish angle of our national security.

It is to the official representatives of the United States abroad that foreign Governments and peoples have the right to look with confidence for the most

* Letter to the editor, January 14, 1954, *The New York Times,* January 17, 1954. Reprinted by permission.

authentic interpretation of American values and the American point of view, and it is upon these same representatives that the President, the Secretary of State and others engaged in formulating our foreign policy must rely for accurate information concerning persons and events abroad.

At present these demands upon the Foreign Service are more exacting than ever before; not only because the events to be reported on have become more complex, more difficult of analysis, but also—and primarily—because the emotional climate at home has made objective reporting unusually difficult.

Recently the Foreign Service has been subjected to a series of attacks from outside sources which have questioned the loyalty and the moral standards of its members. With rare exceptions the justification for these attacks has been so flimsy as to have no standing in a court of law or in the mind of any individual capable of differentiating repeated accusation from even a reasonable presumption of guilt. Nevertheless these attacks have had sinister results.

The conclusion has become inescapable, for instance, that a Foreign Service officer who reports on persons and events to the very best of his ability and who makes recommendations which at the time he conscientiously believes to be in the interest of the United States may subsequently find his loyalty and integrity challenged and may even be forced out of the service and discredited forever as a private citizen after many years of distinguished service. A premium therefore has been put upon reporting and upon recommendations which are ambiguously stated or so cautiously set forth as to be deceiving.

When any such tendency begins its insidious work it is not long before accuracy and initiative have been sacrificed to acceptability and conformity. The ultimate result is a threat to national security. In this connection the history of the Nazi and Fascist foreign services before the Second World War is pertinent.

The forces which are working for conformity from the outside are being reinforced by the present administrative set-up within the Department of State which subordinates normal personnel administration to considerations of security.

It is obvious, of course, that candidates for the Foreign Service should be carefully investigated before appointment and that their work should at all times be under the exacting scrutiny of their professional superiors. But when initial investigation attaches undue importance to such factors as even a temporary departure from conservative political and economic views, casual association with persons holding views not currently in fashion or subscription to a periodical labeled as "liberal"; when subsequent investigation is carried to the point of delaying a promotion list for a year and routine transfers from one post to another; when investigations of individual officers must be kept up to date to within ninety days; when an easy path has been opened to even the anonymous informer; and when the results of these investigations are evaluated not by persons experienced in the Foreign Service or even acquainted at first hand with conditions abroad, but by persons of quite different experience, it is relevant to inquire whether we are not laying the foundations of a Foreign Service competent to serve a totalitarian government rather than the Government of the United States as we have heretofore known it.

Fear is playing an important part in American life at the present time. As a result the self-confidence, the confidence in others, the sense of fair play and the instinct to protect the rights of the nonconformist are—temporarily, it is to be hoped—in abeyance. But it would be tragic if this fear, expressing itself in an exaggerated emphasis on security, should lead us to cripple the Foreign Service, our first line of national defense, at the very time when its effectiveness is essential to our filling the place which history has assigned to us.

— | "We have seen our public life debauched. . . ." *

George F. Kennan in the following essay, presented originally as an address at Radcliffe College in June 1954, condemned the national tendency to expect perfection of foreign policy. It was this illusion that policy need not fail, that the nation could actually have total security, that exposed so many distinguished Americans and estimable organizations, associated with past policies and decisions, to charges of serving the nation badly. To seek perfect security, Kennan warned, would result in the destruction of the considerable security which the country still enjoyed.

ß

. . . There has been much in our domestic life of these recent months that I am sure we should all like to forget; and I hope that we shall soon be permitted to forget a great deal of it. But there are certain overriding facts that ought not to pass too quickly out of our memories. We ought not to forget that we have witnessed in these recent months the spectacle of many millions of Americans unable to put in its place and to assess with any degree of balance and equanimity the time-honored and unexceptional phenomenon of foreign political activity, intrigue, and espionage in our midst—a phenomenon which no great power has ever been spared throughout the course of human history, and from which surely no other great power is immune today. Millions of our people have been unable to accept this normal burden of international leadership at its true worth—have been uncertain as to the value to be assigned to it, uncertain as to what weight to give it in comparison with other problems of our national life. And this uncertainty has given them a peculiar vulnerability—a vulnerability to being taken advantage of, to having their fears exploited, and to being stampeded into panicky, ridiculous, and dangerous attitudes, unworthy of their own national tradition, unworthy of themselves.

Under the sign of this weakness we have seen things that cannot fail to bring deepest concern to any thinking American. We have seen our public life debauched; the faith of our people in great and distinguished fellow citizens

* George F. Kennan, "The Illusion of Security," *The Atlantic,* CXCIV (August 1954), 31–4. Reprinted by permission.

systematically undermined; useful and deserving men hounded thanklessly out
of honorable careers of public service; the most subtle sort of damage done to
our intellectual life; our scholars encouraged to be cautious and unimaginative
in order to escape being "controversial," a pall of anxiety and discouragement
thrown over our entire scientific community, our libraries and forums of knowledge placed on the defensive before the inroads of self-appointed snoopers and
censors, a portion of our youth encouraged to fear ideas on the pretext of
being defended from them.

We have seen the reputations of our great private philanthropic foundations,
with their immense and unique records of contribution to the national life,
recklessly attacked; ingratitude flung in the face of the entire institution of
private benevolence. We have seen our people taught to distrust one another, to
spy, to bear tales, to behave in a manner which is in sharpest conflict with the
American tradition. We have seen our friends in other countries frustrated in
their efforts to help and support us, reduced to an embarrassed and troubled
silence before the calumnies of our enemies upon us, for they were no longer
sure whether these calumnies did not contain some measure of truth. And all of
this in the name of our protection from Communist subversion, and yet every
bit of it agreeable to Communist purposes as almost nothing else could be; and
all of it supported by people who then have the effrontery to come before us
and to say, "Show us one innocent man who has suffered." . . .

I do not mean to overrate these things. I have no doubt that in its superficial
aspects all of this will pass—probably already passing. The names, the idols, the
scapegoats, the stereotypes, the abused words, and the perverted symbols—I have
no doubt that these will all soon disappear, to join the records of the Know-
Nothing movement and the chauvinistic hysteria of 1919 in the unhappier annals
of our public life.

But I think we cannot comfort ourselves too much with this reflection. These
things have happened. We have reacted this way, on this occasion. There must
have been a reason for our doing so. Have we found that reason and learned
from it? Are we going to be better armed to understand the next danger—to
resist the next attempt by the unscrupulous to mobilize us against ourselves
under the banner of our fears?

The causes of these phenomena have undoubtedly been many, and deep, and
complex. One cannot attempt to recount them or to analyze them in the few
brief moments we have at our disposal this morning. But among these possible
causes there is one I should like particularly to mention as perhaps worth your
attention at this time.

In the case of each of these disturbing situations I have spoken of, I wonder
whether an appreciable portion of our difficulty has not been a certain philosophic error to which we twentieth-century Americans, for one reason or another,
are prone. I am referring here to that peculiar form of American extremism
which holds it possible that there should be such a thing as total security, and
attaches overriding importance to the quest for it. A great deal of the impatience
that underlies the growing despair in some quarters over the prospects for

coping with world Communism by means short of large-scale violence seems to me to flow precisely from the illusion, no doubt bred by our nineteenth-century experinece, that there could and should be such a thing as total military security for the United States, and that anything short of this is in the long run intolerable. And similarly, these frenzies many of us seem to have developed with respect to the problem of internal subversion—do they not reflect a belief that it should be possible for a great power to free itself completely from the entire problem of penetration and intrigue in its life by outside forces and, again, that it is intolerable that this should not be done; so intolerable, in fact, that if it is not done, this must be attributed to some stubborn delinquency, if not treason, in the bowels of our public establishment? . . .

There is something about this quest for absolute security that is self-defeating. It is an exercise which, like every form of perfectionism, undermines and destroys its own basic purpose. The French have their wonderful proverb: *Le mieux est l'ennemi du bien*—the absolute best is the enemy of the good. Nothing truer has ever been said. A foreign policy aimed at the achievement of total security is the one thing I can think of that is entirely capable of bringing this country to a point where it will have no security at all. And a ruthless, reckless insistence on attempting to stamp out everything that could conceivably constitute a reflection of improper foreign influence in our national life, regardless of the actual damage it is doing or the cost of eliminating it, in terms of other American values, is the one thing I can think of that could reduce us all to a point where the very independence we are seeking to defend would be meaningless, for we would be doing things to ourselves as vicious and tyrannical as any that might be brought to us from outside.

This sort of extremism seems to me to hold particular danger for a democracy, because it creates a curious area between what is *held* to be possible and what *is* really possible—an area within which government can always be plausibly shown to have been most dangerously delinquent in the performance of its tasks. And this area, where government is always deficient, provides the ideal field of opportunity for every sort of demagoguery and mischief-making. It constitutes a terrible breach in the dike of our national morale, through which forces of doubt and suspicion never cease to find entry. The heart of our problem, here, lies in our assessment of the relative importance of the various dangers among which we move; and until many of our people can be brought to understand that what we have to do is not to secure a total absence of danger but to balance peril against peril and to find the tolerable degree of each, we shall not wholly emerge from these confusions.

Now I renounced, at the outset of these remarks, any intention of peddling personal advice. But perhaps I may be permitted, in conclusion, to observe that these reflections are not without their relevance to the problems of the human individual.

In this personal existence of ours, bounded as it is at both ends by suffering and uncertainty, and constantly attended by the possibility of illness and accident and tragedy, total security is likewise a myth. Here, too, an anxious perfectionism can operate to destroy those real underpinnings of existence, founded in faith, modesty, humor, and a sense of relativity, on which alone a tolerable human existence can be built. The first criterion of a healthy spirit is the ability to walk cheerfully and sensibly amid the congenital uncertainties of existence, to recognize as natural the inevitable precariousness of the human condition, to accept this without being disoriented by it, and to live effectively and usefully in its shadow.

In welcoming you, then—as it is my privilege this morning to do—into the fellowship and responsibility of maturity, let me express the hope that in each of your lives, as individuals and as citizens, *le bien* may be permitted to triumph over its ancient and implacable enemy *le mieux*. And if any of your friends come to you with the message that the problems of public life have become intolerable and require some immediate and total solution, I think you might do well to bear in mind the reply which a distinguished European statesman, Bismarck, once gave to certain of his more impatient and perfectionist contemporaries, who wanted him to solve all his country's problems right away, and entirely. "Let us leave just a few tasks," Bismarck suggested, "for our children to perform; they might be so bored in this world, if they had nothing to do."

## 16 | Truman's Defense of American Policy in the Korean War, April 11, 1951 *

In this address to the nation President Truman repeated the official estimate of the war—that it was part of a greater plan for the Communist conquest of all Asia. In Korea, the President continued, the United States was teaching the Communists that aggression was not cheap or easy. Thus the American effort was defending not only Korea but also the rest of Asia. It was to avoid a general war, however, that the United States refused to bomb Manchuria and China itself. Because General MacArthur disagreed with this policy of limited war, the President, as he explained to the nation, had been forced to relieve him of his command.

⤬

. . . The Communists in the Kremlin are engaged in a monstrous conspiracy to stamp out freedom all over the world. If they were to succeed, the United States would be numbered among their principal victims. It must be clear to everyone that the United States cannot—and will not—sit idly by and await foreign conquest. The only question is: When is the best time to meet the threat and how?

* *The Department of State Bulletin,* XXIV (April 16, 1951), 603-5.

The best time to meet the threat is in the beginning. It is easier to put out a fire in the beginning when it is small than after it has become a roaring blaze.

And the best way to meet the threat of aggression is for the peace-loving nations to act together. If they don't act together, they are likely to be picked off, one by one. . . .

If history has taught us anything, it is that aggression anywhere in the world is a threat to peace everywhere in the world. When that aggression is supported by the cruel and selfish rulers of a powerful nation who are bent on conquest, it becomes a clear and present danger to the security and independence of every free nation.

This is a lesson that most people in this country have learned thoroughly. This is the basic reason why we joined in creating the United Nations. And since the end of World War II we have been putting that lesson into practice— we have been working with other free nations to check the aggressive designs of the Soviet Union before they can result in a third world war. . . .

The aggression against Korea is the boldest and most dangerous move the Communists have yet made.

The attack on Korea was part of a greater plan for conquering all of Asia.

I would like to read to you from a secret intelligence report which came to us after the attack. It is a report of a speech a Communist army officer in North Korea gave to a group of spies and saboteurs last May, one month before South Korea was invaded. The report shows in great detail how this invasion was part of a carefully prepared plot. Here is part of what the Communist officer, who had been trained in Moscow, told his men: "Our forces," he said, "are scheduled to attack South Korean forces about the middle of June. . . . The coming attack on South Korea marks the first step toward the liberation of Asia."

Notice that he used the word "liberation." That is Communist double-talk meaning "conquest."

I have another secret intelligence report here. This one tells what another Communist officer in the Far East told his men several months before the invasion of Korea. Here is what he said: "In order to succesfully undertake the long awaited world revolution, we must first unify Asia. . . . Java, Indochina, Malaya, India, Tibet, Thailand, Philippines, and Japan are our ultimate targets. . . . The United States is the only obstacle on our road for the liberation of all countries in southeast Asia. In other words, we must unify the people of Asia and crush the United States."

That is what the Communist leaders are telling their people, and that is what they have been trying to do. . . .

The question we have had to face is whether the Communist plan of conquest can be stopped without general war. Our Government and other countries associated with us in the United Nations believe that the best chance of stopping it without general war is to meet the attack in Korea and defeat it there.

That is what we have been doing. It is a difficult and bitter task. But so far it has been successful.

So far, we have prevented World War III.

So far, by fighting a limited war in Korea, we have prevented aggression from succeeding and bringing on a general war. And the ability of the whole free world to resist Communist aggression has been greatly improved.

We have taught the enemy a lesson. He has found out that aggression is not cheap or easy. Moreover, men all over the world who want to remain free have been given new courage and new hope. They know now that the champions of freedom can stand up and fight and that they will stand up and fight.

Our resolute stand in Korea is helping the forces of freedom now fighting in Indochina and other countries in that part of the world. It has already slowed down the timetable of conquest.

In Korea itself, there are signs that the enemy is building up his ground forces for a new mass offensive. We also know that there have been large increases in the enemy's available air forces.

If a new attack comes, I feel confident it will be turned back. The United Nations fighting forces are tough and able and well equipped. They are fighting for a just cause. They are proving to all the world that the principle of collective security will work. We are proud of all these forces for the magnificent job they have done against heavy odds. We pray that their efforts may succeed, for upon their success may hinge the peace of the world.

The Communist side must now choose its course of action. The Communist rulers may press the attack against us. They may take further action which will spread the conflict. They have that choice, and with it the awful responsibility for what may follow. The Communists also have the choice of a peaceful settlement which could lead to a general relaxation of tensions in the Far East. The decision is theirs, because the forces of the United Nations will strive to limit the conflict if possible.

We do not want to see the conflict in Korea extended. We are trying to prevent a world war—not to start one. The best way to do that is to make it plain that we and the other free countries will continue to resist the attack.

But you may ask: Why can't we take other steps to punish the aggressor? Why don't we bomb Manchuria and China itself? Why don't we assist Chinese Nationalist troops to land on the mainland of China?

If we were to do these things we would be running a very grave risk of starting a general war. If that were to happen, we would have brought about the exact situation we are trying to prevent.

If we were to do these things, we would become entangled in a vast conflict on the continent of Asia and our task would become immeasurably more difficult all over the world.

What would suit the ambitions of the Kremlin better than for our military forces to be committed to a full-scale war with Red China?

It may well be that, in spite of our best efforts, the Communists may spread the war. But it would be wrong—tragically wrong—for us to take the initiative in extending the war.

The dangers are great. Make no mistake about it. Behind the North Koreans and Chinese Communists in the front lines stand additional millions of Chinese soldiers. And behind the Chinese stand the tanks, the planes, the submarines, the soldiers, and the scheming rulers of the Soviet Union.

Our aim is to avoid the spread of the conflict.

The course we have been following is the one best calculated to avoid an all-out war. It is the course consistent with our obligation to do all we can to maintain international peace and security. Our experience in Greece and Berlin shows that it is the most effective course of action we can follow.

First of all, it is clear that our efforts in Korea can blunt the will of the Chinese Communists to continue the struggle. The United Nations forces have put up a tremendous fight in Korea and have inflicted very heavy casualties on the enemy. Our forces are stronger now than they have been before. These are plain facts which may discourage the Chinese Communists from continuing their attack.

Second, the free world as a whole is growing in military strength every day. In the United States, in Western Europe, and throughout the world, free men are alert to the Soviet threat and are building their defenses. This may discourage the Communist rulers from continuing the war in Korea—and from undertaking new acts of aggression elsewhere.

If the Communist authorities realize that they cannot defeat us in Korea, if they realize it would be foolhardy to widen the hostilities beyond Korea, then they may recognize the folly of continuing their aggression. A peaceful settlement may then be possible. The door is always open.

Then we may achieve a settlement in Korea which will not compromise the principles and purposes of the United Nations.

I have thought long and hard about this question of extending the war in Asia. I have discussed it many times with the ablest military advisers in the country. I believe with all my heart that the course we are following is the best course.

I believe that we must try to limit the war to Korea for these vital reasons: to make sure that the precious lives of our fighting men are not wasted; to see that the security of our country and the free world is not needlessly jeopardized; and to prevent a third world war.

A number of events have made it evident that General MacArthur did not agree with that policy. I have therefore considered it essential to relieve General MacArthur so that there would be no doubt or confusion as to the real purpose and aim of our policy.

It was with the deepest personal regret that I found myself compelled to take this action. General MacArthur is one of our greatest military commanders. But the cause of world peace is more important than an individual.

The change in commands in the Far East means no change whatever in the policy of the United States. We will carry on the fight in Korea with vigor and determination in an effort to bring the war to a speedy and successful conclusion. . . .

In the meantime, I want to be clear about our military objective. We are fighting to resist an outrageous aggression in Korea. We are trying to keep the Korean conflict from spreading to other areas. But at the same time we must conduct our military activities so as to insure the security of our forces. This is essential if they are to continue the fight until the enemy abandons its ruthless attempt to destroy the Republic of Korea.

That is our military objective—to repel attack and to restore peace.

In the hard fighting in Korea, we are proving that collective action among nations is not only a high principle but a workable means of resisting aggression. Defeat of aggression in Korea may be the turning point in the world's search for a practical way of achieving peace and security.

The struggle of the United Nations in Korea is a struggle for peace.

The free nations have united their strength in an effort to prevent a third world war.

That war can come if the Communist rulers want it to come. But this Nation and its allies will not be responsible for its coming.

We do not want to widen the conflict. We will use every effort to prevent that disaster. And in so doing we know that we are following the great principles of peace, freedom, and justice.

## 17 | General Douglas MacArthur's Address to the Congress, April 19, 1951 *

In his analysis of American commitments to the security of the Pacific area, General MacArthur pointed especially to the island chain along the littoral of Asia. He agreed with the decision to defend the American defense line by fighting in Korea. The intervention of the Chinese in November 1950, MacArthur believed, had created a new war that demanded a new strategy. The strategy that he advocated, he declared, was designed to bring victory, swiftly and completely. MacArthur's address was a forceful expression of the traditional Asia-first concept of American foreign policy.

✍

. . . I do not stand here as advocate for any partisan cause, for the issues are fundamental and reach quite beyond the realm of partisan consideration. They must be resolved on the highest plane of national interest if our course is to prove sound and our future protected. I trust, therefore, that you will do me the justice of receiving that which I have to say as solely expressing the considered viewpoint of a fellow American. I address you with neither rancor nor bitterness in the fading twilight of life with but one purpose in mind, to serve my country.

* *Congressional Record*, 82nd Congress, 1st Sess., 4123–5.

The issues are global and so interlocked that to consider the problems of one sector oblivious to those of another is but to court disaster for the whole.

While Asia is commonly referred to as the gateway to Euorpe, it is no less true that Europe is the gateway to Asia, and the broad influence of the one cannot fail to have its impact upon the other.

There are those who claim our strength is inadequate to protect on both fronts, that we cannot divide our effort. I can think of no greater expression of defeatism. If a potential enemy can divide his strength on two fronts, it is for us to counter his effort.

The Communist threat is a global one. Its successful advance in one sector threatens the destruction of every other sector. You cannot appease or otherwise surrender to communism in Asia without simultaneously undermining our efforts to halt its advance in Europe.

Beyond pointing out these general truisms, I shall confine my discussion to the general areas of Asia. Before one may objectively assess the situation now existing there, he must comprehend something of Asia's past and the revolutionary changes which have marked her course up to the present. Long exploited by the so-called colonial powers, with little opportunity to achieve any degree of social justice, individual dignity, or a higher standard of life such as guided our own noble administration of the Philippines, the peoples of Asia found their opportunity in the war just past to throw off the shackles of colonialism and now see the dawn of new opportunity and heretofore unfelt dignity and the self-respect of political freedom.

Mustering half of the earth's population and 60 percent of its natural resources these peoples are rapidly consolidating a new force, both moral and material, with which to raise the living standard and erect adaptations of the design of modern progress to their own distinct cultural environments. Whether one adheres to the concept of colonialization or not, this is the direction of Asian progress and it may not be stopped. It is a corollary to the shift of the world economic frontiers, as the whole epi-center of world affairs rotates back toward the area whence it started. In this situation it becomes vital that our own country orient its policies in consonance with this basic evolutonary condition rather than pursue a course blind to the reality that the colonial era is now past and the Asian peoples covet the right to shape their own free destiny. What they seek now is friendly guidance, understanding, and support, not imperious direction; the dignity of equality, not the shame of subjugation. Their prewar standard of life, pitifully low, is infinitely lower now in the devastation left in war's wake. World ideologies play little part in Asian thinking and are little understood. What the peoples strive for is the opportunity for a little more food in their stomachs, a little better clothing on their backs, a little firmer roof over their heads, and the realization of a normal nationalist urge for political freedom. These political-social conditions have but an indirect bearing upon our own national security, but do form a backdrop to contemporary planning which must be thoughtfully considered if we are to avoid the pitfalls of unrealism.

Of more direct and immediate bearing upon our national security are the changes wrought in the strategic potential of the Pacific Ocean in the course of the past war. Prior thereto, the western strategic frontier of the United States lay on the littoral line of the Americas with an exposed island salient extending out through Hawaii, Midway, and Guam to the Philippines. That salient proved not an outpost of strength but an avenue of weakness along which the enemy could and did attack. The Pacific was a potential area of advance for any predatory force intent upon striking at the bordering land areas.

All this was changed by our Pacific victory. Our strategic frontier then shifted to embrace the entire Pacific Ocean which became a vast moat to protect us as long as we held it. Indeed, it acts as a protective shield for all of the Americas and all free lands of the Pacific Ocean area. We control it to the shores of Asia by a chain of islands extending in an arc from the Aleutians to the Marianas held by us and our free allies.

From this island chain we can dominate with sea and air power every Asiatic port from Vladivostok to Singapore and prevent any hostile movement into the Pacific. Any predatory attack from Asia must be an amphibious effort. No amphibious force can be successful without control of the sea lanes and the air over those lanes in its avenue of advance. With naval and air supremacy and modest ground elements to defend bases, any major attack from continental Asia toward us or our friends of the Pacific would be doomed to failure. Under such conditions the Pacific no longer represents menacing avenues of approach for a prospective invader—it assumes instead the friendly aspect of a peaceful lake. Our line of defense is a natural one and can be maintained with a minimum of military effort and expense. It envisions no attack against anyone nor does it provide the bastions essential for offensive operations, but properly maintained would be invincible defense against aggression.

The holding of this littoral defense line in the western Pacific is entirely dependent upon holding all segments thereof, for any major breach of that line by an unfriendly power would render vulnerable to determined attack every other major segment. This is a military estimate as to which I have yet to find a military leader who will take exception.

For that reason I have strongly recommended in the past as a matter of military urgency that under no circumstances must Formosa fall under Communist control.

Such an eventuality would at once threaten the freedom of the Philippines and the loss of Japan, and might well force our western frontier back to the coasts of California, Oregon, and Washington. . . .

On Formosa, the Government of the Republic of China has had the opportunity to refute by action much of the malicious gossip which so undermined the strength of its leadership on the Chinese mainland.

The Formosan people are receiving a just and enlightened administration with majority representation on the organs of government; and politically, economically, and socially appear to be advancing along sound and constructive lines.

With this brief insight into the surrounding areas I now turn to the Korean conflict. While I was not consulted prior to the President's decision to intervene in the support of the Republic of Korea, that decision from a military stand-point proved a sound one. As I say, a brief and sound one as we hurled back the invaders and decimated his forces. Our victory was complete and our objectives within reach when Red China intervened with numerically superior ground forces. This created a new war and an entirely new situation, a situation not contemplated when our forces were committed against the North Korean invaders, a situation which called for new decisions in the diplomatic sphere to permit the realistic adjustment of military strategy. Such decisions have not been forthcoming.

While no man in his right mind would advocate sending our ground forces into continental China—and such was never given a thought—the new situation did urgently demand a drastic revision of strategic planning if our political aim was to defeat this new enemy as we had defeated the old.

Apart from the military need as I saw it to neutralize sanctuary, protection given to the enemy north of the Yalu, I felt that military necessity in the conduct of the war made necessary:

First, the intensification of our economic blockade against China.

Second, the imposition of a naval blockade against the China coast.

Third, removal of restrictions on air reconnaissance of China's coastal areas and of Manchuria.

Fourth, removal of restrictions on the forces of the Republic of China on Formosa with logistical support to contribute to their effective operation against the Chinese mainland.

For entertaining these views all professionally designed to support our forces committed to Korea and bring hostilities to an end with the least possible delay and at a saving of countless American and Allied lives, I have been severely criticized in lay circles, principally abroad, despite my understanding that from a military standpoint the above views have been fully shared in the past by practically every military leader concerned with the Korean campaign, including our own Joint Chiefs of Staff.

I called for reinforcements, but was informed that reinforcements were not available. I made clear that if not permitted to utilize the friendly Chinese force of some 600,000 men on Formosa; if not permitted to blockade the China coast to prevent the Chinese Reds from getting succor from without; and if there were to be no hope of major reinforcements, the position of the command from the military standpoint forbade victory. We could hold in Korea by constant maneuver and at an approximate area where our supply advantages were in balance with the supply line disadvantages of the enemy, but we could hope at best for only an indecisive campaign, with its terrible and constant attrition upon our forces if the enemy utilized his full military potential. I have constantly called for the new political decisions essential to a solution. Efforts have been made to distort my position. It has been said in effect that I was a warmonger. Nothing could be further from the truth. I know war as few other men now living know it, and nothing to me is more revolting. . . .

But once war is forced upon us, there is no other alternative than to apply every available means to bring it to a swift end. War's very object is victory—

not prolonged indecision. In war, indeed, there can be no substitute for victory.

There are some who for varying reasons would appease Red China. They are blind to history's clear lesson. For history teaches with unmistakable emphasis that appeasement but begets new and bloodier war. It points to no single instance where the end has justified that means—where appeasement has led to more than a sham peace. Like blackmail, it lays the basis for new and successively greater demands, until, as in blackmail, violence becomes the only other alternative. Why, my soldiers asked of me, surrender military advantages to an enemy in the field? I could not answer. Some may say to avoid spread of the conflict into an all-out war with China; others, to avoid Soviet intervention. Neither explanation seems valid. For China is already engaging with the maximum power it can commit and the Soviet will not necessarily mesh its actions with our moves. Like a cobra, any new enemy will more likely strike whenever it feels that the relativity in military or other potential is in its favor on a world-wide basis.

The tragedy of Korea is further heightened by the fact that as military action is confined to its territorial limits, it condemns that nation, which it is our purpose to save, to suffer the devastating impact of full naval and air bombardment, while the enemy's sanctuaries are fully protected from such attack and devastation. Of the nations of the world, Korea alone, up to now, is the sole one which has risked its all against communism. The magnificence of the courage and fortitude of the Korean people defies description. They have chosen to risk death rather than slavery. Their last words to me were "Don't scuttle the Pacific."

I have just left your fighting sons in Korea. They have met all tests there and I can report to you without reservation they are splendid in every way. It was my constant effort to preserve them and end this savage conflict honorably and with the least loss of time and a minimum sacrifice of life. Its growing bloodshed has caused me the deepest anguish and anxiety. Those gallant men will remain often in my thoughts and in my prayers always.

I am closing my 52 years of military service. When I joined the Army even before the turn of the century, it was the fulfillment of all my boyish hopes and dreams. The world has turned over many times since I took the oath on the plain at West Point, and the hopes and dreams have long since vanished. But I since remember the refrain of one of the most popular barrack ballads of that day which proclaimed most proudly that—

"Old soldiers never die; they just fade away." And like the old soldier of that ballad, I now close my military career and just fade away—an old soldier who tried to do his duty as God gave him the light to see that duty.

Good-by.

# XII

## Policy for a Changing World

Containment, whatever the conservatism of its original proponents, evolved into a program of grandiose expectations. The initial military response to Soviet belligerence assumed a direct military threat to the political independence of Western Europe. But the very magnitude and diversity of the Soviet challenge, which appeared to endanger not only Western security but also Western values, rapidly transformed the American mission from one of stabilizing a divided Europe to one of combating Communist tyranny wherever it existed. Nor did this mission seem to exceed Western capabilities. After 1947 it was generally acknowledged by Western leaders that the great democracies, with their capacity to outperform the U.S.S.R. in industrial production, could, through successful containment alone, give the inconsistencies within Russia time to undermine the Soviet structure. Thus merely by preventing further Soviet expansion the policies of the United States would consign communism to eventual oblivion.

Unfortunately, the high hopes of containment slowly disintegrated under the continued search for military supremacy which always seemed to elude the nation. Nor was it certain that any Western military establishment could achieve a universal triumph over Soviet tyranny without war. Perhaps not even war would free the satellites, for the resulting destruction would leave little worth liberating. The United States quickly demonstrated its capacity to maintain the *status quo* in Europe; it did not demonstrate the power to alter it appreciably. Containment, with its military equivalent of stalemate, guaranteed only the continued division of Germany and Korea. But the persistent failure of the nation to dismantle the Soviet empire did not reduce the ends of policy; it merely sent men in frantic search for other, more effective, means to close the gap between the goal of ultimate victory and the experience of limited success.

Those who sought the means whereby American policies might be brought into conformity with established national objectives found them in various forms of psychological warfare. This strategy became the foundation of the policy of boldness that sought to bring liberation to those behind the Iron Curtain and to undermine the Soviet structure through the employment of the rhetoric of freedom. Upholding such methods of psychological warfare, Representative O. K. Armstrong of Missouri declared in February 1952: "Let us realize this great and fundamental truth: That the struggle against communism is the struggle for minds and hearts of mankind. It cannot be won by bombs and guns alone. The strongest weapon that we hold in our hands is truth itself." (*Reading No. 1.*) This strategy conformed to the deep-seated tendency to attribute everything dangerous in a sharply divided world to Soviet ideology, not Soviet power. If the essential contest between the United States and the U.S.S.R. were for the hearts and minds of mankind, then the danger represented no more than a body of ideas. Countering policy, therefore, largely demanded competing thoughts and words, not competing economic and military strength. This explained why those who accepted the new policy of boldness never placed any burden on the national budget.

This burgeoning crusade to undermine Russia's Communist structure and commit the United States to a permanent intervention wherever communism appeared as a military or political factor found its authentic spokesman in John Foster Dulles. More than any other American diplomatist, he possessed both a deep sense of the importance of moral force in international affairs and a supreme confidence in the ultimate triumph of principle. Dulles, who was to become United States Secretary of State in January 1953, entered office from an experience and a family background that seemed to render his appointment inevitable. His grandfather, John W. Foster, and an uncle, Robert Lansing, had been secretaries of state. Dulles's own diplomatic career began as early as 1907, when he served as his grandfather's secretary at the Second Hague Conference. At the close of World War I he was appointed counsel to the American peace commission. He returned to official life in 1945 as a member of the American delegation to the San Francisco Conference and thereafter served the Truman administration repeatedly as a foreign policy adviser. In 1950–51, with the rank of ambassador, he negotiated the peace treaty with Japan as well as the mutual security treaties with the Philippines, Australia, New Zealand, and Japan. Already in the campaigns of 1944 and 1948 he had established himself as Thomas E. Dewey's probable choice for secretary of state.

Detecting the political possibilities in an Eisenhower nomination, he suddenly resigned his position in the government in the spring of 1952. Several weeks later in his article, "A Policy of Boldness," published in *Life*, he developed the thesis that the nation possessed moral resources that could topple the Soviet imperial structure. (*Reading No. 2.*) Containment policy, he charged, was concerned less with eliminating the Soviet peril than with coexisting with it "presumably forever." The time had come to develop a *dynamic* foreign policy that conformed to *moral* principles. American policy must move beyond containment; it must anticipate the "liberation" of those who lived under compulsion behind the Iron Curtain. In the Republican platform of 1952 Dulles promised a program that would "mark the end of the negative, futile and immoral policy of 'containment' which abandons countless human beings to a despotism and Godless terrorism which in turn enables the rulers to forge the captives into a weapon for our destruction." At the time of his appointment to the cabinet in January 1953, Dulles again assured the Senate Foreign Relations Committee that his program of liberation would eventually free the Soviet satellites without war. (*Reading No. 3.*)

Countless Americans, unconcerned by habit with the essential problem of means, accepted the new goal of liberation as both reasonable and legitimate. For Dulles, the superiority of freedom over tyranny in itself assured the ultimate triumph of his principles. To him, the free world, given time, could win the cold war conclusively without great cost to itself, for the Soviet weakness lay fundamentally in the human spirit. If the United States remained strong and at the same time made its own liberty a flaming example to the world, the people under Communist oppression would sense it and demand more of it for themselves. This was the strategy of victory. The concept of liberation demanded above all that the United States shun any settlement with the Kremlin that would recognize Soviet control of alien peoples. Thus liberation in the realm of actual diplomacy varied little from that of containment, for Dulles, as Secretary, possessed no power or authority to liberate eastern Europe not available to the Truman administration.

Dulles's critics regarded his undisclosed program of liberation as so serious an overreaching of American diplomatic capabilities that it could have no meaning for the Iron Curtain countries. Adlai Stevenson, the Democratic candidate in 1952, charged during the presidential campaign that the Republican promise of liberation was nothing but a cynical bid for the eastern European vote in the United States. The London *Economist* declared on August 30, 1952: "Unhappily 'liberation' applied to Eastern Europe—and Asia—means either the risk of war or it means nothing. . . . 'Liberation' entails no risk of war only when it means nothing." In May 1953 the London *Observer* noted that the *status quo* of eastern Europe had been established by Soviet power and would not be altered through Dulles's preachments. The writer suggested that the West, rather than pursue the unachievable, come to terms with the new realities in European politics. (*Reading No. 4.*)

Eventually Dulles, to reconcile his purpose of attaining ultimate victory over communism with the Eisenhower administration's concern for tax reduction, formulated his concept of "massive retaliation." First announced as official United States policy in Dulles' New York speech of January 12, 1954, the "new look" suggested that the United States, through the threatened employment of nuclear retaliation against major enemy targets, could prevent local aggression. The resultant containment of Communist expansion everywhere at reduced cost, Dulles predicted, would produce erosion in the Soviet system and assure its total collapse. (*Reading No. 5.*) Critics charged that the new Dulles policies promised too much for too little, that they were totally inapplicable within the universally accepted context of limited war. They predicted that the danger of escalation would terrify the allies more than the enemy. (*Reading No. 6.*) So profuse were the official explanations of the new look that Walter Lippmann could write in March "that it is almost a career in itself to keep up with them."

When pressed by the Senate Committee on Foreign Relations for an explanation of the alleged innovations in American military policy, Dulles replied:

> Well, I am sorry I cannot go into that here. All I can say to you, and you will have to take it on faith, is that a series of new decisions have been taken by the National Security Council and many have been involved, close, and difficult decisions, but there is today on the record a series of decisions which are largely derived from this basic philosophy which were not there a year and a half ago.

## II

In the Far East the ultimate American purpose demanded nothing less than the return of Chiang Kai-shek to power over all China. Secretary Dulles, quite conscious of the abuse which his predecessor Dean Acheson had suffered at the hands of Chiang's friends in the United States, simply handed control of this area of foreign policy to them. After 1953 Admiral Arthur W. Radford, Chairman of the Joint Chiefs of Staff, Walter S. Robertson, Assistant Secretary of State for Far Eastern Affairs, Senator William F. Knowland of California, chief spokesman for Nationalist China in the Senate, as well as Mr. Dulles himself, perpetuated an attitude of uncompromising antagonism toward the mainland regime. However, though these men and their associates in Congress and the press possessed the power to mould public sentiment, they lacked the power to build a national policy. Their determination to remove the Peiping regime, unfortunately, had no relationship to the means at their disposal, for the simple reason that nothing short of all-out war would guarantee the fulfillment of their intentions toward China.

Too responsible to follow its Far Eastern advisers into military adventures against China, yet too fearful of public opinion to question the optimistic expectations of Chiang's return to the mainland, the Eisenhower administration adopted, in effect, a two-China policy. Unable to return Chiang to power over all China, the administration committed the nation to sustaining the Kuomintang on Formosa and to accepting the doctrine that the island's defense was essential to the security of all Asia. Meanwhile, nonrecognition of the Peiping regime permitted it both to perpetuate the illusion of Chiang's eventual triumph and to co-exist peacefully with Chiang's American friends while actually pursuing a policy of *status quo*. Nothing illustrated more clearly the emptiness of the Eisenhower administration's effort to create the impression of a new Far Eastern policy than its "unleashing" of Chiang Kai-shek in February 1953, by issuing instructions that the Seventh Fleet no longer shield the mainland. Eventually official Washington managed to transform its attitude of contempt toward Peiping into a program which, while imposing no demands on the United States other than economic and military aid for the Republic of China, promised the total destruction of Communist power in the Orient. (*Reading No. 7*.) American policy toward China, Dulles explained, was based on the assumption that "international Communism's rule of strict conformity is, in China, as elsewhere, a passing and not a perpetual phase." Through its continued recognition and support of the Kuomintang on Formosa the United States would speed that passing. To its critics, American behavior toward China lacked all the ingredients of a genuine policy. The expectation of total victory in the Far East with means limited largely to a carefully sustained attitude of contempt could hardly be accepted as serious policy at all. (*Reading No. 8.*)

But the determination to combat and defeat communism wherever it existed in Asia forced American policy into an ever-widening area of commitment. What made the threat of expanding Communist penetration into the under-developed continents appear so acute was the theory that Marxism was anti-thetical to national sovereignty, and that communism, unless destroyed, would gradually undermine all national entities in Asia and create one vast commu-nity under Communist domination. To some American officials Chinese im-perialism was merely the Asiatic agent for the new universalism. "The Soviet leaders, in mapping their strategy for world conquest," Dulles warned in No-vember 1953, "hit on nationalism as a device for absorbing the colonial peoples." The danger, continued his argument, rested in the ability of Communist agi-tators to aggravate the nationalist aspirations of people so that they would rebel violently against the existing order. Before a new stability could be created, the Communists would gain control of the nation and convey it into the Soviet orbit. So pronounced became this interpretation of pressures against the *status quo* in Asia that American policy tended to credit communism, emanating from Peiping and Moscow, rather than nationalism, with stimulating revolu-tionary action against governments friendly to the West.

Impelled by the conviction that freedom everywhere hinged on United States involvement, Washington searched for the hand of the Soviets and Chinese in every remote area of instability. Beginning with the Indochina crisis of 1954, American officials viewed every conflict along the periphery of China as a titanic struggle for mastery of the world. Convinced that all Southeast Asia was at stake in the declining French fortunes, Dulles declared before the Over-seas Press Club in New York on March 29, 1954: "Under the conditions of today the imposition on Southeast Asia of the political system of Communist Russia and its Chinese Communist ally, by whatever means, would be a grave threat to the whole free world community. The United States feels that that possibility should not be possibly accepted, but should be met by united action." Thereafter intervention was measured by the simple scale of communism vs. anti-communism. The American threat to enter the war in Indochina was not designed to rescue the French but to prevent the spread of communism in Asia. Isolated diplomatically by the British refusal to act, the United States eventually failed to secure a united front against the Communist Viet Minh. Yet so thor-oughly was the Eisenhower administration committed to preventing all Com-munist encroachment in Southeast Asia that it refused to sign the Geneva agreement of July 1954, because that document recognized the existence of the Communist state of North Vietnam.

To meet the threat of further Communist aggression in Southeast Asia, the United States government completed its Far Eastern alliance system. At Manila, in September 1954, Dulles negotiated the Southeast Asian Treaty Organization to prevent any further catastrophes such as the fall of north Indochina. SEATO, comprising the United States, England, France, Australia, New Zealand, the Philippines, Thailand, and Pakistan, agreed to act jointly against any danger to the peace in Southeast Asia to the south of Formosa. The formation of this alliance, Dulles explained, rendered the loss of Indochina insignificant. Formerly alliances faced a known enemy with complete mutuality of interest; now it mattered little how distant the allies were from the area of confrontation or how remote from world politics. Under the concept of a universal conflict between freedom and Communist tyranny alliances became meritorious in themselves. They were the assurance that other nations had joined the struggle for freedom.

After 1954 United States policies committed the nation to a state of siege around the entire Soviet-Chinese world, in regions where the combat advantage lay with the powers holding the interior lines of communication. At rare moments in the nineteenth century some editors and politicians had claimed dominance over the North American Continent and even over the hemisphere. But never before had Americans, especially those responsible for national policy, indulged in the belief that the nation possessed the competence or obligation to manage the destiny of all Asia.


### III

What characterized the postwar dichotomy in international politics was less the division of the globe into an area of freedom and an area of tyranny than the clear superiority in military power enjoyed by the United States and the U.S.S.R. This division of the world into two camps reflected specific conditions that could not endure. What held the Soviet bloc together was primarily the power of the Red Army. NATO represented a modest and historic quest of the Western world for security against an Eastern foe. Conservative Western diplomatists regarded its creation as the major triumph of democratic leadership in the postwar era. But nations do not grant to others the ultimate control of their destiny. Those compelled by circumstances to accept the protection and dominance of the two major powers when the cold war began would by the nature of national sovereignty search for roles independent of the Soviet-American conflict. As early as 1950 the tendencies in world politics began to challenge the will and the dogmas of the superpowers.

For the Kremlin it should have been clear that the Soviet Union would not transform the world into the unitary society predicted by Marx, with its headquarters in Moscow. In an uncompromising conflict of national wills, Yugoslavia in 1948 withdrew completely from the Soviet bloc. During the succeeding years the Russians failed to destroy or even weaken the nationalism of the satellite states. Not one square foot of territory could they integrate emotionally or spiritually into the Soviet empire. The East Berlin riots of 1953, followed by major uprisings in Poland and Hungary in 1956, illustrated the repressive nature and tentative character of the Soviet power structure. These events, on the other hand, demonstrated the capacity and determination of the Kremlin to maintain its hegemony over eastern Europe, whatever the attitude of the Western world. If such challenges to the Soviet monolith were the high purpose of American policy, George F. Kennan pleaded in *Harper's* of August 1956 that Washington not pour scorn and ridicule on the Kremlin because it appeared to be accepting change in defiance of its own dogma. (*Reading No. 9.*)

For Secretary Dulles the riots of 1956 were a clear vindication of his concept of liberation. On October 27 he explained to the Dallas Council on World Affairs that the spirit of patriotism and the longing of the captive peoples for freedom would "erode and finally break the iron bonds of servitude." The Secretary invited the Slavic peoples, as they now achieved their independence, to draw upon the United States for aid in adjusting their economies to serve their own needs rather than those of their exploiting masters. (*Reading No. 10.*)

Such boasts that the American-encouraged aspirations for freedom were now rending the Soviet hegemony were drowned out within a week by the crash of Soviet tanks as they slowly ground down the revolutionary forces of Budapest. Some Hungarian leaders cried out for aid, assuming that the American purpose of liberation was more than a moral preachment. They were informed, with stark realism, that any American effort to rescue them would precipitate World War III. In admitting at the moment of greatest urgency that Hungary's independence was not required by the security interests of the United States, American officials rendered the concept of liberation a mockery. Those who expected help from the West recalled in their bitterness the words of the United States delegate at the United Nations declaring that his nation would never desert the people of Hungary. American abstention in the Hungarian revolt demonstrated that even with the support of a major uprising the United States could not and would not change the 1945 line of demarcation. Yet American spokesmen continued to condemn the Soviet posture in eastern Europe, and thus hold out the promise of freedom, while they scrupulously avoided any reference to means. What the verbal adherence to liberation could achieve other than the continued disillusionment of those who took it seriously was not apparent. And yet if no one took it seriously the rhetoric of freedom had no purpose at all.

China evolved into an even greater threat to the unity of the Soviet bloc than did the eastern European satellites, for this Communist nation had never really entered the Soviet hegemony at all. China, at the moment of Communist victory in 1949, became a reluctant ally, drawn to the Soviet Union less by ideology than by a mutual animosity toward the United States and the need of Soviet technological and military aid. At no time after their triumph did the Chinese Communists reveal much more than cold civility toward the Kremlin hierarchy. To maintain some unity in the Communist camp the Chinese supported the Russian efforts to repress Poland and Hungary in 1956, but soon thereafter they embarked on a career of open defiance against both Soviet leadership and Soviet diplomacy, for the latter had grown too conservative. For the Peiping regime, leading a country still in the throes of revolution, Chinese interests lay in belligerence and external chaos. During the years after

1956 the ideological conflict, representing fundamentally a conflict in national interest, increased in pace and intensity. Everywhere the forces of history challenged the concept of a monolithic Communist structure. "From one end of the communist bloc to the other," declared Walt W. Rostow in March 1963, "nationalism and, in certain quarters, the pressure of man for higher degrees of human freedom have weakened the unity of the bloc. Every communist party in the world is trapped in a painful debate over the issues posed in the Sino-Soviet dispute."

Within the Western bloc the tug against bipolarity was even more acute. So completely did the evolution of Western Europe after 1950 destroy the original foundations of the North Atlantic alliance that its continued existence was a tribute to the vigor of its leadership and the capacity of the Kremlin to perpetuate fear and doubt. First, the Soviet achievement of a nuclear stalemate erased the significance of the earlier United States atomic monopoly as the chief source of European security. Second, Khrushchev's new policies of competitive co-existence created a new mood of confidence which modified the early postwar fears of Soviet belligerence. Third, the program of American aid transformed Western Europe by the late 'fifties into a region of enormous productivity and prosperity. If United States aid was still welcome, it was no longer required. What held the Soviet Union at bay was as much the strength of Western Europe as NATO itself.

Increasingly after the mid-'fifties the leading nations of Europe reasserted their independent roles in world politics. Charles de Gaulle, dominated by a sense of grandeur in keeping with France's imperial past, calmly defied the will of the United States and Britain on all fronts and cultivated West Germany as the chief adjunct of his new Europe. He reduced France's commitments to NATO, pursued an independent program of nuclear armament, and demanded equality with the United States and the United Kingdom in the determination of NATO policies. Early in 1963 he defied his allies completely by vetoing the British application for membership in the European Common Market. England also revealed greater independence of action, especially in East-West relations. It was Prime Minister Harold Macmillan who led the Western response to Khrushchev's ultimatum on Berlin after November 1958, filling thereby a vacuum in American leadership created partly by the illness and eventual death of John Foster Dulles, partly by the lack of genuine flexibility in established American policy vis-à-vis the Soviet bloc. For the unquestioned allegiance of West Germany to the alliance the United States refused to alter perceptibly its stand on West Berlin and German unification. That stand was reaffirmed at the Geneva meetings of the Big Four during the summer of 1959 (*Reading No. 11.*)

West Germany, bordering the Iron Curtain without either an adequate military establishment or a nuclear arsenal of its own, found its security in the American commitment to Europe more than did either Britain or France. Yet long-range missile development slowly weakened the mutual interest of the United States and its European allies in the maintenance of the European bases. Somehow the United States appeared much more reliable before it was vulnerable to nuclear attack. The burgeoning concern of European leaders with their own nuclear arsenals reflected in some measure their conviction that they required their own deterrents against Soviet aggression. To counter this tendency in European thought, President John F. Kennedy, in December 1962, proposed a multilateral NATO nuclear defense force which would have the dual effect of reassuring Western Europe of the seriousness of the United States commitment to its defense and of terminating the proliferation of nuclear-armed nations. Washington could conceive of no better program for integrating the power of West Germany into the NATO alliance system. Yet as late as December 1963 both England and France, for reasons of national interest in maintaining their own deterrents, resisted membership in such a multinational and mixed-manned nuclear defense force.

## IV

Somehow the promised victory over the Kremlin proved illusive. The U.S.S.R. did not collapse. In his Reith Lectures over the BBC in 1957, George F. Kennan acknowledged that Soviet political adaptability and technological progress had been greater than he had thought possible ten years earlier. Moreover, much of that nation's expanding industry was still geared to productivity and the manufacture of engines of war. The West did not win the race for military supremacy, and it was clear after the launching of the first Sputnik in 1957 that no conceivable military establishment could gain any declared purpose of American policy, anchored to the principle of self-determination, without war. Contrasted to the Russian past, the daily life of the Russian people had become quite tolerable, and the constant improvement in the quantity and quality of Communist goods available created a sense of progress and the assurance of better tomorrows. The denial of freedom had not challenged the control of the Communist Party over Soviet society. Instead, the Soviet leadership had begun the integration of the rising intellectual and economic elites—the essential components of any successful, complex industrial society—into the governing structure without undermining the concept of one-party rule. The Soviet economic and political system had emerged as a permanent factor in international life.

Nikita S. Khrushchev's new course in international affairs after 1956 reflected his pragmatic evaluation of the world scene. The Soviet leader recognized that Soviet expansion had reached a dead end under the policies of the late Stalin era. Unlike Stalin, Khrushchev was prepared to recognize the legitimacy of neutralism among the Afro-Asian states and to come to terms with their nationalist governments. Fundamentally, Khrushchev's moderation reflected a conviction that military policy had become meaningless under conditions of nuclear stalemate. He declared before the U.N. General Assembly in September 1960 that

> we do not want to impose our order by force upon other countries. Let
> those who determine the policy of states with a social order at differing
> from ours also renounce futile and dangerous attempts at dictating

their will. It is time for them also to recognize that the choice of one way of life or another is a domestic matter for each people. Let us build up our relations, taking into consideration the hard facts of reality. And this will be peaceful coexistence.

In demilitarizing Russian policy Khrushchev gave it an unlimited objective, for nothing had convinced him that the Soviet economic and political system could not outperform the great democracies. What assured the ultimate Communist conquest of the globe, then, was not the limited efficacy of military might or even the gospel of Marx and Lenin, but the superior technology and productivity of the U.S.S.R. Especially troublesome in the new Soviet rhetoric was the identification of co-existence in Asia and Africa with the encouragement of national wars of liberation. Khrushchev's definition of co-existence was scarcely designed to eliminate the cold war from world politics.

For those who took the global threat of Soviet ideology seriously, Khrushchev's new proposals comprised little but a more determined, more varied, and more insidious assault on the free world and its values. Peaceful co-existence, they warned, would not lead to peace, or even co-existence; it would lead to the eventual triumph of the Communist system. (*Reading No. 12.*) This notion of a global Soviet conspiracy demanded that peace, to be genuine, must be total. If one assumed that the U.S.S.R. would never give up its goal of dominating the globe, then the cold war would continue until either freedom or communism were destroyed. Either Russia would be driven back and its victims liberated, or it would steadily and inevitably take over the free world. It was essential, therefore, that United States policy pursue not co-existence, but victory. Senator Barry Goldwater of Arizona, above other American political leaders, popularized this standard of successful national action. (*Reading No. 13.*) Unfortunately no one who advocated victory over the Soviet Union ever suggested the means that would be required to achieve such a limitless objective.

For those Americans who took a more conservative and historical view of world affairs, what mattered was not Soviet intention or even Soviet assumptions regarding the internal collapse of the capitalist world, but rather actual Soviet power and interest and the policies that derived therefrom. For them the burden of American policy rested less in accepting the Soviet definition of the global struggle than in recognizing the varied pressures in world politics that confronted Soviet as well as American ambition. (*Reading No. 14.*) Among American political leaders, Senator J. William Fulbright of Arkansas challenged the goal of total victory as one that exceeded the capability and requirements of the United States. Even a total victory on the battlefield, he warned, would saddle the nation with the unwarranted and crippling burden of providing for and re-educating the hundreds of millions of Chinese and Russian peoples. (*Reading No. 15.*)

Those who expected less than victory of American diplomacy believed that the very stability of a divided Europe offered some prospect for successful East-West negotiation. If the Soviet system possessed an unsuspected resiliency to political change and the technology to compete with the West in the harnessing of destructive power, then liberation would be achieved only on Soviet terms. To alter the *status quo* and bring an element of freedom to the captive nations of eastern Europe, George F. Kennan, in his Reith Lectures, argued for *disengagement* of Soviet and Western forces from a neutralized belt across the heart of Europe. As one concomitant of such an agreement Kennan suggested that NATO agree to the neutralization of Germany. This recommendation of a nuclear-free zone was popularized and expanded by Adam Rapacki, the Foreign Minister of Poland. Disengagement, in short, questioned the fundamental decisions of the past which assumed that desired changes within the Soviet sphere could best be achieved by perpetuating the hard military line of demarcation across Europe. There was no reason why any settlement with the U.S.S.R. must include the total withdrawal of United States armed forces from Europe. Nor was it clear why Western security necessitated a strong West German military commitment to NATO, for the Western powers possessed unquestioned supremacy in nuclear capability, industrial capacity, and manpower resources over the U.S.S.R. and its European satellites. Western leaders, however, preferred the guarantees which military containment, supported by a deep American involvement in Europe's defenses, assured a divided continent, to the more flexible and less predictable concept of disengagement.

As long as the U.S.S.R. possessed the power of mass destruction, the Western world required its full range of military deterrents. Yet it seemed apparent by 1960 that the West had overmilitarized its anti-Soviet response. NATO from the date of its creation remained vastly underprepared, in the personal estimate of its own commanders. After each NATO meeting came the warning that not for another year would the West be prepared to withstand the shock of Soviet conventional capabilities. But the Russians did not march. Year after year they were held in leash by the nuclear power of the United States, and eventually by the strength of reconstructed Europe itself, or else the West had simply overestimated the danger of further Soviet aggression after 1945. Thus much of the effort to rearm Western Europe seemed divorced from reality. The United States had not liberated East-Central Europe; the U.S.S.R. had not subverted the West. Instead the cold war had encouraged a vast arms race which, in its contribution to international anarchy, began to dwarf the problem of Russia itself. Even at that gigantic price the exertion had produced nothing but stalemate. There could be no victory as either the United States or the U.S.S.R. had once conceived it. The world had asserted itself at too many points to permit either of the great powers to have its way.

Those Americans who doubted that the nation possessed the power or the compelling interest to pursue more than the past had demonstrated it could have without war continued to encourage the national leadership to terminate its quest for the unachievable and negotiate with the Russians on the basis of Europe's political and military realities. (*Reading No. 16.*) For them the issue no longer was whether Western or Soviet values would conquer the world, but whether the United States would recognize the pluralistic nature of world politics before it completely lost the power to influence. In many of his addresses, notably those delivered at the University of Washington, Seattle, in

November 1961, and at American University, Washington, in June 1963, President John F. Kennedy accepted the intellectual burden of reminding the American people of the limits of their power to control the affairs of the world. (*Reading No. 17.*) But never was his appeal for moderation quite as incisive as in the address which he had prepared for delivery in Dallas, Texas, November 22, 1963, the day of his assassination:

> In a world of complex and continuing problems, in a world full of frustrations and irritations, America's leadership must be guided by the lights of learning and reason—or else those who confuse rhetoric with reality and the plausible with the possible will gain the popular ascendancy with their seemingly swift and simple solutions to every world problem. There will always be dissident voices heard in the land, expressing opposition without alternatives, finding fault but never favor, perceiving gloom on every side and seeking influence without responsibility. Those voices are inevitable. But today other voices are heard in the land—voices preaching doctrines wholly unrelated to reality, wholly unsuited to the 'sixties, doctrines which apparently assume that words will suffice without weapons, that vituperation is as good as victory and that peace is a sign of weakness.

## V

By extending the cold war into a universal struggle for freedom the United States quickly fell victim to a wide range of fallacies regarding the nature of the non-European world. Unlike the members of NATO, the Asian allies through whom the United States hoped to contain Communist power in the Orient possessed no tradition of political stability or economic predominance. Backward and troubled, without a sense of national cohesion, these nations were often governed by narrow elites if not pure adventurers. The nationalism which guided them was an indigenous movement, its leadership and intent molded by local conditions. For the public at large the dogmas and conflicts of the great powers were remote and incomprehensible. Limited American action, responding purely to indigenous requirements, might have created centers of genuine political stability. Instead, the United States, following the collector's approach, attempted to convert such nations into military allies.

It began with a simple quest for military bases but soon evolved into a massive program of supplying arms, of underwriting large, if useless, armies, and of issuing ubiquitous military guarantees. What the United States might gain from such military arrangements was never made clear. The phraseology of the SEATO pact limited the operation of the alliance primarily, if not exclusively, to foreign aggression, whereas previous Communist encroachment had assumed every conceivable form except open external assault. How could such allies, even if dedicated to the prevention of Communist expansion, find grounds for common action against the open campaigning of legal Communist parties, the subtleties of palace politics, or the slogging military advances of jungle-hidden guerrillas operating day and night? Amid national, religious racial, and local rivalries, and the widespread need for economic and social reforms, the distinction between internal and external aggression against the *status quo* was elusive indeed. The European and Asian members of the alliance system, moreover, had no more enthusiasm for fighting jungle wars than did the United States.

Thus the several American military pacts, conceived as bulwarks against Communist aggression, were too ambitious and too ill-defined to represent any genuine community of interest. In extending the concept of coalition into the Far East, the United States acted as if the mere act of signing an alliance created a mutuality of purpose. Alliances do not hinge on respect for paper arrangements. Unless secured every day by sound policies that identify the enemy in mutually acceptable terms, they do not exist in reality at all. No clear-thinking nation in history has followed another to its own disadvantage simply to fulfill an abstract commitment. In the absence of any genuine military agreement, the United States demanded only that its allies, in exchange for their military and economic aid, profess an allegiance to the anti-Communist cause.

What held the Chinese colossus at bay was not the limited military power that the United States could bring to bear at Quemoy, Laos, Thailand, or South Vietnam, much less the SEATO alliance itself. What contained China were that nation's vast internal problems plus the prospect that open aggression might initiate an all-out war with the United States. Yet it seemed apparent that the over-all weakness of China would in time disappear before the impact of industrialism. If not, there remained the challenge of providing living space for a Chinese population which grew at the rate of fifteen million per year. Against such potentially enormous dangers United States alliance policy had achieved very little actual defense. What remained to perpetuate the *status quo* in Asia against a Chinese assault, other than the threat of large-scale American involvement along China's borders or nuclear retaliation itself, was not clear.

By the late 'fifties it was obvious that the United States had extended its unqualified support to regimes whose political weakness would eventually force it to choose between direct military involvement and an open acknowledgment that its policies of aid and alliance had failed to create the desired political stability. Beginnng with the revolt in Iraq in 1958 and extending through 1960, the world witnessed the total collapse of American-backed regimes in Cuba, Laos, Turkey, and South Korea before more popular and more effective protest movements. The Kuomintang held its own on Formosa only through the ruthless suppression of all political competition. After 1961 the United States faced the unhappy prospect of intervening militarily on an expanding scale in South Vietnam or deserting the recipient of its perennial aid, the inept and increasingly unpopular regime of Ngo Dinh Diem. But perhaps nowhere was the moral and political price which the United States paid for its simplistic anti-Communist approach to the problems of Asia dramatized more forcefully than in the Tokyo riots of June 1960 which forced the cancellation of President Dwight D. Eisenhower's trip to Japan. Following the President's decision, Richard H. Rovere observed in *The New Yorker:* "If there has ever been a moment of national failure and humiliation comparable to the present one, no one in this dazed capital can identify it. . . . Even after the collapse of the summit, it was possible to maintain that our weaknesses had been tactical, rather than strategic. . . . But the feeling one gets now is that the sheer accumulation of errors of application must call into question the validity of the policy itself."

For the important ruling elites of Asia and Africa, representing generally an intense national pride, the concerns and dogmas of the two superpowers had little relevance. What they required was time and opportunity to establish their countries as viable political and economic entities. To avoid what they regarded as an alien quarrel, they refused to align themselves with either the United States or the U.S.S.R. Yet neutralism in itself created less a third force than an increasing diversity in world politics. Indian neutralism took its strength from the pluralism of Hindu thought, which abjured polarity. Accepting good and evil as inseparable ingredients in the human equation, the Indians rejected totally the American notion of a struggle between freedom and tyranny. Nor had they any greater interest in the equally simplistic outlook of the Soviet Union. Arab neutralism, far more emotional but equally effective, reacted violently to all pressures emanating from the older colonial powers. Whether following the Indian or the Arab concept of neutralism, the new nations of Africa were no less determined than the neutrals of Asia and the Middle East to remain aloof from the cold war conflict. As one African diplomat remarked at the 1960 session of the U.N. General Assembly: "Neither side has won us, and we are determined that neither will."

Even without the support of vast military power, the Afro-Asian leadership wielded far greater influence than did the United States or the U.S.S.R. in the backward areas of the world. Arab nationalism, not the Baghdad Pact or the Kremlin, commanded the politics of the Middle East. It was the students of Seoul and Ankara who gave South Korea and Turkey the opportunity for greater national self-determination by overthrowing American-backed regimes. Elsewhere in Asia and Africa the pervading pressures for change were indigenous. Wherever the Communists achieved some success they did so by capturing control of local nationalist sentiment. Clearly the United States had less and less influence over the decisions that mattered. Indeed, all the agonizing effort of the superpowers to command the destiny of mankind appeared quite pointless. Nationalism proved an effective deterrent against the political and ideological assault of the Soviet world. Asian and African socialism represented less an ideological commitment than a normal reaction to a set of precise economic conditions. What resulted would resemble the Soviet economic structure no more than it would the free enterprise system of the United States, for both American capitalism and Soviet communism responded to conditions and traditions so unique as to make both inapplicable to any other region of the world. Perhaps it was time for the United States to accept such limits on its will, to disengage from its single-minded concern for Soviet and Chinese communism, and embrace rather the more genuinely controlling forces in international life.

VI

Illusions die hard. Despite a half-century of experience strewn with the wreckage of lost causes abroad, American leadership continued to assign to diplomacy a variety of political and ideological burdens which it was never designed to carry. Everywhere diplomacy suffered from the degradation of language and the failure to sense the reasonable limits of political action. The historic task of diplomacy—that of conducting relations among nations—became confused in the cold war with the quasi-utopian struggle for the minds of men. The nation adopted the Marxist postulate of a mortal conflict between a free world and a slave world. It behaved as if communism was actually what its proponents claimed it to be—a historic force, supranational in character, which contained the power to create one vast Communist state unmarred by national boundaries. At times national leaders, ignoring the profound diversity in national philosophies and objectives, viewed the entire world as the battleground of the war against communism. President Eisenhower once suggested a global referendum to demonstrate the world's preference for the Western over the Communist way of life. As late as April 1963, President Kennedy, with what had become characteristic phraseology, observed that "two irreconcilable views of the value, the rights and the role of the individual human being confront the peoples of the world." Such notions transformed the historic task of the United States from that of blunting Soviet aggression to that of ridding the world of the final challenge to universal freedom and justice.

Clearly those publicists and politicians who employed such vague and operationally useless concepts as "world domination" to rationalize their demands for total victory possessed political and psychological advantages over those who attempted to place the dangers to national security in true perspective. Since communism represented the antithesis of traditional American middle-class values, those who clamored for the elimination of Peiping and Moscow as significant factors in international affairs readily laid claim to the nation's conservative tradition whereas their entire neglect of means defied every principle which guided the thought and action of all founders of the American diplomatic tradition, from Washington to Theodore Roosevelt. But whatever the utopianism inherent in their program, those who believed victory available for the asking affected profoundly the behavior of government. Responding to their demands for action, Congress from time to time voted unanimously for resolutions, designed ostensibly to dismantle the Iron and Bamboo curtains, which such early leaders as Hamilton, John Quincy Adams, Randolph, and Calhoun would have submitted to such relentless ridicule, characterizing them as either dangerous or dishonest, that they would have had little chance of passage at all.

Too often the Executive, responding to heterogeneous demands that it yield nothing to the nation's enemies, took refuge in framing symmetrical and superficially attractive verbal structures which managed less to define national policies abroad than to assure all potential detractors at home that American purpose squared with their judgment of the nation's capabilities and requirements. If such oft-cited guides to national action as "firmness" and "flexibility" were commendable, they were also mutually exclusive, and Washington never made it clear which would have priority in any specific confrontation. For a democratic leadership each success, no matter how trivial, vindicated the country's entire global posture. Conversely, no demonstrable failure of national purpose in any cold war area, such as China or South Vietnam, could readily effect a policy change, for any serious modification of an established course of action, especially one oversold to sustain popular support, would constitute an admission of erroneous judgment or faulty execution, luxuries no longer permitted the government of the United States. (*Reading No. 18.*)

Realists who expected less than victory of American diplomacy attributed the nation's lack of decision and unwillingness to accept long-range, costly, usually hazardous, and generally imperfect foreign policies—the only kind really available to any country—to the American democratic system. For many analysts the special culprit was the ill-informed and often unreliable public which, in sustaining an active influence at all levels of policy formulation and execution, deranged the normal relationship between government and governed. That mass opinion existed as a powerful determinant even in external decisions was beyond question. Beginning with the administration of George Washington, politicians in search of public recognition repeatedly involved their constituents in questions purely diplomatic—questions whose settlement lay totally outside the existence of any domestic public sentiment. The events of the twentieth century merely accentuated this trend toward public involvement, especially after World War I demonstrated that governments could commit their people to actions which might impose on them heavy ordeals, dangers, and anxieties. Burdened with the gigantic price of victory in that war, even the great democracies of Europe proceeded to popularize their policies by assigning to them some cosmic goal of human betterment which might render the sacrifices acceptable. Many Americans, moreover, adopted the appealing notion that since expertness in foreign affairs existed throughout the populace, the people themselves, acting through their political representatives or pressure groups, should determine the nation's objectives abroad. Through such stages foreign affairs became engrafted to the American democratic process.

But the obligation of government to trim policy to the requirements of popular demand need not have become destructive of prudent national behavior. It did not elsewhere. Public opinion as a factor in policy formulation was never unique to democracy. Cardinal Richelieu, living in an age of undisputed autocracy, contended that no governmental action could succeed without the support of national opinion. Whatever the secretiveness of his methods in managing Europe's diplomacy in the seventeenth century, Richelieu made some effort to convince the French people of the wisdom of his maneuvers and intentions abroad. After his day few astute Western governments, whether democratic or totalitarian, ventured far into foreign entanglements without endeavoring to carry the opinion of their countries with them. Prior to 1898, furthermore, United States diplomacy itself seldom faltered because of the existence of public sentiment. American leadership in the nineteenth century, like that of the other great powers, triumphed over its domestic detractors simply because it remained politically and intellectually sound, guarding as it did the concept of limited objectives and limited power.

American national opinion became destructive of political wisdom in the twentieth century only because it existed in combination with other determining factors. Public sentiment can have no existence except as it is given strength, vitality, and direction by foreign policy elites who possess the power to influence. If the American people were wrong at most critical junctures, it was because the pleasing and inexpensive panaceas they were offered drove them into irrational judgments. Their habit of demanding of the nation's external policies what no government could possibly achieve—perfect security at little cost—represented less the failure than the abuse and exploitation of democratic government. The illusions of omnipotence which characterized the nation's outlook after 1900, and which after mid-century divided the American people so deeply on the issue of the Soviet threat, resulted simply from the refusal of two generations of editors and politicians to identify previous American successes with the genuine elements of power which the nation still enjoyed at the turn of the century. Instead, they attributed the nation's remarkable security, and even the achievements of its diplomacy, to the peculiar qualities of American civilization as they then existed—the American free enterprise system, low taxes, the inexpensive military establishment, and the moral promise of American democracy. If the nation had experienced success in the past without huge cost to itself, ran the perennial assurance, it could, as the world's leading power, continue to do so. That diplomacy could not survive the running of that political gauntlet was obvious enough from the record.

What mattered in the twentieth-century American experience, then, was not the power of public opinion as such, but what the people had been taught to expect of the country's foreign policies and whether those expectations would permit a national leadership the freedom to establish objectives and engage in actions overseas which had some relationship to the nation's irreducible interests and its limited power. Herein lay the core of the American problem, and no official acknowledged it with greater clarity than did Dean Rusk when, a full decade before he became Secretary of State, he wrote:

> There are few fields of human endeavor where wishful thinking and self-delusion are as common, or as dangerous, as in foreign policy. We demand simple answers to the most complex questions confronting human intelligence. We expect consistency in policy, though the facts themselves are full of contradictions. We should like an easy way to carry a heavy burden, an agreeable way to perform disagreeable tasks, a cheap way to bring about an expensive result.

It was this habit of easy overexpectation that eliminated for the American people the necessity of coming to terms realistically with certain external forces, designated as immoral, even when they impinged dramatically on the nation's will. Perhaps it was true that responsible leaders would have found it intellectually and politically impracticable to challenge such philosophical aberrations or

tell American voters the facts of international life. Yet could they really escape
so easily their obligation to the nation and its democratic institutions? As George
Kennan once observed:

> History does not forgive us our national mistakes because they are ex-
> plicable in terms of our domestic politics. If you say that mistakes of
> the past were unavoidable because of our domestic predilections and
> habits of thought, you are saying that what stopped us from being
> more effective than we were was democracy, as practiced in this country.
> And, if that is true, let us recognize it and measure the full seriousness
> of it—and find something to do about it. A nation which excuses its own
> failure by the sacred untouchableness of its own habits can excuse itself
> into complete disaster.

"Diplomacy," Bismarck reputedly observed, "is the art of the possible." As
such it is a utilitarian act. It is not an end but rather the means whereby
nations seek that stability in world affairs which permits the development of the
transcendant arts. The solid record of the past demonstrated that diplomacy
achieved reasonable success only when directed at specific and finite goals. Nations fulfilled their obligations to themselves and to humanity when they defined their interests with balance and precision, accepted diversity and change
as the normal order in international life, and employed their power and diplomacy to circumscribe those changes which endangered the essential environment
in which they lived and had their being. Diplomacy by traditional standards was
a search for compromise that might reconcile conflicting interests among nations.
It was not, Sir Ernest Satow once asserted, a system of moral philosophy. It
comprised rather, he said, "the application of intelligence and taste to the conduct of official relations between the governments of independent states."

For the United States the necessary task of preserving diplomacy's historic
role proved insuperable. After the presidency of Woodrow Wilson it became
the national style to pursue abstract objectives and to engage in exaggerated
political discussion. If such tendencies existed in the nineteenth century, it was
Wilson who first identified America completely with the cause of human freedom and made the quest of such transcendent benefaction a national habit of
mind. Under the repeated assault of a platitudinous sentimentalism United
States diplomacy became divorced from its own remarkable heritage. For the
Founding Fathers, like all genuinely successful statesmen of the modern world,
were realists for whom the principle that commitments be limited by the means
available was as inexorable as the laws of gravity. In large measure the nation
continued to stumble under the burden of its easy successes in the nineteenth
century. Secluded from the doubts and torments which characterized the rise of
other great powers, it entered the world stage without experiencing that anguish
which alone can make even the unthinking conscious of the limits of human
strength and human wisdom. To fulfill the promise of its youth, the country had
no choice but to recapture the humility which again would permit it to come
to terms with the processes of history.

1 | Representative O. K. Armstrong's Speech on
    Psychological Warfare, February 1952 *

In this speech, delivered in Washington, Representative O. K. Armstrong of Missouri reflected the mounting conviction that the United States must win the cold war against communism conclusively or ultimately be destroyed. War itself was not the answer, for this would wreck too much of Western civilization. Containment was inadequate because it was both too costly and too tolerant of the enemy. For Armstrong the surest and easiest response to the challenge of Soviet-based communism lay in psychological warfare which would stimulate resistance to Soviet rule both within the Iron Curtain countries and even within Russia itself.

ⓚ

. . . Our purpose, as set forth by those inviting us to be present and to participate, is as follows:

To focus public attention upon the resistance to Soviet Communist control by peoples now enslaved by its regimes, in the Soviet Union and satellite lands; to make known the potential of this resistance, to discuss ways and means whereby all such resistance movements may be increased and made more effective; to present definite plans of action to aid the oppressed victims of Communist tyranny to the end that they may at the proper time overthrow the Communist regimes and be liberated to establish free and democratic governments, based on the right of self-determination; and to establish a continuing organization to carry out the aims and programs developed in the conference.

Within that framework, let us set up the foundation and structure of a bold, new, effective foreign policy to recommend to our Government and to our friends in other free nations willing to cooperate with us. Let us here launch a crusade for truth and freedom, a crusade for the liberation of all those enslaved by Bolshevik tyranny.

The task is not an easy one. Look at the map of the world. The iron curtain of Soviet Communist control has descended over vast areas and hundreds of millions of people, in Eastern Europe and in Asia, since the close of World War II. It is unspeakably tragic that this should be the case, when it need not have been. After our victory over aggressive forces in that war, the world deserved a just and lasting peace. The Atlantic Charter promised the peoples of the world that they might everywhere enjoy liberty, resources and self-government. Those ideals were discarded for the false hope that if Stalin and his Kremlin conspirators were given the concessions they desired, in territory and domination of peoples, the Bolshevik leaders would cooperate with democratic nations to create an international order of justice and peace. . . .

* Speech of Representative O. K. Armstrong of Missouri before the Conference on Psychological Warfare in the Cold War, Washington, February 22, 1952, *Vital Speeches of the Day*, XVII (April 1, 1952), 381–2.

By every possible means—by insults, denunciations, vicious propaganda in Soviet areas, infiltration of Communist spies and agents into every nation on earth, and actual overthrow of many free governments that made the mistake of collaboration and appeasement, the Kremlin tyrants made clear that our offers of cooperation only increased their arrogance and whetted their enmity toward us. Then our policy shifted to one of containment. Let us contain the Bolshevik movement in the areas it now has enslaved, runs the theory. Let us coexist with the Bolsheviks, in the hope that if we let them alone they will let us alone. Even after Soviet leaders launched a full-scale war of aggression against the people of South Korea, giving notice that this struggle is one of life or death for the free world, the policy of containment and coexistence persists.

The theory is false. The containment policy is a foundation of shifting sand, upon which the structure of international order and peace will crumble to earth. The policy assumes that Bolshevik leaders can be dealt with as you deal with honest diplomats, that their pledged word will be kept, that they recognize honor and justice among men and that they will, if left alone, leave their peace-loving neighbors alone. Surely we have learned that this is not true.

Surely now, my friends, we have learned the true nature of communism. It is a world-wide conspiracy, bent upon dominating the world. . . .

Even if communism could be halted in its present tracks, and even if the Communist regimes indicated that they desire not one more acre of land nor one more victim, and should actually stop further aggression, we cannot shut our eyes to the sight of slave-labor camps nor shut our ears to the screams of tortured men and women. To say that we should coexist with communism so long as communism leaves us alone is to shrug off the fate of 800,000,000 people. Those who follow such a doctrine are abject isolationists. We who are sensitive to the sufferings of humanity cannot do this. It is unworthy of a free man to be callous to the slave status of his brother. Those who love liberty do not love it for themselves alone, but for all mankind.

Surely now we know there can be no collaboration with communism by the free world. It cannot be appeased. It cannot be contained. So long as this world-wide conspiracy exists, it will seek to destroy human liberties. There remains only one conclusion; communism must be defeated. It must be destroyed. Its virus must be eradicated. Its grip upon the people must be broken. Its victims must be liberated. Unless this is done, freedom will die, slowly but inevitably, all over the world.

At this point fearful voices are heard, saying that the only way to overthrow bolshevism is by another major war—a world-wide, atomic war, that would wreck civilization irretrievably. That is false. Indeed, quite the contrary is true. Our present policies will lead—in fact, are leading us—straight into another major war. Our policy of containment is based upon the fallacy that if we pile up huge armaments and make great preparations for war, fear will restrain the Kremlin leaders from further aggression. Pile up more and more atomic bombs, start manufacturing the hydrogen bomb, draft more and more young men into the Armed Forces, build a wall of military strength around Sovietland, and Stalin and his stooges will at last give up the struggle, say our theorists—the same theorists that believed that appeasement would do the trick. Do we not see that this is falling squarely into the Kremlin trap? That we are draining away our resources and manpower until we shall become weak enough that no armaments can protect us? Do we not see that this is a policy of fear, of hopelessness, of reliance upon weapons that will neither prevent nor win future wars?

Let us realize this great and fundamental truth: That the struggle against communism is the struggle for the minds and hearts of mankind. It cannot be won by guns and bombs alone. The strongest weapon that we hold in our hands is truth itself. Our strongest and most valuable asset in the crusade to overthrow communism without war is the burning desire of captive peoples for freedom.

Let us then move boldly to prevent further aggression and war by a crusade to liberate the masses enslaved by communism, in all the captive lands, and in Russia itself. . . .

Let us highly resolve that we will not quit the crusade so long as there is a concentration camp anywhere, so long as bolshevism crushes out religion, liberty, hope, faith, honor, and justice among any people on earth. It was Abraham Lincoln who said, "This Nation cannot exist half slave and half free." Let us recognize that this world cannot exist half slave and half free, and that someday it shall exist wholly free.

Our primary weapons will not be guns, but ideas. Our first task will be to give assurance of hope to the now hopeless millions of captive peoples, that we intend to work unceasingly for their liberation. Our next and continuing task will be to find and employ the best methods of strengthening resistance among the victims of Soviet enslavement, and enlist our governments and our peoples to making those methods effective. . . .

The time is urgent. There are two reasons why we cannot delay indefinitely the use of effective psychological strategy in the cold war.

First, in all areas which the Bolsheviks control, the process of sovietizing goes relentlessly forward. Men disappear singly or in groups. Mass deportations are carried out. The land is collectivized. The native culture is eradicated, and a new culture substituted—the life of the man who lives in terror, without hope of relief. We have but to look to the Baltic States to see what this sovietizing process will do.

Second, the free world is losing the psychological struggle. The enslaved peoples are losing hope, and the neutral peoples are losing faith. Because of the ruinous policies of collaboration, appeasement, and containment, the Soviet prestige has grown stronger and the prestige of the United States and our allies has grown weaker. . . .

Let the timid and the indifferent step aside, while those of us who believe we can overcome this Soviet tyranny and still save our civilization from the horrors of all-out war, stride forward like brave men and women, comrades in a great crusade of truth and freedom for all mankind.

## 2 | John Foster Dulles and the New Policy of Boldness, May 1952 *

Accepting the conviction that United States containment policies were failing to achieve successes commensurate with their cost, John Foster Dulles, in the following article, challenged the validity of the Truman approach to the Soviet problem and assured his readers that another, less costly but far more effective, program was available to them for disposing of the Communist challenge. For him the promise of victory lay within the spiritual weakness of the Soviet system itself.

✍

Soviet Communism confronts our nation with its gravest peril. To meet its long-term strategy of encirclement and strangulation, we have adopted a series of emergency measures which are fantastically costly not only in money but in their warping of our American way of life.

No one would begrudge the cost of what we are doing if, in fact, it was adequate and was ending the peril, and if there was no better way. Actually, our policies are *inadequate* in scope. They are *not* ending the peril. There is a better way.

The costs of our present policies are perilously high in money, in freedom and in friendships.

The Administration's "security policies" would this year cost us, in money, about 60 billion, of which about 99% goes for military purposes and for equipment (which will quickly become obsolete and demand replacement indefinitely). Such gigantic expenditures unbalance our budget and require taxes so heavy that they discourage incentive. They so cheapen the dollar that savings, pensions and Social Security reserves have already lost much of their value.

What is worse, this concentration on military matters is—to use George Washington's words—"inauspicious to liberty." It leads to encroachments on civil rights and transfers from the civilian to the military decisions which profoundly affect our domestic life and our foreign relations.

We are also rapidly expending our friendships and prestige in the world. Increasing numbers turn away from our policies as too militaristic, too costly, too erratic and too inconclusive for them to follow. Our far-flung, extravagant and surreptitious military projects are frightening many who feel that we are conducting a private feud with Russia, which may endanger them, rather than performing a public service for peace. . . .

Our present negative policies will never end the type of sustained offensive

* John Foster Dulles, "A Policy of Boldness," *Life,* May 19, 1952, 146–57. Reprinted by permission.

which Soviet Communism is mounting; they will never end the peril nor bring relief from the exertions which devour our economic, political and moral vitals. Ours are treadmill policies which, at best, might perhaps keep us in the same place until we drop exhausted. . . .

Where do we go from here?

A nation with our resourcefulness should be able to devise better policies. But we cannot take it for granted that better policies will automatically result from a change of Administration. Conceivably policies could be worse rather than better. . . .

Looked at in any impartial way, we are the world's greatest and strongest power. The only commodity in which we seem deficient is faith. In all material things we have a productivity far exceeding that of Russia: our steel production is about three and one half times that of the Soviet Union, and in aluminum, petroleum and electric power our superiority is even greater. Our people have a standard of education, an inventive talent and a technical skill unmatched by any of the peoples under Soviet rule.

On the Soviet side a dozen people in the Kremlin are attempting to rule 800 million human beings—while trying to conquer more. All except a privileged few work under conditions which sternly deny them the "pursuit of happiness." Within Russia itself the discontent can be judged by the 15 million prisoners in forced labor camps—more than twice the membership of the Soviet Communist party. Even the leaders are suspicious of each other as each wonders whether the other plots his purge.

In satellite countries, such as Poland and Czechoslovakia, the situation is worse, because there it is aggravated by the repression of patriotism. Leaders in the Czech Communist party have been liquidated one after another. In China the party tries to frighten the people into subjection by staging wholesale public executions.

All of this reflects not strength but weakness. The "dictatorship of the proletariat" is like other tyrannies that went before. They may present a formidable exterior, but they are "like unto whited sepulchres, which indeed appear beautiful outward, but are within full of dead men's bones and of all uncleanness."

The free should not be numbed by the sight of this vast graveyard of human liberties. It is the despots who should feel haunted. They, not we, should fear the future.

As we stop fretting and start thinking, the first problem to tackle is the strictly military one. It comes in the form of a paradox: for we must seek a military formula more effective than any devised to date—that we may no longer be so overridingly preoccupied with purely military necessity.

The dimensions of the problem are plain: at least 3,000,000 Soviet soldiers regularly under arms, another 3,000,000 to 4,000,000 in the Chinese Red armies. These forces, poised in a central area could strike with massive power east, south or west at any one of more than 20 nations along the 20,000-mile boundary which runs from near Alaska down by Japan, through East Asia and South Asia, along the Middle and Near East to Europe and up through Central Europe to the North Cape. . . .

Those who think only of Western Europe and of making it "impregnable"—without regard to the Near, Middle and Far East and Africa—are just as blind as those who think only of the United States and of making it "impregnable." Policies that do not defend freedom in Asia are fatally defective.

How do we defend it? Obviously, we cannot build a 20,000-mile Maginot Line or match the Red armies, man for man, gun for gun and tank for tank at any particular time or place their general staff selects. To attempt that would mean real strength nowhere and bankruptcy everywhere.

*There is one solution and only one: that is for the free world to develop the will and organize the means to retaliate instantly against open aggression by Red armies, so that, if it occurred anywhere, we could and would strike back where it hurts, by means of our choosing.*

The principle involved is as simple as that of our municipal police forces. We do not station armed guards at every house to stop aggressors—that would be economic suicide—but we deter potential aggressors by making it probable that if they aggress, they will lose in punishment more than they can gain by aggression. . . .

Today atomic energy, coupled with strategic air and sea power, provides the community of free nations with vast new possibilities of organizing a community power to stop open aggression before it starts and reduce, to the vanishing point, the risk of general war. So far these weapons are merely part of national arsenals for use in fighting general war when it has come. If that catastrophe occurs, it will be because we have allowed these new and awesome forces to become the ordinary killing tools of the soldier when, in the hands of the statesmen, they could serve as effective political weapons in defense of the peace.

This does not mean that old ways of defending the peace should be abandoned where they can still be efficacious. The United States should maintain a strong military force of a kind befitting our responsibilities. . . .

But these old methods are quite inadequate to match the 20,000-mile scope of the present military peril; and if we strain to make them adequate, we shall succumb to the twin evils of militarism and bankruptcy. New methods of defense are needed to save the free nations from the dilemma, which present policies impose, of choosing between murder from without or suicide from within.

That is the enlightened and effective way to proceed. It is a way that we can afford to live with, and until there is effective international disarmament, it is the way we cannot afford to live without.

Once the free world has established a military defense, it can undertake what has been too long delayed—a political offense.

It is ironic and wrong that we who believe in the boundless power of human freedom should so long have accepted a static political role. It is also ironic and wrong that we who so proudly profess regard for the spiritual should rely so utterly on material defenses while the avowed materialists have been waging a winning war with social ideas, stirring humanity everywhere.

There are three truths which we need to recall in these times:

1) The dynamic prevails over the static; the active over the passive. We were from the beginning a vigorous, confident people, born with a sense of destiny

and of mission. That is why we have grown from a small and feeble nation to our present stature in the world.

2) Nonmaterial forces are more powerful than those that are merely material. Our dynamism has always been moral and intellectual rather than military or material. During most of our national life we had only a small military establishment and during the last century we had to borrow money abroad to develop our expanding economy. But we always generated political, social and industrial ideas and projected them abroad where they were more explosive than dynamite.

3) There is a moral or natural law not made by man which determines right and wrong and in the long run only those who conform to that law will escape disaster. This law has been trampled by the Soviet rulers, and for that violation they can and should be made to pay. This will happen when we ourselves keep faith with that law in our practical decisions of policy.

We should let these truths work in and through us. We should be *dynamic*, we should use *ideas* as weapons; and these ideas should conform to *moral* principles. That we do this is right, for it is the inevitable expression of a faith— and I am confident that we still do have a faith. But it is also expedient in defending ourselves against an aggressive, imperialistic despotism. For even the present lines will not hold unless our purpose goes beyond confining Soviet Communism within its present orbit.

Consider the situation of the 20-odd non-Western nations which are next door to the Soviet world. . . . Today they live close to despair because the United States, the historic leader of the forces of freedom, seems dedicated to the negative policy of "containment" and "stalemate."

As a matter of fact, some highly competent work is being done, at one place or another, to promote liberation. Obviously such activities do not lend themselves to public exposition. But liberation from the yoke of Moscow will not occur for a very long time, and courage in neighboring lands will not be sustained, *unless the United States makes it publicly known that it wants and expects liberation to occur.* The mere statement of that wish and expectation would change, in an electrifying way, the mood of the captive peoples. It would put heavy new burdens on the jailers and create new opportunities for liberation.

Here are some specific acts which we could take:

1) We could make it clear, on the highest authority of the President and the Congress, that U.S. policy seeks as one of its peaceful goals the eventual restoration of genuine independence in the nations of Europe and Asia now dominated by Moscow, and that we will not be a party to any "deal" confirming the rule of Soviet despotism over the alien peoples which it now dominates.

2) We could welcome the creation in the free world of political "task forces" to develop a freedom program for each of the captive nations. Each group would be made up of those who are proved patriots, who have practical resourcefulness and who command confidence and respect at home and abroad.

3) We could stimulate the escape from behind the Iron Curtain of those who can help to develop these programs.

4) The activities of the Voice of America and such private committees as those

for Free Europe and Free Asia could be coordinated with these freedom programs. The agencies would be far more effective if given concrete jobs to do.

5) We could coordinate our economic, commercial and cultural relations with the freedom programs, cutting off or licensing intercourse as seemed most effective from time to time.

6) We could end diplomatic relations with present governments which are in fact only puppets of Moscow, if and when that would promote the freedom programs.

7) We could seek to bring other free nations to unite with us in proclaiming, in a great new Declaration of Independence, our policies toward the captive nations.

We do not want a series of bloody uprisings and reprisals. There can be peaceful separation from Moscow, as Tito showed, and enslavement can be made so unprofitable that the master will let go his grip. Such results will not come to pass overnight. But we can know, for history proves, that the spirit of patriotism burns unquenched in Poles, Czechs, Hungarians, Romanians, Bulgarians, Chinese and others, and we can be confident that within two, five or 10 years substantial parts of the present captive world can peacefully regain national independence. That will mark the beginning of the end of Soviet despotism's attempt at world conquest. . . .

# 3 | Dulles's Statement on Liberation Policy, January 15, 1953 *

When Dulles appeared before the Senate Committee on Foreign Relations in January 1953, prior to becoming Secretary of State, he insisted again that the liberation of both China and the Soviet satellites could be gained without war or even revolution. Precisely how he hoped to bring this about he never stated, either here or elsewhere. Dulles viewed the entire Communist world as a solid block, controlled by the Soviet Union.

✍

. . . The CHAIRMAN. I am particularly interested in something I read recently, to the effect that you stated you were not in favor of the policy of containment. I think you advocated a more dynamic or positive policy. Can you tell us more specifically what you have in mind? . . . .

Mr. DULLES. There are a number of policy matters which I would prefer to discuss with the committee in executive session, but I have no objection to

* Hearing before the Committee on Foreign Relations, United States Senate, Eighty-Third Congress, First Session, on the Nomination of John Foster Dulles, Secretary of State-Designate, January 15, 1953 (Washington, 1953), 5–6.

saying in open session what I have said before: namely, that we shall never have a secure peace or a happy world so long as Soviet communism dominates one-third of all of the peoples that there are, and is in the process of trying at least to extend its rule to many others.

These people who are enslaved are people who deserve to be free, and who, from our own selfish standpoint, ought to be free because if they are the servile instruments of aggressive despotism, they will eventually be welded into a force which will be highly dangerous to ourselves and to all of the free world.

Therefore, we must always have in mind the liberation of these captive peoples. Now, liberation does not mean a war of liberation. Liberation can be accomplished by processes short of war. We have, as one example, not an ideal example, but it illustrates my point, the defection of Yugoslavia, under Tito from the domination of Soviet communism. Well, that rule of Tito is not one which we admire, and it has many aspects of despotism, itself; but at least it illustrates that it is possible to disintegrate this present monolithic structure which, as I say, represents approximately one-third of all the people that there are in the world.

The present tie between China and Moscow is an unholy arrangement which is contrary to the traditions, the hopes, the aspirations of the Chinese people. Certainly we cannot tolerate a continuance of that, or a welding of the 450 million people of China into the servile instruments of Soviet aggression.

Therefore, a policy which only aims at containing Russia where it now is, is, in itself, an unsound policy; but it is a policy which is bound to fail because a purely defensive policy never wins against an aggressive policy. If our only policy is to stay where we are, we will be driven back. It is only by keeping alive the hope of liberation, by taking advantage of that wherever opportunity arises, that we will end this terrible peril which dominates the world, which imposes upon us such terrible sacrifices and so great fears for the future. But all of this can be done and must be done in ways which will not provoke a general war, or in ways which will not provoke an insurrection which would be crushed with bloody violence, such as was the case, for example, when the Russians instigated the Polish revolt, under General Bor, and merely sat by and watched them when the Germans exterminated those who were revolting.

It must be and can be a peaceful process, but those who do not believe that results can be accomplished by moral pressures, by the weight of propaganda, just do not know what they are talking about.

I ask you to recall the fact that Soviet communism itself, has spread from controlling 200 million people some 7 years ago to controlling 800 million people today, and it has done that by methods of political warfare, psychological warfare and propaganda, and it has not actually used the Red Army as an open aggressive force in accomplishing that.

Surely what they can accomplish, we can accomplish. Surely if they can use moral and psychological force, we can use it; and, to take a negative defeatest attitude is not an approach which is conducive to our own welfare, or in conformity with our own historical ideas. . . .

# 4 | The London *Observer* on the Concept of Liberation, May 1953 *

The following editorial on peace-making began with the assumption that a stalemate had been reached around the world in the struggle between the Western and Communist camps. For that reason, concluded the writer, a settlement would of necessity be based on the *status quo*. He suggested that negotiations include the general recognition of the new government of China as well as the Soviet hegemony in eastern Europe. The challenge, he saw, was that of altering the mentality of conflict in the world to one of conciliation. If the West could not negotiate away its ideological differences with the Soviet bloc, it could at least eliminate some of the precise and foreseeable causes of war.

✦

. . . In every conflict there comes a moment when the true balance of forces is fully tested and established, and nothing can be gained by further hostilities. That is the moment which must be seized if a durable peace is to be made. In both world wars it was missed in the quest for a victory which was to be "total" but only proved totally barren.

In the present world conflict this moment is now upon us. For a year or so now, the balance and limit of the opposed forces have been clearly established, both in Europe and in Asia. No longer, as in the days of the Prague coup, the Greek civil war, and the Berlin blockade, can the Russians hope to extend their area of influence or control in Europe by any forcible means short of war. Neither has the West discovered any effective means, short of war, of forcibly moving or removing the Iron Curtain.

In Asia, too, there is a stalemate and a balance everywhere except in Indo-China. Nothing short of war can unseat the Communist Government in China, undo the Japanese link with America, or unite Korea. Both in Europe and Asia the methods of cold war—propaganda, subversion, boycott, blockade, armed demonstrations, local insurrections—have reached the end of their tether. Since nobody can want a war which would threaten to destroy the world without promising to unite it, the only choice today is between a prolonged military stalemate and a negotiated peace "based on facts."

The Russians have given clear indications that they are prepared to try for the latter alternative, and Britain has now responded to their welcome advances. The most difficult part of the art of peacemaking, however, is the transition from the mentality of conflict to the mentality of conciliation, without which negotiations lead nowhere. What is needed for this transition is, in Sir Winston's words, that "for a while each State looks about for things to do which would be agreeable instead of being disagreeable to each other."

This deliberate effort at agreeableness must be accompanied by the patience

* The London *Observer*, May 17, 1953.

to proceed step by step, for which Mr. Atlee, in his admirable speech for the Opposition, found a striking simile: "When the logs are jammed in the river one must begin by extricating one or two, in the hope that thereby the whole mass might move."

A further requisite of the art of peacemaking is a keen sense of the possible, coupled with constructive imagination. No imaginable peace settlement can remove the deep ideological differences between Communism and Western liberalism—it was Roosevelt's fatal error to believe that this was possible. All that a peace settlement can remove is the forseeable causes of war, and the fear of war, between States. Further, no peace settlement based on the existing balance of power can have as its condition the liberation of the Communist countries in Eastern Europe. It might have as its result some liberalization both in their external relations and in their internal regimes.

The best we can hope for—and this is not a wholly unreasonable or unrealistic hope—is that a period of peace may reduce Russia's iron grip on her neighbors which six years of cold war have merely tightened—just as in Aesop's fable of the gale and the sun betting which of them could strip a wanderer of his coat, the sun succeeded, where all the violent tuggings of the gale had only made the wanderer grip his wrappings more firmly.

# 5 | Dulles's Speech on Massive Retaliation, in New York, January 12, 1954 *

This address to the Council on Foreign Relations comprised a complete statement of Dulles's concept of foreign affairs as they applied to the Soviet Union. Again he was critical of the Truman policies because they had been piecemeal and had always left the initiative to the Kremlin. It was necessary, he said, for the United States to develop long-range policies which would protect the nation's security at reduced cost. He found the answer in "massive retaliation." But his program went far beyond the assurance that the United States could prevent aggression simply by threatening to employ its weapons of mass destruction. In addition he promised that the time gained by preventing aggression would produce erosion within the enemy states and thus eventually give the United States a victory in the cold war. This speech tied the concept of massive retaliation to the concept of peaceful liberation. It not only promised ultimate victory but also promised it at little risk and at reduced expenditure.

* *The Department of State Bulletin*, XXX (January 25, 1954), 107–10.

. . . We live in a world where emergencies are always possible, and our survival may depend upon our capacity to meet emergencies. Let us pray that we shall always have that capacity. But, having said that, it is necessary also to say that emergency measures—however good for the emergency—do not necessarily make good permanent policies. Emergency measures are costly; they are superficial; and they imply that the enemy has the initiative. They cannot be depended on to serve our long-time interests.

This "long time" factor is of critical importance. The Soviet Communists are planning for what they call "an entire historical era," and we should do the same. . . .

In the face of this strategy, measures cannot be judged adequate merely because they ward off an immediate danger. It is essential to do this, but it is also essential to do so without exhausting ourselves.

When the Eisenhower administration applied this test, we felt that some transformations were needed. It is not sound military strategy permanently to commit U.S. land forces to Asia to a degree that leaves us no strategic reserves. It is not sound economics, or good foreign policy, to support permanently other countries; for in the long run, that creates as much ill will as good will. Also, it is not sound to become permanently committed to military expenditures so vast that they lead to "practical bankruptcy." . . . We need allies and collective security. Our purpose is to make these relations more effective, less costly. This can be done by placing more reliance on deterrent power and less dependence on local defensive power.

This is accepted practice so far as local communities are concerned. We keep locks on our doors, but we do not have an armed guard in every home. We rely principally on a community security system so well equipped to punish any who break in and steal that, in fact, would-be aggressors are generally deterred. That is the modern way of getting maximum protection at a bearable cost.

What the Eisenhower administration seeks is a similar international security system. We want, for ourselves and the other free nations, a maximum deterrent at a bearable cost.

Local defense will always be important. But there is no local defense which alone will contain the mighty land-power of the Communist world. Local defenses must be reinforced by the further deterrent of massive retaliatory power. A potential aggressor must know that he cannot always prescribe battle conditions that suit him. Otherwise, for example, a potential aggressor, who is glutted with manpower, might be tempted to attack in confidence that resistance would be confined to manpower. He might be tempted to attack in places where his superiority was decisive. . . .

But before military planning could be changed, the President and his advisers, as represented by the National Security Council, had to take some basic policy decisions. This has been done. The basic decision was to depend primarily upon a great capacity to retaliate, instantly, by means and at places of our choosing. Now the Department of Defense and the Joint Chiefs of Staff can shape our military establishment to fit what is *our* policy, instead of having to try to be ready to meet the enemy's many choices. . . . As a result, it is now possible to get, and share, more basic security at less cost.

Let us now see how this concept has been applied to foreign policy, taking first the Far East. In Korea this administration effected a major transformation. The fighting has been stopped on honorable terms. That was possible because the aggressor, already thrown back to and behind his place of beginning, was faced with the possibility that the fighting might, to his own great peril, soon spread beyond the limits and methods which he had selected. . . .

I have said in relation to Indochina that, if there were open Red Chinese armed aggression there, that would have "grave consequences which might not be confined to Indochina." I expressed last month the intention of the United States to maintain its position on Okinawa. This is needed to insure adequate striking power to implement the collective concept which I describe.

All of this is summed up in President Eisenhower's important statement of December 26. He announced the progressive reduction of the U.S. ground forces in Korea. He pointed out that U.S. military forces in the Far East will now feature "highly mobile naval, air and amphibious units"; and he said in this way, despite some withdrawal of land forces, the United States will have a capacity to oppose aggression "with even greater effect than heretofore." . . .

At the April meeting of the NATO Council, the United States put forward a new concept, now known as that of the "long haul." That meant a steady development of defensive strength at a rate which will preserve and not exhaust the economic strength of our allies and ourselves. This would be reinforced by the striking power of a strategic air force based on internationally agreed positions. . . .

There are still some strategic spots where the local governments cannot maintain adequate armed forces without some financial support from us. In these cases, we take the judgment of our military advisers as to how to proceed in the common interest. For example, we have contributed largely, ungrudgingly, and I hope constructively, to end aggression and advance freedom in Indochina. The technical assistance program is being continued, and we stand ready to meet nonrecurrent needs due to crop failures or like disasters. But, broadly speaking, foreign budgetary aid is being limited to situations where it clearly contributes to military strength. . . .

If we can deter such aggression as would mean general war, and that is our confident resolve, then we can let time and fundamentals work for us. We do not need self-imposed policies which sap our strength. . . . We intend that our conduct and example shall continue, as in the past, to show all men how good can be the fruits of freedom.

If we rely on freedom, then it follows that we must abstain from diplomatic moves which would seem to endorse captivity. That would, in effect, be a conspiracy against freedom. I can assure you that we shall never seek illusory security for ourselves by such a "deal." We do negotiate about specific matters but only to advance the cause of human welfare. . . .

If we persist in the courses I outline we shall confront dictatorship with a task that is, in the long run, beyond its strength. For unless it changes, it must sup-

press the human desires that freedom satisfies—as we shall be demonstrating. If
the dictators persist in their present course, then it is they who will be limited
to superficial successes, while their foundation crumbles under the tread of their
iron boots. . . .

We can be sure that there is going on, even within Russia, a silent test of
strength between the powerful rulers and the multitudes of human beings. Each
individual no doubt seems by himself to be helpless in this struggle. But their
aspirations in the aggregate make up a mighty force. There are signs that the
rulers are bending to some of the human desires of their people. There are
promises of more food, more household goods, more economic freedom.

That des not prove that the Soviet rulers have themselves been converted. It
is rather that they may be dimly perceiving a basic fact, that is that there are
limits to the power of any rulers indefinitely to suppress the human spirit. In
that God-given fact lies our greatest hope. It is a hope that can sustain us. For
even if the path ahead be long and hard, it need not be a warlike path; and we
can know that at the end may be found the blessedness of peace.


## 6 | Hans J. Morgenthau's Observations on Massive Retaliation, March 1954 *

In the following perceptive evaluation of Secretary's Dulles's doctrine of "massive
retaliation," Professor Hans J. Morgenthau of the University of Chicago included most of the standard arguments leveled at the doctrine by American and
British writers during the weeks and months following its announcement. Professor Morgenthau noted that the new concept of national defense, despite the
many explanations of it offered by members of the administration and even
Dulles himself, had to be examined in the form presented on January 12. The
burden of Morgenthau's criticism was that the doctrine, announced within the
context of tax reduction, promised too much for too little. It narrowed the
military choices available to the nation and ignored, in contrast to Dean
Acheson's address of January 1950, the revolutionary and indigenous nature of
change in the Orient which eliminated at the outset the legitimate employment
of atomic weapons.

❧

The "Instant Retaliation" speech of Secretary Dulles, delivered on January
12, was presented as a major redefinition of United States policy for the decade
to come. Its importance, if not its meaning, was confirmed by the debate it has

* Hans J. Morgenthau, "Instant Retaliation: Will It Deter Aggression?" *The New
Republic*, CXXX (March 29, 1954), 11–14. Reprinted by permission.

provoked. Lester Pearson has questioned it; Adlai Stevenson has criticized it; Vice President Nixon has defended it; Sir John Slessor has amplified it; Secretary Wilson has minimized it; Admiral Radford and his colleagues have set out to "explain" it and ended by explaining it away; President Eisenhower has stated that the new doctrine is not a new doctrine at all; Secretary Dulles has reaffirmed its newness in a somewhat more modest form.

Through the confusion of these conflicting statements certain clear lines of argument can be seen. Congress and our allies have asked who will decide on "instant retaliation" and have been assured that their "consent and acquiescence" is necessary. Army and Navy spokesmen have stressed that conventional weapons are still needed and this also is conceded. Objections have been advanced to the rigidity of the Dulles formula and in turn the Secretary of State acknowledges that its application in any given situation will turn on the facts. For all these modifications and qualifications, however, the doctrine itself has not been questioned by those in power. The January 12 speech stands in its essentials, as the expression of a major step by the National Security Council. It outlines a fundamental change that has taken place in United States strategy, and that is affirmed day by day, in important decisions such as those to eliminate three active Army divisions, to reduce naval personnel by 100,000 men, to extend the use of atomic weapons, and at the same time to warn our opponents that, in the event of new aggression in Korea, our counter-action will not stop short at that nation's Northern frontier.

With this in mind let us start over by re-examining the January 12 address, setting aside interpretations of Secretary Dulles' address by his colleagues, and assuming that he meant precisely what he said.

Mr. Dulles makes essentially five points which serve as the keystones of the new policy.

First, "emergency action, imposed on us by our enemies" and exemplified by the Korean War and the Marshall Plan, must be replaced by a long-term plan which provides "a maximum deterrent at a bearable cost."

Second, we shall—and this is "the basic decision" made by the President and the National Security Council—"depend primarily upon a great capacity to retaliate, instantly, by means and at places of our choosing."

Third, as a corollary to "placing more reliance on deterrent power," we shall depend less on "local defensive power."

Fourth, "broadly speaking, foreign budgetary aid is being limited to situations where it clearly contributes to military strength."

Fifth, "if we can deter such aggression as would mean general war . . . then we can let time and fundamentals work for us . . . The fundamental, on our side, is the richness—spiritual, intellectual and material—that freedom can produce and the irresistible attraction it then sets up." Thus "we shall confront dictatorship with a task that is, in the long run, beyond its strength." . . .

The new policy assumes that the threat to the US will take the form of open military aggression to be prevented by the threat, or answered by the reality, of atomic retaliation. With this assumption the new policy reverts to the pattern of the 40's when the American monopoly of the atomic bomb or at least of a stockpile of atomic bombs sufficient to wage successful atomic war stabilized the line of demarcation of 1945 between East and West. The virtual certainty that any step taken by the Soviet Union beyond that line would lead to the outbreak of a third world war, fought only by the US with atomic weapons, may have prevented such a step from being taken. It may seem trite, but in view of the somnambulistic quality of much official argumentation it is not superfluous, to point out that a policy of atomic retaliation is a sure deterrent only if the retaliatory power has a monopoly or at least a vast superiority in the retaliatory weapon. But what if the power to be retaliated against is in a position to retaliate against the retaliation or to make retaliation impossible by prevention?

The new policy is intended in future to make local aggression, Korea-style, impossible; for no government in its senses will embark upon local aggression in the knowledge that its industrial and population centers will be reduced to rubble in retaliation. In other words, the policy of atomic retaliation, by the very fact of its announcement, removes the need for its implementation. However, this is not the end of the story. It is easy to imagine situations where local aggression will not be deterred by the threat of atomic retaliation but will be regarded by the aggressor nation of such vital importance to itself that it must be undertaken in spite of the risk of an atomic war. One can well imagine a situation arising in Central Europe which will induce the Soviet Union to take military measures which come under the heading of local aggression. . . .

The new policy shifts the emphasis from the conventional weapons to the new instruments of atomic power. By doing so, it recognizes what, at least in theory, has not always been recognized before, namely, that the United States has not the resources to oppose more than one local aggression at a time by local means. The United States would not have been able to fight two Korean Wars at the same time. By recognizing these limits of American strength, the new policy also recognizes that there may be local aggressions to which we have no answer at all, *e.g.* Indo-China, or against which our only answer is the atomic bomb. The shift from the traditional weapons of local defense to atomic weapons, then, on the one hand, limits our ability to meet local aggression by local means, as we did in Korea, and, on the other, increases the temptation to use the atomic bomb against local aggression where under the old strategy we might have used traditional weapons. In other words, the new policy tends to limit our choices. Formerly we could have met local aggression by doing nothing, by resisting it locally, or by striking at its source with atomic bombs. The new policy contracts the sphere within which the second alternative can operate. Confronted with a choice between doing nothing at all or dropping an atomic bomb, the new policy increases the incentive for doing the latter. In the words of William Graham Sumner, "For what we prepare for is what we shall get."

Yet the chances that any of these contingencies will actually come to pass may well be small. For the immediate threat to the security of the West arises not from local aggression, Soviet inspired or otherwise, nor from atomic war deliberately embarked upon by the Soviet Union, but from the revolutionary fire which is sweeping through much of Asia, Africa, Western Europe and Latin

America. Atomic retaliation can only be an answer to open military aggression. It stands to reason that to drop atomic bombs on Moscow or Peking is no answer to the threat of Communist revolution in Italy or Indo-China. The crucial problem of national and social revolutions, that Moscow did not create but which it exploits, Mr. Dulles fails to face. The generalities of freedom are offered, of course; it is the specifics of freedom that concern the nations whose futures are now in doubt.

Nothing in the January 12 address shows more clearly the new policy's lack of political sensitivity and imagination and its predominant concern with military matters than Mr. Dulles' assurance that "foreign budgetary aid is being limited to situations where it clearly contributes to military strength." This is a far cry indeed from the promise of Point Four. Yet the full measure of the reduction of American political and military strategy to the threat of atomic retaliation and of its moral, political and even military impoverishment is revealed only if one compares Mr. Dulles' speech with the one Dean Acheson gave exactly four years earlier, painting a vivid picture of the Asiatic revolution and of the role America must play in it.

Perhaps, however, the key to the new policy is to be sought not in such considerations of high political and military policy, but in the fact that in a speech of about 3,500 words there are no less than 15 references to the comparative cost of alternative policies and to the cheapness of the new one. Perhaps it is all a matter of saving money. Perhaps the *London Times* is right in saying: "It is indeed hard to see where and how the great strategic change has taken place, though it is not hard to recognize the economic reason why it has become politically desirable to assume that it has done so."

If the economic interpretation of the new policy is correct, and much in the recent statements of the President and of Mr. Dulles point to its correctness, it may again seem trite, but it is not superfluous, to remind the money savers that a Korean War, even one fought in perpetuity, is cheaper in every respect than an atomic war. . . .

## 7 | Dulles's Defense of United States China Policy, June 28, 1957 *

In this speech, delivered in San Francisco, Dulles repeated the rationale developed by American officials after 1952 to explain and defend American policy toward China. These arguments assumed a pattern which never varied. For that reason one need read only one full defense of that policy to grasp the full argumentation.

✒

* *The Department of State Bulletin*, XXXVII (July 15, 1957), 91–5.

. . . On the China mainland 600 million people are ruled by the Chinese Communist Party. That party came to power by violence and, so far, has lived by violence. It retains power not by will of the Chinese people but by massive forcible repression. It fought the United Nations in Korea; it supported the Communist war in Indochina; it took Tibet by force. It fomented the Communist Huk rebellion in the Philippines and the Communists' insurrection in Malaya. It does not disguise its expansionist ambitions. It is bitterly hateful of the United States, which it considers a principal obstacle in the way of its path of conquest.

In the face of this condition the United States has supported, morally and materially, the free nations of the Western Pacific and Southeast Asia. Our security treaties make clear that the violation of these nations by international communism would be considered as endangering our own peace and safety and that we would act accordingly. Together we constitute a goodly company and a stout bulwark against aggression.

As regards China, we have abstained from any act to encourage the Communist regime—morally, politically, or materially. . . .

United States diplomatic recognition of Communist China would have the following consequences:

(1) The many mainland Chinese, who by Mao Tse-tung's own recent admission seek to change the nature of their government, would be immensely discouraged.

(2) The millions of overseas Chinese would feel that they had no Free China to which to look. Today increasing numbers of these overseas Chinese go to Free China to study. Six years ago there were less than 100 Chinese students from Southeast Asia and Hong Kong studying in Taiwan. Now there are nearly 5,000. . . .

If the United States recognized the Chinese Communist regime, many of the millions of overseas Chinese in free Asian countries would, reluctantly, turn to acceptance of the guiding direction of the Communist regime. This would be a tragedy for them; and it would imperil friendly governments already menaced by Chinese Communist subversion.

(3) The Republic of China, now on Taiwan, would feel betrayed by its friend. That Government was our ally in the Second World War and for long bore alone the main burden of the Far Eastern war. It had many tempting opportunities to compromise with the Japanese on terms which would have been gravely detrimental to the United States. It never did so. . . . We are honorbound to give our ally, to whom we are pledged by a mutual defense treaty, a full measure of loyalty.

(4) The free Asian governments of the Pacific and Southeast Asia would be gravely perplexed. They are not only close to the vast Chinese land mass, but geographically and, to some extent, politically, they are separated as among themselves. The unifying and fortifying influence is, above all, the spirit and resolution of the United States. If we seemed to waver and to compromise with communism in China, that would in turn weaken free Asia resistance to the Chinese Communist regime and assist international communism to score a great success in its program to encircle us.

United States recognition of Communist China would make it probable that the Communist regime would obtain the seat of China in the United Nations. That would not be in the interest either of the United States or of the United Nations. . . . Should a regime which in 7 years has promoted five foreign or civil wars—Korea, Indo-China, Tibet, the Philippines, and Malaya . . . be given a permanent seat, with veto power, in the body which under the charter has "primary responsibility for the maintenance of international peace and security"?

Communist Russia, with its veto power, already seriously limits the ability of the United Nations to serve its intended purposes. Were Communist China also to become a permanent, veto-wielding member of the Security Council, that would, I fear, implant in the United Nations the seeds of its own destruction. . . .

Trade with Communist China is not a normal trade. It does not provide one country with what its people want but cannot well produce for themselves, in exchange for what other people want but cannot well produce themselves. Trade with Communist China is wholly controlled by an official apparatus, and its limited amounts of foreign exchange are used to develop as rapidly as possible a formidable military establishment and a heavy industry to support it. . . .

We also doubt the value of cultural exchanges, which the Chinese Communists are eager to develop. They want this relationship with the United States primarily because, once that example were given, it would be difficult for China's close neighbors not to follow it. These free nations, already exposed to intense Communist subversive activities, could not have the cultural exchanges that the Communists want without adding greatly to their danger.

These are the considerations which argue for a continuance of our present policies. What are the arguments on the other side?

There are some who say that we should accord diplomatic recognition to the Communist regime because it has now been in power so long that it has won the right to that. That is not sound international law. Diplomatic recognition is always a privilege, never a right.

Of course, the United States knows that the Chinese Communist regime exists. We know that very well, for it has fought us in Korea. . . . For nearly 2 years we have been, and still are, dealing with it in an effort to free our citizens and to obtain reciprocal renunciations of force.

But diplomatic recognition gives the recognized regime valuable rights and privileges, and, in the world of today, recognition by the United States gives the recipient much added prestige and influence at home and abroad. . . .

Another argument beginning to be heard is that diplomatic recognition is inevitable, so why not now?

First, let me say emphatically that the United States need never succumb to the argument of "inevitability." We, with our friends, can fashion our own destiny. We do not accept the mastery of Communist forces. . . . The reality is that a governmental system which tolerates diversity has a long life expectancy, whereas a system which seeks to impose conformity is always in danger. That results from the basic nature of human beings. . . .

We always take into account the possibility of influencing the Communist regime to better ways if we had diplomatic relations with it, or if, without that, we had commercial and cultural contacts with it. But the experience of those who now recognize and deal with the Chinese Communist regime convinces us that, under present conditions, neither recognition, nor trade, nor cultural relations, nor all three, would favorably influence the evolution of affairs in China. The probable result, internally, would be the opposite of what we hope for. . . .

Do we see any chance that the potentially great Chinese nation, with its rich and ancient culture and wisdom, will again be able to play a constructive part in the councils of the nations? We confidently answer these questions in the affirmative. Our confidence is based on certain fundamental beliefs. One is a belief in the future of human freedom. . . .

We can confidently assume that international communism's rule of strict conformity is, in China as elsewhere, a passing and not a perpetual phase. We owe it to ourselves, our allies, and the Chinese people to do all that we can to contribute to that passing.

If we believed that this passing would be promoted by trade and cultural relations, then we would have such relations. If we believed that this passing would be promoted by our having diplomatic relations with the present regime, then we would have such relations. If we believed that this passing would be promoted by some participation of the present regime in the activities of the United Nations, then we would not oppose that.

We would be, and we are, constantly testing our policies, to be as certain as we can be that, in the light of conditions as they from time to time are, our policies shall serve the great purposes to which our Nation has been dedicated since its foundation—the cause of peace, justice, and human liberty. . . .

Many free nations seek to coordinate their foreign policies with ours. Such coordination is indeed indispensable if the free world is to have the cohesion needed to make it safe. But United States policies will never serve as rallying points for free peoples if the impression is created that our policies are subject to change to meet Communist wishes for no reason other than that communism does not want to change. If communism is stubborn for the wrong, let us be steadfast for the right.

The capacity to change is an indispensable capacity. Equally indispensable is the capacity to hold fast that which is good. Given those qualities, we can hopefully look forward to the day when those in Asia who are yet free can confidently remain free and when the people of China and the people of America can resume their long history of cooperative friendship.

# 8 | Kenneth Younger's Critique of American China Policy, September 1957 *

Among the many critiques of American China policy which appeared during the 'fifties, none was more perceptive than that of Kenneth Younger, a member of the Labour party in the House of Commons. Many of his arguments were as stereotyped as those offered in defense of the policy. But Mr. Younger, more than most American writers, was concerned with the effort of the United States to isolate mainland China diplomatically in the Orient, for he believed that all Asia would either learn to live with China or become involved in war. Such a war would serve the interests of neither the West nor the countries of Asia.

✍

The controversy over policy towards China, which has now lasted nearly eight years, has centered around three main questions. Should the People's Government in Peking be diplomatically recognized? Should it occupy the Chinese seat in the United Nations? And what should be the trading and cultural relations between Communist China and the Western world?

The arguments used on both sides have, naturally enough, changed somewhat as the years have gone by. The dispute began before the outbreak of the Korean War, but was then widely expected to be settled within a matter of months. Chinese intervention in Korea, while it left the basic attitudes of both sides unaltered, led to the whole question being put into cold storage until the fighting was over. Since then, anxieties about Formosa, or the offshore islands or Indo-China have from time to time focused world opinion upon the issue, but have brought it, apparently, no nearer solution. The mere fact that everyone has become used to living with the problem has tended somewhat to reduce its explosive power. Nevertheless it remains important, as much on account of the embarrassments it causes between allies as for its effect upon relations between the West and the communist powers.

Through all vicissitudes two things have remained constant. The first is that the attitude of the United States has determined that of most of the governments—more than fifty of them—which do not recognize Peking. No one doubts that a change of American policy would reverse the present anti-Peking majority overnight. The second is that throughout the controversy, before and after the Korean fighting, as well as during it, United States government spokesmen have justified their policy in terms appropriate to a state of war.

Communist China, they say, is bent on world domination. It is an aggressor and morally and politically unfit to be a member of the United Nations. There is no point, they assert, in having cultural relations, let along diplomatic ones,

* *Western World*, I (September 1957), No. 5, 30–34. Reprinted by permission of the author.

with such a pariah while any form of trade with it can only have the effect of strengthening a government which must be regarded as an enemy.

Normally one would expect to be at war with a country of which one spoke in such terms; and the United States is, in effect, at war with Communist China in every respect except the one usually regarded as most characteristic of a state of war—it is not fighting China by force of arms. . . .

Quite apart . . . from the question whether it is wise for the West to base its own world policy upon a doctrine of inevitable conflict, which it attributes to and condemns in the communist powers, the American application of the doctrine to China is cruder and less discriminating than that which the communists adopt towards the West, or than the Americans themselves adopt towards the Soviet Union and other communist countries. The communists appreciate, for instance, that if one intends to pursue a policy of implacable hostility throughout a prolonged period of so-called peace, one must be flexible in one's methods. To behave as one would in war, by cutting diplomatic relations, and by forbidding one's citizens to communicate or trade with other countries, at a time when military force is neither in use nor immediately in prospect, is to deprive oneself of the means of waging peace without securing the advantages of waging war.

This is just the unhappy state of frustrated impotence to which the United States has condemned itself in China in recent years. It has avoided this in its dealings with the Soviet Union. . . .

Dulles has recently replied to the obvious query as to why the United States does not treat the Soviet Union as it treats China, by saying that the United States would not have recognized the Soviet government in 1933 if it had then known how the Soviet Union would subsequently behave. Does anyone, however, really think that if the United States had refused all contact with the Soviet Union over the years, this would have advanced the cause of peace? Surely not; and surely this is why Dulles does not choose to break off relations now. Indeed now, when he knows very well how the Soviet Union behaves, he not only maintains diplomatic relations but permits Americans to visit the Soviet Union. . . . At the same time, however, he refuses Mrs. Roosevelt permission to visit China as a journalist.

These striking discrepancies are explicable only in terms of the psychology of certain sections of American opinion, not in terms of objective differences between the Soviet and Chinese communist situations.

Closely linked with diplomatic recognition is the question of China's representation in the United Nations. China is, under the Charter, a member of the organization and a permanent member of the Security Council. The United States, when asked why, in these circumstances, it will not contemplate China being represented in the United Nations by the government which has controlled China for eight years, gives two replies. The first, heard more faintly every year, is that the Peking government's grip on China may be broken at any minute. No one, however, believes this. It is strictly for the record. The second reply is that the Chinese government's behavior unfits it for membership in the world club. . . .

"The United Nations," Dulles magisterially stated the other day, "is not a reformatory for bad governments." Maybe not; but neither is it a Sunday school for good governments. Indeed its main role is not that of a school at all, but of a meeting place where international quarrels may be settled. If the United Nations is to do its job of settling disputes without war, those governments, wicked or virtuous, which are at loggerheads, must be able to meet there. The more they disapprove of each other, the more important it is that their confrontation should take place within the organization. Otherwise they may confront one another on the battlefield. The United Nations exists precisely to prevent this from happening.

By excluding the Peking government, which wields effective power in its country, one damages not Peking but the United Nations, which is thereby ruled out as an effective instrument of international conciliation. . . .

The question of trade relations, which has recently entered a new phase, with Britain leading a breakaway from the United States embargo, has damaged interallied cooperation more than it has held up Chinese development. Just defensible while fighting continued in Korea, the discrimination between the Soviet Union and China in this field ceased to make any sense several years ago. . . . What has caused the ill-feeling among allies is not the scale of the fortunes which businessmen felt they were losing, but the attitude towards the problem of world communism of which the American embargo is a symptom. The American policy could claim to offer useful results only on the assumption that a trial by war is going to occur within a few years; or that the major communist governments can be overturned by external action to prevent a rise in living standards of their peoples. Neither of these propositions is accepted by America's allies, still less can support for them be found among China's Asian neighbors. . . .

Supporters of American policy are entitled to ask what dividends have resulted from recognition of the Peking government, and what could be expected from a switch by the United States or from the admission of the Communist China to the United Nations.

It is true that Britain cannot point to striking benefits to its interests in China, where British business has not been notably better treated than American. Nor have the Chinese ever been willing to exchange ambassadors with Britain.

To some extent this is due to Chinese resentment of the close relations which Britain has with the openly hostile United States. . . .

Other countries, both Asian and European, which have recognized Peking, but are uncommitted to any American alliance have certainly escaped some of Britain's disadvantages.

Moreover some of the benefits, which might have resulted from worldwide recognition of the People's government in 1950, were automatically ruled out when the United States succeeded in excluding it from the United Nations. Britain's policy not having been made effective, one could hardly expect to enjoy the fruits.

This reflection applies even more obviously to the hope which used to be

expressed, that Chinese communists, if gently humored, would avoid close alignment with the Soviet Union and might even "go Titoist." This was probably
always an over-optimistic forecast, though we are already seeing that Chinese
Marxism can show independence of Moscow. Nevertheless, American policy
since 1949 has undoubtedly cemented the Sino-Soviet alliance. A policy which
draws one's supposed adversaries together is not on the face of it an intelligent
one to follow and requires strong compensating advantages to justify it. In this
case they are not easy to find.

To ask what can now be gained by a change is, perhaps, to pose the question
wrongly. No one believes that admission to the United Nations or the general
normalization of relations would transform Peking overnight into a cooperative
regime. Experience with the Soviet Union, which is generally recognized, suggests no such thing. What is more pertinent is to ask what dangers and disadvantages might be avoided.

One has only to go back to the Geneva Conference on Indo-China in 1954 in
order to see the inconvenience and even danger which arises when major powers
will not speak to one another. . . . This was the lowest point of American postwar diplomatic prestige, and it was due directly to the anomalies inherent in
the American attitude to China. It is very important that, if further crises involving China should arise, this tragi-comedy should not have to be repeated.

Quite as important is the effect of United States policies upon the rest of
Asia. The United States has, of course, sufficient power to be able to buy the
acquiescence of a few Asian states who need its military protection, but it is
broadly true to say that no one in Asia except Syngman Rhee and Chiang
Kai-shek comes anywhere near to sharing the American attitude to Peking.

For Asian countries, it is self-evident that they must seek co-existence with
the communist regime in China. China to them looms larger than Russia and
seems a much more permanent factor in the Asian scene than the United
States. They do not believe that Chiang Kai-shek's government will ever see
China again, nor do they expect the collapse of the mainland regime. The
shifts and changes in personnel and policy, which have lately characterized
both Moscow and Peking, lead very few Asians to draw the conclusion Dulles
seems to draw—that continued external pressure may still overturn communism
in China in favor of some more Jeffersonian conception. On the contrary,
pressure of the American kind forces Chinese nationalism into alliance with
the Communist Party inside China, while in the rest of Asia it helps to turn
the spirit of Bandung into something specifically anti-Western.

In all this the United States shows itself surprisingly indifferent to the reactions of the uncommitted countries of Asia whose development and relationship
with the new China are likely to determine the shape which Asia will take a
generation hence. In particular it is curious that Americans, who have been
more closely associated than any other Westerners with the postwar problems of
Japan, should apparently make so little allowance for its future place on the
Asian firmament.

To be simply a part of America's strategic "island chain," the outer perimeter
of California's defenses, facing an ever-developing Sino-Soviet communist main-

land, with whom it is expected to have the minimum of relations—this is surely a prospect which the rising generation of Japanese cannot be expected to accept. It is a restriction upon its economic means of livelihood and an attempt to deny its Asian character. . . .

No one, of course, is asking that the United States should abandon forthwith its painfully acquired positions of strength in the Far East, let alone that it should now contemplate the turning over of Formosa to communist rule. All that is asked is that an attempt should be made to look at the problem of the Far East in the long perspective of Asian development rather than in the short perspective of American strategy.

The interest of the United States in this area is not strikingly different from that of its allies. It is much less a question of the defense of the American continent and much more a question of laying foundations for the co-existence of China and its Asian neighbors than some American strategists can bring themselves to admit.

The interest of America's allies is the same—to find a new equilibrium which minimizes the danger of armed conflict, especially among the great powers, and leaves room for the upsurge of the new revolutionary forces which are so evident on both sides of the Iron Curtain in Asia. These requirements are scarcely met at all by the attitude to China which has so far been dominant in the United States.

From the point of view of mutual confidence within the Western alliance, there is one further urgent need. It is to demonstrate that the United States is now framing its policies in the Far East, as it is already doing in other areas, upon the basis of an honest appraisal of world events and not upon the basis of prejudices deriving from its own domestic situation and its isolationist past.

To base the policy of great nations upon make-believe leads inevitably to deceiving of allies—as the Nationalists in Formosa were deceived about United States backing for a return to the mainland. It leads to the striking of fine attitudes followed by last minute withdrawals—as in the unfulfilled threats of all-out war in Korea or of nuclear intervention after Dien Bien Phu. When the moment of decision arrives, it is the realities which are added up and form the basis of action, but the resulting disillusionment can do a lot of damage.

Worst of all, prolonged dissemination of romantic myths ends by creating a public opinion, rooted in unreality, which itself becomes a stubborn obstacle to statesmanship.

# 9 | George F. Kennan's Observations on the New Soviet Leadership, August 1956 *

In this prize-winning essay George F. Kennan analyzed the changes in the Soviet outlook wrought by the passing of Stalin and the rise to power of Nikita S. Khrushchev. Whereas Kennan doubted that the new Soviet policies would permit much room for relaxation, he believed that the new Soviet rhetoric and the new emphasis on trade and aid were significant and to be welcomed by the American nation. But he urged that these changes in the direction of American purpose not be greeted with boasts that they represented either weakness within the Soviet system or a triumph for United States policies. Lastly, Kennan noted that the apparent gains of Soviet policy in the mid-'fifties resulted as much from American failure as from Soviet wisdom or success.

. . . I would like to make a few observations about the recent changes and the present state of affairs in Russia and the bearing of all this on the problems of American foreign policy.

I think we ought first to have a brief look at what these changes in Russia since Stalin's death have amounted to. And the best way to begin this examination is, I think, by noting one thing they have *not* amounted to.

I refer here to what seems to be a rather common impression that Stalin was a man of war, aiming to launch a military onslaught against the non-Communist world, whereas his successors are men of peace. Proceeding from this assumption people argue that whereas it was right for us, several years ago, to orient our policies exclusively to the danger of war, we now no longer need do so.

This is a great oversimplification. Stalin was not what you would call a nice man, and his intentions toward ourselves were strictly dishonorable. But these intentions, I am convinced, did not include the determination to unleash a third world war in the grand manner. The image of a Stalinist Russia poised and yearning to attack the West, and deterred only by our possession of atomic weapons, was largely a creation of the Western imagination, against which some of us who were familiar with Russian matters tried in vain, over the course of years, to make our voices heard.

In this respect the change that has recently come about has been more a change in the American interpretation of external reality than in that reality itself.

I do not mean to say that there have been *no* significant differences between the outlooks of Stalin and his successors in their bearing on the prospects for

* George F. Kennan, "Overdue Changes in Our Foreign Policy," *Harper's Magazine,* CCXIII (August 1956), 27–33. Reprinted by permission.

war or peace. Stalin, though not desirous of having another world war, was probably more skeptical than some of his successors of the possibility of avoiding one. He was more suspicious, I think, of the Western powers—more cynical about their motives—more incredulous of the possibility of having any relationship with them other than one of the most embittered and deadly and dangerous hostility. Like all truly evil people, he rationalized his own hatred of humanity by cherishing the belief that the rest of mankind were no better than himself. . . .

Against the background of this attitude, Stalin contrived to make of his own regime the most profound and sinister sort of conspiracy—a conspiracy not just against the outside world but also against the Soviet peoples themselves and, in a sense, against the very Communist movement by which he was supported. And by the same token, he contrived to communicate to Russia's relations with the outside world a climate of tightness and fear and antagonism so total and so terrible that it lay for decades, like a great black cloud, over the face of international life, and only the most naïve and wishful of people could bring themselves to hope for any lightening of the atmosphere so long as Stalin remained alive.

This was not a desire for war. It was not an intention to attack the West by force of arms at the earliest moment. It was not to be confused with the reckless plans and military timetables of a Hitler. But it was something so infinitely malicious—so cruel, so relentless, so menacing—that it is small wonder many people were unable to distinguish it from a desire to make war; small wonder the Western world, and this country in particular, responded—once the aftermath of the war had made all this clear—with urgent measures of military defense; small wonder a considerable portion of Western public opinion was brought to the belief that war was inevitable; small wonder the world hovered, for half a decade, in a state of extreme military nervousness and tension.

Are Stalin's successors any better? Do they not also entertain this same deadly hostility toward the outside world? Do not the principles of the political movement from which they have sprung render them just as dangerous, just as unreliable, as Stalin himself? . . .

It is quite true that there has theoretically been no change of objective. But there *has* been a very significant change of method. And this change of method, let us note, is one which, on our standards, we can only approve. There is far less terror, internally. There is a really far-reaching relaxation of the restrictions on cultural activity within Russia. There is much greater liberality with respect to cultural relations with the outside world. There is a much more liberal attitude toward the satellites. There is greater maturity, confidence, and courtesy in the approach to relationships between government, on the diplomatic level; and this, let us remember, is extremely important for the transaction of international business. We are witnessing, in other words, the evolution of the Soviet structure from the most nightmarish sort of modern totalitarianism to something resembling a traditional authoritarian state, oligarchically governed.

What more do we want in three-and-a-half years? Of course the objectives have not changed but the objectives are only the ends; whereas the methods are the means. And who are we to exalt the ends above the means? As a nation bred in the Christian tradition, we should understand something of the importance of method. We, of all people, should know that it is method—not the objective—which, in the last analysis, determines the outcome.

It is true of all of us, I think, that our achievements are more often conditioned by the manner in which we behave ourselves than by the foolish daydreams and illusions we so often accept as our goals in life. This is why manners are of such overriding importance everywhere both in personal life and in the affairs of nations. The individual cannot do anything about the beast in himself; but he can help a lot, and make life more tolerable for his friends and neighbors, by trying to act as though the beast did not exist. Just so the nation may not be able to alter—at least not abruptly—the unreal or absurd or outdated purposes to which it seems to be the habit of nations to be theoretically dedicated; but it can, by its behavior in practice, do much to enhance the prospects for a more stable and peaceful and hopeful world.

Let us not turn up our noses, then, or profess ourselves doubly afraid, over changes in Soviet behavior that are surely in the general direction we should like to see followed by political society at large. Let us not, after having criticized the Russian Communists all these years for being too totalitarian, pour scorn and ridicule upon them the moment they show signs of becoming anything else.

Let us not, in particular, discourage evolution in this new direction by receiving it with wild boasts that it represents the triumph and vindication of our policies and an ignominious defeat for the Soviet leaders who have introduced these changes. The victories of democracy occur not when men are destroyed, but when they are illuminated and made wiser and more tolerant. If greater liberality now comes to the Soviet world, the victory belongs not to us but to the forces of health and hope that live—thank God—in men everywhere; however they may at times be thrust down and discouraged; and if a defeat has been suffered, it was not really by the men who brought about these changes, but by those tendencies within their own system—perhaps within their own minds—that were unworthy of any great people and unresponsive to men's deepest needs. Let us have the humility to recognize these things, let us remember we are the agents, not the authors, of the eternal verities in which we profess to believe, and let us not take personal credit for what is in reality the power of these verities themselves.

What *are* these Soviet objectives that so disturb us? We must learn to distinguish here between the things people would theoretically *like* to do and the things they may reasonably expect to accomplish within their lifetimes. We must also distinguish between a belief that something is bound, by the laws of nature, to occur sooner or later, and a determination to bring that "something" about in the immediate future by one's own efforts.

The present Soviet leaders believe quite sincerely, I think, that the capitalist system is an episode in world history; that it cannot last; that it contains within it contradictions and weaknesses which will eventually prove its undoing; that it must sooner or later make place for a new order, which they call Socialism, and which will be marked primarily by government ownership of the means of production. . . .

Now in addition to having their misguided ideas about what the future is bound to bring, the Soviet leaders are also in business. They are in the business of national power. They have inherited the governmental responsibility for a great state—one of the major traditional units in the contemporary international family—with its people, its history, its traditions, its aspirations, its prejudices, and its rivalries. Like others who are in business, they like to win friends and influence people. They like to do better rather than worse. They like to see their own prestige and fortunes enhanced, their dangers lessened, their security increased, their power augmented. And international life being, like any other business, a competitive matter, it happens that these blessings can often be obtained only to the disadvantage of one's competitors.

Now the Soviet leaders have never concealed the fact that they consider themselves in competition with us; and I must say that I doubt we would let them forget it even if they were inclined to do so. They play, furthermore, a hard game; and they take whatever comes their way. If 30 or 40 per cent of the French electorate choose to believe Soviet propaganda and to be guided by the Soviet political line, the Soviet leaders are certainly not going to rebuff them and tell them to forget it and run along and be good Frenchmen. If large sections of the Asian public entertain the wildest prejudices against America and like to indulge themselves in the belief that the Soviet experiment holds the key to rapid economic development, no one in Moscow is going to rush to disabuse them of these illusions. And if nationalist leaders in the Middle East come to Moscow with soundings for military assistance that seem to offer attractive possibilities for the expansion of Russian influence in that area, these stirrings are certainly not going to be brutally discouraged at the Russian end.

Now this sort of thing is serious, of course, because Russia *is* our competitor and in many ways the strongest of world powers. But I don't think it can be taken as proof of any new or special aggressiveness on the Soviet side—of any aggressiveness that should cause people here to despair of meeting the problem short of war or to embrace panicky and extreme solutions. For one thing, this is all too similar to the way other great powers have behaved and still behave. The differences are relative. But beyond that: the openings—the breaks—of which the Soviet leaders take advantage are all too often ones of our own making, or ones we would have a good chance of closing, and denying to them, if we would only conduct our own affairs to that end.

Just how, after all, and in what ways, are Soviet policies considered to threaten us? What is it we are faced with? I think we would agree on the main items. We are faced, surely, with the peace campaign (which, incidentally, long preceded Stalin's death); with the appeal to the neutrals; with offers of trade, not aid; with the claim to be sincerely interested in economic development and to know how to carry it out; with a merciless exploitation of the colonial issue; with a similar exploitation of the color problem; and, last but not least, with the rapid and effective development of the Soviet military-industrial potential.

These, I repeat, are the things we are faced with on the Soviet side. And we must ask ourselves whether there is a single one of these issues in which we have not led with our chins?

Is it not we who have rendered ourselves vulnerable to the peace campaign by the over-militarization of our entire approach to world problems in these recent years—by our obdurate preoccupation with a war that might or might not come—by a concentration on this possible war so exclusive that it was bound to leave us empty-handed and devoid of suggestion if, in fact, war did not come?

Is it not we who have estranged the neutral world with our self-centeredness, with our lack of understanding for the very principle of neutrality, with our demand that everyone stand up and be counted either on our side or on the side of our adversaries; with our ill-advised efforts to corral all sorts of countries into military pacts—of which the implications were bound to be widely unwelcome to their peoples and the necessity obscure?

Is it not we who have set up the Soviet leaders in their slogan of trade not aid—by our exaggerated efforts to stifle East-West trade—and by our unbending attachment to all these vestigial remnants of protectionism that do so much psychological damage and so little practical good—by our tariffs and subsidies, our "Buy American" acts?

Have we not played into Soviet hands by our overemphasis on military aid to the detriment of economic aid, and by the unfortunate manner in which we have consistently portrayed our economic aid efforts as moves in the cold war— as bribes of sorts, rather than as the expression of a sincere interest in economic development for its own sake? To this day, our officials continue to describe various of our aid programs as efforts to "counter" Soviet moves here and there. How long will it take us to learn that if we wish to be effective in this field we must have the consistency to do things for their own sake and not for ulterior purposes? If we believe that economic development in this or that part of the world would be a good thing and worthy of American support, then let us support it for that reason and not wait for the Russians to frighten us into doing so. And if we do not believe this, let us not be pressured into doing things we don't believe in.

Again, the Russians exploit the colonial issue—yes; and there is much unscrupulousness and much injustice involved in this exploitation. But we can hardly say that the Western world has yet fully faced up to the issues involved. Great stupidities continue to be committed in the name of colonial, or quasi-colonial power, not by ourselves, to be sure, but by our Allies. And I would question whether the great hordes of officials we Americans maintain in the countries emerging from colonialism have yet learned to live there in a manner that does not exasperate in a hundred little ways the sensitivities on which anti-colonialism feeds.

Similarly, the color problem. We are all aware of the vicious distortions and exaggerations peddled by the Communists throughout the world about the state of race relations in this country; and I have no desire to condone the terrible irresponsibility that causes people to try to mislead other men by such means. But can we deny that we are continuing to pour oil on these fires in no small way? I do not mean to suggest that I think this problem susceptible of any easy and quick solution here at home; nor do I mean to make light of the feelings involved on either side of the controversy.

But what do we suppose is the effect on hundreds of millions of colored people in other lands of the direct reports from this country of what goes on here in the field of race relations? . . . Who is poisoning, here, the wells of world opinion? The Russians or ourselves? Both of us, no doubt—we by inadvertence, they by design; but we are doing our share.

Finally, we are faced with the assertion that Soviet military-industrial potential is growing more rapidly than our own. Well, there are—in this proposition —certain over-simplifications and certain exaggerations which I will not go into here. I doubt that the Russians are gaining on us quite so rapidly as some think. I suspect that they have greater troubles ahead than is often supposed. But I am prepared to accept, generally, the judgment of the economic experts that their ability to make war is already beginning to surpass our own in certain ways and will probably continue to grow in the coming period at a rate more rapid than ours.

Once more, I must point out that we are ourselves a vital factor in this disparity. We have in this country the resources that would permit us to outproduce the Russians twice over in military hardware any time we really wished to do so. And the disparities in the respective educational systems, by virtue of which they appear to be outpacing us in scientific and engineering competence, are also ones we have it in our power to overcome in the course of a few years, should we wish to do so.

This disparity is thus in part a matter of our own choice. It is our own habits and predilections, from which we do not wish to depart, that handicap us in this race. Ours is a high-cost country. We like it that way; and we have no intention of having it any other way. And for this reason our armed forces establishment is a high-cost establishment. It will remain that way. One might say that we have priced ourselves out of the race for military pre-eminence.

And our shortage of engineers and the deficiencies of our educational system are reflections of our aversion to every sort of regimentation and of the factors that lie behind the decline of educational standards in this country generally. I am not inveighing here against these weaknesses or arguing, at this point, for their correction. I am merely saying that they exist; that they are relevant to our competition with the Russians; and that we cannot ascribe entirely to Soviet aggressiveness disparities and reverses that are in part attributable to the weaknesses of our own performance.

The fact is, whether we like it or not, that in the Soviet challenge to our world there are two components: one composed of Soviet strength and another composed of our own weaknesses and deficiencies. And I would like to point out that there is none of these weaknesses or deficiencies that did not exist and cry out for attention long before Stalin's death. It should not have taken the very relative subtleties of Khrushchev and Bulganin to bring it home to us that an overmilitarization of approach to the cold war was losing us the sympathies of world opinion; that petty protectionism is foolish; that the race question within our country needs our most prayerful and courageous attention; and that we have a huge problem on our hands in our relations with the undeveloped side of the world.

For these reasons I do not find that the things that have occurred in Russia in these last three or four years change anything very much in the necessities that govern American foreign policy. They merely accentuate and make more urgent the demands that already rested upon us, and leave us less time, and perhaps less room, to do the things we ought long ago to have been doing. . . .

## 10 | Dulles's Address before the Dallas Council on World Affairs, October 27, 1956 *

As Soviet foreign policy in 1955 and 1956 began to reveal an unprecedented flexibility, Secretary Dulles, quite in contrast to the moderation of Kennan's views regarding a proper American attitude, attributed the change to Russian weakness and the success of United States policies. His confidence in the capacity of American rhetoric to destroy the Soviet hegemony in Eastern Europe reached its epitome during the Hungarian revolution of 1956. In the following review of American military and diplomatic policy, the Secretary recounted the sources of American military strength. While Western power held the Communists at bay, he noted, the forces for liberty in Hungary and elsewhere were exposing the true weakness of the Soviet structure. Again as in his previous foreign policy statements, Dulles predicted the achievement of his goal of liberation through the successful operation of the nation's established containment policies.

✍

. . . Let me speak first of our military strength. That we must have. For moral strength alone is not enough. If we were relatively feeble in relation to the vast military power possessed by unscrupulous men, then we would not be the master of our own destiny.

But while it is simple to decide to be militarily strong, it is difficult to decide in what way to be strong. There are many ways—air, army, navy—conventional and atomic weapons—defense and offense. We cannot be equally strong in all ways and at all times and at all places without assuming an intolerable load.

* Department of State, *American Foreign Policy: Current Documents, 1956* (Washington, 1959), 42–9.

Fortunately, it is not necessary for the United States, by itself, to possess all of the military power needed to balance that of the Soviet bloc. We have allies, and they contribute to the common defense. But we do have one special responsibility. We alone have the economic and financial strength and the "know-how" to prevent the world from being dominated by the atomic and nuclear weapons which the Soviet Union is feverishly developing. We must possess a capacity to retaliate on a scale which is sufficient to deter aggression. We must have that capacity, not in the expectation of having to use it but because if we have that capacity we shall probably never have to use it.

But there may be local aggressions, so-called "nibblings," not initially involving the most potent weapons. We and our allies should, between us, have the capacity to deal with these without our action producing a general nuclear war. Furthermore, it would be reckless to risk everything on one form of armament, because no one can forecast with certainty the requirements of a future war.

Thus, we and our allies, in addition to having great nuclear power, should have conventional forces which can help to defend the free world. The combined free-world military strength must be sufficiently balanced, sufficiently flexible, and so deployed that it can deter or defeat both big and little aggressions. . . .

I turn now to a second major area of concern. That is the maintaining and strengthening of our collective security arrangements. . . .

All of these arrangements, in their present form, are the product of a sense of danger born of the aggressive and violent foreign policies of power-hungry dictators—firstly Hitler and then the Soviet and Chinese Communist rulers.

But now that sense of danger is somewhat dissipated. The Soviet Union has continued intensively its efforts to develop military supremacy. But it has also sought—at least until this week—to appear more peace-loving. In consequence, rightly or wrongly, it became widely felt that there was less danger of general war. The cement of fear is not so strong to hold us together as it was to bring us together.

That is not logical, because the basic danger persists—vast military power in the hands of a dictatorship unrestrained by moral principles. We should, therefore, hold fast that which has made us more safe. But we cannot get away from the fact that as people feel less endangered they tend to draw apart—unless they find a basis for unity which transcends that sense of danger. . . .

A third major area of concern relates to the nearly 700 million people who, in 18 new nations, have achieved full independence since World War II.

These new nations are distinctive in many respects. But they are alike in being imbued with national patriotism that won them their freedom. Also they are all inspired by a vision of progress toward well-being.

Some of these newly independent nations realize that their independence can best be assured through such collective security arrangements as we have described. We are proud to be associated with these nations and are determined to justify their confidence. Other newly independent nations prefer not to adhere to collective security pacts. We acknowledge, of course, their freedom of choice.

We have a deep interest in the independence of all of these new nations and we stand ready to contribute, from our store of skills and resources, to help them achieve a solid economic foundation for their freedom.

This is a challenging problem for the free world. For, in the long run, political independence and economic well-being are interdependent. Much has been done, and is being done, to meet the problem. But it is on a piecemeal basis. The search for adequate and dependable processes is still unfinished business.

Surely it is within the capability of the free world to assure that no people dedicated to freedom have to choose between Communist serfdom and economic destitution. . . .

Another intensive concern of our foreign policy is in relation to the captive nations of the world. We had looked upon World War II as a war of liberation. The Atlantic Charter and the United Nations Declaration committed all the Allies to restore sovereign rights and self-government to those who had been forcibly deprived of them, and to recognize the right of all peoples to choose the form of government under which they would live. Unhappily, those pledges have been violated, and in Eastern Europe one form of conquest was merely replaced by another.

But the spirit of patriotism, and the longing of individuals for freedom of thought and of conscience and the right to mold their own lives, are forces which erode and finally break the iron bonds of servitude.

Today we see dramatic evidence of this truth. The Polish people now loosen the Soviet grip upon the land they love. And the heroic people of Hungary challenge the murderous fire of Red Army tanks. These patriots value liberty more than life itself. And all who peacefully enjoy liberty have a solemn duty to seek, by all truly helpful means, that those who now die for freedom will not have died in vain. It is in this spirit that the United States and others have today acted to bring the situation in Hungary to the United Nations Security Council.

The weakness of Soviet imperialism is being made manifest. Its weakness is not military weakness nor lack of material power. It is weak because it seeks to sustain an unnatural tyranny by suppressing human aspirations which cannot indefinitely be suppressed and by concealing truths which cannot indefinitely be hidden.

Imperialist dictatorships often present a formidable exterior. For a time they may seem to be hard, glittering, and irresistible. But in reality they turn out to be "like unto whited sepulchres, which indeed appear beautiful outward, but are within full of dead men's bones and of all uncleanness." They have vulnerabilities not easily seen.

Our Nation has from its beginning stimulated political independence and human liberty throughout the world. Lincoln said of our Declartion of Independence that it gave "liberty not alone to the people of this country, but hope for the world for all future time." During the period when our Nation was founded, the tides of despotism were running high. But our free society and its good fruits became known throughout the world and helped to inspire the subject peoples of that day to demand, and to get, the opportunity to mold their own destinies. Today our Nation continues its historic role. The captive peoples should never have reason to doubt that they have in us a sincere and dedicated friend who shares their aspirations. They must know that they can draw upon our abundance to tide themselves over the period of economic adjustment which is inevitable as they rededicate their productive efforts to the service of their own people, rather than of exploiting masters. Nor do we condition economic ties between us upon the adoption by these countries of any particular form of society.

And let me make this clear, beyond a possibility of doubt: The United States has no ulterior purpose in desiring the independence of the satellite countries. Our unadulterated wish is that these peoples, from whom so much of our national life derives, should have sovereignty restored to them and that they should have governments of their own free choosing. We do not look upon these nations as potential military allies. We see them as friends and as part of a new and friendly and no longer divided Europe. We are confident that their independence, if promptly accorded, will contribute immensely to stabilize peace throughout all of Europe, West and East.

Let me add a word about future relations with the peoples who compose the Union of Soviet Socialist Republics. They, too, can have hope. The spread of education and industrial development create growing demands for greater intellectual and spiritual freedom, for greater personal security through the protection of law, and for greater enjoyment of the good things of life. And there has been some response to those demands.

There is ground to believe that that trend will prove to be an irreversible trend. It may bring the day when the people of the United States can have, with the people of Russia, the relations of fellowship which they would like, and when the governments of our countries can deal with each other as friends. . . .

We all know the obstacles which men face and surmount, in time of war, to secure victory. It seems not to be realized that it is necessary to make comparable efforts, in time of peace, to preserve peace. Peace will never be won so long as men reserve for war their finest effort. Peace has to be waged, just as war has to be waged, and men and nations have to work intensively and sacrificially to overcome the threats to peace and justice.

I see no reason why that should not be done. Surely peace is a goal which deserves to be sought with the same dedication that would be devoted in war to winning victory. Today it is the more important because we now live in a world where, if war comes, there may be no victors.

I am confident that the mood I describe is that of our people and of our political leaders, without regard to party. If that mood be matched by the people and leaders of other lands, then we can see the future as one which, despite its vast perplexities, beckons us hopefully to great tasks of creation.

West Berlin, lying a hundred miles behind the Iron Curtain, became after November 1958 the chief focus of East-West tension in Europe. For the Western nations the legal right of access was essential if the city was to remain outside the Communist world, and as long as the access routes remained open the West was under no compulsion to negotiate with the Kremlin on matters of Germany's future. Late in November 1958, Premier Khrushchev touched off a major crisis when, in a note to the Western powers, he challenged the Allied status in West Berlin. He gave the British, French, and United States governments six months to negotiate the establishment of a demilitarized free city before the Soviet Union would sign a separate peace treaty with the East German government and give it control of the routes into West Berlin. At the Geneva Conference of Foreign Ministers, convened in May 1959 to consider the Berlin question, the Western powers refused to sign away any of their legal rights of access or to recognize the East German regime. In a formal address on June 5, Secretary of State Christian A. Herter made it clear that the United States still anchored its German policy to the principle of self-determination.

✑

. . . The Foreign Minister of the Soviet Union has said that by the term the "Berlin problem" he meant "primarily the ending of the occupation in West Berlin." It seems that this definition minimizes the real dimensions of the Berlin problem. For us, the Berlin problem means maintenance of freedom for more than two million human beings who at the end of the war with the agreement of the Soviet Government came under the occupation authority of the three Western Powers.

Although our rights in Berlin stem from the war, our obligations arise from the trusteeship which we have undertaken to exercise for the people of Berlin until the reunification of their country removed this need for our protection. The past fourteen years have shown that West Berlin is encircled by hostile forces and that its independence and well being are dependent upon the presence of the three Western Powers in the city and in the maintenance of the political and economic links between Berlin and the West.

I think that there is another fundamental difference between the Soviet Union and ourselves on this matter of Berlin. This difference derives from our different attitude toward the reunification of Germany. Although talking about the ideal of German unity and recognizing that German reunification is the real key to the Berlin problem the Soviet Union has openly adopted a two-Germany policy, if not a three-Germany policy.

* Statement of Christian A. Herter, June 5, 1959, Department of State, *Foreign Ministers Meeting, May–August 1959, Geneva* (Washington, 1959), 245–54.

Now how does West Berlin fit into this policy of the permanent partition of Germany? The Soviet Foreign Minister gave us the answer on May 30, in one of the most revealing statements made during the many plenary sessions we have held. . . . I am quoting the Soviet Foreign Minister:

> If we are to speak frankly, the Soviet Government considers the creation of a Free City far from being an ideal solution of the West Berlin question. The most equitable approach to this question would be, of course, the extension to West Berlin of the full sovereignty of the German Democratic Republic. I think that the German Democratic Republic, whose capital the division of the city continues to mutilate, could with the fullest justification demand such a solution of the question.

I am grateful to Mr. Gromyko for his willingness to speak so frankly. We thus have in his own words a clear and valuable statement of the ultimate objective of the Soviet Union regarding West Berlin. . . .

During the course of our talks about Berlin, this conference has clarified at least one important matter. The Western Powers' presence and their access to Berlin are a matter of right—they are not at the sufferance of any other authority—legitimate or otherwise. . . .

The second salient defect in the Soviet plan is that it would in effect compel the Western Powers to grant a measure of recognition to the so-called GDR. No non-communist nation has recognized this instrument of the Soviet Union as an independent nation. I can assure you that we have no intention of recognizing the so-called GDR as the price of a solution to the Berlin problem.

I should point out one other serious defect in the Soviet plan. Although purporting to terminate the occupation it would supplant the present regime by imposing in a real occupation spirit a new political status of the people of West Berlin. The U.S.S.R. in its note of November 27, 1958, formally acknowledged that West Berlin must be granted the right to whatever way of life it wishes for itself—with one qualification "When the foreign occupation is ended." I cannot find any hint or suggestion in the Soviet plan that even though the "foreign occupation" would be ended under the Soviet plan the people of West Berlin would have any real voice in whether or not the proposed new political status should come into existence.

As a matter of fact the West Berliners have by an overwhelming vote endorsed their present way of life—and by that same vote they have in effect rejected the Soviet scheme. They are in a first rate position to judge for themselves the comparative merits of a free system and a communist system.

The U.S.S.R. has vigorously urged that we impose this new unwanted status on West Berliners under the label of a "Free City." Surely by this time the U.S.S.R. should have had enough experience with governments not based upon the consent of the governed! This indeed is a curious proposal coming from the Soviet Foreign Minister who at the same time complains that the West Berliners are now being deprived by the Western Powers of rights contained in the Charter of the United Nations.

One final defect in the Soviet plan should be noted. In addition to the Western military presence, West Berlin owes its viability to its political, economic and social ties with the Federal Republic of Germany.

The entire thrust of the Soviet plan for West Berlin cuts into these ties and is clearly intended to establish a situation which will be but a "way-station" on the road to the preferred Soviet solution—that of annexation of West Berlin by the communist controlled authority in East Germany. . . .

The heart of the Western Peace plan lies in its comprehensive proposal for the gradual reunification of Germany. The plan makes provision as well for European security and concomitant arms control moves—and for an interim Berlin solution. But the continued dangerous division of Germany places great obstacles in the way of real progress on European security, arms control and Berlin. The unification of Germany is still our main task. We are confident that the solution proposed in the Western Peace plan will stand the test of history and will be seen to offer reasonable answers to the great problems raised by the continuing division of Germany.

It seems clear from the worldwide appreciation which the Western Peace plan has received that the Soviets' claim that it is but a device to generate disagreement has met the reception it deserved.

And so let us continue to look at these matters in parallel. In trying to improve the Berlin situation for the interim we must not do anything to put off the day when Germany is reunified. And in our striving for German unity we must not prejudice the position of West Berlin.

What is the interim Berlin proposal contained in the Western Peace Plan? It would in advance of final reunification of Germany permit the unification of the separated parts of Berlin. Free elections would be held throughout the city. The Four Powers would guarantee the freedom of the city and access thereto pending the reunification of Germany. These happy developments would take place in the very first phase of the Western Peace plan. Their accomplishment would be a good harbinger of that greater unity which under our plan would follow shortly thereafter for all of Germany.

The USSR gave short shrift to the whole Western Peace Plan as well as its all-Berlin proposal. . . .

What then is the present situation? The USSR while recognizing existing Western rights in and to Berlin still puts forward its "second preference" plan as unveiled some months ago. It proposes that the Western Powers abandon their present rights in favor of the Soviet plan. This we will not do. We will have no share in imposing a new status on the West Berliners against their will. Such a new regime would make German unity more difficult to achieve since it would establish still a third part of Germany.

However, we recognize our responsibilities for keeping frictions between our two systems to a minimum. We recognize that Berlin, because of its unique situation, can be a source of friction. We are willing to search in good faith with the Soviet Union for some reciprocal improvement in the Berlin situation. However, it should be very clear that any improvement arrangement must meet these criteria: a) respect for existing Western rights of presence and access to Berlin and existing agreements concerning such rights since the Western presence is essential to maintain West Berlin's freedom; b) no recognition of the so-called GDR; c) maintenance of West Berlin's political and economic ties with the West. . . .

Our reading of recent history indicates that the proposed "Free City" would be but a disguise for gradual smothering of West Berliners' present freedom. In 1948 no one was really fooled by the "technical difficulties" alibi. In 1959, no one is being fooled by the fair label "free city."

This is no time to resort to a breach of solemn international agreements under the guise of "relaxation of tensions." If the Soviet Government will exercise the necessary degree of responsibility and recognize the legitimate rights of other nations, the situation in Berlin may develop in a tolerable fashion.

Today the world judges nations by their willingness to stand by their international obligations. The Soviet Government must recognize that Berlin is a solemn testing ground on which its intentions with respect to its international obligations are being watched.

In these troubled times, peace with justice is the greatest goal to which man can aspire. I hope the Soviet Union will be willing to demonstrate, by word and by deed, that it is ready to move toward that great goal. . . .

Innumerable acts of force originating in East Berlin have been carried out against people in West Berlin.

The most sensational of these have been cases of kidnapping. Our own conservative calculations show there have been at least 63 actual cases, 31 attempted kidnappings and 21 probable cases since the end of the war. Although drugs were used in a number of instances, most of these kidnappings involved the use of brute force. A report just completed by the Senate of Berlin confirms our figures.

General subversive activities, incitement to sedition, and attacks on public order, directed from East Berlin comprehend a vast variety of activities. . . .

East Berlin is being misused as the center of an extensive campaign of slanderous personal vilification against the institutions and officials of the Allies and of the German authorities in West Berlin. This involves the frequent use of lies as well as outright forgeries. A good example of this is the current campaign of vilification by press and radio against myself, the Foreign Minister of the Federal Republic, and other leading officials.

The fact that over 500 persons living or working in West Berlin were convicted of treasonable activities in a period from August 30, 1951 to the end of 1958—an average of more than one a week—helps illustrate the scope and purpose of this attempt to subvert the existing order in West Berlin. . . .

I have given an all-too-brief description of a situation which is both scandalous and dangerous. It is a sad commentary on the ethics of the men who conduct these activities. Those men comprise the regime of the so-called German Democratic Republic, and that regime is neither German, nor democratic, nor a republic. More important still, it is a revelation of the determination of these men to achieve their objective by any means at hand. And that objective is to bring West Berlin and the Federal Republic under the control of an ideology which teaches that any means is legal and good which serves to impose it on the other peoples. . . .

— | "Now we can and must be united by the desire to do everything to prevent a revival of German militarism. . . ." *

Andrei Gromyko, representing the Soviet Union at the Geneva Conference, based his argument on power and interest rather than on principle. He denied the validity of self-determination for Germany, the aggressor nation of World War II. He recalled what Hitler's Germany had done to Europe when it enjoyed self-determination. The total failure of the negotiations at the Geneva Conference, which terminated finally in August 1959, illustrated the critical importance of Berlin and Germany in the continuing European cold war.

✍

. . . It was only two days before the opening of this conference that the anniversary of the victory over Hitler Germany and of the cessation of the war in Europe was observed for the fourteenth time. Since the memorable spring of 1945 life has made a big stride forward. In place of the smouldering ruins and debris left by the war, hundreds and thousands of towns and villages have been restored or rebuilt. Humanity has ben enriched by discoveries made by the genius of man which not only enable us to make life on earth better but also pave the way for the conquest of cosmic space. During these years new independent States have emerged in many parts of the world. A new generation was born which at present is preparing to cross the threshold of adult life. . . .

Germany has always occupied one of the leading positions among the European States both for her economic and for her political weight and importance, and her geographical position in the centre of Europe for centuries linked the German people with West and East. It is only natural that as long as the relations between Germany and the States which were the victims of Hitlerite aggression are not cleared of the deposits left by the war, Europe will feel that burden on her shoulders.

Meanwhile, if we approach with sober mind the assessment of the situation that has developed here over the recent years, we cannot fail to see that we are again faced with the fact of a dangerous piling up of inflammable materials in this part of the world where in the course of a quarter of a century the conflagration of war has twice flared up enveloping almost the entire world.

* Statement of Andrei Gromyko at the Geneva Foreign Ministers Meeting, May 15, 1959, ibid. 63–74.

The division of Europe into two opposing military camps, the beginning of which was laid by bringing about a certain military grouping of the Western States, has now reached a dangerous level. Never before have the States of West Europe seen on their territories such accumulations of foreign troops and war equipment, never before has so vast an area of fertile soil been taken away from the peaceful population in order to build on it all kinds of military bases, depots, launching sites, airfields, testing grounds. Never before have the armies come to possess such deadly weapons as hydrogen bombs and missiles.

It would be a profound delusion to think that if all these military preparations are directed against the Soviet Union and other socialist countries, they do not affect other States. The fact is that if world war II involved a far greater number of States than the previous one, world war III may have no bounds at all.

Had a German peace treaty been concluded in time, we would undoubtedly have been faced with a different Germany, and with a different situation in Europe. For it is inconceivable that if a peace treaty had existed there could have taken place such facts as the incorporation of the FRG in NATO, the equipment of the Bundeswehr with atomic and rocket weapons, revanchist pronouncements in West Germany, i.e., everything that has dug a deep trench between the two German States and has brought about the atmosphere of tension which is so typical of the present situation in Germany and in Europe as a whole.

If we are faced today wtih the necessity of taking measures to render harmless such a hotbed of international conflicts as West Berlin has become owing to the unduly prolonged occupation, this is also one of the consequences of the absence of a peace treaty. . . .

But who will be so bold as to maintain—without flying in the face of facts— that the soil which nourished German militarism in the past has now been destroyed in Western Germany too, as the Potsdam Agreement required, or that those who faithfully served the nazi regime are not there enjoying authority and influence, or that a policy of militarizing the country is not undermining the foundations of European security?

Much of the present policy of the Government of the Federal Republic of Germany is designed to aggravate international tension, and this inevitably compels us to be on our guard. How can European States, and especially Germany's neighbours, be free from anxiety when the Government of the Federal Republic of Germany is openly proclaiming its territorial pretensions? It is in Bonn that the voice of blackmail is raised at the first sign of rapprochement between the States concerned, or of the prospect of settling outstanding international questions. We all know what obstacles were raised by certain people in the Federal Republic of Germany against calling this conference. . . .

We realize, of course, that the Soviet Union and the Western Powers have a different approach to the German question, different notions as to the future development of Germany. But our countries have one thing in common which once enabled us to make common cause. During the war we were united by the desire to destroy German militarism and to secure peace for the nations.

Now we can and must be united by the desire to do everything to prevent a revival of German militarism and the possibility of its ever again, either alone or in alliance with anyone, launching a new war, which would again drown Europe and the whole world in blood and turn flourishing cities into ruins.

The main argument advanced by those who oppose the conclusion of a peace treaty with Germany comes to this: that at present there is no government that could sign a peace treaty on behalf of the whole of Germany and ensure that the obligations involved would be fulfilled. But this argument cannot be accepted as either correct or convincing. It proceeds from extremely formal legalistic considerations, than which none could be less appropriate under the existing conditions. It is rooted in a deliberate refusal to recognize the *de facto* situation in Germany, a territory in which two independent sovereign States have long been in existence. Is not the very fact that the official representatives of the Governments of these two States are present in this room convincing proof that it is no longer possible to be blind to the actual state of affairs?

Moreover, if we are to speak of the legal side of the matter, there are examples in the practice of international relations, to show that the existence of the two German States cannot be an obstacle to the conclusion of a peace treaty with Germany. . . .

Taking into account the *de facto* situation, the Soviet Government sees no other possibility but to conclude a peace treaty with the two German States; and, in the event that a German confederation has been formed by the time the peace treaty is signed, to sign the treaty with the German confederation as well as with the GDR and the FRG. To refuse to conclude a peace treaty today means to face still bigger differences between the GDR and the FRG tomorrow, to pander to those extremist circles in West Germany which do not conceive of the unification of Germany in any other way than by their absorbing the GDR, even though this could mean confronting the world with the catastrophe of a new war. If, of course, these circles were able to assess the situation soberly, even they might see the completely illusory and absurd nature of such plans.

Similarly, it is difficult to take seriously the arguments of those who are trying to justify their negative attitude to proposals for a peaceful settlement with Germany by references to the fact that they recognize one German State alone. We know that the social system of the GDR is not to the liking of certain people in the West. In politics, however, it is least of all appropriate to give way to feelings, at the expense of a sober approach to facts, and the facts are that the Government of the GDR has fully acknowledged and accepted all the aims that were proclaimed in the Allied agreements on Germany. . . .

Certain circles in the West are expressing themselves in favour of granting Germany a so-called freedom of choice between the Eastern and the Western military alliances; in fact, what they have in mind here is the future integration of the whole of Germany into NATO; that is, the possibility of using her territory and her resources in material and manpower in the interests of this military alliance. It is known also that such plans meet with support from certain quarters in the FRG, although the latter, of course, are not thinking in terms of the advantages of the Western Powers which today hold the leading position in NATO, but of designs of their own which are prompted by their unwillingness to resign themselves to the defeat of Hitler Germany. . . .

We are also told that the withdrawal of Soviet forces from the GDR would not be equivalent to the withdrawal of the foreign troops from West Germany, since the Soviet armed forces would, they say, still be able to remain somewhere close to Germany. Such arguments are patently artificial and far-fetched. We have only to remember that the armed forces of France, Great Britain, Belgium and other NATO countries would also, in this case, be no farther from Germany than the Soviet troops. Moreover, the critics of the Soviet proposal on the withdrawal of troops from Germany cannot be unaware of the fact that the Soviet Government has long been urging an even more fundamental settlement of the problem of foreign troops in Europe. The Soviet Union is prepared to withdraw its troops not only from Germany but also from Poland and Hungary, where they are at present under the terms of the Warsaw Treaty, provided of course, that the other NATO countries withdraw their forces back within their own frontiers and dismantle their military bases on foreign territories. . . .

The conclusion of a peace treaty would greatly facilitate the unification of Germany in accordance with the national aspirations of the German people. The acceptance and *bona fide* fulfillment of the provisions of the peace treaty by both German States will remove the barriers on the road to a rapprochement between the GDR and the FRG, and will lead to the development of fruitful co-operation between them.

The Soviet Draft Peace Treaty provides for the Contracting Parties to render every assistance to both German States in order that this aim may be achieved, and to refrain from such actions as might hinder the unification of Germany.

The Soviet Government's proposal on the conclusion of a peace treaty with Germany includes a simultaneous solution of the Berlin question; this solution would thereby become an integral part of the general peace settlement with Germany. The quadripartite agreements which determined the procedure for the administration and occupation of Germany, including Berlin, would naturally lapse with the signing of the peace treaty. The occupation regime which is still maintained in West Berlin, would thereby be ended, and the soil which nurtures the very causes of friction between States would be removed. In this connexion there arises the question of the future status of West Berlin, pending the restoration of German unity, and of Berlin's becoming once again the capital of a united German State. The Soviet Government believes that the most appropriate solution would be to give West Berlin the status of a demilitarized Free City. This is the solution of the Berlin question which is envisaged in Article 25 of the Soviet Draft Peace Treaty; it enjoys the full support of the Government of the GDR on whose territory West Berlin is situated.

We are prepared to work out, together with other States concerned, appropriate guarantees to ensure that the proposed status of West Berlin is respected so that there would be no interference in the life of the Free City from any quarter and so that its independence, as well as its commercial, cultural and other ties with the countries of both West and East would be assured. If the proposal for a Free City were put into effect a healthier situation would be created not only in Berlin but also throughout Germany; at the same time, the arrangement would not introduce any changes in the social and economic order which already exists in West Berlin. . . .

## 12 | Bertram D. Wolfe on the Soviet Challenge: Ideology, January 1959 *

Bertram D. Wolfe, the noted writer on Soviet affairs, stood at the forefront of those who interpreted Soviet foreign policy in the light of Soviet ideology—the ideology of Communist victory. In the following essay he viewed the U.S.S.R. as a deadly enemy which never abandoned its two basic aims of remaking man and conquering the world. With such an enemy there could be neither compromise nor co-existence. To reduce tensions would lead to disaster. While criticising past American policies for their failure to contain or to liberate, he did not suggest what American policies might eliminate this ruthless enemy from the international scene.

✿

The Soviet system of power, which is the enemy we face, can only be understood properly with the help of certain theoretical criteria of a socio-historical nature. Very briefly, we may say that the Soviet system is a closed, single-centered, modern totalitarian society, as distinguished from an open, multi-centered society. A *closed society* is one with built-in staying powers which enable it to endure for a very long period of time; it is a self-conserving society, in that any changes that occur are within-system changes that leave the basic structure of power untouched. A *single-centered society* is one in which there is only one focus of power, the state, which does not tolerate the diffusion of power among any other relatively independent social institutions or groups. Finally, a *modern totalitarian society,* as distinguished even from an old-fashioned despotism, is one in which the state seeks to be co-extensive with the whole of society and the whole of life, a society that is perpetually at war with its own people and with the rest of the world, and which uses modern technology and widespread literacy as weapons in that war.

* Bertram D. Wolfe, "The Deadly Enemy We Face," *The New Leader,* XLII (January 26, 1959), 14–18. Reprinted by permission.

Now, the Soviet Union is truly a great power—great in population, great in resources, great in technology, and great in military strength. Secondly, it has a great state machine which is in a condition of permanent semimobilization, and which attempts to keep its people mobilized. Finally, it is an enemy which is resourceful enough, wealthy enough, and determined enough to do what we have not had the determination to do (although we have had the resources in the West in much greater abundance): Namely, to keep simultaneously an atomic striking power and a massive conventional striking force in being. It has a definite advantage over us at this moment because it is geared to both types of warfare. It believes that both types are necessary and that they must be integrated into a single plan. . . .

It is a deadly enemy. It is a deadly enemy because never for a moment does it abandon its two basic aims: to remake man, and to conquer the world. It is particularly our enemy—not because we so choose, but because it has chosen. It regards the strength and the way of life of the United States as the chief obstacle to its plan to remake its own people and to remake the world in the image of its blueprint. We have been picked as Enemy Number One. . . .

Let us not listen to the siren song of those who tell us that we can get release of tensions and a little peace in our time if we only "disengage" ourselves. If we disengage ourselves, we leave another strip to be occupied, a new place from which battle will begin.

They know, to be sure, that they cannot conquer us. They know something about our strength. They do not covet for a moment the risks of all-out war with us. There are two things that they are determined with all of their might to avoid: one is all-out war, the other is all-out peace. They will keep us in between as long as they have the power to do so. They do not wish all-out war because they believe that time and history are on their side. When they consider how their system has been expanding, I must say it seems to them that they have some empirical confirmation for their belief that time is on their side.

Of course, they do not want all-out peace, for their two fundamental aims do not permit them to be at peace either with their own people or with the rest of the world. . . .

The real reason for the Kremlin's endless hostility toward the United States, regardless of what we do, is that they regard us, and rightly, as the main obstacle to their underlying plan. This will not be changed if Khrushchev should come to New York and "see our skyscrapers," or if he should then go to Detroit and see how many automobiles our workingmen have. The Russian leaders are ruthlessly friendly. They talk of "easing of tensions." In our society, "tension" is a bad word. We can thank the Freudians for that, I suppose, for they talk of the "age of anxiety" and the "age of tension." To anybody who comes with a panacea for easing tensions, we open our arms and our hearts. However, if every time they speak of "easing of tensions" you would substitute for the word "tension" the word "concern" (which is a more neutrally or differently colored word), you would see that what they are asking us to do is to *stop concerning ourselves with the freedom of the world and with our own freedom*. Then you would realize that we must hug our "tensions" to our breasts as long as the dangers exist which have caused the concern. . . .

We have tried the gesture of "Let's be friends and see if that won't work"— we have tried it more often than our historical memories permit us to recall. I remember when Franklin Roosevelt said to Frances Perkins: "I really believe that I can get Uncle Joe to go along with me." Well, we tried it. So, at the end of the war, it turned out that there were three kinds of occupation zones. There were countries which Russia occupied ("liberated") exclusively—they lost their freedom and were sucked behind the Iron Curtain. There were the countries which were jointly occupied—all of those except one have been partitioned, and the Soviet-occupied half of each is behind the Iron Curtain (North Korea, East Germany, and so on). One country was occupied exclusively by us, Japan, and there the occupied country is free to criticize and disagree with its occupiers and liberators. If the experience of those three types of occupation does not teach us not to play this costly game of seeing if we cannot hypnotize the men in the Kremlin into abandoning their blueprint or into just being nice, then nothing will ever teach us. In the end we will perish, and deserve to perish, for being fools incapable of learning. . . .

Our policy of containment has not contained; and our policy of liberation has not liberated; as our acceptance of the poison semantics of "peaceful coexistence" and the propaganda circus of "summit conferences" has given us neither genuine conferences for agreement on anything, nor peace, nor "coexistence." All these errors—and, alas, I could enumerate many more like them —come from a failure to understand the difficulties and intricacies of the problems, because of a failure to understand the nature of our enemy, his system, his power, his ruthlessness and unscrupulousness in negotiation and action, his aims, his determination, and the role of his ideology in his efforts to conquer the world and remake man. This failure of vision or understanding is at the root of our failures in action and omission and negotiation. . . .


## 13 | Senator Barry Goldwater's Demand for Total Victory, July 14, 1961 *

In this speech before the Senate, Senator Goldwater asked that the United States government make total victory its objective in the cold war, for anything less than victory would lead to eventual "defeat, degradation, and slavery." He harbored no apparent doubt that victory was available for those who would have it, but neither here nor elsewhere did he suggest what means would be required

* Senator Barry Goldwater's remarks in the Senate, July 14, 1961, *Congressional Record,* 87th Congress, 1st Sess., Vol. 107, No. 118, 11690.

to achieve such a victory other than maintaining a hard, non-compromising posture on all diplomatic fronts. How standing up to the Communist powers would destroy them he did not make clear, for he, like Mr. Dulles before him, attached his program to governmental economy.

⚲

. . . Mr. President, I should like to see us get on the right track, once and for all, in our approach to foreign policy matters. And I believe the first step is for the President of the United States to declare officially that it is our purpose to win the cold war, not merely wage it in the hope of attaining a standoff. Further, I would like to see the chairman of the Senate Foreign Relations Committee urge this action on the President, and back him to the hilt if he agrees.

Mr. President, it is really astounding that our Government has never stated its purpose to be that of complete victory over the tyrannical forces of international communism. I am sure that the American people cannot understand why we spend billions upon billions of dollars to engage in a struggle of world-wide proportions unless we have a clearly defined purpose to achieve victory. Anything less than victory, over the long run, can only be defeat, degradation, and slavery. Are not these stakes high enough for us? Is not this reason enough for us to fight to win?

I suggest that our failure to declare total victory as our fundamental purpose is a measure of an official timidity that refuses to recognize the all-embracing determination of communism to capture the world and destroy the United States. This timidity has sold us short, time and time again. It denied us victory in the Korean war, when victory was there for the taking. It refused General MacArthur the right to prosecute a war for the purpose of winning, and caused him to utter these prophetic words:

> The best that might be said for the policy-makers responsible for these monumental blunders is that they did not comprehend the truism, as old as history itself, that a great nation which voluntarily enters upon war and does not fight it through to victory must ultimately accept all of the consequences of defeat—that in war, there is no substitute for victory.

Mr. President, we would do well to heed those words of General MacArthur, and apply them to the present—apply them to our position in this cold war, for if we engage in this cold war, and do not fight it through to victory, we must be prepared to accept the consequences of defeat. And, the consequences of such a defeat, I can assure you, Mr. President, will be slavery for all the peoples of the world.

In addition to an over-all objective of victory, we need a careful appraisal of what such an effort will cost, and a priority list of essentials to measure against the willy-nilly demands for spending on all sectors. This is a clarification which the American people are demanding. In this respect, I refer to the findings of

Mr. Samuel Lubell, a public opinion expert who recently took samplings in 19 States. He reached these conclusions:

> If President Kennedy is to gain public support for a more intensive cold war effort, two basic reforms seem needed:
> 1. Existing programs must yield better results.
> 2. All of the Government spending effort, domestic and foreign, must be unified into a thought-through, first-things-first system of priorities.

Mr. President, I am not one who ordinarily takes the findings of public-opinion pollsters as the last word in popular sentiment; but I must say that the findings of Mr. Lubell are in keeping with everything which my office mail, as well as conversations I have had with people across the face of this country, have been telling me. There is a great restiveness among our people, because they have the feeling that the administration's programs have been thrown together without sufficient regard for an overall objective or for final costs. They are disturbed at reports that the State Department is toying with a so-called two-China policy; at indications that we may negotiate with Khrushchev on Berlin instead of standing firm; at the possibility that a flimsy, "phony" pretext will be found for diplomatic recognition of Communist Outer Mongolia.

To date, Mr. President, the American people have nothing to which they can point as a positive indication that the New Frontier means to stand up to the forces of international communism, after the fashion of a great world power. They have waited patiently—and in vain—for this Government to resume nuclear testing, against growing evidence that the Soviet Union is already secretly engaged in this vital activity. Let me say that I believe right here is where the New Frontier could act to show us that it does not intend to be hoodwinked forever by Soviet negotiators. I do not think there is any longer a reason for even fixing a deadline for the resumption of these tests. I believe the United States should just pull its representatives back from the test meetings, and begin work—work that has been delayed too long in the face of new and greater Communist threats around the world.

These are things, I believe, that our Nation needs right now, instead of more excuses for inaction and more justifications for an expanding foreign-aid program, which needs drastic alterations before it can yield results. We need a declaration that our intention is victory. We need a careful cost-accounting of what will be required to meet this objective within the framework of our economic ability. And we need an official act, such as the resumption of nuclear testing, to show our own people and the other freedom-loving peoples of the world that we mean business.

These are minimum requirements, Mr. President, in the nature of first steps. But they are essential if we are to chart a positive course aimed at total victory in a struggle for the future of freedom.

## 14 | Louis J. Halle on the Soviet Danger: Power and Interest, June 1959 *

Interpreting Soviet foreign policy and Soviet external objectives in the light of Russia's historic national interests, Louis J. Halle, former State Department officer and well-known student of world affairs, discounted the Marxist concept of world revolution as having any significant influence on Soviet action. Far more fundamental, he believed, was the Stalinist concept of national communism. He concluded, in the following essay, that nationalism would always remain a more powerful force than communism and that even in a communist world the power and authority of Russia would never extend beyond the reach of the Red Army. Perhaps some Russian intellectuals took the dream of world revolution seriously, he admitted, but to him the men who controlled the Kremlin were realists who appreciated the limits of Russian power and Russian ideology. Their concern was the pursuit of Russia's traditional interests and ambitions.

✍

. . . . The men who seized power in Russia in 1917 thought they were inaugurating the world revolution that Marx had predicted. Trotsky, setting up a Commissariat of Foreign Affairs, announced that he would "issue a few revolutionary proclamations to the people of the world and then close up shop." Presumably the people of the world would take care of the rest. And with the spread of the revolution the Russian state and the other nation-states would disappear.

But all this failed to happen. The chain-reaction did not take place. The people of the world did not rise up. When it became evident that the prediction on which the entire Communist program had been based was not being realized, there was nothing to do but adjust the program to that fact. Ideological purists like Trotsky were swept aside by the opportunist, Stalin, who undertook to do what the reality required rather than what the Marxist scriptures directed. With Stalin's proclamation of "socialism in one country," the Russian state, about to be interred, was reprieved and restored.

It would be hard to over-estimate the significance of this return to nationalism in Moscow. With the Russian state once more an accepted fact, to be maintained in a hostile world, the men in the Kremlin found themselves preoccupied with the same problems of state policy as had preoccupied their Czarist predecessors. Their self-appointed role as the representatives of the world's people would become increasingly unreal now, as would the objective of a spontaneous world revolution that went with it. But their role as the Government of the Russian

* Louis J. Halle, "The Basic Aim of the Kremlin," *The New York Times Magazine,* June 28, 1959, 5, 41–3. Copyright © 1959 by The New York Times Company. Reprinted by permission of the author.

state would retain a vivid reality, as would the corresponding objective of Russia's survival and success in the arena of international rivalries. In the circumstances, the Communist movement, with all its apparatus for propaganda and subversion, was bound to become subservient to the national interests of the ancient imperial realm that, for ten centuries, had been steadily growing in greatness. . . .

What the successors of Stalin have inherited today is not so much the revolutionary movement projected in another age by Marx or Lenin, it is the ancient and embattled Russian Empire as expanded by the Red Army under Stalin. With it they have inherited the verbiage and the tactical apparatus of the Communist movement, which serves the purpose of the Russian state by misleading people all over the world and weakening their will to resist that purpose.

One consequence of the restoration of the nation-state called Russia appears not to have been foreseen on either side of the Iron Curtain. When Stalin proclaimed "socialism in one country" he replaced international communism, in effect, with national communism. The far-reaching implications of this replacement began to manifest themselves clearly only when national communism, already existing inside Russia, made its first appearance outside Russia in the form of "Titoism."

To orthodox Marxism, discounting nationalism as it did, international differences among Communists were unthinkable. Stalin and his associates may well have assumed that any country that became Communist would automatically be in the Russian camp, lined up with Mother Russia against the enemy. We in the West made this same assumption. It should be clear now, however, that Moscow's abandonment of its anti-nationalism, its resumption of its role as a national capital, implied an end to the hope that the original Marxists had entertained of one international Communist world.

If Generalissimo Stalin felt himself impelled to put the national interests of Russia first, Marshal Tito would feel himself impelled to put the national interests of Yugoslavia first. And so any national Communist government, beyond easy reach of the Soviet Army, would likewise feel impelled to put its national interests ahead of the interests of any supposedly international cause that had become subservient to the national interests of Russia. Not only could Moscow not command the voluntary allegiance of the workers in non-Communist countries, but even in countries that had been captured by local Communists it could not be sure of commanding the voluntary allegiance of either governments or peoples.

Until his last years, Stalin may not have doubted that, even though other countries were communized by the Soviet Army rather than by spontaneous revolution, once communized they would all stick together under the leadership of Moscow. This would have tempted him to pursue a course of unlimited military expansion aimed at the creation of the one Communist world of Marxist dreams. Until toward the end, he may not have fully grasped the implications of accumulating experience, which were that, even in a world in which capitalism had everywhere been replaced by communism, the supremacy of Moscow could not be expected to extend beyond the reach of the Soviet Army.

A Communist France might be a Titoist France. A Communist United States might be no less hostile to the Soviet Union than a liberal democratic United States. Because its total resources could be more easily mobilized it might, in fact, be distinctly more threatening.

The sequence of developments that have followed the Russian Revolution is so closely matched by the sequence of developments that followed the French Revolution that it may, perhaps, be taken to represent a pattern inherent in the history of such revolutions. In 1793 the forces of the French Revolution set out to liberate the peoples of the world from the bondage in which they supposedly languished. With the passage of time, however, it became apparent that the peoples outside France were opposing the "liberating" forces of the revolution, and opposing them on nationalistic grounds. The program of liberation, therefore, became a program of military conquest under the opportunist Napoleon. Eventually, what happens to every program of unlimited military expansion happened to Napoleon's program: it reached the point of overextension. By 1812 the problem was to draw back to defensible frontiers.

We must guard against carrying this parallel too far, but there is reason to believe that the problem inherited by Stalin's successors was that of eliminating certain weaknesses associated with an overextended position. They found themselves faced with Yugoslavia's successful defiance. They found themselves having to hold down by the intimidation of sheer force the rebellious populations of East Germany, of Poland, of Hungary, and of the other satellites—in circumstances in which an explosion might occur at any time, with incalculable consequences. They found themselves having to worry about the independence of attitude that a Communist China, devoted more to Chinese than to Russian national interests, might be able to afford. They found that they had rather more to control than they could be quite sure of controlling, especially under the conditions of what was still a collective leadership. . . .

Can we say, then, that Moscow still has as a working objective that world revolution that was the objective of Communist intellectuals in another age? It may be that Marx's vision of Utopia is still entertained as a daydream by some Russian Communists. But the men who run things in Moscow are tough, practical operators, gang leaders more than they are intellectuals. However profitable they may find it for their own purposes still to intone in public the old Marxist incantations, they may privately be as cynical as politicians anywhere; and in any case their working objectives are surely of quite a different order. They are the familiar objectives of a great power, to realize its interests and ambitions as one state in a world of rival states.

For ten centuries Russia has been obsessed by military insecurity and the fear of encirclement, as she is still today. This has impelled her to push the danger away by constantly expanding the area under her control. In doing so she has threatened the security of her neighbors, who have repeatedly acted to contain her or to force her retraction.

In a large sense, then, the present "cold war" is simply a continuation of that long struggle in which the Crimean War, a century ago, was one incident. The struggle has become more dangerous to us today on two counts. For one, the development of atomic weapons has made its possible consequences more terrible. For another, the relative power of Russia, greater today than ever before, has been tending to exceed the power that we have been willing to muster, on our side, to balance and contain it. We have depended, hitherto, on our exclusive possession of nuclear weapons to offset the Soviet superiority in other forms of armament. Now Russia's acquisition of a full nuclear capability tends to neutralize our own capability, inhibiting its use, leaving her with a net superiority in military power that she did not have before. Here is where the parallel with Napoleonic France in 1812 breaks down.

If this is a realistic picture of what we confront today, then the objectives of Soviet policy are not hard to understand. They are the classical objectives of an autocratically governed empire that has constituted itself the challenger in an old-fashioned power contest. They are the objectives of achieving security by first increasing the relative power of the state, then forcing changes in the international status quo that reflect the increase.

In the politics of power, an international arrangement is legitimate only as long as it accurately reflects the relative power of the participants. When the power relationships change, then the arrangement itself must be correspondingly changed. . . .

The answer to this prospect is simple, if not easy. Moscow will presumably refrain from repeatedly challenging our strategic positions in the world whenever it has reason to believe that we have built and are maintaining the power to support them. This power must be more than military power. It must include political and economic power, and what we might call cultural strength. It must have a moral basis.

But we should not deceive ourselves with the belief that, as an alternative to military power, we can rely on some putative spiritual power that does not call for material sacrifices by us or interfere with our desire to balance the budget. The military power to back our diplomacy is only one element among others, but it is indispensable. It is indispensable to the achievement of that international stability from which a peaceful world order might at last grow.

## 15 | Senator J. William Fullbright's Remarks on the Concept of Total Victory, July 24, 1961 *

In this reply to Senator Goldwater's speech of ten days earlier, Senator Fulbright posed a realistic evaluation of both the ends and the means involved in a program of total victory over the U.S.S.R. He noted the burden which a total vic-

* Senator J. William Fulbright's remarks in the Senate, July 24, 1961, *Congressional Record*, 87th Congress, 1st Sess., Vol. 107, No. 123, 12280–81.

tory over Russia and China, even if it could be achieved, would actually entail. The two world wars of the twentieth century, Fulbright reminded the Senate, had resulted in total victories, but the results had offered little encouragement. Total victories generated problems of their own. Fulbright concluded his speech with an appeal that the nation's commitments abroad be circumscribed by the interests and capabilities of the United States.

Mr. President, I should like to comment briefly today on certain themes contained in the remarks concerning our foreign policy made by the junior Senator from Arizona [Mr. GOLDWATER] on July 13. The Senator's views are, as usual, forthright and provocative. They are of special significance, in that the Senator is an acknowledged spokesman and leader of opinion in his party.

The Senator says that our fundamental objective must be "total victory" over international communism. I must confess to some difficulty in understanding precisely what "total victory" means in this age of ideological conflict and nuclear weapons. Certainly the term is a stirring one. It has a romantic ring. It quickens the blood like a clarion call to arms, and stimulates the imagination with a vision of brave and gallant deeds.

It would be beneficial and instructive, I think, if those who call for total victory would spell out for us precisely how it might be achieved and, more important, what we would do with a total victory once we had won it. Is it to be won by nuclear war—a war which at the very least would cost the lives of tens of millions of people on both sides, devastate most or all of our great cities, and mutilate or utterly destroy a civilization which has been built over thousands of years?

Or can total victory be won without war—by some brilliant stroke of diplomacy or by arguments of such compelling logic that the Communists will acknowledge the error of their ways and abandon their grand imperialistic design? Perhaps the advocates of total victory believe that we can achieve it by abandoning our efforts toward disarmament and engaging in an unrestricted nuclear arms race, even though such a policy would provoke similar measures by the Communist powers.

The Senator from Arizona suggests that the periphery of freedom "is growing steadily smaller in direct ratio to our failure to act from strength." What would a policy of strength involve? Does it mean a military invasion of Cuba which would destroy the Castro dictatorship, but which would also alienate the rest of Latin America and necessitate the stationing of Marines in Cuba to protect an American-imposed regime against Fidelista rebels and guerillas? Does it mean the commitment of American forces to interminable guerilla warfare in the jungles of Laos, a war in which all the advantages of geography would be on the side of the Communists?

Even more perplexing than the question of how to win a total victory is the problem of what we would do with it once it was won. Would we undertake a military occupation of Russia and China and launch a massive program to re-educate 200 million Russians and 600 million Chinese in the ways of Western democracy?

Political objectives must be framed in terms of time and circumstance. In the Middle Ages, when military combat took the form of jousts between chivalrous knights, total victory was perhaps a reasonable objective. One combatant bested the other with his sword or lance or mace, and that was the end of it. In our own time the chivalrous encounter has been relegated to the football field or the boxing arena, and it is a dangerous illusion to confuse the rules of a college football game with those that apply to the arena of world politics.

We have had total victories in the past, and their examples offer little encouragement. We fought the First World War to make the world safe for democracy, and prosecuted the Second World War to achieve the unconditional surrender of our enemies. Both World Wars ended in total victory, but the world is far less safe for democracy today than it was in 1914, when the current era of upheavals began. One of the principal lessons of two World Wars is that wars, and total victories, generate more problems than they solve. Apparently we have not yet fully accepted the fact that there are no absolute solutions, that we can hope to do little more than mitigate our problems as best we can and learn to live with them.

As I said in my remarks of June 29, there is a double standard in the struggle between communism and the free nations. While Communist tactics include terror, subversion, and military aggression, the world demands a higher order of conduct from the United States. Our policies must be consistent with our objectives, which are those of constructive social purpose and world peace under world law. Were we to adopt the same mischievous tactics as those employed by the Communists, the principal target of these tactics would be our own principles and our own national style.

The Senator says that world opinion "is an area of official concern which has no reason for existing," that world opinion actually countenances international communism. The Senator does an injustice to the hopes and aspirations of peoples throughout the world and he credits communism with a far greater appeal than it actually has. It is not communism which appeals to the hearts and minds of the emergent peoples of Asia, Africa, and Latin America. These people hope for peace, for a decent material life, and for national self-determination. Only insofar as communism succeeds in identifying itself with these aspirations does it win prestige, allegiance, and respect.

World opinion is eminently worth courting—because the hopes of millions of people for world order and for economic and social reform are our hopes as well. Where world opinion seems to us to be feeble or ill-informed, our proper task is to seek to develop and inform it, not to dismiss it as unworthy of our concern.

We have much to learn, as well as to teach, from the opinions of peoples throughout the world. Our own judgments are not infallible, and there is much to be gained by a decent respect for the opinions of mankind.

World opinion is a civilizing force in the world, helping to restrain the great powers from the worst possible consequences of their mutual hostility. To disavow and override the opinions of other peoples because they do not always agree with our own is to destroy a potentially powerful force for peace and to return to the laws of the jungle.

The Senator says that I favor a policy of "nonintervention." I am indeed opposed to policies that would overextend the United States, especially when such policies find little or no support elsewhere in the non-Communist world. By refusing to permit our national strength to be sapped by peripheral struggles, we maximize our power to honor our obligations and commitments all over the world. We are committed to military and political alliances with many nations and we are committed to assist many more nations toward the fulfillment of their legitimate political, economic, and social aspirations. Such policies are the diametric opposite of any doctrine of nonintervention. Their basic concept is one of intervention—but not indiscriminate military intervention in response to every provocation and every disorder, regardless of its character and cause. The latter approach is one of rigid and negative reaction, one which would leave every initiative to our adversaries. The program which I support is one of long-range intervention in depth, one which employs all of the instrumentalities of foreign policy, the political and economic as well as the military. Its object is the realization of our national interests and not merely the piecemeal frustration of Communist ambitions.

There are limitations to foreign policy. We are neither omniscient nor omnipotent, and we cannot aspire to make the world over in our image.

Our proper objective is a continuing effort to limit the world struggle for power and to bring it under civilized rules. Such a program lacks the drama and romance of a global crusade. Its virtue is that it represents a realistic accommodation between our highest purposes and the limitations of human capacity. Its ultimate objective is indeed total victory, not alone for our arms in a nuclear war or for the goal of a world forcibly recast in our image, but rather for a process—a process of civilizing international relations and of bringing them gradually under a world-wide regime of law and order and peaceful procedures for the redress of legitimate grievances.

## 16 | The Bases for Realistic Negotiation with the Soviet Bloc *

Throughout the 'fifties and into the 'sixties many American journalists and scholars concerned with world affairs observed that the lines of demarcation in Europe were established and would not be changed without war. Since the

* *The New York Times,* May 18, 1954. Reprinted by permission of the Estate of Ralph B. Perry.

political division of Europe, whatever its challenge to the principle of self-determination, did not serve Western interests badly, they suggested that the United States negotiate on the basis of the *status quo*. To Professor Ralph Barton Perry of Harvard University, for example, American foreign policy by 1954 had become so antagonistic toward Russia and China that there was too little flexibility left for negotiation. In the following letter to the *New York Times*, Professor Perry recalled that diplomacy always demanded the making of concessions. It required not ideals but working formulas. For the uncompromising state of the American mind he blamed not only members of Congress but also those members of the Executive who dwelt constantly on the magnitude of the Communist threat.

Some years ago the country was persuaded to adopt the policy of "negotiation from strength," and during the interval the strength has been achieved and published at home and abroad. This policy was taken to mean that when it became apparent that our policy was not dictated by weakness the emphasis would be shifted to negotiation. But this is not what has happened. In proportion as our military and industrial power has been increased we have become increasingly disposed to threaten and to lay down ultimata.

In order that their political support may be obtained the American people have been encouraged to believe that they can have their way in the world provided only that they keep ahead in efficiency of atomic weapons and in the size of the stockpile. We are increasingly dictatorial in relation to our associates and increasingly bitter and suspicious toward our opponents. This attitude of mind is unrealistic and fatuous.

The world is likely for some decades to come to be divided into two opposing camps so evenly balanced that open war, implemented by modern technology, would be so devastating as to prevent the realization of the aims of either party. There is no possibility of peace by force in any constructive sense of the term "peace"; in the sense, namely, of a resumption of the social and cultural progress through goodwill and cooperation. The only alternative to a peace by negotiation is a prolonged stalemate or an era of violence in which all parties are ruined together.

Peace by negotiation does not mean the abandonment of principle. It means that the realization of the kind of world which we desire, and rightly desire, must be postponed until it can be realized by peaceful persuasion; as is now, after centuries of wasteful bloodshed, recognized in the sphere of religion. Meanwhile we must live together on the surface of the same planet with those with whom we profoundly disagree and whose creed we hope and believe will ultimately be rejected by the suffrage of mankind.

Peace by negotiation implies that there shall be a flexibility of policy adapted to time, place and circumstance. It implies making concessions as well as demanding them. The door to negotiation is closed by every absolute laid down in advance, such as the nonrecognition of Communist China, or the nonadmission of Communist China to the United Nations, or the nonpartitioning of Korea, Germany or Indochina.

Peace by negotiation implies a residue of comity, patience despite provocations. It implies a will to agree, never silenced or weakened by the acrimony of dispute. Peace by negotiation implies that the initiative and leadership in world affairs pass from the bitter-enders, however strong, and from the utopians, however idealistic, to statesmen who contrive workable formulas of settlement.

Our diplomatic agencies are said to be imprisoned by public opinion and by domestic politics. This is undoubtedly true, but it is often forgotten that these agencies themselves are largely responsible for the imprisonment. Public officials themselves create political forces and popular attitudes. They are the principal instruments not only of political action but of political education. Through their perpetual harping on the menace of communism they have created a political atmosphere in which anti-Communism has become the chief condition of social prestige and of appointment or election to office.

In this atmosphere paramount political power is exercised by full-time career anti-Communists who have no other asset or qualification whatsoever—no ideas, no solutions of problems, no enlightenment, nothing but the tedious reiteration of this negative appeal to fear and suspicion.

Strength means not only bargaining power, but also magnanimity. A powerful America can afford to make concessions without loss of pride. There is a kind of pride which manifests itself in self-congratulation, boasting, or the brandishing of weapons, and which has to be excited by a tribal war dance. This is the pride of the weak. The pride of the strong manifests itself in the steady pursuit of long-range objectives of the sort which can be achieved only by understanding and generosity.

— | "Only by successful negotiations can this dangerous armament race be abated and the prospects of hydronuclear war be postponed." *

At the time that John F. Kennedy entered the White House in January 1961, William R. Mathews, editor of the *Arizona Daily Star,* published the following open letter to the new President in *The Atlantic.* Neither in concept nor proposals was it unique, but it comprised an able and forthright statement of the view that the military policies of the United States had achieved political stability in much of the world. To gain further territory or other advantages would require war. The time had come, believed Mathews, to negotiate on the basis of a divided Europe, even to the recognition of the East German regime. It was essential above all that American diplomacy endeavor to break the

* William R. Mathews, "A Letter to the New President," *The Atlantic,* CCVII (January 1961), 37-9. Reprinted by permission.

cold war deadlock. Nothing less would reduce the tensions which sustained the nuclear arms race. Either the great powers would co-exist or they would destroy each other in war. Between these two long-range alternatives the choice, for him, appeared clear.

✒

DEAR MR. PRESIDENT: As you take office the American people are looking to you for a new approach to our nation's foreign affairs. They are no longer interested in rehashing the mistakes of the past Administration. They are deeply interested in what you are going to do about peace and war in our nuclear age. That is the subject that interests them most.

They have shown by their votes that they believe what you have promised about a stronger nation economically and militarily. The fact that we as a nation will grow stronger prompts the caution that great power used wisely can bring wonderful blessings to a bewildered world. If used recklessly, vainly, or stupidly, it will become a scourge and blight to humanity.

Yet your plea for stronger military defenses has added to the momentum of the most gigantic armament race the world has ever seen. History confirms that every such race, unless moderated, leads to war on a grand scale. The peoples of all nations have sensed this danger with the approval they have given to the idea of disarmament. Fortunately, this growing strength of ours will put you in a better position to negotiate. Only by successful negotiations can this dangerous armament race be abated and the prospects of hydronuclear war be postponed.

If negotiations are to be successful, both sides must be ready to compromise; both sides must expect to give up something in return. Successful negotiations require a temperate atmosphere. That means that, just as Mr. K must stop his bullying, missile rattling, and sending of ultimatums, so might you see to it that our talking generals and admirals are silenced.

Peace cannot be made in an atmosphere where each adversary tries to out-boast, out-denounce, and out-threaten the other. A Summit meeting will be worthless unless its success has been reasonably ensured by previous negotiations. If diplomats at the working level cannot come close to a tentative agreement, you will not be able to come to an agreement at the top level.

Your big job is to prepare the American people to make peace. They are prepared morally and militarily to make war, but they are poorly prepared to make peace. They have been taught to expect a rigid perfection in the conduct of our foreign policy. They need to be told that perfection is not only impossible but dangerous. Although they accept compromises constantly in their everyday domestic lives, they reject them as "appeasement" in our foreign policy.

You can do much to change their present-day thinking that we are always right and the other fellow always wrong, that unless we have victories we will have to suffer humiliating defeats. The people must be persuaded that there can be diplomatic successes where each side profits by making mutual concessions.

A widespread belief prevails that unless we defeat Communism, Communism will take over the whole world, and that if we defeat Communism, our troubles will be over. Therefore, so the reasoning goes, there can be no compromises. The Communist must give in; we must never give in. The resulting deadlock, coupled with the intensified armament race, creates an increasing danger of hydronuclear war.

Badly needed at this time is an explanation that Communism today is a widely accepted belief, but so is our Judaeo-Christian belief in freedom and democracy. Because each one is backed today by political powers that can never be vanquished by military conquest, both will continue to exist for generations, if not centuries.

The big issue before these two giant political powers is whether it might not be best for the leaders of each to try to get along with the other rather than to try to destroy each other. It is better for us to get along just halfway than to expect perfection from each other. That means compromise. That there must be concessions by both sides is scarcely understood. If the American people could see that it is to their own self-interest to make concessions in return for concessions by the Soviets, as a means of avoiding hydronuclear war, a more peaceful climate might result.

This situation requires that you, as President, boldly explode the present-day myth about disarmament or control of armaments, which assumes that agreements about arms can be made without dealing with the conflicting political ambitions that create the necessity to arm.

Surely the time has come for the people of our country and the world to learn that war is a social disease brought on by conflicting political ambitions, which in turn are generated by economic, social, religious, and racial causes. War cannot be abolished by legal edicts. Armaments are a fever of this social disease, not a cause. They will rise and fall with the virulence and scope of the disease. If we are to lower the fever, we must deal with the cause. We can never hope to abolish war completely, but we should hope and work to limit its scope and virulence, just as we have in the case of numerous other diseases.

You should not be expected to perform wonders, such as abolishing war, nor should you insist that our ideals be made to prevail throughout the world. That is the big mistake that President Truman and President Eisenhower have made. They have, unwittingly, promised the impossible in laying down the rigid policy that our ideals of freedom and democracy must be made to prevail "everywhere" by "liberating the enslaved." You can certainly promise the American people that Communist ideas will not be allowed to prevail everywhere. . . .

Because the Berlin issue is acute, it requires your prompt attention, but no President of the United States should ever enter any negotiations under the threat of a time limit. If we can come to a compromise over Berlin that will abate the Soviet Union's justified fears over a third invasion by a united Germany, it may well set a precedent that can be used elsewhere.

If Russia were a parliamentary democracy, its government would be compelled to insist on a divided Germany as a precaution against a third invasion. Americans must bear in mind that the Russian people have twice within a generation suffered terrible invasions by the Germans. Not for decades can any Soviet government give up East Germany.

American policy today is mistaken in insisting on a united Germany. Such a Germany would soon be demanding the return of its "lost provinces" to the east. Any competent observer can continually hear expressions of that ambition in West Germany. The Russians feel safer with a divided Germany, and so do our allies Britain and France. When we call for a united Germany, we play into the hands of the German chauvinists.

We could properly compromise by recognizing the government of East Germany with the provision that we, France, and Britain will continue to maintain our forces in West Berlin with free ingress and egress. This provision we must back with all of our might and power. If the Soviets really want peace, they will agree to it, because to do so will further their own interest.

Of course, Chancellor Adenauer will rage and threaten, and the American people will demur. There is where you will have to speak out and explain that it is to America's self-interest to bring this about. The Germans have caused the United States plenty of trouble in the past forty-five years. If the recognition of the East German government will lessen the armament race and promote the chances of peace, why should the American people object? Once they understand the realities, they will support recognition, provided our interests in Berlin are maintained.

If the agreement provided for the gradual withdrawal of the armed forces of all countries from both Germanies, it would require that the people of East Germany and West Germany look after their own defense and pay for it themselves. NATO should be maintained as a deterrent power, along with our nuclear capabilities on the seas and in the air.

The case of Germany provides you with an opportunity to test not only the sincerity of the Soviet's professed peaceful intentions but also the willingness of the American people to promote a more peaceful world. Unless the rigid stand of the American people, which has been reflected in the diplomatic deadlock of the outgoing Administration, is modified by the skill and courage of your own persuasion, negotiations are doomed to failure.

The case of Germany is significant because it may help to establish two basic principles that should at all times guide our diplomatic conduct. The first is that of self-interest. Treaties that do not respect self-interest of both parties are bound to be violated. Closely associated with this principle is that of respect for the primary interests of the other side. If we want the Kremlin to respect our primary interests in Cuba, the Western Hemisphere, Berlin, Korea, Japan, Formosa, and the Philippines, we must respect Russia's primary interests in eastern Europe.

For more than two hundred years, every Russian government has asserted a primary interest in that area and has been willing to defend it. If the Soviet Union were a parliamentary democracy, its government would have to do the same thing, because national security is at stake in the minds of its people and leaders.

I know that the American people will always respond to the defense of their own self-interest. And I feel sure that they will unite to make effective any policy that reflects that principle. . . .

If successful diplomacy can abate the armament race, funds from it can be diverted to making the world productive. If your diplomacy fails, your whole domestic and foreign program will fail. It cannot succeed unless you prepare the people of our country to make peace. If you can do that, you will have a united nation behind you.

## 17 | President John F. Kennedy's Speech at Seattle, Washington, November 16, 1961 *

In this widely quoted speech, President Kennedy developed the theme that the United States, despite its enormous powers of destruction, was neither omnipotent nor omniscient and that it could not control human destiny. Too many Americans, he said, were fearful of a long twilight struggle and demanded a quick and easy solution immediately. Those who would purchase peace at any price and those who would oppose all negotiation and compromise, he declared, were equally wrong. The nation had better choices than being Red or dead. A foreign policy to be adequate and effective, he saw, required an historic balance between force and the willingness to talk and compromise.

In 1961 world affairs have become even more tangled. One of our former allies has become an adversary, and he has his own adversaries who are not even our allies. Not only are kings removed from their thrones, heroes are even removed from their tombs.

We increase our arms at a heavy cost, primarily to make certain we will never use them. We must face up to the chance of war if we are to have a chance for peace. We must work with certain countries lacking in freedom in order to strengthen the cause of freedom.

We are determined to prevent certain nations from adopting neutrality, and to prevent certain others from abandoning it. And, as the most powerful defender of freedom on earth, we find ourselves unable to escape the responsibilities of power, and yet unable to exercise it without restraints imposed by the very freedoms we seek to protect.

We cannot, as a free nation, compete with our adversaries in tactics of terror, assassination, false promises and counterfeit mobs and crises.

* _The New York Times_, November 17, 1961.

We cannot, under the scrutiny of a free press and public, tell different stories to different audiences, foreign, domestic, friendly, and hostile.

We cannot abandon the slow processes of consulting with our allies to match the swift expediencies of those who merely dictate to their satellites.

We can neither abandon nor control the international organization in which we now cast less than 1 per cent of the General Assembly votes.

We possess weapons of tremendous power, but they are least effective in combating the weapons most often used by freedom's foes: subversion, infiltration and civil disorder.

We can send arms to other peoples, just as we can send them the ideals of democracy, but we cannot send them the will to use those arms or to abide by those ideals.

And while we believe, not only in the force of arms, but in the force of right and reason, we have learned that reason does not always appeal to unreasonable men, that it is not always true that "a soft answer turneth away wrath" and that right does not always make might.

In short, we must face problems which do not lend themselves to easy, quick or permanent solutions. And we must face the fact that the United States is neither omnipotent nor omniscient, that we cannot always impose our will on the other 94 per cent of mankind, that we cannot right every wrong or reverse each adversity, and that therefore there cannot be an American solution for every world problem.

These burdens and frustrations are accepted by most Americans with maturity and understanding. They may long for the days when war meant charging up San Juan Hill, or when our isolation was guarded by two oceans, or when the atomic bomb was ours alone, or when much of the industrialized world depended upon our economic resources and aid. But they know that those days are gone, and that gone with them are the old policies and the old complacency. And they know, too, that we must make the best of our new problems and our new opportunities, whatever the risk and the cost.

But there are others who cannot bear the burden of a long twilight struggle. They lack confidence in our long-run capacity to survive and succeed. They see communism as the wave of the future. And they want some quick and easy and cheap solution, now.

There are two groups of these frustrated citizens, far apart in their views yet very much alike in their approach. On the one hand are those who urge upon us what I regard to be the pathway to surrender—appeasing our enemies, compromising our honor, purchasing peace at any price, disavowing our arms, our friends, our obligations. If their view had prevailed, the world of free choice would be smaller today.

On the other hand are those who urge upon us what I regard to be the pathway to war—equating negotiations with appeasement and substituting rigidity for firmness. If their view had prevailed, we would be at war today, and in more places than one.

It is a curious fact that each of these extreme opposites resembles the other. Each believes that we have only two choices—appeasement or war, suicide or surrender, humiliation or holocaust, to be either Red or dead. Each side sees only hard and soft nations, hard and soft policies, hard and soft men. Each believes that any departure from its own course inevitably leads to the other—one group believes that any peaceful solution means appeasement; the other believes that any arms build-up means war.

One group regards everyone else as warmongers, the other regards everyone else as appeasers. Neither side admits its path will lead to disaster, but neither can tell us how or where to draw the line once we descend the slippery slopes of either appeasement or intervention.

In short, while both extremes profess to be the true realists, neither could be more unrealistic. While both claim to be doing the nation a service, they could do it no greater disservice. For this kind of talk, if believed, could inspire uncertainty among our allies when they must, above all, be united. It could inspire uncertainty among our allies when they must, above all, be confident. And even more dangerously, it could, if believed, inspire doubt among our adversaries when they must, above all, be convinced of our readiness to defend our vital interest.

The essential fact that both of these groups fail to grasp is that diplomacy and defense are not substitutes for one another. Either, alone, would fail. A willingness to resist force, unaccompanied by a willingness to talk, could provoke belligerence, while a willingness to talk, unaccompanied by a willingness to resist force, could invite disaster.

But as long as we know precisely what comprises our vital interest and our long-range goals, we have nothing to fear from negotiations at the appropriate time, and nothing to gain by refusing them. At a time when a single clash could escalate overnight into a holocaust of mushroom clouds, a great power does not prove its firmness by leaving the task of exploring the other's intentions to sentries or those without full responsibility. Nor can ultimate weapons rightfully be employed, or the ultimate sacrifice rightfully demanded of our citizens, until every reasonable solution has been explored.

"How many wars," Winston Churchill has written, "have been averted by patience and persisting good will . . . how many wars have been precipitated by firebrands."

If vital interests under duress can be preserved by peaceful means, negotiations will find that out. If our adversary will accept nothing less than a concession of our rights, negotiations will find that out. And if negotiations are to take place, this nation cannot abdicate to its adversaries the task of choosing the forum and framework.

For there are carefully defined limits within which any serious negotiations must take place. With respect to any future talks on Germany and Berlin, for example, we cannot, on the one hand, confine our proposals to a list of concessions we are willing to make. Nor can we, on the other hand, advance any proposals which compromise the security of free Germans and West Berliners, or endanger their ties with the West.

No one should be under the illusion that negotiations for the sake of negotiations always advance the cause of peace. If, for lack of preparation or respect, they break up in bitterness, the prospects of peace have been endangered. If they are made a mere forum for propaganda or a cover for aggression, the processes of peace have been abused.

But it is a test of our national maturity to accept the fact that negotiations are not a contest spelling victory or defeat. They may succeed, they may fail. But they are likely to be successful only if both sides reach an agreement which both regard as preferable to the status quo, an agreement in which each side can consider that its own situation has been improved.

But, while we shall negotiate freely, we will never negotiate freedom. Our answer to the classic question of Patrick Henry is still no. Life is not so dear and peace is not so precious "as to be purchased at the price of chains and slavery." And that is our answer, even though, for the first time since the ancient battles between Greek city-states, war entails the threat of total annihilation, of everything we know, of society itself. For to save mankind's future freedom, we must face up to any risk that is necessary. We will always seek peace, but we will never surrender.

In short, we are neither warmongers nor appeasers, neither hard nor soft. We are Americans, determined to defend the frontiers of freedom by an honorable peace, if peace is possible, but by arms if arms are used against us.

And if we are to move forward in that spirit, we shall need all the calm and thoughtful citizens our great universities can produce, all the light they can shed, all the wisdom they can bring to bear. It is customary, both here and around the world, to regard life in these United States as easy. Our advantages are many. But more than any other people in the world, we bear burdens and accept risks unprecedented in their size and duration, not for ourselves alone but for all who wish to be free. No other generation of free men in a single nation has ever faced so many and such difficult challenges, not even those who lived in the dark days of 1861, when this great university was founded.

This nation was then torn by war. This territory had only the rudest elements of civilization. And this city had barely begun to function. But a university was one of their earliest thoughts, and they summed it up in the motto they adopted: "Let There be Light." What more can be said today regarding all the dark and tangled problems we face: Let there be light.

18 | Senator Fulbright's Address before the Senate, March 1964 *

By 1964 it had become obvious that the national habit of overdemanding in external affairs had subjected United States foreign policy to a series of easily predictable embarrassments. If it was true, as the Sacramento *Morning News* insisted early in March, that Charles de Gaulle of France, in his open defiance

* *The New York Times,* March 26, 1964.

of American purpose in Europe, China, and South Vietnam, was making a "confused tangle of American diplomacy," one could ask in good conscience why the national leadership remained wedded to policies which could be so easily tangled. It was only a matter of time before Democratic spokesmen themselves would challenge the absence of realism in many American positions abroad, especially since it was their political opposition, stimulated too often by a thoughtless partisanship, who had forced on the United States government a variety of unachievable objectives. To attempt to attach to American policy the goal of victory, they saw, was either meaningless or dangerous. As George F. Kennan observed in November 1963, "People who expect the capitulation of Communist power are talking about something so unrealistic that they really want war." Senators Mike Mansfield of Montana and Frank Church of Idaho assumed command of those who sought some limitation of United States ambitions for Southeast Asia which might permit the establishment of a balance between the national goal of political stability and the price which the country appeared willing to pay. President Lyndon B. Johnson, following the lead of President Kennedy, declared on March 24 that since war was unthinkable it was essential that United States policies be adjusted to the realities on the world scene. Leading Democrats, often disagreeing among themselves on specific issues, shared an uneasiness about the status of American foreign policy.

This tendency toward introspection and self-appraisal culminated in the speech of Senator J. William Fulbright of Arkansas before the United States Senate on March 25, 1964. Developing the theme of "Old Myths and New Realities," Fulbright challenged the ubiquitous American assumptions of a bipolar world. He charged that any policy was unrealistic which did not recognize the infinite variety of interests and objectives among nations of all power blocs. It was the business of the United States to concern itself with the power and external ambitions of other nations, not with their domestic institutions. The Senator pointed specifically to the inflexibility and lack of imagination in United States attitudes toward Eastern Europe and mainland China, the two perennial areas of high tension in the cold war. But he suggested as well that the United States close the gap between objectives and power in American Cuban and Southeast Asian policies, either by reducing the goals or by augmenting the means to be employed.

There is an inevitable divergence, attributable to the imperfections of the human mind, between the world as it is and the world as men perceive it. As long as our perceptions are reasonably close to objective reality, it is possible for us to act upon our problems in a rational and appropriate manner. But when our perceptions fail to keep pace with events, when we refuse to believe something because it displeases or frightens us, or is simply startlingly unfamiliar, then the gap between fact and perception becomes a chasm and actions become irrelevant and irrational.

There has always—and inevitably—been some divergence between the realities of foreign policy and our ideas about it. This divergence has in certain respects been growing rather than narrowing and we are handicapped, accordingly, by policies based on old myths rather than current realities. This divergence is, in my opinion, dangerous and unnecessary—dangerous because it can reduce foreign policy to a fraudulent game of imagery and appearances, unnecessary because it can be overcome by the determination of men in high office to dispel prevailing misconceptions by the candid dissemination of unpleasant but inescapable facts.

Before commenting on some of the specific areas where I believe our policies are at least partially based on cherished myths rather than objective facts, I should like to suggest two possible reasons for the growing divergence between the realities and our perceptions of current world politics. The first is the radical change in relations between and within the Communist and the free worlds and the second is the tendency of too many of us to confuse means with ends and, accordingly, to adhere to prevailing practices with a fervor befitting immutable principles. Although it is too soon to render a definitive judgment, there is mounting evidence that events of recent years have wrought profound changes in the character of East-West relations. . . .

It seems reasonable . . . to suggest that the character of the cold war has, for the present at least, been profoundly altered: by the drawing back of the Soviet Union from extremely aggressive policies; by the implicit repudation by both sides of a policy of "total victory," by the establishment of an American strategic superiority which the Soviet Union appears to have tacitly accepted because it has been accompanied by assurances that it will be exercised by the United States with responsibility and restraint. These enormously important changes may come to be regarded by historians as the foremost achievements of the Kennedy administration in the field of foreign policy. Their effect has been to commit us to a foreign policy which can accurately—though perhaps not pru-dently—be defined as one of "peaceful co-existence."

Another of the results of the lowering of tensions between East and West is that each is now free to enjoy the luxury of accelerated strife and squabbling within its own domain. The ideological thunderbolts between Washington and Moscow which until a few years ago seemed a permanent part of our daily lives have become a pale shadow of their former selves. Now instead, the United States waits in fascinated apprehension for the Olympian pronouncements that issue from Paris at six-month intervals while the Russians respond to the crude epithets of Peking with almost plaintive rejoinders about "those who want to start a war against everybody." These astonishing changes in the configuration of the postwar world have had an unsettling effect on both public and official opinion in the United States. One reason for this, I believe, lies in the fact that we are a people used to looking at the world, and indeed at ourselves, in moral-istic rather than empirical terms. We are predisposed to regard any conflict as a clash between good and evil rather than as simply a clash between conflicting interests. . . .

We are confronted with a complex and fluid world situation and we are not adapting ourselves to it. We are clinging to old myths in the face of new realities and we are seeking to escape the contradictions by narowing the permissible bounds of public discussion, by relegating an increasing number of ideas and viewpoints to a growing category of "unthinkable thoughts.". . .

The master myth of the cold war is that the Communist bloc is a monolith composed of governments which are not really governments at all but organized conspiracies, divided among themselves perhaps in certain matters of tactics, but all equally resolute and implacable in their determination to destroy the free world. I believe that the Communist world is indeed hostile to the free world in its general and long-term intentions but that the existence of this animosity in principle is far less important for our foreign policy than the great variation in its intensity and character both in time and among the individual members of the Communist bloc.

Only if we recognize these variations, ranging from China which poses imme-diate threats to the free world to Poland and Yugoslavia which pose none, can we hope to act effectively upon the bloc and to turn its internal differences to our own advantage and to the advantage of those bloc countries which wish to maximize their independence. It is the responsibility of our national leaders, both in the Executive Branch and in Congress, to acknowledge and act upon these realities, even at the cost of saying things which will not win immediate wide-spread enthusiasm. For a start, we can acknowledge the fact that the Soviet Union, though still a most formidable adversary, has ceased to be totally and implacably hostile to the West. . . .

If we are to do these things effectively, we must distinguish between Commu-nism as an ideology and the power and policy of the Soviet state. It is not Communism as a doctrine, or Communism as it is practiced within the Soviet Union or within any other country, that threatens us. How the Soviet Union organizes its internal life, the gods and doctrines that it worships, are matters for the Soviet Union to determine. It is not Communist dogma as espoused within Russia but Communist imperialism that threatens us and other peoples of the non-Communist world. Insofar as a great nation mobilizes its power and re-sources for aggressive purposes, that nation, regardless of ideology, makes itself our enemy. Insofar as a nation is content to practice its doctrines within its own frontiers, that nation, however repugnant its ideology, is one with which we have no proper quarrel. We must deal with the Soviet Union as a great power, quite apart from differences of ideology. To the extent that the Soviet leaders abandon the global ambitions of Marxist ideology, in fact if not in words, it becomes possible for us to engage in normal relations with them, relations which probably cannot be close or trusting for many years to come but which can be gradually freed of the terror and the tensions of the cold war. . . .

Important opportunities have been created for Western policy by the develop-ment of "polycentrism" in the Communist bloc. . . . The choices open to the satellite states are limited but by no means insignificant. They can adhere slav-ishly to Soviet preferences or they can strike out on their own, within limits, to enter into mutually advantageous relations with the West. Whether they do so, and to what extent, is to some extent at least within the power of the West to determine. If we persist in the view that all Communist regimes are equally hostile and equally threatening to the West, and that we can have no policy toward the "captive nations" except the eventual overthrow of their Communist regimes, then the West may enforce upon the Communist bloc a degree of unity which the Soviet Union has shown itself to be quite incapable of imposing—just as Stalin in the early postwar years frightened the West into a degree of unity that it almost certainly could not have attained by its own unaided efforts. If, on the other hand, we are willing to re-examine the view that all Communist regimes are alike in the threat which they pose for the West—a view which had a certain validity in Stalin's time—then we may be able to exert an important influence on the course of events within a divided Communist world. . . .

There are numerous areas in which we can seek to reduce the tensions of the cold war and to bring a degree of normalcy into our relations with the Soviet Union and other Communist countries—once we have resolved that it is safe and wise to do so. . . .

Free world trade with Communist countries has been increasing at a steady but unspectacular rate and it seems unlikely to be greatly accelerated because of the limited ability of the Communist countries to pay for increased imports. A modest increase in East-West trade may nonetheless serve as a modest instrument of East-West détente—provided that we are able to overcome the myth that trade with Communist countries is a compact with the devil and to recognize that, on the contrary, trade can serve as an effective and honorable means of advancing both peace and human welfare. Whether we are able to make these philosophic adjustments or not, we cannot escape the fact that our efforts to devise a common Western trade policy are a palpable failure and that our allies are going to trade with the Communist bloc and the bloc countries are showing themselves to be reliable customers. Since 1958 Western Europe has been increasing its exports to the East at the rate of about seven per cent a year, which is nearly the same rate at which its over-all world sales have been increasing. . . .

There is little in history to justify the expectation that we can either win the cold war or end it immediately and completely. These are favored myths, respectively, of the American Right and of the American Left. They are, I believe, equal in their unreality and in their disregard for the feasibilities of history. We must disabuse ourselves of them and come to terms, at last, with the realities of a world in which neither good nor evil is absolute and in which those who move events and make history are those who have understood not how much but how little it is within our power to change. . . .

Latin America is one of the areas of the world in which American policy is weakened by a growing divergency between old myths and new realities. The crisis over the Panama Canal has been unnecessarily protracted for reasons of domestic politics and national pride and sensitivity on both sides—for reasons, that is, of only marginal relevance to the merits of the dispute. . . . It is important for us to remember that the issue over the canal is only one of a great many in which the United States is involved, and by no means the most important. For Panama, on the other hand, a small nation with a weak economy and an unstable government, the canal is the pre-eminent factor in the nation's economy and in its foreign relations. Surely in a confrontation so unequal, it is not unreasonable to expect the United States to go a little farther than half way in the search for fair settlement. . . .

We would also do well to disabuse ourselves of the myth that there is something morally sacred about the Treaty of 1903. The fact of the matter is that the treaty was concluded under circumstances that reflect little credit on the United States. It was made possible by Panama's separation from Colombia, which probably could not have occurred at that time without the dispatch of the United States warships to prevent the landing of Colombian troops on the isthmus to put down the Panamanian rebellion. . . . I see no reason—certainly no reason of "weakness" or "dishonor"—why the United States cannot put an end to the semantic debate over whether treaty revisions are to be "negotiated" or "discussed" by stating positively and clearly that it is prepared to negotiate revisions in the canal treaty and to submit changes as are made to the Senate for its advice and consent. I think it is necessary for the United States to do this even though a commitment to revise the treaty may be widely criticized at home. . . .

The problem of Cuba is more difficult than that of Panama, and far more heavily burdened with the dead weight of old myths and prohibitions against "unthinkable thoughts." I think the time is overdue for a candid re-evaluation of our Cuban policy even though it may lead to distasteful conclusions. There are and have been three options open to the United States with respect to Cuba: first, the removal of the Castro regime by invading and occupying the island; second, an effort to weaken and ultimately bring down the regime by a policy of political and economic boycott; and, finally, acceptance of the Communist regime as a disagreeable reality and annoyance but one which is not likely to be removed in the near future because of the unavailability of acceptable means of removing it. . . .

The approach which we have adopted has been the second of those mentioned, an effort to weaken and eventually bring down the Castro regime by a policy of political and economic boycott. This policy has taken the form of extensive restrictions against trade with Cuba by United States citizens, of the exclusion of Cuba from the inter-American system and efforts to secure Latin-American support in isolating Cuba politically and economically, and of diplomatic efforts, backed by certain trade and aid sanctions, to persuade other free world countries to maintain economic boycotts against Cuba. This policy, it now seems clear, has been a failure, and there is no reason to believe that it will succeed in the future. Our efforts to persuade our allies to terminate their trade with Cuba have been generally rebuffed. The prevailing attitude was perhaps best expressed by a British manufacturer who, in response to American criticism of the sale of British buses to Cuba, said: "If America has a surplus of wheat, we have a surplus of buses.". . .

The boycott policy has not failed because of any "weakness" or "timidity" on the part of our government. This charge, so frequently heard, is one of the most pernicious myths to have been inflicted on the American people. The boycott policy has failed because the United States is not omnipotent and cannot be. The basic reality to be faced is that it is simply not within our power to compel our allies to cut off their trade with Cuba, unless we are prepared to take drastic sanctions against them, such as closing our own markets to any foreign company that does business in Cuba. . . . The prospects of bringing down the Castro regime by political and economic boycott have never been very good. Even if a general free-world boycott were successfully applied against Cuba, it is unlikely that the Russians would refuse to carry the extra financial burden and thereby permit the only Communist regime in the Western Hemisphere to collapse. We are thus compelled to recognize that there is probably no way of bringing down the Castro regime by means of economic pressures unless we are prepared to impose a blockade against nonmilitary shipments from the Soviet Union. . . .

Communist Cuba has been a disruptive and subversive influence in Venezuela and other countries of the hemisphere and there is no doubt that both we and our Latin-American partners would be better off if the Castro regime did not exist. But it is important to bear in mind that, despite their best efforts, the Cuban Communists have not succeeded in subverting the hemisphere and that in Venezuela, for example, where Communism has made a major effort to gain power through terrorism, it has been repudiated by a people who in a free election have committed themselves to the course of liberal democracy. . . . I think we are bound to conclude that Castro is a nuisance but not a grave threat to the United States and that he cannot be gotten rid of except by means that are wholly disproportionate to the objective. . . .

The policy of the United States with respect to Latin America as a whole is predicated on the assumption that social revolution can be accomplished without violent upheaval. This is the guiding principle of the Alliance for Progress and it may in time be vindicated. We are entitled to hope so and it is wise and necessary for us to do all that we can to advance the prospects of peaceful and orderly reform. At the same time we must be under no illusions as to the extreme difficulty of uprooting long-established ruling oligarchies without disruptions involving lesser or greater degrees of violence. . . .

The Far East is another area of the world in which American policy is handicapped by the divergence of old myths and new realities. Particularly with respect to China, an elaborate vocabulary of make-believe has become compulsory in both official and public discussion. We are committed, with respect to China and other areas of Asia, to inflexible policies of long standing from which we hesitate to depart because of the attribution to these policies of an aura of mystical sanctity. . . . The point is that, whatever the outcome of a rethinking of policy might be, we have been unwilling to undertake it because of the fear of many Government officials, undoubtedly well founded, that even the suggestion of new policies toward China or Vietnam would provoke a vehement public outcry.

I do not think that the United States can or should recognize Communist China or acquiesce in its admission to the United Nations under present circumstances. It would be unwise to do so because there is nothing to be gained by it so long as the Peking regime maintains its attitude of implacable hostility toward the United States. I do not believe, however, that this state of affairs is necessarily permanent. As we have seen in our relations with Germany and Japan, hostility can give way in an astonishingly short time to close friendship; and as we have seen in our relations with China, the reverse can occur with equal speed. It is not impossible that in time our relations with China will change again, if not to friendship then perhaps to "competitive co-existence.". . .

French recognition of Communist China, though untimely and carried out in a way that can hardly be considered friendly to the United States, may nonetheless serve a constructive long-term purpose by unfreezing a situation in which many countries, none more than the United States, are committed to inflexible policies by long-established commitments and the pressures of domestic public opinion. One way or another, the French initiative may help generate a new situation in which the United States, as well as other countries, will find it possible to re-evaluate its basic policies in the Far East.

The situation in Vietnam poses a far more pressing need for a re-evaluation of American policy. Other than withdrawal, which I do not think can be realistically considered under present circumstances, there are three options open to us in Vietnam: first, the continuation of the anti-guerrilla war within South Vietnam along with renewed American efforts to increase the military effectiveness of the South Vietnamese army and the political effectiveness of the South Vietnamese Government; second, an attempt to end the war through negotiations for the neutralization of South Vietnam or of both North and South Vietnam; and, finally, the expansion of the scale of the war, either by the direct commitment of large numbers of American troops or by equipping the South Vietnamese army to attack North Vietnamese territory, possibly by means of commando-type operations from the sea or air.

It is difficult to see how a negotiation, under present military circumstances, could lead to the termination of the war under conditions that would preserve the freedom of South Vietnam. It is extremely difficult for a party to a negotiation to achieve by diplomacy objectives which it has conspicuously failed to win by warfare. The hard fact of the matter is that our bargaining position is at present a weak one. . . .

Recent initiatives by France calling for the "neutralization" of Vietnam have tended to confuse the situation without altering it in any fundamental way. France could perhaps play a constructive mediating role if she were willing to consult and co-operate with the United States. . . .

It seems clear that there are only two realistic options open to us in Vietnam in the immediate future: the expansion of the conflict in one way or another or a renewed effort to bolster the capacity of the South Vietnamese to prosecute the war successfully on its present scale. . . . Whatever specific policy decisions are made, it should be clear to all concerned that the United States will continue to meet its obligations and fulfill its commitments with respect to Vietnam. . . .

In all the issues which I have discussed, American policy has to one degree or another been less effective than it might have been because of our national tendency to equate means with ends and therefore to attach a mythological sanctity to policies and practices which in themselves have no moral content or value except insofar as they contribute to the achievement of some valid national objective. I believe that we must try to overcome this excessive moralism, which binds us to old myths and blinds us to new realities and, worse still, leads us to regard new and unfamiliar ideas with fear and mistrust. We must dare to think about "unthinkable" things. We must learn to explore all of the options and possibilities that confront us in a complex and rapidly changing world. . . .

If Congress and public opinion are unduly susceptible to "shock," the Executive Branch, and particularly the Department of State, is subject to the malady of chronic and excessive caution. An effective foreign policy is one which concerns itself more with innovation abroad than with conciliation at home. . . . It is sometimes necessary for leaders to do unpleasant and unpopular things, because, as Burke pointed out, the duty of the democratic politician to his constituents is not to comply with their every wish and preference but to give them the benefit of, and to be held responsible for, the exercise of his own best judgment. We must dare to think about "unthinkable things," because when things become "unthinkable," thinking stops and action becomes mindless. . . .